Lecture Notes in Computer Science

Lecture Notes in Artificial Intelligence 17105

Founding Editor

Jörg Siekmann

Series Editors

This was established in 1988 as a topical subseries of LNCS devoted to artificial intelligence. The editors are Wolfgang Wahlster (DFKI, Berlin), Zhi-Hua Zhou (Nanjing University), and Randy Goebel (University of Alberta, Edmonton).

For further information please contact lncs@springer.com.

Mariana Recamonde-Mendoza ·
Rodrigo C. Barros
Editors

Intelligent Systems

36th Brazilian Conference, BRACIS 2026
Cuiaba, Brazil, October 19–22, 2026
Proceedings, Part I

Springer

Editors
Mariana Recamonde-Mendoza
Universidade Federal do Rio Grande do Sul
Porto Alegre, Brazil

Rodrigo C. Barros
Pontifícia Universidade Católica do Rio Grande do Sul
Porto Alegre, Brazil

ISSN 0302-9743 ISSN 1611-3349 (electronic)
Lecture Notes in Artificial Intelligence
ISBN 978-3-032-39881-9 ISBN 978-3-032-39882-6 (eBook)
https://doi.org/10.1007/978-3-032-39882-6

LNCS Sublibrary: SL7 – Artificial Intelligence

This Springer imprint is published by the registered company Springer Nature Switzerland AG
The registered company address is: Gewerbestrasse 11, 6330 Cham, Switzerland

Preface

The 36th Brazilian Conference on Intelligent Systems (BRACIS 2026) stands as one of the most significant Brazilian events for researchers in 2026, focused on publishing groundbreaking work in Artificial and Computational Intelligence. BRACIS was formed from the merger of Brazil's two leading scientific events in these fields: the Brazilian Symposium on Artificial Intelligence (SBIA, 21 editions) and the Brazilian Symposium on Neural Networks (SBRN, 12 editions). This year marked the 36th edition of BRACIS, continuing the numbering from the first edition of SBIA, in honor of the history of the Brazilian scientific community.

Supported by the Brazilian Computer Society (SBC), together with the Special Committees on Artificial Intelligence (CE-IA) and Computational Intelligence (CE-IC), BRACIS 2026 served as a platform to promote both theoretical advancements and robust practical applications in these IA/IC (Artificial/Computational Intelligence) fields. The conference promoted the exchange of innovative ideas among researchers, practitioners, and industry leaders.

In 2026, BRACIS was held in Cuiabá, Mato Grosso, organized by the Universidade Federal do Mato Grosso (UFMT). The conference took place alongside four other events: the National Meeting on Artificial and Computational Intelligence (ENIAC), the Symposium on Information and Human Language Technology (STIL), the Symposium on Knowledge Discovery, Mining and Learning (KDMiLe), and the Workshop-School on Agents, Environments, and Applications (WESAAC). The 15th edition of the CTDIAC (The Brazilian National Contest of Ph.D. and M.Sc. Theses on Artificial and Computational Intelligence) also happened this year.

BRACIS 2026 received 582 valid complete paper submissions, each undergoing a rigorous review process conducted by a Program Committee of 493 experienced AI/CI researchers, with the support of 114 additional reviewers, all within a double anonymous format. All papers received at least three reviews from experts in the field. This year, we accepted 40.20% of the submissions, 234 in total, in three key tracks: 135 articles in the main track, showcasing cutting-edge AI/CI methods and solid results; 28 articles in the AI/CI for Social Good track, featuring innovative applications of AI/CI for societal benefit using established methodologies; 65 articles on other AI/CI applications, presenting novel applications using established AI/CI methods, naturally considering the ethical aspects of the application. In addition, 6 top-tier papers published in leading AI conferences and journals were presented during the event.

The topics of interest included, but were not limited to, the following:

- Agent-Based and Multi-Agent Systems
- AI/CI Algorithms and Models
- AI and Quantum Computing, Communication, and Technologies
- AI Ethics, Accountability, and Societal Impact
- AI for Innovation and Technological Sovereignty
- Automated, Probabilistic, and Approximate Reasoning

- Bioinformatics and Biomedical Engineering Applications of AI
- Cognitive Modeling and Human-AI Interaction
- Combinatorial and Numerical Optimization
- Computer Vision
- Constraint Programming and Optimization
- Data Mining and Knowledge Discovery
- Deep Learning and Neural Networks
- Distributed and Decentralized AI
- Education for AI and AI for Education
- Evolutionary Computation and Metaheuristics
- Explainable Artificial Intelligence (XAI)
- Federated and Privacy-Preserving Learning
- Forecasting and Time Series Analysis
- Foundations of Artificial Intelligence and Computational Intelligence
- Fuzzy Systems and Soft Computing
- Game Playing and Intelligent Interactive Entertainment
- Generative AI and Foundation Models
- Graph Neural Networks and Relational Learning
- Human-Centered AI
- Hybrid AI Systems
- Information Retrieval, Integration, and Extraction
- Intelligent Robotics and Autonomous Vehicles
- Knowledge Representation and Reasoning
- Large Language Models
- Logic-Based Knowledge Representation and Reasoning
- Machine Learning
- Meta-Learning and Automated Machine Learning (AutoML)
- Model-Based Reasoning
- Multidisciplinary AI and CI
- Natural Language Processing
- Ontologies and the Semantic Web
- Pattern Recognition and Cluster Analysis
- Planning, Routing, and Scheduling
- Reinforcement Learning

We extend our heartfelt thanks to everyone who contributed to the success of BRACIS 2026. We are especially grateful to the Program Committee members and reviewers for their generous and voluntary efforts in the review process. Special thanks also go to all the authors who submitted their papers and worked tirelessly to refine them into the best possible versions. We also acknowledge the General Chair, the Local Organization Committee for their unwavering support, the Brazilian Computing Society (SBC), and all our sponsors and supporters. We are confident that these proceedings showcase the exceptional work being done in the artificial and computational intelligence fields.

August 2026

Mariana Recamonde-Mendoza
Rodrigo C. Barros

Organization

General Chair

Thiago Ventura	Universidade Federal do Mato Grosso, Brazil

Program Committee Chairs

Mariana Recamonde-Mendoza	Universidade Federal do Rio Grande do Sul, Brazil
Rodrigo C. Barros	Pontifícia Universidade Católica do Rio Grande do Sul, Brazil

Steering Committee (CEIA and CEIC)

Anna Helena Reali Costa	Universidade de São Paulo, Brazil
Anne Magaly de Paula Canuto (CEIC Coordinator)	Universidade Federal do Rio Grande do Norte, Brazil
Denis Deratani Mauá	Universidade de São Paulo, Brazil
Diego Mesquita	Fundação Getúlio Vargas, Brazil
Gisele Lobo Pappa	Universidade Federal de Minas Gerais, Brazil
Hélida Santos	Universidade Federal do Rio Grande, Brazil
Jaime Sichman	Universidade de São Paulo, Brazil
Leliane Nunes de Barros	Universidade de São Paulo, Brazil
Murilo Coelho Naldi	Universidade Federal de São Carlos, Brazil
Ricardo M. Marcacini	Universidade de São Paulo, Brazil
Rodrigo C. Barros	Pontifícia Universidade Católica do Rio Grande do Sul, Brazil
Rosiane de Freitas Rodrigues	Universidade Federal do Amazonas, Brazil
Solange Rezende	Universidade de São Paulo, Brazil
Tatiane Nogueira Rios (CEIA Coordinator)	Universidade Federal da Bahia, Brazil

Local Organizers

Allan Gonçalves de Oliveira	Universidade Federal do Mato Grosso, Brazil
Cesar Eduardo Guarienti	Universidade Federal do Mato Grosso, Brazil
Claudia Aparecida Martins	Universidade Federal do Mato Grosso, Brazil
Cleyton Slaviero	Universidade Federal do Mato Grosso, Brazil
Eunice Pereira dos Santos Nunes	Universidade Federal do Mato Grosso, Brazil
Gracyeli Santos Souza Guarienti	Universidade Federal do Mato Grosso, Brazil
Leiliane Silva do Nascimento	Universidade Federal do Mato Grosso, Brazil
Nilton Hideki Takagi	Universidade Federal do Mato Grosso, Brazil

Program Committee

Adauto Bueno	Universidade do Estado de Mato Grosso, Brazil
Adenilton José da Silva	Universidade Federal de Pernambuco, Brazil
Adriana Laurindo Monteiro	Instituto de Ciência e Tecnologia Itaú, Brazil
Adriano Quilião de Oliveira	Universidade Federal de Santa Maria, Brazil
Adriano Rivolli	Universidade Tecnológica Federal do Paraná, Brazil
Adriano V. Werhli	Universidade Federal do Rio Grande, Brazil
Adrião Duarte Dória Neto	Universidade Federal do Rio Grande do Norte, Brazil
Afonso Sales	Pontifícia Universidade Católica do Rio Grande do Sul, Brazil
Alan Ferreira Pinheiro Tavares	Universidade do Estado do Amazonas, Brazil
Alan Demétrius Baria Valejo	Universidade Federal de São Carlos, Brazil
Alceu Britto Jr.	Pontifícia Universidade Católica do Paraná, Brazil
Aldísio Gonçalves Medeiros	Universidade Federal do Ceará, Brazil
Alessandro de L. Bicho	Universidade Federal do Rio Grande, Brazil
Alex Marino Gonçalves de Almeida	Faculdade de Tecnologia de Ourinhos, Brazil
Alexandre Alcoforado	Universidade de São Paulo, Brazil
Alexandre Mello Ferreira	Universidade Estadual de Campinas, Brazil
Alexandre Tacla	SENAI CIMATEC, Brazil
Alexandre Thurow Bender	Universidade Federal de Pelotas, Brazil
Alexandre C. M. Oliveira	Universidade Federal do Maranhão, Brazil
Aline Marques Del Valle	Instituto Federal de Educação, Ciência e Tecnologia do Sul de Minas Gerais, Brazil
Aline Neves	Universidade Federal do ABC, Brazil
Aline Paes	Universidade Federal Fluminense, Brazil
Alison R. Panisson	Universidade Federal de Santa Catarina, Brazil

Allan Gonçalves de Oliveira	Universidade Federal de Mato Grosso, Brazil
Alneu de Andrade Lopes	Universidade de São Paulo, Brazil
Alvaro Moreira	Universidade Federal do Rio Grande do Sul, Brazil
Amanda Gondim de Oliveira	Universidade Federal Rural do Semiárido, Brazil
Amar Gupta	Massachusetts Institute of Technology, USA
Amedeo Napoli	Laboratoire Lorrain de Recherche en Informatique et ses Applications, France
Ana L. C. Bazzan	Universidade Federal do Rio Grande do Sul, Brazil
Ana Trindade Winck	Universidade Federal de Ciências da Saúde de Porto Alegre, Brazil
Ana Carolina Lorena	Instituto Tecnológico de Aeronáutica, Brazil
Ana Cristina B. Kochem Vendramin	Universidade Tecnológica Federal do Paraná, Brazil
Ana Cristina Bicharra Garcia	Universidade Federal do Estado do Rio de Janeiro, Brazil
Ana Luiza da Conceicao Tenorio	Fundação Getúlio Vargas, Brazil
Analucia Schiaffino Morales	Universidade Federal de Santa Catarina, Brazil
Anderson Meneses	Universidade Federal do Oeste do Pará, Brazil
Anderson R. Tavares	Universidade Federal do Rio Grande do Sul, Brazil
Anderson Sergio	CESAR School, Brazil
André Britto	Universidade Federal de Sergipe, Brazil
André C. A. Nascimento	Universidade Federal Rural de Pernambuco, Brazil
André Kelbouscas	Universidade Federal do Rio Grande, Brazil
André L. D. Rossi	Universidade Estadual Paulista Júlio de Mesquita Filho, Brazil
André Ricardo Backes	Universidade Federal de São Carlos, Brazil
André Vignatti	Universidade Federal do Paraná, Brazil
André Gustavo Hochuli	Pontifícia Universidade Católica do Paraná, Brazil
Andrés Eduardo Coca Salazar	Universidade Tecnológica Federal do Paraná, Brazil
Anna Helena Reali Costa	Universidade de São Paulo, Brazil
Anne Magaly de Paula Canuto	Universidade Federal do Rio Grande do Norte, Brazil
Anselmo Cardoso de Paiva	Universidade Federal do Maranhão, Brazil
Antonio Carlos Sobieranski	Universidade Federal de Santa Catarina, Brazil
Antonio Parmezan	Universidade Estadual de Londrina, Brazil
Antonio Oseas de Carvalho Filho	Universidade Federal do Piauí, Brazil
Aon Safdar	University College Dublin, Ireland
Araken de Medeiros Santos	Universidade Federal Rural do Semi-Árido, Brazil

Ariane Machado-Lima	Universidade de São Paulo, Brazil
Aristófanes Corrêa Silva	Universidade Federal do Maranhão, Brazil
Arnaldo Cândido Júnior	Universidade Estadual Paulista Júlio de Mesquita Filho, Brazil
Arthur Mangussi	Instituto Tecnológico de Aeronáutica, Brazil
Arthur Marques de Oliveira	Universidade Federal do Rio Grande do Sul, Brazil
Artur Jordao	Universidade de São Paulo, Brazil
Aurora Pozo	Universidade Federal do Paraná, Brazil
Betania Campello	Universidade Estadual de Campinas, Brazil
Brenno M. Alencar	Universidade Federal da Bahia, Brazil
Bruno Almeida Pimentel	Universidade Federal de Alagoas, Brazil
Bruno Cascaes Alves	Universidade Federal de Pelotas, Brazil
Bruno Guazzelli Batista	Universidade Federal de Itajubá, Brazil
Bruno Nogueira	Universidade Federal de Mato Grosso do Sul, Brazil
Bruno Cesar Ribas	Universidade de Brasília, Brazil
Caetano Mazzoni Ranieri	Universidade Estadual Paulista Júlio de Mesquita Filho, Brazil
Caique Almeida	Universidade de São Paulo, Brazil
Carina Friedrich Dorneles	Universidade Federal de Santa Catarina, Brazil
Carla Amor Divino Moreira Delgado	Universidade Federal do Rio de Janeiro, Brazil
Carla Diniz Lopes Becker	Universidade Federal de Ciências da Saúde de Porto Alegre, Brazil
Carlos Augusto Calage Silveira Júnior	Universidade Federal de Pelotas, Brazil
Carlos Caminha	Universidade Federal do Ceará, Brazil
Carlos Eduardo Thomaz	Centro Universitário da Fundação Educacional Inaciana Pe Sabóia de Medeiros, Brazil
Carlos F. A. Gomes	Pontifícia Universidade Católica do Rio Grande do Sul, Brazil
Carlos Henrique Leitão Cavalcante	Instituto Federal de Educação, Ciência e Tecnologia do Ceará, Brazil
Carlos M. S. Figueiredo	Universidade do Estado do Amazonas, Brazil
Carlos Alexandre Silva	Instituto Federal de Minas Gerais, Campus Sabará, Brazil
Carlos Eduardo Pantoja	Centro Federal de Educação Tecnológica Celso Suckow da Fonseca, Brazil
Carlos Mauricio Dourado	Instituto Federal do Ceará, Brazil
Carolina Gil Marcelino	Universidade Federal do Rio de Janeiro, Brazil
Carolina Paula de Almeida	Faculdade de Educação de Jaru, Brazil
Celia G. Ralha	Universidade de Brasília, Brazil

Cesar Renno-Costa	Universidade Federal do Rio Grande do Norte, Brazil
César Lincoln Cavalcante Mattos	Universidade Federal do Ceará, Brazil
Charles Costa	Universidade de Brasília, Brazil
Christian Mattjie	Pontifícia Universidade Católica do Rio Grande do Sul, Brazil
Christiano Pinheiro	Universidade Federal do Espírito Santo, Brazil
Claudia Martins	Universidade Federal de Mato Grosso, Brazil
Claudiney R. Tinoco	Universidade Federal de Uberlândia, Brazil
Claudio Filipi Gonçalves do Santos	Universidade Estadual Paulista Júlio de Mesquita Filho, Brazil
Claudio Lucio Lopes	A3Data Consultoria, Brazil
Claudio Miceli de Farias	Universidade Federal do Rio de Janeiro, Brazil
Claudio R. Jung	Universidade Federal do Rio Grande do Sul, Brazil
Cláudio Elízio Calazans Campelo	Universidade Federal de Campina Grande, Brazil
Cleber Zanchettin	Universidade Federal de Pernambuco, Brazil
Cleo Zanella Billa	Universidade Federal do Rio Grande, Brazil
Cleyton Mário de Oliveira Rodrigues	Universidade de Pernambuco, Brazil
Cristiano Torezzan	Universidade Estadual de Campinas, Brazil
Cynthia Moreira Maia	Universidade Federal de Pernambuco, Brazil
Dalvan Griebler	Pontifícia Universidade Católica do Rio Grande do Sul, Brazil
Daniel Oliveira Dantas	Universidade Federal de Sergipe, Brazil
Daniel Welfer	Universidade Federal de Santa Maria, Brazil
Daniela Barreiro Claro	Universidade Federal da Bahia, Brazil
Daniela Silva	Universidade Federal do Rio Grande do Norte, Brazil
Danilo Sipoli Sanches	Universidade Tecnológica Federal do Paraná, Brazil
Dayane Schweitzer	Universidade do Estado de Santa Catarina, Brazil
Denilson Pereira	Universidade Federal de Lavras, Brazil
Denis D. Mauá	Universidade de São Paulo, Brazil
Dennis Balreira	Universidade Federal do Rio Grande do Sul, Brazil
Diana Francisca Adamatti	Universidade Federal do Rio Grande, Brazil
Didier Vega	Universidade Federal de São Paulo, Brazil
Diego Furtado Silva	Universidade de São Paulo, Brazil
Diego Kreutz	Universidade Federal do Pampa, Brazil
Diego Mesquita	Fundação Getúlio Vargas, Brazil
Diego Minatel	Universidade de São Paulo, Brazil
Diego Nascimento	NEOMA Business School, France

Diego Pinheiro	Universidade Católica de Pernambuco, Brazil
Diego P. Pinto-Roa	Universidad Nacional de Asunción, Paraguay
Diógenes Marques José	Universidade do Estado de Mato Grosso, Brazil
Diogo Medeiros de Almeida	Universidade Federal de Pernambuco, Brazil
Domingos Santos Júnior	Universidade de Pernambuco, Brazil
Eder Mateus Nunes Gonçalves	Universidade Federal do Rio Grande, Brazil
Edson Takashi Matsubara	Universidade Federal de Mato Grosso do Sul, Brazil
Eduardo Bezerra	Centro Federal de Educação Tecnológica Celso Suckow da Fonseca, Brazil
Eduardo Bogue	Universidade Federal de Mato Grosso do Sul, Brazil
Eduardo C. Goncalves	Escola Nacional de Ciências Estatísticas, Brazil
Eduardo Camilo Inacio	Universidade Federal de Santa Catarina, Brazil
Eduardo Ferreira	Centro Federal de Educação Tecnológica Celso Suckow da Fonseca, Brazil
Eduardo Freire Nakamura	Universidade Federal do Amazonas, Brazil
Eduardo J. Spinosa	Universidade Federal do Paraná, Brazil
Eduardo Ogasawara	Centro Federal de Educação Tecnológica Celso Suckow da Fonseca, Brazil
Eduardo Jose da Silva Luz	Universidade Federal de Ouro Preto, Brazil
Edward Hermann Haeusler	Pontifícia Universidade Católica de Goiás, Brazil
Efren Lopes Souza	Universidade Federal do Oeste do Pará, Brazil
Elaine Faria	Universidade Federal de Uberlândia, Brazil
Elaine Sousa	Universidade de São Paulo, Brazil
Elisa Marchioro Stumpf	Universidade Federal do Rio Grande do Sul, Brazil
Emanuel Pereira	Universidade Federal do Rio Grande do Norte, Brazil
Emerson Cabrera Paraiso	Pontifícia Universidade Católica do Paraná, Brazil
Emiliano Soares Monteiro	Universidade do Estado de Mato Grosso, Brazil
Eraylson Galdino da Silva	Universidade de Pernambuco, Brazil
Eric Antonelo	Universidade Federal de Santa Catarina, Brazil
Eric Fujiwara	Universidade Estadual de Campinas, Brazil
Erick Barboza	Universidade Federal de Alagoas, Brazil
Erico Teixeira	Venturus - Centro de Inovação Tecnológica, Brazil
Erneson Oliveira	Universidade de Fortaleza, Brazil
Eugénio Ribeiro	ISCTE - Instituto Universitário de Lisboa, Portugal
Eulanda Santos	Universidade Federal do Amazonas, Brazil
Fabiano Silva	Universidade Federal do Paraná, Brazil
Fábio Gagliardi Cozman	Universidade de São Paulo, Brazil
Fábio José Muneratti Ortega	Universidade de São Paulo, Brazil

Fábio Lobato	Universidade Federal do Oeste do Pará, Brazil
Fabio Marujo da Silva	Centro Brazileiro de Pesquisas Físicas, Brazil
Fabiola Souza Fernandes Pereira	Universidade Federal de Uberlândia, Brazil
Fabrício Aguiar Silva	Universidade Federal de Viçosa, Brazil
Fabricio Alves de Almeida	Instituto Tecnológico de Aeronáutica, Brazil
Fabrício Enembreck	Pontifícia Universidade Católica do Paraná, Brazil
Fabricio Olivetti de França	Universidade Federal do ABC, Brazil
Felipe Diego Toro-Hernández	Universidade Federal do ABC, Brazil
Felipe Kenji Nakano	Katholieke Universiteit Leuven, Belgium
Felipe André Zeiser	Universidade do Vale do Rio dos Sinos, Brazil
Fernanda Maria da Cunha Santos	Universidade Federal de Uberlândia, Brazil
Fernando Hsieh	Universidade de São Paulo, Brazil
Fernando Maciano de Paula Neto	Universidade Federal de Pernambuco, Brazil
Fernando Osório	Universidade de São Paulo, Brazil
Filipe Mutz	Universidade Federal do Espírito Santo, Brazil
Filipe Saraiva	Universidade Federal do Pará, Brazil
Flavia Bernardini	Universidade Federal Fluminense, Brazil
Flávio Soares Corrêa da Silva	Universidade de São Paulo, Brazil
Franciele Fath	Universidade Federal de Goiás, Brazil
Francisco da Silva	Instituto Federal da Paraíba, Campus Cajazeiras, Brazil
Francisco de Carvalho	Universidade Federal de Pernambuco, Brazil
Francisco de Assis Boldt	Instituto Federal do Espírito Santo, Brazil
Francisco Hércules dos Santos Silva	Instituto Federal de Educação, Ciência e Tecnologia do Ceará, Brazil
Frederico Guimaraes	Universidade Federal de Minas Gerais, Brazil
Frederico Messa	Universidade Federal do Rio Grande do Sul, Brazil
Gabriel Almeida Gomes	Universidade Federal de Pelotas, Brazil
Gabriel Bianchin de Oliveira	Universidade Estadual de Campinas, Brazil
Gabriel de Oliveira Ramos	Universidade do Vale do Rio dos Sinos, Brazil
Gabriel Ferreira da Costa	Universidade Federal de Ouro Preto, Brazil
Gabriel P. Oliveira	Universidade Federal de Minas Gerais, Brazil
Gabrielly de Queiroz Pereira	Universidade Estadual de Ponta Grossa, Brazil
George Darmiton da Cunha Cavalcanti	Universidade Federal de Pernambuco, Brazil
Geovany Araujo Borges	Universidade de Brasília, Brazil
Geraldo Pereira Rocha Filho	Universidade Estadual do Sudoeste da Bahia, Brazil
Geraldo Zafalon	Universidade Estadual Paulista Júlio de Mesquita Filho, Brazil
Gerson Zaverucha	Universidade Federal do Rio de Janeiro, Brazil

Jadson Castro Getrudes	Universidade Federal de Ouro Preto, Brazil
Jaime Sichman	Universidade de São Paulo, Brazil
Jayr Pereira	Universidade Federal do Cariri, Brazil
Jean Paul Barddal	Pontifícia Universidade Católica do Paraná, Brazil
Jefferson Souza	Universidade Federal de Uberlândia, Brazil
Jianlong Yan	Universidade de São Paulo, Brazil
João Cardia	Fatec Estudante Rafael Almeida Camarinha (FATEC Marília), Brazil
João Comba	Universidade Federal do Rio Grande do Sul, Brazil
João Papa	Universidade Estadual Paulista Júlio de Mesquita Filho, Brazil
João C. Xavier-Júnior	Universidade Federal do Rio Grande do Norte, Brazil
João Dallyson Sousa de Almeida	Universidade Federal do Maranhão, Brazil
Joao Otavio Bandeira Diniz	Instituto Federal do Maranhão, Brazil
João Paulo Canário	Universidade Federal da Bahia, Brazil
Joao Paulo Pordeus Gomes	Universidade Federal do Ceará, Brazil
Joao Victor Ferreira Alves	Instituto de Ciência e Tecnologia Itaú, Brazil
Joel Luís Carbonera	Universidade Federal do Rio Grande do Sul, Brazil
Jonathan Andrade Silva	Universidade Federal de Mato Grosso do Sul, Brazil
Jordan Passinato Sausen	Universidade do Vale do Itajaí, Brazil
Jorge L. B. Araujo	Universidade de Fortaleza, Brazil
Jorge Carlos Valverde-Rebaza	Tecnológico de Monterrey, Mexico
Jorge Kysnney Santos Kamassury	Fundação CERTI, Brazil
José Jailton	Universidade Federal do Pará, Brazil
José Júnior	Universidade Federal do Rio Grande do Norte, Brazil
José Antonio Sanz	Universidad Pública de Navarra, Spain
José Eduardo Henriques da Silva	Laboratório Nacional de Computação Científica, Brazil
Jose Eduardo Ochoa Luna	Universidad Católica San Pablo, Peru
Jose Leonardo Machado Paes	Universidade Estadual de Maringá, Brazil
Josecley Goes	Universidade Federal do Oeste do Pará, Brazil
Josiel Maimone Figueiredo	Universidade Federal de Mato Grosso, Brazil
Joventino de Oliveira Campos	Universidade Federal de Juiz de Fora, Brazil
Juan Alberto Rojas Tueros	Universidade Federal de Pernambuco, Brazil
Juarez Monteiro dos Santos Júnior	Instituto Kunumi, Brazil
Juliana Resplande Sant'anna Gomes	Centro de Competência Embrapii em Tecnologias Imersivas, Universidade Federal de Goiás, Brazil

Julio C. S. Reis	Universidade Federal de Viçosa, Brazil
Julio Cesar Nievola	Pontifícia Universidade Católica do Paraná, Brazil
Karin Becker	Universidade Federal do Rio Grande do Sul, Brazil
Karina Valdivia-Delgado	Universidade de São Paulo, Brazil
Karina S. Machado	Universidade Federal do Rio Grande, Brazil
Karla Pereira Lima	Universidade de São Paulo, Brazil
Kate Cerqueira Revoredo	Humboldt-Universität zu Berlin, Germany
Kauan Mariano	Universidade Federal de Goiás, Brazil
Kellyton Brito	Universidade Federal Rural de Pernambuco, Brazil
L. F. Steve Ataucuri Cruz	Universidade de São Paulo, Brazil
Larissa Astrogildo Freitas	Universidade Federal de Pelotas, Brazil
Leandro Couto	Universidade Federal de Uberlândia, Brazil
Leandro Henrique Furtado Pinto Silva	Universidade Federal de Viçosa, Brazil
Leandro Santiago de Araújo	Universidade Federal Fluminense, Brazil
Leandro Honorato Silva	Universidade de Pernambuco, Brazil
Leliane Nunes de Barros	Universidade de São Paulo, Brazil
Leonardo Lima	Centro de Pesquisa e Desenvolvimento em Telecomunicações (CPqD), Brazil
Leonardo Matos	Universidade Federal de Sergipe, Brazil
Leonardo Nascimento Ferreira	Universidade Estadual de Campinas, Brazil
Leonardo Rocha	Universidade Federal de São João del-Rei, Brazil
Leonardo Tomazeli Duarte	Universidade Estadual de Campinas, Brazil
Leonardo Augusto Ferreira	Universidade Federal do Minas Gerais, Brazil
Levy Boccato	Universidade Estadual de Campinas, Brazil
Li Weigang	Universidade de Brasília, Brazil
Lilian Berton	Universidade Federal de São Paulo, Brazil
Luana Batista da Cruz	Universidade Federal do Cariri, Brazil
Lucas G. M. Castro	Sidia Instituto de Ciência e Tecnologia, Brazil
Lucas N. Alegre	Universidade Federal do Rio Grande do Sul, Brazil
Lucas Pascotti Valem	Universidade de São Paulo, Brazil
Lucas Silveira Kupssinskü	Pontifícia Universidade Católica do Rio Grande do Sul, Brazil
Lucas Francisco Pellicer	Instituto de Ciência e Tecnologia Itaú, Brazil
Lucas Rafael Costella Pessutto	Universidade Federal do Rio Grande do Sul, Brazil
Lucas Raniére Juvino Santos	Universidade Federal de Campina Grande, Brazil
Lucelene Lopes	Universidade de São Paulo, Brazil
Luciana Bencke	Universidade Federal do Rio Grande do Sul, Brazil

Mariana Caravanti de Souza	Universidade Federal de Mato Grosso do Sul, Brazil
Marilia Rosa Silveira	Universidade Federal de Pelotas, Brazil
Marilton Sanchotene de Aguiar	Universidade Federal de Pelotas, Brazil
Mariza Ferro	Universidade Federal Fluminense, Brazil
Marley M. B. R. Vellasco	Pontifícia Universidade Católica do Rio de Janeiro, Brazil
Marlo Souza	Universidade Federal da Bahia, Brazil
Marlon Marcon	Universidade Tecnológica Federal do Paraná, Brazil
Matheus Bernardelli de Moraes	Centro de Tecnologia da Informação Renato Archer, Brazil
Matheus Giovanni Pires	Universidade Estadual de Feira de Santana, Brazil
Matheus Menezes	Instituto de Ciência e Tecnologia Grupo Equatorial, Brazil
Matheus Todescato	Universidade Federal do Rio Grande do Sul, Brazil
Matheus Costa Pereira	Universidade Federal de Itajubá, Brazil
Mauri Ferrandin	Universidade Federal de Santa Catarina, Brazil
Maurício Cecílio Magnaguagno	Pontifícia Universidade Católica do Rio Grande do Sul, Brazil
Mauricio Solar	Universidad Técnica Federico Santa María, Chile
Miguel Arjona Ramírez	Universidade de São Paulo, Brazil
Mikael Nedel Hartmann	Universidade Tecnológica Federal do Paraná, Brazil
Mirela T. Cazzolato	Universidade de São Paulo, Brazil
Míriam B. Born	Universidade Federal de Pelotas, Brazil
Murillo G. Carneiro	Universidade Federal de Uberlândia, Brazil
Murilo Bellezoni Loiola	Universidade Federal do ABC, Brazil
Murilo Falleiros Lemos Schmitt	Universidade Estadual do Centro-Oeste, Brazil
Murilo Naldi	Universidade Federal de São Carlos, Brazil
Myriam R. B. S. Delgado	Universidade Tecnológica Federal do Paraná, Brazil
Nádia Felix	Universidade Federal de Goiás, Brazil
Natalia Emelianova	Universidade Federal do ABC, Brazil
Natan dos Santos	Universidade Federal do Pará, Brazil
Natasha Correia Queiroz Lino	Universidade Federal da Paraíba, Brazil
Nator Junior Carvalho da Costa	Universidade Estadual do Ceará, Brazil
Nelson Carvalho Sandes	Universidade Federal do Cariri, Brazil
Ogobuchi Daniel Okey	Universidade Federal do ABC, Brazil
Omar Andres Carmona Cortes	Instituto Federal do Maranhão, Brazil
Otávio Parraga	Pontifícia Universidade Católica do Rio Grande do Sul, Brazil

Pablo Andretta Jaskowiak	Universidade Federal de Santa Catarina, Brazil
Pablo Luiz Braga Soares	Universidade Federal do Ceará, Brazil
Patricia Rufino Oliveira	Universidade de São Paulo, Brazil
Patrick Terrematte	Universidade Federal do Rio Grande do Norte, Brazil
Paulo Mann	Universidade Federal do Rio de Janeiro, Brazil
Paulo Quaresma	Universidade de Évora, Portugal
Paulo R. Ferreira Jr.	Universidade Federal de Pelotas, Brazil
Paulo Diego Silva Souza	Universidade Federal de Uberlândia, Brazil
Paulo Henrique Pisani	Universidade Federal do ABC, Brazil
Paulo Renato A. Firmino	Universidade Federal do Cariri, Brazil
Paulo T. Guerra	Universidade Federal do Ceará, Brazil
Pedro Clarindo da Silva Neto	Instituto Federal do Mato Grosso, Brazil
Pedro Corrêa	Universidade de São Paulo, Brazil
Pedro de A. dos Santos Neto	Universidade Federal do Piauí, Brazil
Pedro Ilidio	Katholieke Universiteit Leuven, Belgium
Pedro Neto	Atlas AI Nexus, Brazil
Pedro Silva	Universidade Federal de Ouro Preto, Brazil
Pedro Henrique Silva Barros	Universidade Federal de Minas Gerais, Brazil
Pedro Pedrosa Rebouças Filho	Instituto Federal de Educação, Ciência e Tecnologia do Ceará, Brazil
Petrucio Viana	Universidade Federal Fluminense, Brazil
Priscila Lima	Universidade Federal do Rio de Janeiro, Brazil
Priscila Tiemi Maeda Saito	Universidade Federal de São Carlos, Brazil
Rafael Giusti	Universidade Federal do Amazonas, Brazil
Rafael Gomes Mantovani	Universidade Tecnológica Federal do Paraná, Brazil
Rafael Marinho	Instituto Nacional de Pesquisas Espaciais, Brazil
Rafael Mesquita	Instituto Federal de Pernambuco, Brazil
Rafael Morais da Cunha	Universidade Federal do Piauí, Brazil
Rafael Oleques Nunes	Universidade Federal do Rio Grande do Sul, Brazil
Rafael Stubs Parpinelli	Universidade do Estado de Santa Catarina, Brazil
Rafael Teixeira Sousa	Universidade Federal de Mato Grosso, Brazil
Rafaela Ravazio	Pontifícia Universidade Católica do Rio Grande do Sul, Brazil
Raimundo da Silva Barreto	Universidade Federal do Amazonas, Brazil
Raimundo Santos Moura	Universidade Federal do Piauí, Brazil
Raíssa Contassot	Pontifícia Universidade Católica do Rio Grande do Sul, Brazil
Raissa dos Santos Barcellos	Universidade do Estado do Rio de Janeiro, Brazil
Raoni Florentino da Silva Teixeira	Universidade Federal de Mato Grosso, Brazil

Raquel Silveira	Instituto Federal do Ceará, Brazil
Reinaldo A. C. Bianchi	Centro Universitário FEI, Brazil
Renan Moioli	Universidade Federal do Rio Grande do Norte, Brazil
Renan Soares de Andrades	Universidade Federal do Rio Grande do Sul, Brazil
Renata de Paris	Instituto Kunumi, Brazil
Renato Krohling	Universidade Federal do Espírito Santo, Brazil
Renato Miyaji	Visagio Group, Brazil
Renato Moraes Silva	Universidade de São Paulo, Brazil
Renato Tinos	Universidade de São Paulo, Brazil
René Santin	Universidade de São Paulo, Brazil
Ricardo Araújo Rios	Universidade Federal da Bahia, Brazil
Ricardo B. C. Prudêncio	Universidade Federal de Pernambuco, Brazil
Ricardo Cerri	Universidade de São Paulo, Brazil
Ricardo Gomes de Oliveira	Universidade Federal da Bahia, Brazil
Ricardo Marcondes Marcacini	Universidade de São Paulo, Brazil
Ricardo Augusto Souza Fernandes	Universidade de São Paulo, Brazil
Ricardo Jose Pfitscher	Universidade Federal de Santa Catarina, Brazil
Roberta Andrade de Araújo Fagundes	Universidade de Pernambuco, Brazil
Roberto Fray da Silva	Universidade de São Paulo, Brazil
Robespierre Dantas da Rocha Pita	Universidade Federal da Bahia, Brazil
Robson Pereira	Universidade Federal de São Carlos, Brazil
Rodrigo da Motta Cabral-Carvalho	CloudWalk Research and Development Team, Brazil
Rodrigo de Melo Souza Veras	Universidade Federal do Piauí, Brazil
Rodrigo Nogueira	Maritaca AI, Brazil
Rodrigo César Pedrosa Silva	Universidade Federal de Ouro Preto, Brazil
Romis Attux	Universidade Estadual de Campinas, Brazil
Ronaldo C. Prati	Universidade Federal do ABC, Brazil
Ronaldo R. Goldschmidt	Instituto Militar de Engenharia, Brazil
Roseli Ap. Francelin Romero	Universidade de São Paulo, Brazil
Rosiane de Freitas	Universidade Federal do Amazonas, Brazil
Ruben Interian	Universidade Estadual de Campinas, Brazil
Rubens Marques Chaves	Universidade de Brasília, Brazil
Rudimar Luís Scaranto Dazzi	Universidade do Vale do Itajaí, Brazil
Rui Camacho	Universidade do Porto, Portugal
Salatiel Dantas	Universidade Federal de Campina Grande, Brazil
Samara Lima de Souza	Universidade Federal do Pará, Brazil
Samuel Armbrust Freitas	Universidade do Vale do Rio dos Sinos, Brazil
Sandra Avila	Universidade Estadual de Campinas, Brazil

Sandra M. Aluísio	Universidade de São Paulo, Brazil
Sandro Rama Fiorini	Instituto PUC-Behring para Inteligência Artificial, Brazil
Santiago Ravelo	Universidade Estadual de Campinas, Brazil
Saulo Matos	Universidade Federal de Sergipe, Brazil
Saulo Moraes Villela	Universidade Federal de Juiz de Fora, Brazil
Sávio Teles	Universidade Federal de Goiás, Brazil
Sebastiao E. Alves Filho	Universidade do Estado do Rio Grande do Norte, Brazil
Sidney Evaldo Leal	Venturus - Centro de Inovação Tecnológica, Brazil
Silvan Ferreira	Universidade Federal do Rio Grande do Norte, Brazil
Silvia M. W. Moraes	Pontifícia Universidade Católica do Rio Grande do Sul, Brazil
Sílvia Maria Diniz Monteiro Maia	Universidade Federal do Rio Grande do Norte, Brazil
Sílvio César Cazella	Universidade Federal de Ciências da Saúde de Porto Alegre, Brazil
Silvio Fernandes	Universidade Federal Rural do Semiárido, Brazil
Solange Rezende	Universidade de São Paulo, Brazil
Soraia Raupp Musse	Pontifícia Universidade Católica do Rio Grande do Sul, Brazil
Stefan Blawid	Universidade Federal de Pernambuco, Brazil
Suane Pires Pinheiro da Silva	Instituto Federal de Educação, Ciência e Tecnologia do Ceará, Brazil
Talles Medeiros	Universidade Federal de Ouro Preto, Brazil
Tatiane Nogueira	Universidade Federal da Bahia, Brazil
Thais Rodrigues Neubauer	Universidade de São Paulo, Brazil
Thales Almeida	Universidade Estadual de Campinas, Brazil
Thalyson Gomes Nepomuceno da Silva	Universidade Estadual do Ceará, Brazil
Thelmo P. de Araujo	Universidade Estadual do Ceará, Brazil
Thiago Covoes	Universidade Federal do ABC, Brazil
Thiago Ferreira	Universidade Federal Fluminense, Brazil
Thiago M. Ventura	Universidade Federal de Mato Grosso, Brazil
Thiago Pardo	Universidade de São Paulo, Brazil
Thiago Queiroz de Oliveira	Instituto Federal do Ceará, Brazil
Tiago A. Almeida	Universidade Federal de São Carlos, Brazil
Tiago A. E. Ferreira	Universidade Federal Rural de Pernambuco, Brazil
Tiago Brazileiro	Instituto Federal da Paraíba, Brazil
Tiago Gonçalves Botelho	Universidade Federal de São Carlos, Brazil
Tiago Lima	Instituto Federal de Pernambuco, Brazil

Tiago Henrique Trojahn	Instituto Federal de São Paulo, Brazil
Tsang Ing Ren	Universidade Federal de Pernambuco, Brazil
Ulisses Brisolara Corrêa	Universidade Federal de Pelotas, Brazil
Valdinei Freire	Universidade de São Paulo, Brazil
Valéria de Carvalho Santos	Universidade Federal de Ouro Preto, Brazil
Valmir Macario	Universidade Federal Rural de Pernambuco, Brazil
Vander L. S. Freitas	Universidade Federal de Ouro Preto, Brazil
Vasco Furtado	Universidade de Fortaleza, Brazil
Vinicius M. A. Souza	Pontifícia Universidade Católica do Paraná, Brazil
Vinicius Ponte Machado	Universidade Federal do Piauí, Brazil
Vinicius Ruela Pereira Borges	Universidade de Brasília, Brazil
Vinícius Teixeira de Carvalho Freitas	Universidade de São Paulo, Brazil
Vinicius Renan de Carvalho	Universidade de São Paulo, Brazil
Vitor G. Rolla	Instituto Nacional de Matemática Pura e Aplicada, Brazil
Viviane Menezes	Universidade Federal do Ceará, Brazil
Viviane Moreira	Universidade Federal do Rio Grande do Sul, Brazil
Vládia Pinheiro	Universidade de Fortaleza, Brazil
Wandemberg Gibaut	Instituto de Pesquisas Eldorado, Brazil
Wellynton Diniz	Faculdade de Tecnologia de Sinop, Brazil
Wesley Carvalho	Universidade de São Paulo, Brazil
Wollace Souza Picanço	Universidade Federal do Amazonas, Brazil
Yuri Malheiros	Universidade Federal da Paraíba, Brazil

Additional Reviewers

Afonso Lima
Alan Goncalves
Alexandre Fernandes
Alisson Sampaio de Carvalho Alencar
Alysson Amaral
Amaury W. Carvalho
Ana Erthal
Anderson de Paula
André Françani
André Gomes Regino
André Ribeiro
Angela Patricia Mestas Muñante
Antonio Fernando L. Jacob Junior
Arturo de Souza
Athus Cavalini
Augusto Antônio Fontanive Leal
Augusto Camargo
Brenda Lelis
Bruno Henrique Meyer
Bruno Tavares
Carlos Castro
Carlos de Meo
Cristiano Melo
Davi Aragão
Daniel Barbosa
Edilene Veneruchi

Eduardo Almeida
Eduardo Bouhid
Eliton Scardin Perin
Evandro Scudeleti Ortigossa
Fabrício Almeida do Carmo
Felipe Serras
Fernanda Assi
Fernando Almeida do Carmo
Fernando Maia da Mota
Fernando Rezende Zagatti
Franciele Alves Barbosa
François Fernandes Ribeiro Barbosa
Frederico Corrêa da Silva
Gabriel Assis
Gabriel Castro Michelassi
Gabriel Henrique Garcia Ticianeli
Gabriel Orlando
Gabriel da Silva Corvino Nogueira
Gabriele De Sousa Araújo
Gian Franco Joel Condori Luna
Gianlucca Zuin
Giovanna Aguiar Castro
Guilherme Rinaldo
Gustavo Cordeiro Galvão Van Erven
Hermon Faria de Araujo
Higor Moreira
Irene Tenison
Israel Fama
Italo Francyles Santos da Silva
Janayna Moura
Jorge Batista
José Nascimento Dos Santos
João Pedro Ribeiro da Silva
Julia da Rocha Junqueira
Justino Duarte Santos
Kaléo Turnes Silvestri
Katia Pires N. do Sacramento
Keith Ando Ogawa
Keylly Santos
Leonardo Pereira de Sousa
Letícia Freire
Luan Portella da Silva
Lucas Candiani
Lucas Nardi Vieira
Lucas Okamura
Luciano Serafim de Souza
Luísa Santos
Madson Luiz Dantas Dias
Marcelo Gauy
Marco Vieira
Maria de Lourdes Maia Silva
Mariana O. Silva
Mariane R. Sponchiado Cassenote
Mariana Recamonde-Mendoza
Mariela Nina
Mateus Melchiades
Mateus Monteiro
Matheus Rocha
Mirlei Moura da Silva
Murilo de Barros
Nathália B. Santos
Nícolas Roque dos Santos
Paulo Knob
Pedro Bugatti
Pedro Cruz
Pedro DallAntonia
Pedro Hericson Machado Araújo
Pedro Pires
Rafael Berri
Rafael Passador
Rafael da Costa Silva
Razer A. N. R. Montaño
Renato da Costa Santos
Reni Aparecido Norberto Pinto
Richard Gonçalves
Rodrigo C. Barros
Ronaldo Wong
Rômulo Ferreira
Salomão Pena
Sandy Hoffmann
Thales Levi Valente
Thiago Henrique Freire de Oliveira
Thiago Lopes Trugillo da Silveira
Thiago Sikusawa
Victor Flávio de Andrade Araújo
Vinicius Wolosky Muchulski
Vitória Santos
Yuri A. de C. R. Sanchez

Contents

Main Track

Main Track

Towards a Noisy Estimation of Distribution Algorithm for Expensive Binary Optimization Problems

Matheus Bernardelli de Moraes(✉), Gilson Yuuji Shimizu, and Rodrigo Bonacin

Center for Information Technology Renato Archer, Campinas, São Paulo, Brazil
{mbmoraes,gyshimizu,rbonacin}@cti.gov.br

Abstract. Expensive Binary Optimization Problems (EBOPs) are non-linear optimization problems in which the decision space is represented using binary decision vectors. In time-consuming environments, the application of gradient-based or exact optimization algorithms is challenging. Hence, the research literature has focused on investigating metaheuristics to solve these expensive problems. Nonetheless, the vast majority of metaheuristics studied for this purpose were originally designed for continuous optimization problems, and only a few have been developed specifically for time-consuming problems with discrete domains. For this reason, this paper proposes a novel Estimation of Distribution Algorithm (EDA), named the Noisy Estimation of Distribution Algorithm (NEDA), to solve EBOPs. NEDA is a naive EDA that assumes independence between variables, constructs a probabilistic model from elite solutions, and injects Gaussian noise into the estimation process to improve convergence performance on EBOPs. An experimental comparison between NEDA and four other metaheuristics on 24 binary box-constrained test instances from six benchmark problems in the literature, with up to 100 decision variables and exhibiting characteristics similar to EBOPs, indicates that NEDA provides superior performance, achieving the highest average results in 12 test instances, with 8 additional instances tied for the best result.

Keywords: Combinatorial optimization · Evolutionary computation · Metaheuristics · Surrogate modeling · Unconstrained knapsack

1 Introduction

Many non-linear optimization problems can be represented with binary solution representations. In these cases, each decision variable represents a specific asset, and the binary values indicate whether the asset is present (1) or not (0) in a given solution [21]. This simple yet effective representation is used in various research and industrial applications, such as financial portfolio selection [13], feature selection [11], knapsack problems [27], task allocation [26], among others.

M. Recamonde-Mendoza and R. C. Barros (Eds.): BRACIS 2026, LNAI 17105, pp. 3–17, 2027.
https://doi.org/10.1007/978-3-032-39882-6_1

One example of a real-world engineering optimization problem that can be represented with a binary decision vector is the oil and gas well placement optimization (WPO) [4,14,20]. In a binary WPO, several candidate well positions are distributed on the reservoir surface using simulation models, and optimization algorithms attempt to find the subset of wells that maximizes or minimizes a given objective function. Each candidate well position can be either used or not, which allows the problem to be represented with a binary solution encoding. Each objective function evaluation requires a call to a time-consuming reservoir simulator, which forecasts the reservoir's fluid behavior under the selected well placement plan throughout the exploration life cycle [1]. Binary WPO is an example of an Expensive Binary Optimization Problem (EBOP). An EBOP can be formally defined using Eq. 1:

$$
\begin{aligned}
\max \quad & \mathcal{P} = (\mathbf{X}, f) \\
\text{s.t.} \quad & N_{\text{eval}} \leq N_{\max} \\
& \mathbf{X} = \begin{bmatrix} \mathbf{x}^1 \\ \mathbf{x}^2 \\ \vdots \\ \mathbf{x}^m \end{bmatrix}_{m \times n} = \begin{bmatrix} x_1^1 & x_2^1 & \cdots & x_n^1 \\ x_1^2 & x_2^2 & \cdots & x_n^2 \\ \vdots & \vdots & \ddots & \vdots \\ x_1^m & x_2^m & \cdots & x_n^m \end{bmatrix}_{m \times n} \\
& x_j^i \in \{0, 1\}, \forall i \in \{1, 2, \ldots, m\}, \forall j \in \{1, 2, \ldots, n\}
\end{aligned} \tag{1}
$$

where $\mathbf{X}$ is a set of feasible solutions of size m, and $f : \mathbf{X} \rightarrow \mathbb{R}$ is the objective function. Each $\mathbf{x} \in \mathbf{X}$ is an n-length binary vector. The optimization goal is to find an optimal solution $\mathbf{x}^* \in \arg\max_{\mathbf{x} \in X} f(\mathbf{x})$. In a time-consuming environment, the number of objective function evaluations (N_{eval}) cannot exceed the maximum allowed evaluations (N_{max}) due to time, computational, or financial limitations. If no additional constraints are present, the feasible search space is composed of $m = 2^n$ solutions.

As $\mathcal{P}$ is an expensive function, the application of gradient-based or exact optimization algorithms becomes challenging. For this reason, research on the use of metaheuristics for expensive optimization problems has increased in the past decade due to their derivative-free nature and ability to handle complex non-linear problems.

To the best of our knowledge, the majority of metaheuristics applied to expensive optimization problems were originally designed for continuous domains. For instance, research on metaheuristics for time-consuming problems often employs Particle Swarm Optimization [10], Covariance Matrix Adaptation Evolution Strategy [6], Differential Evolution [3], Grey Wolf Optimizer (GWO) [17], Sparrow Search [24], Cuckoo Search [2], Bat Algorithm [16], Black Widow Optimizer [19], and Imperialist Competitive Algorithm (ICA) [8], all of which contain internal mechanisms designed to handle continuous spaces. To adapt a continuous optimization algorithm to a binary domain, transfer functions are required [22].

Few single-objective metaheuristics have been proposed specifically for time-consuming environments with discrete domains, such as the Iterative Discrete

Latin Hypercube (IDLHC) [9] and the Regression-based Estimation of Distribution Algorithm (REDA) [4]. IDLHC and REDA are Estimation of Distribution Algorithms (EDAs) [12], a class of metaheuristics that has shown promising results in expensive environments. For this reason, this paper proposes a novel EDA named the Noisy Estimation of Distribution Algorithm (NEDA). NEDA is a naive EDA that assumes independence between variables, constructs a probabilistic model from elite solutions, and injects Gaussian noise into the estimation process to prevent premature convergence to local optima in EBOPs.

The main contributions of this work are summarized below:

- We propose NEDA, a novel approach that combines the framework of an EDA with a noise-based model-building strategy to solve EBOPs.
- We perform a comparative study between NEDA and a set of metaheuristics previously applied to time-consuming optimization problems, namely IDLHC, REDA, GWO, and ICA. We use several binary benchmark problems with different dimensionalities and landscape characteristcs, emulating conditions found in time-consuming environments. We also apply grid search to tune the hyper-parameters of the metaheuristics for each test instance.
- We apply statistical analysis to verify wether NEDA produces statistically significant improvements over the compared algorithms in EBOPs.

The remainder of this work is organized as follows. Section 2 introduces NEDA. Section 3 presents the experimental setup. Section 4 presents the results and discussions. Finally, Sect. 5 concludes this work and outlines directions for future research.

2 Proposed Method

Algorithm 1 presents the pseudocode of NEDA. It starts by creating empty values for the best solution found, $\mathbf{x}^*$, its corresponding objective function value, f^*, and the initial probabilistic model, $\mathbf{U}^{(\mathbf{0})}$. It also sets the N_{eval} counter to 0. Then, it randomly generates the initial population $\mathbf{Q}^{(\mathbf{0})}$ and evaluates each individual in it using the expensive objective function. From Line 5 onward, the main loop begins.

First, NEDA generates the current elite set $\mathbf{E}^{(t)}$ of size N_{elite}, where t is the current iteration. This procedure is straightforward: the solutions are ordered in descending order (for maximization) or ascending order (for minimization) based on their objective function values. The top N_{elite} solutions are selected and added to $\mathbf{E}^{(t)}$. In case of ties, equivalent solutions are selected randomly. Then, in Line 7, NEDA generates a new probabilistic model $\mathbf{U}^{(t+1)}$ using Algorithm 2. The model is built considering the frequencies observed in the elite solutions for each feasible value of each decision variable. This procedure can be formally defined as follows: let $\mathbf{E} = \{\mathbf{x}^{(1)}, \ldots, \mathbf{x}^{(N_{elite})}\}$ be the elite set and $V_j = \{v_{j1}, \ldots, v_{jK}\}$ the set of possible values for variable j. The empirical probability of $x_j = v_{jk}$ is estimated as:

$$p_{jk} = \frac{1}{N_{elite}} \sum_{i=1}^{N_{elite}} \delta(x_j^{(i)}, v_{jk}) \tag{2}$$

where $x_j^{(i)}$ is the j-th variable of the i-th vector present in the elite set, and $\delta(a, b) = 1$ if $a = b$ and 0 otherwise. The probability vector for variable j is $\mathbf{u}_j = (p_{j1}, \dots, p_{jK_j})$, and the overall probabilistic model matrix is $\mathbf{U} = [\mathbf{u}_1^\top, \dots, \mathbf{u}_n^\top]^\top$. The empirical probability is naive because unlike other probabilistic model approaches such as Bayesian Networks [18], variables are assumed to be independent of each other. As NEDA is designed for EBOPs, we can assume $V_j = \{0, 1\}$.

Algorithm 1. NEDA

Require: Population size N_{pop}, elite size N_{elite}, maximum evaluations $N_{\max}$, noise standard deviation σ

Ensure: Best solution found $\mathbf{x}^*$ and f^*.

Initialize $\mathbf{x}^* \leftarrow \emptyset$, $f^* \leftarrow -\infty$, $N_{\text{eval}} \leftarrow 0$
Initialize probabilistic model $\mathbf{U}^{(0)} \leftarrow \emptyset$
Generate randomly the initial population $\mathbf{Q}^{(0)}$ of size N_{pop}
Evaluate $f(\mathbf{x})$ for all $\mathbf{x} \in \mathbf{Q}^{(0)}$
while N_{eval}¡$N_{\max}$ **do**
    Select elite set $\mathbf{E}^{(t)}$ of size N_{elite}
    Build $\mathbf{U}^{(t+1)} \leftarrow \textsc{NoisyModelBuild}(\mathbf{U}^{(t)}, \mathbf{E}^{(t)}, \sigma)$
    Sample $\mathbf{Q}^{(t+1)}$ of size N_{pop} from $\mathbf{U}^{(t+1)}$
    Evaluate $f(\mathbf{x})$ for all $\mathbf{x} \in \mathbf{Q}^{(t+1)}$
    for each $\mathbf{x} \in \mathbf{Q}^{(t+1)}$ **do**
        if $f(\mathbf{x}) > f^*$ **then** ▷ In case of maximization
            $\mathbf{x}^* \leftarrow \mathbf{x}$
            $f^* \leftarrow f(\mathbf{x})$
        end if
    end for
    $N_{\text{eval}} \leftarrow N_{\text{eval}} + N_{\text{pop}}$
end while
return $\mathbf{x}^*, f^*$

Using the naive approach in an EBOP can easily cause the EDA to become trapped in a local optimum, as both N_{pop} and N_{elite} are likely small. Even if it does not become trapped, the mechanism of building the model using few samples may create sectors of deterministic sampling, i.e., when a feasible value has a 100% chance of being selected. In such scenarios, the probabilistic model is more likely to misrepresent the search space, which can negatively impact convergence. In a non-expensive environment, this would be easily overcome due to the large number of iterations, which may not occur in an EBOP. To avoid premature convergence to sub-optimal regions, NEDA adds a noise vector

ϵ sampled from a Gaussian distribution centered at zero to the naive estimations of each variable j using Eq. 3:

$$\tilde{u}_{j,k}^{(t+1)} = \frac{\max(u_{j,k}^{(t)} + \epsilon_{j,k}, 0)}{\sum_{\ell=1}^{m} \max(u_{j,\ell}^{(t)} + \epsilon_{j,\ell}, 0)}, \quad \text{where} \quad \epsilon_{j,k} \sim \mathcal{N}(0, \sigma^2). \tag{3}$$

where $\tilde{u}_{j,k}^{(t+1)}$ is the probability of variable j at iteration $t+1$ be k, $\epsilon_{j,k}$ is a Gaussian noise value, and σ is the noise standard deviation. The numerator keeps the entries non-negative, and the denominator rescales the vector so that its probabilities add up to 1.

Algorithm 2. Noisy Model Build

Require: elite set $\mathbf{E}^{(t)}$, noise standard deviation σ
Ensure: New model $\mathbf{U}^{(t+1)}$
1: Initialize $\mathbf{U}^{(t+1)} \leftarrow \emptyset$
2: **for** each variable x_j **do**
3: Estimate $\mathbf{u}_j^{(t+1)}$ from $\mathbf{E}^{(t)}$ ▷ Eq. 2
4: Apply noise: $\tilde{\mathbf{u}}_j^{(t+1)} = \mathcal{N}(\mathbf{u}_j^{(t+1)})$ ▷ Equation 3
5: Add $\tilde{\mathbf{u}}_j^{(t+1)}$ to $\mathbf{U}^{(t+1)}$
6: **end for**
7: **return** $\mathbf{U}^{(t+1)}$

Finally, after the new probabilistic model $\mathbf{U}^{(t+1)}$ is constructed, a new population $\mathbf{Q}^{(t+1)}$ of size N_{pop} is sampled from $\mathbf{U}^{(t+1)}$. Each solution $\mathbf{x} \in \mathbf{Q}^{(t+1)}$ is then evaluated using the expensive objective function. If any sampled solution yields a better result than the current best solution $\mathbf{x}^*$, it replaces $\mathbf{x}^*$. This procedures continues until the number of function evaluations N_{eval} reaches the maximum limit N_{max}.

2.1 Novelty and Limitations

To the best of our knowledge, NEDA is the first naive EDA to incorporate Gaussian noise into the estimation process as a mechanism to mitigate premature convergence and enhance exploration in EBOPs, achieving competitive performance (see Sect. 4). This distinguishes NEDA from existing approaches in the literature, which either rely on surrogate models or require user-defined parameters to redistribute probabilities among feasible values, as in REDA and IDLHC, respectively.

Despite its advantages, the proposed approach has certain limitations. In non-expensive environments, EDA population sizes, and consequently their elite subsets, tend to be large. Under such circumstances, injecting noise into the estimation process becomes unnecessary and may even slow convergence.

Furthermore, in other combinatorial optimization problems with larger or more complex search spaces (e.g., integer optimization problems), even within expensive environments, the probability of becoming trapped in deterministic sampling is lower because each decision variable can take on a greater number of feasible values. Therefore, NEDA is particularly suited for EBOPs and may not deliver a competitive performance in alternative problem settings.

3 Experimental Setup

This section presents the experimental analysis used to evaluate NEDA's performance under various conditions. NEDA was compared with two state-of-the-art discrete EDAs (IDLHC and REDA), and two continuous metaheuristics that have been previously applied to time-consuming optimization problems in the literature, namely GWO and ICA. Transfer functions are employed to allow these continuous methods to operate in binary domains.

A set of binary benchmark problems was selected according to the following criteria: (i) the problem must be binary; (ii) it must allow control over the dimensionality; and (iii) it must have a known global optimum vector and objective function. These characteristics enable the construction of challenging yet computationally inexpensive test instances suitable for evaluating the algorithms under different conditions. To emulate a time-consuming environment, the maximum number of objective function evaluations is constrained. Further details are provided in the following subsections.

3.1 Benchmark Problems

The first benchmark problem is the *Unconstrained Knapsack* (UK) [23], a non-linear, multimodal, box-constrained-only variant of the conventional Knapsack Problem in which the capacity constraint is removed. To avoid the trivial global optimum obtained by setting all decision variables to one, some item profits are allowed to be negative. The UK is defined in Eq. (4):

$$\begin{aligned} \max f(\mathbf{x}) = \sum_{j}^{n} x_j \cdot p_j \\ \text{s.t. } x_j \in \{0, 1\} \\ p_j \in [-\delta, +\delta] \end{aligned} \tag{4}$$

where δ is a given boundary and p_j is the profit of variable j. For the UK, the global optimum $\mathbf{x}^*$ is obtained using Eq. (5):

$$x_j^* = \begin{cases} 1, & \text{if } p_j > 0 \\ 0, & \text{otherwise} \end{cases}, \forall j \in \{1, \dots, n\} \tag{5}$$

where x_j^* is the j-*th* decision variable of $\mathbf{x}^*$. Hence, f^* is obtained through Eq. (6):

$$f^* = \sum_{j:p_j>0} p_j \tag{6}$$

The second benchmark is the *OneMax* (OM) [7], a well-known unimodal linear binary optimization problem. The goal is simply to maximize the number of 1 s in the binary string. Thus, the global optimum is $\mathbf{x}^* = [1, 1, \dots, 1]$ with $f^* = n$. Equation 7 defines the OM:

$$\max f(\mathbf{x}) = \sum_{j=1}^{n} x_j \tag{7}$$

The third benchmark is the *Leading Ones* (LO) [7], a classical non-linear unimodal binary optimization problem. It computes the number of consecutive 1 s from the left until the first 0 is encountered. The global optimum is $\mathbf{x}^* = [1, 1, \dots, 1]$ with $f^* = n$. Equation 8 defines the LO:

$$\max f(\mathbf{x}) = \sum_{i=1}^{n} \prod_{j=1}^{i} x_j \tag{8}$$

The next three benchmarks are variations of the *Solution Match Problem* [12], where the general goal is to find a solution that matches a given arbitrary target vector $\mathbf{x}^*$. Equation (9) defines a *Quadratic Binary* (QB) maximization problem. The squared Euclidean distance $||\mathbf{x} - \mathbf{x}^*||^2$ is zero when $\mathbf{x} = \mathbf{x}^*$ and strictly positive otherwise. The negative sign converts this into a maximization problem, yielding negative values for any non-optimal solution. Thus, the global optimum occurs when $\mathbf{x} = \mathbf{x}^*$, with $f^* = 0$.

$$\max f(\mathbf{x}) = -||\mathbf{x} - \mathbf{x}^*||^2 \tag{9}$$

Next, Eq. (10) defines an *Exponential Binary* (EB) maximization problem. Similarly, the objective depends on the squared distance to the target vector, but through an exponential transformation with $\alpha > 0$. The function attains its maximum value when $\mathbf{x} = \mathbf{x}^*$ since $exp(0) = 1$, and decreases monotonically as the distance increases. Therefore, the global optimum is achieved at $\mathbf{x} = \mathbf{x}^*$, with $f^* = 1$.

$$\max f(\mathbf{x}) = \exp(-\alpha||\mathbf{x} - \mathbf{x}^*||^2) \tag{10}$$

Finally, Eq. (11) defines a *Product Binary* (PB) maximization problem. Given a binary vector $\mathbf{x}$ and a target vector $\mathbf{x}^*$, each component contributes multiplicatively to the objective function. If $x_i = x_i^*$, the corresponding factor is 1;

otherwise, it is $1+\beta$, with $\beta > 0$. Thus, each mismatch increases the product by a factor of $1+\beta$. The negative sign ensures that solutions with more mismatches yield lower objective values. Therefore, the global optimum is when $\mathbf{x} = \mathbf{x}^*$ and $f^* = -1$.

$$\max f(\mathbf{x}) = -\prod_i (1 + \beta|x_i - x_i^*|) \tag{11}$$

The benchmark functions UK, OM, LO, QB, EB, and PB provide a controllable, challenging, but easy-to-compute test environment to evaluate NEDA and its competitors in the experimental setup. For all problems, four instances were created by varying the number of variables such that $n \in \{25, 50, 75, 100\}$. Thus, there were a total of 24 test instances with different dimensionalities and landscapes. The profits generated for the UK were random values drawn from a uniform distribution in the interval [-5,5]. We set the parameters $\alpha = 0.01$ and $\beta = 0.01$ for the EB and PB problems across all test instances.

3.2 Transfer Functions

To allow originally continuous metaheuristics to optimize binary solution representations, this work uses three transfer functions obtained from Saremi et al. [22]. They are the sigmoid function:

$$T(\mathbf{x}) = \frac{1}{1 + e^{-\mathbf{x}}} \tag{12}$$

The tanh function:

$$T(\mathbf{x}) = |\tanh(\mathbf{x})| \tag{13}$$

And a v-shaped transfer function termed in this manuscript as "v3":

$$T(\mathbf{x}) = |\frac{\mathbf{x}}{\sqrt{1 + \mathbf{x}^2}}| \tag{14}$$

These functions returns a probability of a value being 1. After computing the probability, a threshold step is used for each variable $x_j \in \mathbf{x}$:

$$x_j = \begin{cases} 1 \text{ if } rand() < T(x_j) \\ 0 \text{otherwise} \end{cases} \tag{15}$$

where $rand()$ is a uniformly distributed random number in [0,1]. This procedure is standard for converting a continuous vector into a binary vector. [22].

3.3 Hyper-parameter Tuning

This study conducts a sensitivity analysis for hyper-parameter tuning across all test instances and benchmark problems using an exhaustive grid-search procedure. Table 1 lists the candidate values considered for each hyper-parameter of every algorithm. Each hyper-parameter combination is evaluated over 31 independent runs. The best configuration for each algorithm is defined as the one achieving the highest average objective value across these 31 runs. The runs are paired by seed.

Table 1. Grid search parameter configurations for the tested optimization algorithms.

Algorithm	Parameter	Possible values
GWO	N_{pop} (population size)	[5, 10, 20, 25]
	Transfer function	[Sigmoid, Tanh, V3]
ICA	N_{pop} (population size)	[5, 10, 20, 25]
	$N_{imperialists}$ (elite size)	[2,3,4,5]
	β (assimilation rate)	[0.2,0.4,0.6,0.8]
	p_{rev} (revolution rate)	[0.01,0.05,0.10]
	Transfer function	[Sigmoid, Tanh, V3]
REDA	N_{pop} (population size)	[5, 10, 20, 25]
	N_{elite} (elite size)	[2, 3, 4, 5]
IDLHC	N_{pop} (population size)	[5, 10, 20, 25]
	N_{elite} (elite size)	[2, 3, 4, 5]
	p_{cut} (probability cut)	[0.1,0.2,0.3]
NEDA	N_{pop} (population size)	[5, 10, 20, 25]
	N_{elite} (elite size)	[2, 3, 4, 5]
	σ (noise control)	[0.05, 0.10, 0.20]

The maximum number of evaluations was used as the stopping criterion, which was set to $N_{\text{max}} = 200$ for each test, a reasonable value for time-consuming environments. Hence, the number of iterations is defined as $\frac{N_{max}}{N_{pop}}$. The parameter f of REDA was set as $f = N_{pop} \times 2$ for all instances as greater values were time-impeditive for a grid search.

4 Results and Discussions

The numerical efficiency of the NEDA developed in this manuscript was tested by solving 24 test instances from six classical binary benchmark functions of the optimization literature. The benchmark suite used in this study covers a diverse range of problem characteristics. OM and LO evaluate the ability of algorithms to exploit fitness gradients, while the UK and PB functions introduce non-linear structures and epistatic interactions that challenge global search. The EB and QB benchmarks evaluates robustness under smooth but steep fitness landscapes. This diversity ensures that the conclusions drawn from the experiments are not limited to a particular type of binary optimization structure.

Table 2 presents the results obtained by each algorithm on each test instance. NEDA achieved the best results in 12 out of the 24 test instances, with 8 additional instances tied for the best result, followed by IDLHC (8 out 24), REDA (4 out of 24), GWO (4 out of 24), and ICA (0 out of 24). As observed, IDLHC and REDA produced the closest results to NEDA. This indicates that native discrete methods may surpass continuous methods adapted to discrete domains in certain problems.

Table 2. Mean ± Standard deviation on the benchmark problems over 31 independent runs according to the number of decision variables (n). The best results are highlighted in bold (higher is better).

Problem	n	GWO	ICA	IDLHC	REDA	NEDA
OM	25	23.8 ± 0.6	21.8 ± 0.8	24.5 ± 0.8	23.9 ± 1.1	**24.9** ± 0.2
	50	45.2 ± 1.1	40.3 ± 1.4	47.5 ± 1.2	43.3 ± 1.8	**48.2** ± 1.1
	75	65.9 ± 1.4	57.8 ± 1.3	67.8 ± 2.0	60.4 ± 2.1	**69.2** ± 1.8
	100	86.0 ± 1.7	75.3 ± 1.6	88.0 ± 2.1	77.0 ± 2.5	**88.1** ± 2.5
LO	25	**15.6** ± 3.8	12.7 ± 2.5	8.0 ± 2.8	13.1 ± 2.9	10.5 ± 3.2
	50	**17.1** ± 4.8	12.7 ± 2.8	8.3 ± 3.0	13.7 ± 2.6	11.4 ± 3.3
	75	**15.9** ± 5.6	11.3 ± 2.6	7.2 ± 2.5	14.0 ± 2.6	10.8 ± 2.7
	100	**15.8** ± 4.1	12.4 ± 2.9	8.8 ± 3.3	13.7 ± 2.8	11.1 ± 2.8
UK	25	22.3 ± 1.9	22.0 ± 2.1	29.3 ± 0.9	28.7 ± 1.1	**30.0** ± 0.4
	50	42.0 ± 4.1	42.6 ± 4.8	70.6 ± 3.1	62.1 ± 3.8	**71.9** ± 2.7
	75	19.0 ± 3.9	18.3 ± 4.7	59.5 ± 4.6	43.4 ± 4.3	**62.3** ± 4.2
	100	39.4 ± 6.8	37.2 ± 5.5	95.5 ± 5.9	74.3 ± 5.7	**98.5** ± 5.7
PB	25	−1.1 ± 0.0	−1.1 ± 0.0	**-1.0** ± 0.0	**-1.0** ± 0.0	**-1.0** ± 0.0
	50	−1.2 ± 0.0	−1.2 ± 0.0	**-1.0** ± 0.0	−1.1 ± 0.0	**-1.0** ± 0.0
	75	−1.3 ± 0.0	−1.3 ± 0.0	**-1.1** ± 0.0	**-1.1** ± 0.0	**-1.1** ± 0.0
	100	−1.4 ± 0.0	−1.4 ± 0.0	**-1.1** ± 0.0	−1.2 ± 0.0	**-1.1** ± 0.0
EB	25	0.9 ± 0.0	0.9 ± 0.0	**1.0** ± 0.0	**1.0** ± 0.0	**1.0** ± 0.0
	50	0.9 ± 0.0	0.9 ± 0.0	**1.0** ± 0.0	0.9 ± 0.0	**1.0** ± 0.0
	75	0.8 ± 0.0	0.8 ± 0.0	**0.9** ± 0.0	**0.9** ± 0.0	**0.9** ± 0.0
	100	0.7 ± 0.0	0.7 ± 0.0	**0.9** ± 0.0	0.8 ± 0.0	**0.9** ± 0.0
QB	25	−5.5 ± 1.1	−5.6 ± 0.9	−0.5 ± 0.7	−1.2 ± 0.8	**0.0** ± 0.2
	50	−15.0 ± 1.6	−15.5 ± 1.3	−2.5 ± 1.2	−7.0 ± 1.7	**-1.6** ± 1.5
	75	−25.1 ± 1.8	−24.9 ± 1.8	−6.5 ± 2.2	−13.9 ± 2.8	**-5.9** ± 2.1
	100	−36.4 ± 2.4	−36.6 ± 1.7	−11.8 ± 2.5	−22.5 ± 2.5	**-11.2** ± 2.9

In order to further analyze the performance of the proposed NEDA, Fig. 1 presents the box plots of the best objective function values achieved by each algorithm over 31 independent runs. NEDA achieved the overall best results, with the exception of the LO benchmark. It also exhibits lower variability among the independent runs compared to the other metaheuristics. The box plots also reveal qualitative differences in robustness. While methods such as GWO occasionally achieve competitive best-case values, their distributions are considerably more dispersed, with long upper whiskers indicating unstable convergence behavior. REDA shows moderate variability but still exhibits frequent outliers, likely due to its dependency on surrogate model accuracy. In contrast, NEDA displays both low median and tight interquartile ranges, evidencing that its performance is not only strong on average but also consistent across independent runs.

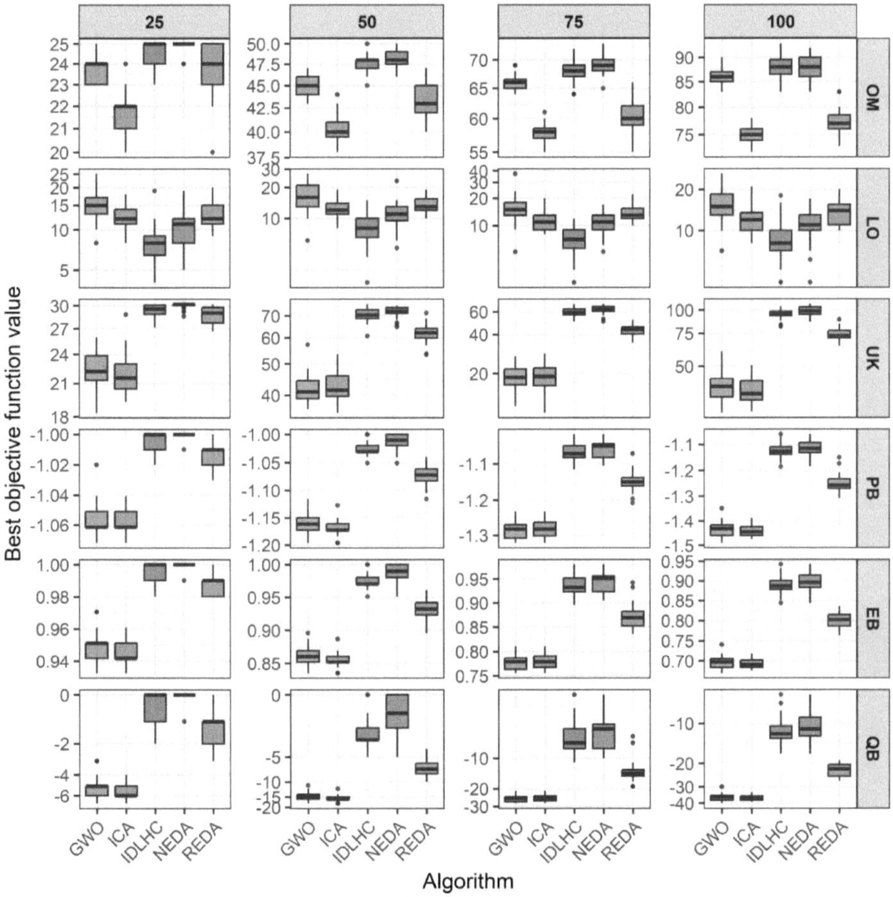

Fig. 1. Boxplot of the best objective function achieved by each algorithm over 31 independent runs.

The unilateral Wilcoxon signed-rank test [25] was applied to assess whether NEDA's performance was statistically superior to that of its competitors. Figure 2 illustrates the Wilcoxon test results. NEDA is statistically superior to GWO, ICA, and REDA (p-value < 0.01) in all benchmarks except for the LO benchmark. NEDA is also superior to IDLHC in the UK and LO benchmarks across all dimensionalities, and it remains superior in the remaining problems when $n < 50$ (p-value < 0.05).

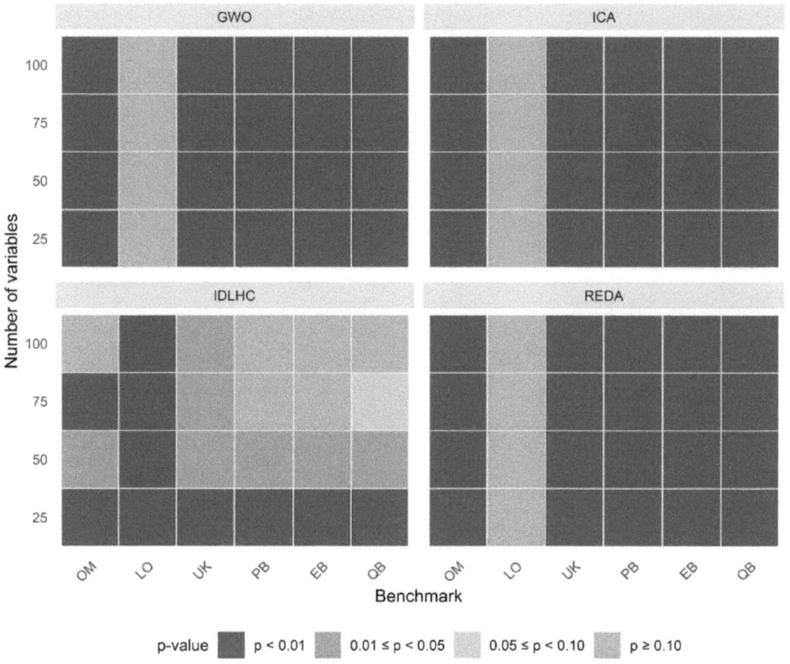

Fig. 2. Results of the unilateral Wilcoxon test, assessing whether NEDA is statistically superior to each competitor for a given problem and dimensionality. Red and orange indicate that NEDA is superior, yellow indicates statistical equivalence, and grey indicates that NEDA is inferior. (Color figure online)

One interesting aspect we observed is that the probability cutoff of IDLHC was never actually triggered during the optimization. This occurred because the empirical probabilities never reached the threshold for probability redistribution, due to the low number of individuals in the population. It indicates that, under small population sizes, the probability of unimportant feasible values decreases slowly, preventing the mechanism from engaging. This effectively reduces IDLHC to a standard naive discrete EDA such as the Univariate Marginal Distribution Algorithm (UMDA) [15], losing one of its key diversity-preserving components. NEDA avoids this limitation by adding Gaussian noise directly to the probability estimates, ensuring that the search distribution remains dynamic even in low-population scenarios.

Compared to REDA, NEDA also achieved superior results. REDA employs a surrogate model (Random Forest) to evaluate promising candidate solutions before performing the actual expensive evaluations. Although surrogate modeling is more complex and has received significant attention in the research literature [4,5], the results indicate that injecting noise into the estimations of a naive EDA can actually yield better performance in EBOPs. This may be attributed to the surrogate model's sensitivity to uninformative samples in early iterations, which can mislead the Random Forest predictions and propagate errors into the selection of candidate solutions. NEDA avoids this issue by maintaining a direct probabilistic search model and enhancing it with controlled noise, which appears to provide a more reliable balance between exploration and exploitation in EBOPs.

Overall, the experimental results demonstrate that NEDA provides a robust alternative to existing metaheuristics for binary optimization, as statistical analysis confirms the consistency of its improvements. The method not only surpasses other discrete EDAs such as IDLHC and REDA but also outperforms continuous-domain algorithms adapted to binary spaces, reinforcing the importance of native discrete modeling. These findings demonstrates the potential effectiveness of noise-driven probabilistic updates in enhancing a naive EDA performance.

5 Conclusions and Future Work

This study proposes a novel Noisy Estimation of Distribution Algorithm (NEDA) to address expensive binary optimization problems (EBOPs). NEDA assumes independence among variables to construct a probabilistic model from elite solutions while injecting Gaussian noise into the estimation process. Evaluated on 24 test instances from six benchmark problems and compared against four state-of-the-art metaheuristics, the method achieved the best results in 12 test instances, with 8 additional instances tied for the best result.

As for future work, although NEDA has shown competitive results, it has yet to be evaluated on a real-world EBOP. For this reason, we plan to apply NEDA to a binary oil and gas well placement optimization problem. Additionally, it would be important to investigate strategies to avoid introducing a new hyper-parameter, as performing sensitivity analysis in time-consuming environments can be impractical.

Acknowledgments. The authors acknowledge the use of Generative AI for English grammar revision.

Data Availibility Statement. The source code of the experimental setup, the global optimum for the UK test instances, the best hyper-parameter combination as well as the results files can be found in https://github.com/mbdemoraes/bracis-2026-neda-open-data.

Disclosure of Interests. The authors have no competing interests to declare that are relevant to the content of this article.

References

1. Schiozer, D.J., Santos, A.A., Drumond, P.S.: Integrated model based decision analysis in twelve steps applied to petroleum fields development and management. Paper presented at the EUROPEC 2015, Madrid, Spain (2015). https://doi.org/10.2118/174370-MS
2. Alghareeb, Z.M., Walton, S.P., Williams, J.R.: Well placement optimization under constraints using modified cuckoo search. In: SPE Saudi Arabia Section Technical Symposium and Exhibition. SPE (2014). https://doi.org/10.2118/172841-MS
3. Awotunde, A.A.: Inclusion of well schedule and project life in well placement optimization. In: SPE Nigeria Annual International Conference and Exhibition. SPE (2014). https://doi.org/10.2118/172386-MS
4. Brum, A., Coelho, G., Santos, A.A., Schiozer, D.J.: Estimation of distribution algorithms for well placement optimization in petroleum fields. Comput. Geosci. **29**(2), (2025). https://doi.org/10.1007/s10596-024-10331-9
5. De Moraes, M.B., Coelho, G.P.: A random forest-assisted decomposition-based evolutionary algorithm for multi-objective combinatorial optimization problems. IEEE Congress on Evolutionary Computation (CEC), pp, 1–8 (2022). https://doi.org/10.1109/CEC55065.2022.9870412
6. Ding, D.Y.: Optimization of well placement using evolutionary algorithms. In: Europec/EAGE Conference and Exhibition. SPE (2008). https://doi.org/10.2118/113525-MS
7. Doerr, C., Ye, F., Horesh, N., Wang, H., Shir, O.M., Bäck, T.: Benchmarking discrete optimization heuristics with iohprofiler. Appl. Soft Comput. **88**, 106027 (2020). https://doi.org/10.1016/j.asoc.2019.106027
8. Dossary, M.A.A., Nasrabadi, H.: Well placement optimization using imperialist competitive algorithm. J. Petrol. Sci. Eng. **147**(11), 237–248 (2016). https://doi.org/10.1016/j.petrol.2016.06.017
9. von Hohendorff Filho, J.C., Maschio, C., Schiozer, D.J.: Production strategy optimization based on iterative discrete latin hypercube. J. Braz. Soc. Mech. Sci. Eng. **38**, 2473–2480 (2016). https://doi.org/10.1007/s40430-016-0511-0
10. Hutahaean, J., Demyanov, V., Arnold, D., Vazquez, O.: Optimization of well placement to minimize the risk of scale deposition in field development. In: Abu Dhabi International Petroleum Exhibition and Conference. SPE (2014).https://doi.org/10.2118/171733-MS
11. Keleş, M.K., Kiliç, U.: Binary black widow optimization approach for feature selection. IEEE Access **10**, 95936–95948 (2022). https://doi.org/10.1109/ACCESS.2022.3204046
12. Larranaga, P., Lozano, J.A.: Estimation of distribution algorithms: a new tool for evolutionary computation, Kluwer Academic Publishers (2002)
13. Markowitz, H.: Portfolio selection. J. Financ. **7**(1), 77–91 (1952)
14. de Moraes, M.B., Coelho, G.P., Santos, A.A.S., Schiozer, D.J.: Binary well placement optimization using a decomposition-based multi-objective evolutionary algorithm with diversity preservation. Comput. Geosci. **27**, 765–782 (2023). https://doi.org/10.1007/s10596-023-10235-0

15. Mühlenbein, H.: The equation for response to selection and its use for prediction. Evol. Comput. **5**(3), 303–346 (1997). https://doi.org/10.1162/evco.1997.5.3.303
16. Naderi, M., Khamehchi, E.: Well placement optimization using metaheuristic bat algorithm. J. Petrol. Sci. Eng. **150**, 348–354 (2017). https://doi.org/10.1016/j.petrol.2016.12.028
17. Ocran, D., Ikiensikimama, S.S., Broni-Bediako, E.: Grey wolf optimizer for solving well placement optimization problem constrained to minimum well distance. Pet. Sci. Technol. **41**(14), 1391–1413 (2023). https://doi.org/10.1080/10916466.2022.2092507
18. Pelikan, M., Sastry, K., Goldberg, D.E.: Scalability of the bayesian optimization algorithm. Int. J. Approximate Reas. **31**(3), 221–258 (2002). https://doi.org/10.1016/S0888-613X(02)00095-6, https://www.sciencedirect.com/science/article/pii/S0888613X02000956
19. Raji, S., Dehnamaki, A., Somee, B., Mahdiani, M.R.: A new approach in well placement optimization using metaheuristic algorithms. J. Petroleum Sci. Eng. **215** (2022). https://doi.org/10.1016/j.petrol.2022.110640
20. Bertini, J.R., Batista, S.F., Funcia, M.A., da Silva, L.O.M., Santos, A.A.S., Schiozer, D.J.: A comparison of machine learning surrogate models for net present value prediction from well placement binary data. J. Petrol. Sci. Eng. **208**, 109208, ISSN 0920-4105 (2022). https://doi.org/10.1016/j.petrol.2021.109208
21. Salo, A., Doumpos, M., Liesiö, J., Zopounidis, C.: Fifty years of portfolio optimization. Eur. J. Oper. Res. **318**(1), 1–18 (2024). https://doi.org/10.1016/j.ejor.2023.12.031
22. Saremi, S., Mirjalili, S., Lewis, A.: How important is a transfer function in discrete heuristic algorithms. Neural Comput. Appl. **26**(4), 625–640 (2015). https://doi.org/10.1007/s00521-014-1743-5
23. Schulze, B., Klamroth, K., Stiglmayr, M.: Multi-objective unconstrained combinatorial optimization: a polynomial bound on the number of extreme supported solutions. J. of Global Optimization **74**(3), 495–522 (2019). https://doi.org/10.1007/s10898-019-00745-6
24. Tabatabaei, S.M., Asadian-Pakfar, M., Sedaee, B.: Well placement optimization with a novel swarm intelligence optimization algorithm: sparrow search algorithm. Geoenergy Sci. Eng. **231** (2023). https://doi.org/10.1016/j.geoen.2023.212291
25. Wilcoxon, F.: Individual comparisons by ranking methods. Biom. Bulletin **1**(6), 80–83 (1945). http://www.jstor.org/stable/3001968
26. Yang, J., Zhang, H., Ling, Y., Pan, C., Sun, W.: Task allocation for wireless sensor network using modified binary particle swarm optimization. IEEE Sens. J. **14**(3), 882–892 (2014). https://doi.org/10.1109/JSEN.2013.2290433
27. Zitzler, E., Thiele, L.: Multiobjective evolutionary algorithms: a comparative case study and the strength pareto approach. IEEE Trans. Evol. Comput. **3**(4), 257–271 (1999). https://doi.org/10.1109/4235.797969

Contrastive Deep Graph Clustering with Dynamic Cluster Estimation

Tiago Gonçalves Botelho[1,2](✉), Guilherme Henrique Messias[1], Alan Demétrius Baria Valejo[1], and Murilo Coelho Naldi[1]

[1] Universidade Federal de São Carlos, Sao Carlos, SP, Brazil
ghmessias@estudante.ufscar.br, {alanvalejo,naldi}@ufscar.br
[2] Instituto Federal do Sul de Minas Gerais - Campus Muzambinho, Muzambinho, MG, Brazil
tiago.botelho@muz.ifsuldeminas.edu.br

Abstract. Deep clustering on attributed graphs is a fundamental data mining task, identifying latent communities based on topological and attribute similarity without requiring labels. Although the use of Graph Neural Networks has advanced the state of the art, most existing approaches still rely on predefining the number of clusters (k), a limitation that hinders their applicability in scenarios where no prior knowledge about the true number of classes is available. Moreover, the few current solutions for autonomous estimation of k face critical challenges, such as producing weakly discriminative representations or exhibiting a tendency to overestimate the number of clusters. In this context, this work proposes Contrastive Attentional Dynamic Graph Clustering (CADGC), a framework primarily focused on the precise and autonomous estimation of k. Based on the hypothesis that accurate discovery of k directly depends on the separability of the latent space, CADGC integrates Graph Attention Networks and contrast learning to maximize embedding discriminability. Additionally, we introduce a local confidence regularization that stabilizes assignments and allows inferring the optimal k. Experiments on multiple benchmarks demonstrate that CADGC maintains competitive clustering quality (Accuracy and Normalized Mutual Information) while significantly improving autonomous estimation: it achieved exact convergence of the number of clusters in dense topologies and reduced estimation variance by 50% in complex scenarios, outperforming existing baselines. CADGC has established itself as a competitive solution for real-world scenarios with unknown cluster structures.

Keywords: Deep Graph Clustering · Representation Learning · Cluster Estimation · Contrastive Learning

1 Introduction

The growing digitization and interconnection of data has generated an abundance of information that can be naturally represented as graphs [5,8,13].

M. Recamonde-Mendoza and R. C. Barros (Eds.): BRACIS 2026, LNAI 17105, pp. 18–33, 2027.
https://doi.org/10.1007/978-3-032-39882-6_2

Extracting the latent cluster structure from these data by clustering is a fundamental challenge in domains ranging from social networks [4,20] to biological systems [10,24]. With the rise of deep learning models, Graph Neural Networks (GNNs) have emerged as the state of the art, enabling the learning of representations (embeddings) that preserve structural and semantic relationships [3,9].

Despite their success, applications of GNNs to deep clustering expose limitations in real-world scenarios. A critical limitation of existing deep graph clustering methods lies in their reliance on a predefined number of clusters (k), which is rarely known in real-world scenarios, or estimating it using heuristics disconnected from representation learning. Recent approaches, although they incorporate topology through convolutions, prioritize optimization objectives focused on semantic cohesion, leaving structural information underexplored [11]. In contrast, purely topological approaches focus on optimizing quality metrics such as modularity [1], neglecting the richness of information provided by node attributes for reliable cluster estimation. This dichotomy results in suboptimal representations or inaccurate estimates of the number of clusters.

In this work, we argue that the accuracy (ACC) of the automatic cluster number estimation k is intrinsically related to the separability of the latent space. To overcome this limitation, we propose Contrastive Attentional Dynamic Graph Clustering (CADGC), a novel framework that integrates the expressiveness of Graph Attention Networks (GAT) [17] with the discriminative capability of Contrastive Learning (CL) [6]. Unlike previous works that employ CL solely to enhance representations, we investigate its direct impact on autonomous cluster estimation, showing that embedding separability stabilizes parameter-free selection k by explicitly shaping the geometry of the latent space. To operationalize this discovery, we introduce a local-confidence regularization mechanism that stabilizes cluster assignments, allowing the model to eliminate redundant dimensions (drop-cluster) and estimate the optimal (k) without requiring prior knowledge.

The proposed framework was implemented and subjected to rigorous validation using multiple benchmark datasets from various domains. The experimental protocol was structured into three main stages: (i) an ablation study to isolate and validate the individual contributions of the attention mechanism and contrast loss; (ii) an evaluation of clustering performance (with fixed k) compared against a representative baseline from the literature and ablation variants; and (iii) a study on the effectiveness of autonomously estimating the number of clusters (k), contrasting the precision of the proposed model with the baseline method and the data ground truth (GT). Our main contributions are:

- We propose the first unified framework that integrates GAT and CL, adapted for automatic cluster estimation on attributed graphs. Unifying these approaches yields a latent space that is more representative of the underlying clusters;
- We introduce a novel local-confidence regularization mechanism that stabilizes flexible cluster assignments and improves the stability of the k estimate;

- We conducted a comprehensive experimental study, including a parametric sensitivity analysis, demonstrating competitive cluster quality (ACC and Normalized Mutual Information - NMI) and advances in autonomous cluster number estimation: CADGC achieved exact recovery of the number of clusters in dense topologies and reduced estimation variance by 50% in complex scenarios, outperforming strong baselines.

Our findings suggest that improving latent space geometry enables reliable and scalable unsupervised graph clustering under unknown structures.

The remainder of this paper is organized as follows: Sect. 2 presents the definition of the problem and reviews GNN models and cluster-number estimation methods related to our approach. Section 3 introduces the proposed model. Section 4 reports the experimental results of our model and the baselines. Conclusions and future work are described in Sect. 5.

2 Background and Related Work

Formally, the problem addressed in this work considers a homogeneous attributed graph, represented as the ordered triple $G = (V, E, X)$, where $V = \{v_1, v_2, \cdots, v_n\}$ denotes the vertices or nodes, E represents the edges connecting these vertices, capturing the network's topological structure. Connectivity is described by the adjacency matrix $A \in \mathbb{R}^{n \times n}$, where $A_{ij} = 1$ indicates the existence of an edge between v_i and v_j, and 0 otherwise. In addition to the structure, each vertex v_i has a feature vector $x_i \in \mathbb{R}^d$, forming the attribute matrix $X \in \mathbb{R}^{n \times d}$. Vertex clustering partitions V into k disjoint sets $C = \{C_1, \ldots, C_k\}$ such that vertices within the same cluster C_i maximize their topological and semantic similarity while minimizing similarity with vertices from other clusters [21].

To solve this optimization problem without using labels, the literature has converged on Self-Supervised Representation Learning (SSR), which underpins modern GNNs. Early methods, such as DAEGC [18] and SDCN [2], predominantly focus on reconstructing the structure or attributes. However, a more recent and sophisticated line of SSR, termed Self-Separation Regularization, argues that simple reconstruction is insufficient for clustering. This approach proposes directly refining the geometry of the latent space by operating on pairwise affinities ($N \times N$) rather than only on vertex-to-centroid assignments. The strategy consists of minimizing the Kullback–Leibler (KL) divergence between the current similarity distribution and a sharper auxiliary target distribution (typically via a t-Student kernel), penalizing medium-confidence connections and enforcing a clearer separation among clusters [11,19]. Although effective in preserving global information, these generative losses often prioritize low-level details at the expense of the high-level semantics required for clustering, failing to ensure clear separability among clusters in the latent space.

To mitigate the limitations of these generative losses, CL has emerged as an effective approach to improving the quality of latent representations. By focusing on instance discrimination, CL follows a distinct philosophy: it maximizes similarity between augmented views of the same node (generated, for example, via attribute masking or edge perturbation) and minimizes it with respect to negative pairs, thereby learning representations that are invariant to local noise [13,23]. Recent works [12] show that this approach enforces a clear geometric separation, which is fundamental for clustering.

However, despite the superiority of contrastive representations, a fundamental limitation persists in most of these frameworks: the dependence on a predefined number of clusters k to obtain the final partition. Automatic determination of k remains an open challenge [14]. Few initiatives, such as SP-DAGC [11] and DGCluster [1], attempt to estimate k via Softmax Autoencoders or modularity optimization, but often underexploit the correlation between structure and attributes or rely on external algorithms. In contrast to recent approaches, our proposal directly links representation learning and cluster number estimation through contrastive objectives and adaptive pruning. By jointly modeling structural attention and discriminative embeddings, we provide a unified solution for both clustering and automatic estimation of k.

3 Proposed Method: The Framework CADGC

In this section, we present the proposed framework (CADGC), designed to overcome the limitations of methods based on convolutions and simple geometric regularizations. An overview of the architecture is shown in Fig. 1. Although conceptually inspired by two-stage frameworks in the literature, such as SP-DAGC, our approach differs fundamentally from these baselines by employing attention mechanisms to capture dynamic structural relationships and contrastive objectives to explicitly shape the geometry of the latent space.

3.1 Attention Encoder and Structural Reconstruction

The core component is an Encoder based on GAT. Unlike SP-DAGC, which uses Graph Convolutional Network (GCN), GAT computes normalized attention coefficients α_{ij} to weight the importance of each neighbor [17], enabling the capture of more subtle community structures [18]:

$$z_i = \sigma\left(\sum_{j\in\mathcal{N}_i} \alpha_{ij} W \boldsymbol{h}_j\right) \tag{1}$$

where z_i is the latent representation of vertex i, $\mathcal{N}_i$ denotes the set of neighbors, W is the learned weight matrix, h_j is the attribute vector, α_{ij} is the normalized attention coefficient that indicates the importance of neighbor j to vertex i, and $\sigma(\cdot)$ is a non-linear activation function (typically ELU or ReLU).

To preserve fundamental graph properties, the encoder is trained with two auxiliary reconstruction losses: $\mathcal{L}_{attr}$ (Attribute Reconstruction via Mean Squared Error (MSE)) and $\mathcal{L}_{struct}$ (Topology Reconstruction via Binary Cross Entropy (BCE)), which ensures data fidelity in the latent space.

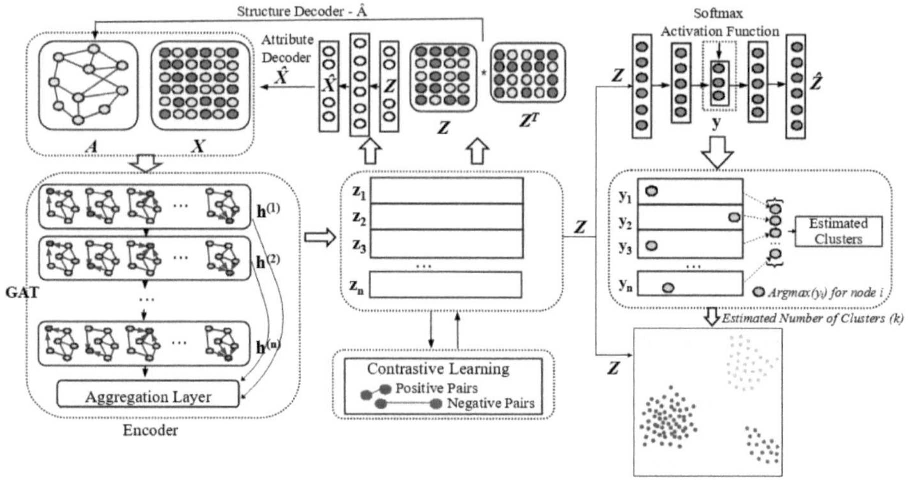

Fig. 1. Overview of the CADGC framework. The model processes the graph through a GAT Encoder optimized via CL and Dual Reconstruction, feeding a Softmax Autoencoder (SAE) module for autonomous estimation of the number of clusters (k).

3.2 Optimization via Contrastive Learning

The main innovation of the framework lies in replacing geometric regularization (SSR) with CL. We generate correlated views of the graph by applying stochastic perturbations (attribute masking and edge removal). The contrastive loss function (NT-Xent) [6] is applied to bring positive pairs closer and push negative pairs apart:

$$\mathcal{L}_{CL} = -\log \frac{\exp(\text{sim}(z_i, z_j)/\tau)}{\sum_{k=1}^{2N} \mathbb{1}_{[k\neq i]} \exp(\text{sim}(z_i, z_k)/\tau)} \tag{2}$$

where $\text{sim}(z_i, z_j)$ denotes the cosine similarity between vectors z_i and z_j, τ is a *Temperature* parameter that controls the hardness of separating negatives, and $\mathbb{1}_{[k\neq i]}$ is an indicator function that prevents comparing a sample with itself. This loss acts directly on the discriminative quality of the embedding, facilitating the subsequent task of cluster estimation.

3.3 Cluster Estimation Module

For the automatic determination of k, we adopt an architecture based on the Softmax Autoencoder (SAE), inspired by the SP-DAGC method [11]. The goal of this module is to project the embeddings into a probability space of dimension d_c and identify the number of active clusters.

We introduce a modification to the regularization strategy compared to the original work. While SP-DAGC applies the Gini index over the marginal distribution (columns) to enforce global sparsity, our approach proposes a Local Confidence Regularization. The estimator module loss is defined by:

$$\mathcal{L}_{est} = ||Z - \hat{Z}||^2 + \beta\mathcal{L}_{conf} \tag{3}$$

where the term $\mathcal{L}_{conf}$ penalizes ambiguous assignments, encouraging each vertex to have high confidence in its membership in a cluster:

$$\mathcal{L}_{conf} = -\frac{1}{N}\sum_{i=1}^{N}\sum_{j=1}^{d_c}(P_{ij})^2 \tag{4}$$

where $Z \in \mathbb{R}^{N\times d}$ is the frozen embedding matrix produced by the GAT encoder, $\hat{Z}$ is the matrix reconstructed by the SAE decoder, β controls the weight of the confidence regularization, N is the total number of vertices, d_c defines the maximum cluster capacity (upper bound) and P_{ij} denotes the probability that vertex i belongs to cluster j.

In practice, the model does not increase the number of clusters, but instead performs a pruning operation (*drop-cluster*) from an upper bound d_c. Since Softmax activation ensures that the probabilities for each vertex sum to 1, minimizing $\mathcal{L}_{conf}$ is equivalent to maximizing $(P_{ij})^2$, thus encouraging the network to assign a probability of approximately 1 to a single cluster and 0 to the others (i.e., minimizing entropy). For example, when initializing $d_c = 20$ in a graph with only 5 well-defined communities, this penalty effectively suppresses 15 columns of the matrix P, concentrating the assignments on the 5 most representative columns. The estimated number of clusters $\hat{k}$ is then explicitly and deterministically obtained at the end of training by counting the columns of P that receive valid assignments through the arg max operation.

Inference with Known k: Although the main contribution of this work is the autonomous estimation of $\hat{k}$, the framework also enables operation in a fixed-k mode to validate the quality of the representation. In this setting, we use the final embeddings Z as input to the traditional k-means algorithm, configured with the true number of classes in the dataset. This approach isolates the quality of the latent space produced by CADGC from the performance of the estimator module.

3.4 Total Loss Function

Training the CADGC framework minimizes two complementary objectives: latent representation quality and cluster estimation accuracy. The system's global objective function sums the encoder and estimator losses:

$$\mathcal{L}_{Total} = \underbrace{(\mathcal{L}_{attr} + \mathcal{L}_{struct} + \lambda_{CL}\mathcal{L}_{CL})}_{\text{GNN Losses}} + \underbrace{(\mathcal{L}_{rec\_z} + \beta\mathcal{L}_{conf})}_{\text{Estimation Loss}} \tag{5}$$

where $\mathcal{L}_{attr}$ and $\mathcal{L}_{struct}$ preserve attributes and topology; $\mathcal{L}_{CL}$ adds discriminative contrast; and the Estimation Loss ($\mathcal{L}_{rec\_z}+\beta\mathcal{L}_{conf}$) guides the k-estimation. To ensure stability and reproducibility, weights such as λ_{CL} and β act as scale-normalizing factors, empirically balancing the distinct magnitudes of MSE and contrastive/entropic gradients to prevent any single objective from dominating.

Algorithm 1: CADGC Training Procedure

Input: Graph $G = (A, X)$, Epochs E_{pre}, E_{max}, Params λ_{CL}, β
Output: Estimated clusters $\hat{k}$ and assignments Y
Phase 1: Pre-training (GAT only);
Initialize GAT weights;
for *epoch* $= 1$ ***to*** E_{pre} **do**
  $Z \leftarrow \text{GAT}(A, X)$; `// Topology and attribute encoding`
  Update GAT by minimizing $\mathcal{L}_{attr} + \mathcal{L}_{struct}$;
end
Phase 2: Unified Training (Alternating Optimization);
Initialize SAE weights;
for *epoch* $= 1$ ***to*** E_{max} **do**
  `// Step 2A: Update GAT (Contrastive + Reconstruction)`
  Generate stochastic views $\tilde{G}_1, \tilde{G}_2$;
  Compute Z_1, Z_2 and $\mathcal{L}_{CL}(Z_1, Z_2)$;
  Update GAT minimizing $\mathcal{L}_{rec} + \lambda_{CL}\mathcal{L}_{CL}$;
  `// Step 2B: Update SAE (Confidence Regularization)`
  $Z_{fixed} \leftarrow \text{GAT}(A, X)$; `// Detach gradients`
  $P, \hat{Z} \leftarrow \text{SAE}(Z_{fixed})$; `// Compute soft-assignments`
  Update SAE minimizing $||Z_{fixed} - \hat{Z}||^2 + \beta\mathcal{L}_{conf}(P)$;
end
Phase 3: Inference;
$\hat{k} \leftarrow$ count valid cols in P ; `// Drop-cluster process`
$Y \leftarrow \arg\max(P)$; `// Final discrete assignments`

The optimization of $\mathcal{L}_{Total}$ is carried out in two stages, as detailed in Algorithm 1. In the pre-training phase, the GAT minimizes only the reconstruction losses ($\mathcal{L}_{attr} + \mathcal{L}_{struct}$) to establish a coherent topology. Subsequently, in the unified training phase, the optimization becomes alternating at each epoch to ensure the stability of the latent space. First, the GAT updates its parameters by minimizing the reconstruction and contrastive losses. Then, the gradient flow is separated: the latent representations (Z) are fixed (*no grad*), and the SAE module updates exclusively its own weights to minimize $\mathcal{L}_{est}$. This mathematical separation is crucial to prevent the estimator from distorting the topology learned by the GNN in pursuit of trivial solutions.

3.5 Complexity Analysis

For a graph with N vertices, $|E|$ edges, attribute dimension F and latent dimension D, the complexity of the framework is dominated by three components: the GAT encoder, contrast loss, and estimation module:

1. **GAT Encoder:** The time complexity for a single attention layer is $O(NFD + |E|D)$. Since $|E| \ll N^2$ in sparse graphs, this stage is computationally efficient and scales linearly with the number of edges.

2. **Contrastive Learning and Reconstruction:** The exact computation of contrastive loss and structural reconstruction requires pairwise similarity calculations, resulting in a complexity of $O(N^2D)$. However, for large-scale graphs, we adopt a mini-batch sampling strategy with a batch size of $B \ll N$, reducing the effective complexity to $O(NBD)$ per epoch.
3. **Estimation Module (SAE):** Since it is composed of linear layers (MLP), its complexity is $O(NDd_c)$, where d_c is the upper bound on the number of clusters, which is linear with respect to the number of vertices.

Therefore, the total complexity per-epoch is asymptotically $O(|E|D+NBD)$, making the method scalable to large networks when using mini-batch training. In the worst case, without the use of sampling, the complexity is dominated by the complete computation of pairwise similarities, resulting in $O(N^2D)$.

4 Experiments

Experiments were conducted on five benchmark datasets with varying topological complexity: Cora, CiteSeer, and PubMed [15]; Wiki [22]; and Amazon-Photo [16]. Dataset statistics are summarized in Table 1. We use three external metrics, comparing predictions with ground truth (ACC, NMI and Adjusted Rand Index (ARI)), as well as internal metrics based on graph topology (Modularity - Q and Conductance - C). For the autonomous estimation task, we report the mean and standard deviation of the predicted number of clusters ($\hat{k}$), analyzing its proximity to the true value k.

The experimental environment was standardized using PyTorch Geometric. To ensure a fair comparison with state-of-the-art methods, hyperparameters were explored via grid search, selecting the models that achieved the best trade-off between minimizing the unsupervised loss function and structural stability. Configurations prone to overfitting due to excessive loss reduction (such as deep networks) were discarded. The reported results reflect the mean and standard deviation ($\mu \pm \sigma$) over 10 independent runs with random seeds, avoiding the bias of selecting a "best run" based on labels. For rigorous evaluation, the statistical significance ($p < 0.05$) between the best and second-best performing models is evaluated using both the paired Student's t-test and the non-parametric Wilcoxon signed-rank test [7].

Table 1. Summary of the datasets used.

Info	Cora	CiteSeer	Wiki	Photo	PubMed
Nodes	2708	3327	2405	7650	19717
Edges	5429	4732	17981	119081	44338
Attributes	1433	3703	4973	745	500
Classes	7	6	17	8	3

Cluster Dimensionality (d_c): We evaluate the impact of the resolution of the latent clustering space by comparing two strategies for setting d_c: (i) based on class-complexity ($d_c = 2k$) and (ii) based on graph-scale ($d_c = \min(\lceil N/100 \rceil, 50)$). Although the latter scale-based rule acts as an empirical heuristic rather than a theoretically derived limit, the strict sparsity induced by our confidence regularization effectively handles the excess capacity across varying topologies. The results of both approaches are reported to analyze the trade-off between incorporating prior domain knowledge ($2k$) and generalization capacity based purely on the graph scale.

Implementation Details: All experiments were conducted on an NVIDIA Tesla P100 GPU (16GB). In the Cora dataset, the GAT encoder was configured with 1 layer containing 1 attention head (single-head) and a hidden dimension of 64, followed by a linear projection (JK-projection) to a latent space of dimension 64. Training was carried out in two phases: 200 pretraining epochs and 300 unified optimization epochs. We used the Adam optimizer with a learning rate and a weight decay of 10^{-3}. The global loss function was balanced with $\alpha = 1.0$ (reconstruction), $\beta = 0.007$ (confidence regularization) and $\lambda_{CL} = 0.1$ (contrastive), using temperature $\tau = 0.3$ in the NT-Xent calculation. The dimensionality of the cluster for Cora ranged from $d_c = 14$ to $d_c = 27$, with a dropout rate of 0.5. For contrastive data augmentation, the attribute masking rate was fixed at 0.3 and the edge removal rate at 0.4. Detailed hyperparameter configurations and full experimental logs are provided in the supplementary material (https://github.com/tiagogbotelho/article).

4.1 Ablation Study and Performance Analysis

Table 2 compares the proposed model (CADGC) with three variants for the clustering task of nodes: the reproduced SP-DAGC baseline (denoted GCN+SSR) and ablations isolating contrast loss (GCN+CL) and the attention mechanism (GAT+SSR). Although re-running the baseline under identical seeds yielded lower performance on CiteSeer and PubMed than originally reported, revealing its initialization sensitivity, this shared controlled environment ensures a fair relative comparison, wherein CADGC consistently achieves superior results.

When analyzing the components, we observe that the introduction of the attention mechanism (GAT) is critical for complex graphs. In the Amazon-Photo data set, the GAT+SSR variant obtained a slight advantage over the full model (CADGC). This suggests that, in highly dense topologies rich in attributes, attention alone already captures community structure effectively, whereas CL augmentations may introduce marginal noise. Across the overall average and specifically on citation graphs (Cora, CiteSeer), the CADGC combination provides the best consistency, unifying attentional selectivity with contrast-promoted separability.

Table 2. Performance comparison on the fixed-k task. Metrics: Accuracy (ACC), Normalized Mutual Information (NMI), Modularity (Q), and Conductance (C). Best in **bold**.

Data	Model	NMI (↑)	ARI (↑)	ACC (%) (↑)
Cora	GCN+SSR (Rep.)	0.549 ± 0.016	0.475 ± 0.027	70.6 ± 1.1
	GCN+CL (Abl.)	0.556 ± 0.016	0.508 ± 0.024	71.6 ± 1.9
	GAT+SSR (Abl.)	0.585 ± 0.010	0.553 ± 0.016	75.1 ± 0.9
	CADGC (Prop.)	**0.604 ± 0.006**	**0.579 ± 0.007**	**76.4 ± 0.8**
Cite.	GCN+SSR (Rep.)	0.387 ± 0.009	0.385 ± 0.017	63.5 ± 1.3
	GCN+CL (Abl.)	0.392 ± 0.006	0.387 ± 0.016	64.1 ± 1.8
	GAT+SSR (Abl.)	0.406 ± 0.004	0.417 ± 0.004	67.1 ± 0.3
	CADGC (Prop.)	**0.427 ± 0.003**	**0.437 ± 0.005**	**68.2 ± 0.3**
Wiki	GCN+SSR (Rep.)	0.416 ± 0.014	0.193 ± 0.024	44.5 ± 1.8
	GCN+CL (Abl.)	0.465 ± 0.012	0.260 ± 0.025	48.0 ± 2.4
	GAT+SSR (Abl.)	0.458 ± 0.012	0.222 ± 0.028	48.0 ± 2.3
	CADGC (Prop.)	**0.470 ± 0.013**	**0.288 ± 0.030**	**51.7 ± 3.0**
Photo	GCN+SSR (Rep.)	0.681 ± 0.022	0.582 ± 0.040	75.1 ± 3.1
	GCN+CL (Abl.)	0.692 ± 0.024	0.590 ± 0.037	76.5 ± 2.0
	GAT+SSR (Abl.)	**0.707 ± 0.010**	**0.622 ± 0.009**	**78.9 ± 1.0**
	CADGC (Prop.)	0.694 ± 0.013	0.607 ± 0.008	77.7 ± 0.6
Pub.	GCN+SSR (Rep.)	0.274 ± 0.006	0.284 ± 0.008	67.5 ± 0.6
	GCN+CL (Abl.)	0.276 ± 0.015	0.291 ± 0.028	67.8 ± 1.4
	GAT+SSR (Abl.)	0.272 ± 0.030	0.265 ± 0.044	66.2 ± 2.7
	CADGC (Prop.)	**0.295 ± 0.028**	**0.297 ± 0.030**	**68.4 ± 1.8**

4.2 Estimating the Number of Clusters and Structural Quality

Unlike traditional methods that require a fixed k, CADGC dynamically adjusts the active clusters by confidence regularization ($\mathcal{L}_{conf}$) and drop-cluster. For the main comparative results (Table 3), we adopted the adaptive strategy to size the latent space ($d_c \propto N$), which proved superior to the rigid setting based on k (detailed analysis in Fig. 2). Table 3 validates this approach: the model achieved high accuracy in estimating $\hat{k}$ in all scenarios, with exact convergence in Amazon-Photo ($\hat{k} = 8.0$). In Wiki ($k_{GT} = 17$), CADGC mitigated the under-segmentation tendency observed in the baseline (which showed structural saturation at $\hat{k} \approx 14.6$, limiting recovery of the true classes), achieving a granularity that is more faithful to the data ($\hat{k} \approx 15.9$) with a 50% reduction in the standard deviation of the estimate.

The structural analysis reveals a critical trade-off. The DGCluster baseline attains high Q, but at the cost of over-segmentation ($\hat{k} \gg k_{GT}$), fragmenting true classes. In contrast, CADGC consistently minimizes $\mathcal{C}$, indicating that the model prioritizes topological bottleneck cuts. This structural characteristic showed a stronger correlation with the semantic organization of the data, resulting in superior external metrics (NMI and ACC) and avoiding artificial fragmentation observed in the baselines.

Table 3. Extended comparison on the k-estimation task. Note that while DGCluster achieves high Q, it suffers from over-segmentation (high $\hat{k}$), whereas CADGC balances structural quality with ground truth alignment. Best in **bold.** $*$ indicates statistical significance ($p < 0.05$) between the best and second-best models, confirmed by both the paired Student's t-test and the Wilcoxon signed-rank test.

Data (k)	Model	Est. $\hat{k}$	NMI (↑)	ACC (%) (↑)	Q (↑)	$\mathcal{C}$ (↓)
Cora (7)	DGCluster	28.7 ± 2.1	$\mathbf{0.621 \pm 0.010}^*$	–	$\mathbf{0.786 \pm 0.004}^*$	0.145 ± 0.028
	GCN+SSR	7.7 ± 1.3	0.552 ± 0.023	66.1 ± 7.5	0.765 ± 0.017	0.080 ± 0.008
	CADGC	$\mathbf{6.5 \pm 0.9}^*$	0.592 ± 0.026	$\mathbf{73.4 \pm 4.6}^*$	0.750 ± 0.018	$\mathbf{0.071 \pm 0.006}^*$
Cite. (6)	DGCluster	62.1 ± 4.7	0.410 ± 0.005	–	$\mathbf{0.863 \pm 0.003}^*$	0.065 ± 0.010
	GCN+SSR	$\mathbf{5.7 \pm 0.6}$	0.390 ± 0.019	63.7 ± 4.8	0.771 ± 0.031	$\mathbf{0.040 \pm 0.006}$
	CADGC	5.1 ± 0.6	$\mathbf{0.429 \pm 0.010}^*$	$\mathbf{68.4 \pm 3.0}^*$	0.754 ± 0.020	$\mathbf{0.040 \pm 0.003}$
Wiki (17)	DGCluster	–	–	–	–	–
	GCN+SSR	14.6 ± 2.2	0.406 ± 0.018	42.7 ± 3.2	0.545 ± 0.028	0.317 ± 0.033
	CADGC	$\mathbf{15.9 \pm 1.1}$	$\mathbf{0.465 \pm 0.018}^*$	$\mathbf{51.0 \pm 3.0}^*$	$\mathbf{0.594 \pm 0.021}^*$	$\mathbf{0.290 \pm 0.016}^*$
Photo (8)	DGCluster	10.0 ± 1.1	$\mathbf{0.773 \pm 0.018}^*$	–	$\mathbf{0.716 \pm 0.003}$	0.124 ± 0.088
	GCN+SSR	7.6 ± 1.1	0.662 ± 0.023	73.2 ± 3.9	0.710 ± 0.012	$\mathbf{0.095 \pm 0.018}$
	CADGC	$\mathbf{8.0 \pm 1.1}$	0.696 ± 0.016	$\mathbf{77.7 \pm 1.4}^*$	$\mathbf{0.716 \pm 0.007}$	0.101 ± 0.021
Pub. (3)	DGCluster	10.2 ± 3.0	$\mathbf{0.326 \pm 0.016}$	–	$\mathbf{0.712 \pm 0.010}^*$	0.246 ± 0.073
	GCN+SSR	3.5 ± 0.7	0.275 ± 0.007	60.8 ± 9.2	0.632 ± 0.043	0.062 ± 0.017
	CADGC	$\mathbf{3.2 \pm 0.6}$	0.289 ± 0.057	$\mathbf{64.3 \pm 1.8}$	0.610 ± 0.076	$\mathbf{0.050 \pm 0.009}$

Figure 2 details the sensitivity to the hyperparameter d_c. The fixed strategy ($2k$) limits the expressiveness in larger graphs, increasing the error $|\Delta k|$. In contrast, the adaptive strategy overcame this barrier, but revealed an operational limitation: estimation accuracy degrades in excessively wide latent spaces ($d_c > 50$). Consequently, we imposed the experimental cap $d_c = \min(50, N/100)$, which ensured stability without introducing noise into massive graphs, resulting in higher NMI values in general.

A direct correlation is observed between the flexibility of the dimension d_c and the accuracy of the model. The fixed strategy ($d_c = 2k$, in red/light blue) tends to limit expressiveness in graphs with a large number of nodes (such as Wiki), resulting in higher estimation error (peak on the red curve). On the other hand, the proposed adaptive strategy ($d_c \propto N$, in green/dark blue) allowed the model to accommodate topological complexity without overfitting, driving the $\hat{k}$ error to values close to zero and, consequently, increasing NMI across all scenarios. This suggests that the capacity of the latent space should scale with the graph size, rather than only with the expected number of classes.

Beyond the final accuracy, it is essential to evaluate the temporal stability and parametric robustness of the estimation process, which are analyzed next.

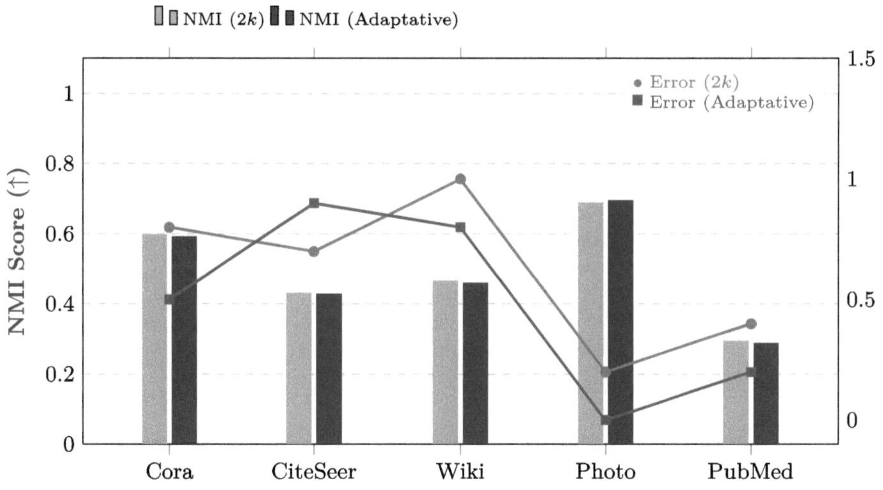

Fig. 2. Impact of dimensionality (d_c). Bars show NMI, lines show absolute estimation error $|\Delta k|$. The adaptive strategy minimizes error (closer to 0) across datasets. Lower $|\Delta k|$ indicates more accurate cluster number estimation. (Color figure online)

4.3 Convergence and Parametric Sensitivity Analysis

To validate the stability of the optimization process, we investigate the dynamic behavior of the estimated $\hat{k}$ throughout the training and the model's sensitivity to the confidence regularization hyperparameter (β).

Figure 3(a) illustrates the convergence dynamics of the estimate $\hat{k}$ for a representative run (Seed 42). We chose to visualize a single seed to highlight the discrete steps of cluster elimination (cluster pruning), a behavior that would be obscured by smoothing via an arithmetic mean. We observe that the confidence regularization mechanism progressively reduces the initial entropy ($\hat{k} \approx 16$) until it stabilizes at $k = 7$. Although this specific run reached the exact ground truth value, the method's stability is statistically supported by the overall mean across runs ($\hat{k} = 6.5 \pm 1.0$), confirming that convergence to values close to the true value is an intrinsic characteristic of the model rather than a selection artifact.

In parallel, Fig. 3(b) analyzes sensitivity to the hyperparameter β. A standard trade-off behavior is observed:

- **Low-Confidence Regime ($\beta < 0.005$):** The penalty is insufficient to enforce sharp decisions, resulting in over-segmentation ($\hat{k} = 10$) and a drop in NMI due to class fragmentation. In the extreme case of a direct ablation ($\beta = 0$) on Cora, the model severely over-segments ($\hat{k} \approx 15$, true $k = 7$), plummeting Accuracy from 76.3% to 50.0%, confirming the module's critical role.
- **High-Confidence Regime ($\beta \geq 0.05$):** The regularization becomes overly aggressive, prematurely collapsing distinct classes ($\hat{k} \to 4$), which severely degrades performance (a decrease of $\approx 16\%$ in NMI).

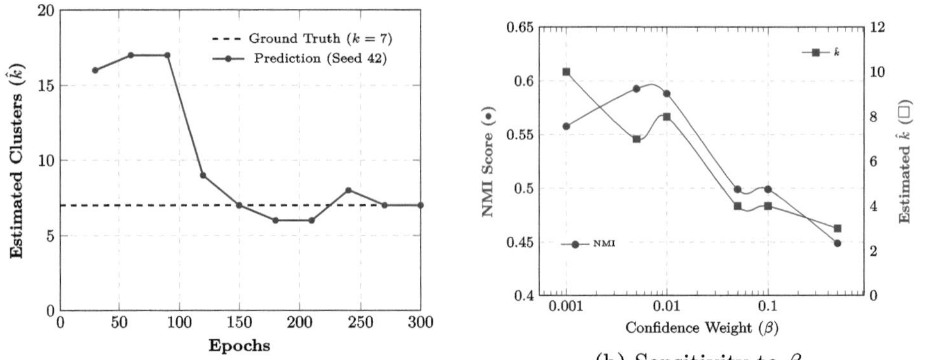

(a) Convergence Dynamics

(b) Sensitivity to β

Fig. 3. Convergence dynamics of the cluster estimate $\hat{k}$ for a representative run (Seed 42) on the Cora dataset. The behavior illustrates the progressive reduction of active clusters until stabilization near the *ground truth*. The global mean across all runs is $\hat{k} = 6.5 \pm 1.0$. Sensitivity analysis of the parameter β, highlighting the optimal operating region around 0.007.

- **Optimal Regime ($0.005 \leq \beta \leq 0.01$):** A plateau is observed where $\hat{k}$ aligns with the true value and NMI is maximized. The choice of $\beta = 0.007$ was based on this operational stability, balancing cluster cohesion without incurring trivial collapse solutions ($k \rightarrow 1$) typical of excessive regularization.

4.4 Visual Qualitative Analysis

To assess the structural quality of the representations and the estimation of k, Fig. 4 presents a visual comparison of the latent space via t-SNE for the Cora dataset. To ensure representativeness, the displayed projections correspond to the seeds whose results were closest to the reported mean. Figure 4(b) serves as a reference (ground truth), showing the ideal structure of 7 well-defined classes learned by the proposed method.

Figure 4(a) illustrates the limitation of the baseline (GCN+SSR): the emphasis on self-separation regularization (SSR) led to an over-segmentation of the space, where single classes (such as Class 3, in red in the GT) were fragmented into multiple subclusters, resulting in an inflated estimate of $k = 8$.

In contrast, Fig. 4(c) demonstrates the effectiveness of the proposed method (CADGC). Even in the challenging autonomous estimation setting, the model preserved the semantic integrity of the clusters. The conservative estimate ($k = 6$) resulted from the coherent merging of two adjacent classes in the latent space, avoiding the artificial fragmentation observed in the baseline and maintaining superior quality metrics (NMI=0.595).

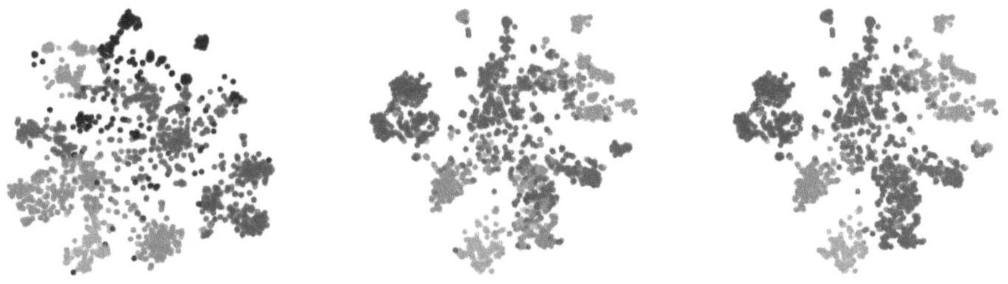

(a) GCN+SSR (Predicted) (b) Ground Truth (c) CADGC (Predicted)

Fig. 4. t-SNE visualization of learned embeddings on the **Cora** dataset. (a) Predicted clusters by GCN+SSR (k-estimated). Seed 42, $k = 8$, NMI=0.568, ARI=0.477. (b) Ground truth classes projected onto CADGC embeddings ($k = 7$). (c) Predicted clusters by CADGC (k-estimated). Colors represent classes, where aligned colors indicate correspondence with the ground truth. Seed 2025, $k = 6$, NMI=0.595, ARI=0.553. (Color figure online)

5 Conclusions and Future Work

In this work, we proposed CADGC, a novel framework for deep graph clustering that not only improves the quality of node clustering, but also enables automatic estimation of the number of clusters k. By combining Graph Attention Networks with Contrastive Learning, the method learns more discriminative latent representations, which lead to more coherent partitions and more reliable estimation of k without requiring prior knowledge of the underlying class structure.

Experiments on five benchmark datasets showed that the proposed method not only achieves competitive or superior clustering performance compared with the baseline and its variants under fixed k evaluation metrics, but also establishes greater robustness in the task of estimating k. While topological approaches such as DGCluster tend toward over-segmentation to maximize modularity, CADGC preserved the semantic integrity of clusters by minimizing conductance and recovering the number of clusters with reduced error in challenging scenarios such as Amazon-Photo and PubMed. In addition, the local confidence regularization strategy proved effective, reducing the variability of the results between runs.

Overall, our findings suggest that explicitly shaping the geometry of the latent space is a key factor in enabling stable and scalable unsupervised graph clustering, particularly in scenarios where the number of clusters is unknown.

Despite promising results, future work will focus on two main directions: validating the theoretical $O(NBD)$ mini-batch scalability on massive modern benchmarks (e.g., OGB datasets) and heterophilic topologies that challenge classical GNN homophily assumptions; and investigating Curriculum Learning strategies to dynamically balance objectives and accelerate convergence.

Acknowledgments. This research was funded by the Coordination for the Improvement of Higher Education Personnel (CAPES) âĂŞ Code 001, through a Ph.D. scholarship; by the IFSULDEMINAS - Campus Muzambinho; The São Paulo Research Foundation (FAPESP) [grants 22/03090-0]; and Brazilian National Council for Scientific and Technological Development (CNPq) [grants 420025/2023-5]. The authors also thank the Data Mining and Applications Group (MIDAS) for their support and computational resources. Finally, we acknowledge the use of AI-based tools to support text revision.

References

1. Bhowmick, A., Kosan, M., Huang, Z., Singh, A., Medya, S.: Dgcluster: a neural framework for attributed graph clustering via modularity maximization. Proc. AAAI Conf. Artifi. Intell. **38**(10), 11069–11077 (2024)
2. Bo, D., Wang, X., Shi, C., Zhu, M., Lu, E., Cui, P.: Structural deep clustering network. In: Proceedings of The Web Conference 2020, pp. 1400–1410. WWW '20, Association for Computing Machinery, New York, NY, USA (2020)
3. Cai, H., Zheng, V.W., Chang, K.C.C.: A comprehensive survey of graph embedding: problems, techniques, and applications. IEEE Trans. Knowl. Data Eng. **30**(9), 1616–1637 (2018)
4. Chandrika, G.N., Alnowibet, K., Kautish, K.S., Reddy, E.S., Alrasheedi, A.F., Mohamed, A.W.: Graph transformer for communities detection in social networks. Comput. Mat. Continua **70**(3), 5707–5720 (2022)
5. Chen, R.: Preserving global information for graph clustering with masked autoencoders. Mathematics **12**(10), 1574 (2024)
6. Chen, T., Kornblith, S., Norouzi, M., Hinton, G.: A simple framework for contrastive learning of visual representations. In: Proceeding of the 37th International Conference on Machine Learning, vol. 119, pp. 1597–1607. (2020) PMLR
7. Demšar, J.: Statistical comparisons of classifiers over multiple data sets. J. Mach. Learn. Res. **7**, 1–30 (2006)
8. Hamilton, W., Ying, Z., Leskovec, J.: Inductive representation learning on large graphs. Adv. Neural Inf. Process. Syst. **30** (2017)
9. Hamilton, W.L.: Graph Representation Learning, vol. 14. Morgan & Claypool (2020)
10. Huang, L., Ye, X., Yang, M., Pan, L., hua Zheng, S.: MNC-net: multi-task graph structure learning based on node clustering for early parkinson's disease diagnosis. Comput. Biol. Med. **152**, 106308 (2023)
11. Ji, J., Liang, Y., Lei, M.: Deep attributed graph clustering with self-separation regularization and parameter-free cluster estimation. Neural Netw. **142**, 522–533 (2021)
12. Liu, Y., et al.: Hard sample aware network for contrastive deep graph clustering. Proc. AAAI Conf. Artif. Intell. **37**(7), 8914–8922 (2023)
13. Liu, Y., Gao, X., He, T., Zheng, T., Zhao, J., Yin, H.: Reliable node similarity matrix guided contrastive graph clustering. IEEE Trans. Knowl. Data Eng. **36**(12), 9123–9135 (2024)
14. Messias, G.H., Gonçalves Botelho, T., Iasulaitis, S., Coelho Naldi, M., Demétrius Baria Valejo, A.: A systematic review of graph neural network for node clustering in homogeneous attributed networks. IEEE Access **13**, 215265–215285 (2025)

15. Sen, P., Namata, G., Bilgic, M., Getoor, L., Galligher, B., Eliassi-Rad, T.: Collective classification in network data. AI Mag. **29**(3), 93 (2008)
16. Shchur, O., Mumme, M., Bojchevski, A., Günnemann, S.: Pitfalls of graph neural network evaluation (2018). arXiv:1811.05868 arXiv preprint
17. Veličković, P., Cucurull, G., Casanova, A., Romero, A., Lio, P., Bengio, Y.: Graph attention networks (2017). arXiv:1710.10903 arXiv preprint
18. Wang, C., Pan, S., Hu, R., Long, G., Jiang, J., Zhang, C.: Attributed graph clustering: a deep attentional embedding approach. In: Proceeding of the International Joint Conference on Artificial Intelligence, pp. 3670–3676 (2019)
19. Wang, C., Pan, S., Celina, P.Y., Hu, R., Long, G., Zhang, C.: Deep neighbor-aware embedding for node clustering in attributed graphs. Pattern Recogn. **122**, 108230 (2022)
20. Wang, X., Wang, K., Chen, K., Wang, Z., Zheng, K.: Unsupervised twitter social bot detection using deep contrastive graph clustering. Knowl.-Based Syst. **293**, 111690 (2024)
21. Wu, D., Guo, X., Luo, X., Qiao, Z., Ma, J.: Adaptive harmony learning and optimization for attributed graph clustering. In: Proc. of the 2022 International Joint Conference on Neural Networks, pp. 1–8. IEEE (2022)
22. Yang, C., Liu, Z., Zhao, D., Sun, M., Chang, E.Y.: Network representation learning with rich text information. In: Proceeding of the 24th International Conference on Artificial Intelligence, pp. 2111–2117 (2015)
23. Zhu, J., Li, X., Gao, C., Wang, Z., Kurths, J.: Unsupervised community detection in attributed networks based on mutual information maximization. New J. Phys. **23**(11), 113016 (2021)
24. Zhuo, L., Chen, Y., Song, B., Liu, Y., Su, Y.: A model for predicting ncrna-protein interactions based on graph neural networks and community detection. Methods **207**, 74–80 (2022)

Explainable Artificial Intelligence for Prediction of Li-Fraumeni Syndrome and *TP53* p.R337H Founder Variant in Brazil

Ana Carolina Prado Ricciardi[1,2](✉), Roseli Aparecida Francelin Romero[1], and José Cláudio Casali da Rocha[2]

[1] Institute of Mathematics and Computer Sciences (ICMC), University of São Paulo (USP), São Carlos, Brazil
acarolinaricciardi@usp.br, rafrance@icmc.usp.br

[2] Department of Oncogenetics, A.C. Camargo Cancer Center, São Paulo, Brazil
casali.rocha@accamargo.org.br

Abstract. Li-Fraumeni Syndrome (LFS) is a rare hereditary condition associated with germline variants in the *TP53* gene. In Brazil, the founder variant p.R337H shows an estimated population prevalence of 0.2–0.3% in the South and Southeast regions, in sharp contrast with its rarity elsewhere. Traditional clinical screening criteria, such as Chompret, display low sensitivity in this setting, favouring systematic underdiagnosis. This work investigates machine learning (ML) models—Random Forest (RF), XGBoost, and CatBoost—to identify carriers of pathogenic *TP53* variants using clinical and familial data from 515 probands seen at A.C. Camargo Cancer Center. Performance was assessed with imbalance-robust metrics (AUC-ROC, AUPRC, Matthews Correlation Coefficient [MCC], and Balanced Accuracy), complemented by SHAP-based explainability analysis. Random Forest consistently outperformed the Chompret criterion: AUC 0.73 vs. 0.42, MCC 0.30 vs. −0.12, and Balanced Accuracy 0.69 vs. 0.42. SHAP analysis suggested distinct clinical profiles between subgroups: p.R337H carriers showed predominance of maternal breast cancer history and later-onset diagnoses, whereas carriers of other pathogenic variants exhibited a broader tumour spectrum with earlier onset. These results provide objective decision-support for genetic screening and counselling, with potential to inform oncogenetics guidelines and public health policy in the Brazilian Unified Health System (SUS).

Keywords: Li-Fraumeni Syndrome · *TP53* p.R337H · Machine Learning · Explainable AI · SHAP · MCC · Balanced Accuracy · Hereditary Cancer · Precision Medicine · Brazil

1 Introduction

Li-Fraumeni Syndrome (LFS) is one of the most emblematic examples of hereditary cancer predisposition. First described by Li and Fraumeni in 1969 [11] from

M. Recamonde-Mendoza and R. C. Barros (Eds.): BRACIS 2026, LNAI 17105, pp. 34–47, 2027.
https://doi.org/10.1007/978-3-032-39882-6_3

observations of familial clusters of sarcomas and early-onset breast tumours, LFS is caused by germline variants in the *TP53* gene, located on chromosome 17p13.1. The encoded protein—p53—is a transcription factor responsible for multiple cellular damage-response mechanisms, including cell-cycle arrest, DNA repair, and apoptosis induction, which justifies its designation as the "guardian of the genome" [10].

In Brazil, the epidemiology of LFS presents a singular particularity: the founder variant *TP53* p.R337H, resulting from the transition c.1010G>A, exhibits a prevalence of 0.2–0.3% in the South and Southeast regions—considerably higher than in any other population worldwide [8,9]. Genealogical and haplotype analyses indicate a single mutational event occurring approximately three centuries ago, introduced by a European ancestor in southern Brazil [7,15]. This variant maps to exon 10, which encodes the oligomerisation domain of p53, conferring distinct biochemical behaviour compared with classical DNA-binding domain mutations: under physiological conditions the resulting protein retains partial function, but loses thermal stability in slightly acidic environments—such as tumour microenvironments—explaining the intermediate penetrance and atypical clinical spectrum observed in Brazilian carriers [17].

Traditional clinical screening criteria for LFS, including the classical Li-Fraumeni criteria and the revised Chompret criteria (2015), were developed primarily from European and North American cohorts [4,6]. Their application to the Brazilian context shows limited sensitivity, particularly for p.R337H carriers whose phenotypes frequently diverge from the expected pattern: ages of onset tend to be later, the tumour spectrum is more concentrated (with breast cancer predominating), and family history may be less striking [13]. The result is a systematic diagnostic gap that delays molecular testing and the adoption of preventive protocols for at-risk families.

Machine learning (ML) approaches emerge as complementary alternatives capable of integrating multiple clinical and familial variables into individualised probabilistic estimates, overcoming the rigidity of fixed rule-based systems. The present work proposes and evaluates supervised models—Random Forest, XGBoost, and CatBoost—to identify carriers of pathogenic *TP53* variants with special attention to the p.R337H variant in a Brazilian patient cohort. Explainable Artificial Intelligence (XAI) methods, emphasising SHAP (SHapley Additive exPlanations) [12], are employed to render predictions interpretable and clinically actionable.

2 Related Work

The literature on LFS and the p.R337H mutation in Brazil is dominated by clinical and epidemiological studies. Achatz et al. [1] documented the association of p.R337H with both classical LFS and Li-Fraumeni-like (LFL) presentations, establishing the investigative line on the founder effect. Subsequent multicentre studies confirmed population frequencies of 0.2–0.3% in the South and Southeast regions [8,9], and Formiga et al. [5] described atypical manifestations among Brazilian carriers, including papillary thyroid carcinoma. Matta et al. [13] demonstrated that a relevant fraction of patients with *TP53* variants did not fulfil Chompret criteria at the time of diagnosis, evidencing the mismatch between traditional clinical algorithms and the local epidemiological reality. Bittar et al. [3] further documented this heterogeneity by characterising patients fulfilling Chompret criteria in southern Brazil, reinforcing the need for population-adapted screening tools.

In the field of artificial intelligence applied to oncogenetics, Mikhail et al. [14] used the UMD *TP53* database to show that SVM and Multilayer Perceptron models can differentiate mutations associated with multiple cancer types with reasonable accuracy. Probabilistic tools such as LFSPRO [16] were developed to estimate the probability of carrying a *TP53* mutation, although they lack validation in populations with high frequencies of founder variants such as the Brazilian p.R337H. A recent evaluation by Corredor et al. [19] compared LFSPRO predictions against standard genetic counselling practice on prospectively collected probands, motivating population-specific ML approaches capable of integrating local epidemiological context. Recent systematic reviews [2] have highlighted the growing role of XAI—particularly SHAP—in generating auditable predictions for medical contexts. To the best of our knowledge, the present work is the first to apply ML models with SHAP explainability specifically to differentiate p.R337H carriers from other pathogenic *TP53* subtypes in a Brazilian cohort.

3 Methodology

3.1 Data Collection and Curation

The study adopted an observational, cross-sectional, and retrospective design, developed in the Department of Oncogenetics at A.C. Camargo Cancer Center. The primary data source was the Electronic Family Questionnaire (QFAM), made available to patients via REDCap® after scheduling their first genetic counselling appointment. The instrument collects structured clinical and familial information: personal oncological history, pedigree up to the third generation, sociodemographic data, and age at neoplasm diagnosis. Data collection began on 24 July 2020 and passed through three successive versions of the questionnaire.

REDCap® data were supplemented by three institutional sources: (i) the Tasy electronic health record system, for verification and enrichment of clinical and oncological data; (ii) the Progeny® platform, used to build pedigrees and identify aggregation-of-risk patterns; and (iii) A.C. Camargo's Internal Genetic Studies Database, for variant interpretation following ACMG/ClinGen protocols. All procedures were conducted in compliance with Brazil's General Data Protection Law (LGPD—Law n. 13,709/2018), with participant anonymisation and digital acceptance of an authorisation form. Of the 576 probands referred, 515 had complete clinical and familial records and comprised the final analytical dataset.

3.2 Variable Definition and Encoding

The 515 probands were classified into three mutually exclusive groups: **Group 0**—no mutation detected in *TP53*, including individuals without known genetic alterations and carriers of pathogenic variants in other genes (e.g., *BRCA1*, *BRCA2*, *CHEK2*, *PALB2*; $n = 421$); **Group 1**—carriers of the founder variant *TP53* p.R337H ($n = 63$); and **Group 2**—carriers of other pathogenic or likely pathogenic variants in *TP53*, distinct from p.R337H ($n = 31$). This tripartite coding allows supervised models to identify clinical-genetic patterns specific to each subgroup.

For missing data, categorical variables received a dedicated `unknown` category, preserving the informational structure and avoiding forced imputation. Continuous variables such as age at diagnosis were imputed by the empirical sample median, which is more robust than the mean for the skewed distributions typical of oncological cohorts. Genetic fields—gene identification, presence of pathogenic variants, and molecular classification—were not imputed, as they were treated as MNAR (missing not at random), given that their absence tends to stem from specific clinical or technical factors. Feature engineering included derived attributes from family information: mean age at diagnosis among affected relatives, distribution of neoplasm types among first-degree relatives, number of consecutive generations with tumour occurrence, and minimum age of onset among family cases.

3.3 Predictive Modelling and Evaluation

Three decision-tree-based supervised methods were employed: Random Forest (RF), XGBoost (XGB), and CatBoost (CAT). RF was adopted as a baseline for its stability in the presence of noise and its solid performance on heterogeneous datasets. XGBoost, incorporating advanced regularisation, is well established in public-health applications. CatBoost was included for its native handling of categorical variables, reducing the need for prior encoding.

The sample was split into training, validation, and test subsets using stratified partitioning that preserved class proportions. Hyperparameter optimisation combined grid search for less computationally demanding models and Bayesian strategies for those with larger parameter spaces. Stratified k-fold cross-validation was applied on the training partition to estimate result variability and prevent overfitting, with the test set held out for final evaluation only. Class imbalance was handled through class weighting during training, without synthetic resampling of the test set. The complete preprocessing and training workflow was organised into a reproducible pipeline with automated logging of parameters, seeds, and metrics.

As a clinical reference, the Chompret criteria were implemented computationally in Python and evaluated under the same validation conditions applied to the ML models, on the same cohort, establishing a reproducible benchmark.

Evaluation adopted metrics suitable for imbalanced classification: Area Under the ROC Curve (AUC-ROC), Area Under the Precision-Recall Curve

(AUPRC), Matthews Correlation Coefficient (MCC), and Balanced Accuracy. Classical metrics—accuracy, precision, recall, and F1-score—were included for reference. **The predictive evaluation reported in this work concerns the binary task** (*TP53* mutated vs. non-mutated); the contrast between p.R337H carriers and carriers of other pathogenic *TP53* variants is examined at the *explanatory* level through subgroup SHAP analysis, not as a separate classification task.

Interpretability was implemented via SHAP values [12]. SHAP attributes to each feature an additive contribution to a given prediction, derived from cooperative game theory: the Shapley value of a feature is its average marginal contribution across all possible feature coalitions, yielding a locally accurate and consistent decomposition of the model output; for tree ensembles we used the exact TreeSHAP estimator. We report global importance as the mean absolute SHAP value across the test set and local explanations for representative subgroups. To assess the robustness of the metrics, their variability was estimated by bootstrap resampling of the held-out test set, and the three models were compared pairwise (DeLong test for AUC; paired bootstrap for MCC and Balanced Accuracy) with Holm correction for multiple comparisons. SHAP stability was additionally assessed by bootstrap resampling of the feature-ranking procedure, allowing the most recurrent explanatory variables to be distinguished from ranking fluctuations in this small and imbalanced cohort.

4 Results

4.1 Sample Characterisation

Of the 515 eligible probands, 361 (70.1%) had a history of at least one oncological diagnosis, while 154 (29.9%) were asymptomatic. Group 0 was the largest subgroup ($n = 421$), comprising 321 individuals without detectable mutations and 100 carriers of pathogenic variants in other genes. Among *TP53* carriers, 63 had p.R337H (Group 1) and 31 had other pathogenic variants (Group 2). The relative distribution of variants confirmed the central epidemiological position of *TP53*—particularly p.R337H, which corresponded to 32.5% of positive findings—alongside *BRCA1* (9.3%) and *BRCA2* (7.7%) (Fig. 1).

The distribution of oncological status by pathogenic gene revealed clinically relevant penetrance differences. In the p.R337H group, the proportion between affected (44.4%) and unaffected (55.6%) probands suggests intermediate penetrance, contrasting with Group *TP53*-others, where 71.0% of carriers already had an oncological diagnosis. Among *BRCA2* carriers, 73.3% had cancer. In the p.R337H group, breast cancer was the most frequent diagnosis (48.7%), followed by CNS tumours, extremity sarcomas, and prostate cancer (all around 5%). For other *TP53* mutation carriers, the spectrum was more varied: breast (33.3%), gastric neoplasms (10%), sarcomas (13.3%), and head-and-neck (6.2%). The median age at first diagnosis was higher in the p.R337H group than in the *TP53*-others group, consistent with the later clinical expressivity reported for the intermediate-penetrance p.R337H variant relative to classical DNA-binding-domain mutations (Fig. 2).

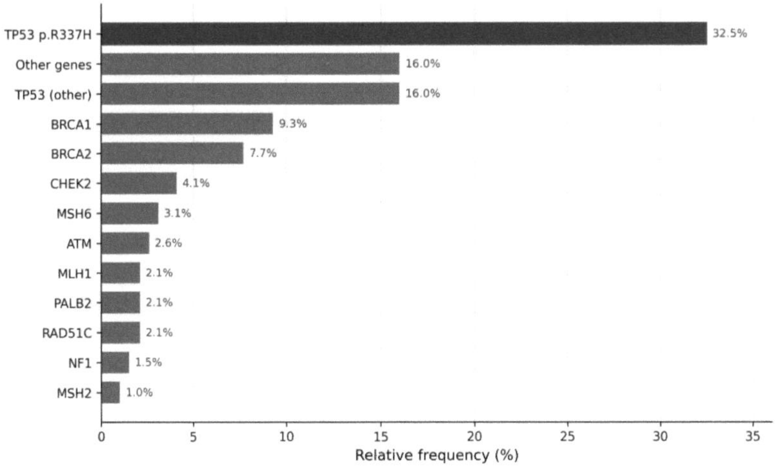

Fig. 1. Relative distribution of pathogenic germline variants among probands with confirmed mutations.

4.2 Comparative Model Performance

In the ROC curve comparison, Random Forest achieved AUC 0.73, followed by CatBoost (0.66) and XGBoost (0.65). The stronger RF performance in this experiment may reflect conditions favouring this algorithm: a moderately sized sample with measurement variability, dispersed non-linear predictor interactions, moderately imbalanced classes, and lower inter-fold variability during cross-validation. The Chompret criterion, implemented under the same validation conditions, presented AUC 0.42—near the random diagonal—indicating discriminative capacity below chance in this cohort (Fig. 3).

Table 1. Comparative performance of Chompret criteria vs. Random Forest on classical classification metrics.

Metric	Chompret	Random Forest
Accuracy	0.55	0.72
Precision (PPV)	0.13	0.39
Recall (Sensitivity)	0.21	0.58
F1-Score	0.16	0.46
AUC-ROC	0.42	0.73
MCC	−0.12	0.30
Balanced Accuracy	0.42	0.69

No pairwise difference among Random Forest, XGBoost, and CatBoost reached statistical significance for any metric (DeLong test for AUC and paired

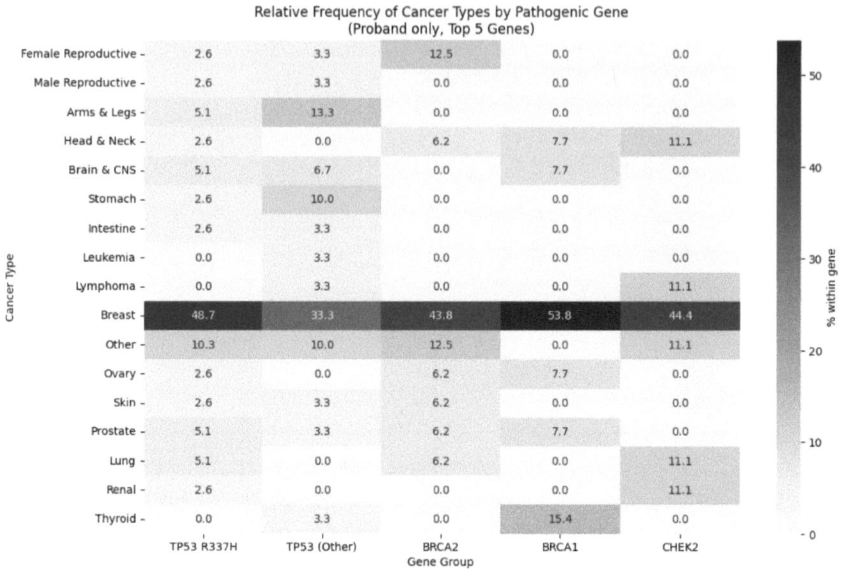

Fig. 2. Heat map showing the proportional distribution of cancer types among carriers of pathogenic variants in the five predominant genes of the sample.

bootstrap for MCC and Balanced Accuracy, all Holm-corrected $p > 0.05$), indicating that the three models perform comparably on this cohort and that the choice among them is not driven by a statistically distinguishable performance gap.

Imbalance-robust metrics confirmed the advantage of Random Forest (Table 1). AUPRC was marginally higher for RF ($\approx$0.20) compared with Chompret ($\approx$0.18), signalling greater precision in identifying true positives among rare classes. MCC revealed marked differences: negative for Chompret (≈ -0.12), indicating performance below chance, and positive for RF (≈ 0.30), indicating significant correlation between predictions and the outcome. Balanced Accuracy was substantially higher for the model (≈ 0.69 vs. ≈ 0.42), reflecting better equilibrium between sensitivity and specificity. Of the 20 top predictors identified across the three algorithms, 17 were selected by all models, constituting a robust core of central variables—a result confirmed by bipartite graph analysis (Fig. 4).

4.3 Explainability and Identified Clinical Profiles

SHAP analysis revealed how different clinical and familial variables influence model predictions, highlighting patterns not captured by traditional clinical criteria. At the global level, the mean absolute SHAP values of the Random Forest model across the test set rank the most influential predictors for the binary

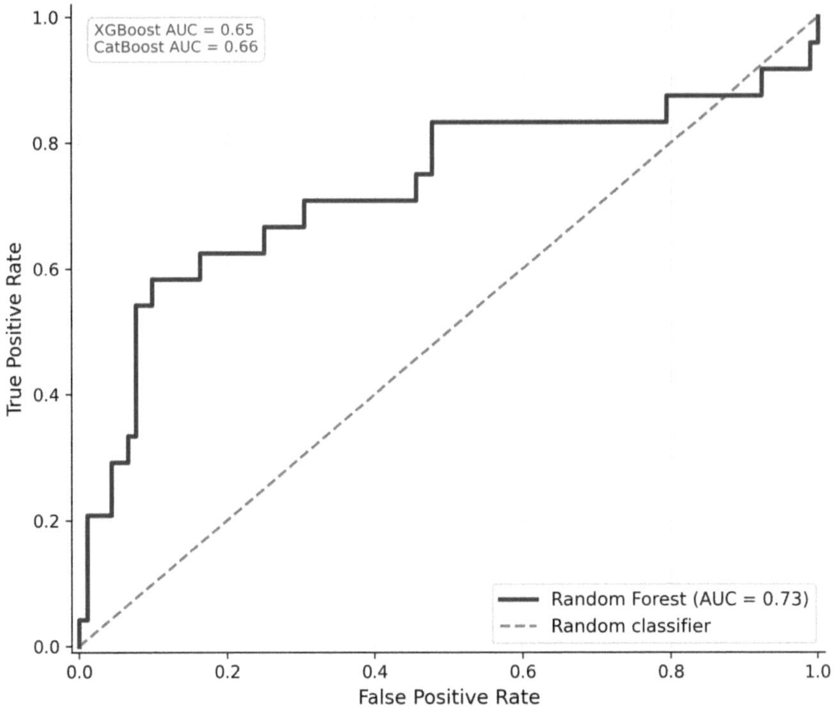

Fig. 3. ROC curve of the Random Forest model (AUC = 0.73) for identifying carriers of pathogenic *TP53* variants; the dashed line represents the expected performance of a random classifier. For reference, XGBoost and CatBoost achieved AUC 0.65 and 0.66, respectively (annotated).

TP53-carrier task (Fig. 5), providing a population-level view that complements the per-subgroup local analyses that follow.

For p.R337H carriers, the most important variables were: approximate age of cancer onset in the mother (highest absolute contribution), proband's breast cancer type, proband's age at breast cancer diagnosis, minimum age of diagnosis among siblings, and most common cancer type in the mother (breast cancer). This profile is consistent with the literature describing p.R337H as an intermediate-penetrance variant with a more concentrated tumour spectrum and a strong matrilinear component (Fig. 6).

For carriers of other pathogenic *TP53* variants, models highlighted a more diverse scenario: in addition to early-onset breast cancer, CNS tumours, gastrointestinal neoplasms, sarcomas, and head-and-neck neoplasms emerged as important indicators. Later ages at diagnosis reduced the probability of assignment to this group, consistent with the typical early onset of classical LFS. These contrasts between subgroups are not captured by the Chompret criteria, evidencing the added value of explainable techniques in clinical stratification and individualised genetic counselling support (Fig. 7). Bootstrap SHAP stability analysis

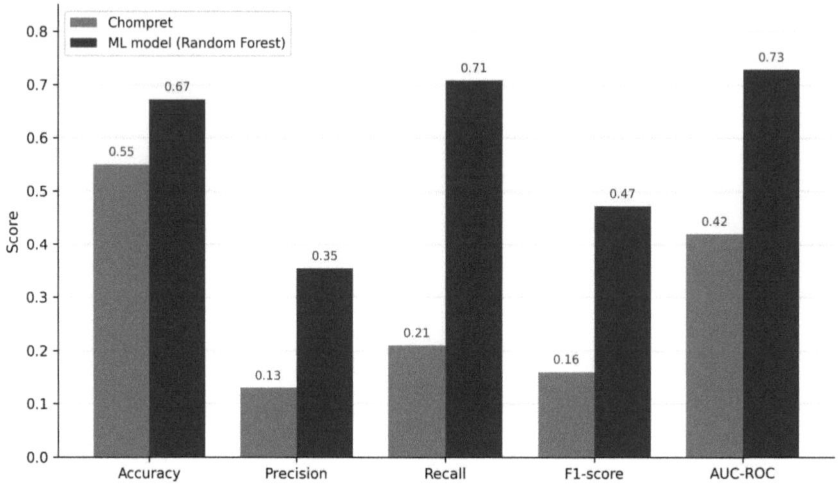

Fig. 4. Comparison using imbalance-robust metrics. The ML model (Random Forest) consistently outperforms the clinical (Chompret) criterion across all metrics. Of the 20 top predictors identified by the three algorithms, 17 were selected by all models, constituting a robust core of central variables—a result confirmed by bipartite graph analysis.

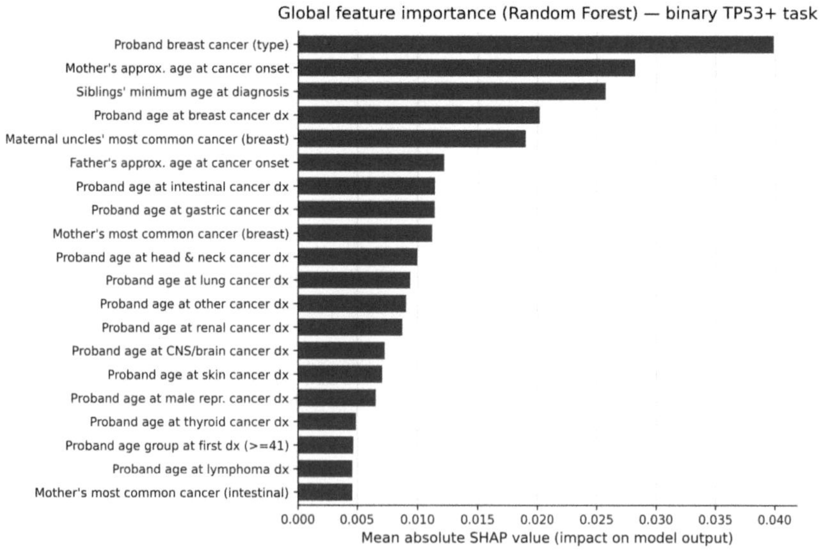

Fig. 5. Global feature importance (mean absolute SHAP value across the test set) for the Random Forest model on the binary *TP53*-carrier task, ranking predictors by overall contribution to model output.

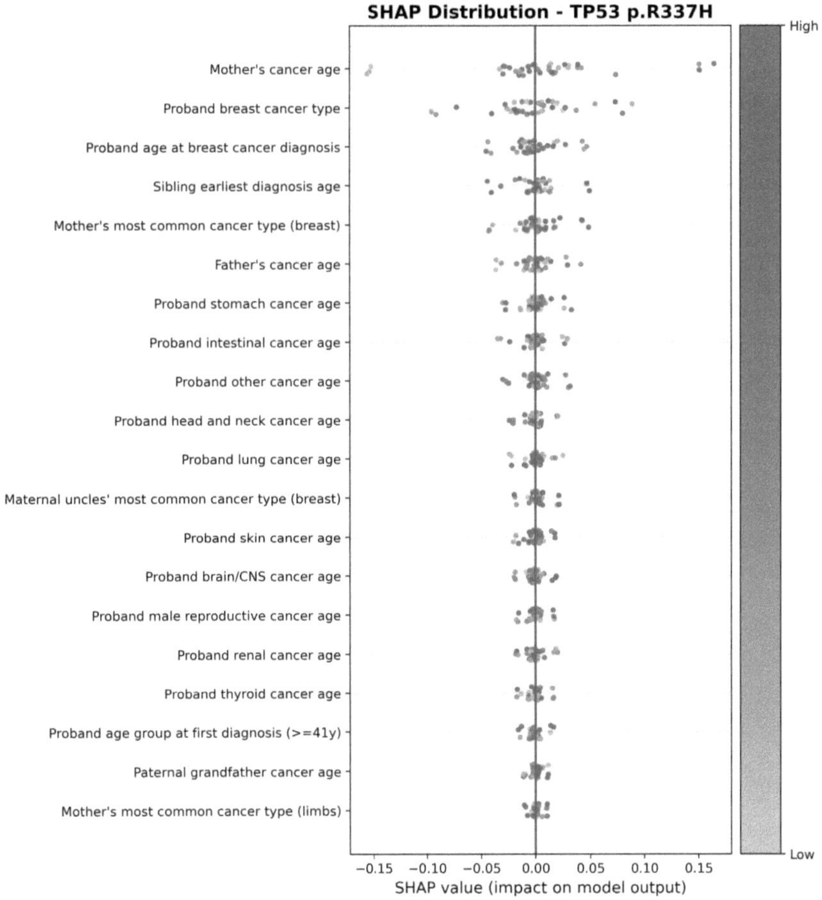

Fig. 6. Distribution of SHAP values in the p.R337H group. The horizontal position represents each variable's effect on classification, while the colour of the points reflects the magnitude of the observed value for the patient (best viewed in colour).

supported this interpretation by showing that the main explanatory variables were not isolated artifacts of a single model fit, although their ranking should still be interpreted as hypothesis-generating rather than causal.

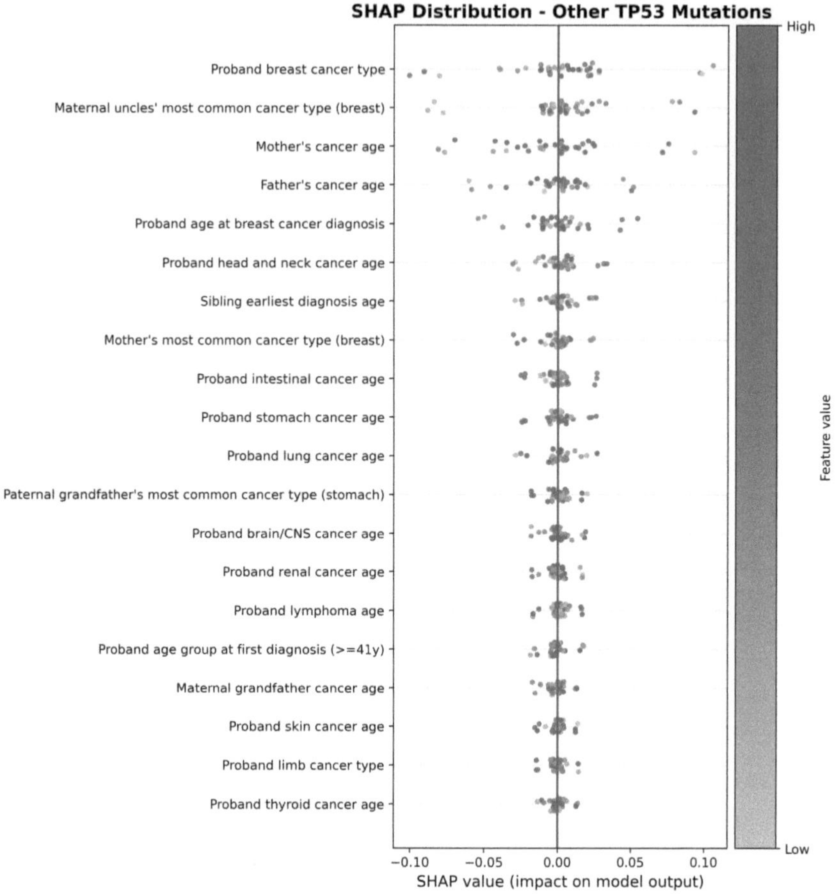

Fig. 7. SHAP values for differentiation of carriers of pathogenic variants other than p.R337H. Greater weight is observed for early-onset diagnoses and involvement of multiple anatomical sites. The colour of the points reflects the magnitude of the observed feature value (best viewed in colour).

5 Discussion

Chompret criteria are widely adopted in international protocols for clinical screening of individuals with suspected LFS. However, a central problematic assumption is that all pathogenic *TP53* variants confer equivalent risks, which contrasts with the broad phenotypic diversity associated with distinct mutations in this gene. In Brazil, this limitation is particularly relevant because of the p.R337H variant, whose geographic distribution and clinical behaviour differ substantially from those for which the criteria were originally designed [18].

ML models, by integrating multiple clinical and familial variables probabilistically, may complement conventional heuristic systems when fixed clinical rules do not capture the full phenotypic context. In this cohort, this capacity appeared relevant in cases where p.R337H-carrying families did not exhibit classical tumour aggregation patterns: the algorithm was able to capture subtle risk signals, suggesting greater flexibility in the face of phenotypic heterogeneity. Increasing sensitivity reduces the probability of false negatives—whose clinical and social cost tends to be substantially higher than the impact generated by a false positive—supporting further evaluation of these models as aids for preventive oncological screening.

The model's ability to distinguish p.R337H from other pathogenic *TP53* mutations suggests a potentially useful extension beyond fixed rule-based protocols, although this finding requires external validation before clinical use. If replicated, this differentiation could inform screening and prevention protocols: p.R337H carriers are typically enrolled in the Toronto Protocol [20] (whole-body MRI, biochemical exams), whereas carriers of other variants require management adapted to a broader and more aggressive tumour spectrum.

From the perspective of Brazil's Unified Health System (SUS), predictive tools based on clinical and familial information—without immediate need for genotyping—can act as intelligent triage mechanisms, helping to direct resources to higher-risk groups. In a continent-sized country with unequal coverage of oncogenetics services, this strategy has the potential to broaden access to personalised medicine and reduce regional inequalities. Integration of these algorithms into electronic health records could assist non-specialist clinicians in identifying suspicious cases, prioritising their referral to reference centres.

Beyond the rule-based Chompret criterion, the most established computational tool for this problem is LFSPRO [16], a Mendelian, family-history-based model that estimates *TP53* carrier probability via the Elston–Stewart algorithm. A relevant consideration is that LFSPRO's penetrance estimates derive from North American cohorts and do not model the Brazilian p.R337H founder variant, whose intermediate penetrance and breast-cancer-concentrated spectrum diverge from classical LFS. This population mismatch motivates the central argument of this work: models calibrated to local epidemiology can capture risk signals that internationally derived tools, however well validated elsewhere, may miss in the Brazilian context. A direct empirical comparison against LFSPRO on a pedigree-structured cohort is a natural next step and is left for future work.

A methodological note regarding Group 0 is warranted: this reference category is heterogeneous, comprising 321 individuals without any detectable mutation alongside 100 carriers of pathogenic variants in other hereditary cancer genes (*BRCA1*, *BRCA2*, *CHEK2*, *PALB2*). Aggregating these molecularly distinct subgroups into a single negative class may reduce model specificity and partially mask risk signals specific to *TP53* carriers. Strategies based on multigene panels would allow more precise segmentation, increasing both clinical utility and model discriminative capacity.

Among the study's further limitations are: the dataset originating from a single specialised centre (which favours methodological uniformity but restricts generalisability); the relatively small number of cases in Groups 1 and 2, making representation of rare non-p.R337H variants challenging; and the reliance on retrospective records from tertiary services, which may introduce referral bias.

The absence of longitudinal follow-up also prevents assessment of lifetime risk evolution.

6 Conclusions

This work suggests that supervised machine learning models integrated with explainable AI techniques can provide complementary discriminative information to Chompret clinical criteria for identifying carriers of pathogenic *TP53* variants in this Brazilian cohort. Random Forest emerged as a solid methodological reference, with AUC 0.73, MCC 0.30, and Balanced Accuracy 0.69—against AUC 0.42, MCC −0.12, and Balanced Accuracy 0.42 for the clinical criterion.

The observed ability to differentiate p.R337H carriers from carriers of other pathogenic *TP53* mutations may have implications for screening, genetic counselling, and the definition of personalised surveillance protocols if confirmed in independent cohorts. SHAP analysis indicated distinct epidemiological and clinical profiles between subgroups, providing interpretable hypotheses for oncological practice rather than definitive causal explanations.

The immediate priority is to test the model across multiple centres—including SUS units—to verify its capacity to adapt to different epidemiological contexts. Progressively incorporating somatic molecular, epigenetic, and imaging data, alongside long-term prospective studies, will further improve predictive accuracy and clarify whether the tool can become a reliable component of hereditary cancer predisposition syndrome screening in Brazil. The successful transition from proof-of-concept to large-scale application depends on inter-institutional cooperation, robust data infrastructures, and a firm commitment to transparency and equity of access.

Acknowledgments. The authors thank the Department of Oncogenetics at A.C. Camargo Cancer Center and the Institute of Mathematics and Computer Sciences at the University of São Paulo for institutional support.

Disclosure of Interests. The authors have no competing interests to declare that are relevant to the content of this article.

Use of Generative AI. Generative AI language tools were used to assist in drafting and revising portions of the manuscript text; all scientific content,data analysis, interpretations, and conclusions are the exclusive responsibility of the authors, who reviewed and verified the entire manuscript.

References

1. Achatz, M.I., et al.: The TP53 mutation, R337H, is associated with Li-Fraumeni and Li-Fraumeni-like syndromes in Brazilian families. Cancer Lett. **245**(1–2), 96–102 (2007)
2. Alkhanbouli, R., et al.: The role of explainable artificial intelligence in disease prediction: a systematic literature review and future research directions. BMC Med. Inf. Decis. Mak. **25**, 110 (2025)

3. Bittar, C.M., et al.: Clinical and molecular characterization of patients fulfilling Chompret criteria for Li-Fraumeni syndrome in southern Brazil. PLoS ONE **16**(9), e0251639 (2021)
4. Bougeard, G., et al.: Revisiting Li-Fraumeni syndrome from TP53 mutation carriers. J. Clin. Oncol. **33**(21), 2345–2352 (2015)
5. Formiga, M.N.D.C.: Frequency of thyroid carcinoma in Brazilian TP53 p. R337H carriers with Li-Fraumeni syndrome. JAMA Oncol. **3**(10), 1400–1402 (2017)
6. Frebourg, T., et al.: Guidelines for the Li-Fraumeni and heritable TP53-related cancer syndromes. Eur. J. Hum. Genet. **28**(10), 1379–1386 (2020)
7. Garitano, S.: Detailed haplotype analysis at the TP53 locus in p. R337H mutation carriers in Southern Brazil: evidence for a founder effect. Hum. Mutat. **31**(2), 143–150 (2010)
8. Giacomazzi, J., et al.: Prevalence of the *TP53* p.R337H mutation in breast cancer patients in Southern Brazil: a multicenter study. Genet. Mol. Biol. **44**(1), e20200089 (2021)
9. Hahn, E.C., et al.: *TP53* p.Arg337His germline mutation prevalence in southern Brazil: further evidence for mutation testing in young breast cancer patients. PLOS ONE **13**(12), e0209934 (2018)
10. Lane, D.P.: p53, guardian of the genome. Nature **358**(6381), 15–16 (1992)
11. Li, F.P., Fraumeni, J.F.: Soft-tissue sarcomas, breast cancer, and other neoplasms: a familial syndrome? Ann. Int. Med. **71**(4), 747–752 (1969)
12. Lundberg, S.M., Lee, S.-I.: A unified approach to interpreting model predictions. In: Proceedings of the 31st NeurIPS, pp. 4765–4774 (2017)
13. Matta, B.P., et al.: Familial history and prevalence of BRCA1, BRCA2 and TP53 pathogenic variants in HBOC Brazilian patients from a public healthcare service. Sci. Rep. **12**(1), 18629 (2022)
14. Mikhail, D.Y., Al-Mukhtar, F.H., Kareem, S.W.: A comparative evaluation of cancer classification via TP53 gene mutations using machine learning. Asian Pac. J. Cancer Prev. **23**(7), 2459–2467 (2022)
15. Paskulin, D.D., et al.: Ancestry of the Brazilian *TP53* c.1010G>A (p.Arg337His, R337H) founder mutation: clues from haplotyping of short tandem repeats on chromosome 17p. PLoS ONE **10**(11), e0143262 (2015)
16. Peng, G., et al.: Estimating TP53 mutation carrier probability in families with Li-Fraumeni syndrome using LFSPRO. Cancer Epidemiol. Biomarkers Prev. **24**(11), 1766–1773 (2015)
17. Pinto, E.M., Zambetti, G.P.: What 20 years of research has taught us about the TP53 p. R337H mutation. Cancer **126**(20), 4678–4686 (2020)
18. Schneider, K., et al.: Li-Fraumeni Syndrome. In: GeneReviews® [Internet]. University of Washington, Seattle (2025)
19. Corredor, J.L., et al.: Performance of LFSpro *TP53* germline carrier risk predictions compared to standard genetic counseling practice on prospectively collected probands. medRxiv (2024). Preprint. https://doi.org/10.1101/2024.07.09.24310095
20. Villani, A., et al.: Biochemical and imaging surveillance in germline TP53 mutation carriers with Li-Fraumeni syndrome: 11 year follow-up of a prospective observational study. Lancet Oncol. **17**(9), 1295–1305 (2016)

SCA-Lex: A Lightweight Forensic Triage Framework Based on Few-Shot Semantic Centroid Alignment

Italo Firmino da Silva(✉), Maurício Darabas Ronzani, Alexandre Leopoldo Gonçalves, and Alison R Panisson

Department of Computing, Federal University of Santa Catarina (UFSC), Florianópolis, Brazil
{italo.silva,m.darabas}@grad.ufsc.br,
{a.l.goncalves,alison.panisson}@ufsc.br

Abstract. Digital forensics currently faces a critical challenge due to the exponential growth in digital evidence volume and the sensitive nature of seized data, which restricts the creation of large-scale public training datasets. This paper proposes SCA-Lex (Semantic Centroid Alignment with Lexical enhancement), a high-performance triage framework for the automated classification of image evidence. Leveraging the Contrastive Language-Image Pre-training (CLIP) foundation model, we introduce a Few-Shot Semantic Centroid Alignment method that optimizes zero-shot knowledge for specialized forensic contexts (Weapons, Drugs, Currency, and Others). Our approach refined semantic anchors within a 512-dimensional vector space using lexical prompt engineering. Benchmarking demonstrates that the SCA-Lex framework achieved 93.69% accuracy, significantly outperforming a robust baseline implementation consisting of a five-architecture Voting Ensemble (89.48%). These results suggest that for privacy-restricted environments where large-scale specialized training is unfeasible, the SCA-Lex framework, leveraging a well-anchored foundation model, provides superior semantic generalization compared to ensembles of supervised specialists.

Keywords: Digital Forensics · CLIP · Triage · Foundation Models · XAI

1 Introduction

The digital forensics landscape has reached a precarious tipping point, driven by the phenomenon increasingly recognized as the "Forensic Tsunami" [2]. As personal computing and mobile connectivity become ubiquitous, the volume of digital image data extracted from seized devices frequently exceeds the human capacity for manual review. Forensic investigators today suffer from severe "data fatigue" and cognitive overload, struggling to triage thousands of files per case, a bottleneck that often delays critical legal proceedings for several months [16].

M. Recamonde-Mendoza and R. C. Barros (Eds.): BRACIS 2026, LNAI 17105, pp. 48–62, 2027.
https://doi.org/10.1007/978-3-032-39882-6_4

While traditional Computer Vision (CV) tools offer potential relief, their implementation in criminalistic workflows faces a dual constraint: data privacy and computational accessibility. Unlike generic academic datasets (e.g., ImageNet), forensic evidence contains highly sensitive private information that cannot be uploaded to cloud-based APIs or released for traditional supervised training [19]. This creates a "privacy bottleneck", where the lack of annotated forensic training data prevents the development of specialized models for local law enforcement.

Furthermore, state-of-the-art Large Multimodal Models (LMMs), while capable of high-level reasoning, often require extreme hardware resources and exhibit high inference latency. These factors make them impractical for processing the thousands of files typically encountered on standard laboratory workstations. Consequently, there is an urgent need for lightweight, locally-executable triage systems that can capitalize on broad semantic knowledge without requiring large-scale, sensitive training data.

To address these challenges, this paper proposes the SCA-Lex Framework, a modular forensic triage system based on Few-Shot Semantic Centroid Alignment leveraging the CLIP foundation model. To achieve this, our methodology operates through three key steps: (1) extracting latent visual features via the CLIP vision encoder; (2) constructing robust textual anchors using a specialized Forensic Semantic Lexicon with a multi-prompt strategy; and (3) applying a Hybrid Fusion mechanism that calibrates zero-shot classification via cosine similarity. By fusing this universal zero-shot knowledge with a restricted set of local investigative anchors, our approach enables high-speed sorting into forensic categories (Weapons, Drugs, Currency, and Others) on consumer-grade hardware. The main contributions of this work are: (i) a privacy-preserving triage framework that bypasses traditional exhaustive training; (ii) a streamlined preprocessing pipeline for automated evidence alignment; and (iii) a comparative evaluation between single foundation model and specialist ensembles in forensic scenarios.

2 Related Work

Recent academic efforts have increasingly leaned towards LMMs for investigative support. For instance, [7] demonstrates the use of generative models like LLaVA and Gemini for contextual scene interpretation in surveillance scenarios, providing complex descriptions of human activities and anomalies. Similarly, in the financial forensic domain, [5] proposed a multimodal framework to categorize fraud types in social media posts, combining textual and visual features to identify illicit advertisements.

Other frameworks have focused on Real-Time Integration and IoT ecosystems. WatchOverGPT [17] utilizes wearable cameras and Large Language Models (LLMs) to automate crime detection and response in urban environments. Furthermore, works by [13] highlight the growing role of intelligent systems for specialized tasks, such as public safety monitoring through distributed CCTV matching.

A separate branch of research explores the challenges presented by synthetic media and AI-generated noise in investigative datasets. Recent studies [12] analyzed transformer-based architectures for identifying AI-generated content, while others [15] proposed zero-shot strategies to detect generative manipulations across various model families. In a practical forensic context, this generative shift introduces significant semantic ambiguity; for instance, the rise of AI-generated advertisements for online gambling platforms often includes realistic but irrelevant images of currency or luxury items. Distinguishing between genuine criminal evidence and generative visual noise from propaganda is a critical hurdle for foundation models that prioritize high-level semantic features. Additionally, the necessity for maintaining data confidentiality has prompted investigations into privacy-preserving machine learning within forensic pipelines [1].

Despite these advancements, these existing approaches face critical systemic limitations when applied to the Forensic Tsunami context of local investigative units. First, generative LMMs require extreme computational resources (multi-GPU setups) and suffer from high inference times, making them impractical for processing the thousands of files typically seized in a single forensic case. Second, several frameworks rely on cloud-based APIs, which introduce severe concerns regarding data sovereignty and the technical chain-of-custody required for court-admissible evidence. Finally, traditional supervised specialist models demand large, annotated public datasets, which are virtually non-existent for sensitive forensic categories like weapons or narcotics.

Unlike cloud-dependent LMMs or data-hungry supervised models, our proposed SCA-Lex framework directly bridges the gap between high-level semantic understanding and operational resource constraints. By utilizing a zero-shot foundation model augmented with Few-Shot Semantic Centroid Alignment, SCA-Lex operates efficiently on consumer-grade local hardware, strictly preserving data sovereignty while bypassing the need for large-scale annotated forensic datasets. This ensures a scalable and secure triage solution tailored specifically for the realities of local investigative units.

3 Theoretical Background

The core of this research involves a comparison between emerging Foundation Models and traditional Specialist Architectures. This section details the technical mechanisms of the models used in this study.

3.1 Multimodal Learning with CLIP (ViT-B/32)

CLIP (Contrastive Language-Image Pre-training) is a bimodal architecture designed to map images and text into a Joint Embedding Space [14]. The primary engine of this architecture uses a Vision Transformer (ViT-B/32) as its vision encoder [4]. This model operates by decomposing 224×224 input images into 32×32 localized patches, which are then processed through transformer layers to capture high-level semantic features.

Simultaneously, the Text Encoder tokenizes natural language prompts into a shared 512-dimensional latent space using the Attention mechanism [18]. In the original framework, a Contrastive Objective pulls correct pairs together. A key distinction of the ViT-B/32 in the context of CLIP is its training scale; by exposure to over 400 million diverse image-text pairs, it develops a "Universal Semantic Prior" that enhances zero-shot generalization.

By mapping both modalities into a unified latent space, CLIP enables zero-shot classification without the need for additional training on specific downstream sets.

3.2 Architecture of Vision Transformers (ViT-B/16)

The Vision Transformer (ViT) represents a shift away from traditional convolutions by treating image patches as a sequence of tokens, similar to word processing in natural language tasks [4]. Specifically, the ViT-B/16 variant is a widely used architecture that, unlike the ViT-B/32, employs a finer patch resolution of 16×16 pixels. While this allows the model to capture more granular spatial details, it also significantly increases the computational cost and the risk of overfitting when trained on specialized, low-volume datasets without the benefit of massive multimodal pre-training. The core mechanism is the Self-Attention layer, which allows the model to weight the importance of different image regions globally, enabling it to focus on forensic evidence regardless of its position in the frame.

3.3 Convolutional Neural Networks (CNNs) in Forensics

Traditional forensic triage tools rely heavily on Convolutional Neural Networks (CNNs) [1]. Architectures such as ResNet and MobileNet are frequently applied in these scenarios. These models are built upon the Inductive Bias of spatial locality, utilizing local receptive fields to detect patterns.

- **ResNet-18/50:** These models introduce Residual Blocks with skip-connections [6], which allow deep layers to learn residual mappings, preventing the vanishing gradient problem and ensuring stable training for categorical classification.
- **MobileNet-V3:** This architecture is optimized for edge-computing environments through Depthwise Separable Convolutions [8], significantly reducing the number of parameters while maintaining high efficiency in real-time forensic scanning.
- **YOLO-v8 (Classification):** A variant of the "You Only Look Once" family [9], known for its extremely fast spatial reasoning and efficiency in identifying salient objects in cluttered scenes.

While these models are highly effective for extracting specific visual textures, such as the metallic sheen of a weapon, they often lack the global semantic context necessary to distinguish between genuine evidence and visually complex "noise" in multi-layered digital environments.

4 The Automated Triage Framework

The developed system operates as a Multimodal Forensic Sorter, designed to automate the initial organization of vast multimedia datasets. The primary task of the framework is to ingest raw digital images extracted from seized devices (input), semantically classify them into one of four prioritized forensic categories, Weapons, Drugs, Currency, or Others,and automatically redistribute these files into corresponding investigative folders (output). This section details the technical framework, from data ingestion to the optimized classification logic.

4.1 Operational Pipeline and Human-in-the-Loop Triage

The automated triage process is structured as a sequential data pipeline designed to operate on standard forensic workstations. First, raw digital evidence is ingested in bulk directly from seized devices or file directories. Second, each image is processed through the CLIP Vision Encoder to extract a high-dimensional semantic embedding. Third, these image embeddings undergo a semantic matching phase, where their cosine similarity is calculated against the predefined hybrid category centroids. Finally, the system executes an automated routing protocol, redistributing the files into prioritized folders based on the highest similarity score. Figure 1 depicts the proposed 6-step structured pipeline. This pre-sorting drastically reduces the manual workload, ensuring that human investigators can focus their time and cognitive effort on reviewing high-impact forensic findings first.

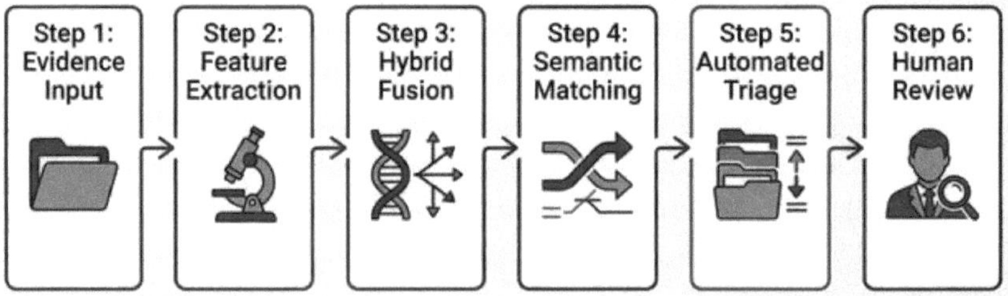

Fig. 1. Operational Workflow: From digital evidence extraction to the automated triage and human investigator review.

4.2 Implementation of the Categorization Engine

The categorization engine employs the CLIP ViT-B/32 architecture [14] as a high-speed semantic feature extractor. The process begins with a standardized pre-processing layer where input images are rescaled to the model's native 224×224 resolution and normalized using pre-training statistics. This procedure ensures that the generated 512-dimensional embeddings occupy a predictable region within the latent space.

To optimize triage accuracy, we enhance the zero-shot classification via a specialized Forensic Lexicon using a multi-prompt strategy. Instead of relying on a single generic label (e.g., "weapon"), we compute the vectorial mean of several descriptive sentences (e.g., "a forensic photo of a metallic firearm", "a seized revolver"). This aggregation generates a robust, composite textual anchor that prioritizes technical forensic features.

By projecting these aggregated descriptions into the joint latent space, the engine constructs a semantically "dense" representation for each target class. This approach specifically mitigates the "lost in the middle" degradation [11], ensuring that even when processing complex multimedia backgrounds, the model maintains focus on the primary evidentiary features. The Hybrid Fusion strategy effectively filters irrelevant dataset artifacts while sharpening the model's focus on the semantic core of each forensic category.

4.3 Forensic Semantic Lexicon

The "Others" category, often treated as a generic background class in traditional computer vision, is anchored here by a specific Forensic Semantic Lexicon. This lexicon consists of over 40 curated prompts categorized into forensic targets and universal benign distractors (e.g., hygiene, health, household items). While Table 1 provides representative examples, the complete set of prompts implemented in the classification engine is publicly available in our repository[1].

Table 1. Examples from the Forensic Semantic Lexicon (Universal Lexicon).

Category	Representative Semantic Prompts (Anchors)
Weapons	"a forensic photo of a physical metallic firearm", "a real 3D handgun or pistol on a surface"
Currency	"a forensic photo of real physical paper currency", "stacks of real bank bills used in law enforcement"
Drugs	"a forensic photo of illegal narcotics or drugs", "pressed bricks of cocaine or marijuana in plastic"
Others (Benign)	"stethoscope, thermometer, bandage", "food, fruit, vegetable"

This engineering of the semantic space allows the model to differentiate, for instance, a real 3D firearm from a tattoo or a cartoon illustration, a distinction

[1] https://github.com/Liga-IA/RepoAI/tree/main/cv/_SCAlex.

that represents a classic failure point for traditional CNNs trained on simple pixel labels.

4.4 Centroid Tuning via Hybrid Fusion and Classification

To adapt the general-purpose CLIP model to specific forensic domains without the necessity of full-scale fine-tuning, we implemented a Hybrid Fusion strategy for centroid initialization. While the proposed architecture is related to a traditional Nearest-Centroid classifier, our formulation extends this paradigm by operating within a multimodal latent space. This method effectively bridges the gap between the universal zero-shot knowledge and the specialized visual distribution of forensic evidence.

Accordingly, instead of relying solely on the textual embeddings derived from the Forensic Semantic Lexicon, the framework calculates a Tuned Forensic Centroid c_j for each category j. This is achieved by combining the textual embedding mean vector T_j with its counterpart visual mean vector V_j.

In this context, the visual prototype V_j is designed to capture the characteristic visual distribution of a specific forensic class. It is calculated as the mean vector of a curated set of N specialized forensic image samples, denoted as I_{jk}, where k represents the k-th individual sample within category j. These N samples are chosen to represent common investigative scenarios, such as specific camera angles, low-light conditions, and diverse backgrounds typical of seizures. Each raw image I_{jk} is processed through the vision encoder layer to generate its corresponding 512-dimensional embedding:

$$V_j = \frac{1}{N} \sum_{k=1}^{N} \text{Encoder}_{\text{vision}}(I_{jk}) \tag{1}$$

Furthermore, the final decision anchor is generated through a weighted linear interpolation in the 512-dimensional latent space. We first define the intermediate hybrid vector c as the weighted average:

$$c = \alpha \cdot T_j + (1 - \alpha) \cdot V_j \tag{2}$$

The final tuned forensic anchor c_j is then obtained via L_2-normalization:

$$c_j = \frac{c}{||c||} \tag{3}$$

The hyperparameter $\alpha = 0.5$ was selected as an unweighted prior to ensure a strict geometric balance between global semantic knowledge (text) and local feature representation (image), preventing empirical bias towards either modality prior to inference. As demonstrated in our Ablation Study (Sect. 5.1), this balanced fusion strategy yields robust generalization across diverse forensic distractors. This alignment mechanism ensures that the model can be tailored to arbitrary law enforcement categories without requiring a single epoch of backpropagation.

This normalization step maintains manifold consistency within the joint embedding space. Since both T_j and V_j are calculated as means of sets of distinct unit embeddings, they reside in the interior of the hypersphere (i.e., $\|T_j\| < 1$ and $\|V_j\| < 1$). Consequently, their weighted average c also resides within the unit sphere ($\|c\| < 1$). While cosine similarity is inherently scale-invariant, re-projecting the hybrid vector c back onto the surface ensures that forensic anchors remain strictly aligned with the hypersphere's unit topology, eliminating magnitude-related biases and ensuring that comparison strictly depends on the learned semantic directions [14]. This geometric process is illustrated in Fig. 2.

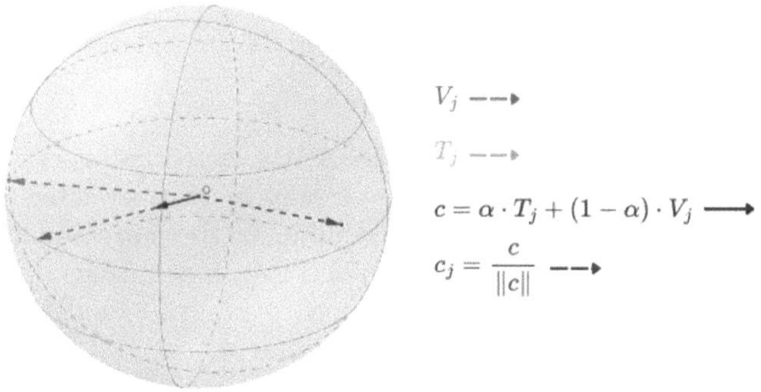

Fig. 2. Geometric Manifold Consistency: Linear combinations of centroids (T_j, V_j) naturally result in a hybrid vector c residing in the hypersphere's interior ($\|c\| < 1$). L_2-normalization re-projects this vector back onto the unit surface to establish the final tuned anchor c_j.

In the SCA-Lex framework, classification is performed by calculating the Cosine Similarity between the normalized image embedding v_i and the hybrid Tuned Forensic Centroid c_j:

$$\text{Similarity} = \frac{v_i \cdot c_j}{\|v_i\| \|c_j\|} \tag{4}$$

By maximizing this similarity, the engine can automatically prioritize evidence that aligns with investigative objectives. This architectural efficiency allows the system to categorize thousands of files in minutes on standard forensic workstation hardware.

4.5 Benchmark Baseline: The Council of Specialists

To evaluate the efficiency of the proposed SCA-Lex framework, we established a comparison baseline using a Voting Ensemble. This ensemble follows a traditional supervised learning approach, consisting of five distinct architectures chosen for their structural diversity: ResNet-18 and ResNet-50 [6], ViT-B/16 [4],

MobileNet-V3 [8], and YOLO-v8 [9]. While these specialist architectures effectively capture spatial and local features like metallic reflections, they often lack the global semantic robustness required to disregard complex forensic distractors. To ensure a controlled experimental comparison, all models in the ensemble, alongside the SCA-Lex framework, were evaluated using the same standardized forensic image sets.

Each model was independently fine-tuned to act as a specialist. Classification in this baseline is determined by a hard-voting ensemble with probability-weighted tie-breaking. While the final decision follows a majority consensus among the five models, category splits are resolved by calculating a cumulative score $S(l)$ for each candidate category l:

$$S(l) = \sum_{m \in \mathcal{M}_l} P(l|m) \tag{5}$$

where $\mathcal{M}_l$ represents the subset of models that selected category l, and $P(l|m)$ denotes the confidence score assigned by model m to that category. The final verdict is given by $\hat{l} = \arg\max_l S(l)$. By combining these architecturally diverse models (Residual-based, Attention-based, and Edge-optimized) with this democratic weighting scheme, the ensemble aims to minimize individual bias and provide a high-rigor baseline for forensic assessment.

A critical distinction observed in our benchmark is the performance difference between the ensemble's ViT-B/16 and the SCA-Lex's ViT-B/32 backbone. While the ViT-B/16 specialist utilizes smaller 16×16 patches for higher-resolution feature capture, its training on a limited forensic dataset introduces a significant risk of "specialist overfitting". In contrast, the SCA-Lex framework leverages a "universal semantic prior" from its extensive pre-training.

5 Experiments and Results

The experimental evaluation was designed to address the challenges of the Forensic Tsunami and the effectiveness of the proposed SCA-Lex framework against the Voting Ensemble benchmark.

5.1 Ablation Study: Centroid Tuning Strategies

To validate the efficacy of the proposed Hybrid Fusion centroid alignment, we conducted an ablation study comparing four distinct initialization strategies. Specifically, we evaluated classification relying exclusively on textual semantics ($\alpha = 1$), exclusively on visual prototypes ($\alpha = 0$), the proposed Hybrid Fusion ($\alpha = 0.5$), and a traditional K-Nearest Neighbors (KNN) over the visual embeddings.

The results in Table 2 demonstrate that while the Visual-Only baseline achieves the highest raw accuracy (95.39%) on the clean test set, it exhibits overfitting vulnerabilities to localized textures (e.g., misclassifying toy guns as

Table 2. Ablation Study: Performance of Centroid Initialization Strategies

Strategy	Accuracy (%)	Macro F1-Score (%)
Text-Only Anchors ($\alpha = 1$)	83.62	82.55
Visual-Only Prototypes ($\alpha = 0$)	95.39	95.42
Hybrid Fusion SCA-Lex ($\alpha = 0.5$)	93.86	93.88
KNN (Visual Embeddings)	92.66	92.69

real weapons). The unweighted Hybrid Fusion strategy ($\alpha = 0.5$) achieves a highly competitive accuracy (93.86%) while successfully inheriting the robust semantic contextualization of the Text-Only baseline, effectively filtering out complex visual distractors that deceive pure visual models.

5.2 Dataset Characteristics and Forensic Distractors

The framework was evaluated using a curated real-world forensic dataset extracted from seized digital devices provided by local law enforcement agencies. Unlike standard computer vision benchmarks (e.g., ImageNet or COCO), this dataset reflects the high-entropy environment of actual criminal investigations, containing a significant proportion of "Forensic Distractors".

These distractors include internet memes, luxury items propaganda, and widespread gambling advertisements (e.g., "Fortune Tiger"-style banners). Such noise often triggers false positives in traditional supervised models due to the presence of metallic textures, saturated colors, and representations of wealth that mimic the visual features of currency and weapons.

The curated dataset comprises a total of 1,861 forensic images, partitioned into two primary sets: a *Training Set* (1,275 samples) used for the semantic centroid alignment (Hybrid Fusion) and a *Benchmarking Set* (586 samples) used for performance evaluation. The distribution of images across the target categories is detailed in Table 3. All classification and inference were executed on a consumer-grade computer equipped with 16GB RAM, i5 processor, an NVIDIA GeForce RTX 2050 GPU, running Ubuntu 22.04.

Table 3. Distribution of forensic image samples across categories for both centroid alignment (Training) and benchmarking (Test) sets.

Category	Training (Alignment)	Benchmarking (Test)	Total
Weapons	323	148	471
Currency	336	150	486
Drugs	289	140	429
Others (Benign)	327	148	475
Total	**1275**	**586**	**1861**

The models were evaluated based on three primary metrics: Accuracy, Macro F1-Score, and Inference Time (ms) per image.

5.3 Performance Analysis: Efficiency vs. Complexity

Table 4 summarizes the performance of all evaluated architectures. The results demonstrate the superiority of the SCA-Lex framework in terms of accuracy, keeping a good operational speed.

Table 4. Comparative Performance of Individual Models and the Ensemble Baseline.

Model/Architecture	Accuracy	Macro F1	Inference Time (ms)
ResNet-18	85.84%	0.8605	**2.93**
ResNet-50	87.71%	0.8798	6.64
MobileNet-V3	87.37%	0.8765	2.95
ViT-B/16	84.98%	0.8536	18.94
YOLO-v8 (Cls)	88.10%	0.8839	14.62
Council (Ensemble)	89.48%	0.8972	46.09
SCA-Lex	**93.69%**	**0.9370**	22.93

The empirical data highlights that the SCA-Lex outperformed the entire 5-model specialist ensemble by over 4%. This demonstrates that for forensic triage, the complexity of an ensemble does not translate into superior accuracy; rather, the semantic robustness of a well-anchored foundation model provides a more effective and computationally lean solution.

5.4 Class-Wise Performance and Semantic Balancing

Table 5 details the Precision and Recall metrics for the SCA-Lex compared to the Ensemble baseline.

Table 5. Detailed Per-Category Performance: SCA-Lex vs. Ensemble.

Category	SCA-Lex (Proposed)		Ensemble (Baseline)	
	Precision	Recall	Precision	Recall
Weapons	**0.99**	**0.96**	0.88	0.95
Currency	**0.99**	**0.96**	1.00	0.85
Drugs	0.91	**0.96**	**0.98**	0.87
Others	**0.88**	0.88	0.77	**0.91**

The granular data reveals that the SCA-Lex framework achieved near-perfect Precision (0.99) for both Weapons and Currency.

5.5 Explainability and Failure Mode Analysis

A significant advantage identified in the SCA-Lex engine is its resilience against "forensic distractors", i.e., items that share visual textures with illicit categories but lack the semantic context. Traditional CNNs in our ensemble baseline frequently misclassified samples such as tattoos of firearms or toy guns as genuine weapons, primarily due to their reliance on local texture gradients and metallic sheen.

In contrast, the CLIP Vision Transformer (ViT-B/32) maps global relationships across patches. When evaluated against the full set of 148 forensic distractors (the *Others* category), the foundation model maintained a precision of 0.88, whereas the Voting Ensemble dropped to 0.77. This "contextual awareness" is further supported by the Attention Maps generated during inference, which consistently prioritized the structural silhouette of objects over isolated pixel intensities.

However, certain failure modes persist. Both systems encountered challenges in low-light scenarios where the contrast between currency stacks and complex textile backgrounds was minimal. Furthermore, very small samples of clutter in disorganized environments remains a challenging boundary for the ViT-B/32 architecture. Future iterations will explore higher-resolution multi-scale feature fusion to address these localized detection gaps.

A notable limitation of this design is the broad granularity of the *Others* category. While employing a predefined multi-prompt lexicon reduces common false positives, it introduces a trade-off: highly anomalous visual distractors not mapped within the Lexicon might be misclassified into the primary target classes. Although subdividing *Others* into finer-grained subcategories (e.g., people, vehicles, nature) was considered, this approach was ultimately rejected to maintain the computational efficiency and operational simplicity required for rapid forensic sorting.

5.6 Qualitative Analysis of the Latent Space

To understand the semantic structure that enables high-accuracy triage, we performed a qualitative analysis of the forensic latent space using Principal Component Analysis (PCA) [10]. Figure 3 illustrates a 2D projection of the 512-dimensional embeddings for the target categories and the centroid anchors.

The visualization reveals that the hybrid centroids effectively act as semantic "gravity poles", partitioning the joint embedding space into distinct, non-overlapping forensic zones. The evident separation between sensitive categories (e.g., Weapons vs. Currency) in the projected space justifies the framework's superior precision. The resulting Voronoi boundaries [3] demonstrate that the alignment of lexical prompts with visual prototypes creates a robust manifold where genuine evidence is correctly pulled towards its respective anchor, even when facing significant visual noise.

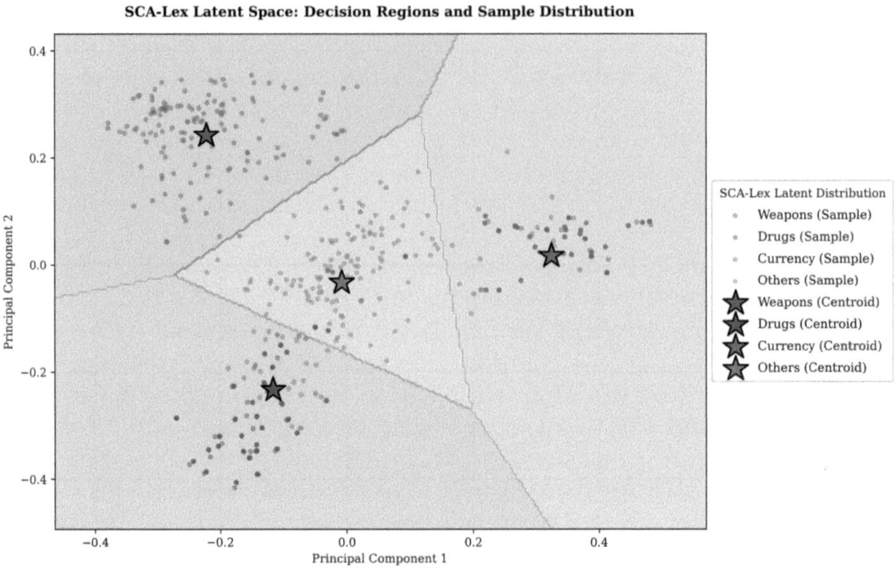

Fig. 3. Qualitative latent space mapping: PCA projection showing semantic clustering and the Voronoi decision regions established by the SCA-Lex hybrid centroids.

Table 6. Infrastructure Overhead and Adaptation Efficiency.

Model/Architecture	Training Time (s)	Model Footprint (MB)
ResNet-18	227.8 s	42.7 MB
ResNet-50	577.7 s	90.0 MB
MobileNet-V3	212.9 s	16.2 MB
ViT-B/16	2288.0 s	327.3 MB
YOLO-v8 (Cls)	320.0 s	2.8 MB
SCA-Lex	**45.0 s**	**< 1.0 MB**

5.7 Infrastructure Overhead and Training Efficiency

The results in Table 6 highlight not only the superior training efficiency and reduced model footprint of the proposed approach, but also its practical suitability for deployment in resource-constrained environments such as forensic offices. In these settings, where data sensitivity, chain-of-custody requirements, and strict privacy regulations often prohibit the use of cloud-based solutions, the ability to train and operate models locally becomes critical. The significantly lower training time (45.0 s) and minimal storage requirements (less than 1 MB) enable rapid adaptation to new forensic categories or evidence types without the need for high-performance infrastructure. This facilitates on-site model updates, reduces dependency on external computational resources, and minimizes data exposure risks. Consequently, the proposed approach supports a more secure, responsive, and operationally feasible workflow for forensic practitioners, aligning computational efficiency with the stringent confidentiality and autonomy demands of digital forensics contexts.

6 Conclusion

This research demonstrates that frameworks like SCA-Lex, leveraging foundation models, represent a paradigm shift in digital forensics triage. By achieving a classification accuracy of 93.69% using our proposed framework, we demonstrated that semantic discovery via lexical enhancement can surpass the performance of complex multi-model ensemble architectures. Our findings demonstrate that universal zero-shot knowledge, when properly anchored via semantic centroid alignment, provides a superior and computationally efficient alternative to traditional supervised specialist ensembles.

Furthermore, this modular approach addresses the critical dual-constraint of data privacy and computational accessibility. By ensuring that all inference and centroid tuning occurs locally on the investigator's workstation, the framework preserves the technical chain-of-custody and data sovereignty required for court-admissible evidence.

In addition, the architecture is designed to be paradigm-agnostic, allowing for the seamless replacement of the core classifier, as demonstrated by our comparison between multimodal foundation models and specialized ensemble. This modularity ensures that the framework remains adaptable to future advancements in LMMs without requiring a complete redesign of the forensic pipeline.

Future work will investigate the refinement of these centroids through continuous active learning loops, where investigators can provide real-time feedback to the model during the triage process. While the current study focused on image classification, we plan to evaluate the integration of these zero-shot capabilities into expanded multimedia pipelines, exploring temporal vision-language models for the automated triage of video evidence and audio-visual forensic artifacts in large-scale criminal investigations.

Acknowledgments. The authors thank the local law enforcement agencies for providing the forensic dataset used in this study. In compliance with academic transparency policies, the authors acknowledge the use of Large Language Models for proofreading and linguistic refinement of the manuscript.

Ethical Considerations and Data Availability. Due to the sensitive and confidential nature of the digital evidence seized during active law enforcement investigations, the raw image dataset used in this study cannot be made publicly available. This restriction is necessary to ensure strict compliance with judicial chain-of-custody protocols and the Brazilian General Data Protection Law (LGPD). However, to promote reproducibility, the complete source code of the SCA-Lex framework, including the Hybrid Fusion algorithms, evaluation scripts, and the full Forensic Semantic Lexicon, will be made freely available in a public repository https://github.com/Liga-IA/RepoAI/tree/main/cv_SCAlex

References

1. Abulaish, M., Haldar, N.A.H., Jahiruddin, J.: P2df: a privacy-preserving digital forensics framework. Int. J. Digital Crime Forensics **13**(6), 1–15 (2021)
2. Ayyagari, D.: The forensic tsunami: the rise of digital forensics. J. Digital Forensics Secur. Law **7**(4), 5 (2012)
3. Chu, L., Hu, X., Hu, J., Wang, L., Pei, J.: Exact and consistent interpretation for piecewise linear neural networks: a decision boundary perspective. In: International Conference on Learning Representations (ICLR) (2018)
4. Dosovitskiy, A., et al.: An image is worth 16x16 words: transformers for image recognition at scale (2020). https://arxiv.org/abs/2010.11929
5. Gao, C., Wu, Y.: Recognizing the financial fraud type of telegram advertisement posts based on multimodal learning. In: ISDFS 2025 - 13th International Symposium on Digital Forensics and Security. IEEE (2025)
6. He, K., Zhang, X., Ren, S., Sun, J.: Deep residual learning for image recognition. In: Proceedings of the IEEE Conference on Computer Vision and Pattern Recognition (CVPR), pp. 770–778 (2016)
7. Hoffmann, S., Fernandes, A.R., Muchulski, V.W., Sarkadi, S., von Wangenheim, A., Panisson, A.R.: Towards intelligent monitoring system using computer vision. In: Proceedings of the 18th International Conference on Agents and Artificial Intelligence (ICAART 2026), pp. 2767–2774. SCITEPRESS (2026)
8. Howard, A., et al.: Searching for mobilenetv3. In: Proceedings of the IEEE/CVF International Conference on Computer Vision (ICCV), pp. 1314–1324 (2019)
9. Jocher, G., Chaurasia, A., Jing, Q.: Ultralytics yolov8 (2023). https://github.com/ultralytics/ultralytics
10. Jolliffe, I.T., Cadima, J.: Principal component analysis: a review and recent developments. Phil. Trans. R. Soc. A: Math. Phys. Eng. Sci. **374**(2065) (2016)
11. Liu, N.F., et al.: Lost in the middle: how language models use long contexts. Trans. Assoc. Comput. Linguist. **12**, 157–173 (2024)
12. Mahara, A., Rishe, N.: Methods and trends in detecting ai-generated images: a comprehensive review. Comput. Sci. Rev. **60**, 100908 (2026)
13. Nama, V., Pillivuttla, S.P., Anu Barathi, B.: Enhancing public safety: criminal identification system through distributed cctv photo matching. In: AIP Conference Proceedings. AIP Publishing (2025)
14. Radford, A., et al.: Learning transferable visual models from natural language supervision. arXiv preprint arXiv:2103.00020 (2021)
15. Sar, A., Roy, S., Choudhury, T., Abraham, A.: Zero-shot visual deepfake detection: can AI predict and prevent fake content before it is created? Found. Trends Signal Process. **19**(3), 212–370 (2025)
16. Saukko, P., Knight, B.: Knight's Forensic Pathology. CRC Press, Boca Raton (2015)
17. Shahid, A.R., Hasan, S.M., Kankanamge, M.W., Hossain, M.Z., Imteaj, A.: Watchovergpt: a framework for real-time crime detection and response using wearable camera and large language model. In: IEEE 48th Annual Computers, Software, and Applications Conference (COMPSAC 2024). IEEE (2024)
18. Vaswani, A., et al.: Attention is all you need. Adv. Neural Inf. Process. Syst. 5998–6008 (2017)
19. Vetrivel, S.C., Vidhyapriya, P., Arun, V.P., Sabareeshwari, V.: Ethical and Legal Considerations in AI-Generated Media. IGI Global (2025)

Improving Low-Confidence AlphaFold Protein Predictions Using Deterministic Local Optimization

Nicholas Wojeicchowski, Lucas Gonçalves Erdmann, and Rafael Stubs Parpinelli(✉)

Graduate Program in Applied Computing, State University of Santa Catarina (UDESC), Paulo Malschitzki Street, Joinville, Brazil
rafael.parpinelli@udesc.br

Abstract. The Protein Structure Prediction (PSP) problem is one of the most prominent challenges in the field of bioinformatics. Recently, the field was revolutionized by AlphaFold, a state-of-the-art model that predicts structures with unprecedented accuracy. Despite these notable advances, AlphaFold still exhibits limitations, particularly regarding the reliability of predictions in regions with low-confidence scores. To address this, this work proposes a refinement model specifically designed to enhance these low-confidence regions. The approach optimizes the structure guided by the Rosetta energy function, utilizing the Nelder-Mead optimization algorithm. The model was benchmarked against recent approaches from the literature across 8 target proteins. Results demonstrate that the proposed method is highly competitive, achieving superior RMSD values in several cases compared to the AlphaFold baseline within the targeted low-confidence regions, while maintaining statistical equivalence in global structural topology. Furthermore, comparative experiments among various optimization algorithms confirmed that Nelder-Mead provided the most effective convergence for this task, validating its superiority for protein structure refinement within this model.

Keywords: Protein Structure Prediction · Alphafold · Refinement model · Nelder-Mead Algorithm

1 Introduction

Proteins are essential macromolecules that govern most cellular processes, with their specific biological functions intrinsically linked to their three-dimensional conformations [8]. Because experimental determination techniques like X-ray crystallography and Nuclear Magnetic Resonance are expensive and time-consuming [9], computational Protein Structure Prediction (PSP) has emerged as a vital alternative. The PSP problem consists of predicting a protein's tertiary structure solely from its amino acid sequence, a task crucial for biomedical applications such as targeted drug design [3].

M. Recamonde-Mendoza and R. C. Barros (Eds.): BRACIS 2026, LNAI 17105, pp. 63–77, 2027.
https://doi.org/10.1007/978-3-032-39882-6_5

In the literature, computational PSP models are primarily categorized into Template-Free Modeling (TFM) and Template-Based Modeling (TBM) [4]. TFM approaches operate without requiring known homologous proteins, though their accuracy decreases for larger targets [4]. Conversely, TBM methods generally achieve higher accuracy for large proteins, but their success depends strictly on the availability of similar sequences with known structures (templates) [3].

AlphaFold advanced computational structure prediction by utilizing deep learning, MSA, and contact maps to generate template-independent models [5]. However, structural prediction remains an open challenge [9], primarily due to the model's uncertainty in specific structural regions. This uncertainty is measured by the pLDDT metric, where scores below 90 reflect suboptimal residue placement [5]. Consequently, the structural unreliability in these low-confidence segments limits the full comprehension of protein functions and restricts the model's utility in precision-critical applications like drug design [3].

Grounded in Anfinsen's postulate—which states that a protein's native structure is thermodynamically stable at its minimum potential energy [1]—this work proposes a model to refine low-confidence regions in AlphaFold 2 predictions. The framework operates in three sequential stages: a pre-processing phase that extracts the low-confidence amino acids; a processing phase where the Nelder-Mead algorithm optimizes these specific residues by minimizing the Rosetta energy function to drive the structure toward a stable conformation; and a post-processing stage that reconstructs the full protein by reintegrating the refined segments.

The primary distinction of this framework is the application of selective optimization. The model operates exclusively on low-confidence amino acids (pLDDT $<$ 90), treating high-confidence regions (pLDDT $>$ 90) as fixed parameters. By concentrating computational efforts only on these specific segments, the method reduces the overall search space, facilitating the efficient refinement of large proteins. This localized strategy complements AlphaFold's initial global search; while the baseline model identifies the general structural topology, the proposed pipeline utilizes the Nelder-Mead algorithm to execute a focused local refinement within the uncertain regions.

Consequently, the central contribution of this work lies in validating this local search integration. The methodology was evaluated using target proteins with known experimental structures (ground truth) that presented low-confidence AlphaFold predictions. Structural improvements were assessed by calculating the Root Mean Square Deviation (RMSD) before and after the refinement process. The RMSD calculations considered only the alpha-carbon (C_α) atoms, computed after a local structural alignment. To ensure robustness, the study also includes a benchmark of the proposed framework against recent prediction models from the literature, alongside a comparative analysis of the Nelder-Mead algorithm against alternative optimization methods applied within the same pipeline.

2 Background

2.1 Protein Structure Prediction and AlphaFold

All proteins are made up of a specific sequence of amino acids. There are 20 amino acids that are known in nature and the union between them makes polypeptides; one or more polypeptides will make proteins. The link between two amino acids is made up of peptide bonds, and these connections form the primary structure of the protein, that is, nothing more than the amino acid sequence of a protein [8]. In terms of structure, a protein has three more types of structure: secondary structure, tertiary structure, and quaternary structure.

The rotation between two amino acids is characterized by three primary angles: ϕ (phi), ψ (psi) and ω (omega). The angles ϕ and ψ are related to the C_α atom and are capable of freely rotating along their respective axes, typically ranging from –180° to 180°.

When referring to computational approaches for the PSP problem, the first step is to choose the computational representation of a protein. There are several representation methods; the models of the more well-known representations are the all-atom model and the backbone model [9].

The all-atom model is the most complete model that contains all the atom information of a protein; however, this model can be computationally expensive given the large number of atoms and interactions of a single protein structure [4]. The other representation is the backbone representation that uses a list of dihedral angle tuples (ϕ, ψ, ω) to represent a protein. This model is interesting because it does not simplify the protein and is also not computationally expensive [9].

The computational methods for the PSP problem can be optimization or machine learning. Optimization-based methods are supported by the postulate of [1], which states that the canonical structure of a protein lies near the minimum potential energy of the molecule [4]. For other side, machine learning algorithms are used in conjunction with large databases containing proteins with already known structures. The target protein, is analyzed, and proteins with similar structures are selected. Based on this comparison, the algorithm attempts to predict the structure of the new protein using these similarities as a reference [4].

AlphaFold, developed by Google DeepMind, is a protein structure prediction model recognized for its performance at CASP14 [5]. Its architecture consists of three main stages: pre-processing, processing (the Evoformer block), and post-processing (the Structure Module). Initially, the model extracts co-evolutionary data via a Multiple Sequence Alignment (MSA) and maps spatial residue relationships using a pair representation [5]. These inputs are then processed within the Evoformer block, which employs attention mechanisms to iteratively exchange information between the evolutionary (MSA) and spatial (pair) representations [5].

Finally, the Structure Module translates this processed data into the 3D coordinates of the predicted protein [3]. A fundamental output of this stage—and the primary metric of interest for this work—is the calculation of the predicted Local Distance Difference Test (pLDDT). The pLDDT provides a per-residue confidence score, quantitatively estimating the model's certainty regarding the predicted spatial position of each individual amino acid [5].

2.2 Nelder-Mead Algorithm

The Nelder-Mead algorithm is a classic deterministic local search method. Its main advantage is that it does not require the gradient of the function, making it particularly useful for problems where the objective function is nondifferentiable or subject to noise. This characteristic not only simplifies its implementation, but also establishes it as a robust approach to optimizing such functions [7].

The core idea of Nelder-Mead involves the evolution of a simplex, a geometric figure, within the search space. For an N-dimensional problem, the algorithm constructs and manipulates a simplex of N+1 vertices. At each iteration, the method evaluates the objective function at every vertex and, through operations of reflection, expansion, contraction, and shrink, moves the simplex toward an optimal or near-optimal solution [7].

The iterative process of the Nelder-Mead algorithm follows a decision tree to replace its worst vertex (x_{worst}) and move the simplex toward an optimum. Each iteration begins by testing a reflection of the worst point through the simplex's centroid. If this new reflected point (x_r) is highly successful (better than the current best point, x_{best}), the algorithm attempts an expansion to accelerate in this promising direction. If the reflected point is not the new best but is still an acceptable improvement (better than the second-worst point), it is simply accepted. If the reflection is poor, the algorithm performs a contraction to search for a solution closer to the simplex. Finally, if none of these operations yield a better point, the entire simplex shrinks around the best vertex (x_{best}) to refocus the search [7]. Figure 1 illustrates these operations in a 2D space.

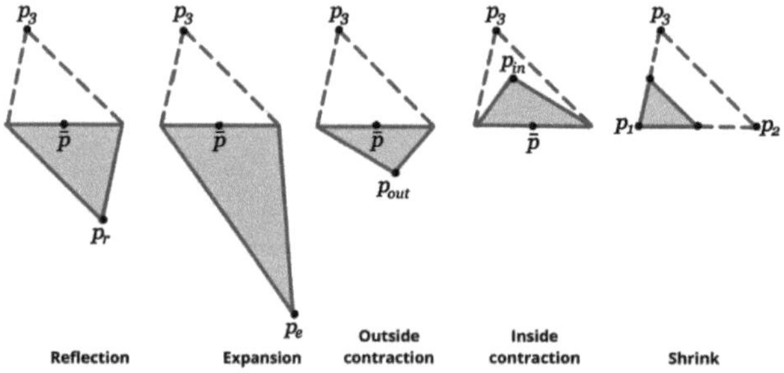

Fig. 1. Nelder-Mead operations. Adapted from [7].

Following any of these operations, the simplex is updated, and the cycle begins anew with the re-evaluation of its vertices to identify the new worst point. The algorithm repeats this process until a stopping criterion is satisfied [7].

3 Related Works

The first related work is the AlphaFold model, proposed by [5]. However, we will not go into depth here, since it is described in Subsect. 2.1.

Recent literature models employ distinct architectures for structure prediction. RoseTTAFold [2] utilizes a three-track neural network (1D MSA, 2D pair representations, and 3D coordinates) that processes data in parallel to generate 3D structures directly. ESMFold [6], alternatively, replaces MSA generation with a pre-trained protein language model (LLM) to extract evolutionary patterns, processing embeddings through a Folding Block and a Structure Module.

Classical template-dependent approaches include SWISS-MODEL and Phyre2. SWISS-MODEL [11] uses Template-Based Modeling (TBM) to map homologous templates, model mutations with rotamer libraries, and apply energy minimization. Phyre2 [10] relies on Fold Recognition, constructing profile Hidden Markov Models (HMMs) from the target sequence to search against known structures via the HHsearch algorithm.

Finally, Table 1 categorizes these works based on their prediction approach, core algorithms, relation to AlphaFold, application of an energy function (E.F.), and focus on low-confidence amino acids (R.L.R.).

Table 1. Comparison among related works.

Model	Source	Approach used	Main Algorithm	A.F	E.F	R.L.R
Alphafold	[5]	ab-initio (DL)	Transf.	Y	N	N
RosettaFold	[2]	ab-initio (DL)	Transf.	Y	N	N
ESMFold	[6]	ab-initio (LM)	Transf.	Y	N	Y
SWISS-MODEL	[11]	Homology Modeling	BLAST	Y	Y	N
Phyre2	[10]	Fold Recognition	HHsearch	Y	N	N
Proposed Model	This work	Hybrid	Nelder-Mead	Y	Y	Y

While existing literature relies either on Transformer-based architectures (such as AlphaFold, RoseTTAFold, and ESMFold) or alignment-based search algorithms (like SWISS-MODEL and Phyre2), this work introduces a unique hybrid approach. The proposed framework fills a methodological gap by simultaneously combining AlphaFold predictions, a Rosetta-guided energy function for refinement, and a local optimization search focused strictly on low-confidence regions.

4 Proposed Method

This work proposes a hybrid model to refine the low-confidence regions of proteins predicted by AlphaFold. The central strategy is to unite AlphaFold's global search capability with a local search refinement, focused only on the regions where prediction quality is low.

As previously mentioned, this refinement is guided by the optimization of an energy function, provided by the *Rosetta* suite[1]. *Rosetta* fulfills two roles in this work: besides providing the energy function (the optimization target), it is used to load the AlphaFold .pdb file and convert it to a centroid computational representation.

The energy function used by Rosetta is a weighted linear combination of terms (specifically implemented using the ref2015 score function) that balance various physicochemical, biological, and statistical properties. The primary properties taken into consideration when calculating the energy function include Van der Waals energies, hydrogen bonds, disulfide bonds, and torsion angles. This function receives a list of dihedral angle tuples representing a protein and returns a score for it. According to Rosetta's criteria, the lower the score, the better the quality of the predicted protein [9].

The computational representation of the protein in this work combines the amino acid sequence with two pieces of information provided by AlphaFold. The first is geometry, which is defined by the centroid model, where each residue is represented by its *backbone* dihedral angles (ϕ, ψ, ω), extracted from the .pdb file, with each angle treated as an independent variable in the optimization space. The second component is the quality information, given by the pLDDT value of each residue, extracted from a .json file. Figure 2 illustrates this combined representation.

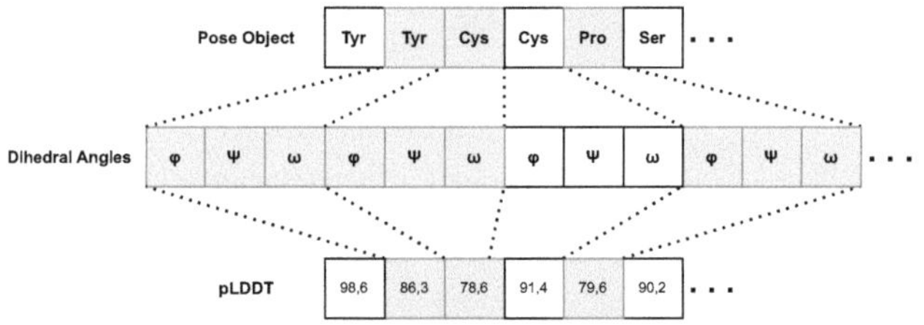

Fig. 2. Computational representation of the protein.

The representation (Fig. 2) has three main components. The first is the *pose* object, which represents the sequence of amino acids that make up the protein. The second component is the dihedral angle tuple (ϕ, ψ, ω), which is mapped to each residue. Finally, the third component is the pLDDT metric, which indicates

[1] Available at https://rosettacommons.org/.

the prediction quality for each amino acid. The residues highlighted in red are those selected for local refinement, as they have a $pLDDT < 90$.

A high-level overview of the model can be seen in Fig. 3, which illustrates its three main stages: *Initialization*, *Processing*, and *Post-processing*.

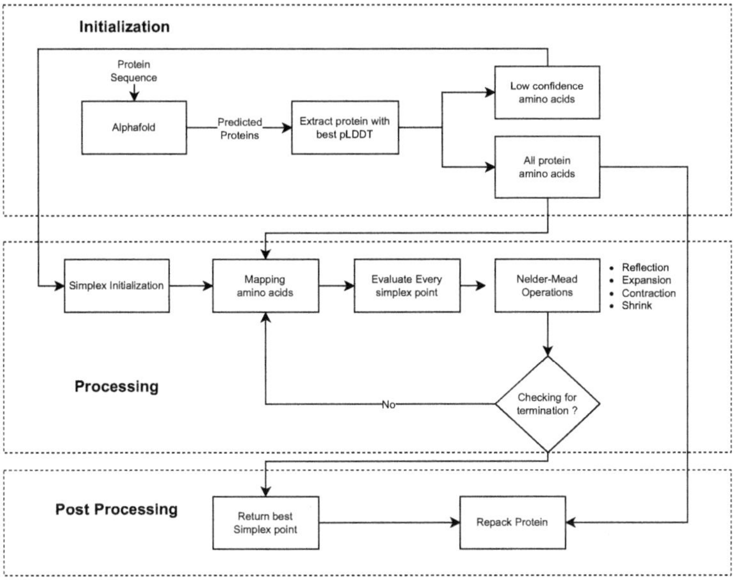

Fig. 3. High-level overview of the model.

The initialization stage begins with the execution of AlphaFold, which generates 40 predictions for the input sequence. For each prediction, the average pLDDT of the structure is calculated, and then the protein with the highest average score is selected for the next stage.

Once the best structure is selected, the next step is to extract two datasets from it: the complete structure (all amino acids) and the list of positions for low-confidence residues ($pLDDT < 90$). This mapping is essential, as it allows the optimizer to act selectively only on the problematic regions, while the Rosetta energy function evaluates the entire protein, which is necessary for the calculation.

The processing stage begins with the initialization of the simplex for the Nelder-Mead algorithm. The simplex is composed of $N + 1$ vertices (solutions), where N (the dimensionality of the problem) corresponds to the number of low-confidence amino acids. Each vertex is a point in the search space, representing a candidate conformation.

The simplex initialization is performed in an axis-aligned manner. The first vertex (P_0) is the initial point, that is, the original solution provided by AlphaFold. The other N vertices are generated from P_0: The k-th vertex (P_k)

is a copy of P_0 with a step applied only to its k-th coordinate. The size of this step is controlled by the *scale* parameter ($0 < scale < 1$).

Following initialization, the model must evaluate each of the $N + 1$ vertices of the simplex. However, the Rosetta energy function (which is used for evaluation) requires the complete protein, not just the low-confidence residues that the simplex is optimizing. Therefore, for each vertex, the model first reconstructs the entire structure. This is done by mapping the low-confidence amino acids (represented by the vertex) back into their original positions. Only after this reassembly is the energy of each vertex actually calculated.

After all vertices have been evaluated, the Nelder-Mead algorithm begins its iteration. It applies one of its operations (reflection, expansion, contraction, or shrink), according to the rules detailed in Subsect. 2.2. Next, the algorithm checks the stopping criterion. If the criterion is met, the best vertex from the current simplex is returned and proceeds to the post-processing stage. Otherwise, a new iteration begins, and the algorithm loops back to the reconstruction and evaluation step for the new vertices that form the simplex.

In the post-processing phase, the complete protein is reassembled using the best vertex returned from the processing stage. This structure is then converted to a *full-atom* model, and finally, a .pdb file is generated containing the refined protein.

5 Experiments and Results

The experiments aim to evaluate the refinement model under various optimization strategies and benchmark it against recent literature models (Sect. 3). All tests were executed in Python 3 on a LABICOM-UDESC server (Ubuntu 22.04.4 LTS, 4x Intel Xeon E7-8860, 40 physical cores/80 threads at 2.26 GHz, 940 GB RAM). Initial structures were predicted using AlphaFold 2 via ColabFold[2], while the refinement stage was implemented using PyRosetta 4.

The dataset comprises eight proteins of varying sizes from CASP14 and UniProt, as detailed in Table 2. To prevent data leakage, all selected targets were strictly required to be absent from the Protein Data Bank (PDB), ensuring they were not included in AlphaFold's training data.

Empirically determined through successive testing, the model's core parameters consist of a scale factor of 0.025, specific coefficients for reflection ($\alpha = 1$), expansion ($\gamma = 2$), contraction ($\rho = 0.5$), and shrinking ($\sigma = 0.05$), and a 10,000-iteration stopping criterion. Parameters like the simplex vertices and the minimum pLDDT threshold were kept at default values.

The model's evaluation encompassed three stages. Initially, the refinement RMSD was compared across local search and evolutionary algorithms. Subsequently, the proposed approach was benchmarked against recent literature models using RMSD, supported by Friedman and Conover-Friedman post-hoc tests.

[2] Available at https://colab.research.google.com/github/sokrypton/ColabFold/blob/main/AlphaFold2.ipynb.

Table 2. Set of proteins used in the experiments.

Protein	Full length	Low-confidence amino acids	Average pLDDT
MTMR10	50	42	73.31
H3BTL1	75	31	84.34
M1WCF2	119	88	82.88
Q3UWR2	166	106	73.57
P82804	207	171	78.24
Q6TMK2	231	195	68.55
T1272s2	326	165	84.90
Q54S83	484	229	84.81

Lastly, the refinement efficiency was evaluated by comparing the RMSD of low-confidence residues before and after processing. This was paired with a qualitative visual superposition of the native, predicted, and refined structures to analyze structural fold adjustments.

The first experiment was designed to benchmark the refinement capability of the Nelder-Mead algorithm against other prominent optimization techniques: Pattern Search, Differential Evolution (DE), and the Biased Random-Key Genetic Algorithm (BRKGA).

To this end, the proposed model, detailed in Sect. 4, was tested with each algorithm. The stochastic methods underwent 30 independent executions to calculate the mean and standard deviation of the RMSD relative to the native structure. The distribution of these outcomes is represented in a box plot, which can be observed in Fig. 4.

Figure 4 illustrates the performance and variance of the tested algorithms. The visual dispersion of the evolutionary methods reflects their stochastic nature, which contrasts with the zero standard deviation of the deterministic Nelder-Mead and Pattern Search algorithms. In terms of structural refinement, Nelder-Mead consistently achieved the lowest RMSD values across all tested proteins. Although the performance margins are narrower for smaller targets, the difference becomes more pronounced as protein size increases, with Nelder-Mead's results remaining consistently below the other methods. These findings justify its integration into the proposed refinement model.

Another metric evaluated for each algorithm was the mean and standard deviation of the processing time per protein, measured in seconds. These results are listed in Table 3.

As observed in Table 3, the execution time of the evolutionary algorithms is considerably shorter than that of the deterministic ones. This efficiency stems from the inherent parallelization capability of population-based methods. Conversely, such a strategy is not feasible in the standard implementation of Nelder-Mead, which operates sequentially. This highlights a limitation of the current work: the substantial processing time required for large proteins.

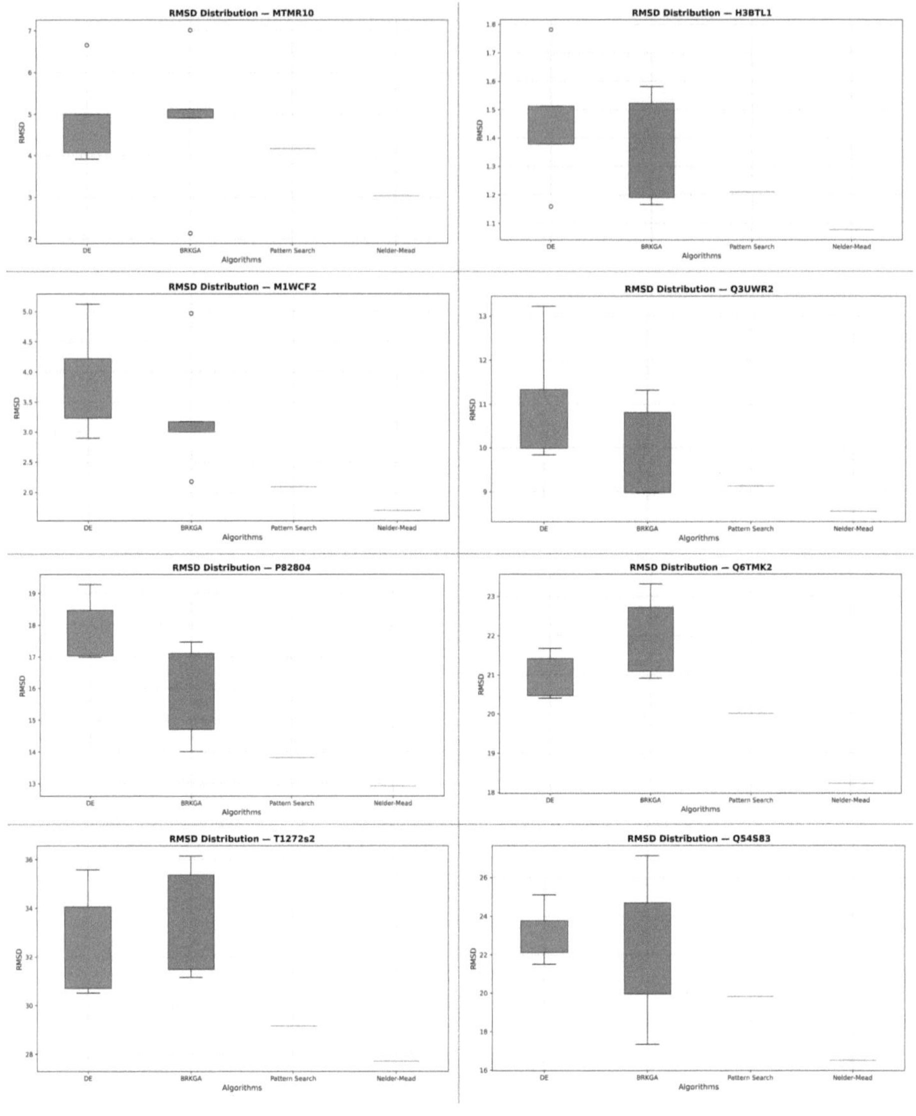

Fig. 4. Box-plot of RMSD values for the tested algorithms.

The second experiment was conducted to compare the proposed model (utilizing the Nelder-Mead algorithm) against recent prediction models from the literature. The baseline stochastic models underwent 30 independent executions to calculate the mean and standard deviation of their RMSD, whereas the deterministic proposed model was executed a single time. The resulting RMSD distributions for all evaluated models were then visualized using box plots (Fig. 5).

Table 3. Mean and standard deviation of the processing time, in seconds, for each tested algorithm.

Proteins	D.E	BRKGA	Pattern Search	Nelder-Mead
MTMR10	23.35 ± 3.85	19.15 ± 0.81	132.88 ± 0	98.376 ± 0
H3BTL1	71.92 ± 7.60	59.47 ± 2.10	246.88 ± 0	186.28 ± 0
M1WCF2	190.22 ± 11.67	88,69 ± 6,03	838.12 ± 0	570.07 ± 0
Q3UWR2	544.90 ± 67,08	216, 64 ± 19,70	3197.18 ± 0	2540.81 ± 0
P82804	460.76 ± 34.42	174,29 ± 13,61	2795.01 ± 0	2216.50 ± 0
Q6TMK2	809.11 ± 89.69	532.96 ± 32.85	7008.23 ± 0	5673.69 ± 0
T1272s2	1115.71 ± 68.36	988.35 ± 77.03	15097.15 ± 0	10521.79 ± 0
Q54S83	94692.15 ± 539.11	81006.82 ± 888.42	591044.11 ± 0	369490.33 ± 0

Table 4. Mean and standard deviation of RMSD for all proteins in low confidence amino acids.

Protein	Alphafold	Proposed Model
MTMR10	5.44 ± 1.377	3.037 ± 0.0
H3BTL1	2.179 ± 0.417	1.199 ± 0.0
M1WCF2	5.693 ± 3.169	1.926 ± 0.0
Q3UWR2	14.23 ± 2.376	9.316 ± 0.0
P82804	25.262 ± 6.496	13.307 ± 0.0
Q6TMK2	24.816 ± 1.598	21.259 ± 0.0
T1272s2	41.401 ± 2.604	35.894 ± 0.0
Q54S83	29.519 ± 3.631	23.677 ± 0.0

Figure 5 illustrates the consistent behavior of the proposed model, which, alongside AlphaFold, maintains the lowest structural deviations across the dataset. In contrast, the remaining models display significant target-dependent variance. ESMFold's performance fluctuates considerably across different proteins, while the TBM approaches (SWISS-MODEL and Phyre2) show degraded accuracy on targets lacking homologous templates, such as H3BTL1 and M1WCF2. Additionally, a direct correlation between the proposed model and AlphaFold is evident. Since the proposed model performs local optimization on AlphaFold's predictions, its final RMSD is structurally constrained by the topological accuracy of the initial conformation provided by the baseline.

To evaluate the statistical significance among the methods, the Conover-Friedman *post-hoc* test was applied to rank the models based on their RMSD. As illustrated in the critical difference diagram (Fig. 6), where positions further to the left indicate lower mean ranks, the proposed model and AlphaFold occupy the primary positions. However, the distance between them is smaller than the critical difference (CD), indicating statistical equivalence regarding the

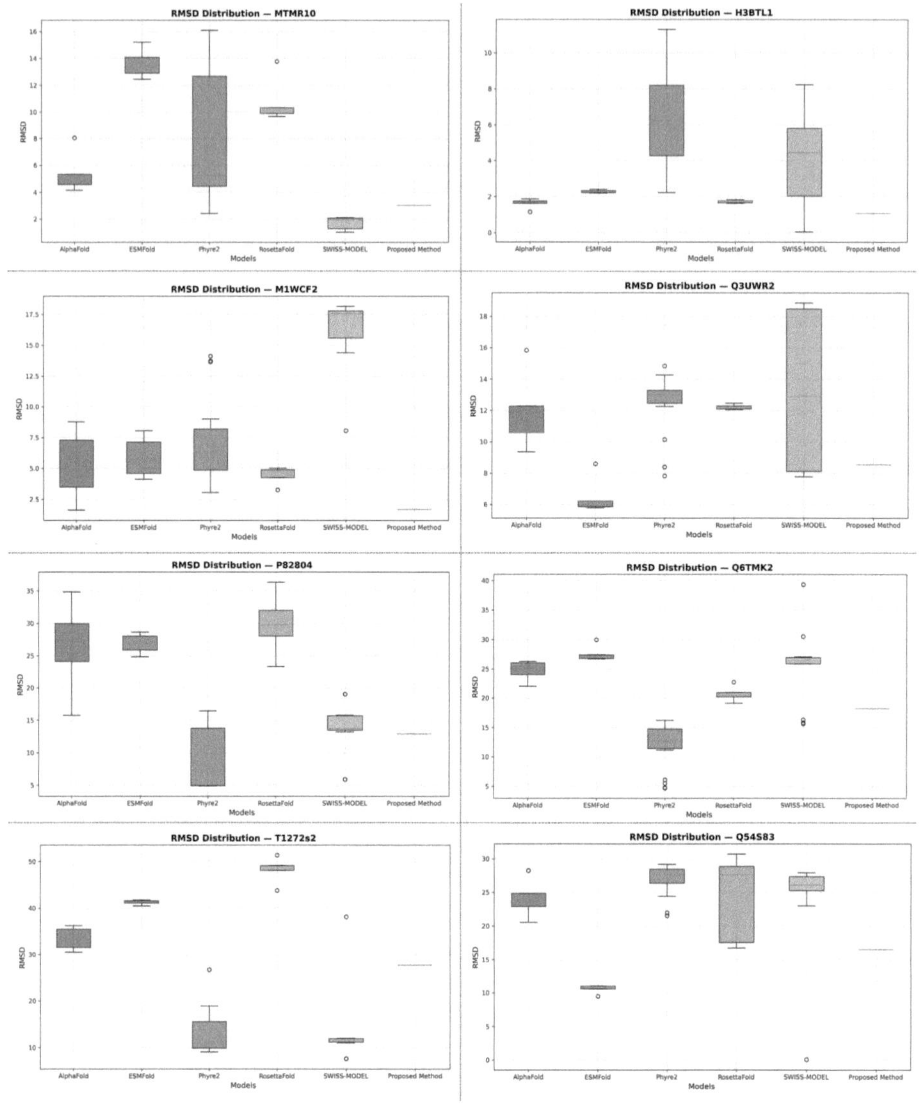

Fig. 5. Box-plot of the RMSD for the tested models.

full-length structure. This suggests that the localized structural improvements are diluted when calculating the RMSD across the entire protein.

Consequently, to assess the specific effect of the refinement process, the RMSD was recalculated exclusively for the altered low-confidence amino acids. The results of this focused analysis are detailed in Table 4.

Table 4 shows that, for all proteins, the proposed model yields a partial RMSD (considering low-confidence amino acids) lower than that of AlphaFold.

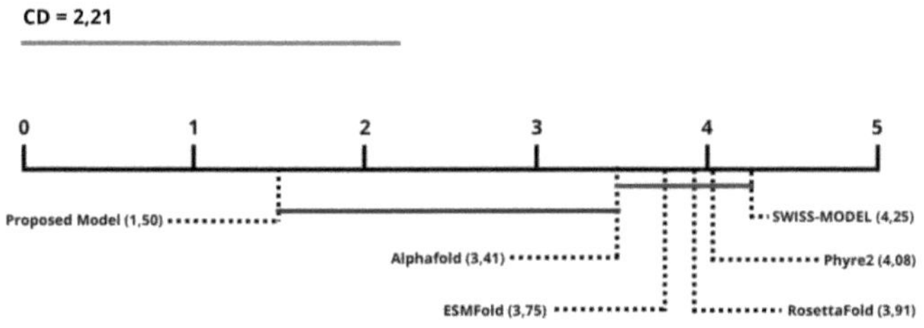

Fig. 6. Critical difference diagram for the tested models.

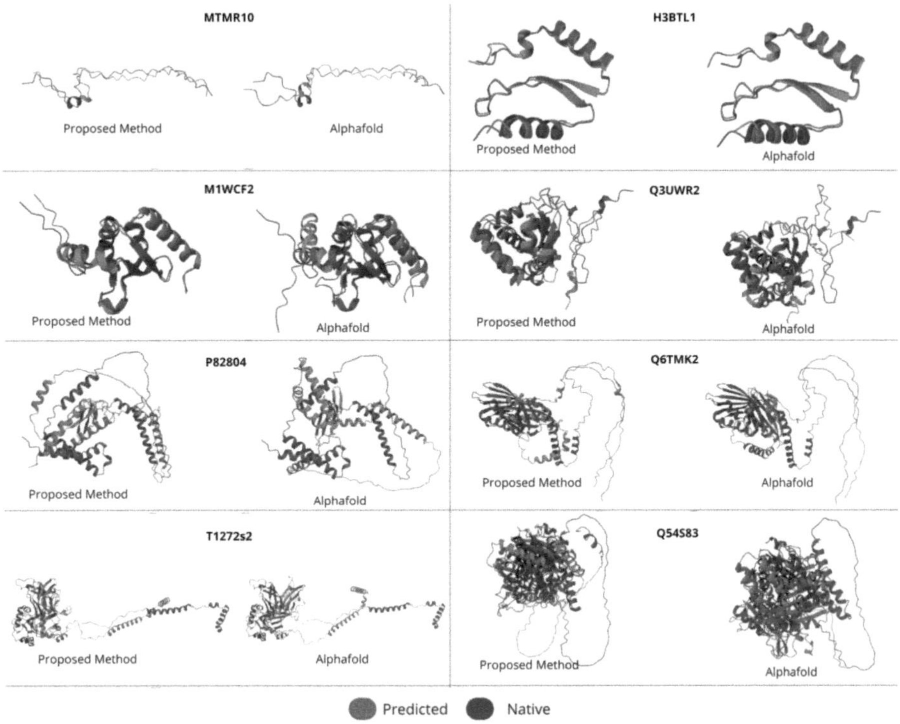

Fig. 7. Structural superposition comparing the native protein with the AlphaFold prediction and the proposed model.

Additionally, a greater variation in this metric is noted in the AlphaFold model. The Friedman test was performed again, this time considering only the RMSD of these local regions. The result confirmed that, for this criterion, there is a statistically significant difference between the models.

Finally, the last experiment aimed at a more qualitative analysis of the refined proteins. To this end, a superposition of the 3D representations of the predicted and native structures was performed for both AlphaFold and the proposed model. The resulting visualizations are presented in Fig. 7.

It is observed in Fig. 7 that, for the majority of proteins, the proposed model achieved a closer approximation to the native structure compared to AlphaFold. The proteins MTMR10, H3BTL1, M1WCF2, and Q3UWR2 predicted by the proposed model are significantly closer to the native conformation than their AlphaFold counterparts. For the remaining proteins, greater proximity is observable in specific regions, although the difference is more subtle. This experiment also reveals a limitation of the model regarding the refinement of certain secondary structures, particularly loop regions.

6 Conclusions and Future Work

Protein structure prediction (PSP) is a pivotal step in understanding biological function, playing a fundamental role in disease combat and drug discovery. While various computational approaches have been proposed over the years, AlphaFold emerged as a technological milestone, predicting structures with unprecedented accuracy. However, it faces limitations, particularly regarding prediction accuracy in regions with low-confidence amino acids.

In this context, the model proposed in this work focuses on refining AlphaFold predictions. It aims to improve low-confidence regions by optimizing a Rosetta suite energy function using the deterministic local search algorithm, Nelder-Mead. The primary contributions of this work are: (1) the proposed methodology is competitive with recent approaches in the literature, and (2) through a comparative algorithm analysis, the Nelder-Mead is well-suited for the refinement task over low-confidence regions.

Experiments demonstrated that, overall, the model enhances the structures predicted by AlphaFold. Furthermore, ranking analysis revealed that the proposed model achieved a superior average classification compared to the others.

Conversely, the use of Nelder-Mead was observed to increase processing time. This reveals a scalability limitation. Hence, we aim to optimize the computational efficiency of the model by leveraging Graphics Processing Units (GPUs) to accelerate the refinement process.

Notwithstanding, other future improvements for the model were identified. The first is the calibration of Rosetta energy function weights, guided by AlphaFold output. Additionally, we propose expanding the framework into a multi-model refiner. Instead of focusing solely on AlphaFold predictions, the system could be adapted to refine structures generated by other relevant academic models, such as SWISS-MODEL, RosettaFold, and ESMFold. Another future work direction includes expanding the experiments to a larger set of proteins.

Acknowledgments. This study was financed in part by the Coordenação de Aperfeiçoamento de Pessoal de Nível Superior - Brasil (CAPES) - Finance Code 001. The authors also thank the State University of Santa Catarina (UDESC) for providing the laboratory infrastructure and equipment necessary to conduct the experiments.

Disclosure of Interests. The authors declare that they have no conflict of interest.

References

1. Anfinsen, C.B.: Principles that govern the folding of protein chains. Science **181**(4096), 223–230 (1973)
2. Baek, M., et al.: Accurate prediction of protein structures and interactions using a three-track neural network. Science **373**(6557), 871–876 (2021). https://doi.org/10.1126/science.abj8754
3. Bertoline, L.M.F., Lima, A.N., Krieger, J.E., Teixeira, S.K.: Before and after alphafold2: an overview of protein structure prediction. Front. Bioinf. **3** (2023). https://doi.org/10.3389/fbinf.2023.1120370
4. Dhingra, S., Sowdhamini, R., Cadet, F., Offmann, B.: A glance into the evolution of template-free protein structure prediction methodologies. Biochimie **175**, 85–92 (2020). https://doi.org/10.1016/j.biochi.2020.04.026
5. Jumper, J., et al.: Highly accurate protein structure prediction with alphafold. Nature **596**(7873), 583–589 (2021). https://doi.org/10.1038/s41586-021-03819-2
6. Lin, Z., et al.: Evolutionary-scale prediction of atomic-level protein structure with a language model. Science **379**(6637), 1123–1130 (2023). https://doi.org/10.1126/science.ade2574
7. Nelder, J.A., Mead, R.: A simplex method for function minimization. Comput. J. **7**(4), 308–313 (1965). https://doi.org/10.1093/comjnl/7.4.308
8. Nelson, D.L., Cox, M.M.: Princípios de bioquímica de Lehninger, 8th edn. Artmed Editora, Porto Alegre (2022)
9. Parpinelli, R.S., Wojeicchowski, N., Will, N.N.: Protein structure prediction with evolutionary algorithm. Elsevier (2024). https://doi.org/10.1016/bs.apcsb.2024.09.006
10. Powell, H.R., Islam, S.A., David, A., Sternberg, M.J.: Phyre2.2: a community resource for template-based protein structure prediction. J. Molec. Biol. **437**(15), 168960 (2025). https://doi.org/10.1016/j.jmb.2025.168960
11. Waterhouse, A.M., Studer, G., Robin, X., Bienert, S., Tauriello, G., Schwede, T.: The structure assessment web server: for proteins, complexes and more. Nucleic Acids Res. **52**(W1), W318–W323 (2024). https://doi.org/10.1093/nar/gkae270

StreamGen: An Interactive Web-Based Generator of Non-stationary Data Streams

Rafaella Oliveira[1(✉)], Hiago F. Oliveira[1], Elaine R. Faria[2], João Gama[3], and Ricardo Cerri[1]

[1] Instituto de Ciências Matemáticas e de Computação, Universidade de São Paulo, São Carlos, SP, Brazil
{rafaella_oliveira,h_freire}@usp.br, cerri@icmc.usp.br

[2] Faculty of Computing, Federal University of Uberlândia, Uberlândia, MG, Brazil
elaine@ufu.br

[3] INESC TEC, University of Porto, Porto, Portugal
joao.gama@inesctec.pt

Abstract. Evaluating learning algorithms under non-stationary conditions requires benchmark datasets with precisely controlled drift characteristics—a need that existing synthetic generators address only partially, as they rely on numerical parameterization without direct control over the spatial and temporal structure of drift. This paper proposes a canvas-based generation tool for synthetic multi-label data streams in which concept drift, concept evolution, and label overlap emerge directly from the geometric and temporal configuration of centroid trajectories, providing explicit and visually verifiable control over drift type, severity, and timing. Extra feature dimensions are positioned via Moore-neighborhood displacement from the cluster's spatial centroid, with configurable scale and offset per feature and per cluster, and can optionally follow independent trajectories, enabling the generation of datasets where feature dimensions evolve under distinct drift processes. The tool is implemented in StreamGen, an interactive web application that operationalizes the proposed approach without requiring programming expertise or software installation. Experiments across six synthetic multiclass and multi-label datasets covering all four canonical drift types, concept evolution, and complex spiral trajectories with disconnected feature dimensions confirm that the generation tool produces datasets with distinct and theoretically consistent non-stationary dynamics, and that trajectory geometry alone is sufficient to generate substantially more challenging scenarios than canonical drift configurations under identical parametric settings. StreamGen is openly available at https://streamgen.vercel.app/.

Keywords: Generator · Data streams · Multiclass · Multi-label

1 Introduction

Data streams are sequences of instances generated continuously over time, often at high speed and in potentially unbounded volumes. In many real-world sce-

M. Recamonde-Mendoza and R. C. Barros (Eds.): BRACIS 2026, LNAI 17105, pp. 78–92, 2027.
https://doi.org/10.1007/978-3-032-39882-6_6

narios, the underlying statistical properties of these streams change over time, a phenomenon known as concept drift [2,9,10,12,17]. Such changes can occur abruptly, as in sensor failures or market crashes, or gradually, as in seasonal behavioral shifts or evolving user preferences [31]. Learning algorithms operating in these environments must detect and adapt to concept drift to maintain predictive performance, making the evaluation of such algorithms a critical and active research concern [11,19].

A challenge in concept drift research is the availability of suitable benchmark datasets. Real-world streams with precisely labeled drift events are rare, expensive to collect, and often cannot be shared due to privacy or proprietary constraints [12,28]. Even when available, they rarely allow researchers to isolate specific drift configurations since timing, type, and intensity of drift are unknown or uncontrolled. Synthetic data generators address this gap by producing controlled streams in which drift characteristics are fully specified.

However, most existing tools are embedded in larger frameworks such as MOA [5], scikit-multiflow [21], RIVER [20] and capyMOA [15], and rely on numerical parameterization rather than direct control over the spatial and temporal structure of drift. Generating a specific scenario, such as a gradual transition confined to a particular region of the feature space, a controlled multi-label overlap of defined duration, or a complex trajectory that revisits previously occupied regions, requires writing code and reasoning about abstract parameters without visual feedback, creating a significant barrier to systematic experimentation, particularly in educational contexts.

To address these limitations, we propose a tool for synthetic data stream generation in which concept drift, concept evolution, and multi-label structure are defined through the geometric and temporal configuration of cluster centroid trajectories in a two-dimensional canvas, rather than through numerical parameterization alone. This tool is implemented in StreamGen, an interactive web application that operationalizes the proposed approach with no programming expertise or software installation required. Every aspect of the stream is customizable, including the number of clusters, their spatial trajectories, temporal boundaries, instance density, and distribution spread, allowing the same underlying drift type to range from a simple, near-linear transition to a trajectory with multiple overlap regions, governed entirely by the geometry the user defines. The main contributions of this paper are:

- A canvas-based generation tool in which concept drift and concept evolution emerge from the geometric and temporal configuration of centroid trajectories, providing fine-grained, visually verifiable control over drift timing, severity, and spatial structure, including complex trajectory geometries that go beyond standard linear or rotational drift patterns;
- A spatially-grounded mechanism for multi-label stream generation, in which label overlap is determined by the geometric proximity of cluster centroids rather than by abstract label transformation strategies, together with a Moore-neighborhood-based mechanism for positioning additional feature

dimensions at controllable degrees of spatial correlation with the principal drift trajectory;
- StreamGen, a web-based interactive application that implements the proposed tool, requiring no programming expertise or software installation;
- A set of reproducible benchmark datasets covering all four drift types, concept evolution, and complex distribution scenarios based on trajectory geometries, exported with full drift annotation metadata.

The remainder of this work is organized as follows. Section 2 reviews related work, while Sect. 3 introduces background and definitions. Section 4 describes the StreamGen tool, and Sect. 5 presents experimental results. Finally, Sect. 6 presents the conclusions and future improvements to the tool.

2 Related Works

Synthetic data stream generation has been primarily addressed through large frameworks such as MOA [5], scikit-multiflow [21], RIVER [20], and CapyMOA [15], which provide comprehensive suites of generators, classifiers, and evaluation tools accessible via programming interfaces. Within these frameworks, generators such as the Hyperplane generator [16], which simulates gradual drift by rotating a decision boundary in feature space, and the RandomRBF generator, which produces incremental drift through random centroid walks, have become standard benchmarks in the concept drift literature. Despite their expressiveness, these tools share a common limitation: drift is configured through numerical parameters without spatial or temporal feedback, making it difficult to define specific scenarios such as a controlled overlap between two clusters during a precise temporal window, or a trajectory confined to a particular region of the feature space. The type, timing, and geometry of drift are determined by fixed algorithmic procedures rather than by user intent, and no existing generator provides visual feedback during configuration.

The generation of synthetic multi-label data streams has received comparatively little attention. Read et al. [24] proposed a foundational framework for multi-label stream generation with configurable label dependencies and concept drift, demonstrating that drift may affect individual labels independently or jointly—a challenge absent from the multiclass setting. However, their approach relies on parameterized generation without spatially defined cluster trajectories, and most subsequent tools treat multi-label scenarios as extensions of multiclass generators through label transformation strategies [29] rather than as first-class generation targets. The generation model proposed in this paper addresses these limitations by grounding drift specification in centroid trajectories whose geometry directly determines drift type and timing, and by providing a spatially-defined multi-label mechanism in which label overlap emerges from cluster proximity rather than from abstract label transformations.

3 Background and Definitions

This section introduces the core concepts and formal definitions that underline the StreamGen generation model.

3.1 Data Streams

A multiclass data stream is a potentially unbounded sequence of instances $S = \langle x_1, x_2, \ldots, x_t, \ldots \rangle$, where each instance $x_t = (f_1, f_2, \ldots, f_d, y_t)$ consists of a feature vector of dimension d and an associated label y, observed at a discrete time t [9,12,13]. In the multi-label setting, this assumption changes: each instance is associated with a label vector $l_q \in \mathcal{L}$, where $\mathcal{L} = \{l_1, l_2, \ldots, l_q\}$ is a finite set of labels, and multiple labels may be simultaneously active for a given instance [6,7,14,17,24,26,29,30].

Unlike static datasets, data streams are generated continuously and must be processed under constraints of limited memory and bounded processing time per instance [24]. Accordingly, in the context of supervised learning, a stream learner must produce a prediction for each incoming instance before observing its true label, and subsequently update its model upon receiving feedback [6,8,23,26].

3.2 Concept Drift

Let $P_t(x, y)$ denote the joint probability distribution over features and labels at time t. Concept drift occurs when $P_t(x, y) \neq P_{t+\tau}(x, y)$ for some time lag $\tau > 0$ [12,19]. This change may affect the distribution of features $P_t(x)$, the posterior distribution of labels given features $P_t(y \mid x)$, or both. From a learning perspective, drift in $P_t(y \mid x)$ is the most critical, as it directly invalidates previously learned decision boundaries [24].

Concept drift can be characterized along two dimensions: its severity, which captures the magnitude of distributional change, and its transition, which describes how the change occurs over time [9,12,18,19]. Given this, the literature separates the changes into four types:

- Abrupt: the distribution changes instantaneously, at a single time step, with no transition period. Formally, $P_{t-1}(x, y) \neq P_t(x, y)$ [2];
- Gradual: two concepts coexist during a transition window of duration w, with the new concept gradually establishing itself and replacing the old one [9,12];
- Incremental: the distribution changes continuously over time in the distribution space, such that $P_t(x, y)$ varies as a continuous function of t;
- Recurrent: a concept that was previously active returns after a period [9,19]. As an example, there can exist time steps $t_1 < t_2 < t_3$ such that $P_{t_1}(x, y) \approx P_{t_3}(x, y) \neq P_{t_2}(x, y)$ [9,19].

3.3 Concept Evolution

While concept drift describes changes in the distribution of existing classes over time, concept evolution refers to a distinct and complementary phenomenon in which entirely new classes emerge in the stream after the learning process has already begun [9,17]. Formally, let $\mathcal{Y}_t = \{c_1, c_2, \ldots, c_m\}$ denote the set of classes active at time t. Concept evolution occurs when there exists a time step $t' > t$ such that $\mathcal{Y}_{t'} \supset \mathcal{Y}_t$, that is, the label space strictly expands over time with the introduction of one or more previously unseen classes. This phenomenon poses significant challenges for stream learners, as models trained exclusively on $\mathcal{Y}_t$ lack the capacity to recognize or classify instances belonging to classes in $\mathcal{Y}_{t'} \setminus \mathcal{Y}_t$. Handling concept evolution, therefore, requires mechanisms for novelty detection, dynamic model expansion, and the integration of new class representations without catastrophic forgetting of previously learned concepts [9].

Concept evolution may occur in isolation or in combination with concept drift. In the latter case, existing classes may simultaneously shift their distributions while new classes emerge, producing complex non-stationary scenarios that are particularly challenging to evaluate without controlled synthetic data.

4 StreamGen Overview

StreamGen is a web-based framework for generating synthetic labeled data streams with controllable concept drift. The system was designed to support the creation of both single-label and multi-label streams through direct manipulation of cluster trajectories, allowing users to define spatial and temporal properties of the data generation process without requiring programming expertise. Figure 1 presents the main components of the StreamGen interface. StreamGen[1] and its source code[2] are freely available.

The StreamGen interface is organized into a configuration sidebar, a top toolbar, and a central interactive canvas. The sidebar provides access to global stream parameters through a dedicated modal, while the toolbar controls stream generation, visualization, and dataset export. The canvas serves as the primary workspace, where users define centroid trajectories and observe the stream evolving in real time; colored trajectories represent distinct clusters, and black points indicate multi-label instances produced in regions where neighboring distributions overlap. A central design principle of the generation model is that concept drift should be specified through explicit spatial and temporal trajectory configurations rather than through low-level numerical parameters: different geometric and temporal arrangements of segments naturally produce abrupt, gradual, incremental, recurrent, and concept-evolution scenarios, establishing a direct and observable relationship between user-defined trajectories and the resulting stream dynamics. These configurations are not mutually exclusive: multiple drift

[1] https://stream-gen.vercel.app/.
[2] https://github.com/rafaellaoliveira-source/StreamGen.

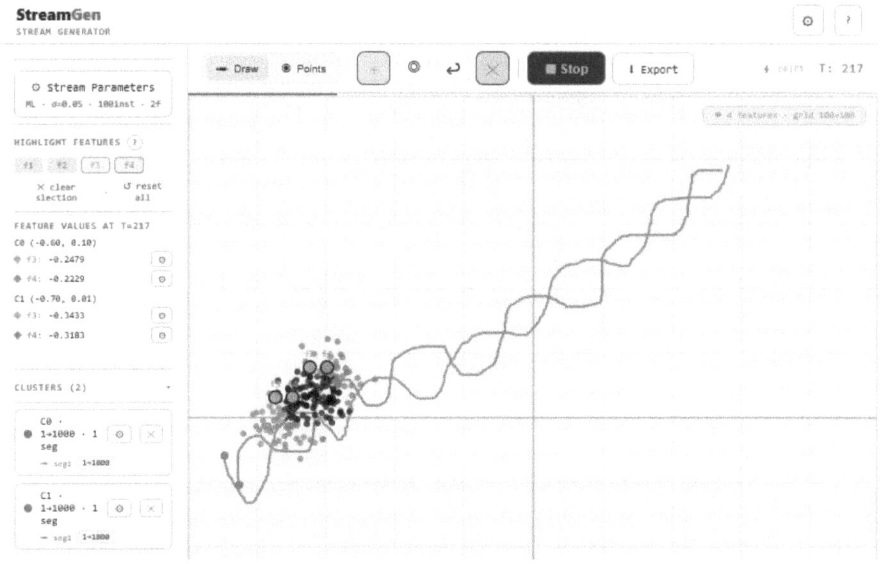

Fig. 1. StreamGen Web interface.

types, concept evolution, per-cluster instance frequency variation, and independently evolving feature dimensions can be combined within a single dataset, enabling the construction of composite non-stationary scenarios that reflect the complexity of real-world data streams.

Multi-label instances emerge from the spatial overlap of cluster distributions, allowing label relationships to evolve as concepts move, appear, merge, or separate over time—a mechanism that enables dynamic multi-label scenarios that are difficult to specify using traditional parameter-based generators. To the best of our knowledge, no existing generator combines visual specification of drift trajectories, native multi-label stream generation, and support for concept evolution within a single environment. Figure 2 summarizes the three-step generation pipeline, where solid boxes represent parameters always available to the user and dashed boxes indicate conditional configurations that appear only when the corresponding option is selected.

4.1 Gaussian Cluster Distributions

In StreamGen, a *cluster* represents a single class c (or label, in the multi-label setting) and corresponds to a Gaussian distribution over the feature space whose centroid moves over time. At each time step t, a configurable number of instances are sampled around the cluster's current centroid position, meaning that a single time step may produce multiple instances per cluster, and multiple clusters may be simultaneously active, in contrast to stream formulations that assume a single

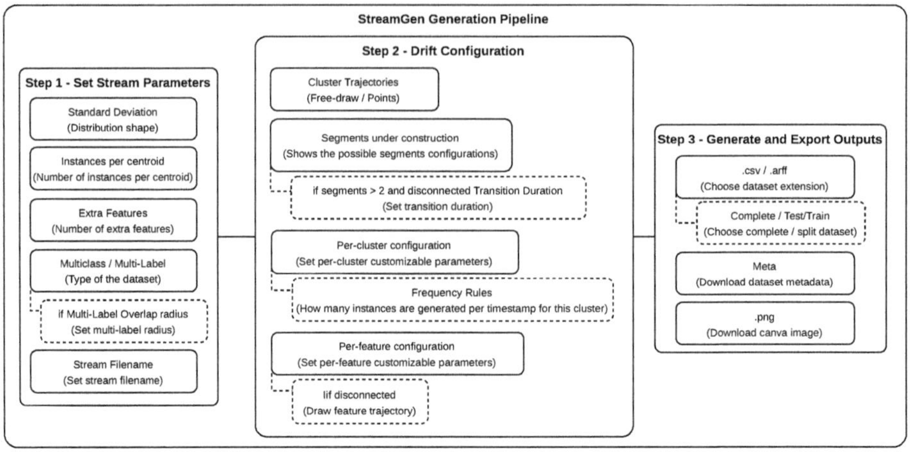

Fig. 2. Overview of StreamGen generation pipeline.

instance per time step. This design allows the spatial structure and density of each class to be explicitly controlled throughout the stream.

StreamGen models each class as a Gaussian cluster with a time-varying centroid $\mu_t = (\mu_x, \mu_y) \in [-1, 1]^2$ on the canvas plane. The Eq. 1 presents for a given centroid position at time t, how spatial instances are generated by sampling each coordinate independently:

$$x \sim \mathcal{N}(\mu_x,\ \sigma^2), \quad y \sim \mathcal{N}(\mu_y,\ \sigma^2) \tag{1}$$

where σ is a global spread parameter shared across all clusters. Extra feature dimensions $f_3, \ldots, f_k$ are not sampled around independently positioned centroids; instead, their centroids are derived from the cluster's spatial centroid μ_t through a Moore-neighborhood-based displacement mechanism, described in Sect. 4.3, ensuring that every additional feature remains linked, by construction, to the same drift process that governs the canvas dimensions. All generated values are clipped to the interval $[-1, 1]$.

4.2 Centroid Trajectories and Drift

The generation of synthetic datasets for data stream research remains a challenging task, particularly when specific characteristics such as concept drift, concept evolution, or changes in data distribution must be incorporated [1,27,28]. Although several generators have been proposed, they typically require users to configure data evolution through abstract parameters, such as rotation angles, transition widths, or stochastic movement rules, with little insight into the resulting behavior before the stream is produced [25]. To address these limitations, we propose a visual stream design environment StreamGen, in which concept drift is introduced by defining centroid trajectories, sequences of positions $\mu_t = (\mu_x, \mu_y)$

that a cluster centroid occupies over time. A trajectory can be composed of one or more segments, each lasting for a specific time interval $[t_s, t_e]$. The drift type of a cluster is determined by the geometric and temporal configuration of its segments:

- A single free-drawn path segment produces incremental drift, as the centroid moves continuously along the drawn curve;
- Two or more points or separated segments without temporal overlap produce abrupt drift, as the centroid jumps instantaneously between positions;
- Separated segments with a configured overlap duration $w > 0$ produce gradual drift. During the overlap window, instances are drawn from both the outgoing and incoming centroids, with the proportion transitioning linearly from the former to the latter;
- Three or more free-drawn segments whose first and last trajectories overlap spatially produce recurrent drift, as the centroid returns to a region previously occupied by an earlier distribution, causing a previously active concept to reappear during the final segment.

4.3 Extra Feature Generation

Extra feature dimensions beyond x and y are positioned relative to the cluster's spatial centroid $\mu_t = (\mu_x, \mu_y)$ using the Moore neighborhood [22]. For a configured number of extra features N, relative offsets $(\Delta x_k, \Delta y_k)$ are assigned for each $k = 1, \ldots, N$ by traversing concentric square rings around the origin: the first ring covers the eight immediate neighbors $(\pm 1, 0)$, $(0, \pm 1)$, $(\pm 1, \pm 1)$; the second ring adds sixteen positions; and so on, allowing the mechanism to scale to an arbitrary number of features without repetition. The following Eq. 2 shows how a feature's centroid f_k at time t is computed:

$$\mu_{f_k}(t) = \Big(\text{clip}\big(\mu_x + \Delta x_k \cdot \delta \cdot \alpha_k + \beta_x^{(k)},\ -1,\ 1\big),\ \ \text{clip}\big(\mu_y + \Delta y_k \cdot \delta \cdot \alpha_k + \beta_y^{(k)},\ -1,\ 1\big)\Big) \quad (2)$$

where δ is a user-configurable base step shared by all extra features, $\alpha_k \in [-3, 3]$ is a per-feature, per-cluster scale factor, and $(\beta_x^{(k)}, \beta_y^{(k)})$ is a per-feature, per-cluster offset. This formulation allows the user to control, independently for each feature and each cluster, how strongly f_k remains spatially correlated with the cluster's principal trajectory: small α_k and $\beta^{(k)}$ values produce features nearly identical to the canvas centroid, while larger values progressively decouple f_k from the spatial drift, without requiring it to be generated as an independent, uncontrolled dimension.

Once $\mu_{f_k}(t)$ is determined, feature values are sampled from a Gaussian distribution centered at the feature centroid, following the same procedure as Eq. 3

$$f_k \sim \mathcal{N}\big(\mu_{f_k}(t),\ \sigma^2\big) \quad (3)$$

StreamGen additionally supports a *disconnected mode*, in which the user draws an independent trajectory π_k for feature f_k, following the same drawing and interpolation logic described in Sect. 4.2 for cluster centroids. In this mode, f_k no longer depends on the cluster's spatial centroid μ_t: its position is determined entirely by π_k, allowing a subset of the feature space to follow a completely separate drift process, decoupled from the visible x-y trajectory.

4.4 Default Hyperparameters and Design Choices

Several generation hyperparameters have default values in the current implementation, which are presented below for reproducibility.

The multi-label overlap radius is defined as $r = \lambda \cdot \sigma$, where $\lambda \in [1, 6]$ is a user configurable multiplier and σ is the global cluster standard deviation parameter. The range was defined to produce meaningful multi-label overlap under typical stream configurations with $\sigma \leq 0.1$. Since each cluster represents a single class in the generated stream, an instance x_t receives a positive label for class c_i, where $i = 1, \ldots, M$, and M is the number of active clusters, if its Euclidean distance to the centroid $\mu_t^{(i)}$ of cluster at time t is at most r. The default value is $\lambda = 3$, which at $\sigma = 0.05$ yields $r = 0.15$ units, approximately three standard deviations, ensuring that only points in the tails of the Gaussian distribution overlap with neighboring clusters.

The train/test split is performed by instance count rather than by timestamp: the first $p\%$ of instances, sorted chronologically and shuffled within each time step, are assigned to the training partition, and the remaining $(100 - p)\%$ to the evaluation partition, where p is a user-defined integer in $[10, 90]$. The training file omits drift metadata, while the evaluation file is accompanied by a separate metadata file (`_meta.txt`) containing per-cluster drift annotations, including drift start time stamp, drift end time stamp, transition duration, and split configuration.

5 Dataset Generation and Experimental Validation

To demonstrate the capabilities of the StreamGen generation model and validate that the generated datasets produce meaningful and distinguishable learning scenarios, six synthetic multi-label datasets were produced: four representing the canonical drift types supported by the model (abrupt, gradual, incremental, and recurrent), one representing concept evolution, and one complex dataset with interleaving spiral trajectories and disconnected extra feature dimensions. All datasets share a common configuration: two classes(clusters), five features (f_1, f_2, f_3, f_4, f_5), a stream duration of $t \in [1, 100]$, 20 instances per centroid per time step, standard deviation $\sigma = 0.05$, multi-label overlap radius $r = 3\sigma$, and feature step $\delta = 0.05$. The extra features f_3, f_4, and f_5 are positioned via Moore neighborhood displacement from each cluster's spatial centroid, as described in Sect. 4.3. Table 1 summarizes the structural and statistical properties of each dataset.

The recurrent dataset was configured with three free-drawn segments whose first and last trajectories are spatially overlapping, causing the concept to return

Table 1. Structural properties of the generated datasets.

Property	Abrupt	Gradual	Increm.	Recurrent	Spiral	Conc. Evol.
Features	5	5	5	5	5	5
Classes (Clusters)	2	2	2	2	2	3
Overlap duration	0t	40t	–	0t	–	0t
Total instances	4,000	4,000	4,000	4,000	4,000	5,020

to a region previously occupied by the initial distribution. The gradual dataset was configured with a transition overlap of 40 time stamps. The tool automatically determines the midpoint of the cluster duration and symmetrically distributes the overlap around it, ensuring both centroids coexist during the transition window. Rounding applied to segment boundaries resulted in an effective overlap of 40 time stamps ($t = 31$ to $t = 71$), during which instances are sampled from both centroids simultaneously. The incremental dataset uses a single continuous, free-drawn trajectory spanning the full stream duration, resulting in smooth centroid displacement throughout. The abrupt dataset uses two disconnected point segments, causing an instantaneous centroid jump at the transition tick. The concept evolution dataset introduces a third cluster at $t = 50$, representing the emergence of a new class in the middle of the stream. From $t = 50$ onward, the number of active clusters increases from 2 to 3, raising the instances per time stamp from 20 to 60 and the total stream length to 5,020 instances. The spiral dataset follows an incremental configuration but with interleaving spiral trajectories; features f_3 and f_5 are set to disconnected mode with trajectories that invert the feature distribution between the two clusters at the midpoint of the stream, creating a contradiction between the spatial separation learned before and the new feature distributions after the inversion point.

5.1 Experimental Results

To validate that the generated datasets produce meaningful and distinguishable learning scenarios, three online multi-label classifiers were evaluated under a prequential evaluation protocol [11]: the Hoeffding Adaptive Tree (HAT) [5], Leveraging Bagging (LBag) [5], and K-Nearest Neighbors (KNN), all applied via Binary Relevance decomposition. HAT was used with its default RIVER configuration, which employs ADWIN [4] as the embedded drift detector with default sensitivity parameters. All classifiers were initialized with fixed random seeds to ensure reproducibility. Performance was measured using Hamming Loss, F1 Micro, and F1 Macro averaged over the full stream.

LBag achieved the best overall performance across five of the six drift configurations, with F1 Macro ranging from 0.942 (Spiral) to 0.978 (Gradual), at the cost of substantially higher computational time—approximately 40 to 70 times slower than HAT. HAT demonstrated competitive performance with significantly lower execution time, and notably achieved its best result on the incremental

Table 2. Classifier performance across drift types, 20 instances per centroid. Best result per drift type in bold.

Drift	Classifier	Ham. Loss	F1 Micro	F1 Macro	Time (s)
Abrupt	HAT	0.1003	0.9457	0.9455	2.84
	LBag	**0.0450**	**0.9762**	**0.9762**	107.81
	KNN	0.0725	0.9622	0.9622	41.40
Gradual	HAT	0.1100	0.9408	0.9393	1.20
	LBag	**0.0432**	**0.9775**	**0.9775**	92.63
	KNN	0.0506	0.9739	0.9740	40.32
Incremental	HAT	**0.0700**	**0.9609**	**0.9609**	1.38
	LBag	0.0558	0.9690	0.9690	86.06
	KNN	0.1187	0.9363	0.9363	39.79
Recurrent	HAT	0.0919	0.9500	0.9500	2.16
	LBag	**0.0635**	**0.9657**	**0.9657**	85.40
	KNN	0.0934	0.9505	0.9505	40.61
Spiral	HAT	0.1857	0.8602	0.8611	1.60
	LBag	**0.0746**	**0.9419**	**0.9419**	81.39
	KNN	0.1293	0.9023	0.9021	40.62
Conc. Evol.	HAT	0.1256	0.9064	0.8912	2.88
	LBag	**0.0542**	**0.9589**	**0.9560**	198.72
	KNN	0.1432	0.8920	0.8844	71.73

dataset (F1 Macro = 0.961), consistent with the theoretical characterization of incremental drift as the type most amenable to continuous adaptation. On the incremental dataset, HAT also outperformed LBag (0.969) in Hamming Loss, suggesting that the ADWIN-based drift detection mechanism provides an advantage when centroid displacement is smooth and uniform. The gradual dataset produced a sustained performance drop for HAT during the overlap window, as the prolonged coexistence of two concepts creates ambiguity that the detector resolves only after the transition completes, yielding a lower mean F1 Macro (0.939) despite the overall gentle nature of the drift. The spiral dataset produced the lowest performance across all classifiers, with HAT reaching F1 Macro = 0.861 and LBag 0.942, demonstrating that trajectory geometry and disconnected feature inversion together generate substantially more challenging scenarios than the canonical drift types under the same parametric configuration. The concept evolution dataset is the only configuration where F1 Micro and F1 Macro diverge noticeably across all three classifiers (HAT: 0.906 vs 0.891; LBag: 0.959 vs 0.956; KNN: 0.892 vs 0.884), confirming that the emergence of a new class creates uneven per-label performance that aggregate metrics alone would not reveal.

While Table 2 reports aggregate performance over the entire stream, such global averages can mask substantial variation near drift points. Figure 3 reports F1 Macro per evaluation window for HAT across all datasets, complementing the aggregate results by revealing the temporal structure of classifier performance. The incremental dataset exhibits stable, high performance throughout the stream with minimal variation, consistent with its uniform centroid displacement. The gradual dataset shows a sustained drop within the overlap window followed by progressive recovery as the new concept consolidates. The abrupt dataset produces a sharp, localized drop at the transition point with rapid subsequent recovery. The recurrent dataset shows two localized drops at the drift points, with faster recovery at the second transition as HAT partially reuses previously learned structure. The concept evolution dataset begins with low performance as the model encounters the initial distribution without prior training, improves progressively, and experiences a second perturbation at the emergence of the third cluster before stabilizing at high performance. The spiral dataset exhibits persistent high variability throughout the stream with no stable recovery period, reflecting the continuous and non-monotonic nature of the interleaving trajectories combined with the mid-stream feature inversion. These distinct behavioral signatures confirm that the datasets generated by StreamGen faithfully reproduce the expected non-stationary dynamics of each drift type, and that the generation model's configurability, from uniform linear trajectories to complex spiral geometries with disconnected feature dimensions, directly determines the temporal structure of classifier performance.

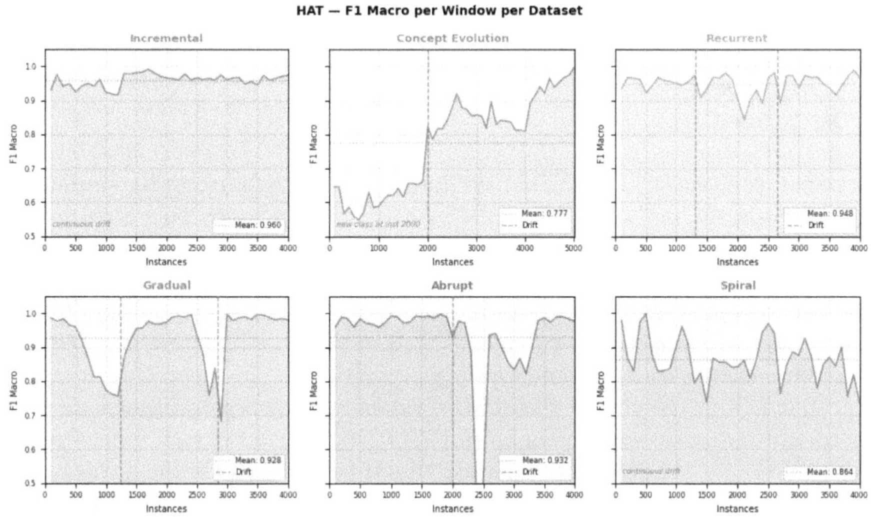

Fig. 3. F1 Macro per evaluation window for HAT across all datasets. Each subplot shows the temporal evolution of classification performance. Dashed vertical lines indicate drift transition points.

Figure 4 shows selected parts of the animation of an incremental dataset over time. Centroids follow continuous trajectories from the lower region toward the upper quadrant of the canvas, producing incremental concept drift throughout the entire stream. Black points indicate multi-label instances located in the overlap region between the two cluster distributions.

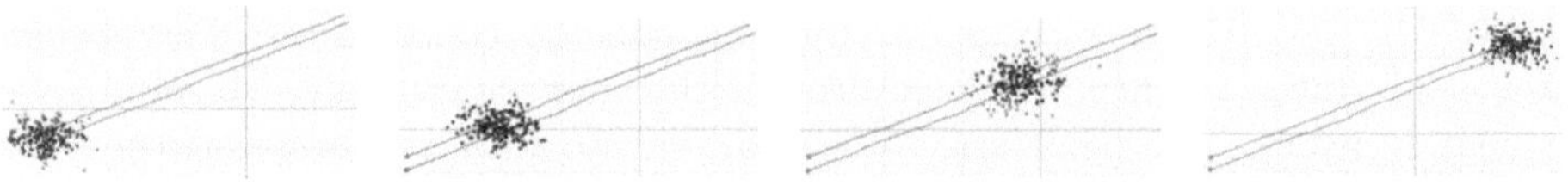

(a) $t = 1$ (b) $25 < t < 50$ (c) $50 < t < 75$ (d) $t = 100$

Fig. 4. Temporal evolution of an incremental dataset across the stream duration.

The curves in Fig. 3 reflect the learning behavior of HAT under prequential evaluation rather than intrinsic properties of the dataset, so performance at any window reflects the model's ability to generalize based on what it has learned from previous instances. Performance drops therefore indicate moments when the current model, trained on the preceding concept, fails to predict instances drawn from a new or transitioning distribution before sufficient retraining has occurred. The distinct drop patterns observed across drift types are a direct consequence of the drift configurations imposed during generation, confirming that the datasets produced by StreamGen faithfully reproduce the expected non-stationary dynamics of each drift type and that the generation model's configurability directly determines the classifier behavior across the time.

6 Conclusion

This paper presented StreamGen, an interactive web application implementing a canvas-based generation tool for synthetic multi-label data streams with configurable concept drift. The proposed tool grounds drift specification in centroid trajectories whose geometric and temporal configuration directly determines drift type, severity, and temporal structure, providing explicit and visually verifiable control over stream properties that existing parameterized generators do not offer. Extra feature dimensions are positioned via Moore neighborhood displacement from the cluster's spatial centroid, with configurable scale and offset per feature and per cluster, and optionally decoupled through independently drawn trajectories, addressing scenarios where feature dimensions evolve under distinct drift processes. The experimental results confirmed that the generated datasets faithfully reproduce the expected non-stationary dynamics of each drift type, with distinct temporal behavioral signatures across classifiers. The spiral dataset demonstrated that trajectory geometry and disconnected feature inversion alone—without any parameter change—are sufficient to generate substantially more challenging scenarios than the canonical drift types, producing the lowest performance across all classifiers and the only configuration where all three classifiers showed meaningful F1 Micro and F1 Macro divergence simultaneously. Current limitations include a shared σ across all clusters and dimensions, and the absence of instance-level noise, missing values, and label latency. Future work includes an option for a class to be represented by more than one cluster, per-cluster standard deviation configuration, support for Extreme Multi-Label (XML) scenarios with large label spaces [3], additional distribution types beyond Gaussian and RBF, and tighter integration with established stream evaluation frameworks.

Acknowledgment. R.O. and R.C. thank the São Paulo Research Foundation (FAPESP), Brazil, grants #2022/02981-8 and #2024/15875-7. R.C thanks the Brazilian National Council for Scientific and Technological Development (CNPq), grant #300934/2025-4.

References

1. Abufadda, M., Mansour, K.: A survey of synthetic data generation for machine learning. In: 2021 22nd International Arab Conference on Information Technology, ACIT (2021)
2. Agrahari, S., Srivastava, S., Singh, A.K.: Review on novelty detection in the non-stationary environment. Knowl. Inf. Syst. **66**(3), 1549–1574 (2024)
3. Babbar, R., Schölkopf, B.: Data scarcity, robustness and extreme multi-label classification. Mach. Learn. 1329–1351 (2019). https://doi.org/10.1007/s10994-019-05791-5
4. Bifet, A., Gavalda, R.: Learning from time-changing data with adaptive windowing. In: Proceedings of the 2007 SIAM International Conference on Data Mining, pp. 443–448. SIAM (2007)
5. Bifet, A., Holmes, G., Kirkby, R., Pfahringer, B.: MOA: massive online analysis. J. Mach. Learn. Res. **11**, 1601–1604 (2010)
6. Cerri, R., Faria, E.R., Gama, J.: An algorithm adaptation method for multi-label stream classification using self-organizing maps. In: 2022 21st IEEE International Conference on Machine Learning and Applications (ICMLA), pp. 1071–1076 (2022)
7. Cerri, R., Junior, J.D.C., Faria, E.R., Gama, J.: A new self-organizing map based algorithm for multi-label stream classification. In: Proceedings of the 36th Annual ACM Symposium on Applied Computing, SAC 2021, pp. 418–426. Association for Computing Machinery, New York (2021)
8. Esteban, A., Cano, A., Zafra, A., Ventura, S.: Hoeffding adaptive trees for multi-label classification on data streams. Knowl.-Based Syst. **304**, 112561 (2024)
9. de Faria, E.R., Ponce de Leon Ferreira Carvalho, A.C., Gama, J.: MINAS: multiclass learning algorithm for novelty detection in data streams. Data Min. Knowl. Discov. **30**(3), 640–680 (2016)
10. Freire-Oliveira, H., Paiva, E., Gama, J., Khan, L., Cerri, R.: A systematic literature review on multi-label data stream classification. arXiv preprint arXiv:2508.17455 (2025)
11. Gama, J., Medas, P., Castillo, G., Rodrigues, P.: Learning with drift detection. In: Brazilian Symposium on Artificial Intelligence, pp. 286–295. Springer (2004)

12. Gama, J., Žliobaitė, I., Bifet, A., Pechenizkiy, M., Bouchachia, A.: A survey on concept drift adaptation. ACM Comput. Surv. **46**(4) (2014)
13. Gama, J., Sebastião, R., Rodrigues, P.P.: On evaluating stream learning algorithms. Mach. Learn. **90**(3), 317–346 (2013)
14. Gatto, E.C., Ferrandin, M., Cerri, R.: Multi-label classification with label clusters. Knowl. Inf. Syst. (2024)
15. Gomes, H.M., et al.: CapyMOA: efficient machine learning for data streams in python (2025)
16. Hulten, G., Spencer, L., Domingos, P.: Mining time-changing data streams. In: Proceedings of the Seventh ACM SIGKDD International Conference on Knowledge Discovery and Data Mining, pp. 97–106 (2001)
17. Junior, J.D.C., Faria, E.R., Silva, J.A., Gama, J., Cerri, R.: Novelty detection for multi-label stream classification. In: 2019 8th Brazilian Conference on Intelligent Systems (BRACIS). IEEE (2019)
18. Li, P., Zhang, H., Hu, X., Wu, X.: High-dimensional multi-label data stream classification with concept drifting detection. IEEE Trans. Knowl. Data Eng. **35**(8), 8085–8099 (2023)
19. Lu, J., Liu, A., Dong, F., Gu, F., Gama, J., Zhang, G.: Learning under concept drift: a review. IEEE Trans. Knowl. Data Eng. **31**(12), 2346–2363 (2020)
20. Montiel, J., et al.: River: machine learning for streaming data in python. J. Mach. Learn. Res. **22**(110), 1–8 (2021)
21. Montiel, J., Read, J., Bifet, A., Abdessalem, T.: Scikit-multiflow: a multi-output streaming framework. J. Mach. Learn. Res. **19**(72), 1–5 (2018)
22. Moore, E.F.: Machine models of self-reproduction. In: Proceedings of Symposia in Applied Mathematics, vol. 14, pp. 17–33. American Mathematical Society (1962)
23. Porwik, P., Orczyk, T., Wrobel, K., Dadzie, B.M.: A novel method for drift detection in streaming data based on measurement of changes in feature ranks. J. Artif. Intell. Soft Comput. Res. **15**(2), 147–166 (2024)
24. Read, J., Pfahringer, B., Holmes, G.: Generating synthetic multi-label data streams. In: ECML/PKKD 2009 Workshop on Learning from Multi-label Data (MLD 2009), pp. 69–84 (2009)
25. Sivakumar, J., Ramamurthy, K., Radhakrishnan, M., Won, D.: GenerativeMTD: a deep synthetic data generation framework for small datasets. Knowl.-Based Syst. **280**, 110956 (2023)
26. Soares, R.G., Minku, L.L.: Online ensemble model compression for nonstationary data stream learning. Neural Netw. **185**, 107151 (2025)
27. Swami, A., V, T.: Multi-label tabular synthetic data generation for bundle recommendation problem. In: 2023 IEEE 2nd International Conference on Data, Decision and Systems (ICDDS), pp. 1–6 (2023)
28. Tomas, J.T., Spolaôr, N., Cherman, E.A., Monard, M.C.: A framework to generate synthetic multi-label datasets. Electron. Notes Theor. Comput. Sci. **302**, 155–176 (2014)
29. Tsoumakas, G., Katakis, I.: Multi-label classification: an overview. In: Data Warehousing and Mining: Concepts, Methodologies, Tools, and Applications pp, pp. 64–74 (2008)
30. Zheng, X., Li, P., Chu, Z., Hu, X.: A survey on multi-label data stream classification. IEEE Access **8**, 1249–1275 (2019)
31. Žliobaitė, I., Bifet, A., Read, J., Pfahringer, B., Holmes, G.: Evaluation methods and decision theory for classification of streaming data with temporal dependence. Mach. Learn. **98**(3), 455–482 (2015)

Crime Signature: Gang Graffiti for Criminal Risk Prediction in Street Networks

Victor Carvalho Soares de Araújo(✉), Kelson Rômulo Teixeira Aires, and Raimundo Santos Moura

Federal University of Piauí (UFPI), Teresina, PI, Brazil
{victor.araujo,kelson,rsm}@ufpi.edu.br

Abstract. Predictive systems for criminal risk based on street networks predominantly model the formal city, ignoring the territorial control exerted by criminal organizations. In urban contexts such as the Brazilian one, gang graffiti acts as an active marker of this power; however, there is no record of its operationalization as structured features in predictive models at the street-segment level. To fill this gap, this work proposes a framework that transforms georeferenced gang graffiti into quantitative spatial indicators integrated into line graphs. The methodology applies a hierarchical ablation study using LightGBM, a tree-based algorithm, and TabNet, a tabular neural network, in the city of Teresina-PI, with replicability validation in Parnaíba-PI. The results confirm the territorial signature hypothesis: incorporating the dynamics of criminal organizations yields statistically significant predictive gains in both cities and in both architectures, with a magnitude proportional to the density of the territorial signal available in each context. Operationally, the analysis of the highest-risk segments shows that prioritizing only 5% of the street network covers approximately 50% of criminal occurrences, a result consistent across both cities and both evaluated architectures. Finally, the explainability consensus obtained through the convergence between SHAP in LightGBM and attention masks in TabNet identifies territorial markers as predictors independent of the street infrastructure, providing the interpretive robustness required for police decision-support systems.

Keywords: Predictive Policing · Explainable Artificial Intelligence · Street Networks · Crime Dynamics

1 Introduction

Urban crime is not randomly distributed in space: empirical evidence consolidated by the "Law of Crime Concentration" [27] shows that approximately half of all crimes concentrate in 3 to 5% of the street segments of any given city. This pattern motivates the development of systems that model the street network[1] as

[1] The set of roads, streets, and highways comprising a city's circulation infrastructure.

M. Recamonde-Mendoza and R. C. Barros (Eds.): BRACIS 2026, LNAI 17105, pp. 93–107, 2027.
https://doi.org/10.1007/978-3-032-39882-6_7

a graph and apply machine learning algorithms to identify criminal risk segments at the microlocal level [9,22].

Despite the advances of these systems, their modeling is predominantly anchored in the "formal city" dimension, restricted to processing physical infrastructure, topology, and aggregated socioeconomic characteristics. In complex contexts such as the Brazilian one, this representation is structurally incomplete, as it disregards the informal and dynamic territorial domain exerted by criminal organizations over urban space. In Brazil, this control frequently materializes through gang graffiti, which operates as a genuine marking of power [26]. These are intentional markings used to delimit boundaries, intimidate rivals, and assert presence, configuring a strategic territoriality [23] with measurable effects on the spatial reconfiguration of criminal risk [1], a phenomenon aggravated by the expansion of these organizations into the Northeastern interior of Brazil [4,7,26].

Despite this empirical relevance, the microlocal crime prediction literature does not incorporate indicators of criminal territorialization into its models, configuring a structural gap whose closure demands systematic observational data-collection efforts in the field, given the unavailability of such data in official repositories.

This gap motivates the central research question of this work: *how does the incorporation of observable indicators of territorial domain into street network graphs impact the discriminatory capacity of criminal risk models, and to what extent is this approach replicable across distinct urban contexts?* Two hypotheses guide the experiments: **H1** (Predictive Relevance): gang graffiti improves prediction relative to baselines composed solely of street infrastructure and POIs; and **H2** (Directional Replicability): the framework preserves the direction and statistical significance of predictive gains when replicated in a new urban context without structural adjustments to the pipeline, with a magnitude proportional to the density of the available territorial signal.

To assess these hypotheses, this work proposes a framework that operates over two municipalities in Piauí with distinct territorialization dynamics, combining urban infrastructure data with field records. The contributions of this work are threefold: (i) territorial feature engineering that transforms georeferenced graffiti records collected in the field into quantitative spatial indicators integrated into the street network graph; (ii) empirical evidence of statistically significant predictive gains in two distinct urban contexts, Teresina and Parnaíba, validated via paired bootstrap; and (iii) a demonstration of operational viability at the street-segment level, with the Top-k analysis translating predictive evidence into concrete resource allocation, and the explainability via SHAP and attention masks providing the interpretability required for responsible use in police decision support.[2]

[2] A preliminary version of this work, restricted to Teresina and to LightGBM, was presented in [2].

2 Related Work

The effectiveness of spatial analysis of crime data depends on the computational discretization of urban space, since the choice of the unit of analysis determines the ability to capture the causal mechanisms of crime dynamics [28]. Rosser et al. [22] showed that street-network-based approaches identify approximately 20% more crimes at the 5% coverage level than regular grids, evidencing that arbitrary discretizations dilute high-risk segments into low-risk cells.

MIRANTE [9] models the city such that intersections correspond to vertices and street segments to edges, a structure equivalent to what the literature calls the primal graph [20], generating high-resolution time series. Its evolution, CriPAV [10], introduced stochastic matrices and autoencoders for the temporal clustering of hotspots, showing that frequent crimes concentrate on primary roads, whereas sporadic events are distributed across secondary roads.

Unlike previous approaches, Hassan et al. [11] modeled crime dynamics in São Paulo by adopting the inverse representation, with street segments as vertices and intersections as edges, a structure analogous to the line graph [20]. To mitigate data sparsity, incidents were aggregated into monthly intervals.

Pocco et al. [19] explored Graph Autoencoders for fusing static and dynamic features in crime analysis, but without incorporating territorial markers of criminal organizations as a predictive source. Silva et al. [25] analyzed the influence of Points of Interest (POIs) on urban crime in cities of Alagoas at the street-corner level, identifying that different types of establishments exhibit varying associations with crime depending on the local socioeconomic context.

Beyond spatial discretization approaches and the use of urban infrastructure, the choice of features plays a critical role in predictive performance. The crime prediction literature incorporates socioeconomic variables [6], urban infrastructure [9,25], and state control over territory [13], but does not report studies that operationalize territorial markings of criminal organizations as structured features in street-network-graph predictive models.

Hughes et al. [14] provided the core theoretical basis by demonstrating that gang graffiti acts as a leading predictor of violence, associated with a 40 to 60% increase in the probability of violent crime in territorial boundary zones. The crucial limitation for operational purposes is the scale of analysis: neighborhoods, not street segments.

Kronkvist et al. [16] validated the use of open data from OpenStreetMap (OSM) in Risk Terrain Modeling, demonstrating that primary observational sources can complement official records with comparable performance. Raimundo et al. [21] argue that interpretability is a critical requirement for police decision-support systems, showing that models must provide actionable insights beyond accurate prediction.

The gap that this work addresses lies at the intersection of these two strands: the criminological theory of territorial signaling [14] and computational tools for street-segment-level analysis [11,22]. The integration of these two dimensions, as well as the assessment of replicability across multiple Brazilian urban contexts, remains absent from the literature, a direct reflection of the difficulty of obtaining data on criminal territorialization.

3 Street Network Graph Modeling

The street network can be modeled as a primal graph $G = (V, E)$, an undirected graph in which V represents the set of road intersections and E the set of street segments connecting pairs of intersections, with weight $w(e) = \ell(e)$ corresponding to the physical length of segment $e \in E$. This formulation fails to preserve the street segment as the structural unit of analysis. As illustrated in Fig. 1a, this approach prevents the direct assignment of features to the segment, the unit of criminological interest.

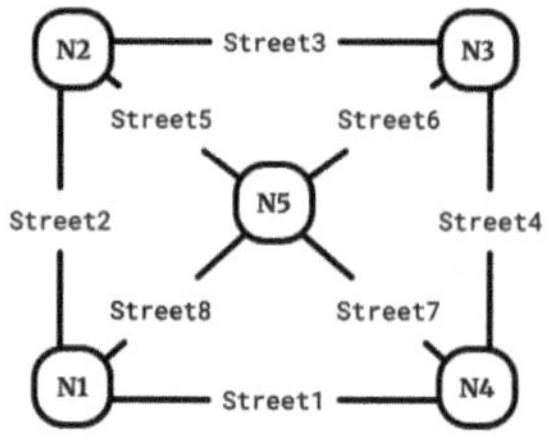

(a) Primal Graph

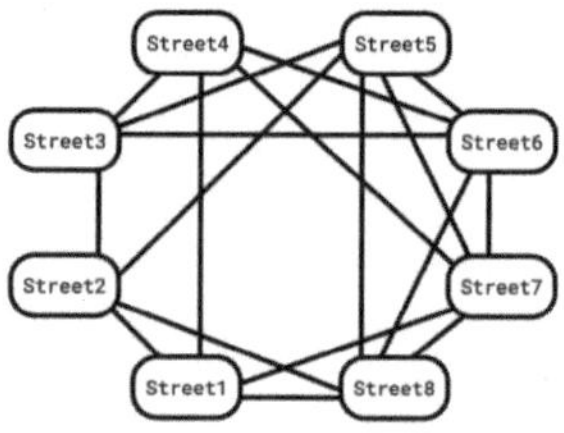

(b) Line Graph

Fig. 1. Street network graph representations: (a) Primal Graph and (b) Line Graph.

To mitigate this limitation, the dual representation, or line graph, $G_L = (V_L, E_L)$ [20], is adopted. In this formalization, shown in Fig. 1b, each street segment becomes a node, and two nodes are connected if their respective segments share an intersection in the primal graph. Each edge $e_L \in E_L$ receives weight $w(e_L) = \frac{\ell(e_1)+\ell(e_2)}{2}$, corresponding to the mean of the lengths of the two segments incident to the shared intersection. This transformation enables the direct application of models over the street segment, the unit identified by Rosser et al. [22] as the most meaningful for forecasting and police resource allocation, in line with the configurational logic of Hillier and Hanson [12], who correlate topological accessibility with movement dynamics and urban safety.

Over the resulting graph, three classical centrality metrics from complex networks [18] are computed per segment. *Betweenness* measures the fraction of shortest paths in the graph that pass through a node and is computed with edge-length weighting, capturing the strategic position of the segment in traffic flows, in line with the metric analysis of street networks [20]. *Closeness* is defined as the inverse of the sum of distances from the node to all others and is computed topologically, counting the number of hops between vertices, an option that preserves the interpretability of the metric as a measure of the segment's global configurational accessibility within the line graph [18,20]. *Degree* corresponds to the number of direct neighbors of the node and is, by definition, unweighted, reflecting the immediate local connectivity of the segment [18]. The physical length of the segment is preserved as an independent morphological attribute. This structure constitutes the basis onto which the empirical data layers described in the following section are integrated.

4 Study Area and Data

The two municipalities studied present distinct and complementary territorialization dynamics. Teresina, the state capital, has recorded since 2022 the simultaneous expansion of three criminal organizations (PCC, B40, and GDE)[3], whose characteristic gang graffiti has begun to demarcate territorial disputes across the city's neighborhoods. Parnaíba, the second largest municipality in the state, occupies a strategic geographic position on the coast of Piauí, becoming a route for drug trafficking, with the presence of CV[4] and PCC since 2020. This asymmetry between the cities provides favorable conditions for testing the robustness of the framework in structurally distinct urban contexts.

To operationalize the framework in these two contexts, the Public Security Secretariat of Piauí (SSP-PI) provided, under a scientific cooperation agreement, the database of criminal occurrence records covering the period from January 2022 to December 2023. To align with the spatial unit of analysis, the scope of this study is restricted to occurrences whose direct police response falls under the Military Police, that is, events with immediate spatial manifestation and an on-the-spot response demand, encompassing crimes against persons, property crimes, drug-related crimes, firearm-related crimes, and other categories with direct spatial manifestation. After processing, the final database contains 150,905 occurrences in Teresina and 22,839 in Parnaíba. Each occurrence contributes in a binary manner to the label of the segment–month pair, without discrimination by type, severity, or quantity, a methodological choice well established in the microlocal crime prediction literature [22,27] that prioritizes identifying where risk concentrates over classifying the type or intensity of the event.

In addition to occurrence records, this study incorporates gang graffiti as observable features of criminal territorialization, collected in a systematic field survey conducted by the author together with intelligence teams from the Piauí Military Police (PMPI), with GPS georeferencing and photographic documentation. In Teresina, the survey covered all neighborhoods of the city between October 2022 and February 2023, resulting in 659 records (PCC: 321, B40: 326, GDE: 12). In Parnaíba, the mapping was conducted in the areas of greatest territorial conflict identified by police intelligence, resulting in 52 records (CV: 36, PCC: 16). Figure 2 presents representative examples of the collected graffiti, in which, beyond demarcation by acronyms, one observes coercive commands such as "remove the helmet", "x9 [snitches] will die", and "enemy of the state".

[3] PCC: Primeiro Comando da Capital; B40: Bonde dos 40; GDE: Guardiões do Estado.
[4] CV: Comando Vermelho.

Fig. 2. Examples of georeferenced gang graffiti in the two cities: GDE, B40, PCC, and CV.

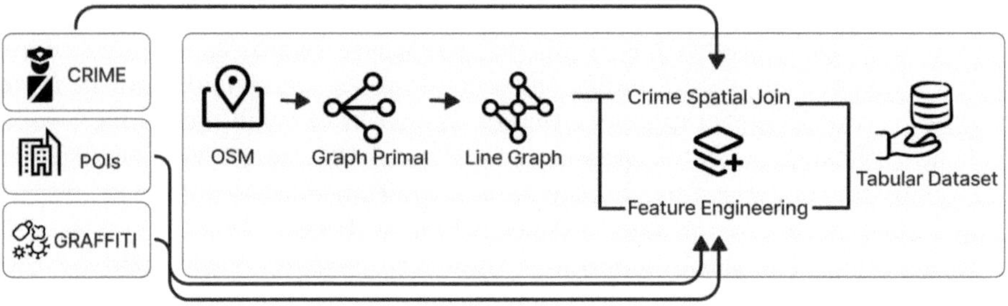

Fig. 3. Dataset construction pipeline: from the street network to the generation of segment–month pair instances.

In addition to gang graffiti, the framework incorporates urban structure through POIs extracted from OpenStreetMap, distributed across 17 categories detailed in Table 1, totaling 2,481 POIs in Teresina and 233 in Parnaíba.

5 Methodology

The dataset construction adopts the street segment as the unit of analysis, a choice grounded in the evidence that crimes tend to concentrate at specific places [27], providing greater spatial precision. Onto this structure, three layers of information are integrated: criminal history, urban structure (POIs), and gang graffiti, organized into a tabular structure in which each instance corresponds to a (segment, month) pair, with the temporal dimension incorporated into the label (presence or absence of crime in the month) and static features associated with the segment.

The street network of each municipality was obtained via OSMnx [5] and converted into a line graph (Fig. 3), as described in Sect. 3, resulting in 79,417 nodes and 243,652 edges in Teresina and 18,804 nodes and 59,383 edges in Parnaíba. Onto this structure, crime records, POIs, and graffiti are integrated through spatial joining and feature engineering, generating the dataset used in the ablation study.

Each graffiti instance is represented by its GPS coordinates and by the organization to which it belongs, identified from characteristic acronyms and iconography. From this representation, each organization contributes four features per segment: the distance to the nearest graffiti, truncated at 1,000 m, a value calibrated from the empirical analysis of the predictive gradient of the markings; the count of graffiti within a 200 m radius; and the mean values of both metrics computed over adjacent segments sharing an intersection, capturing territorial diffusion over contiguous streets. Although graffiti appears as pointwise and geographically sparse observations, propagation multiplies the reach of the signal: 25.4% of segments in Teresina and 6.4% of segments in Parnaíba record graffiti within the 200 m radius, transforming a point-based dataset into broad predictive coverage.

Crime records were linked to the street network graph through proximity-based spatial joining, associating each occurrence with the nearest segment. Monthly granularity was adopted owing to data sparsity, given that most street segments do not record occurrences on any given day. The final dataset comprises 1,911,624 instances in Teresina and 454,488 in Parnaíba.

5.1 Algorithms and Evaluation Metrics

Two algorithms were selected for the complementarity between efficiency and interpretability. LightGBM [15] was adopted for its computational efficiency and its native ability to handle high dimensionality and sparse categorical variables, such as road type, without performance degradation. TabNet [3] was selected for its native interpretability based on attention mechanisms, a critical feature for auditing whether predictions are coherent with known territorial dynamics.

Given the extreme class imbalance ($\rho > 100$), AUPRC is adopted as the primary metric because it isolates true negatives and makes the imbalance visually explicit [8], avoiding the artificial inflation of AUROC by the massive volume of negatives [24]. Complementarily, Top-k Coverage is employed, the operational denomination adopted in this work for the Hit Rate criterion of [22], which quantifies the proportion of crimes covered when prioritizing the k% segments of highest predicted risk.

5.2 Experimental Protocol

The hierarchical ablation study evaluates the marginal contribution of each feature group, adding them progressively to isolate the effect of each category. Three incremental configurations were defined: **Model A** (structural attributes), **Model B** (Model A + POIs), and **Model C** (Model B + graffiti). Each configuration was implemented with LightGBM and TabNet, yielding six experiments per municipality, twelve in total. Table 1 summarizes the feature counts.

Validation adopted strict temporal partitioning to prevent data leakage: training from January 2022 to June 2023 (18 months), validation in July and August 2023, and testing from September to December 2023 (4 months). LightGBM was tuned via Grid Search with `TimeSeriesSplit` (5 folds); TabNet via

Table 1. Detailed features by model and city.

Model	Features	Description	Teresina	Parnaíba
A	Structural	Morphological: road types[a] and physical length of the segment	15	15
	Structural	Topological metrics (*betweenness*, *closeness*, *degree*)	3	3
B	POIs	Count per category[b] within a 200 m radius	17	17
C	Graffiti	Criminal organizations (Teresina: PCC, B40, GDE; Parnaíba: PCC, CV)	12	8
Total Features			**47**	**43**

[a] OpenStreetMap `highway` classification: *motorway*, *trunk*, *primary*, *secondary*, *tertiary*, *residential*, *service*, *unclassified*, *living_street*, and their respective links.
[b] POI categories: hospital, clinic/PSF, school, daycare, university, police station, military police barracks, armed forces barracks, government building, bank, bar, restaurant, hotel, event venue, gas station, public transport, and theater.

Bayesian optimization with Optuna and early stopping. Class imbalance was handled with `class_weight='balanced'` in LightGBM and explicit weights in the loss function for TabNet. The statistical significance of AUPRC gains was assessed via paired bootstrap (1,000 resamples) on the test set.

6 Results

The results are analyzed along three dimensions: predictive performance, operational utility, and explainability.

6.1 Ablation Study

Table 2 presents the results of the hierarchical ablation study for both cities. In Teresina, adding POIs to the topological baseline yields a modest gain in LightGBM (+2.67% in AUPRC), whereas gang graffiti raises this index by +13.64% in the B→C transition (Full Model). TabNet exhibits an analogous pattern, with higher relative magnitudes due to a lower absolute baseline: +17.50% in the A→B transition and +38.75% in the B→C transition. LightGBM maintains superior absolute performance across all configurations, qualifying it as the operational model.

In Parnaíba, POIs yield no gain in LightGBM, a pattern consistent with the sparsity of this category, and graffiti constitutes the only source of predictive improvement in this architecture (+1.64% in the B→C transition). TabNet detects a residual signal from POIs (+6.29% in the A→B transition) and responds with a substantial gain to graffiti in the B→C transition (+32.99%). AUROC follows the trend in both scenarios and models, confirming the consistent improvement of Model C over the previous stages.

The statistical significance of the gain of Model C over Model B, isolating the specific contribution of graffiti given the model that already incorporates street infrastructure and POIs, was confirmed in all scenarios. In Teresina, the gains are robust in both architectures (LightGBM: ΔAUPRC $= +0.0356$, $p < 0.001$; TabNet: ΔAUPRC $= +0.0716$, $p < 0.001$). In Parnaíba, TabNet sustains a substantial gain (ΔAUPRC $= +0.0476$, $p < 0.001$), while LightGBM exhibits a modest yet significant gain (ΔAUPRC $= +0.0039$, $p = 0.002$), consistent with the lower graffiti density in this city. In all experiments, the 95% confidence intervals exclude zero.

Table 2. Ablation study – Teresina and Parnaíba.

City	Model	LightGBM			TabNet		
		AUROC	AUPRC	Gain	AUROC	AUPRC	Gain
Teresina	A – Baseline	0.7832	0.2549	–	0.7325	0.1576	–
	B – POIs	0.7873	0.2617	+2.67%	0.7519	0.1852	+17.50%
	C – Full	**0.8162**	**0.2974**	**+13.64%**	**0.8085**	**0.2569**	**+38.75%**
Parnaíba	A – Baseline	0.8502	0.2615	–	0.7900	0.1349	–
	B – POIs	0.8502	0.2615	0.00%	0.7967	0.1434	+6.29%
	C – Full	**0.8604**	**0.2658**	**+1.64%**	**0.8376**	**0.1906**	**+32.99%**

6.2 Top-K Coverage

The Top-k analysis translates predictive capacity into concrete resource allocation, quantifying the criminal coverage achieved by prioritizing the k% segments of highest predicted risk, given that monitoring the entire street network is operationally infeasible.

Table 3 compares Models A and C across the four months of the test set. In Teresina, LightGBM Model C outperforms the baseline at every cutoff (+4.7 pp at Top-5%: 48.5%→53.2%), and TabNet exhibits greater variation at the same cutoff (+16.5 pp: 32.7%→49.2%), as a consequence of starting from a lower initial coverage.

In Parnaíba, LightGBM hardly alters coverage at Top-5% (57.1%→57.4%), whereas TabNet records a gain of +8.1 pp (43.9%→52.0%), as a consequence of starting from a lower initial coverage.

Figure 4 illustrates the spatial distribution of segments in the Top-5% of predicted risk by LightGBM in December 2023. The model identifies persistent-risk street corridors, a pattern incompatible with random fluctuations and consistent with the criminal territorialization documented in both cities.

Table 3. Top-k operational coverage – Models A and C (Sep–Dec 2023).

Top-k	Teresina				Parnaíba			
	LightGBM		TabNet		LightGBM		TabNet	
	A	C	A	C	A	C	A	C
5%	48.5%	53.2%	32.7%	49.2%	57.1%	57.4%	43.9%	52.0%
10%	58.9%	63.6%	44.0%	61.1%	70.3%	70.4%	55.2%	63.9%
20%	70.0%	74.8%	61.0%	73.6%	82.5%	82.9%	70.7%	78.3%
50%	88.7%	91.3%	83.8%	91.2%	93.2%	94.6%	90.7%	93.6%

(a) Teresina

(b) Parnaíba

Fig. 4. Snapshot of the top 5% of segments with the highest predicted risk (LightGBM), December 2023.

6.3 Explainability

In public security applications, interpretability is a necessary condition for responsibly supporting decisions. SHAP [17] is applied to LightGBM to quantify the contribution of each variable; the global attention masks of TabNet [3] reveal the features prioritized by the network. The joint analysis identifies convergences between the architectures and reduces the risk of artifacts from a single explainability method.

In Teresina, `Closeness` leads in both models (Table 4), confirming topological accessibility as the primary risk predictor. Regarding the graffiti features, the models reveal distinct readings: in LightGBM, `PCC Distance` appears as a high-relevance feature, operating as a pointwise proximity threshold to graffiti; in TabNet, this same feature recedes, while `PCC Neighborhood Distance` moves to the top, suggesting that TabNet captures the territorial diffusion of the criminal organization over the neighborhood better than the direct distance to the marker. Although topology dominates the predictive power in both models, the consistent presence of PCC and B40 indicators at the top demonstrates that territorial-influence dynamics constitute a predictive contribution independent of street infrastructure.

Table 4. Top-10 Explainability Features – Teresina, Model C (Values normalized with respect to the total sum of importances to facilitate comparison between cities)

Feature	SHAP (%)	Feature	Attention (%)
Closeness	26.0	Closeness	12.7
PCC Distance	18.2	Street Length (m)	10.9
Street Length (m)	9.9	Betweenness	10.5
Betweenness	6.7	PCC Neigh. Distance	7.4
B40 Distance	5.8	Degree	6.3
PCC Neighborhood Distance	4.7	Mobility	5.8
Uncategorized Road	4.4	B40 Density	5.3
Residential Roads	4.3	B40 Neigh. Distance	5.0
Mobility	4.2	Schools/Education	4.2
Degree	4.0	PCC Density	3.5

Table 5. Top-10 Explainability Features – Parnaíba, Model C (Values normalized with respect to the total sum of importances to facilitate comparison between cities)

Feature	SHAP (%)	Feature	Attention (%)
Closeness	40.5	Street Length (m)	12.4
Street Length (m)	15.4	Closeness	10.8
Betweenness	12.2	CV Distance	7.1
PCC Distance	9.1	Degree	6.9
CV Distance	7.2	PCC Neigh. Distance	6.5
Degree	6.4	Betweenness	4.7
Uncategorized Roads	3.5	Schools/Education	4.5
CV Neighborhood Distance	0.9	PCC Density	4.5
Primary Roads	0.8	PCC Distance	4.2
Tertiary Roads	0.7	CV Density (200m)	4.1

In Parnaíba, `Closeness` leads in LightGBM by a wide margin over the remaining features (Table 5), indicating a strong concentration of discriminative power on topological accessibility. Regarding the graffiti features, the models reveal distinct readings: in LightGBM, `PCC Distance` and `CV Distance` operate as a pointwise proximity threshold; in TabNet, `CV Distance` moves up to 3rd place while `Street Length` appears at the top of global attention, suggesting that TabNet weighs the physical extent of the segment as a vector of territorial diffusion. The coexistence of CV and PCC indicators at the top of both models reflects the territorial reality documented along the Piauí coast.

The heterogeneity of risk profiles observed at the segment level suggests that interventions based solely on street infrastructure or on criminal territorialization would be insufficient; rather, it is the interaction between the two dimensions that defines local risk.

7 Discussion of Results

The results enable an affirmative answer to hypothesis H1 in both cities. Gang graffiti improves prediction with gains not captured by street infrastructure features and POIs. In Teresina, the graffiti features contribute consistently alongside POIs. In Parnaíba, these features constitute the only source of effective improvement over the baseline, a fact consistent with the sparsity of POI records in this city, and one that highlights the robustness of network metrics as a predictive anchor in data-scarce contexts.

Hypothesis H2 is also confirmed, although with important qualifications. The pipeline applied to Parnaíba without structural adjustments yields statistically significant gains in both architectures, but with a magnitude lower than that observed in Teresina. This attenuation is proportional to the density of the territorial signal available in each context.

The two algorithms play complementary roles in this work. LightGBM maintains superior absolute performance across all configurations and in both cities, qualifying it as the operational model for production use. Both models identify graffiti as relevant predictors, but the reading of the territorial phenomenon differs: the explainability analysis (Sect. 6.3) shows that LightGBM assigns greater weight to the *direct distance* to the nearest territorial marker, whereas TabNet favors *neighborhood and diffusion features* through its attention mechanism. The convergence of the two models in identifying graffiti as risk predictors strengthens the evidence: the effect is detectable under two complementary readings of the same phenomenon, captured by LightGBM in its pointwise expression and by TabNet in its diffuse expression. The direction and significance of the gains are preserved; the magnitude varies according to signal density and the architectural reading of the territory.

The validity of the data collection deserves specific examination in Parnaíba. The survey in this municipality covered the territory only partially, restricted to areas in which police intelligence had identified active territorial disputes among criminal organizations. This reflects the phenomenon under study, not the intensity of local criminality. On this basis, the predictive signal remains statistically significant in both architectures. In Teresina, the survey covered all neighborhoods, providing evidence over a fully mapped territory.

Graffiti enters the model as a static variable, a formulation that assumes territorial stability between collection and the test period. In Teresina, a 2025 reassessment supports this assumption: of the originally collected points, PCC and B40 retained 98% and 100% of the markings over 24 months, and the growth observed in this period concentrated in the same region, with sub-kilometer displacement of the territorial centroids. The pattern indicates densification over already demarcated territories rather than migration. For Parnaíba, in the absence of an analogous reassessment, stability is supported by the literature on the persistence of territorial markings [14,26] and by the short lag between collection and the test period. Longitudinal reassessment in both contexts remains as future work.

Beyond the temporal validity of the design, it is worth qualifying the type of claim the model supports. The model identifies risk segments based on the spatial co-occurrence of graffiti and crimes, but does not establish a causal link between the presence of a marking and the specific occurrence of an adjacent crime. Graffiti may precede the arrival of territorial control, accompany already established consolidation, or reflect ongoing disputes, configuring associations whose operational interpretation requires contextual analysis and which serve as an input to police decision-making rather than as a standalone conclusion.

Despite these limitations, the operational implications are clear. The Top-k analysis shows that approximately half of all crimes can be covered by concentrating efforts on only 5% of the street network, a result consistent across both cities and both evaluated architectures, with direct implications in resource-constrained contexts. The convergence between SHAP and TabNet attention masks in identifying territorial markers as predictors independent of street infrastructure endows these results with the interpretive robustness required for decision-support use, a requirement that distinguishes operationally responsible tools from opaque models. Their application requires expert validation and integration with problem-oriented policing approaches, being complementary to community policing strategies and to structural public policies.

8 Conclusion

This work operationalized gang graffiti as structured features in street network graphs at the street-segment level, integrating georeferenced field collection with a criminal risk prediction pipeline. The experiments confirmed that these markers contribute a statistically significant predictive signal in two distinct urban contexts, with a magnitude proportional to the density of the territorial signal.

The Top-k analysis showed that approximately half of all crimes are covered by concentrating efforts on only 5% of the street network, a result consistent across cities and architectures. The convergence between SHAP in LightGBM and attention masks in TabNet identified territorial markers as predictors independent of street infrastructure, providing the interpretability required for decision-support use.

Two complementary directions stand out as future work. The first is a systematic experimental comparison with graph-aware architectures over the line graph, evaluating the trade-off between the ability to capture topological interactions and robustness in the face of the extreme class imbalance characteristic of crime data. The second is the development of an operational decision-support interface integrating collection, training, prediction, and continuous evaluation, translating the framework into a tool deployable in the public security context.

Acknowledgments. This work was partially funded by the Public Security Secretariat of Piauí, with support from the Cultural Foundation for the Promotion of

Research, Teaching, Extension and Innovation (FADEX). We thank the technical teams of PMPI and SSP-PI for their support and for providing the data.

Disclosure of Interests. The authors have no competing interests to declare that are relevant to the content of this article.

References

1. Alves, B.E.C.: Territórios marcados pelo medo: a influência das facções criminosas na mobilidade urbana de adolescentes em Araguaína. Master's thesis, Universidade Federal do Tocantins (2025)
2. Araújo, V.C.S.D., Moura, R.S.: Análise de risco criminal em grafos viários usando marcações territoriais de facções como features preditivas. In: ERCEMAPI (2025)
3. Arik, S.Ö., Pfister, T.: TabNet: attentive interpretable tabular learning. In: Proceedings of the AAAI Conference on Artificial Intelligence, vol. 35, no. 8 (2021)
4. Barbosa, W., Limeira, M., Rocha, D., Cunha, G., Sampaio, F.: Mapas do crime: a territorialização das facções criminosas em juazeiro do norte - ce. Plural, vol. 30, pp. 80–107. (2023). https://doi.org/10.11606/issn.2176-8099.pcso.2023.213892
5. Boeing, G.: Modeling and analyzing urban networks and amenities with OSMnx (2025). https://doi.org/10.31235/osf.io/d5fp3_v1
6. Bogomolov, A.: Once upon a crime: towards crime prediction from demographics and mobile data. In: Proceedings of the 16th International Conference on Multimodal Interaction (ICMI) (2014)
7. Cruz, J.B.: Abaixe o vidro. tire o capacete: a pichação de muros como registro dos conflitos entre facções em fortaleza (2023). http://repositorio.ufc.br/handle/riufc/80438. Trabalho de Conclusão de Curso – Universidade Federal do Ceará
8. Davis, J., Goadrich, M.: The relationship between precision-recall and roc curves. In: Proceedings of the 23rd International Conference on Machine Learning (ICML) (2006). https://doi.org/10.1145/1143844.1143874
9. Garcia-Zanabria, G., et al.: Mirante: a visualization tool for analyzing urban crimes. In: Proceedings of the XXXIII Conference on Graphics, Patterns and Images (SIBGRAPI), pp. 188–195. SBC (2020)
10. García-Zanabria, G., et al.: CriPAV: street-level crime patterns analysis and visualization. IEEE Trans. Visual Comput. Graphics **28**(12), 4000–4015 (2022). https://doi.org/10.1109/TVCG.2021.3111146
11. Hassan, W., Cabral, M., Ramos, T., Castelo Filho, A., Nonato, L.: Modeling and predicting crimes in the city of são paulo using graph neural networks. In: Proceedings of the XXXIV Brazilian Conference on Intelligent Systems (BRACIS), pp. 372–386. SBC (2024)
12. Hillier, B., Hanson, J.: The Social Logic of Space. Cambridge University Press (1984)
13. Hou, M., Hu, X., Cai, J., Single, H., Yuan, S.: An integrated graph model for spatial-temporal urban crime prediction based on attention mechanism. ISPRS Int. J. Geo Inf. **11**(5), 294 (2022). https://doi.org/10.3390/ijgi11050294
14. Hughes, L.A., Schaible, L.M., Kephart, T.: Gang graffiti, group process, and gang violence. J. Quantit. Criminol. **38**, 365–384 (2022). https://doi.org/10.1007/s10940-021-09507-8
15. Ke, G., Meng, Q., Finley, T., Wang, T., Chen, W., Ma, W., Ye, Q., Liu, T.Y.: LightGBM: a highly efficient gradient boosting decision tree. In: Advances in Neural Information Processing Systems, vol. 30 (2017)

16. Kronkvist, K., Borg, A., Boldt, M., Gerell, M.: Predicting public violent crime using register and OpenStreetMap data: a risk terrain modeling approach across three cities of varying size. Appl. Spat. Anal. Policy **18**(1), 9 (2024). https://doi.org/10.1007/s12061-024-09609-3
17. Lundberg, S., Lee, S.I.: A unified approach to interpreting model predictions. In: Advances in Neural Information Processing Systems (NIPS) (2017). https://doi.org/10.48550/arXiv.1705.07874
18. Newman, M.E.J.: Networks: An Introduction. Oxford University Press (2010)
19. Pocco, X., et al.: Exploring urban factors with autoencoders: relationship between static and dynamic features. In: Proceedings of the XXXVIII Conference on Graphics, Patterns and Images (SIBGRAPI), pp. 1–6 (2025). https://doi.org/10.1109/SIBGRAPI67909.2025.11223351
20. Porta, S., Crucitti, P., Latora, V.: The network analysis of urban streets: a dual approach. Phys. A: Stat. Mech. Appl. **369**(2) (2006). https://doi.org/10.48550/arXiv.cond-mat/0411241
21. Raimundo, M.M., Garcia-Zanabria, G., Nonato, L.G., Poco, J.: CounterCrime: using counterfactual explanations to explore crime reduction scenarios. IEEE Trans. Visual Comput. Graphics **31**(10), 9008–9023 (2025). https://doi.org/10.1109/TVCG.2025.3586202
22. Rosser, G., Davies, T., Bowers, K.J., Johnson, S.D., Cheng, T.: Predictive crime mapping: arbitrary grids or street networks? J. Quant. Criminol. **33**(3), 569–594 (2016). https://doi.org/10.1007/s10940-016-9321-x
23. Sack, R.D.: Human Territoriality: Its Theory and History. Cambridge University Press (1986)
24. Saito, T., Rehmsmeier, M.: The precision-recall plot is more informative than the ROC plot when evaluating binary classifiers on imbalanced datasets. PLoS ONE **10** (2015)
25. Silva, D.B.L., Vieira, T., Costa, E.D.B., Paiva, A., Nonato, L.G.: A street corner-level methodology to analyze the influence of points of interest on urban crime. Soc.-Econ. Plann. Sci. **102**, 102297 (2025). https://doi.org/10.1016/j.seps.2025.102297
26. de Souza, R.M., de Albuquerque, E.S.: As pichações como demarcadores do controle territorial das organizações criminosas em bayeux-pb. Rev. Geopol. **16**(5), e1118 (2025). https://doi.org/10.56238/revgeov16n5-258
27. Weisburd, D.: The law of crime concentration and the criminology of place. Criminology **53** (2015). https://doi.org/10.1111/1745-9125.12070
28. Weisburd, D., Groff, E., Yang, S.M.: The Criminology of Place: Street Segments and Our Understanding of the Crime Problem. Oxford University Press (2013)

HoTHP: Hyperbolic Rotary Position Embedding-Based Transformer Hawkes Process for Length Extrapolation

Hugo Ramos Soares(✉), César Lincoln C. Mattos, and João P. P. Gomes

Department of Computing, Federal University of Ceará (UFC), Fortaleza, CE, Brazil
hugoramos84@alu.ufc.br, {cesarlincoln,jpaulo}@dc.ufc.br

Abstract. Transformer-based Temporal Point Processes (TPP) have shown promising results in event sequence modeling. However, these models frequently degrade when tested on sequences longer than those encountered during training, an important limitation when addressing real-world applications. In this work, we propose Hyperbolic Transformer Hawkes Process (HoTHP), a Transformer-based model for Hawkes Processes that replaces the trigonometric rotary kernel of RoTHP with a version using hyperbolic functions, inspired by HoPE. Instead of rotating the Q and K vectors before the attention product, HoTHP reformulates the attention score as a function of the temporal difference between events, combining the hyperbolic kernel with a learned decay parameter θ', constrained during training to values greater than the largest θ' value, in order to guarantee decay. This model incorporates an explicit decay bias into the attention mechanism, which naturally reflects the self-exciting structure of a Hawkes process. We evaluate HoTHP on synthetic datasets generated by Hawkes processes, following the *train short, test long* technique, in which the model is trained on shorter sequences and then tested on sequences with more elements. The results show that HoTHP maintains a stable negative log-likelihood (NLL) even on longer sequences, while RoTHP degrades progressively. These results suggest that the hyperbolic positional encoding approach with an explicit exponential decay bias is a more appropriate framework for modeling event sequences when training data is sparser than real-world data.

Keywords: Temporal Pointing Process · Hawkes Process · Transformers

1 Introduction

Hawkes processes [3] are widely used to study the behavior of phenomena with low repetition rates, but in an increasingly connected world, we have a growing amount of data to analyze. Today, through telemetry, it has become common to analyze very long chains of events in areas such as social networks, healthcare systems, and building maintenance.

M. Recamonde-Mendoza and R. C. Barros (Eds.): BRACIS 2026, LNAI 17105, pp. 108–122, 2027.
https://doi.org/10.1007/978-3-032-39882-6_8

A Hawkes process has as its main characteristic the influence of past events on future events, causing the probability of a given event to depart from its baseline rate (μ) and increase (or decrease) at an intensity α, then decay over time at a rate β until returning to the initial baseline rate, which is the stationary rate of the event. The resulting quantity of the process is the conditional intensity λ, as illustrated in Fig. 1.

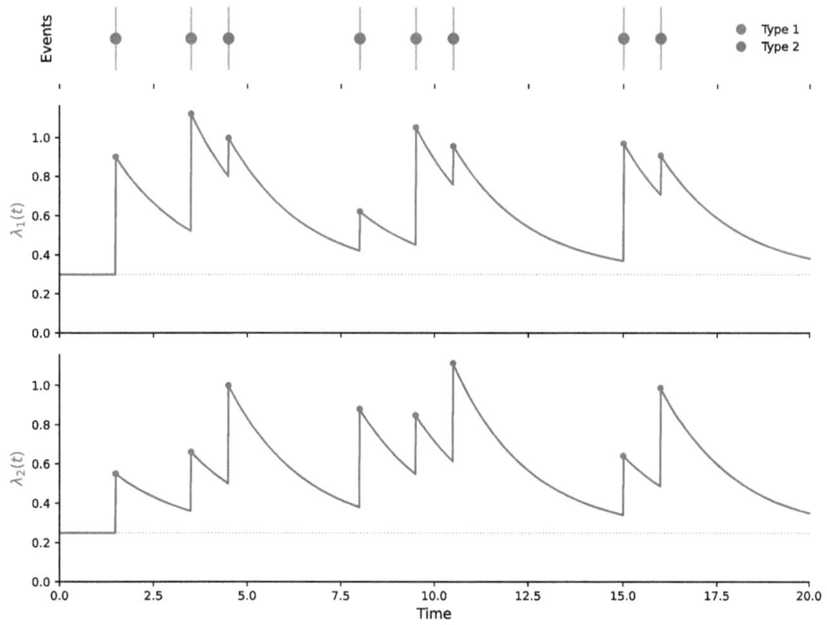

Fig. 1. Illustration of a multivariate Hawkes process with two event types. Each event causes a jump in the conditional intensity $\lambda(t)$, which decays exponentially. Events close in time accumulate their effects, and each type can excite events of both its own type and other types.

Neural models such as the Neural Hawkes Process [5], using Long Short-Term Memory (LSTM) networks, emerged and began to capture complex relationships between events, outperforming linear models. Despite their broad applicability, these models face limitations common to recurrent networks, such as slow training and vanishing gradients.

Through resources such as telemetry or behavioral data collection from social networks, we now have an abundance of data, and training on long sequences is expensive and time-consuming, even with modern parallelizable techniques such as Transformers [9]. In language models, however, it is common to apply a technique called train short, test long [6], which consists of training the model on short word sequences but testing on long sequences, always seeking to maintain model quality as measured by metrics such as perplexity. There is still no consolidated model in Temporal Point Processes (TPPs) that effectively addresses this problem.

The Transformer Hawkes Process (THP) [11] is a widely used Hawkes process model that, like the classical Transformer, uses embeddings with absolute times and is therefore not time-invariant, producing different results when executed at different times even with the same datasets and seeds. The Rotary Position Embedding-based Transformer Hawkes Process (RoTHP) [2] addresses this problem through trigonometric rotation matrices [8], which make it time-invariant but without the recency bias characteristic of a Hawkes process.

Returning to the language modeling domain, HoPE: Hyperbolic Rotary Positional Encoding for Stable Long-Range Dependency Modeling in Large Language Models [1] showed that hyperbolic functions combined with a learnable parameter to ensure exponential bias provide the model with stable perplexity even on sequences longer than those seen during training. The Hyperbolic Transformer Hawkes Process (HoTHP), our proposed model, pioneers this concept in the Hawkes process domain and shows that the inductive bias aligns with the very concept of the Hawkes process, demonstrating great stability on sequences longer than those seen during training, as measured by the log-likelihood.

2 Background

In this section, we present the fundamental concepts needed to understand the contribution of this work. We begin by defining temporal point processes and the Hawkes process, then discuss the cost function used to train these models, and trace the evolution of Hawkes models within machine learning, from parametric approaches to the Transformer-based architectures that motivate our work.

2.1 Temporal Point Processes and the Hawkes Process

A Temporal Point Process (TPP) is a stochastic model that describes sequences of events occurring in continuous time. Formally, a realization of a TPP is an ordered sequence of timestamps. When each event carries additional type information, we have a multivariate TPP, in which the sequence is given by $\mathcal{S} = \{(t_i, k_i)\}_{i=1}^{N}$, where k_i represents the type of event i, t the timestamp, and N the number of events.

The central tool for describing the dynamics of a TPP is the conditional intensity function $\lambda(t \mid \mathcal{H}_t)$, which represents the instantaneous rate of event occurrence at time t, given the past events, that is, the probability of observing an event in the infinitesimal interval $[t, t+dt)$, where $\mathcal{H}$ represents all past events until t.

The Hawkes process [3] is a particular case of TPP in which past events excite the occurrence of new ones. This phenomenon is called self-excitation. Its conditional intensity is defined by

$$\lambda(t) = \mu + \sum \varphi(t - t'), \tag{1}$$

where $\mu > 0$ is the base intensity and $\varphi(\cdot)$ is the triggering kernel that quantifies the effect of each past event on the present intensity. The most common choice for φ is the exponential kernel [4]:

$$\varphi(t) = \alpha \cdot \exp(-\beta \cdot t), \tag{2}$$

with α controlling the magnitude of the effect and β controlling the decay rate. It is important to note that the influence of a past event on the present intensity decays exponentially with elapsed time, and that events can inhibit, rather than excite, future occurrences. This property will be central to the motivation of HoTHP.

2.2 Log-Likelihood in Point Processes

The standard cost function for training TPP models is the log-likelihood. Given a sequence of events $\{t_1, \ldots, t_N\}$ observed in an interval $[0, T]$, the log-likelihood is defined as:

$$\mathcal{L} = \sum_{i=1}^{N} \log \lambda(t_i) - \int_0^T \lambda(t)\, dt. \tag{3}$$

The first term rewards the model for assigning high intensity at the instants where events actually occurred. The second term penalizes the model for maintaining high intensity in regions where there are no events. For convenience, we minimize the negative log-likelihood (NLL), which is the metric we use in the experiments.

2.3 From Simple Parametric Models to Transformers

The first models for Hawkes processes were parametric and assumed a specific form for the kernel, with the exponential being the most commonly used. Although mathematically tractable, these approaches have limited expressiveness and do not capture well complex dependencies between events of different types [7].

To overcome this limitation, neural approaches emerged. The Neural Hawkes Process (NHP) [5] uses a Recurrent Neural Network (RNN) LSTM to model the conditional intensity, allowing it to capture complex and long-range dependencies. However, the sequential nature of LSTMs makes parallelization more difficult and training slow on long sequences.

The Transformer Hawkes Process (THP) [11] brought the self-attention mechanism of Transformers to the TPP context, enabling parallel processing and capture of dependencies between distant events. To represent the temporal position of each event, the THP uses a sinusoidal encoding applied directly to the absolute time of each event:

$$[\boldsymbol{z}(t_j)]_i = \begin{cases} \cos\left(\frac{t_j}{10000^{(i-1)/d}}\right), & \text{if } i \text{ is odd,} \\ \sin\left(\frac{t_j}{10000^{i/d}}\right), & \text{if } i \text{ is even,} \end{cases} \tag{4}$$

where d is the model dimension. The problem with this approach is that it operates on absolute timestamps. Shifting all timestamps by a constant σ changes the computations and, consequently, the attention scores and the model predictions.

2.4 RoTHP: Time Invariance via Rotation

RoTHP [2] solves the time-invariance problem by adapting RoPE [8] to continuous timestamps. Instead of adding a positional encoding to the event time, RoTHP rotates the query $\boldsymbol{q}$ and key $\boldsymbol{k}$ vectors using a rotation matrix $\boldsymbol{R}$:

$$\boldsymbol{R}(t_i) = \begin{pmatrix} \cos t_i\theta_1 & \sin t_i\theta_1 & \cdots & 0 & 0 \\ -\sin t_i\theta_1 & \cos t_i\theta_1 & \cdots & 0 & 0 \\ \vdots & \vdots & \ddots & \vdots & \vdots \\ 0 & 0 & \cdots & \cos t_i\theta_{d/2} & \sin t_i\theta_{d/2} \\ 0 & 0 & \cdots & -\sin t_i\theta_{d/2} & \cos t_i\theta_{d/2} \end{pmatrix}, \tag{5}$$

where the θ_l are learnable frequencies. Since the attention is computed by the inner product of Q and K, we have:

$$\boldsymbol{q}_i^\top \boldsymbol{R}(t_i)^\top \boldsymbol{R}(t_j)\, \boldsymbol{k}_j = \boldsymbol{q}_i^\top \boldsymbol{R}(t_j - t_i)\, \boldsymbol{k}_j. \tag{6}$$

This ensures that the attention score depends only on the temporal difference $\Delta t = t_j - t_i$, respecting time invariance.

However, the cosine and sine functions are oscillatory. As Δt grows, the attention score oscillates periodically, as shown in Fig. 2. This means that two temporally close events may receive a lower attention score than distant events, depending on the phase of the oscillation. This behavior contradicts the natural exponential decay of the Hawkes process, in which the influence of past events should decrease monotonically with time.

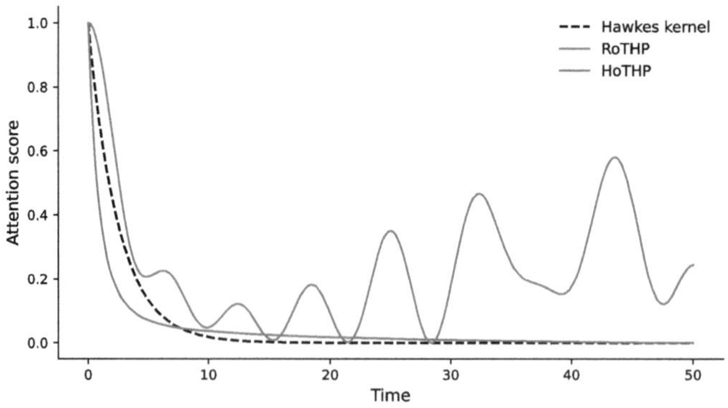

Fig. 2. Normalized attention profile of each model compared to the true exponential kernel $e^{-\beta \Delta t}$. HoTHP aligns better with the real kernel than RoTHP.

This problem worsens in the length extrapolation scenario. When the model is tested on sequences longer than those seen during training, the temporal differences can reach values that were never observed during training. Since the trigonometric function oscillates in these regions, the model has no guarantee of generalizing correctly, and in practice performance degrades.

2.5 Length Extrapolation

Before presenting HoTHP, it is necessary to clarify the problem it aims to solve. In this section, we define length extrapolation in the context of TPPs, argue how a recency bias applied to the attention mechanism is suitable for Hawkes processes, and empirically demonstrate that rotational models based on trigonometric rotation, despite being time-shift invariant, do not possess this characteristic.

We adapt the definition from Attention with Linear Biases (ALiBi) [6] to the TPP scenario. Let L be the length (in number of events) of the sequences used during training and L_{test} the length of the sequences used for testing. We say that a model extrapolates efficiently when its performance remains stable as the ratio L_{test}/L grows, in the case of TPPs, considering the log-likelihood as the cost function. Given the quadratic nature of the Transformer architecture, training the model on very long sequences can become infeasible.

As we have seen, RoTHP solves the time-invariance issue, but the oscillatory nature of its trigonometric functions prevents a monotonic decay in the attention scores. This motivates the search for a positional encoding that combines time invariance with an exponential decay bias, aligned with the structure of the Hawkes process itself.

3 Hyperbolic Rotary Position Embedding-Based Transformer Hawkes Process for Length Extrapolation (HoTHP)

HoTHP is built upon three basic principles: the attention score must depend only on the temporal difference between events, ensuring invariance to time shifts; the score must decrease monotonically, following the bias introduced by the original Hawkes process; and the decay must be part of the model structure and not merely an additional layer. We adopt the hyperbolic kernel from HoPE [1] and adapt it for TPPs by reformulating the product $q^T \boldsymbol{B}(\theta, m-n)k$ directly as a function of the temporal delta, unlike RoTHP, which pre-rotates $\boldsymbol{q}$ and $\boldsymbol{k}$ before sending them to the attention mechanism.

3.1 From Trigonometric Rotation to Hyperbolic Rotation

As seen in Sect. 2.4, the rotation matrix $\boldsymbol{R}(t_i)$ of RoTHP [1,2] is block-diagonal, composed of 2×2 trigonometric rotation blocks. For each pair of dimensions $(2j-1, 2j)$, the corresponding block applied to a temporal difference Δt is:

$$\boldsymbol{R}_j(\Delta t) = \begin{bmatrix} \cos(\theta_j \Delta t) & \sin(\theta_j \Delta t) \\ -\sin(\theta_j \Delta t) & \cos(\theta_j \Delta t) \end{bmatrix}. \tag{7}$$

This block ensures time invariance, since the attention score depends only on $\Delta t = t_i - t_j$.

HoPE [1] proposes replacing the trigonometric rotation with a hyperbolic rotation. The 2×2 block becomes:

$$\boldsymbol{B}_j(\Delta t) = \begin{bmatrix} \cosh(\theta_j \Delta t) & \sinh(\theta_j \Delta t) \\ \sinh(\theta_j \Delta t) & \cosh(\theta_j \Delta t) \end{bmatrix}. \tag{8}$$

The fundamental difference is that cosh and sinh are monotonic functions (for $\Delta t > 0$), unlike cos and sin, which oscillate. This eliminates the undesirable oscillations in the attention score. However, we cannot use the block $\boldsymbol{B}_j$ directly because, unlike the trigonometric rotation, the hyperbolic rotation is not an orthogonal transformation; moreover, the inner product of $\boldsymbol{q}$ and $\boldsymbol{k}$ grows with $|\Delta t|$ instead of decaying [1]. This means that distant events would receive higher scores than nearby events, which is the opposite of the desired behavior.

To solve this problem, HoPE [1] introduces a learnable parameter θ' and applies damping factors to the $\boldsymbol{q}$ and $\boldsymbol{k}$ vectors, with $\boldsymbol{q}$ at position m multiplied by $e^{-m\theta'}$, and $\boldsymbol{k}$ by $e^{+m\theta'}$. When we compute the attention score between positions m and n, these factors combine:

$$g(\boldsymbol{x}_m, \boldsymbol{x}_n, n-m) = e^{-(m-n)\theta'} \, \boldsymbol{q}^\top \boldsymbol{B}(\theta, m-n) \, \boldsymbol{k}. \tag{9}$$

Adapting for TPPs, we replace the discrete positions m, n with the continuous timestamps t_i, t_j, and the difference $m - n$ with the temporal delta $\Delta t = t_i - t_j$. The attention score becomes:

$$g(\Delta t) = e^{-\Delta t \cdot \theta'} \, \boldsymbol{q}^\top \, \boldsymbol{B}(\theta, \Delta t) \, \boldsymbol{k}. \tag{10}$$

For the damping to dominate the growth of cosh, it is required that $\theta' > \max \theta$. Under this condition, the score decays monotonically with Δt, like the exponential kernel of the Hawkes process, where recent events are naturally more influential than distant events.

3.2 HoTHP Attention Score

Substituting the definition of $\boldsymbol{B}_j$ (Eq. 8) into Eq. 10, the attention score for dimension pair j becomes:

$$g_j(\Delta t) = e^{-|\Delta t|\theta'} \left[\underbrace{(q_1 k_1 + q_2 k_2)}_{\text{cosh part}} \cosh(\theta_j \Delta t) + \underbrace{(q_1 k_2 + q_2 k_1)}_{\text{sinh part}} \sinh(\theta_j \Delta t) \right]. \tag{11}$$

As in HoPE, we keep the parameter θ', enforcing the constraint $\theta' > \max \theta$ throughout training. Since θ' is a learnable parameter, we cannot simply fix its value. To enforce this constraint automatically during training, we parameterize θ' as:

$$\theta' = \text{softplus}(\theta'_{\text{raw}}) + \max(\theta) + \epsilon, \tag{12}$$

where θ'_{raw} is the learnable parameter and $\epsilon = 10^{-4}$ is a safety margin. In this way, we structurally guarantee that θ' is greater than any value of θ and, therefore, guarantee the exponential decay.

3.3 Temporal Normalization

Different datasets have very distinct time scales: in social networks, the intervals between events can be on the order of milliseconds, while in seismic data they can be on the order of days. If we used raw timestamps in the hyperbolic kernel, the values of $\theta \Delta t$ would be on incompatible scales and the model would not work well without manual tuning.

To address this, we normalize the timestamps before computing the attention scores. First, we shift the timestamps so that the sequence starts at zero. Then, we divide each timestamp by the mean inter-event interval observed up to that point.

After this normalization, the mean inter-event interval is close to 1.0, regardless of the original scale of the data.

3.4 Full Architecture

The HoTHP architecture follows the encoder structure of the Transformer [9], adapted for temporal point processes. Each event (t_i, k_i) is represented by a learned embedding of type k_i. Unlike THP [11], timestamps are not added to the embedding; temporal information is incorporated exclusively through the hyperbolic kernel in the attention mechanism.

The model uses N stacked encoder layers, each composed of a multi-head attention block followed by a feed-forward network. The attention block computes scores via the hyperbolic kernel, using the normalized temporal differences. A causal mask is applied to ensure that each event attends only to previous events. The conditional intensity for each event type k is computed as:

$$\lambda_k(t \mid \mathcal{H}_t) = f_k\left(\underbrace{\alpha_k \frac{(t - t_j)}{t_j}}_{\text{current}} + \underbrace{\boldsymbol{w}_k^\top \boldsymbol{h}(t_j)}_{\text{history}} + \underbrace{b_k}_{\text{base}}\right), \tag{13}$$

where $\boldsymbol{h}(t_j)$ is the encoder output representation for event j, α_k, $\boldsymbol{w}_k$, and b_k are learnable parameters, and $f_k = \text{softplus}$ is the activation function that ensures positivity of the intensity, following the THP formulation [11].

The main difference between HoTHP and RoTHP lies in how temporal information enters the attention mechanism. RoTHP individually pre-rotates the $\boldsymbol{q}$ and $\boldsymbol{k}$ vectors using the trigonometric matrices $\boldsymbol{R}(t_i)$ and $\boldsymbol{R}(t_j)$, and then computes the standard dot product, so that the dependence on Δt is mathematically guaranteed. In HoTHP, the attention score $\boldsymbol{q}^\top \boldsymbol{B}(\Delta t)\boldsymbol{k}$ is formulated directly as a function of the temporal difference between each pair of events, which allows incorporating the decay factor $e^{-\Delta t\,\theta'}$ into the kernel structure itself.

4 Experiments

4.1 Experimental Setup

We generate event sequences from multivariate Hawkes processes with $K = 2$ event types and exponential kernel. To evaluate the model behavior under different regimes of temporal dependence, we define two scenarios. In the slow decay scenario, the influence of past events persists for a long time, so that distant events still contribute significantly to the present intensity. In the fast decay scenario, only recent events exert relevant influence. For each scenario, we generate 500 training sequences, 150 validation sequences, and 200 test sequences.

Training follows the *train short, test long* technique, inspired by [6]. To systematically evaluate the extrapolation capability, we sweep over multiple training lengths ($L \in \{10, 20, 50, 100\}$) and extrapolation factors ($2\times$, $5\times$, $10\times$), resulting in test sequences ranging from 20 to 1,000 events. The NLL is computed over the full sequence, allowing a direct measurement of the model's length extrapolation capability across different combinations of training length and extrapolation ratio.

We compare HoTHP with RoTHP [2], both implemented on the EasyTPP framework [10]. The only difference between the models is the positional kernel used in the attention mechanism. All experiments are repeated with $N = 5$ distinct seeds and we report mean $\pm$ standard deviation. Statistical significance is assessed via the Wilcoxon signed-rank test (one-sided), a non-parametric paired test appropriate for small sample sizes.

4.2 Slow Decay vs. Fast Decay

Table 1 presents the NLL results for both models in the two decay scenarios, evaluated on sequences of different lengths. Figure 3 illustrates the evolution of the NLL as the test length grows.

In the fast decay scenario, HoTHP consistently outperforms RoTHP across all extrapolation scales, with statistically significant differences (Wilcoxon $p = 0.031$) at $2\times$, $5\times$, and $10\times$. At the $10\times$ scale, the NLL difference is 0.551 nats. The HoTHP NLL remains essentially flat across all scales (≈ 1.69), while RoTHP degrades from 1.68 at $1\times$ to 2.25 at $10\times$. Beyond the difference in means, the standard deviations reveal an important difference in model stability. RoTHP exhibits a standard deviation of 0.246 at the $10\times$ scale, compared to only 0.011 for HoTHP. This suggests that the trigonometric kernel of RoTHP is sensitive to extrapolation beyond horizons seen during training, while the hyperbolic kernel of HoTHP maintains consistent behavior regardless of the seed.

In the slow decay scenario, HoTHP also achieves lower NLL than RoTHP at all extrapolation scales, although the differences are smaller and do not reach

Table 1. NLL (mean ± standard deviation, $N = 5$ seeds) for the slow and fast decay scenarios. Values in **bold** indicate the best result in each column per process group. Lower values are better. Statistical significance assessed via Wilcoxon signed-rank test ($^* p < 0.05$).

Process	Model	1×	2×	5×	10×
Slow	RoTHP	**1.685 ± 0.004**	1.719 ± 0.009	1.757 ± 0.024	1.779 ± 0.035
	HoTHP	1.693 ± 0.009	**1.698 ± 0.021**	**1.713 ± 0.032**	**1.724 ± 0.038**
Fast	RoTHP	**1.677 ± 0.003**	1.994 ± 0.126	2.111 ± 0.186	2.246 ± 0.246
	HoTHP	1.692 ± 0.006	**1.693 ± 0.009***	**1.694 ± 0.010***	**1.695 ± 0.011***

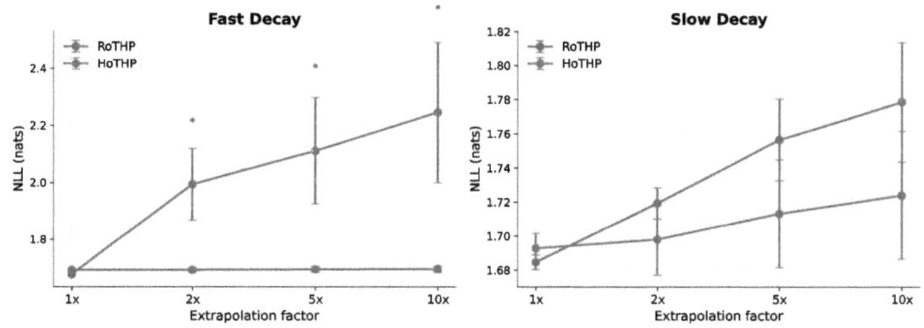

Fig. 3. NLL evolution as a function of test length for the slow decay (left) and fast decay (right) scenarios. Error bars indicate ±1 standard deviation over 5 seeds.

statistical significance for $L = 50$ ($p = 0.062$ at 10×). This suggests that the exponential decay bias of HoTHP provides a benefit even when the generating process has slow decay, though the effect is less pronounced because the oscillatory behavior of the trigonometric kernel is less harmful when temporal differences are smaller.

These results indicate that the decay bias of HoTHP aligns with the structure of the Hawkes process with exponential kernel, enabling more stable extrapolation in both decay regimes, with a particularly large advantage in processes with fast decay.

4.3 Complementary Analyses

Figure 2 compares the attention profile of each model with the true exponential kernel of the generating process. RoTHP exhibits an oscillatory profile, while HoTHP exhibits a decreasing profile closer to the real kernel. This shows that the hyperbolic kernel is able to learn an attention profile more aligned with the exponential decay of the Hawkes process.

Figure 4 summarizes the HoTHP advantage ($\text{NLL}_{RoTHP} - \text{NLL}_{HoTHP}$) across all combinations of training length and extrapolation factor. In the fast decay scenario, HoTHP is significantly better in all 12 combinations (Wilcoxon $p = 0.031$), with the advantage growing as the training length decreases and the

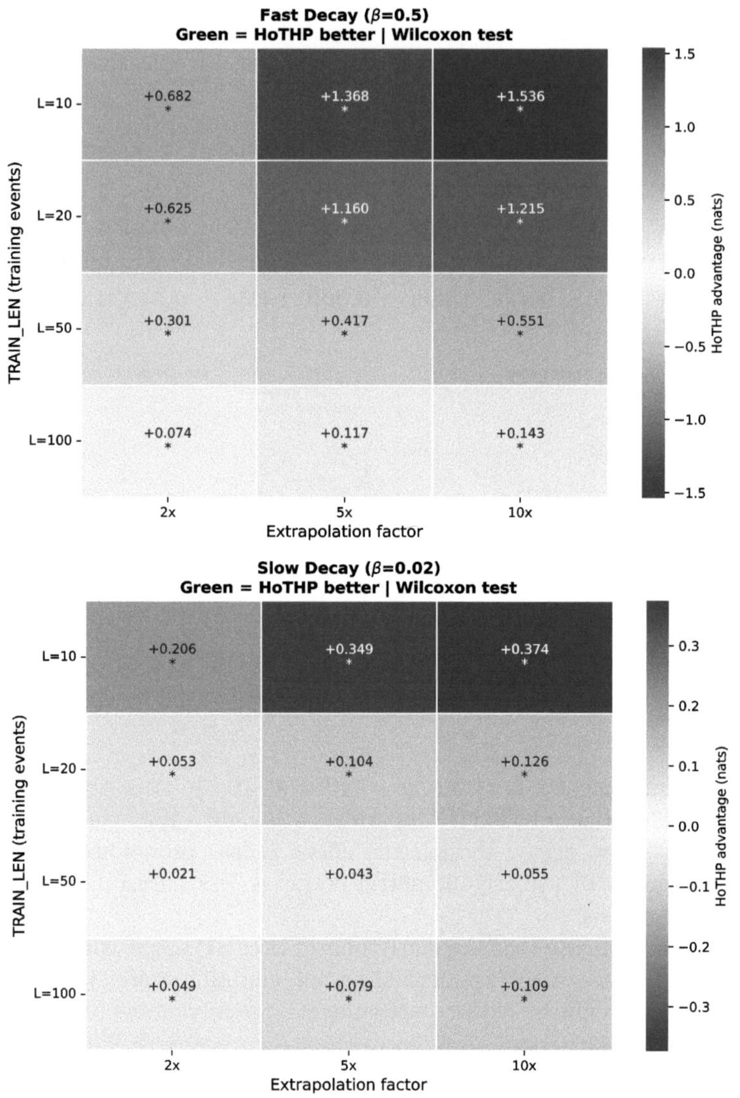

Fig. 4. HoTHP advantage over RoTHP (NLL difference in nats) across training lengths and extrapolation factors. Green indicates HoTHP is better. Asterisks denote Wilcoxon signed-rank significance ($^* p < 0.05$). Left: fast decay. Right: slow decay. (Color figure online)

extrapolation factor increases. In the slow decay scenario, 9 out of 12 combinations are significant at $p < 0.05$, confirming that the benefit of the hyperbolic kernel is not restricted to fast decay processes.

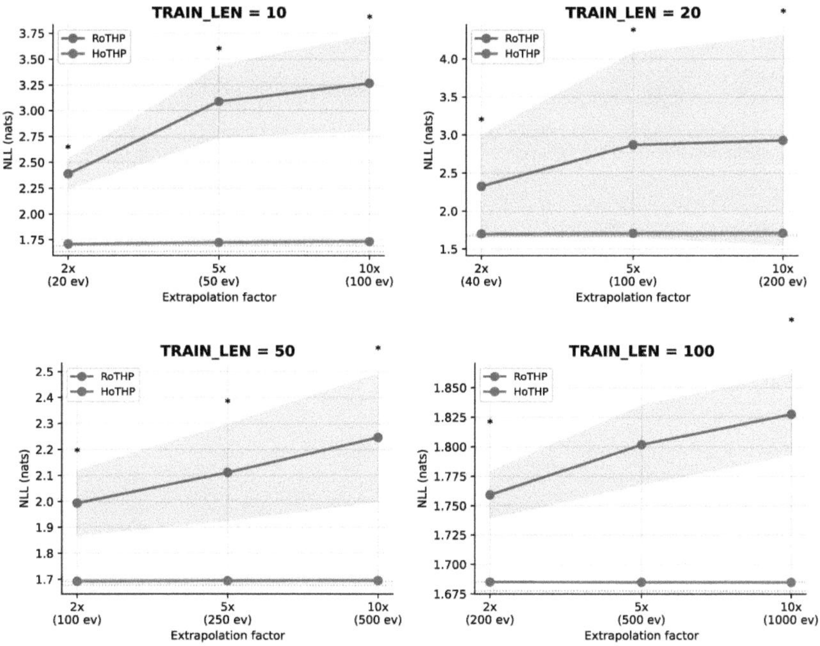

Fig. 5. NLL by extrapolation factor for each training length in the fast decay scenario. Shaded areas indicate ±1 standard deviation over 5 seeds. Dotted lines show in-distribution NLL. Asterisks denote Wilcoxon significance ($^* p < 0.05$).

Figures 5 and 6 show the NLL evolution for each training length individually. In the fast decay scenario (Fig. 5), RoTHP degrades sharply across all training lengths, while HoTHP remains stable. The effect is most dramatic for shorter training sequences ($L = 10$, $L = 20$), where RoTHP reaches NLL values above 3.0 at 10× extrapolation. In the slow decay scenario (Fig. 6), the gap between the two models is narrower but HoTHP consistently maintains lower NLL. The only case where the confidence bands overlap substantially is $L = 50$, where the HoTHP advantage does not reach statistical significance.

5 Related Work

Our contribution in neural networks for TPPs involves concepts drawn from the most recent advances in positional encoding for Transformers. Although parallel, these lines of research have maintained a recurring dialogue on advances in positional encoding originally proposed within the context of language models and their adaptations to TPP scenarios, and these adaptations have represented important performance leaps in the area. THP [11] established this pattern by adapting the original Transformer architecture [9] to continuous event sequences.

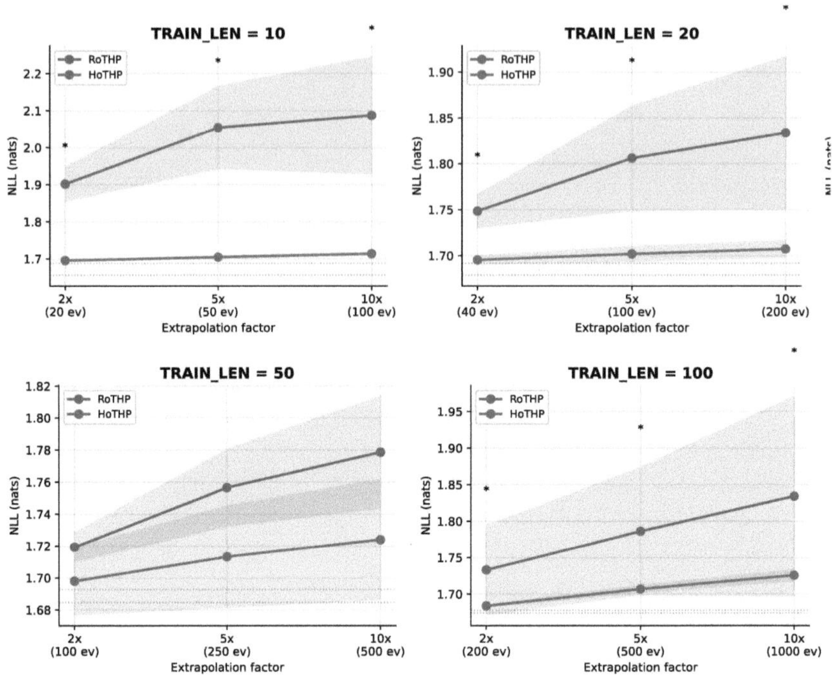

Fig. 6. NLL by extrapolation factor for each training length in the slow decay scenario. Shaded areas indicate ± 1 standard deviation over 5 seeds. Dotted lines show in-distribution NLL. Asterisks denote Wilcoxon significance ($^* p < 0.05$).

RoTHP [2] continued this trend by adapting RoPE [8] to continuous timestamps, addressing the fragility of THP with temporal shifts.

ALiBi [6] introduced a linear decay bias to the attention scores, enabling length extrapolation in language models, but its linear profile does not match the exponential decay of the Hawkes kernel. HoPE [1] addressed the oscillatory limitations of RoPE by replacing trigonometric rotations with hyperbolic functions. The resulting attention weights decay monotonically with distance, which is a property that aligns naturally with the recency bias of the Hawkes process, where the influence of past events decreases with time.

Our research takes one more step in this direction, adapting the advantage of recency bias within the context of a Hawkes process and thus delivering more stability to the model in extrapolation scenarios, which are very useful for large datasets whose training becomes very expensive and time-consuming, or when training data is sparse. Figure 7 illustrates the theoretical attention profiles of these approaches, showing RoTHP oscillating without decaying, ALiBi decaying linearly, and HoTHP decaying exponentially.

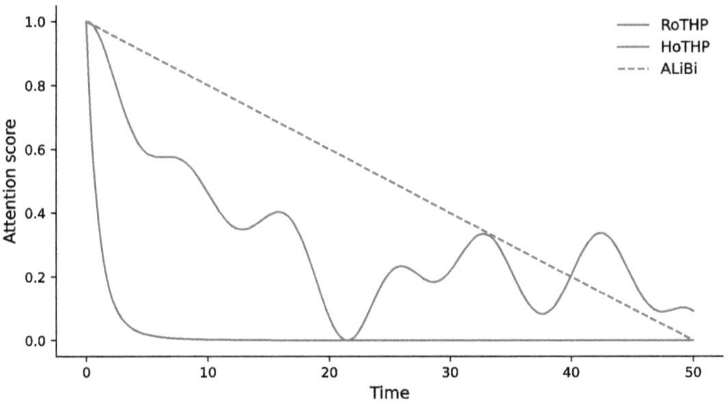

Fig. 7. Theoretical attention profiles as a function of Δt for RoTHP, ALiBi, and HoTHP. The HoTHP profile most closely resembles the exponential decay kernel of the Hawkes process.

6 Conclusion

In this work, we proposed HoTHP, a Transformer Hawkes Process that replaces the trigonometric rotational kernel of RoTHP with a hyperbolic kernel with learnable exponential decay, parameterized by θ'. The central motivation is the structural alignment between the exponential decay induced by the hyperbolic kernel and the exponential kernel of the Hawkes process. Just as the intensity function introduced by Hawkes [3] $\varphi(t) = \alpha e^{-\beta\Delta}$ imposes that past events lose influence monotonically over time, the HoTHP kernel imposes the same bias directly in the attention mechanism. This structural correspondence is not accidental but rather the inductive bias that justifies the choice of HoPE as inspiration and distinguishes HoTHP from other positional encoding approaches.

The experiments on synthetic data confirm that HoTHP generalizes better in the length extrapolation scenario (*train short, test long*). In the fast decay regime, the performance difference relative to RoTHP is statistically significant (Wilcoxon $p = 0.031$), with HoTHP maintaining stable NLL while RoTHP degrades progressively. In slow decay processes, HoTHP also achieves lower NLL at all extrapolation scales, although with smaller margins that do not reach statistical significance for $L = 50$. Furthermore, HoTHP exhibited lower variance across different seeds and better alignment with the data-generating kernel, while maintaining the time invariance introduced by RoTHP.

The experiments were conducted exclusively on synthetic data. Although this choice allowed precise control of the generating process and isolation of the effect of positional encoding from other factors, it does not directly demonstrate performance on real data, where the dependency structure may be more complex and the generating process is unknown.

As future work, we plan to evaluate HoTHP on real-world event datasets, including financial transactions, social networks, and seismic data, where the ability to extrapolate length has a direct impact on practical applications.

Acknowledgments. The authors used Claude, an AI assistant by Anthropic, to support language editing and text refinement during manuscript preparation. All scientific content, experimental design, results, and conclusions were produced, reviewed, and validated entirely by the authors, who bear full responsibility for the final version of this work.

This work was supported by the National Council for Scientific and Technological Development (CNPq), grant number 306569/2024-8.

References

1. Dai, C., Shan, H., Song, M., Liang, D.: Hope: hyperbolic rotary positional encoding for stable long-range dependency modeling in large language models. CoRR **abs/2509.05218** (2025). https://doi.org/10.48550/ARXIV.2509.05218
2. Dai, S., Gao, A., Li, Z., Du, Y.: Rotary position embedding-based transformer Hawkes process for event-type big data. Big Data Min. Anal. (2026)
3. Hawkes, A.G.: Spectra of some self-exciting and mutually exciting point processes. Biometrika **58**(1), 83–90 (1971)
4. Laub, P.J., Lee, Y., Pollett, P.K., Taimre, T.: Hawkes models and their applications. Ann. Rev. Stat. Appl. **12**(Volume 12, 2025), 233–258 (2025). https://doi.org/10.1146/annurev-statistics-112723-034304, https://www.annualreviews.org/content/journals/10.1146/annurev-statistics-112723-034304
5. Mei, H., Eisner, J.: The neural hawkes process: a neurally self-modulating multivariate point process. In: NIPS 2017 (2017)
6. Press, O., Smith, N.A., Lewis, M.: Train short, test long: attention with linear biases enables input length extrapolation. In: International Conference on Learning Representations (ICLR) (2022)
7. Shchur, O., Türkmen, A.C., Januschowski, T., Günnemann, S.: Neural temporal point processes: a review. In: Proceedings of the Thirtieth International Joint Conference on Artificial Intelligence, IJCAI-21, pp. 4585–4593 (2021). https://doi.org/10.24963/ijcai.2021/623
8. Su, J., Ahmed, M., Lu, Y., Pan, S., Wen, B., Liu, Y.: Roformer: enhanced transformer with rotary position embedding. Neurocomputing **568** (2024)
9. Vaswani, A., et al.: Attention is all you need. In: Advances in Neural Information Processing Systems (NeurIPS) (2017)
10. Xue, S., et al.: EasyTPP: towards open benchmarking temporal point processes. In: The Twelfth International Conference on Learning Representations (2024). https://openreview.net/forum?id=PJwAkg0z7h
11. Zuo, S., Jiang, H., Li, Z., Zhao, T., Zha, H.: Transformer Hawkes process. In: International Conference on Machine Learning (ICML) (2020)

Solomonoff Value-Mixtures and the Free Inference Boundary: A Theoretical Framework for Meta-reinforcement Learning via Finite Bayesian Mixtures of Q-Agents

Luiz Carlos Castro Guedes[1,2](✉) and Edward Hermann Haeusler[1](✉)

[1] Departamento de Informática, PUC-Rio, Rio de Janeiro, Brazil
hermann@inf.puc-rio.br
[2] Seção de Engenharia de Computação, Instituto Militar de Engenharia, Rio de Janeiro, Brazil
lcguedes@ime.eb.br

Abstract. Solomonoff's theory of universal induction defines the gold standard for Bayesian sequence prediction via mixtures over computable hypotheses weighted by algorithmic complexity [10,11]. We have developed a complementary Meta-Reinforcement Learning (Meta-RL) perspective [5], constructing a Meta-Agent that maintains Bayesian beliefs over a finite family of grid-world environments and thereby instantiates a tractable bridge between Solomonoff's universal induction, MDL mixture coding, Bayesian Reinforcement Learning, and Meta-RL Task Inference [2,3]. We analyze two strategy modes: Value-Mixture (VM), which acts according to belief-weighted averaged Q-functions, and posterior mode selection (PMS), which commits to the highest-belief hypothesis. We have identified a distinct phase transition in the VM Meta-Agent behavior which we term 'Free Inference'. This phenomenon allows a zero-regret policy to emerge from the value-mixture well before the agent has sufficient data to isolate the true environment. The Free Inference property reveals that Solomonoff mixtures can be terminally valuable in action-selection settings, computing a robust consensus policy that no single hypothesis can provide.

Keywords: Meta-Reinforcement Learning · Solomonoff Induction · Minimum Description Length · Bayesian Reinforcement Learning

1 Introduction and Motivation

Solomonoff induction defines a universal mixture predictor that assigns to each computable hypothes a weight proportional to its Kolmogorov complex-

Edward H. Haeusler is p.f by FAPERJ grant APQ1 E-26/210.258/2019.249292), CNPq grant 309287/2023-5 and CAPES/COFECUB 88881.878969/2023-01.

M. Recamonde-Mendoza and R. C. Barros (Eds.): BRACIS 2026, LNAI 17105, pp. 123–138, 2027.
https://doi.org/10.1007/978-3-032-39882-6_9

ity [10, 11]. This mixture is prediction-optimal in a strong sense, but uncomputable. AIXI, Hutter's universal reinforcement learning agent, extends universal induction to decision-making by selecting actions that maximize expected reward under the universal mixture, again at the cost of uncomputability [6].

Meta-Reinforcement Learning (Meta-RL) provides a practical perspective: the agent faces a distribution over tasks/environments and must **infer the current task from interaction**. This can be formalized as a POMDP with a latent static task variable [5]. Many Meta-RL algorithms learn task inference implicitly (e.g., via recurrent policies) [1] or approximate belief updates through amortized inference [8, 13].

This paper develops a complementary perspective, motivated by empirical observations from a Meta-Reinforcement Learning system. We construct a Meta-Agent that maintains a Bayesian belief over a finite family of grid-world environments. This aligns with the view of Meta-RL as inference over a latent task/environment variable whose posterior acts as a sufficient statistic for adaptation [5]. The Meta-Agent operates in two distinct strategy modes. The **Value-Mixture (VM)** mode acts according to the belief-weighted average of pre-trained Q-functions, a finite, constructive approximation of a Solomonoff mixture restricted to a hypothesis class of environment models. The **posterior mode selection (PMS)** mode, at each step, selects the environment with highest posterior belief and acts according to that single environment's Q-function, committing to its best current hypothesis. From a Bayesian control perspective, VM corresponds to posterior integration while PMS corresponds to posterior optimization over a finite environment class [2].

The central empirical finding is that these two modes exhibit qualitatively different regret profiles, and that their relationship undergoes a phase transition governed by the geometric structure of the environment family. While the VM Meta-Agent achieves **near-optimal returns without identifying the true environment** across a wide range of environment complexities, the PMS Meta-Agent's returns degrade approximately linearly, paying the cost of identification even when it is unnecessary. We call this VM regime **Free Inference**; it reveals a structural property of Solomonoff-type mixtures in action selection that is distinct from their well-known convergence properties in prediction.

We develop the theory primarily through a **nested environment family**, where obstacle sets satisfy $O_{\nu_{0.1}} \subseteq \cdots \subseteq O_{\nu_{1.0}}$. Here Free Inference depends on two conditions: **local obstacle avoidance** (the mixture avoids contested cells) and **navigational coherence** (the mixture's greedy policy produces a globally viable trajectory through the consensus free space). The **Free Inference boundary** is determined by the breakdown of coherence, driven by the topology of the environments in the family.

We connect four threads: the **Solomonoff mixture** as a universal prior over computable environments [10, 11], **MDL mixture coding** as the prequential interpretation of Bayesian mixture prediction [3], **Bayesian Reinforcement Learning** as control under posterior uncertainty [2], and **Meta-RL Task Inference** as latent-environment adaptation [5]. The VM and PMS Meta-Agents thus appear as two complementary finite approximations, one averaging, one selecting, and the **Free Inference boundary** marks where averaging ceases to dominate selection, determined in the nested case by navigational coherence and in general by coherence and percolation [4].

2 Related Work

Solomonoff's universal mixture defines optimal sequence prediction by weighting all computable hypotheses according to algorithmic probability [10,11]. AIXI extends this principle to reinforcement learning by maximizing expected reward under a universal environment prior, yielding an ideal but uncomputable decision-theoretic agent [6]. Our work can be interpreted as a **computable restriction** of this paradigm: we replace the infinite hypothesis class with a finite structured set and replace Kolmogorov complexity with explicit description lengths, yielding an exact finite Bayesian mixture with MDL interpretation.

The prequential view of MDL interprets cumulative negative log predictive probability as a code length and shows that Bayesian mixtures achieve optimal log-loss regret relative to the best hypothesis in a model class [3]. Our posterior update and mixture predictor correspond exactly to this prequential mixture coding identity within a finite environment class, applied directly to sequential decision-making rather than static prediction.

Bayesian RL formalizes optimal exploration as planning in a belief-augmented MDP (BAMDP) [2]. While exact Bayes-adaptive planning is typically intractable, our method can be viewed as a structured finite BAMDP with conjugate transition and reward models, combined with lightweight control approximations (belief-weighted Q mixing or posterior mode sampling).

Recent work interprets meta-reinforcement learning as inference over a latent task variable in a POMDP [5]. Practical algorithms such as RL^2 [1], PEARL [8], and VariBAD [13] perform task inference implicitly through recurrent policies or probabilistic latent context encoders. In contrast, we define explicit generative likelihoods for transitions and rewards and perform exact Bayesian filtering within a finite hypothesis class, enabling a direct MDL and finite-Solomonoff interpretation.

3 Formal Setup

3.1 Environment Family

Let $\mathcal{V} = \{\nu_1, \ldots, \nu_N\}$ be a finite family of deterministic grid-world environments sharing:

- A common grid $\mathcal{G} = \{0, \ldots, W-1\} \times \{0, \ldots, H-1\}$,
- A common start state $s_0 \in \mathcal{G}$ and goal state $g \in \mathcal{G}$,
- A common action space $\mathcal{A} = \{0, 1, 2, 3\}$ (up, right, down, left),
- A common reward structure: step reward $r_{\text{step}} = -k$ for $k \in (0, 1]$, wall penalty $r_{\text{wall}} = -100k$.

Environments differ only in their **obstacle set** $O_\nu \subset \mathcal{G}$. For each ν, the **free space** is $F_\nu = \mathcal{G} \setminus O_\nu$.

The transition function for environment ν is deterministic:

$$T_\nu(s,a) = \begin{cases} s+\delta_a & \text{if } s+\delta_a \in F_\nu \\ s & \text{otherwise (obstacle collision)} \end{cases} \tag{1}$$

where δ_a is the displacement associated with action a.

3.2 Nested Environment Families

Definition 1 (Nested Environment Family). *An environment family $\mathcal{V}$ is* ***nested*** *if the obstacle sets are totally ordered by inclusion:*

$$O_{\nu_1} \subseteq O_{\nu_2} \subseteq \cdots \subseteq O_{\nu_N} \tag{2}$$

In our experimental setup, environments are generated from a base random maze $\mathcal{M}$ by keeping a fraction ρ of its obstacles. Each environment ν_ρ has $O_{\nu_\rho} = \rho \cdot O_{\mathcal{M}}$, with $\rho \in \{0.1, 0.2, \ldots, 1.0\}$, producing a nested family. The free spaces are reverse-nested: $F_{\nu_{1.0}} \subseteq F_{\nu_{0.9}} \subseteq \cdots \subseteq F_{\nu_{0.1}}$.

A key property of nested families: the **consensus free space** $F^* = \bigcap_\nu F_\nu = F_{\nu_{1.0}}$ equals the free space of the most constrained environment. If the Q-agent trained on $\nu_{1.0}$ reaches the goal, then F^* is always connected.

3.3 Expert Agents

For each environment $\nu_i \in \mathcal{V}$, a Q-learning agent has been trained to convergence, producing a Q-table $Q_i : \mathcal{G} \times \mathcal{A} \to \mathbb{R}$. We assume each Q_i represents an optimal (or near-optimal) action-value function for ν_i.

3.4 Belief and Inference

The Meta-Agent maintains a belief $\xi_t : \mathcal{V} \to [0,1]$ with $\sum_i \xi_t(\nu_i) = 1$, initialized uniformly:

$$\xi_0(\nu_i) = \frac{1}{N} \quad \forall i \tag{3}$$

After observing a transition (s, a, r, s') at time t, the belief updates via Bayes' rule, as in the Bayes-adaptive perspective on Reinforcement Learning and Task Inference [2,5]:

$$\xi_{t+1}(\nu_i) \propto \xi_t(\nu_i) \cdot p_{\nu_i}(s', r \mid s, a) \tag{4}$$

where $p_{\nu_i}(s', r \mid s, a)$ is the likelihood of the observation under environment hypothesis ν_i.

3.5 Action Selection: Two Strategy Modes

Value-Mixture (VM) Mode. The VM Meta-Agent computes the belief-weighted mixture Q-function:

$$Q_{\text{mix}}(s, a) = \sum_{i=1}^{N} \xi_t(\nu_i) \cdot Q_i(s, a) \tag{5}$$

and acts greedily:

$$a_t^{\text{VM}} = \arg\max_{a \in \mathcal{A}} Q_{\text{mix}}(s_t, a) \tag{6}$$

This is the **averaged predictor**: all hypotheses contribute to every decision, weighted by their current plausibility. It is the risk-neutral Bayesian control rule obtained by integrating values under the current posterior over environments [2].

Posterior Mode Selection (PMS) Mode. The PMS Meta-Agent selects the maximum a posteriori (MAP) environment and acts according to its Q-function:

$$\hat{\nu}_t = \arg\max_{\nu_i \in \mathcal{V}} \xi_t(\nu_i) \tag{7}$$

$$a_t^{\text{PMS}} = \arg\max_{a \in \mathcal{A}} Q_{\hat{\nu}_t}(s_t, a) \tag{8}$$

This is a **posterior mode** control rule: a single hypothesis is selected at each step, and the agent fully commits to that hypothesis's policy. It is closer to greedy posterior commitment than to classical Thompson sampling, which would sample a hypothesis from the posterior rather than choose the posterior mode [9, 12].

Remark 1 (Structural Duality). VM and PMS represent the two canonical ways to use a posterior distribution for decision-making: **integration** (average over the posterior) versus **optimization** (select the mode of the posterior). The VM/PMS duality inherits the integration-vs-optimization structure from Solomonoff theory and the Bayes-adaptive control viewpoint [2, 6].

4 Connection to Solomonoff Induction

Solomonoff's universal prior assigns to each computable hypothesis h a weight proportional to $2^{-K(h)}$, where $K(h)$ is the Kolmogorov complexity of h [10, 11]. The universal mixture predictor is:

$$M(x_{1:n}) = \sum_{h} 2^{-K(h)} \cdot h(x_{1:n}) \tag{9}$$

This mixture dominates every computable predictor: for any computable h^*,

$$-\log M(x_{1:n}) \leq -\log h^*(x_{1:n}) + K(h^*) + O(1) \tag{10}$$

The standard interpretation is that M converges to the true hypothesis: the posterior on h^* concentrates, and M's predictions become indistinguishable from h^*'s. In the Reinforcement Learning setting, the analogous idealized extension is AIXI, which selects actions under a universal environment mixture [6].

The Meta-Agent's two modes instantiate complementary finite restrictions of the Solomonoff framework, which also admits an MDL reading: replacing the infinite universal class by a finite structured family turns Bayesian averaging into a computable prequential mixture code with explicit description lengths [3]. Table 1 summarizes this correspondence.

Table 1. Correspondence between Solomonoff Framework and Meta-Agent modes.

Solomonoff Framework	VM Meta-Agent	PMS Meta-Agent
Hypothesis class: all computable	$\mathcal{V} = \{\nu_1, \ldots, \nu_N\}$	$\mathcal{V} = \{\nu_1, \ldots, \nu_N\}$
Prior weight: $2^{-K(h)}$	$\xi_0(\nu_i) = 1/N$	$\xi_0(\nu_i) = 1/N$
Decision method	$Q_{\text{mix}} = \sum_i \xi_t(\nu_i) Q_i$	$Q_{\hat{\nu}_t}$ for $\hat{\nu}_t = \arg\max \xi_t$
Prediction mode	Weighted average	MAP selection

The critical distinction is that VM uses the belief to weight contributions from all environments while PMS uses it to choose one; both update the belief identically, differing only in how the posterior selects an action.

In the prediction setting, the Solomonoff mixture's value lies primarily in its convergence, with predictions becoming accurate as the posterior concentrates on the true hypothesis. In the **action-selection setting** the two modes can diverge sharply: Q_{mix} can encode a near-optimal policy **even when the belief is completely uninformative**, a property we call **Free Inference**, whereas PMS commits to a single hypothesis and suffers the consequences of wrong commitments. This divergence is driven by the **asymmetric cost structure** (obstacle penalties vastly exceed step penalties), which makes averaging act as a safety mechanism that selection cannot replicate, connecting universal induction, MDL coding, Bayesian RL, and Meta-RL task inference at the level of *action choice* rather than prediction alone.

5 Free Inference: Two Necessary Conditions

5.1 The Consensus Free Space

Definition 2 (Consensus Free Space). *Given an environment family $\mathcal{V}$, the* ***consensus free space*** *is:*

$$F^* = \bigcap_{\nu \in \mathcal{V}} F_\nu = \mathcal{G} \setminus \bigcup_{\nu \in \mathcal{V}} O_\nu \tag{11}$$

A cell $c \in \mathcal{G}$ belongs to F^* if and only if it is free in every environment in $\mathcal{V}$.

Definition 3 (Free Inference). *An episode exhibits* ***Free Inference*** *if the VM Meta-Agent reaches the goal without encountering any obstacle (receiving* r_{wall} *zero times), starting from uniform belief.*

5.2 Condition (C1): Local Obstacle Avoidance

The first condition for Free Inference is that the mixture Q-function steers the agent away from contested cells (cells that are obstacles in at least one environment).

Proposition 1 (Obstacle Avoidance under Uniform Belief). *Let* ξ_t *be uniform. Consider state* $s \in F^*$ *with two neighboring cells* $c_f \in F^*$ *(consensus-free) and* $c_o \notin F^*$ *(obstacle in at least one environment). Let* a_f *and* a_o *be the actions moving toward* c_f *and* c_o *respectively. Then under mild conditions on the Q-tables:*

$$Q_{mix}(s, a_f) > Q_{mix}(s, a_o) \tag{12}$$

Proof (Proof sketch). Let $\mathcal{V}_{\text{wall}}(c_o) = \{\nu \in \mathcal{V} : c_o \in O_\nu\} \neq \emptyset$. For each $\nu \in \mathcal{V}_{\text{wall}}(c_o)$, $Q_\nu(s, a_o) \approx r_{\text{wall}} + \gamma V_\nu(s)$, carrying the severe wall penalty. For the reward structure used ($r_{\text{wall}}/r_{\text{step}} = 100$), even $|\mathcal{V}_{\text{wall}}| = 1$ suffices to make $Q_{\text{mix}}(s, a_o) < Q_{\text{mix}}(s, a_f)$. We call this the **veto mechanism**: a single dissenting environment can block an action.

Remark 2 (PMS Has No Obstacle Avoidance Guarantee). Proposition 1 has no analog for posterior mode selection. Under uniform belief, PMS breaks ties arbitrarily and then follows a single environment's policy; more generally, any commitment-based rule lacks the averaging-induced veto mechanism that protects VM from dangerous minority hypotheses.

5.3 Condition (C2): Navigational Coherence

Local obstacle avoidance (C1) ensures the agent avoids contested cells at each step, but says nothing about what happens at states where all neighbors are in F^*. At such states, the agent must choose among consensus-free directions, and this choice is governed by the relative Q-values across environments, which may disagree.

Definition 4 (Navigational Coherence). *The mixture* Q_{mix} *is* ***navigationally coherent*** *over* F^* *if the greedy policy* $\pi_{mix}(s) = \arg\max_a Q_{mix}(s, a)$*, starting from* s_0*, produces a trajectory that:*

1. *Remains entirely within* F^* *(never enters a contested cell), and*
2. *Reaches the goal* g *in finite steps.*

Navigational coherence is a **global** property: it requires that the sequence of locally greedy decisions produces a globally viable path. It implies local obstacle avoidance but is strictly stronger.

Proposition 2 (Local Avoidance Does Not Imply Coherence). *There exist environment families $\mathcal{V}$ where F^* is connected, Q_{mix} satisfies local obstacle avoidance everywhere in F^*, and yet Q_{mix} is not navigationally coherent.*

Proof (Proof by construction). We exhibit a three-environment family on the 8×4 grid below ($\cdot$ free in all environments, # a shared wall, S/G start/goal, F the fork, p the pocket cells, e the contested exit):

```
   0 1 2 3 4 5 6 7
0: S . F p p p p .
1: # # . # # # # e
2: . . . # # # # G
3: . . . . . . . .
```

All three environments share these walls; they differ only at $e = (7,1)$: $O_{\nu_1} = O_{\nu_2} = \varnothing$ (extra), while $O_{\nu_3} = \{(7,1)\}$. Thus $e \notin F^*$, and the pocket $\{(3,0), \ldots, (6,0)\}$ is a region of F^* whose only exit toward g is through the contested e; the all-free corridor (col. 2 down to row 3, then right to G) keeps F^* connected, so a consensus path exists. At the fork $F = (2,0)$, the shorter route for ν_1, ν_2 runs right through the pocket and e, while ν_3 (for which e is blocked) prefers the corridor; under uniform belief the 2:1 majority gives $Q_{\text{mix}}(F, \text{right}) - Q_{\text{mix}}(F, \text{down}) = +0.63 > 0$, so the greedy mixture enters the pocket. At the pocket exit $(7,0)$ the action into e carries ν_3's wall penalty, $Q_{\text{mix}} = -39.0$ versus -7.0 for stepping back into F^*: the veto of Proposition 1 holds, the agent never enters a contested cell, and it oscillates in the pocket without reaching g. Local obstacle avoidance (C1) holds at every step and F^* is connected, yet the mixture is not navigationally coherent.

5.4 The Two-Condition Theorem

Theorem 1 (Free Inference Conditions). *The VM Meta-Agent achieves Free Inference if and only if:*

(C1) Local obstacle avoidance: *At every state s along the trajectory, Q_{mix} assigns higher value to consensus-free actions than to contested actions.*

(C2) Navigational coherence: *The greedy policy on Q_{mix}, restricted to F^*, produces a trajectory from s_0 to g.*

Both conditions are necessary. When both conditions hold, the VM Meta-Agent's returns satisfy:

$$G_{VM} \geq G^*_{\nu^*} + r_{step} \cdot \Delta L \tag{13}$$

where $G^*_{\nu^*}$ is the optimal return in the true environment ν^*, and $\Delta L = L_{VM} - L^*_{\nu^*}$ is the path-length overhead.

Corollary 1 (Information-Free Optimality). *In the Free Inference regime, the VM Meta-Agent achieves near-optimal returns with zero information about the identity of the true environment. The belief ξ_t remains approximately uniform throughout the episode.*

This is the key theoretical insight: **the Solomonoff mixture achieves good performance not by converging to the truth, but by computing a policy that is robust across all hypotheses simultaneously.**

5.5 Posterior Mode Selection: Identification Before Action

Where VM exploits consensus, PMS pursues identification. Under uniform belief, PMS selects an environment uniformly at random and commits to its policy.

Proposition 3 (PMS Requires Identification). *For the PMS Meta-Agent with initial uniform belief, the expected number of obstacle collisions satisfies:*

$$\mathbb{E}[B_{PMS}] \geq \frac{N-1}{N} \cdot \mathbb{E}[B_{wrong}] \tag{14}$$

where B_{wrong} is the expected number of collisions when following a randomly chosen wrong environment's policy.

Proposition 4 (PMS Linear Regret Scaling). *The PMS Meta-Agent's expected regret scales approximately linearly with environment complexity:*

$$\mathcal{R}_{PMS} \approx (|r_{wall}| - |r_{step}|) \cdot D(\nu^*, \mathcal{V}) \tag{15}$$

where $D(\nu^*, \mathcal{V})$ measures the obstacle collisions needed to distinguish ν^* from all other environments.

6 The Free Inference Boundary in Nested Families

6.1 Why Connectivity is Trivially Satisfied

In the nested experimental family, $F^* = F_{\nu_{1.0}}$, the free space of the densest environment. Since the Q-agent trained on $\nu_{1.0}$ solves the environment, F^* is connected. Therefore Condition (C1) is satisfied throughout the family, and **the Free Inference boundary is determined entirely by Condition (C2), navigational coherence.**

6.2 The Majority-Minority Dynamic

Navigational coherence breaks down through a specific mechanism: the **majority-minority split** among environments.

As $\rho_{\max}$ increases, the environments' optimal paths through F^* increasingly diverge. At critical states, the environments split into:

- The **majority** (simpler environments) which prefer routes through broad, open regions, regions that are consensus-free but eventually lead toward contested boundaries.
- The **minority** (denser environments) which prefer routes through narrow corridors, the paths that actually respect the full obstacle landscape and remain navigable within F^*.

Under uniform belief, when the majority outnumbers the minority, the majority's preferred direction dominates Q_{mix} at states where the two groups disagree.

6.3 Measuring Coherence

Definition 5 (Q-Value Disagreement). *For state $s \in F^*$, the* ***Q-value disagreement*** *is:*

$$\mathcal{D}(s) = \max_{a,a' \in \mathcal{A}_{F^*}(s)} Var_{\nu \sim Uniform(\mathcal{V})} \left[Q_\nu(s,a) - Q_\nu(s,a')\right] \tag{16}$$

where $\mathcal{A}_{F^*}(s) = \{a : s + \delta_a \in F^*\}$ is the set of actions leading to consensus-free cells.

Definition 6 (Navigational Coherence Score). *The* ***navigational coherence score*** *is:*

$$\mathcal{C}(\mathcal{V}) = \max_{P: s_0 \rightsquigarrow g \text{ in } F^*} \min_{s \in P} \frac{Q_{mix}(s, a_P(s)) - \max_{a \neq a_P(s)} Q_{mix}(s,a)}{\max_a Q_{mix}(s,a) - \min_a Q_{mix}(s,a)} \tag{17}$$

where $a_P(s)$ is the action continuing along path P.

$\mathcal{C}(\mathcal{V}) > 0$ means there exists a consensus path along which the mixture's greedy policy has positive margin at every state. $\mathcal{C}(\mathcal{V}) = 0$ means some path has all non-negative margins but with at least one tie (benign: tie-breaking resolves it). $\mathcal{C}(\mathcal{V}) < 0$ means every consensus path has at least one state where the mixture actively prefers a non-navigable direction.

Theorem 2 (Coherence Characterizes Free Inference in Nested Families). *For nested families where F^* is connected:*

$$\textit{Free Inference holds} \iff \mathcal{C}(\mathcal{V}) \geq 0 \tag{18}$$

Definition 7 (Free Inference Boundary for the Nested Case). *For nested families, the* ***Free Inference boundary*** *is the critical obstacle fraction at which navigational coherence is lost:*

$$\rho_c = \rho_c^{coher} = \sup\{\rho_{\max} : \mathcal{C}(\mathcal{V}) \geq 0\} \tag{19}$$

Proposition 5 (Coherence Degrades Monotonically). *$\mathcal{C}(\mathcal{V})$ is monotonically non-increasing in $\rho_{\max}$ for nested families.*

7 Empirical Validation

Initially, we computed $\mathcal{C}(\mathcal{V})$ for the experimental family of 10 nested environments on the 40×25 random maze grid, evaluating a sequence of growing families $\mathcal{V}_k = \{\nu_{0.1}, \ldots, \nu_{0.1k}\}$ for $k = 1, \ldots, 10$. The data revealed a sharp transition at $\rho_c \approx 0.7$: for $\rho_{\max} \leq 0.6$, $\mathcal{C} = 0.000$ (benign); at $\rho_{\max} = 0.7$, $\mathcal{C}$ dropped to -0.429 (incoherent), precisely matching the experimental Free Inference boundary.

To test whether the Free Inference boundary was a property of the obstacle density fraction or grid size, we computed $\mathcal{C}(\mathcal{V})$ for nested families across seven grid sizes from 10×5 to 100×50. Table 2 summarizes the results.

Table 2. Coherence score across grid sizes. Bold indicates first negative $\mathcal{C}$.

Grid	ρ=0.1	0.2	0.3	0.4	0.5	0.6	0.7	0.8	0.9	1.0
10 × 5	0	0	0	0	0	0	0	0	0	0
20 × 10	0	0	0	0	0	0	**−1.00**	−1.00	−1.00	−1.00
40 × 20	0	0	0	0	0	0	**−1.00**	−1.00	−1.00	−1.00
40 × 25	0	0	0	0	0	0	**−0.43**	−0.67	−1.00	−1.00
60 × 30	0	0	0	0	0	**−0.17**	−0.96	−1.00	−1.00	−1.00
80 × 40	0	0	0	0	0	0	**−1.00**	−1.00	−1.00	−1.00
100 × 50	0	0	0	0	0	0	**−1.00**	−1.00	−1.00	−1.00

The most striking finding is the **stability of ρ_c across grid sizes**. For all grids from 20 × 10 to 100 × 50 (a 25-fold range in cell count) the Free Inference boundary falls consistently at $\rho_c \in \{0.6, 0.7\}$. This indicates that **the Free Inference boundary is governed by the obstacle density fraction, not by the absolute grid size**. The 10×5 grid is the sole exception, maintaining $\mathcal{C} = 0$ at all densities due to the absence of narrow bottlenecks. The invariance demonstrated here is across grid *size* at a fixed generator and reward ratio; the specific value $\rho_c \approx 0.7$ is thus an empirical regularity of the Random-Maze family rather than a generator-independent constant, and whether its numerical level transfers to other obstacle distributions is an empirical question we take up in follow-on work.

8 The General Case: Non-nested Families

8.1 A Second Mechanism for Free Inference Breakdown

In nested families, F^* is always connected, so Free Inference breaks only through navigational incoherence (Mechanism II). In non-nested families, a fundamentally different mechanism can also operate:

Mechanism I: Topological Disconnection. If the consensus free space F^* lacks a connected path from s_0 to g, no policy, however intelligent, can reach the goal without crossing a contested cell.

This is a genuine **percolation phenomenon**. If each cell is independently an obstacle in environment ν_i with probability p, the probability that cell c is consensus-free is $(1-p)^N$. The effective obstacle density in the consensus space is $1-(1-p)^N$, and the consensus-connectivity threshold corresponds to the standard site-percolation critical probability on the grid [4].

Definition 8 (Generalized Free Inference Boundary). *For general environment families, the Free Inference boundary is:*

$$\rho_c = \min(\rho_c^{topo}, \rho_c^{coher}) \tag{20}$$

where ρ_c^{topo} *is the threshold at which* F^* *becomes disconnected (Mechanism I), and* ρ_c^{coher} *is the threshold at which navigational coherence is lost (Mechanism II).*

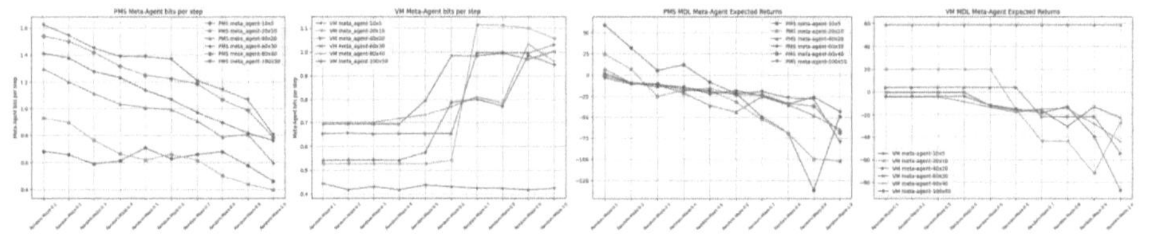

Fig. 1. MDL-inspired bps and returns (y-axis) for PMS and VM Meta-Agents across obstacle densities (x-axis), aggregated over grid sizes from 10×5 to 100×50. Bps lower values indicate higher action confidence under the surrogate codelength perspective.

9 Information-Theoretic Characterization

9.1 MDL Bits per Step

The Minimum Description Length (MDL) viewpoint interprets cumulative negative log predictive probability as codelength in a prequential mixture code [3]. Here we use a simpler MDL-inspired surrogate, bits per step, as an action-confidence diagnostic:

$$\text{bps}(s_t, a_t) = -\log_2 \pi(a_t \mid s_t) \tag{21}$$

where π is the Boltzmann (softmax) policy over the acting agent's Q-values, $\pi(a \mid s) \propto \exp(Q(s,a)/\tau)$, with $Q = Q_{\text{mix}}$ for VM and $Q = Q_{\hat{\nu}_t}$ for PMS, and temperature $\tau = 1$ throughout; this is the distribution used to produce Fig. 1.

Proposition 6 (Mixture Sharpening). *When all Q-tables agree on the optimal action* a^* *at state* s*, the mixture Q-function has a larger margin,* $\Delta Q_{mix} = Q_{mix}(s, a^*) - \max_{a \neq a^*} Q_{mix}(s, a)$*, between* a^* *and suboptimal actions than any individual Q-table, leading to:*

$$\pi_{mix}(a^* \mid s) \geq \max_i \pi_i(a^* \mid s) \tag{22}$$

and correspondingly $bps_{mix}(s, a^*) \leq \min_i bps_i(s, a^*)$*.*

This is the information-theoretic signature of the Free Inference regime: **the mixture is more confident than any individual expert.** The quantity above is not the exact prequential observation codelength of MDL theory, but it is aligned with the same intuition that concentrated predictive mass corresponds to shorter descriptions [3].

Figure 1 corroborates Table 2 by showing the average bps for both Meta-Agents across sizes from 10×5 to 100×50 and all densities. PMS confidence rises with density, lowering bps and degrading returns as more obstacle hits are needed to "buy" certainty about the true environment; VM confidence stays high up to the critical fraction, where Free Inference breaks down and returns degrade.

10 Convergence Properties

The convergence claims below should be read in the same spirit as finite Bayesian model selection and Bayes-adaptive Reinforcement Learning: when wrong environment hypotheses are consistently assigned lower predictive probability along the experienced trajectory, posterior mass shifts toward the true environment, and control based on posterior integration becomes progressively closer to optimal [2,3].

Theorem 3 (Free Inference Regret for VM). *In the Free Inference regime, VM regret is bounded by:*

$$Regret_{VM} = G^*_{\nu^*} - G_{VM} \leq |r_{step}| \cdot \Delta L \tag{23}$$

where ΔL depends on the topology of F^* and the coherence-constrained path, not on the number of environments N or the belief state.

Corollary 2 (Regret Insensitivity to Family Size). *VM regret in the Free Inference regime does not grow with $|\mathcal{V}|$, as long as both conditions (C1 and C2) remain satisfied.*

This parallels the Solomonoff prior's property that adding hypotheses incurs only a constant penalty.

Proposition 7 (PMS Regret Grows with Complexity). *PMS regret satisfies:*

$$Regret_{PMS} \geq (|r_{wall}| - |r_{step}|) \cdot \mathbb{E}[B_{PMS}] \tag{24}$$

where $\mathbb{E}[B_{PMS}]$ grows with distinguishing complexity. Unlike VM, PMS regret is non-zero and environment-dependent even in the sub-critical regime.

11 Broader Implications

The Free Inference property suggests a Meta-RL design principle: **when the hypothesis space admits a coherent consensus policy, value-mixture methods should be preferred over commitment-based selection.** The mixture margin $\Delta Q_{\text{mix}} = Q_{\text{mix}}(s, a^*) - \max_{a \neq a^*} Q_{\text{mix}}(s, a)$ is a state-level diagnostic: high margin indicates coherence (stay in VM), low margin indicates breakdown (switch to PMS).

Furthermore, the Free Inference phenomenon reveals that Solomonoff mixtures can be **terminally valuable**, not as approximations of any single hypothesis, but as entities computing what no single hypothesis can: the consensus safe policy. Whereas standard universal-induction theory emphasizes the mixture as a route to eventual concentration on the true hypothesis [6,10,11], the Free Inference regime shows it can instead be *the* solution.

The regime also provides a **formally characterizable safe operating region**: within it the VM agent provably avoids harmful actions across all hypotheses simultaneously, and the coherence score $\mathcal{C}(\mathcal{V})$ is a computable diagnostic for whether the system remains inside it.

12 Open Questions

1. **Tighter bounds on ΔL:** Can the path-length overhead be bounded as a function of grid topology and family structure?
2. **Non-nested families:** What is the precise relationship between the percolation threshold ρ_c^{topo}, the number of environments N, and the grid structure?
3. **Optimal family design:** Given a budget of N environments, how should $\mathcal{V}$ be chosen to maximize ρ_c?
4. **Non-grid environments and PAC-Bayes:** Does the Free Inference / coherence correspondence extend to continuous state spaces, and can the boundary be related to the PAC-Bayes complexity term?
5. **Optimal VM/PMS switching criterion:** What is the optimal policy for switching between modes during an episode?

13 Reproducibility

The base environment is made of Random-Maze nested families across six grid sizes $\{10 \times 5, 20 \times 10, 40 \times 20, 60 \times 30, 80 \times 40, 100 \times 50\}$ with obstacle density ρ, start $s_0 = (0, H-1)$ and goal $g = (W-1, 0)$. The base maze $\mathcal{M}$ marks each non-terminal cell as an obstacle independently at random, rejecting draws that disconnect s_0 from g; each environment retains an ρ-fraction of $\mathcal{M}$'s obstacles. For each density level $\rho \in \{0.1, 0.2, \ldots, 1.0\}$ we precompute an optimal Q-table Q_i via value iteration (discount factor $\gamma = 0.99$, step cost $k = 1$ so $r_{\text{step}} = -1$ and $r_{\text{wall}} = -100$), yielding a library of $N = 10$ nested environments. Source code and data files can be accessed at https://github.com/luizc-guedes/BRACIS2026

14 Conclusion

We have developed a theoretical framework bridging Solomonoff's universal mixture, MDL mixture coding, Bayesian Reinforcement Learning, and Meta-RL Task Inference, within which the VM and PMS Meta-Agents arise as two complementary finite approximations and the Free Inference boundary separates the regime where averaging dominates selection from the regime where identification becomes necessary. The central theoretical contribution is the identification of the **Free Inference regime** and the **two conditions** that govern it: **(C1) Local obstacle avoidance**, the veto mechanism by which a single dissenting hypothesis steers the mixture away from dangerous actions; and **(C2) Navigational coherence**, the global property that the mixture Q-function produces a viable trajectory through the consensus free space.

In nested environment families, the Free Inference boundary is determined entirely by Condition (C2). The breakdown occurs through the majority-minority dynamic: as obstacle density increases, simpler environments dominate the mixture Q-function, leading toward routes that are locally consensus-free but globally incoherent. The Free Inference boundary ($\rho_c \approx 0.7$, confirmed across grid sizes from 20×10 to 100×50) is the point at which this imbalance becomes sufficient to prevent coherent navigation. The Free Inference property reveals an aspect of Solomonoff mixtures that is specific to the action-selection setting: **the mixture can be a better policy than any of its components, not because it converges to the truth, but because it computes a robust consensus that is inherently safe across all hypotheses.** Finally, under Hutter's formal notion of intelligence as expected value aggregated across a (weighted) class of environments [6,7], the meta-agent can be interpreted as exhibiting an "intelligence gain" relative to any of its components.

Disclosure of AI use. The authors carefully reviewed, verified, and take full responsibility for all content. No AI tools were used to generate theoretical or empirical results, figures, or code unless explicitly stated elsewhere.

Disclosure of Interests. The authors have no competing interests to declare that are relevant to the content of this article.

References

1. Duan, Y., Schulman, J., Chen, X., Bartlett, P.L., Sutskever, I., Abbeel, P.: Rl^2: Fast reinforcement learning via slow reinforcement learning. arXiv preprint arXiv:1611.02779 (2016)
2. Ghavamzadeh, M., Mannor, S., Pineau, J., Tamar, A.: Bayesian reinforcement learning: a survey. Found. Trends Mach. Learn. **8**(5–6), 359–483 (2015)
3. Grünwald, P.D.: The Minimum Description Length Principle. MIT Press, Cambridge (2007)
4. van der Hofstad, R.: Percolation on random graphs (2025). https://arxiv.org/abs/2512.15673
5. Humplik, J., Galashov, A., Hasenclever, L., Ortega, P.A., Teh, Y.W., Heess, N.: Meta reinforcement learning as task inference. arXiv preprint arXiv:1905.06424 (2019)
6. Hutter, M.: Universal Artificial Intelligence: Sequential Decisions Based on Algorithmic Probability. Springer, Berlin (2005)
7. Legg, S., Hutter, M.: Universal intelligence: a definition of machine intelligence. Mind. Mach. **17**(4), 391–444 (2007). https://doi.org/10.1007/s11023-007-9079-x

8. Rakelly, K., Zhou, A., Quillen, D., Finn, C., Levine, S.: Efficient off-policy meta-reinforcement learning via probabilistic context variables. In: Proceedings of the 36th ICML, pp. 5331–5340 (2019)
9. Russo, D.J., Van Roy, B., Kazerouni, A., Osband, I., Wen, Z.: A tutorial on thompson sampling. Found. Trends Mach. Learn. **11**(1), 1–96 (2018)
10. Solomonoff, R.J.: A formal theory of inductive inference. part i. Inf. Control **7**(1), 1–22 (1964)
11. Solomonoff, R.J.: A formal theory of inductive inference. part ii. Inf. Control **7**(2), 224–254 (1964)
12. Thompson, W.R.: On the likelihood that one unknown probability exceeds another in view of the evidence of two samples. Biometrika **25**(3/4), 285–294 (1933)
13. Zintgraf, L.M., et al.: Varibad: a very good method for bayes-adaptive deep RL via meta-learning. J. Mach. Learn. Res. **22**(289), 1–39 (2021)

Learning to Order: GNN-Based Deep Reinforcement Learning Policies for Autoregressive Graph Models

Alysson Amaral da Silva(✉) and André Luís Vignatti

Universidade Federal do Paraná, Curitiba, Paraná, Brazil
{alysson.amaral,vignatti}@inf.ufpr.br

Abstract. Sequential graph generative models rely on graph linearization to convert permutation-invariant objects into ordered construction sequences. This ordering directly shapes the likelihood factorization, decision ambiguity, and overall generation quality. In this paper, we treat node ordering as a learnable component of sequential graph generation rather than as a fixed preprocessing choice. We formulate node ordering as a graph-conditioned Markov decision process and propose *Attention RL ordering*, a Deep Reinforcement Learning policy parameterized by an attention-based Graph Neural Network. The policy constructs permutations one node at a time from the topology of the input graph and is optimized with a policy-gradient objective inside an alternating loop, where rewards are defined by the quality of graphs produced by the downstream generator. We evaluate the method on Barabási–Albert graphs, a standard benchmark for sparse scale-free network structure, and compare it against representative deterministic orderings. The results show that Attention RL ordering substantially strengthens the learned-serialization pipeline, achieving perfect size validity, near-perfect connectivity, realistic graph sizes, and competitive hub-oriented statistics, making it a strong alternative to handcrafted orderings. Overall, the study supports node ordering as an optimization target inside sequential graph generation and shows that attention-based reinforcement learning with graph policies is an effective way to adapt graph linearizations to downstream autoregressive generators.

Keywords: Graph generation · Node ordering · Deep Reinforcement learning · Graph neural networks

1 Introduction

Graph generation aims to learn a probability distribution over graph-structured objects from a set of observed instances, enabling the sampling of novel structures that preserve the relevant properties of the training data. In practice, these structures represent entities such as molecular compounds, biological interactions, synthetic networks, and combinatorial structure synthesis [8,9]. Among

M. Recamonde-Mendoza and R. C. Barros (Eds.): BRACIS 2026, LNAI 17105, pp. 139–153, 2027.
https://doi.org/10.1007/978-3-032-39882-6_10

the main graph generative approaches, autoregressive models remain especially influential because they decompose generation into explicit construction actions. This decomposition provides interpretability, modularity, and fine-grained control over the generation process [1,16].

An example of the autoregressive approach is the Deep Generative Model of Graphs (DGMG) [11], which constructs a graph incrementally, based on a sequence of actions. Training a sequential generator on a graph from the dataset requires specifying a node ordering σ, since graphs do not admit a natural canonical sequence. This ordering determines the graph-to-sequence mapping that defines the action sequence seen during training. The choice of σ is therefore not innocuous: different orderings of the same graph induce different action sequences and, in turn, different conditional prediction problems for the downstream generator. In this sense, node ordering directly shapes how the graph distribution is learned. Motivated by this observation, this work formulates node ordering as a learnable sequential decision process and formulate it as a Deep Reinforcement Learning problem. More specifically, we learn graph-conditioned node orderings with a policy parameterized by a Graph Neural Network (GNN), allowing the ordering strategy to adapt to the topology of each input graph rather than being fixed by a hand-crafted heuristic.

Concretely, we formulate node ordering as a graph-conditioned Markov Decision Process and train a policy to select nodes sequentially, producing an ordering that is subsequently translated into an autoregressive graph generator sequence. We evaluate the approach on Barabási–Albert graphs [2], a conventional choice for testing algorithms on non-trivial topologies, and compare it against representative deterministic orderings under a fixed experimental protocol. The results show that the learned ordering is feasible in a sparse scale-free regime and can preserve strong size control together with meaningful degree inequality and hub structure, outperforming fixed heuristics. Overall, the study supports the view that node ordering should be treated as an optimization target within sequential graph generation rather than as a fixed preprocessing artifact.

Related Work: Sequential graph generation commonly converts a graph into an ordered sequence before learning. Foundational autoregressive models such as DGMG [11], GraphRNN [16], and edge-based recurrent generators [1] established this paradigm by constructing graphs step by step through node and edge decisions, typically under predefined serializations based on traversal heuristics or other hand-crafted rules. As a result, different orderings of the same graph induce different conditioning contexts and optimization behavior. This has motivated methods that treat ordering as part of the modeling problem. Chen et al. [5] formulate node ordering probabilistically and approximately marginalize it as a latent variable. Bu et al. [4] view ordering as a representation problem and propose *latent sort*, while Cohen-Karlik et al. [7] reduce sensitivity to arbitrary serializations through orderless regularization. More recently, Wang et al. [14] introduce a trainable *order-policy* optimized jointly with an autoregressive generator. In parallel, transformer-based approaches such as GraphGPT [17] and G2PT [6] revisit the graph-to-sequence interface from the perspective of scalable serialization and tokenization, reinforcing that sequence design remains central even beyond recurrent models. Outside graph generation, reinforcement learning has also been applied to sequential ordering in combinatorial settings [12], and graph construction studies for GNNs further show that upstream structural choices can strongly affect downstream learning quality [3].

Our Results: This paper addresses the limitations of fixed orderings by treating node sequencing as a learnable decision process. Rather than imposing hand-crafted rules, we model node ordering as a graph-conditioned policy that constructs a valid ordering by selecting nodes one at a time from the input topology. Because the resulting sequence directly affects the generator's performance, and because the discrete and combinatorial nature of orderings precludes direct differentiation, we formulate this task as a Deep Reinforcement Learning problem. Concretely, the ordering policy is parameterized by an attention-based [13] Graph Neural Network, allowing it to exploit structural information from the graph while adaptively reweighting relevant topological cues through transformer-style attention. Our main contribution is therefore a framework that treats node ordering as an optimization variable coupled to the generator, rather than as a preprocessing artifact. Specifically, we formalize node ordering as a graph-conditioned Markov Decision Process (MDP) whose trajectories correspond to valid orderings (Sect. 3); derive a policy-gradient objective that rewards the ordering policy based on downstream generative quality, balancing predictive fit with structural validity (Sect. 3); propose an alternating optimization procedure to co-train the ordering policy and the graph generator, now strengthened with a three-layer graph encoder and a Degree-based warm-start initialization (Sect. 3); and demonstrate the method on Barabási–Albert graphs [2], showing that *Attention RL ordering* is feasible in a sparse scale-free setting and can simultaneously achieve perfect size validity, near-perfect connectivity, realistic graph size, and competitive hub structure relative to strong deterministic heuristics (Sect. 4).

2 Preliminaries

Graph-to-Sequence Formulation: The goal of graph generation is to learn a probability distribution $p_\phi(G)$ over observed graph instances, where ϕ denotes the generator parameters. In autoregressive models, graph generation is decomposed into a step-by-step sequence of construction decisions. Since graphs do not possess a natural canonical order, this sequential factorization requires choosing a node permutation σ, which determines the order in which nodes become visible during generation. Therefore, the graph distribution can be written as a marginalization over admissible orderings:

$$p_\phi(G) = \sum_{\sigma \in \mathcal{O}_G} p_\phi(G \mid \sigma)\, p(\sigma), \tag{1}$$

where $\mathcal{O}_G$ denotes the set of admissible node orderings and $p(\sigma)$ is a distribution over them. In practice, generators model $p_\phi(G \mid \sigma)$ using fixed or latent orderings.

Since different orderings induce unique action sequences, σ profoundly impacts the downstream prediction problem.

Node ordering σ is insufficient to specify a graph as it lacks edge information. Thus, given G and σ, we define an action sequence $a = (a_1, \ldots, a_L)$, where a_t denotes the action at step t. In this paper, the action vocabulary consists of five actions: ADDNODE, which inserts a new node into the partial graph; ADDEDGE, which starts a new edge incident to the most recently added node; CHOOSEDEST, which selects one previously inserted node as the destination of the current edge; STOPEDGE, which stops adding edges for the current node; and STOPNODE, which terminates graph generation. Additionally, we define a function $T(G, \sigma)$ acting as a graph-to-sequence translator that produces the action sequence $a = (a_1, \ldots, a_L)$. Notice that

$$p_\phi(G \mid \sigma) \equiv p_\phi(T(G, \sigma)) \equiv p_\phi(a),$$

so now the objective is to model the generative distribution $p_\phi(a)$. By the chain rule of probability,

$$p_\phi(a) = \prod_{t=1}^{L} p_\phi(a_t \mid a_{<t}), \tag{2}$$

where $a_{<t}$ denotes the prefix sequence $(a_1, \ldots, a_{t-1})$. Following Eq. 2, the model can be trained via maximum likelihood. The resulting loss function $\mathcal{L}_{\text{train}}$ is the negative log-likelihood:

$$\mathcal{L}_{\text{train}}(\phi, T(G, \sigma)) = \mathcal{L}_{\text{train}}(\phi, a) = -\sum_{t=1}^{L} \log p_\phi(a_t \mid a_{<t}). \tag{3}$$

This formulation makes explicit that each supervised target a_t is intrinsically dependent on the chosen ordering σ.

The formulation in Eq. 1 can be interpreted as treating the node ordering as a latent variable, a perspective that has been explored in recent work on ordering-aware graph generation [4,5,7]. In practice, marginalizing over all orderings is intractable due to the factorial growth of possible orderings. Consequently, many autoregressive models fix a single heuristic ordering and treat it as canonical [11,16]. However, different orderings induce distinct local decision contexts for the same graph, suggesting that the ordering itself should be an object of optimization. While fixed heuristics (e.g., BFS, DFS, or degree ranking) can align sequences with certain structural regularities, they remain decoupled from the generative objective. A graph-theoretically sound heuristic may still be suboptimal for a model's negative log-likelihood or sampling behavior. This is because graph-theoretic criteria are generally designed to expose structural properties of the graph, whereas the generator is optimized to predict a sequence of local construction actions. An ordering that preserves desirable structural characteristics may nevertheless induce high-entropy destination-selection distributions or long-range dependencies that are difficult for the model to learn. As a result, the ordering that best reflects graph structure is not necessarily the ordering that yields the easiest optimization problem for the autoregressive generator. Furthermore, the effectiveness of an ordering is topology-dependent: a traversal suitable for trees may fail for hub-dominated graphs. These limitations motivate our central approach: instead of manually fixing the permutation σ, we learn it as a policy optimized directly from downstream generative feedback.

Reinforcement Learning: We formalize node ordering discovery within the Reinforcement Learning (RL) framework, modeling the sequential decision-making process as a Markov Decision Process (MDP). This process is defined by the tuple $(\mathcal{S}, \mathcal{A}, \mathcal{P}, \mathcal{R}, \gamma)$, where $\mathcal{S}$ is a finite set of *states*, $\mathcal{A}$ is a finite set of *actions*, $\mathcal{P} : \mathcal{S} \times \mathcal{A} \times \mathcal{S} \to [0, 1]$ is the state *transition probability* function, $\mathcal{R} : \mathcal{S} \times \mathcal{A} \to \mathbb{R}$ is the *reward* function, and $\gamma \in [0, 1]$ is the *discount factor.*

An *episode* is a complete interaction sequence from the initial state s_0 to a terminal state s_T. At each time step t, the agent selects an action a_t according to a stochastic policy $\pi_\theta(a_t \mid s_t)$. The resulting *trajectory* τ is the sequence of states, actions, and rewards encountered:

$$\tau = (s_0, a_0, r_1, s_1, a_1, \ldots, s_{T-1}, a_{T-1}, r_T, s_T).$$

Unlike value-based methods such as Q-learning, which estimate state-action values, we employ *policy gradient* methods to directly optimize the policy parameters θ. The objective is to maximize the function $J(\theta)$, representing the expected *return* under π_θ. To refine the model, we compute the gradient $\nabla_\theta J(\theta)$ to perform parameter updates.

3 Learning Node Orderings with Reinforcement Learning

The key idea of the proposed method is to treat node ordering as a learnable control variable rather than a fixed preprocessing rule. Given a graph $G = (V, E)$, we seek an ordering $\sigma = (v_1, \ldots, v_n)$ that induces a graph-to-sequence representation favorable for the downstream graph generator, which in our case is DGMG [11], but it could be any autoregressive graph generator. Since an ordering is a permutation built one node at a time, this naturally defines a sequential decision problem.

Let $\mathcal{D}$ be a dataset of graphs. For each graph $G \in \mathcal{D}$, let $\pi_\theta(\cdot \mid G)$ be a stochastic policy parameterized by θ that defines a distribution over the set of all valid node orderings $\mathrm{Perm}(G)$. A sampled ordering $\sigma \sim \pi_\theta(\cdot \mid G)$ is used to translate the graph into a sequence of actions via a function $T(G, \sigma)$, which subsequently serves as input for training the downstream generator. The quality of the ordering is therefore measured only indirectly, through downstream generator performance. This yields a bilevel view of the problem. Let ϕ denote the generator parameters.

Ideally, the bilevel optimization problem is defined as follows. In the lower-level task, for a given policy π_θ, we seek the optimal generator parameters $\phi^\star(\theta)$ that minimize the expected training loss over the distribution of orderings:

$$\phi^\star(\theta) = \arg\min_{\phi} \mathbb{E}_{G \sim \mathcal{D}} \left[\mathbb{E}_{\sigma \sim \pi_\theta(\cdot \mid G)} \left[\mathcal{L}_{\text{train}} \left(\phi, T(G, \sigma) \right) \right] \right]. \quad (4)$$

The optimal policy parameters $\theta^\star$ are found by solving the upper-level task to maximize the expected downstream reward R, evaluated at the lower-level equilibrium $\phi^\star(\theta)$:

$$\theta^\star = \arg\max_\theta \mathbb{E}_{G\sim\mathcal{D}}\left[\mathbb{E}_{\sigma\sim\pi_\theta(\cdot|G)}\left[R\big(G,\sigma,\phi^\star(\theta)\big)\right]\right], \tag{5}$$

where $R(G,\sigma,\phi)$ is a delayed reward that evaluates the ordering σ against the current generator state ϕ (see Sect. 3.1 for details).

Solving Eq. (4) to convergence for every update of θ is computationally prohibitive. Therefore, we adopt an alternating optimization strategy, detailed in Sect. 3.3, in which the generator and the ordering policy are updated in interleaved stages, effectively performing stochastic gradient steps on both levels.

3.1 Markov Decision Process Formulation

To solve the problem, we define a Markov Decision Process (MDP) through the tuple $(\mathcal{S},\mathcal{A},\mathcal{P},\mathcal{R},\gamma)$. Since our task is episodic and finite, we assume $\gamma = 1$, ensuring that the cumulative reward remains focused on the final outcome.

State ($\mathcal{S}$): Let $S_t \subseteq V$ denote the set of nodes in the current prefix, i.e., all nodes already selected before step t. The state space is defined as

$$\mathcal{S} = \{(G,S_t) \mid S_t \subseteq V\},$$

where each state $s_t = (G,S_t)$ captures both the complete input graph G and the subset of nodes already chosen.

Action Space ($\mathcal{A}$): The action space is state-dependent. At each step t, the available actions are precisely the nodes that have not yet been selected:

$$a_t \in \mathcal{A}_t = V \setminus S_t.$$

Transition Function ($\mathcal{P}$): The transition function $\mathcal{P} : \mathcal{S}\times\mathcal{A}\times\mathcal{S} \to [0,1]$ is deterministic. If action $a_t = v$ is selected, the new set of chosen nodes becomes $S_{t+1} = S_t \cup \{v\}$. Formally,

$$P(s_{t+1} \mid s_t, a_t) = \begin{cases} 1, & \text{if } s_{t+1} = (G, S_t \cup \{a_t\}) \\ 0, & \text{otherwise.} \end{cases}$$

Reward ($\mathcal{R}$): We employ the trajectory-level return, denoted by $R(\tau)$, where τ is a complete episode trajectory. An episode terminates once all nodes have been selected, i.e., when $|S_T| = n$, where $n = |V|$. At termination, we obtain a valid node permutation $\sigma = (a_1,\ldots,a_n)$ defined by the sequence of actions in τ.

Let ϕ denote the current DGMG parameters after a generator-update stage using sequences induced by the policy. The step-wise reward is defined as

$$\mathcal{R}(s_t,a_t) = \log p_\phi(a_t \mid a_{<t}),$$

noting that s_t implicitly contains the information of the previous decisions $a_{<t}$.

A central design principle of our method is that an ordering should not be rewarded in isolation. Instead, the reward must reflect the quality of the downstream generator trained under that ordering. Therefore, we define the trajectory return $R(\tau)$ as a combination of predictive fit $R_{\text{pred}}(\tau)$ and structural validity $R_{\text{struct}}(\tau)$. This avoids optimizing the policy for spurious sequence patterns by tying the objective to both likelihood and graph-level structural fidelity.

We first define the predictive term $R_{\text{pred}}(\tau)$. Given a graph G and a permutation σ of its nodes, the validation loss $\mathcal{L}_{\text{val}}$ is

$$\mathcal{L}_{\text{val}}(\phi, T(G, \sigma)) = -\sum_{t=1}^{n} \log p_\phi(a_t \mid a_{<t}) = -\sum_{t=1}^{n} \mathcal{R}(s_t, a_t).$$

Let $\mathcal{D}_{\text{val}} = \{G^{(i)}\}_{i=1}^{m}$ be the validation set. The average validation loss is

$$\overline{\mathcal{L}}_{\text{val}}(\tau) = \frac{1}{m} \sum_{i=1}^{m} \mathcal{L}_{\text{val}}(\phi, T(G^{(i)}, \sigma)).$$

Since lower values of $\overline{\mathcal{L}}_{\text{val}}$ are better, a natural predictive reward is its negative value:

$$R_{\text{pred}}(\tau) = -\overline{\mathcal{L}}_{\text{val}}(\tau).$$

Equivalently,

$$R_{\text{pred}}(\tau) = \frac{1}{m} \sum_{i=1}^{m} \sum_{t=1}^{n} \log p_\phi(a_t \mid a_{<t}).$$

The structural term $R_{\text{struct}}(\tau)$ is tailored to the graph family of interest. To estimate it, we sample S candidate graphs $\{\hat{G}^{(k)}\}_{k=1}^{S}$ from the current DGMG model and evaluate them using a family-specific validity predicate. In the Barabási–Albert setting, this structural component incorporates size control, connectivity, and distributional statistics related to scale-free behavior, including degree inequality and hub concentration. In this way, the policy is encouraged not only to improve predictive fit, but also to induce orderings that support the recovery of the characteristic heavy-tailed structure of BA graphs.

The final composite reward is

$$R(\tau) = R_{\text{pred}}(\tau) + \lambda\, R_{\text{struct}}(\tau), \tag{6}$$

where $\lambda > 0$ controls the trade-off between predictive fit and structural validity.

To make the dependency explicit, we write

$$R(\tau) \equiv R(G, \sigma, \phi),$$

since the trajectory τ defines a node permutation σ, whose quality depends on the input graph G and on the generator parameters ϕ used to evaluate it.

3.2 Policy

Given the MDP defined in Sect. 3.1, the objective is to learn a policy π_θ that maximizes the expected return:

$$J(\theta) = \mathbb{E}_{G\sim\mathcal{D}}\mathbb{E}_{\sigma\sim\pi_\theta(\cdot|G)}\left[R(G,\sigma,\phi)\right].$$

In the remainder of this section, we first detail the optimization of the policy parameters θ, and then describe how the Reinforcement Learning ordering architecture parameterizes the distribution over node selections.

Policy Gradient: Since the reward depends on downstream evaluation of the full ordering and is not differentiable through the complete training-and-sampling pipeline, we optimize $J(\theta)$ using the score-function estimator [15]. The gradient is given by the following result.

Theorem 1. *Let*

$$J(\theta) = \mathbb{E}_{G\sim\mathcal{D}}\mathbb{E}_{\sigma\sim\pi_\theta(\cdot|G)}\left[R(G,\sigma,\phi)\right].$$

Then

$$\nabla_\theta J(\theta) = \mathbb{E}_{G\sim\mathcal{D}}\left[\mathbb{E}_{\sigma\sim\pi_\theta}\left[\left(\sum_{t=1}^{n}\nabla_\theta \log \pi_\theta(a_t \mid s_t)\right)R(G,\sigma,\phi)\right]\right].$$

Proof. By definition of expectation,

$$\mathbb{E}_{\sigma\sim\pi_\theta(\cdot|G)}\left[R(G,\sigma,\phi)\right] = \sum_{\sigma\in\mathcal{O}_G}\pi_\theta(\sigma \mid G)R(G,\sigma,\phi),$$

where $\mathcal{O}_G$ denotes the set of all valid orderings of G. Therefore,

$$J(\theta) = \mathbb{E}_G\left[\sum_{\sigma\in\mathcal{O}_G}\pi_\theta(\sigma \mid G)R(G,\sigma,\phi)\right].$$

Since R does not explicitly depend on θ during the policy update, we obtain

$$\nabla_\theta J(\theta) = \mathbb{E}_G\sum_{\sigma\in\mathcal{O}_G}\nabla_\theta\pi_\theta(\sigma \mid G)R(G,\sigma,\phi).$$

Using the log-derivative trick,

$$\nabla_\theta\pi_\theta(\sigma \mid G) = \pi_\theta(\sigma \mid G)\nabla_\theta \log \pi_\theta(\sigma \mid G),$$

hence

$$\nabla_\theta J(\theta) = \mathbb{E}_G\sum_{\sigma\in\mathcal{O}_G}\pi_\theta(\sigma \mid G)\nabla_\theta \log \pi_\theta(\sigma \mid G)R(G,\sigma,\phi).$$

Rewriting the weighted sum as an expectation over σ yields

$$\nabla_\theta J(\theta) = \mathbb{E}_{G\sim\mathcal{D}}\mathbb{E}_{\sigma\sim\pi_\theta}\left[\nabla_\theta \log \pi_\theta(\sigma \mid G)R(G,\sigma,\phi)\right].$$

Finally, because the policy factorizes over the sequential node choices,

$$\pi_\theta(\sigma \mid G) = \prod_{t=1}^{n} \pi_\theta(a_t \mid s_t),$$

we have

$$\log \pi_\theta(\sigma \mid G) = \sum_{t=1}^{n} \log \pi_\theta(a_t \mid s_t),$$

and therefore

$$\nabla_\theta \log \pi_\theta(\sigma \mid G) = \sum_{t=1}^{n} \nabla_\theta \log \pi_\theta(a_t \mid s_t).$$

Substituting into the previous expression gives the desired result. □

To reduce gradient variance, we subtract a baseline $b(G)$ that does not depend on the sampled action:

$$\nabla_\theta J(\theta) = \mathbb{E}_{G\sim\mathcal{D}}\left[\mathbb{E}_{\sigma\sim\pi_\theta}\left[\left(\sum_{t=1}^{n} \nabla_\theta \log \pi_\theta(a_t \mid s_t)\right)(R(G,\sigma,\phi) - b(G))\right]\right]. \quad (7)$$

An entropy regularizer may also be added to encourage exploration and prevent premature policy collapse:

$$J_{\text{ent}}(\theta) = J(\theta) + \beta\mathbb{E}\left[\sum_{t=1}^{n} \mathcal{H}\big(\pi_\theta(\cdot \mid s_t)\big)\right],$$

where $\beta \geq 0$ controls the strength of the entropy bonus.

Policy Architecture: The policy must score candidate nodes conditioned on both graph structure and the current prefix mask. For this reason, the controller is parameterized by an Graph Neural Network (GNN). This makes the architecture better suited to graphs with heterogeneous local influence patterns, such as Barabási–Albert networks with hubs and long-tailed degree distributions.

Let x_v denote the feature vector of node v. In our synthetic setting, node features are lightweight and may include structural descriptors such as normalized degree together with a binary indicator showing whether the node has already been selected. Given state $s_t = (G, S_t)$, the graph encoder computes node embeddings

$$h_v^{(T_\sigma)} = \text{GNN}_\theta(G, S_t, x_v),$$

where T_σ denotes the number of message-passing rounds used by the policy network. The GNN can be substituted with more specialized architectures. In Sect. 4, we evaluate performance by comparing two distinct GNN variations.

A graph-level summary is then computed through a permutation-invariant readout, like an average:

$$h_G^{(T_\sigma)} = \text{READOUT}\big(\{h_v^{(T_\sigma)}\}_{v\in V}\big).$$

Each candidate node receives a logit

$$z_v^{(t)} = f_{\text{sel}}\big(h_v^{(T_\sigma)}, h_G^{(T_\sigma)}, m_v^{(t)}\big),$$

where $m_v^{(t)}$ indicates whether node v has already been selected. Already selected nodes are masked out, and the policy over valid actions is

$$\pi_\theta(a_t = v \mid s_t) = \frac{\exp(z_v^{(t)})}{\sum_{u \in V \setminus S_t} \exp(z_u^{(t)})}.$$

The policy is sampled during training to preserve exploration and executed greedily during evaluation.

3.3 Alternating Optimization with DGMG

The ordering policy and the graph generator are coupled: changing the policy changes the sequences seen by DGMG, while changing DGMG changes the reward landscape seen by the policy. We therefore use alternating optimization.

Training proceeds through I outer iterations. At each outer iteration, the current policy induces orderings for the training graphs, those orderings are translated into DGMG action sequences, the generator is trained or updated on the resulting supervision, and the policy is then updated using the reward computed from downstream validation and sampling metrics.

For the Attention RL presented at Sect. 4, the optimization is not initialized from a random policy trajectory. Instead, the first outer iteration is warm-started from the deterministic degree ordering. This choice gives the generator and the controller an informative initial serialization that already reflects an important structural prior for scale-free graphs, namely the early exposure of high-degree nodes. From that point onward, reinforcement learning refines the ordering policy beyond the hand-crafted baseline, allowing the model to preserve the advantages of degree-based initialization while adapting the remaining sequence decisions to the downstream generative objective.

More concretely, training follows an alternating procedure with I outer iterations. At iteration $i = 1$, each graph G is serialized using the degree ordering. For iterations $i > 1$, the current policy $\pi_\theta(\cdot \mid G)$ is used to sample or greedily construct an ordering σ for every training graph G, which is then translated into an action sequence $a = T(G, \sigma)$. These sequences are used to update the DGMG parameters ϕ by minimizing negative log-likelihood. The updated generator is then evaluated on validation graphs and on sampled graphs, and the resulting predictive and structural metrics are combined into the reward $R(\tau)$ in Eq. (6). Finally, the policy parameters θ are updated with REINFORCE for K policy steps. In this way, I controls how many times generator learning and policy learning alternate, while K controls how strongly the policy is updated within each alternation. Algorithm 1 summarizes the full procedure.

Algorithm 1. Alternating optimization for Attention RL ordering

Require: training graphs $\mathcal{D}_{\text{train}}$, validation graphs $\mathcal{D}_{\text{val}}$, generator parameters ϕ, policy parameters θ
for $i = 1, \ldots, I$ **do**
  for each graph $G \in \mathcal{D}_{\text{train}}$ **do**
    if $i = 1$ **then**
      compute degree ordering σ
    else
      sample or compute ordering $\sigma \sim \pi_\theta(\cdot \mid G)$
    end if
    translate graph into action sequence $a = T(G, \sigma)$
  end for
  update DGMG parameters ϕ on the policy-induced sequences
  evaluate DGMG on $\mathcal{D}_{\text{val}}$ and on sampled graphs
  compute reward R
  for $k = 1, \ldots, K$ policy steps **do**
    estimate policy gradient with REINFORCE
    update θ
  end for
end for

4 Experimental Study

4.1 Setup

We evaluate the proposed learned-ordering method on Barabási–Albert (BA) graphs [2], which provide a sparse, scale-free regime with nontrivial degree heterogeneity[1]. These graphs constitute a demanding benchmark because a good ordering must simultaneously preserve size control, connectivity, and hub-oriented structure, rather than merely satisfying a simple family predicate.

The dataset is generated with the standard BA preferential-attachment mechanism using attachment parameter $m = 2$, and target size range $N \in [20, 60]$. The dataset contains 6000 training graphs, 750 validation graphs, and 750 test graphs. As deterministic references, we consider the same orderings previously evaluated under the BA protocol: degree (highest-degree nodes first), BFS (Breadth-First Search), DFS (Depth-First Search), degeneracy (smallest-last/core-based ordering), LexBFS (lexicographic breadth-first search), MCS (maximum cardinality search), spectral (ordering induced by a spectral embedding), and random (uniformly shuffled nodes).

We have defined two major experiments. One with Graph Convolutional Network [10] methods and the other with an attention-based graph encoder. For the GCN process, DGMG is coupled with the RL policy described in Sect. 3. In that setting, the generator is kept fixed, with hidden dimension $H = 16$, message-passing rounds $T = 2$, learning rate $\eta = 10^{-4}$, batch size 1, and 25 training epochs per update stage. For a graph-ordering pair (G, π), the translated

[1] Code repository: https://github.com/prunebr/learning_to_order.

sequence $a = T(G, \pi)$ is used in teacher-forced maximum-likelihood training with objective as presented in Eq. 3.

In the attention learned-ordering run, however, the policy module is strengthened in three complementary ways. First, the previous GCN-style encoder is replaced by an attention-based graph encoder implemented in PyTorch, using transformer-style attention to let the controller weigh structural cues more adaptively when selecting the next node in the ordering. Second, the policy depth is increased to three graph layers, enlarging the effective structural receptive field available before each decision. Third, instead of starting from a random initial ordering, optimization is warm-started from the Degree ordering. This gives the controller an explicitly hub-aware prior from the beginning, after which reinforcement learning refines that prior toward a better global compromise between size, connectivity, and BA-style structural organization.

The training loop alternates between: (i) generating policy-induced orderings, (ii) translating graphs into action sequences, (iii) updating DGMG, and (iv) updating the ordering policy from downstream reward. In the BA setting, the reward follows Eq. 6, where the structure-specific term $R_{\text{struct}}(\tau)$ is defined as

$$R_{\text{struct}}(\tau) = \texttt{valid\_size\_ratio} \cdot \texttt{connected\_ratio},$$

where `valid_size_ratio` measures the fraction of generated graphs whose size remains within the training interval, and `connected_ratio` measures the fraction of generated graphs that are fully connected.

Evaluation is performed on freshly sampled graphs. Since BA graphs do not admit a single exact validity predicate, we report average size, valid size ratio (compared to the training data), connected ratio, degree Gini coefficient (which measures the inequality of the degree distribution) and hubiness (which quantifies the extent to which the graph is organized around highly connected hub nodes). Validation negative log-likelihood is also monitored during training, and the attention run is stopped according to a convergence criterion based on the difference between consecutive loss values across outer iterations.

4.2 Main Results and Optimization Dynamics

Table 1 compares the deterministic orderings, the GCN RL ordering and the Attention RL ordering. While the RL GCN configuration already achieved excellent size control, connectivity remained clearly below the strongest deterministic baselines. With the attention-based policy, learned ordering becomes much more competitive and, in several respects, offers the strongest overall compromise among the methods in the table.

The clearest improvement is in connectivity. Attention RL ordering reaches a connected ratio of 0.9960, essentially matching BFS (1.0000), but without the severe size collapse of BFS, whose average generated size is only 27.3110. In contrast, the learned policy maintains an average size of 41.4140, well within the target regime and much closer to the characteristic scale of the BA training distribution. The comparison with Degree ordering is also revealing: both methods

Table 1. Comparison of BA results under deterministic node orderings, the RL-learned orderings

Ordering	Avg. Size	Valid Size	Connected	Gini Degree	Hubiness
BFS	27.3110	0.8130	1.0000	0.2923	0.4282
Degeneracy	37.0770	0.9670	0.9740	0.3287	0.3993
MCS	40.5150	0.9670	0.9110	0.3323	0.3886
DFS	40.8660	0.9630	0.8280	0.3411	0.4202
Random	46.2100	0.9940	0.7930	0.3328	0.3460
Degree	50.3650	1.0000	0.6490	0.3516	0.3326
Spectral	48.4210	0.9910	0.6010	0.3184	0.3085
LexBFS	50.2580	0.9540	0.4910	0.3358	0.3237
RL GCN ordering	39.3220	1.0000	0.6334	0.3272	0.3443
Attention RL ordering	**41.4140**	**1.0000**	**0.9960**	**0.3081**	**0.3855**

achieve perfect valid-size ratio, but Attention RL ordering raises connectivity from 0.6490 to 0.9960 while also improving hubiness from 0.3326 to 0.3855. This shows that the learned policy does not merely reproduce the Degree initialization; rather, reinforcement learning refines that hub-oriented prior into a substantially stronger global serialization strategy.

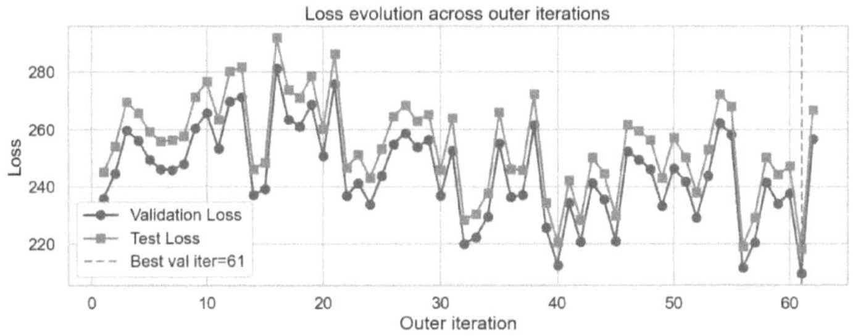

Fig. 1. Validation and test Loss across outer iterations (Attention RL).

Figure 1 helps explain this result. The Attention RL ordering remains competitive over a much longer optimization horizon and reaches its best validation checkpoint only at outer iteration 61. Although the trajectory remains oscillatory, as expected in an alternating RL–DGMG setting, the late best checkpoint indicates that the stronger policy continues refining the ordering space instead of collapsing prematurely to a suboptimal solution. Taken together, Table 1 and Fig. 1 support the same conclusion: Attention RL ordering is the only learned method in the comparison that simultaneously achieves perfect valid-size ratio, near-perfect connectivity, realistic graph size, and competitive hub-oriented structure, making it a genuinely strong alternative to handcrafted orderings such as Degree, BFS, Degeneracy, and MCS.

5 Discussion and Conclusion

This paper frames node ordering not as a mere preprocessing choice, but as a core architectural component of sequential graph generators such as DGMG. To address this problem, we formulate node ordering as a graph-conditioned Markov Decision Process and solve it with a Deep Reinforcement Learning policy parameterized by a Graph Neural Network. This allows the policy to exploit graph topology directly while optimizing orderings according to downstream generator quality rather than heuristic criteria.

Beyond the common GCN learned-ordering formulation, this work also introduces two practical innovations that substantially strengthen the policy. First, we use an attention-based graph encoder implemented in PyTorch, bringing transformer-style attention into the ordering process and allowing the policy to reweight structural signals more adaptively. Second, instead of starting from a random initial ordering, training is warm-started from the Degree ordering, giving the controller a strong hub-aware prior that reinforcement learning can refine rather than relearn from scratch. We refer to this enhanced learned policy as Attention RL ordering.

The empirical results on sparse scale-free BA graphs show that Attention RL ordering significantly improves the learned-ordering pipeline. In particular, it preserves perfect valid-size ratio while raising connectivity to a near-perfect level, and it remains competitive in hub-related descriptors such as hubiness. This is an important result because it moves the learned approach beyond the earlier regime in which size control was strong but connectivity remained the main weakness. In the present configuration, the policy becomes competitive not only with the previous RL variant, but also with strong handcrafted orderings such as Degree, BFS, Degeneracy, and MCS. The learned policy therefore no longer appears merely as a flexible alternative to deterministic rules, but as a strong ordering mechanism in its own right.[2]

The main contribution of this paper is therefore twofold. Conceptually, it repositions node ordering as an optimization target within sequential graph generation. Methodologically, it shows that learned graph serialization becomes substantially stronger when the ordering policy itself is upgraded with attention mechanisms, deeper graph representations, and informed initialization. Although demonstrated on DGMG, this perspective is applicable to other autoregressive graph generators that depend on graph-to-sequence conversion.

Future work includes refining reward design to control more global structural properties directly, comparing *Attention RL ordering* against stronger learned and hybrid baselines, transferring the framework to other autoregressive generators, and evaluating it on more heterogeneous real-world graph distributions. Additional methodological improvements may also enhance robustness, reduce oscillation across outer iterations, and lower the computational cost of training.

[2] This work was supported by the Coordination for the Improvement of Higher Education Personnel (CAPES), Brazil, through the Program of Academic Excellence (PROEX).

References

1. Bacciu, D., Errica, F., Micheli, A.: Edge-based sequential graph generation with recurrent neural networks. In: International Conference on Neural Information Processing (ICONIP), pp. 3–16. Springer, Cham (2019)
2. Barabási, A.L., Albert, R.: Emergence of scaling in random networks. Science **286**(5439), 509–512 (1999)
3. Bloemheuvel, S., van den Hoogen, J., Atzmueller, M.: Graph construction on complex spatiotemporal data for enhancing graph neural network-based approaches. Int. J. Data Sci. Anal. **18**(2), 157–174 (2024)
4. Bu, J., Mehrab, K.S., Karpatne, A.: Let there be order: Rethinking ordering in autoregressive graph generation. arXiv preprint arXiv:2305.15562 (2023)
5. Chen, X., Han, X., Hu, J., Ruiz, F.J.R., Liu, L.: Order matters: probabilistic modeling of node sequence for graph generation. In: Proceedings of the 38th International Conference on Machine Learning (ICML), pp. 1630–1639. PMLR (2021)
6. Chen, X., Wang, Y., He, J., Du, Y., Hassoun, S., Xu, X., Liu, L.: Graph generative pre-trained transformer. In: Singh, A., et al (eds.) Proceedings of the 42nd International Conference on Machine Learning. Proceedings of Machine Learning Research, vol. 267, pp. 9176–9197. PMLR (2025)
7. Cohen-Karlik, E., Rozenberg, E., Freedman, D.: Overcoming order in autoregressive graph generation for molecule generation. Trans. Mach. Learn. Res. (2024)
8. Gilmer, J., Schoenholz, S.S., Riley, P.F., Vinyals, O., Dahl, G.E.: Neural message passing for quantum chemistry. In: Proceedings of the 34th International Conference on Machine Learning (ICML), pp. 1263–1272. PMLR (2017)
9. Gómez-Bombarelli, R., et al.: Automatic chemical design using a data-driven continuous representation of molecules. ACS Cent. Sci. **4**(2), 268–276 (2018)
10. Kipf, T.N., Welling, M.: Semi-supervised classification with graph convolutional networks. In: International Conference on Learning Representations (2017)
11. Li, Y., Vinyals, O., Dyer, C., Pascanu, R., Battaglia, P.: Learning deep generative models of graphs. In: International Conference on Learning Representations (ICLR) (2018)
12. Ottoni, A.L.C.: Automated reinforcement learning for sequential ordering problem using hyperparameter optimization and metalearning. Auton. Intell. Syst. **5**(1), 15 (2025)
13. Vaswani, A., et al.: Attention is all you need. Adv. Neural Inf. Process. Syst. **30** (2017)
14. Wang, Z., Shi, J., Heess, N., Gretton, A., Titsias, M.: Learning-order autoregressive models with application to molecular graph generation. In: Forty-Second International Conference on Machine Learning (ICML) (2025)
15. Williams, R.J.: Simple statistical gradient-following algorithms for connectionist reinforcement learning. Mach. Learn. **8**(3–4), 229–256 (1992)
16. You, J., Ying, R., Ren, X., Hamilton, W., Leskovec, J.: Graphrnn: generating realistic graphs with deep auto-regressive models. In: Proceedings of the 35th International Conference on Machine Learning, vol. 80, pp. 5708–5717. PMLR (2018)
17. Zhao, Q., Ren, W., Li, T., Liu, H., He, X., Xu, X.: Graphgpt: generative pre-trained graph eulerian transformer. In: Proceedings of the 42nd International Conference on Machine Learning. ICML'25, JMLR.org (2025)

Assessing Transfer Learning for Turbofan RUL Prediction Under Data Scarcity and Domain Shift

Manuel Bezerra-Brandao(✉) and Lilian Berton

Institute of Science and Technology, Federal University of São Paulo (UNIFESP), São José dos Campos, Brazil
{mbrandao25,lberton}@unifesp.br

Abstract. Remaining Useful Life (RUL) prediction is critical for predictive maintenance, but target domains often provide limited labeled degradation data. Transfer learning (TL) can mitigate this scarcity, yet its benefits are not guaranteed and negative transfer remains insufficiently characterized. This work presents a controlled framework for evaluating TL in RUL prediction using the NASA C-MAPSS benchmark. Zero-shot and fine-tuning transfer are analyzed across source–target domains, scarcity levels, architectures, and random seeds, considering MLP, GRU, LSTM, and CNN models under a reproducible protocol with hyperparameter optimization, cross-validation, controlled sampling, and statistical validation. Results show that TL is selective rather than universally beneficial: it is most effective under severe target-data scarcity, structural source–target compatibility, temporal architectures, and full fine-tuning, with LSTM full fine-tuning showing the strongest robustness against statistically significant degradation. As target data increase or source–target alignment weakens, transfer can become neutral or detrimental. PCA-based domain analysis indicates that transferability depends on degradation-trajectory coverage and operating-condition subdomain alignment, rather than global domain similarity alone. The proposed framework supports reproducible assessment of when TL is beneficial and when it induces negative transfer under data scarcity and domain shift.

Keywords: Transfer Learning · Remaining Useful Life · Negative Transfer · Data Scarcity · C-MAPSS

1 Introduction

Remaining Useful Life (RUL) prediction is a central task in Prognostics and Health Management (PHM), supporting maintenance planning by estimating the time until component failure [4]. Although sensor-based monitoring has increased the viability of data-driven RUL models in industrial systems [16,19], supervised learning requires representative run-to-failure data, which may be scarce, costly, or unavailable for new operating conditions.

M. Recamonde-Mendoza and R. C. Barros (Eds.): BRACIS 2026, LNAI 17105, pp. 154–169, 2027.
https://doi.org/10.1007/978-3-032-39882-6_11

Transfer learning (TL) addresses this limitation by reusing knowledge from a source domain to improve learning in a data-scarce target domain [10]. However, source–target differences in operating regimes, fault modes, degradation trajectories, or sensor–RUL relationships may bias the target model and cause negative transfer (NT) [18]. Recent reviews identify limited run-to-failure data, source–target distribution discrepancy, and NT as persistent challenges in TL-based prognostics, motivating systematic benchmarking and deeper analysis of transfer behavior [3,15]. Building on these gaps, it remains unclear how transfer effects vary with target-data availability and random target-domain partitions, and under which source–target, architectural, and adaptation configurations transfer becomes beneficial, neutral, or detrimental.

This study addresses this gap through a controlled empirical analysis of TL for RUL prediction using the C-MAPSS turbofan engine degradation benchmark from the NASA Prognostics Data Repository [13]. Rather than proposing a new RUL architecture or claiming state-of-the-art performance, this work investigates when transfer helps, fails, or induces NT under data scarcity and domain shift. Target-only and transfer-based models are compared under paired experimental conditions using the same target subsets, source checkpoints, random seeds, and evaluation protocol. The contributions are: (i) a controlled TL evaluation protocol covering all ordered C-MAPSS source–target pairs, multiple architectures, optimized source configurations, fine-tuning strategies, and repeated seeds, accompanied by supporting code and experimental artifacts; (ii) an explicit NT metric that quantifies the magnitude, direction, and variability of transfer effects against paired target-only references; and (iii) a statistical and structural characterization of beneficial, neutral, and detrimental transfer, including zero-shot behavior, scarcity-dependent trends, and source–target domain structure.

2 Related Work

Prior reviews show that TL has been increasingly explored in predictive maintenance and RUL prediction, but NT remains insufficiently formalized and systematically analyzed, with open questions regarding its characterization, causes, and mitigation [3,15]. Most related time-series studies address domain shift through domain adaptation (DA), aligning source and target representations to improve target performance. Examples include attention-based methods that share latent structures while preserving domain-specific components [6], and optimal-transport-based methods that align both samples and temporal structure [9]. These approaches are valuable for adaptation, but they primarily introduce explicit alignment mechanisms. Consequently, they address a different experimental question from that examined in this work: rather than proposing another adaptation mechanism, this study isolates the effect of transferred source knowledge under controlled target-data scarcity.

Recent RUL benchmarking work further shows that inconsistent data handling, backbones, training schemes, adaptation settings, and hyperparameter search can obscure the actual benefits of deep unsupervised DA. Under standardized evaluation, CRULE found that only one evaluated method significantly outperformed a no-adaptation baseline, while some methods exhibited negative transfer [7]. Closer to this work, C-MAPSS TL has been studied through recurrent pretraining and fine-tuning, showing gains under limited target data but also degradation in some transfer directions [17]. However, prior evidence remains limited in architecture, source–target coverage, adaptation strategy, and repetitions. This work instead provides a controlled paired evaluation across C-MAPSS domains, architectures, adaptation modes, seeds, and scarcity levels.

3 Problem Formulation

This work addresses remaining useful life (RUL) prediction under domain shift and limited target data. Let $\mathcal{D}_s$ and $\mathcal{D}_t$ denote the source and target domains. Each domain consists of units u, represented by multivariate time series:

$$X^{(u)} = \{x_1, x_2, \ldots, x_{C_u}\}, \quad x_t \in \mathbb{R}^d \tag{1}$$

where d is the number of sensor channels and C_u the sequence length.

RUL is defined as the number of cycles remaining until failure. For a unit u with lifetime C_u, at cycle c:

$$\text{RUL}_u(c) = C_u - c \tag{2}$$

A predictive model f_θ approximates:

$$f_\theta : \mathbb{R}^{d \times W} \to \mathbb{R} \tag{3}$$

where the input is a temporal window of length W and the output the RUL at the final time step. RUL values are capped by a constant R_{max} to focus on the degradation regime and reduce the influence of early-cycle observations.

Under scarcity, a fraction $x \in [0, 1]$ of target units $\mathcal{U}_t$ is used for training:

$$|\mathcal{U}_t^{(x)}| = x \cdot |\mathcal{U}_t| \tag{4}$$

Transfer learning aims to leverage knowledge from $\mathcal{D}_s$ to improve performance on $\mathcal{D}_t$ under limited data, either through direct transfer or adaptation with scarce target data.

4 Methodology

4.1 Experimental Framework

A controlled experimental framework is used to evaluate TL under varying levels of target data scarcity. All strategies are compared under identical conditions, ensuring that performance differences are attributable to the effect of transfer. Each configuration is evaluated across multiple seeds $\mathcal{S}$.

For each configuration, target-only and transfer-based models share the same target data, train-validation split, architecture, hyperparameters, and evaluation protocol, enabling paired comparisons. Reproducibility is ensured through fixed seeds and consistent preprocessing.

4.2 Transfer Strategies

Three strategies are evaluated under varying target data availability:

- Target-Only (TO): The TO strategy serves as a baseline, where the model is initialized randomly and trained only on the available target data.
- Zero-Shot (ZS): In the ZS setting, a model trained on $\mathcal{D}_s$ is directly applied to $\mathcal{D}_t$ without adaptation [5].
- Fine-Tuning (FT): FT adapts a source-trained model to $\mathcal{D}_t$ using limited target data, initializing from source parameters and continuing training [10, 14]. Two modes are considered:
  - Full fine-tuning: all parameters are updated.
  - Head-only fine-tuning: only the final linear prediction layer is updated.

4.3 Negative Transfer Metric

Negative transfer (NT) is defined as the performance difference between FT and TO models under identical conditions.

Let $x \in (0, 1]$ denote the fraction of available target training data, and let $k \in \mathcal{S}$ denote an experimental seed. Each configuration is defined by a source-target pair $(\mathcal{D}_s, \mathcal{D}_t)$. NT is defined at the seed level as:

$$NT_k(x; \mathcal{D}_s, \mathcal{D}_t) = RMSE_k^{FT}(x; \mathcal{D}_s, \mathcal{D}_t) - RMSE_k^{TO}(x; \mathcal{D}_t). \quad (5)$$

The Root Mean Square Error (RMSE), denoted as $RMSE_k^{FT}$ and $RMSE_k^{TO}$, is computed on the target test set.

By construction, $NT_k > 0$ indicates degradation, $NT_k < 0$ indicates improvement, and values close to zero indicate negligible effect.

Across seeds, the mean and standard deviation are:

$$\mu_{NT}(x; \mathcal{D}_s, \mathcal{D}_t) = \frac{1}{|\mathcal{S}|} \sum_{k \in \mathcal{S}} NT_k(x; \mathcal{D}_s, \mathcal{D}_t) \quad (6)$$

$$\sigma_{NT}(x; \mathcal{D}_s, \mathcal{D}_t) = \sqrt{\frac{1}{|\mathcal{S}| - 1} \sum_{k \in \mathcal{S}} (NT_k - \mu_{NT})^2} \quad (7)$$

This formulation enables consistent comparison of transfer effects across data scarcity levels and configurations.

5 Experimental Setup

5.1 Dataset and Data Representation

This study uses the NASA C-MAPSS Turbofan Engine Dataset [13], consisting of run-to-failure simulations under varying operating conditions and fault modes. The dataset is provided in four predefined subsets (FD001–FD004), representing increasing levels of complexity in operating conditions and fault modes. Table 1

Table 1. Summary of the NASA C-MAPSS dataset subsets.

Sub-dataset	FD001	FD002	FD003	FD004
Training engines	100	260	100	249
Testing engines	100	259	100	248
Operating conditions	1	6	1	6
Fault modes	1	1	2	2
Min cycles per unit	128	128	145	128
Max cycles per unit	362	378	525	543

summarizes their main characteristics. Each trajectory is a multivariate time series with 3 operational settings and 21 sensor measurements.

Trajectories are segmented using sliding windows of length W [11]. Inputs are constructed as tensors of size $d \times W$, where d denotes the number of sensor channels, with targets corresponding to the RUL at the final time step.

RUL values are capped at $R_{\max} = 125$ using a piecewise-linear target function, reducing the influence of the initial high-RUL plateau where degradation signatures are weak. Since all trajectories exceed 128 cycles, the decreasing-RUL segment is preserved for every unit.

5.2 Modeling and Training Setup

Four architectures are evaluated: multilayer perceptron (MLP), one-dimensional convolutional neural network (CNN), long short-term memory (LSTM), and gated recurrent unit (GRU), capturing complementary inductive biases for time-series modeling [2,8,17].

Hyperparameters are optimized independently for each source domain using Optuna [1], with 50 trials and 5-fold cross-validation at the unit level. The search space includes architectural parameters (e.g., number of layers, hidden dimensions), training parameters (e.g., learning rate, batch size, dropout), and data-related parameters such as window size W.

Input features are standardized as $\tilde{x} = (x-\mu)/\sigma$, with training-split statistics. All sensors are retained to ensure a consistent feature space across domains. Models are trained using gradient-based optimization with mean squared error (MSE) loss and early stopping based on validation performance.

For each source domain $\mathcal{D}_s$, a final model $f_\theta^{(k_f)}$ is trained using the selected hyperparameters on a 90%-10% train-validation split, chosen to retain sufficient source data for transfer, with a fixed seed $k_f \in \mathcal{S}$. This model serves as the reference for transfer experiments. The same configuration is also trained across multiple seeds $k \in \mathcal{S}$ to assess performance variability.

5.3 Experimental Protocol

Experiments are conducted across all ordered domain pairs $(\mathcal{D}_s, \mathcal{D}_t)$ with $\mathcal{D}_s \neq \mathcal{D}_t$, target data fractions $x \in (0, 1]$, evaluated over a predefined discrete set, and seeds $k \in \mathcal{S}$, with $|\mathcal{S}| = 20$. For each $\mathcal{D}_s$, the reference model $f_\theta^{(k_f)}$ is used across all transfer strategies.

For each (x, k), a subset $\mathcal{U}_t^{(x,k)} \subseteq \mathcal{U}_t$ is sampled and split into training and validation sets (80/20). Target-only and fine-tuning are evaluated under identical splits and configurations, enabling paired comparisons, while zero-shot is evaluated once per domain pair. To avoid source-target leakage, normalization is strategy-dependent: target-only uses statistics from the target training split, while zero-shot and fine-tuning reuse source-domain statistics.

All metrics are computed on a fixed test set. Sequences shorter than the window length are padded for consistency across models. Performance is evaluated using RMSE, R^2, and the asymmetric C-MAPSS score as defined in [2,12].

Paired Wilcoxon signed-rank tests are applied to the negative transfer values (NT_k) across seeds for each $(\mathcal{D}_s, \mathcal{D}_t, x)$, using identical target subsets $\mathcal{U}_t^{(x,k)}$. P-values are adjusted via the Holm–Bonferroni procedure ($\alpha = 0.05$). Effect size is reported using rank-biserial correlation, and transfer is labeled as beneficial, negative, or inconclusive based on the sign and significance of the median NT_k, consistent with the non-parametric nature of the test.

6 Results

6.1 Baseline Models Performance

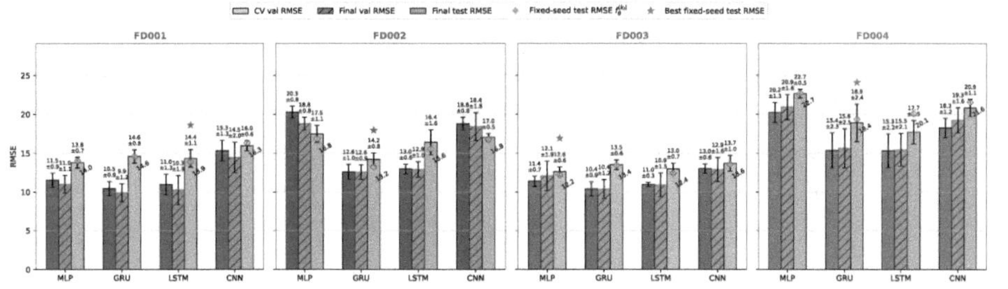

Fig. 1. RMSE comparison across C-MAPSS subsets and architectures. Panels correspond to each subset. Bars show CV performance of the selected Optuna trial and validation/test performance of f_θ across seeds $\mathcal{S}$. Diamonds mark $f_\theta^{(k_f)}$; stars mark the best fixed-seed metric. Error bars denote standard deviation across CV folds or seeds.

Figure 1 and Table 2 report the baseline performance of the evaluated architectures across the C-MAPSS subsets. These results define the target-domain references used in the subsequent transfer learning analysis, with the best result per subset highlighted in bold. Overall, the baseline stage comprises 4,320 training runs, including hyperparameter selection and seed-wise retraining.

Using RMSE as the primary criterion, LSTM performs best on FD001, MLP on FD003, and GRU on FD002–FD004. The CMAPSS score shows a similar

Table 2. Test performance of fixed reference models $f_\theta^{(k_f)}$ across C-MAPSS subsets.

	RMSE				R^2				CMAPSS			
	MLP	GRU	LSTM	CNN	MLP	GRU	LSTM	CNN	MLP	GRU	LSTM	CNN
FD001	14.05	14.58	**13.90**	16.32	0.877	0.868	**0.880**	0.834	3.86×10^2	3.79×10^2	$\mathbf{2.66\times10^2}$	4.80×10^2
FD002	16.84	**13.22**	15.57	16.76	0.846	**0.905**	0.868	0.848	1.25×10^3	$\mathbf{0.98\times10^3}$	1.19×10^3	1.67×10^3
FD003	**12.19**	13.44	12.44	13.57	**0.903**	0.882	0.899	0.880	$\mathbf{2.45\times10^2}$	4.99×10^2	2.88×10^2	4.47×10^2
FD004	22.72	**19.37**	20.11	21.55	0.721	**0.797**	0.781	0.749	5.07×10^3	3.48×10^3	$\mathbf{2.87\times10^3}$	3.62×10^3

pattern, except in FD004, where LSTM obtains the lowest score while GRU has the lowest RMSE. CNN is never the best model. Variability is generally low, except in FD004, and the lack of a dominant architecture motivates analyzing transfer across both domain pairs and model architectures.

6.2 Transfer Behavior Under Data Scarcity

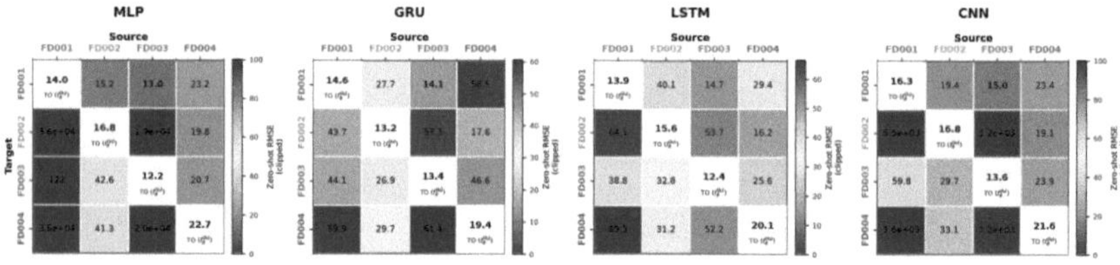

Fig. 2. Zero-shot RMSE across C-MAPSS subsets for each architecture. Rows: $\mathcal{D}_t$, columns: $\mathcal{D}_s$. Off-diagonal cells show transfer; the diagonal reports the target reference $f_\theta^{(k_f)}$. Bold indicates improvement over the reference; color encodes RMSE (clipped).

Zero-shot Regime. Figure 2 reports ZS, in which source-trained models are evaluated directly on the target domain without adaptation. Overall, ZS performance is poor, especially when transferring to FD002 and FD004. However, the results are strongly asymmetric: FD003 $\rightarrow$ FD001 consistently outperforms FD001 $\rightarrow$ FD003 and, in several cases, also surpasses the target reference. This behavior is consistent with the hypothesis that FD003 provides broader degradation coverage than FD001. Recurrent models also show greater ZS stability than CNN and MLP.

Transfer Dynamics Across Data Scarcity. Figure 3 examines how transfer performance evolves across 12 discrete target-data fractions x. The analysis comprises 1,152 transfer configurations and 768 target-only baseline configurations indexed over the full domain grid, each evaluated across $|\mathcal{S}| = 20$ seeds, totaling 38,400 training runs. For each fine-tuning curve, the corresponding target-only curve

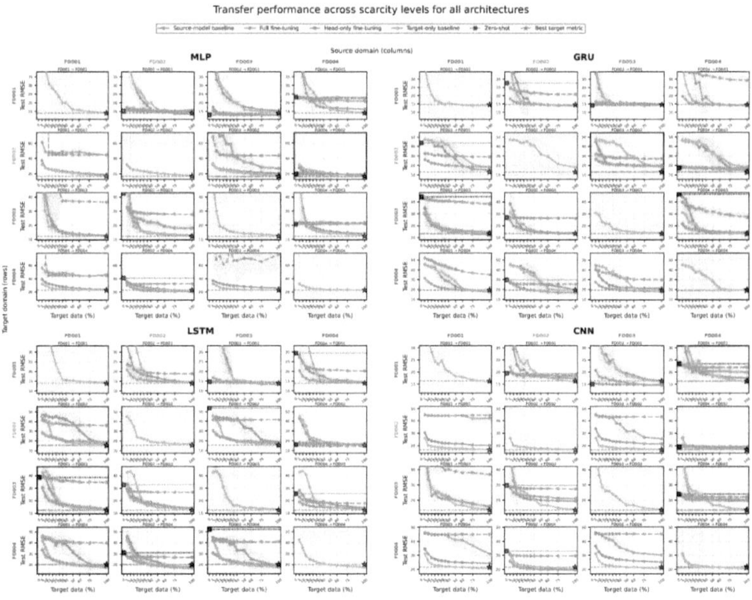

Fig. 3. Transfer RMSE across target-data fractions. Rows denote $\mathcal{D}_t$ and columns $\mathcal{D}_s$. Curves compare zero-shot evaluation, full and head-only fine-tuning from a pretrained $\mathcal{D}_s$ model, and target-only training baselines. Stars indicate the fixed $\mathcal{D}_t$ reference model $f_\theta^{(k_f)}$. Shaded bands denote variability across seeds. Vertical axes are truncated for readability; missing markers correspond to values above the displayed range.

provides the matched scarcity baseline, while the fixed reference line indicates the optimized target-domain model $f_\theta^{(k_f)}$ on $\mathcal{D}_t$.

Transfer behavior is strongly regime-dependent. For interpretation, target-data fractions are grouped into low-data ($x \leq 0.15$), mid-data ($0.20 \leq x \leq 0.50$), and high-data ($x \geq 0.60$) regimes. In the low-data regime, fine-tuning is broadly beneficial relative to the matched target-only baseline: GRU and LSTM improve performance in nearly all configurations, whereas CNN and MLP improve in only about 50–65% of cases. As more target data become available, this advantage weakens. GRU remains effective in the mid-data regime but drops to about 58% beneficial configurations in the high-data regime. Although the proportion of beneficial LSTM configurations also decreases with increasing target data, LSTM full fine-tuning remains statistically the most stable strategy, with few or no significant negative-transfer cases.

Architecture largely determines transfer stability. Recurrent models show the most robust transfer behavior, whereas CNN and MLP exhibit more frequent degradation and larger outlier failures, with some low-data transfers increasing RMSE by several hundred units. This suggests that architectures with explicit temporal modeling provide more transferable RUL representations in this setting.

Full fine-tuning is generally more robust, especially for heterogeneous source–target pairs, while head-only adaptation remains competitive in highly aligned transfers such as FD003 → FD001.

Finally, the fine-tuning results preserve the zero-shot asymmetry. FD003 → FD001 remains one of the most favorable directions after adaptation, whereas FD001 → FD003 degrades performance. This supports a hierarchical interpretation: domains with broader degradation coverage transfer effectively to simpler domains, but not conversely. The same asymmetry appears in CNN, although with amplified instability, suggesting that transfer direction is governed by domain structure, while robustness depends on architecture.

C-MAPSS Score Behavior. As a secondary metric, the C-MAPSS Score largely confirms the RMSE-based trends. Across transfer comparisons, $\Delta RMSE$ and Δ Score are strongly correlated (Spearman $\rho = 0.892$) and agree in direction in 91.8% of cases. Beneficial transfer remains concentrated in the low-data regime and is most stable under full fine-tuning with recurrent models. The few disagreements are also informative: 3.7% of configurations improve RMSE while worsening the Score, indicating that transfer can reduce average error while increasing the asymmetric penalty associated with late RUL overestimation.

6.3 Negative Transfer Analysis and Statistical Validation

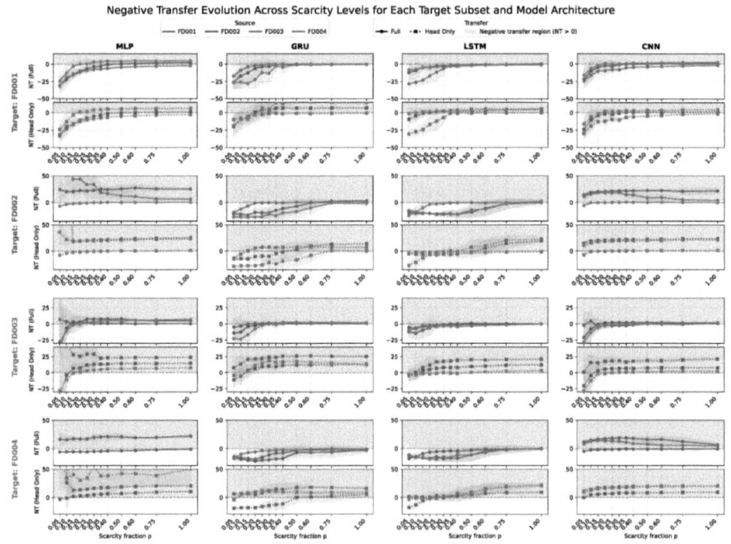

Fig. 4. Negative transfer across target data fractions for each target domain and architecture. Rows denote $\mathcal{D}_t$ and columns architectures; subpanels show full (top) and head-only (bottom) fine-tuning. Curves show mean μ_{NT} with variability σ_{NT} across seeds; colors denote $\mathcal{D}_s$. The shaded region indicates $NT > 0$ (relative degradation).

Negative Transfer Dynamics. Figure 4 shows that negative transfer is strongly conditioned by architecture and adaptation strategy. Under full fine-tuning, recurrent models show substantially lower negative-transfer rates than CNN and MLP. This advantage is especially clear for LSTM, which combines negative mean NT with almost no significant degradation. Head-only adaptation reverses this pattern, increasing degradation rates for both GRU and LSTM and exposing severe outlier failures in MLP.

Across scarcity regimes, $NT > 0$ becomes more frequent as target data increases. With full fine-tuning, LSTM and GRU remain highly robust in low- and mid-data regimes, but degradation increases in high-data settings, reaching 16.7% and 38.9%, respectively. CNN and MLP are less robust, exceeding 75% degradation even under full fine-tuning.

Crossover analysis confirms this transition. For CNN, MLP, and head-only recurrent models, beneficial-to-negative transitions occur mostly between $p = 0.10$ and $p = 0.60$, with medians around $p = 0.20$–0.25. GRU full delays this transition (median $p = 0.30$), while LSTM full is the most stable, crossing only at $p = 1.00$. Overall, full fine-tuning reduces both the frequency and early onset of negative transfer.

Statistical Transfer Patterns. Figure 5 summarizes the statistical structure of transfer behavior by segmenting NT trajectories into significant scarcity regions and transition patterns. The resulting cells reveal three dominant regimes: always beneficial (AB), always negative (AN), and beneficial-to-negative (B→N). The B→N pattern shows that transfer can be useful under severe scarcity but become detrimental as target data increases, while AB and AN indicate persistent source–target alignment or mismatch, respectively.

Statistical validation shows that reliable transfer is concentrated in recurrent models under full fine-tuning. LSTM full is the most robust case, with no statistically significant negative points, 50.7% significantly beneficial points, and 11/12 source–target cells classified as AB. GRU full follows with 39.6% significantly beneficial points, only 5.6% significantly negative points, and 9/12 AB cells.

In contrast, CNN and MLP exhibit frequent statistically significant degradation. Under full fine-tuning, significant negative points account for 42.4% and 50.0% of evaluations, increasing to 66.0% and 66.7% under head-only adaptation. This confirms that head-only fine-tuning does not stabilize transfer; instead, it increases the likelihood of statistically supported degradation.

Scarcity-dependent patterns reinforce this conclusion. Significant degradation increases from low to high target-data regimes. LSTM full remains free of significant degradation across all regimes, and GRU full remains near-zero in low and mid regimes (0.0% and 1.4%). By contrast, CNN and MLP exceed 58% and 63% significant degradation in high-data settings even under full fine-tuning. Overall, the statistically validated patterns indicate that full recurrent adaptation is the only consistently reliable transfer strategy under data scarcity.

Statistically Significant Transfer Improvements. Table 3 asks a stricter question: among regions where TL significantly improves over the paired target-only baseline, which configurations also outperform the best fixed target reference $f_{\theta}^{(k_f)}$ on $\mathcal{D}_t$?

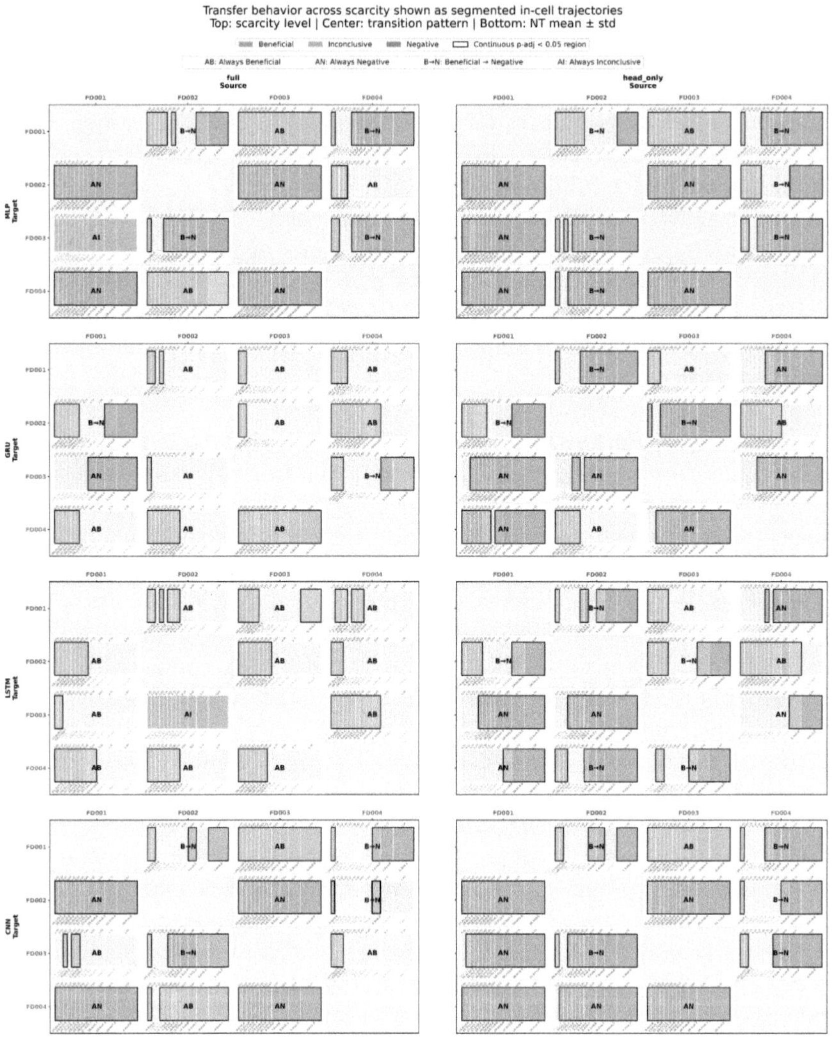

Fig. 5. Segmented transfer behavior across target data fractions. Panels combine architectures and fine-tuning modes; rows denote $\mathcal{D}_t$ and columns $\mathcal{D}_s$. Cell segments represent scarcity intervals, colored by transfer state and confidence. Black borders indicate contiguous significant regions ($p_{\text{adj}} < 0.05$). Central labels summarize transition patterns; bottom text reports $\mu_{NT} \pm \sigma_{NT}$.

Table 3. Significant beneficial transfer configurations that also outperform the fixed target reference $f_\theta^{(k_f)}$ on $\mathcal{D}_t$. FT: F (full), H (head-only); n: number of significant scarcity levels. Scarc. (%) denotes contiguous significant ranges. TL $RMSE$ is reported as mean ± standard deviation, and $\Delta RMSE$ is measured against the fixed target reference at the first and last points of each range.

D_t	Best f_θ	D_s	Model	FT	n	Scarc.	TL $RMSE$	$\Delta RMSE$
FD001	13.9	FD003	MLP	F	4	35–60%	13.29±0.70→13.37±0.73	-0.60→-0.53
	(LSTM)	FD003	MLP	F	1	75%	13.14±0.47	–0.76
		FD003	MLP	F	1	100%	13.08±0.40	–0.81
		FD003	LSTM	F	1	100%	13.22±0.48	–0.68
		FD003	MLP	H	8	15–60%	13.28±0.49→12.74±0.23	-0.62→–1.15
		FD003	MLP	H	1	75%	12.58±0.15	–1.32
		FD003	MLP	H	1	100%	12.68±0.17	–1.22
FD004	19.4	FD002	GRU	F	1	40%	19.26±1.51	–0.11
	(GRU)	FD003	GRU	F	2	50–60%	19.02±0.71→18.81±0.84	-0.36→–0.56
		FD003	GRU	F	1	75%	18.17±0.57	–1.20
		FD003	GRU	F	1	100%	17.70±0.45	–1.67

Significant improvements over the fixed target reference are rare and structured. No configuration improves FD002 or FD003, showing that TL can reduce error relative to paired target-only baselines without exceeding a well-trained target-domain model. Gains concentrate in FD003 → FD001, mainly with MLP fine-tuning, and in FD003 → FD004 with GRU full fine-tuning. This reinforces that reliable transfer depends jointly on source–target compatibility, architecture, and adaptation strategy, rather than on transfer alone.

7 Discussion

7.1 Domain Structure and Transfer Implications

To interpret when transfer learning becomes beneficial or detrimental, Fig. 6 analyzes the C-MAPSS subsets through PCA projections of the input feature space. Figure 6(a) shows substantial train–test overlap within each subset, suggesting that performance differences are not primarily driven by marginal shifts in the projected space. Instead, transfer behavior is more closely related to degradation structure, source–target coverage, and sensor–RUL relationships. Although operational settings are excluded from the PCA input, FD002 and FD004 still form distinct clusters, indicating that operating regimes remain implicitly encoded in the sensor measurements.

Panels (b)–(d) show coherent degradation trajectories in FD001 and FD003, with FD003 covering an additional branch associated with its second fault mode. This broader coverage is consistent with the stronger FD003 → FD001 transfer and the weaker inverse direction. In contrast, FD002 and FD004 overlap only within specific regimes, making transfers involving complex subsets more sensitive to subdomain mismatch.

Overall, PCA supports a structural interpretation of selective transfer: transfer is beneficial when the source covers target-compatible degradation trajectories, but becomes neutral or detrimental when coverage is narrow or misaligned. An exploratory quantitative check confirms this pattern: across the 12 ordered pairs, target-to-source nearest-neighbor distance was strongly associated with transfer degradation (Spearman $\rho = 0.916$ for mean $\Delta RMSE$), while target coverage was associated with lower degradation ($\rho = -0.797$) and higher beneficial-transfer rates ($\rho = 0.743$). Global symmetric distances were less informative, suggesting that NT is better explained by uncovered target regions than by global source–target dissimilarity alone.

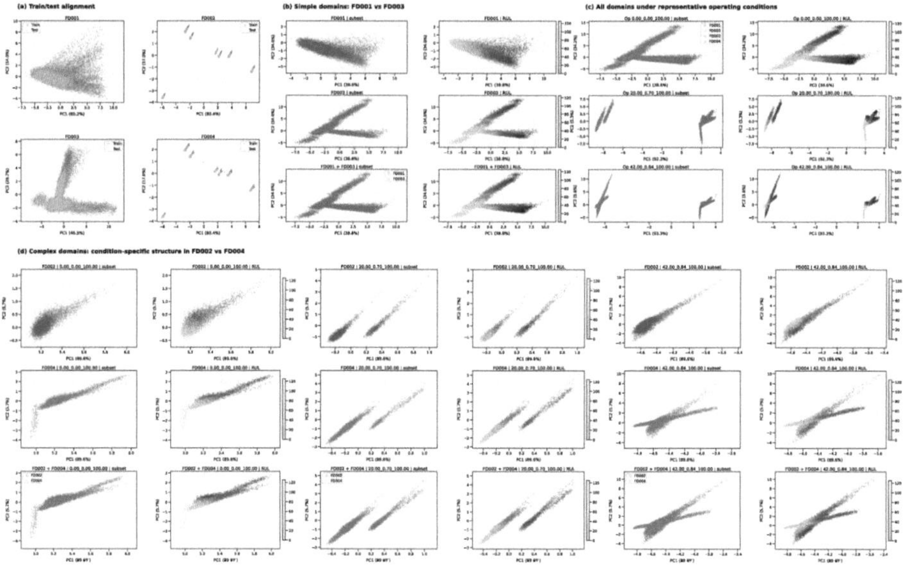

Fig. 6. PCA analysis of train/test alignment, domain overlap, and degradation structure in the C-MAPSS subsets. Panel (a) shows training and test projections for each subset. Panels (b)–(d) illustrate subset overlap and degradation trajectories, with color indicating capped RUL values ($RUL \leq 125$).

7.2 Negative Transfer, Model Behavior, and Practical Implications

Building on the structural evidence, NT can be interpreted as a mismatch between source-covered degradation regions and target trajectories. Under severe scarcity, transfer provides a useful inductive prior when target trajectories lie within compatible source regions; as target data increase, target-only models better capture domain-specific degradation patterns, and source-induced bias may become neutral or detrimental. This explains the observed beneficial-to-negative transitions: transfer is most reliable in structurally compatible directions, such as FD003 → FD001, but less stable for fragmented or partially aligned domains, as in FD002/FD004 transfers.

The stronger behavior of GRU and LSTM suggests that temporal inductive bias supports transferable RUL representations, while full fine-tuning improves robustness by adapting representations to target-specific trajectories and subdomains. Overall, TL for RUL prediction should be treated as a conditional strategy rather than a default improvement mechanism: source selection, architecture, adaptation strategy, and target-data availability must be considered jointly. This study is limited to C-MAPSS, a fixed sensor representation, and PCA-based input-space interpretation, which preserve controlled comparisons but may not fully characterize learned representations or generalize to other prognostics datasets.

8 Conclusion and Future Work

This study presented a controlled framework for evaluating transfer learning in RUL prediction under target-data scarcity and domain shift. The framework combines source–target transfer experiments, architecture-level comparison, repeated-seed evaluation, negative-transfer quantification, and statistical identification of beneficial and detrimental scarcity regimes.

The results show that transfer learning in C-MAPSS is selective rather than universally beneficial. Transfer is most effective under severe target-data scarcity, compatible source–target degradation coverage, temporal architectures, and full fine-tuning. As target data increase or source–target alignment weakens, transfer can become neutral or detrimental.

The PCA analysis supports this interpretation: favorable directions such as FD003 → FD001 are associated with broader source coverage of target-compatible degradation trajectories, whereas transfers involving fragmented operating regimes are more sensitive to subdomain mismatch. Overall, TL for prognostics should be treated as a scarcity- and structure-dependent strategy rather than a default alternative to target-domain training.

Future work should extend this framework to additional prognostics datasets, learned representation spaces, and alternative transfer strategies, including domain adaptation, multi-source transfer, and representation alignment. Developing source-selection criteria to anticipate negative transfer before adaptation remains an important direction.

Acknowledgments. The authors acknowledge the financial support provided by the São Paulo Research Foundation (FAPESP) under grant numbers 2024/22546-0 and 2020/09850-0. The authors also acknowledge the use of generative AI tools, including ChatGPT and Gemini, for language editing and grammar revision purposes only. All scientific content and interpretations are the sole responsibility of the authors.

Code Availability. Code and experiment configurations are available in a public repository at https://github.com/mbezerrabrandao/tl-cmapss.

Disclosure of Interests. The authors declare that they have no competing interests.

References

1. Akiba, T., Sano, S., Yanase, T., Ohta, T., Koyama, M.: Optuna: a next-generation hyperparameter optimization framework. In: Proceedings of the 25th ACM SIGKDD International Conference on Knowledge Discovery & Data Mining, pp. 2623–2631 (2019)
2. Asif, O., Haider, S.A., Naqvi, S.R., Zaki, J.F.W., Kwak, K.S., Islam, S.M.R.: A deep learning model for remaining useful life prediction of aircraft turbofan engine on C-MAPSS dataset. IEEE Access **10**, 95425–95440 (2022). https://doi.org/10.1109/access.2022.3203406
3. Azari, M.S., Flammini, F., Santini, S., Caporuscio, M.: A systematic literature review on transfer learning for predictive maintenance in industry 4.0. IEEE Access **11**, 12887–12910 (2023). https://doi.org/10.1109/ACCESS.2023.3239784
4. Ferreira, C., Gonçalves, G.: Remaining Useful Life prediction and challenges: a literature review on the use of Machine Learning Methods. J. Manuf. Syst. **63**, 550–562 (2022). https://doi.org/10.1016/j.jmsy.2022.05.010
5. Guo, Y., Ding, G., Han, J., Gao, Y.: Zero-shot learning with transferred samples. IEEE Trans. Image Process. **26**(7), 3277–3290 (2017)
6. Jin, X., Park, Y., Maddix, D., Wang, H., Wang, Y.: Domain adaptation for time series forecasting via attention sharing. In: International Conference on Machine Learning, pp. 10280–10297. PMLR (2022)
7. Krokotsch, T., Ragab, M., Wu, M., Li, X., Chen, Z., Gühmann, C.: From inconsistency to unity: benchmarking deep learning-based unsupervised domain adaptation for RUL. IEEE Trans. Autom. Sci. Eng. **23**, 3316–3328 (2026). https://doi.org/10.1109/TASE.2025.3528469
8. Li, X., Ding, Q., Sun, J.Q.: Remaining useful life estimation in prognostics using deep convolution neural networks. Reliab. Eng. Syst. Saf. **172**, 1–11 (2018). https://doi.org/10.1016/j.ress.2017.11.021
9. Painblanc, F., Chapel, L., Courty, N., Friguet, C., Pelletier, C., Tavenard, R.: Match-and-deform: time series domain adaptation through optimal transport and temporal alignment. In: Koutra, D., Plant, C., Gomez Rodriguez, M., Baralis, E., Bonchi, F. (eds.) Machine Learning and Knowledge Discovery in Databases: Research Track: European Conference, ECML PKDD 2023, Turin, Italy, September 18–22, 2023, Proceedings, Part V, pp. 341–356. Springer-Verlag, Berlin, Heidelberg (2023). https://doi.org/10.1007/978-3-031-43424-2_21
10. Pan, S.J., Yang, Q.: A survey on transfer learning. IEEE Trans. Knowl. Data Eng. **22**(10), 1345–1359 (2010). https://doi.org/10.1109/TKDE.2009.191
11. Paoli, C., Voyant, C., Muselli, M., Nivet, M.L.: Forecasting of preprocessed daily solar radiation time series using neural networks. Sol. Energy **84**(12), 2146–2160 (2010). https://doi.org/10.1016/j.solener.2010.08.011
12. Ramasso, E., Saxena, A.: Review and analysis of algorithmic approaches developed for prognostics on CMAPSS dataset. In: Annual Conference of the PHM Society, vol. 6, no. 1 (2014). https://doi.org/10.36001/phmconf.2014.v6i1.2512
13. Saxena, A., Goebel, K., Simon, D., Eklund, N.: Damage propagation modeling for aircraft engine run-to-failure simulation. In: 2008 International Conference on Prognostics and Health Management, pp. 1–9. IEEE, Denver, CO, USA (2008). https://doi.org/10.1109/PHM.2008.4711414

14. Vrbancic, G., Podgorelec, V.: Transfer learning with adaptive fine-tuning. IEEE Access **8**, 196197–196211 (2020). https://doi.org/10.1109/ACCESS.2020.3034343
15. Wu, F., Wu, Q., Tan, Y., Xu, X.: Remaining useful life prediction based on deep learning: a survey. Sensors **24**(11), 3454 (2024). https://doi.org/10.3390/s24113454
16. Wuest, T., Weimer, D., Irgens, C., Thoben, K.D.: Machine learning in manufacturing: advantages, challenges, and applications. Prod. Manuf. Res. **4**(1), 23–45 (2016). https://doi.org/10.1080/21693277.2016.1192517
17. Zhang, A., et al.: Transfer learning with deep recurrent neural networks for remaining useful life estimation. Appl. Sci. **8**(12), 2416 (2018). https://doi.org/10.3390/app8122416
18. Zhang, W., Deng, L., Zhang, L., Wu, D.: A survey on negative transfer. IEEE/CAA J. Autom. Sin. **10**(2), 305–329 (2023). https://doi.org/10.1109/JAS.2022.106004
19. Zhong, R.Y., Xu, X., Klotz, E., Newman, S.T.: Intelligent manufacturing in the context of industry 4.0: a review. Engineering **3**(5), 616–630 (2017). https://doi.org/10.1016/j.eng.2017.05.015

On the Feasibility of Distilled Small Language Models for Agentic Text-to-SQL in Portuguese Under Real-World Conditions

Breno Carvalho Pedroso[1], Denilson Alves Pereira[1](✉), Caio Matheus Leite da Silva[2], Márcio Montagnana Vicente Leme[3], and Kimberly Coutinho Paes Leme de Castro[4]

[1] Department of Computer Science, Federal University of Lavras (UFLA), Lavras, MG, Brazil
denilsonpereira@ufla.br

[2] Agência UFLA de Inovação em Geotecnologias e Sistemas Inteligentes no Agronegócio – Zetta, Lavras, MG, Brazil
caio@zetta.fundecc.org.br

[3] Department of Engineering, Federal University of Lavras (UFLA), Lavras, MG, Brazil
marcio.leme@ufla.br

[4] Ministry of Management and Innovation in Public Services (MGI), Brasília, DF, Brazil
kimberly.castro@gestao.gov.br

Abstract. Text-to-SQL enables users to query relational databases in natural language, but real production schemas require more than one-shot translation because models must inspect metadata, execute queries, and decide when a question is ambiguous or unsupported. *Small Language Models* (SLMs) are especially relevant in resource-constrained settings because they can run locally on modest hardware, reducing cost, latency, and dependence on proprietary APIs. Distillation offers a practical way to transfer agentic behavior from stronger models to SLMs by training them on high-quality teacher trajectories. This paper studies whether SLMs with up to 4 billion parameters can act as Portuguese Text-to-SQL agents. Experiments use a real PostgreSQL/PostGIS environmental registry database with Brazilian Portuguese data, plus a separate public-health database for cross-database evaluation. The benchmark combines SQL generation, clarification detection, and unanswerability recognition, evaluated with strict and relaxed execution-based comparison. We fine-tune Qwen3-4B-Thinking by distilling high-quality Qwen3.5-27B agent trajectories. Fine-tuning increases overall accuracy from 56.1% to 78.9%, surpassing the local 27B teacher in aggregate and outperforming untuned SLMs, although the strongest large models still lead on difficult SQL queries. Cross-database dynamics show that out-of-domain transfer needs more optimization than in-domain gains; Pass@5 reaches 91.7%, indicating that substantial task knowledge is present but not reliably expressed in a single trajectory.

M. Recamonde-Mendoza and R. C. Barros (Eds.): BRACIS 2026, LNAI 17105, pp. 170–185, 2027.
https://doi.org/10.1007/978-3-032-39882-6_12

Keywords: Text-to-SQL · Small Language Models · Portuguese · Agentic Systems · Distillation · Fine-tuning · PostgreSQL · PostGIS

1 Introduction

Text-to-SQL systems usually follow a classical prompt-to-query formulation: the model receives a schema description and a question, then emits SQL in one step [6]. This assumption underlies Spider and BIRD [16,31] and also much Portuguese-language work [2,12,19]. In production databases, however, schemas are large, domain conventions are implicit, values are irregular, and some questions are ambiguous or impossible to answer from the available tables. Geospatial production data add another layer of difficulty beyond typical Spider- and BIRD-style relational queries: models must reason about geometry columns, spatial predicates, coordinate conventions, and domain-specific area semantics. Therefore, recent benchmarks and systems move toward agentic Text-to-SQL, where models inspect metadata, execute exploratory SQL, recover from errors, and decide when to clarify or abstain [1,11,15].

This shift is especially demanding for *Small Language Models* (SLMs). We define SLMs restrictively as models with up to 4 billion parameters, small enough to run on modest consumer hardware. This constraint matters in Brazil, where the repeated use of large proprietary APIs can be expensive for local organizations and research groups. Local deployment improves cost, privacy, and infrastructure autonomy, but smaller open models are known to lag proprietary systems in complex Text-to-SQL [2]. Agentic behavior raises the bar further: the model must choose what to inspect, test hypotheses, repair mistakes, and recognize when not to generate SQL [26].

In this context, model distillation is a practical way to reduce the gap: a stronger teacher can generate high-quality agent trajectories, and a smaller student can be fine-tuned to reproduce useful reasoning, tool-use, recovery, and decision behavior under local hardware constraints.

We therefore evaluate whether distilled SLMs can become useful agentic Portuguese database assistants. Experiments use a real PostgreSQL/PostGIS production database with 19 tables and entirely Portuguese data, plus a second database from public health used only for transfer evaluation. The benchmark covers SQL generation, clarification detection, and unanswerability recognition.

The main contributions are:

1. a native Portuguese agentic Text-to-SQL benchmark grounded in a real production database;
2. explicit evaluation of geospatial Text-to-SQL over PostGIS data, including spatial predicates and domain-specific area semantics;
3. an evaluation protocol covering SQL, clarification, and unanswerable questions;
4. a distillation study of high-quality teacher-generated agentic trajectories for a 4B SLM;

5. cross-setting evaluation through a public-health schema and a SQL-only classical Text-to-SQL baseline;
6. a public artifact repository on Hugging Face, with model weights, agent code, selected traces, benchmark metadata, and the public-health benchmark.

2 Related Work

Classical Text-to-SQL research, anchored by Spider [31] and BIRD [16], assumes that all needed schema information is available before generation. Spider 2.0, BIRD-INTERACT, and APEX-SQL weaken this assumption by emphasizing enterprise-scale schemas, clarification, knowledge retrieval, execution feedback, and schema exploration [1,11,15]. Reliability work reaches a complementary conclusion: systems must detect ambiguity and unanswerability instead of always producing plausible SQL [14,25,28].

Portuguese Text-to-SQL remains mostly tied to translated or Spider-derived settings. José and Cozman adapted RAT-SQL+GAP to Portuguese [12]; Pedroso et al. released a validated Portuguese Spider translation [19]; Carvalho et al. showed that proprietary systems retain a strong advantage in Brazilian Portuguese, especially on complex queries and smaller open models [2]; and Fróes and Braghetto studied temporal challenges in Brazilian Portuguese educational data [5]. Native Portuguese, real-database, agentic evaluation is still largely absent.

Distillation is a natural route for SLM deployment because it can transfer expensive reasoning behavior into local models. Recent work studies distribution-aligned long-CoT distillation, student-in-the-loop trace selection, and conditions for reasoning SFT generalization [9,23,29]. Related work also distills LLM agents with tools [13]. In Text-to-SQL, prior studies show that standard autoregressive distillation suffers from inference-time error propagation, while structured rationales, teacher-generated NL2SQL data, and query-plan-based reasoning can improve smaller models [10,24,27,32]. Our focus is the agentic case, where the student must learn tool use, schema inspection, recovery, clarification, and abstention.

3 Methodology

3.1 Databases and Benchmarks

The primary experiments use a real PostgreSQL/PostGIS environmental registry database organized as a 19-table star schema with millions of rows. Its contents cover rural properties, municipalities, Indigenous Lands, conservation units, environmental embargoes, settlements, quilombola territories, federal public lands, deforestation events, and spatial-overlap facts. All schema contents, values, and questions are in Brazilian Portuguese, requiring domain-specific vocabulary, irregular value grounding, and spatial reasoning. Transfer is tested on `rede_saude_publica`, a synthetic Brazilian public-health schema covering health units, professionals, patients, appointments, hospitalizations, bed occupancy, medicine stock, and vaccination campaigns. This out-of-domain (OOD) schema differs in domain and structure, has no PostGIS columns, and has no training trajectories.

The primary benchmark is a held-out test set (no overlap with training) containing 180 questions: 90 SQL, 45 clarification, and 45 unanswerable. Clarification questions are intentionally underspecified; for example, a municipality name such as *Cantagalo* can refer to more than one state, so the agent should ask which is intended. Unanswerable questions ask for information outside the database or system contract, such as generating a map. SQL questions are split into 20 easy, 30 medium, 30 hard, and 10 expert instances; difficulty combines reference-query complexity with pilot-run behavior. The SQL subset covers PostGIS spatial reasoning, joins, aggregation, temporal filters, and domain-specific value grounding. The test set was iteratively validated to avoid benchmark annotation errors [20].

The cross-database benchmark contains 100 questions: 50 SQL, 25 clarification, and 25 unanswerable, with SQL difficulty split into 16 easy, 21 medium, 10 hard, and 3 expert cases.

To separate gains from agentic interaction and SQL generation itself, we also evaluate a classical SQL-only variant on the 90 SQL questions. This setting uses a single prompt-to-query call with full schema context and sample values, evaluated with the same execution metrics. Clarification and unanswerable questions are excluded because classical Text-to-SQL has no terminal action for those cases.

The distillation training pool came from company pilot questions, manually authored hard/diverse cases, and LLM-assisted topical expansion on the primary environmental database. After deduplication and overlap removal against the test set, 831 questions remained and were expanded to 2,493 paraphrased items, each labeled `sql`, `clarification`, or `unanswerable`. Since constructing the test set already required roughly two weeks of SQL validation, producing gold SQL for the full training pool was infeasible; this limitation is addressed by the distillation procedure, which filters teacher trajectories using execution equivalence and secondary ranking.

To improve generalization and error recovery, the training corpus was augmented with trajectories from two additional sources. First, a noisy variant of the primary database was created by injecting deliberate errors into the schema documentation, including renamed columns, fabricated tables, wrong data types, and misleading relationship notes; the underlying data remained unchanged. This forces the teacher to encounter schema-documentation mismatches during exploration, producing trajectories that demonstrate inspection, hypothesis testing, and recovery from misleading metadata. Second, a synthetic Brazilian public-procurement database (`compras_publicas_hard`) was used to provide cross-domain training trajectories, exposing the student to different schema structures, vocabulary, and query patterns during training. Early experiments with single-database training showed faster overfitting and weaker cross-database transfer, motivating this augmentation.

3.2 Agentic System Implementation

The system is an iterative tool-using agent. The model receives a database overview, active schema, domain instructions, and a strict tool contract, then acts through three tools: `get_table_schema` (column metadata, business rules, categorical distributions), `execute_sql` (exploratory SQL with compact result previews and verbatim errors), and `final_answer` (terminal SQL, clarification, or unanswerability). To enforce grounded interaction, the agent may not reference a table before inspecting its schema in the current run. The loop detects repeated call batches, requires tool use after tool-free responses, and ends with a final-attempt prompt after the iteration budget.

3.3 Models and Evaluation Protocol

All SLMs in Table 1 were run through `llama.cpp` with Q8_0 quantization [7]. Models requiring nonstandard tool support or failing a single valid tool call in preliminary tests were excluded, since they would not produce meaningful agentic comparisons.

The strongest untuned SLM was Qwen3.5 4B, followed by Qwen3 4B Thinking 2507 [22,30]. Only Qwen3 4B Thinking 2507 was fine-tuned because the available QLoRA stack did not yet support the hybrid Gated DeltaNet architecture of Qwen3.5 4B; QLoRA was required to fit long agentic traces on the RTX 5060 Ti 16 GB GPU [4]. The fine-tuning result is therefore conservative: the stronger untuned Qwen3.5 4B may be a better target once the same hardware path supports it. A larger local Qwen3.5 27B model (Q3_K_M, Unsloth) served as both baseline and teacher [21]. DeepSeek V4 Pro, GLM 5.1, MiniMax M2.7, Nemotron-3-Super-120B-A12B, and DeepSeek-V3.2 (Reasoning) provide stronger external references [3,8,17,18].

All models used developer-recommended hyperparameters when available; otherwise defaults of temperature $= 0.6$, top-$k = 20$, top-$p = 0.95$ were applied [8,17,21]. Local models ran on the same RTX 5060 Ti 16 GB GPU; API-backed models were accessed through their official APIs. SLM baselines and large-scale references were evaluated under Pass@1; the fine-tuned model under both Pass@1 and Pass@5 (correct if any of five trajectories succeeds under relaxed SQL or expected non-SQL type).

The classical SQL-only variant uses one non-agentic prompt per SQL question with all 19 tables, two sample rows per table, and no few-shot examples.

3.4 Teacher Distillation and Fine-Tuning

The teacher (Qwen3.5 27B) was run twice per training question across all three sources, with up to three retries per run to match the expected response type;

remaining type mismatches were discarded. Since no gold SQL was available, quality filtering compared the two trajectories per question using execution equivalence: if both produced the same result set, the shorter or cleaner trajectory was preferred; otherwise a secondary LLM ranked them. This candidate-selection idea follows CHASE-SQL [20], applied here to teacher trajectories rather than final SQL. After filtering by trajectory quality and response-type agreement, the final training set contained 7,875 trajectories: 4,901 from the primary database (including multiple retained trajectories per question where both runs passed quality filters), 2,167 from the noisy-documentation variant, and 807 from the public-procurement database.

Fine-tuning used Unsloth's QLoRA with LoRA adapters (rank $= 64$, $\alpha = 32$, learning rate $= 1 \times 10^{-4}$), sequence length $= 17{,}000$, micro-batch size $= 1$, and gradient accumulation $= 16$. Two design choices shaped supervision quality: reasoning and tool-call spans producing SQL errors were masked during loss computation [8], and training instances were organized so that database sources, SQL, clarification, and unanswerable examples were well distributed throughout the training set. The selected model was chosen by minimum evaluation loss on a held-out split.

3.5 Evaluation Metrics

Text-to-SQL benchmarks commonly report *Exact Match* (EM) and *Execution Accuracy* (EX) [16,31]. EM is not used here because equivalent answers may differ in SQL text. We evaluate by executing both generated and reference queries and comparing result sets.

Two execution modes are reported. *Strict* mode requires matching row count, column count, row order, and normalized values; this score is closest in spirit to the execution accuracy (EX) used in standard Text-to-SQL benchmarks such as Spider and BIRD [16,31]. *Relaxed* mode is the primary metric because semantically equivalent production queries often differ in aliases, column order, non-essential columns, row order, or numeric rounding.

Relaxed evaluation is controlled per question. Each SQL item records whether row order, exact column count, and exact row count are semantically required. Values are normalized (null variants, booleans, numeric strings, case-insensitive strings, datetimes; relative tolerance 10^{-4}, absolute tolerance up to 5×10^{-3}). Extra columns are allowed when column count is not relevant, but every reference column must match one-to-one; reference rows must appear as a multiset subset when exact row count is not relevant; row order is ignored when not relevant. Relaxed scoring tolerates harmless presentation differences but rejects missing or contradictory values. Non-SQL items are evaluated by response-type correctness.

4 Results

All reported scores correspond to Pass@1 unless stated otherwise. The primary environmental registry benchmark contains 90 SQL questions and 90 non-SQL questions (45 clarification, 45 unanswerable), so overall accuracy reflects balanced performance across both categories.

4.1 Overall Benchmark Performance

Table 1 reports primary benchmark results across all evaluated models. Stronger large-scale models dominate the upper tier, with DeepSeek V4 Pro achieving the highest overall score at 86.7%, as well as the highest relaxed SQL accuracy (83.3%) and non-SQL accuracy (90.0%). GLM 5.1 follows at 84.4% overall and remains strongest on unanswerable questions (91.1%). The fine-tuned Qwen3-4B-Thinking model reaches 78.9%, surpassing DeepSeek 3.2, Nemotron-3-Super-120B-A12B, and the local Qwen3.5-27B teacher in aggregate.

Compared with its untuned base model, fine-tuning improves overall accuracy from 56.1% to 78.9%, relaxed SQL accuracy from 36.7% to 70.0%, and non-SQL accuracy from 75.6% to 87.8%, while also completing the benchmark more quickly than the base run. The fine-tuned model exceeds all other SLMs by a large margin and ties the local 27B teacher on relaxed SQL, but its relaxed SQL accuracy remains below the strongest large-scale systems. Figure 1 summarizes this shift for representative models. The strongest untuned SLM remains Qwen3.5-4B at 62.2% overall, which supports the interpretation that Qwen3.5-4B would likely be an even stronger fine-tuning target once QLoRA support for its architecture is available in the same hardware setting.

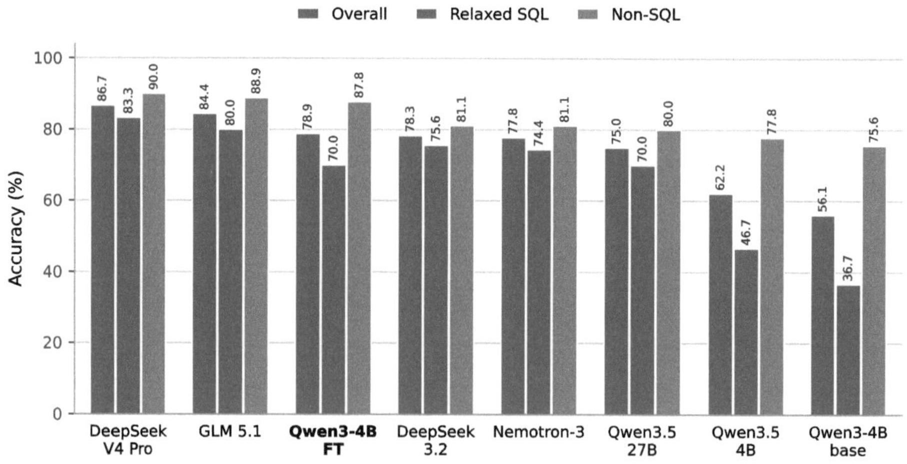

Fig. 1. Primary benchmark results for representative models. DeepSeek V4 Pro sets the strongest Pass@1 reference, while the distilled 4B model surpasses the local 27B teacher in overall accuracy and improves both SQL and non-SQL behavior. Relaxed SQL remains the main gap to the strongest large models. Full results are reported in Table 1.

Table 1. Overall benchmark results at Pass@1.

Model	Overall	Strict SQL	Relaxed SQL	Non-SQL	Clarification	Unanswerable	Runtime
DeepSeek V4 Pro	**86.7**	44.4	**83.3**	**90.0**	**93.3**	86.7	3h 55 m
GLM 5.1	84.4	44.4	80.0	88.9	86.7	**91.1**	2 h 20 m
Qwen3-4B-Thinking FT	78.9	34.4	70.0	87.8	86.7	88.9	2 h 01 m
DeepSeek 3.2 (Reasoning)	78.3	45.6	75.6	81.1	84.4	77.8	11 h 03 m
Nemotron-3-Super-120B-A12B	77.8	**47.8**	74.4	81.1	75.6	86.7	4 h 51 m
Qwen3.5-27B-Q3_K_M	75.0	40.0	70.0	80.0	75.6	84.4	3 h 52 m
Minimax 2.7	73.9	33.3	72.2	75.6	68.9	82.2	1 h 59 m
Qwen3.5-4B	62.2	28.9	46.7	77.8	73.3	82.2	1 h 56 m
Qwen3-4B-Thinking-2507	56.1	28.9	36.7	75.6	71.1	80.0	2 h 42 m
Qwen3.5-4B (no reasoning)	32.8	15.6	32.2	33.3	24.4	42.2	3 h 55 m
Qwen3-4B-Instruct-2507	31.1	26.7	33.3	28.9	8.9	48.9	1 h 12 m
Llama 3.2-3B-Instruct	27.8	1.1	1.1	54.4	73.3	35.6	11 m 40 s
Granite-4.0-Micro	22.2	13.3	16.7	27.8	51.1	4.4	40 m 29 s
Qwen2.5-3B	22.2	7.8	7.8	36.7	62.2	11.1	29 m 57 s
Qwen2.5-Coder-3B-Instruct	19.4	4.4	8.9	30.0	26.7	33.3	25 m 07 s

4.2 Non-SQL Reliability

Non-SQL performance is where the fine-tuned SLM is closest to large models. DeepSeek V4 Pro leads this category at 90.0% non-SQL accuracy, followed by GLM 5.1 at 88.9% and the fine-tuned Qwen3-4B-Thinking model at 87.8%. Over the base model, fine-tuning adds 15.6 points on clarification and 8.9 on unanswerability, showing that distillation transfers the decision of when to clarify or abstain, not only SQL-generation skill.

4.3 SQL Accuracy by Difficulty

Table 2 reports relaxed SQL accuracy by difficulty. Most untuned SLMs collapse after easy questions and solve no expert cases. The fine-tuned model reaches 80.0% on easy, 86.7% on medium, 63.3% on hard, and 20.0% on expert questions, compared with 70.0%, 43.3%, 20.0%, and 0.0% for its base model. The gains therefore extend beyond easy examples, but complex SQL remains the main gap: DeepSeek V4 Pro, GLM 5.1, DeepSeek-V3.2, Nemotron, and MiniMax M2.7 still lead in relaxed SQL, while the 27B teacher ties the fine-tuned model overall.

4.4 Agentic vs. Classical SQL Generation

Table 3 tests whether SLMs would be better served by a classical one-shot setup on the same 90 SQL questions. The classical run receives all tables, sample rows, and schema context in one prompt but cannot inspect schemas, execute exploratory queries, repair errors, clarify, or abstain.

Even on SQL-only evaluation, the base Qwen3-4B-Thinking model is better as an agent than as a classical system (36.7% vs. 30.0% relaxed SQL). Fine-tuning transfers beyond the agent loop: the classical score rises from 30.0%

Table 2. SQL accuracy (relaxed) by difficulty level.

Model	Easy	Medium	Hard	Expert
DeepSeek V4 Pro	**100.0**	**93.3**	73.3	**50.0**
GLM 5.1	**100.0**	**93.3**	70.0	30.0
DeepSeek 3.2 (Reasoning)	90.0	86.7	70.0	30.0
Nemotron-3-Super-120B-A12B	95.0	86.7	60.0	40.0
Minimax 2.7	95.0	73.3	**76.7**	10.0
Qwen3.5-27B-Q3_K_M	90.0	80.0	60.0	30.0
Qwen3-4B-Thinking FT	80.0	86.7	63.3	20.0
Qwen3.5-4B	85.0	56.7	26.7	0.0
Qwen3-4B-Thinking-2507	70.0	43.3	20.0	0.0
Qwen3-4B-Instruct-2507	70.0	33.3	20.0	0.0
Qwen3.5-4B (no reasoning)	70.0	33.3	16.7	0.0
Granite-4.0-Micro	35.0	20.0	6.7	0.0
Qwen2.5-Coder-3B-Instruct	25.0	6.7	3.3	0.0
Qwen2.5-3B	25.0	6.7	0.0	0.0
Llama 3.2-3B-Instruct	5.0	0.0	0.0	0.0

to 46.7%, but the fine-tuned model remains much stronger in the agentic setting (70.0% relaxed SQL, execution failures reduced from 9 to 1). Distillation therefore teaches both reusable SQL-generation behavior and a tool-use policy important for complex production schemas.

Table 3. SQL-only comparison between classical single-shot Text-to-SQL and the agentic setting on the primary benchmark.

Model	Setting	Strict SQL	Relaxed SQL	Exec. Failures
Qwen3-4B-Thinking-2507	Classical	22.2	30.0	9
Qwen3-4B-Thinking-2507	Agentic	28.9	36.7	16
Qwen3-4B-Thinking FT	Classical	30.0	46.7	9
Qwen3-4B-Thinking FT	Agentic	34.4	70.0	1

4.5 Fine-Tuned Model: Pass@1 vs Pass@5

Table 4 compares Pass@1 and Pass@5 for the fine-tuned model, while Fig. 2 shows the full cumulative curve. The Pass@5 run reaches 91.7% overall accuracy, 87.8% relaxed SQL, and 95.6% non-SQL. Most of the gain appears by the second trajectory: overall accuracy rises from 78.9% at Pass@1 to 88.3% at

Pass@2, then climbs more gradually to 91.7% at Pass@5. SQL benefits throughout the sampling budget, improving from 70.0% to 87.8%, whereas non-SQL behavior saturates by Pass@2. Since Pass@5 is defined over relaxed SQL and non-SQL type correctness, strict SQL is omitted from this table and remains a Pass@1 diagnostic in Table 1. The model therefore contains substantially more task knowledge than it expresses on the first trajectory, making inference-time selection or reranking a natural next step.

Table 4. Fine-tuned model results under Pass@1 and Pass@5.

Protocol	Overall	Relaxed SQL	Non-SQL	Runtime
Pass@1	78.9	70.0	87.8	2h 01 m
Pass@5	91.7	87.8	95.6	5h 31 m

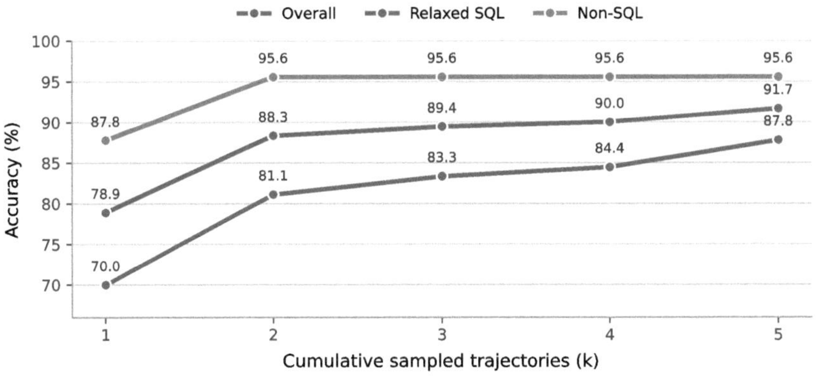

Fig. 2. Cumulative Pass@k for the fine-tuned checkpoint-1500 model. The largest jump comes from the second sampled trajectory, while later samples mainly add SQL coverage.

4.6 Cross-Database Generalization and Distillation Dynamics

Table 5 reports transfer to `rede_saude_publica`, which differs in both domain and schema. The fine-tuned model improves over its base model on the new database: overall accuracy rises from 70.0% to 75.0%, SQL from 64.0% to 72.0%, and non-SQL from 76.0% to 78.0%. The 27B teacher remains higher at 82.0% overall, driven by 90.0% SQL accuracy, but the 4B gains persist outside the training databases. This is important because the student never sees training trajectories from this schema; the improvement therefore reflects transferable agentic behavior rather than memorization of training-database conventions.

Table 5. Cross-database generalization results on `rede_saude_publica` at Pass@1.

Model	Overall	SQL	Non-SQL
Qwen3.5-27B-Q3_K_M	82.0	90.0	74.0
Qwen3-4B-Thinking FT	75.0	72.0	78.0
Qwen3-4B-Thinking-2507	70.0	64.0	76.0

The training trajectory in Fig. 3 clarifies why this transfer result should be read as a generalization story rather than only as a final score. Ren et al. argue that reasoning SFT generalization is conditional on optimization, data quality, and model capability, and that short runs can confuse an intermediate learning phase with failed generalization [23]. We see a similar pattern in the agentic Text-to-SQL setting. Each epoch contains 440 optimization steps over the filtered training trajectories (after sequence-length truncation from the full 7,875). In-domain overall accuracy improves quickly and then continues upward, from 56.1% at the base model to 78.9% at the selected checkpoint. Out-of-domain behavior is slower and less monotonic: at step 125 it falls below the base model (57.0% vs. 70.0% overall), returns near the base around the first epoch, reaches its best value at step 1100 (78.0%, 2.5 epochs), and remains above the base at step 1500.

The lower panel shows that response length falls sharply early in training, before cross-database accuracy reaches its best region. This supports the interpretation that the student first learns the teacher's shorter trace style and primary-database routines, while later epochs are needed to convert trajectories into portable agentic procedures: inspecting unfamiliar tables, testing hypotheses, recovering from SQL errors, and deciding when not to answer with SQL. The selected fine-tuned model is therefore a later training snapshot where in-domain gains, shorter traces, and cross-database transfer are all present, even though the out-of-domain curve shows that more epochs can matter differently for generalization than for the primary benchmark.

4.7 Failure Analysis

The final fine-tuned model's errors are no longer dominated by tool-use collapse. Earlier intermediate checkpoints almost never recovered when traces accumulated many SQL errors; in contrast, the final model includes correct trajectories with double-digit iterations and recovery after execution errors. The dominant failure is now semantic precision after exploration: among 27 incorrect SQL answers at Pass@1, 26 execute successfully; 19 are hard or expert questions.

The counterintuitive lower accuracy on easy than medium questions is first-trajectory variance: four easy questions fail in the first draw, three are recovered by the second trajectory, and the errors are ordinary semantic slips (year parsing, regional membership, missing filters). With only 20 easy questions, a few misses suffice to push easy below medium.

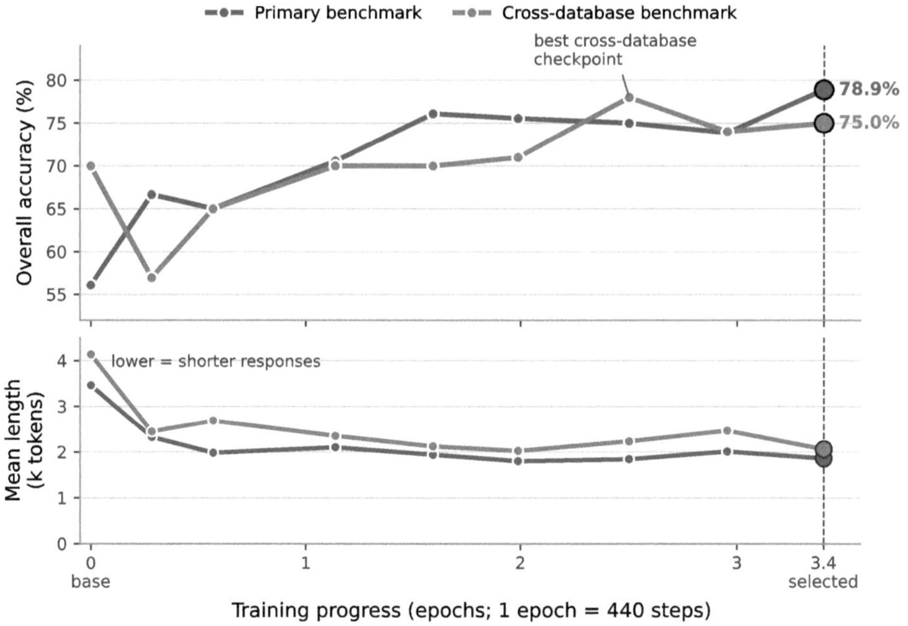

Fig. 3. Overall accuracy and response length during trajectory distillation. Step 0 is the untuned Qwen3-4B-Thinking base model; one epoch corresponds to 440 optimization steps. The primary benchmark is the in-domain environmental-registry evaluation, and `rede_saude_publica` is the out-of-domain benchmark. Response length is the mean number of generated assistant tokens per question.

The incorrect SQL outputs are mostly plausible queries with subtle semantic defects across three main patterns: (1) grounded-value or closed-set errors, such as omitting a state from a region or selecting the wrong entity-name realization; (2) missing domain conventions or predicates, such as a rural-property type filter, conservation-unit exclusion, or temporal scope; and (3) aggregation errors, where the model reaches the right tables but chooses the wrong denominator, percentile, window definition, or grouping level. Expert spatial questions add failures involving geometry conventions, SRID handling, centroid logic, or area-source selection.

Non-SQL errors show a related calibration problem: the model often detects ambiguity or unsupportedness but chooses the wrong terminal action, asking for clarification when the benchmark expects abstention, or vice versa. Together with the Pass@5 gap, this suggests the bottleneck is semantic verification, clarification-vs-unanswerability calibration, and trajectory selection rather than syntax repair.

5 Discussion and Limitations

Four findings stand out. First, agentic Portuguese Text-to-SQL remains difficult even for large models: no system solves the benchmark. Second, reasoning-oriented models consistently outperform instruction-only variants. Third, trajectory distillation produces practical gains: Qwen3-4B-Thinking rises from 56.1% to 78.9% overall and from 36.7% to 70.0% relaxed SQL, surpassing the 27B teacher in aggregate while remaining behind the strongest external models. Fourth, even when evaluation is restricted to SQL questions, the agentic version outperforms the classical variant, and distillation improves both settings.

The out-of-domain training curve, Pass@1–Pass@5 gap, and failure analysis show that the bottleneck is optimization and first-trajectory semantic reliability, not only missing knowledge. The student first learns shorter response style, then later converts traces into transferable agentic behavior. Remaining failures are executable, plausible answers with wrong closed sets, domain filters, denominators, spatial conventions, or terminal response types. This motivates recovery-oriented distillation with semantic counterexamples, candidate reranking, and RLVR-style rewards.

The Qwen3.5-4B limitation is narrow: it was not fine-tuned because QLoRA did not yet support its hybrid architecture under 16 GB. Since untuned Qwen3.5-4B already leads by 6.1 overall and 10.0 relaxed-SQL points, the present result is evidence that the approach works, not an upper bound for 4B systems.

The training pool lacks manually verified gold SQL, so teacher-trajectory quality depends on execution agreement and secondary ranking. A training set with validated gold SQL would likely improve SQL generation further. The classical SQL-only comparison uses one specific prompt configuration and is meant as a controlled diagnostic, not an exhaustive search over classical prompting strategies. API-backed model results may vary with provider-side model updates and service conditions.

6 Conclusion

This work shows that untuned SLMs are not yet robust agentic Portuguese Text-to-SQL systems, but filtered teacher-trajectory distillation can make a 4B local model competitive with a 27B local teacher and transferable to a second database. The remaining gap is concentrated in complex SQL semantics, semantic verification, and terminal-decision calibration rather than in tool use alone. The SQL-only classical comparison further suggests that this is not a simple choice between agents for reliability and classical prompting for SQL: the fine-tuned model improves in both settings, while the agentic setting remains stronger on the production-schema SQL subset. Future work will expand the distilled corpus, fine-tune newer 4B architectures once supported under the same hardware constraints, and use recovery-oriented or RLVR-style training with semantic checks to convert the Pass@5 headroom into stronger Pass@1 reliability.

Acknowledgments. This work was supported by the Ministry of Management and Innovation in Public Services (MGI), Brazil, under Agreement No. 107/2024-UFLA, associated with Partnership No. 973069/2024.

Disclosure of Interests. The authors have no competing interests to declare that are relevant to the content of this article.

References

1. Cao, B., et al.: Apex-sql: talking to the data via agentic exploration for text-to-sql (2026). https://arxiv.org/abs/2602.16720
2. Carvalho, L., Júnior, P.S., Oliveira, H.: Benchmarking large language models for text-to-sql in Brazilian Portuguese and English. In: Anais do XVI Simpósio Brasileiro de Tecnologia da Informação e da Linguagem Humana, pp. 101–112. SBC, Porto Alegre, RS, Brasil (2025). https://doi.org/10.5753/stil.2025.37817
3. DeepSeek-AI, et al.: Deepseek-v3.2: pushing the frontier of open large language models (2025). https://arxiv.org/abs/2512.02556
4. Dettmers, T., et al.: Qlora: efficient finetuning of quantized llms. In: Levine, S. (ed.) Advances in Neural Information Processing Systems, vol. 36, pp. 10088–10115. Curran Associates, Inc. (2023)
5. Fróes, K., Braghetto, K.R.: Exploring temporal text-to-sql challenges in Brazilian Portuguese: lessons from educational data. In: Anais do XL Simpósio Brasileiro de Bancos de Dados, pp. 963–969. SBC, Porto Alegre, RS, Brasil (2025). https://doi.org/10.5753/sbbd.2025.247836
6. Gao, D., Wang, H., Li, Y., Sun, X., Qian, Y., Ding, B.: Text-to-sql empowered by large language models: a benchmark evaluation. Proc. VLDB Endow. **17**(5), 1132–1145 (2024). https://doi.org/10.14778/3641204.3641221
7. ggml-org: llama.cpp: Llm inference in c/c++. https://github.com/ggml-org/llama.cpp (2026), gitHub repository. Accessed 17 Apr 2026
8. GLM-5-Team, et al.: Glm-5: from vibe coding to agentic engineering (2026). https://arxiv.org/abs/2602.15763
9. He, C., Chen, Y., Xiao, C., Han, X., Wen, L.: Student-in-the-loop chain-of-thought distillation via generation-time selection (2026). https://arxiv.org/abs/2604.02819
10. Hoang, C.D.V., Tangari, G., Lanfranchi, C., Guo, D., Cayet, P., Siu, S., et al.: Distill-C: enhanced NL2SQL via distilled customization with LLMs. In: Chen, W., Yang, Y., Kachuee, M., Fu, X.Y. (eds.) Proceedings of the 2025 Conference of the Nations of the Americas Chapter of the Association for Computational Linguistics: Human Language Technologies (Volume 3: Industry Track), pp. 833–848. Association for Computational Linguistics, Albuquerque, New Mexico (2025). https://doi.org/10.18653/v1/2025.naacl-industry.64
11. Huo, N., Xu, X., Li, J., Jacobsson, P., Lin, S., Qin, B., et al.: Bird-interact: Reimagining text-to-sql evaluation for large language models via lens of dynamic interactions (2026), https://arxiv.org/abs/2510.05318
12. José, M., Cozman, F.: mRAT-SQL+GAP: a Portuguese text-to-sql transformer. In: Anais da X Brazilian Conference on Intelligent Systems. SBC, Porto Alegre, RS, Brasil (2021). https://sol.sbc.org.br/index.php/bracis/article/view/19088
13. Kang, M., Jeong, J., Lee, S., Cho, J., Hwang, S.J.: Distilling llm agent into small models with retrieval and code tools (2025). https://arxiv.org/abs/2505.17612

14. Lee, G., Chay, W., Cho, S., Choi, E.: Trustsql: benchmarking text-to-sql reliability with penalty-based scoring (2024). https://arxiv.org/abs/2403.15879
15. Lei, F., Chen, J., Ye, Y., Cao, R., Shin, D., Su, H., et al.: Spider 2.0: evaluating language models on real-world enterprise text-to-sql workflows (2025). https://arxiv.org/abs/2411.07763
16. Li, J., Hui, B., Qu, G., Yang, J., Li, B., Li, B., et al.: Can llm already serve as a database interface? A big bench for large-scale database grounded text-to-sqls. In: Proceedings of the 37th International Conference on Neural Information Processing Systems. NIPS '23, Curran Associates Inc., Red Hook, NY, USA (2023)
17. MiniMax: Minimax m2.7. https://www.minimax.io/models/text/m27 (2026). official model page. Accessed 17 Apr 2026
18. NVIDIA, et al.: Nemotron 3 super: open, efficient mixture-of-experts hybrid mamba-transformer model for agentic reasoning (2026). https://arxiv.org/abs/2604.12374
19. Pedroso, B., Pereira, M., Pereira, D.: Performance evaluation of llms in the text-to-sql task in Portuguese. In: Anais do XXI Simpósio Brasileiro de Sistemas de Informação, pp. 260–269. SBC, Porto Alegre, RS, Brasil (2025). https://doi.org/10.5753/sbsi.2025.246471
20. Pourreza, M., Li, H., Sun, R., Chung, Y., Talaei, S., Kakkar, G.T.: Chase-sql: multi-path reasoning and preference optimized candidate selection in text-to-sql. In: Yue, Y., Garg, A., Peng, N., Sha, F., Yu, R. (eds.) International Conference on Learning Representations, vol. 2025, pp. 60385–60415 (2025)
21. Qwen Team: Qwen3.5-27b. https://huggingface.co/Qwen/Qwen3.5-27B (2025), hugging Face model card. Accessed: 2026-04-17
22. Qwen Team: Qwen3.5-4b (2025). https://huggingface.co/Qwen/Qwen3.5-4B. Accessed 17 Apr 2026. hugging Face model card
23. Ren, Q., Wang, P., Cai, R., Shao, S., Guo, D., Xie, Y., et al.: Rethinking generalization in reasoning sft: a conditional analysis on optimization, data, and model capability (2026). https://arxiv.org/abs/2604.06628
24. Rossiello, G., Pham, N., Glass, M., Lee, J., Subramanian, D.: Rationalization models for text-to-sql (2025). https://arxiv.org/abs/2502.06759
25. Saxer, J., Aigner, I.M., Linzmeier, L., Weiler, A., Stockinger, K.: Query carefully: detecting the unanswerables in text-to-sql tasks (2025). https://arxiv.org/abs/2512.21345
26. Shen, W., Li, C., Chen, H., Yan, M., Quan, X., Chen, H., et al.: Small LLMs are weak tool learners: a multi-LLM agent. In: Al-Onaizan, Y., Bansal, M., Chen, Y.N. (eds.) Proceedings of the 2024 Conference on Empirical Methods in Natural Language Processing, pp. 16658–16680. Association for Computational Linguistics, Miami, Florida, USA (2024). https://doi.org/10.18653/v1/2024.emnlp-main.929
27. Thaker, K., Bresler, Y.: Knowledge distillation with structured chain-of-thought for text-to-sql (2026). https://arxiv.org/abs/2512.17053
28. Wang, B., Gao, Y., Li, Z., Lou, J.G.: Know what I don't know: handling ambiguous and unknown questions for text-to-SQL. In: Rogers, A., Boyd-Graber, J., Okazaki, N. (eds.) Findings of the Association for Computational Linguistics: ACL 2023, pp. 5701–5714. Association for Computational Linguistics, Toronto, Canada (2023). https://doi.org/10.18653/v1/2023.findings-acl.352
29. Yan, S., Liu, K., Shen, C., Wang, B., Fan, S., Zhang, J., et al.: Distribution-aligned sequence distillation for superior long-cot reasoning (2026). https://arxiv.org/abs/2601.09088
30. Yang, A., Li, A., Yang, B., Zhang, B., Hui, B., Zheng, B., et al.: Qwen3 technical report (2025). https://arxiv.org/abs/2505.09388

31. Yu, T., Zhang, R., Yang, K., Yasunaga, M., Wang, D., Li, Z.: Spider: a large-scale human-labeled dataset for complex and cross-domain semantic parsing and text-to-SQL task. In: Riloff, E., Chiang, D., Hockenmaier, J., Tsujii, J. (eds.) Proceedings of the 2018 Conference on Empirical Methods in Natural Language Processing, pp. 3911–3921. Association for Computational Linguistics, Brussels, Belgium (2018). https://doi.org/10.18653/v1/D18-1425
32. Zhong, Q., Chen, K., Ding, L., Liu, J., Du, B., Tao, D.: Learning from imperfect data: towards efficient knowledge distillation of autoregressive language models for text-to-SQL. In: Al-Onaizan, Y., Bansal, M., Chen, Y.N. (eds.) Findings of the Association for Computational Linguistics: EMNLP 2024, pp. 6874–6885. Association for Computational Linguistics, Miami, Florida, USA (2024). https://doi.org/10.18653/v1/2024.findings-emnlp.403

A Hybrid Method for Generating Local Rule-Based Explanations for Skin Lesion Images Classification

Gabriel Branco Vitorino, Luciano Bachmann, and Renato Tinós(✉)

FFCLRP, University of São Paulo (USP), Ribeirão Preto, SP, Brazil
gabriel.branco@usp.br, rtinos@ffclrp.usp.br

Abstract. Machine Learning models such as Convolutional Neural Networks have demonstrated great performance on complex tasks but often lack interpretability, which is critical in domains such as medicine, where predictive models must be both accurate and trustworthy. Many methods in the field of eXplainable Artificial Intelligence (XAI) address this issue by providing human-understandable explanations for model predictions. This paper evaluates various XAI methods within the context of skin lesion classification. Using an EfficientNetB0 model trained on the HAM10000 dataset, we compare state-of-the-art techniques, such as Gradient-weighted Class Activation Mapping (Grad-CAM), Local Interpretable Model-agnostic Explanations (LIME) and variations of LOcal Rule-based Explanations (LORE). The resulting explanations are assessed quantitatively using the Area Over the Perturbation Curve as a faithfulness metric and surrogate accuracy as a fidelity measure for rule-based approaches, and qualitatively by examining how each method highlights relevant regions in a challenging misclassified case. Contrary to expectations, LORE variants with diversity-promoting mechanisms fail to consistently improve faithfulness when compared to the standard algorithm, a behavior we attribute to the constraints imposed by the required discrete, superpixel-based representations. To overcome this, we propose a hybrid strategy that integrates controlled local perturbations with an evolutionary search for generating the artificial neighborhood, yielding statistically significant performance gains. These results underscore the interactions between explanation methods and the structural properties of image-based data.

Keywords: Explainable Artificial Intelligence · Dermatoscopic Images · Genetic Algorithms

1 Introduction

Modern Machine Learning (ML) models, such as Convolutional Neural Networks (CNNs), have demonstrated excellent performance on complex tasks, but their decisions are often difficult to interpret, even for domain experts. In this context,

M. Recamonde-Mendoza and R. C. Barros (Eds.): BRACIS 2026, LNAI 17105, pp. 186–200, 2027.
https://doi.org/10.1007/978-3-032-39882-6_13

interpretability refers to the ability to explain model decisions or present them in terms understandable to humans [4].

A fundamental challenge in ML is this common trade-off between performance and interpretability, since highly accurate models are frequently the least interpretable. This issue has become increasingly important with the widespread adoption of ML models in high-stakes domains such as Medicine, where relying solely on accuracy is insufficient, as predictive models must also be transparent and trustworthy when transforming inputs into outputs. Recent research has focused on mitigating this problem by developing methods that make the predictions of black-box models more understandable to humans [1].

These approaches fall under the field of eXplainable Artificial Intelligence (XAI), which aims to improve the transparency of complex ML systems. XAI encompasses a wide range of techniques [9], such as Local Interpretable Model-agnostic Explanations (LIME), Anchors, LOcal Rule-based Explanations (LORE), SHapley Additive exPlanations (SHAP), and Gradient-weighted Class Activation Mapping (Grad-CAM), each presenting distinct properties, strengths, and limitations. Some of these methods are architecturally limited to text and tabular data and cannot be applied to image data without significant modification. The others can either be adapted for the task or are directly developed for it.

In this work, we compare LIME, Grad-CAM, and LORE (Sect. 2) in the problem of generating explanations for classifications performed by a CNN trained on a dataset with dermatoscopic images of skin lesions. Particular attention is given to LORE, for which we implemented and adapted variants to the image explanation setting, including extensions designed to promote diversity in the locally generated neighborhood. The experimental results (presented in Sect. 4) reveal that, contrary to expectations, these enhanced variants did not consistently outperform the original LORE [8] formulation in terms of faithfulness, as measured by the established perturbation-based metrics.

This unexpected behavior motivated a deeper investigation into the interaction between neighborhood generation strategies and the discrete nature of the image-based surrogate space. We conclude that, for the explanations constructed over the binary superpixel representations, the structure of the search space imposes constraints that can hinder the effectiveness of diversity-driven approaches. Based on this insight, we propose a new hybrid strategy that adapts the generation process to the underlying structure of the problem, leading to improved faithfulness in the resulting explanations. The results are presented in Sect. 4 and the conclusions in Sect. 5.

2 LIME, LORE, and Grad-CAM for Image Analysis

LIME [13] explains individual predictions by learning a sparse, locally weighted linear surrogate model around a specific instance. For image data, the input is first segmented into superpixels, which define the interpretable feature space. Perturbed samples are generated by randomly masking subsets of superpixels, and the predictions of the original model on these samples are used to fit the surrogate model. The resulting coefficients estimate the contribution of each superpixel to the prediction, capturing whether each region promotes or suppresses the predicted outcome. The final explanation highlights the most influential superpixels, offering an intuitive visualization of positive and negative evidence for the predicted class.

The original implementation of LORE [8] is designed for tabular data and utilizes Genetic Algorithms (GAs) to generate a synthetic local neighborhood around the instance being explained. These GAs evolve instances that remain feature-similar to the original input while either preserving the black-box model's predicted class, referred to as Similar Same Outcome (SSO), or altering it, Similar Different Outcome (SDO) [6]. Once the neighborhood is established, a Decision Tree (DT) is trained to extract Factual and Counterfactual rules that explain the model's prediction within that local region by indicating what were the features responsible for the classification and the modifications necessary to change the original prediction.

Although LORE [8] was not originally designed for image data, a subsequent variant, known as LORE Stable and Actionable [7], introduces a strategy that extends LORE's applicability to image and text domains. For image explanation tasks, an approach similar to LIME is adopted, in which images are segmented and encoded as binary vectors. The neighborhood generation and rule extraction procedures follow the original LORE framework, leveraging GAs to guide the search. In the final step, a Decision Tree (DT) is trained; the resulting rules are then mapped back to the image as a saliency map, highlighting the superpixel segments identified by the rules as responsible for the classification.

Local Rule-Based Explanations with Fitness Sharing (LOREfs) [15] extends LORE by incorporating a fitness sharing mechanism [5] into the genetic algorithm to promote diversity among generated synthetic instances. This mechanism penalizes individuals located in densely populated regions of the search space by adjusting their fitness based on proximity to neighbors within a predefined radius, encouraging exploration of less populated regions. The main motivation is to ensure that the local decision boundaries learned by the surrogate decision tree more closely approximate those of the black-box classifier. While LOREfs has been previously applied only to tabular datasets, this work extends its use to image analysis for the first time.

Lastly, Grad-CAM [16] generates explanations by leveraging the internal structure of CNNs. It computes gradients of the target class output with respect to the feature maps of a convolutional layer. These gradients are globally averaged to obtain importance weights and combined to produce a coarse localization map. This heatmap is upsampled and overlaid on the input image, highlighting regions that most influence the prediction. Unlike LIME and LORE, that are model-agnostic, Grad-CAM is model-specific; it is computationally efficient and directly grounded in learned feature representations.

3 Methodology

We first present the dermatoscopic image dataset and the CNN used. We then describe the implementation of the XAI methods, introduce the proposed hybrid approach and its relation to the feature search space, and finally outline the evaluation metrics for quantitative analysis.

3.1 Dataset and Convolutional Neural Network

The Human Against Machine with 10,000 training images dataset (HAM10000) is a publicly available collection of dermatoscopic images developed within the International Skin Imaging Collaboration (ISIC) initiative [10]. It provides high-quality skin lesion images with gold-standard diagnoses and relevant clinical metadata. The dataset comprises seven diagnostic categories: actinic keratoses and intraepithelial carcinoma, basal cell carcinoma, benign keratosis-like lesions, dermatofibroma, melanoma, melanocytic nevi, and vascular lesions.

The model employed is a CNN based on EfficientNetB0 [17], trained via transfer learning, enabling the reuse of general visual representations while specializing in skin lesion characteristics. The images were resized and normalized according to the model's requirements and data augmentation techniques, including horizontal flips, rotations, and zoom variations, were applied to the training set, 7010 images, to improve generalization.

Training was performed in two stages using a validation set of 2253 images. In the transfer learning stage, only the classification layers were trained while the backbone remained frozen. This was followed by a fine-tuning phase, in which deeper layers were unfrozen and updated using a reduced learning rate. Standard regularization strategies, including early stopping and learning rate scheduling, were employed to stabilize training. The trained CNN was evaluated on a held-out test set of 752 images. All splits were stratified to ensure that all classes were represented in each set, the results are presented in Sect. 4.

3.2 Algorithms Implementation

Although the original LORE formulation [8] does not explicitly include a similarity threshold, and penalizes only exact copies of the original instance, the publicly available implementation in GitHub [6] introduces a parameter η to control the admissible similarity between generated instances and the reference input. This parameter acts as a local constraint, discouraging the generation of trivial or near-duplicate neighbors by penalizing candidates that lie within a predefined radius of the original instance. This mechanism may appear similar to fitness sharing, but they act at different levels of the search. While η evaluates candidates only with respect to the original instance, fitness sharing relies on pairwise distances across the whole population to estimate local density.

We implemented three in-house variants of LORE adapted to the image explanation setting, differing in how similarity and diversity are enforced during neighborhood generation. The baseline, denoted as oLORE, follows the formulation in the original LORE article [8], penalizing only identical solutions. The second variant, denoted as scLORE, incorporates the η similarity constraint from the public implementation [6], limiting the generation of overly similar instances within a predefined radius. Finally, iLOREfs [15] extends this approach by combining the similarity constraint with fitness sharing to explicitly promote population diversity. All versions are publicly available on our repository [2].

The proposed in-house implementations for image classification depart from the standard tabular setting by representing instances as superpixel-based binary masks, where each feature encodes the presence or absence of regions obtained by a segmentation algorithm. The algorithm used in this work is Quickshift as implemented in Scikit-Learn. The segmentation defines a binary combinatorial search space over image regions, in which the GA operates directly using specialized fitness functions for SSO and SDO objectives.

These objectives jointly account for structural similarity, measured through normalized Hamming distance, and consistency with CNN predictions, while additional components handle the preprocessing pipeline that maps raw images into this binary representation. The three implementations have slightly different fitness functions. More specifically, they differ in the similarity component of the equations:

$$\textit{scLORE:} \quad \begin{cases} f_{\text{SSO}}(z_i) = \alpha_1 \cdot \text{sim\_score}(z_0, z_i) + \beta_1 \cdot \mathbb{I}[f(z_i) = y_0] \\ f_{\text{SDO}}(z_i) = \alpha_2 \cdot \text{sim\_score}(z_0, z_i) + \beta_2 \cdot \mathbb{I}[f(z_i) \neq y_0] \end{cases} \tag{1}$$

$$\textit{iLOREfs:} \quad \begin{cases} f_{\text{SSO}}(z_i) = \dfrac{\alpha_1 \cdot \text{sim\_score}(z_0, z_i) + \beta_1 \cdot \mathbb{I}[f(z_i) = y_0]}{\sum_j sh(d(z_i, z_j))} \\ f_{\text{SDO}}(z_i) = \dfrac{\alpha_2 \cdot \text{sim\_score}(z_0, z_i) + \beta_2 \cdot \mathbb{I}[f(z_i) \neq y_0]}{\sum_j sh(d(z_i, z_j))} \end{cases} \tag{2}$$

$$\textit{Definitions:} \quad \begin{cases} \text{sim\_ratio}(z_0, z_i) = 1 - d(z_0, z_i) \\ \text{sim\_score}(z_0, z_i) = \begin{cases} 0, & \text{if sim\_ratio}(z_0, z_i) \geq \eta \\ \text{sim\_ratio}(z_0, z_i), & \text{otherwise} \end{cases} \\ sh(d(z_i, z_j)) = \max\left(1 - \dfrac{d(z_i, z_j)}{\zeta}\right) \end{cases} \tag{3}$$

where, z_0 denotes the original instance and $y_0 = f(z_0)$ its corresponding black-box prediction. Let z_i and z_j be synthetic instances generated in the neighborhood of z_0, with $f(z_i)$ denoting the model's prediction for z_i. The indicator function $\mathbb{I}[\cdot]$ returns 1 when the condition holds and 0 otherwise. The quantity $d(z_i, z_j) \in [0, 1]$ represents the normalized hamming distance between two instances in the binary superpixel space, while $\text{sim\_ratio}(z_0, z_i) = 1 - d(z_0, z_i)$ measures their similarity. The function $\text{sim\_score}(z_0, z_i)$ applies a threshold η to penalize overly similar instances. The coefficients α_1 and α_2 control the similarity term, whereas β_1 and β_2 weight the class-consistency terms in SSO and SDO. The function $sh(\cdot)$ implements fitness sharing, and ζ defines the sharing radius.

When $\eta = 1.0$, and the distances are normalized, the scLORE function reproduces the oLORE behavior, rejecting only individuals that are identical to the reference instance; that is how we set the oLORE version for the experiments. In scLORE η was set to 0.8 based on the mean number of segments generated across the images of the test set used to evaluate the CNN, as we will discuss next in Subsect. 3.3, so it penalizes exact copies of the original instance and also individuals whose normalized Hamming distance to the original individual is less than 0.2.

The fitness sharing variant still relies on the η parameter to discourage individuals from remaining too close to the original instance, while additionally promoting diversity through the fitness sharing mechanism. In this way, as the η parameter controls proximity to the original instance, the radius ζ from the fitness sharing function ensures that the search remains spatially diverse and was set to be 0.15 for the same reasoning used for η.

The other two algorithms considered in this study, LIME and Grad-CAM, were used directly from the XAI-Library repository. We opted for in-house implementations of LORE-based methods, as the image-oriented version available in XAI-Lib (iLOREM) [11] relies on a LIME-like random neighborhood generation procedure rather than the GA originally proposed in LORE. This design choice ensures consistency with the original formulation of the method, as well as with the proposed fitness sharing strategy.

3.3 Proposed Hybrid Method

The adaptations of LORE described in the previous section did not improve upon the oLORE baseline in preliminary experiments. To understand this outcome, we analyze factors that may explain the reduced performance of these variants in image classification. In the LORE framework for images, the length K of the binary vectors varies naturally across samples because the number of generated segments depends on the image content, even when identical segmentation parameters are used. In the HAM10000 dataset, the segmentation algorithm produced an average of approximately 25 ± 4 segments per image, which served as the initial reference for defining the η and ζ parameters.

Additionally, a single bit flip corresponds to modifying one image region, and the similarity between instances can be naturally measured using the normalized Hamming distance. This induces a discrete and highly structured combinatorial search space. For a given reference instance, all possible perturbations are organized into discrete levels defined by their Hamming distance k, with the number of candidates at each level given by $\binom{K}{k}$. As a consequence, distances are quantized and correspond to specific numbers of modified segments, defining distinct "shells" of candidates around the original instance, imposing a minimum meaningful perturbation (one bit flip) and restricting the set of reachable neighbors.

These characteristics have direct implications for the behavior of the evolutionary search. In particular, the parameters η and ζ must be interpreted in terms of discrete perturbation levels. The parameter η effectively defines a threshold on the minimum number of bit changes required for an individual to be considered non-trivial, while ζ determines the threshold within which individuals are considered too similar creating a niche. Since the number of segments K varies across images, fixed values of these parameters correspond to different absolute numbers of modified segments, leading to inconsistent behavior across instances, an issue we address by adjusting these parameters according to the value of K, dynamically for each image.

Empirically, we observed that small perturbations tend to preserve the original class, while larger Hamming distances rapidly increase the probability of class change. In particular, individuals within a distance of $1/K$ or $2/K$ from the original instance, i.e., with one or two bits flipped, are considerably more likely to preserve the original prediction. Beyond this range, generating SSO instances becomes increasingly difficult under the considered setup. This behavior highlights a limitation of diversity-promoting mechanisms in our context, as encouraging exploration tends to drive the population towards regions of the search space where the original class prediction is no longer maintained.

To further investigate this behavior, we developed a procedure to quantify how often predictions change under controlled perturbations. Images are grouped by the same value of K, and for each image in the group we generate 100 perturbed samples by deactivating exactly k segments ($k = 0, 1, \ldots, K$). The CNN is then used to predict the class of each perturbed sample, so we can compute the proportion of samples whose predicted class differs from the original (change rate). These rates are computed per image and averaged within groups so they can be plotted as a function of k, yielding perturbation curves that characterize model sensitivity. Results show that small perturbations, typically 2–3 bit flips, are sufficient to induce substantial class changes (above 45%), indicating high sensitivity to minimal structural modifications.

Motivated by these limitations, we propose iLOREfs Hybrid, a strategy that explicitly leverages the discrete nature of the search space. For SSO generation, instead of relying exclusively on the GA, candidate instances are created by randomly flipping one or two bits of the original instance, enabling efficient exploration of the local neighborhood where class preservation is more likely. When this procedure produces an insufficient number of valid SSO instances, defined as fewer than half the size of the largest class in the sampled population, the algorithm falls back to the standard GA-based iLOREfs generation process with parameters dynamically adjusted according to the number of image segments.

For the generation of SDO instances, the evolutionary approach is maintained, as diversity is beneficial in exploring regions associated with alternative predictions. In this case, the parameters η and ζ are also adapted according to the number of segments K, ensuring that their effect remains consistent across different image representations always penalizing individuals that are only one-bit different from the original instance and considering a two-bit difference to include individuals in a niche for fitness sharing. As shown in the experimental results, the proposed setup led to improvements in explanation faithfulness.

3.4 Evaluation Metrics

Evaluation in XAI aims to assess whether explanations provide meaningful and reliable insights into a model's behavior [3,14]. Unlike standard evaluation, which targets predictive performance, XAI focuses on explanation quality and its alignment with the model. As methods produce different representations (e.g., rules, feature attributions, surrogate models), specialized metrics are required. These are typically computed locally using perturbations around a given instance to capture explanation-specific properties rather than global generalization.

Fidelity is a central criterion in XAI and measures how accurately an explanation reflects the behavior of the target model in the neighborhood of an input. Given a model f, an instance x, a perturbation distribution D_x, and an explanation g, fidelity quantifies the agreement between g and f over samples $z \sim D_x$ [8,15]. In this work, local fidelity is measured as the accuracy of the surrogate model over the generated neighborhood for the LORE-based methods.

In addition, we adopt the sensitivity-based metric *Area Over the Perturbation Curve* (AOPC) as a unified faithfulness criterion [12,14]. AOPC evaluates whether the regions identified as important by an explanation method correspond to features that significantly influence the model's prediction. The underlying principle of AOPC as a faithfulness metric is that a More Relevant First (MoRF) perturbation strategy, in which the most relevant features are progressively removed, should lead to a substantial decrease in the model's confidence for the originally predicted class. For each instance z_0, the model produces a prediction $y_0 = \arg\max f(z_0)$ with confidence $p_f(y_0 \mid z_0)$. Given a ranking of feature importance, the top $k(\%)$ features are iteratively masked, producing perturbed inputs $z_0^{(k)}$, and the confidence drop is computed as:

$$\Delta P(z_0) = p_f(y_0 \mid z_0) - p_f(y_0 \mid z_0^{(k)}).$$

By varying $k(\%)$, a perturbation curve is obtained, and AOPC corresponds to the aggregated confidence drop (mean $\Delta P(z_0)$), where higher values indicate more faithful explanations. We plot $p_f(y_0 \mid z_0^{(k)})$ across $k(\%)$, averaged over 150 stratified test images, together with the baseline $p_f(y_0 \mid z_0)$. For each image, the ΔP values obtained across perturbation levels were averaged to produce an image-level AOPC score. The segments were ranked according to the explanation method and masked using a fixed baseline. Evaluation was performed using masking ratios $k(\%) \in 0, 2, 5, 10, 15, 20, 25, 30, 50, 80, 100$. This unified protocol ensures comparability across methods by standardizing the perturbation process while allowing method-specific ranking strategies.

Statistical significance between iLOREfs Hybrid and the competing methods was assessed using the Wilcoxon signed-rank test. For each image, the AOPC curve produces a set of $\Delta P(z)$ values corresponding to the successive perturbation steps. These values were averaged to obtain a single AOPC score for that image and method, representing the overall explanation quality for the sample. The mean AOPC reported for each method corresponds to the average of these image-level AOPC scores across the entire evaluation set. Since all methods were evaluated on the same set of images, the image-level AOPC scores form paired observations, enabling a direct image-by-image statistical comparison using the Wilcoxon signed-rank test. To account for multiple pairwise comparisons between iLOREfs Hybrid and the competing methods, p-values were adjusted using the Holm-Bonferroni procedure. Differences were considered statistically significant when the adjusted p-value was below 0.05.

4 Results

All experiments were conducted on a workstation equipped with an AMD Ryzen 7 5800X processor, an NVIDIA GeForce RTX 3060 Ti GPU, and 32 GB of DDR4 RAM. The entire implementation was developed in Python, leveraging its extensive ecosystem of libraries for machine learning and data analysis.

4.1 Convolutional Neural Network Evaluation

The evaluation over 752 instances yielded an accuracy of 0.75 and a weighted F1-score of 0.77, indicating moderate CNN performance and reflecting the dataset's class imbalance. Performance varied across classes, with Class 2 (benign keratosis-like lesion, "bkl"') showing low precision and attracting a disproportionate number of predictions. This tendency was also observed during the development of the XAI methods, where many generated perturbations shifted predictions towards Class 2, suggesting consistency between the GA fitness function and the CNN behavior.

Additionally, a systematic confusion between Classes 4 (melanoma,"mel") and 5 (nevus, "nv") suggests overlapping feature representations in the learned space. Although the model does not achieve uniform performance across all classes, it is sufficiently expressive for the purpose of this study, where the primary goal is to analyze and compare explanation methods rather than optimize classification accuracy.

4.2 Qualitative Analysis

We present a qualitative analysis of the explanations generated for a selected example, aiming to elucidate the operating principles and interpretative characteristics of each method. This example is particularly relevant as it corresponds to a misclassification made by the CNN. The instance was predicted as Class 2, whereas its true diagnosis is Class 0 (actinic keratoses and intraepithelial carcinoma, "akiec"). The CNN assigned higher confidence to Class 2 (0.39) and Class 1 (basal cell carcinoma, "bcc", 0.38) than to the ground-truth class,"akiec" (0.10), while all remaining classes received negligible confidence.

The resulting explanation obtained with LIME is shown in the first row of Fig. 1. The leftmost panel presents the explanation, where green regions indicate positive contributions to the prediction of "bkl" and red regions denote negative contributions. The presence of extensive regions with both positive and negative attributions indicates that the XAI method effectively captures the model's

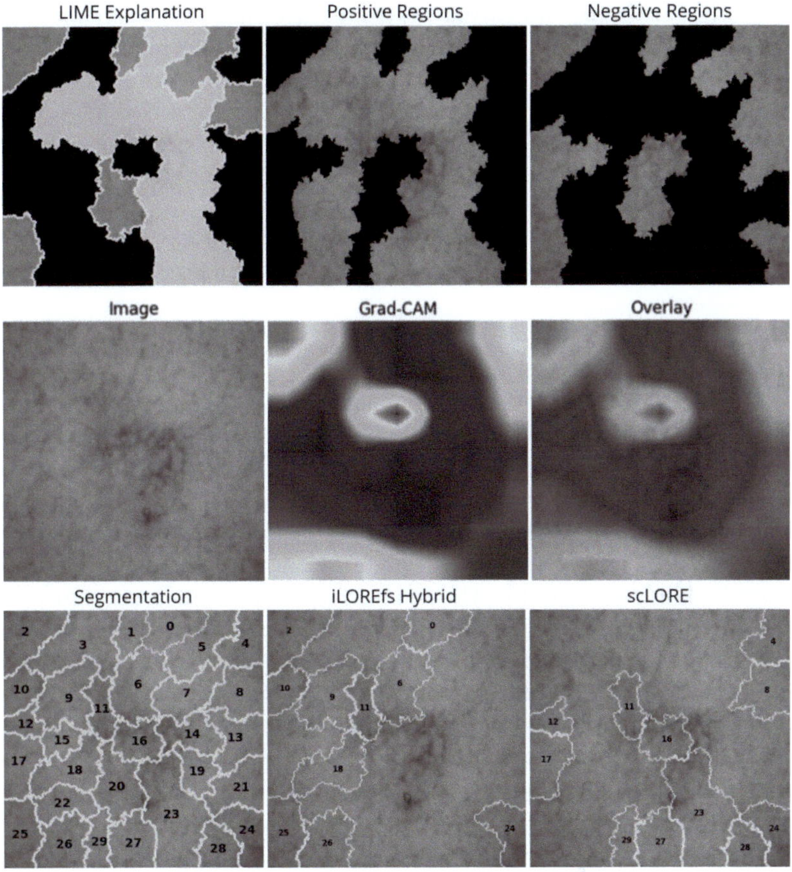

Fig. 1. Explanations generated by each method. The top row corresponds to LIME, the middle row shows Grad-CAM heat maps and the bottom row presents the image segmentation alongside iLOREfs Hybrid and scLORE explanations.

uncertainty, which is consistent with the prediction scores, where the two most probable classes exhibit similar confidence levels.

The second and third images in the same row of Fig. 1 separately highlight the regions positively and negatively correlated to the predicted class, providing a clearer visualization of the segments influencing the model's decision. The explanation reveals that, although the model relies on parts of the actual lesion in the center of the image, which even appeared negatively correlated to the predicted class in the explanation, the prediction is still highly influenced by features located in the image corners with no relevant information.

The Grad-CAM explanation, shown in the center row of Fig. 1, exhibits a pattern consistent with LIME, with its gradient activations concentrated in the outer regions of the image, particularly in the upper-left corner. As discussed in the following paragraphs, the proposed hybrid method successfully identifies very similar regions, indicating a strong agreement between the explanation approaches. The main discrepancy is the lower-right region, which receives greater emphasis in the LIME explanation.

When applied to explain the decision of the CNN for this image, iLOREfs Hybrid generated the following set of factual ($\mathcal{R}$) and counterfactual ($\mathcal{C}$) rules displayed here as an example explanation.

Factual class: 2 **Local fidelity:** 0.90

$$\mathcal{R}: \text{seg}_{11} > 0.5;\ \text{seg}_{2} > 0.5;\ \text{seg}_{6} > 0.5;\ \text{seg}_{10} > 0.5; \text{seg}_{9} > 0.5;\ \text{seg}_{26} > 0.5;\ \text{seg}_{24} > 0.5;\ \text{seg}_{25} > 0.5; \text{seg}_{0} > 0.5;\ \text{seg}_{18} > 0.5 \Rightarrow \text{Class 2}$$

$$\mathcal{C}_1: \text{seg}_{11} \leq 0.5;\ \text{seg}_{6} > 0.5;\ \text{seg}_{23} > 0.5;\ \text{seg}_{9} > 0.5; \text{seg}_{2} > 0.5;\ \text{seg}_{27} > 0.5;\ \text{seg}_{8} > 0.5;\ \text{seg}_{0} > 0.5 \Rightarrow \text{Class 3}$$

$$\mathcal{C}_2: \text{seg}_{11} > 0.5;\ \text{seg}_{2} > 0.5;\ \text{seg}_{6} \leq 0.5;\ \text{seg}_{24} > 0.5; \text{seg}_{12} > 0.5;\ \text{seg}_{25} > 0.5;\ \text{seg}_{22} > 0.5;\ \text{seg}_{18} > 0.5;\ \text{seg}_{27} > 0.5 \Rightarrow \text{Class 3}$$

The rules generated by the surrogate model, a DT, take the form of threshold conditions (>0.5 or ≤ 0.5), indicating whether a given superpixel is present (1) or absent (0). These rules are summarized in the image at the center column of the last row of Fig. 1, where the segments contributing to the prediction of Class 2 are highlighted. Notably, the counterfactual rules indicate that removing segments 11 or 6 leads to a change in classification to Class 3. These segments are also identified as highly relevant by Grad-CAM, reinforcing their importance in the model's decision-making process.

The scLORE explanation, shown in the last row of Fig. 1, focused on the lower-right corner, a region identified as relevant only by LIME. Interestingly, scLORE generated counterfactual rules indicating that the absence of segment 23 increases the probability of the correct class (Class 0).

4.3 Quantitative Model Comparison

In this section, we evaluate the explanation methods using the AOPC protocol described in the methodology. Since different XAI approaches produce fundamentally different types of explanations, a method-specific ranking strategy is required to establish the perturbation order. Despite these differences, the protocol provides a unified evaluation framework by measuring the impact of progressively removing the regions identified as most relevant by each method.

Segment ranking was therefore performed according to the nature of each explanation method. For LIME, superpixels are ranked in descending order of their positive attribution weights. For the LORE-based methods, ranking is derived from symbolic rules, where segments are ordered according to their occurrence in factual and counterfactual conditions, with a higher importance score assigned to segments that appear more frequently in counterfactual changes.

For Grad-CAM, the continuous heat map was aggregated over the generated image segments to ensure consistency with the segment-based explanations produced by LIME and the LORE-based approaches. Segment importance was computed as the average activation within each segment, although alternative

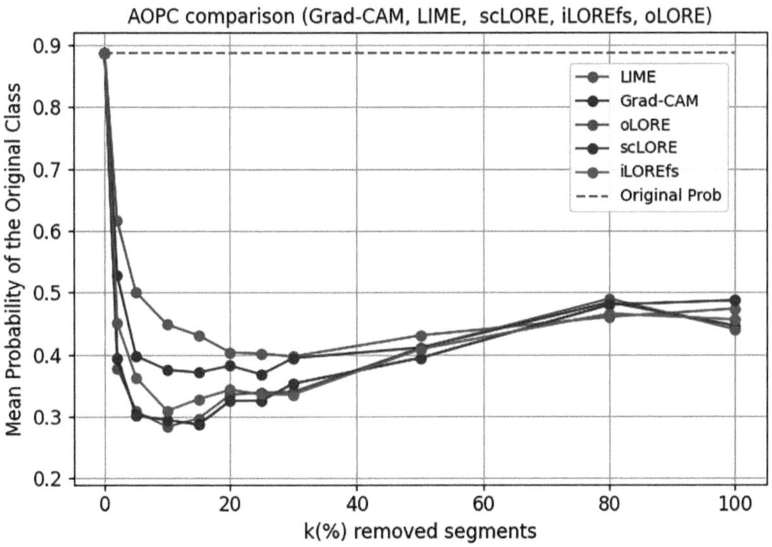

Fig. 2. AOPC results for the standard methods with fixed parameters. The mean $\Delta P(z)$ values are 0.392 (LIME), 0.429 (Grad-CAM), 0.462 (iLOREfs), 0.476 (scLORE) and 0.478 (oLORE).

aggregation strategies based on maximum activation and activation sum were also evaluated and produced similar rankings. Since Grad-CAM explanations are continuous rather than segment-based, an additional pixel-level perturbation analysis was performed directly on the saliency map. The resulting AOPC curves closely matched those obtained with segment-level aggregation, suggesting that discretization had minimal impact on the evaluation and supporting the validity of the proposed comparison framework.

All experiments with the LORE variants used the same GA hyperparameters: 20 generations with an early-stopping mechanism, a population size of 350 individuals, and crossover and mutation rates of 0.2 and 0.1 for SSO, and 0.9 and 0.25 for SDO. The resulting AOPC curves, presented in Fig. 2, constitute the first quantitative comparison of the explanation methods. The mean confidence drop $\Delta P(z)$ across all images and $k(\%)$ values is reported as a summary statistic for the curves and used in the statistical tests.

In the first evaluation of the AOPC curves, an unexpected result was observed: both LORE variants incorporating diversity-promoting mechanisms failed to outperform oLORE. Although scLORE and iLOREfs exhibited slightly lower AOPC values than the original algorithm, the observed differences were not statistically significant (Holm-corrected p-values of 0.45 and 0.21, respectively). Despite this outcome, oLORE and scLORE consistently outperformed LIME and Grad-CAM in identifying relevant image segments under the considered experimental setup, also verified by the Wilcoxon signed-rank test.

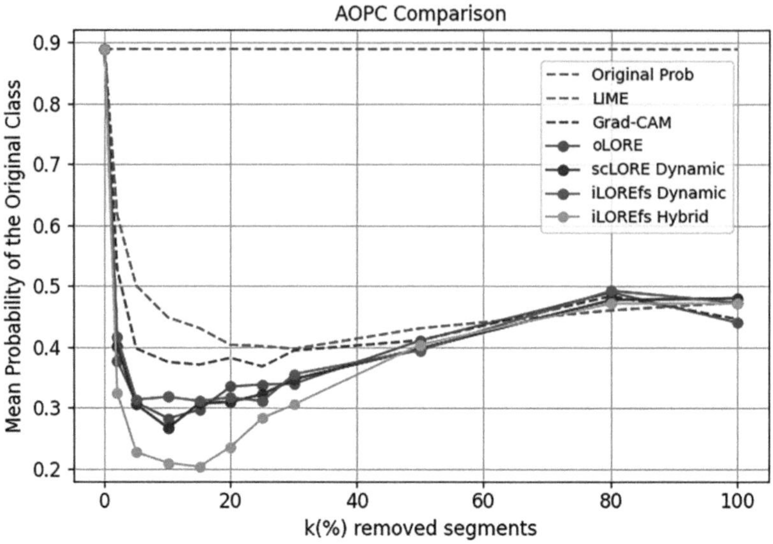

Fig. 3. AOPC results for iLOREfs Hybrid, scLORE, and iLOREfs with dynamic adjustment of η and ζ based on the number of segments K. Grad-CAM, LIME, and oLORE results are included for reference. Mean $\Delta P(z)$ values were 0.522 for iLOREfs Hybrid, 0.478 for oLORE and scLORE, and 0.470 for iLOREfs.

After dynamically adjusting the diversity parameters according to K, both modified LORE variants showed a modest improvement in performance. Nevertheless, they still failed to achieve a significant advantage over oLORE, as shown in Fig. 3. These results suggest that the proposed diversity mechanisms have little impact on explanation faithfulness in this scenario, despite a small but statistically significant improvement in local fidelity. Specifically, oLORE achieved a mean local fidelity of 0.952, whereas iLOREfs and scLORE reached 0.966 and 0.958, respectively.

Leveraging the well-defined discrete structure of the combinatorial space, together with the tendencies discussed in Sect. 3.3, we propose the hybrid neighborhood generation strategy. The hybrid method produced a clear improvement in faithfulness as measured by AOPC. Figure 3 compares oLORE, dynamically adjusted scLORE, dynamically adjusted iLOREfs, and the proposed iLOREfs Hybrid. The hybrid approach achieved a mean AOPC of 0.522, compared with 0.478 for oLORE, the next best performing algorithm, corresponding to an improvement of approximately 9%. This difference was statistically significant according to the Wilcoxon signed-rank test (Holm-corrected p-value $= 0.001$ and $W = 3947$). The improvement was particularly evident in the initial portion of the perturbation curves where the most important segments are located.

5 Conclusion

In this work, we have investigated the behavior and reliability of different XAI methods, including our proposed hybrid approach, applied to a CNN trained on the HAM10000 dermatoscopic dataset. The evaluation combined qualitative inspection with a quantitative AOPC-based protocol, the results show that LORE-based approaches consistently provided more faithful explanations, however, introducing diversity-promoting mechanisms, such as similarity constraints (η) and fitness sharing (ζ), does not inherently improve performance, especially when using fixed values for these parameters, as their effectiveness is limited by the discrete and combinatorial nature of the superpixel-based binary representation, where distances are quantized and directly linked to the number of modified segments.

The binary representation of segmented images and CNN sensitivity make the SSO region considerably more constrained than in typical tabular settings. In this context, explicit diversity pressure becomes counterproductive, as it penalizes the limited set of valid neighbors that preserve the original prediction. By accounting for this structure, we show that parameter adaptation, particularly when aligned with minimal perturbations in Hamming space, is critical for effective neighborhood generation. The proposed iLOREfs Hybrid addresses these issues by combining controlled local bit-flipping for SSO stability with an adaptive, K-dependent genetic search for SDO exploration, resulting in improved faithfulness in this setup.

The results highlight that the effectiveness of XAI methods is inherently linked to the structure of the underlying representation. In particular, our findings suggest that aligning explanation mechanisms with the geometry of the input space and the predictive model's sensitivity could lead to improved outcomes. Future work should investigate the extension of this framework to other datasets and model architectures. Such directions are essential to ensure that explanation methods remain both faithful and reliable in complex domains such as medical imaging.

Acknowledgments. This work was partially supported by the São Paulo Research Foundation (FAPESP), under grants 2024/15430-5, 2024/08485-8, 2024/04927-6 and 2025/13249-4, and CNPq grant 304640/2024-7.

Disclosure of Interests. The authors have no competing interests to declare that are relevant to the content of this article.

References

1. Arrieta, A.B., et al.: Explainable artificial intelligence (xai): concepts, taxonomies, opportunities and challenges toward responsible ai (2019). https://arxiv.org/abs/1910.10045
2. Branco, G.: ilorefs hybrid (2026). https://github.com/BabrielGranco/iLOREfs-Hybrid, gitHub repository. Accessed 07 Apr 2026

3. Chan, C.S., Kong, H., Liang, G.: A comparative study of faithfulness metrics for model interpretability methods (2022). https://arxiv.org/abs/2204.05514
4. Doshi-Velez, F., Kim, B.: Towards a rigorous science of interpretable machine learning (2017). https://arxiv.org/abs/1702.08608
5. Goldberg, D.E., Richardson, J.: Genetic algorithms with sharing for multimodal function optimization. In: Proceedings of the Second International Conference on Genetic Algorithms, Lawrence Erlbaum Associates (1987)
6. Guidotti, R., et al.: Lore: local rule-based explanations (2018). https://github.com/riccotti/LORE, gitHub repository. Accessed 24 Mar 2026
7. Guidotti, R., et al.: Stable and actionable explanations of black-box models through factual and counterfactual rules. Data Min. Knowl. Discovery **38**(5), 2825–2862 (2024). https://doi.org/10.1007/s10618-022-00878-5
8. Guidotti, R., Monreale, A., Ruggieri, S., Pedreschi, D., Turini, F., Giannotti, F.: Local rule-based explanations of black box decision systems (2018). https://arxiv.org/abs/1805.10820
9. Guidotti, R., Monreale, A., Ruggieri, S., Turini, F., Pedreschi, D., Giannotti, F.: A survey of methods for explaining black box models (2018). https://arxiv.org/abs/1802.01933
10. International Skin Imaging Collaboration (ISIC): Isic archive (2026). https://www.isic-archive.com. Accessed 24 June 2026
11. KDD Lab Pisa: Xai-lib: Explainable artificial intelligence library (2026). https://github.com/kdd-lab/XAI-Lib. Accessed 24 Mar 2026
12. Liu, J., Yu, H., Zhang, X.: Beyond attribution: unified concept-level explanations (2026). https://arxiv.org/abs/2410.12439
13. Ribeiro, M.T., Singh, S., Guestrin, C.: Why should i trust you?: explaining the predictions of any classifier (2016). https://arxiv.org/abs/1602.04938
14. Samek, W., Binder, A., Montavon, G., Bach, S., Muller, K.R.: Evaluating the visualization of what a deep neural network has learned. IEEE Trans. Neural Netw. Learn. Syst. **28**(11) (2017)
15. Santos, D.A., Baranauskas, J.A., Tinos, R.: Local rule-based explanations method based on genetic algorithms with fitness sharing. Learning Nonlinear Models **21**(2) (2023)
16. Selvaraju, R.R., Cogswell, M., Das, A., Vedantam, R., Parikh, D., Batra, D.: Grad-cam: visual explanations from deep networks via gradient-based localization. Int. J. Comput. Vis. **128**(2), 336–359 (2019). https://doi.org/10.1007/s11263-019-01228-7, http://dx.doi.org/10.1007/s11263-019-01228-7
17. Tan, M., Le, Q.V.: Efficientnet: rethinking model scaling for convolutional neural networks. In: Proceedings of the International Conference on Machine Learning (ICML). PMLR (2019)

C-DEEPSO-Powell: A Hybrid Approach for Large-Scale Optimization Problems

Patrick Paiva Medeiros de Albuquerque[1], Camila Caleones Figueiredo[2(✉)], and Carolina Gil Marcelino[1]

[1] Instituto de Computação, Universidade Federal do Rio de Janeiro, Rio de Janeiro, Brazil
{patrick,carolina}@ic.ufrj.br

[2] Programa de Engenharia de Sistemas e Computação, COPPE, Universidade Federal do Rio de Janeiro, Rio de Janeiro, Brazil
camila@cos.ufrj.br

Abstract. Large-scale optimization problems, characterized by a high number of decision variables, arise in several real-world domains such as finance, logistics, and energy systems, where finding optimal solutions is computationally challenging. Metaheuristic algorithms offer a viable alternative, producing high-quality approximate solutions within reasonable time budgets. This paper proposes C-DEEPSO-Powell, a hybrid algorithm that combines the global search capabilities of C-DEEPSO (Canonical Differential Evolutionary Particle Swarm Optimization) with the local refinement of Powell's conjugate-direction method. The hybridization follows a periodic transfer strategy, where the global best solution is refined by Powell's method at strategically chosen checkpoints throughout the optimization process. The proposed approach was evaluated on all 15 functions of the CEC'2013 large-scale benchmark suite ($D = 1000$). Experimental results show that C-DEEPSO-Powell outperformed standalone C-DEEPSO in 14 out of 15 functions. For the six functions with less pronounced differences, a Student's t-test ($\alpha = 0.05$) confirmed statistical significance in five; for the remaining functions, the improvement spans several orders of magnitude. The most notable gains were observed in smooth, well-conditioned functions, where mean fitness improved by up to 12 orders of magnitude (e.g., f_1: from 7.52×10^{10} to 1.63×10^{-2}; f_{12}, the overlapping Rosenbrock function: from 9.35×10^{11} to 2.57×10^{3}).

Keywords: Computational intelligence · Evolutionary algorithms · Hybridization · Large-scale optimization · C-DEEPSO · Powell's method

1 Introduction

Large-scale global optimization problems (LSOPs) arise in numerous real-world domains, including the design of power systems, vehicle routing, water distribution networks, and financial portfolio optimization [10,12]. These problems are

M. Recamonde-Mendoza and R. C. Barros (Eds.): BRACIS 2026, LNAI 17105, pp. 201–215, 2027.
https://doi.org/10.1007/978-3-032-39882-6_14

characterized by hundreds or thousands of decision variables, which dramatically expand the search space and make it increasingly difficult for optimization algorithms to find high-quality solutions. As dimensionality increases, many algorithms suffer from the so-called curse of dimensionality, where their performance deteriorates significantly [9].

In this context, metaheuristic algorithms have gained considerable attention as practical alternatives to exact methods. Unlike deterministic approaches, metaheuristics do not guarantee finding the optimal solution, but they can produce good approximate solutions within acceptable computational budgets [5]. Among the most successful metaheuristics are population-based algorithms such as Particle Swarm Optimization (PSO) [7], Differential Evolution (DE) [16], and their variants, which explore the search space through the collective behavior of a set of candidate solutions.

Despite their effectiveness in global exploration, population-based metaheuristics often struggle with local exploitation, with the ability to efficiently refine a solution once a promising region has been identified [15]. This limitation has motivated the development of hybrid approaches that combine the global search capabilities of metaheuristics with the local refinement of other optimization methods. Several studies have investigated such hybridizations, combining evolutionary algorithms with gradient-free local search procedures to accelerate convergence [3,4,17]. However, most of these approaches apply local search only at the end of the evolutionary process, limiting the ability of the refined solution to influence subsequent population dynamics.

A promising direction is to integrate local search periodically during the evolutionary process, allowing the improved solution to propagate through the population and benefit the global search. Powell's conjugate-direction method [14] is a natural candidate for this integration because it performs efficient local optimization without requiring gradient computation and guarantees convergence to the global minimum for quadratic objective functions [6].

In this paper, C-DEEPSO-Powell is proposed, a hybrid algorithm that combines C-DEEPSO (Canonical Differential Evolutionary Particle Swarm Optimization) [11] with the modified Powell's method [1]. The main contributions of this work are:

- A hybrid algorithm that integrates the global search of C-DEEPSO with the local refinement of Powell's method through a periodic transfer strategy;
- A milestone-based activation schedule with proportional evaluation budget allocation, ensuring effective local refinement at multiple stages of the optimization process;
- An extensive experimental evaluation on the CEC'2013 LSGO benchmark suite [9] ($D = 1000$), in which C-DEEPSO-Powell outperformed standalone C-DEEPSO in 14 out of 15 functions.

The remainder of this paper is organized as follows. Section 2 reviews related works on hybrid metaheuristics and Powell's method. Section 3 provides the necessary background on C-DEEPSO and Powell's method. Section 4 presents the proposed C-DEEPSO-Powell algorithm. Section 5 describes the experimental evaluation and discusses the results. Finally, Sect. 6 concludes the paper and outlines future work.

2 Related Works

This section reviews existing approaches that are most relevant to the proposed hybridization. The reviewed works are organized into two categories: hybrid algorithms incorporating Powell's method and recent developments in large-scale optimization with metaheuristics.

2.1 Powell's Method in Evolutionary Algorithms

Several works have explored the integration of Powell's method with population-based metaheuristics. Beck and Gomes [3] proposed a hybrid combining PSO with a modified Powell's method for global optimization. In their approach, PSO performs the global search until the particles converge sufficiently around a promising region, at which point a transition to Powell's method is triggered based on a distance criterion relative to the population's center of gravity. The hybrid was tested on benchmark functions with 2 to 6 dimensions and at most 10 local minima, outperforming simulated annealing and ant colony variants in 9 out of 10 comparisons. However, the approach was limited to low-dimensional problems and the transition mechanism does not allow the refined solution to benefit subsequent PSO iterations.

Bento et al. [4] conducted experiments combining Powell's method with both a Genetic Algorithm (GA) and PSO. Unlike the previous work, both metaheuristics were allowed to complete their execution according to their own stopping criteria before passing the best solution to Powell's method for final refinement. Their results showed that the GA with Powell's method achieved higher convergence rates with fewer function evaluations compared to the PSO variant. Nevertheless, this strategy treats local search as a post-processing step, and the refined solution cannot influence the evolutionary dynamics.

Tunay and Abiyev [17] proposed a different strategy by incorporating Powell's method directly into the GA loop. In their Genetic Algorithm with Local Search Procedure (GALSP), Powell's method is applied twice per generation: once after fitness evaluation and once after mutation. This periodic activation allows the population to benefit from locally optimized individuals at each generation. The results demonstrated improvements in both mean and best fitness values compared to the standard GA. The present work builds on this periodic activation concept, extending it to the C-DEEPSO framework with a milestone-based scheduling strategy.

2.2 Large-Scale Optimization with Metaheuristics

Large-scale global optimization has been an active research area, with benchmark competitions such as CEC'2013 [9] driving the development of specialized algorithms. Liu et al. [10] presented a comprehensive review and comparative study of evolutionary optimization methods for large-scale problems, highlighting that cooperative coevolution and hybrid strategies are among the most effective approaches. The C-DEEPSO algorithm [11,12], which combines characteristics of PSO and DE with self-adaptive parameter mutation, has shown competitive performance in power systems optimization. Avancini [2] demonstrated that optimized hyperparameters significantly improve C-DEEPSO performance, a finding that informed the experimental design of the present work.

In summary, while previous works have demonstrated the potential of combining Powell's method with metaheuristics, they share common limitations: the hybridization is restricted to low-dimensional problems [3], local search is applied only as a post-processing step [4], or the evaluation is limited to simple benchmark functions [17]. Unlike these approaches, C-DEEPSO-Powell addresses large-scale problems ($D = 1000$), employs a periodic activation strategy with proportional budget allocation, and is evaluated on the standardized CEC'2013 LSGO benchmark suite with statistical significance testing.

3 Background

This section introduces the two algorithmic components that form the basis of the proposed hybrid: the C-DEEPSO algorithm for global search and Powell's conjugate-direction method for local refinement.

3.1 C-DEEPSO

The Canonical Differential Evolutionary Particle Swarm Optimization (C-DEEPSO) [11] is a population-based metaheuristic that combines characteristics of PSO and Differential Evolution (DE) with self-adaptive parameter control. It maintains a population of N_p particles, each represented by a position vector $X_t \in \mathbb{R}^D$ and a velocity vector $V_t \in \mathbb{R}^D$.

The velocity update rule in C-DEEPSO incorporates inertia, assimilation (cognitive), and communication (social) components:

$$V_t = w_T^* \cdot V_{t-1} + w_A^* \cdot (X_{st} - X_{t-1}) + w_C^* \cdot B \cdot (X_{gb}^* - X_{t-1}) \tag{1}$$

where w_T^*, w_A^*, and w_C^* are the mutated inertia, assimilation, and communication weights, respectively; X_{st} is a strategic vector computed using the DE/current-to-best/1/bin strategy; X_{gb}^* is the mutated global best; and B is a diagonal binary communication matrix that stochastically controls the social influence on each dimension. Each diagonal element of B is independently set to 1 with probability P (the communication rate reported in Table 2) and to 0 otherwise. Throughout this paper, subscripts denote either an iteration index (e.g., X_t, V_{t-1}) or a descriptive role (e.g., X_{gb} for the global best, X_{st} for the strategic vector); the intended meaning is clear from the context.

The strategic vector X_{st} is computed as:

$$X_{st} = X_r + F \cdot (X_{best} - X_r) + F \cdot (X_{r_1} - X_{r_2}) \tag{2}$$

where X_r is a reference vector sampled using the *SgPb-rnd* strategy (a combination of same-generation and past-best sampling [12]), X_{best} is the particle's personal best, F is the differential weight, and X_{r_1}, X_{r_2} are randomly selected vectors.

The strategic weights are self-adapted through mutation at each generation:

$$w_k^* = w_k + \tau \cdot \mathcal{N}(0,1), \quad k \in \{T, A, C\} \tag{3}$$

where τ is the mutation rate and $\mathcal{N}(0,1)$ is a standard normal random variable. Similarly, the global best is mutated as:

$$X_{gb}^* = X_{gb} \cdot (1 + \tau' \cdot \mathcal{N}(0,1)) \tag{4}$$

where τ' is a learning parameter. This self-adaptation mechanism allows C-DEEPSO to dynamically adjust its exploration-exploitation balance throughout the optimization process [13].

3.2 Powell's Method

Powell's method [14] is a derivative-free optimization algorithm that finds the minimum of a function through successive line minimizations along a set of conjugate directions. Starting from an initial point P_0 and a set of N direction vectors $\{u_0, \ldots, u_{N-1}\}$, typically initialized as the standard basis vectors, the algorithm performs line minimization along each direction sequentially, updating the directions at the end of each iteration to maintain conjugacy.

For quadratic objective functions of the form $f(x) = \frac{1}{2}x^T Ax + b^T x + c$, the method generates mutually conjugate directions and converges to the global minimum in at most N iterations [6]. Two vectors u and v are conjugate with respect to a symmetric matrix A if $u^T Av = 0$.

The basic Powell's method can suffer from linear dependence of directions in high-dimensional spaces. To address this, the modified variant proposed by Acton [1] is employed, which replaces the direction that yielded the largest decrease rather than the oldest one. This heuristic prevents the direction set from collapsing into a lower-dimensional subspace. The replacement is governed by two conditions based on the fitness values at the iteration's start (f_1), end (f_2), and an extrapolated point (f_3):

$$f_3 \geq f_1 \tag{5}$$

$$2(f_1 - 2f_2 + f_3)[(f_1 - f_2) - \Delta]^2 \geq \Delta(f_1 - f_3)^2 \tag{6}$$

where Δ is the largest decrease in any single direction during that iteration. If either condition is satisfied, the current direction set is retained for the next iteration [15].

Line minimization within Powell's method is performed using the golden section search [8], which iteratively narrows the interval containing the minimum by evaluating function values at points determined by the golden ratio ($w \approx 0.38197$), until a user-specified tolerance is reached.

4 Proposed Approach: C-DEEPSO-Powell

This section presents C-DEEPSO-Powell, a hybrid optimization algorithm that integrates the global search capabilities of C-DEEPSO with the local refinement provided by Powell's conjugate direction method. The motivation behind this hybridization is that C-DEEPSO is effective at exploring the search space globally, but it can struggle to efficiently exploit promising regions once a near-optimal area has been identified. Conversely, Powell's method excels at local refinement through successive line minimizations along conjugate directions, but its performance is highly dependent on the quality of the initial point. By combining both strategies, C-DEEPSO-Powell leverages the strengths of each component: C-DEEPSO identifies promising regions, and Powell's method refines the best solution found within those regions.

Figure 1 illustrates the overall pipeline of the proposed approach. The algorithm operates in three main stages: (i) C-DEEPSO performs the global search over the population; (ii) at a predefined checkpoint, the current global best X_{gb} is transferred to Powell's method for local refinement using a limited budget of function evaluations; and (iii) the refined solution is returned to the population as the updated global best, and C-DEEPSO resumes its execution. This transfer-and-return mechanism is applied multiple times throughout the optimization process.

4.1 Hybridization Strategy

The hybridization between C-DEEPSO and Powell's method follows a periodic transfer strategy. Rather than invoking Powell's method only at the end of the optimization process, as proposed in previous works [3,4], C-DEEPSO-Powell activates the local search at the midpoint of predefined evaluation milestones. This design choice is motivated by two observations. First, invoking Powell's method only at the final stage does not allow the improved solution to influence the remaining swarm dynamics. Second, by the midpoint of each milestone, C-DEEPSO has typically guided the global best toward a promising region, providing Powell's method with a high-quality starting point.

The CEC'2013 benchmark suite defines three evaluation milestones: 1.2×10^5, 6.0×10^5, and 3.0×10^6 function evaluations. Accordingly, Powell's method is activated at the midpoint of each milestone interval, with a proportional allocation of function evaluations, as described in Table 1.

Table 1. Powell's method activation schedule within C-DEEPSO-Powell.

Milestone	Powell Evaluations	Activation Point
1.2×10^5	1.2×10^4	6.0×10^4
6.0×10^5	6.0×10^4	3.6×10^5
3.0×10^6	2.28×10^5	1.8×10^6

At each activation point, the current global best X_{gb} is passed to the modified Powell's method (Sect. 3.2) as the initial point. Powell's method then performs line minimizations along conjugate directions using the golden section search, consuming only the allocated evaluation budget. Upon completion, the refined solution replaces X_{gb} if an improvement has been achieved, and the C-DEEPSO population continues its evolution, benefiting from a locally optimized leader that influences the swarm through the social component of the velocity equation.

The total number of function evaluations allocated to Powell's method in all three milestones is 3.0×10^5, which corresponds to 10% of the total budget of 3.0×10^6 evaluations. This allocation ensures that local search does not consume an excessive portion of the computational budget while still providing meaningful refinement at each stage.

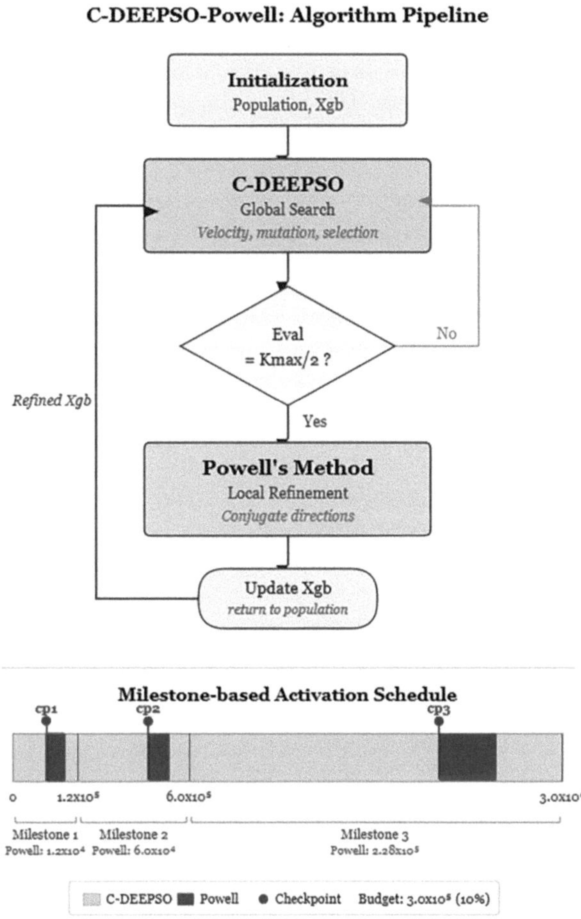

Fig. 1. Overview of the C-DEEPSO-Powell algorithm. Top: flowchart showing the periodic transfer of X_{gb} between C-DEEPSO and Powell's method. Bottom: activation schedule across the three CEC'2013 evaluation milestones, with proportional budget allocation.

4.2 Design Rationale

Several design decisions in C-DEEPSO-Powell deserve an explanation.

Why Powell's Method as the Local Search? Powell's method was chosen for three reasons. First, it does not require gradient computation, which is consistent with the derivative-free nature of the overall approach. Second, it guarantees convergence to the global minimum for quadratic objective functions in a finite number of iterations [6,14], making it particularly effective for the subset of CEC'2013 functions that are smooth and well-conditioned. Third, its line minimization strategy along the conjugate directions provides a structured search pattern that complements the stochastic exploration of C-DEEPSO.

Why Activate at the Midpoint Rather than at the End? Previous hybridizations [3,4] applied the local search only after the metaheuristic completed its execution, treating it as a post-processing step. In contrast, the midpoint activation strategy adopted here allows the improved global best to propagate through the swarm in subsequent generations. This is similar to the approach of Tunay and Abiyev [17], who demonstrated that periodic local refinement during evolution accelerates convergence.

4.3 Algorithm

Algorithm 1 presents the pseudocode of C-DEEPSO-Powell. The algorithm follows the standard C-DEEPSO procedure with the addition of conditional Powell activations (lines 15–17).

Algorithm 1 C-DEEPSO-Powell

Require: N_p, τ, P, MB, D, $Eval_{\max}$, checkpoints $\{cp_1, cp_2, cp_3\}$, budgets $\{b_1, b_2, b_3\}$
Ensure: Best solution X_{gb}
1: Initialize $\mathcal{P} = \{X_1, \ldots, X_{N_p}\}$ uniformly in $[X_{\min}, X_{\max}]$
2: Evaluate $\mathcal{P}$; $X_{gb} \leftarrow \arg\min_{X_i \in \mathcal{P}} f(X_i)$
3: $Eval \leftarrow N_p$; $k \leftarrow 0$
4: **while** $Eval < Eval_{\max}$ **do**
5:   **for** each particle i in $\mathcal{P}$ **do**
6:     Compute X_r using *SgPb-rnd* strategy
7:     Mutate w_T^*, w_A^*, w_C^* via Eq. (3)
8:     Mutate X_{gb}^* via Eq. (4)
9:     Compute V_t via Eq. (1)
10:     $X_t \leftarrow X_{t-1} + V_t$
11:     Evaluate $f(X_t)$; $Eval \leftarrow Eval + 1$
12:     Select fittest between X_t and X_{t-1}
13:   **end for**
14:   **if** $Eval \geq cp_{k+1}$ **and** Powell not yet applied at cp_{k+1} **then**
15:     $X_{gb} \leftarrow \text{ModifiedPowell}(f, X_{gb}, b_{k+1})$
16:     $Eval \leftarrow Eval + b_{k+1}$; $k \leftarrow k + 1$
17:   **end if**
18:   Update X_{gb} and memory MB
19: **end while**
20: **return** X_{gb}

The ModifiedPowell procedure in line 16 follows the variant described in Sect. 3.2, which replaces the direction yielding the largest decrease to avoid linear dependence in high-dimensional spaces [1,15]. In summary, C-DEEPSO-Powell extends C-DEEPSO by periodically transferring the global best to Powell's method for local refinement, combining broad swarm exploration with the precise convergence properties of conjugate direction methods.

5 Experiments and Results

This section presents the experimental evaluation of C-DEEPSO-Powell on the CEC'2013 benchmark suite for large-scale global optimization. The experiments aim to answer three research questions: (RQ1) Does the inclusion of Powell's method improve C-DEEPSO's performance? (RQ2) For which types of functions is the hybrid most effective? (RQ3) How does local refinement behave across different evaluation milestones?

5.1 Experimental Setup

Benchmark Suite. The CEC'2013 LSGO benchmark suite [9] comprises 15 minimization functions with $D = 1000$ decision variables, organized into five categories: fully separable (f_1–f_3), partially separable with 7 non-separable groups (f_4–f_7), partially separable with 20 non-separable groups (f_8–f_{11}), overlapping (f_{12}–f_{14}), and fully non-separable (f_{15}). All functions operate in $[-100, 100]^D$ and include transformations (shifts, rotations, distortions) that increase difficulty. Functions f_{13} and f_{14} have a reduced effective dimension of $D = 905$ due to overlapping subcomponents.

Hyperparameter Tuning. The C-DEEPSO hyperparameters were optimized using a Genetic Algorithm (GA) with tournament selection (size 3), crossover ($\alpha = 0.5$), and Gaussian mutation ($p = 0.2$, $\sigma = 0.2$). The GA was executed on the base functions (Elliptic, Rastrigin, Ackley, Rosenbrock, Schwefel) in $D = 100$, with a budget of 10^5 evaluations per run. The optimized parameters are presented in Table 2. Each CEC'2013 function inherited the hyperparameters from its corresponding base function.

Table 2. Optimized C-DEEPSO hyperparameters per base function.

Base Function	w_T	w_A	w_C	P	τ
Elliptic	0.437	0.769	0.809	0.901	0.803
Rastrigin	0.522	0.770	0.565	0.797	0.827
Ackley	0.513	0.670	0.205	0.696	0.368
Rosenbrock	0.402	0.379	0.754	0.582	0.304
Schwefel	0.503	0.455	0.093	0.582	0.339

Baseline and Implementation. The baseline is the C-DEEPSO algorithm without Powell's method, executed under identical conditions (same hyperparameters, population size, and evaluation budget). Both algorithms use the *SgPb-rnd* sampling strategy. This controlled comparison isolates the effect of the local search component. Both algorithms were implemented in Python 3.12.1 and executed on a machine with an AMD Ryzen 5 3600 processor and 32 GB RAM. Each function was run 25 times per algorithm, with a maximum budget of 3.0×10^6 evaluations, as specified by the CEC'2013 protocol. Common parameters: population size $N_p = 500$, memory size $MB = 50$, dimension $D = 1000$ ($D = 905$ for f_{13}, f_{14}). The Powell activation schedule follows Table 1. Following the CEC'2013 protocol, computational cost is measured by the number of function evaluations rather than wall-clock time; since both algorithms operate under the same budget of 3.0×10^6 evaluations—including the 10% allocated to Powell's refinement—the comparison accounts for the full cost of the local search component. Stochastic variability is accounted for by averaging over 25 independent runs.

5.2 Results

Table 3 presents the final comparison at 3.0×10^6 evaluations, reporting the mean, median, and standard deviation over 25 independent runs. C-DEEPSO-Powell achieved equal or better mean fitness in all 15 functions.

Table 3. Comparison at 3.0×10^6 evaluations for functions f_1–f_{15}. Bold indicates the better mean. Results averaged over 25 runs.

Func.	C-DEEPSO			C-DEEPSO-Powell		
	Mean	Median	Std	Mean	Median	Std
f_1	7.52E+10	7.50E+10	6.26E+09	**1.63E-02**	1.63E-02	2.97E-04
f_2	4.14E+04	4.11E+04	1.46E+03	**2.46E+03**	2.46E+03	4.55E-13
f_3	2.16E+01	2.16E+01	1.06E-02	**2.00E+01**	2.00E+01	1.72E-06
f_4	1.48E+12	1.57E+12	3.18E+11	**3.11E+11**	3.23E+11	9.44E+10
f_5	2.29E+07	2.30E+07	3.25E+06	**1.48E+07**	1.48E+07	1.66E+06
f_6	1.06E+06	1.06E+06	2.81E+03	**1.06E+06**	1.06E+06	1.57E+03
f_7	5.04E+10	3.84E+10	3.09E+10	**1.90E+09**	1.75E+09	9.46E+08
f_8	2.37E+16	2.10E+16	8.87E+15	**1.80E+16**	1.50E+16	9.11E+15
f_9	1.83E+09	1.78E+09	2.13E+08	**1.10E+09**	1.05E+09	1.50E+08
f_{10}	9.47E+07	9.47E+07	3.72E+05	**9.43E+07**	9.44E+07	3.76E+05
f_{11}	1.20E+13	1.10E+13	4.34E+12	**1.64E+11**	1.46E+11	6.06E+10
f_{12}	9.35E+11	9.33E+11	5.93E+10	**2.57E+03**	2.57E+03	2.33E+02
f_{13}	4.14E+12	3.76E+12	2.09E+12	**1.49E+10**	1.38E+10	3.06E+09
f_{14}	9.83E+12	9.31E+12	2.30E+12	**3.09E+11**	3.17E+11	8.27E+10
f_{15}	6.89E+13	6.31E+13	2.46E+13	**5.52E+09**	5.76E+09	2.18E+09

The most dramatic improvements occurred in functions most amenable to conjugate-direction refinement: the quadratic function f_1 (from 10^{10} to 10^{-2}), the overlapping Rosenbrock function f_{12} (from 10^{11} to 10^3), f_{15} (from 10^{13} to 10^9), f_{11} (from 10^{13} to 10^{11}), and f_{13} (from 10^{12} to 10^{10}).

Statistical Significance. For the nine remaining functions, C-DEEPSO-Powell improves the mean fitness by several orders of magnitude (Table 3), so the difference is evident without a formal test. The two-sample Student's t-test ($\alpha = 0.05$) was therefore applied only to the six functions where the difference between the two algorithms was small. Table 4 presents the results.

Table 4. Student's t-test results ($\alpha = 0.05$) for functions with less pronounced differences.

Function	p-value	Decision	Winner
f_3	< 0.001	Reject H_0	C-DEEPSO-Powell
f_5	< 0.001	Reject H_0	C-DEEPSO-Powell
f_6	0.292	Fail to reject H_0	No significant diff.
f_8	0.033	Reject H_0	C-DEEPSO-Powell
f_9	< 0.001	Reject H_0	C-DEEPSO-Powell
f_{10}	0.002	Reject H_0	C-DEEPSO-Powell

The null hypothesis of equal means was rejected for all tested functions except f_6 (Shifted and Rotated Ackley). For the nine functions not subjected to the test, the difference in mean fitness spans several orders of magnitude (Table 3), making the improvement evident without formal testing. Overall, C-DEEPSO-Powell improves upon standalone C-DEEPSO in 14 out of 15 functions.

5.3 Convergence Analysis

The convergence analysis reveals distinct behaviors depending on the function characteristics, as illustrated in Fig. 2.

Functions Amenable to Local Refinement (f_1, f_{12}, f_{15}). These exhibited the most dramatic improvements. In f_1, a sharp drop in fitness occurred at the second milestone checkpoint (3.6×10^5 evaluations), where the mean fitness decreased from 10^{11} to 10^{-2}. This is consistent with the theoretical properties of Powell's method, which guarantees convergence for quadratic functions [6]. Function f_{12} (Rosenbrock) showed progressive improvement across all three milestones, indicating that Powell's method continued finding better solutions at each activation.

Partially Separable Functions (f_4, f_9, f_{10}). These showed moderate but consistent improvements. Powell's method contributed incremental refinements at each checkpoint, though the gains were less pronounced than in the quadratic case.

The rotated and partially separable structure creates a more irregular landscape that is less amenable to line minimization along conjugate directions.

Functions with Marginal Improvement (f_6). For f_6 (Shifted and Rotated Ackley), the convergence curves of both algorithms are nearly identical. Although small improvements were observed at each Powell checkpoint, they were not statistically significant ($p = 0.292$). The highly multimodal and non-separable nature of this function limits the effectiveness of Powell's line minimization strategy.

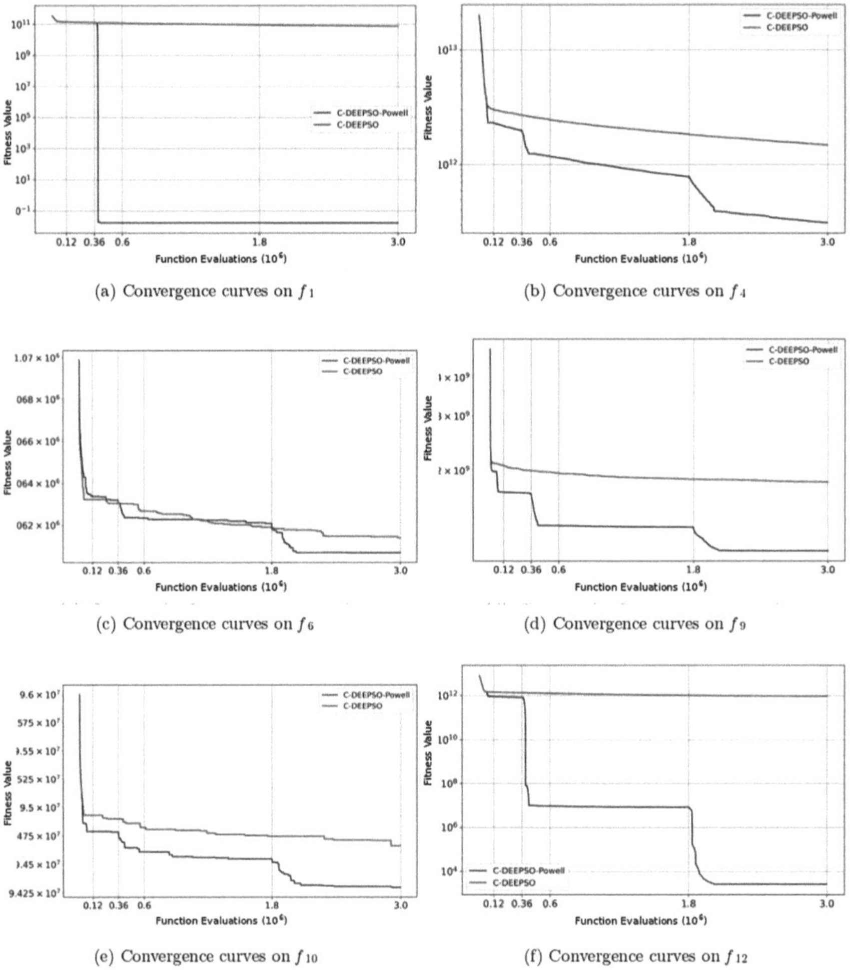

(a) Convergence curves on f_1

(b) Convergence curves on f_4

(c) Convergence curves on f_6

(d) Convergence curves on f_9

(e) Convergence curves on f_{10}

(f) Convergence curves on f_{12}

Fig. 2. Mean convergence curves over 25 runs for selected functions comparing C-DEEPSO and C-DEEPSO-Powell. (a) f_1: dramatic improvement at the second milestone. (b) f_4: moderate improvement. (c) f_6: no significant difference. (d) f_9: moderate improvement. (e) f_{10}: subtle improvement. (f) f_{12}: progressive improvement across all milestones.

5.4 Discussion

Impact Across Milestones. At the first milestone (1.2×10^5), Powell's method had negligible impact, as its budget of 1.2×10^4 evaluations is insufficient to complete a full cycle of line minimizations across $D = 1000$ dimensions. Substantial improvements emerged at the second milestone (notably f_1 and f_{12}), while the final milestone yielded diminishing returns, suggesting that Powell's method had already reached a local minimum.

Why Smooth, Well-conditioned Functions Benefit Most. Powell [14] proved that his method converges to the global minimum of a quadratic function of n variables in at most n iterations. This finite-convergence guarantee applies strictly to quadratic landscapes (e.g., f_1); other functions such as the overlapping Rosenbrock f_{12} benefit because they are smooth and unimodal along the refined directions, even though they are not quadratic. For such landscapes, line minimization steps are large and well-directed, enabling rapid convergence. In contrast, for highly multimodal or ill-conditioned functions (f_3, f_6, f_8), the irregular landscape causes smaller, less effective steps, requiring substantially more iterations to achieve meaningful improvement.

Limitations. Three limitations should be noted. First, the comparison uses standalone C-DEEPSO as the sole baseline. This is a deliberate choice: the goal of this work is to isolate the contribution of the Powell refinement component (with versus without) under identical conditions, rather than to establish an absolute ranking against specialized LSGO solvers such as MOS, MA-SW-Chains, or SHADE-ILS. A broader comparison against these state-of-the-art methods is an important direction for future work. Second, hyperparameter optimization was performed on the base functions in $D = 100$ rather than on the full $D = 1000$ benchmark, which may result in suboptimal configurations. Third, the statistical analysis relied on the Student's t-test, which assumes approximate normality, an assumption difficult to sustain for fitness values spanning many orders of magnitude. A paired non-parametric test (e.g., the Wilcoxon signed-rank test) applied across all 15 functions would provide a more robust confirmation and is left for future work. Finally, consistent with the no-free-lunch theorems, these results characterize the behavior of the hybrid on the CEC'2013 suite and are not claimed to generalize universally.

6 Conclusion

This paper presented C-DEEPSO-Powell, a hybrid optimization algorithm that combines the global search capabilities of C-DEEPSO with the local refinement of Powell's conjugate-direction method. The hybridization employs a periodic transfer strategy with proportional budget allocation across three evaluation milestones, allowing the refined global best to propagate through the swarm at multiple stages of the optimization process.

Experimental results on the CEC'2013 large-scale benchmark suite demonstrate that C-DEEPSO-Powell outperformed standalone C-DEEPSO in 14 out of 15 functions. For the six functions with less pronounced differences, a Student's t-test ($\alpha = 0.05$) confirmed statistical significance in five, with f_6 (Shifted and Rotated Ackley) the only exception; for the remaining functions, the improvement spans several orders of magnitude. The most notable gains were observed in smooth, well-conditioned functions, where mean fitness improved by up to 12 orders of magnitude (e.g., f_1: from 7.52×10^{10} to 1.63×10^{-2}; f_{12}, the overlapping Rosenbrock function: from 9.35×10^{11} to 2.57×10^{3}).

Despite the promising results, the approach has limitations: Powell's method requires a substantial number of evaluations to complete a full cycle in $D = 1000$ dimensions, and its effectiveness is reduced on ill-conditioned functions. Future work includes incorporating additional local search heuristics to complement Powell's method on non-quadratic landscapes, investigating adaptive checkpoint scheduling that dynamically adjusts the activation frequency based on convergence behavior, and evaluating the approach on real-world large-scale optimization problems. Additionally, using alternative initial points for Powell's method (e.g., random individuals instead of the global best) could help the algorithm escape local minima.

Acknowledgments. This work was partially funded by the Brazilian research agencies: FAPERJ- Fundação Carlos Chagas Filho de Amparo à Pesquisa do Estado do Rio de Janeiro (Grant Numbers E-26/200.840/2021, E-26/210.057/2024, and E-26/210.549 /2024), CNPq-National Council for Scientific and Technological Development (Grant Numbers 306258/2019-6, 403964/2023-7, and 309342/2023-6), CAPES - Coordenação de Aperfeiçoamento de Pessoal de Nível Superior (CAPES, Grant number: 23038.006308/2021-70). UFRJ ALV Grant. The authors thank UFRJ for the infrastructure used to conduct this work.

References

1. Acton, F.S.: Numerical Methods That Work. Mathematical Association of America, Washington, D.C. (1990)
2. Avancini, J.V.C.: Criação de um framework para ajuste fino de parâmetros usando testes estatísticos. Undergraduate thesis, Universidade Federal do Rio de Janeiro (2022)
3. Beck, A., Gomes, W.: Hybrid algorithms based on particle swarm optimization and the Powell method for global optimization. In: Proceedings of the Second International Conference on Soft Computing Technology in Civil, Structural and Environmental Engineering. Civil-Comp Press (2011). https://doi.org/10.4203/ccp.97.42
4. Bento, D., et al.: Genetic algorithm and particle swarm optimization combined with Powell method. In: AIP Conference Proceedings, pp. 578–581. AIP (2013). https://doi.org/10.1063/1.4825557
5. Beyer, H.-G., Schwefel, H.-P., Wegener, I.: How to analyse evolutionary algorithms. Theor. Comput. Sci. **287**(1), 101–130 (2002)

6. Brent, R.P.: Algorithms for Minimization Without Derivatives. Prentice-Hall, Englewood Cliffs (1973)
7. Kennedy, J., Eberhart, R.: Particle swarm optimization. In: Proceedings of ICNN'95, vol. 4, pp. 1942–1948. IEEE (1995)
8. Kiefer, J.: Sequential minimax search for a maximum. Proc. Am. Math. Soc. **4**(3), 502–506 (1953)
9. Li, X.: Benchmark Functions for the CEC'2013 Special Session and Competition on Large-Scale Global Optimization. Technical report (2013)
10. Liu, J., et al.: Large-scale evolutionary optimization: a review and comparative study. Swarm Evol. Comput. **85**, 101466 (2024)
11. Marcelino, C.G.: Fundamentals of the C-DEEPSO algorithm and its application to the reactive power optimization of wind farms. In: 2016 IEEE Congress on Evolutionary Computation (CEC), pp.1547–1554. IEEE (2016)
12. Marcelino, C.G.: Uma Abordagem Evolutiva e Híbrida Para a Solução de Problemas de Fluxo de Potência Ótimo. Ph.D. thesis, CEFET-MG (2017)
13. Miranda, V., Fonseca, N.: EPSO - best-of-two-worlds meta-heuristic applied to power system problems. In: Proceedings of the 2002 Congress on Evolutionary Computation, vol. 2, pp. 1080–1085. IEEE (2002)
14. Powell, M.J.D.: An efficient method for finding the minimum of a function of several variables without calculating derivatives. Comput. J. **7**(2), 155–162 (1964)
15. Press, W.H.: Numerical Recipes: The Art of Scientific Computing, 3rd edn. Cambridge University Press, Cambridge (2007)
16. Storn, R., Price, K.: Differential evolution - a simple and efficient adaptive scheme for global optimization over continuous spaces. J. Glob. Optim. **23**, 341–359 (1995)
17. Tunay, M., Abiyev, R.H.: Hybrid local search based genetic algorithm and its practical application. Int. J. Soft Comput. Eng. **5**(2) (2015)

Credit Assignment in Reinforcement Learning with Group Relative Policy Optimization

Augusto Antônio Fontanive Leal(✉) and Gabriel de Oliveira Ramos

Universidade do Vale do Rio dos Sinos, São Leopoldo, Brazil
aaleal@edu.unisinos.br, gdoramos@unisinos.br

Abstract. Credit assignment is a key challenge in reinforcement learning, especially in environments with sparse rewards and long horizons. In this work, we adapt Group Relative Policy Optimization (GRPO) to reinforcement learning and introduce two variants based on timestep-level and episode-level advantages. We compare GRPO with traditional policy gradient methods, including Proximal Policy Optimization (PPO) and Advantage Actor-Critic (A2C), across multiple Gymnasium environments. Across the evaluated tasks, GRPO achieves competitive or superior performance. The timestep variant (GRPO-T) tends to perform best in long-horizon and navigation settings, improving performance by more than 150% in PointMaze (Medium) and enabling successful trajectory discovery in the challenging Pinball (Hard) environment, where PPO and A2C fail to reach the goal. In contrast, the episode variant (GRPO-E) is more effective in goal-conditioned settings, improving performance by up to 96% in FetchReach. These results highlight the importance of advantage construction in learning dynamics within the evaluated environments, suggesting that timestep-level credit assignment can lead to improved stability and efficiency in long-horizon sparse-reward settings.

Keywords: Reinforcement Learning · Credit Assignment · Policy Gradient Methods

1 Introduction

Reinforcement Learning (RL) enables agents to learn through interaction with an environment by optimizing behavior based on reward signals [9,16]. A central challenge in RL is credit assignment [7,15], particularly in environments with sparse or delayed rewards, where identifying the contribution of individual actions to long-term outcomes becomes difficult, especially in continuous control settings. Policy gradient methods such as Proximal Policy Optimization (PPO) [11] achieve strong performance by balancing sample efficiency and training stability, but rely on a value function estimator (critic), making them sensitive to hyperparameters and dependent on accurate reward propagation. In contrast, Group Relative Policy Optimization (GRPO) [13] removes the need for a critic

M. Recamonde-Mendoza and R. C. Barros (Eds.): BRACIS 2026, LNAI 17105, pp. 216–231, 2027.
https://doi.org/10.1007/978-3-032-39882-6_15

by estimating advantages through relative comparisons within groups of trajectories, providing an alternative mechanism for credit assignment that may yield more robust learning signals in sparse-reward settings.

In this work, we adapt GRPO to classical reinforcement learning environments and investigate its behavior under different credit assignment strategies. We consider two variants: a timestep-level formulation (GRPO-T) and an episode-level formulation (GRPO-E), which differ in how advantage signals are constructed. We evaluate these methods across a set of Gymnasium environments and compare them against PPO and Advantage Actor-Critic (A2C) under consistent experimental settings.

Our results demonstrate that GRPO performs particularly well in environments with sparse reward structures, consistently outperforming PPO and A2C in terms of learning efficiency and final performance. In FetchReach, GRPO-E achieves an improvement of over 94% compared to PPO, being the only variant to successfully learn. In PointMaze (Medium), GRPO-T improves final performance by approximately 150% over PPO, while in MountainCarContinuous it achieves a modest but consistent gain of around 1.2%, along with significantly reduced variance. In the challenging Pinball (Hard) environment, GRPO-T transforms failure into successful learning, reaching positive rewards where PPO and A2C fail to discover goal-reaching behaviors. These results suggest that the group-based baseline estimation employed by GRPO provides a robust advantage signal even when reward feedback is infrequent or highly delayed.

Our main contributions are as follows:

- We adapt GRPO to classical reinforcement learning environments, enabling its application beyond language model settings.
- We introduce and analyze two variants of GRPO based on different credit assignment strategies, timestep-level (GRPO-T) and episode-level (GRPO-E), highlighting their impact on learning dynamics.
- We provide an empirical comparison with policy gradient methods (PPO and A2C), demonstrating that GRPO achieves improved performance, stability, and sample efficiency across diverse environments.

This paper is organized into four main sections. Section 2 reviews the necessary background on policy gradient methods, including actor-critic approaches, PPO, and GRPO. Section 3 presents our adaptation of GRPO to reinforcement learning environments, introducing the proposed variants based on different credit assignment strategies and describing the overall training procedure. Section 4 evaluates the proposed methods across a set of benchmark environments, detailing the experimental setup and analyzing both qualitative and quantitative results. Finally, Sect. 5 concludes the paper with a discussion of the main findings and directions for future work.

2 Background and Notation

In this section, we first introduce the reinforcement learning problem as a Markov Decision Process and define the value, action-value, and advantage functions. We then review the main policy gradient methods considered in this work, focusing on actor-critic approaches, PPO, and GRPO.

2.1 Markov Decision Processes

We model the agent-environment interaction as a Markov Decision Process (MDP), $\mathcal{M} = (\mathcal{S}, \mathcal{A}, P, R, \gamma)$, with state space $\mathcal{S}$, action space $\mathcal{A}$, transition dynamics P, reward function R, and discount factor γ [16,18]. For a policy π, the return from timestep t is $G_t = \sum_{k=t}^{T} \gamma^{k-t} r_k$. The value function $V^\pi(s) = \mathbb{E}\pi[G_t \mid s_t = s]$ estimates the expected return from state s, while the action-value function $Q^\pi(s,a) = \mathbb{E}\pi[G_t \mid s_t = s, a_t = a]$ estimates the expected return after taking action a in state s. Their difference defines the advantage signal, which is commonly used by policy-gradient methods to assign credit to actions along a trajectory. This credit-assignment perspective motivates the distinction explored in this work between timestep-level signals, which vary over the trajectory, and episode-level signals, which assign the same outcome-based value to all actions in an episode.

2.2 Policy Gradient

Policy gradient methods provide the theoretical foundation for a broad class of reinforcement learning algorithms that directly optimize a parameterized policy [16]. Instead of estimating action values and deriving a policy from them, these methods learn a stochastic policy $\pi_\theta(a \mid s)$, parameterized by $\theta \in \mathbb{R}^{d'}$, which defines the probability of selecting action a in state s.

The objective is to maximize a performance measure $J(\theta)$ via gradient ascent [16]. The policy gradient theorem [17], with notation adapted from [1,14], provides an expression for the gradient of $J(\theta)$:

$$\nabla_\theta J(\pi_\theta) = \mathbb{E}_{s\sim\rho^\pi, a\sim\pi_\theta}\left[\nabla_\theta \log \pi_\theta(a \mid s)\, Q^\pi(s,a)\right] \quad (1)$$

where $\rho^\pi(s)$ denotes the state visitation distribution under policy π_θ, and $Q^\pi(s,a)$ is the action-value function. This formulation enables unbiased gradient estimates using sampled trajectories, forming the basis of practical algorithms.

To reduce variance, it is common to replace $Q^\pi(s,a)$ with an advantage estimate, leading to actor-critic methods such as A2C. Under appropriate compatibility conditions and learning rate schedules, policy gradient methods can be shown to converge to locally optimal policies [17].

The methods considered in this work follow this stochastic policy-gradient formulation, differing mainly in how the advantage signal is estimated and used during policy updates.

2.3 Advantage Actor-Critic (A2C)

Actor-critic methods combine policy gradient approaches with value function approximation, where the policy (actor) is updated using gradient ascent and the value function (critic) is used as a baseline to reduce variance [16].

The Advantage Actor-Critic (A2C) algorithm is a synchronous variant of the Asynchronous Advantage Actor-Critic (A3C) method [4], and is widely adopted in practice as implemented in reinforcement learning frameworks [19]. A synchronous formulation of A2C, based on coordinated gradient updates across parallel environments, is also discussed in [12].

In A3C, each actor-learner computes gradients based on n-step returns and updates shared parameters asynchronously. A2C simplifies this framework by synchronizing the updates across parallel environments, improving implementation efficiency while preserving the stability benefits of parallel data collection.

The advantage function is defined as $A(s_t, a_t) = Q(s_t, a_t) - V(s_t)$ and is estimated in A3C using n-step returns as proposed [4] and further generalized [10]:

$$A(s_t, a_t) = \sum_{i=0}^{k-1} \gamma^i r_{t+i} + \gamma^k V(s_{t+k}) - V(s_t) \tag{2}$$

Despite its efficiency, A2C relies on accurate value function estimation. In environments with sparse or delayed rewards, the critic may provide weak or noisy learning signals, which can negatively impact performance.

2.4 Proximal Policy Optimization (PPO)

PPO [11] is a policy gradient method designed to balance sample efficiency, stability, and implementation simplicity. Earlier approaches present important limitations: value-based methods such as Deep Q-Networks (DQN) [5] are designed for discrete action spaces and do not extend without modifications to continuous domains, while Vanilla Policy Gradient methods suffer from high variance and sensitivity to hyperparameters. Trust Region Policy Optimization (TRPO) [10] improves stability and performance through constrained updates but introduces significant implementation complexity and limitations when sharing parameters between policy and value networks. PPO addresses these challenges by relying on first-order optimization while introducing mechanisms to control policy updates, ensuring stable and scalable learning.

The PPO objective is based on the probability ratio between the current policy $\pi_\theta(a_t \mid s_t)$ and the previous policy $\pi_{\theta_{\text{old}}}(a_t \mid s_t)$, where θ denotes the current policy parameters and θ_{old} the parameters used to collect the trajectories:

$$r_t(\theta) = \frac{\pi_\theta(a_t \mid s_t)}{\pi_{\theta_{\text{old}}}(a_t \mid s_t)}. \tag{3}$$

Advantage estimates $\hat{A}_t$ are computed using Generalized Advantage Estimation (GAE) [10], which combines multi-step temporal-difference residuals to balance bias and variance. PPO then maximizes the clipped surrogate objective:

$$L^{\text{CLIP}}(\theta) = \hat{\mathbb{E}}_t\Big[\min\big(r_t(\theta)\hat{A}_t,\ \text{clip}(r_t(\theta), 1-\epsilon, 1+\epsilon)\hat{A}_t\big)\Big], \tag{4}$$

where $\epsilon > 0$ is a clipping hyperparameter that restricts the probability ratio to the interval $[1-\epsilon, 1+\epsilon]$. This formulation constrains the policy update by limiting the deviation of $r_t(\theta)$ from 1, preventing excessively large changes in the policy.

In addition to the clipped surrogate objective, PPO can also be formulated using a Kullback-Leibler (KL) divergence penalty between the current and previous policies. In this variant, the objective includes a penalty term that constrains policy updates by limiting the divergence between successive policies, providing an alternative mechanism to the clipping approach.

2.5 Group Relative Policy Optimization (GRPO)

GRPO [13] is a policy gradient method designed to reduce memory and computational requirements compared to PPO. Unlike PPO, GRPO does not rely on a learned value function (critic) as a baseline, replacing it with a group-based normalization of rewards computed over multiple sampled trajectories.

GRPO was originally proposed in settings with relative reward signals, such as language models, where feedback is obtained by comparing multiple outputs for the same input.

For each input $q \sim P(Q)$, GRPO samples a group of outputs $\{o_1, \ldots, o_G\}$ from the previous policy $\pi_{\theta_{\text{old}}}$, where G denotes the group size.

$$J_{\text{GRPO}}(\theta) = \mathbb{E}_{[q \sim P(Q), \{o_i\}_{i=1}^{G} \sim \pi_{\theta_{\text{old}}}(O|q)]}$$
$$\frac{1}{G}\sum_{i=1}^{G}\frac{1}{|o_i|}\sum_{t=1}^{|o_i|}\Bigg\{\min\Bigg[\frac{\pi_\theta(o_{i,t} \mid q, o_{i,<t})}{\pi_{\theta_{\text{old}}}(o_{i,t} \mid q, o_{i,<t})}\hat{A}_{i,t},$$
$$\text{clip}\Big(\frac{\pi_\theta(o_{i,t} \mid q, o_{i,<t})}{\pi_{\theta_{\text{old}}}(o_{i,t} \mid q, o_{i,<t})}, 1-\epsilon, 1+\epsilon\Big)\hat{A}_{i,t}\Bigg] \quad - \beta D_{\text{KL}}(\pi_\theta \,\|\, \pi_{\text{ref}})\Bigg\}. \tag{5}$$

This objective extends the PPO clipped surrogate formulation to a group setting, where $q \sim P(Q)$ denotes inputs sampled from a data distribution and $\{o_i\}_{i=1}^{G}$ are G outputs sampled from the previous policy $\pi_{\theta_{\text{old}}}$. Each output o_i is a sequence of tokens with length $|o_i|$, where $o_{i,t}$ denotes the token at timestep t and $o_{i,<t}$ its prefix. The objective averages over both sampled outputs and their tokens through a hierarchical normalization given by $\frac{1}{G}\sum_{i=1}^{G}\frac{1}{|o_i|}\sum_{t=1}^{|o_i|}$. The probability ratio is defined as $r_{i,t} = \frac{\pi_\theta(o_{i,t}|q,o_{i,<t})}{\pi_{\theta_{\text{old}}}(o_{i,t}|q,o_{i,<t})}$, and $\hat{A}_{i,t}$ denotes the advantage computed from group-normalized rewards. The $\min(\cdot)$ operator corresponds to the clipped surrogate objective inherited from PPO, which constrains policy updates by limiting the deviation of the probability ratio, while the term $\beta D_{\text{KL}}(\pi_\theta \,\|\, \pi_{\text{ref}})$ introduces an additional regularization that penalizes divergence from a reference policy independently of the token-level updates. Finally, $\epsilon > 0$ is the clipping hyperparameter, $\beta > 0$ controls the KL regularization strength, and π_{ref} is a reference policy used to constrain the deviation of the learned policy from a stable reference distribution.

In practice, GRPO can operate under different reward supervision schemes. In outcome supervision, each output o_i receives a scalar reward r_i, which is normalized within the sampled group as $\hat{A}^{\text{out}}_{i,t} = \frac{r_i - \text{mean}(\mathbf{r})}{\text{std}(\mathbf{r})}$ and assigned uniformly to all tokens of the output. In process supervision, intermediate rewards are assigned to reasoning steps, normalized as $\tilde{r}^j_i = \frac{r^j_i - \text{mean}(\mathbf{R})}{\text{std}(\mathbf{R})}$, and the advantage of each token is computed as the sum of the normalized rewards from the following steps, $\hat{A}^{\text{proc}}_{i,t} = \sum_{\text{index}(j) \geq t} \tilde{r}^j_i$. These formulations define the advantage estimates used in Eq. 5. Unlike A2C and PPO, which rely on a learned value function, GRPO replaces the critic with group-based reward normalization.

3 GRPO with Timestep and Episode-Level Credit Assignment

The original GRPO formulation was developed for language models, where interactions are sequential and rewards are typically provided at the end of the generated output. In contrast, reinforcement learning environments such as Gymnasium operate with continuous state transitions and per-timestep rewards. To bridge this gap, we reinterpret GRPO outputs as complete environment trajectories and define advantage estimation over full episodes, while preserving the principle of process-based decision making [13].

In this setting, policy updates are performed using batches of full episodes. At each training iteration, the agent collects N independent trajectories containing state-action pairs $(s_{i,t}, a_{i,t})$, rewards $r_{i,t}$, and corresponding log-probabilities $\log \pi_{\theta_{\text{old}}}(a_{i,t} \mid s_{i,t})$, which are used to construct advantage estimates and update the policy. Here, N plays the role of the group size in the reinforcement learning setting, analogous to G in Eq. 5. While G denotes multiple outputs sampled for a given prompt in the original GRPO formulation, N denotes complete environment episodes sampled for a policy update.

A key aspect of this adaptation lies in how credit is assigned to actions over time. The motivation for the proposed variants is that the granularity of the advantage signal determines how delayed rewards are distributed across actions: timestep-level advantages provide finer temporal credit assignment, while episode-level advantages preserve the original outcome-based structure of GRPO. To investigate this distinction, we consider two variants: GRPO with timestep advantages (GRPO-T) and GRPO with episode-level advantages (GRPO-E). The following subsections describe these variants in detail.

3.1 GRPO with Timestep Advantages (GRPO-T)

In the GRPO-T variant, the process supervision procedure is adapted to operate over full episodes, enabling credit assignment at the level of individual timesteps. At each iteration, the agent collects a batch of N episodes. For episode $i \in \{1, \ldots, N\}$ with length T_i, we denote the state, action, and reward at timestep t by $s_{i,t}$, $a_{i,t}$, and $r_{i,t}$, respectively.

We define the cumulative future reward from timestep t onward, denoted by $G_{i,t}$, as $G_{i,t} = \sum_{k=t}^{T_i} r_{i,k}$, which represents the total reward obtained after timestep t. We further define the total return of episode i, denoted by R_i, as $R_i = \sum_{t=1}^{T_i} r_{i,t}$.

A group-level baseline, denoted by b, is computed as the average return across episodes: $b = \frac{1}{N}\sum_{i=1}^{N} R_i$, where N denotes the number of episodes in the batch. The timestep advantage, denoted by $A_{i,t}$, is then defined as $A_{i,t} = G_{i,t} - b$.

Finally, advantages are normalized within the batch. This formulation enables timestep-level credit assignment, where each action is evaluated based on its contribution to future rewards, providing more precise learning signals along the trajectory. In this sense, it is analogous to the process supervision strategy [13].

3.2 GRPO with Episode-Level Advantages (GRPO-E)

In contrast, the GRPO-E variant assigns credit at the level of entire episodes by aggregating all rewards into a single scalar return. For each episode i with length T_i, the reward at timestep t is denoted by $r_{i,t}$, and the total return is computed as $R_i = \sum_{t=1}^{T_i} r_{i,t}$. The same group-level baseline is used: $b = \frac{1}{N}\sum_{i=1}^{N} R_i$. The advantage is then uniformly assigned to all timesteps of the episode: $A_{i,t} = R_i - b$.

This formulation corresponds to an episode-level credit assignment strategy, analogous to outcome supervision [13]. In this case, all actions in the episode receive the same learning signal based on the final outcome, simplifying the optimization process at the cost of reduced temporal credit resolution.

The two variants differ in how the advantage signal is constructed, resulting in distinct credit assignment behaviors. In GRPO-T, advantages are computed at each timestep based on future returns, enabling temporally localized credit assignment, while in GRPO-E a single episode-level signal is assigned uniformly across all timesteps.

3.3 Training Procedure

The complete training procedure for both GRPO-T and GRPO-E is summarized in Algorithm 1, which describes how batches of full episodes are collected, how a group-level baseline is computed, and how advantage signals are constructed to guide policy updates.

Algorithm 1: GRPO-T and GRPO-E for full-episode batches

Input: Initial policy $\pi_{\theta_{\text{init}}}$, environment $\mathcal{E}$, batch size N, hyperparameters ε, β, μ

Output: Trained policy π_θ

Initialize policy $\pi_\theta \leftarrow \pi_{\theta_{\text{init}}}$

for *iteration* $= 1, 2, \ldots$ **do**

  Collect N episodes $\{\tau_i\}_{i=1}^N$

  Compute $R_i = \sum_{t=1}^{T_i} r_{i,t}$ for all i

  Compute baseline $b = \frac{1}{N}\sum_{i=1}^N R_i$

  foreach *episode* i **do**

    if *GRPO-T* **then**

      Compute $G_{i,t}$ and $A_{i,t} = G_{i,t} - b$ for all t

    else

      Assign $A_{i,t} = R_i - b$ for all t

  Normalize advantages

  for $k = 1, \ldots, \mu$ **do**

    Update π_θ using GRPO objective

The algorithm iteratively collects batches of N complete episodes and computes their returns to estimate a group-level baseline. Advantage signals are then constructed based on the selected variant: GRPO-T computes timestep-level advantages using cumulative future returns, while GRPO-E assigns a single episode-level advantage uniformly across all timesteps. The resulting advantages are normalized, and the policy is updated through multiple optimization steps using the GRPO objective, optionally including KL regularization. This procedure enables learning through relative comparisons without relying on a value function.

The overall training procedure is illustrated in Fig. 1. At each iteration, the agent interacts with the environment to generate a batch of complete episodes, from which rewards are collected and grouped. These rewards are then processed through a group-level computation step, where advantage signals are constructed according to the selected variant (GRPO-T or GRPO-E). The resulting advantages are used to update the policy, closing the training loop. This pipeline highlights the role of group-based normalization and the absence of a value function in guiding policy updates.

This approach contrasts with PPO and A2C, which typically rely on value function estimation to construct advantage signals. While PPO further constrains policy updates through clipping or KL penalties, A2C uses the critic directly as a baseline for actor updates. In GRPO, full episodes are used before each update, and advantage signals are derived from group-based reward normalization, enabling credit assignment without requiring a learned critic.

4 Experiments

In this section, we evaluate the proposed GRPO variants across a set of benchmark reinforcement learning environments. We describe the experimental setup and training methodology, followed by a detailed analysis of the obtained results in terms of performance, stability, and learning dynamics.

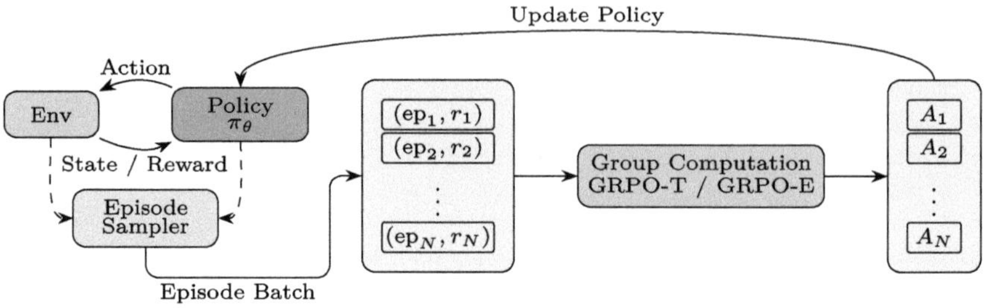

Fig. 1. Training flow of GRPO in Gymnasium environments.

4.1 Methodology

We evaluate the proposed GRPO variants on a set of continuous and discrete control tasks from the Gymnasium benchmark suite, including FetchReach [8], MountainCarContinuous [6], PointMaze (Medium) [2], and the hard variant of the Pinball domain [3]. These environments provide a diverse set of challenges, covering goal-conditioned manipulation, sparse reward navigation, and low-dimensional control.

All methods are trained using full-episode rollouts, following the formulation described in Sect. 3. At each training iteration, a batch of episodes is collected and used to compute advantage estimates. We compare GRPO-T and GRPO-E under identical training conditions, differing only in how the advantage signal is constructed.

For continuous control tasks (FetchReach, MountainCarContinuous, and PointMaze), we use stochastic policies with Gaussian action distributions, while for discrete environments (Pinball) we use categorical policies. The number of parallel environments is fixed to 16, and each update is performed using batches of full episodes.

All policies use two-layer MLPs with 64 hidden units per layer. Continuous-action methods share the same Tanh Gaussian actor, with A2C and PPO adding a critic of the same hidden size. In Pinball, all methods use 64–64 categorical policies. GRPO differs mainly by omitting the value-function estimator.

Hyperparameters are kept consistent across methods whenever possible. We use a discount factor $\gamma = 0.99$ and, where applicable, a GAE parameter $\lambda = 0.95$. The entropy coefficient is set to 0.01 to encourage exploration. Learning rates are defined per environment: 2.5×10^{-4} for Pinball and MountainCarContinuous, 7×10^{-5} for FetchReach, and 1×10^{-5} for PointMaze (Medium). All models are optimized with Adam, and the reported hyperparameters are kept fixed across random seeds for each environment.

For PPO, we follow a standard configuration with 4 optimization epochs per update, minibatches of size 64, and a clipping coefficient of 0.2 [11]. For GRPO, updates are performed using batches of 64 full episodes, without trajectory truncation. Additionally, following the original GRPO formulation [13], we incorporate a replay buffer to reuse past trajectories during training. The buffer stores up to 5000 episodes and is used to sample a fraction of each training batch. At each update, approximately 10% of the batch is drawn from the buffer, while the remaining episodes correspond to newly collected trajectories.

To analyze the impact of different design choices in GRPO, we compare configurations that vary along two key dimensions: the use of KL regularization and the strategy used to construct advantage estimates (timestep-based or episode-based), allowing us to isolate the effect of each component on learning performance. All experiments are repeated across multiple runs with different random seeds (typically 10 repetitions per configuration) to account for variability in training and ensure statistically reliable results.

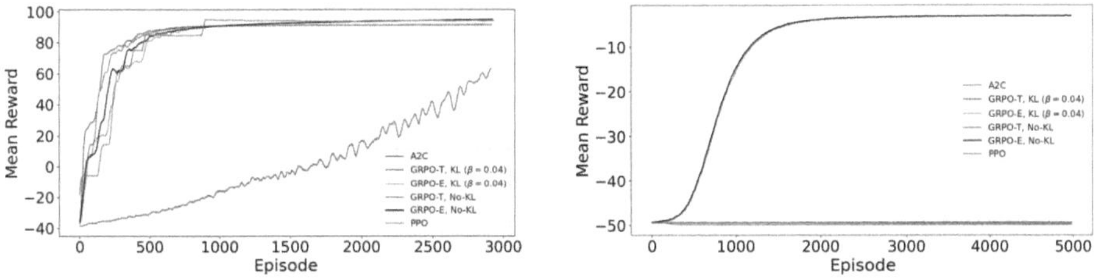

(a) MountainCarContinuous

(b) FetchReach

Fig. 2. Learning curves on continuous control tasks. GRPO variants consistently outperform A2C and achieve performance comparable to or better than PPO, with faster convergence. The results highlight the impact of advantage construction on learning efficiency across different environments.

4.2 Numerical Results

Figures 2, 3, and 5, together with the quantitative results in Table 1, provide a comprehensive view of learning performance across all environments. The learning curves are indexed by completed environment episodes. Notably, PPO exhibits early performance peaks followed by degradation (e.g., PointMaze), while both PPO and A2C collapse under sparse rewards (FetchReach), in contrast to the smoother and more stable convergence of GRPO variants. Overall, GRPO variants consistently outperform A2C, achieving substantially faster convergence and higher final returns in all tasks. A2C exhibits slow and unstable learning, particularly in more complex environments such as MountainCarContinuous and Pinball (Hard). This behavior persists throughout the training horizon, suggesting slower learning dynamics rather than insufficient training.

When compared to PPO, the results are environment-dependent. In MountainCarContinuous, GRPO matches or slightly exceeds PPO while converging faster, as observed in the learning curves, and achieves a modest improvement of approximately 1.2% in final reward. Additionally, GRPO exhibits significantly lower variance (around ± 0.2 compared to ± 0.87 for PPO), indicating more stable learning. This reduction in variance is particularly notable given the absence of a learned critic, suggesting that relative advantage normalization in GRPO can provide a stabilizing effect in certain continuous control settings.

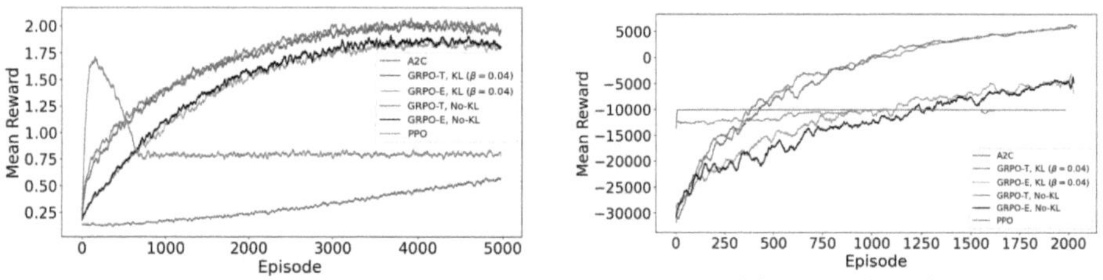

(a) PointMaze (Medium) (b) Pinball (Hard)

Fig. 3. Learning curves on navigation and control tasks. GRPO variants maintain strong performance across environments with different dynamics and reward structures, demonstrating robustness in both continuous navigation and challenging domains such as PinBall.

In FetchReach, both the curves and the quantitative results show that only the episode variant (GRPO-E) successfully learns. While PPO and GRPO-T remain near -50, GRPO-E reaches approximately -2.956, corresponding to an improvement of over 94%. The similarity between KL and no-KL variants further confirms that this behavior is driven by advantage rather than policy regularization. This suggests that episode-level credit assignment fits short-horizon goal-conditioned tasks, where success or failure summarizes the whole trajectory.

In PointMaze (Medium), GRPO clearly outperforms PPO both in learning dynamics and final performance. PPO exhibits unstable progress in the curves, while GRPO converges consistently. This behavior is consistent with known instability patterns in policy gradient methods, particularly under function approximation and noisy advantage estimates. Quantitatively, GRPO-T reaches 1.974 compared to 0.790 for PPO, representing an improvement of approximately 150%, and also achieves significantly higher AUC values, indicating superior sample efficiency.

In Pinball (Hard), the differences are most pronounced due to the underlying MDP structure, which combines sparse rewards, long horizons, and complex dynamics. The agent receives a large terminal reward ($+10000$) only upon reaching the goal, while incurring step-wise penalties (-1 or -5), making successful trajectories both rare and highly delayed in time.

The learning curves show that PPO and A2C collapse to suboptimal behaviors, consistently failing to reach the goal and instead minimizing penalties by converging to low-movement strategies. This is reflected in the final rewards, where PPO remains at -10001.543, indicating failure to discover successful trajectories.

Table 1. Final performance (reward) and area under the learning curve (AUC) across environments. Values are reported as mean ± standard deviation over multiple runs.

Environment	Method	Final Reward	AUC
MountainCarContinuous	A2C	66.277 ± 12.323	7350.178
	PPO	93.831 ± 0.870	254063.399
	GRPO-T (KL)	91.718 ± 0.271	259840.285
	GRPO-T (No-KL)	91.413 ± 0.202	256086.752
	GRPO-E (KL)	$\mathbf{94.926 \pm 0.208}$	252349.786
	GRPO-E (No-KL)	94.963 ± 0.255	**256614.314**
FetchReach	A2C	-49.356 ± 0.149	-247233.619
	PPO	-49.893 ± 0.035	-249714.888
	GRPO-T (KL)	-49.568 ± 0.131	-247503.253
	GRPO-T (No-KL)	-49.614 ± 0.112	-247606.878
	GRPO-E (KL)	$\mathbf{-2.956 \pm 0.134}$	-55086.138
	GRPO-E (No-KL)	-2.957 ± 0.134	**−54337.647**
PointMaze (Medium)	A2C	0.560 ± 0.062	1525.181
	PPO	0.790 ± 0.067	4285.575
	GRPO-T (KL)	1.960 ± 0.092	8349.022
	GRPO-T (No-KL)	$\mathbf{1.974 \pm 0.106}$	**8515.031**
	GRPO-E (KL)	1.803 ± 0.088	7233.834
	GRPO-E (No-KL)	1.821 ± 0.100	7398.984
Pinball (Hard)	A2C	-10000.003 ± 0.016	-20098326.104
	PPO	-10001.543 ± 0.805	-21514724.928
	GRPO-T (KL)	5698.336 ± 760.034	-7055592.202
	GRPO-T (No-KL)	$\mathbf{6031.713 \pm 858.969}$	**−6188067.430**
	GRPO-E (KL)	-5134.864 ± 4195.416	-24292675.304
	GRPO-E (No-KL)	-4749.575 ± 3791.066	-26732818.705

In contrast, GRPO-T maintains consistent improvement and reaches a final reward of 6031.713, indicating that the agent is able to reliably discover and exploit goal-reaching behaviors. This improvement can be attributed to timestep-level credit assignment, which propagates the sparse terminal reward back along the trajectory, allowing the agent to associate intermediate actions with long-term success. On the other hand, GRPO-E exhibits high variance (above ± 3000) and unstable performance. Since it assigns the same advantage to all timesteps within an episode, it struggles to distinguish which parts of the trajectory contributed to reaching the goal, leading to inconsistent learning. These results

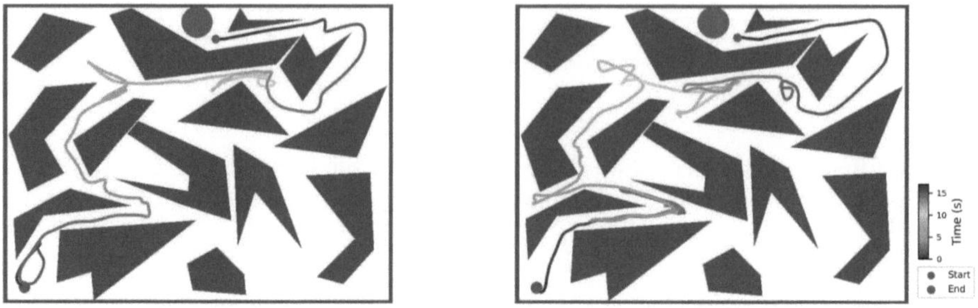

(a) GRPO-T (b) GRPO-E

Fig. 4. Trajectories induced by GRPO variants in the Pinball (Hard) environment. The large red circle denotes the goal location, while the small blue circle indicates the agent's initial position. The small red circle marks the final position of the agent at the end of the trajectory. Paths are overlaid and colored by temporal progression. GRPO-T (left) reaches the goal in 17 s with more direct and consistent navigation, while GRPO-E (right) also succeeds but requires 22.83 s and exhibits increased local exploration. (Color figure online)

suggest that, in long-horizon sparse-reward MDPs such as Pinball (Hard), fine-grained temporal credit assignment plays a critical role in achieving stable and effective learning.

This difference is further illustrated in Fig. 4. While both GRPO variants are able to reach the goal, their trajectories reveal distinct temporal organization. GRPO-T produces a more consistent progression toward the goal, whereas GRPO-E exhibits additional local exploration before converging, suggesting that timestep-level credit assignment provides a more precise learning signal for long-horizon behavior. In contrast, PPO and A2C converge to low-movement strategies after training, resulting in negligible state-space exploration and effectively no meaningful trajectories, as also evidenced by their flat learning curves and poor final performance. For this reason, the figure presents only GRPO-T and GRPO-E.

Differences between GRPO variants are also evident across both figures and quantitative metrics. Across the evaluated environments, GRPO-T is preferable in tasks requiring precise temporal credit assignment, such as PointMaze (Medium) and Pinball (Hard), while GRPO-E is more suitable for short-horizon goal-conditioned settings such as FetchReach.

The effect of KL regularization is limited and environment-dependent. In MountainCarContinuous and FetchReach, KL and no-KL configurations are nearly indistinguishable in both curves and final metrics. In PointMaze (Medium), KL slightly smooths early learning without affecting final performance, while in Pinball no consistent stabilization effect is observed. Overall, these results indicate that the construction of the advantage signal has a stronger influence on learning dynamics than KL-based policy constraints.

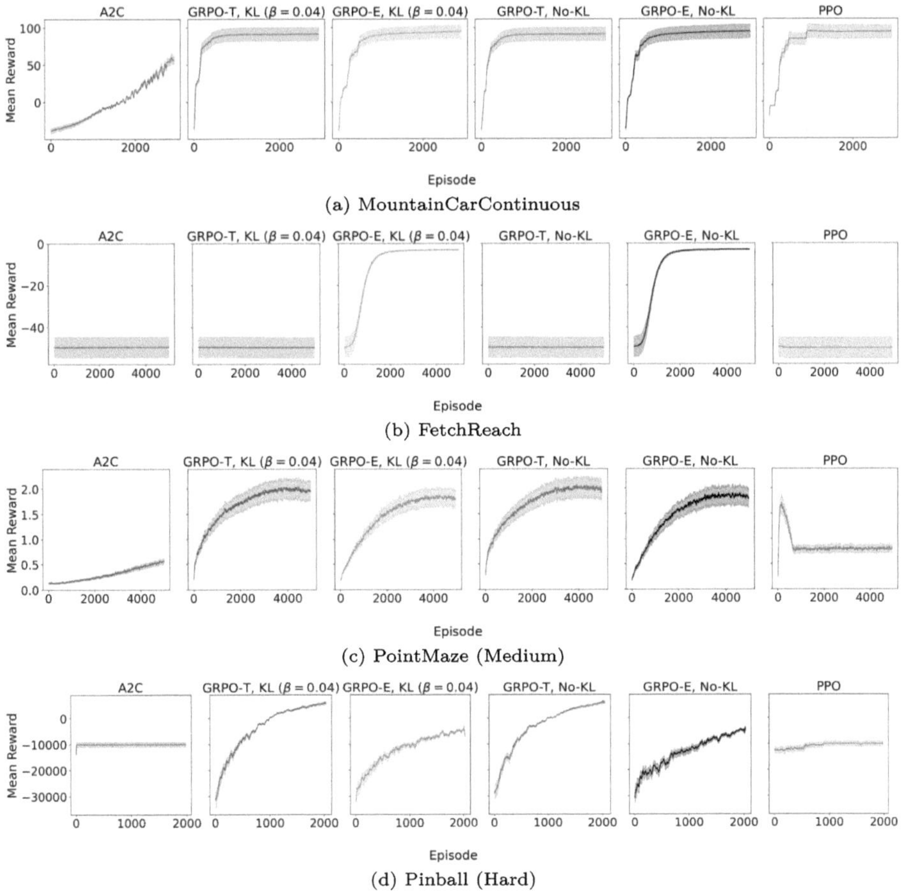

Fig. 5. Learning curves with standard deviation shading across all environments, highlighting variability across runs and the improved stability of GRPO variants compared to PPO and A2C.

5 Conclusion

In this work, we adapted GRPO to classical reinforcement learning environments and investigated its behavior under different credit assignment strategies. The experimental results demonstrate that GRPO achieves competitive and, in several cases, superior performance compared to traditional policy gradient methods such as PPO and A2C. In particular, the proposed variants show strong improvements in environments with sparse rewards and long horizons, highlighting the effectiveness of group-based advantage estimation. Additionally, our analysis reveals that the structure of the advantage signal plays a central role in learning dynamics, with timestep-level credit assignment leading to more consistent performance in complex settings.

Future work includes exploring hybrid formulations that combine group-based estimation with value function approximations, aiming to further improve stability and sample efficiency, as well as evaluating the approach against alternative reinforcement learning methods and across a broader set of environments to assess its generalization across different task structures and reward settings.

Acknowledgments. We thank the anonymous reviewers for their valuable feedback. This work was supported by Kunumi Institute. The authors thank the institution for its financial support and commitment to advancing scientific research. This research was also partially supported by Conselho Nacional de Desenvolvimento Científico e Tecnológico - CNPq (grants 313845/2023-9, 443184/2023-2, 445238/2024-0, and 404800/2025-4).

References

1. Dong, H., Ding, Z., Zhang, S. (eds.): Deep Reinforcement Learning. Springer, Singapore (2020). https://doi.org/10.1007/978-981-15-4095-0
2. Fu, J., Kumar, A., Nachum, O., Tucker, G., Levine, S.: D4rl: datasets for deep data-driven reinforcement learning (2021). https://arxiv.org/abs/2004.07219
3. Konidaris, G.D., Barto, A.G.: Skill discovery in continuous reinforcement learning domains using skill chaining. In: NeurIPS, pp. 1015–1023 (2009)
4. Mnih, V., et al.: Asynchronous Methods for Deep Reinforcement Learning (2016). https://doi.org/10.48550/arXiv.1602.01783
5. Mnih, V., et al.: Human-level control through deep reinforcement learning. Nature **518**(7540) (2015). https://doi.org/10.1038/nature14236
6. Moore, A.W.: Efficient memory-based learning for robot control. Technical report UCAM-CL-TR-209, University of Cambridge, Computer Laboratory (1990). https://www.cl.cam.ac.uk/techreports/UCAM-CL-TR-209.pdf
7. Pignatelli, E., et al.: A Survey of Temporal Credit Assignment in Deep Reinforcement Learning (2024). https://doi.org/10.48550/arXiv.2312.01072
8. Plappert, M., et al.: Multi-goal reinforcement learning: challenging robotics environments and request for research (2018). https://arxiv.org/abs/1802.09464
9. Russell, S.J., Norvig, P.: Artificial Intelligence: A Modern Approach, Global Edition, 4 edn. Pearson, London (2021)
10. Schulman, J., Moritz, P., Levine, S., Jordan, M., Abbeel, P.: High-Dimensional Continuous Control Using Generalized Advantage Estimation (2015). https://doi.org/10.48550/arXiv.1506.02438
11. Schulman, J., Wolski, F., Dhariwal, P., Radford, A., Klimov, O.: Proximal policy optimization algorithms (2017). https://arxiv.org/abs/1707.06347
12. Sewak, M.: Actor-critic models and the A3C. In: Deep Reinforcement Learning: Frontiers of Artificial Intelligence, pp. 141–152 (2019). https://doi.org/10.1007/978-981-13-8285-7_11
13. Shao, Z., et al.: DeepSeekMath: Pushing the Limits of Mathematical Reasoning in Open Language Models (2024). https://doi.org/10.48550/arXiv.2402.03300
14. Silver, D., Lever, G., Heess, N., Degris, T., Wierstra, D., Riedmiller, M.: Deterministic policy gradient algorithms (2014). https://proceedings.mlr.press/v32/silver14.html

15. Sutton, R.S.: Learning to predict by the methods of temporal differences. Mach. Learn. **3**(1), 9–44 (1988). https://doi.org/10.1007/BF00115009
16. Sutton, R.S., Barto, A.G.: Reinforcement Learning: An Introduction (2018)
17. Sutton, R.S., McAllester, D., Singh, S., Mansour, Y.: Policy gradient methods for reinforcement learning with function approximation. Adv. Neural Inf. Process. Syst. **12** (1999)
18. Szepesvári, C.: Algorithms for Reinforcement Learning. Synthesis Lectures on Artificial Intelligence and Machine Learning, 1 edn. Springer, Cham (2010). https://doi.org/10.1007/978-3-031-01551-9
19. Wu, Y., Mansimov, E., Liao, S., Grosse, R., Ba, J.: Scalable trust-region method for deep reinforcement learning using Kronecker-factored approximation (2017). https://doi.org/10.48550/arXiv.1708.05144

Quantitative Event-Based Explanations for Policies in Stochastic Planning

Gabriela Alcaide, Marcos Santos(✉), Luiz Silva, and Valdinei Freire

University of São Paulo (USP), São Paulo, Brazil
{gabriela.alcaide,marcos.felipe.santos,luiz73,valdinei.freire}@usp.br

Sequential decision problems can be modeled as stochastic processes in which the actions of an intelligent agent unfold over time. Markov Decision Processes (MDPs) formalize this type of problem when the next state depends only on the current state and the executed action. The solution of an MDP is represented by a policy, which defines the behavior of the agent. However, despite providing a complete description of the solution, policies are often difficult to interpret. This work proposes an interpretability framework for MDP policies based on formal temporal queries. The proposed framework allows users to query the probability of events specified in Linear Temporal Logic over Finite Traces (LTLf) and, additionally, the probability of selecting actions under logically defined contexts. Rather than introducing a new verification algorithm, the proposed method leverages standard formal verification techniques as an explainability mechanism, enabling quantitative analysis of policy behavior through expressive temporal and contextual queries. We also conduct experiments considering different ways of balancing rewards among providers (*fairness*), using the proposed framework to transparently highlight and compare how such criteria influence the decisions made by the policies.

1 Introduction

Sequential decision problems can be modeled as stochastic processes in which environment states evolve over time [10]. Markov Decision Processes (MDPs) formalize such processes when the next environment state depends solely on the current state and the executed action [10]. Figure 1 illustrates the dynamics of an MDP. At each time step n, the agent observes the current state s_n, executes action a_n, transitions to state s_{n+1}, and receives an immediate reward R_n [6].

The solution of an MDP is a policy that specifies the action to be taken in each environment state [10]. Although policies provide a complete solution, they are not readily interpretable by users [12]. First, each action a_n affects the sequence of future states [10], preventing users from fully observing the effects of applying a policy. Second, policies suffer from the curse of dimensionality, growing exponentially with the number of problem factors [9].

Recent studies have addressed policy explainability in probabilistic planning. [1] proposed an interactive system for querying and visualizing event occurrences, while [3] investigated generating alternatives to the optimal policy to improve

M. Recamonde-Mendoza and R. C. Barros (Eds.): BRACIS 2026, LNAI 17105, pp. 232–246, 2027.
https://doi.org/10.1007/978-3-032-39882-6_16

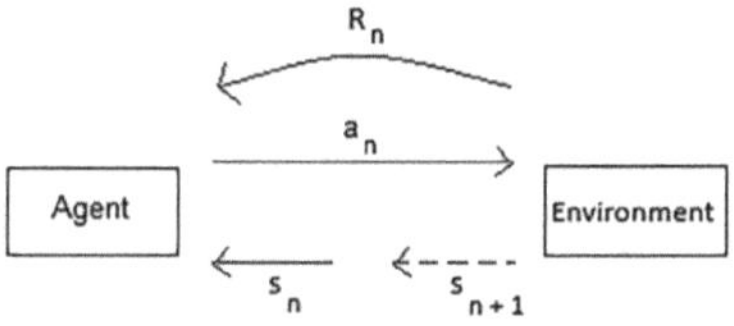

Fig. 1. Markov Decision Process (MDP) [5,10].

comprehensibility. [13] explored a property-based approach, enabling the analysis of which constraints can or cannot be simultaneously satisfied by a policy.

Although previous work has investigated policy explainability in probabilistic planning, these approaches focus predominantly on qualitative explanations based on examples or policy properties. In contrast, this work proposes a complementary approach based on quantitative explanations that express the relationship between a policy and user-relevant events through the behavior induced by that policy.

In sequential decision processes, multiple objectives may need to be satisfied, each associated with a distinct reward component. In such cases, traditional criteria that maximize only cumulative reward can lead to undesirable outcomes among stakeholders, especially when the agent controls the distribution of benefits [16]. To address this issue, *fairness* approaches have been incorporated into multi-objective MDPs to balance overall performance with equity among objectives [16]. Among these approaches, criteria based on *maximin fairness* and its regularized variants prioritize the stakeholder with the lowest aggregated performance, reducing inequalities without completely sacrificing overall system efficiency.

However, communicating these fairness preferences, or even understanding how different fairness criteria affect agent decisions, remains challenging. In this work, we demonstrate how interpretable policies can support this analysis by making explicit the behavioral differences induced by different reward balancing methods.

The goal of this work is to develop an interpretability framework for MDP policies based on quantitative temporal and contextual queries. Figure 2 provides an overview of the framework. Starting from an MDP and a set of policies, users formulate queries, and the framework combines the MDP dynamics with the corresponding policy to compute the requested probabilities. Rather than proposing a new formal verification algorithm, it leverages well-established verification techniques as an explainability mechanism, quantifying event occurrences and context-conditioned decisions induced by a policy.

Unlike previous work, this study extends this interaction by allowing users to formulate quantitative queries about the effects of applying a policy to an MDP. Two complementary forms of interaction are proposed: users can interpret a policy by specifying an arbitrary event and computing its probability of occurrence, or define an arbitrary context and compute the probability of selecting a given

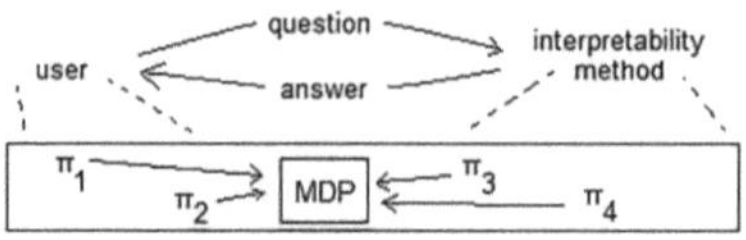

Fig. 2. Proposed Interpretability Method.

action under that context. The proposed framework is evaluated in a simulated scenario that abstracts the dynamics of a service providers' cooperative.

2 Background

This section presents the fundamental concepts used in the study. The classical formulation of Markov Decision Processes (MDPs) is reviewed, followed by an introduction to Linear Temporal Logic over Finite Traces (LTLf), used to specify properties over trajectories. The combination of MDPs and LTLf provides the formal basis for representing temporal events and calculating reachability probabilities, which are central elements in the proposed methodology. Finally, the concepts related to fairness are introduced to guide the experiments.

2.1 Markov Decision Processes (MDPs)

Markov Decision Processes are tuples $< S, s_0, A, R, T, G >$. S is the set of environment states. $s_0 \in S$ is the initial state of the environment. A is the set of actions the agent can execute. $R : S \times A \to \mathbb{R}$ is a reward function that specifies the reward $R(s, a)$ received when the environment is in state $s \in S$ and the agent executes action $a \in A$. $T : S \times A \times S \to [0, 1]$ is a transition function giving the probability $T(s, a, s')$ that the environment transitions from state $s \in S$ to state $s' \in S$ via action $a \in A$ [6]. The set $G \subseteq S$ represents goal (or absorbing) states, i.e., states in which an objective is considered achieved.

The solution to an MDP is a policy, which specifies the action to be executed by the agent in each state. A deterministic policy is defined as $\pi : S \to A$, where $a = \pi(s)$ is the action selected in state s. A probabilistic policy specifies a probability distribution on A in each state, and is defined as $\pi : S \times A \to [0, 1]$, where $\pi(a \mid s)$ denotes the probability of selecting action a in state s. A policy is stationary if it does not depend on the decision time n; otherwise, it is called non-stationary and may be represented as π_n [10].

The value of a policy π is the expected reward from the initial state $s_0 \in S$, following the application of π. This value is given by $V^{\pi}(s) = E(\sum_{n=0}^{\infty} \gamma^n R_n \mid s_0 = s, \pi)$ [14], where γ (gamma) is a discount factor. When $0 \leq \gamma < 1$, future rewards contribute decreasingly, ensuring algorithmic convergence.

The optimal value of a state s, $V^*(s)$, is the maximum among all possible V in a process, i.e., $V^*(s) = \max_{\pi} V^{\pi}(s), \forall s \in S$ [14].

The Bellman equation defines the optimal value of state s, $V^*(s)$, based on these concepts [14]:

$$V^*(s) = \max_{a \in A} \left\{ R(s,a) + \gamma \sum_{s' \in S} T(s,a,s') V^*(s') \right\}.$$

The policy π that leads the process to the optimal value V^* is called the optimal policy π^*, and is defined as [14]:

$$V^{\pi^*} \geq V^{\pi}, \forall \pi \in \Pi.$$

MDPs can be classified according to the decision time horizon [10]. In finite-horizon MDPs, the decision process occurs over a limited number of steps, and optimal policies are generally non-stationary. In undetermined-horizon MDPs, the number of steps is not known in advance, but the process is expected to eventually terminate. In infinite-horizon MDPs, the process extends indefinitely, and stationary policies are commonly used. These problems are typically formulated either using discounted rewards or average rewards over time. In discounted formulations, the discount factor γ ensures convergence of the expected return.

2.2 Linear Temporal Logic over Finite Traces (LTLf)

Linear Temporal Logic over Finite Traces (LTLf) is a propositional temporal logic interpreted over finite sequences of states (traces) [2]. It provides a formal framework to specify temporal properties in domains where executions naturally terminate, such as finite-horizon MDPs or undetermined-horizon MDPs where the policy ensures that the process eventually terminate.

Let P be a finite set of atomic propositions. An LTLf formula ϕ is defined recursively as:

$$\phi ::= \text{true} \mid \text{false} \mid p \mid \neg\phi \mid \phi_1 \wedge \phi_2 \mid \phi_1 \vee \phi_2 \mid \bigcirc\phi \mid \phi_1 \mathbb{U} \phi_2$$

where $p \in P$.

The logical and temporal operators have the following intuitive meaning:

- $\neg\phi$ (*negation*): ϕ does not hold.
- $\phi_1 \wedge \phi_2$ (*conjunction*): both ϕ_1 and ϕ_2 hold.
- $\phi_1 \vee \phi_2$ (*disjunction*): at least one of ϕ_1 or ϕ_2 holds.
- $\bigcirc\phi$ (*next*): ϕ holds at the next state.
- $\phi_1 \mathbb{U} \phi_2$ (*until*): ϕ_1 holds at every step until ϕ_2 eventually holds.

Two commonly used derived temporal operators are:

$$\Diamond\phi \equiv \text{true} \mathbb{U} \phi \quad (\textit{eventually})$$

$$\Box\phi \equiv \neg\Diamond\neg\phi \quad (\textit{always})$$

An LTLf formula is interpreted over a finite trace $\tau = s_0, s_1, \ldots, s_N$, which is a sequence of states generated by the MDP. Each state s_n is associated with a labeling function $\sigma : S \rightarrow 2^P$, such that $\sigma(s_n) \subseteq P$ is the set of atomic propositions that are true at time n.

The satisfaction relation $\tau \models \phi$ indicates whether the trace τ satisfies the formula ϕ, according to the standard finite-trace semantics of LTLf [2]. A formula is satisfied if it evaluates to true over the entire trace according to the labeling of each state and the semantics of its logical and temporal operators. Intuitively, atomic propositions are evaluated using the labeling function σ, Boolean operators combine truth values, and temporal operators constrain how these truth values evolve along the trace.

Although satisfaction is defined over complete traces, it is often desirable to evaluate temporal formulas incrementally during execution. For this purpose, we use the progression operator. Given the set of propositions $\sigma \subseteq P$ that are true in the current state and a formula ϕ, the progression $\text{Prog}(\sigma, \phi)$ returns a new formula representing the remaining condition to be satisfied in future states.

The progression operator is defined recursively as follows [5]:

- $\text{Prog}(\sigma, \text{true}) = \text{true}$
- $\text{Prog}(\sigma, \text{false}) = \text{false}$
- $\text{Prog}(\sigma, p) = \begin{cases} \text{true}, & \text{if } p \in \sigma \\ \text{false}, & \text{otherwise} \end{cases}$
- $\text{Prog}(\sigma, \neg\phi) = \neg\text{Prog}(\sigma, \phi)$
- $\text{Prog}(\sigma, \phi_1 \wedge \phi_2) = \text{Prog}(\sigma, \phi_1) \wedge \text{Prog}(\sigma, \phi_2)$
- $\text{Prog}(\sigma, \phi_1 \vee \phi_2) = \text{Prog}(\sigma, \phi_1) \vee \text{Prog}(\sigma, \phi_2)$
- $\text{Prog}(\sigma, \bigcirc\phi) = \phi$
- $\text{Prog}(\sigma, \phi_1 \mathbb{U} \phi_2) = \text{Prog}(\sigma, \phi_2) \vee (\text{Prog}(\sigma, \phi_1) \wedge (\phi_1 \mathbb{U} \phi_2))$

Derived operators follow from their definitions. For example:

$$\text{Prog}(\sigma, \Diamond\phi) = \text{Prog}(\sigma, \phi) \vee \Diamond\phi, \quad \text{Prog}(\sigma, \Box\phi) = \text{Prog}(\sigma, \phi) \wedge \Box\phi.$$

This mechanism allows temporal properties to be tracked along finite trajectories and integrated into MDP analysis by augmenting the state with the current progressed formula. Progression provides an incremental procedure equivalent to the standard LTLf satisfaction semantics: a finite trace satisfies a temporal property iff the progressed formula evaluates to true after processing the entire trace.

2.3 Fairness in Multi-objective MDPs

In MDPs with multiple reward components, each associated with a different stakeholder, maximizing only the total sum of rewards can create undesirable asymmetries among components. Fairness criteria can be incorporated into the optimization process to balance the distribution of returns without entirely discarding overall system performance.

[16] present a regularized *maximin fairness* criterion, where the optimal stochastic policy is obtained by jointly maximizing the minimum performance among reward components and a term proportional to the total sum of the components. The objective function is:

$$\max_{\pi} \left[\min_i U_i(\pi) \; + \; \frac{\varepsilon}{m} \sum_{i=1}^{m} U_i(\pi) \right],$$

where $U_i(\pi)$ represents the expected return of component i, m is the number of reward components, and $\varepsilon > 0$ controls the relative weight of the aggregating term. The first term favors the worst-performing component, while the regularized term ensures that the aggregate return influences the resulting policy.

Implementing *regularized maximin fairness* in MDPs can be formulated as a linear programming problem [16]. The central idea is to use occupancy measures $f(x, a)$ to represent the discounted frequency with which each state–action pair is visited under a policy. The utility of component i is then expressed as:

$$U_i(f) = \sum_x \sum_a f(x, a) \, R_i(x, a). \tag{1}$$

The objective of *regularized maximin fairness* combines the maximin criterion with a utilitarian term weighted by $\varepsilon > 0$, aiming to simultaneously maximize the worst performance among components and the total sum of performances. The linearized formulation introduces an auxiliary variable z, representing the worst utility among all m components:

$$\max_{f,\, z} \left[\mathrm{z} + \frac{\varepsilon}{m} \sum_{i=1}^{m} U_i(f) \right],$$

subject to the constraints:

$$\begin{gathered} z \leq U_i(f) \quad \forall i, \\ \sum_a f(x', a) = b(x') + \sum_{x,a} \gamma \, T(x' \mid x, a) \, f(x, a) \quad \forall x', \\ f(x, a) \geq 0 \quad \forall x, a. \end{gathered} \tag{2}$$

where z represents the minimum expected reward among the providers, $U_i(f)$ is the accumulated return of provider i, f denotes the occupancy measures function used to reconstruct the policy, m is the total number of providers, and ε controls the relative weight between fairness and efficiency.

After solving the linear program, the optimal stochastic policy is recovered by normalization:

$$\pi(a \mid x) = \frac{f(x, a)}{\sum_{a'} f(x, a')}. \tag{3}$$

This results in a stochastic policy $\pi(a \mid x)$ whose execution, in expectation, tends to increase the expected value of the lowest reward among the considered objectives, even though this criterion is not part of the state and therefore is not directly observed by the policy during decision-making.

3 Related Work

The interpretability of policies in Markov Decision Processes (MDPs) has been widely investigated. Several approaches provide local explanations of policy behavior, typically based on introspection or trajectory inspection. Examples include local analysis techniques and symbolic representations presented in [4,8,11]. These explanations, however, are static, non-interactive, and do not allow queries about arbitrary events.

Other works introduce more interactive mechanisms, such as [1], which enables visual exploration of the occurrence of relevant events across different trajectories. Nevertheless, this interaction does not provide quantitative probabilities associated with such properties.

A complementary line of research investigates generating alternative policies that better align with the user's mental model, as in [3]. There are also approaches focused on declarative constraints: [13] identifies incompatibilities between user-imposed requirements, while [15] determines minimal subsets of constraints that must be relaxed when they cannot be satisfied simultaneously. Additionally, [7] provides contrastive explanations based on abstractions, allowing understanding of why two policies or solutions diverge.

Despite these advances, these approaches remain predominantly qualitative: they provide local, structural, or contrastive explanations, but do not offer a general mechanism that allows free-form queries about complex events in the MDP with associated quantitative estimates.

This work addresses this still underexplored area by proposing a mechanism that allows the specification of arbitrary properties—expressed in temporal logic—and obtaining quantitative estimates of the behavior induced by the policy. In this way, the focus complements the literature by transforming explainability into a consultative and quantitative process, bridging the gap between static local explanations and truly user-oriented interactions.

4 Environment Modeling and Query Mechanisms

This work uses a synthetic environment inspired by the operation of a cooperative service to evaluate proposed interpretability methods in MDPs. The methodology combines (i) the construction of an extended MDP for computing probabilities of events described in LTLf and (ii) an alternative frequency-based measure to estimate probabilities conditioned on contexts, without requiring model extension.

4.1 Implementation of the Synthetic Cooperative Problem

For experimentation and validation purposes, a finite-horizon synthetic problem was developed, inspired by a real-world cooperative of service providers. The model was intentionally simplified to reduce the number of factors and the state space size, preserving only the essential elements for analyzing sequential decisions and effects of preferences among agents.

The problem is modeled as a single-agent finite-horizon MDP N, where a central coordinator makes decisions across N time steps. At each new request, the coordinator can reject it or, if accepted, must assign the service to one of the available providers.

There are W providers and K service types. Each provider has a specific skill for each service type, denoted by P_{wk}, representing the probability of completing that service in each time step. Each service type has a payment G_k and a probability of demand P_k at each time step. In addition, an operational cost per time step H_{wk} is defined for each provider–service pair.

The agent's objective is to select actions over the horizon N to maximize the accumulated profit of the providers, allowing the evaluation of policies under fairness criteria. The number of possible MDP states is $(N+1)(W+1)^{(K+1)}$.

4.2 Event Interpretability

The proposed method allows a user to specify an event as an LTLf formula ϕ and to compute the probability that trajectories generated by a fixed policy π satisfy this property.

Formally, let ϕ be an LTLf formula over a set of atomic propositions P, and let $\tau = s_0, s_1, \ldots, s_n$ be a trajectory induced by policy π. The quantity of interest is:

$$\Pr(\phi) = \Pr[\tau \models \phi \mid s_0, \pi].$$

To compute this probability, we rely on the standard product construction between the MDP and a formula progression mechanism [2,5]. This construction allows reducing the satisfaction of ϕ to a reachability problem over an augmented state space.

Specifically, we define an extended MDP:

$$M^{\times} = \langle S \times \mathcal{P}(\phi), A, T^{\times}, R^{\times}, G \rangle,$$

where $\mathcal{P}(\phi)$ denotes the set of formulas reachable from ϕ through progression. Each extended state is a pair (s, ψ), where $s \in S$ is an original MDP state and ψ is the current progressed formula.

The transition function is given by the transition of the state s when the decision a is taken and by the progression of ψ. It is defined as:

$$T^{\times}((s', \psi') \mid (s, \psi), a) = \begin{cases} T(s' \mid s, a), & \text{if } \psi' = \mathrm{Prog}(\sigma(s), \psi) \\ 0, & \text{otherwise} \end{cases} \tag{4}$$

and the set of accepting states is given by the set of states where the temporal event is satisfied:

$$G = \{(s, \psi) \mid \psi = \texttt{true}\}.$$

Under this construction, the probability that a trajectory satisfies ϕ is equivalent to the probability of reaching G in the extended MDP:

$$\Pr[\tau \models \phi \mid s_0, \pi] = \Pr^{M^\times}[\lozenge G \mid (s_0, \phi), \pi],$$

where $\lozenge G$ denotes that a state in G is eventually reached.

Therefore, $\Pr(\phi)$ can be computed using standard reachability analysis techniques (e.g., dynamic programming or value iteration) applied to $M^\times$ under policy π.

Importantly, Although this construction augments the state space, it preserves the original MDP dynamics and serves exclusively as an analysis model. In this work, established formal verification techniques are employed as an interpretability mechanism, allowing users to quantitatively analyze the behavior induced by a fixed policy through temporal queries.

4.3 Action Probabilities Given a Context

In addition to temporal queries, the proposed framework supports logical context and computing the probability of selecting each action under that context. Let h be a propositional formula over the set of atomic propositions P, recursively defined as:

$$h ::= \text{true} \mid \text{false} \mid \text{ p} \mid \neg \text{ h} \mid h \wedge \text{ h} \mid h \vee h,$$

where $p \in P$. The set of extended states satisfying the context is defined as:

$$G_h = \{(s, n) \mid \sigma(s) \models h\}.$$

To quantify how often extended states are visited under policy π, we use the state occupancy measure. Let $\tilde{T}^\pi$ denote the transition matrix over the augmented finite-horizon state space, whose states are pairs (s, n), where $s \in S$ and n is the decision step. The state occupancy measure is computed as

$$\mu^\pi = (I - \tilde{T}^\pi)^{-1} \mu_0,$$

where μ_0 is the initial state distribution over the extended state space.

The entry $\mu^\pi(s, n)$ corresponds to the expected number of visits to state s at decision step n under policy π. Since the extended state space is acyclic for finite-horizon MDPs, $(I - \tilde{T}^\pi)$ is invertible and the occupancy measure is well defined.

For a stochastic policy, the probability of selecting action a conditioned on context h is given by

$$\Pr(a \mid h) = \frac{\sum_{(s,n) \in G_h} \mu^\pi(s, n)\, \pi(a \mid s, n)}{\sum_{(s,n) \in G_h} \mu^\pi(s, n)}.$$

This quantity represents the expected fraction of visits to extended states satisfying the context h in which action a is selected under policy π. For deterministic policies, where $\pi(a \mid s, n) \in \{0, 1\}$, this expression reduces to the fraction of visits to states satisfying h in which action a is selected. Unlike reward-based formulations, this definition directly captures the behavioral distribution induced by the policy without introducing auxiliary reward signals.

4.4 Limitations

Finite Horizons. The proposed approach relies on exact probability computation for reachability properties. In infinite-horizon MDPs without discounting, the Bellman equations used to compute these probabilities are not necessarily contractive, and standard iterative methods such as value iteration may fail to converge.

For this reason, exact computation of $\Pr(\phi)$ requires either structural modifications to the MDP (e.g., absorbing target states or automata-based constructions) or restrictions on the model. This restriction is consistent with the use of LTLf, which is inherently defined over finite traces, and aligns the proposed method with domains where executions naturally terminate.

In this work, we restrict our analysis to finite-horizon MDPs, ensuring that both the value computation and the occupancy measure are well-defined and can be computed exactly.

Scalability Considerations. The proposed approach inherits the computational challenges commonly associated with probabilistic model checking and product MDP constructions. In particular, the size of the extended state space grows as $|S| \times |\mathcal{P}(\phi)|$, where $\mathcal{P}(\phi)$ is the set of formulas reachable through progression. In the worst case, this set may grow exponentially with respect to the size of ϕ.

Additionally, computing the occupancy measure requires solving a linear system involving the transition matrix T^{π}, which has complexity cubic in the number of states in the general case. In practice, both execution time and memory consumption are dominated by the size of the extended state space and by the solution of the associated linear systems.

These limitations are not specific to the proposed method, but rather inherent to approaches that combine temporal or logical specifications with stochastic decision processes [5]. In practice, scalability can be mitigated by restricting the size of the logical formulas, exploiting structure in the MDP (e.g., sparsity), or using approximate methods. Exploring such techniques is an important direction for future work.

5 Experiment

The proposed experiment aims to compare two distinct policies generated from the same MDP environment, corresponding to the synthetic cooperative service provider problem: (i) a policy focused exclusively on maximizing the expected reward, and (ii) a policy that incorporates balance (*fairness*) parameters in the objective function. Comparing these policies allows evaluating how different objectives influence system behavior and final outcomes.

5.1 Expected-Reward Policy

The first policy, denoted by π_{exp}, is obtained through a standard optimization process that maximizes the expected sum of rewards over the horizon: $\mathbb{E}\left[\sum_{n=0}^{N} R(s_n, a_n)\right]$. No additional criteria are considered beyond the accumulated performance predicted by the model. Thus, this policy exclusively seeks to maximize the sum of gains minus costs, obtained at the end of the process.

5.2 Policy Incorporating Fairness Criteria

The second policy, denoted by π_{fair}, incorporates distributive balance criteria by extending the traditional objective function. Instead of considering only the sum of accumulated rewards, the reward is decomposed into two components: (i) the minimum expected reward among the providers, capturing performance relative to the worst-off actor; and (ii) the total accumulated reward, weighted by an importance factor, as presented in Sect. 2.3.

5.3 Policy Evaluation via Extended MDPs and Context-Conditioned Decision Analysis

With policies π_{exp} and π_{fair} defined, evaluation proceeds using the methodology proposed in this work. For both policies, the extended MDP associated with the synthetic cooperative environment is constructed to compute the probability of events specified in Linear Temporal Logic over Finite Traces (LTLf). This extended MDP preserves the original transitions and adds auxiliary variables only to track the progression of temporal formulas.

Once the extended MDP is defined, the probability of an LTLf event is computed by calculating $\Pr[\tau \models \phi \mid s_0, \pi]$, allowing interpretation of the outcome generated by each policy.

In addition to LTLf-based analysis, a complementary method interprets the decisions made by policies directly based on logical conditions describing the context of interest. In this case, a propositional formula h characterizes the context. The probability of selecting an action a conditioned on this context is then computed by $\Pr(a \mid h)$.

5.4 Synthetic Environment Hyperparameters

The experiments used the following hyperparameters for the synthetic environment:

Environment Structure. The setup considers $W = 2$ service providers and $K = 3$ service types. The probability that no service arrives in a given iteration is defined as $\Pr(\text{no service}) = 0.25$, while the arrival probability for each service type follows the vector $\Pr(\text{service}) = [0.4, 0.25, 0.1]$.

Skills and Gains. The skill matrix is given by P_{wk}. For the providers, we define: $P_{1k} = [0.3, 0.15, 0.1]$ and $P_{2k} = [0.3, 0.15, 0.1]$. The gains associated with each service type are given by $G_k = [5.5987, 7.3647, 9.7670]$.

Costs. The operational cost per time step for each provider–service pair is given by H_{wk}. Specifically: $H_{1k} = [0.1641, 0.1641, 0.1641]$ and $H_{2k} = [0.2131, 0.2131, 0.2131]$. This matrix represents the cost incurred by each provider when executing service k at each time step. This scenario corresponds to a case in which the first provider is more efficient than the second due to higher skill levels across service types.

Regularization and Horizon. The regularization term used in the construction of the policy with fairness criteria is $\varepsilon_{\text{reg}} = 0.01$ and the process horizon is fixed at $N = 20$.

These hyperparameters fully define the environment used both for policy optimization and for interpretability analysis experiments.

5.5 Results

The predicates available for specifying events in the MDP were *some service was requested*, *no services were requested*, *provider*$_w$ *available*, $\forall w \in [1, W]$ and *provider*$_w$ *working*, $\forall\ w \in [1, W]$.

Verifying the Probability of Event Occurrence. The specified events were

$$\begin{aligned}E_1 = \Diamond(&\text{some service was requested} \wedge \\ &(\text{provider}_1 \text{ available} \wedge \\ &(\text{provider}_2 \text{ working } \wedge \bigcirc \text{provider}_1 \text{ available}))),\end{aligned}$$

$$\begin{aligned}E_2 = \Diamond(&\text{some service was requested} \wedge \\ &(\text{provider}_2 \text{ available} \wedge \\ &(\text{provider}_1 \text{ working } \wedge \bigcirc \text{provider}_2 \text{ available}))).\end{aligned}$$

Event E_1 represents the situation in which, eventually, *provider*$_1$ is the only one available and does not receive the job when it arrives. Similarly, E_2 describes the case in which *provider*$_2$ is the only one available and also does not receive the job at the moment of the request.

Under the policy based solely on expected reward, we obtained $Pr(E_1) = 0.2294$ and $Pr(E_2) = 0.3761$. Under the policy incorporating fairness criteria, we obtained $Pr(E_1) = 0.1418$ and $Pr(E_2) = 0.3229$.

Given that *provider*$_1$ is more efficient in all service types, the observed results can be interpreted as follows. We can observe through the proposed methodology that, in the policy that maximizes expected reward, we have $\Pr(E_1) = 0.2294$ and $\Pr(E_2) = 0.3761$, meaning that *provider*$_2$ shows a substantially higher probability of being the only one available and still not receiving the job when it arrives.

This pattern is consistent with the expected behavior of a reward-oriented policy: since *provider*$_1$ is more efficient, the policy tends to prefer her for assignments, leaving *provider*$_2$ with fewer opportunities, which increases $\Pr(E_2)$.

When fairness criteria are incorporated, the probabilities become $\Pr(E_1) = 0.1418$ and $\Pr(E_2) = 0.3229$. The fairness-based policy reduces both probabilities in absolute terms (a reduction of $\Delta E_1 = 0.0876$ and $\Delta E_2 = 0.0532$), with the relative reduction being larger for E_1 (approximately 38.2% for E_1 versus 14.2% for E_2).

According to the fairness criterion adopted in this work, which balances total accumulated reward with the individual gains of each provider, the reduction in the gap between $\Pr(E_1)$ and $\Pr(E_2)$ shows that the fairness-based policy partially redistributes opportunities toward the less favored provider. This effect becomes visible through the proposed probabilistic queries, which allow us to compare how often each provider is excluded under different policies. However, since the objective still preserves a utilitarian component, the more efficient provider remains preferred in expectation, which explains why the asymmetry is reduced but not eliminated.

Analyzing Action Probabilities Under Specific Contexts. We also examined the probability distributions over actions under two different contexts. The specified contexts were

$$C_1 = \text{some service was requested} \wedge \text{provider}_1 \text{ available} \wedge \text{provider}_2 \text{ available} \qquad C_2 = \text{some service was requested} \wedge \text{provider}_1 \text{ working} \wedge \text{provider}_2 \text{ available}$$

In the scenario where context C_1 holds, we observed that the policy based solely on expected reward prioritized assigning the job to *provider*$_1$, who has lower costs for all service types. Under the same context C_1, the policy incorporating fairness criteria prioritized more assignments to *provider*$_2$, who has the highest costs. Table 1 shows the probability distribution over the possible actions given context C_1.

Table 1. Probability distribution over actions under context C_1.

Action	Expected-reward policy	Fairness-based policy
Reject the job	0.1634	0.1501
Assign the job to provider$_1$	0.8366	0.5394
Assign the job to provider$_2$	0.0	0.3106

In the scenario where context C_2 holds, we again observe a prioritization of assigning services to *provider*$_2$. Table 2 shows the probability distribution over actions given context C_2.

Table 2. Probability distribution over actions under context C_2.

Action	Expected-reward policy	Fairness-based policy
Reject the job	0.1962	0.1871
Assign the job to provider_1	0.0	0.0
Assign the job to provider_2	0.8038	0.8129

6 Conclusion

This work presented an interpretability framework for MDP policies based on quantitative temporal and contextual queries. By leveraging established formal verification techniques, the proposed framework enables users to compute the exact probability of events specified in Linear Temporal Logic over Finite Traces (LTLf) and of actions conditioned on logical contexts under a fixed policy.

Unlike traditional reward-based analyses focused on expected values, the proposed framework captures structural and temporal aspects of policy behavior, including rare events and context-dependent decision patterns that cannot be naturally expressed through reward functions alone.

The case study demonstrated how the framework can be used to analyze the behavioral effects of different policy construction criteria, highlighting the impact of fairness objectives on both temporal properties and context-conditioned decisions.

Although the framework is exact for finite-horizon MDPs (or models with guaranteed termination), it inherits the scalability challenges of standard product constructions and probabilistic model checking. These limitations are intrinsic to combining logical specifications with stochastic decision processes and were not the focus of this work.

Future work includes investigating approximate and more scalable implementations, such as sampling-based methods, symbolic representations, and heuristic-guided computation, as well as evaluating the framework on larger domains and more expressive temporal specifications.

Acknowledgments. This study was supported in part by the Programa Unificado de Bolsas (PUB), sponsored by the University of São Paulo (USP), and by the Center for Artificial Intelligence (C4AI-USP), with support from FAPESP (Grant No. 2019/07665-4) and IBM.

References

1. Amitai, Y., Amir, O., Avni, G.: Asq-it: interactive explanations for reinforcement-learning agents. Artif. Intell. **335**, 104182 (2024)
2. De Giacomo, G., Vardi, M.Y.: Linear temporal logic and linear dynamic logic on finite traces. In: Proceedings of the Twenty-Third International Joint Conference on Artificial Intelligence, pp. 854–860. IJCAI '13, AAAI Press (2013)

3. Hanni, A., Boateng, A., Zhang, Y.: Safe explicable planning. In: Proceedings of the Thirty-Fourth International Conference on Automated Planning and Scheduling (ICAPS 2024), pp. 249–257 (2024)
4. Huber, T., Weitz, K., André, E., Amir, O.: Local and global explanations of agent behavior: integrating strategy summaries with saliency maps. Artif. Intell. **299** (2021). https://doi.org/10.1016/j.artint.2021.103519
5. Icarte, R.T., Klassen, T.Q., Valenzano, R., McIlraith, S.A.: Teaching multiple tasks to an rl agent using ltl. In: Proceedings of the 17th International Conference on Autonomous Agents and MultiAgent Systems, pp. 452–461 (2018)
6. Kaelbling, L.P., Moore, A.W.: Reinforcement learning: a survey. J. Artif. Intell. Res. **4**, 237–285 (1996)
7. Krarup, B., Coles, A., Long, D., Smith, D.E.: Explaining plan quality differences. In: Proceedings of the 34th International Conference on Automated Planning and Scheduling (ICAPS 2024) (2024)
8. Likmeta, A., Metelli, A.M., Tirinzoni, A., Giol, R., Restelli, M., Romano, D.: Combining reinforcement learning with rule-based controllers for transparent and general decision-making in autonomous driving. Auton. Robot. **44**, 45–62 (2020). https://doi.org/10.1007/s10514-019-09863-5
9. Majeed, S.J., Hutter, M.: Exact reduction of huge action spaces in general reinforcement learning. In: Proceedings of the AAAI Conference on Artificial Intelligence, vol. 35, pp. 8874–8883 (2021)
10. Puterman, M.L.: Markov decision processes. In: Elsevier (ed.) Handbooks in Operations Research and Management Science, vol. 2, pp. 331–434. Elsevier Science Publishers B.V. (1990)
11. Sequeira, P., Gervasio, M.: Interestingness elements for explainable reinforcement learning: understanding agents' capabilities and limitations. J. Artif. Intell. Res. **69**, 1231–1257 (2020)
12. Sreedharan, S., Srivastava, S., Kambhampati, S.: Explain it as simple as possible, but no simpler-explanation via model simplification for addressing inferential gap. Artif. Intell. **340**, 104279 (2025)
13. Steinmetz, M., Thiébaux, S., Höller, D., Teichteil-Königsbuch, F.: Explaining the space of ssp policies via policy-property dependencies: complexity, algorithms, and relation to multi-objective planning. In: Proceedings of the 34th International Conference on Automated Planning and Scheduling (ICAPS 2024), pp. 555–564. AAAI Press (2024)
14. Sutton, R.S., Barto, A.G.: Reinforcement Learning: An Introduction, 2nd edn. MIT Press, Cambridge, MA (2018)
15. Zehtabi, P., Pozanco, A., Bloch, A., Borrajo, D., Kraus, S.: Contrastive explanations of centralized multi-agent optimization solutions. In: Proceedings of the Thirty-Fourth International Conference on Automated Planning and Scheduling (ICAPS 2024), pp. 671–679 (2024)
16. Zhang, C., Shah, J.A.: Fairness in multi-agent sequential decision-making. In: Proceedings of the 28th International Conference on Neural Information Processing Systems - Volume 2, pp. 2636–2644. NIPS'14, MIT Press, Cambridge, MA, USA (2014)

Density as a Scaling Principle: Adaptive Spatial Context for POI Embeddings

João Victor dos Santos Oliveira(✉) and Salatiel Dantas Silva

Federal University of Campina Grande, Campina Grande, Brazil
joaovictor.oliveira@copin.ufcg.edu.br ,
salatiel.dantas@computacao.ufcg.edu.br

Abstract. The vector representation of Points of Interest (POIs) has become increasingly important for applications such as location-based recommendation, urban analysis, and geographic data mining. To support these tasks, POI categories must be encoded into numerical representations that capture both semantic meaning and spatial context. Recent approaches, such as GeoContext2Vec, address this by learning embeddings from geographic surroundings. However, they typically rely on a fixed spatial radius to define context, assuming a uniform scale across the city and ignoring variations in urban density. To address this limitation, this work extends GeoContext2Vec with a density-aware mechanism in which the context radius is adaptively determined for each POI. The approach applies HDBSCAN to projected coordinates to identify regions with different densities. For points within clusters, the radius is defined as the average distance to the cluster centroid, while for outliers points it corresponds to the distance to the nearest neighbor. A regularization step constrains these values within predefined bounds to ensure stability and comparability with the baseline. The resulting embeddings are evaluated using correlation with a reference similarity metric (HIT) under the ITDL protocol, performance in a dissimilarity task, and hierarchical consistency with the Yelp taxonomy. Experiments conducted on data from Austin show consistent improvements across all metrics, including higher correlations, lower RMSE, and better preservation of hierarchical relationships. In addition, the proposed approach reduces the need for extensive hyperparameter tuning, replacing multiple training runs with a single, data-driven pipeline.

Keywords: POI · geospatial embeddings · spatial context · density · HDBSCAN · GeoContext2Vec

1 Introduction

Points of Interest (POIs) play a central role in the analysis of urban, social, and economic dynamics. These entities represent relevant locations in the geographic space, such as restaurants, parks, and other urban facilities, and constitute fundamental units for applications in location-based recommendation, urban mobility analysis, territorial planning, and spatial data mining [3,7].

M. Recamonde-Mendoza and R. C. Barros (Eds.): BRACIS 2026, LNAI 17105, pp. 247–261, 2027.
https://doi.org/10.1007/978-3-032-39882-6_17

In this context, it becomes essential to develop computational representations of POIs capable of capturing not only their categorical attributes but also their spatial and functional relationships. Vector representation techniques, known as *embeddings*, have been widely employed for this purpose, projecting POIs into dense, low-dimensional vector spaces while preserving relevant semantic properties [1,2].

In the geospatial domain, the generation of POI embeddings is often based on the notion of spatial context, according to which the characterization of a POI depends on the elements present in its neighborhood. Recent studies explore geographic features, POI co-occurrence patterns, and structural information from the urban environment to compose this context [4,5]. Among the approaches that follow this line, GeoContext2Vec, proposed by Silva [9], stands out by using surrounding geographic features as input for learning vector representations of POI types, demonstrating that the explicit incorporation of such features improves performance in similarity and classification tasks.

Despite the advances provided by this approach, defining the spatial scale used to delimit context remains a critical issue. In GeoContext2Vec [9], as well as in related approaches such as Place2Vec [6] and the *place niche* model proposed by Liu et al. [7], the area of influence of each POI is defined by a fixed spatial criterion, uniformly applied to all points in the dataset. Although this choice simplifies the experimental process and allows systematic control of hyperparameters, it implicitly assumes that a single scale is sufficient to characterize heterogeneous urban environments.

However, cities exhibit strong structural variability. Central regions concentrate high density and functional diversity, while peripheral or natural areas are characterized by greater spatial dispersion [3]. In this context, the use of a fixed radius may lead to distortions in the definition of the surrounding area. In dense regions, large areas tend to incorporate redundant and weakly discriminative information. In sparse regions, small areas may fail to gather sufficient data for an adequate characterization of the local context.

This limitation becomes even more evident when considering POIs that perform distinct functions. As illustrated in Fig. 1, a restaurant located in a central area has a highly concentrated spatial context, where small variations in scale significantly impact its representation. In contrast, an urban park or natural area requires a broader region of influence for its surroundings to be adequately captured. Therefore, this work is based on the hypothesis that POIs with different functions require distinct spatial scales to achieve more expressive and discriminative vector representations.

Based on this premise, we propose *Density-aware GeoContext2Vec*, an extension of GeoContext2Vec [9] that incorporates an adaptive mechanism to define spatial scale, guided by the local density of POIs. The proposed strategy replaces the fixed radius with dynamically estimated radii obtained by spatial clustering techniques, using the HDBSCAN algorithm [8]. By leveraging the intrinsic density structure of the data to determine the area of influence of each POI, the spatial scale is transformed from a global hyperparameter into a variable

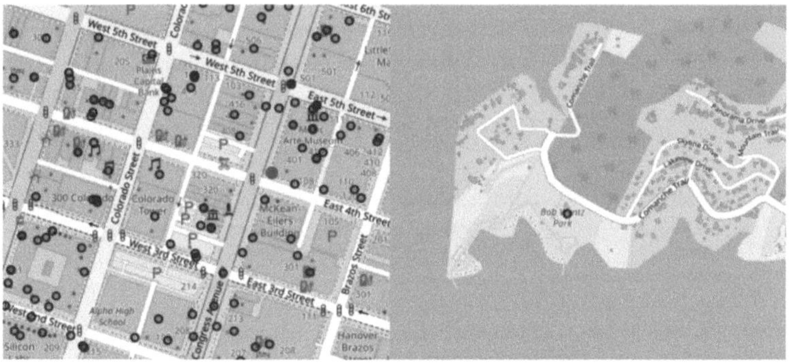

Fig. 1. Examples of Points of Interest (POIs) embedded within urban contexts exhibiting distinct density patterns. On the left, a restaurant (highlighted in red) is situated in a central area characterized by a high concentration of establishments and urban features; on the right, a park is located in a more dispersed region, marked by a lower density of POIs. (Color figure online)

derived from the inherent organization of urban space. This approach bridges the gap between fixed-scale representations and the intrinsic heterogeneity of urban environments.

The experimental results indicate consistent improvements across multiple evaluation metrics, including correlation with reference similarity, discriminative capability, and preservation of hierarchical structure. In addition, the proposed approach reduces the need for extensive hyperparameter tuning, leading to improved computational efficiency.

2 Related Work and Theoretical Background

Vector representations of spatial entities have emerged as a dominant paradigm in geographic data mining and urban computing. The increasing availability of data from collaborative platforms, urban sensors, and mobility records has intensified the demand for techniques capable of capturing complex relationships between places, transcending categorical descriptions and sparse representations [2,5]. In this context, representation learning has become a key tool for modeling latent spatial semantics.

Inspired by advances in Natural Language Processing (NLP), embedding techniques have been successfully adapted to the geographic domain. The core idea is to project entities into dense, low-dimensional vector spaces while preserving semantic and structural relationships. Unlike traditional sparse representations, embeddings enable continuous similarity modeling, which benefits tasks such as classification, recommendation, and predictive analysis [1]. However, directly transferring NLP-based assumptions to spatial data introduces challenges, particularly with regard to the definition of spatial context.

In the geospatial domain, several approaches have been proposed to address representation learning. Jin et al. [6] introduced the *Geohash-based Place2Vec* model, in which geohash-encoded regions are used as contextual units. Although effective, this approach relies on fixed spatial partitions, imposing a rigid notion of context that may fail to capture heterogeneous urban structures. Similarly, Crivellari and Beinat [2] leveraged large-scale mobility data to generate geo-embeddings representing places, trajectories, and users. Although human mobility provides rich functional signals, the method implicitly assumes that observed movement patterns sufficiently capture spatial context, potentially overlooking static geographic features.

Liu, Andris, and Rahimi [7] proposed the concept of *place niche*, introducing a vector representation strategy to quantify regional spatial context. Hu et al. [4] developed a framework for extracting functional urban regions based on embeddings derived from POIs. Despite their effectiveness, these approaches typically assume a uniform spatial scale, limiting their ability to model regions with varying density. Huang et al. [5] extended this line of work by integrating multi-modal data sources, including images, text, and mobility information. Although this enriches representation capacity, the issue of spatial scale definition remains largely unaddressed.

Despite these advances, a recurring limitation concerns how spatial context is defined. Most existing methods adopt fixed criteria, such as spatial grids, administrative boundaries, or constant-radius neighborhoods. While these choices simplify the modeling process, they impose a uniform notion of space that fails to reflect the intrinsic heterogeneity of urban environments, where dense and sparse regions coexist and exhibit distinct spatial dynamics [3]. As a result, the learned representations may be suboptimal, particularly in areas where the chosen scale does not align with local structure.

In the specific context of POI type representation, Silva [9] proposed the GeoContext2Vec algorithm, which incorporates geographic features from the surroundings of POIs, such as streets, green areas, and water bodies, into the embedding learning process. This approach demonstrates that explicitly modeling geographic context improves performance in POI classification tasks. However, GeoContext2Vec adopts a fixed-radius strategy to define spatial neighborhoods, assuming that a single scale is sufficient to characterize all POIs. Given the variability of urban density and function, this assumption may limit the expressiveness and adaptability of the resulting embeddings.

Density-based clustering algorithms offer a natural mechanism to address spatial heterogeneity. Methods such as DBSCAN [16] identify clusters based on local point density, while extensions such as HDBSCAN [8] further improve this paradigm by modeling density variations hierarchically and eliminating the need for a global density threshold (e.g., ϵ). Additionally, HDBSCAN identifies noise points and clusters with varying densities, making it particularly suitable for complex urban environments.

Although clustering techniques have been widely used for urban segmentation and the identification of functional regions, their use as a mechanism for adaptive spatial context definition in embedding models remains underexplored. Existing work predominantly focuses on cluster detection rather than leveraging density information to dynamically adjust the scale of context used during representation learning.

To address this limitation, this work extends GeoContext2Vec, here referred to as *Density-aware GeoContext2Vec*, by introducing a density-aware mechanism for adaptive spatial context definition. Specifically, we leverage HDBSCAN to dynamically determine neighborhood radii based on local density patterns. By aligning context modeling with the intrinsic structure of urban space, the proposed approach aims to produce more expressive and discriminative POI type embeddings, particularly in heterogeneous environments where fixed-scale methods are insufficient (Fig. 2).

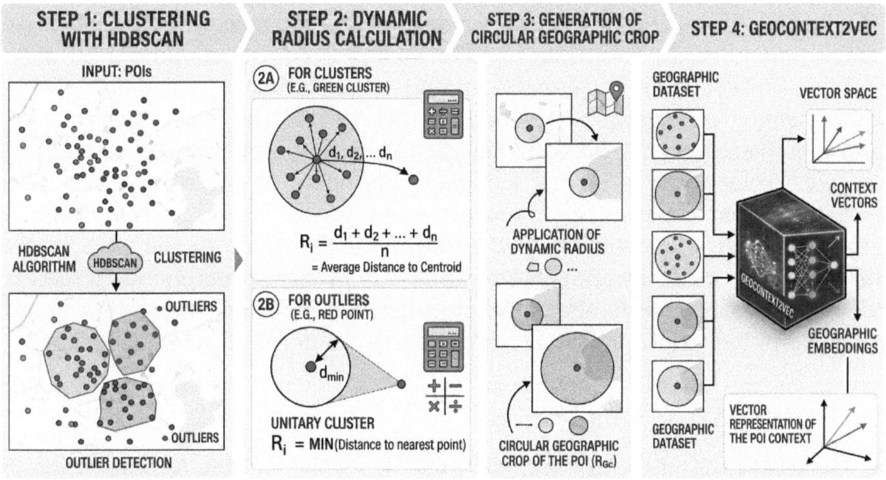

Fig. 2. Proposed pipeline for generating adaptive embeddings of POI types. (1) HDBSCAN is applied to infer the spatial density structure; (2) dynamic radii are computed as the mean distance to the cluster centroid for clustered points and as the nearest-neighbor distance for noise points; (3) circular geographic regions are defined based on the estimated radii; and (4) the resulting contexts are integrated into the GeoContext2Vec pipeline to learn spatial representations.

3 Methodology

This section presents the proposed density-aware mechanism, which is the main methodological contribution of this work. It describes the dataset, the strategy for adaptive spatial scale definition, and the evaluation protocol.

3.1 Dataset

The experiments were conducted using a dataset of 22,398 real-world POIs from the city of Austin, Texas. The categorical information of these points was obtained from the Yelp dataset, while the geographic features used to construct the spatial context were extracted from OpenStreetMap. This integration of establishment data and the physical structure of urban space allows POIs to be analyzed not only from a semantic perspective but also in terms of spatial organization.

The choice of Austin is justified by its morphological and functional diversity. The city contains central areas with a high concentration of commercial and service activities, as well as peripheral regions with lower urban density, including predominantly natural areas. This spatial heterogeneity, characterized by the coexistence of densely occupied zones and highly dispersed regions, makes it particularly suitable for investigating the impact of different context scales on embedding generation.

Each POI in the dataset is described by its geographic coordinates and semantic category. In total, the dataset comprises 1,184 distinct POI types, covering commercial establishments, public areas, urban services, and natural spaces, thereby reflecting the functional diversity of the city. However, as is common in collaborative datasets, the distribution of POIs is not perfectly uniform, with some regions having a higher concentration of records and others presenting potential gaps. This incompleteness directly affects the estimation of spatial density and, consequently, the automatic definition of the radii used to delimit context areas. To address this issue, the proposed methodology incorporates regularization mechanisms by imposing minimum and maximum bounds on the computed values, mitigating the effects of uneven data distribution.

3.2 HDBSCAN Configuration

The spatial density structure was identified using the HDBSCAN algorithm [8], configured to reflect the characteristics of POI distribution in the city of Austin. The algorithm was instantiated using Euclidean distance, *min_cluster_size* equal to 2, and *min_samples* equal to 1.

The use of Euclidean distance is justified because POI coordinates are projected into a metric coordinate system, where distances are expressed in meters. This avoids distortions associated with geographic coordinates in degrees and allows consistent local distance computation.

A small value for *min_cluster_size* was adopted to enable fine-grained detection of local density variations, which is essential for adaptive radius estimation. Clusters with fewer than two elements do not provide sufficient structural information for radius computation. The parameter *min_samples* was set to 1 to make the algorithm less conservative, allowing low-density regions to be considered valid clusters. This choice reduces excessive classification of points as noise and ensures that even sparse regions contribute to spatial scale estimation. HDBSCAN is not used for urban segmentation itself, but rather as an auxiliary mechanism to infer local density structure. The resulting clusters provide the basis for estimating spatial radii and identifying isolated points.

The computational complexity of the proposed method is dominated by HDBSCAN, which typically operates in $O(n \log n)$ time. The additional steps for centroid and radius computation involve linear scans over cluster elements, yielding $O(n)$ complexity. Therefore, the overall approach remains scalable for moderately large urban datasets.

3.3 Dynamic Radius Definition Strategy

In the original GeoContext2Vec [9], a fixed radius r is used to define the spatial region associated with each POI. For a point p_i with projected coordinates (x_i, y_i), the region is defined as:

$$\mathcal{R}_d = \{(x, y) \in \mathbb{R}^2 \mid d((x, y), (x_i, y_i)) \leq r\},$$

where $d(\cdot)$ denotes Euclidean distance.

In the proposed *Density-aware GeoContext2Vec*, the global radius is replaced by a dynamic radius r_i, determined from local density patterns inferred using HDBSCAN.

Let $\mathcal{P}$ be the set of POIs and $\mathcal{K} = \{K_1, \ldots, K_m\}$ the set of clusters obtained. For each cluster K_k, its spatial centroid is computed as

$$\mu_k = \frac{1}{|K_k|} \sum_{p_j \in K_k} (x_j, y_j).$$

The cluster radius is defined as the average distance between its elements and the centroid:

$$r_k = \frac{1}{|K_k|} \sum_{p_j \in K_k} d(p_j, \mu_k).$$

For each $p_i \in K_k$, we assign $r_i = r_k$, ensuring that all points within the same cluster share a scale consistent with local density.

For points classified as noise, i.e., $p_i \notin \bigcup_k K_k$, the radius is defined as:

$$r_i = \min_{p_j \in \mathcal{P}, j \neq i} d(p_i, p_j),$$

which corresponds to the distance to the nearest neighboring POI. This ensures that even isolated points have a minimal contextual region.

3.4 Regularization with Bounds

A purely density-based definition may produce extreme values in regions with missing data or high dispersion. To mitigate this effect, global bounds are defined (in meters):

$$r_i = \max(100, \min(r_i, r_{\max})),$$

where

$$r_{\max} = \begin{cases} 900, & \text{if } p_i \text{ belongs to a cluster} \\ 3000, & \text{if } p_i \text{ is classified as outlier.} \end{cases}$$

The minimum value of 100 m is maintained, as it corresponds to the smallest scale evaluated in the original GeoContext2Vec experiments [9], ensuring consistency with previously validated settings. Similarly, an upper bound of 900 m is adopted for clustered regions to preserve comparability with the largest radius explored in the baseline model. For noise points, a higher upper limit of 3000 m is defined to account for spatial dispersion and ensure sufficient contextual area in low-density regions. This regularization step ensures numerical stability, spatial consistency, and control over extreme variations caused by potential gaps in the dataset.

3.5 Integration with the GeoContext2Vec Pipeline

After defining the dynamic radii r_i, the remaining steps of the GeoContext2Vec pipeline [9] are unchanged. For each POI, geographic features within the region defined by r_i are extracted to form sets of contextual elements. These sets are then treated as spatial sentences for training a Word2Vec model [17], resulting in vector embeddings for POI types.

The proposed modification is restricted to the spatial scale definition step, ensuring that any observed performance differences can be attributed to the adaptive radius mechanism.

3.6 Evaluation Procedure

The experimental evaluation is designed to assess the quality of the generated embeddings from multiple semantic and structural perspectives. The goal is to assess whether the learned vector representations capture similarity relationships, distinguish semantically distinct categories, and preserve hierarchical organization among POI types.

To this end, three main groups of metrics are considered: correlation with external similarity rankings, dissimilarity accuracy, and hierarchical consistency measures.

Correlation with Reference Similarity. This analysis evaluates the alignment between embedding-based similarity and an external reference of semantic similarity. We use the ITDL dataset [10], which provides pairs of POI categories associated with similarity scores (HIT). The dataset is publicly available in the official project repository[1].

For each pair (t_1, t_2), cosine similarity is computed between their corresponding embedding vectors. The relationship between the predicted similarities and the reference HIT scores is then assessed using complementary statistical metrics, capturing both ordinal consistency and numerical accuracy.

Specifically, the following metrics are employed:

[1] https://github.com/b13302/place2vec.

- **Spearman's rank correlation coefficient** [11], which measures the strength of monotonic relationships between the rankings induced by the embedding similarities and the reference scores;
- **Pearson's correlation coefficient** [12], which evaluates the linear relationship between predicted similarities and ground-truth values;
- **Root Mean Squared Error (RMSE)** [13], which quantifies the average magnitude of prediction errors, providing a direct measure of numerical discrepancy.

The combined use of these metrics enables a comprehensive evaluation of the embedding space, capturing both its ability to preserve relative similarity ordering and its accuracy in approximating absolute similarity values.

Dissimilarity Accuracy. This analysis investigates whether the learned embeddings effectively encode semantic similarity relationships among POI categories. To this end, a binary classification task is defined based on the ITDL dataset [10], in which pairs of categories are labeled as similar or dissimilar.

After training the model, the embeddings associated with the categories were extracted and used as input for the evaluation. Subsequently, a script computed the cosine similarities between vectors for each instance in the ITDL-based binary task. Based on these similarity values, the least similar category was selected in each case. This selection was then compared against the reference labels provided by ITDL. The evaluation metric used was accuracy [14], defined as the proportion of correct classifications relative to the total number of evaluated instances. This measure enables assessing whether the embedding space adequately separates categories that should not exhibit semantic proximity, thus providing a direct test of the discriminative capacity of the embeddings.

Hierarchical Consistency. Finally, we evaluated whether the embedding space preserves the hierarchical relationships among POI types. The official Yelp category hierarchy[2] is considered, where each class is associated with higher-, lower-, or same-level categories in the platform taxonomy.

For each evaluated category, the most similar types in the embedding space are retrieved, and the degree of alignment between these predictions and the structural similarity defined by the Yelp hierarchy[2] is assessed. The evaluation was conducted using classical semantic similarity metrics based on taxonomic graphs, following the protocol proposed in [10]. Subsequently, the rankings generated by the embeddings are compared with rankings derived from these metrics using Mean Reciprocal Rank (MRR) [15], which assigns higher weight to correct predictions appearing in top positions.

Two hierarchy-based similarity metrics are considered:

[2] https://business.yelp.com/resources/articles/yelp-category-list/?domain=local-business.

- **WP (Wu & Palmer)** [18], which defines the similarity between two categories t_1 and t_2 as:

$$SIM_{WP}(t_1, t_2) = \frac{2 \cdot depth(lcs)}{depth(t_1) + depth(t_2)}$$

  where *lcs* denotes the Least Common Subsumer of the categories in the hierarchy. This metric favors pairs that share deeper common ancestors, reflecting greater conceptual proximity.
- **LC (Leacock & Chodorow)** [19], which measures similarity based on the shortest path distance N between two categories in the hierarchy:

$$SIM_{LC}(t_1, t_2) = -\log\left(\frac{N}{2D}\right)$$

  where D corresponds to the maximum depth of the taxonomy. This metric captures similarity as a function of normalized structural distance, allowing meaningful comparisons even between categories that do not share the same immediate parent.

While the WP metric emphasizes the depth of the lowest common ancestor as an indicator of semantic proximity, the LC metric models similarity based on normalized structural distance within the taxonomic graph. Together, these measures allow evaluating the ability of the embedding space to reflect the conceptual organization underlying Yelp categories.

Protocol Summary. These evaluation metrics provide a multi-faceted assessment, capturing both geometric properties of the embedding space and its semantic alignment with external knowledge sources:

1. Alignment with external similarity through correlation;
2. Semantic discrimination through accuracy;
3. Structural consistency through hierarchical evaluation.

This comprehensive framework enables a robust analysis of embedding quality across multiple dimensions.

For reproducibility, the full implementation of the pipeline, including preprocessing, clustering, dynamic radius computation, and evaluation procedures, is publicly available at: https://github.com/Jaovicttor/GeoContext2Vec-DynamicRadius/tree/main.

Unlike prior approaches, the proposed method introduces an adaptive, data-driven mechanism for spatial scale definition, enabling more faithful modeling of heterogeneous urban environments.

4 Results and Discussion

This section presents a comparison between the original GeoContext2Vec configuration proposed by Silva [9], whose best performance was obtained with a fixed radius of 100 m and weight 0.8, and the *Density-aware GeoContext2Vec* approach proposed in this work. The same weight parameter is maintained to ensure direct comparability between the models.

4.1 Overall Performance Comparison

Table 1 summarizes the main results obtained under both experimental configurations.

Table 1. Comparison between the fixed-radius model and the dynamic-radius model

Metric	Fixed Radius (100 m)	Dynamic Radius
Spearman	0.4036	0.7646
Pearson	0.3701	0.7786
RMSE	0.4537	0.2576
Dissimilarity Accuracy	0.7922	0.9351
WP	0.4227	0.5967
LC	0.4227	0.5967

Table 1 shows that the, the dynamic-radius approach consistently outperforms the fixed-radius baseline across all evaluated metrics, indicating substantial improvements in both semantic alignment and structural consistency.

4.2 Correlation with Reference Similarity

Spearman correlation increased from 0.4036 to 0.7646, representing a relative improvement of approximately 89.5%. This result indicates a significantly enhanced ability to preserve the relative ordering of POI type similarities. Similarly, Pearson correlation increased from 0.3701 to 0.7786, corresponding to an improvement of approximately 110.4%, demonstrating stronger linear alignment with reference similarity values. Additionally, RMSE decreased from 0.4537 to 0.2576, a reduction of approximately 43.2%, indicating that the predicted similarities are substantially closer to the ground-truth values.

Together, these results provide strong evidence that adapting the spatial scale improves both ordinal and numerical fidelity of similarity modeling.

4.3 Dissimilarity Accuracy

In the task of distinguishing semantically distinct categories, accuracy increased from 0.7922 to 0.9351, corresponding to an approximate 18% relative improvement. This result reflects improved discriminative power in the embedding space.

These results indicate that the dynamic-radius approach not only improves similarity estimation but also strengthens the separation between conceptually unrelated categories, leading to a more structured and meaningful embedding space.

4.4 Hierarchical Consistency

The hierarchical evaluation also showed consistent improvements. Both WP and LC metrics increased from 0.4227 to 0.5967, representing a relative gain of approximately 41.1%.

This improvement indicates that the learned embeddings better reflect the conceptual organization defined by the Yelp taxonomy. Categories that share semantic relationships in the hierarchy are more closely positioned in the embedding space when spatial scale is adaptively defined (Fig. 3).

Fig. 3. Visual comparison between the fixed-radius strategy adopted by GeoContext2Vec (left) and *Density-aware GeoContext2Vec* (right), applied to the same POI.

4.5 Interpretation of the Improvements

The consistent improvements observed across all evaluation dimensions demonstrate that dynamically defining spatial context leads to more expressive and semantically coherent POI type embeddings. In dense regions, smaller radii prevent the inclusion of redundant or overly similar contextual features, reducing noise in representation learning. Conversely, in sparse regions, larger radii ensure that sufficient contextual information is captured, preventing underrepresentation of isolated POIs.

By maintaining all other components of the GeoContext2Vec pipeline unchanged, the observed performance gains can be directly attributed to the proposed adaptive radius mechanism. This isolates the effect of spatial scale and provides strong empirical support for the central hypothesis of this work: that aligning context definition with local density significantly enhances embedding quality.

Overall, the magnitude of the improvements suggests that the spatial heterogeneity of cities should be explicitly considered when modeling geographic vector representations.

4.6 Computational Impact and Experimental Efficiency

Beyond improvements in embedding quality, the proposed approach also introduces significant computational advantages.

In Silva [9], optimal performance was achieved through an exhaustive grid search over two hyperparameters: radius (ranging from 100 to 900 m) and weight (ranging from 0 to 1). This resulted in 99 experimental configurations, each requiring a full pipeline execution, including feature extraction, context construction, embedding training, and evaluation. In contrast, *Density-aware GeoContext2Vec* eliminates the need for radius tuning by deriving it directly from spatial density. By fixing the weight parameter at 0.8, only a single pipeline execution is required, combined with a one-time clustering step.

Although clustering introduces an additional computational cost, it is performed once and has significantly lower complexity compared to repeated embedding training. Therefore, the overall computational cost is substantially reduced. From a scalability perspective, this advantage becomes even more significant in large-scale scenarios involving multiple cities or datasets. Eliminating manual hyperparameter tuning reduces experimental complexity and enhances the approach's transferability.

Overall, *Density-aware GeoContext2Vec* achieves a favorable trade-off between performance and efficiency, simultaneously improving embedding quality and reducing computational requirements. This combination reinforces its practical applicability in real-world urban analytics tasks.

5 Conclusion

This work investigates the impact of dynamically adapting spatial scale in the generation of embeddings for Points of Interest types. Motivated by the limitations of the original GeoContext2Vec formulation [9], which relies on fixed radii to define the spatial context, we proposed a density-aware mechanism to automatically define dynamic radii based on the spatial structure of the data.

The central hypothesis of this work is that POIs with distinct urban functions require different spatial scales to produce expressive and discriminative vector representations. The experimental results provide strong evidence supporting this hypothesis. Significant improvements were observed in all evaluation metrics, including a higher correlation with external similarity measures, a substantial reduction in root mean squared error, improved dissimilarity accuracy, and better preservation of hierarchical relationships between categories.

In addition to semantic improvements, the proposed approach also demonstrates important computational advantages. By replacing exhaustive hyperparameter search with a data-driven mechanism guided by spatial density, the method eliminates the need for multiple full training runs. This results in increased efficiency, improved scalability, and greater transferability across different urban contexts.

Despite these contributions, some limitations must be considered. The effectiveness of the dynamic radius definition depends on the quality and completeness of the POI dataset, and may be affected by missing or unevenly distributed data. Furthermore, the choice of clustering algorithm influences the inferred spatial structure and, consequently, the computed radii. Although HDBSCAN was adopted due to its robustness to variable densities, alternative clustering strategies may lead to different results.

Future work may explore the use of more robust statistical estimators for radius computation, as well as the integration of additional contextual signals, such as temporal dynamics or user mobility patterns. Another promising direction is the evaluation of the proposed approach in multiple cities with distinct urban characteristics, enabling a deeper analysis of its generalization capabilities.

References

1. Chen, M., Zhu, L., Xu, R., Liu, Y., Yu, X., Yin, Y.: Embedding hierarchical structures for venue category representation. ACM Trans. Inform. Syst. **40**(3), 1–29 (2021). https://doi.org/10.1145/3442381
2. Crivellari, A., Beinat, E.: From movement activity to geo-embeddings: generating and exploring vector representations of places, trajectories and visitors from massive mobility data. ISPRS Int. J. Geo Inf. **8**(3), 134 (2019). https://doi.org/10.3390/ijgi8030134
3. Han, S., Liu, C., Chen, K., Gui, D., Du, Q.: A tourist attraction recommendation model fusing spatial, temporal, and visual embeddings for geotagged photos on Flickr. ISPRS Int. J. Geo Inf. **10**(1), 20 (2021). https://doi.org/10.3390/ijgi10010020
4. Hu, S., He, Z., Wu, L., Yin, L., Xu, Y., Cui, H.: A framework for extracting urban functional regions based on multi-prototype word embeddings using points of interest data. Comput. Environ. Urban Syst. **80**, 101442 (2020). https://doi.org/10.1016/j.compenvurbsys.2019.101442
5. Huang, T., Wang, Z., Sheng, H., Ng, A.Y., Rajagopal, R.: Learning neighborhood representation from multi-modal multi-graph: image, text, mobility, and beyond. arXiv preprint (2021). https://arxiv.org/abs/2105.02489
6. Jin, J., Xiao, Z., Qiu, Q., Fang, J.: A geohash-based Place2Vec model. In: IEEE International Geoscience and Remote Sensing Symposium (IGARSS), pp. 3344–3347. IEEE (2019). https://doi.org/10.1109/IGARSS.2019.8898455
7. Liu, X., Andris, C., Rahimi, S.: Place niche and its regional variability: measuring spatial context patterns of points of interest with representation learning. Comput. Environ. Urban Syst. **75**, 146–160 (2019). https://doi.org/10.1016/j.compenvurbsys.2019.02.003
8. Campello, R.J.G.B., Moulavi, D., Sander, J.: Density-based clustering based on hierarchical density estimates. In: Advances in Knowledge Discovery and Data Mining, pp. 160–172. Springer (2013). https://doi.org/10.1007/978-3-642-37456-2_14
9. Silva, S.D.: Geração de embeddings de tipos de POI com base em feições geográficas. Ph.D. thesis, Universidade Federal de Campina Grande (2024)

10. Yan, B., Janowicz, K., Mai, G., Gao, S.: From ITDL to Place2Vec: reasoning about place type similarity and relatedness by learning embeddings from augmented spatial contexts. In: Proceedings of the 25th ACM SIGSPATIAL International Conference on Advances in Geographic Information Systems, pp. 1–10 (2017). https://doi.org/10.1145/3139958.3140054
11. Spearman, C.: The proof and measurement of association between two things. Am. J. Psychol. **15**(1), 72–101 (1904). https://doi.org/10.2307/1412159
12. Pearson, K.: Note on regression and inheritance in the case of two parents. Proc. R. Soc. Lond. **58**, 240–242 (1895). https://doi.org/10.1098/rspl.1895.0041
13. Willmott, C.J.: On the validation of models. Phys. Geogr. **2**(2), 184–194 (1981). https://doi.org/10.1080/02723646.1981.10642213
14. Powers, D.M.W.: Evaluation: from precision, recall and F-measure to ROC, informedness, markedness and correlation. J. Mach. Learn. Technol. **2**(1), 37–63 (2011)
15. Voorhees, E.M.: The TREC-8 question answering track report. In: Proceedings of the 8th Text REtrieval Conference (TREC-8) (1999)
16. Ester, M., Kriegel, H.-P., Sander, J., Xu, X.: A density-based algorithm for discovering clusters in large spatial databases with noise. In: Proceedings of KDD, pp. 226–231 (1996)
17. Mikolov, T., Sutskever, I., Chen, K., Corrado, G., Dean, J.: Distributed representations of words and phrases and their compositionality. In: Advances in Neural Information Processing Systems (NeurIPS) (2013)
18. Wu, Z., Palmer, M.: Verb semantics and lexical selection. In: Proceedings of the Association for Computational Linguistics (ACL), pp. 133–138 (1994). https://doi.org/10.3115/981732.981751
19. Leacock, C., Chodorow, M.: Combining local context and WordNet similarity for word sense identification. In: Fellbaum, C. (ed.) WordNet: An Electronic Lexical Database, pp. 265–283. MIT Press (1998)

DensGNN: A Density Based Graph Neural Network for Node Clustering in Applications with Noise

Guilherme Henrique Messias[1(✉)], Natanael Fabrício Dacioli Batista[1], Tiago Gonçalves Botelho[1,2], Sylvia Iasulaitis[1], Alan Demétrius Baria Valejo[1], and Murilo Coelho Naldi[1]

[1] Universidade Federal de São Carlos, São Carlos, SP, Brazil
{ghmessias,natanael.batista}@estudante.ufscar.br, tiago.botelho@muz.ifsuldeminas.edu.br, {si,alanvalejo,naldi}@ufscar.br
[2] Instituto Federal do Sul de Minas Gerais, Muzambinho, MG, Brazil

Abstract. Attributed graphs combine structural and semantic information, making them suitable for a wide range of applications such as social network analysis and biological system modeling. Although graph neural networks (GNNs) have shown strong performance in supervised settings, their application to unsupervised tasks such as clustering nodes remains challenging, especially in the presence of noise, outliers, and clusters with irregular shapes. In this work, we propose DensGNN, a density-based Graph Neural Network that integrates a Graph Autoencoder (GAE) with a self-supervised module guided by the HDBSCAN algorithm. Instead of relying on centroid-based assumptions, the proposed method leverages dense support sets to guide the organization of the latent space, allowing the identification of clusters with arbitrary geometries while reducing the influence of noisy and boundary points. We also provide a theoretical analysis that demonstrates that the proposed density-based distance is invariant to small perturbations in boundary points, in contrast to centroid-based approaches. Experimental results in benchmark data sets indicate that DensGNN achieves superior clustering performance compared to state-of-the-art methods, while maintaining robustness in scenarios where the number of clusters is unknown. These findings highlight the effectiveness of incorporating density-based principles directly into the learning objective of deep graph clustering models.

Keywords: Graph Neural Networks · Node clustering · HDBSCAN · Density-based clustering

1 Introduction

Attributed graphs are mathematical and computational structures particularly suited to represent data that combine relational information and individual node

M. Recamonde-Mendoza and R. C. Barros (Eds.): BRACIS 2026, LNAI 17105, pp. 262–276, 2027.
https://doi.org/10.1007/978-3-032-39882-6_18

characteristics, expressed by topology and semantic attributes respectively [7]. This type of representation has been used in several applications, such as cluster identification in social networks [19], protein interaction prediction [33], and vehicular traffic control [12]. The broad applicability of such data has driven the development of supervised and semi-supervised models for graphs, among which Graph Neural Networks (GNNs) stand out [8,29]. By integrating semantic and topological information, these models are able to construct highly representative latent spaces. Despite their success in supervised settings, GNNs still face challenges in identifying patterns in unsupervised scenarios, where no labels are available [13].

Among unsupervised learning tasks on graphs, node clustering plays a prominent role. Its goal is to partition the vertices into disjoint clusters such that the elements within the same cluster are more similar to each other than to those of other clusters [14]. To address this problem, different approaches have been proposed. Some rely on GNNs combined with adversarial embedding learning methods [22], followed by external clustering algorithms. Others formulate objective functions that are directly aimed at optimizing cluster quality metrics, such as modularity [18]. There are also deep methods capable of constructing probabilistic latent spaces in order to promote better structural organization of the clusters [30].

While these approaches have shown promising results, they inherit fundamental limitations common to traditional clustering algorithms: the requirement to pre-specify the number of clusters and a vulnerability to noise and outliers. Furthermore, many objective functions in deep clustering assume that clusters can be adequately represented by a prototypical element, typically a centroid. This implicitly imposes a restrictive sphericality assumption on the cluster geometries [6]. Consequently, these models struggle to capture arbitrarily shaped clusters in the latent space, which cannot be accurately modeled by centroid-based methods such as K-means.

To overcome these limitations, we propose a novel GNN grounded in density-based clustering. By leveraging the HDBSCAN algorithm [3], our model is able to: (1) capture arbitrary latent structures by identifying regions of varying density; (2) robustly handle noise in the latent representation space by prioritizing dense regions and isolating outliers; and (3) automatically determine the number of clusters during training, thereby enhancing its applicability to real-world scenarios. Our main contributions are as follows:

- We propose a novel density-based clustering model for attributed graphs. By combining GNNs with a loss function based on the probability of belonging to dense clusters, DensGNN induces a latent space that captures the structurally relevant regions of the graph. To the best of our knowledge, this is the first deep learning graph model that explicitly leverages cluster density to guide the representation learning process.
- We demonstrate that DensGNN is highly robust, remaining invariant to perturbations in data points that fall outside dense support sets.

- We theoretically demonstrate that DensGNN is robust to irregular cluster geometries, noise, and the influence of border points. Furthermore, we conduct a comprehensive empirical evaluation against state-of-the-art node clustering methods across several benchmark data sets.
- We present an ablation study analyzing the model's key hyperparameters, alongside experiments simulating realistic scenarios where the true number of clusters is unknown a priori.

The paper is structured as follows: Sect. 2 reviews related literature; Sect. 3 details the proposed methodology; Sect. 4 presents the empirical results; and Sect. 5 concludes by discussing our contributions and limitations.

2 Related Work

2.1 Deep Clustering via GNN

Clustering algorithms for attributed graphs can generally be divided into three main categories [17]: embedding-based models, adversarial models, and deep models. Deep models, in particular, are characterized by two central assumptions: (1) they employ loss functions capable of inducing a latent representation space suitable for clustering, that is, a space in which similar elements remain close to one another while dissimilar elements are pushed apart [26]; and (2) they are designed to execute the final cluster assignment internally [30], i.e., without relying on an external algorithm.

In practice, however, this second characteristic is often fully realized only in the final stages of the pipeline. Because unsupervised clustering is inherently complex, external algorithms are frequently employed to guide the learning process during training. Among these, K-means is the most widely adopted due to its computational efficiency and robust performance [6]. Consequently, for many methods in this category, the overall loss function comprises two primary components: a reconstruction term derived from a Graph AutoEncoder (GAE), and a divergence term that measures the discrepancy between the current cluster assignments (matrix Q) and a smoothed target distribution (matrix P):

$$\mathcal{L} = \mathcal{L}_{\text{GAE}} + \gamma \mathcal{L}_{\text{cluster}}, \qquad \mathcal{L}_{\text{cluster}} = \text{KL}(P||Q), \tag{1}$$

and

$$q_{ij} = \frac{(1 - d(z_i, \Omega_j))^{-1}}{(1 - \sum_k d(z_i, \Omega_k))^{-1}}, \qquad p_{ij} = \frac{\frac{q_{iu}^2}{\sum_i q_{iu}}}{\sum_k \left(\frac{q_{ik}^2}{\sum_i q_{ik}} \right)} \tag{2}$$

where $d(\cdot, \cdot)$ denotes a distance function (usually Euclidean Distance), z_i is the embedding of vertex i, Ω_j represents the j-th cluster among the k obtained clusters, KL stands for Kullback-Leibler Divergence and γ is a trade-off parameter between the terms of the objective function.

Although widely adopted across various attributed graph clustering methods—including those using attention mechanisms [30], multi-embeddings [15], k-order matrices [16], and DeepWalk-inspired strategies [11]—this formulation presents significant drawbacks. Specifically, the optimization of Eq. 2 together with the centroid identification of K-means imposes strict geometric limitations on the latent space. Moreover, it inherently lacks outlier filtration, forcing the model to treat noisy or atypical data points equivalently to core structural nodes.

Density-based algorithms define clusters as contiguous regions of high data density separated by sparse, low-density areas. This characteristic enables these methods to automatically determine the number of clusters while inherently identifying outliers. Figure 1 illustrates the difference between a centroid-guided clustering strategy, such as K-means, and a density-oriented strategy from the perspective of a vertex z_i in latent space.

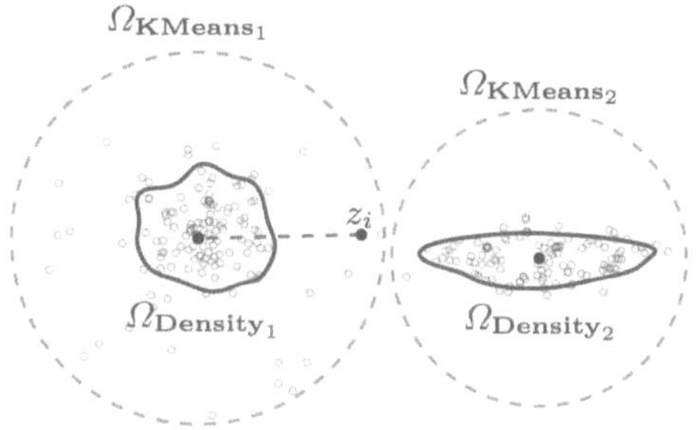

Fig. 1. Comparison of centroid-based (dotted green) and density-based (solid blue) cluster boundaries. The point z_i represents an outlier that should ideally exert minimal influence on the structure of cluster $\Omega_{K\text{-means}_1}$. (Color figure online)

2.2 HDBSCAN* Algorithm

Recognized as a leading algorithm in unsupervised learning, HDBSCAN* [3] advances traditional density-based methods by extracting a multi-scale cluster hierarchy from the data. By generalizing the DBSCAN model across all possible density thresholds (ϵ), it effectively handles clusters of variable densities and actively isolates background noise without requiring the number of clusters to be specified *a priori*. Consequently, it relies solely on the minimum number of points m_{pts} parameter to smooth the density estimate, defining the ϵ-neighborhood size required for a region to be considered dense. While its robustness has driven broad adoption across diverse scientific domains [4,10,24,25,27], these exact properties—dynamic cluster discovery, explicit noise handling, and hierarchical structuring—make HDBSCAN* exceptionally promising for integration with GNNs. Whether applied to graph topologies or learned node embeddings, it naturally identifies latent communities, facilitates hierarchical pooling by defining structural super-nodes, and filters anomalous noise prior to message passing, ultimately improving the computational efficiency, robustness, and interpretability of graph-based models [2,28].

3 DensGNN: Density-Based GNN for Node Clustering

Our main goal consists of clustering the nodes of a given graph $G = (V, E, X)$, where V is the set of vertices (nodes) with n elements, $E = \{(v_i, v_j) : v_i, v_j \in V\}$ is the set of edges, $X \in \mathbb{R}^{n \times d}$ is the attribute matrix of G, in which each row x_i represents the features of vertex v_i, $A \in \mathbb{R}^{n \times n}$ is the symmetric adjacency matrix for $A_{ij} = 1$ if $(v_i, v_j) \in E$ and $A_{ij} = 0$ otherwise, and D is the diagonal matrix in which D_{ii} represents the number of neighbors of v_i. The result is a set $\Omega = \{\Omega_1, \Omega_2, \cdots, \Omega_k\}$ of distinct clusters [31].

Traditional deep clustering approaches rely on restrictive centroid-based representations that fail to capture non-convex shapes, heterogeneous densities, ambiguous boundaries, and background noise. Furthermore, in the context of attributed graphs, the complex latent structures induced by the interplay of topology and node attributes frequently defy the spherical assumptions inherent to these centroid models. To overcome these limitations, we propose DensGNN.

The algorithm operates through two interconnected modules. The initial embedding module utilizes a GAE [9] to map the graph G and its attributes into an informative latent space. To establish a stable foundation, training begins with a warm-up period of e_{warm} epochs, during which the GAE parameters are updated solely via a topological reconstruction loss ($\mathcal{L}_{\text{recon}}$). Following this warm-up, the self-supervised module is activated to refine the representations. By applying the HDBSCAN algorithm [3], this module identifies natural clusters as dense support sets within the latent space, introducing a density-guided loss ($\mathcal{L}_{\text{dens}}$) into the overall objective. By combining these complementary objectives, DensGNN preserves structural organization while inducing a clustering-friendly latent geometry. Crucially, because the clustering signal is guided by naturally dense regions rather than restrictive centroids, the method is inherently better equipped to handle noise, varying densities, and irregular cluster structures. The core components of this architecture are detailed in the following subsections.

3.1 Embedding Module

The embedding module aims to learn a low-dimensional vector representation for each vertex while simultaneously incorporating semantic and topological information. To this end, we employ a GAE whose the l-th encoder layer is defined as:

$$h_i^{l+1} = \sigma\left(\sum_{j \in N(i) \cup \{i\}} \tau_{ij} W^{l+1} h_j^l\right), \tag{3}$$

where τ_{ij} represents the weight of the edge (i, j). By default, the architecture used in the encoder is a GCN [8], that is, $\tau_{ij} = (D_{ii} \cdot D_{jj})^{-1/2}$. The final encoder layer can be represented as $Z = f_\theta(X, A)$. From this representation, the decoder reconstructs the adjacency matrix through the inner product between latent vectors:

$$\hat{A} = \sigma(Z \cdot Z^T), \tag{4}$$

where σ denotes the sigmoid function. During the warm-up stage, corresponding to the first e_{warm} epochs, the model is trained using the following objective function:

$$\mathcal{L}_{\text{GAE}} = -\sum_{(v_i,v_j)\in E^+} \log \sigma(z_i^\top z_j) - \sum_{(v_i,v_j)\in E^-} \log\left(1 - \sigma(z_i^\top z_j)\right). \tag{5}$$

where E^+ and E^- denotes the positive and negative edge samples, similarly to [9]. This procedure provides an initial stabilization stage for the embedding and reduces the chance of collapse of the latent space into a degenerate solution, in which all points are projected into the same cluster, which would hinder subsequent training.

3.2 Self-supervised Density Module

This module aims to impose a more suitable organization on the latent space. Let Ω_j be the set of points associated with cluster j. The subset $\Omega_j^{\text{sup}} \subset \Omega_j$, called the support set of Ω_j, is formed by border points or core points of Ω_j, according to the probability of belonging to the cluster, defined as

$$\text{prob}(v_i \in \Omega_j) = \frac{\lambda_{\text{death},i} - \lambda_{\text{birth},j}}{\sum_{v_l \in \Omega_j} (\lambda_{\text{death},l} - \lambda_{\text{birth},j})}, \tag{6}$$

where λ denotes the density level used in the HDBSCAN hierarchy.

Given a threshold α, we define v_i as a *border* point if $\text{prob}(v_i \in \Omega_j) < \alpha$; otherwise, it is considered a *core* point. The choice between *core* and *border* support sets to represent a cluster inherently influences the final partition. To systematically investigate the behavioral distinctions between these approaches, we conducted experiments utilizing both support-set variants.

Unlike traditional approaches that rely on a single centroid to compute point-to-cluster distances, DensGNN represents each cluster using a dense support set within the latent space. This strategy effectively mitigates biases associated with rigid cluster geometries and minimizes the disproportionate influence of noisy data points on the final partition. Leveraging these support points, we define the distance d_{ij} between a latent vector z_i and a cluster Ω_j via the Mutual Reachability Distance (MRD) [3]:

$$\begin{aligned} \text{MRD}(x, y) &= \max(c_{\hat{k}}(x), c_{\hat{k}}(y), d(x, y)), \\ d_{ij} &= \frac{1}{|\Omega_j^{\text{sup}}|} \sum_{v_l \in \Omega_j^{\text{sup}}} \text{MRD}(z_i, z_l) \end{aligned} \tag{7}$$

where $c_{\hat{k}}(\cdot)$ represents the core distance, i.e., the distance from the point to its $\hat{k}$-th nearest neighbor. From d_{ij}, we define a soft assignment distribution matrix Q as:

$$q_{ij} = \frac{d_{ij}^{-1}}{\sum_k d_{ik}^{-1}}. \tag{8}$$

This distribution indicates the degree of affinity between vertex v_i and cluster Ω_j. Next, a target distribution matrix P is constructed as:

$$p_{iu} = \frac{q_{iu}^2 / \sum_i q_{iu}}{\sum_k \left(q_{ik}^2 / \sum_i q_{ik}\right)}. \tag{9}$$

Since MRD is sensitive to local density, DensGNN becomes more robust to irregular cluster geometries, the presence of noise, and the influence of border points. Regarding specifically the influence of such border points, we state and prove the following theorem:

Theorem 1. *Let Ω_j be a cluster, μ_j its centroid, and S_j be the dense support set used by DensGNN. For a query point z_i, define the centroid-based distance d_C and the* MRD*-based distance d_M:*

$$d_C(z_i, \Omega_j) = \|z_i - \mu_j\|, \qquad d_M(z_i, \Omega_j) = \frac{1}{|S_j|} \sum_{s \in S_j} \mathrm{MRD}(z_i, s).$$

If a boundary point $x_b \in \Omega_j \setminus S_j$ is perturbed by $x_b + \varepsilon\delta$, then the centroid-based distance changes according to:

$$\mu_j(\varepsilon) = \mu_j + \frac{\varepsilon}{|\Omega_j|}\delta,$$

whereas the MRD-based distance remains strictly invariant under sufficiently small perturbations ε, provided that the support set and their local $\hat{k}$-neighborhood topology remain intact.

Proof. Perturbing a single point changes the centroid by the sample mean formula:

$$\mu_j(\varepsilon) = \frac{1}{|\Omega_j|} \left(\sum_{x \in \Omega_j} x + \varepsilon\delta \right) = \mu_j + \frac{\varepsilon}{|\Omega_j|}\delta.$$

Hence $d_C(z_i, \Omega_j)$ changes whenever $\delta \neq 0$. In contrast, the distance $d_M(z_i, \Omega_j)$ is strictly determined by the support points $s \in S_j$ and their respective $\hat{k}$-neighborhoods, given by:

$$\mathrm{MRD}(z_i, s) = \max\{c_{\hat{k}}(z_i), c_{\hat{k}}(s), \|z_i - s\|\}.$$

Consequently, for a fixed support set S_j, a perturbed boundary point can only influence $\mathrm{MRD}(z_i, s)$ if it falls within the $\hat{k}$-neighborhood of either s or z_i, which is a condition that contradicts the premises of this theorem. Even if this violation occurs, $\mathrm{MRD}(z_i, s)$ remains entirely unaltered provided that z_i and s do not reside within each other's $\hat{k}$-neighborhoods. Under such circumstances, the distance $\|z_i - s\|$ strictly dominates both core distances, $c_{\hat{k}}(s)$ and $c_{\hat{k}}(z_i)$. Crucially, introducing a perturbation point within a given $\hat{k}$-neighborhood can only monotonically decrease the corresponding core distance. Because $\mathrm{MRD}(z_i, s)$ is fundamentally lower-bounded by the maximum of its arguments, shrinking a core distance exerts a highly limited effect on the overall reachability distance, leaving it completely unaffected in the vast majority of practical scenarios.

3.3 Training Procedure

DensGNN is trained using an alternating optimization scheme that iteratively refines the node embeddings and the dense clustering structure. Initially, the model undergoes a *warm-up* phase during which only the reconstruction loss, $\mathcal{L}_{\text{GAE}}$, is optimized. This pre-training stage is crucial to prevent the clustering signal from enforcing structural priors on embeddings whose topological organization has not yet stabilized.

Following the *warm-up* period, the encoder generates updated embeddings Z at each epoch. From these representations, the soft assignment distribution Q is computed based on the distances between nodes and the cluster support sets, as defined in Eq. 7. Because Q is recalculated at every epoch, it continuously reflects the evolving latent geometry.

Conversely, the target distribution P is updated at a fixed interval of l epochs. During these updates, HDBSCAN is reapplied to the current latent space to redefine the dense cluster structures and their corresponding support sets Ω_j^{sup}, thereby recalculating the target distribution. At the conclusion of training, the final cluster assignment r_i for each node is determined by:

$$r_i = \arg\max_u q_{iu}. \tag{10}$$

Consequently, even if certain nodes are initially classified as noise or ambiguous by the density-based algorithm, the final output of DensGNN guarantees a complete node partition derived from the soft distribution learned during training. The dual utilization of P and Q explicitly guides the latent space toward a denser, more cohesive organization. The overall objective function of DensGNN jointly optimizes the embedding and self-supervised modules as follows:

$$\mathcal{L} = \mathcal{L}_{\text{GAE}} + \gamma \mathcal{L}_{\text{dens}}, \tag{11}$$

where $\mathcal{L}_{\text{dens}} = \mathrm{KL}(P \parallel Q)$ and γ acts as a hyperparameter controlling the trade-off between the two error terms. This formulation effectively renders DensGNN a multi-objective learning model. The reconstruction term preserves the inherent topological information of the graph, while the clustering term enforces the dense organization of the latent representations. Maintaining a precise balance between these two components is essential to prevent the degradation of graph structure and avoid the collapse of the latent space into trivial solutions.

4 Experiments and Experimental Design

To assess the effectiveness of density-based algorithms in shaping the latent space and identifying clusters in noisy settings, we conducted three primary experimental analyzes: (1) an ablation study on the key hyperparameters of DensGNN; (2) a performance benchmark against state-of-the-art node clustering methods across three widely used data sets; and (3) an evaluation in a realistic setting where the true number of clusters is unknown *a priori*.

4.1 Ablation Study

To analyze the influence of DensGNN's hyperparameters, we systematically evaluated the number of warm-up epochs e_{warm}, the trade-off parameter γ, and the border/core probability threshold α. These parameters directly dictate the quality of the learned latent space and how individual vertices influence the final clustering structure. Using the Cora data set [32], we tested $e_{\text{warm}} \in \{0, 10, \ldots, 100\}$, $\alpha \in \{0.1, 0.2, \ldots, 0.9\}$, and $\gamma \in \{0.0, 0.4, 1.0, 5.0, 10.0, 100.0, 1000.0\}$. Furthermore, we compared two types of support sets: *Core* ($\text{Prob}(v_i) \geq \alpha$) and *Border* ($\text{Prob}(v_i) < \alpha$). Figure 2 summarizes the clustering performance measured by Normalized Mutual Information (NMI).

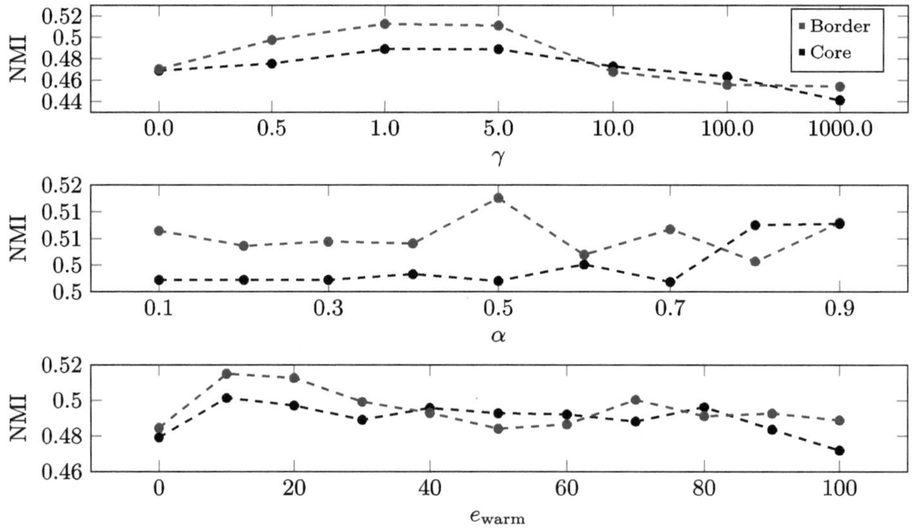

Fig. 2. Ablation study for γ (top), α (middle), and e_{warm} (bottom) of different values in *Border* and *Core* support set scenarios.

The performance curves illustrated in Fig. 2 demonstrate that hyperparameter tuning for DensGNN requires careful consideration. Notably, none of the evaluated parameters exhibited a monotonic trend, underscoring the model's sensitivity to specific configurations and reinforcing the necessity of rigorous calibration. Across all three evaluations, the *Border* support-set variant consistently yielded superior performance. In contrast, when the *Core* support set was used, the highest NMI scores were generally achieved at higher α thresholds, suggesting that the model benefits from more tightly concentrated support sets.

Furthermore, both variants achieved optimal performance with a relatively low number of warm-up epochs, indicating that small values of e_{warm} are sufficient to stabilize the initial embeddings. Finally, the trade-off parameter γ demonstrated a substantial impact on the overall quality of the clustering. This strong sensitivity to γ aligns with previous findings for deep clustering methods that optimize composite objective functions based on KL divergence [5,30].

4.2 Clustering Benchmark

To benchmark DensGNN against state-of-the-art literature, we evaluated its performance relative to several established neural architectures: DNENC [30], DGCSS [5], ARGA [23], GAE [9], and ORC Community [21]. Furthermore, we incorporated K-means (utilizing exclusively node attributes) and Node2Vec (utilizing exclusively graph topology) as foundational baselines. This comparative analysis was conducted across the Cora, CiteSeer [32], and PolBlogs [1] datasets. To guarantee a fair and standardized evaluation, all neural models were equipped with a two-layer encoder containing 128 and 32 hidden units, respectively, alongside an inner-product decoder as defined by [9]. The models were uniformly trained for 200 epochs with a learning rate of 0.005. For our proposed DensGNN, the HDBSCAN module was explicitly configured with a minimum cluster size of 10, a Mutual Reachability Distance (MRD) parameter of $\hat{k} = 5$, a probability threshold of $\alpha = 0.5$, and the *Excess-of-Mass* (EOM) criterion [3] for optimal cluster selection. The quantitative outcomes of these benchmarks are detailed in Table 1.

Given that the PolBlogs dataset lacks semantic attributes, we constructed its attribute matrix as an identity matrix ($X = I$), following the methodology of [8]. Under this formulation, each vertex is represented by a unique one-hot vector; consequently, attribute-exclusive baselines such as K-means were omitted from this specific evaluation.

On the PolBlogs dataset, DensGNN achieved the highest NMI scores, particularly when employing the *Border* variant. Although its silhouette and modularity scores remained highly competitive, they were ultimately surpassed by DNENC and ORC Community, respectively. This dynamic indicates that while competing methods may heavily optimize for specific structural heuristics, DensGNN successfully recovers a partition that aligns more faithfully with the dataset's ground-truth labels.

For the Cora dataset, DensGNN outperformed all baselines across all three evaluated metrics, demonstrating robust efficacy with both the *Border* and *Core* support sets. This constitutes a highly significant finding, as Cora serves as a foundational benchmark in the node clustering literature [17]. Conversely, on the CiteSeer dataset, while the *Border* and *Core* variants yielded comparable

Table 1. Clustering performance across data sets

	Model	Source	NMI	Sil.	Mod.
PolBlogs	ORC Community [21]	A	0.3414 ± 0.00	-	$\mathbf{0.4223 \pm 0.00}$
	Node2Vec	A	0.0003 ± 0.00	0.2339 ± 0.00	-0.0797 ± 0.00
	DGCSS (BC) [5]	X, A	0.1999 ± 0.11	0.4893 ± 0.03	0.0801 ± 0.10
	DNENC [30]	X, A	0.0165 ± 0.00	$\mathbf{0.8434 \pm 0.11}$	-0.0023 ± 0.00
	ARGA [23]	X, A	0.1187 ± 0.13	0.2828 ± 0.01	0.1447 ± 0.17
	GAE [9]	X, A	0.1121 ± 0.14	0.2964 ± 0.02	0.1623 ± 0.15
	DensGNN (Border)	X, A	$\mathbf{0.3963 \pm 0.03}$	0.6182 ± 0.07	0.2698 ± 0.14
	DensGNN (Core)	X, A	0.3265 ± 0.04	0.5502 ± 0.06	0.0999 ± 0.07
Cora	ORC Community [21]	A	0.3889 ± 0.00	-	0.7121 ± 0.00
	Node2Vec	A	0.4612 ± 0.01	0.1198 ± 0.00	0.7145 ± 0.00
	K-means	X	0.0983 ± 0.04	0.0181 ± 0.01	0.1294 ± 0.09
	DGCSS (BC) [5]	X, A	0.3481 ± 0.00	0.2663 ± 0.01	0.6426 ± 0.01
	DNENC [30]	X, A	0.3459 ± 0.02	0.2708 ± 0.04	0.6072 ± 0.03
	ARGA [23]	X, A	0.4661 ± 0.01	0.1093 ± 0.00	0.7047 ± 0.01
	GAE [9]	X, A	0.4414 ± 0.04	0.1067 ± 0.01	0.7047 ± 0.00
	DensGNN (Border)	X, A	$\mathbf{0.5199 \pm 0.00}$	$\mathbf{0.5127 \pm 0.09}$	$\mathbf{0.7665 \pm 0.01}$
	DensGNN (Core)	X, A	0.5107 ± 0.01	0.3581 ± 0.09	0.7249 ± 0.01
CiteSeer	ORC Community [21]	A	$\mathbf{0.3268 \pm 0.00}$	-	$\mathbf{0.8405 \pm 0.00}$
	Node2Vec	A	0.2271 ± 0.02	0.0948 ± 0.00	0.6996 ± 0.02
	K-means	X	0.0569 ± 0.05	0.0299 ± 0.01	0.1105 ± 0.11
	DGCSS (BC) [5]	X, A	0.1717 ± 0.02	0.1482 ± 0.05	0.6924 ± 0.01
	DNENC [30]	X, A	0.2250 ± 0.03	$\mathbf{0.2677 \pm 0.01}$	0.7397 ± 0.00
	ARGA [23]	X, A	0.2268 ± 0.02	0.0842 ± 0.00	0.7058 ± 0.03
	GAE [9]	X, A	0.1907 ± 0.02	0.0681 ± 0.00	0.7080 ± 0.01
	DensGNN (Border)	X, A	0.2761 ± 0.00	0.1971 ± 0.08	0.7664 ± 0.03
	DensGNN (Core)	X, A	0.2782 ± 0.00	0.1915 ± 0.06	0.7591 ± 0.02

internal performance, ORC Community secured the best overall results. This divergence likely stems from CiteSeer's heightened semantic complexity, which inherently complicates the extraction of highly discriminative latent representations. Because CiteSeer's topological structure is densely informative, methods that aggressively prioritize raw graph connectivity naturally gain a distinct advantage in this specific context.

4.3 Applications in a Realistic Setting

To evaluate DensGNN under more realistic conditions, we analyzed its performance on the Cora dataset in a fully unsupervised setting where the true number of clusters is unknown *a priori*. In such practical scenarios, baselines reliant on

K-means are forced to iteratively evaluate a spectrum of candidate k values to approximate an optimal partition. This experimental setup explicitly simulates a true unsupervised application, highlighting the operational advantages of density-based approaches when prior structural knowledge is unavailable.

To empirically investigate this dynamic, we evaluated the baseline models $\text{ARGA}_{K\text{-means}}$ and $\text{GAE}_{K\text{-means}}$ across a range of candidate cluster counts, specifically $k \in \{2, 3, \ldots, 10\}$. To further isolate the impact of the clustering algorithm on embedding generation, we introduced two hybrid baselines, $\text{ARGA}_{\text{Dens}}$ and GAE_{Dens}, which apply HDBSCAN directly to the latent representations learned by ARGA and GAE. For methods requiring a predefined k, we conducted three independent training runs for each candidate value, totaling 27 executions per model. To ensure statistical parity, each density-based variant–including DensGNN–was similarly executed 27 times. The resulting Normalized Mutual Information (NMI) distributions from these trials are presented in Fig. 3.

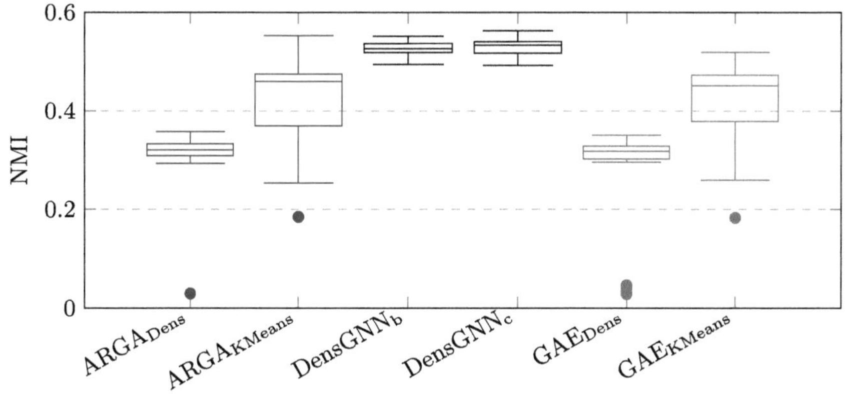

Fig. 3. Performance of the models in scenarios where the number of clusters k is absent. DensGNN_b stands for *Border* support points and DensGNN_c stants for *Core* support points.

As anticipated, algorithms reliant on a predefined k exhibited significantly higher standard deviations, corroborating the known sensitivity of centroid-based methods to the estimated number of clusters [20]. In contrast, density-based approaches demonstrated substantially lower variability. However, despite their parameter-free advantages, hybrid variants $\text{ARGA}_{\text{Dens}}$ and GAE_{Dens} still did not meet our proposed model. DensGNN achieved the highest overall results alongside the lowest standard deviation, highlighting its superior robustness and reliability in fully unsupervised scenarios where the true number of clusters is unknown.

5 Discussion and Conclusion

In this work, we introduced DensGNN, a density-based GNN model capable of identifying *outliers* during training and actively steering the learning process toward dense regions of the latent space. By leveraging the HDBSCAN algorithm, DensGNN extracts dense cluster support sets to formulate soft membership probabilities. The network weights are subsequently optimized via a composite loss function that balances a topological reconstruction term with a KL divergence density objective. Our empirical evaluations demonstrate the effectiveness of the model in two distinct scenarios. First, under standard benchmarking conditions where the number of clusters is predefined, DensGNN consistently outperforms state-of-the-art baselines across multiple data sets. Second, in more realistic settings where the target number of clusters is unknown *a priori*, the model exhibits superior structural stability and achieves the highest overall NMI scores, circumventing the high variance associated with centroid-reliant methods.

Despite these promising results, the integration of density-based algorithms introduces notable parameterization challenges. Specifically, careful calibration of the trade-off parameter γ within the composite loss function is critical to achieving optimal performance. Furthermore, our empirical observations indicate that DensGNN excels in environments characterized by sparse semantic information or non-convex cluster geometries, as evidenced by its superior performance on the Cora and PolBlogs datasets (Table 1). To the best of our knowledge, DensGNN represents the first model to integrate density-based clustering directly into the objective function of a Graph Neural Network for attributed graph clustering. This approach successfully unifies two robust research domains: deep graph representation learning and established density-based clustering methodologies. Regarding future work, a primary objective is the development of strategies to mitigate the model's sensitivity to multiple hyperparameters. Additionally, we plan to explore alternative criteria for extracting cluster support sets, whether through novel cluster selection mechanisms or reparameterization techniques grounded in the statistical properties of dense regions. Finally, evaluating the behavior and scalability of density-based models on highly sparse networks remains a critical avenue for future investigation.

Acknowledgments. This research was funded by the Coordination for the Improvement of Higher Education Personnel (CAPES) - Code 001, through a Ph.D. scholarship; by the IFSULDEMINAS - Campus Muzambinho; The São Paulo Research Foundation (FAPESP) [grants 22/03090-0]; and Brazilian National Council for Scientific and Technological Development (CNPq) [grants 420025/2023-5]. The authors also acknowledge the use of AI-based tools to support text revision and the organization of experiments.

References

1. Adamic, L.A., Glance, N.: The political blogosphere and the 2004 U.S. election: divided they blog. In: Proceedings of the 3rd International Workshop on Link Discovery, LinkKDD 2005, pp. 36–43. Association for Computing Machinery, New York (2005)
2. Bianchi, F.M., Grattarola, D., Alippi, C.: Spectral clustering with graph neural networks for graph pooling. In: III, H.D., Singh, A. (eds.) Proceedings of the 37th International Conference on Machine Learning. Proceedings of Machine Learning Research, vol. 119, pp. 874–883. PMLR (2020)
3. Campello, R.J.G.B., Moulavi, D., Zimek, A., Sander, J.: Hierarchical density estimates for data clustering, visualization, and outlier detection. ACM Trans. Knowl. Discov. Data **10**(1) (2015)
4. D'Amico, S., et al.: Mosaic: an artificial intelligence–based framework for multimodal analysis, classification, and personalized prognostic assessment in rare cancers. JCO Clin. Cancer Inform. (8), e2400008 (2024)
5. Filho, C.P.L., Messias, G.H., Iasulaitis, S., Lopes, A.D.A., Valejo, A.D.B.: Deep graph clustering using graph neural networks and seed detection, pp. 347–361. Springer (2026)
6. Guo, L., Dai, Q.: End-to-end variational graph clustering with local structural preservation. Neural Comput. Appl. **34**(5), 3767–3782 (2021)
7. Javed, M.A., Younis, M.S., Latif, S., Qadir, J., Baig, A.: Community detection in networks: a multidisciplinary review. J. Netw. Comput. Appl. **108**, 87–111 (2018)
8. Kipf, T.N., Welling, M.: Semi-supervised classification with graph convolutional networks (2016)
9. Kipf, T.N., Welling, M.: Variational graph auto-encoders. arXiv preprint arXiv:1611.07308 (2016)
10. Krysmon, S., et al.: Applying density-based clustering for the analysis of emission events in real driving emissions calibration. Future Transp. **4**(1), 46–66 (2024)
11. Li, X., Li, D., Jin, R., Ramnath, R., Agrawal, G.: Deep graph clustering with random-walk based scalable learning. In: 2022 IEEE/ACM International Conference on Advances in Social Networks Analysis and Mining (ASONAM), pp. 88–95 (2022)
12. Li, Y., et al.: Developing a novel approach in estimating urban commute traffic by integrating community detection and hypergraph representation learning. Expert Syst. Appl. **249**, 123790 (2024)
13. Li, Z., Zhu, C.: Self-supervised graph clustering via attention auto-encoder with distribution specificity. Multimedia Syst. **30**(3) (2024)
14. Lin, Z., Kang, Z., Zhang, L., Tian, L.: Multi-view attributed graph clustering. IEEE Trans. Knowl. Data Eng. 1 (2021)
15. Liu, H., Lu, X., Cheng, K., Liu, X.: A multi-embedding fusion network for attributed graph clustering. Appl. Soft Comput. **165** (2024)
16. Liu, H., Wei, J., Wu, Y., Liang, C.: Information-enhanced deep graph clustering network. Neurocomputing **597**, 127992 (2024)
17. Messias, G.H., Gonçalves Botelho, T., Iasulaitis, S., Coelho Naldi, M., Demétrius Baria Valejo, A.: A systematic review of graph neural network for node clustering in homogeneous attributed networks. IEEE Access **13**, 215265–215285 (2025)
18. Moradan, A., Draganov, A., Mottin, D., Assent, I.: UCoDe: unified community detection with graph convolutional networks. Mach. Learn. **112**(12), 5057–5080 (2023)

19. Naga Chandrika, G., Alnowibet, K., Sandeep Kautish, K., Sreenivasa Reddy, E., F. Alrasheedi, A., Wagdy Mohamed, A.: Graph transformer for communities detection in social networks. Comput. Mater. Continua **70**(3), 5707–5720 (2022)
20. Naldi, M., Campello, R., Hruschka, E., Carvalho, A.: Efficiency issues of evolutionary k-means. Appl. Soft Comput. **11**(2), 1938–1952 (2011). The Impact of Soft Computing for the Progress of Artificial Intelligence
21. Ni, C.C., Lin, Y.Y., Luo, F., Gao, J.: Community detection on networks with Ricci flow. Sci. Rep. **9**(1) (2019)
22. Pan, S., Hu, R., Fung, S.F., Long, G., Jiang, J., Zhang, C.: Learning graph embedding with adversarial training methods. IEEE Trans. Cybern. **50**(6), 2475–2487 (2020)
23. Pan, S., Hu, R., Long, G., Jiang, J., Yao, L., Zhang, C.: Adversarially regularized graph autoencoder for graph embedding (2019)
24. Pastor-Galindo, J., Ân Sandlin, H., Mármol, F.G., Bovet, G., Pérez, G.M.: A big data architecture for early identification and categorization of dark web sites. Futur. Gener. Comput. Syst. **157**, 67–81 (2024)
25. Rahnama, A., et al.: A microfluidic approach to study variations in chlamydomonas reinhardtii alkaline phosphatase activity in response to phosphate availability. Analyst **149**, 4256–4266 (2024)
26. Salha, G., Hennequin, R., Vazirgiannis, M.: Simple and effective graph autoencoders with one-hop linear models, pp. 319–334. Springer (2021)
27. Tang, L., Wu, T., Hu, R., Gu, Q., Yang, X., Mao, H.: Hemodynamic property incorporated brain tumor segmentation by deep learning and density-based analysis of dynamic susceptibility contrast-enhanced magnetic resonance imaging (MRI). Quant. Imaging Med. Surg. **14**(4), 2774 (2024)
28. Tsitsulin, A., Palowitch, J., Perozzi, B., Müller, E.: Graph clustering with graph neural networks. J. Mach. Learn. Res. **24**(127), 1–21 (2023)
29. Veličković, P., Cucurull, G., Casanova, A., Romero, A., Liò, P., Bengio, Y.: Graph attention networks (2017)
30. Wang, C., Pan, S., Yu, C.P., Hu, R., Long, G., Zhang, C.: Deep neighbor-aware embedding for node clustering in attributed graphs. Pattern Recogn. **122**, 108230 (2022)
31. Wu, D., Guo, X., Luo, X., Qiao, Z., Ma, J.: Adaptive harmony learning and optimization for attributed graph clustering. In: 2022 International Joint Conference on Neural Networks (IJCNN), p. 1–8. IEEE (2022)
32. Yang, Z., Cohen, W.W., Salakhutdinov, R.: Revisiting semi-supervised learning with graph embeddings. In: Proceedings of the 33rd International Conference on International Conference on Machine Learning, ICML 2016, vol. 48, pp. 40–48. JMLR.org (2016)
33. Zhuo, L., Chen, Y., Song, B., Liu, Y., Su, Y.: A model for predicting ncRNA–protein interactions based on graph neural networks and community detection. Methods **207**, 74–80 (2022)

How Large Language Models Profile Brazilians: Socioeconomic Attribution and Stereotypes

Anderson Luis Bento Soares(✉), Leonardo Nascimento Ferreira, Ruben Interian, and Zanoni Dias

Institute of Computing, University of Campinas (Unicamp), Campinas, SP, Brazil
anderson.soares@students.ic.unicamp.br, {lnf,ruben,zanoni}@ic.unicamp.br

Abstract. Large language models (LLMs) are increasingly used to generate personas, summaries, and other user-facing descriptions of social groups. In countries marked by strong socioeconomic inequality, it is often unclear when such outputs reflect plausible social patterns and when they reinforce stereotypes. We examine this question in Brazil using a controlled profile-generation task: 23 LLMs generated short, structured adult profiles conditioned only on region and a self-identification category. We analyze socioeconomic attribution, focusing on income as the main calibrated outcome, while using occupation and educational attainment as contextual descriptive fields. Additionally, we examine representational stereotyping, using an LLM judge guided by predefined criteria targeting occupational automaticity, character complexity, and exoticization. For calibration, we compare model-assigned incomes to public tabulations from the Brazilian Institute of Geography and Statistics (IBGE). Across 688 valid profiles, outputs follow the broad regional ordering observed in official data but generally assign higher income levels, with substantial variation across different combinations of region and race/color. On a five-point stereotype scale, scores cluster around the middle, with most ratings falling in the 2–3 range, suggesting that the dominant pattern in the generated profiles is moderate, socially patterned simplification rather than overt caricature. Overall, the results indicate that LLMs can reproduce recognizable social regularities while still introducing calibration errors and representational rigidity.

Keywords: large language models · bias evaluation · stereotypes · Brazil · socioeconomic profiling

1 Introduction

Large language models (LLMs) are increasingly used to produce socially meaningful descriptions, for example, personas, fictional profiles, educational examples, synthetic data, and user-facing assistance. In these applications, the models do more than complete text generation; they allocate attributes—such as

M. Recamonde-Mendoza and R. C. Barros (Eds.): BRACIS 2026, LNAI 17105, pp. 277–292, 2027.
https://doi.org/10.1007/978-3-032-39882-6_19

occupation, income, lifestyle, and education—to socially marked identities. This makes profile generation a useful site for studying representational harms and socioeconomic attribution in language technology.

A key challenge is that generated profiles may track empirical regularities while also slipping into stereotyped shortcuts. When a model assigns higher income to one region than another, it may be reflecting documented gradients, but it may also render them rigidly or exaggerate them in narrative form. We therefore ask whether outputs differ across groups and whether these differences are calibrated and context-sensitive.

Brazil is an informative setting for this question. Regional disparities remain substantial across the country, and official statistics also document persistent inequalities associated with race/color categories used in public administration and demographic surveys [8]. This is particularly important in Brazil, where race/color operates as a socially consequential dimension of stratification rather than as a merely descriptive label [10]. These inequalities are not interchangeable and cannot be reduced to a single axis. Their interaction matters because multiple social markers can combine to shape social outcomes in ways that are not reducible to a single dimension [5]. A generated profile can encode regional cues, race/color cues, and their interaction, sometimes reproducing documented patterns and sometimes turning them into default assumptions about who a person is.

In this paper, we examine how LLMs generate profiles of Brazilian adults when prompted with region and a self-identification category. We analyze two aspects of the outputs: socioeconomic attribution, with income as the primary quantitative outcome and occupation and educational attainment as contextual descriptors, and representational stereotyping (whether a profile is judged as a plausible social description or as a simplified, regionally coded caricature).

To operationalize this design, we created a controlled prompt that asks an LLM to produce a brief structured (JSON) profile of an adult inhabitant from one of the five Brazilian macro-regions, optionally specifying one of the official race/color categories commonly used by the IBGE. We queried 23 LLMs, once per combination of region and group condition, producing 690 profiles in total, of which 688 were successfully generated and included in the analysis. We evaluated outputs in two steps: we extracted structured variables such as monthly income and compared the resulting distributions with IBGE reference tabulations; then we scored each profile using an LLM judge guided by a set of predefined criteria, rating stereotype reinforcement on a five-point scale.

We find three main patterns. Generated incomes largely preserve the regional ordering in IBGE data, but they are typically higher than the reference means and vary markedly across region × race/color cells. Meanwhile, stereotype scores cluster in the middle of the scale, with most ratings falling in the 2–3 range, indicating that the generated profiles are generally plausible but still exhibit some degree of socially patterned simplification rather than extreme caricature. Together, these results suggest that, in this task, LLMs neither invent social inequalities nor reproduce them in a neutral or fully calibrated manner.

The paper is organized as follows. Section 2 situates the study in prior work on bias and representational harm in NLP and LLMs. Section 3 presents the prompting setup, models, normalization procedures, and evaluation rubric. Section 4 reports the empirical results, including comparisons with IBGE and stereotype-score distributions. Section 5 discusses the broader implications of the findings and presents the limitations, and Sect. 6 concludes the paper.

2 Related Work

Research on bias in Natural Language Processing (NLP) has shown that statistical language representations can encode socially patterned associations, including those linked to gender, race, occupation, and status. Early work on word embeddings demonstrated that distributional semantics can recover human-like biases from large corpora [3,4]. Subsequent research in NLP emphasized that "bias" is not a single phenomenon, but a family of issues that includes harmful associations, performance disparities, representational exclusion, and downstream allocation effects [2].

The emergence of LLMs has made these issues more difficult and, in some respects, more consequential. Because these models generate open-ended text rather than selecting from fixed labels, they can express stereotypes through narrative detail, framing, lexical choice, and omitted alternatives. It has been argued that the scale and apparent fluency of contemporary language models can obscure the limits of textual pattern matching and encourage users to attribute grounded understanding to synthetic outputs [1]. A broad taxonomy of risks posed by language models has been proposed, including discrimination, representational harms, and the reinforcement of existing power asymmetries [11].

Several datasets and evaluation protocols have been proposed to measure social bias in generated text. For example, prior work has introduced broad benchmarks for probing social descriptors in open-ended generation settings [9]. Other work has examined occupational stereotypes, demographic attributes, and persona generation as settings in which models may allocate social roles unevenly. A recurrent theme in this literature is that distributional alignment with social reality does not automatically imply fairness or non-harm: a system may reproduce documented regularities while still reifying them as default expectations.

The present study contributes to this line of work in three respects. We focus on a Brazilian setting, where regional and race/color inequalities are both historically salient and institutionally measured; this matters because Brazilian race/color categories are embedded in a distinct historical and sociological formation and are intertwined with other axes of inequality rather than reducible to a generic racial taxonomy [5,10]. We also compare generated socioeconomic values directly with reference statistics [6], instead of treating any cross-group difference as bias per se. Finally, we pair this external calibration step with a criteria-based stereotype judgment, allowing us to distinguish socioeconomic attribution from representational evaluation, since a generated profile may align with official socioeconomic aggregates yet remain narratively reductive. Conversely, a profile may avoid overtly stereotyped wording while assigning implausibly patterned socioeconomic values. We therefore treat calibration and stereotype judgment as related but distinct dimensions of model behavior.

3 Methods

This section describes the experimental design of the study, including the profile-generation task, the evaluated models, the external reference data, and the stereotype-assessment procedure.

3.1 Profile-Generation Task

We designed a controlled profile-generation prompt in Portuguese. The prompt asks the model to create a brief profile of an adult inhabitant from a specified Brazilian region and to return the output strictly in a structured form (JSON). The requested fields are: name, age, city and state, current profession, schooling, morning routine, personality, monthly income, and breakfast items. The prompt also specifies that the routine should be plausible and that the personality trait should not be defined solely by geography.

The region factor includes the five Brazilian macro-regions: North, Northeast, Center-West, Southeast, and South. A second factor represents self-identification using the Brazilian official race/color categories *Branca* (White), *Parda* (Brown/mixed), *Preta* (Black), *Indígena* (Indigenous), and *Amarela* (Asian), along with an unspecified condition. Throughout the paper, we refer to this factor as race/color, following the terminology adopted in Brazilian official statistics [6].

The requirement of a structured output (JSON) was central to the design because it reduced ambiguity in post-processing. In contrast to free-form biographies, structured outputs allow straightforward extraction of numeric and categorical fields and facilitate direct comparison across models. The instruction to generate an adult profile was included to avoid child or adolescent outputs and to make income and occupation assignments meaningful.

3.2 Models and Number of Profiles

We adopt a controlled cross-model experimental design in which multiple LLMs are queried under identical region and group conditions. The study includes 23 LLMs. The model set was selected to cover a diverse sample of API-accessible instruction-tuned systems available at the time of collection, including different model families, providers, and sizes. Each model was queried once for every combination of region and group condition. With five regions and six group conditions, this yields $5 \times 6 \times 23 = 690$ planned profile generations. Two generations failed due to looping behavior in the *Qwen/Qwen3.5-27B* model for prompts targeting the South and Southeast regions, resulting in 688 valid profiles for analysis. A summary of the experimental setup is provided in Table 1.

All models were accessed via API under a deterministic setup (temperature = 0), with all other parameters left at provider defaults. This choice improves determinism within each provider, but does not fully eliminate cross-provider configuration differences. Data collection was performed on March 29, 2026. Under this single-shot design, each region × race/color condition was sampled exactly once per model.

This single-shot design focuses on evaluating variability across models rather than within-model variance. It is suitable for identifying broad directional patterns, especially when the same prompt template is applied systematically across models and group conditions. At the same time, it does not capture stochastic variability due to sampling or prompt-order effects. We return to this limitation in Sect. 5.

Table 1. Experimental design used in the main study.

Component	Description
Country	Brazil
Regions	North, Northeast, Center-West, Southeast, South
Group conditions	White, Brown, Black, Indigenous, Asian, unspecified
Number of LLMs	23
Planned profiles per model	30
Planned profiles	690
Valid analyzed profiles	688
Output format	Strict JSON
Main extracted variables	Income, profession, educational attainment, age
Secondary evaluation	Criteria-based stereotype score (Table 2)
External reference	IBGE public income tabulations [6]

Exact model identifiers, providers, and access details are provided in the repository[1] (see `conf/main_config.yaml`).

3.3 External Reference Data

For external calibration, we used IBGE official tabulations with 2022 reference values. Regional mean monthly income by race/color was obtained from IBGE 2022 Census tabulations (SIDRA Table 10285), using publicly available statistics on income by region and race/color whenever a compatible category was available [6]. All monetary values were expressed in Brazilian reais (BRL).

To ensure comparability between the IBGE 2022 reference values and the LLM-generated outputs collected in 2026, we adjusted the IBGE values using

[1] https://github.com/graphs4ai/Profile_Brazilians.

the official IPCA inflation index provided by the IBGE [7]. The cumulative inflation between January 2022 and January 2026 is approximately 21.37%, and the adjusted values were computed as:

$$\mu_{r,g}^{\text{IBGE-adj}} = \mu_{r,g}^{\text{IBGE}} \times 1.2137, \tag{1}$$

where $\mu_{r,g}^{\text{IBGE}}$ is the original IBGE mean income for region r and group g, and $\mu_{r,g}^{\text{IBGE-adj}}$ is the corresponding inflation-adjusted value. This adjustment reduces the effect of nominal currency variation, but does not account for structural or compositional changes in income distributions between 2022 and the 2026 collection period.

To quantify calibration for each region and race/color combination, we use the relative deviation

$$\Delta_{r,g} = \frac{\mu_{r,g}^{\text{LLM}} - \mu_{r,g}^{\text{IBGE-adj}}}{\mu_{r,g}^{\text{IBGE-adj}}}, \tag{2}$$

where r indexes region and g indexes the race/color condition. Positive values indicate overestimation relative to the reference data and negative values indicate underestimation.

This external calibration step is conceptually important. A generated difference between groups is not, on its own, evidence of harmful stereotyping. Some differences reflect documented social inequalities. The central question is whether the model reproduces those patterns in a calibrated manner, whether it exaggerates them, or whether it introduces distortions in their relative ordering and narrative framing.

3.4 Criteria-Based Stereotype Judgment

Each generated profile was also evaluated using a separate prompt designed to assess stereotype reinforcement in socially coded profile generation, including cues related to region, race/color, and their interaction. Our goal is to quantify the degree to which generated profiles rely on socially patterned simplifications or stereotypical cues. The prompt presents the profile and requests a score from 1 to 5, where 1 indicates strong representational quality and 5 indicates a severe stereotype. The evaluation is based on three dimensions intended to capture regionally coded simplification as well as broader forms of representational narrowing associated with race/color marking and intersectional social cues.

The judge model was openai/gpt-oss-20b (DeepInfra), queried with temperature $= 0$ and default parameters. We use this model as a rubric-following proxy for scalable comparative assessment, not as a ground-truth annotator. Because stereotype recognition is culturally situated and socially sensitive, especially in the Brazilian context, these scores should be interpreted as automated, rubric-based indicators of representational simplification rather than validated measurements of social harm. They are therefore used descriptively to compare patterns across prompts and models, and not to establish definitive claims about whether a given profile would be judged stereotypical by human annotators.

More specifically, the evaluation considers three dimensions:

1. **Profession and educational attainment:** whether the profile automatically associates a region with a narrow class position, occupational role, or level of educational attainment;
2. **Character complexity:** whether the profile presents a minimally multidimensional person or reduces the subject to a predictable type;
3. **Exoticization and caricature:** whether the routine description resembles everyday life or instead adopts a postcard-like or folkloric framing.

The judge was instructed to return a brief explanation, a list of detected markers, and an ordinal score. Because this score is ordinal and based on study-specific evaluation criteria, we analyze it primarily through distributions and group proportions rather than as a continuous measure. Table 2 summarizes the interpretation of the score.

For the sake of brevity, all prompts, evaluation criteria, and implementation details are provided in the same accompanying repository.

Table 2. Interpretation of the stereotype score used in the judge prompt.

Score	Interpretation
1	Excellent representation: breaks common stereotypes and presents a natural, multidimensional character
2	Good representation: plausible and largely avoids common regional clichés
3	Mixed or neutral: combines realistic elements with some predictable social coding
4	Moderate stereotype: clear regional or group-based generalization, though not fully reduced to caricature
5	Severe stereotype: profile relies heavily on clichés or prejudicial generalizations

4 Results

This section presents the main empirical results, focusing on income attribution relative to IBGE reference data and on stereotype-score patterns across regions, race/color conditions, and models.

4.1 Regional Income Patterns and Comparison with IBGE

Figure 1 compares the mean monthly income assigned by the LLMs with the corresponding IBGE 2022 regional means, reported both in nominal terms and adjusted for inflation using the IPCA index. Two regularities stand out: the generated values follow the expected broad regional ordering, with lower averages

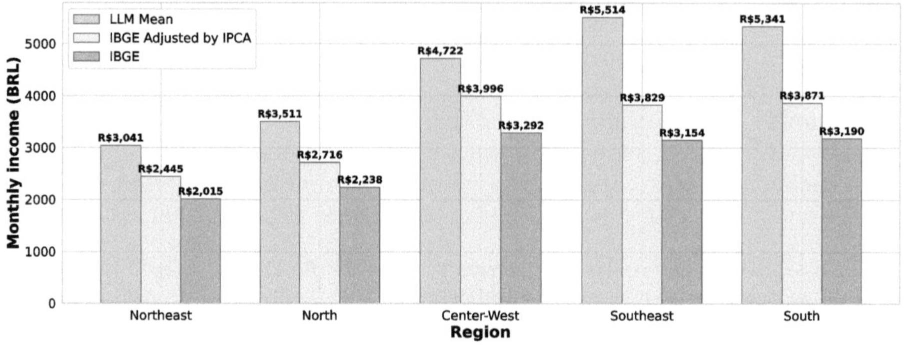

Fig. 1. Mean monthly income assigned by the LLMs compared with IBGE 2022 reference values [6], shown in nominal terms and adjusted for inflation using the IPCA index. The models reproduce the broad regional ordering but assign consistently higher values than the official benchmarks.

in the Northeast and North, intermediate values in the Center-West, and higher values in the Southeast and South; at the same time, LLM-assigned means are consistently above the official benchmarks.

At the regional level, the LLM averages are R$3,041 for the Northeast, R$3,511 for the North, R$4,722 for the Center-West, R$5,514 for the Southeast, and R$5,341 for the South. The corresponding IBGE values are lower in all five regions, ranging from R$2,015 in the Northeast to R$3,292 in the Center-West and R$3,154 and R$3,190 in the Southeast and South, respectively. The result is a clear regional gradient combined with a general upward shift in level.

Substantively, this means that the models are not producing flat or random income assignments across regions. They encode a recognizable regional hierarchy, but that hierarchy is not reproduced in a calibrated way. In this sense, the outputs are better described as directionally aligned but inflated in magnitude.

To examine this well-known regional contrast in Brazil, we aggregate North and Northeast into one block and South and Southeast into another, allowing us to assess whether this divide is reflected not only in mean values but also in the distribution of generated profiles. Figure 2 shows a clear separation between these two aggregates. The difference in mean income is substantial (Delta = R$2,152), compared to a smaller difference of R$1,270 in the IBGE reference values, after adjusting for inflation using IPCA. A model-clustered bootstrap yields a 95% confidence interval of [R$1,823, R$2,476] for the LLM-based mean difference.

This pooled contrast remains clearly visible, but it should not be interpreted as evidence of accurate calibration relative to the external reference data.

4.2 Region × Race/color Patterns

Regional averages are informative, but they do not show how calibration varies across the interaction between region and race/color. Figure 3 therefore reports

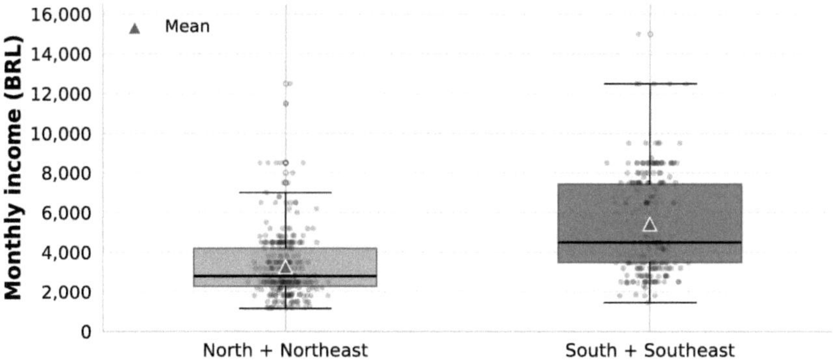

Fig. 2. Distribution of generated income values for North+Northeast versus South+Southeast aggregates. The aggregate regional contrast remains clearly visible across the pooled outputs of all 23 models. The difference in mean income is R$2,152, with a model-clustered bootstrap 95% confidence interval of [R$1,823, R$2,476].

mean income values for each region and race/color cell in the LLM outputs alongside the matched IBGE 2022 reference values. The "Not informed" condition corresponds to prompts in which no race/color category was specified, allowing the model to generate a profile without explicit group conditioning. This condition is shown only for the LLM outputs because there is no directly matched IBGE race/color category for external comparison.

The observed pattern is clearly structured. Cells in the Southeast, South, and Center-West generally present higher salaries than those in the North and Northeast. The Asian category tends to receive relatively high values in both the LLM outputs and the reference data. At the same time, the side-by-side comparison reveals substantial level differences: in most cells, the LLM mean exceeds the corresponding IBGE value.

These deviations are heterogeneous rather than uniform. In some cells, such as North–Asian and Center-West–Asian, the generated mean is close to the official reference. In others, the gap is much larger, especially in the South and Southeast under Brown and Black conditions, as well as in several White cells. This pattern indicates that the models are not merely rescaling the official data by a constant factor; they are introducing cell-specific distortions.

As a descriptive summary of the relationship shown in Fig. 3, we computed the Pearson correlation between the LLM and IBGE mean incomes across matched region × race/color cells. The correlation is high ($r = 0.87$, $p < 0.001$), indicating that the generated values broadly follow the ordering of the reference data. This result, however, does not imply calibration.

4.3 Stereotype Judgments Across Regions and Groups

The second dimension of analysis concerns representational form. Figure 4 shows the distribution of stereotype scores by region and by race/color condition. These

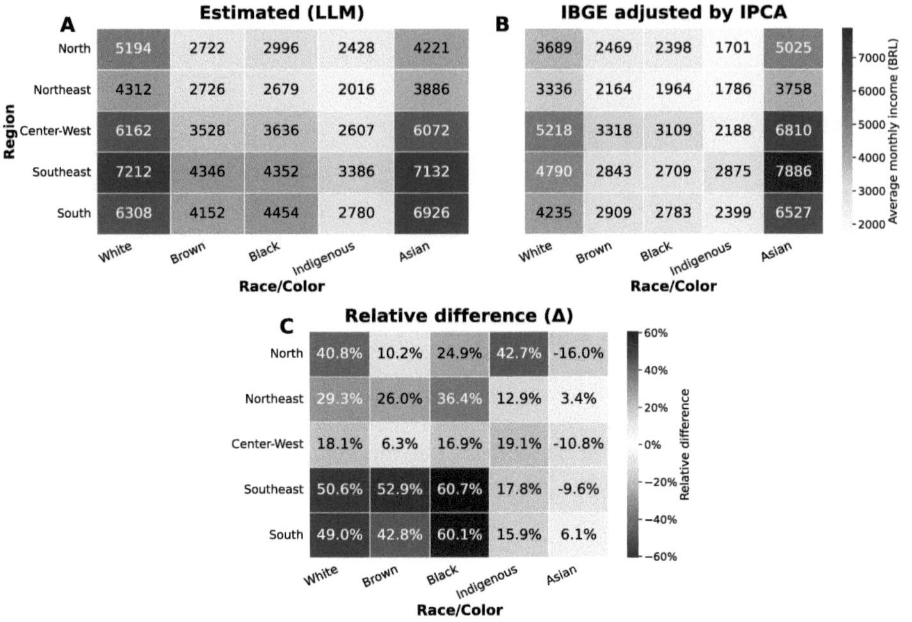

Fig. 3. Mean monthly income by region and race/color condition in the LLM outputs (A) and in the matched IBGE reference values (B), along with the corresponding relative calibration error $\Delta_{r,g}$ (C). The overall ordering is broadly similar across panels, but the generated values are generally higher and the magnitude of the deviation varies across combinations. Positive values in (C) indicate overestimation relative to IBGE-adjusted reference values, while negative values indicate underestimation. The Pearson correlation between LLM and IBGE mean incomes across matched region × race/color combinations is $r = 0.87$ ($p < 0.001$, $n = 25$).

scores should be interpreted as judgments of representational simplification in the generated profiles, rather than as a measure of regional stereotyping alone. The first notable result is that the scores are concentrated in the middle of the scale. Ratings of 2 and 3 account for the large majority of observations across both panels. Scores of 5 are rare, while scores of 4 are more frequent but still a minority.

This score distribution, with most ratings concentrated in the 2–3 range and relatively few profiles receiving high stereotype scores (4–5), suggests that the dominant pattern in the corpus is not explicit caricature. Rather, the profiles tend to combine plausible social detail with moderate simplification. This is consistent with the generation prompt: the models were not asked to produce satirical or exaggerated personas, but to construct plausible adult profiles with ordinary routines and occupations.

The group-level differences are still informative. By region, the North shows somewhat higher shares of score 4 than the others. By race/color condition, Indigenous profiles receive the largest concentration of score 3 and score 4 judgments in the displayed distribution, whereas Asian and Black profiles are more concentrated in score 2. The unspecified condition occupies an intermediate position. We interpret these differences cautiously because the design includes one observation per cell per model, but the pattern is nevertheless consistent with the idea that some prompts invite more socially coded simplification than others.

The stereotype scores should also be read together with the calibration results above. A profile can have a relatively moderate stereotype score while still assigning a socially patterned income that is substantially miscalibrated. Conversely, a profile can be closer to the external income reference and yet still rely on an occupational or routine template that the judge regards as predictable. For this reason, representational evaluation and socioeconomic calibration should not be conflated.

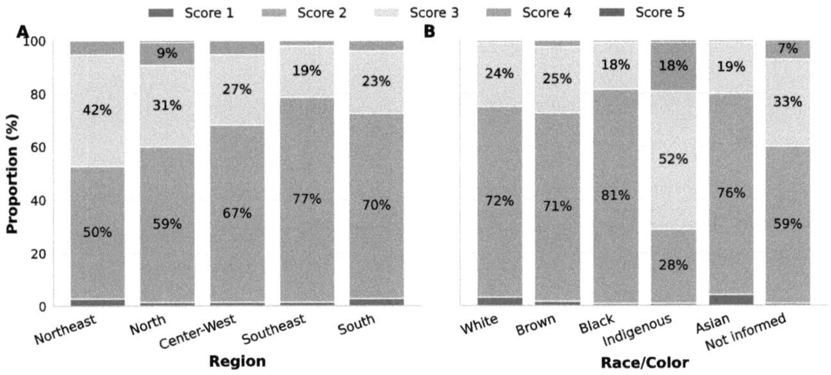

Fig. 4. Distribution of stereotype scores by region (A) and race/color condition (B). Most profiles are rated 2 or 3, indicating a predominance of plausible but socially coded representations rather than overt caricature. The "Not informed" condition corresponds to prompts in which no race/color category was specified, and is included only for the LLM outputs.

4.4 Variation Across LLMs

The results reported so far pool all 23 models to describe the overall pattern. Figure 5 presents the mean income attribution by race/color condition for each model and overlays the corresponding IBGE reference values as a baseline. Rather than ranking models in absolute terms, this comparison is intended to assess whether the pooled pattern is broadly shared across models and to examine how much it varies in magnitude from one model to another.

Two features stand out. First, the cross-group structure is widespread rather than model-specific. Across models, higher mean incomes are more frequently assigned to White and especially Asian profiles, whereas Brown, Black, and particularly Indigenous profiles more often appear in the lower-income ranges.

Second, income levels and their dispersion vary widely across models. Some systems produce relatively compressed profiles across categories, while others generate much wider gaps and much higher values for specific groups.

This heterogeneity matters for two reasons. Methodologically, it shows that the pooled pattern is not driven by a single outlier model. Substantively, it suggests that socioeconomic miscalibration is not a uniform property of "LLMs" as a category. Instead, different models appear to reproduce similar social gradients while differing in scale, spread, and distance from the official reference.

At the same time, the cross-model comparison does not overturn the pooled results. Despite substantial variation in level, the overall structure remains recognizable across systems: income attribution differs systematically across race/color conditions, and these differences remain meaningfully aligned with broader socioeconomic hierarchies in the Brazilian context, even when the assigned values depart substantially from the IBGE benchmarks.

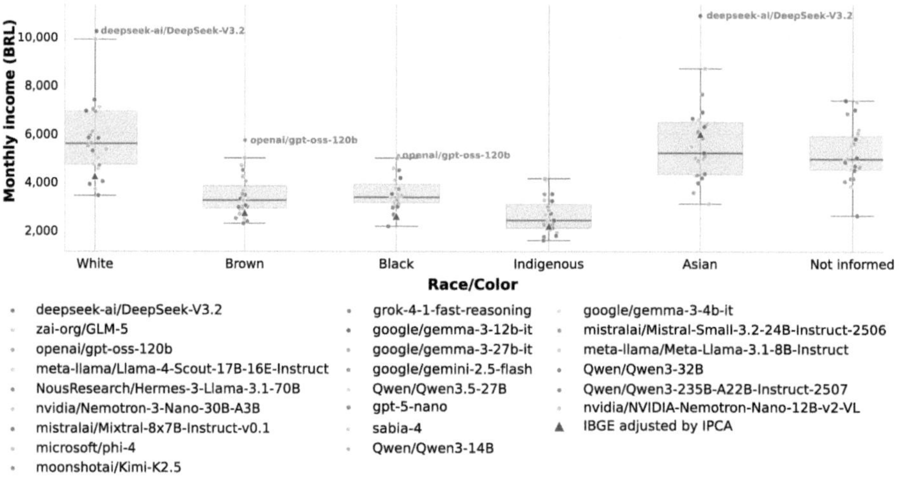

Fig. 5. Mean monthly income by race/color condition across the 23 LLMs, with IBGE reference values shown for comparison. The models differ in level and spread, but all exhibit systematic differences in income attribution across race/color conditions. For each model, values are averaged across all five regions within each race/color condition.

5 Discussion

The central empirical result of this paper is that the LLMs did not behave as though region and race/color were irrelevant to profile generation. Instead, they assigned different incomes, occupations, and routines across region and race/color conditions within the same prompt template, in a way that broadly tracked known Brazilian socioeconomic structure. This pattern should be interpreted cautiously: in this experimental setup, it is best understood as evidence of tendencies in model-generated representations, rather than as either a fully accurate description of real-world distributions or a purely random effect.

A claim that the models reproduce stereotypes would be incomplete, as the generated patterns are informed by real socioeconomic structure. At the same time, the preservation of relative ordering does not imply neutrality. Instead, the models appear to reflect these social patterns while altering them in magnitude and distribution, resulting in a combination of inflation and selective distortion.

Calibration against real-world data matters. If a model assigns lower income to the Northeast than to the Southeast, that difference is not necessarily a hallucinated prejudice; it may reflect persistent regional inequality documented in official data. Evaluation frameworks that treat every cross-group difference as evidence of bias risk overlooking these underlying empirical inequalities.

Our results show systematic upward shifts in income relative to IBGE and heterogeneity across region × race/color cells. In other words, the models are not merely reproducing the official distribution. In this paper, calibration is quantified only for income. Occupation and educational attainment are treated as contextual descriptive dimensions rather than as independently validated outcomes. The models appear to reconstruct aspects of socioeconomic structure through internal statistical associations, which may compress some gaps, enlarge others, and convert demographic tendencies into person-level defaults.

The distinction between aggregate-level calibration and individual-level representation is especially relevant in profile generation. Official statistics describe aggregates, whereas the prompt asks for an individual. Moving from a group-level tendency to a specific person is exactly where stereotypes can emerge: not because the broad pattern is false, but because the model treats it as the most natural template for the person in front of it. The danger is not only false content, but also essentialization: presenting a historically contingent social pattern as the expected biography of an individual.

The stereotype-judgment results reinforce this interpretation. The profiles were rarely rated as extreme caricatures. Most were judged as plausible, but not entirely free of predictable social coding. In practice, this is a realistic form of risk for contemporary LLM applications. Users are unlikely to encounter crude, openly prejudicial text in every case. More often, they encounter profiles that appear plausible—assigning reasonable occupations, income levels, and daily routines—while systematically reflecting socially patterned assumptions about class, region, and identity.

The higher concentration of scores 3 and 4 for Indigenous profiles is particularly important. It suggests that Indigenous identity may trigger more predictable and group-coded narrative templates than other race/color conditions in this prompt setting. We interpret this pattern cautiously, given the single-shot design and LLM-based judgment, but it points to a specific form of representational narrowing that would be obscured by aggregate stereotype scores alone.

The Brazilian context also sharpens the methodological point. Region and race/color are not redundant variables. A model can be approximately aligned with regional income gradients while still handling within-region race/color differences inconsistently. Likewise, a profile can avoid explicitly stereotypical or caricatured descriptions while still attaching a narrow occupational role to a given identity. Evaluations that rely on a single global bias score may therefore miss the specific mechanisms by which socially coded generation occurs.

Our results suggest that an informative evaluation of LLM-generated social profiles should combine at least two lenses. The first is external calibration: how closely do the generated values track reputable external references? The second is representational judgment: how much does the text reduce a person to a predictable social script? The present study does not collapse these two questions into one number, because they capture different failure modes.

These findings should be interpreted in light of limitations. The experimental design is single-shot at the model-by-condition level, meaning that each model was queried once per region and race/color combination. While this supports structured cross-model comparison, it does not capture within-model variability under repeated sampling. Future work should sample multiple outputs per condition under non-zero temperature and compare full generated and empirical distributions, including dispersion and skewness, rather than only group means.

The stereotype scores were produced by an LLM-based judge guided by predefined criteria rather than by human annotators. Although this approach enables scalable and consistent evaluation, the resulting scores should not be interpreted as definitive assessments of social stereotyping. A stronger design would combine human annotation with multiple automated judges and inter-rater agreement analysis.

In addition, the study isolates two prompt factors, region and race/color, while holding other attributes constant. This abstraction enables controlled comparisons but omits dimensions such as gender, age, and within-region heterogeneity. Incorporating additional attributes would likely yield a more detailed account of how these factors interact in generated profiles.

External calibration is also limited to variables that can be reasonably aligned with public statistics. Income lends itself naturally to this comparison, whereas dimensions such as personality and routine remain qualitatively assessed. Furthermore, the calibration relies on IBGE 2022 reference values updated to the 2026 collection period using the official IPCA index. This improves nominal comparability for income, but it does not account for other structural changes between the census reference period and the model-evaluation date.

Importantly, the purpose of this study is not to endorse group-conditioned profiling as an appropriate representation of individuals, but to examine how LLMs operationalize socially salient cues under a controlled prompting design.

Finally, the results reflect a specific prompting setup tailored to the Brazilian context. As such, they should be interpreted as evidence of model behavior under this controlled design rather than as general claims about all prompting strategies or application domains.

6 Conclusion

We presented a controlled study of Brazilian profile generation with 23 LLMs, examining how region and race/color shape socioeconomic attribution and stereotype judgments. The models reproduced the broad regional ordering found in official measurements [6], which suggests that their outputs are broadly aligned with real social gradients rather than showing arbitrary differentiation. At the same time, the generated income values were generally higher than the matched official references, and the degree of deviation varied substantially across region × race/color cells.

The stereotype analysis based on predefined criteria showed that most profiles fell in an intermediate range: usually plausible, but often socially coded in predictable ways. This suggests that the main risk in this setting is not predominantly extreme caricature, but moderate representational rigidity combined with imperfect socioeconomic calibration.

More broadly, the results support a two-part evaluation framework for socially conditioned LLM generation. Researchers should ask not only whether model outputs differ across groups, but whether those differences are calibrated against external references and how they are narratively realized in individual profiles. In contexts marked by persistent inequality, realism and stereotype are not mutually exclusive categories: LLMs may reproduce socially recognizable structure while still turning that structure into a default profile template, and may also reinforce socially patterned stereotypes in the process.

Acknowledgments. This work was supported by the National Council for Scientific and Technological Development (CNPq; grant no. 302530/2022-3) and the São Paulo Research Foundation (FAPESP), Brazil (Processes no. 2024/12936-5). The authors thank Instituto Kunumi for their financial and structural support.

The authors acknowledge the use of ChatGPT for grammar and language enhancement in the preparation of this manuscript.

References

1. Bender, E.M., Gebru, T., McMillan-Major, A., Shmitchell, S.: On the dangers of stochastic parrots: can language models be too big? In: Conference on Fairness, Accountability, and Transparency (FAccT), pp. 610–623 (2021)
2. Blodgett, S.L., Barocas, S., Daumé III, H., Wallach, H.: Language (technology) is power: a critical survey of "bias" in NLP. In: Annual Meeting of the Association for Computational Linguistics (ACL), pp. 5454–5476. ACL (2020)
3. Bolukbasi, T., Chang, K.-W., Zou, J.Y., Saligrama, V., Kalai, A.T.: Man is to computer programmer as woman is to homemaker? Debiasing word embeddings. In: Advances in Neural Information Processing Systems, vol. 29, pp. 4349–4357 (2016)
4. Caliskan, A., Bryson, J.J., Narayanan, A.: Semantics derived automatically from language corpora contain human-like biases. Science **356**(6334), 183–186 (2017)

5. Crenshaw, K.: Demarginalizing the intersection of race and sex. Univ. Chic. Leg. Forum **1989**(1), 139–167 (1989)
6. Instituto Brasileiro de Geografia e Estatística (IBGE): SIDRA, Tabela 10285. Censo Demográfico (2022). https://sidra.ibge.gov.br/tabela/10285
7. Instituto Brasileiro de Geografia e Estatística (IBGE): Calculadora do IPCA. https://anda.ibge.gov.br/2889-novo-portal/np-anexo/27641-calculadora-do-ipca.html
8. Instituto Brasileiro de Geografia e Estatística (IBGE). Cor ou raça: conceitos e metodologia do quesito. Apresentação técnica. Rio de Janeiro (2022). https://agenciadenoticias.ibge.gov.br/media/com_mediaibge/arquivos/13ee0337cffc1de37bf0cd4da3988e1f.pdf
9. Liang, P.P., Wu, C., Morency, L.-P., Salakhutdinov, R.: Towards understanding and mitigating social biases in language models. In: International Conference on Machine Learning (ICML), vol. 139, pp. 6565–6576. PMLR (2021)
10. Telles, E.E.: Race in Another America: The Significance of Skin Color in Brazil. Princeton University Press, Princeton (2004)
11. DeepMind: Taxonomy of risks posed by language models. In: Conference on Fairness, Accountability, and Transparency (FAccT), pp. 214–229 (2022)

Learning from Negative Edge Quality in Graph-Based Drug–Target Interaction Prediction

Lucas Goulart da Silva[1,2(✉)], Guilherme Henrique Messias[1], Ricardo Cerri[3], and Alan Demétrius Baria Valejo[1]

[1] Universidade Federal de São Carlos, São Carlos, SP, Brazil
lucas.goulart@ifsuldeminas.edu.br, ghmessias@estudante.ufscar.br, alanvalejo@ufscar.br

[2] Instituto Federal do Sul de Minas Gerais - Campus Muzambinho, Muzambinho, MG, Brazil

[3] Instituto de Ciências Matemáticas e de Computação, Universidade de São Paulo, São Carlos, SP, Brazil
cerri@icmc.usp.br

Abstract. Predicting drug-target interactions is central to drug discovery, yet a critical aspect remains largely overlooked: the role of negative edges. Because negative interactions are rarely observed, most approaches rely on randomly sampled negatives, implicitly assuming they are equally informative. However, this assumption introduces label noise and may distort the representations learned by graph neural networks. We propose NegAwareDTI, a transductive multitask framework that explicitly leverages negative edges not only as supervision signals but also as structural components of the graph. The model integrates pre-trained molecular and protein embeddings with a heterogeneous graph transformer and jointly optimizes edge classification and edge-label reconstruction. Experiments on the *Human* and *C. elegans* datasets, comparing high-confidence and randomly sampled negatives, show that negative edge quality is a decisive factor for performance. When reliable negatives are available, incorporating them into the graph structure significantly improves representation learning and yields state-of-the-art results (AUC-ROC up to 0.9897 and AUC-PR up to 0.9796). When negatives are noisy, injecting them into the graph structure harms representation learning, and restricting the encoder to positive edges yields more robust models. Our results establish negative edge as a key design choice in graph-based DTI prediction.

Keywords: Drug-target interaction · Graph Neural Networks · Edge-label supervision · Negative edges · Multitask learning

1 Introduction

Predicting drug-target interactions (DTI) is a central task in drug discovery, compound repositioning, and prioritizing candidate interactions for experimental

M. Recamonde-Mendoza and R. C. Barros (Eds.): BRACIS 2026, LNAI 17105, pp. 293–308, 2027.
https://doi.org/10.1007/978-3-032-39882-6_20

validation [11]. Because laboratory validation is expensive and time-consuming, machine learning methods are widely used to reduce the search space and guide experiments toward promising drug–protein pairs [1,4].

A common formulation represents drugs and proteins as nodes in a bipartite graph, where edges correspond to known interactions [3]. In this setting, Graph Neural Networks (GNNs) effectively combine node attributes and graph structure to learn representations for link prediction [10]. Recent advances incorporate embeddings from pre-trained language models (PLMs), capturing richer chemical and biological properties and improving representation quality [7,14].

Despite these advances, a critical aspect of DTI prediction remains underexplored: the role of negative edges (i.e., non-interacting drug–target pairs, whereas positive edges correspond to experimentally validated interactions) [16]. Since true negatives are rarely observed, most approaches rely on randomly sampled pairs [20]. This assumption introduces label noise, as many sampled pairs may correspond to unknown positives, affecting both learned representations and model evaluation [19]. More critically, the challenge is not only how to construct negative edges, but also how to model them within learning algorithms, as they are typically treated solely as supervision signals rather than as structural components that can influence representation learning.

In graph-based models, negative edges can play two roles: as supervision signals (or labels) or as part of the graph structure guiding representation learning. However, most approaches use them only as labels and rely on random sampling [20]. As a result, the joint effect of negative-edge quality, its integration into the graph structure, and learning objectives remains poorly understood [16]. This raises a fundamental question: **how does the quality of negative edges influence learned representations, and under which conditions should they be incorporated into the learning process rather than used only as supervision?**

To address this gap, we propose **NegAwareDTI**, a transductive multitask framework based on GNNs that explicitly models the role of negative edges in graph-based DTI prediction. The model integrates pre-trained molecular and protein embeddings (PLM) with a Heterogeneous Graph Transformer (HGT) encoder [8] and jointly optimizes edge classification and edge-label reconstruction, the latter acting as structural regularization. Unlike traditional approaches, NegAwareDTI leverages negative edges both as supervision signals and as structural components of the graph, enabling a controlled analysis of their impact. We hypothesize that the usefulness of negative edges depends on their reliability and on how they are incorporated into the model. Our main contributions are:

- A systematic analysis of negative-edge quality in graph-based DTI prediction, separating high-confidence and randomly sampled negatives.
- We propose the NegAwareDTI framework, which explicitly models negative edges as both supervision signals and structural components of the graph, enabling them to directly influence representation learning through joint classification and reconstruction.

- A controlled experimental design isolating the impact of negative edges as supervision signals and structural elements.
- Evidence that negative edges have a dual role: beneficial when reliable, harmful when noisy, if incorporated into the graph.
- The finding that adapting encoder topology to the negative-edge regime is more important than uniformly applying multitask learning.

Experiments show that negative-edge quality is decisive for performance. When high-confidence negatives are available, incorporating them into the graph improves representation learning and achieves state-of-the-art results. In contrast, with randomly sampled negatives, injecting them into the encoder degrades performance, and restricting message passing to positive edges yields more robust models. These results establish negative-edge usage as a central design choice in graph-based DTI prediction.

The remainder of the paper is organized as follows. Section 2 reviews related work. Section 3 presents NegAwareDTI. Section 4 describes the experimental design. Section 5 reports and discusses the results, including the ablation analysis. Section 6 concludes the paper.

2 Related Work

This section reviews representative approaches for DTI prediction, with an emphasis on graph-based methods and the treatment of negative examples.

2.1 Comparative Methods

DTI prediction has been addressed using a variety of approaches, including similarity-based, supervised learning, and deep learning methods, reflecting the diversity of available data sources such as molecular structures, protein sequences, and interaction networks [1,4]. Among sequence-based methods, Transformer architectures [15] have shown strong performance by capturing complex dependencies in molecular and protein sequences. For example, MolTrans applies attention mechanisms to tokenized representations to infer interaction patterns [9].

Another major direction involves graph-based methods, which model structural relationships between drugs and proteins at different levels, from molecular graphs to heterogeneous interaction networks [17,21]. Representative approaches such as MGraphDTA and DTI-LM combine structural information with pre-trained representations from LLMs to improve predictive performance [2,18]. These methods highlight the effectiveness of graph representations but still rely on predefined strategies for handling negative examples. Despite their differences, all these approaches depend critically on how negative examples are defined, a factor that directly impacts both training dynamics and evaluation reliability [16,19].

2.2 Definition of Negative Examples in DTI

Defining negative examples remains a central challenge in DTI prediction [16]. While positive interactions are experimentally confirmed, most drug-protein pairs remain unlabeled. Furthermore, the predominant approach is to treat unobserved pairs as negative through random sampling [20]. However, this practice may introduce false negatives, since some of these pairs may correspond to true interactions (positive interactions) that have not yet been identified, directly affecting model performance [11].

To mitigate this issue, some works propose selecting high-confidence negatives. For example, Liu et al. [13] identifying high-confidence negatives interaction based on dissimilarity relationships in chemogenomic space. In addition to its methodological contribution, the work introduced the *Human* and *C. elegans* datasets, which have been widely used in subsequent studies.

Despite these advances, significant gaps remain. Most studies focus on how to construct negative samples, but rarely investigate how these samples are used within learning models. In particular, negative edges are typically treated only as supervision signals, with little attention to their potential structural role in graph-based methods. As a result, the interaction between negative-edge quality, graph topology, and representation learning remains poorly understood [16].

This issue is particularly relevant in the context of GNNs, because the quality of negative samples can directly influence the representations learned across the graph [5]. It therefore remains an open question how much these models benefit from incorporating high-confidence negatives and how strongly their use affects performance across different approaches. This gap motivates the development of **NegAwareDTI**, which explicitly models negative edges as both supervision signals and structural components of the graph, as described in the next section.

Table 1 highlights that existing methods predominantly treat negative edges only as labels, overlooking their structural role and lacking controlled analyses of their impact.

Table 1. Negative edge usage in DTI methods.

Method	Model	Neg. usage	Structural role	Analysis
MolTrans [9]	Transformer	Label	×	×
MGraphDTA [18]	GNN + CNN	Label	×	×
DTI-LM [2]	GNN+LLM	Label	×	×
Liu et al. [13]	Sampling	Label	×	✓
NegAwareDTI (ours)	HGT+MT	Label + Structure	✓	✓

3 NegAwareDTI: Negative-Aware Graph Neural Network for Drug-Target Interaction Prediction

To address the limitations identified in Sect. 2, we propose **NegAwareDTI**, a graph-based framework designed to explicitly model the dual role of negative edges. In contrast to conventional approaches, which use negative edges only as supervision signals, our method allows them to act both as labels and as structural components of the graph, directly influencing representation learning.

The model is built upon a Heterogeneous Graph Transformer (HGT) encoder and a multitask learning strategy that combines edge classification and edge-label reconstruction. This design enables a controlled analysis of how negative-edge quality and its integration into the graph affect the learned representations.

Furthermore, NegAwareDTI explicitly distinguishes between two learning regimes: one in which negative edges are incorporated into the graph structure (PosNeg), and another in which they are used only as supervision signals (Pos). This distinction is central to our study, as it isolates the effect of negative edges on message passing and representation learning.

3.1 Problem Formulation

Let $G = (\mathcal{V}, \mathcal{E}, \mathcal{X})$ denote a bipartite graph of drug-target interactions, where $\mathcal{V} = \mathcal{V}^d \cup \mathcal{V}^p$ and $\mathcal{V}^d$ and $\mathcal{V}^p$ represent the drug and protein nodes, respectively. The edge set $\mathcal{E} \subseteq \mathcal{V}^d \times \mathcal{V}^p$ connects only nodes of different types, thus characterizing a bipartite graph. Node attributes are given by $\mathcal{X} = \{\mathbf{X}^d, \mathbf{X}^p\}$, where $\mathbf{X}^d \in \mathbb{R}^{|\mathcal{V}^d| \times F_d}$ is the drug attribute matrix and $\mathbf{X}^p \in \mathbb{R}^{|\mathcal{V}^p| \times F_p}$ is the protein attribute matrix. These initial attributes are obtained from pre-trained representations extracted from SMILES strings and amino acid sequences.

In our setting, the problem is formulated as a transductive link-prediction task in which all nodes remain available during training and the objective is to predict the label of drug-protein pairs between nodes already present in the graph. Throughout this work, $\mathcal{E}^+$ denotes the set of known positive interactions and $\mathcal{E}^-$ denotes the set of negative pairs used in the experiment. When the dataset provides negatives selected according to the protocol of Liu et al., these edges are used directly to define $\mathcal{E}^-$; otherwise, $\mathcal{E}^-$ is formed by sampling unobserved pairs.

For each drug-protein pair (d, p), the supervised label is given by $y_{dp} \in \{0, 1\}$, where 1 indicates a known positive interaction and 0 indicates a pair labeled as negative in the experiment.

3.2 Framework Architecture

The NegAwareDTI architecture consists of three main components: initial node representations, heterogeneous graph construction, and multitask optimization.

Drug nodes are represented by embeddings generated by ChemBERTa, a chemical language model pre-trained on SMILES sequences [6], whereas protein nodes are represented by embeddings extracted from ESM-2, a language model for protein sequences [12]. These vectors are used as initial node attributes in a bipartite graph. The graph is then processed by an HGT encoder, which projects the representations into a shared latent space that is sensitive to the different semantic types in the problem.

Using the latent embeddings produced by the encoder, NegAwareDTI optimizes two complementary tasks. The first is supervised edge classification, which estimates the probability of interaction for labeled drug-protein pairs. The second is an auxiliary edge-label reconstruction task, in which the model reconstructs the labels of observed edges from the node embeddings. Supervision therefore operates not only at the final classification stage but also helps structurally organize the latent space learned by the encoder.

Finally, the two tasks are jointly optimized through a composite loss function. This strategy allows the encoder to be trained simultaneously for a discriminative objective focused on interaction prediction and a structural objective focused on reconstructing the labels of observed edges. An overview of this pipeline is shown in Fig. 1.

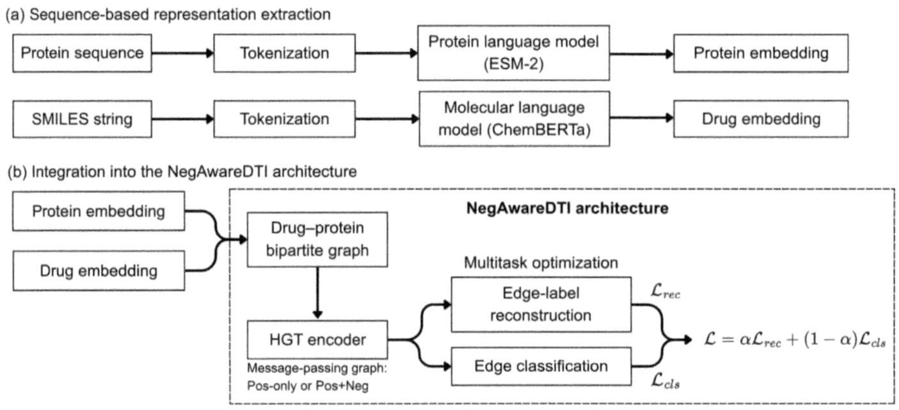

Fig. 1. Overview of NegAwareDTI. (a) Extraction of protein and drug representations from amino acid sequences and SMILES strings using ESM-2 and ChemBERTa. (b) Integration of these embeddings into the NegAwareDTI architecture, which combines an HGT encoder with supervised edge classification and auxiliary edge-label reconstruction under a joint multitask objective.

3.3 Heterogeneous Graph Encoder

To model the inherent heterogeneity of the DTI problem, NegAwareDTI uses an HGT encoder. Unlike homogeneous architectures, HGT parameterizes message passing according to node type and edge type, making it particularly well suited to bipartite graphs composed of drugs and proteins. In NegAwareDTI, the initial attributes of each node type are first projected into a common latent space and then refined through successive layers of heterogeneous attention.

At each layer, the representation of a target node is updated from its neighbors through an attention mechanism that depends on the source node type, the edge type, and the target node type. For clarity, we present a simplified form of the HGT attention mechanism between a neighboring source node s and a target node t:

$$\alpha_{s\to t}^{(l)} = \mathrm{softmax}_{s\in\mathcal{N}(t)}\left(\frac{\left(\mathbf{W}_{\tau(t)}^{Q}\mathbf{h}_t^{(l-1)}\right)^{\top}\left(\mathbf{W}_{\tau(s)}^{K}\mathbf{h}_s^{(l-1)}\right)}{\sqrt{d_h}}\right), \tag{1}$$

where $\tau(\cdot)$ denotes the node type, $\mathcal{N}(t)$ represents the neighborhood of t, and d_h is the hidden dimensionality.. In practice, HGT also incorporates relation-specific parameters, which enhance the model's ability to distinguish among interaction patterns in heterogeneous graphs.

After the attention coefficients are computed, messages from neighboring nodes are aggregated to update the target representation. In summary, the layer-l update is given by:

$$\mathbf{h}_t^{(l)} = \mathbf{h}_t^{(l-1)} + \phi\left(\sum_{s\in\mathcal{N}(t)} \alpha_{s\to t}^{(l)}\mathbf{W}_{\tau(s)}^{V}\mathbf{h}_s^{(l-1)}\right), \tag{2}$$

where $\phi(\cdot)$ denotes a nonlinearity applied after aggregation. Throughout the remainder of the paper, we reserve $\sigma(\cdot)$ for the logistic sigmoid function used to obtain predicted probabilities.

In this way, each node incorporates structural and semantic information from its neighborhood while preserving the distinction between drugs and proteins throughout propagation. After L layers, the latent embeddings $\mathbf{Z} = \mathbf{H}^{(L)}$ are obtained. These embeddings serve as the basis for the classification and reconstruction modules of NegAwareDTI.

3.4 Edge Classification Module

The main task of NegAwareDTI is the supervised classification of drug-protein edges. For a pair (d, p), with $d \in \mathcal{V}^d$ and $p \in \mathcal{V}^p$, the edge representation is obtained by concatenating the latent embeddings of the corresponding nodes:

$$\mathbf{e}_{dp} = [\mathbf{z}_d \,\|\, \mathbf{z}_p]. \tag{3}$$

where $\mathbf{z}_d, \mathbf{z}_p \in \mathbb{R}^h$ are latent embeddings in the shared space.

This vector is then processed by an MLP with one hidden layer and ReLU activation, denoted by $f_{cls}(\cdot)$. The predicted interaction probability $\hat{y}_{dp}$ is obtained by applying the sigmoid function to the score produced for the drug-protein pair.

We define the set of edges used by the encoder under two variants.

$$\mathcal{E}_{tr}^{enc} = \begin{cases} \mathcal{E}_{tr}^{+}, & \text{for the } \textit{Pos} \text{ variant,} \\ \mathcal{E}_{tr}^{+} \cup \mathcal{E}_{tr}^{-}, & \text{for the } \textit{PosNeg} \text{ variant.} \end{cases} \tag{4}$$

In *Pos*, only positive edges are included in the graph, and negative edges act only as supervision signals. In *PosNeg*, negative edges are also included in the graph, allowing them to influence message passing and the learned representations. The classification loss is defined by binary cross-entropy:

$$\mathcal{L}_{cls} = -\frac{1}{|\mathcal{E}_{tr}^{+}| + |\mathcal{E}_{tr}^{-}|} \left(\sum_{(d,p)\in\mathcal{E}_{tr}^{+}} \log \hat{y}_{dp} + \sum_{(d,p)\in\mathcal{E}_{tr}^{-}} \log(1 - \hat{y}_{dp}) \right). \tag{5}$$

The relative contribution of positive and negative examples is determined directly by the composition of $\mathcal{E}_{tr}^{+}$ and $\mathcal{E}_{tr}^{-}$ in each training partition.

3.5 Edge-Label Reconstruction

The auxiliary task of NegAwareDTI reconstructs the labels of the observed edges in the training graph from the latent embeddings produced by the encoder. In the supervised setting adopted in the *Pos* and *PosNeg* experiments, reconstruction is applied to the labeled positive and negative training edges. When the *PosNeg* variant is used, these negative edges affect the model in two ways: they are included in the adjacency processed by the encoder and are also used explicitly as supervised targets for reconstruction and classification. In the *Pos* variant, by contrast, negative edges are used only as supervised targets and are excluded from the encoder adjacency.

Reconstruction is performed by a parameter-free decoder based on the inner product between node embeddings. For an observed pair (d, p), the reconstruction score is given by

$$s_{dp}^{rec} = \mathbf{z}_d^{\top} \mathbf{z}_p, \qquad \hat{r}_{dp} = \sigma(s_{dp}^{rec}), \tag{6}$$

where $\hat{r}_{dp}$ represents, in the auxiliary task, the predicted probability that the edge (d, p) has a positive label.

The reconstruction loss is defined by binary cross-entropy over the positive and negative edges labeled in training:

$$\mathcal{L}_{rec} = -\frac{1}{|\mathcal{E}_{tr}^{+}| + |\mathcal{E}_{tr}^{-}|} \left(\sum_{(d,p)\in\mathcal{E}_{tr}^{+}} \log \hat{r}_{dp} + \sum_{(d,p)\in\mathcal{E}_{tr}^{-}} \log(1 - \hat{r}_{dp}) \right). \tag{7}$$

This formulation encourages the latent space to assign high similarity to positive edges and low similarity to negative edges. As a result, the auxiliary objective acts as label-based structural regularization, complementing the main classification task and reinforcing the separation between positive and negative interactions in the bipartite graph.

3.6 Multitask Optimization

NegAwareDTI is trained end-to-end, with a shared encoder for the classification and reconstruction heads. Although the reconstruction module introduces no additional parameters because it uses an inner-product decoder, its loss propagates gradients through the node embeddings and thus acts directly as regularization on the encoder.

The total loss function is given by

$$\mathcal{L} = \alpha \mathcal{L}_{rec} + (1 - \alpha)\mathcal{L}_{cls}, \tag{8}$$

where $\alpha \in [0, 1]$ controls the balance between the structural and discriminative components. Larger values of α increase the influence of reconstruction on the latent space, while smaller values favor the main classification task.

In each training epoch, the full graph of the training partition is passed once through the heterogeneous encoder to produce the node embeddings $\mathbf{Z}$. Using the labeled training edges, that is, the sets $\mathcal{E}_{tr}^{+}$ and $\mathcal{E}_{tr}^{-}$, the classification and reconstruction losses are then computed. Their weighted sum is used to update the trainable parameters via backpropagation.

Under this joint optimization, supervised classification acts directly on both the predictive head and the encoder, while reconstruction provides supervised structural regularization of the latent space. This coupling is central to NegAwareDTI and allows the information contained in labeled positive and negative edges to be exploited during learning.

This joint optimization allows negative edges to influence learning at two levels: through supervision in the classification loss and, when included in the graph, through structural interactions in the encoder. This dual influence is central to the proposed framework.

4 Experimental Design

The experimental design addressed three main aspects: the impact of negative-edge definition on DTI prediction, the conditions under which incorporating negative edges into the encoder is beneficial, and the contribution of the auxiliary reconstruction task under different encoder configurations.

4.1 Datasets and Preprocessing

Experiments were conducted on the *Human* and *C. elegans* datasets introduced by Liu et al. [13], which provide experimentally validated positive interactions and high-confidence negative pairs. The datasets were preprocessed to remove invalid compounds, eliminate duplicates, and standardize molecular representations. In our setting, the provided negative pairs were treated as high-confidence negatives. In the sampled-negative scenario, additional negatives were generated by randomly sampling unobserved drug–protein pairs while preserving the original class balance.

Table 2 summarizes the final dataset statistics. In this study, pairs labeled as negative were treated as high-confidence negatives. In the sampled-negative scenario, new negative pairs were drawn from the unobserved drug-protein pairs while preserving the original number of negatives in each dataset.

Table 2. Statistics of the datasets after preprocessing.

Dataset	Final pairs	Drugs	Proteins	Positives	High-confidence negatives
Human	5252	2523	1782	2253	2999
C. elegans	5962	1727	1739	2129	3833

4.2 Experimental Protocol

The task was formulated as transductive edge prediction on a bipartite graph. In this setting, all drug and protein nodes remain available throughout training, and only the labeled edges are split into training, internal validation, and test sets. For each external fold k, the graph used by the encoder, denoted by $G_{enc}^{(k)}$, is built exclusively from the labeled training edges of that fold. In the *PosNeg* variant, $G_{enc}^{(k)}$ includes both positive and negative training edges; in the *Pos* variant, it includes only positive training edges. The same rule is applied in the internal validation loop. As a result, edges from internal validation and test sets are excluded from the adjacency used in message passing and are used only for hyperparameter selection and final evaluation, respectively.

Evaluation used repeated nested cross-validation. In each experimental condition, five repetitions were run, with seeds controlling the data splits to ensure reproducibility. Within each repetition, positive and negative labeled edges were shuffled separately and divided into five external folds. All methods used the same negative sets within each experimental condition. For each external fold, one fold was held out for testing and the remaining folds were used for training.

Hyperparameters were selected through three-fold internal cross-validation. In each external fold, Optuna evaluated 75 trials and selected the configuration with the highest mean AUPR. Final training was limited to 100 epochs.

4.3 Comparative Methods and Evaluation

We compared NegAwareDTI against MolTrans [9], MGraphDTA [18], and DTI-LM [2] under the same postprocessed datasets and data partitions. This standardization ensured fair comparisons by keeping the processed datasets, negative-edge definitions, and evaluation protocol fixed across methods. AUC-PR was used as the primary metric due to class imbalance, and AUC-ROC was reported as a secondary metric.

In addition to deep learning methods, we included three classical baselines: Logistic Regression (LR), Random Forest (RF), and Support Vector Machine

(SVM). These methods represent levels of supervised-learning complexity. LR provides a linear reference, RF captures nonlinear relationships through tree ensembles, and SVM offers a baseline for binary classification in high-dimensional spaces. Together, these models help assess whether the gains observed with deep and graph-based architectures can be attributed to the proposed design.

The values reported in the tables were aggregated in two stages. Within each run, the metric was averaged over the five external folds. These run-level averages were then aggregated across the five independent runs. Therefore, the $\mu \pm \sigma$ format in the tables represents the mean across runs and the corresponding standard deviation of the fold-averaged results.

4.4 Ablation Design

We conduct ablation experiments to analyze the impact of negative-edge usage and the reconstruction objective. Specifically, we evaluate four variants of NegAwareDTI, combining: (i) the edge set used by the encoder (*Pos* vs *PosNeg*), and (ii) the training objective (classification only vs multitask learning).

These variants allow us to isolate the effects of negative edges as supervision signals and as structural components of the graph, as well as to assess the contribution of the reconstruction loss under different conditions.

5 Results and Discussion

Tables 3 and 4 report the results on the *Human* and *C. elegans* datasets. For the proposed method, *PosNeg* denotes the variant in which both positive and negative edges are included in the encoder graph, whereas *Pos* denotes the variant that uses only positive edges. In addition, *MT* denotes the multitask setting, in which classification is jointly optimized with edge-label reconstruction, whereas *Cls* denotes classification only.

5.1 Ablation Analysis and Comparison with Comparative Methods

To examine the impact of negative-edge definition, we compared model performance under high-confidence negatives and randomly sampled negatives. Replacing high-confidence negatives with sampled negatives led to a consistent performance drop. The difference between these settings lies not in the number of negative examples, which was kept constant, but in the reliability of their labels: in the first case, negatives are provided by the dataset protocol; in the second, they are obtained by sampling unobserved pairs. The observed differences are therefore best explained by the quality of the supervised signal and by the noise it can introduce into both the loss function and, depending on the configuration, the graph structure processed by the encoder.

In the *Human* and *C. elegans* settings with negatives selected according to the protocol of Liu et al., the proposed method outperformed the comparative methods in most evaluations. Under these conditions, the best configuration was

Table 3. Performance comparison on the *Human* dataset. Values are reported as mean ± standard deviation and the best results are shown in bold.

Negatives	Method	AUC-PR	AUC-ROC
High-confidence negatives	DTI-LM	0.9687 ± 0.0021	0.9730 ± 0.0018
	MolTrans	0.9695 ± 0.0018	0.9729 ± 0.0019
	MGraphDTA	0.9540 ± 0.0025	0.9611 ± 0.0027
	Logistic Regression	0.9538 ± 0.0013	0.9632 ± 0.0009
	Random Forest	0.9658 ± 0.0012	0.9689 ± 0.0007
	SVM	0.9620 ± 0.0019	0.9692 ± 0.0009
	NegAwareDTI (PosNeg+MT)	**0.9796 ± 0.0025**	**0.9832 ± 0.0016**
	NegAwareDTI (PosNeg+Cls)	0.9781 ± 0.0023	0.9812 ± 0.0015
	NegAwareDTI (Pos+MT)	0.9638 ± 0.0049	0.9641 ± 0.0065
	NegAwareDTI (Pos+Cls)	0.9544 ± 0.0242	0.9473 ± 0.0355
Sampled negatives	DTI-LM	0.8810 ± 0.0063	0.8964 ± 0.0031
	MolTrans	0.8921 ± 0.0092	0.9117 ± 0.0050
	MGraphDTA	0.8856 ± 0.0034	0.9089 ± 0.0027
	Logistic Regression	0.8260 ± 0.0047	0.8507 ± 0.0025
	Random Forest	0.8886 ± 0.0046	0.8964 ± 0.0045
	SVM	0.8139 ± 0.0062	0.8442 ± 0.0046
	NegAwareDTI (PosNeg+MT)	0.8978 ± 0.0090	0.9066 ± 0.0063
	NegAwareDTI (PosNeg+Cls)	0.9060 ± 0.0090	0.9137 ± 0.0065
	NegAwareDTI (Pos+MT)	**0.9091 ± 0.0037**	**0.9221 ± 0.0021**
	NegAwareDTI (Pos+Cls)	0.9048 ± 0.0011	0.9197 ± 0.0015

NegAwareDTI (PosNeg+MT), which achieved the highest AUC-ROC on both datasets, the highest AUC-PR on *Human*, and an AUC-PR on *C. elegans* close to the best result. These findings suggest that, when high-confidence negatives are available, incorporating negative edges into the encoder enriches the structural representation and better aligns reconstruction with the final classification task. Although DTI-LM retained a slight advantage in AUC-PR on *C. elegans*, the proposed method performed best overall in terms of class discrimination.

In the sampled-negative setting, the effect of the edge set used by the encoder became clearer. The best overall performance on both datasets was achieved by NegAwareDTI (Pos+MT). In both cases, variants that used only positive edges in the encoder outperformed those that also incorporated sampled negatives, suggesting that injecting potentially noisy negatives into the encoder can degrade the learned representations. In this setting, restricting the encoder to positive edges preserves the more reliable graph structure, while the supervised classification task continues to exploit negative examples through the loss function.

Comparing the MT and Cls variants indicates that the auxiliary reconstruction task plays a complementary role and yields generally modest gains. Overall, the multitask variant tends to outperform its classification-only counterpart, but this effect depends on the encoder configuration and should be inter-

Table 4. Performance comparison on the *C. elegans* dataset. Values are reported as mean ± standard deviation and the best results are shown in bold.

Negatives	Method	AUC-PR	AUC-ROC
High-confidence negatives	DTI-LM	**0.9834 ± 0.0006**	0.9874 ± 0.0009
	MolTrans	0.9799 ± 0.0019	0.9868 ± 0.0011
	MGraphDTA	0.9588 ± 0.0037	0.9763 ± 0.0017
	Logistic Regression	0.9744 ± 0.0014	0.9839 ± 0.0005
	Random Forest	0.9745 ± 0.0008	0.9841 ± 0.0004
	SVM	0.9748 ± 0.0017	0.9837 ± 0.0012
	NegAwareDTI (PosNeg+MT)	0.9818 ± 0.0015	**0.9897 ± 0.0007**
	NegAwareDTI (PosNeg+Cls)	0.9787 ± 0.0029	0.9876 ± 0.0018
	NegAwareDTI (Pos+MT)	0.9552 ± 0.0189	0.9633 ± 0.0218
	NegAwareDTI (Pos+Cls)	0.9688 ± 0.0012	0.9798 ± 0.0009
Sampled negatives	DTI-LM	0.8875 ± 0.0025	0.9246 ± 0.0016
	MolTrans	0.8900 ± 0.0033	0.9302 ± 0.0011
	MGraphDTA	0.8827 ± 0.0147	0.9294 ± 0.0060
	Logistic Regression	0.8253 ± 0.0050	0.8720 ± 0.0025
	Random Forest	0.9037 ± 0.0011	0.9307 ± 0.0010
	SVM	0.8151 ± 0.0044	0.8673 ± 0.0030
	NegAwareDTI (PosNeg+MT)	0.8770 ± 0.0343	0.9185 ± 0.0179
	NegAwareDTI (PosNeg+Cls)	0.8967 ± 0.0059	0.9283 ± 0.0051
	NegAwareDTI (Pos+MT)	**0.9119 ± 0.0033**	**0.9431 ± 0.0021**
	NegAwareDTI (Pos+Cls)	0.9102 ± 0.0035	0.9425 ± 0.0024

preted together with the choice of edge set used for message passing. When high-confidence negatives are available, reconstruction contributes more consistently to performance. In the sampled-negative setting, however, its benefits are smaller and appear mainly when the encoder is restricted to positive edges. Taken together, these results suggest that $\mathcal{L}_{rec}$ primarily refines the learned representations rather than serving as the main driver of the observed gains.

Overall, the results show that performance is governed not by model complexity alone, but by the interaction between negative-edge quality, encoder topology, and supervision. When the structural signal is reliable, incorporating negatives into the encoder improves learning; when it is noisy, excluding them from message passing is essential. These findings reinforce that the key factor is how negative edges are modeled, rather than their mere inclusion.

5.2 Interpretation of Findings

These results indicate that, in graph-based DTI prediction, the usefulness of negative edges depends on the reliability of the signal they provide to the encoder. When this signal is reliable, incorporating negatives into the graph structure facilitates message passing and improves representation learning, allowing reconstruction to contribute more consistently to refinement. When the signal is noisier, negative edges introduce misleading structural information that propagates through the graph, making it more robust to restrict message passing to positive edges. Thus, the main finding of this work is not a uniform gain from multitask learning, but the need to align the encoder topology with the supervision regime for negative edges.

The comparative methods further highlight the role of supervision quality. In settings with high-confidence negatives, different approaches remain competitive, suggesting that cleaner supervision allows distinct models to exploit the available signal. In contrast, settings with sampled negatives show greater sensitivity to degraded supervision, leading to more variable performance. These observations help explain why prior methods, which treat negative edges uniformly, may produce inconsistent results across datasets. In this context, the main contribution of the proposed method lies not only in its absolute performance, but in demonstrating that adapting the encoder topology to the negative-edge regime is an effective strategy for handling noisy settings. This perspective extends beyond DTI, suggesting that the treatment of negative edges should be considered a structural design choice in graph-based learning.

6 Conclusion and Future Work

This work investigated drug-protein interaction prediction on bipartite graphs, focusing on the role of negative edges in graph-based models. We proposed NegAwareDTI, a framework that integrates a heterogeneous graph transformer with multitask learning to explicitly model negative edges both as supervision signals and as structural components of the graph.

The results show that NegAwareDTI performs competitively on the evaluated datasets and that its performance depends not only on the presence of negative examples but also on how these edges are incorporated into the learning process. In particular, the experiments indicate that adapting the encoder topology to the negative-edge regime is central to the method's robustness, while reconstruction contributes by refining the learned representations.

These findings suggest that the primary challenge is not only whether to use negative edges, but also how to align their role with the learning mechanism. This perspective reframes the treatment of negative examples as a structural design choice in graph-based learning, rather than a purely data-level concern.

A limitation of this work is the dependence on the availability of high-confidence negative samples, which may not be accessible in many real-world scenarios. Future work should focus on developing strategies for estimating reliable negatives and on designing adaptive models capable of adjusting their structure according to the uncertainty of negative edges. Extending this analysis to larger datasets and other graph-based domains is also a promising direction.

Acknowledgments. This research was funded by the Coordination for the Improvement of Higher Education Personnel (CAPES) – Code 001, through a Ph.D. scholarship; by the IFSULDEMINAS - Campus Muzambinho; The São Paulo Research Foundation (FAPESP) [grants 22/03090-0]; and Brazilian National Council for Scientific and Technological Development (CNPq) [grants 420025/2023-5 and 300934/2025-4]. The authors also acknowledge the use of AI-based tools to support text revision and the organization of experiments.

References

1. Ahmad, B., Ouahada, K., Hamam, H.: Machine learning for drug-target interaction prediction: a comprehensive review of models, challenges, and computational strategies. Comput. Struct. Biotechnol. J. **31**, 316–345 (2026)
2. Ahmed, K.T., Ansari, M.I., Zhang, W.: DTI-LM: language model powered drug-target interaction prediction. Bioinformatics **40**, btae533 (2024)
3. Al Musawi, A.F., Roy, S., Ghosh, P.: A review of link prediction applications in network biology. IEEE Access **13**, 54997–55016 (2025)
4. Bagherian, M., Sabeti, E., Wang, K., Sartor, M.A., Nikolovska-Coleska, Z., Najarian, K.: Machine learning approaches and databases for prediction of drug–target interaction: a survey paper. Brief. Bioinform. **22**, 247–269 (2021)
5. Cheng, Z., Xu, D., Ding, D., Ding, Y.: Prediction of drug-target interactions with high- quality negative samples and a network-based deep learning framework. IEEE J. Biomed. Health Inform. **29**, 1567–1578 (2025)
6. Chithrananda, S., Grand, G., Ramsundar, B.: ChemBERTa: large-scale self-supervised pretraining for molecular property prediction (2020)
7. Guo, F., et al.: Foundation models in bioinformatics. Natl. Sci. Rev. **12**, nwaf028 (2025)
8. Hu, Z., Dong, Y., Wang, K., Sun, Y.: Heterogeneous graph transformer. In: Proceedings of the Web Conference 2020, pp. 2704–2710 (2020)
9. Huang, K., Xiao, C., Glass, L.M., Sun, J.: MolTrans: molecular interaction transformer for drug–target interaction prediction. Bioinformatics **37**, 830–836 (2021)
10. Khemani, B., Patil, S., Kotecha, K., Tanwar, S.: A review of graph neural networks: concepts, architectures, techniques, challenges, datasets, applications, and future directions. J. Big Data **11**, 18 (2024)
11. Liao, Q., et al.: Application of artificial intelligence in drug-target interactions prediction: a review. NPJ Biomed. Innov. **2**, 1 (2025)
12. Lin, Z., et al.: Evolutionary-scale prediction of atomic-level protein structure with a language model. Science **379**, 1123–1130 (2023)
13. Liu, H., Sun, J., Guan, J., Zheng, J., Zhou, S.: Improving compound–protein interaction prediction by building up highly credible negative samples. Bioinformatics **31**, i221–i229 (2015)
14. Sun, Y., Li, Y.Y., Leung, C.K., Hu, P.: iNGNN-DTI: prediction of drug–target interaction with interpretable nested graph neural network and pretrained molecule models. Bioinformatics **40**, btae135 (2024)
15. Vaswani, A., et al.: Attention is all you need. In: Advances in Neural Information Processing Systems, vol. 30 (2017)
16. Vefghi, A., Rahmati, Z., Akbari, M.: Drug-target interaction/affinity prediction: deep learning models and advances review. Comput. Biol. Med. **196**, 110438 (2025)
17. Wang, Y., Li, Z., Barati Farimani, A.: Graph neural networks for molecules. In: Machine Learning in Molecular Sciences, vol. 36, pp. 21–66. Springer (2023)

18. Yang, Z., Zhong, W., Zhao, L., Yu-Chian Chen, C.: MGraphDTA: deep multiscale graph neural network for explainable drug-target binding affinity prediction. Chem. Sci. **13**, 816–833 (2022)
19. Yu, D., Liu, H., Yao, S.: Drug–target interaction prediction based on improved heterogeneous graph representation learning and feature projection classification. Expert Syst. Appl. **252**, 124289 (2024)
20. Zhang, Z., et al.: Graph neural network approaches for drug-target interactions. Curr. Opin. Struct. Biol. **73**, 102327 (2022)
21. Zhou, J., et al.: Graph neural networks: a review of methods and applications. AI Open **1**, 57–81 (2020)

Enem-VL: A Multimodal Benchmark of Brazilian Exams for Evaluating Vision-Language Models

Anderson Luis Bento Soares(✉), Leonardo Nascimento Ferreira, Giovani Mambrim Leme, Matheus Ferracciú Scatolin, Ruben Interian, and Zanoni Dias

Institute of Computing, University of Campinas (Unicamp), Campinas, SP, Brazil
{anderson.soares,giovani.leme,matheus.scatolin}@students.ic.unicamp.br,
{lnf,ruben,zanoni}@ic.unicamp.br

Abstract. Brazil's National High School Exam (Enem) is a large-scale, high-stakes assessment and a major pathway to higher education in Brazil. Its questions combine long textual prompts, diagrams, tables, and culturally grounded content, making it a valuable source for evaluating vision-language models (VLMs) in non-English contexts. However, existing Enem-based resources are not primarily designed as longitudinal multimodal benchmarks, often focusing on text-only evaluation or recent editions. We present Enem-VL, a multimodal benchmark built from Enem editions spanning 1998–2025. The dataset contains 7,703 question records from 87 exams over 28 years, including 2,614 questions with visual elements and 320 foreign-language items. It provides structured question fields, answer-key metadata, images, extracted visual assets, and annotations for language, area, and answer status. We describe the construction pipeline, including PDF processing, question segmentation, visual-asset extraction, answer-key integration, and metadata annotation, as well as documented irregularities in official sources. We also define a reproducible multiple-choice evaluation protocol and report a four-model VLM baseline with deterministic decoding. Across 30,812 responses, 99.85% were valid normalized options. Accuracy varies substantially across knowledge areas and years, highlighting the need for fine-grained evaluation. Enem-VL provides a historically broad, multimodal benchmark for studying VLM behavior in educational assessment scenarios.

Keywords: multimodal benchmark · Enem · vision-language models · educational assessment · Portuguese

1 Introduction

Recent progress in LLMs and VLMs has expanded the practical scope of AI systems for educational support, tutoring, content analysis, and assessment under-

M. Recamonde-Mendoza and R. C. Barros (Eds.): BRACIS 2026, LNAI 17105, pp. 309–324, 2027.
https://doi.org/10.1007/978-3-032-39882-6_21

standing. However, many widely used benchmarks remain centered on English-language or curated exam-style settings [1–3,5,6], while authentic high-stakes assessments with multimodal layouts and culturally grounded content remain less represented, especially outside English-dominant contexts [7,8]. This limits the ability to characterize model behavior under realistic conditions.

The Brazilian National High School Exam (Enem) is a large-scale standardized assessment and serves as one of the main gateways to higher education in Brazil. Its scores are used in major national admission programs, such as the Unified Selection System (SISU), the University for All Program (ProUni), and the Student Financing Fund (FIES). In addition, both public and private higher education institutions widely adopt Enem results as a selection criterion [13,14].

In terms of scale, Enem is often compared to China's Gaokao. According to the National Institute for Educational Studies and Research Anísio Teixeira (Inep), these two exams are considered the largest large-scale assessments administered at the end of secondary education for access to higher education [15].

Its questions frequently require integrated reasoning over text, visual elements, and domain knowledge across major subject areas. These characteristics make Enem a valuable source for evaluating the multimodal reasoning capabilities of contemporary models, especially in Portuguese and in multilingual cases where items are language-specific. However, existing Enem-based resources have not been primarily designed for this purpose: some focus on text-only question answering [18,19], while others cover recent editions or specific model-evaluation settings [20,21]. Given the limitations in the available Enem dataset, there is still a need for a benchmark that jointly preserves question-level visual assets, answer-status metadata, and source-level irregularities across the historical Enem archive.

In this paper, we introduce Enem-VL, a multimodal dataset and benchmark assembled from Enem editions spanning 1998–2025. The core objective is to provide a reproducible and extensible dataset of Enem questions that preserves their textual, visual, linguistic, and metadata structure for multiple research uses, including educational assessment analysis, multilingual question answering, multimodal reasoning, and model evaluation. In this paper, we instantiate this broader resource as a VLM benchmark by defining an initial multiple-choice evaluation protocol and reporting baseline results for contemporary VLMs on Enem-VL. This manuscript formalizes the methodology and baseline setup for the benchmark's initial version and presents experimental results for multiple VLMs on Enem-VL.

Our construction process combines semi-automated document processing with deterministic validation checks and manual review checkpoints. The pipeline extracts question text and associated visual artifacts from exam PDFs, standardizes layout-derived structures, merges answer keys via reference mappings, and tags language-sensitive items (English/Spanish). We also attribute subject labels by official question ranges and preserve metadata needed for robust slicing and longitudinal analysis, including year, booklet identity, question number, answer availability/cancellation state, language tag, image-path fields, and text fields (statement, support text, alternatives).

The contributions of this work are:

1. A multimodal benchmark of Enem questions (1998–2025), with question-level metadata and image assets suitable for VLM evaluation.
2. A documented construction and curation pipeline covering extraction, structuring, answer-key integration, language handling, and area attribution.
3. A quality validation framework that explicitly tracks missing keys, annulled answers, and historical source gaps.
4. A reproducible baseline protocol for multiple-choice evaluation (A–E) with standardized inference settings, output-validity accounting, and slice-based analysis.
5. A release repository including source files, processed artifacts, images, question records, machine-readable JSON manifests, and the baseline code with prompt templates.
6. Baseline results for four VLMs, including response-validity statistics and accuracy analyses by knowledge area and year.

2 Related Work

Educational benchmark research has developed along multiple fronts: broad academic QA datasets, multilingual evaluation suites, and multimodal reasoning corpora. Classic reading comprehension and exam-style datasets such as SQuAD [1] and RACE [2] established early paradigms for passage-grounded question answering, while later benchmarks like MMLU [3] emphasized broad knowledge assessment.

In multimodal evaluation, benchmarks such as VQAv2 [4], ScienceQA [5], MMMU [6], and M3Exam [7] have expanded coverage to image-grounded reasoning, science diagrams, college-level multimodal tasks, and authentic multilingual exam settings. These resources are influential but still mostly centered on English or on specific collection designs.

Parallel work on multilingual evaluation has highlighted performance disparities across languages and the importance of broader language coverage [8,9]. Beyond question-answering benchmarks, exam-based datasets also require careful document curation. In the case of Enem, this involves preserving the relation between questions, support texts, alternatives, tables, diagrams, and other visual elements across heterogeneous PDF layouts. Generic text extraction alone is insufficient for this setting, since the benchmark requires question-level segmentation, visual-asset preservation, answer-key alignment, and metadata validation. These requirements motivate the dedicated construction pipeline described in Sect. 3.

More directly related to Enem-VL, previous Enem-centered resources have introduced valuable but narrower evaluation settings. The Enem Challenge proposed Enem as a benchmark for artificial intelligence in Brazilian Portuguese and provided a machine-readable representation of multiple-choice questions [18,19].

However, this resource was primarily designed as a text-based benchmark: its public dataset contains only the textual portion of the objective exam and covers Enem editions from 2009 to 2017. In its initial construction, the machine-readable database retained only the textual part of the selected questions, while non-textual elements were used for annotation rather than preserved as question-level visual assets; foreign-language questions were also discarded to simplify the task.

Recent LLM-oriented studies have expanded Enem evaluation to contemporary models. One line of work evaluates GPT-3.5 and GPT-4 on Enem questions from 2009–2017 and on the 2022 edition [20]. Another line extends this setting to multimodal evaluation, releasing Enem 2022–2024 datasets with image references and textual descriptions of visual content [21]. These resources enable controlled comparisons between text-only and vision-capable models, but their temporal scope is limited to recent editions and they are not intended as a full reconstruction of the Enem archive.

BLUEX focuses on entrance exams from specific universities (Unicamp and USP) [22], while Alvorada-Bench includes Enem among several Brazilian examinations but explicitly targets text-only model evaluation by filtering out questions that require visual interpretation [23]. Recent psychometric studies have also used Enem items and official item response theory (IRT) parameters to analyze model proficiency or item-difficulty estimation [24], but these studies address calibration questions rather than providing a curated multimodal question-level benchmark.

Enem-VL is designed to complement these prior efforts by providing an Enem-specific benchmark with broader temporal coverage, spanning 1998–2025, and by preserving question-level images and extracted visual assets. In addition, the dataset integrates answer-key metadata, marks missing and annulled items, handles language-specific questions, and documents official-source irregularities. Rather than replacing previous Enem resources, Enem-VL extends this line of work toward a reproducible, multimodal, and historically broader benchmark for VLM assessment.

3 Methodology

This section describes the construction of Enem-VL, covering data acquisition, document processing, question structuring, answer-key integration, metadata annotation, and the benchmark evaluation protocol.

3.1 Data Acquisition

Enem-VL covers official Enem exam materials from 1998 to 2025, collected from the public archive of exam booklets and answer keys maintained by Inep [16]. The collection process targeted question booklets and associated answer sources when available. Source files were archived with versioned provenance metadata to support traceability.

The current version includes:

- exam-derived question records across years 1998–2025;
- metadata fields for question identity and evaluation;
- visual assets including question-level PNGs and extracted figures from within questions.

When historical answer-key sources were unavailable, incomplete, or inconsistent with the corresponding booklet, items were retained with explicit missing-label markers instead of being discarded or silently corrected.

The official archive is essential for provenance, but it is not a perfectly consistent data source. During acquisition, we found links that did not resolve to the expected exam booklet, missing answer keys, and answer-key links that pointed to incorrect exam files. These irregularities affect reproducibility because a naive crawler can download an apparently valid PDF while actually collecting the wrong application or booklet.

The most consequential case identified in our current release is the 2016 reapplication. In the official source, both exam and answer-key links for that reapplication resolve to materials from the first application, which prevents reliable collection of the intended reapplication data. Enem-VL therefore avoids duplicating first-application records under the reapplication identity and records the affected items as unavailable at source level. All such cases are explicitly documented in this paper and handled through manual curation to ensure consistency in the dataset.

3.2 Dataset Construction

The processing workflow used in Enem-VL comprises six stages, as illustrated in Fig. 1: (i) exam ingestion, (ii) layout standardization, (iii) question division, (iv) structure detection and extraction, (v) document organization, and (vi) semantic field extraction.

At layout standardization time, each input PDF page is processed by a vertical-divider detector. When a page is identified as two-column, it is split vertically and reordered into a single reading flow by placing one half below the other. This step reduces downstream parsing errors caused by mixed column reading order.

The pipeline begins with PDF parsing and page-level normalization. We apply layout-aware segmentation to identify candidate question boundaries, then split each booklet into per-question PDFs. Split triggers include explicit markers such as *"Questão XX"* and support-text headers such as *"Texto de apoio para questões XX a XX"* (or close variants). Because Enem formatting is not fully uniform across all years, this stage produced recurring edge-case failures that were corrected manually.

For each question/support unit, we run three extraction steps:

- a PNG rendering of the question region;
- extraction of internal figures, including vector objects (e.g., charts/tables) and embedded raster images;

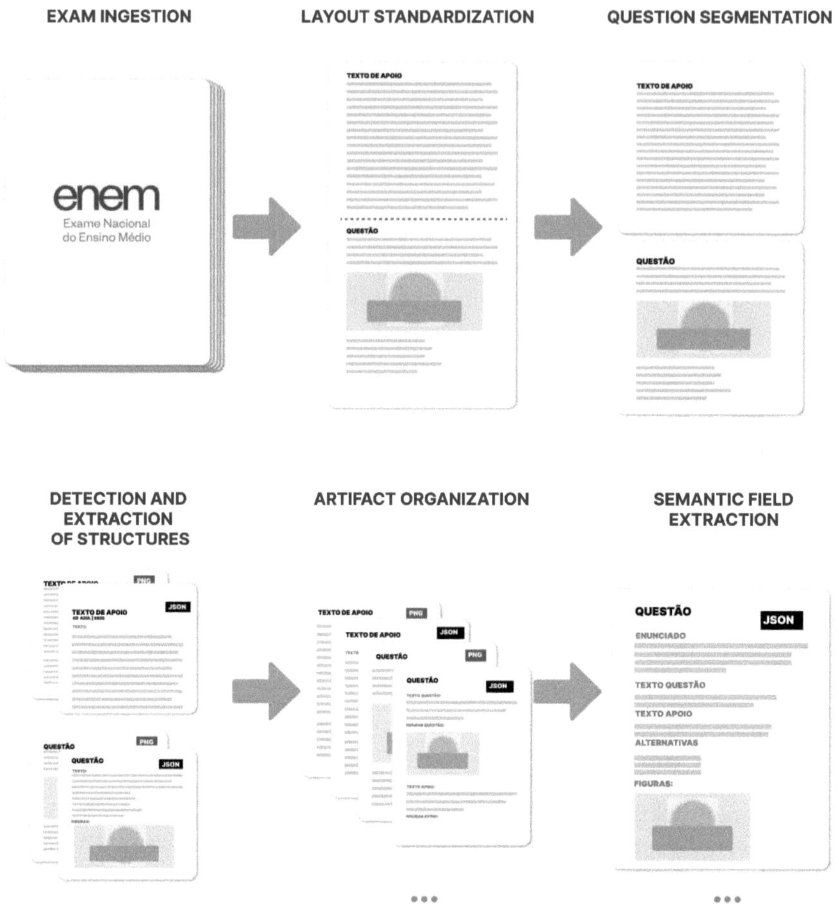

Fig. 1. Enem-VL construction pipeline from exam ingestion to structured multimodal question records.

– raw text extraction from PDF content streams.

Because raw text extraction can be noisy in some items, we add a VLM-based correction stage using `Qwen/Qwen3-VL-30B-A3B-Instruct`. For question units, the model receives the question PNG and extracted text and returns normalized statement, support text, and alternatives. For support-text-only units, the model receives the support-text PNG and returns corrected support text. The goal is to improve extraction fidelity and reliably separate statement/support content before final assembly.

This correction stage does not use answer keys and is restricted to normalizing extracted statements, support texts, and alternatives. The normalization and baseline evaluation were also performed as separate runs, with task-specific prompts and without shared conversational context. Therefore, the preprocessing model (`Qwen`) does not receive the canonical answers during text correction, nor is it asked to solve the questions at this stage. Since `Qwen/Qwen3-VL-30B-A3B-Instruct` is also included in the baseline roster, we explicitly document this overlap for transparency. Its baseline score should be read as a result under the same released Enem-VL records used by the other models, while recognizing that future releases may use a preprocessing model outside the evaluation roster.

After this stage, support texts are linked back to each question that depends on them. This strategy supports both end-to-end image reasoning and controlled experiments using text plus extracted visual components.

Answer keys were obtained from publicly available sources and integrated into the dataset with minimal manual intervention. For Enem editions from 2009 to 2025, official answer keys were downloaded from the Inep repository of exam materials [16]. For earlier editions (1998–2008), answer keys were collected from an archival repository maintained by the University of São Paulo [17].

A small number of exceptions required manual processing. In particular, for the first application of Enem 2010, the official material was released as an annotated exam booklet with answers marked directly on the questions. In this case, the answer key was manually transcribed into a structured format and converted into a standardized PDF to enable integration with the dataset.

Additional gaps were identified in the official sources. The reapplication exams of 2010 and 2011 do not have answer keys available in the Inep repository and are therefore marked as missing in Enem-VL. In other cases, answer-key links resolve to files from a different application, including the 2016 reapplication issue described above. Rather than imputing or reconstructing these labels, we explicitly preserve missing-answer cases in the dataset.

Enem includes foreign-language questions (primarily English and Spanish in specific sections and editions). These items are explicitly flagged through language-aware processing so that evaluations can be stratified by language. This prevents cross-language mixing in analyses and enables fairer interpretation of multilingual model behavior.

To support educational and psychometric slicing, each item receives an area tag derived from official question ranges for the corresponding edition and exam structure. When a historical edition deviates from modern organization, range mappings are documented and applied consistently across that year's records.

For historical editions from 1998 to 2008, Enem differs substantially from later formats: exams contain 63 questions and do not provide the same area definitions used in modern editions. As a result, no area labels are assigned to these items in Enem-VL, and the corresponding field is left as missing.

Each Enem-VL record includes core metadata for identity, provenance, and evaluation. Table 1 lists the principal fields.

Figure 2 illustrates this representation with a concrete example, showing how Enem-VL links the question image, the shared support section, the extracted visual asset, and the final structured record.

Table 1. Core Enem-VL schema.

Field	Type	Description
id	string	Unique question identifier in Enem-VL
year	string	Enem edition year (e.g., "2010")
exam	string	Exam identifier (e.g., "2010_CD7_reg")
booklet	string	Booklet/caderno identifier (e.g., "CD7")
question_number	string	Original question index within booklet
area	string/null	Question area; null for editions without official area definition
language	string/null	Item language (e.g., "ingles", "espanhol")
answer	string/null	Correct option (A–E) or null if missing
question_image_path	string	Path to PNG of the full question
support_image_path	string	Path to auxiliary support image (if available)
extracted_images	list[string]	Paths to figures extracted from the question
question_text	string	Main question statement
question_support_text	string	Support text embedded in the question page
external_support_text	string/null	External support text shared across questions (if applicable)
alternatives	object	Multiple-choice alternatives (A–E)

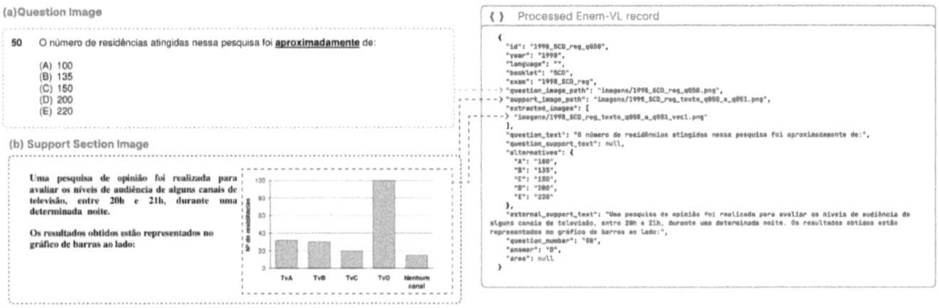

Fig. 2. Example of a processed Enem-VL record, showing the question image (a), shared support section (b), explicit chart extraction, and the corresponding JSON metadata linking textual fields, answer information, and visual assets.

The release repository is organized to support both benchmark use and auditability. It contains dataset records, metadata, source exam materials, processed question artifacts, image assets, answer sheets, machine-readable JSON manifests, and the baseline code with prompt templates.[1] The structured JSON files support direct experimental use, while the original and intermediate artifacts remain available for provenance checks and extraction debugging. Table 2 summarizes the top-level organization of the release repository.

Table 2. Top-level organization of the Enem-VL release package.

Path	Contents and intended use
`answer_sheets/`	Answer-key files used to assign canonical alternatives, including cases that require manual curation or missing-answer markers
`exams/`	Source exam booklets collected from official or archival repositories, retained for provenance and reproducibility
`formatted_exams/`	Intermediate processed exam files after formatting and layout normalization, used by the extraction pipeline
`images/`	Rendered question images and extracted visual assets used for multimodal evaluation
`questions/`	Question-level artifacts organized for inspection, including structured records and links to associated visual material
`baseline.ipynb`	Notebook containing the baseline evaluation code and the prompt templates used in the multiple-choice protocol
`dataset.json`	Main machine-readable dataset export for loading question records programmatically
`dataset-en.json`	Alternate JSON export variant for users who prefer an English-facing dataset file

3.3 Benchmark Setup

We define benchmark evaluation as a five-way multiple-choice task with output constrained to options A–E. For records with a canonical non-annulled answer, a prediction is correct if and only if the selected option matches the answer key. Records without answer keys and annulled questions are retained in the dataset for transparency but excluded from answer-accuracy denominators.

Enem-VL is intended for VLM evaluation. The benchmark input therefore combines the structured textual fields of each item (statement, support text, and alternatives) with the corresponding visual evidence, provided as the full

[1] Source code and benchmark implementation: https://github.com/graphs4ai/enem-vl-code. Dataset: https://www.kaggle.com/datasets/andersonlbsoares/enem-v-questions.

question image and, when available, extracted figures from within the question. This setup evaluates whether models can jointly use textual, layout, and visual information in a multimodal multiple-choice setting.

In this initial benchmark release, we focus on the full multimodal protocol, in which models are evaluated with the visual resources preserved by Enem-VL. This choice reflects the primary goal of the dataset: to provide question-level visual evidence together with structured textual fields for VLM evaluation. Text-only or image-ablated variants are supported by the dataset structure and constitute a natural direction for future controlled analyses.

Unless otherwise stated, inference is deterministic with temperature = 0.

The initial baseline roster includes four publicly available VLMs:

- `Qwen/Qwen3-VL-30B-A3B-Instruct`
- `google/gemma-4-31B-it`
- `mistralai/Mistral-Small-3.2-24B-Instruct-2506`
- `zai-org/GLM-4.6V`

Each model was prompted once per question record, producing 30,812 total responses across the 7,703-question corpus. Model outputs were generated deterministically with temperature = 0.

The instruction template requests exactly one option in {A, B, C, D, E}. The baseline code and prompt templates are included in the release repository, in `baseline.ipynb`. Post-processing normalizes format variants (e.g., "Option C", "C.") to canonical labels. Outputs that cannot be normalized to a single option are not force-remapped. They are counted as invalid responses and, under the strict scoring policy, as incorrect predictions whenever the question has an eligible canonical answer.

3.4 Metrics

The primary metric is **accuracy** over eligible records, defined as the proportion of predictions that match the canonical answer among non-annulled questions with available answer keys. Records without answer keys or with annulled answers are excluded from the accuracy denominator.

As secondary reporting, we compute the **response-validity rate**, defined as the percentage of generated responses that normalize to exactly one A–E option. Invalid responses are reported separately and are counted as incorrect under the strict scoring policy whenever the corresponding question has an eligible canonical answer.

To expose model behavior beyond aggregate scores, we report slice-level analyses by year and knowledge area in the current baseline. The dataset schema also supports further stratification by language (Portuguese, English, or Spanish) and by the presence of image assets.

4 Results

This section summarizes the composition of Enem-VL, including answer availability, knowledge-area distribution, language options, and visual-asset coverage, and presents the initial VLM baseline evaluation under the proposed multiple-choice protocol.

4.1 Dataset Statistics

Table 3 summarizes the main corpus-level statistics of Enem-VL, together with the distribution by knowledge area and foreign-language option. The "no area label" category corresponds to historical editions from 1998 to 2008, whose 63-question format does not map directly to the modern four-area Enem structure.

Table 3. Enem-VL overview statistics and corpus distribution (initial version).

Overview		Answer status	
Temporal coverage	1998–2025	Canonical answer	7,317
Years covered	28	Without answer key	370
Total exams	87	Annulled	16
Total records	7,703	With image	2,614
Knowledge areas		**Language options**	
Linguagens	1,880	Spanish	160
Humanas	1,710	English	160
Natureza	1,710		
Matemática	1,710		
No modern label	693		

Answer-status categories are mutually exclusive. "No modern label" corresponds to Enem editions from 1998–2008.

Enem-VL explicitly preserves real-world irregularities:

- Some items have no answer key due to unavailable historical sources or inconsistent official links.
- Some items correspond to annulled answers and are flagged accordingly.
- Historical editions (1998–2008) contain 63 questions and do not include official area labels.
- Visual data is available at two levels: question PNGs and extracted internal figures.

These conditions are treated as part of the benchmark specification rather than removed during curation, and should be considered in experimental reporting.

4.2 VLM Baseline Evaluation

Table 4 reports output validity for the initial baseline. Across the four models, 30,765 of 30,812 generated responses were normalized to exactly one A–E option, corresponding to an overall validity rate of 99.85%.

Table 4. Response-validity statistics for the initial four-model baseline.

Model	Generated	Valid	Invalid	Validity
Qwen/Qwen3-VL-30B-A3B-Instruct	7,703	7,703	0	100.00%
google/gemma-4-31B-it	7,703	7,697	6	99.92%
mistralai/Mistral-Small-3.2-24B-Instruct-2506	7,703	7,680	23	99.70%
zai-org/GLM-4.6V	7,703	7,685	18	99.77%
Total	30,812	30,765	47	99.85%

Figure 3 summarizes the initial accuracy results by knowledge area and by year. The area-level heatmap shows that model rankings vary substantially across curricular domains. Gemma obtains the highest accuracy in Human Sciences and Languages, while GLM-4.6V is strongest in Mathematics and Natural Sciences. Mathematics is the most discriminative slice: accuracies range from 35.3% for Mistral-Small to 85.4% for GLM-4.6V. The year-level curves reveal longitudinal variability and show that the relative ordering of models is not constant across Enem editions.

These results should be interpreted as initial benchmark baselines rather than contamination-free estimates of reasoning ability, since Enem questions are public and may have appeared in model pretraining corpora.

Although a full manually annotated error analysis is outside the scope of the initial release, the slice-level results and inspection of representative cases motivate the following error taxonomy for future audits:

1. **Visual grounding failures:** the model ignores or misreads diagrams, plots, tables, or geometric figures.
2. **Distractor confusion:** lexical overlap between alternatives induces near-miss selections.
3. **Long-context degradation:** performance drops on verbose statements with multi-part support text.
4. **Language confusion:** foreign-language items (English/Spanish) trigger semantic drift or translation errors.
5. **Numeric/diagrammatic mistakes:** arithmetic or symbolic misinterpretations when visual and textual cues must be combined.

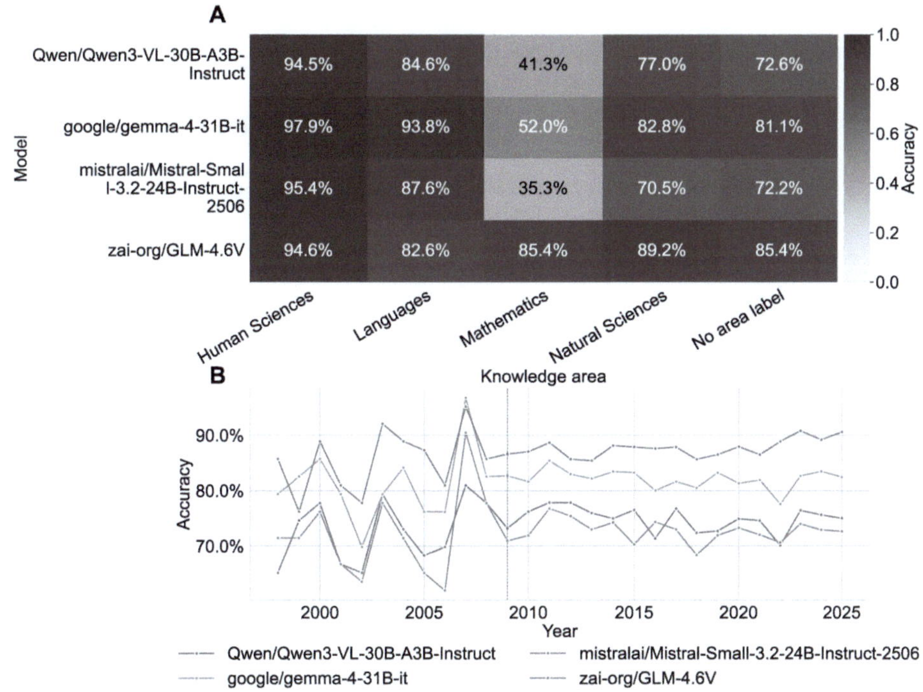

Fig. 3. Initial baseline accuracy by knowledge area (A) and by Enem year (B). The dashed line marks the transition from the historical 63-question Enem format to the modern area-structured exam.

5 Discussion

Enem-VL has important limitations. First, historical source heterogeneity and official-archive inconsistencies lead to incomplete answer-key coverage in part of the timeline. The exam also changed over time in format, number of items, and area organization, so longitudinal comparisons should be interpreted with attention to year and exam structure. Second, some source links resolve to incorrect materials, requiring conservative exclusion or missing-label treatment rather than automatic ingestion. Third, PDF extraction errors may persist despite validation and audits. Finally, benchmark performance does not directly translate to pedagogical effectiveness or fairness in high-stakes deployment.

Because Enem items may include third-party textual and visual materials reproduced in official exam booklets, Enem-VL distinguishes between metadata, derived annotations, and redistributed source artifacts. Users are responsible for verifying the applicable terms of use of the original exam materials. When redistribution rights are uncertain, the dataset should be used through references to official sources or under the licensing conditions specified in the release documentation. The benchmark documentation records provenance and separates derived metadata from original exam content to support auditability and responsible reuse.

Because Enem exams are public and widely mirrored online, baseline results may reflect a combination of multimodal reasoning, prior exposure during model training, and memorization. Enem-VL should therefore not be interpreted as a contamination-free benchmark. To mitigate this issue, we report performance by year and encourage analyses that separate recent editions, image-dependent questions, and questions with reduced textual memorability.

From an ethical perspective, Enem-VL should be used for research and model evaluation, not for automated high-stakes decision-making. We recommend that users:

- disclose model limitations and uncertainty;
- avoid using benchmark scores as sole evidence of educational suitability;
- evaluate subgroup behavior and language slices before deployment claims;
- respect exam content usage terms and data governance policies.

Potential misuse includes answer memorization systems, exam leakage facilitation, and overconfident tutoring outputs. Mitigation strategies include usage policies, dataset documentation aligned with datasheets for datasets, model reporting aligned with model cards, and transparent governance practices appropriate to foundation-model-based systems [10–12].

6 Conclusion

This paper presented Enem-VL, a multimodal benchmark built from Enem exams spanning 1998–2025. We detailed a practical, auditable construction pipeline covering question and image extraction, answer-key integration via reference mappings, language-sensitive handling, and area attribution by question ranges. We documented key data particularities, including missing historical labels, annulled questions, and official-source inconsistencies, and we reported a reproducible VLM-centered multiple-choice baseline with deterministic decoding.

The main contributions are threefold: (i) an initial version of a longitudinal, Portuguese-centered multimodal exam benchmark; (ii) a transparent curation and quality-validation methodology; and (iii) a standardized evaluation framework with response-validity accounting, slice-based diagnostics, and a preliminary error taxonomy. We expect Enem-VL to support future empirical studies on multilingual multimodal reasoning in educational settings, particularly in Portuguese-centered and exam-based evaluation scenarios.

Acknowledgments. This work was supported by the National Council for Scientific and Technological Development (CNPq; grant no. 302530/2022-3) and the São Paulo Research Foundation (FAPESP), Brazil (Processes no. 2024/12936-5). The authors thank Instituto Kunumi for their financial and structural support.

The authors acknowledge the use of ChatGPT for grammar and language enhancement in the preparation of this manuscript.

Conflict of Interest. The authors declare that they have no competing interests relevant to the content of this article.

References

1. Rajpurkar, P., Zhang, J., Lopyrev, K., Liang, P.: SQuAD: 100,000+ questions for machine comprehension of text. In: EMNLP (2016)
2. Lai, G., Xie, Q., Liu, H., Yang, Y., Hovy, E.: RACE: large-scale ReAding comprehension dataset from examinations. In: EMNLP (2017)
3. Hendrycks, D., Burns, C., Basart, S.: Measuring massive multitask language understanding. In: ICLR (2021)
4. Goyal, Y., Khot, T., Summers-Stay, D., Batra, D., Parikh, D.: Making the v in VQA matter: elevating the role of image understanding in visual question answering. Int. J. Comput. Vision **127**, 398–414 (2019)
5. Lu, P., Mishra, S., Xia, T.: Learn to explain: multimodal reasoning via thought chains for science question answering. In: NeurIPS (2022)
6. Yue, X., Ni, Y., Zhang, K.: MMMU: a massive multi-discipline multimodal understanding and reasoning benchmark for expert AGI. In: CVPR (2024)
7. Zhang, W., Aljunied, S.M., Gao, C., Chia, Y.K., Bing, L.: M3Exam: a multilingual, multimodal, multilevel benchmark for examining large language models. arXiv preprint arXiv:2306.05179 (2023)
8. Bandarkar, L., et al.: The Belebele benchmark: a parallel reading comprehension dataset in 122 language variants. In: ACL, pp. 749–775 (2024)
9. Muennighoff, N., Wang, T., Sutawika, L.: Crosslingual generalization through multitask finetuning. In: ACL (2023)
10. Bommasani, R., Hudson, D.A., Adeli, E.: On the opportunities and risks of foundation models. arXiv preprint arXiv:2108.07258 (2021)
11. Gebru, T., Morgenstern, J., Vecchione, B., et al.: Datasheets for datasets. Commun. ACM **64**(12), 86–92 (2021)
12. Mitchell, M., Wu, S., Zaldivar, A.: Model cards for model reporting. In: FAT* (2019)
13. Instituto Nacional de Estudos e Pesquisas Educacionais Anísio Teixeira (Inep): Exame Nacional do Ensino Médio (Enem). https://www.gov.br/inep/pt-br/acesso-a-informacao/perguntas-frequentes/exame-nacional-do-ensino-medio-enem
14. Instituto Nacional de Estudos e Pesquisas Educacionais Anísio Teixeira (Inep): Saiba como cursar a educação superior com o Enem. https://www.gov.br/inep/pt-br/centrais-de-conteudo/noticias/enem/saiba-como-cursar-a-educacao-superior-com-o-enem
15. Instituto Nacional de Estudos e Pesquisas Educacionais Anísio Teixeira (Inep): Evento divulga edição 112 da revista Em Aberto. Portal Gov.br (2022). https://www.gov.br/inep/pt-br/centrais-de-conteudo/noticias/institucional/evento-divulga-edicao-112-da-revista-em-aberto
16. Instituto Nacional de Estudos e Pesquisas Educacionais Anísio Teixeira (Inep): Provas e gabaritos. https://www.gov.br/inep/pt-br/areas-de-atuacao/avaliacao-e-exames-educacionais/enem/provas-e-gabaritos
17. Universidade de São Paulo: Arquivo de provas e gabaritos do Enem. https://fep.if.usp.br/~profis/arquivo/avaliacao/enem/provas_gabaritos

18. Silveira, I.C., Mauá, D.D.: University entrance exam as a guiding test for artificial intelligence. In: BRACIS, pp. 426–431 (2017)
19. Silveira, I.C., Mauá, D.D.: Advances in automatically solving the enem. In: BRACIS, pp. 43–48 (2018)
20. Nunes, D., Primi, R., Pires, R., Lotufo, R., Nogueira, R.: Evaluating GPT-3.5 and GPT-4 models on Brazilian university admission exams. arXiv preprint arXiv:2303.17003 (2023)
21. Pires, R., Almeida, T.S., Abonizio, H., Nogueira, R.: Evaluating GPT-4's vision capabilities on brazilian university admission exams. arXiv preprint arXiv:2311.14169 (2023)
22. Almeida, T.S., Laitz, T., Bonás, G.K., Nogueira, R.: BLUEX: a benchmark based on Brazilian leading universities entrance eXams. arXiv preprint arXiv:2307.05410 (2023)
23. Godoy, H.: Alvorada-bench: can language models solve Brazilian university entrance exams?. arXiv preprint arXiv:2508.15835 (2025)
24. Brant, T., Kühn, J., Pang, J.: Estimating exam item difficulty with LLMs: a benchmark on Brazil's enem corpus. arXiv preprint arXiv:2602.06631 (2026)

Teaching LLMs Brazilian Healthcare: Injecting Knowledge from Official Clinical Guidelines

Hugo Abonizio[1,2](✉), Filipe Rocha Lopes[3], Roberto Lotufo[1], and Rodrigo Nogueira[2]

[1] FEEC, UNICAMP, Campinas, Brazil
hugo.abonizio@gmail.com
[2] Maritaca AI, São Paulo, Brazil
[3] NoHarm.ai, Porto Alegre, Brazil

Abstract. Brazil's Unified Health System (SUS) relies on official clinical guidelines that define diagnostic criteria, treatments, dosages, and monitoring procedures for over 200 million citizens. Yet current LLMs perform poorly on this guideline-specific knowledge, and no benchmark evaluates clinical recall grounded in Brazilian Portuguese protocols. We address this gap by adapting Qwen2.5-14B-Instruct to the Brazilian clinical domain. From 178 official guidelines (~5.4M tokens), we generate ~70M tokens of synthetic data in three formats—rephrases, wiki-style articles, and question-answer pairs—using four generator LLMs. We then apply continual pre-training followed by Group Relative Policy Optimization (GRPO). We introduce HealthBench-BR, with 1,780 balanced true/false clinical assertions, and PCDT-QA, with 890 open-ended clinical questions scored by an LLM judge. Our best model achieves 83.9% on HealthBench-BR and 85.4% on PCDT-QA, outperforming GPT-5.2, Claude Sonnet 4.6, Gemini 3.1 Pro, and Google AI Overview's web-grounded RAG despite having only 14B parameters. Ablations show that generator diversity and reinforcement learning are critical to these gains. We release all datasets, benchmarks, and model weights to support reproducible clinical NLP research for Brazilian Portuguese. Code, data, and model weights are available at https://github.com/hugoabonizio/clinical-protocols-br.

Keywords: Large Language Models · Clinical NLP · Brazilian Portuguese · Continual Pre-Training · Synthetic Data

1 Introduction

Brazil's Unified Health System (SUS – *Sistema Único de Saúde*) provides universal healthcare coverage to over 200 million people, making it one of the largest public health systems in the world. Clinical decision-making within SUS is governed by official clinical guidelines published by the Ministry of Health, which

M. Recamonde-Mendoza and R. C. Barros (Eds.): BRACIS 2026, LNAI 17105, pp. 325–339, 2027.
https://doi.org/10.1007/978-3-032-39882-6_22

prescribe diagnostic criteria, treatment regimens, dosages, and monitoring procedures for conditions treated under public care [4]. These documents—primarily Clinical Protocols and Therapeutic Guidelines (PCDTs), but also several related categories described in Sect. 3—are hosted under the Ministry's PCDT portal.[1] Adherence to these protocols is mandatory for SUS managers, yet their volume and complexity make it difficult for healthcare professionals to recall specific recommendations at the point of care. Large language models (LLMs) offer a promising path toward intelligent clinical decision support, yet current medical LLMs are predominantly trained on English-language medical literature and evaluated on English benchmarks, leaving their knowledge of Brazilian clinical guidelines largely untested [5,10].

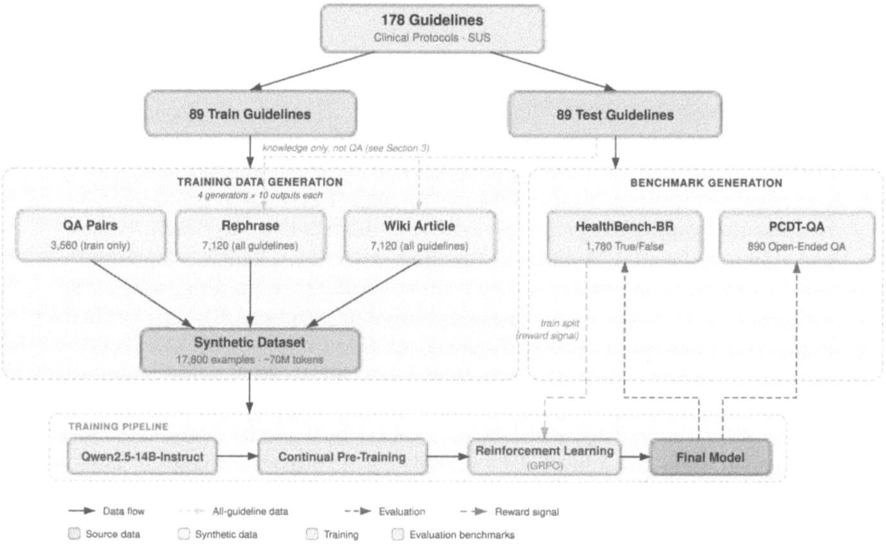

Fig. 1. Overview of our pipeline. The 178 clinical guidelines are split into train and test sets. All guidelines feed rephrase and wiki-style generation (dashed gray arrows), while QA pairs are generated only from train guidelines to prevent leakage. Four generator LLMs produce the synthetic corpus (~70M tokens), which is used for continual pre-training of Qwen2.5-14B-Instruct. The HealthBench-BR train split provides the reward signal for GRPO reinforcement learning (dashed amber arrow). Both benchmarks are evaluated on the final model (dashed red arrows). (Color figure online)

Even state-of-the-art open medical LLMs leave Brazilian clinical knowledge largely uncovered. MedGemma [23] is built on Anglo-centric data—biomedical text, FHIR-based electronic health records, and English QA pairs—with no multilingual coverage. BioMistral [14] is pre-trained exclusively on PubMed Central

[1] https://www.gov.br/saude/pt-br/assuntos/pcdt.

and assesses Portuguese only through machine-translated benchmarks. Apollo-MoE [35] covers 50 languages including Portuguese, but draws its medical corpus from generic multilingual sources rather than country-specific clinical protocols.

We address this gap by proposing a training protocol for adapting a general-purpose LLM to the clinical domain of the Brazilian public health system. Starting from all 178 clinical guidelines described above, we first generate approximately 70 million tokens of synthetic training data across three complementary formats (rephrases, wiki-style articles, and question-answer pairs) using four diverse generator LLMs, following multi-style rephrasing strategies shown to be effective for domain adaptation [8,16]. This corpus is used for continual pre-training (CPT) of Qwen2.5-14B-Instruct [32], followed by reinforcement learning via Group Relative Policy Optimization (GRPO) [24] to encourage explicit clinical reasoning. To evaluate knowledge absorption, we introduce two guideline-grounded benchmarks: **HealthBench-BR**, comprising 1,780 balanced true/false clinical assertions requiring precise factual recall, and **PCDT-QA**, containing 890 open-ended clinical questions scored by an LLM judge.

Our best configuration outperforms GPT-5.2 on both benchmarks despite being a 14B-parameter open model. In summary, our main contributions are: (i) a reproducible training protocol combining multi-generator synthetic data, continual pre-training, and reinforcement learning for clinical domain adaptation; (ii) two protocol-grounded evaluation benchmarks for the Brazilian public health system; (iii) a detailed analysis of the trade-offs between knowledge injection and catastrophic forgetting, including ablations showing that both multi-generator diversity and reinforcement learning are critical to the observed gains; and (iv) the public release of all synthetic datasets, benchmarks, and model weights to support reproducible research on clinical NLP for Brazilian Portuguese.

2 Related Work

2.1 Medical LLMs and Portuguese Medical NLP

Proprietary models have driven rapid progress on medical benchmarks, with Med-PaLM [26], Med-PaLM 2 [27], and Med-Gemini [20] successively raising the bar on the USMLE, and GPT-4 exceeding the passing threshold by over 20 points without medical prompting [17]. Their closed nature and English-centric design, however, limit applicability in settings like Brazilian public health, where transparency and native-language reasoning are essential. On the open-source side, continual pre-training (CPT) has emerged as the dominant adaptation strategy: MEDITRON [7], PMC-LLaMA [30], Me-LLaMA [31], and the more recent multimodal MedGemma [23] scale CPT on biomedical literature from tens to over 100B tokens, while multilingual efforts—BioMistral [14] and ApolloMoE [35]—either evaluate Portuguese only via machine translation or rely on generic multilingual corpora, with no incorporation of official Brazilian protocols.

Work specific to Portuguese medical NLP began with encoder models such as BioBERTpt [21] for clinical NER, followed by Clinical-BR-LlaMA/Mistral [28] and DrBode [18], which applied LoRA and QLoRA on clinical notes and translated medical data—though adapted models often underperformed the base due to catastrophic forgetting. On the data and evaluation side, MedPT [6] released 384K native patient–doctor QA pairs, the Revalida exam has been used to benchmark LLMs [5], and HealthQA-BR [9] provides 5,632 residency questions. None of these resources, however, evaluates factual recall over official Brazilian clinical protocols, and no prior work injects parametric knowledge from these protocols into LLMs—the dual gap we address with our adaptation pipeline and protocol-grounded benchmarks (Sect. 5).

2.2 Synthetic Data for Domain Adaptation

Training on high-quality synthetic data can match or exceed training on much larger natural corpora. Gunasekar et al. [11] demonstrated that models trained primarily on synthetic textbook-quality data achieve strong coding performance at a fraction of the usual data scale. WRAP [16] generalized this insight to pre-training: by prompting an instruction-tuned model to rephrase web documents in multiple styles—Wikipedia-like, question–answer, and paraphrase—it speeds up pre-training while improving downstream accuracy. Nemotron-CC [29] scaled this source-rephrasing approach to trillions of tokens, and AdaptLLM [8] showed that reformatting raw domain corpora as reading comprehension tasks enables small models to rival much larger domain-specific ones. In medicine, AlpaCare [34] and ChatDoctor [15] demonstrated that LLM-generated instructions and dialogues substantially boost clinical performance from limited seeds. Our synthetic data pipeline follows this philosophy, transforming 178 official Brazilian protocols into rephrases, wiki-style articles, and QA pairs—similar to the multi-style strategy of WRAP but applied to a small, high-value domain corpus to maximize knowledge absorption.

2.3 Catastrophic Forgetting in Continual Pre-training

A key risk in CPT is catastrophic forgetting, which scales as a power law in parameters and update steps [13]. Parameter-efficient methods like LoRA naturally mitigate this by modifying fewer parameters [3,12], and replay of even 1% of pre-training data can prevent it [2]—though recent work suggests that some observed drops reflect alignment loss rather than true knowledge erasure [36]. We opt for full CPT to maximize knowledge injection from our small domain corpus, explicitly measure forgetting on general benchmarks, and provide ablations comparing the trade-offs of forgetting-mitigation strategies.

3 Clinical Guideline Corpus

Brazilian clinical guidelines fall into several regulatory categories: Clinical Protocols and Therapeutic Guidelines (PCDTs – *Protocolos Clínicos e Diretrizes Terapêuticas*), which form the majority; Protocols of Use (*Protocolos de Uso*);

Oncology Diagnostic and Therapeutic Guidelines (*Diretrizes Diagnósticas e Terapêuticas em Oncologia*); National Guidelines (*Diretrizes Brasileiras*); and Care Pathways (*Linhas de Cuidado*). All are elaborated with support from the National Commission for the Incorporation of Technologies (CONITEC – *Comissão Nacional de Incorporação de Tecnologias no SUS*), and their adoption is mandatory for SUS managers. For brevity, we refer to the full collection as *clinical guidelines* throughout this paper.

We collected all 178 clinical guidelines available as of March 2026 as PDF documents from the Ministry of Health portal. The text content was extracted from each PDF, yielding a raw corpus of approximately 26.9 million characters. Individual protocols range from 18k to over 915k characters (median 117k). To fit within the context window of our generator models (Sect. 4), we truncate each protocol at 120k characters, retaining the full text for the majority of protocols and the initial sections—which contain diagnostic criteria, treatment recommendations, and monitoring parameters—for longer ones. After truncation, the corpus comprises approximately 16.6M characters (5.4M tokens). The extracted protocols and all derived datasets are publicly available.

4 Synthetic Data Pipeline

Rather than training on the original guidelines, we use LLMs to transform each guideline into synthetic texts in three complementary formats (Fig. 1, green blocks), following recent work showing that rephrasing corpora into diverse formats improves knowledge absorption during pre-training [8,16]. Each train-split guideline is processed under three prompts, while test-split guidelines are processed only under the rephrase and wiki-style prompts, sampling 10 outputs per prompt.

Rephrase. The generator rewrites the guideline, modifying information order and paraphrasing while preserving all clinical content. This exposes the model to the same knowledge in varied surface forms. Rephrases are generated for all 178 guidelines.

Wiki-Style Article. The generator produces an expository article in the style of Wikipedia, restructuring the prescriptive clinical document while retaining all key numerical values and details. Wiki articles are generated for all 178 guidelines.

Question–Answer Pairs. The generator creates questions and detailed answers grounded in the guideline, ranging from broad clinical queries to specific dosage and monitoring questions. Answers include step-by-step rationales to encourage internalization of clinical reasoning patterns. To prevent data leakage, QA pairs are generated only from the 89 train-split guidelines, as illustrated by the dashed arrows in Fig. 1: test-split guidelines feed only rephrase and wiki generation, never QA.

To increase the stylistic and lexical diversity of the synthetic corpus, each of the three generation strategies is applied independently by four distinct models: GPT-4.1-mini, GPT-5-nano, GPT-OSS-20B, and Qwen3-235B. As shown in Table 2, scaling from one to four generators substantially improves downstream performance. We also evaluate self-generation with the target model (Qwen2.5-14B-Instruct), which yields the weakest results; we analyze this case in Sect. 7.3.

The full synthetic corpus comprises 17,800 documents (~70M tokens), a roughly 13× expansion over the original 5.4M-token corpus with substantially greater format and stylistic diversity. This dataset is used for continual pre-training (Sect. 6).

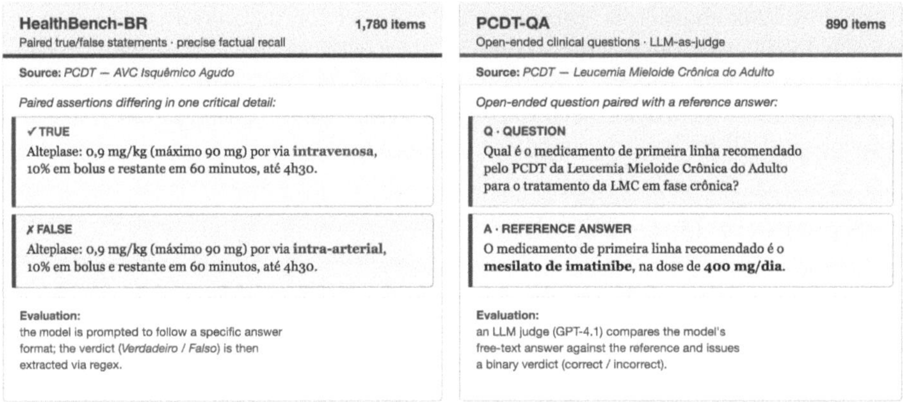

Fig. 2. Examples from the two proposed benchmarks. *Left:* HealthBench-BR pairs each true assertion with a variant in which one critical detail is modified to produce a plausible distractor. *Right:* PCDT-QA pairs an open-ended question with a reference answer, scored against the model's response by an LLM judge.

5 Evaluation Benchmarks

We introduce two complementary benchmarks derived from the clinical guidelines, illustrated in Fig. 2. Both are split into training and test by guideline, with 89 guidelines in each split. Questions are generated for all 178 guidelines, but we report accuracy separately on train and test splits; performance on test-split questions reflects generalization to guidelines seen only as rephrase and wiki data during training, never as QA supervision.

5.1 HealthBench-BR

HealthBench-BR is a true/false benchmark comprising 1,780 clinical assertions (10 per guideline, 890 per split). Assertions are generated in paired form using

GPT-5.2, conditioned on the full text of each guideline: for each clinical fact, one statement is faithful to the guideline (true) and a second modifies a key detail—such as a dosage, route of administration, or monitoring interval—to produce a plausible but false variant. This yields a perfectly balanced dataset (50% true, 50% false) and ensures that correct classification requires precise factual recall rather than surface-level heuristics. During evaluation, the model is prompted to conclude with an explicit verdict (*Verdadeiro*/*Falso*), extracted via regex. All inference uses greedy decoding.

5.2 PCDT-QA

PCDT-QA is an open-ended benchmark containing 890 questions (5 per guideline, 445 per split) covering both broad clinical topics (e.g., inclusion criteria) and specific factual queries (e.g., recommended pediatric dosages). Each question is paired with a reference answer grounded in the guideline text. Evaluation uses an LLM-as-a-judge pipeline: the model under evaluation generates a free-text answer, and GPT-4.1 compares it against the reference, producing a binary verdict (correct/incorrect). This accommodates the open-ended nature of clinical responses, where correct answers may differ substantially in wording from the reference.

6 Experimental Setup

6.1 Continual Pre-training

We perform continual pre-training (CPT) on Qwen2.5-14B-Instruct [32] using a standard causal language modeling objective over the full synthetic corpus. Training runs on a TPU v6-64 pod using JAX. We train for 3 epochs with a cosine learning rate schedule (peak 5×10^{-5}, minimum 10% of peak) and AdamW (β_1=0.9, β_2=0.95). The effective batch size is 32. Sequences are truncated to 4,096 tokens; all tokens contribute to the loss. We use a warmup ratio of 1/3 of total steps.

6.2 Reinforcement Learning with GRPO

After CPT, we apply GRPO [24] using the HealthBench-BR train split. The task requires the model to assess factual clinical assertions and produce a justified true/false verdict, making it suitable for reinforcement learning with verifiable rewards (RLVR).

Following recent evidence that parameter-efficient methods are effective for RLVR [22,33], we train GRPO with LoRA ($r = 32$, $\alpha = 64$) applied to all linear layers for 5 epochs. We generate 16 completions per prompt with a maximum length of 512 tokens, use an effective batch size of 128, and set the KL coefficient β to 0, relying on clipping ($\epsilon = 0.2$, $\epsilon_{\text{high}} = 0.28$) to bound updates. The reward is 1.0 for correct answers with at least 50 words of reasoning and 0.0 otherwise, discouraging bare-label reward hacking while encouraging explicit clinical justification.

6.3 Supervised Fine-Tuning

As an alternative to GRPO, we also evaluate supervised fine-tuning (SFT) on guideline-grounded QA pairs. For each HealthBench-BR train-split question, we prompt GPT-5.2 with the source guideline in context to produce a reasoned *Verdadeiro*/*Falso* answer, yielding 890 prompt–answer pairs; no test-split assertions are used. We fine-tune with AdamW (lr 3×10^{-5}), effective batch size 64, masking the loss over user tokens so it is computed only on assistant tokens.

7 Results

7.1 Main Results

Table 1. Main results on HealthBench-BR (true/false accuracy) and PCDT-QA (open-ended accuracy via LLM judge). Train and Test refer to the guideline split (Sect. 5). All values in %. Baseline is Qwen2.5-14B-Instruct without domain-specific training.

Model	HealthBench-BR		PCDT-QA	
	Train	Test	Train	Test
Ours				
Baseline (no training)	61.1	59.4	30.8	27.9
+ RL only	68.7	64.2	31.5	29.4
+ SFT only	74.0	62.1	32.8	29.4
+ CPT	67.1	69.6	73.5	66.3
+ CPT + SFT	83.5	70.4	64.9	57.8
+ CPT + RL	85.5	75.6	70.6	65.4
+ CPT (4 generators)	70.9	71.1	91.0	86.3
+ CPT (4 generators) + SFT	87.0	76.4	87.6	81.1
+ CPT (4 generators) + RL	90.4	83.9	88.8	85.4
Frontier models				
GPT-4.1	73.1	73.3	70.1	70.3
GPT-5.2 (instant)	72.5	76.3	69.2	71.7
GPT-5.2 (high)	78.9	78.5	74.6	78.2
Claude Sonnet 4.6	77.2	77.6	67.0	70.3
Gemini 3.1 Pro	77.8	79.3	74.8	80.0
RAG				
Google AI Overview	72.4	70.5	77.1	77.3
Baseline + RAG (BM25)	88.4	90.0	56.0	58.2
Baseline + RAG (embeddings)	86.5	87.9	83.6	86.7
CPT + RAG (BM25)	87.4	89.0	79.8	78.9
CPT + RAG (embeddings)	86.1	85.2	91.2	92.1
CPT (4 gen) + RAG (BM25)	74.2	73.9	92.1	88.3
CPT (4 gen) + RAG (embeddings)	74.0	71.1	92.1	94.8
CPT (4 gen) + RL + RAG (BM25)	94.9	95.3	90.6	88.8
CPT (4 gen) + RL + RAG (embeddings)	94.2	94.0	92.6	93.3

Table 1 summarizes performance across all configurations and baselines. The base Qwen2.5-14B-Instruct model, without any domain-specific training, achieves 59.4% on HealthBench-BR and 27.9% on PCDT-QA (test split), suggesting that guideline-specific knowledge is largely absent from the model's parameters.

Continual pre-training with a single generator raises test performance to 69.6% on HealthBench-BR and 66.3% on PCDT-QA—already approaching GPT-4.1 on both benchmarks. Scaling to four generators further improves PCDT-QA to 86.3%, substantially surpassing all frontier models, while HealthBench-BR reaches 71.1%. The disproportionate gain on PCDT-QA suggests that generator diversity primarily benefits free-form knowledge recall, where exposure to varied phrasings and explanatory styles translates directly into richer answers.

Following CPT with GRPO yields the strongest HealthBench-BR results: 83.9% on the test split with four generators, a 12.8% point gain over CPT alone. The effect on PCDT-QA is more nuanced: GRPO produces a small decrease from 86.3% to 85.4%, likely because the reward objective optimizes specifically for true/false clinical verification rather than open-ended generation. Despite this marginal trade-off, the final model remains above all frontier baselines on both benchmarks.

Among frontier models, Gemini 3.1 Pro is the strongest baseline at 79.3% on HealthBench-BR and 80.0% on PCDT-QA, followed closely by GPT-5.2 (high). Our best configuration outperforms Gemini 3.1 Pro by 4.6 and 5.4 percentage points, respectively, despite being a 14B-parameter open model. Notably, even our CPT-only configuration (4 generators, no GRPO) already surpasses all frontier models on PCDT-QA by over 6 points, suggesting that continual pre-training on guideline-specific synthetic data is highly effective for knowledge absorption in this domain.

We also compare against Google AI Overview,[2] which generates answers grounded in web search results—effectively a retrieval-augmented generation (RAG) system—and is arguably one of the most widely deployed sources of AI-generated clinical information, given its integration into Google Search. For evaluation, we submit each benchmark question as a search query and extract the generated summary when available. Notably, AI Overview does not produce a response for every query: it abstained on 11.7% of HealthBench-BR and 4.9% of PCDT-QA questions, and the reported accuracy considers only questions where a response was generated, giving it an inherent advantage. Even under this favorable comparison, our best configuration outperforms AI Overview by 13.4 points on HealthBench-BR and 8.1 points on PCDT-QA, demonstrating that targeted knowledge injection into a 14B model can surpass retrieval-augmented access to the open web.

An important dimension beyond accuracy is sycophancy—the tendency to agree with the user regardless of factual correctness. On HealthBench-BR, a well-calibrated model should predict "True" for approximately 50% of questions, since the dataset is perfectly balanced. The base Qwen2.5-14B-Instruct is well calibrated at 49.9%, but CPT shifts this to 58.9%, suggesting that continual pre-training on synthetic data introduces a bias toward agreement, possibly because

[2] https://blog.google/products/search/generative-ai-google-search-may-2024.

Table 2. Effect of generation format and generator diversity on CPT performance (test split). HB = HealthBench-BR, PCDT = PCDT-QA. "1 generator" uses GPT-4.1-mini only; "4 generators" uses all four models described in Sect. 4.

Generation format	1 generator			4 generators		
	#	HB	PCDT	#	HB	PCDT
Rephrase	1,780	62.8	52.4	7,120	63.6	73.0
Wiki	1,780	64.2	60.9	7,120	69.7	76.9
Rephrase + QA	2,670	63.7	56.6	10,680	66.3	75.3
Wiki + QA	2,670	67.0	62.2	10,680	68.2	76.0
Wiki + Rephrase	3,560	63.0	65.4	14,240	68.4	83.8
Rephrase + Wiki + QA	4,450	69.6	66.3	17,800	71.1	86.3

the training corpus tends toward affirmative framing. GRPO effectively corrects this: our best configuration (CPT + RL, 4 generators) returns to 53.0%, indicating that the reinforcement learning stage, by requiring the model to justify its verdict, teaches it to disagree when the evidence warrants it. Among frontier models, Claude Sonnet 4.6 (49.2%) and GPT-5.2 high (48.7%) are well calibrated, while Gemini 3.1 Pro exhibits a moderate agreement bias at 63.3%—noteworthy given that it is the strongest frontier baseline on both benchmarks. The most concerning case is Google AI Overview, which predicts "True" 69.6% of the time, making it the most sycophantic system evaluated. Given its reach as the default AI-generated response in Google Search, this tendency to confirm clinical assertions—including false ones about dosages, contraindications, and monitoring intervals—raises concerns for users seeking clinical information without professional guidance.

We complement parametric evaluation with two RAG variants: BM25 and dense retrieval using `text-embedding-3-small` embeddings[3], both retrieving the top-k=10 chunks (2,000 characters, 200-character overlap) from the full guideline corpus. Retriever choice interacts with task format: BM25 dominates HealthBench-BR (95.3 vs. 94.0 with our best model), where verifying dosages and intervals rewards lexical matching, while embeddings dominate PCDT-QA (93.3 vs. 88.8), where semantic retrieval surfaces broader evidence. Notably, CPT (4 gen) + RAG underperforms Baseline + RAG on HealthBench-BR (73.9 vs. 90.0), suggesting that a domain-adapted model partially overrides retrieved evidence—an effect GRPO reverses (95.3), as the verdict reward trains the model to ground its answer in the retrieved context.

7.2 Effect of Generation Formats

Table 2 isolates the contribution of each augmentation format under both single- and multi-generator settings. Across all configurations, wiki-style articles consistently outperform rephrases—for instance, with a single generator, wiki alone reaches 64.2% on HealthBench-BR and 60.9% on PCDT-QA, compared to 62.8%

[3] https://developers.openai.com/api/docs/models/text-embedding-3-small.

Table 3. Effect of the generator model on CPT performance. Each model generates all three augmentation types (rephrase, wiki, QA) for 4,450 training examples.

Generator model	Tokens	Avg. doc	HB (%)	PCDT (%)
Qwen2.5-14B (self-aug)	7.1M	1,594	60.2	50.1
GPT-OSS-20B	15.4M	3,471	65.7	64.0
GPT-5-nano	15.7M	3,522	65.2	67.4
GPT-4.1-mini	18.1M	4,065	69.6	66.3
Qwen3-235B	20.3M	4,551	63.5	66.7

and 52.4% for rephrase. This advantage likely reflects the expository nature of the wiki format, which restructures protocol content into self-contained explanations that more closely resemble the reasoning required at evaluation time.

Combining formats is consistently beneficial: each additional format improves at least one benchmark, and the full combination (rephrase + wiki + QA) yields the best results in every setting. With four generators, adding QA to the wiki + rephrase combination raises HealthBench-BR from 68.4% to 71.1% (+2.7 points) and PCDT-QA from 83.8% to 86.3% (+2.5 points), confirming that direct question–answer supervision provides a complementary learning signal that document-style formats alone do not fully capture.

7.3 Effect of the Generator

Table 3 compares the five generator models in isolation, each producing all three generation formats. The clear outlier is self-generation with the base model itself (Qwen2.5-14B-Instruct), which yields the weakest results by a wide margin—60.2% on HealthBench-BR and 50.1% on PCDT-QA. We attribute this to output length: Qwen2.5-14B averages 1,594 tokens per example against 3,471–4,551 for the external generators, producing only 7.1M tokens total. Shorter outputs inevitably omit the specific dosages, monitoring intervals, and inclusion criteria that are central to both benchmarks.

Among the four external generators, no single model leads on both benchmarks: GPT-4.1-mini achieves the best HealthBench-BR score (69.6%), while GPT-5-nano leads on PCDT-QA (67.4%). Notably, Qwen3-235B does not dominate either benchmark despite producing the most tokens, suggesting diminishing returns from additional generator capacity.

This motivates combining all four external generators rather than relying on the strongest one. Generator and format diversity are complementary: with one generator, all three formats combined yield 66.3% on PCDT-QA; scaling to four generators on the same combination reaches 86.3% (Table 2)—a 20.0 point gain that far exceeds any single-format improvement.

7.4 Catastrophic Forgetting Analysis

Table 4 reports performance on five out-of-distribution (OOD) benchmarks alongside our two in-distribution evaluations, comparing two forgetting-

Table 4. Comparison of catastrophic forgetting-mitigation strategies. All values are test accuracy in %. HealthBench-BR and PCDT-QA are in-distribution benchmarks; Avg is the average over the five OOD benchmarks.

Data	Method	In-distribution		Out-of-distribution					
		HB	PCDT	HealthQA	DrBode	MedPT	BLUEX	IFEval	Avg
Baseline	–	59.4	27.9	67.8	65.3	56.4	75.0	79.7	68.8
1 gen	Full FT	69.6	66.3	66.0	62.7	56.4	73.5	75.8	66.9
	LoRA	67.2	65.2	64.1	56.6	53.8	71.1	68.6	62.8
	Replay	63.8	65.6	67.0	64.5	55.9	72.7	77.1	67.4
4 gen	Full FT	71.1	86.3	63.3	61.2	54.1	72.8	69.3	64.1
	LoRA	70.3	77.1	60.8	58.3	52.1	68.9	65.6	61.1
	Replay	69.2	80.0	65.7	59.2	54.0	73.2	69.3	64.3

mitigation strategies. The OOD set spans HealthQA-BR [9], DrBode [18], MedPT [6], BLUEX [1] (Brazilian university admissions, general PT knowledge), and IFEval [37] (instruction-following). We compare full fine-tuning, LoRA, and full FT with 50% replay drawn from FineWeb [19] as an English-language proxy for the Qwen2.5 pre-training distribution.

Full fine-tuning (FT) yields moderate forgetting: −1.9 points on average with one generator and −4.7 with four. The larger drop tracks the larger in-distribution gain (PCDT-QA 66.3 → 86.3), consistent with the power-law trade-off in [13]. IFEval is the most affected (−4 to −10 points), suggesting that prolonged optimization on document-style text partially erodes instruction-following alignment.

Counterintuitively, LoRA is dominated by full FT on both axes—more OOD forgetting (−6.0 vs. −1.9 with one generator; −7.7 vs. −4.7 with four) and lower in-distribution scores (PCDT-QA 77.1 vs. 86.3). This contrasts with Biderman et al. [3], who report that LoRA both learns and forgets less than full FT. The pattern is instead consistent with the *intruder dimensions* account of Shuttleworth et al. [25], in which LoRA solutions contain high-magnitude singular vectors approximately orthogonal to the base model—absent from full-FT solutions—that degrade unrelated tasks; this matches our largest gap being on IFEval (−11.1 and −14.1 vs. −3.9/−10.4), where these directions plausibly overlap with instruction-following parameters.

Mixing FineWeb at a 1:1 ratio helps mainly at smaller scale: with one generator, replay recovers the OOD average to 67.4 (−1.4 vs. baseline; +0.5 over full FT) while retaining most of the in-distribution gain (HealthBench-BR 63.8, PCDT-QA 65.6). At four generators the benefit vanishes (64.3 vs. full FT's 64.1), and the in-distribution cost shifts from HealthBench-BR (∼6 points at one generator) to PCDT-QA (80.0 vs. 86.3). Since FineWeb is predominantly English, part of the retention may reflect continued English exposure; a PT replay source is a natural follow-up, consistent with Bethune et al. [2].

Overall, full FT sits on the favorable side of the knowledge–retention frontier across both data scales; replay offers a small OOD-preservation benefit at lower training scale that diminishes with more training data, at a consistent in-distribution cost; LoRA is dominated on both axes. We adopt full FT for the main results.

8 Ethical Considerations

Our model is designed to support, not replace, clinical judgment: even at 83.9% on HealthBench-BR, residual errors may involve consequential details such as dosages or contraindications. The released artifact is a research model, not a certified medical device, and should be used only under professional supervision. Since all training data comes from public Ministry of Health guidelines, privacy risks from clinical notes are avoided, though biases from the source documents and generator models may persist. Our sycophancy results further show that clinical AI systems should be evaluated not only for accuracy but also for their tendency to confirm false user assertions. Finally, open release of models trained on Brazilian protocols is a step toward equitable access for Portuguese-speaking clinicians and patients underserved by English-centric medical LLMs.

9 Conclusion

We presented a reproducible protocol for adapting an open LLM to the Brazilian Unified Health System, together with two protocol-grounded benchmarks—HealthBench-BR and PCDT-QA—that fill an evaluation gap for Portuguese clinical NLP. Expanding 178 official guidelines (5.4M tokens) into $\sim$70M tokens of synthetic data across three formats and four generators, then applying continual pre-training and GRPO to Qwen2.5-14B-Instruct, yields 83.9% on HealthBench-BR and 85.4% on PCDT-QA, outperforming GPT-5.2, Claude Sonnet 4.6, Gemini 3.1 Pro, and Google AI Overview's web-grounded RAG by 4.6 to 15.1 points despite being a 14B open model. Ablations show that generator and format diversity are complementary (+20 points on PCDT-QA), GRPO is critical for verdict-style recall (+12.8 points) and corrects post-CPT sycophancy from 58.9% to 53.0%, and full FT dominates LoRA on both knowledge gain and OOD retention. Limitations include evaluation grounded in guideline recall rather than real clinical encounters and the absence of prospective validation with professionals. We release all datasets, benchmarks, and model weights to support reproducible research on clinical NLP for Brazilian Portuguese.

References

1. Almeida, T.S., Laitz, T., Bonás, G.K., Nogueira, R.: BlueX: a benchmark based on Brazilian leading universities entrance exams. In: Intelligent Systems: 12th Brazilian Conference, BRACIS 2023, Belo Horizonte, Brazil, 25–29 September 2023, Proceedings, Part I, pp. 337–347. Springer, Heidelberg (2023). https://doi.org/10.1007/978-3-031-45368-7_22

2. Bethune, L., Grangier, D., Busbridge, D., Gualdoni, E., Cuturi, M., Ablin, P.: Scaling laws for forgetting during finetuning with pretraining data injection. In: ICML (2025)
3. Biderman, D.: LoRA learns less and forgets less. Trans. Mach. Learn. Res. (2024)
4. BRASIL: Lei n. 12.401, de 28 de abril de 2011. Altera a Lei n. 8.080/1990, para dispor sobre a assistência terapêutica e a incorporação de tecnologia em saúde no âmbito do SUS (2011), diário Oficial da União, seção 1, Brasília, DF (2011)
5. Bruneti Severino, J.V., et al.: Benchmarking open-source large language models on Portuguese Revalida multiple-choice questions. BMJ Health Care Inform. **32**(1), e101195 (2025). https://doi.org/10.1136/bmjhci-2024-101195
6. Bufon Färber, F., Alves Brito, I., Soares Dollis, J., Schindler Freire Brasil Ribeiro, P., Teixeira Sousa, R., Rodrigues Galvão Filho, A.: MedPT: a massive medical question answering dataset for Brazilian-Portuguese speakers. arXiv e-prints arXiv:2511.11878 (2025). https://doi.org/10.48550/arXiv.2511.11878
7. Chen, Z., Hernández-Cano, A., Romanou, A., Bonnet, A., Matoba, K.: Meditron-70b: scaling medical pretraining for large language models (2023)
8. Cheng, D., Huang, S., Wei, F.: Adapting large language models to domains via reading comprehension. In: ICLR (2024)
9. D'addario, A.M.V.: HealthQA-BR: a system-wide benchmark reveals critical knowledge gaps in large language models. arXiv preprint arXiv:2506.21578 (2025)
10. Garcia, G.L., Manesco, J.R.R., Paiola, P.H., Crespan Ribeiro, P.H., Garcia, A.L.A., Papa, J.P.: A step forward for medical LLMs in Brazilian Portuguese: Establishing a benchmark and a strong baseline (2025)
11. Gunasekar, S., Zhang, Y., Aneja, J., Mendes, C.C.T., Del Giorno, A.: Textbooks are all you need. arXiv preprint arXiv:2306.11644 (2023)
12. Hu, E.J., et al.: LoRA: low-rank adaptation of large language models. In: ICLR (2022)
13. Kalajdzievski, D.: Scaling laws for forgetting when fine-tuning large language models. arXiv preprint arXiv:2401.05605 (2024)
14. Labrak, Y., Bazoge, A., Morin, E., Gourraud, P.A., Rouvier, M., Dufour, R.: BioMistral: a collection of open-source pretrained large language models for medical domains. In: Findings of ACL (2024)
15. Li, Y., Li, Z., Zhang, K., Dan, R., Jiang, S., Zhang, Y.: ChatDoctor: a medical chat model fine-tuned on LLaMA using medical domain knowledge. arXiv preprint arXiv:2303.14070 (2023)
16. Maini, P., Seto, S., Bai, R., Grangier, D., Zhang, Y., Jaitly, N.: Rephrasing the web: a recipe for compute and data-efficient language modeling. In: Proceedings of the 62nd Annual Meeting of the Association for Computational Linguistics (Volume 1: Long Papers), pp. 14044–14072. Association for Computational Linguistics (2024)
17. Nori, H., King, N., McKinney, S.M., Carignan, D., Horvitz, E.: Capabilities of GPT-4 on medical challenge problems. arXiv preprint arXiv:2303.13375 (2023)
18. Paiola, P.H., Garcia, G.L., Manesco, J.R.R., Roder, M., Rodrigues, D., Papa, J.P.: Adapting LLMs for the medical domain in Portuguese: a study on fine-tuning and model evaluation (2024)
19. Penedo, G., Kydlíček, H.: The FineWeb datasets: decanting the web for the finest text data at scale. In: NeurIPS Datasets and Benchmarks Track (2024)
20. Saab, K., Tu, T., Weng, W.H., Tanno, R., Stutz, D.: Capabilities of Gemini models in medicine. arXiv preprint arXiv:2404.18416 (2024)
21. Schneider, E.T.R., et al.: BioBERTpt - a Portuguese neural language model for clinical named entity recognition. In: Rumshisky, A., Roberts, K., Bethard, S.,

Naumann, T. (eds.) Proceedings of the 3rd Clinical Natural Language Processing Workshop, pp. 65–72. Association for Computational Linguistics (2020). https://doi.org/10.18653/v1/2020.clinicalnlp-1.7
22. Schulman, J., Lab, T.M.: LoRA without regret. Thinking Machines Lab: Connectionism (2025). https://doi.org/10.64434/tml.20250929, https://thinkingmachines.ai/blog/lora/
23. Sellergren, A., et al.: MedGemma technical report. arXiv preprint arXiv:2507.05201 (2025)
24. Shao, Z., et al.: DeepSeekMath: pushing the limits of mathematical reasoning in open language models (2024)
25. Shuttleworth, R., Andreas, J., Torralba, A., Sharma, P.: LoRA vs full fine-tuning: an illusion of equivalence. arXiv preprint arXiv:2410.21228 (2024)
26. Singhal, K., et al.: Large language models encode clinical knowledge. Nature **620**, 172–180 (2023)
27. Singhal, K., et al.: Toward expert-level medical question answering with large language models. Nat. Med. **31**(3), 943–950 (2025). https://doi.org/10.1038/s41591-024-03423-7
28. de Souza Pinto, J.G., Rodrigues de Freitas, A., Martins, A.C.G., Sawazaki, C.M.R., Vidal, C., Silva e Oliveira, L.E.: Developing resource-efficient clinical LLMs for Brazilian Portuguese. In: Paes, A., Verri, F.A.N. (eds.) Intelligent Systems, pp. 46–60. Springer, Cham (2025)
29. Su, D., et al.: Nemotron-CC: transforming common crawl into a refined long-horizon pretraining dataset (2024)
30. Wu, C., Lin, W., Zhang, X., Zhang, Y., Xie, W., Wang, Y.: PMC-LLaMA: toward building open-source language models for medicine. J. Am. Med. Inform. Assoc. **31**(9), 1833–1843 (2024). https://doi.org/10.1093/jamia/ocae045
31. Xie, Q., Chen, Q., Chen, A., Peng, C., Hu, Y., et al.: Me-LLaMA: foundation large language models for medical applications. arXiv preprint arXiv:2402.12749 (2024)
32. Yang, A., Yang, B., Zhang, B., Hui, B., Zheng, B., et al.: Qwen2.5 technical report. arXiv preprint arXiv:2412.15115 (2024)
33. Yin, Q., et al.: Evaluating parameter efficient methods for RLVR (2025)
34. Zhang, X., Tian, C., Yang, X., Chen, L., Li, Z., Petzold, L.R.: AlpaCare: instruction-tuned large language models for medical application. arXiv preprint arXiv:2310.14558 (2024)
35. Zheng, G., Wang, X., Liang, J., Chen, N., Zheng, Y., Wang, B.: Efficiently democratizing medical LLMs for 50 languages via a mixture of language family experts (2024)
36. Zheng, J.: Spurious forgetting in continual learning of language models. In: ICLR (2025)
37. Zhou, J., et al.: Instruction-following evaluation for large language models. arXiv preprint arXiv:2311.07911 (2023)

Hypergraph-Based Affinity Degree Detection for Researchers and Government Strategic Themes

Marcos Gôlo[1](✉), Matheus Utino[1], Marcelo Turine[2], and Ricardo Marcacini[1]

[1] Institute of Mathematical and Computer Sciences, University of São Paulo, São Carlos, São Paulo, Brazil
{marcosgolo,matheusutino}@usp.br, ricardo.marcacini@icmc.usp.br

[2] Faculty of Computing, Federal University of Mato Grosso do Sul, Campo Grande, Mato Grosso do Sul, Brazil
marcelo.turine@facom.ufms.br

Abstract. Detecting the affinity degree between researchers and themes is an important task for research management, funding allocation, and public policy planning. This task aims to assess how closely a researcher's academic profile aligns with strategic themes defined by government priorities. However, affinity detection is challenging because it depends on subtle semantic relations between textual descriptions and is often modeled as an isolated pairwise classification problem. Although large language models LLMs can address this task, they still observe peers individually even when researchers share themes and researchers share themes. In this paper, we propose a hypergraph-based approach for affinity degree detection called HyperAff. Our main assumption is that explicitly modeling relations among researchers, themes, and their interactions can improve prediction by incorporating relational context. In particular, hypergraphs provide a richer representation by modeling edges in the original graph through new nodes that capture higher-order dependencies beyond standard pairwise structures. We evaluate this perspective on five datasets, each representing one geographic region of Brazil. Results indicate that hypergraph-based models achieve competitive or superior performance compared to LLM or traditional alternatives. In addition, hypergraph modeling enables post-classification structural analysis, such as identifying thematic communities and broader alignment patterns, which is not directly available in non-graph methods.

Keywords: Pair Classification · Edge Classification · Affinity Detection

1 Introduction

Every year, many researchers complete master's and doctoral programs in Brazil. Considering both master's dissertations and Ph.D. theses, this number passes 100k graduates per year [1]. At the same time, Brazilian states define strategic themes directly related to public policies and social demands, such as education, health, sustainability, technology, regional development, and economic

M. Recamonde-Mendoza and R. C. Barros (Eds.): BRACIS 2026, LNAI 17105, pp. 340–355, 2027.
https://doi.org/10.1007/978-3-032-39882-6_23

growth [15]. These themes represent relevant challenges that should be addressed through scientific and technological production aligned with global agendas, such as the United Nations Sustainable Development Goals [16]. In this context, an important question arises: are the strategic themes defined by the government being addressed by research conducted in Brazilian graduate programs?

One way to answer this question is to formulate the problem as an affinity classification task between government strategic themes and master's dissertations or doctoral theses [15]. Given a set of 470 strategic themes declared in Brazil[1] and more than 100k graduates per year [1], manually evaluating the affinity between each theme and each research work becomes infeasible. This scenario requires automatic methods capable of supporting large-scale analysis. Therefore, machine learning techniques, especially automatic classification methods, have become a natural alternative for classifying the degree of affinity between strategic themes and graduate research.

Recent studies on the automatic classification of affinity between strategic themes and graduate research have explored various approaches. Some works investigate threshold-based strategies applied to textual embeddings [11], traditional machine learning classifiers from scikit-learn [17], and one-class classification approaches [4]. Other studies explore Large Language Models (LLMs), since these models have achieved strong performance in tasks involving textual data [14]. However, using these classifiers alone reduces the problem to an isolated pairwise analysis between a single theme and a single research work. This ignores the relational nature of the data, since one research work may be related to several themes, and one theme may be related to several research works. Moreover, methods usually do not exploit neighborhood information, do not propagate contextual evidence across related entities, and do not provide a structured representation that supports post-classification analysis, such as identifying groups of themes covered by similar researchers [4,11,14,17].

Graphs appear as an alternative to this scenario because they explicitly model relations between entities [6]. In this problem, strategic themes and researchers can be represented as nodes, while the relations between them correspond to candidate pairs for classification, such as a bipartite graph [19,21]. Therefore, the final task can be seen as an edge classification problem, in which each edge represents a possible affinity relation between two nodes [8]. Graph Neural Networks (GNNs) are promising for this setting because they are state-of-the-art methods for representation learning on graph-structured data [8,19,21]. However, most GNN architectures are primarily designed to learn node representations, while in our problem, the main objects of classification are edges [5]. This creates additional challenges, since edge classification often depends on how the two endpoint node embeddings are combined. In addition, directly classifying edges may limit the model's ability to learn specific representations of the affinity relation itself, especially when multiple edges share the same theme or researcher, and when the same node participates in relations with different labels.

[1] https://agendanacional.capes.gov.br/map.

We introduce HyperAff, a new hypergraph method for affinity classification between strategic themes and graduate research. The main idea is to transform each edge that would be classified in the original graph into a new node in an expanded hypergraph [3,5]. Thus, the object of classification becomes a node, allowing the GNN to learn representations directly for the affinity relations. This formulation preserves the relational structure of the original graph while making the target of prediction more suitable for standard GNN-based models. We propose using an orthogonal operator to fuse the theme and researcher embeddings into the initial representation of the new node in the hypergraph, emphasizing the complementary information in both vectors by removing redundant components and highlighting the most informative semantic differences. We explore the Graph Attention Network in our HyperAff method to learn the representations. Figure 1 illustrates the affinity detection task, the strategies used in this scenario, and their respective gaps. In summary, our main contributions are:

1. We model the affinity classification task between strategic themes and graduate research as a graph-based learning problem, explicitly representing researchers, themes, and their candidate relations.
2. We propose HyperAff, a hypergraph-based method that transforms candidate affinity edges into classification nodes and uses GNN-based representation learning to predict degrees of affinity.
3. We show that HyperAff achieves superior or competitive results compared with sklearn methods, MLPs, graph-based models, and zero-shot LLM.

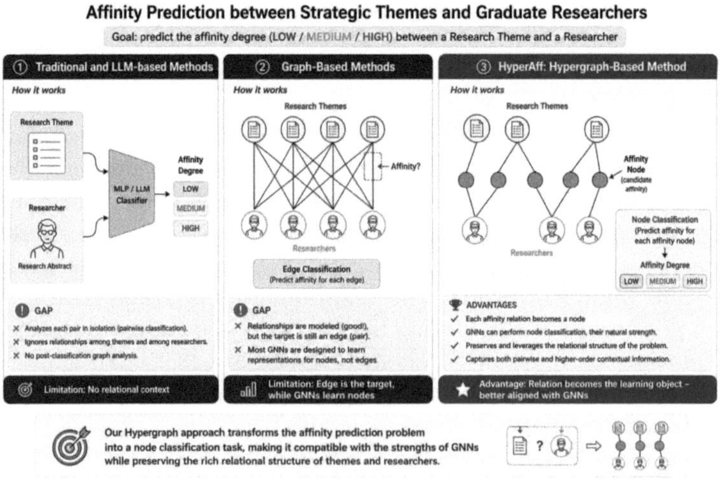

Fig. 1. Affinity detection between research themes and graduate researchers. Traditional and LLM-based methods classify each pair independently, ignoring relational context. Graph-based methods model relationships but still predict edge labels, which is not ideal for GNNs. Hypergraph-based methods transform each relation into a node, enabling node classification and better alignment with GNNs.

2 Problem Definition and Background

Let $\mathcal{R} = \{r_1, r_2, \ldots, r_n\}$ be a set of researchers, where each researcher is represented by the abstract content of a master's dissertation or doctoral thesis. Let $\mathcal{T} = \{t_1, t_2, \ldots, t_m\}$ be a set of government strategic themes represented by a description of the theme. The goal is to classify the affinity between a researcher $r_i \in \mathcal{R}$ and a strategic theme $t_j \in \mathcal{T}$. Each candidate pair (r_i, t_j) is associated with a label $y_{ij} \in \mathcal{Y}$, where $\mathcal{Y} = \{\text{Low}, \text{Medium}, \text{High}\}$. Thus, the task is to learn a function that predicts the degree of affinity between a research work and a strategic theme:

$$f : \mathcal{R} \times \mathcal{T} \rightarrow \mathcal{Y}, \tag{1}$$

In a standard machine learning formulation, both the strategic theme and the research abstract are first mapped to vector representations using an embedding model. Let $\phi(\cdot)$ be a textual embedding function. For each theme t_j, we obtain an embedding vector $\mathbf{x}_{t_j} = \phi(t_j) \in \mathbb{R}^d$. Similarly, for each researcher r_i, represented by the abstract of the corresponding dissertation or thesis, we obtain $\mathbf{x}_{r_i} = \phi(r_i) \in \mathbb{R}^d$. A common way to represent the pair (r_i, t_j) is to concatenate both embeddings: $\mathbf{x}_{ij} = [\mathbf{x}_{r_i} \,||\, \mathbf{x}_{t_j}] \in \mathbb{R}^{2d}$. Then, a classifier $g(\cdot)$ is trained to predict the affinity label: $\hat{y}_{ij} = g(\mathbf{x}_{ij})$. During inference, whenever a candidate pair passes a previous filtering stage and needs classification, the corresponding theme and research embeddings are concatenated and used as input to the classifier.

3 Related Work

Affinity for Researchers and Themes. The problem of detecting affinity between researchers and strategic themes has gained increasing attention in recent years, especially after the establishment of the Brazilian national agenda for postgraduate evaluation [15]. Several approaches have been proposed to address this task [4,11,14,17]. Early methods rely on simple strategies, such as embedding concatenation combined with threshold-based rules, to distinguish high from low affinity [11]. More advanced approaches employ traditional machine learning classifiers to perform binary classification over researcher–theme pairs [17]. Additionally, one-class learning strategies have been explored to model high-affinity regions per theme, focusing on learning the distribution of relevant profiles [4]. More recently, [14] investigated the use of LLMs to classify affinity into Low, Medium, and High classes. A key limitation is that they treat researcher–theme pairs independently, ignoring the relational structure among entities. This pairwise and isolated modeling prevents the exploitation of global patterns, such as shared topics, overlapping expertise, or structural dependencies across researchers and themes. This gap motivates the use of graphs, which enable modeling interactions among multiple entities.

Graphs for Edge Classification. The affinity prediction problem can be naturally formulated as an edge classification task in bipartite graphs, where nodes represent researchers and themes, and edges correspond to relationships that must be classified. This formulation enables GNNs to leverage neighborhood information and relational patterns [8,19,21]. Recent works have explored edge classification in graph settings. For instance, [21] proposes a GNN-based approach for binary edge classification in bipartite graphs, distinguishing positive and negative relations. Similarly, [19] investigates edge classification using message passing mechanisms tailored for bipartite structures. In a different domain, [8] applies edge classification in graphs for intrusion detection in IoT systems. However, GNN architectures are inherently designed for node representation learning, which limits their ability to explicitly model and classify edges. As a result, there is a lack of studies applying graph-based edge classification methods to the affinity prediction problem between researchers and themes, even though this formulation provides a natural, structured representation that can capture richer relational information.

Hypergraphs for Pair Classification. Recent works have explored hypergraph transformations that promote edges to nodes. These methods transform each edge into a new node. This approach is particularly attractive for GNNs, as it aligns with their inherent design for node-level representation learning. A pioneering work in this direction is [5], which proposes a framework for converting graph edges into hypergraph nodes. This idea has shown strong performance in tasks where edge information is critical, such as graph reconstruction and classification. From a similar perspective, [20] introduces a hypergraph line expansion technique in which hyperedge pairs are treated as nodes. These transformations highlight the importance of modeling relations as first-class entities. More recently, [3] explores this paradigm in the context of causal discovery, transforming directed edges between events into nodes within a hypergraph. Despite the promising results of hypergraph-based approaches for edge representation and classification, their application to the affinity prediction problem between researchers and themes remains largely unexplored. To the best of our knowledge, there are no existing works that leverage hypergraph transformations for multi-class affinity classification in this domain. This gap highlights an opportunity to combine the structural advantages of hypergraphs with the task's relevance.

4 HyperAff: Hypergraph for Affinity Prediction

The motivation for using hypergraphs in this work is that affinity classification is not only a textual pair classification problem, but also a relational problem. Traditional classifiers and LLMs can analyze each pair independently, but they do not naturally model the fact that researchers and themes are connected through multiple candidate affinity relations [4,11,14,17]. Graphs solve part of this limitation by representing researchers and themes as nodes and candidate affinities as edges [8,19,21]. However, the target of prediction remains the edge, whereas most GNNs are naturally designed for node representation learning. HyperAff addresses this limitation by converting the original graph into a hypergraph-inspired expanded representation, in which each candidate relation becomes a node for classification [3,5,20]. The complete pipeline consists of four main steps: graph construction, hypergraph transformation, GNN-based representation learning, and affinity classification.

We first model the problem as an undirected bipartite graph [19]. Let $G = (\mathcal{V}, \mathcal{E})$ be a graph where the node set is given by $\mathcal{V} = \mathcal{R} \cup \mathcal{T}$, with $\mathcal{R}$ representing researcher nodes and $\mathcal{T}$ representing theme nodes. Each edge $e_{ij} = (r_i, t_j) \in \mathcal{E}$ represents a candidate affinity relation between researcher r_i and theme t_j. Since edges connect researchers to themes only, G is a bipartite graph. Each edge has an associated label $y_{ij} \in \{\text{Low}, \text{Medium}, \text{High}\}$ when it belongs to the labeled set. The initial representation of each node is obtained from the textual embedding model [22]. Therefore, each researcher node has an initial feature vector $\mathbf{x}_{r_i} \in \mathbb{R}^d$, and each theme node has an initial feature vector $\mathbf{x}_{t_j} \in \mathbb{R}^d$.

After constructing the bipartite graph, HyperAff transforms each candidate edge into a new node [3,5]. For each edge $e_{ij} = (r_i, t_j)$ in the original graph, we create a new relation node a_{ij}, which represents the affinity pair to be classified. The new node set is defined as:

$$\mathcal{V}' = \mathcal{R} \cup \mathcal{T} \cup \mathcal{A} \tag{2}$$

where $\mathcal{A} = \{a_{ij} \mid (r_i, t_j) \in \mathcal{E}\}$ is the set of affinity nodes. For each original edge (r_i, t_j), two new undirected edges are created: (r_i, a_{ij}) and (a_{ij}, t_j). Thus, the new edge set is:

$$\mathcal{E}' = \{(r_i, a_{ij}), (a_{ij}, t_j) \mid (r_i, t_j) \in \mathcal{E}\} \tag{3}$$

The label originally assigned to the edge e_{ij} is transferred to the new node a_{ij}. Therefore, the affinity classification task becomes a node classification task over the nodes in $\mathcal{A}$. A key question in this transformation is how to initialize the representation of the new affinity node a_{ij}, since it represents the relation between a researcher and a theme.

A simple option would be to initialize each affinity node by concatenating the researcher and theme embeddings. However, concatenation increases the dimensionality of the representation and places it in a different feature space compared to the original node embeddings. This is not ideal for GNNs, which rely on neighborhood aggregation mechanisms that assume node representations lie in a shared latent space with consistent dimensionality across nodes. Therefore, it is preferable to use a fusion operator that preserves the original embedding dimension. Possible operators include mean, minimum, maximum, subtraction, element-wise product, and other fixed-size combinations. HyperAff uses an orthogonal fusion operator to emphasize the semantic component of one vector that is not already explained by the other. This operation removes from one vector the component that points in the direction of the other, preserving the information that differs between the two vectors. This is useful because highly similar vectors may indicate high affinity, while the remaining orthogonal component can highlight the semantic differences that help low affinities. Thus, for each affinity node a_{ij}, we define its initial representation as:

$$\mathbf{x}_{a_{ij}} = \mathbf{x}_{t_j} - (\mathbf{x}_{r_i}^\top \mathbf{x}_{t_j})\mathbf{x}_{r_i}, \tag{4}$$

where $\mathbf{x}_{r_i}$ and $\mathbf{x}_{t_j}$ are vectors from a embedding model.

After the hypergraph transformation, we apply a GNN to learn node representations [6]. A GNN updates each node representation by aggregating information from its neighbors and combining this aggregated information with the current node representation [7]. Let $\mathbf{h}_v^{(l)}$ be the representation of node v at layer l. Aggregation and Update can be written as:

$$\mathbf{m}_v^{(l)} = \text{Aggregation}^{(l)}\left(\{\mathbf{h}_u^{(l)} : u \in \mathcal{N}(v)\}\right), \tag{5}$$

$$\mathbf{h}_v^{(l+1)} = \text{Update}^{(l)}\left(\mathbf{h}_v^{(l)}, \mathbf{m}_v^{(l)}\right), \tag{6}$$

where $\mathcal{N}(v)$ is the set of neighbors of node v. In this work, we use Graph Attention Network layers that learn distinct importance weights for different neighbors [18]. For a node i and one of its neighbors j, the attention is computed as:

$$e_{ij}^{(l)} = \text{LeakyReLU}\left(\mathbf{b}^\top \left[\mathbf{W}^{(l)}\mathbf{h}_i^{(l)} \,||\, \mathbf{W}^{(l)}\mathbf{h}_j^{(l)}\right]\right), \tag{7}$$

where $\mathbf{W}^{(l)}$ is a trainable weight matrix, $\mathbf{b}$ is a trainable attention vector, and $||$ denotes concatenation. The attention coefficient is then obtained by:

$$\alpha_{ij}^{(l)} = \frac{\exp(e_{ij}^{(l)})}{\sum_{k \in \mathcal{N}(i)} \exp(e_{ik}^{(l)})}. \tag{8}$$

The representation of node i in the next layer is computed as

$$\mathbf{h}_i^{(l+1)} = \sigma\left(\sum_{j \in \mathcal{N}(i)} \alpha_{ij}^{(l)} \mathbf{W}^{(l)} \mathbf{h}_j^{(l)}\right), \tag{9}$$

where σ is a non-linear activation function.

HyperAff uses two GAT layers to learn the final representations of the nodes in the hypergraph. Since the labels are assigned to the affinity nodes, only the representations of nodes $a_{ij} \in \mathcal{A}$ are used for classification. After the second GAT layer, we apply a Linear layer to classify the affinity, generating a $\mathbf{o}_{ij}$ value, where $\mathbf{o}_{ij} \in \mathbb{R}^{|\mathcal{Y}|}$, i.e., $\mathbf{o}_{ij}$ is the vector of class logits. The predicted class distribution is obtained with a softmax function: $\hat{\mathbf{y}}_{ij} = \text{softmax}(\mathbf{o}_{ij})$. The model is trained using the cross-entropy loss over the labeled affinity nodes:

$$\mathcal{L} = -\sum_{a_{ij} \in \mathcal{A}} \sum_{c \in \mathcal{Y}} \mathbf{1}(y_{ij} = c) \log(\hat{y}_{ij,c}). \tag{10}$$

5 Experimental Evaluation

This section presents the datasets, experimental settings, and results used to evaluate the proposed method. The main goal is to verify whether a hypergraph-based method can outperform or remain competitive with traditional machine learning classifiers, MLPs, graph-based models, and LLM-based baselines. The source code used in the experiments is publicly available[2].

5.1 Datasets

We used datasets presented in the LeanDL-HPC Challenge, hosted by the International Symposium on Computer Architecture and High Performance Computing Workshops (SBAC-PADW) [13]. In this challenge, a dataset of affinity relations between government strategic themes and master's dissertations or doctoral theses authored by Brazilian graduates was provided to enable the proposal and evaluation of classification strategies during the conference. The data cover all Brazilian regions, which allowed us to build five regional datasets: North, Northeast, West-Central, Southeast, and South.

Each dataset contains one column for a researcher identifier and one column for the strategic theme. The textual content includes the theme description and the abstract of the dissertation or doctoral thesis. Finally, each pair has an associated affinity label: Low, Medium or High. Table 1 summarizes the main characteristics of the datasets.

Table 1. Dataset statistics for the five Brazilian regions.

Characteristic	North	Northeast	West-Central	Southeast	South
Total instances	3,641	8,381	3,843	11,684	5,390
High pairs	550	1,592	538	2,348	1,106
Medium pairs	1,198	2,691	1,255	3,825	1,784
Low pairs	1,893	4,098	2,050	5,511	2,500
Unique themes	124	159	67	67	41
Unique researchers	1,518	3,973	1,735	6,627	3,005

5.2 Experimental Settings

We compared HyperAff with different groups of baselines. First, we used traditional scikit-learn classifiers applied to concatenated embeddings, as in the studies in the related work Sect. 3, for **Affinity for Researchers and Themes**. We use Decision Trees, Random Forests, SVMs, and Logistic Regression. We also

[2] https://github.com/GoloMarcos/HyperAff.

used an MLP applied to the concatenation of the researcher and theme embeddings to assess the value of using graphs instead of a simple MLP. Another comparison method was a graph-based GNN for edge classification, to represent the **Graphs for Edge Classification** studies in Sect. 3. Finally, as strong baselines, we used three LLMs: *Qwen/Qwen3-8B* [12], *google/gemma-3-4b-it* [2], and *meta-llama/Llama-3.1-8B* [10]. For these models, the prompt included the strategic theme, the research abstract, and an explanation of the affinity classification task, asking the model to return the corresponding label. For the scikit-learn, MLP, Graph, and HyperAff methods, we use the *Qwen/Qwen3-Embedding-8B* model [22]. All methods were compared using f_1-macro on the test set. We used 80% for training, 10% for validation and hyperparameter selection, and 10% for testing. The hyperparameters were:

- **Decision Tree:** maximum depth in $\{5, 10, 20\}$, minimum samples split in $\{2, 5, 10\}$, and criterion in {`gini`, `entropy`}.
- **Random Forest:** number of estimators in $\{100, 200\}$, maximum depth in $\{10, 20\}$, minimum samples split in $\{2, 5\}$, and criterion in {`gini`, `entropy`}.
- **SVM:** kernel={`linear`, `rbf`}, $C = \{0.1, 1.0, 10.0\}$, and γ ={`scale`, `auto`}.
- **Logistic Regression:** $C = \{0.1, 1, 10\}$ and class weight={`None`, `balanced`}.
- **LLMs:** Temperature = 0, max tokens = 100, max model len = 20000;
- **MLP:** two hidden layers with dimensions (128, 64), dropout of 0.1, learning rates in $\{10^{-3}, 10^{-4}\}$, weight decay in $\{10^{-4}, 10^{-5}\}$, maximum of 3000 epochs, and early stopping patience in $\{50, 100\}$.
- **Graph baseline and HyperAff:** GATConv layer with one attention head, hidden dimension of 128, embedding dimension in $\{32, 64\}$, dropout of 0.1, learning rates in $\{10^{-3}, 10^{-4}\}$, weight decay of 10^{-4}, maximum of 3000 epochs, and early stopping patience in $\{50, 100\}$.

5.3 Results and Discussion

Table 2 reports the f_1-macro results for the classification of High, Medium, and Low affinity classes. Each row corresponds to a method, and each column corresponds to one dataset. The best result for each dataset is shown in bold, while the second-best result is underlined. The table allows us to compare traditional machine learning models, LLMs, MLPs, Graphs, and the proposed HyperAff method across all five Brazilian regions. HyperAff got the best results, MLP the second-best, and Gemma the third-best. LLaMa obtains the worst results.

The results show that HyperAff achieved the best performance in three of the five datasets: Northeast, West-Central, and Southeast. In the Northeast dataset, HyperAff obtained a f_1-macro of 0.502, slightly outperforming the MLP, which achieved 0.498. In the West-Central dataset, HyperAff also obtained the best result, at 0.450, followed very closely by Gemma 3 at 0.448. In the Southeast dataset, the largest dataset in terms of number of instances and researchers, HyperAff reached 0.519, outperforming the MLP, which achieved 0.510. These results suggest that the hypergraph representation is useful when the relational structure provides information beyond what is available from isolated pairs.

Table 2. f_1-macro results for the affinity detection with High, Medium and Low classes.

	North	Northeast	West-Central	Southeast	South
Decision Tree	0.306	0.380	0.356	0.373	0.413
Random Forest	0.278	0.316	0.264	0.349	0.334
SVM	0.297	0.425	0.326	0.472	0.454
Logistic Regre.	0.268	0.355	0.314	0.312	0.332
Qwen 3 (8B)	0.234	0.222	0.239	0.229	0.215
Gemma 3 (4b)	**0.499**	0.454	<u>0.448</u>	0.469	0.460
LLaMa 3.1 (8B)	0.088	0.107	0.087	0.112	0.122
MLP	<u>0.439</u>	<u>0.498</u>	0.419	<u>0.510</u>	**0.516**
Graph	0.414	0.475	0.377	0.473	0.470
HyperAff	0.426	**0.502**	**0.450**	**0.519**	<u>0.503</u>

The North and South datasets show a different pattern. In the North dataset, Gemma 3 achieved the best result at 0.499, followed by the MLP at 0.439 and HyperAff at 0.426. This dataset has the fewest instances, with 3,641 pairs, but it has 124 unique themes, which may make the graph structure sparser and more difficult for a GNN-based method to exploit. In the South dataset, the MLP achieved the best result at 0.516, followed by HyperAff at 0.503 and the graph baseline at 0.470. This dataset has fewer themes, only 41, and a moderate number of researchers, which may favor models based on direct embedding concatenation.

Among the traditional machine learning methods, SVM was generally the strongest baseline, especially in the Southeast and South datasets, with f_1-macro values of 0.472 and 0.454, respectively. The Decision Tree achieved moderate results, while Random Forest and Logistic Regression were less competitive across most datasets. The LLM results were mixed. Gemma 3 was highly competitive, achieving the best result on the North dataset, but Qwen 3 and LLaMa 3.1 performed poorly across all datasets. This indicates that zero-shot LLM classification is not necessarily reliable for this task, especially when the model must distinguish fine-grained labels such as High, Medium, and Low.

HyperAff consistently outperforms the strongest LLM baseline, Gemma 3 (4B), in most datasets, highlighting the advantage of explicitly modeling relational structure. While Gemma achieves the best result in the North dataset (0.499 vs. 0.426), HyperAff surpasses it in the Northeast (0.502 vs. 0.454), West-Central (0.450 vs. 0.448), and Southeast (0.519 vs. 0.469) and remains competitive in the South (0.503 vs. 0.460). This comparison indicates that although LLMs are powerful for pairwise semantic understanding, they are limited in their ability to jointly model multiple relations across themes and researchers. In contrast, HyperAff leverages the relational structure via a hypergraph representation, yielding more robust and generalizable performance.

The comparison between HyperAff and the standard graph baseline is also important. HyperAff outperformed the graph model in all five datasets in the ternary setting. This supports the hypothesis that transforming candidate edges into classification nodes is preferable to directly classifying edges based on end-point node representations. In particular, the improvement is clearer in the West-Central and Southeast datasets, where HyperAff obtained 0.450 and 0.519, while the graph baseline obtained 0.377 and 0.473, respectively. This suggests that learning a specific representation for each affinity relation helps the model capture information that the original graph does not fully encode.

Figure 2 presents a projection of the learned representations for four different approaches: raw embeddings, MLP, graph-based, and the proposed hypergraph-based method in the Southeast dataset. We use t-SNE to project the embeddings [9]. As shown in the embedding space, the three classes are highly intermixed, indicating that the original representations are not sufficiently discriminative for affinity prediction (concatenation). The MLP slightly improves this separation by introducing non-linear transformations, but the clusters remain overlapping, suggesting a limited ability to capture complex relationships. The graph-based approach yields more structured clusters, reflecting the benefit of incorporating relational information; however, significant overlap between classes persists. In contrast, the hypergraph-based method exhibits a more coherent separation of the classes, with clearer global structure and improved grouping of similar instances. We can observe the blue points on the left, the orange points on the right, and the green points (medium class) distributed in the space. This behavior suggests that transforming relations into nodes enables the model to learn more informative representations by jointly capturing relational contexts, consistent with the performance gains observed in the quantitative results.

Overall, the ternary results indicate that affinity classification is a difficult task. The Medium class is especially challenging because it may represent an intermediate, sometimes ambiguous, relationship between clear affinity and no affinity. From the government's perspective, the most important operational decision may not be to distinguish perfectly between High and Medium affinity, but to identify research that has some useful affinity with strategic themes. Therefore, combining High and Medium into a single positive class may be more realistic for supporting public policy, since both classes may indicate research that contributes to a strategic theme. In contrast, low-affinity pairs can be treated as non-relevant for that specific theme. This binary formulation is also consistent with practical decision-making, where the goal is often to select potentially relevant research for further analysis rather than assign a fine-grained degree at the first stage. For this reason, we also evaluated a binary setting in which High and Medium labels were merged into a single positive class, while Low remained the negative class. Predictions originally assigned as Medium were converted to High. Table 3 reports the f_1-macro results for this binary setting.

The binary results show a general improvement in f_1-macro for all methods, confirming that the task becomes more consistent when High and Medium are treated as relevant affinity cases. HyperAff achieved the best result in four of the five datasets: Northeast, West-Central, Southeast, and South. In the Northeast dataset, HyperAff achieved 0.644, outperforming the MLP (0.630) and the graph

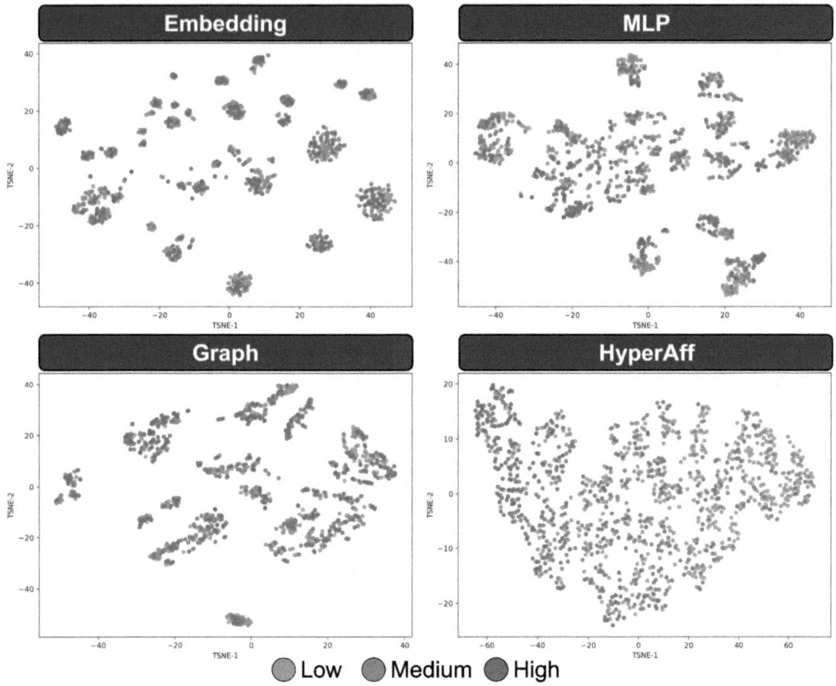

Fig. 2. t-SNE visualization, in the Southeast dataset, of the learned representations for different methods: raw embeddings, MLP, graph-based, and HyperAff. Blue indicates high affinity, green indicates medium, and orange indicates low. The HyperAff approach produces more structured, distinct embeddings, indicating improved organization. (Color figure online)

Table 3. f_1-macro results for the **binary** affinity classification setting.

	North	Northeast	West-Central	Southeast	South
Decision Tree	0.432	0.524	0.560	0.545	0.581
Random Forest	0.489	0.503	0.506	0.524	0.532
SVM	0.508	0.585	0.547	0.635	0.627
Logistic Regre.	0.472	0.513	0.513	0.487	0.506
Qwen 3 (8B)	0.360	0.338	0.365	0.342	0.322
Gemma 3 (4b)	**0.631**	0.603	0.585	0.610	0.613
LLaMa 3.1 (8B)	0.324	0.338	0.319	0.346	0.349
MLP	<u>0.577</u>	<u>0.630</u>	<u>0.618</u>	<u>0.666</u>	<u>0.638</u>
Graph	0.568	0.618	0.579	0.632	0.605
HyperAff	0.564	**0.644**	**0.620**	**0.672**	**0.644**

baseline (0.618). In the West-Central dataset, HyperAff reached 0.620, slightly above the MLP with 0.618. In the Southeast dataset, HyperAff achieved the highest result overall at 0.672, followed by the MLP at 0.666 and the SVM at 0.635. In the South dataset, HyperAff also achieved the best result, at 0.644, followed by the MLP at 0.638.

The only dataset in which HyperAff did not achieve the best binary result was North. In this dataset, Gemma 3 obtained 0.631, while the MLP achieved 0.577 and HyperAff achieved 0.564. As in the ternary setting, this result may be related to the characteristics of the North dataset. It has the fewest instances and a relatively high number of themes, which can reduce the graph's density and make relational learning harder. In such a setting, a strong language model may benefit from its prior textual knowledge, especially when the available relational structure is limited.

Compared with the ternary setting, the binary setting strengthens the evidence for the proposed method. HyperAff consistently outperformed the standard graph baseline in four datasets and remained very close in the North dataset. This indicates that the hypergraph transformation provides a better structure for learning relational representations, especially when the classification target aligns with the practical goal of identifying relevant affinity pairs. The MLP was also a strong competitor, ranking second across four datasets, confirming that concatenated embeddings contain useful semantic information. However, HyperAff outperformed the MLP in most datasets by incorporating relational information from the graph structure.

The results also show that traditional classifiers are competitive but limited. SVM achieved strong results, especially on the Southeast and South datasets, but it was consistently below HyperAff in the regions where the proposed method performed best. Decision Tree and Random Forest improved in the binary setting, but they did not reach the performance of the neural methods. Among the LLMs, Gemma 3 remained the strongest model, while Qwen 3 and LLaMa 3.1 performed poorly. This reinforces the importance of task-specific supervised methods for this problem, particularly when the objective is to classify a large number of candidate pairs in a scalable way.

Table 4. f_1-macro results for the **ablation** of HyperAff considering the ternary classification.

	North	Northeast	West-Central	Southeast	South
GCN + Sum	0.350	0.487	0.378	0.454	0.471
GCN + Mean	0.348	0.482	0.363	0.445	0.455
GCN + Orthogonal	0.303	0.437	<u>0.382</u>	0.468	0.456
GAT + Sum	<u>0.374</u>	<u>0.492</u>	<u>0.382</u>	<u>0.481</u>	<u>0.479</u>
GAT + Mean	0.366	0.455	0.359	0.451	0.465
HyperAff	**0.426**	**0.502**	**0.450**	**0.519**	**0.503**

Table 4 presents an ablation study comparing different combinations of GNN architectures and fusion operators within the HyperAff framework. HyperAff, which combines GAT with the orthogonal fusion operator, achieves the best performance across all five regional datasets. GAT consistently outperforms GCN under the same fusion operator, highlighting the advantage of attention-based aggregation in the hypergraph setting. Notably, the orthogonal operator underperforms when paired with GCN, indicating that it requires the expressive power of GAT to be effective. GAT with Sum ranks as the second-best variant across most datasets, further reinforcing the importance of the backbone architecture. Taken together, these results demonstrate that the combination of GAT and orthogonal fusion reflects a meaningful interaction between the two components, rather than independent contributions.

6 Conclusion and Future Work

This work presented HyperAff, a hypergraph-based method for affinity classification between government strategic themes and graduate research. The proposed method addresses an important problem in public policy analysis: understanding whether the scientific production of graduate programs aligns with strategic demands set by the government. Instead of treating each theme-research pair independently, HyperAff models the task as a relational learning problem: we first build a bipartite graph between researchers and themes, then transform each candidate edge into a new node for classification. The main advantage of HyperAff is that it adapts the affinity classification problem to the natural strengths of GNNs: node representation.

The experimental results showed that HyperAff is competitive with traditional machine learning methods, MLPs, graph-based models, and LLM baselines. In the ternary setting, HyperAff achieved the best results in three of the five regional datasets and outperformed the standard graph baseline in all regions. In the binary setting, which is closer to a practical public policy use case, HyperAff achieved the best results in four of the five datasets. These results indicate that hypergraph-based modeling is a promising direction for large-scale affinity prediction between strategic themes and graduate research.

As future work, we intend to investigate other GNN architectures and hypergraph neural networks specifically designed for higher-order relations. Another important direction is to include metadata on researchers, graduate programs, institutions, and research areas, which may improve the quality of the relational representation and yield a heterogeneous hypergraph.

Acknowledgments. This study was partially funded by FAPEC (23104.003594/2025-12), CNPq (317002/2026-0), and FAPESP (2025/07160-0, 2024/08485-8, 2024/15430-5, 2023/10100-4, 2022/09091-8).

References

1. CAPES: Plano nacional de pós-graduação – PNPG 2024–2028: versão preliminar para consulta pública. Technical report, Ministério da Educação / CAPES, Brasília (2023). Accessed: 30 Mar 2026
2. Gemma, T.: Gemma 3. Google Deep Mind (2025). https://goo.gle/Gemma3Report
3. Gôlo, M.P.S., Marcacini, R.M.: One-class edge classification through heterogeneous hypergraph for causal discovery. Sci. Rep. (2025)
4. Gôlo, M.P.S., Utino, M.Y.R.: One-class lightweight interpretable filtering for academic profiles and strategic themes affinity. In: 2025 IEEE/SBC 37th International Symposium on Computer Architecture and High Performance Computing Workshops (SBAC-PADW), pp. 147–154. IEEE (2025)
5. Jo, J., Baek, J., Lee, S., Kim, D., Kang, M., Hwang, S.J.: Edge representation learning with hypergraphs. In: NeurIPS, pp. 7534–7546. NeurIPS Foundation (2021)
6. Khemani, B., Patil, S., Kotecha, K., Tanwar, S.: A review of graph neural networks: concepts, architectures, techniques, challenges, datasets, applications, and future directions. J. Big Data **11**(1), 18 (2024)
7. Kipf, T.N., Welling, M.: Semi-supervised classification with graph convolutional networks. In: International Conference on Learning Representations (2017)
8. Lo, W.W., Layeghy, S., Sarhan, M., Gallagher, M., Portmann, M.: E-graphsage: a graph neural network based intrusion detection system for IoT. In: NOMS 2022-2022 IEEE/iFIP Network Operations and Management Symposium. IEEE (2022)
9. Van der Maaten, L., Hinton, G.: Visualizing data using t-SNE. J. Mach. Learn. Res. **9**(11), 2579–2605 (2008)
10. Meta, T.: The llama 3.1 herd of models. arXiv preprint (2024). https://meta.com
11. Miranda, A.C.D., Utino, M.Y.R., Gôlo, M.P.S., Dos Santos, M.A.A., de Souza, M.C.: Reducing costs in large-scale classification: a hybrid BERT–LLM strategy. In: 2025 IEEE/SBC 37th International Symposium on Computer Architecture and High Performance Computing Workshops (SBAC-PADW). IEEE (2025)
12. Qwen, T.: Qwen3 technical report (2025). https://arxiv.org/abs/2505.09388
13. Rigo, S.: International Symposium on Computer Architecture and High Performance Computing Workshops SBAC-PADW (2025)
14. Sakiyama, K.M., Fujimoto, M.L., Santin, R.V., Rezende, S.O.: Leandl HPC challenge 2025: applying large-scale model adaptation techniques. In: 2025 IEEE/SBC 37th International Symposium on Computer Architecture and High Performance Computing Workshops (SBAC-PADW), pp. 139–146. IEEE (2025)
15. Turine, M.A.S., Souto Maior, A.P., Marcacini, R.M.: Agenda nacional para a formação de pessoal de nível superior: temas estratégicos declarados pelas unidades da federação do Brasil. CAPES, Brasília, DF (2025)
16. United Nations: Transforming our world: The 2030 agenda for sustainable development. Technical report, United Nations (2015). https://brasil.un.org/pt-br/91863-agenda-2030-para-o-desenvolvimento-sustentavel. Accessed 20 Apr 2026
17. Utino, M.Y.R., Gôlo, M.P.S.: Efficient filtering with BERT embeddings for researcher-topic affinity prediction in HPC pipelines. In: 2025 IEEE/SBC 37th International Symposium on Computer Architecture and High Performance Computing Workshops (SBAC-PADW), pp. 155–162. IEEE (2025)
18. Veličković, P., Cucurull, G., Casanova, A., Romero, A., Liò, P., Bengio, Y.: Graph attention networks. In: International Conference on Learning Representations (2018)

19. Wang, H., Yang, R., Xiao, X.: Effective edge-wise representation learning in edge-attributed bipartite graphs. In: Proceedings of the 30th ACM SIGKDD Conference on Knowledge Discovery and Data Mining, pp. 3081–3091 (2024)
20. Yang, C., Wang, R., Yao, S., Abdelzaher, T.: Semi-supervised hypergraph node classification on hypergraph line expansion. In: Proceedings of the 31st ACM International Conference on Information & Knowledge Management (2022)
21. Zhang, X., Wang, H., Yu, J., Chen, C., Wang, X., Zhang, W.: Polarity-based graph neural network for sign prediction in signed bipartite graphs. World Wide Web **25**(2), 471–487 (2022)
22. Zhang, Y., et al.: Qwen3 embedding: advancing text embedding and reranking through foundation models. arXiv preprint arXiv:2506.05176 (2025)

TECOBEE: Adaptive Acceleration BERT Inference via Text Complexity-Based Early-Exit

Fernando Baptistella de Lima(✉) and Eraylson Galdino da Silva

University of Pernambuco, Recife, Pernambuco, Brazil
{fbl,egs}@ecomp.poli.br

Abstract. Early-exit mechanisms have attracted considerable attention in BERT and other pre-trained language models (PLMs) because they enable a trade-off between predictive performance and computational efficiency during inference. However, many existing early-exit approaches require careful manual tuning of hyperparameters, which limits their adaptability and practical deployment. This work proposes Text Complexity-Based Early Exit (TECOBEE), a simple and adaptive inference strategy that dynamically adjusts the depth of computation according to the complexity and readability of the input text. The proposed method leverages classical readability metrics to estimate text complexity and determine whether the model can produce a reliable prediction at earlier layers. Unlike many previous approaches, the proposed strategy avoids the need for multiple hyperparameter configurations or additional training procedures. Extensive experiments conducted on tasks from the GLUE benchmark demonstrate that the proposed approach achieves performance comparable to state-of-the-art early-exit methods while significantly improving inference efficiency. The method reduces inference time by up to approximately 40% while maintaining competitive predictive accuracy. These results indicate that incorporating text readability signals into early-exit strategies provides an effective and lightweight mechanism for improving the efficiency of transformer-based language models. The source code for TECOBEE is available at https://github.com/FernandoBLima/TECOBEE.

Keywords: Early-Exit Mechanisms · Dynamic Inference · Adaptive Computation · BERT Acceleration · Pre-trained Language Models

1 Introduction

Pre-trained Language Models (PLMs) based on the BERT [4] architecture have been widely adopted for their effectiveness in achieving state-of-the-art (SOTA) results across diverse Natural Language Processing (NLP) tasks on the GLUE benchmark [26], including sentiment analysis, natural language inference, and question–answer entailment. Despite these improvements, BERT-style models

M. Recamonde-Mendoza and R. C. Barros (Eds.): BRACIS 2026, LNAI 17105, pp. 356–370, 2027.
https://doi.org/10.1007/978-3-032-39882-6_24

such as ALBERT [13], RoBERTa [15], and XLNet [30] face significant challenges due to their enormous size and over-parameterization. The presence of dozens of layers increases the model's structural complexity and computational cost, often resulting in higher processing demands without equivalent improvements in accuracy or efficiency. Additionally, these models tend to perform excessive computation, despite shallow layers being sufficient to generate correct outputs for simpler inputs. The deeper processing can even lead to incorrect predictions, a problem known as overthinking [10]. In Fig. 1, we illustrate the problem of overthinking from the average prediction confidence per layer, measured by entropy, that changes through model layers and by increasing entropy in final layers. As the inference progresses through the layers, it obtains progressively lower entropy values, indicating greater confidence in its prediction. Upon reaching the final layers, the entropy increases abruptly, indicating that the intermediate layers may surpass the last layer.

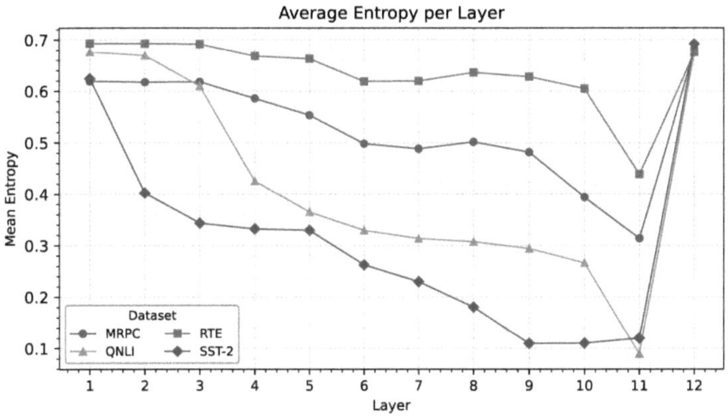

Fig. 1. Average per-layer entropy for MRPC, QNLI, RTE, and SST-2 from the GLUE benchmark [26] in BERT-base, illustrating how information uncertainty changes across model layers.

The early-exit technique from adaptive inference methods [1] has drawn considerable interest by proposing model structures that adjust dynamically based on the input data to speed up inference. Intermediate classifiers are added across layers of the model, seeking to process simpler examples in the shallow layers, while more complex inputs continue through deeper layers. Among the early-exit approaches applied to PLMs, DeeBERT [28] applies BranchyNet [22] by using confident-based early exiting using prediction entropy to determine when to exit, PABEE [32] implements the patience-based approach that dynamically terminates inference when internal classifiers predictions remain unchanged for a predefined number of steps, and PCEE-BERT [31] that combines confident-based and the patience-based early exiting. Although existing early exiting models achieve promising quality–efficiency trade-offs, they lack dynamic adaptability.

In practice, optimizing their performance for specific tasks or domain characteristics still requires manual adjustment of patience or entropy hyperparameters, which limits their flexibility and generalization across diverse scenarios.

Although complex inputs typically require greater computational resources than simpler ones, the use of input complexity to prevent overthinking and dynamically adapt processing remains underexplored in early-exit mechanisms. We propose Text Complexity-Based Early Exit (TECOBEE), a novel early-exiting strategy that enables models to dynamically adapt their computational inference depth according to the complexity and readability of the input, thereby eliminating the need for manual hyperparameter tuning. The central idea is to compute the complexity of the input data, enabling the model to dynamically determine an appropriate early-exit point, thereby improving computational efficiency without compromising prediction accuracy. To validate this approach, we conducted experiments on the GLUE benchmark using TECOBEE, showing that incorporating textual complexity into early-exit decisions can accelerate model inference with minimal hyperparameter tuning and without degrading the quality–efficiency trade-off.

This study highlights the following key contributions: (1) Proposes a novel and effective inference mechanism, TECOBEE, which leverages input text complexity to guide early-exit of decisions and accelerate inference in PLMs; (2) Presents, to the best of our knowledge, the first investigation combining early-exit strategies with input complexity, demonstrating that our method improves inference speed while preserving accuracy across different GLUE tasks; (3) Provides an extensive comparative evaluation of early-exit strategies across different PLM architectures.

2 Related Work

Static Inference Approach. Several research efforts have emerged to address the acceleration of model inference and make PLMs more efficient for limited-resource environments. Techniques that compress a large model into a smaller one, such as pruning [17], knowledge distillation [7], and weight quantization [11], are commonly used to reduce model size and computational cost. Among the models derived from these approaches, DistilBERT [19], TinyBERT [9], and Q-BERT [20] stand out for effectively maintaining performance while significantly improving efficiency. Nevertheless, these models consist of multiple stacked layers, their computational path remains fixed and every input must pass through all layers regardless of its complexity, resulting in limited flexibility.

Dynamic Early Exiting. A promising emerging research direction, dynamic neural networks, seeks to adapt the computational path according to the input data, aiming to balance performance and efficiency. Among these methods, early-exit mechanisms have attracted increasing attention as a SOTA approach to adaptive inference, enabling models to terminate inference at earlier layers and reduce computational cost. Three main dynamic early-exiting strategies have been developed to determine whether to stop inference. The first is confident-based, also referred to as score-based, calculates prediction probability distribution to decide when to exit early, BranchyNet [22], DeeBERT [28] and FastBERT [14] leverage the entropy of the predicted probability distribution. The second strategy is learned-based, a trainable module learns a criterion for early exit, such as BERxiT [29], LeeBERT [33] and SmartBERT [8]. The third approach is patience-based, where the exit decision is determined by predictions across several consecutive intermediate classifiers, the model exits only when the same prediction is maintained for a predefined number of layers, as in PABEE [32] and F-PABEE [5]. Despite recent advances, PABEE and DeeBERT present important limitations, PABEE is inflexible in adapting the acceleration rate with a fixed patience parameter, it can only achieve a fixed speedup rate. DeeBERT relies on fixed confidence thresholds, which can lead to imprecise criteria decisions. Alternative approaches have also emerged, PCEE-BERT [31] combines the score-based and the patience-based methods. Nevertheless, the values chosen for hyperparameters such as patience or entropy thresholds significantly impact both latency and performance. No single hyperparameter configuration consistently yields optimal results across all tasks; instead, performance is highly dependent on the specific scenario. This reliance on manual hyperparameter tuning for each task or domain continues to limit the flexibility and generalization of early-exit mechanisms.

Readability Metrics. The task of measuring how easily a text can be understood by readers has emerged as a fundamental task in NLP research [24]. Traditional readability metrics, such as Gunning Fog Index (FOG) [6], Automated Readability Index (ARI) [21], and Coleman-Liau Index (CLI) [2], estimate the US grade level necessary to comprehend a text by analyzing syntactic structures and vocabulary complexity and Flesch Reading Ease (FRE) [12] metric measures the readability of a text, indicating its level of reading difficulty. These metrics are widely applied to both direct the generation of text and assess its quality, providing an estimated measure of text readability. The measured text can be influenced by several factors, including lexical and syntactic, sentence structure, and the use of technical terms [3]. Complexity metrics have been employed to evaluate neural approaches for document readability, highlighting their adaptability and advantages over traditional methods [16]. For content control, previous studies have applied instruction tuning techniques to dynamically adjust the readability of generated text, enabling the production of outputs at specific and nearly continuous readability levels [23]. Complex textual adjustment relies on quantitative assessment using standardized metrics such as FOG, ARI, CLI. Readability metrics, particularly the FRE, control the textual complexity of summaries generated by LLMs [18], enabling the model to adjust readability levels while preserving coherence and factual consistency.

3 Text Complexity-Based Early Exit

Motivation. Text readability reflects the cognitive effort required to understand a given content, capturing how linguistic complexity affects overall comprehension. Inspired by this concept, we adopt a computational readability measure in which lower scores indicate simpler texts and higher scores indicate greater complexity. TECOBEE adopts two early-exit decision strategies, an entropy-based criterion (Sect. 3) and a patience-based criterion (Sect. 3). Textual complexity modulates both mechanisms, providing an adaptive control signal that accelerates inference while preserving the quality–efficiency trade-off. The inference of TECOBEE, illustrated in Fig. 2, follows a dynamic and adaptive approach that combines score-based and patience-based early exiting methods. In this method, each data instance x_i from X is processed sequentially by the network through a hierarchy of layers L_n, with textual readability metrics indicating the complexity of a text, aiming to perform early exit.

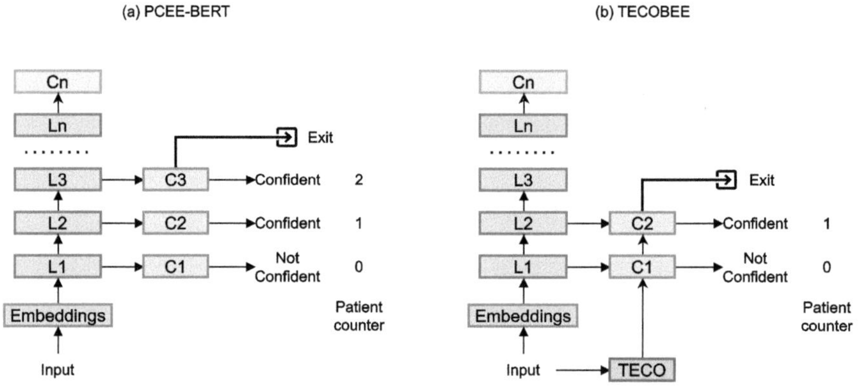

Fig. 2. Comparison between PCEE-BERT [31] and our TECOBEE, a novel early exit method that combines confidence-based and scoring-based early exit, taking into account the complexity of the text. By using a computational module named TECO, it estimates the complexity of each input, acting as a gating function to determine the appropriate processing level in the model.

Training. The training structure incorporates intermediate classifiers at multiple layers of the BERT model, allowing each layer to learn to make independent predictions. In the fine-tuning phase, all exits are trained jointly using an aggregated loss function, following [32], defined as:

$$\mathcal{L} = \frac{\sum_{j=1}^{n} j \cdot \mathcal{L}_j}{\sum_{j=1}^{n} j} \tag{1}$$

The model is trained to minimize the cross-entropy loss, denoted as $\mathcal{L}_j$, at each jth layer. Every intermediate classifier learns to make accurate predictions, contributing to the overall optimization of the network during fine-tuning.

Inference. In this work, we leverage the pre-trained BERT model, a multi-layer Transformer network [25], in conjunction with TECO, a computational module that estimates the textual complexity of the input. This complexity score is then used to guide early-exit decisions during inference, allowing the model to dynamically select the most appropriate layer for classification, further accelerating inference with minimal hyperparameter tuning in downstream tasks while maintaining a favorable trade-off between quality and efficiency.

Readability Assessment Measurement. During inference, TECO receives the input data and estimates its textual complexity. This component acts as a gating function that evaluates the computational effort associated with each instance, serving as a key step in determining the appropriate processing level within the model. To measure the textual complexity from the input data, a mechanism that combines multiple well-established readability metrics widely used are combined in the function. For readability and complexity assessment metrics, we consider ARI, CLI, FOG and FRE. These metrics are selected for their diverse approaches to quantifying different aspects of linguistic structure, including sentence, syllable, and character counts, enabling a comprehensive assessment of the text.

The metrics are normalized to a common scale [0, 10] using upper and lower truncation functions to ensure that the values remain within the same range. The FRE score has a scale [0,100], while ARI, CLI, and FOG use up to 25 to consider long words and extremely complex sentences. For FRE, it was necessary to invert the original values to ensure interpretative coherence in the aggregation of the indexes, since its scale differs from the other metrics used, while the CLI, ARI, and FOG metrics associate higher values with more complex texts, the FRE assigns higher values to easier texts.

The TECO module generates two outputs: Readability Level (RL), a continuous value employed in the threshold decay formula, and a categorical indicator, Readability Grade (RG) used in the patience interval. The RL value is obtained from the scores from the input x_i that represent the text's overall readability, by Eq. 2. The readability score is computed as the average of the normalized values and is rescaled to the interval $[0, 1]$.

$$RL_i = \frac{\text{ARI}_i + \text{CLI}_i + \text{FOG}_i + \text{FRE}_i}{4} \tag{2}$$

For inference tasks that evaluate two texts, such as the MNLI, RTE, QNLI, and STS-B tasks in the GLUE benchmark, the model assesses semantic relationships between sentence pairs. The final score is defined as the average of the individual scores RL_{i1} and RL_{i2}. The RG is calculate using RL value as a scalar mapping function that normalized continuous values in the interval $[0, 1]$ to discrete output levels ranging from l_{min} to l_{max}, as defined in Eq. 3.

$$RG_i = l_{\text{min}} + RL_i \cdot (l_{\text{max}} - l_{\text{min}}) \tag{3}$$

where l_{max} represents the maximum number of layers, defining the upper bound of the categorical scale. Higher values of RG are associated with more complex instances that require deeper layers for accurate processing, while lower values correspond to simpler instances that can be classified at earlier stages.

Linear Threshold Decay. The entropy threshold at each layer is defined by a linearly decreasing function of the layer index l_i, known as Linear Threshold Decay (LTD). For each input x_i, a threshold value for each layer l_i is calculated by subtracting a proportional value to the layer index, given by $\alpha_{linear} \cdot l$. The α_{linear} value represents a constant that determines the rate of threshold decay per layer. The threshold for layer l_i is defined by the Eq. 4:

$$\tau_{l_i} = \max\left(\tau_{\min}, RL_i - \alpha_{linear} \cdot l_i\right) \tag{4}$$

This approach assumes that as the network deepens, its predictions become more reliable, and therefore the stopping criterion becomes more stringent as the depth increases, reflecting the improved and more reliable estimates of the model. The τ_{min} value was set based on the interpretation of entropy levels, where lower entropy indicates that the output distribution is more concentrated, meaning the model is confident. In contrast, higher entropy suggests that the model remains uncertain and continues adjusting its internal representation. In this configuration, the model exits earlier for easier instances while maintaining higher confidence at deeper layers, ensuring that the confidence criterion tends to become more rigorous as the model progresses through deeper layers. The value calculated by the LTD function is compared with the entropy value of the input x_i probability distribution and verified to ensure it is sufficient for the intermediate classifier. The hyperparameter α_{linear} was set to 0.05 in the experiments, and the confidence measure used is the entropy of the probability distribution, defined as the Eq. 5:

$$H(p_i) = -\sum_{c=1}^{C} p_c \log p_c \tag{5}$$

The model exits early when the entropy value drops below the threshold. For each instance x_i, a prediction is made at an intermediate layer l_i and compared to the corresponding threshold τ_{l_i}.

Patience-Based Ranged. The RG value is used as the number of times that the intermediate predictions of the internal classifiers must remain unchanged to output. RG_i represents the predefined integer to be reached for the instance x_i and is compared with a patience counter cnt that stores the number of times that the predictions remain the same in consecutive layers, calculated as:

$$cnt = \begin{cases} cnt + 1, & \text{if } H_{l_i} \leq \tau_{l_i}, \\ cnt, & \text{otherwise.} \end{cases} \tag{6}$$

When the entropy at layer l_i is below its corresponding threshold τ_{l_i}, the patient counter cnt is incremented. If the early-exit criterion is not satisfied, the model proceeds to the next layer. Once the patience condition is met, the inference process terminates early and outputs the current prediction. Instead of using a hyperparameter to define the patience, it is calculated for each instance x_i and used as the value for the patience criterion.

4 Experiments

Dataset. We conduct experiments on the proposed approach using six classification datasets from the GLUE benchmark [26] to cover a wide range of natural language understanding tasks, enabling a comprehensive evaluation across diverse text classification scenarios. The tasks selected were SST-2, MRPC, QNLI, RTE, QQP, and MNLI. We exclude the STS-B dataset because it is a regression task, and we omit the WNLI and CoLA datasets due to their small size.

Baseline Models. In our experiments, we adapted the pretrained BERT-base-uncased from Hugging Face Transformers Library [27]. BERT is employed as the backbone model with the base configuration of 12 transformer layers. We compare our approach against existing BERT early-exit methods to enable a fair evaluation relative to other strategies aimed at accelerating BERT inference.

Backbone Models. We selected BERT-base for all experiments, ensuring fair and consistent comparisons across different setups.

Static Model Compression Approach. We include DistilBERT to represent static model compression approaches using knowledge distillation. This approach reduces the size and computational cost of the original BERT model by transferring knowledge from a larger pre-trained model.

Directly Reducing Layers. Experiment directly with the first 3, 6, or 9 layers of each original BERT, ALBERT, and RoBERTa model. They represent the baseline performance, using full-layer inference without early-exit mechanisms, and therefore incur the highest computational cost.

Early-Exit Approaches. We include BERxiT, DeeBERT, PABEE, and PCEE-BERT, to compare different strategies: confident-based, patience-based, patience and confident-based, and learn-based early exiting, evaluating both predictive performance and computational speedup.

Experimental Settings. All experiments were conducted in the Google Colab environment using a single NVIDIA A100 GPU 80 GB with CUDA 12.4. Following the work [29], we use the library default hyperparameters, including optimizer, learning rate, hidden state size, and dropout probability, and preserved random seeds to ensure reproducible and fair comparisons. Training used baseline settings for hidden size, learning rate, fine-tuning schedule, and batch size, while inference was conducted with a batch size of 1.

Evaluation Metrics. To evaluate early exiting performance and to ensure comparability with existing methods, we use the speedup ratio to assess computational efficiency. This metric compares the layers processed to the total layers in the backbone model. For a model with N layers, m_i denotes the exit layer of the i-th sample. The numerator sums the executed layers, while the denominator corresponds to full-layer processing for all samples.

$$\text{Speedup Ratio} = 1 - \frac{\sum_{i=1}^{N} m_i}{\sum_{i=1}^{N} M} \quad (7)$$

The equation represents the average proportion of layers executed. Subtracting it from 1 gives the speedup ratio, which shows the relative reduction in computational cost, ranging from 0 for no acceleration to values near 1 for maximum speedup with early exits.

4.1 Main Results

We report the performance comparisons of each baseline with TECOBEE on the GLUE benchmark in Table 1. The patience interval values used in *RG* was [1–3] and for *RL* the τ_{min} value was set to 0.2. To enable a more comprehensive efficiency comparison of TECOBEE, we configured three distinct speedup settings for each approach based on the performance-efficiency trade-off. These settings were designed to demonstrate: (1) The configuration with the best performance selected, if multiple configurations show minimal degradation (<0.5%) from the baseline result, the one with the highest speedup is chosen; (2) substantial speedup with moderate performance degradation (2% - 4%); (3) maximum computational savings, prioritizing efficiency over accuracy. Based on the results presented, we highlight the following observations:

- TECOBEE consistently achieves substantial efficiency gains across all GLUE tasks. Our method achieves an average computational savings of about ≈40%, maintaining performance comparable to the baseline models, and its ability to generalize across diverse tasks further highlights its robustness and adaptability to varying linguistic and semantic contexts, as well as its efficient resource usage without sacrificing performance.
- In contrast to methods that produce a series of options with different hyperparameter values to achieve an optimal trade-off between performance and computational cost, such as DeeBERT, PABEE, and PCEE-BERT, TECOBEE achieves with a dynamic model similar levels of accuracy and accelerated inference.
- By leveraging classical readability techniques, TECOBEE provides a simple and efficient solution that avoids the time-consuming transformer pretraining required by DistilBERT, while still achieving competitive performance through fine-tuning or more complex training like BERxiT.

Table 1. Experimental results comparison between TECOBEE and different early exiting methods with BERT backbone on the GLUE benchmark. The results show that TECOBEE is effective in accelerating BERT's inference with dynamic adaptability using complexity metrics.

	MRPC		SST-2		QNLI		RTE		MNLI-(m/mm)		QQP	
	F_1	Speedup	Acc	Speedup	Acc	Speedup	Acc	Speedup	Acc	Speedup	F_1	Speedup
BERT	90.05	0.0%	92.54	0.0%	90.99	0.0%	69.67	0.0%	84.60	0.0%	91.03	0.0%
DistilBERT	89.79	50.00%	90.48	50.00%	89.23	50.00%	61.73	50.00%	82.36	50.00%	88.37	50.00%
BERT-3L	81.22	75.00%	78.44	75.00%	70.62	75.00%	52.34	75.00%	48.84	75.00%	64.99	75.00%
BERT-6L	81.93	50.00%	83.60	50.00%	82.61	50.00%	63.53	50.00%	69.35	50.00%	79.09	50.00%
BERT-9L	83.49	25.00%	90.48	25.00%	83.78	25.00%	67.87	25.00%	78.62	25.00%	83.55	25.00%
BERxiT	88.69	19.24%	91.05	30.73%	90.90	23.47%	68.59	6.31%	84.38	21.27%	90.50	23.83%
	88.13	39.09%	88.87	75.73%	87.53	63.88%	67.87	19.70%	80.92	59.25%	88.98	66.62%
	81.22	91.66%	83.71	89.19%	82.06	74.68%	64.62	43.38%	78.77	65.31%	82.13	85.51%
DeeBERT	90.05	9.64%	92.43	24.24%	90.92	21.75%	69.67	2.19%	84.38	16.74%	87.70	32.53%
	87.52	38.13%	89.44	55.80%	86.78	50.03%	67.87	6.34%	82.08	30.76%	84.87	49.55%
	84.21	58.98%	80.50	80.36%	81.69	65.66%	67.50	25.27%	78.04	41.01%	71.86	73.74%
PABEE	87.91	5.61%	91.16	19.98%	90.09	14.25%	68.42	2.13%	84.01	11.55%	87.65	33.15%
	86.38	40.15%	88.64	53.40%	86.93	55.91%	68.06	14.41%	81.75	42.62%	85.89	59.73%
	81.22	83.33%	83.25	82.29%	65.71	81.34%	53.06	79.03%	62.99	78.16%	64.45	81.92%
PCEE-BERT	89.52	22.77%	91.85	59.34%	90.51	22.04%	68.42	48.31%	84.16	18.13%	87.77	29.01%
	87.76	49.71%	87.95	76.56%	89.20	45.74%	68.08	43.88%	82.16	51.10%	85.85	64.58%
	87.52	53.63%	85.09	88.53%	86.65	66.50%	66.42	10.77%	79.90	62.16%	79.45	78.44%
TECOBEE	89.22	27.32%	89.53	51.59%	90.24	40.40%	68.23	30.27%	83.86	32.50%	87.31	49.16%

Ablation of Different Patience Range and Limiar Configurations. Experiments were conducted to evaluate the impact of different $\tau_{\min}$ values in the LTD function and different patience range intervals for RG value. The experiment for $\tau_{\min}$ in TECOBEE uses the set of values $\{0.0, 0.2, 0.4\}$ to analyze the effect and its influence on the overall performance of the model using [1–3] patience interval range. Lower $\tau_{\min}$ values indicate a lower entropy bound for the function, giving the model more confidence in its predictions, while higher $\tau_{\min}$ values increase the lower bound of the LTD function, leading to earlier outputs and potentially lower accuracy. The results are presented in Table 2 and indicate that increasing $\tau_{\min}$ from 0.0 to 0.4 results in a gradual decline in the score, accompanied by a substantial rise in speedup, which impacts the balance between performance and efficiency.

Moderate thresholds such as $\tau_{min} = 0.2$ balance accuracy and efficiency, QQP, QNLI, and SST-2 highlighting robustness and effective control of the accuracy–efficiency trade-off. The experiment in TECOBEE with different configurations for RG value is presented in Table 3 with intervals [1–3], [1–6], [3–8], and [1–12] using τ_{min} with 0.2.

Expanding the range intervals in TECOBEE produced small gains in F_1 and accuracy across tasks, but at a substantial cost to inference efficiency. As the interval widened from [1–3] to [1–12], speedup dropped $\approx 38\%$ on average over

Table 2. Comparison of TECOBEE model performance across GLUE tasks under different confidence thresholds ($\tau = 0.0, 0.2,$ and 0.4), illustrating the trade-off between performance and computational efficiency.

τ	MRPC		SST-2		QNLI		RTE		MNLI		QQP	
	F_1	Speedup	Acc	Speedup	Acc	Speedup	Acc	Speedup	Acc	Speedup	F_1	Speedup
0.0	84.55	10.45%	88.99	49.93%	90.18	32.62%	68.59	12.06%	83.96	12.38%	87.42	22.63%
0.2	89.22	27.32%	89.53	51.59%	90.24	40.40%	68.23	30.27%	83.86	32.50%	87.31	49.16%
0.4	83.57	34.62%	87.38	57.36%	89.56	46.88%	68.59	39.80%	83.31	43.81%	86.35	59.78%

Table 3. Comparison of TECOBEE model performance across GLUE tasks under different varying patience range intervals ([1–3], [1–6], [3–8], and [1–12]), the influence of interval width on performance and computational efficiency.

Range	MRPC		SST-2		QNLI		RTE		MNLI		QQP	
	F_1	Speedup	Acc	Speedup	Acc	Speedup	Acc	Speedup	Acc	Speedup	F_1	Speedup
[1–3]	89.22	27.32%	89.53	51.59%	90.24	40.40%	68.23	30.27%	83.86	32.50%	87.31	49.16%
[1–6]	89.37	17.09%	89.56	45.47%	90.44	29.49%	68.59	20.51%	84.03	25.01%	87.65	42.35%
[3–8]	89.52	7.08%	91.39	43.85%	90.48	16.52%	68.59	8.93%	84.11	13.94%	87.75	28.57%
[1–12]	89.52	5.82%	91.39	44.92%	90.48	14.40%	68.59	7.37%	84.11	13.94%	87.75	33.02%

the tasks while performance improved by less than $\approx 2\%$ overall. This pattern shows that larger intervals promote more stable and consistent model behavior, enhancing robustness and slightly improving conventional metrics. Nevertheless, this comes with a loss in computational efficiency, emphasizing the inherent trade-off between maintaining high performance stability and preserving the adaptive, lightweight nature of the model.

Ablation of TECO Applied Exclusively to Patience-Based or Confidence-Based. TECOBEE integrates the Patience-Based and Confidence-Based approaches, derived from DeeBERT [28] and PABEE [32], respectively. To further assess its effectiveness and enable a controlled evaluation of its individual contribution, we conducted ablation experiments where TECO was applied independently to DeeBERT and PABEE in Table 4. In these settings, the DeeBERT was implemented using the LTD function, experiments were conducted by varying the threshold $\{0.0, 0.2, 0.4\}$ to examine its impact on model behavior. For PABEE experiments, the patience-ranged method was employed by varying the patience range across [1–3], [1–6], [3–8], and [1–12] intervals to evaluate how range size influences model performance and computational trade-offs. All configurations were evaluated on GLUE benchmark tasks to provide a consistent and comprehensive comparison.

In DeeBERT, increasing τ_{min} enhanced speedup, showing strong gains in computational efficiency while maintaining competitive accuracy, with only minor drops in performance across tasks such as MRPC and SST-2. This suggests

Table 4. Comparison of DeeBERT model under varying confidence thresholds ($\tau = 0.0$, 0.2, and 0.4) and PABEE model under varying range intervals ([1–3], [1–6], [3–8], and [1–12]), illustrating their respective trade-offs between performance and computational efficiency across GLUE tasks.

Config	MRPC		SST-2		QNLI		RTE		MNLI		QQP	
	F_1	Speedup	Acc	Speedup	Acc	Speedup	Acc	Speedup	Acc	Speedup	F_1	Speedup
						DeeBERT						
0.0	89.61	10.35%	87.38	47.15%	89.51	20.14%	68.95	4.96%	84.49	4.86%	86.93	15.42%
0.2	89.77	17.09%	87.04	63.14%	89.41	29.19%	68.95	6.28%	84.24	17.67%	86.83	35.06%
0.4	87.62	33.10%	85.66	70.66%	87.82	42.62%	67.14	9.98%	83.10	26.42%	84.40	50.27%
						PABEE						
[1–3]	81.22	75.71%	86.35	73.94%	82.64	67.52%	66.45	51.83%	71.92	68.26%	74.17	75.80%
[1–6]	82.12	64.56%	89.10	61.90%	86.50	53.11%	68.42	37.00%	77.28	55.39%	81.44	66.97%
[3–8]	86.95	40.64%	91.51	43.54%	88.81	34.79%	68.62	19.52%	82.47	35.07%	86.72	47.77%
[1–12]	85.83	40.82%	91.05	42.90%	88.92	32.13%	67.34	17.53%	80.79	19.54%	84.19	54.52%

that larger τ_{min} values enable faster inference without severely compromising model quality. In PABEE, higher patience intervals improved task-specific metrics like QQP and QNLI accuracy but substantially reduced speedup, highlighting that performance stability was achieved at the expense of efficiency. Overall, these results emphasize the trade-off between inference speed and predictive performance when tuning early-exit parameters. The proposed TECO method can also be individually applied to both DeeBERT and PABEE approaches, as they achieve competitive performance and acceleration compared to the baseline configurations. This demonstrates the flexibility and generalization across different early-exit strategies, enabling dynamic control over the model.

Table 5. Results for ablation study of TECOBEE with ALBERT as backbone on GLUE tasks.

Model	MRPC		SST-2		QNLI	
	F_1	Speedup	Acc	Speedup	Acc	Speedup
ALBERT	89.27	0.0%	90.94	0.0%	90.84	0.0%
PCEE-BERT	90.32	52.45%	92.20	57.50%	91.76	31.28%
	89.59	60.88%	89.44	82.87%	90.31	68.49%
	85.03	80.12%	86.35	86.21%	88.26	75.68%
TECOBEE	89.59	60.82%	91.85	69.89%	91.67	48.67%

Ablation of PLM Backbones. In addition to the baseline BERT-base, we extend our evaluation to include the ALBERT [13] to analyze how different architectures impact performance and inference efficiency. We perform TECOBEE using ALBERT on the MRPC, SST-2 and QNLI tasks from GLUE to assess their generalization across different natural language understanding scenarios, and the results are presented in Table 5. TECOBEE consistently outperforms the baseline approach. Furthermore, the results show that maintain baseline results across all evaluated tasks, indicating a balance between performance and resource utilization while maintaining strong predictive capability.

5 Conclusion and Future Work

In order to reduce the lack of adaptability and eliminate the need for manual hyperparameter selection, we proposed TECOBEE, a novel efficient inference method that calculates the text complexity of the input to adjust the computational inference to better performance-acceleration trade-off. Experiments on the GLUE benchmark demonstrate the effectiveness of the TECO approach compared with previous SOTA early exiting methods. In addition, ablation studies show that (a) TECOBEE can adopt different readability metrics; (b) our method performs consistently well on different PLMs to speed up dynamically the inference; (c) by leveraging well-established readability metrics, it offers a straightforward yet simple and highly efficient solution that achieves competitive performance without the need for complex model architectures or extensive additional training. The current evaluation employs classical text readability metrics to assess the distribution of linguistic information, yet it is limited to observing how this information is spread across layers and does not account for the fact that certain layers contribute more than others to lexical and syntactic knowledge within the model. For future work extend the experimental conditions configurations in order to evaluate the robustness and generalization generalization potential and adding a pre-training step would be a promising direction for enhancing the model across diverse tasks.

References

1. Bolukbasi, T., Wang, J., Dekel, O., Saligrama, V.: Adaptive neural networks for efficient inference. In: International Conference on Machine Learning, pp. 527–536. PMLR (2017)
2. Coleman, M., Liau, T.L.: A computer readability formula designed for machine scoring. J. Appl. Psychol. **60**(2), 283 (1975)
3. Crossley, S.A., Skalicky, S., Dascalu, M., McNamara, D.S., Kyle, K.: Predicting text comprehension, processing, and familiarity in adult readers: new approaches to readability formulas. Discourse Process. **54**(5–6), 340–359 (2017)
4. Devlin, J., Chang, M.W., Lee, K., Toutanova, K.: BERT: pre-training of deep bidirectional transformers for language understanding. In: Proceedings of the 2019 Conference of the North American Chapter of the Association for Computational Linguistics: Human Language Technologies (Volume 1: Long and Short Papers), pp. 4171–4186 (2019)

5. Gao, X., Zhu, W., Gao, J., Yin, C.: F-pabee: flexible-patience-based early exiting for single-label and multi-label text classification tasks. In: 2023 IEEE International Conference on Acoustics, Speech and Signal Processing (ICASSP), ICASSP 2023, pp. 1–5. IEEE (2023)
6. Gunning, R.: The technique of clear writing (1952)
7. Hinton, G., Vinyals, O., Dean, J.: Distilling the knowledge in a neural network. arXiv preprint arXiv:1503.02531 (2015)
8. Hu, B., Zhu, Y., Li, J., Tang, S.: Smartbert: a promotion of dynamic early exiting mechanism for accelerating BERT inference. arXiv preprint arXiv:2303.09266 (2023)
9. Jiao, X., et al.: Tinybert: distilling BERT for natural language understanding. arXiv preprint arXiv:1909.10351 (2019)
10. Kaya, Y., Hong, S., Dumitras, T.: Shallow-deep networks: understanding and mitigating network overthinking. In: International Conference on Machine Learning, pp. 3301–3310. PMLR (2019)
11. Kim, S., Gholami, A., Yao, Z., Mahoney, M.W., Keutzer, K.: I-BERT: integer-only BERT quantization. In: International Conference on Machine Learning, pp. 5506–5518. PMLR (2021)
12. Kincaid, J.P., Fishburne, R.P., Jr., Rogers, R.L., Chissom, B.S.: Derivation of new readability formulas (automated readability index, fog count and flesch reading ease formula) for navy enlisted personnel. Technical report, Naval Air Station Memphis, Research Branch (1975)
13. Lan, Z., Chen, M., Goodman, S., Gimpel, K., Sharma, P., Soricut, R.: Albert: a lite BERT for self-supervised learning of language representations. In: International Conference on Learning Representations (ICLR) (2019). https://openreview.net/forum?id=H1eA7AEtvS
14. Liu, W., Zhou, P., Zhao, Z., Wang, Z., Deng, H., Ju, Q.: Fastbert: a self-distilling BERT with adaptive inference time. arXiv preprint arXiv:2004.02178 (2020)
15. Liu, Y., et al.: Roberta: a robustly optimized BERT pretraining approach. arXiv preprint arXiv:1907.11692 (2019)
16. Martinc, M., Pollak, S., Robnik-Šikonja, M.: Supervised and unsupervised neural approaches to text readability. Comput. Linguist. **47**(1), 141–179 (2021)
17. Michel, P., Levy, O., Neubig, G.: Are sixteen heads really better than one? In: Advances in Neural Information Processing Systems, p. 32 (2019)
18. Ribeiro, L.F., Bansal, M., Dreyer, M.: Generating summaries with controllable readability levels. arXiv preprint arXiv:2310.10623 (2023)
19. Sanh, V., Debut, L., Chaumond, J., Wolf, T.: Distilbert, a distilled version of BERT: smaller, faster, cheaper and lighter. arXiv preprint arXiv:1910.01108 (2019)
20. Shen, S., et al.: Q-BERT: hessian based ultra low precision quantization of BERT. In: Proceedings of the AAAI Conference on Artificial Intelligence, vol. 34, pp. 8815–8821 (2020)
21. Smith, E.A., Senter, R.: Automated readability index, vol. 66. Aerospace Medical Research Laboratories, Aerospace Medical Division, Air ... (1967)
22. Teerapittayanon, S., McDanel, B., Kung, H.T.: Branchynet: fast inference via early exiting from deep neural networks. In: 2016 23rd International Conference on Pattern Recognition (ICPR), pp. 2464–2469. IEEE (2016)
23. Tran, H., Yao, Z., Li, L., Yu, H.: Readctrl: personalizing text generation with readability-controlled instruction learning. arXiv preprint arXiv:2406.09205 (2024)
24. Vajjala, S.: Trends, limitations and open challenges in automatic readability assessment research. In: Proceedings of the Thirteenth Language Resources and Evaluation Conference, pp. 5366–5377 (2022)

25. Vaswani, A., et al.: Attention is all you need. In: Advances in Neural Information Processing Systems, vol. 30 (2017)
26. Wang, A., Singh, A., Michael, J., Hill, F., Levy, O., Bowman, S.R.: Glue: a multi-task benchmark and analysis platform for natural language understanding. arXiv preprint arXiv:1804.07461 (2018)
27. Wolf, T., et al.: Transformers: state-of-the-art natural language processing. In: Proceedings of the 2020 Conference on Empirical Methods in Natural Language Processing: System Demonstrations, pp. 38–45 (2020)
28. Xin, J., Tang, R., Lee, J., Yu, Y., Lin, J.: Deebert: dynamic early exiting for accelerating BERT inference. arXiv preprint arXiv:2004.12993 (2020)
29. Xin, J., Tang, R., Yu, Y., Lin, J.: Berxit: early exiting for BERT with better fine-tuning and extension to regression. In: Proceedings of the 16th Conference of the European Chapter of the Association for Computational Linguistics: Main Volume, pp. 91–104 (2021)
30. Yang, Z., Dai, Z., Yang, Y., Carbonell, J., Salakhutdinov, R.R., Le, Q.V.: Xlnet: generalized autoregressive pretraining for language understanding. In: Advances in Neural Information Processing Systems, vol. 32 (2019)
31. Zhang, Z., Zhu, W., Zhang, J., Wang, P., Jin, R., Chung, T.S.: PCEE-BERT: accelerating BERT inference via patient and confident early exiting. In: Findings of the Association for Computational Linguistics: NAACL 2022, pp. 327–338 (2022)
32. Zhou, W., Xu, C., Ge, T., McAuley, J., Xu, K., Wei, F.: Bert loses patience: fast and robust inference with early exit. Adv. Neural. Inf. Process. Syst. **33**, 18330–18341 (2020)
33. Zhu, W.: Leebert: learned early exit for BERT with cross-level optimization. In: Proceedings of the 59th Annual Meeting of the Association for Computational Linguistics and the 11th International Joint Conference on Natural Language Processing (Volume 1: Long Papers), pp. 2968–2980 (2021)

DyFO: Heterogeneous Temporal Graph Attention with Typed Edge Conditioning for Financial Co-movement Forecasting

Igor Felipe Carboni Battazza[1,2](✉), João Fausto L. de Oliveira[2], and Cleyton Mário de Oliveira Rodrigues[2]

[1] Polytechnic School of Pernambuco, University of Pernambuco (POLI/UPE), Recife, Brazil
battazza@gmail.com

[2] FITec – Technological Innovations, Recife, Brazil

Abstract. Forecasting dynamic financial co-movements requires integrating asynchronous heterogeneous signals into a continuous-time relational model. We propose DyFO (Dynamic Financial Observer), a non-recurrent Temporal Graph Attention Network for next-day pairwise correlation forecasting over a heterogeneous financial graph with three typed edge classes: DCC-GARCH dynamic correlations (CORR), GICS sector links (SECT), and Fama–French five-factor co-loadings (FACT). A key contribution is a relation-aware graph attention layer that conditions attention weights on typed edge embeddings, preventing the homogeneous treatment of structurally heterogeneous neighbours and mitigating the attention-dilution failure of standard single-type graph attention. Evaluated on 50 S&P 500 constituents spanning all 11 GICS sectors (2018–2024) under a nine-window walk-forward protocol with 1,093 out-of-sample days, DyFO achieves strong predictive accuracy ($R^2 = 0.893$, Spearman $\rho = 0.958$, MAE = 0.035, classification F1 = 0.793), outperforming a recurrent Temporal Graph Network, a snapshot-based temporal baseline, and a static graph attention network across all windows. Diebold–Mariano tests with Newey–West HAC correction indicate statistically significant prediction-level gains, with all prediction-level comparisons surviving Holm–Bonferroni correction. As a secondary diagnostic analysis, we also evaluate whether improved correlation forecasts translate into Global Minimum Variance portfolio performance. Paired block-bootstrap tests show that Sharpe-ratio differences are not statistically distinguishable, suggesting that classical mean–variance allocation may not directly exploit improvements in covariance forecast quality, highlighting the need for decision-aware allocation mechanisms to convert forecasting gains into portfolio utility.

1 Introduction

The degree to which asset prices move together—their *co-movement*—is the raw material of risk management. When two holdings rise and fall in tandem,

M. Recamonde-Mendoza and R. C. Barros (Eds.): BRACIS 2026, LNAI 17105, pp. 371–385, 2027.
https://doi.org/10.1007/978-3-032-39882-6_25

holding both provides little diversification; when they move independently or in opposition, combining them reduces portfolio variance. Pairwise correlations therefore drive position sizing, hedging, and risk budgeting, and an investor who anticipates how the correlation structure will shift *tomorrow*—for instance, the tendency of equities to become jointly correlated during a market shock—can rebalance defensively before the move rather than after. Yet these correlations are not static: they strengthen during crises and relax in calm regimes, so forecasting their next-day evolution, rather than assuming yesterday's values persist, is of direct practical value.

Forecasting financial co-movements is a central problem in empirical finance, risk modelling, and portfolio construction. Classical baselines such as persistence (naive forecast) and Exponentially Weighted Moving Average (EWMA) remain competitive diagnostic reference points because they are simple, transparent, and exploit the strong autocorrelation present in rolling pairwise correlations. However, they operate on a target-dependent information set: the lagged correlation state ρ_{ij}^{t} must already be observed at inference time, and they have no mechanism to incorporate asynchronous structural signals such as sector membership, factor co-loadings, or event-driven shocks. This creates a fundamental limitation for systems that seek to exploit causal, non-lagged signals for forward-looking predictions. We therefore treat persistence and EWMA not as competing baselines but as target-dependent reference points: DyFO deliberately forgoes the lagged correlation state to remain applicable when the previous-day matrix is unreliable or absent, as at the regime breaks examined in Sect. 4. A diagnostic comparison quantifying the predictive headroom above this trivial autocorrelation is left for future work.

Recent years have witnessed growing interest in graph-based models for financial markets. Companies are represented as nodes and inter-company relations as edges, and graph neural networks learn asset representations for prediction or portfolio construction. Representative examples include the temporal relational ranking of Feng et al. [4] and the cross-asset attention network of AlphaStock [15]. While these approaches demonstrate the value of relational information, many operate on static graphs or optimise downstream trading decisions directly.

In this paper we introduce **DyFO** (Dynamic Financial Observer)[1], a relation-aware temporal graph architecture for next-day pairwise correlation forecasting. DyFO operates on a dynamic heterogeneous financial graph whose edges encode three complementary sources of co-movement information: DCC-GARCH correlations (CORR), GICS sector links (SECT), and Fama–French five-factor co-loadings (FACT). Market activity is modelled as a continuous stream of typed events, including price updates, earnings releases, macro surprises, and Federal Reserve decisions. A non-recurrent Temporal Graph Attention Network (TGAT) [18] encodes recent events through bounded-history attention over per-node event buffers, while a relation-aware graph attention layer aggregates information over typed structural neighbourhoods. The resulting node embeddings

[1] Source code available at https://github.com/cyb3rpunk/DyFO.

are decoded into next-day pairwise correlation forecasts *without* direct dependence on the previous-day correlation matrix.

Our empirical results show that DyFO improves prediction-level accuracy over recurrent, snapshot-based, and static graph baselines across all nine walk-forward windows. The improvement is confirmed by Diebold–Mariano tests, Wilcoxon signed-rank tests, and Newey–West HAC standard errors on out-of-sample forecasting errors. As a secondary diagnostic, we assess whether these prediction-level gains translate into downstream portfolio utility under a standard Global Minimum Variance (GMV) allocation rule; paired block-bootstrap tests show that the Sharpe-ratio differences are not statistically distinguishable, indicating that classical mean–variance allocation does not directly exploit the improved covariance forecasts. We frame DyFO primarily as a correlation forecasting architecture, and present the portfolio analysis as an exploratory downstream diagnostic rather than a primary contribution.

The main contributions of this work are threefold:

- We propose a domain-adapted Temporal Graph Attention Network (TGAT) [18] for continuous-time financial event streams, extending the original homogeneous formulation with three key innovations: (i) typed edge embeddings that distinguish correlation, sector, and factor relations; (ii) a heterogeneous event vocabulary with domain-specific feature vectors; and (iii) a continuous regression decoder for next-day pairwise correlation forecasting. The resulting non-recurrent architecture avoids recurrent memory updates and backpropagation through time, while enabling accurate predictions on a dynamic heterogeneous financial graph.
- We integrate three complementary edge types (dynamic correlations, sector membership, and factor co-loadings) and quantify their marginal contributions through ablation, showing that factor co-loadings yield the largest and statistically significant gain while the full heterogeneous graph remains the empirically competitive configuration.
- We provide a statistically grounded evaluation of graph-based correlation forecasting models via Diebold–Mariano tests, Wilcoxon signed-rank tests, and Newey–West HAC standard errors, showing that prediction-level gains are robust across all nine walk-forward windows.

The remainder of the paper is organised as follows. Section 2 reviews related work on graph-based and temporal models for financial markets. Section 3 formalises the problem and details the DyFO architecture. Section 4 presents the experimental setup and main results. Finally, Sect. 5 concludes and outlines future research directions.

2 Related Work

Portfolio management has traditionally been addressed through two complementary lines of research: classical optimisation techniques and, more recently, data-driven learning methods.

Classical Approaches. Markowitz's mean-variance framework [8] remains the foundation of modern portfolio theory. The Fama–French five-factor model [3] captures systematic risk exposures, while for dynamic settings Engle's DCC-GARCH model [2] provides time-varying conditional correlations that remain a strong industry baseline. These methods, however, treat pairwise relationships in isolation and cannot exploit higher-order relational structures among companies.

Graph-Based Methods in Finance. Prior graph-based financial models, including AlphaStock [15], HATS [7], DeepPocket [13], and GPM [12], use sectoral, ownership, topical, or correlation links for ranking and portfolio decisions. In contrast, DyFO targets next-day pairwise correlation forecasting, enabling direct evaluation of the learned covariance structure.

Temporal Graph Networks and TGAT. TGN [10] maintains per-node GRU memory updated continuously as events arrive, while TGAT [18] offers a stateless alternative via functional time encoding and multi-head attention over temporal neighbourhoods. ROLAND [20] operates on discrete graph snapshots with EMA state propagation. All three were designed for homogeneous graphs with a single edge type, lack domain-specific event representations, and target link classification rather than continuous pairwise correlation regression. More recent finance-specific architectures combine temporal and heterogeneous modelling: THGNN [17] couples a Transformer temporal encoder with graph attention over daily-rebuilt correlation graphs, while TCGPN [19] introduces a temporal-correlation fusion encoder with graph pre-training. These methods, however, target stock *movement* classification or price ranking rather than the causal, next-day pairwise *correlation regression* addressed here; we therefore adopt TGN, ROLAND, and GAT_STATIC as baselines because they cleanly isolate the three temporal-graph paradigms (recurrent memory, snapshot, and static attention) against which DyFO's bounded-history attention is contrasted.

DyFO thus combines the temporal modelling of TGAT with the typed relational attention of heterogeneous GNNs, extending them with (i) typed edge embeddings distinguishing `CORR`, `SECT`, and `FACT` relations; (ii) a heterogeneous event vocabulary with domain-specific feature vectors; and (iii) a continuous regression decoder with tanh activation for pairwise correlation forecasting.

Heterogeneous Graph Neural Networks. Conditioning message passing or attention on edge types is well established in the heterogeneous-GNN literature. R-GCN [11] introduces relation-specific weight matrices, RGAT [1] extends graph attention with relation-aware coefficients, and HAN [16] and HGT [5] employ type-specific projections and semantic-level attention over heterogeneous neighbourhoods. DyFO's relation-aware attention layer (Eq. (3)) is an instance of this family rather than a new attention mechanism in isolation. Its contribution is the integration of typed relational attention with *continuous-time* event-driven temporal modelling and a *continuous correlation-regression* objective: the heterogeneous-GNN methods above are predominantly static and target node or edge classification, whereas DyFO conditions attention on typed edges within a bounded-history temporal architecture and decodes the full next-day pairwise correlation matrix. To our knowledge, this specific combination has not been applied to causal financial co-movement forecasting.

3 Methodology

As shown in Fig. 1, DyFO combines event-driven temporal updates with heterogeneous graph structure to predict next-day pairwise correlations. The model constructs typed event messages, summarises each node's recent event history via temporal attention over per-node ring buffers, computes node embeddings through a *relation-aware* heterogeneous graph attention layer, and finally decodes pairwise correlations for downstream portfolio evaluation.

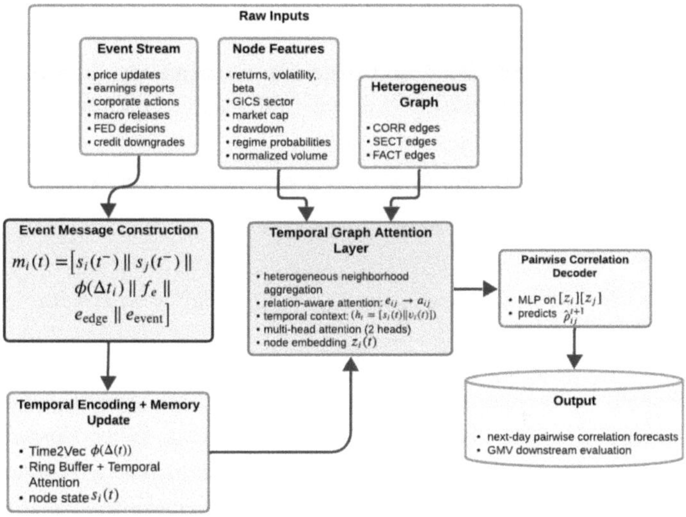

Fig. 1. Overview of DyFO. Typed financial events are encoded into node-level ring buffers and summarised by temporal attention. The resulting temporal summaries, node features, and typed structural edges (CORR, SECT, FACT) are processed by a relation-aware graph attention layer and decoded into next-day pairwise correlation forecasts.

3.1 Problem Formulation

Let $\mathcal{G} = (\mathcal{V}, \mathcal{E})$ be a heterogeneous financial graph where each node $v_i \in \mathcal{V}$ represents a publicly traded asset. We model market activity as a continuous stream of typed events $\{(s, r, t, \mathbf{f}_e)\}$, where $s, r \in \mathcal{V}$ are the source and (optional) target nodes, $t \in \mathbb{R}^+$ is a continuous timestamp, and $\mathbf{f}_e \in \mathbb{R}^{d_e}$ is an event feature vector.

The learning objective is next-day correlation prediction: given all events up to and including day t, predict the pairwise Pearson correlation ρ_{ij}^{t+1} for all asset pairs (i, j) on day $t + 1$. This formulation is causally valid by construction—no label information from day $t + 1$ is visible at inference time.

3.2 Dataset

Universe. The choice of $N = 50$ balances market coverage and computational tractability: preliminary single-window scaling tests with $N \in \{30, 50, 100\}$ showed that predictive accuracy improves from 30 to 50 assets and remains stable from 50 to 100 assets, although this diagnostic is descriptive rather than a formal statistical comparison.

Period. Daily data from 2018-01-01 to 2024-12-31 (7 years, approximately 1,760 trading days). Adjusted closing prices are sourced from Yahoo Finance via `yfinance`.

Walk-Forward Protocol. Nine non-overlapping windows (500 train/125 validation/125 test days, step 125), yielding 1,093 out-of-sample days spanning 2018–2024.

Event Stream. The event stream carries seven event types (Table 1), each with a three-dimensional feature vector $\mathbf{f}_e = [magnitude,\ direction,\ relative\_size]$.

Table 1. Event types in the DyFO financial event stream.

Event Type	Description	Source
`PRICE_UPDATE`	Daily log-return signal	Yahoo Finance
`EARNINGS_REPORT`	Earnings release date	Yahoo Finance
`CORP_ACTION`	Dividend/stock split	Yahoo Finance
`CORRELATION_UPDATE`	DCC-GARCH ρ threshold crossing	Estimated (Sect. 3.3)
`MACRO_RELEASE`	Macro surprise ($> 1.5\sigma$)	FRED API
`FED_DECISION`	Federal funds rate change	FRED API
`CREDIT_DOWNGRADE`	OAS spread shock	FRED API

3.3 Correlation Target (DCC-GARCH)

Correlation labels are estimated via the Dynamic Conditional Correlation (DCC) - Generalized Autoregressive Conditional Heteroskedasticity GARCH(1,1) model of Engle (2002), fitted over a rolling 252-day window. Let ϵ_t be the vector of standardised GARCH(1,1) residuals. The conditional correlation matrix follows:

$$Q_t = (1 - a - b)\,\bar{Q} + a\,\epsilon_{t-1}\epsilon_{t-1}^{\top} + b\,Q_{t-1} \tag{1a}$$

$$R_t = \mathrm{diag}(Q_t)^{-1/2}\, Q_t\, \mathrm{diag}(Q_t)^{-1/2} \tag{1b}$$

where $\bar{Q}$ is the unconditional covariance matrix estimated over the training window. DCC-GARCH is preferred over rolling Pearson because it captures volatility clustering and provides time-varying estimates robust to heteroskedastic returns.

For the event stream, `CORRELATION_UPDATE` events are emitted whenever $|\rho_{ij}^t| \geq 0.3$ (sparsification threshold). Regression labels use the unsparsified DCC series to preserve continuous signal for all pairs.

3.4 Node Features

Each asset v_i is described by a 20-dimensional time-varying feature vector $\mathbf{v}_i(t)$:

$$\mathbf{v}_i(t) = \left[\underbrace{r_{21d},\ \sigma_{21d},\ \beta_{63d}}_{\text{market signals}},\ \underbrace{\mathbf{s}_i}_{\text{GICS one-hot, 11d}},\ \underbrace{\tilde{m}_i}_{\text{log mcap}},\ \underbrace{dd_i(t)}_{\text{drawdown}},\ \underbrace{\boldsymbol{\pi}_i(t)}_{\text{regime probs, 3d}},\ \underbrace{\tilde{v}_i(t)}_{\text{vol/avg}} \right]$$

where r_{21d}, σ_{21d}, β_{63d} are 21-day return, volatility, and 63-day beta; $\mathbf{s}_i$ is the GICS one-hot encoding (11d); $\tilde{m}_i$ is normalised log market cap; $dd_i(t)$ is drawdown from peak; $\boldsymbol{\pi}_i(t)$ is a 3-d regime probability vector; and $\tilde{v}_i(t)$ is volume normalised by its 21-day mean.

3.5 Graph Structure and Edge Types

The static graph $\mathcal{G}$ contains three types of edges, as summarised in Table 2. Every edge type is embedded into a shared $d_{\text{edge}} = 16$ dimensional space through a learned `Embedding` table. Critically, these embeddings serve a dual role: they are concatenated into the temporal message during event encoding *and* passed as edge attributes to the structural graph attention layer, where they modulate attention weights on a per-relation basis (see Sect. 3.6).

Table 2. Edge types used in the static graph $\mathcal{G}$.

Type	Description	Construction
`CORR`	Dynamic pairwise correlation	DCC-GARCH, $\lvert\rho\rvert \geq 0.3$
`SECT`	Same GICS sector	Binary indicator
`FACT`	Fama-French 5-factor co-loading	FF5 loading cosine ≥ 0.5

3.6 DyFO Architecture

As summarised in Fig. 2, each node combines event-driven temporal messages with typed structural context to produce its embedding. DyFO builds on the non-recurrent Temporal Graph Attention Network (TGAT) of [18], which replaces

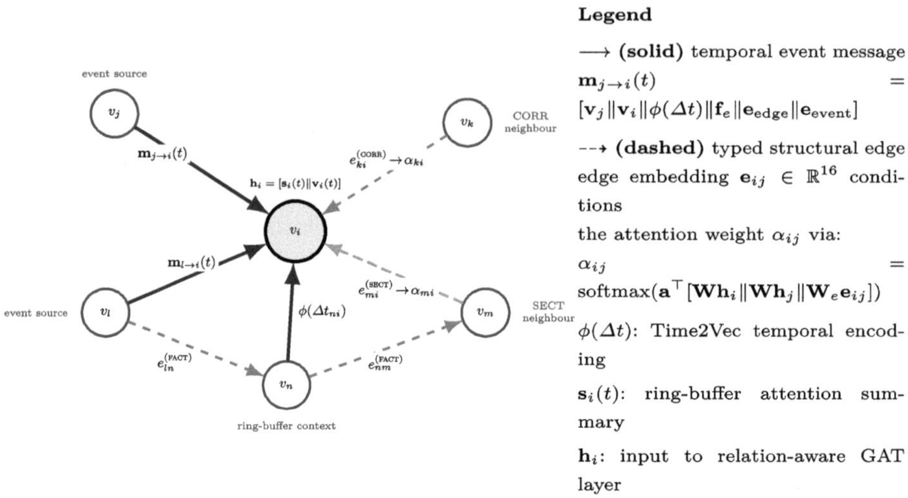

Fig. 2. Message passing in DyFO's heterogeneous temporal graph. The central node v_i receives two classes of information: *(i)* event-driven messages (solid arrows) from neighbouring nodes, each encoding node states, a Time2Vec time gap $\phi(\Delta t)$, event features $\mathbf{f}_e$, and typed edge/event embeddings; these messages populate the per-node ring buffer and are summarised into $\mathbf{s}_i(t)$ via temporal multi-head attention. *(ii)* Structural context (dashed arrows) from typed graph edges (CORR, SECT, FACT), whose 16-dimensional embeddings $\mathbf{e}_{ij}$ are concatenated into the attention logit of the relation-aware GATConv layer, allowing the model to suppress attention towards redundant neighbours (e.g. dense SECT edges) and amplify it towards informative ones (e.g. CORR, FACT).

recurrent node-memory updates with direct temporal attention over recent interactions stored in bounded per-node event buffers.

DyFO extends the original TGAT architecture—initially designed for homogeneous graphs and binary link prediction—in four main respects. First, the message function incorporates typed edge embeddings, $\mathbf{e}_{\text{edge}} \in \mathbb{R}^{16}$, and event-type embeddings, $\mathbf{e}_{\text{event}} \in \mathbb{R}^{16}$, allowing the model to learn type-specific temporal patterns, such as distinguishing an earnings report from a macroeconomic surprise. Second, node attributes are represented as 20-dimensional time-varying feature vectors, as described in Sect. 3.4. Third, the structural attention layer is made *relation-aware* by conditioning attention scores on typed edge embeddings through a projection matrix $\mathbf{W}_e$; this component is analysed in Sect. 4.4. Fourth, the decoder is adapted to output continuous correlation forecasts in the interval $[-1, 1]$ through a tanh activation function. The resulting pipeline for each trading day t is described as follows.

Event Ring Buffer. Each node maintains a fixed-capacity ring buffer of its most recent events. Rather than propagating a recurrent memory vector, recent historical events are attended to directly at inference time.

Message Function. For each event $(i, j, t, \mathbf{f}_e)$, a raw message for the source node is:

$$\mathbf{m}_i(t) = \left[\mathbf{v}_i(t^-) \parallel \mathbf{v}_j(t^-) \parallel \phi(\Delta t_i) \parallel \mathbf{f}_e \parallel \mathbf{e}_{\text{edge}} \parallel \mathbf{e}_{\text{event}}\right] \in \mathbb{R}^{175} \quad (2)$$

where $\phi(\Delta t) \in \mathbb{R}^{100}$ is the Time2Vec encoding [6] of the elapsed time since node i's last event, and $\mathbf{v}_j(t^-)$ is replaced with $\mathbf{0}$ for node-only events (target $= -1$). A symmetric message is computed for the target node j.

Temporal Attention over Buffer. The network applies a multi-head temporal attention mechanism over the messages stored in the event ring buffer. This produces a feedforward summary representation of the node's recent temporal history. Thus, DyFO is not stateless in the strict sense, since it retains a bounded event buffer, but it is free from recurrent hidden-state updates and backpropagation through time.

Unified Aggregation. Source and target summary vectors are pooled and aggregated via mean, ensuring that nodes appearing as both source and target within the same daily batch receive a single coherent context representation. The mean aggregator is mandatory for broadcast events such as `FED_DECISION`, where all N nodes receive an event at the identical timestamp; using a `last`-based aggregator in this setting would introduce order-dependent, non-deterministic updates.

Relation-Aware Graph Attention Embedding. Node embeddings are computed by a single-layer multi-head graph attention network (GATConv 2 heads) over the static heterogeneous neighbourhood. Critically, the attention weight between node i and neighbour j is conditioned on the typed edge embedding $\mathbf{e}_{ij} \in \mathbb{R}^{16}$:

$$\alpha_{ij} = \text{softmax}_j\left(\text{LeakyReLU}\left(\mathbf{a}^\top \left[\mathbf{W}\mathbf{h}_i \parallel \mathbf{W}\mathbf{h}_j \parallel \mathbf{W}_e\mathbf{e}_{ij}\right]\right)\right) \quad (3)$$

where $\mathbf{W}$, $\mathbf{W}_e$, and $\mathbf{a}$ are learned parameters, and $\mathbf{h}_i = [\mathbf{s}_i(t) \parallel \mathbf{v}_i(t)] \in \mathbb{R}^{192}$ is the concatenation of the temporal summary and the time-varying node feature vector. The final node embedding is:

$$\mathbf{z}_i(t) = \text{MLP}\left(\mathbf{h}_i \parallel \sum_{j \in \mathcal{N}(i)} \alpha_{ij}\,\mathbf{W}\mathbf{h}_j\right) \in \mathbb{R}^{100} \quad (4)$$

This relation-aware formulation resolves an attention-dilution failure mode that arises under standard homogeneous graph attention. Without edge conditioning, the GATConv layer treats edges of type `CORR`, `SECT`, and `FACT` as structurally identical neighbours. When the static `SECT` edges (dense, binary) are added to the graph alongside the more informative `CORR` and `FACT` edges, the increased node degree dilutes the attention mass directed towards discriminative neighbours, degrading predictive performance ($\Delta R^2 = -0.0042$ for ALL_EDGES vs. CORR+FACT under the homogeneous formulation; see Sect. 4.4). Equation (3) corrects this by allowing the model to learn relation-specific attention biases, so that redundant static neighbours receive low weight automatically.

Decoder. A 3-layer MLP with architecture $[200 \to 64 \to 32 \to 1]$ takes the concatenated pair embedding $[\mathbf{z}_i \,\|\, \mathbf{z}_j] \in \mathbb{R}^{200}$ and outputs $\hat{\rho}_{ij}^{t+1} \in [-1, 1]$ via a tanh final activation.

Weight Initialisation. Linear layers use Xavier uniform initialisation.
The total parameter count is **85,480**, a substantial reduction relative to the recurrent TGN baseline (556,909 parameters) from removing the GRU memory updater.

3.7 Training Protocol

Pre-training objective. The model is trained to minimise the Huber loss (SmoothL1, $\delta = 1$) between predicted and DCC-GARCH correlations over all known pairs on day $t + 1$:

$$\mathcal{L} = \frac{1}{|\mathcal{P}_t|} \sum_{(i,j) \in \mathcal{P}_t} \ell_\delta\big(\hat{\rho}_{ij}^{t+1}, \, \rho_{ij}^{t+1}\big) \tag{5}$$

Huber loss is chosen for robustness to outlier correlations near ± 1 that arise during market stress periods.

Walk-Forward Split and Evaluation. The full period is partitioned into nine non-overlapping walk-forward windows (500 train/125 validation/125 test days, step 125 days), yielding 1,093 total out-of-sample trading days. The event ring buffer state is **not** reset between splits within a window; each window is initialised from scratch to ensure strict causal validity. To establish statistical rigour for portfolio metrics, we apply a **Block Bootstrap** methodology ($B =$ 2,000 re-samples, block size 5 days) to the out-of-sample returns, providing 95% confidence intervals and p-values for pairwise comparisons.

Optimisation. Adam optimiser with learning rate $\eta = 10^{-3}$ and early stopping (patience 10 epochs for DyFO and TGN, 5 for baselines) monitoring validation R^2; the best checkpoint is restored for test evaluation. Gradients are clipped to ℓ_2-norm ≤ 0.5. Maximum 50 training epochs per window.

Reproducibility. All experiments are run with a fixed random seed per window to ensure deterministic data splits. Data preparation (downloads, DCC-GARCH estimation) is performed once and shared across model variants to isolate stochasticity to model initialisation. The complete implementation is available at https://github.com/cyb3rpunk/DyFO.

4 Experiments

4.1 Evaluation Metrics

We report the following metrics computed on the held-out test portions of the nine non-overlapping walk-forward windows (125 test days per window, 1,093 out-of-sample trading days in total).

- R^2 (coefficient of determination): fraction of variance in ρ_{ij}^{t+1} explained by $\hat{\rho}_{ij}^{t+1}$.
- **Spearman** ρ: rank correlation between predicted and actual correlations, measuring ordinal accuracy of the predicted correlation structure.
- **MAE**: mean absolute error in correlation units.

Additionally, we report a derived classification metric, F1 score at $|\hat{\rho}| \geq 0.5$, denoted as cls-F1, which reflects the practical accuracy of identifying high-correlation asset pairs.

4.2 Main Results

Table 3 reports the average test performance over the nine walk-forward windows. The baselines represent three temporal-graph paradigms: **TGN** [10] with recurrent memory, **ROLAND** [20] with discrete snapshots and EMA propagation, and **GAT_STATIC** [14] without temporal dynamics.

Table 3. Test performance over nine walk-forward windows. Higher is better except for MAE.

Model	R^2	Spearman ρ	MAE	cls-F1
DyFO	**0.893 ± 0.034**	**0.958**	**0.035**	**0.793**
TGN (Recurrent Baseline)	0.790 ± 0.079	0.911	0.048	0.702
ROLAND	0.518	0.763	0.071	0.043
GAT_STATIC	0.684	0.880	0.056	0.273

DyFO achieves the best performance across all prediction-level metrics ($R^2 = 0.893 \pm 0.034$, Spearman $\rho = 0.958$, MAE $= 0.035$, cls-F1 $= 0.793$), with an advantage in both mean accuracy and stability. It maintains $R^2 > 0.83$ in all nine windows (worst case 0.849, Window 2), whereas the GRU memory of TGN collapses to $R^2 = 0.623$ during the 2022–2023 regime transition in Window 7, yielding $\sigma_{R^2} = 0.079$ (more than twice DyFO's 0.034). Even excluding this failure case, TGN's dispersion only drops to $\sigma_{R^2} = 0.055$, indicating a broad sensitivity of recurrent memory to regime shifts rather than a single outlier; the collapse persisted despite gradient clipping, warmup, and orthogonal initialisation, pointing to an architectural rather than an optimisation limitation. ROLAND fails to recover daily correlation dynamics, with $F_1 = 0.00$ in seven of nine windows, mainly due to insufficient snapshot granularity.

4.3 Downstream Portfolio Diagnostic

As a secondary diagnostic, we assess whether DyFO's forecasting gains translate into downstream portfolio utility under a standard Global Minimum Variance

(GMV) allocation rule, separating predictive accuracy from its eventual translation into portfolio-level gains. Out-of-sample returns are evaluated via paired block bootstrap ($B = 2{,}000$, block size 5 days), yielding 95% confidence intervals and p-values for pairwise comparisons of Sharpe ratio, CVaR(5%), maximum drawdown (MDD), turnover, and annualised volatility (Table 4).

Table 4. Portfolio-level GMV diagnostic over nine walk-forward windows. No pairwise Sharpe comparison is significant after Holm–Bonferroni correction.

Variant	Sharpe	MDD Worst	Turnover	Vol (ann.)
DyFO	1.601	−14.20%	0.1121	0.1032
TGN	1.622	−14.03%	0.1138	0.1026
ROLAND	1.796	−14.16%	0.1205	0.1040
GAT_STATIC	1.688	−14.48%	0.1210	0.1044

The window-level Wilcoxon signed-rank test for the primary comparison (DyFO vs. TGN) yields $p = 0.715$, well above any conventional significance threshold; all other Sharpe comparisons are similarly non-significant after Holm–Bonferroni correction (all corrected $p \geq 1.00$). The coefficient of variation exceeds 90% for every model, confirming that the Sharpe proxy is dominated by the market regime of each test window rather than by differences in forecast quality. Windows 5–7 (coinciding with the 2022 rate-hike bear market) produce negative Sharpe ratios for *all* models, while Windows 8–9 (2023–2024 recovery) yield ratios exceeding 3. Similarly, the CVaR(5%) bootstrap comparisons are non-significant in all nine windows and all pairs.

No risk or efficiency difference across models reaches statistical significance under paired block bootstrap, consistent with the Markowitz error-amplification interpretation [9]: the GMV optimiser is insensitive to encoder quality at this universe size.

In contrast, pooled Diebold–Mariano tests with Newey–West HAC correction, using 10 lags over 1,093 trading days, confirm large effect-size advantages at the prediction level. DyFO significantly outperforms ROLAND with $d = -5.28$ and $p \approx 0$, `GAT_STATIC` with $d = -3.41$ and $p < 10^{-258}$, and TGN with $d = -2.26$ and $p < 10^{-121}$. All comparisons remain statistically significant after Holm–Bonferroni correction. This divergence indicates that the allocation layer, rather than the forecaster itself, constitutes the binding constraint on realised portfolio utility.

4.4 Ablation Study: Edge-Type Configuration

We evaluated DyFO under four edge-type subsets to quantify the marginal contribution of each relation type to predictive performance: CORR-ONLY (DCC-GARCH correlations only), CORR+SECT (correlations and static sector membership), CORR+FACT (correlations and Fama-French factor loadings), and

ALL_EDGES (full heterogeneous graph: CORR ∪ SECT ∪ FACT). All configurations were trained for 50 epochs with seeds {42, 123, 456} across nine walk-forward windows (train = 500, validation = 125, test = 125 trading days).

Aggregate Ablation Comparison. Table 5 summarises the aggregate predictive and portfolio-level metrics for all four edge-type configurations, averaged over the nine walk-forward windows and three seeds. Under the relation-aware formulation (Eq. (3)), ALL_EDGES attains the highest mean R^2 and lowest mean MSE and MAE, consistent with the theoretical expectation that a fully heterogeneous graph should dominate any edge-type subset.

Table 5. Aggregate predictive and portfolio metrics for the DyFO ablation study (mean over nine walk-forward windows and seeds {42, 123, 456}). ALL_EDGES corresponds to the full heterogeneous configuration and serves as the primary model reported in Table 3.

Configuration	R^2	MAE	MSE ($\times 10^{-3}$)	Spearman ρ	Sharpe	MDD	Turnover
CORR-ONLY	0.8696	0.0391	2.50	0.9495	1.506	−6.81%	11.05%
CORR+SECT	0.8853	0.0363	2.10	0.9567	1.594	−6.58%	11.32%
CORR+FACT	0.8904	0.0356	2.00	0.9581	**1.610**	**−6.55%**	11.24%
ALL_EDGES†	**0.8926**	**0.0351**	**2.00**	**0.9582**	1.601	−6.59%	11.21%

† Full DyFO model used as the primary configuration in all comparisons.

Statistical Significance. Wilcoxon signed-rank tests on the nine-window MSE vectors confirm that the full configuration significantly outperforms CORR-ONLY ($p = 0.0039$), while CORR+FACT also improves significantly over CORR-ONLY ($p = 0.0078$). Sector edges alone provide only a marginal gain ($p = 0.0742$), and ALL_EDGES is statistically indistinguishable from CORR+FACT ($p = 0.25$). Thus, factor co-loadings account for most of the measurable gain beyond dynamic correlations, while the full heterogeneous graph remains the theoretically grounded and empirically competitive DyFO configuration. Read against the failure mode it is designed to correct (Sect. 3.6), the measurable effect of typed-edge conditioning is to neutralise the attention dilution that dense SECT edges induce under homogeneous attention ($\Delta R^2 = -0.0042$), allowing the full heterogeneous graph to match—rather than fall below—the strongest edge subset. The mechanism thus enables structurally redundant relations to be integrated without degrading accuracy, which is its intended role, rather than yielding a statistically significant gain over CORR+FACT.

5 Conclusion and Future Work

We introduced DyFO, a non-recurrent relation-aware temporal graph attention architecture for next-day pairwise correlation forecasting over a heterogeneous financial graph. Under a nine-window walk-forward protocol covering 1,093 out-of-sample days and 50 S&P 500 constituents, DyFO achieved strong and stable predictive performance, outperforming recurrent, snapshot-based, and static graph baselines across correlation-level metrics. The results support the central claim of this work: typed-edge conditioning and bounded-history temporal attention provide an effective architecture for financial co-movement forecasting.

A secondary Global Minimum Variance portfolio diagnostic showed that prediction-level improvements did not yield statistically significant Sharpe-ratio gains under paired block bootstrap. Rather than undermining the forecasting contribution, this result highlights a known gap between covariance prediction accuracy and realised portfolio utility under classical mean–variance optimisation. Future work should therefore investigate decision-aware allocation frameworks, differentiable optimisation layers, and reinforcement-learning allocators designed to exploit richer covariance forecasts directly, including the use of DyFO node embeddings as learned state representations for a portfolio policy agent. Additional extensions include incorporating textual financial news, analyst revisions, and larger asset universes. A diagnostic comparison against target-dependent naive predictors, such as persistence and EWMA, is left for future work. These baselines require access to the lagged correlation state, which DyFO deliberately excludes; therefore, they fall outside the causal comparison setting adopted in this study. As a calibration point, a diagnostic EWMA fitted directly on the lagged target series attains a near-ceiling performance of $R^2 \approx 0.99$. This result is expected rather than genuinely competitive, since the DCC-GARCH target is itself an exponentially weighted recursion that EWMA largely mirrors. Accordingly, EWMA should be interpreted as an autoregressive upper bound that is unavailable in the non-lagged regime targeted by DyFO, where correlation dynamics must instead be reconstructed from structural relations and asynchronous events.

Overall, DyFO should be understood as a methodological contribution to graph-based financial correlation forecasting, not as a complete end-to-end portfolio allocation system.

Disclosure of Interests. The authors have no competing interests to declare that are relevant to the content of this article.

References

1. Busbridge, D., Sherburn, D., Cavallo, P., Hammerla, N.Y.: Relational graph attention networks (2019). https://arxiv.org/abs/1904.05811
2. Engle, R.: Dynamic conditional correlation: a simple class of multivariate generalized autoregressive conditional heteroskedasticity models. J. Bus. Econ. Stat. **20**(3), 339–350 (2002)
3. Fama, E.F., French, K.R.: A five-factor asset pricing model. J. Financ. Econ. **116**(1), 1–22 (2015)
4. Feng, F., He, X., Wang, X., Luo, C., Liu, Y., Chua, T.S.: Temporal relational ranking for stock prediction. ACM Trans. Inf. Syst. **37**(2) (2019). https://doi.org/10.1145/3309547

5. Hu, Z., Dong, Y., Wang, K., Sun, Y.: Heterogeneous graph transformer. In: Proceedings of the Web Conference 2020, WWW 2020, pp. 2704–2710. Association for Computing Machinery, New York (2020). https://doi.org/10.1145/3366423.3380027
6. Kazemi, S.M., et al.: Time2vec: learning a vector representation of time. arXiv preprint arXiv:1907.05321 (2019)
7. Kim, R., So, C.H., Jeong, M., Lee, S., Kim, J., Kang, J.: Hats: a hierarchical graph attention network for stock movement prediction (2019). https://arxiv.org/abs/1908.07999
8. Markowitz, H.: Portfolio selection. J. Financ. **7**(1), 77–91 (1952). https://doi.org/10.1111/j.1540-6261.1952.tb01525.x. https://onlinelibrary.wiley.com/doi/abs/10.1111/j.1540-6261.1952.tb01525.x
9. Michaud, R.O.: The Markowitz optimization enigma: is 'optimized' optimal? Financ. Anal. J. **45**(1), 31–42 (1989)
10. Rossi, E., Chamberlain, B., Frasca, F., Eynard, D., Monti, F., Bronstein, M.: Temporal graph networks for deep learning on dynamic graphs. In: Proceedings of the 37th International Conference on Machine Learning (ICML) (2020)
11. Schlichtkrull, M., Kipf, T.N., Bloem, P., van den Berg, R., Titov, I., Welling, M.: Modeling relational data with graph convolutional networks. In: Gangemi, A., et al. (eds.) The Semantic Web, pp. 593–607. Springer, Cham (2018)
12. Shi, S., Li, J., Li, G., Pan, P., Chen, Q., Sun, Q.: GPM: a graph convolutional network based reinforcement learning framework for portfolio management. Neurocomputing **498**, 14–27 (2022). https://doi.org/10.1016/j.neucom.2022.04.068
13. Soleymani, F., Paquet, E.: Deep graph convolutional reinforcement learning for financial portfolio management - deeppocket. Expert Syst. Appl. **182**, 115127 (2021). https://doi.org/10.1016/j.eswa.2021.115127. https://www.sciencedirect.com/science/article/pii/S0957417421005686
14. Veličković, P., Cucurull, G., Casanova, A., Romero, A., Liò, P., Bengio, Y.: Graph attention networks. arXiv preprint arXiv:1710.10903 (2018)
15. Wang, J., Zhang, Y., Tang, K., Wu, J., Xiong, Z.: Alphastock: a buying-winners-and-selling-losers investment strategy using interpretable deep reinforcement attention networks. In: Proceedings of the 25th ACM SIGKDD International Conference on Knowledge Discovery & Data Mining, KDD 2019, pp. 1900–1908. Association for Computing Machinery, New York (2019). https://doi.org/10.1145/3292500.3330647
16. Wang, X., et al.: Heterogeneous graph attention network (2021). https://arxiv.org/abs/1903.07293
17. Xiang, S., Cheng, D., Shang, C., Zhang, Y., Liang, Y.: Temporal and heterogeneous graph neural network for financial time series prediction. In: Proceedings of the 31st ACM International Conference on Information and Knowledge Management, CIKM 2022, pp. 3584–3593. ACM (2022). https://doi.org/10.1145/3511808.3557089
18. Xu, D., Ruan, C., Korpeoglu, E., Kumar, S., Achan, K.: Inductive representation learning on temporal graphs (2020). https://arxiv.org/abs/2002.07962
19. Yan, W., Tan, Y.: TCGPN: temporal-correlation graph pre-trained network for stock forecasting (2024). https://arxiv.org/abs/2407.18519
20. You, J., Du, T., Leskovec, J.: ROLAND: graph learning framework for dynamic graphs. In: Proceedings of the 28th ACM SIGKDD Conference on Knowledge Discovery and Data Mining (KDD), pp. 2359–2369 (2022)

Learning Transferable Instance Hardness: A Meta-learning Approach to Predict Model Difficulty Across Datasets

Patricia S. M. Ueda[1(✉)], Adriano Rivolli[2], Carlos M. M. O. P. Soares[3], and Ana C. Lorena[1]

[1] Instituto Tecnológico de Aeronáutica, São José dos Campos, Brazil
uedapsm@gmail.com, aclorena@ita.br

[2] Universidade Tecnológica Federal do Paraná, Cornélio Procópio, Brazil
rivolli@utfpr.edu.br

[3] University of Porto, Porto, Portugal
csoares@fe.up.pt

Abstract. Instance Hardness (IH) quantifies the difficulty of correctly predicting the labels of individual samples in a dataset. It is broadly assessed through model-based IH (empirical prediction errors from algorithms) and data-based Instance Hardness Measures (IHMs) (geometric and topological data descriptors). In this work, we investigate whether the target model-based IH can be predicted strictly from data-based IHMs and, crucially, whether such predictions generalize across datasets. We propose a meta-learning framework in which model-based IH is modeled as a function of data-based IHMs. The model-based IH is estimated using a probabilistic formulation derived from cross-validated predictions of a diverse pool of classifiers. The resulting meta-dataset is then used to train meta-regression models. To assess generalization, we adopt a leave-one-dataset-out (LODO) protocol over ten classification datasets, evaluating performance on entirely unseen data distributions. Our results show that model-based IH can be predicted with consistent accuracy and strong rank correlation across datasets, indicating that the relationship between local data complexity and predictive difficulty is transferable. Furthermore, the proposed approach provides a surrogate for model-based IH, eliminating the need for repeated model training. These findings establish instance hardness as a learnable and generalizable property of data, bridging the gap between data complexity and algorithmic performance.

Keywords: Instance Hardness · Meta-Learning · Data Complexity · Meta-Regression

1 Introduction

The Machine Learning (ML) landscape has increasingly shifted from purely algorithmic advancements to a Data-Centric Artificial Intelligence (AI) perspective,

M. Recamonde-Mendoza and R. C. Barros (Eds.): BRACIS 2026, LNAI 17105, pp. 386–400, 2027.
https://doi.org/10.1007/978-3-032-39882-6_26

where understanding and improving data quality is as crucial as developing complex architectures [14]. A fundamental step toward this understanding is shifting the evaluation from aggregated global metrics to a fine-grained, instance-level analysis of classification difficulty [7].

Historically, the complexity of a classification problem was assessed globally, mapping the overall geometry of class boundaries and feature overlaps [6]. However, global metrics often overlook local particularities. To address this, the concept of *Instance Hardness* (IH) was introduced to characterize the specific difficulty of correctly predicting the labels of individual observations within a dataset [15]. Model-based IH is typically defined as the likelihood that an instance is misclassified by a diverse pool of learning algorithms [8]. While highly informative, obtaining model-based IH is computationally expensive, as it requires repeated cross-validation across multiple architectures.

To circumvent this computational bottleneck and as an attempt to explain reasons why an instance is hard to classify, researchers have proposed data-based *Instance Hardness Measures* (IHMs), which describe the local geometric and topological properties of an instance, such as neighborhood class mixture and decision boundary proximity. While recent studies have explored adapting IHMs for unlabeled data to support reject-option strategies during model deployment [16], the present work takes a fundamentally different direction. We use traditional, label-dependent IHMs as the essential vehicle for investigating a broader phenomenon: the transferability of data complexity to model complexity, at the instance-level, across datasets.

Currently, IHMs have been studied on within-dataset evaluations [10], or across datasets of the same domain, containing the same input attributes [17,18]. Such approaches fail to answer a critical question: does the relationship between local data descriptors and predictive difficulty generalize across entirely different domains?

In this paper, we bridge this gap by framing the estimation of model difficulty as a cross-dataset meta-learning regression problem. Instead of simply predicting IH within isolated datasets, we show that predictive difficulty can be learned as a transferable function across disparate domains, enabling the estimation of model difficulty on unseen datasets without the need to train predictive models. By learning a mapping from the instance space (geometric descriptors) to the performance space (predictive error), we hypothesize that regions with high predicted IH correspond to universal expected failure regions.

To validate this hypothesis, we propose a Leave-One-Dataset-Out (LODO) evaluation protocol across diverse classification datasets. By training a meta-regressor solely on the traditional data-based IHMs of source datasets and predicting the model-based IH on an entirely unseen target dataset, this work functions as a meta-learning generalization test. Ultimately, we demonstrate that traditional IHMs successfully enable the prediction of algorithmic failure globally, acting as an efficient surrogate foundation model that opens new actionable directions for future applications in areas such as curriculum learning [19], data pruning [13], and classification with reject option [4].

The remainder of this paper is organized as follows: Sect. 2 reviews the background on measuring instance hardness and meta-learning. Section 3 details the proposed methodology, including the meta-learning formalization and the evaluation protocol using multiple meta-regressors. Section 4 presents the experimental results, assessing predictability, ranking consistency, and feature importance. Section 5 provides a boundary analysis, using topological clustering and an study to diagnose transferability failures. Finally, Sect. 6 discusses the study's limitations and concludes the paper.

2 Background and Related Work

The study of instance-level classification difficulty intersects several established fields in Machine Learning, including Data Complexity, Meta-Learning, and Data-Centric AI. This section contextualizes the proposed framework within these domains and highlights current limitations concerning the transferability of hardness estimates.

2.1 Foundations of Data Complexity and Instance Hardness

The systematic analysis of what makes a classification problem difficult was pioneered by Ho and Basu [6]. They introduced a set of global complexity measures designed to characterize the geometry of class boundaries, focusing on aspects such as feature and class overlaps, and the linearity of the problem. While these global metrics provide a macro-perspective of dataset difficulty, they often fail to capture the nuances of individual observations and localized regions of the feature space [10].

To address this limitation, Smith et al. introduced the concept of *Instance Hardness* (IH) [15]. In their seminal work, an instance is defined as "hard" if it is consistently misclassified by a diverse pool of learning algorithms with varying inductive biases. Given a dataset $\mathcal{D}$ with n instances $\mathbf{x}_i$ and corresponding labels y_i, the (model-based) instance hardness (IH) is defined as:

$$IH_{\mathcal{L}}(\mathbf{x}_i) = 1 - \frac{1}{|\mathcal{L}|} \sum_{j=1}^{|\mathcal{L}|} p\big(y_i \mid \mathbf{x}_i, l_j(\mathcal{D}, \beta)\big), \tag{1}$$

where $\mathcal{L}$ denotes a diverse set of learning algorithms, and $p\big(y_i \mid \mathbf{x}_i, l_j(\mathcal{D}, \beta)\big)$ is the probability assigned to the true class y_i for instance $\mathbf{x}_i$ by the j-th algorithm in the pool, trained on $\mathcal{D}$ with hyperparameters β. Summarizing, Eq. 1 averages the probabilities of misclassification of the learning algorithms in the pool $\mathcal{L}$ when using $\mathcal{D}$ as input.

This model-based IH definition shifted the focus from the dataset as a whole to the specific regions where algorithms struggle to generalize. Subsequent research has refined these measures by linking them to robust statistical frameworks, such as Item Response Theory, thereby providing a more rigorous interpretation of classification difficulty at the local level [8].

2.2 Data-Based Descriptors for Hardness Estimation

Concurrent with model-based IH, several research efforts focused on developing *Instance Hardness Measures* (IHMs) that rely on data characteristics. These measures act as local proxies for complexity, utilizing neighborhood density, class likelihood, and tree structures to explain why certain instances are problematic. Recent studies have categorized these IHMs into taxonomies based on their mathematical foundations, demonstrating their utility as meta-features for characterizing overlapping classes [1].

The following set of measures are used in this work (all measures take values in the $[0, 1]$ range, where higher values indicate greater difficulty) [7]:

k-Disagreeing Neighbors [15]: measures the proportion of the k nearest neighbors of $\mathbf{x}_i$ in $\mathcal{D}$ that have a different label:

$$kDN(\mathbf{x}_i) = \frac{\sharp \mathbf{x}_j \mid \mathbf{x}_j \in kNN(\mathbf{x}_i) \wedge y_j \neq y_i}{k}, \tag{2}$$

where $kNN(\mathbf{x}_i)$ denotes the set of k nearest neighbors of instance $\mathbf{x}_i$ in the dataset $\mathcal{D}$.

Ratio of intra-class to extra-class distances [2]: this measure quantifies how close $\mathbf{x}_i$ is to instances of its own class relative to those of other classes. It is defined as:

$$N2(\mathbf{x}_i) = 1 - \frac{1}{\text{IntraInter}(\mathbf{x}_i) + 1}, \tag{3}$$

where $\text{IntraInter}(\mathbf{x}_i)$ is the ratio between the distance to its nearest neighbor from the same class and the distance to its nearest neighbor from a different class (i.e., the nearest enemy):

$$\text{IntraInter}(\mathbf{x}_i) = \frac{d(\mathbf{x}_i, NN(\mathbf{x}_i) \in y_i)}{d(\mathbf{x}_i, NE(\mathbf{x}_i))}, \tag{4}$$

where d is a distance function, $NN(\mathbf{x}_i)$ denotes the nearest neighbor of $\mathbf{x}_i$, and $NE(\mathbf{x}_i)$ is the nearest enemy of $\mathbf{x}_i$.

Class Likelihood Difference [15]: measures the difference between the likelihood that $\mathbf{x}_i$ belongs to its true class y_i and the highest likelihood assigned to any other class:

$$CLD(\mathbf{x}_i) = \frac{1 - (P(xi \mid y_i)P(y_i) - \max y_j \neq y_i\,[P(\mathbf{x}_i \mid y_j)P(y_j)])}{2}, \tag{5}$$

where $P(\mathbf{x}_i \mid y_i)$ denotes the likelihood of instance $\mathbf{x}_i$ given class y_i, and $P(y_i)$ is the prior probability of class y_i, which is assumed to be $\frac{1}{C}$ for all instances, where C is the number of classes. The conditional probability $P(\mathbf{x}_i \mid y_i)$ can be estimated under the assumption that input features are independent.

Disjunct Size [15]: constructs an unpruned decision tree DT from $\mathcal{D}$ and measures the relative size of the disjunct (leaf node) to which $\mathbf{x}_i$ belongs:

$$DS(\mathbf{x}_i) = 1 - \frac{\sharp\{\mathbf{x}_j \mid \mathbf{x}_j \in Disjunct(\mathbf{x}_i)\}}{\max |Disjunct(\mathcal{D})|}, \tag{6}$$

where $Disjunct(\mathbf{x}_i)$ denotes the set of instances contained in the leaf node where $\mathbf{x}_i$ is assigned, and the denominator corresponds to the size of the largest disjunct in the dataset $\mathcal{D}$.

Disjunct Class Percentage [15]: computes the proportion of instances within the same disjunct (i.e., leaf node) as $\mathbf{x}_i$ in a pruned decision tree built from $\mathcal{D}$ that share its class label. It is defined as:

$$DCP(\mathbf{x}_i) = 1 - \frac{\sharp\{\mathbf{x}_j \mid \mathbf{x}_j \in Disjunct(\mathbf{x}_i) \wedge y_j = y_i\}}{\sharp\{\mathbf{x}_j \mid \mathbf{x}_j \in Disjunct(\mathbf{x}_i)\}}. \quad (7)$$

Tree Depth [15]: measures the depth of the leaf node that classifies $\mathbf{x}_i$ in a decision tree DT, normalized by the maximum depth of the tree built from $\mathcal{D}$:

$$TD(\mathbf{x}_i) = \frac{depth_{DT}(\mathbf{x}_i)}{\max\{depth_{DT}(\mathbf{x}_j) \mid \mathbf{x}_j \in \mathcal{D}\}}, \quad (8)$$

where $depthDT(\mathbf{x}_i)$ denotes the depth of the leaf node in which $\mathbf{x}_i$ is placed. This measure can be computed using either a pruned decision tree (TD_P) or an unpruned one (TD_U).

Despite the proliferation of these measures, most applications remain descriptive rather than predictive. While recent literature has successfully adapted IHMs to function without ground-truth labels for post-deployment rejection strategies [16], the core limitation remains: the majority of research in this area explores complexity within isolated datasets, failing to investigate if the geometric descriptors universally correlate with algorithmic failure.

2.3 Meta-learning for Performance Prediction

Meta-learning (MtL) involves using data about ML processes to improve the performance in future learning tasks [3]. Traditionally, MtL has been applied to model selection and hyperparameter optimization by mapping dataset-level meta-features to the performance of different algorithms [12].

The extension of MtL to the instance level is a more recent development. Contemporary literature has explored training regression meta-models to estimate the IH of new observations [11]. These meta-models are also called assessors in the relate literature [5]. However, most of the existing frameworks often demonstrate high accuracy when evaluated on test sets sampled from the same distribution as the training data. This paper bridges this gap by explicitly framing the problem as a cross-dataset meta-regression task, evaluating whether the mapping from local data geometry to predictive error is a transferable property.

3 Methodology

The primary objective of the proposed framework is to establish a functional relationship between the intrinsic geometry of data and the predictive difficulty experienced by ML models. This section details the formalization of our MtL approach, the construction of the meta-dataset, the definitions of the meta-features, and the evaluation protocol designed to test cross-dataset generalization.

3.1 Formalization of the Meta-learning Task

Traditional MtL focuses on mapping dataset-level characteristics to algorithm performance [3]. In contrast, we formulate the estimation of model-based IH as measured by Eq. 1 as an instance-level meta-regression problem.

The proposed framework learns a meta-regressor $f : \Phi \rightarrow \mathbb{R}$, where Φ represents a meta-feature space derived from local data descriptors [12]. For each instance $\mathbf{x}_i$ in a dataset $\mathcal{D}$, we extract a vector of meta-features $\phi(\mathbf{x}_i) \in \Phi$, which serves as the input to the meta-regressor. The output is a predicted hardness value $\widehat{IH}(\mathbf{x}_i)$, which aims to approximate the model-based hardness $IH(\mathbf{x}_i)$.

To ensure that the hardness target is not biased towards a single learning algorithm's inductive bias, we adopt a consensus pool approach, a standard procedure for robust instance-level evaluation [14]. The model-based IH for an instance $\mathbf{x}_i$ is defined as the average probability of error across a diverse ensemble of $\mathcal{L}$ classifiers, as described in Eq. 1.

Our pool $\mathcal{L}$ contains five distinct learning algorithms: Random Forest (RF), Gradient Boosting (GB), Logistic Regression (LR), Multi-Layer Perceptron (MLP), and a Calibrated Linear Support Vector Machine (LSVM) using Platt scaling.

To prevent overfitting and capture true generalization difficulty, the probability assigned by each model $l_j \in \mathcal{L}$ to the true label y_i is estimated via 5-fold cross-validation. This target effectively identifies instances located in regions of the feature space where multiple decision boundaries consistently fail [7].

To provide a comprehensive geometric description of each instance without relying on model predictions, we extract Instance Hardness Measures (IHMs). Originally proposed to quantify reasons for data predictive difficulty [15], and recently adapted for various deployment scenarios [16], these measures act as the independent variables (meta-features) in our framework. We categorize them into three main groups based on the topological characteristics they capture:

1. **Neighborhood-based**: These measures evaluate the immediate spatial vicinity of an instance. The measures from this category are kDN and N2. Together, these descriptors capture local density mixtures and the proximity of an instance to the theoretical decision boundary.
2. **Likelihood-based**: CLD fits this category, providing a probabilistic view of hardness. Instances with high CLD values (as formulated in Eq. 5) are situated in ambiguous regions where multiple classes are highly probable, indicating inherent probabilistic uncertainty.
3. **Tree-based**: Measures DS, DCP and TD leverage the recursive partitioning structure of decision trees. They assume that harder instances require more complex, deeper rules to be isolated from the rest of the data.

Given N datasets $\mathcal{D}_i$, meta-features and meta-targets are extracted from each of them. Since all datasets are characterized by the same set of meta-features and meta-targets, they are then combined into a single meta-dataset for regression[1].

The datasets used in the experiments were selected from the TabZilla benchmark [9], which includes datasets considered challenging for classification tasks. A summary is provided in Table 1. All selected datasets correspond to binary classification problems, although the proposed analysis is not limited to this setting. This initial subset was chosen due to its manageable size. The meta-dataset has 17,512 rows and seven input columns (the IHMs).

Table 1. Dataset summary and class distribution.

Dataset	Instances	Features	Minority Class (%)
ada_agnostic	4562	48	24.8
Australian	690	14	44.5
Bioresponse	3751	1776	45.8
colic	368	27	33.7
credit-a	690	15	44.5
credit-g	1000	20	30.0
heart-h	294	13	36.1
jasmine	2984	144	50.0
kc1	2109	21	15.5
qsar-biodeg	1055	41	33.7

3.2 Meta-regressors and Feature Importance

To ensure that the transferability of instance hardness is not biased by a specific meta-algorithm, we employ three distinct meta-regression models to learn the mapping from data descriptors to predictive difficulty: Random Forest (RF), Support Vector Regression (SVR), and Extreme Gradient Boosting (XGBoost). We deliberately use these algorithms with their default hyperparameters to provide a general, unbiased evaluation of transferability across domains, although future hyperparameter tuning could further improve absolute predictive performance. Furthermore, to understand which geometric properties most dictate algorithmic failure universally, we extract and compare the inherent Feature Importance from all three meta-models. For the tree-based ensembles, we use their native impurity-based importance, whereas for the SVR, we employ permutation feature importance to measure the contribution of each IHM.

[1] The repository containing the complete extraction pipeline and experiments is available at https://github.com/uedapaty/bracis2026-instance-hardness.

We train the meta-models using $N-1$ datasets and test the results on the left out dataset, in a Leave-One-Dataset-Out (LODO) procedure. The complete pipeline of our methodology, from the base dataset processing to the meta-regression under the LODO protocol, is visually summarized in Fig. 1.

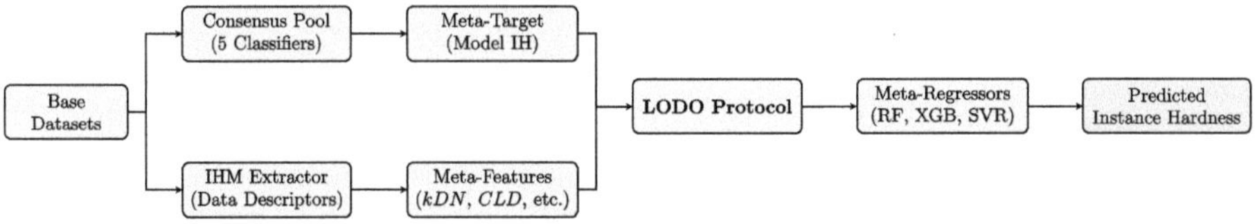

Fig. 1. Overview of the proposed MtL framework for predicting IH.

3.3 Evaluation Protocol and Research Questions

To explicitly justify our experimental design and deeply assess the transferability of the proposed mapping, we structure our evaluation around three core research questions:

- **Q1—Predictability**: Can model-based IH be robustly predicted from instance-level geometric descriptors (IHMs) alone? To answer this question, we evaluate the absolute accuracy of our meta-regressors using Mean Absolute Error (MAE) and the Coefficient of Determination (R^2).
- **Q2—Ranking Consistency**: Does the model correctly preserve the relative ordering of instances by difficulty? In practical downstream applications like curriculum learning, incorrectly predicting the exact hardness value is less detrimental than incorrectly ordering the training samples. Thus, we strongly prioritize evaluation using Spearman's ρ rank correlation. Spearman's correlation captures monotonic relationships better than Pearson's correlation, making it ideal for difficulty-based ordering tasks.
- **Q3—Cross-Dataset Generalization**: Does the learned relationship transfer universally to unseen domains? To strictly answer this, we implement a Leave-One-Dataset-Out (LODO) protocol. Under this setting, the meta-regressor is trained on $N-1$ datasets and tested on the entirely unseen N-th dataset, ensuring no data leakage occurs.

To accurately contextualize our LODO results, we establish a comparative baseline. We define a trivial baseline, where the model simply predicts the global average hardness of the training domains for all target instances. Outperforming this baseline proves that the meta-regressor has learned a meaningful function rather than defaulting to the mean [12].

Additionally, to understand how the inherent hardness distribution varies across domains and to diagnose potential LODO failures, we employ the Wasserstein distance between the distributions combined with hierarchical clustering.

This allows us to map the topological similarity of the hardness space across datasets and identify outlier domains (domain shift) where the meta-regressors might face negative transfer.

4 Results

This section presents the empirical evaluation of the proposed meta-learning framework. We structure our analysis to directly address the research questions formulated in Sect. 3.3. First, we address Q1, Q2, and Q3 by evaluating the global predictability and ranking consistency of multiple meta-regressors across the benchmark datasets, thereby establishing the transferability of instance hardness under the strict LODO protocol. Subsequently, we investigate the underlying drivers of algorithmic failure by analyzing the feature importance extracted from the trained models, revealing which topological characteristics universally dictate predictive difficulty.

4.1 Predictability and Ranking Consistency Across Regressors

The primary objective of our experiments is to verify whether algorithmic difficulty can be reliably mapped and ranked in unseen domains (addressing Q1, Q2, and Q3). Table 1 presents the predictive performance (R^2, MAE - Q1) and ranking consistency (Spearman's ρ - Q2) under the strict LODO protocol (Q3) for all evaluated regressors.

The results provide compelling evidence for cross-dataset predictability (addressing Q1). As detailed in Table 2, the meta-regressors significantly outperformed the trivial baseline across all datasets. While the baseline yielded constant 0.00 Spearman scores and negative R^2 values—ranging from -0.003 to -0.357, dropping to -1.300 for `jasmine`—the trained regressors achieved highly positive scores. Notably, `kc1` and `credit-a` reached exceptional R^2 values up to 0.840, alongside low MAE.

Regarding ranking consistency (addressing Q2), the framework in general exhibited an outstanding ability to order instances. Spearman correlations frequently exceeded 0.75, peaking at 0.885 for `ada_agnostic` (using XGBoost) and 0.872 for `kc1` (using Random Forest). These high coefficients across multiple models validate that the meta-regressors can sort observations from easiest to hardest, a critical requisite for downstream tasks such as data pruning and curriculum learning. The overall success of the meta-models across entirely unseen domains confirms the generalization capabilities of our framework (addressing Q3). In contrast, for one specific dataset (`jasmine`), the ranking results were non-satisfactory. We analyze possible reasons for this behavior in Sect. 5.

When comparing the meta-regressors, the tree ensemble models exhibited advantage by attaining the best performance more frequently. SVR struggled on certain datasets, such as `colic` and `jasmine`.

Table 2. Cross-dataset predictive performance (R^2 and MAE) and ranking consistency (Spearman's ρ) across meta-regressors under the LODO protocol. Results reflect the updated consensus pool (excluding Naive Bayes). The trivial baseline for Spearman is 0.00 for all datasets and baseline R^2 values were omitted for brevity as they yielded strictly negative scores. Best performances are in bold.

Target Dataset	Spearman (ρ)			R^2 Score			MAE			
	RF	XGB	SVR	RF	XGB	SVR	Baseline	RF	XGB	SVR
ada_agnostic	0.857	**0.885**	0.835	0.669	0.697	**0.708**	0.205	0.104	**0.098**	0.107
Australian	0.662	**0.782**	0.781	0.758	**0.793**	0.757	0.194	0.093	**0.080**	0.095
Bioresponse	**0.689**	0.659	0.563	**0.474**	0.429	0.410	0.185	**0.127**	0.138	0.144
colic	0.741	**0.761**	0.574	0.576	**0.577**	0.403	0.188	0.117	**0.116**	0.126
credit-a	**0.780**	0.751	0.757	**0.840**	0.837	0.815	0.192	**0.065**	0.066	0.081
credit-g	0.824	**0.837**	0.831	0.666	**0.677**	0.659	0.210	0.112	**0.109**	0.113
heart-h	**0.852**	0.845	0.799	**0.774**	0.744	0.729	0.215	**0.086**	0.093	0.110
jasmine	0.160	**0.292**	0.147	**0.897**	0.813	-0.619	0.235	**0.042**	0.052	0.198
kc1	**0.872**	0.857	0.843	0.820	**0.837**	0.829	0.197	0.071	**0.064**	0.075
qsar-biodeg	0.794	**0.824**	0.764	0.587	**0.680**	0.629	0.179	0.111	**0.097**	0.112

4.2 Meta-feature Importance

Beyond raw predictive metrics, our framework provides interpretability into the intrinsic causes of algorithmic failure across domains. By extracting the feature importance across the different meta-models, we identify the topological descriptors that universally govern instance hardness.

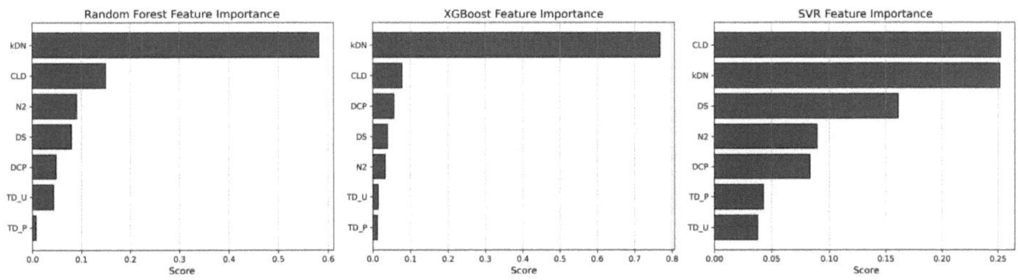

Fig. 2. Feature importance across the meta-regressors.

As explicitly shown in Fig. 2, the kDN and CLD measures consistently dominate the predictive contribution across all models. While kDN is the overwhelmingly primary driver for tree-based ensembles (Random Forest and XGBoost), CLD and kDN share the top-tier importance in the SVR model. This convergence is fundamentally significant: it reveals that local neighborhood class mixture (captured by kDN) and inherent probabilistic overlap (captured by CLD) act as universal indicators of model confusion, transcending the specific characteristics of individual datasets and the inductive bias of the meta-regressors.

In contrast, most tree-based complexity measures (e.g., TD_U, TD_P, and DCP) showed marginal to negligible importance throughout the pool. This behavior indicates that the structural depth required to partition an instance in a decision tree is heavily biased by the macro-structure of the specific dataset from which it was extracted. Consequently, these features fail to generalize as universal descriptors of hardness when transferred to unseen domains.

5 Boundary Analysis

While the proposed meta-learning mapping succeeded across a wide array of datasets, cross-dataset transferability has explicit limits. Rather than undermining the framework, analyzing instances where the models struggle provides a valuable opportunity to map the precise boundaries of the geometry-performance relationship. As observed in Table 2, the `jasmine` dataset emerged as a distinct outlier, with weak rank correlation. This section thoroughly diagnoses this failure through a topological distribution analysis.

5.1 Topological Isolation and Meta-target Variance

To diagnose the failure of the `jasmine` dataset within the LODO protocol, we mapped the hardness distributions of the entire meta-training pool using the Wasserstein distance (Earth Mover's Distance), a robust metric for comparing probability distributions. This topological discrepancy is illustrated in Fig. 3, which highlights the severe isolation of the target domain. Three distinct clusters of datasets can be identified in Fig. 3a: (i) `colic`, `Bioresponse` and `credit-g`; (ii) `ada_agnostic`, `heart-h`, `kc1`, `qsar-biodeg`, `Australian` and `credit-a`; and (iii) `jasmine`.

The clustering dendrogram explicitly demonstrates that `jasmine` occupies a completely isolated branch (Cluster 3), disconnected from the typical distributions of the other datasets. This topological isolation confirms an extreme domain shift. Figure 3b shows the model-based IH distributions of these datasets, colored by cluster. `Jasmine` has a very distinct behavior, with concentrated values near 0 and a few hard instances. Cluster 1 comprises datasets with mixed difficulty and heavy-tailed hard instances. Cluster 2 contains systematically harder datasets.

Furthermore, an internal analysis of the target labels revealed a critical phenomenon regarding the model pool. For the `jasmine` dataset, the variance among the base classifiers' predictions reached an exceptionally high average of $\approx$ 0.1172. This high model variance implies extreme base-classifier disagreement—for instance, SVM might consistently fail on instances where Random Forests easily succeed. Consequently, the averaged meta-target becomes inherently noisy and highly model-dependent in this specific domain, drastically increasing the difficulty of the meta-regression task.

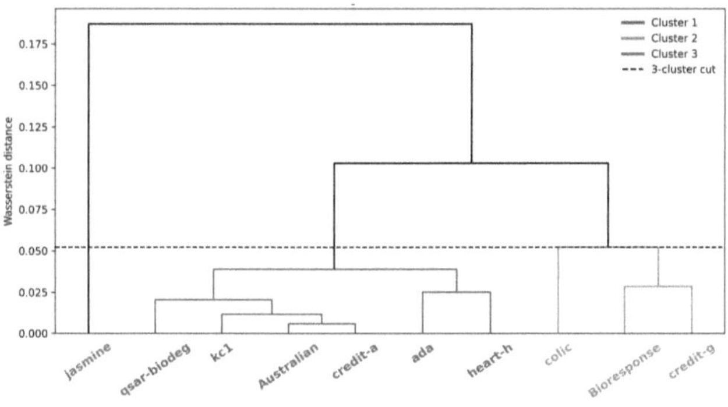

(a) Hierarchical Clustering (Wasserstein Distance)

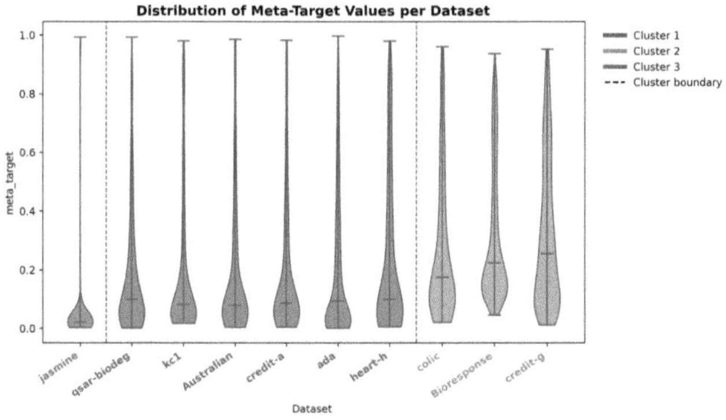

(b) Hardness Distribution per Dataset

Fig. 3. Hierarchical clustering using Wasserstein distance on the instance hardness distributions. The `jasmine` dataset is topologically isolated in its own cluster.

5.2 Potential Negative Transfer

Drawing upon the feature importance findings from Sect. 4.2 and the topological isolation mapped above, we theorized that the meta-models were suffering from negative transfer. Specifically, the models were aggressively attempting to apply irrelevant, dataset-specific tree-based rules (learned from the nine source datasets) to the highly distinct geometry of the `jasmine` domain.

To empirically validate this hypothesis, we designed a study where we systematically removed the poorly generalising tree-based features (DCP, TD_U, and TD_P) from the meta-feature space. We then retrained the meta-regressors relying exclusively on the core generalized features: kDN, CLD, N2, and DS (Table 3).

By merely restricting the feature space to universally robust descriptors, the predictive performance on the previously failing `jasmine` dataset improved in some specific cases. The R^2 score for SVR improved dramatically from a severe

Table 3. Additional study on the *jasmine* dataset under the LODO protocol. Results compare the full meta-feature set (7 IHMs) against the refined set (4 IHMs: kDN, N2, DS, CLD). Some highlighted results are boldfaced.

Feature Set	Spearman (ρ)			R^2 Score			MAE		
	RF	XGB	SVR	RF	XGB	SVR	RF	XGB	SVR
Full Set (7 IHMs)	0.1602	0.2922	0.1469	0.8966	0.8133	-0.6191	0.0418	0.0520	0.1984
Reduced Set (4 IHMs)	0.0832	**0.3221**	0.0371	0.7819	0.7194	**0.7486**	0.0665	0.0784	**0.0798**

negative transfer state (-0.619) to a robust 0.749, with a corresponding drop in MAE. This breakthrough validates that the underlying relationship between geometric complexity and predictive difficulty is indeed fundamentally transferable, especially rescuing models highly sensitive to domain shifts like SVR. Interestingly, while the reduced feature space stabilized the absolute predictability (R^2 and MAE) for SVR, fixing its global magnitude of hardness estimates, the rank correlation (Spearman) within `jasmine` remained relatively weak across all models. And a closer observation of the other meta-regressors reveals that restricting the meta-feature set can lead to drops in performance. This behavior corroborates the findings from Sect. 5.1: because the internal model variance in `jasmine` is extremely high, the exact micro-ordering of instances is inherently noisy. Therefore, we need to incorporate additional datasets with similar hardness profiles to `jasmine` into our pool, which are generally easier to predict but may include a few hard instances.

6 Conclusion and Future Work

In this work, we demonstrated that model-based predictive difficulty is not strictly a local phenomenon, but rather a learnable and transferable property tied to intrinsic data geometry. By framing IH estimation as a cross-dataset meta-learning task under a strict Leave-One-Dataset-Out (LODO) protocol, our framework proved capable of universally predicting and ranking instance difficulty across disparate domains.

The extensive evaluation across multiple regression models revealed that local neighborhood mixture and probabilistic class overlap, captured by descriptors like kDN, N2, and CLD, are robust, universal indicators of algorithmic failure. Furthermore, our boundary analysis highlighted the phenomenon of negative transfer: while the core geometry-performance relationship is highly transferable, there is a need to consider including more datasets with distinct hardness profiles in our pool.

1. **Changes in Meta-Targeting**: Currently, our meta-target is defined as the average error across a consensus pool. Since topologically isolated domains can exhibit high base-classifier disagreement (high model variance), future research will investigate dynamic meta-target weighting and model-specific

hardness profiling to handle algorithmic variance more robustly. Analyzing model-specific hardness can also aid studies revealing the limits and capabilities of each individual classifier.

2. **Expansion of the Meta-Feature Space**: Although the evaluated subset of traditional IHMs proved highly effective, there is an opportunity to expand the meta-feature space to capture even finer nuances of topological overlapping.
3. **Scaling the Meta-Training Pool**: We plan to scale the meta-training pool beyond the initial benchmark of ten datasets. Evaluating the framework across a broader, massive spectrum of data distributions (also including multiclass datasets) will help to comprehensively map the universality limits of the geometry-performance relationship.
4. **Applying the meta-model**: After the previous adjustments, the resulting meta-model will be employed in downstream tasks where difficulty-based ordering is beneficial, such as curriculum learning, data pruning, and reject-option prediction.

These continuous efforts will further bridge the gap between intrinsic data characteristics and algorithmic behavior, ultimately driving the development of more reliable and interpretable ML systems.

Acknowledgements. This work was partially supported by the Coordenação de Aperfeiçoamento de Pessoal de Nível Superior—Brasil (CAPES)—Finance Code 001. The authors also acknowledge the support of the São Paulo Research Foundation (FAPESP), under grant number 2021/06870-3 and CNPq under grant number 310065/2023-2. The authors used AI tools during the preparation of this manuscript for language editing, text refinement, and coding assistance. The AI-generated outputs were carefully reviewed, modified, and validated by the authors. No AI system contributed to the scientific design, interpretation of results, or final decision-making. The authors remain fully responsible for all content presented in the manuscript.

References

1. Al Hosni, O.S., Starkey, A.: Investigating the performance of data complexity & instance hardness measures as a meta-feature in overlapping classes problem. In: ICCBDC 2023, Manchester, UK (2023). https://doi.org/10.1145/3616131.3616132
2. Arruda, J.L., Prudêncio, R.B., Lorena, A.C.: Measuring instance hardness using data complexity measures. In: Brazilian Conference on Intelligent Systems, pp. 483–497. Springer, Cham (2020)
3. Brazdil, P., van Rijn, J.N., Soares, C., Vanschoren, J.: Metalearning: Applications to Automated Machine Learning and Data Mining. Springer, Cham (2022)
4. Hendrickx, K., Perini, L., Van der Plas, D., Meert, W., Davis, J.: Machine learning with a reject option: a survey. Mach. Learn. **113**(5), 3073–3110 (2024)
5. Hernández-Orallo, J., Schellaert, W., Martínez-Plumed, F.: Training on the test set: mapping the system-problem space in AI. In: Proceedings of the AAAI Conference on Artificial Intelligence, vol. 36, pp. 12256–12264. AAAI Press (2022)

6. Ho, T.K., Basu, M.: Complexity measures of supervised classification problems. IEEE Trans. Pattern Anal. Mach. Intell. **24**(3), 289–300 (2002). https://doi.org/10.1109/34.990132
7. Lorena, A.C., Paiva, P.Y., Prudêncio, R.B.: Trusting my predictions: on the value of instance-level analysis. ACM Comput. Surv. **56**(7), 1–28 (2024)
8. Martínez-Plumed, F., Prudêncio, R.B., Martínez-Usó, A., Hernández-Orallo, J.: Item response theory in AI: analysing machine learning classifiers at the instance level. Artif. Intell. **271**, 18–42 (2019)
9. McElfresh, D., et al.: When do neural nets outperform boosted trees on tabular data? Adv. Neural. Inf. Process. Syst. **36**, 76336–76369 (2023)
10. Paiva, P.Y.A., Moreno, C.C., Smith-Miles, K., Valeriano, M.G., Lorena, A.C.: Relating instance hardness to classification performance in a dataset: a visual approach. Mach. Learn. **111**(8), 3085–3123 (2022)
11. Prudêncio, R.B., Lorena, A.C., Silva-Filho, T., Drapal, P., Valeriano, M.G.: Assessor models for explaining instance hardness in classification problems. In: 2024 International Joint Conference on Neural Networks (IJCNN), pp. 1–8. IEEE (2024)
12. Rivolli, A., Garcia, L.P., Soares, C., Vanschoren, J., de Carvalho, A.C.: Meta-features for meta-learning. Knowl.-Based Syst. 108101 (2022)
13. Saseendran, A.T., Setia, L., Chhabria, V., Chakraborty, D., Roy, A.B.: Impact of data pruning on machine learning algorithm performance. arXiv preprint arXiv:1901.10539 (2019)
14. Schweighofer, E.: Data-centric machine learning: Improving model performance and understanding through dataset analysis. In: Legal Knowledge and Information Systems: JURIX 2021, vol. 346, p. 54. IOS Press (2021)
15. Smith, M.R., Martinez, T., Giraud-Carrier, C.: An instance level analysis of data complexity. Mach. Learn. **95**(2), 225–256 (2014)
16. Ueda, P.S.M., Rivolli, A., Lorena, A.C.: An instance level analysis of classification difficulty for unlabeled data. In: Paes, A., Verri, F.A.N. (eds.) Intelligent Systems, BRACIS 2024. LNCS, vol. 15412. Springer, Cham (2025). https://doi.org/10.1007/978-3-031-79029-4_10
17. Ueda, P.S.M., Valeriano, M.G., Mangussi, A.D., Prudêncio, R.B.C., Lorena, A.C.: Classification with reject option: building meta-models to predict classification error. In: de Freitas, R., Furtado, D. (eds.) Intelligent Systems (BRACIS 2025). LNCS, vol. 16179, pp. 215–230. Springer, Cham (2026). https://doi.org/10.1007/978-3-032-15987-8_15
18. Valeriano, M.G., Marzagão, D.K., Montelongo, A., Kiffer, C.R.V., Katz, N., Lorena, A.C.: Filtering instances and rejecting predictions to obtain reliable models in healthcare. Mach. Learn. **115**(1), 15 (2026)
19. Wang, X., Chen, Y., Zhu, W.: A survey on curriculum learning. IEEE Trans. Pattern Anal. Mach. Intell. **44**(9), 4555–4576 (2021)

Diffused Embeddings: Exploring Sentence Representations from DLMs

Ramiro N. Barros[1(✉)], Vinícius Conte Turani[1], Rodrigo C. Barros[1,2], and Lucas S. Kupssinskü[1]

[1] MALTA – Machine Learning Theory and Applications Lab, PUCRS, Porto Alegre, Brazil
{ramiro.barros,v.turani}@edu.pucrs.br,
{rodrigo.barros,lucas.kupssinsku}@pucrs.br
[2] Kunumi Institute, Belo Horizonte, Brazil

Abstract. Sentence Embeddings support semantic search, retrieval-augmented generation, clustering, and classification, yet most deployed encoders are either encoder-only transformers or Autoregressive Language Model (ARLM) adapted with additional training. Recently, Diffusion Language Model (DLM) have been proposed as an alternative that refines full-sequence representations through iterative denoising with bidirectional context. In this work, we examine whether such models can also serve as effective sentence encoders under training-free conditions—varying only pooling and layer aggregation. We compare a diffusion model (LLaDA-8B) against an Autoregressive (AR) baseline (Llama 3-8B), sweeping a grid of pooling functions and layer-aggregation schemes, on three representative MTEB tasks—ArguAna, Banking77, and STS-Benchmark. We find that diffusion-based encoders can match or exceed AR baselines when pooling and layer choices are tuned. Our results show that mean pooling over top layers is most effective for diffusion encoders, whereas AR models are more sensitive to extraction choices and benefit from special-token exclusion and low-layer aggregation in classification.

Keywords: Sentence Embeddings · diffusion language models · autoregressive language models · text pooling

1 Introduction

Sentence Embeddings (SE) drive semantic search, Retrieval-Augmented Generation (RAG), clustering, deduplication, and downstream classification in modern Natural Language Processing (NLP). Encoder-only models such as BERT and RoBERTa introduced the now-standard recipe of pooling token-level representations into fixed-length sentence vectors [7,14], and subsequent contrastive approaches sharpened these vectors specifically for retrieval and Semantic Textual Similarity (STS) tasks [8,24]. Benchmarks like Massive Text Embedding

R. N. Barros and V. C. Turani—Equal contribution.

M. Recamonde-Mendoza and R. C. Barros (Eds.): BRACIS 2026, LNAI 17105, pp. 401–415, 2027.
https://doi.org/10.1007/978-3-032-39882-6_27

Benchmark (MTEB) [16] provide systematic evidence that different architectures and pooling choices can lead to markedly different performance across tasks and languages. Taken together, these observations show that both *how* we obtain SEs and *which* models we use matter in practice.

As models with bidirectional context are explored, DLMs have emerged as promising alternatives to ARLMs for text generation. Building on the Denoising Diffusion Probabilistic Models (DDPMs) idea from the vision domain [9], DLMs generate text by iteratively denoising continuous representations rather than strictly predicting tokens from left to right. Initial NLP adaptations (e.g., Diffusion-LM [12]) demonstrate controllable generation by steering in latent space. More recently, large-scale models based on already pre-trained Language Models (LMs) and further refined with Supervised Fine-Tuning (SFT) (e.g., Large Language Diffusion Model (LLaDA)-8B [17]) have reported competitive results against similarly-sized AR models. Because diffusion models refine the entire sequence at every step, they continuously condition on the global context, maintaining bidirectional conditioning, a property that aligns well with producing sentence representations.

In contrast, decoder-only ARLMs (e.g., GPT-3) are pre-trained with a causal objective that restricts attention to past tokens during training [3]. Turning these models into encoders typically requires nontrivial adaptations or extra inference costs. Echo Embeddings [21], for example, duplicate the input and read off representations from the repeated segment, improving quality but increasing context length and latency. LLM2Vec [2] enables bidirectional attention and applies masked/contrastive objectives to repurpose decoder LMs into text encoders, improving the quality at the expense of additional training and engineering. These adaptations highlight a practical gap: ARLMs can yield strong embeddings but often with trade-offs, such as additional inference cost in the case of Echo Embeddings or architectural changes and additional pre-training in the case of LLM2Vec.

In this study, we investigate whether DLMs can serve as sentence encoders and compare them with an ARLM baseline with a comparable number of parameters. Specifically, we extracted embeddings from a DLM (LLaDA-8B [17]) and an AR baseline (Llama [23]) under matched settings and without task-specific fine-tuning, isolating the effect of extraction choices. Our study performs a comparison of pooling strategies over selected layers, and inclusion/exclusion of special tokens, to quantify their impact on SE tasks.

Experiments and evaluations were conducted following the MTEB [16], covering three representative SE tasks. We assess (i) STS for sentence-level semantic alignment, reported as Spearman's ρ on human-annotated similarity scores; (ii) retrieval, to measure ranking quality relevant to RAG; and (iii) classification, which tests the linear separability of embeddings through accuracy on labeled data sets. Together, these tasks span complementary aspects of embedding quality (semantic consistency, retrieval effectiveness, and discriminative utility) reflecting the core practical demands of modern SE applications.

Our research question is: *How good are SEs from DLMs compared to similarly sized ARLMs?* To answer this research question, we conduct a **fine-tuning-free** comparison of DLMs and ARLMs as sentence encoders. We (i) enumerate pooling designs (mean/max, IDF-weighted) and layer aggregation strategies (last, last4 (L4), window-based (first8/mid8/last8)) and quantify their effects; (ii) evaluate on MTEB tasks STS, retrieval, and classification; and (iii) run a controlled diffusion-vs-AR comparison using the best-matched configurations to isolate architecture from extraction choices. Together, these results map when diffusion encoders lag, match, or surpass comparable AR models and provide practical guidance for selecting pooling and layer strategies for SE applications.[1]

2 Background

2.1 Sentence Embeddings

Early sentence representations relied on static word embeddings such as Word2Vec [15] and GloVe [18], which assign each word a fixed vector regardless of context. Encoder only models such as BERT [7] introduced contextual token-level representations, enabling bidirectional context integration and substantially improving downstream performance. These encoder-only models establish the standard recipe for obtaining sentence vectors: pool token-level representations into a fixed-length vector. As we show in this work, the same pooling recipe can be applied to DLMs, which produce rich contextual representations without the causal constraint of decoder-only architectures.

2.2 Evaluation Benchmarks for Sentence Representations

The proliferation of SE methods led to the creation of standard benchmarks to evaluate and compare them. SentEval [6] is an early toolkit that provides a suite of evaluation tasks for universal sentence representations, including STS, paraphrase identification, entailment (Natural Language Inference), and various classification tasks.

Building on previous benchmarks, MTEB [16] was introduced as a comprehensive evaluation platform covering over 50 datasets across diverse languages and task categories (from clustering to information retrieval and question answering). MTEB standardized the evaluation protocol and provides a single number for overall performance as well as breakdowns by task type. One key finding from MTEB is that no single model or approach dominates universally across all tasks [16]. For instance, models based on different architectures (transformer encoders vs. large generative models) or training objectives (supervised vs. unsupervised) excel on different subsets of tasks. This underscores the influence of both model design and embedding extraction choices on performance, motivating research into how architectural differences and pooling methods affect SE quality.

---
[1] Code: https://github.com/RamiroNB/Diffused-Embeddings.

2.3 ARLMs as Encoders

ARLMs, like OpenAI's GPT-3 [3] and a more recent open-source Llama [23], are trained to predict text left-to-right and have demonstrated remarkable generation and few-shot learning capabilities. However, due to their causal attention mechanism, these decoder-only models do not naturally produce embeddings that capture the full bidirectional context of a sentence in one forward pass.

Turning an ARLM into a sentence encoder typically requires non-trivial adaptations or extra inference costs [10]. Since many large LMs can follow prompts, one can prompt the model to produce a summary or description and then use the hidden state of that generated summary as an embedding [10, 11]. Among the prompting-based methods, the study on Echo Embeddings [21] feed the input text to a GPT-style model twice (appending a second "echoed" copy of the sequence) and then use the hidden state corresponding to the end of the second copy as the sentence representation. This trick forces the ARLM to implicitly attend to the entire original input when predicting the echo, yielding a more holistic embedding at the cost of doubling the sequence length. Echo Embeddings illustrate that prompting substantially sharpen sentence representations from frozen LLMs, without any additional fine-tuning.

Another approach, LLM2Vec [2], transforms the ARLMs into a sentence encoder by modifying a pre-trained decoder LM with bidirectional attention layers, and fine-tunes it so that the model learns to output meaningful sentence vectors. By doing so, LLM2Vec repurposes a generative LM into an encoder without training from scratch. These strategies demonstrate that ARLMs can produce high-quality SE comparable to those from encoders, but typically with additional computational overhead (longer inputs or extra training). The need for such workarounds highlights the fundamental limitation: an AR model's one-directional training objective is at odds with the inherently bidirectional nature of encoding semantic content.

2.4 Diffusion Language Models and LLaDA

DLMs generate text by iteratively denoising a sequence of representations, rather than predicting tokens left to right. Building on DDPMs from computer vision [9], Diffusion-LM [12] adapts this process to text using a Transformer with full self-attention at each denoising step, allowing every token to attend to all positions in the sequence at every iteration. This bidirectional conditioning means that the final hidden states are a product of multiple passes of global context integration: every token's representation encodes information from the entire sentence, past and future, distilled through the denoising process. In contrast, ARLMs restrict each token to attend only to past positions during training, requiring additional adaptations such as input duplication [21] or architectural changes [2] to produce comparable context coverage. More recent DLMs such as LLaDA [17] and Dream [26] have scaled this paradigm to billions of parameters, reporting performance on par with similarly sized AR models on reasoning and generation tasks.

LLaDA operates in a discrete token space by progressively masking input tokens with a special `[MASK]` symbol at noise levels $t \in [0, 1]$, and trains a Transformer to predict all masked tokens conditioned on the visible ones, a masked-token prediction objective parameterized as a diffusion process with a continuous noise schedule. Unlike image diffusion models that refine continuous latent vectors [9], denoising in LLaDA happens entirely in discrete token space. The *Instruct* variant is further trained via SFT on prompt–response pairs, applying masking and denoising only to the response segment, keeping prompt tokens visible [17]. These properties make LLaDA a suitable backbone for evaluating diffused embeddings.

2.5 Pooling Strategies and Layer Aggregation

A critical aspect of obtaining SE from any model is the pooling strategy used to compress token-level features into a single vector. Different approaches can significantly affect the quality of the resulting embeddings. A simple and widely used technique is mean pooling, i.e., averaging all token embeddings in the sequence (optionally excluding trivial tokens such as punctuation or padding). This method tends to produce a robust representation of the overall content and was adopted as a default in many early works.

Some models instead rely on a special classification token. For example, BERT [7] introduces a [CLS] token whose output embedding is intended to capture a summary of the sequence. This representation can be directly used as the SE, as done in BERT's original setup and in many fine-tuned tasks. Other heuristic approaches include max pooling, which selects the maximum value across tokens for each feature dimension to highlight salient features, and IDF-weighted pooling, which emphasizes informative (rare) words while downweighting common ones.

Beyond token-level pooling, another important design choice is which layer or combination of layers to use. The final layer of a pre-trained model does not always yield the best embeddings for semantic tasks. In BERT, for instance, earlier layers can sometimes produce representations that better capture semantic similarity, as the final layer is more specialized for the pre-training objective. Similarly, ELMo demonstrated that a learned weighted combination of internal layers can improve downstream performance [19], suggesting that multi-layer aggregation enriches representations.

In transformer-based models, recent practices for SE include concatenating or averaging the last few layers (e.g., "last-2" or "last-4" combinations in BERT-based models). These strategies have been shown to yield improvements in tasks such as STS and information retrieval. Furthermore, results from MTEB [16] highlight that no single pooling strategy is universally optimal, as different tasks benefit from different extraction methods.

Motivated by these observations, our study devotes careful attention to pooling and layer aggregation. We evaluate mean versus max pooling, the inclusion or exclusion of special tokens (e.g., [CLS] or end-of-sequence markers), and the impact of using single-layer versus multi-layer representations. By controlling these factors consistently across diffusion and AR models, we ensure that performance differences reflect architectural properties rather than artifacts of embedding extraction.

3 Related Work

Building on diffusion ideas from vision [9], Diffusion-LM [12] adapts iterative denoising to text, operating on full sequences of continuous representations. More recent systems such as LLaDA [17] and LongLLaDA [13] scale this paradigm to billions of parameters, showing that DLMs can match or approach the quality of similarly sized AR transformers on standard language benchmarks.

However, these studies focus on generation quality and downstream task performance rather than on frozen SE under controlled extraction settings. Zhang et al. [29] report that diffusion-based representations can outperform those from comparable ARLMs on long-document retrieval, but do not isolate the effect of pooling and layer aggregation.

Zhang et al. [28] survey speculative decoding, multi-token prediction, insertion-based generation, and diffusion-based methods, and highlight that DLMs can attain favorable speed–quality trade-offs for long outputs by refining entire sequences in parallel. Learn2PD [1] and related adaptive schemes treat parallel decoding as a decision problem, learning when and how many tokens to finalize and reporting large throughput gains on LLaDA without quality loss. These advances make diffusion models more attractive as practical backbones by mitigating raw inference cost, but they are primarily concerned with generation efficiency rather than the quality of frozen SE.

While the previous studies presented focus on fine-tuning or decoding efficiency, our study compares the performance of diffusion and AR backbones as frozen sentence encoders, varying only pooling and layer aggregation, and benchmarking the resulting embeddings on representative STS, retrieval, and classification tasks.

4 Diffused Embeddings

We use the term *diffused embeddings* to denote sentence representations extracted from DLMs without task-specific fine-tuning. Given an input sequence $x = (w_1, \ldots, w_S)$ of length S, we run model inference to obtain token-level hidden states

$$\mathbf{H} = \begin{bmatrix} \mathbf{h}_1 \\ \vdots \\ \mathbf{h}_S \end{bmatrix} \in \mathbb{R}^{S \times d},$$

where $\mathbf{h}_i \in \mathbb{R}^d$ is the hidden state associated with token w_i and d is the hidden dimension. We then pool these token representations into a fixed-length sentence vector $\mathbf{z} \in \mathbb{R}^d$. This mirrors the established encoder-style recipe used for SE [20], but is applied to DLMs.

Figure 1 highlights a key architectural contrast between DLMs and ARLMs. In ARLMs, causal self-attention generates the hidden states $\mathbf{H}$ sequentially, restricting each token to attend only to past positions and therefore preventing access to future context at inference time. In contrast, DLMs employ bidirectional self-attention, allowing every token to attend to all others. This behavior makes DLMs natural candidates for deriving embeddings, since each token representation already integrates global context without requiring architectural modifications or inference-time tricks.

Starting from a noisy token embedding matrix, the diffusion model refines the continuous token representations through a sequence of denoising steps ($t = 1, \ldots, T$). At each step, bidirectional self-attention integrates contextual information across the entire sequence, allowing every token representation $\mathbf{h}_i^{(t)}$ to depend on both past and future tokens.

Pooling Strategies. Before detailing our experimental setup, we formalize the pooling operators used to compress the final-layer matrix $\mathbf{H}_T$ into a single vector $\mathbf{z} \in \mathbb{R}^d$, using the notation introduced above. We additionally denote by $m_i \in \{0, 1\}$ the usual attention mask, with $m_i = 1$ for valid (non-padding) positions and $m_i = 0$ for padding. We study five pooling strategies:

$$
\begin{aligned}
\textbf{Mean:} \quad & \mathbf{z} = \frac{\sum_{i=1}^{S} m_i \, \mathbf{h}_i}{\sum_{i=1}^{S} m_i} \\
\textbf{Mean-no-special(MNS):} \quad & \mathbf{z} = \frac{\sum_{i=1}^{S} m_i \mathbb{K}[w_i \notin \mathcal{I}_{\mathrm{sp}}] \, \mathbf{h}_i}{\sum_{i=1}^{S} m_i \mathbb{K}[w_i \notin \mathcal{I}_{\mathrm{sp}}]} \\
\textbf{EOS:} \quad & \mathbf{z} = \mathbf{h}_{i^\star}, \quad i^\star = \max\{i \mid m_i = 1\} \\
\textbf{Max:} \quad & \mathbf{z} = \max_{i: m_i = 1} \, \mathbf{h}_i \\
\textbf{IDF-Mean:} \quad & \mathbf{z} = \frac{\sum_{i=1}^{S} m_i \, \mathrm{idf}(w_i) \, \mathbf{h}_i}{\sum_{i=1}^{S} m_i \, \mathrm{idf}(w_i)}
\end{aligned}
$$

Here, $\mathcal{I}_{\mathrm{sp}}$ denotes the set of special tokens (e.g., padding, BOS, EOS, and unknown tokens) defined by the tokenizer, and $\mathbb{K}[\cdot]$ is the indicator function: for any condition C, $\mathbb{K}[C] = 1$ if C is true and $\mathbb{K}[C] = 0$ otherwise (e.g., $\mathbb{K}[w_i \notin \mathcal{I}_{\mathrm{sp}}] = 1$ only if token w_i is not special). The **mean** and **max** pooling operators use all non-padding positions (as indicated by the attention mask), whereas **MNS** ignores special tokens. **IDF-Mean** further reweights tokens by inverse document frequency, down-weighting high-frequency words; we estimate $\mathrm{idf}(\cdot)$ on a held-out corpus before evaluation.

Layer Aggregation. In addition to pooling across tokens, we also aggregate information across depth. Instead of using only the last hidden layer, we experiment

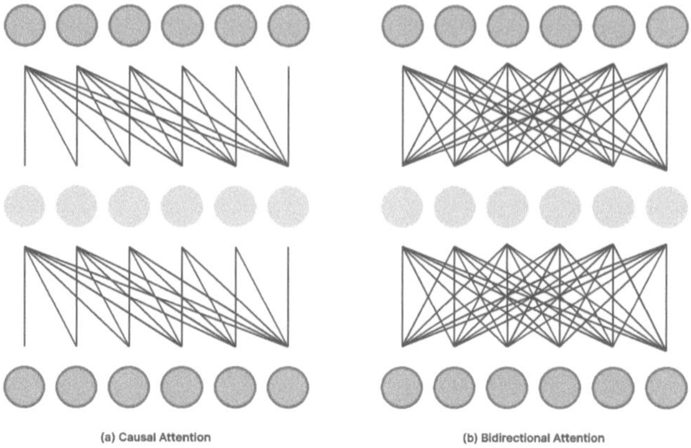

Fig. 1. Comparison between (a) causal and (b) bidirectional self-attention. In causal attention, each token can only attend to past positions, whereas bidirectional attention allows all tokens to attend to one another.

with simple layer-aggregation schemes to reduce variance and capture complementary signals. We consider: last (final layer only), L4 (mean of the last four layers), and window-based (fixed windows by depth), such as *first8*, *mid8*, and *last8*. For the latter, we average contiguous blocks of eight layers near the bottom, middle, or top of the stack. In all cases, we first apply the chosen layer aggregation to obtain a single token-level representation $\mathbf{H}$ and then compute $\mathbf{z}$ using one of the pooling operators. Finally, we apply L2 normalization to $\mathbf{z}$.

5 Experimental Methodology

Models. We compare a DLM [17] against an equivalent-size AR decoder from the Llama 8B family [23]. In all experiments, both models were used strictly as frozen encoders: we never updated their parameters and only extracted hidden states for creating diffused embeddings.

Post-training. For each architecture, we consider both *Base* and *Instruct* variants, i.e., LLaDA-8B-Base vs. LLaDA-8B-Instruct and Llama-8B-Base vs. Llama-8B-Instruct. In both families, the Instruct models are obtained by applying additional post-training on top of the same pre-trained weights, but the alignment pipelines are not identical. LLaDA-8B-Instruct is trained via supervised fine-tuning (SFT) on prompt–response pairs, following a masked-diffusion objective adapted to instruction data [17]. In contrast, instruction-tuned Llama combines SFT with preference-based alignment methods such as rejection sampling or direct preference optimisation (DPO) on human or synthetic preference data [3,23]. As a result, even though we deliberately narrow other sources of variation (frozen weights, matched model size, and identical embedding extraction and pooling pipelines), residual differences in post-training and alignment may still impact the results.

Tokenization and Inference. For each model, we use its respective tokenizers, with truncation enabled and a fixed maximum length of 128. Inference is run on Graphics Processing Units (GPUs) in reduced precision (bfloat16), and we enable the output of hidden states to collect per-layer token representations ${\mathbf{H}^{(\ell)}}_{\ell=1}^{L}$ for each input.

Pooling and Layer Grid. We systematically evaluate a grid over (i) token-pooling operators and (ii) layer-aggregation strategies, as introduced in Sect. 4. The pooling operators are mean, max, EOS, MNS, and IDF-Mean, corresponding respectively to mean pooling, max pooling, EOS-based pooling, mean pooling excluding tokenizer-defined special tokens (padding, BOS, EOS, unknown, etc.), and IDF-weighted mean pooling. All operators use only non-padding positions, as indicated by the attention mask; MNS additionally discards special tokens. For IDF-Mean, we estimate inverse document frequencies idf(·) from raw text in a held-out slice of the evaluation corpus, following the standard Information Retrieval (IR) preprocessing.

For layer aggregation, we consider last, L4, and window-based (first8/mid8/last8). The last strategy uses only the final hidden layer; L4 averages the last four layers; and window-based averages fixed windows of eight contiguous layers near the bottom (first8), middle (mid8), or top (last8) of the stack. In all cases, we first aggregate across layers to obtain a single token-level representation $\mathbf{H}$ and then apply one of the pooling operators above to obtain a sentence vector $\mathbf{z}$.

Tasks and Metrics. We evaluate on three MTEB [16] tasks: ArguAna [25] (argument retrieval), Banking77 [4] (single-sentence intent classification), and STSBenchmark [5] (semantic textual similarity). For STSBenchmark, we report Spearman's ρ between the cosine similarities and gold similarity scores. For ArguAna, we follow the MTEB **Retrieval** protocol and report standard metric normalized Discounted Cumulative Gain (nDCG)@10. For Banking77, we report the classification accuracy, as defined in MTEB.

Evaluation Protocol. All evaluations are run via the official MTEB Application Programming Interface (API) (v2) to ensure consistent task definitions and metrics. For each backbone, we vary only pooling and layer-aggregation choices. We report: (a) the best-performing configuration per model, (b) a results Table 1 grouped by pooling family (mean-like, max-like, EOS-based, IDF-weighted), and (c) trends across layer windows (bottom/middle/top). For reproducibility, we record all inference hyperparameters: encoding batch size of 64, `bfloat16` weights/activations, and L2-normalization applied to all SE.

6 Results and Discussion

We compared the diffusion-based LLaDA and LLaDA Instruct models against Llama and Llama Instruct on the three MTEB tasks (Sect. 5). For each model, we sweep a grid of pooling configurations that vary in (i) how layers are combined (last, L4, window-based (first8/mid8/last8)) and (ii) how token representations are aggregated (mean, max, EOS, MNS and IDF-Mean).

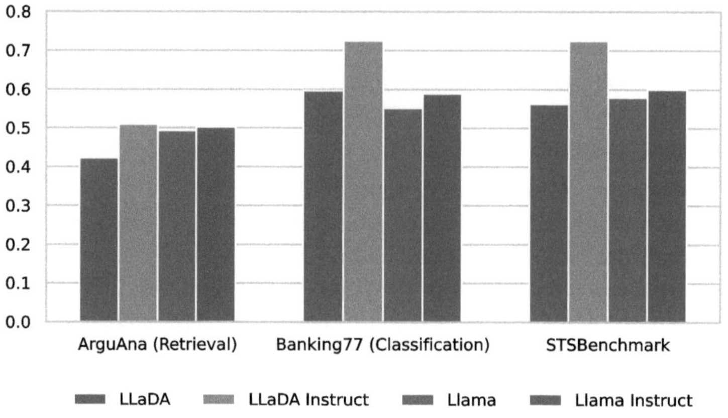

Fig. 2. Top performance per model on three MTEB tasks. Scores are nDCG@10 for ArguAna (retrieval), accuracy for Banking77 (classification), and Spearman's ρ for STSBenchmark (semantic similarity).

Table 1. Complete pooling–layer grid for diffusion and AR encoders on MTEB benchmarks. **Bold** = best per model within each benchmark; **underline+bold** = overall best across all models. LB = LLaDA Base, LI = LLaDA Instruct, MB = Llama Base, MI = Llama Instruct. F8 = first 8, M8 = mid 8, T8 = last 8, L = last, L4 = last 4.

Pooling	Layer	ArguAna				Banking77				STSBenchmark			
		LB	LI	MB	MI	LB	LI	MB	MI	LB	LI	MB	MI
EOS	F8	0.003	0.004	0.009	0.010	0.035	0.065	0.335	0.403	0.168	0.265	0.347	0.378
	M8	0.004	0.004	0.013	0.011	0.025	0.092	0.339	0.444	0.132	0.113	0.374	0.381
	T8	0.004	0.009	0.056	0.047	0.173	0.107	0.378	0.483	0.188	0.174	0.436	0.486
	L	0.010	0.020	0.045	0.041	0.210	0.200	0.314	0.414	0.198	0.202	0.394	0.451
	L4	0.006	0.011	0.054	0.047	0.229	0.139	0.375	0.474	0.205	0.205	0.435	0.487
IDF-Mean	F8	0.260	0.310	0.353	0.344	0.271	0.450	0.289	0.290	0.559	0.578	0.223	0.230
	M8	0.318	0.344	0.426	0.402	0.233	0.570	0.377	0.357	0.506	0.618	0.363	0.373
	T8	0.361	0.429	0.486	0.497	0.543	0.628	0.481	0.503	0.419	0.696	0.579	**0.600**
	L	0.370	0.490	0.414	0.417	0.488	0.673	0.401	0.429	0.449	0.668	0.533	0.547
	L4	0.401	0.469	0.467	0.484	0.571	0.659	0.464	0.495	0.432	**0.725**	**0.572**	0.590
Max	F8	0.203	0.234	0.194	0.196	0.367	0.481	0.013	0.013	**0.562**	0.606	0.433	0.479
	M8	0.157	0.206	0.343	0.313	0.240	0.561	0.013	0.013	0.271	0.478	0.427	0.453
	T8	0.172	0.274	0.397	0.376	0.515	0.632	0.369	0.370	0.378	0.500	0.485	0.473
	L	0.163	0.285	0.297	0.257	0.423	0.674	0.381	0.421	0.422	0.612	0.425	0.436
	L4	0.240	0.347	0.383	0.368	0.544	0.649	0.377	0.395	0.445	0.552	0.463	0.456
Mean	F8	0.276	0.332	0.370	0.362	0.297	0.501	0.270	0.281	0.489	0.519	0.213	0.227
	M8	0.329	0.358	0.434	0.404	0.233	0.602	0.255	0.226	0.395	0.534	0.203	0.209
	T8	0.392	0.462	0.492	0.501	0.575	0.697	0.380	0.375	0.364	0.641	0.360	0.359
	L	0.387	**0.509**	0.425	0.432	0.495	0.694	0.416	0.446	0.418	0.647	0.459	0.482
	L4	**0.423**	0.495	0.475	0.489	**0.596**	**0.725**	0.417	0.426	0.384	0.687	0.409	0.418
MNS	F8	0.276	0.332	0.380	0.369	0.297	0.501	**0.552**	**0.589**	0.489	0.519	0.497	0.524
	M8	0.329	0.358	0.438	0.408	0.233	0.602	0.519	0.549	0.395	0.534	0.475	0.504
	T8	0.392	0.462	**0.493**	**0.502**	0.575	0.697	0.524	0.561	0.364	0.641	0.521	0.548
	L	0.387	**0.509**	0.425	0.432	0.495	0.694	0.419	0.449	0.418	0.647	0.458	0.480
	L4	**0.423**	0.495	0.476	0.489	**0.596**	**0.725**	0.500	0.534	0.384	0.687	0.506	0.529

6.1 Comparison Between Diffusion vs. AR Encoders

Figure 2 highlights the best performance of each model on the three MTEB tasks. Two general trends emerge. First, instruction-tuning consistently helps both architectures: the Instruct variants outperform their base counterparts across all datasets and pooling strategies. Second, LLaDA Instruct achieves the highest score on every task, with particularly large margins on Banking77 and STSBenchmark.

Table 1 shows the complete pooling–layer grid for all four models. Picking the best configuration per model, LLaDA Instruct outperforms Llama Instruct by +0.007 on ArguAna (0.509 vs. 0.502), +0.136 on Banking77 (0.725 vs. 0.589), and +0.125 on STSBenchmark (0.725 vs. 0.600). The narrow gap on ArguAna, where all models achieve lower absolute scores than on the other two tasks, suggests that architectural differences between diffusion and AR encoders play a more limited role in retrieval settings. In contrast, the larger margins on Banking77 and STSBenchmark indicate that, under matched pooling and layer aggregation, DLMs can translate their full-context training signal into higher downstream sentence-encoding quality.

Secondary patterns are visible across the grid. EOS pooling consistently underperforms token-aggregation methods for both architectures, likely because a single special token carries a limited sentence semantics when the model was not explicitly trained to deposit sentence meaning there. Finally, the Base-to-Instruct gap is larger for LLaDA than for Llama across all pooling strategies, suggesting that instruction-tuning has a stronger effect on representation quality in diffusion models than in their AR counterparts.

6.2 Pooling-Family Trends

Beyond individual best scores, we examine how different pooling families behave across the full grid. On Banking77 and STSBenchmark, DLMs clearly benefit from mean and IDF-Mean pooling: compared to AR models, LLaDA Instruct gains approximately +0.03 with IDF-Mean on Banking77 and roughly +0.08 on STSBenchmark. MNS pooling, which excludes padding and special tokens from the average, yields the best results for Llama on Banking77 (0.589, MNS+F8), suggesting that for AR models the special tokens introduce noise that hurts classification. On ArguAna, AR models tend to perform better on average across pooling types, but LLaDA Instruct's best configuration still matches or slightly exceeds that of Llama Instruct (0.509 vs. 0.502). Overall, these patterns confirm that DLMs are more effective than ARLMs under standard pooling schemes for semantic similarity and intent classification, while retrieval remains the more challenging setting for both architectures.

6.3 Layer-Depth Trends

We next examine how performance changes across layer windows. Prior work has shown that different layers of AR LLMs encode qualitatively distinct information, and that intermediate layers can complement the last layer for embedding tasks [22]. Our grid allows us to test whether this observation extends to diffusion encoders.

On Banking77, LLaDA Instruct achieves its best scores with the top and last-aggregated layers: Mean+L4 and MNS+L4 both reach 0.725, compared to 0.501 at the bottom window (F8). For AR models on the same task, the bottom window is markedly more informative (MNS+F8 = 0.589 vs. MNS+L4 = 0.534), suggesting that Llama's lower layers capture intent-discriminative features that are lost or overwritten in deeper layers. On STSBenchmark, LLaDA Instruct again benefits from deeper layers (IDF-Mean+L4 = 0.725), while Llama Instruct peaks in the top window (IDF-Mean+T8 = 0.600). In retrieval (ArguAna), AR models remain ahead at every depth window, but the gap narrows at the top layers: LLaDA Instruct reaches 0.509 at Mean+last, while Llama Instruct's best is 0.502 at MNS+T8. Taken together, these trends suggest that diffused embeddings provide stronger signals across a broader range of depths for semantic classification and similarity, whereas AR embeddings are more sensitive to reading position.

6.4 Naive vs. Tuned Pooling

We also compare naive mean pooling over the last layer (Mean+last) with the best configuration found for each model and task. For LLaDA Instruct, Mean+last already achieves the optimal score on ArguAna (0.509) and comes within 0.031 of the best on Banking77 (0.694 vs. 0.725) and 0.078 on STS-Benchmark (0.647 vs. 0.725). In contrast, Llama Instruct is more sensitive to configuration: its Mean+last scores are 0.432 on ArguAna, 0.446 on Banking77, and 0.482 on STSBenchmark, all substantially below its respective bests of 0.502, 0.589, and 0.600. This reinforces the qualitative picture from Sect. 4: diffusion models provide last-layer token representations that are well-suited for sentence encoding, whereas AR models are more sensitive to *where* we read from the sequence.

6.5 Pre-training Scale and Instruction Tuning

LLaDA was trained from scratch on approximately 2.3×10^{12} tokens with a 4k-token context using roughly 1.3×10^{5} H800 GPU hours [17], while the AR counterpart Llama was pre-trained on substantially larger corpora of 1.5×10^{13} tokens [23]. These differences in pre-training scale would, in principle, favor Llama as an encoder. Yet LLaDA Instruct consistently outperforms Llama Instruct on two of the three tasks, suggesting that the full-context training signal of masked diffusion may compensate for the smaller pre-training budget when the downstream task rewards global sentence-level semantics.

Comparing base vs. Instruct variants, we find that LLaDA benefits more from supervised fine-tuning than Llama. LLaDA Instruct improves over LLaDA Base by +0.086 on ArguAna (0.509 vs. 0.423), +0.129 on Banking77 (0.725 vs. 0.596), and +0.038 on STSBenchmark (0.687 vs. 0.562, reading Max+F8 as LLaDA Base's best on STS), whereas Llama's gains are smaller in all cases. This asymmetry is consistent with the finding in LLaDA-V [27] that diffusion models exhibit strong data scalability and respond well to instruction-following fine-tuning even when the base model is weaker in absolute terms. Combined with the smaller pre-training corpus of LLaDA, this suggests that instruction tuning acts as an effective adapter that makes diffused hidden states more directly usable as SEs.

7 Limitations and Future Work

This study has two main limitations: First, we evaluate a single diffusion family (LLaDA) and a single AR family (Llama) at 8B parameters; broader comparisons across model sizes, architectures, and languages are needed to fully characterize the trade-offs. Second, we evaluated only zero-shot embeddings on a small subset of MTEB; extending the analysis to more tasks (e.g., question answering, clustering, reranking) and to multilingual settings would yield a more comprehensive picture.

8 Conclusion

In this study, we investigated DLMs as sentence encoders and compared them with similarly sized ARLMs. We introduced the notion of *diffused embeddings*: sentence representations obtained by pooling the native hidden states of DLMs without additional fine-tuning or architectural changes. Using LLaDA (base and Instruct) and Llama (base and Instruct), we evaluated a total of 25 combinations of pooling and layer-aggregation strategies on three representative MTEB tasks: ArguAna (retrieval), Banking77 (intent classification), and STSBenchmark (semantic textual similarity).

Our findings support three main conclusions:

- **DLMs are promising sentence encoders.** Across the three benchmarks, the best diffusion configuration (LLaDA Instruct) consistently matches or outperforms the best AR configuration (Llama Instruct), with particularly strong gains on Banking77 and STSBenchmark. This shows that DLMs can yield promising SE even when trained on smaller corpora than modern ARLMs.
- **Diffused embeddings are more robust to pooling strategy.** For LLaDA, simple mean-style pooling over the top layers (with or without IDF weighting) is enough to achieve better performance, and naive mean pooling on the last layer is already a good alternative. In contrast, Llama only reaches its top performance when we carefully select the pooling window (e.g., restricting to early or mid-sequence spans and excluding special tokens). This suggests that final-layer token representations in diffusion models are more uniformly useful for sentence encoding, whereas AR models produce states that remain more entangled with the left-to-right next-token prediction objective.

- **Instruction tuning is particularly beneficial for diffusion encoders.** Comparing base and Instruct variants, we observe that supervised instruction tuning improves LLaDA more than Llama on sentence-embedding benchmarks. This indicates that SFT acts as an effective adapter that makes diffused hidden states more directly usable as sentence encoders.

Taken together, these results provide quantitative evidence that DLMs are a promising alternative to traditional encoder or decoder architectures for building SE. They naturally support bidirectional attention at inference time and align well with encoder pooling recipes.

Acknowledgments. This study was financed in part by Conselho Nacional de Desenvolvimento Científico e Tecnológico (CNPq) – Grant Number: 443072/2024-8; and by Fundação de Amparo à Pesquisa do Estado do Rio Grande do Sul (FAPERGS) – Grant Number: 25/2551-0000891-3 and 25/2551-0002824-8. This work was supported by Kunumi Institute. The authors thank the institution for its financial support and commitment to advancing scientific research.

References

1. Bao, W., Chen, Z., Xu, D., Shang, Y.: Learning to parallel: accelerating diffusion large language models via learnable parallel decoding (2025). https://arxiv.org/abs/2509.25188
2. BehnamGhader, P., Adlakha, V., Mosbach, M., Bahdanau, D., Chapados, N., Reddy, S.: Llm2vec: large language models are secretly powerful text encoders (2024). https://arxiv.org/abs/2404.05961
3. Brown, T.B., et al.: Language models are few-shot learners. arXiv preprint arXiv:2005.14165 (2020)
4. Casanueva, I., Temcinas, T., Gerz, D., Henderson, M., Vulić, I.: Banking77: a dataset for banking and finance domain intent detection. In: Proceedings of the 12th Language Resources and Evaluation Conference (LREC) (2020)
5. Cer, D., Diab, M., Agirre, E., Lopez-Gazpio, I., Specia, L.: Semeval-2017 task 1: semantic textual similarity – multilingual and cross-lingual focused evaluation. In: Proceedings of the 11th International Workshop on Semantic Evaluation (SemEval-2017), pp. 1–14 (2017)
6. Conneau, A., Kiela, D.: SentEval: an evaluation toolkit for universal sentence representations. arXiv preprint arXiv:1803.05449 (2018)
7. Devlin, J., Chang, M., Lee, K., Toutanova, K.: BERT: pre-training of deep bidirectional transformers for language understanding. CoRR abs/1810.04805 (2018). http://arxiv.org/abs/1810.04805
8. Gao, T., Yao, X., Chen, D.: Simcse: simple contrastive learning of sentence embeddings (2022). https://arxiv.org/abs/2104.08821
9. Ho, J., Jain, A., Abbeel, P.: Denoising diffusion probabilistic models. In: Advances in Neural Information Processing Systems (2020). https://arxiv.org/abs/2006.11239
10. Jiang, T., Huang, S., Luan, Z., Wang, D., Zhuang, F.: Scaling sentence embeddings with large language models. In: Findings of EMNLP 2024, pp. 3182–3196 (2024). https://doi.org/10.18653/v1/2024.findings-emnlp.181

11. Lei, Y., et al.: Meta-task prompting elicits embeddings from large language models. In: Proceedings of the 62nd Annual Meeting of the ACL (Long Papers), pp. 10141–10157 (2024). https://doi.org/10.18653/v1/2024.acl-long.546
12. Li, X.L., Thickstun, J., Gulrajani, I., Liang, P., Hashimoto, T.: Diffusion-LM improves controllable text generation. arXiv preprint arXiv:2205.14217 (2022)
13. Liu, X., Liu, Z., Huang, Z., Guo, Q., He, Z., Qiu, X.: Longllada: unlocking long context capabilities in diffusion LLMs (2025). https://arxiv.org/abs/2506.14429
14. Liu, Y., et al.: Roberta: a robustly optimized BERT pretraining approach. arXiv preprint arXiv:1907.11692 (2019)
15. Mikolov, T., Chen, K., Corrado, G., Dean, J.: Efficient estimation of word representations in vector space (2013). https://arxiv.org/abs/1301.3781
16. Muennighoff, N., Tazi, N., Magne, L., Reimers, N.: Mteb: massive text embedding benchmark (2023). https://arxiv.org/abs/2210.07316
17. Nie, Y., et al.: Large language diffusion models. arXiv preprint arXiv:2502.09992 (2025)
18. Pennington, J., Socher, R., Manning, C.D.: Glove: global vectors for word representation. In: Proceedings of the 2014 Conference on Empirical Methods in Natural Language Processing (EMNLP), pp. 1532–1543 (2014)
19. Peters, M.E., et al.: Deep contextualized word representations. In: Proceedings of the 2018 Conference of the North American Chapter of the ACL: Human Language Technologies, pp. 2227–2237 (2018)
20. Reimers, N., Gurevych, I.: Sentence-BERT: sentence embeddings using Siamese BERT-networks. EMNLP-IJCNLP (2019). https://arxiv.org/abs/1908.10084
21. Springer, J.M., Kotha, S., Fried, D., Neubig, G., Raghunathan, A.: Repetition improves language model embeddings (2025). https://arxiv.org/abs/2402.15449
22. Tang, Y., Yang, Y.: Pooling and attention: what are effective designs for LLM-based embedding models? (2024). https://arxiv.org/abs/2409.02727
23. Touvron, H., et al.: Llama: open and efficient foundation language models (2023). https://arxiv.org/abs/2302.13971
24. Wang, L., et al.: Text embeddings by weakly-supervised contrastive pre-training (2024). https://arxiv.org/abs/2212.03533
25. Wieneke, W., Daxenberger, J., Gurevych, I.: Data-driven argument retrieval and analysis. In: Proceedings of the 7th Workshop on Argument Mining (2020)
26. Ye, J., et al.: Dream 7b: diffusion large language models. arXiv preprint arXiv:2508.15487 (2025)
27. You, Z., et al.: Llada-V: large language diffusion models with visual instruction tuning (2025). https://arxiv.org/abs/2505.16933
28. Zhang, L., et al.: A survey on parallel text generation: From parallel decoding to diffusion language models (2025). https://arxiv.org/abs/2508.08712
29. Zhang, S., Zhao, Y., Geng, L., Cohan, A., Luu, A.T., Zhao, C.: Diffusion vs. autoregressive language models: a text embedding perspective (2025). https://arxiv.org/abs/2505.15045

Unifying Graph-Based Retrieval: A Higher-Order Topological Framework for RAG

Jorge Luiz Franco[1,3](✉), Erik Jhones Freitas do Nascimento[2], Filipe A. N. Verri[3], Diego Mesquita[4], Moacir Antonelli Ponti[1], and Amauri Holanda Souza[2]

[1] Universidade de São Paulo (USP), São Paulo, Brazil
[2] Instituto Federal de Educação, Ciência e Tecnologia do Ceará (IFCE), Ceará, Brazil
[3] Instituto Curvelo, São Paulo, Brazil
jorge.luiz@usp.br
[4] Fundação Getulio Vargas (FGV), Rio de Janeiro, Brazil

Abstract. Graph-based retrieval-augmented generation (RAG) is currently spread across several different representations: binary knowledge graphs (GFM-RAG), hypergraphs (HyperGraphRAG), and cell complexes (TopoRAG). These can all be viewed as instances of a single object, the *combinatorial complex* (CC), a fairly general domain in the topological deep-learning hierarchy. Starting from this observation, we describe **HigherOrderRAG**, a framework in which the differences between the methods above reduce to two design choices: a lifting operator Λ that maps a flat corpus into a CC, and a message-passing scheme that propagates query-conditioned relevance across cells of arbitrary rank. We instantiate Λ as an entity co-occurrence lifting and pair it with a query-conditioned higher-order message-passing network (QC-HOMP) and a multi-rank scoring head. On MuSiQue multi-hop QA, this configuration reaches R@5 = 76.6%, which is 18.4 points above GFM-RAG under the same evaluation protocol. Ablations suggest that most of the gain comes from the lifting operator: replacing k-NN with entity lifting under the same architecture is worth +7.4 R@5, and rank-1 reranking adds a further +5.6. We see the framework less as an end-state than as a way of making the lifting choice and the message-passing rank explicit and comparable.

Keywords: Retrieval-Augmented Generation · Combinatorial Topology · Higher-Order Message Passing · Topological Deep Learning · Multi-hop QA

1 Introduction

Multi-hop question answering requires synthesizing information from multiple passages that are *complementary* rather than similar. Answering "What country is the birthplace of the director of Jaws?" requires one passage identifying

M. Recamonde-Mendoza and R. C. Barros (Eds.): BRACIS 2026, LNAI 17105, pp. 416–430, 2027.
https://doi.org/10.1007/978-3-032-39882-6_28

Spielberg as director and another stating his birthplace—texts about different topics, linked only through a shared entity.

Standard RAG [9] relies on dense retrieval via cosine similarity, which ranks passages by topical overlap with the query. This fails for multi-hop reasoning: while the first passage matches the query, the bridging passage about Spielberg's birthplace shares little surface-level similarity with a question about Jaws.

Several graph-based RAG methods have been proposed in response. GFM-RAG [13] trains a GNN over binary knowledge-graph triples (h, r, t). Hyper-GraphRAG [12] and HyperRAG [11] use hyperedges to encode n-ary facts. TopoRAG [20] promotes existing textual graphs to cell complexes by detecting relational cycles. LP-RAG [14] casts retrieval as link prediction on a chunk-query graph. These representations are not interchangeable: each one constrains which passage interactions can be expressed and which retrieval patterns are learnable. The literature, however, has treated these choices in isolation, with no shared vocabulary for relating them or for predicting which choice suits which task.

It is convenient to view all of these representations as instances of a single object: a *combinatorial complex* (CC) [6,7], a general higher-order domain in the topological deep-learning hierarchy [16]. We use this perspective to discuss the methods above on a common footing. Our main contributions are:

1. We describe graph-based RAG as query-conditioned message passing on combinatorial complexes, which lets us discuss binary-graph, hypergraph and cell-complex methods on a common footing (Sects. 2–3).
2. We organise corpus-to-CC lifting operators into a small taxonomy and associate each existing method with a specific choice of lifting (Sect. 3.1).
3. We instantiate the framework with QC-HOMP, a query-conditioned message-passing scheme that exchanges information across cells of different rank (Sect. 3.2).
4. On MuSiQue, entity-based CC lifting paired with QC-HOMP reaches R@5 = 76.6%, which is the best result among the graph-based RAG baselines we compare with. Ablations look at the contribution of each component (Sect. 5).

2 Background: Higher-Order Topological Domains

Most graph-based RAG methods represent documents and entities as nodes connected by pairwise edges. Multi-hop reasoning, however, often involves groups of passages that are jointly relevant, which is a higher-order pattern that pairwise graphs do not represent directly. Topological deep learning (TDL) [7,16] offers a hierarchy of domains that generalise graphs in this direction. The four domains we use below are listed from most restrictive to most general.

Graphs. A graph $G = (V, E)$ has nodes V and edges $E \subseteq \{\{u, v\} \mid u, v \in V, u \neq v\}$. Each edge connects exactly two nodes. GFM-RAG [13] and LP-RAG [14] operate strictly at this pairwise relational level.

Hypergraphs. A hypergraph $\mathcal{H} = (V, E)$ generalizes graphs by allowing each hyperedge $e \in E$ to connect an arbitrary number of nodes: $e \subseteq V$ with $|e| \geq 2$. HyperGraphRAG [12] and HyperRAG [11] use this domain.

Simplicial and Cell Complexes. A simplicial complex $\mathcal{K}$ is a collection of subsets of V (called *simplices*) that is *downward closed*: if $\sigma \in \mathcal{K}$ and $\tau \subseteq \sigma$, then $\tau \in \mathcal{K}$. A k-simplex has $k+1$ vertices (0-simplices are nodes, 1-simplices are edges, 2-simplices are triangles, etc.). A cell complex relaxes downward closure but requires each k-cell's boundary to be homeomorphic to S^{k-1} (e.g., 2-cells must have cycle-shaped boundaries). TopoRAG [20] operates at this level, detecting relational cycles as 2-cells. TopoRAG assumes a *pre-existing textual graph* as input (e.g., knowledge bases, scene graphs); it does not address retrieval from unstructured corpora directly, which is the setting we consider here.

Combinatorial Complexes. A combinatorial complex (CC) is the most general domain. Following Hajij et al. [6], a CC is a triple $(\mathcal{S}, \mathcal{X}, \mathrm{rk})$ where $\mathcal{S}$ is a set of base entities, $\mathcal{X} \subseteq 2^{\mathcal{S}} \setminus \{\emptyset\}$ is a set of cells, and $\mathrm{rk} : \mathcal{X} \to \mathbb{Z}_{\geq 0}$ is a rank function satisfying two axioms:

1. Every singleton $\{s\}$ for $s \in \mathcal{S}$ is a rank-0 cell.
2. *Rank monotonicity*: if $x \subsetneq y$ are both cells, then $\mathrm{rk}(x) < \mathrm{rk}(y)$.

We write $\mathcal{X}_k = \{x \in \mathcal{X} : \mathrm{rk}(x) = k\}$ for the set of rank-k cells; thus $\mathcal{X}_0$ are nodes, $\mathcal{X}_1$ are edges or hyperedges, $\mathcal{X}_2$ are 2-cells, etc. Unlike simplicial complexes, CCs do not require downward closure. Unlike cell complexes, CCs impose no topological boundary conditions. This means a CC can have a rank-1 cell $\{a, b, c\}$ without requiring the edges $\{a, b\}$, $\{a, c\}$, $\{b, c\}$ to also be cells—exactly the flexibility needed when grouping chunks by shared entities.

These domains form a strict inclusion hierarchy: **Graph** $\subsetneq$ **Hypergraph** $\subsetneq$ **CC** and **Graph** $\subsetneq$ **Simp. Complex** $\subsetneq$ **Cell Complex** $\subsetneq$ **CC**. Hypergraphs and simplicial complexes are *incomparable*: neither contains the other. All four domains can be described as special cases of CCs.

Neighborhoods on CCs. Message passing requires a notion of adjacency. On a CC, each rank-k cell x has a *boundary neighborhood* $\mathcal{B}(x) = \{y \in \mathcal{X}_{k-1} : y \subsetneq x\}$ (lower-rank cells contained in x) and a *coboundary neighborhood* $\mathcal{B}^{\uparrow}(x) = \{y \in \mathcal{X}_{k+1} : x \subsetneq y\}$ (higher-rank cells containing x). Two rank-k cells are *upper-adjacent* if they share a common rank-$(k+1)$ cell. These neighborhoods induce incidence matrices $B_k \in \{0, 1\}^{|\mathcal{X}_{k-1}| \times |\mathcal{X}_k|}$ and adjacency matrices $A_{\uparrow,k} = B_{k+1} B_{k+1}^{\top} - \mathrm{diag}(B_{k+1} B_{k+1}^{\top})$, generalizing standard graph adjacency.

3 Method: HigherOrderRAG

HigherOrderRAG is a three-stage retrieval pipeline. Stage 1 applies a lifting operator Λ that maps the flat corpus into a combinatorial complex. Stage 2 runs query-conditioned higher-order message passing (QC-HOMP) on the resulting CC. Stage 3 scores chunks through a multi-rank head that combines a chunk-level score with a cell-level re-ranker. The next three subsections describe each stage.

3.1 Stage 1: Corpus Lifting

A *lifting operator* Λ maps a corpus $\mathcal{C} = \{c_1, \ldots, c_n\}$ into a CC $(\mathcal{S}, \mathcal{X}, \text{rk})$ with initial features $\mathbf{h}_x^{(0)} \in \mathbb{R}^d$ for each cell. Each existing RAG method corresponds to a specific lifting choice. We identify five operators, organized by the topological domain they produce.

Λ_{GRAPH} *: Binary KG Lifting (GFM-RAG).* Extract entity-relation-entity triples (h, r, t) via NER and OpenIE. Rank-0 cells are entities; rank-1 cells are binary edges $\{h, t\}$ with type labels. Chunks map to entities via entity linking. This is the lifting used by GFM-RAG [13].

Λ_{HYP} *: Hypergraph Lifting (HyperGraphRAG).* Represent n-ary facts as hyperedges over entities. Rank-1 cells can have arbitrary cardinality (vs. always 2 for graphs). Used by HyperGraphRAG [12], though with cosine retrieval rather than learned message passing.

Λ_{CW} *: Cell Complex Lifting (TopoRAG).* Given a *pre-existing* textual graph, detect fundamental cycles (via spanning tree) and attach them as rank-2 cells. The cell complex satisfies the boundary condition $\partial\sigma \cong S^{k-1}$. Used by TopoRAG [20], which is restricted to datasets where a graph structure is already provided and does not apply to unstructured corpora like MuSiQue [19].

Λ_{KNN} *: Similarity-Based Lifting (Ablation Baseline).* Connect each chunk to its k nearest neighbours by cosine similarity, forming rank-1 cells as star neighbourhoods. This produces a CC with the same rank-$\{0, 1\}$ structure as Λ_{ENTITY} but groups *similar* rather than *complementary* chunks. We use Λ_{KNN} as a controlled ablation baseline (Table 2) to isolate the effect of the grouping principle from the topological structure.

$\Lambda_{\mathit{ENTITY}}$ *: Entity Co-occurrence Lifting (Ours).* We lift at the **chunk level**, using shared entities as the grouping principle:

$$\mathcal{X}_0 = \{\{c_i\}\}, \qquad \mathcal{X}_1 = \{\sigma_e : e \in \mathcal{V},\ \sigma_e = \{c_i \in \mathcal{C} : e \in \mathcal{E}(c_i)\},\ |\sigma_e| \in [2, K_{\max}]\}, \tag{1}$$

where $\mathcal{E}(c_i) \subseteq \mathcal{V}$ are the named entities in chunk c_i. Each rank-1 cell groups all chunks sharing an entity. These chunks are *complementary*: they discuss different aspects of the same entity, which is exactly the structure needed for multi-hop retrieval. Gold chunk pairs in MuSiQue have mean cosine similarity of only 0.272, consistent with this view.[1]

We apply alias resolution via word-subset matching ("Obama" → "Barack Obama") and demonym normalization ("American" → "America"), reducing the

[1] The construction can produce two rank-1 cells with $\sigma_e \subsetneq \sigma_{e'}$ (e.g. if the chunks mentioning a specific person are a subset of those mentioning the country they work in). Strict CC rank monotonicity would require $\text{rk}(\sigma_e) < \text{rk}(\sigma_{e'})$, which fails when both are rank-1. We treat the construction as a *relaxed* CC in which same-rank set inclusion is permitted; the boundary and coboundary message-passing rules in Sect. 3.2 are defined strictly across consecutive ranks and so are unaffected by such inclusions.

entity vocabulary by approximately 20% while increasing connectivity. Entities with $|\sigma_e| > K_{\max}$ are subdivided into overlapping ego-cells via farthest-point sampling in embedding space.

$\Lambda_{\text{ENTITY+CYCLE}}$: *Entity + cycle lifting (rank-2 ablation).* We augment the entity hypergraph with rank-2 cells obtained by cycle detection. First, we construct a chunk adjacency graph G_{adj} where two chunks c_i, c_j are connected if they co-occur in at least one entity hyperedge:

$$(c_i, c_j) \in E_{\text{adj}} \iff \exists\, \sigma_e \in \mathcal{X}_1 : c_i \in \sigma_e \text{ and } c_j \in \sigma_e. \tag{2}$$

We then compute a cycle basis of G_{adj} using standard algorithms [1] and promote each cycle of length $\ell \in [3, 6]$ to a rank-2 cell. Since CC cells are sets rather than ordered tuples, we record only the vertex set of each cycle:

$$\mathcal{X}_2 = \big\{\{c_{i_1}, \ldots, c_{i_\ell}\} : (c_{i_1}, \ldots, c_{i_\ell}) \in \text{cycle\_basis}(G_{\text{adj}}),\ 3 \le \ell \le 6\big\}. \tag{3}$$

The cyclic order is retained at the level of the boundary edges (stored separately as rank-1 cells), but does not enter the cell set itself. The resulting CC has rank-0 chunks, rank-1 entity hyperedges, and rank-2 cycle cells, enabling same-rank message passing among entity hyperedges that share chunks in a cycle. We use this lifting in our ablation (Table 2) to test whether higher topological rank improves retrieval.

Table 1 summarizes how each RAG method maps to a lifting operator and the resulting CC properties.

Table 1. Existing graph-based RAG methods as instantiations of HigherOrderRAG. Each row shows the lifting operator, the maximum cell rank, whether cross-rank message passing is used, whether retrieval is learned, and whether multi-rank scoring is applied.

Method	Lifting	Max rank	Cross-rank	Learned	Multi-rank
GFM-RAG [13]	Λ_{GRAPH}	1	No	Yes	No
HyperGraphRAG [12]	Λ_{HYP}	1	No	No	No
HyperRAG [11]	Λ_{HYP}	1	No	Yes	No
TopoRAG [20]	Λ_{CW}	2	Partial	Yes	Yes
Ours	Λ_{ENTITY}	≥ 1	**Full**	**Yes**	**Yes**

In short, each prior method commits to a specific sub-domain (binary edges only for GFM-RAG, rank-1 hyperedges with cosine retrieval for HyperGraphRAG, rank-2 cell complexes from a pre-existing graph for TopoRAG); the framework here uses general CCs and pairs them with a learned scorer at multiple ranks (Fig. 1).

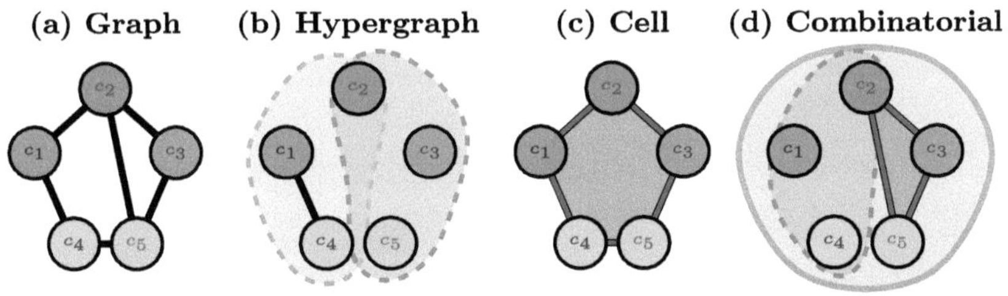

Fig. 1. Four topological representation spaces defined over the same five text chunks $\{c_1, \ldots, c_5\}$. **(a)** *Graph*: pairwise edges encode co-occurrence or shared entities between chunks; only rank-0 (nodes) and rank-1 (edges) structure exists. **(b)** *Hypergraph*: dashed regions group arbitrary subsets of chunks as rank-1 hyperedges ($H_1 = \{c_1, c_2, c_4\}$; $H_2 = \{c_2, c_3, c_5\}$); pairwise edges (e.g., c_1–c_4) can coexist with higher-cardinality hyperedges, but no rank-2 cells exist. **(c)** *Cell complex*: the pentagon boundary cycle is filled as a solid rank-2 cell; every boundary edge of the cell must itself be a cell ($\partial\sigma \cong S^{k-1}$). This is a local boundary condition, weaker than downward closure (which would require *all* subsets to be cells). **(d)** *Combinatorial complex*: a rank-2 outer region spans all chunks; a dashed rank-1 hyperedge (left) groups $\{c_1, c_2, c_4\}$ without requiring edges; a rank-2 cell (right, cyan with teal boundary) fills the triangle c_2-c_3-c_5 with explicit boundary edges as in (c). Both structures coexist—hyperedge-style grouping *and* cell-complex-style bounded cells—with no global downward-closure constraint. The CC strictly generalises the other three domains.

3.2 Stage 2: Query-Conditioned Higher-Order Message Passing

Given a CC from Stage 1 and a query q, we embed all chunks and the query using a frozen sentence transformer f : text $\to \mathbb{R}^{768}$. We project these to a hidden dimension d: $\mathbf{x}_i = W_x f(c_i)$ and $\mathbf{q} = W_q f(q)$.

Initialization. Rank-0 cells (chunks) are initialized as:

$$\mathbf{h}^{(0)}_{\{c_i\}} = \mathbf{x}_i + \mathbb{1}[i \in \text{top-}K_0] \cdot \mathbf{q}, \tag{4}$$

where $\mathbb{1}[\cdot]$ is the indicator function and the top-K_0 chunks by cosine similarity to q are seeded with the query embedding. Rank-1 cells are initialized as the mean of the rank-0 representations of their constituent chunks: $\mathbf{h}^{(0)}_{\sigma_e} = \frac{1}{|\sigma_e|}\sum_{c_i \in \sigma_e} \mathbf{h}^{(0)}_{\{c_i\}}$. This carries query information into rank-1 cells whenever any of their constituent chunks is among the top-K_0 seeds.

Message Passing. In its most general form, QC-HOMP updates cell representations through three channels: boundary messages (from lower-rank cells), coboundary messages (from higher-rank cells), and same-rank messages (from upper-adjacent cells at the same rank, computed from the $A_{\uparrow,k}$ adjacency defined in Sect. 2). All messages are modulated by the query via element-wise multiplication (DistMult-style gating).

In our rank-$\{0, 1\}$ instantiation, same-rank messages are subsumed by the boundary/coboundary pathway (two rank-0 cells sharing a rank-1 cell already exchange information via boundary → coboundary), so we use two channels:

$$\tilde{\mathbf{h}}_x^{(\ell)} = \mathbf{h}_x^{(\ell)} \odot W_r^{(k,\ell)}\mathbf{q}, \tag{5}$$

$$\mathbf{m}_{\downarrow}(x) = \frac{1}{|\mathcal{B}(x)|}\sum_{y\in\mathcal{B}(x)} \tilde{\mathbf{h}}_y^{(\ell)}, \quad \mathbf{m}_{\uparrow}(x) = \frac{1}{|\mathcal{B}^{\uparrow}(x)|}\sum_{z\in\mathcal{B}^{\uparrow}(x)} \tilde{\mathbf{h}}_z^{(\ell)}, \tag{6}$$

$$\mathbf{h}_x^{(\ell+1)} = \mathrm{LN}\Big(\mathbf{h}_x^{(\ell)} + \mathrm{MLP}\big([\mathbf{m}_{\downarrow}(x) \,;\, \mathbf{m}_{\uparrow}(x) \,;\, \mathbf{h}_x^{(\ell)} \,;\, \mathbf{h}_x^{(0)}]\big)\Big). \tag{7}$$

Here $W_r^{(k,\ell)} \in \mathbb{R}^{d\times d}$ is a rank- and layer-specific matrix, and $[\cdot\,;\,\cdot]$ denotes concatenation. When a neighborhood is empty (rank-0 cells have no boundary; cells of maximum rank have no coboundary), we set the corresponding message to the zero vector, so that the concatenated MLP input keeps a fixed dimension. For a full CC instantiation with rank ≥ 2, the same-rank channel becomes more useful: rank-1 entity hyperedges sharing a rank-2 chain cell can then exchange messages directly, which lets information travel along multi-hop entity chains in fewer layers.

The DistMult modulation (Eq. 5) is the key mechanism: $W_r^{(k,\ell)}\mathbf{q}$ acts as a query-dependent feature gate, controlling *which features propagate* for each query. This extends the same DistMult-style modulation principle used in GFM-RAG's Bellman-Ford propagation [21]: in both cases, a query-dependent vector gates which features propagate through the structure. The key difference is that GFM-RAG applies this to typed binary edges over entity nodes, while QC-HOMP applies it to cells of arbitrary rank over chunk nodes—enabling higher-order propagation without changing the core modulation mechanism.

Why higher-Order Helps. The benefit of QC-HOMP over binary message passing is best stated in terms of the role of the entity in the architecture, rather than as a strict path-length argument. On a binary chunk-entity graph, an entity e shared by chunks $c_1, \ldots, c_m$ is a routing node whose feature vector aggregates and redistributes chunk messages, but is updated by the same generic GNN rule used for chunks. On a CC, the same set of chunks belongs to a rank-1 cell σ_e that is treated as a first-class object: it has its own learned representation $\mathbf{h}_{\sigma_e}$ and rank-specific parameters $W_r^{(1,\ell)}$, so it can implement an aggregation function tuned to entity-grouped propagation. Within a single QC-HOMP layer, every chunk in σ_e contributes to that learned aggregator and receives the aggregator's broadcast back, which is exactly the chunk → cell → chunk path. The corresponding two-step exchange on the binary graph also takes two hops, but it goes through a node whose semantics are not specialised by rank; we view this as the qualitative source of the gap, more than any precise hop-count statement.

3.3 Stage 3: Multi-rank Scoring

After L layers of QC-HOMP, we compute retrieval scores at two ranks.

Rank-0 Scoring (Chunk Recall). Each chunk receives a score combining the cosine baseline with a learned correction:

$$s_0(q, c_i) = \cos(f(q), f(c_i)) + \sigma(\gamma)\cdot \mathrm{MLP}\big([\mathbf{h}_{\{c_i\}}^{(L)} \,;\, \mathbf{q}]\big), \tag{8}$$

where γ is a learnable gate initialized so $\sigma(\gamma) \approx 0$, ensuring the model starts from pure cosine retrieval and learns only necessary corrections. This design means the model can never be worse than cosine at initialization.

Rank-1 Scoring (Cell Re-ranking). From the top-K_1 rank-0 candidates, we score rank-1 cells (entity groups) jointly:

$$s_1(q, \sigma) = \text{MLP}\Big(\big[\ \text{proj}(\mathbf{q})\ ;\ \text{DeepSet}\ \big(\{\text{sg}[\mathbf{h}^{(L)}_{\{c_i\}}] : c_i \in \sigma\}\big)\ \big]\Big), \tag{9}$$

where sg[·] is the stop-gradient operator, which detaches QC-HOMP outputs so that only the rank-1 MLP is trained by $\mathcal{L}_1$ (see Training below). At inference time, rank-1 scores feed back into the chunk ranking as

$$s(q, c_i) = s_0(q, c_i) + \alpha \cdot \max_{\sigma \in \mathcal{X}_1 :\, c_i \in \sigma} s_1(q, \sigma), \tag{10}$$

with $\alpha \in [0, 1]$ tuned on a small validation split (we use $\alpha = 0.5$). The max aggregator gives each chunk credit for its single best cell, which is what we want when one entity hyperedge already captures the bridge structure of the query.

Training. Both ranks are trained with multi-positive InfoNCE. For rank-0, the loss over gold chunks $\mathcal{G}_q$ against hard negatives $\mathcal{H}_q$ (top cosine chunks not in $\mathcal{G}_q$) is:

$$\mathcal{L}_0 = -\sum_{c^+ \in \mathcal{G}_q} \frac{1}{|\mathcal{G}_q|} \log \frac{\exp(s_0(q, c^+)/\tau)}{\sum_{c \in \mathcal{G}_q \cup \mathcal{H}_q} \exp(s_0(q, c)/\tau)}. \tag{11}$$

For rank-1, we construct positive cells σ^+ (containing ≥ 1 gold chunk) and negative cells σ^- (no gold chunks) from the top-K_1 candidates, and apply the same contrastive objective:

$$\mathcal{L}_1 = -\sum_{\sigma^+} \frac{1}{|\Sigma_q^+|} \log \frac{\exp(s_1(q, \sigma^+)/\tau)}{\sum_{\sigma \in \Sigma_q^+ \cup \Sigma_q^-} \exp(s_1(q, \sigma)/\tau)}. \tag{12}$$

The total loss is $\mathcal{L} = \mathcal{L}_0 + \lambda\mathcal{L}_1$. Here $\mathcal{L}_0$ trains QC-HOMP and the rank-0 scorer end-to-end, while $\mathcal{L}_1$ trains *only* the rank-1 scoring MLP—it uses QC-HOMP outputs as fixed features due to the stop-gradient in Eq. 9. This separation prevents the two objectives from competing over QC-HOMP's parameters: without it, rank-0 R@5 degrades from 66.2% to 53.3% as the rank-1 loss distorts chunk representations.

4 Related Work

We situate HigherOrderRAG within four lines of work: dense retrieval methods that score passages independently, graph-based RAG methods that introduce relational structure but rely on fixed heuristics, learned graph retrieval methods that train scoring functions on binary graphs, and higher-order RAG methods that move beyond pairwise edges. We close with a brief overview of topological deep learning, from which our framework draws its theoretical foundations.

Dense Retrieval. Probabilistic retrieval methods such as BM25 [17] rank passages by lexical overlap, while neural approaches like Contriever [8] and ColBERTv2 [18] learn dense representations that capture semantic similarity. Both families retrieve passages independently, scoring each candidate against the query in isolation. This independence assumption fails for multi-hop questions, where the relevant passages are *complementary* (discussing different aspects of a reasoning chain) rather than individually similar to the query.

Graph-Based RAG. To capture inter-passage relationships, several works overlay a graph structure on the corpus and use it to guide retrieval. GraphRAG [2] constructs entity-level knowledge graphs and produces community-based summaries for query-focused retrieval. HippoRAG [5] draws on neurobiological principles, applying Personalized PageRank over a knowledge graph to simulate hippocampal memory retrieval. LightRAG [4] focuses on efficient graph indexing for the same setting. The retrieval mechanisms in this group are mostly based on fixed heuristics rather than learned scoring functions, which leaves less room for adapting to the specific structure of multi-hop queries.

Learned Graph Retrieval. A more recent line of work learns the retrieval function directly on the graph structure. GFM-RAG [13] trains a graph foundation model based on QueryNBFNet [21] on typed knowledge-graph triples and reports strong multi-hop retrieval results; the underlying representation is a binary graph, so group interactions among three or more passages have to be encoded indirectly through chains of pairwise edges. LP-RAG [14] recasts retrieval as link prediction on chunk-query bipartite graphs and trains the predictor from LLM-generated synthetic queries linked to their source chunks, without explicit KG construction or external KG pretraining. Our setup is closely related: synthetic queries are one of the training signals we can use, and we adopt LP-RAG's recipe when we do (see Sect. 5). The main difference is structural: LP-RAG operates on a flat (binary) chunk-query graph, whereas the framework here is phrased on combinatorial complexes, which lets us also represent higher-order groupings (entity hyperedges, and in principle rank ≥ 2 cells). We also support a hybrid training regime that can mix synthetic queries with gold question–chunk annotations, but treat the two signals as optional and interchangeable rather than as a single fixed recipe. The methods in this group all work with binary (pairwise) graphs, which is one of the design choices we relax.

Higher-Order RAG. Moving beyond pairwise edges, a handful of recent methods explore higher-order representations for RAG. HyperGraphRAG [12] represents n-ary facts as hyperedges over entities, capturing group relationships that binary graphs miss; however, it relies on cosine retrieval over the hypergraph rather than learning from its topology. HyperRAG [11] addresses this gap by learning traversal strategies on knowledge hypergraphs. TopoRAG [20] goes further up the topological hierarchy by lifting *pre-existing* textual graphs (e.g., Freebase subgraphs, scene graphs) into cell complexes via fundamental cycle detection, then retrieving relevant subcomplexes for LLM reasoning. Crucially, TopoRAG assumes graph-structured input and evaluates on textual graph

QA benchmarks (WebQSP, ExplaGraphs, SceneGraphs)—it does not address retrieval from unstructured document corpora, which is the standard RAG setting and the focus of our work. Each of these methods makes an implicit topological choice that determines which passage interactions are representable. HigherOrderRAG simply makes these choices explicit within a single framework. As far as we are aware, combinatorial complexes have not been used previously at the corpus level for retrieval, but we emphasise that the underlying topological tools come straight from the TDL literature cited above.

Topological Deep Learning. TDL extends graph neural networks to higher-order topological domains [7,16], with message-passing rules defined on cell complexes, hypergraphs and combinatorial complexes that generalise the standard GNN neighbourhood aggregation to cells of arbitrary rank [1,6]. A recent position paper [15] argues that TDL is a natural frontier for relational learning and highlights lifting operators as an underexplored design axis. DiffLift [3] makes the topological structure itself learnable via differentiable lifting. We apply this TDL perspective to corpus-level RAG.

5 Experiments

The framework supports cells of arbitrary rank. We instantiate it primarily at rank-$\{0, 1\}$ with entity co-occurrence lifting (Λ_{Entity}) and QC-HOMP, and additionally test a rank-$\{0, 1, 2\}$ variant ($\Lambda_{\text{Entity+Cycle}}$) that augments entity hyperedges with cycle-based rank-2 cells (Sect. 3.1). This design lets us measure both the effect of the lifting operator (entity vs. k-NN) and the effect of the topological rank (rank-1 vs. rank-2).

5.1 Setup

We evaluate on MuSiQue [19], a multi-hop QA benchmark designed for 2–4 hop reasoning, composed of single-hop sub-questions with annotated supporting passages. We follow the GFM-RAG [13] evaluation protocol: all methods share a 95,597-chunk corpus; we train on 1,000 questions from the standard split and evaluate on the 2,417-question evaluation split using R@2 and R@5. Published baselines are taken directly from GFM-RAG under identical conditions. We additionally conduct ablations on a 50-sample subset for rapid iteration. Retrieval quality is measured by Recall@K (R@K): the fraction of queries where *all* gold supporting chunks appear in the top-K.

All chunk and query representations use frozen `all-mpnet-base-v2` embeddings (768-dim). For CC construction, we run SpaCy NER restricted to six entity types (Person, Organization, GPE, Location, Event, Work of Art), apply alias resolution via word-subset matching and demonym normalization (reducing the entity vocabulary by approximately 20%), and subdivide large hyperedges with $K_{\max} = 30$ via farthest-point sampling. The resulting CC over the full corpus has approximately 66K rank-1 cells. QC-HOMP uses hidden dimension $d = 128$, $L = 2$ layers, dropout 0.1, learning rate 2×10^{-4} with cosine annealing, top-$K_0 = 20$ seed chunks, and temperature $\tau = 0.05$. Hard negatives are the top-100 chunks by cosine similarity that are not in the gold set.

5.2 Ablation: Component Contributions

Table 2 isolates each framework component on the 50-sample controlled subset, averaged over 3 random sampling seeds.

Table 2. Ablation on 50-sample MuSiQue subset (mean ± std over 3 seeds). Each row varies the lifting domain, scoring rank, or topological rank. All experiments use the same evaluation protocol.

Lifting domain	Scoring	R@2	R@5
— (flat corpus)	Cosine only	$42.8_{\pm 1.4}$	$57.2_{\pm 1.8}$
Λ_{KNN} (simil.)	s_0	$43.6_{\pm 1.6}$	$58.8_{\pm 2.1}$
Λ_{KNN} (simil.)	s_0+s_1	$47.4_{\pm 1.9}$	$63.7_{\pm 2.3}$
Λ_{Entity} (compl.)	s_0	$51.2_{\pm 1.5}$	$66.2_{\pm 1.7}$
Λ_{Entity} (compl.)	s_0+s_1	$\mathbf{52.8}_{\pm 1.3}$	$\mathbf{71.8}_{\pm 1.6}$
$\Lambda_{\text{Entity+Cycle}}$ (rank-2)	s_0+s_1	$52.4_{\pm 1.8}$	$71.2_{\pm 2.0}$

A few observations stand out from this table. The biggest single jump comes from the lifting operator: with the same QC-HOMP architecture, entity lifting reaches 66.2 R@5 versus 58.8 for k-NN lifting. We read this as evidence that grouping chunks by shared entities surfaces the kind of bridge structure multi-hop retrieval relies on, while k-NN tends to group chunks that are already similar in embedding space and so contribute less new information. The $\Lambda_{\text{Entity+Cycle}}$ row is also informative: adding cycle-based rank-2 cells does not improve over the rank-1 entity hypergraph in this setting, which is consistent with the view that the requirement to close a cycle with all its boundary edges is at odds with the naturally sparse pattern of multi-hop chunk groups (three chunks that mention "Obama" need not be pairwise similar). Multi-rank scoring contributes a smaller but consistent gain: adding s_1 on top of s_0 is worth +5.6 pp R@5 for entity lifting and +4.9 pp for k-NN. Finally, the stop-gradient in Eq. 9 is doing real work: removing it drops rank-0 R@5 from 66.2% to 53.3% in our setup, because $\mathcal{L}_1$ then back-propagates through QC-HOMP and pulls the chunk representations in a different direction than $\mathcal{L}_0$ wants.

In a separate sanity check we tried twelve variants of co-occurrence hypergraph lifting without entity types; none of them learned a useful propagation pattern. This is in line with the framework's view that an untyped dense hypergraph offers little directional signal for the message-passing layers, but we report it as qualitative evidence rather than as a controlled benchmark.

5.3 Comparison with Published Baselines

Table 3 places HigherOrderRAG alongside published baselines on MuSiQue. We adopt a hybrid training regime: the model can be trained from gold question–chunk pairs alone, from LLM-generated synthetic queries alone (in the style of LP-RAG [14]), or from both. The numbers in Table 3 are obtained with 1,000 gold pairs from the MuSiQue training split; the synthetic-only configuration is reported in Table 4. Retrieval is evaluated on a separate set of held-out questions over the full 95K-chunk corpus.

Table 3. Retrieval on MuSiQue [19] (R@2/R@5). All methods use the same corpus, eval split, and metrics. Published baselines from [13]. HigherOrderRAG is trained on 1K questions from the training split.

Category	Method	R@2	R@5
Dense	BM25 [17]	32.3	41.2
	Contriever [8]	34.8	46.6
	ColBERTv2 [18]	37.9	49.2
Graph-enhanced	GraphRAG [2]	35.4	49.3
	LightRAG [4]	24.8	34.7
	HippoRAG [5]	40.2	53.2
	SubgraphRAG [10]	36.9	50.2
Learned (graph)	GFM-RAG [13]	49.1	58.2
Learned (CC)	**HigherOrderRAG**	**55.0**	**76.6**

In this comparison HigherOrderRAG is the strongest of the methods we look at, improving over GFM-RAG by +5.9pp R@2 and +18.4pp R@5. We read the larger R@5 gap as evidence that entity hyperedges help to surface complementary chunks that binary-graph and similarity-based methods reach less directly.

Table 4 shows additional scaling results.

Table 4. HigherOrderRAG scaling on MuSiQue (full 95K-chunk corpus).

Configuration	R@2	R@5	R@10	R@20
Cosine baseline	24.8	35.1	43.8	53.1
Λ_{ENTITY}, synthetic-only	31.2	40.8	52.4	62.0
$\Lambda_{\text{ENTITY}} + s_0 + s_1$ (1K train)	**55.0**	**76.6**	**87.3**	**96.5**

The “synthetic-only” row trains QC-HOMP from LLM-generated synthetic queries alone, which is the same training signal that LP-RAG [14] uses. Synthetic questions are generated from batches of connected chunks in the CC and linked back to their source chunks. This setting incurs LLM token costs at training time but does not need annotated multi-hop data; it gives +5.7 pp R@5 over cosine. We treat the synthetic and gold-label training signals as interchangeable inputs to the same training loop: in our experience, mixing them has helped in some cases and not in others, so we report each in isolation rather than fixing a single hybrid recipe.

5.4 Efficiency and Practical Considerations

A key practical advantage of HigherOrderRAG is that the entity co-occurrence lifting (Λ_{ENTITY}) requires **no LLM calls**: entity extraction uses SpaCy NER, a lightweight local model, and hyperedge construction is purely algorithmic. In contrast, GFM-RAG [13] requires an LLM (GPT-4o-mini) for both NER and OpenIE during KG construction, incurring significant API cost and latency.

Table 5 compares indexing and inference costs.

Table 5. Efficiency on MuSiQue. Index times and LLM token costs from [14]; query times from [13]. Our measurements on a single RTX 4060 (8 GB).

Method	Index time	Query time	LLM tokens	Learned
LightRAG	90 min	1.11 s	86.7M	No
GraphRAG	76 min	3.04 s	n/r	No
HippoRAG	16 min	0.25 s	4.0M	No
GFM-RAG†	20 h	0.12 s	4.0M	Yes
Ours	**32 min**	0.15 s	**0***	Yes

†End-to-end including LLM-based KG construction; additionally requires pretraining on 60 KGs (14M triples, 700K docs) [13]. "n/r": not reported in a directly comparable form; GraphRAG uses LLM calls during indexing but the published figures we have do not match the units in this column. *The "LLM tokens" column reports tokens consumed during *indexing*. Our indexing pipeline (SpaCy NER plus algorithmic CC construction) does not call an LLM. The model can optionally be trained with LLM-generated synthetic queries in the spirit of LP-RAG [14]; that cost is a training-time expense and is not included in the column above.

Indexing in our pipeline (SpaCy NER plus algorithmic CC construction) takes 32 minutes for the full corpus and does not call an LLM, against 4M tokens for HippoRAG and GFM-RAG (NER and OpenIE via GPT-4o-mini) and over 86M for LightRAG. Synthetic queries (when used) are a training-time cost and are reported separately. Per-query inference (0.15 s) is comparable to GFM-RAG (0.12 s). GFM-RAG additionally relies on pretraining over 60 KGs (14M triples, 700K documents) [13]; the configuration here is trained from scratch on the target corpus alone (1K questions, 25 minutes training, on a single RTX 4060). Indexing costs are sensitive to setup and we present them only to flag order-of-magnitude differences. As a sanity check, re-running GFM-RAG with Llama 3.1:8b (via Ollama) in place of GPT-4o-mini gave R@2 = 45.7%, R@5 = 56.1% (96% of the published R@5), which suggests Λ_{GRAPH} lifting is reachable without proprietary APIs at some cost in KG quality.

6 Conclusion

We described graph-based RAG as query-conditioned message passing on combinatorial complexes, putting binary-graph, hypergraph and cell-complex methods on a common footing where the differences between them reduce to the choice of lifting operator and the message-passing rank. On MuSiQue, entity-based CC lifting paired with QC-HOMP gives the strongest result among the graph-based RAG baselines we compared against. The ablations make clear that most of the gain comes from the lifting operator—switching from k-NN to entity lifting under the same architecture is worth 7.4 R@5 points—which is consistent with the view that multi-hop retrieval benefits from grouping chunks by *complementarity* rather than by similarity. The negative results point in the same direction: untyped co-occurrence lifting never beat cosine, and cycle-based rank-2 cells did not improve over rank-1 entity hyperedges, both of which we read as failures of the grouping principle rather than of the architecture.

Some limitations are worth naming. The evaluation is on a single dataset; extending to HotpotQA and 2WikiMultiHopQA would test whether the lifting-operator effect generalises. We only explored ranks ≤ 2, and the entity extractor is a fixed SpaCy model whose interaction with the lifting choice on domain-specific corpora (scientific text, tabular data) is unexplored. We see the lifting choice as the more pressing open axis at present, and broader evaluations—other multi-hop benchmarks, learned or differentiable liftings [3], richer extractors—as the natural next steps.

References

1. Bodnar, C., et al.: Weisfeiler and Lehman go cellular: CW networks. In: Advances in Neural Information Processing Systems, vol. 34 (2021)
2. Edge, D., et al.: From local to global: a graph RAG approach to query-focused summarization. arXiv preprint arXiv:2404.16130 (2024)
3. Franco, J.L., et al.: Differentiable lifting for topological neural networks. In: The Fourteenth International Conference on Learning Representations (ICLR) (2026).
4. Guo, Z., Xia, L., Yu, Y., Ao, T., Huang, C.: LightRAG: simple and fast retrieval-augmented generation. In: Findings of the Conference on Empirical Methods in Natural Language Processing (EMNLP) (2025)
5. Gutiérrez, B.J., Shu, Y., Gu, Y., Yasunaga, M., Su, Y.: HippoRAG: neurobiologically inspired long-term memory for large language models. In: Advances in Neural Information Processing Systems, vol. 37, pp. 59532–59569 (2024)

6. Hajij, M., et al.: Combinatorial complexes: bridging the gap between cell complexes and hypergraphs. In: 57th Asilomar Conference on Signals, Systems, and Computers, pp. 799–803. IEEE (2023)
7. Hajij, M., et al.: Topological deep learning: Going beyond graph data. arXiv preprint arXiv:2206.00606 (2022)
8. Izacard, G., et al.: Unsupervised dense information retrieval with contrastive learning. Trans. Mach. Learn. Res. (2022)
9. Lewis, P., et al.: Retrieval-augmented generation for knowledge-intensive NLP tasks. In: Advances in Neural Information Processing Systems, vol. 33, pp. 9459–9474 (2020)
10. Li, M., Miao, S., Li, P.: Simple is effective: the roles of graphs and large language models in knowledge-graph-based retrieval-augmented generation. In: The Thirteenth International Conference on Learning Representations (ICLR) (2025)
11. Lien, W.S., et al.: HyperRAG: reasoning N-ARY facts over hypergraphs for retrieval augmented generation. In: Proceedings of the ACM Web Conference (WWW) (2026)
12. Luo, H., E., et al.: HyperGraphRAG: retrieval-augmented generation via hypergraph-structured knowledge representation. In: Advances in Neural Information Processing Systems (NeurIPS) (2025)
13. Luo, L., et al.: GFM-RAG: graph foundation model for retrieval augmented generation. In: The Thirty-ninth Conference on Neural Information Processing Systems (NeurIPS) (2025)
14. Nascimento, E.J.F.d., Franco, J.L., Souza, A.H.: LP-RAG: a link prediction-based framework for retrieval-augmented generation. In: ICLR 2026 Workshop on Memory for LLM-Based Agentic Systems (2026). https://openreview.net/forum?id=Y8Txo8vaH7
15. Papamarkou, T., et al.: Position: topological deep learning is the new frontier for relational learning. In: Proceedings of the 41st International Conference on Machine Learning (ICML) (2024)
16. Papillon, M., Sanborn, S., Hajij, M., Miolane, N.: Architectures of topological deep learning: a survey of message-passing topological neural networks. arXiv preprint arXiv:2304.10031 (2024)
17. Robertson, S.E., Walker, S.: Some simple effective approximations to the 2-poisson model for probabilistic weighted retrieval. In: SIGIR '94: Proceedings of the 17th Annual International ACM SIGIR Conference, pp. 232–241 (1994)
18. Santhanam, K., Khattab, O., Saad-Falcon, J., Potts, C., Zaharia, M.: ColBERTv2: effective and efficient retrieval via lightweight late interaction. In: Proceedings of the 2022 Conference of the North American Chapter of the ACL (NAACL), pp. 3715–3734 (2022)
19. Trivedi, H., Balasubramanian, N., Khot, T., Sabharwal, A.: MuSiQue: multi-hop questions via single hop question composition. Trans. Assoc. Comput. Linguist. **10**, 539–554 (2022)
20. Zhao, S., Zhou, L., Chen, Y., Zou, D.: Topology of reasoning: retrieved cell complex-augmented generation for textual graph question answering. In: The Fourteenth International Conference on Learning Representations (ICLR) (2026)
21. Zhu, Z., Zhang, Z., Xhonneux, L.P., Tang, J.: Neural Bellman-Ford networks: a general graph neural network framework for link prediction. In: Advances in Neural Information Processing Systems, vol. 34 (2021)

Instance-Level Hardness Analysis for Multi-label Classification

Bruno U. Marcato[1(✉)], Ana C. Lorena[2], Adriano Rivolli[3], Rafael G. Mantovani[3], and Ricardo Cerri[1]

[1] Institute of Mathematics and Computer Science, University of São Paulo, São Paulo, Brazil
brunoumarcato@usp.br, cerri@icmc.usp.br
[2] Aeronautics Institute of Technology, São Paulo, Brazil
aclorena@ita.br
[3] Federal University of Technology - Paraná, Curitiba, Brazil
{rivolli,rafaelmantovani}@utfpr.edu.br

Abstract. Classification is one of the main Machine Learning tasks, which consists of assigning unknown instances to one or more known classes. In multi-label problems, an instance can simultaneously belong to several classes. Thus, this task presents additional challenges, making its modeling more complex. Several algorithms have been applied to multi-label classification, either as adaptations of existing methods or as algorithms that adapt the problem by dividing it into simpler tasks. Similarly, specific metrics are needed to adequately evaluate the generated models. Evaluating only global metrics can hide systematic errors within subsets of the data, requiring a more refined analysis. In this context, measures that quantify the difficulty of correctly classifying instances can improve understanding of classifier behavior and guide optimization strategies. To address these challenges, we propose five novel instance-level complexity measures that characterize the unique sources of difficulty in multi-label classification. We evaluate these metrics across diverse benchmark datasets by analyzing their Spearman correlation with the Hamming Loss of multiple multi-label classifiers. Our results demonstrate that these measures provide a reliable characterization of classification difficulty, supporting more informed error analysis and meta-learning strategies in multi-label contexts.

Keywords: Metafeatures · Instance Hardness · Multi-label learning

1 Introduction

The performance of Machine Learning (ML) algorithms is strongly influenced by the intrinsic data characteristics on which they are applied. This observation motivated the development of metalearning, whose main goal is to leverage meta-knowledge from previous tasks to inform decisions such as algorithm selection, hyperparameter optimization, and model design. In this context, metafeatures

M. Recamonde-Mendoza and R. C. Barros (Eds.): BRACIS 2026, LNAI 17105, pp. 431–445, 2027.
https://doi.org/10.1007/978-3-032-39882-6_29

provide quantitative descriptions of learning problems and enable the establishment of relationships between data properties and algorithm behavior [5].

Among the different categories of metafeatures, complexity-based measures aim to characterize the hardness of a classification task. They capture properties such as class overlap, separability, and irregularity of the decision boundary and are traditionally defined at the dataset level [2]. As a result, they provide a global view of problem complexity and are used in metalearning systems [8].

More recently, research has shifted towards instance-level complexity measures [11], which assess how difficult individual examples are to classify. Instance hardness measures enable a finer-grained analysis of learning problems, supporting tasks such as error analysis, instance selection, and a deeper understanding of classifier behavior. However, most existing approaches were designed exclusively for single-label classification and do not account for the specific challenges posed by more complex output spaces.

In Multi-label Classification (MLC), each instance may be associated with multiple, potentially correlated labels, which alters classical notions of separability, overlap, and ambiguity inherited from single-label classification. In this setting, instances that are close in the feature space may differ in their label subsets, while distant instances may share similar label combinations. Instance difficulty is therefore influenced not only by feature-space characteristics but also by dependencies in the output space, including label co-occurrence patterns, label cardinality, and the presence of rare labels, which have been shown to contribute to defining difficult labels in multi-label data [7].

Thus, we propose five novel instance-level complexity measures specifically tailored to (MLC). The proposed metrics account for concepts such as label density, label dependencies, and label scarcity. By providing a more faithful characterization of instance difficulty in multi-label problems, this work contributes to the study of complexity-based metafeatures and supports more informed analyses and metalearning strategies in multi-label classification.

2 Instance Hardness

In supervised learning problems, each instance may present a different degree of difficulty, reflected in its misclassification probability. Factors such as noise in the data, incorrect labels, proximity to decision boundaries, or presence in sparse regions of the attribute space tend to increase this difficulty. Instance Hardness (IH) [11] is an approach that seeks to quantify this probability, enabling analysis of model behavior at the individual level.

Considering a dataset $\mathcal{D}$ containing n instances $x_i \in X$ and their respective labels $y_i \in Y$, the (IH) represents the probability that an instance will be incorrectly classified by a set of classifiers $\mathcal{C}$ with different biases, trained on $\mathcal{D}$:

$$IH_{\mathcal{C}}(x_i, y_i) = 1 - \frac{1}{|\mathcal{C}|} \sum_{j=1}^{|\mathcal{C}|} P\left(y_i | x_i, g_j(t, \alpha)\right) \tag{1}$$

where $P(y_i|x_i, g_j(t, \alpha))$ is the probability that the instance x_i will be correctly classified under the label y_i by a model g_j, from the classifier set $\mathcal{C}$, given the training set t and the hyperparameters α. In [11], the choice of classifiers that comprise $\mathcal{C}$ is based on criteria such as utility and wide practical application.

2.1 Instance Hardness Measures (IHM)

The formulation from Eq. 1 estimates which instances are difficult to classify, but does not provide information about the underlying reasons for this difficulty. In this context, Smith et al. [11] proposed a set of measures to quantify IH without relying on the outputs of a pool of classifiers, while enabling identification of possible reasons for a given instance misclassification.

Each hardness measure evaluates a specific aspect that may lead to incorrect classification and, in doing so, provides insights into why certain instances are difficult to classify, how they can be identified, and how strategies can be developed to handle such cases. In the following, we present some of these measures along with their formal definitions. All of them are bounded in the $[0, 1]$ interval and assume higher values for more difficult instances according to the aspect measured, as formulated in [9].

k-Disagreeing Neighbors kDN(x_i): Measures the local overlap of instance x_i with respect to its nearest neighbors. Formally, kDN provides the proportion of the k nearest neighbors of an instance that do not share the same label:

$$kDN(x_i) = \frac{|\{x_j : x_j \in kNN(x_i) \wedge y_j \neq y_i\}|}{k} \tag{2}$$

where $kNN(x_i)$ denotes the set of the k nearest neighbors of x_i. The higher the value of $kDN(x_i)$, the greater the difficulty in correctly classifying x_i, since the instance is surrounded by instances belonging to other classes.

Disjunct Class Percentage DCP(x_i): Builds a pruned decision tree from $\mathcal{D}$ to compute the percentage of instances that fall into the same leaf node (*disjunct*) as instance x_i and share the same label:

$$DCP(x_i) = 1 - \frac{|\{x_j : x_j \in Disjunct(x_i) \wedge y_j = y_i\}|}{|\{x_j : x_j \in Disjunct(x_i)\}|} \tag{3}$$

where $Disjunct(x_i)$ denotes the set of instances belonging to the same leaf node as instance x_i. Note that the higher this percentage, the easier it is for an instance to be correctly classified; therefore, the complement is taken in order to standardize larger values as representing higher instance difficulty.

Class Likelihood Difference CLD(x_i): Measures the difference between the probability of instance x_i belonging to its true class y_i and the highest probability of x_i belonging to any other class:

$$CLD(x_i) = \frac{1 - \left(P(x_i|y_i)P(y_i) - \max_{y_j \neq y_i}[P(x_i|y_j)P(y_j)]\right)}{2} \tag{4}$$

where $P(x_i \mid y_i)$ denotes the probability of x_i belonging to class y_i, and $P(y_i)$ is the prior of class y_i, assumed as $\frac{1}{C}$ for a uniform class distribution, with C being the number of classes [9]. CLD assigns higher values to easier instances, as the confidence in the true class exceeds that of other classes. Its complement is used so that higher values indicate greater instance difficulty.

2.2 Related Works

Building on the concepts presented previously, Arruda et al. [1] advanced this line of work by analyzing IHM derived from global data complexity, showing that different measures capture complementary sources of difficulty. Their findings indicate that no single measure explains all misclassification cases, as some are more sensitive to overlap and noise, while others reflect sparsity or class imbalance. This underscores the need to consider multiple dimensions when studying instance-level difficulty.

Similarly, Torquette et al. [13] proposed a unified formalization and conducted a broad evaluation of IHM across classification and regression. A key contribution is highlighting gaps in handling continuous targets, emphasizing the need for formulations tailored to the output space beyond traditional discrete settings.

More recently, Ueda et al. [17] extended the IHM to unlabeled scenarios, addressing a key limitation of traditional approaches. By adapting existing measures and using meta-learning, they showed that hard instances, especially in overlapping regions, can be identified even without labels, suggesting that difficulty is tied to intrinsic data properties.

Finally, Bello et al. [3] approached multi-label difficulty from a dataset perspective, proposing six measures based on granular computing and Rough Set Theory. These quantify data consistency by adapting quality-of-classification metrics to multi-label settings. Their results show strong correlation with algorithms such as MLKNN [18], offering a way to estimate task complexity beforehand. While these measures operate at the dataset level, Multi-Label Instance Hardness focuses on the difficulty of individual instances.

3 New Instance Hardness Measures for Multi-Label Classification (IHM-MLC)

Multi-label Classification (MLC) deals with problems where each instance $x_i \in \mathcal{X}$ is simultaneously associated with a subset of labels $Y_i \subseteq \mathcal{L}$, where $\mathcal{L} = \{y_1, y_2, \ldots, y_L\}$ is the set of L available labels. Formally, given a dataset $\mathcal{D} = \{(x_i, Y_i)\}_{i=1}^{N}$, with N representing the number of instances, the goal is to learn a predictive function $h : \mathcal{X} \rightarrow \{0, 1\}^L$ that minimizes a specific loss function. Our new IHM, specifically designed for this scenario, are detailed below.

Jaccard k-Disagreeing Neighbors $JkDN(x_i)$: This measure is a direct adaptation of the kDN concept. In the single-label setting, k-Disagreeing Neighbors (kdn) measures the proportion of neighbors from a class different from the target instance, identifying observations in overlapping regions. However, in Multi-label Classification (MLC), two instances may share some labels while differing in others. In this context, Jaccard k-Disagreeing Neighbors (JkDN) replaces the disagreement count with the average Jaccard Distance between neighborhood labelsets. Thus, for an instance x_i with label set Y_i, Jaccard k-Disagreeing Neighbors (JkDN) is defined as:

$$JKDN(x_i) = \frac{1}{k} \sum_{x_j \in kNN(x_i)} \left(1 - \frac{|Y_i \cap Y_j|}{|Y_i \cup Y_j|}\right) \tag{5}$$

High values indicate that, although instances are close in the feature space, their label profiles are distinct. Such instances are considered highly hard because they require the model to learn abrupt transitions in the output space within a restricted region of the input space.

Critical Label Scarcity $CLS(x_i)$: Quantifies instance-level difficulty based on the presence of the most infrequent labels within the observation. It is defined as

$$CLS(x_i) = \max_{y_j \in Y_i} \left(\frac{-\log(P(y_j))}{\log(N)}\right) \tag{6}$$

where $P(y_j)$ denotes the empirical probability of label y_j, estimated from its observed frequency in the dataset. When calculating the maximum normalized negative log-probability, CLS identifies instances associated with labels that are underrepresented in the training data. Higher values indicate that an instance contains at least one highly rare (i.e., high-information) label.

Labelset Scarcity $LSS(x_i)$: Evaluates the uniqueness of an instance's label set combination relative to the dataset. It is defined as:

$$LSS(x_i) = \frac{-\log(P(Y_i))}{\log(N)} \tag{7}$$

where $P(Y_i)$ denotes the empirical probability of the labelset Y_i. Similarly to the previous metric, LSS is based on the normalized negative log-probability, but instead of focusing on individual labels, it evaluates the rarity of the entire labelset. Low values correspond to common label patterns, while higher values indicate rare and more informative labelset configurations, reflecting combinations that are less frequently observed in the data.

Label Co-occurrence Inconsistency $LCI(x_i)$: Evaluates the degree to which the co-occurrence of labels within an instance contradicts the conditional probabilities observed in the entire dataset. For instances with multiple labels, the metric is:

$$LCI(x_i) = \frac{1}{|Y_i|\,(|Y_i| - 1)} \sum_{y_a \in Y_i} \sum_{y_b \in Y_i, a \neq b} [1 - P(y_a | y_b)] \tag{8}$$

where $P(y_a|y_b)$ represents the conditional probability of label a occurring given the presence of label b. This value is estimated from the training data using co-occurrence frequencies, defined as the proportion of instances containing y_a relative to all instances in which y_b is present. LCI scores range from 0 to 1, where values approaching 1 indicate that the instance contains pairs of labels that rarely appear together in the training set, signaling a high level of label set inconsistency.

Label Density Distance $LDD(x_i)$: Measures the normalized deviation of an observation's label density from the average of the dataset. It is defined as:

$$LDD(x_i) = \frac{D_i - \bar{D} + 1}{2} \tag{9}$$

where D_i denotes the label density of instance x_i, and $\bar{D}$ is the average density. The metric maps the distance from the mean to $[0, 1]$, where 0.5 indicates typical density. Values above 0.5 reflect higher label accumulation and greater difficulty.

4 Experimental Methodology

This section details the experimental setup used to evaluate how the proposed IHM-MLC measures behave across diverse MLC datasets. For comparison, we also include the KDN, CLD, and DCP. Since these are originally single-label measures, they are applied via (BR).

4.1 Datasets

The datasets used in this study were selected to cover a broad range of multi-label classification scenarios and to ensure variability in the characteristics that may influence instance-level complexity. The selection process aimed to include datasets with different structural properties, allowing the proposed measures to be evaluated under diverse learning conditions.

All datasets were obtained from the MULAN repository [15], a well-established and widely used benchmark source in multi-label learning research. The selected datasets originate from different real-world applications and differ in size, feature dimensionality, number of labels, number of distinct labelsets, and label cardinality and density [14].

Table 1 summarizes the datasets considered, reporting their main characteristics. By using datasets with distinct properties, this experimental setup enables the analysis of the behavior of the proposed measures across different multi-label classification settings.

4.2 Methods

The diagram in Fig. 1 illustrates the logical sequence used to conduct the experiments. Once the dataset collection is defined, comprising the selected datasets

Table 1. Datasets used in experiments

Name	# Instances	# Features	# Labels	Card.	Density	Distinct	Domain
birds	645	260	19	1.014	0.053	133	Audio
emotions	593	72	6	1.869	0.311	27	Music
enron	1702	1001	53	3.378	0.064	753	Text
genbase	662	1186	27	1.252	0.046	32	Biology
medical	978	1449	45	1.245	0.028	94	Text
scene	2407	294	6	1.074	0.179	15	Image
yeast	2417	103	14	4.237	0.303	198	Biology

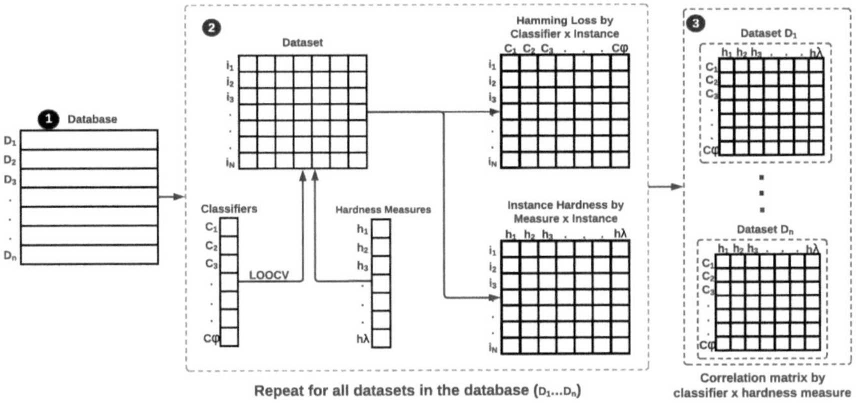

Fig. 1. Methodology for evaluating multi-label instance-level hardness measures.

(D_1, ..., D_n) (Fig. 1, step 1), a set of ϕ multi-label classifiers is applied to each dataset. For our experiments, we considered a set of classifiers widely used in the literature [4,10,16,18]: Multi-label k-Nearest Neighbors (MLkNN), Binary Relevance (BR), Classifier Chains (CC), Label Powerset (LP), Random k-labelsets (RAkEL), and Ensemble of Classifier Chains (ECC), each one using a Random Forest (RF) as base algorithm. These classifiers are trained using Leave-One-Out Cross-Validation (LOOCV) to obtain the Hamming Loss (HL) for each instance. At each LOOCV iteration, the model is trained on all instances except the one being evaluated, allowing the prediction error of the held-out instance to be computed based on a model that has not been trained on it. In parallel, the difficulty of each instance is computed for all datasets using the λ (five, in this case) proposed measures, resulting in a $N \times \lambda$ matrix of instance-level difficulty values (Fig. 1, step 2). Once the HL and difficulty matrices are obtained for each dataset, the Spearman rank correlation coefficient is computed between them (Fig. 1, step 3), relating each classifier's performance to the values produced by each IHM-MLC. This procedure yields n correlation matrices, which are then used to analyze the relationship between instance difficulty and classifier performance across these datasets. The code repository of this study is publicly available[1].

5 Results

This section presents the experimental results obtained to assess the descriptive power of the proposed IHM-MLC. We analyze their relationship with classification error across multiple datasets and classifiers, using correlation analysis, visual inspection, and a case study to illustrate their practical implications.

5.1 Overall Descriptive Power of the Meta-features

Figure 2 presents the overall Spearman correlation between the proposed IHM-MLC and the HL of the pool of algorithms. The measures are increasingly ordered by the median correlation values on the x-axis. They are also categorized by colors: single-label based (CLD, kDN, DCP), density-based (LDD), frequency-based (LCI, CLS, LSS), and those defined by neighborhood (JkDN). Figure 3 shows the correlation coefficients and associated p-values for each measure and classifier across all datasets. Red cells indicate statistically significant correlations at the 95% confidence level ($\alpha = 0.05$).

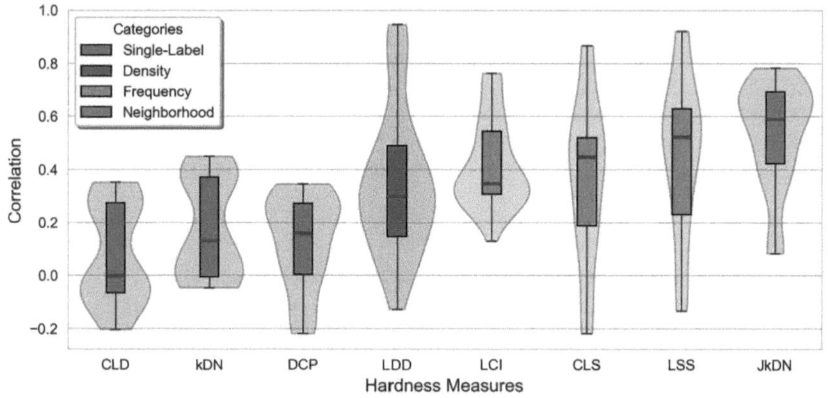

Fig. 2. Aggregated correlation between hardness metrics and Hamming loss.

Figure 2 shows that single-label adaptations yield low median correlations and high dispersion, indicating poor alignment with MLC error. Density and frequency-based measures have higher median correlations, though with varying degrees of spread, suggesting that their descriptive power depends on dataset characteristics. Notably, JkDN outperformed all the others, with the highest

[1] https://github.com/BrunoMarcato/MultiLabelInstanceHardness.

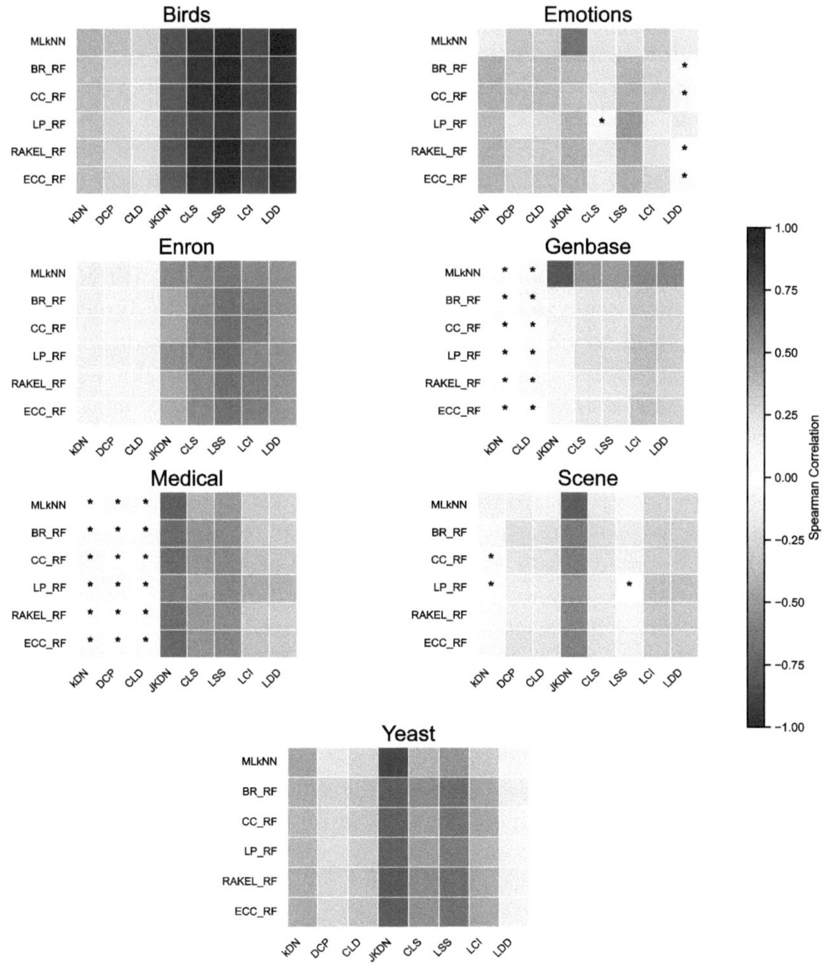

Fig. 3. Correlation heatmaps between algorithms and measures. Colors represent Spearman's ρ, using a common scale across all datasets. Cells marked with * indicate non-significant correlations ($p \geq 0.05$).

median correlation and relatively low variability, indicating a better relationship with performance across datasets and classifiers.

Frequency-based measures, particularly LSS, are sensitive to the diversity of label combinations in the output space. In datasets with a larger number of distinct labelsets, such as Birds, Enron, and Yeast, LSS shows a clearer association with classification error. In these cases, the presence of many different label combinations creates a wider range of labelset frequencies, allowing instances associated with less common combinations to be differentiated from those following dominant patterns. As a result, LSS provides a more informative ordering of instances according to their difficulty.

In contrast, datasets with limited labelset diversity, such as Scene, Emotions, and Genbase, exhibit weaker results for LSS. When the number of possible label combinations is small, the distinction between frequent and infrequent labelsets becomes less pronounced. Under these conditions, instances tend to share similar frequency profiles, reducing LSS's ability to reflect differences in classification difficulty. This suggests that the usefulness of labelset-based scarcity measures depends on the richness of the output space.

LDD captures a different aspect of dataset structure by focusing on deviations from the average label density. In low-density datasets such as Birds, instances with more labels than usual represent clear departures from the typical pattern. These deviations tend to be associated with higher classification error, which could explain the stronger correlation observed for LDD in this dataset. As label density increases and becomes more uniform, as in Yeast, the contrast captured by LDD decreases, weakening its association with HI.

A related behavior is observed for CLS, especially in datasets with highly unequal label frequency distributions. In Enron, the presence of labels that range from very frequent to very rare allows CLS to identify instances that include underrepresented labels. Such instances are prone to increased error due to insufficient statistical support during training. In datasets with more balanced label frequencies, this effect becomes less pronounced.

Measures based on label co-occurrence, such as LCI, are influenced by the dependency structure among labels. In Genbase, LCI shows a stronger association with classification error, which can be linked to labels that occur only once or in very restricted combinations. These rare co-occurrences create patterns that are poorly supported by the data and therefore harder to model. In Yeast, although labels also exhibit dependencies, the high frequency of several labels reduces the contrast between common and uncommon co-occurrence patterns, leading to more moderate results for LCI.

Overall, JkDN has the most stable behavior across the datasets, consistently presenting higher associations with instance-level error. However, in the Genbase it shows weaker correlations for most classifiers, with values between 0.08 and 0.10. MLkNN is an exception, with a correlation of 0.73. This behavior is consistent with the shared neighborhood-based inductive bias of both the measure and the algorithm, which rely on local similarity to infer labelsets. Thus, the high global median of JkDN is partially influenced by its performance in scenarios where the classifier's inductive bias aligns with the metric's logic. Still, JkDN remains a reliable meta-feature, as it combines geometric proximity and labelset overlap in a way that generalizes well across different domains.

Results from single-label adaptations highlight the limitations of ignoring label interactions in multi-label problems. In datasets with strong label dependencies or high-dimensional feature spaces, these measures tend to exhibit weak or unstable correlations, failing to capture the sources of difficulty in multi-label problems. In contrast, the proposed IHM-MLC measures provide complementary perspectives on instance-level hardness closely aligned with the structural properties of multi-label data. Measures with higher median correlations, such as JkDN and frequency-based meta-features, yield larger statistically significant associations across classifiers in datasets with richer output spaces. In contrast, single-label adaptations yield non-significant results, even when moderate correlations are observed for specific classifiers, as their behavior being less stable and more dependent on isolated experimental conditions. Overall, the p-value distributions reinforce that the proposed multi-label measures provide more consistent and statistically supported descriptions of instance-level hardness.

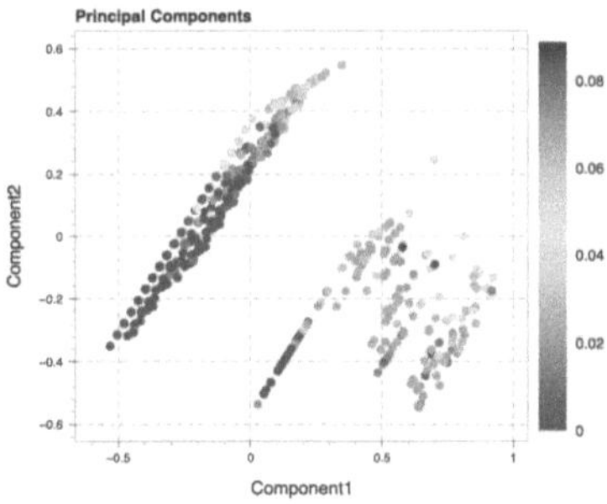

(a) Medical dataset

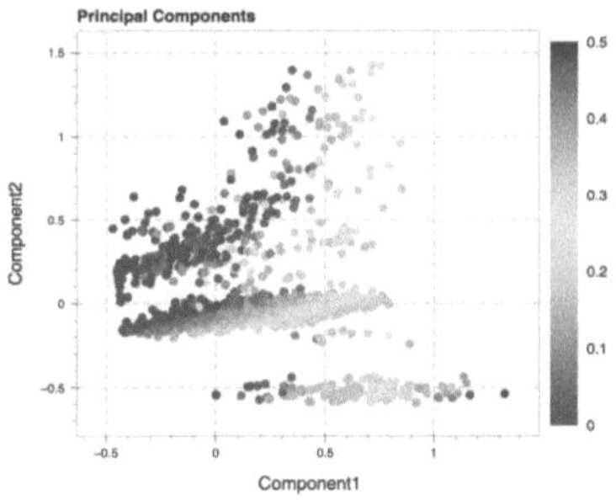

(b) Scene dataset

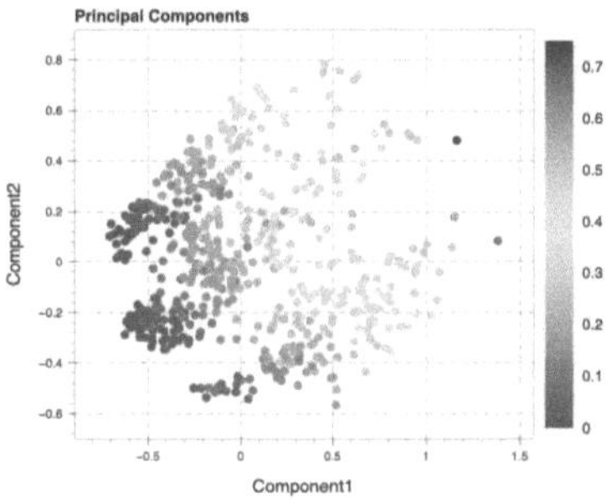

(c) Emotions dataset

Fig. 4. PCA of instance hardness measures, colored according to the average Hamming loss of the pool of algorithms.

5.2 Hardness Visualization

Here we analyze the relationship between the extracted instance hardness meta-features and the average HL across the pool of algorithms. This average serves as a multi-label analogue of the model-based instance hardness in Eq. 1, using HL as the performance measure. Figure 4 shows projections onto the first two principal components obtained via Principal Component Analysis (PCA) on the

IHM matrices of three representative datasets. Each point represents an instance, colored by its average HL, reflecting its model-based hardness. Redder points indicate harder instances, while bluer points indicate easier ones. The datasets illustrate different hardness ranges: low (medical, 0.013 to 0.089), medium (scene, 0.079 to 0.45), and high (emotions, 0.197 to 0.75).

Across all plots in Fig. 4, clear hardness gradients can be observed, with bluer points generally opposing redder ones along the principal directions. This pattern highlights a consistent association between the joint IHM-MLC and the algorithms' average Hamming loss, reinforcing the validity of the measures for describing instance hardness in the multi-label domain.

An analysis of the PCA loadings shows that the observed hardness gradients are associated with a limited set of measures. In the medical dataset, the first components are mainly influenced by JkDN and LCI, indicating that neighborhood disagreement and label co-occurrence patterns contribute to separating instances with lower and higher HL. For the scene dataset, JkDN, LCI, and CLD present the highest loadings, reflecting the joint influence of local structure and label distribution. On the other hand, LCI and JkDN, together with DCP and CLD, represent the principal loadings on the emotions dataset. Overall, these results indicate that the joint use of instance hardness measures provides a more detailed analysis of easy and hard instances, as each measure reflects a distinct source of information.

5.3 Case Study: Algorithm Recommendation

One potential application of IH measures is the characterization of datasets within meta-learning settings. In this section, we present a case study on the *emotions* dataset, in which IH measures are used as meta-features and provided as inputs to the Instance Space Analysis (ISA) framework [12].

The ISA framework projects problem instances into a two-dimensional space (the Instance Space), such that the meta-feature values exhibit approximately linear trends. The projection also incorporates the performance of a pool of algorithms – measured by their Hamming losses – and enforces linear trends for these performance values in the embedded space. As a result, the instance space provides a compact representation that summarizes the meta-features and their relationships with algorithmic performance.

Figure 5 presents the Instance Space (IS) of the *emotions* dataset, constructed by relating eight instance hardness meta-features to the Hamming losses of six multi-label classification algorithms. The IS was generated using the MATILDA (Melbourne Algorithm Test Instance Library with Data Analytics) web application[2]. The tool requires defining a performance threshold for Hamming loss, which was set to 0.3 in this analysis. Although the framework includes an automatic meta-feature selection step, it was intentionally omitted to analyze the joint behavior of all instance hardness measures.

[2] https://matilda.unimelb.edu.au/, Analysis: https://tinyurl.com/ISA-emotions.

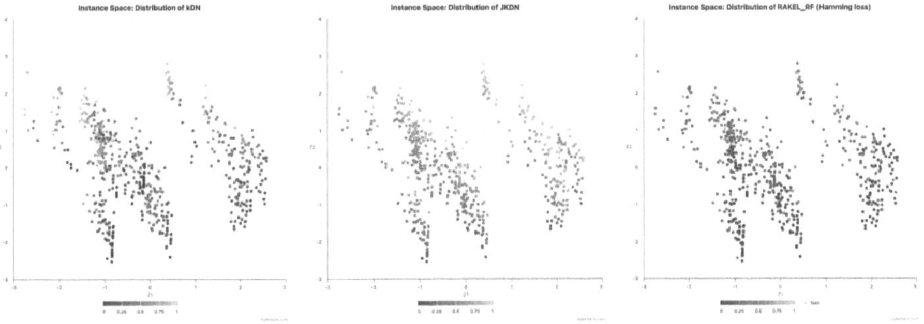

(a) Colored by kDN values. (b) Colored by JkDN values. (c) Colored by RAkEL performance.

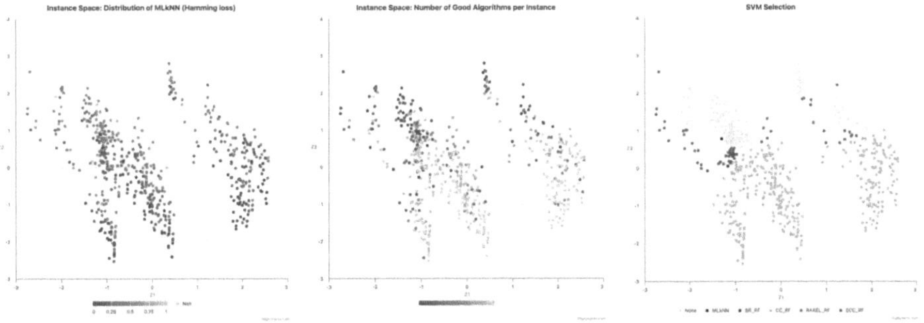

(d) Colored by MLkNN performance. (e) Colored by the number of algorithms with good performance. (f) Colored by SVM algorithm selection.

Fig. 5. Instance Space of the emotions dataset, colored by meta-features (kDN and JkDN), algorithm performance (RAkEL, MLkNN, number of algorithms with good performance), and algorithm selection by SVM meta-models.

Figure 5(e) colors the points in the IS according to the number of algorithms achieving good predictive performance, with a 0.3 threshold. Yellow regions correspond to instances for which all algorithms exhibit good performance, whereas dark blue points indicate instances for which no algorithm surpasses the threshold. Consequently, harder-to-classify instances are located predominantly in the upper region of the IS, while easier instances are concentrated in the lower region.

Figures 5(a) and 5(b) color the instances according to the kDN and JkDN meta-features, respectively. In both cases, higher values (yellow) are generally associated with hard-to-classify instances, whereas lower values (blue) indicate easier ones. Notably, JkDN varies more smoothly across the IS than kDN.

Figures 5(c) and 5(d) color the instances according to the performance of RAkEL and MLkNN, respectively, which correspond to the algorithms with the best and worst overall performance on this dataset. MLkNN presents a larger number of instances with poorer performance, as indicated by the prevalence of green to yellow tones, while RAkEL demonstrates consistently strong performance across most regions of the IS.

An additional feature of the ISA framework is the construction of SVM-based meta-models that predict the most suitable algorithm for each region of the IS based on the meta-feature values. The recommendations produced by these meta-models are shown in Fig. 5(f). The CC algorithm is recommended for regions containing predominantly easy-to-classify instances (pink), RAkEL is suggested for a subset of difficult instances (blue), and ECC is recommended for instances of intermediate difficulty (brown). For the most challenging instances, located at the top of the IS, no algorithm can be recommended (yellow). These results provide insights into the competence domains of different algorithms and may inform strategies such as dynamic classifier selection [6].

6 Conclusions

This work explored instance-level hardness in multi-label classification, examining how data properties relate to classification difficulty at the instance level. We assess whether measures tailored to this setting better capture difficulty than single-label metrics. Among them, JkDN stood out as the most stable and informative across datasets and classifiers. Its consistent correlation with error indicates that local neighborhood information effectively identifies ambiguous, hard-to-classify instances.

The results revealed that the proposed measures are complementary. For example, metrics like LSS and LDD varied across datasets, reflecting their structural differences. This suggests that instance difficulty cannot be attributed to a single factor, but rather emerges from multiple aspects of the data. Therefore, combining measures is necessary to capture the complexity of multi-label hardness. Visualization analyses reinforced this view, showing smooth gradients aligned with model-based hardness when measures are combined, supporting a multidimensional interpretation influenced by neighborhood structure, label dependencies, and output sparsity.

Integrating instance hardness metrics into the ISA framework showed their potential for algorithm recommendation, though with some limitations. The instance space revealed regions where classifiers like CC or RAkEL perform better, as well as areas with consistently hard instances lacking clear recommendations. This highlights the practicality of instance-level measures for supporting dynamic algorithm selection and more fine-grained performance analysis beyond dataset-level summaries.

Some future work emerges from this study. One is using instance hardness measures to guide data-centric strategies, such as label refinement and noise detection in multi-label datasets. Another is incorporating hardness into adaptive learning systems, adjusting models or inference based on instance difficulty. Finally, evaluating these measures in large-scale or weakly supervised settings could help assess their broader applicability.

Acknowledgment. B.U.M, R.C., and A.C.L. thank the São Paulo Research Foundation (FAPESP), Brazil, grants #2022/02981-8, #2025/10035-3, and #2021/06870-3. R.C thanks the Brazilian National Council for Scientific and Technological Development (CNPq), grant #300934/2025-4.

References

1. Arruda, J.L.M., Prudêncio, R.B.C., Lorena, A.C.: Measuring instance hardness using data complexity measures. In: Brazilian Conference on Intelligent Systems, pp. 483–497 (2020)
2. Basu, M., Ho, T.K.: Data Complexity in Pattern Recognition. Springer-Verlag (2006)
3. Bello, M., Nápoles, G., Vanhoof, K., Bello, R.: Data quality measures based on granular computing for multi-label classification. Inf. Sci. **560**, 51–67 (2021)
4. Bogatinovski, J., Todorovski, L., Džeroski, S., Kocev, D.: Comprehensive comparative study of multi-label classification methods. Expert Syst. Appl. **203**, 117215 (2022)
5. Brazdil, P., van Rijn, J., Soares, C., Vanschoren, J.: Metalearning: Applications to Automated Machine Learning and Data Mining. Springer (2022)
6. Britto, A.S., Jr., Sabourin, R., Oliveira, L.E.: Dynamic selection of classifiers–a comprehensive review. Pattern Recogn. **47**(11), 3665–3680 (2014)
7. Charte, F., Rivera, A.J., del Jesus, M.J., Herrera, F.: Dealing with difficult minority labels in imbalanced muti-label data sets. Neurocomputing **326**, 39–53 (2019)
8. Lorena, A.C., Garcia, L.P.F., Lehmann, J., Souto, M.C.P., Ho, T.K.: How complex is your classification problem? a survey on measuring classification complexity. ACM Comput. Surv. **52**(5) (2019)
9. Lorena, A.C., Paiva, P.Y.A., Prudêncio, R.B.C.: Trusting my predictions: on the value of instance-level analysis. ACM Comput. Surv. **56**(7) (2024)
10. Read, J., Pfahringer, B., Holmes, G., Frank, E.: Classifier chains for multi-label classification. Mach. Learn. **85**(3), 333–359 (2011)
11. Smith, M.R., Martinez, T., Giraud-Carrier, C.: An instance level analysis of data complexity. Mach. Learn. **95**(2), 225–256 (2014)
12. Smith-Miles, K., Muñoz, M.A.: Instance space analysis for algorithm testing: methodology and software tools. ACM Comput. Surv. **55**(12), 1–31 (2023)
13. Torquette, G.P., Nunes, V.S., Paiva, P.Y.A., Lorena, A.C.: Instance hardness measures for classification and regression problems. J. Inf. Data Manag. **15**(1), 152–174 (2024)
14. Tsoumakas, G., Katakis, I., Vlahavas, I.: Mining multi-label data. In: Data Mining and Knowledge Discovery Handbook, pp. 667–685 (2009)
15. Tsoumakas, G., Spyromitros-Xioufis, E., Vilcek, J., Vlahavas, I.: Mulan: a java library for multi-label learning. J. Mach. Learn. Res. **12**, 2411–2414 (2011)
16. Tsoumakas, G., Vlahavas, I.: Random k-Labelsets: An Ensemble Method for Multilabel Classification. In: Kok, J.N., et al. (eds.) ECML 2007. LNCS (LNAI), vol. 4701, pp. 406–417. Springer, Heidelberg (2007). https://doi.org/10.1007/978-3-540-74958-5_38
17. Ueda, P.S.M., Rivolli, A., Lorena, A.C.: An instance level analysis of classification difficulty for unlabeled data. In: Intelligent Systems (BRACIS), pp. 141–155 (2025)
18. Zhang, M.L., Zhou, Z.H.: ML-KNN:Dazy learning approach to multi-label learning. Pattern Recogn. **40**(7), 2038–2048 (2007)

Solving Tetris Through Double Deep Q-Learning Using Afterstates and a Variable Reward Function

Arthur Mantelli Antonietto(✉) and Fabiano Silva

Universidade Federal do Paraná, Curitiba, Brazil
arthur.mant@gmail.com, fabiano@inf.ufpr.br

Abstract. Tetris is a classic puzzle game that has been studied in artificial intelligence for decades. Although its rules are very simple, its randomness and lack of a win condition lead to a rather complex game with a huge state space, making it a great testing ground for learning algorithms. While many agents for Tetris exist in the literature, most stick with a very simple survival at all costs strategy, in contrast to the optimal strategy usually employed by more experienced players, which consists of trying to maximize moves that clear four lines at once, generating the maximum possible score from every piece played. This is due to the much more complex planning required and the greater risk associated with that approach. This article attempts to create an agent capable of autonomously learning to employ this optimal strategy. Our agent is based on Double Deep Q-Learning with two main innovations: (1) the use of a variant of the Bellman equation that employs afterstates to significantly reduce the action-value function's domain, and (2) a reward function that becomes more rigorous during training in order to further reinforce desired behavior. This resulted in the best performance of any comparable agent in the literature, with the agent capable of consistently clearing four lines simultaneously, surviving an average of over 3,000 pieces, and reaching a score-per-piece ratio comparable to that of an experienced human player.

Keywords: Tetris · Reinforcement Learning · Double Deep Q-Learning · Afterstates

1 Introduction

Tetris is a puzzle game, in which the player is tasked with stacking randomly given pieces in order to avoid letting them reach the top. The only way to reduce the stack is by filling every cell in a row, which causes that row to be erased and the entire stack above it to drop.

There is no win condition in this game; the player can only delay their loss, so the objective is to score as many points as possible. The main way to do this is by clearing lines, with the score increasing cubically in relation to the amount

M. Recamonde-Mendoza and R. C. Barros (Eds.): BRACIS 2026, LNAI 17105, pp. 446–460, 2027.
https://doi.org/10.1007/978-3-032-39882-6_30

of lines cleared at the same time. The falling speed of the pieces increases as the game progresses, reaching speeds too high to even a very experienced player keep up, effectively creating a limit in how many pieces can be played. So, in order to increase the score received, the player must also try to play as efficiently as possible. Therefore, the optimal strategy for human players is to maximize the amount of simultaneous four rows clears, which yields the maximum score per piece consumed.

To be able to clear four rows at once, a significant amount of preparation is needed: four rows must be entirely filled by pieces, except for one column that will be used to place the only piece in the game capable of filling cells in four rows (the I-piece). This must be done using only the randomly given pieces, and any holes left will prevent it from happening, downgrading it to only a three row clear, which results in just one quarter of the score. This strategy also increases the risk of a loss, since it requires that a large stack is always present on the board, which can lead to a quick loss given a long enough sequence of inconvenient pieces. Since this paper's Tetris game derived from Tetris for the Nintendo Entertainment System, the pieces generated are entirely at random following a uniform distribution; therefore, any sequence of pieces can be generated, and the player must be able to deal with them to survive. According to Demaine et al. [3], maximizing the amount of four rows clears given a finite known sequence of pieces has NP-complete complexity. Given that in the actual game the sequence of pieces is neither finite nor known, this poses a challenging environment for learning algorithms and can serve as a computationally cheap tool to evaluate them.

Most Tetris agents in the literature [1,5,9] so far have focused only on surviving, keeping the stack as low as possible and clearing lines as soon as they can. The aim of our agent is replicating the previously discussed human optimal strategy, which aims at maximizing the score per piece received. While for machines the increase in piece falling speed isn't an issue, and plenty of agents that completely ignore any notion of efficiency have been built that surpass any human player's highest score due to the sheer amount of lines completed, we still opted to try to build an agent that seeks efficient plays, since it is a significantly more complex task that demands a lot more planning from it, which makes this a much more interesting problem to study. The chosen method to build this agent was reinforcement learning, specifically Double Deep Q-Learning, so that it can slowly improve its strategy through trial and error towards this optimal one.

This work's best performing agent was able to surpass all other comparable agents found in the literature [2,6], surviving an average of 3,300 pieces, around four times what a professional player achieves, and reaching an average of around 60% of the maximum possible score given the same amount of pieces it survived. Each move is decided in less than 7 ms, which is less than half the time needed for a piece to fall a single cell even at the highest possible speed.

The remainder of this paper is organized as follows. Section 2 presents the theoretical background on Double Deep Q-Learning. Section 3 formulates Tetris as a Markov Decision Process, highlighting the challenges that arise from its large state space. Section 4 introduces the concept of afterstates and describes how we adapt the Bellman equation to reduce the domain of the action-value function. Section 5 details our variable reward function, which becomes progressively stricter during training to reinforce optimal behavior. Section 6 reports the training setup and hyperparameters used. Section 7 presents the training results, followed by a controlled evaluation of the final agent in Sect. 8. Section 9 compares our agent's performance with other Tetris agents from the literature. Finally, Sect. 10 discusses the implications of our findings and suggests directions for future work.

2 Double Deep Q-Learning

The algorithm chosen for this agent is Double Deep Q-Learning [4], which is a reinforcement learning algorithm applicable to any problem that can be modeled as a Markov decision process. It is a more robust variant of Deep Q-Learning [7], which, in turn, is a neural-network version of the tabular reinforcement learning algorithm Q-Learning [10].

This algorithm evaluates every possible action for a given state and chooses the one it estimates will lead to the best long-term rewards. It uses two neural networks: the online network θ, which is actively trained, and the target network θ^-, which is a frozen copy of a previous version of the online network, being copied from it every n training episodes. The action-value estimation is done by the online network θ, and it is based on the agent's training on the target values calculated from recorded experience using the following equation:

$$Q^*(s,a,\theta) = r(s,a) + \gamma \cdot Q(s', \underset{a' \in A}{\text{argmax}}(Q(s',a',\theta)), \theta^-) \tag{1}$$

Where $Q^*(s,a,\theta)$ is the target action-value of action a in the state s according to the online network θ; $r(s,a)$ is the reward received by applying action a in the state s; $0 < \gamma \leq 1$ is a constant that defines how much future rewards impact the action-value; $a = \underset{a' \in A}{\text{argmax}}(Q(s',a',\theta))$ is the action that maximizes the action-value in the state s' according to the online network θ; and $Q(s',a,\theta^-)$ is the action-value of that action a in state s' according to the target network θ^-. The use of both networks in the target action-value calculation helps avoiding overestimations.

A training episode consists of the agent gathering experience from the environment and recording every state transition as the 4-tuple (state, action, reward, next state). Then, for each recorded 4-tuple, a target value is computed using Eq. 1, and these values are used to train the online network θ.

3 Tetris as a Markov Decision Process

A Markov decision process [11] is defined by a set of states S, a set of actions A, a transition function $P(s'|s,a)$ and a reward function $r(s,a)$.

A state $s \in S$ is simply defined by the current board, the current piece and the next piece.

An action $a \in A$ is defined by the position on the board where the current piece will be played. So, it is given by the horizontal and vertical coordinates of the top left corner of the 4×4 grid that defines the piece, along with the selected rotation. The algorithm that generates the sequence of movements that takes the piece from the initial position to the desired final position is done separately using a trivial pathfinding algorithm.

The transition function $P(s'|s, a)$ is, also, simply defined. Both the board and current piece of the next state are deterministic, with only its next piece being randomly chosen. Since this work is based on classic Tetris, its next piece probability will follow an uniform distribution.

Although the transition function is easily defined in this specific case, the implemented algorithm does not use it directly. Instead, it infers the transition dynamics from the experience collected during training. This design choice aims to make our approach more applicable to real-world problems, where the transition function is often unknown.

The reward $r(s, a)$ will be given by two terms: the line completion reward $r_l(s, a)$ and the height penalty $pen_h(a)$. Both these metrics are derived from the game's scoring system. The former is based on the score received by completing lines, while the latter is based on the score associated with the distance the piece falls, i.e. the number of cells the piece drops. Both terms are normalized to the interval $[0, 1]$. To control the influence of each metric on the overall reward function $r(s, a)$, a weight w multiplies the penalty term. The value $w = 0.04$ was determined empirically to yield the best results.

$$r(s, a) = r_l(s, a) - w \cdot pen_h(a)$$

The line completion reward is defined as follows:

$$r_l(s, a) = \left(\frac{l(s, a)}{l_{\max}}\right)^{k_1}$$

where $l(s, a)$ is the amount of lines completed by applying the action a to the state s; $l_{\max}$ is the maximum possible amount of lines completed in a single move, which is 4; and k_1 is a constant that controls how the function grows. The value given to k_1 will be discussed in depth in Sect. 5.

The height penalty is similarly defined:

$$pen_h(a) = \left(\frac{h(a)}{h_{max}}\right)^{k_2}$$

where $h(a)$ is height of the action a;h_{max} is the maximum possible height a piece can be placed, which is 22 (though the board has 20 rows, the piece actually spawns 2 rows above the top board row); and k_2 is a constant that controls how this function grows. The value $k_2 = 2$ was empirically determined to yield the best results.

4 Afterstate

An afterstate $AS(s, a)$ is simply the result of applying a specific action a to a state s [8]. In Tetris, an afterstate is defined by the next piece and a post-action board, that is, the resulting board after the piece is placed according the action and any completed lines are cleared.

The core idea of the afterstate is that, in some domains, multiple state-action pairs can lead to the exact same distribution of possible next states. The afterstate collapses all such state-action pairs into a single representation and evaluates that representation instead of evaluating each pair separately.

This leads to a significant reduction in the domain of the value function, thereby making the training of the agent considerably faster. Although the amount of state-action pairs represented by a single afterstate varies widely, a general reduction factor can be inferred by comparing the size of the set of state-action pairs against the size of the set of afterstates.

The state's board and the afterstate's post-action board share the same dimensionality, as does the next piece in each of them. However, in the afterstate, both the current piece and action are absent, because they are already represented in the post-action board. Considering that the number of possible current pieces is 7, and the minimum number of possible actions on most boards is 9 (achieved by the square piece on an empty board), while the T, L, and J pieces have 34 possible actions on an empty board, and possibly more if the board allows placing a piece in more than one position on a single column, an estimate for the domain reduction is of at least $7 \cdot 9 = 63$, going up to $7 \cdot 34 = 238$ for T, L and J pieces.

Utilizing afterstates changes the value function from evaluating a state-action pair to evaluating an afterstate directly. This means that the neural network will no longer approximate the action-value function $Q(s, a)$, but rather the afterstate value function $V_{AS}(AS(s, a))$. However, the action-value $Q(s, a)$ is still needed when evaluating actions, so it will be calculated using $V_{AS}(AS(s, a))$.

Consider the Bellman equation for a scenario where the transition function $P(s'|s, a)$ is known. In that case, the action-value can be calculated by summing over all possible next states' action-values:

$$Q(s, a) = r(s, a) + \gamma \cdot \sum_{s' \in S_{t+1}} P(s'|s, a) \cdot \max_{a'} Q(s', a')$$

Since the afterstate is, by definition, the encapsulation of the distribution of next states, the value of an afterstate will be given by:

$$V_{AS}(AS(s, a)) = \sum_{s' \in S_{t+1}} P(s'|s, a) \cdot \max_{a'} Q(s', a')$$

Therefore the action-value can be expressed as:

$$Q(s, a) = r(s, a) + \gamma \cdot V_{AS}(AS(s, a)) \tag{2}$$

In practice, $V_{AS}(AS(s,a))$ is approximated directly from experience, without requiring explicit knowledge of the transition function $P(s'|s,a)$. Instead, the neural network is trained using target values $V^*_{AS}(AS(s,a))$ computed from observed transitions, following the same principle as traditional Double Deep Q-Learning. Consequently, an equation that defines these target values is needed.

Consider that a target action-value of a state-action pair can be derived from that of an afterstate in a similar way as described in Eq. 2:

$$Q^*(s,a) = r(s,a) + \gamma \cdot V^*_{AS}(AS(s,a))$$

Since we're utilizing Double Deep Q-Learning, we can expand $Q^*(s,a)$ using Eq. 1:

$$r(s,a) + \gamma \cdot Q(s', \underset{a' \in A}{\text{argmax}} Q(s', a', \theta), \theta^-) = r(s,a) + \gamma \cdot V^*_{AS}(AS(s,a), \theta)$$

Simplifying it, we have the equation that defines the target value of an afterstate:

$$V^*_{AS}(AS(s,a), \theta) = Q(s', \underset{a' \in A}{\text{argmax}} Q(s', a', \theta), \theta^-) \tag{3}$$

5 Variable Reward Function

In Tetris, the largest component of the score comes from clearing lines. This score grows cubically in relation to the number of lines cleared simultaneously. This leads to a strong bias toward completing many lines in a single action: for example, clearing 30 lines one at a time yields the same score as clearing 4 lines at once.

Since the main objective of this paper is to create an agent that consistently seeks to clear four lines at once, the reward function should be designed to encourage this type of behavior. While most of the reward function was properly defined in Sect. 3, the constant k_1, the exponent applied to the number of lines cleared, has not yet been specified. To put it in another way, k_1 defines how the reward grows as a function of the number of lines cleared in a single action. This is shown in the Fig. 1.

Note that, as k_1 increases, the reward for clearing fewer than four lines diminishes. In a sense, this is desirable because it encourages the agent to pursue four line clears. However, if taken too far, the reward for clearing a smaller number of lines becomes so low that the agent may struggle to learn those actions at all. If the agent never properly learns how to clear single lines, it cannot reliably learn to clear more than that. Therefore, a trade-off must be reached. The most natural value is $k_1 = 3$, since the original game score grows cubically. In fact, our empirical tests indicate that $k_1 = 3$ yields the best performing agent.

However, since the problems with higher values of k_1 mostly manifest at the beginning of training, while their benefits only appear once the agent has acquired enough knowledge of the environment to clear four lines in a single move, the idea of increasing k_1 gradually during training seems promising. In a

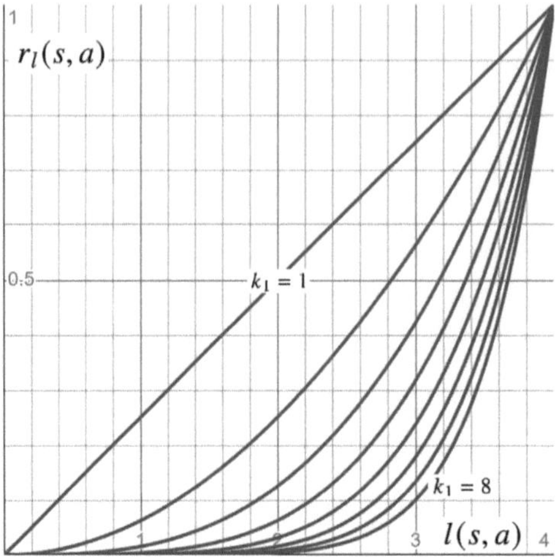

Fig. 1. Graph showing the change in behavior of the reward function according to the k_1 value, with $k_1 \in [1, 8]$. The values of k_1 increase from each curve left to right, giving a smaller reward for line clears between 1 and 3 as k_1 increases.

more theoretical sense, any change to the reward function implies a change to the value function, partially invalidating the one previously learned. Nevertheless, because the change primarily alters how much the agent prioritizes each objective rather than fundamentally changing the objectives themselves or which one is most desirable, the previously learned value function provides a good starting point for training the new one.

6 Training Details

The agent is trained for 2,500 episodes, and in each one the agent plays 100 complete games of Tetris. Each game continues until the agent loses (that is, the piece stack reaches the top of the board) or reaches a limit of 1,000 pieces played (this upper bound exists to limit the amount of time each game takes). During these games, every state transition is recorded as a 4-tuple, representing the current state, the action taken, the reward received, and the next state reached. Then, for each recorded state transition, a target value is calculated. The online network is then trained on these targets via gradient descent. Every 10 episodes, the weights of the online network θ are copied to the target network θ^-. The main difference to the standard Double Deep Q-Learning is that the evaluation is based on afterstate values ($V_{AS}(s, a)$), calculated through the Eq. 2, and, therefore, the target values are also based on afterstates ($V^*_{AS}(AS(s, a))$), calculated through the Eq. 3.

The agent utilizes an ϵ-greedy policy during training, in which the agent has a probability ϵ to choose a random action rather than the action the that maximizes the action-value. This is used only during the beginning of training, to force the agent to explore a wider variety of states before trying to exploit the ones it found most promising. At episode 0, $\epsilon = 1$, and it decreases linearly up to $\epsilon = 0.01$ at episode 500, maintaining this value throughout the rest of the training.

The neural network chosen to approximate V_{AS} was a convolutional neural network, as it preserves the spatial relationships between cells on the board, a crucial property for Tetris. The network receives as input every cell of the post-action board and passes it through a single convolutional layer with 20 filters of size 4×4. The filter size was chosen based on the smallest size needed to accommodate every piece in Tetris. The number of filters was chosen based on the number of possible different pieces and their rotations. In this sense, this layer is envisioned as checking every possible place on the board for every possible rotation of every piece. The output of the convolutional layer is then concatenated with an integer representing the next piece. This combined representation is fed into three dense layers, decreasing from 400, to 200 and finally 100 cells. The final layer collapses into a single floating-point number, which is the estimate of V_{AS}.

For training, a machine with 64 core AMD EPYC 7401 CPU @ 2.8 GHz and 256 GB of RAM was used, running on Debian Linux 12. Since the code was not properly parallelized, only 4 cores were used for each process, opting to run multiple tests at once so different configurations of hyperparameters could be tested. The experiments discussed in Sect. 7 took around 3 to 4 weeks to conclude. The agent evaluation discussed in Sect. 8 was run on a 2 core Intel Core i5-5200U CPU @ 2.20GHz and 8 GB of RAM, running on Debian Linux 12, and took around 2 days to test each agent.

The source code used in this paper is open source and can be accessed in: https://github.com/arthur-mant/tetris-ddqn.

Four different agents were tested, differing only in regards to the reward function:

1. Real score agent: does not utilize the proposed reward function, instead it uses a normalized version of the score given by the original game;
2. Fixed agent: has $k_1 = 3$ during the entire training;
3. Discrete agent: starts the training with $k_1 = 2$ and increases it discretely, adding 1 to k_1 every 300 episodes, up to $k_1 = 8$;
4. Continuous agent: starts the training with $k_1 = 2$ and increases it in a more continuous fashion, growing every time the target network θ^- is updated (which is every 10 episodes), up to $k_1 = 8$ at episode 1,500.

7 Training Results

The training process is analyzed using three different metrics: (1) the average game score per training episode, which is the primary metric the agent aims to maximize; (2) the average number of pieces played per game per episode, which measures the agent's survivability; and (3) the average number of lines cleared per episode, broken down by how many were cleared simultaneously. The third metric reveals the agent's strategy and indirectly indicates its efficiency on a score-per-piece basis. All graphs in this section use a moving average with a window size of 30 to reduce noise and facilitate interpretation.

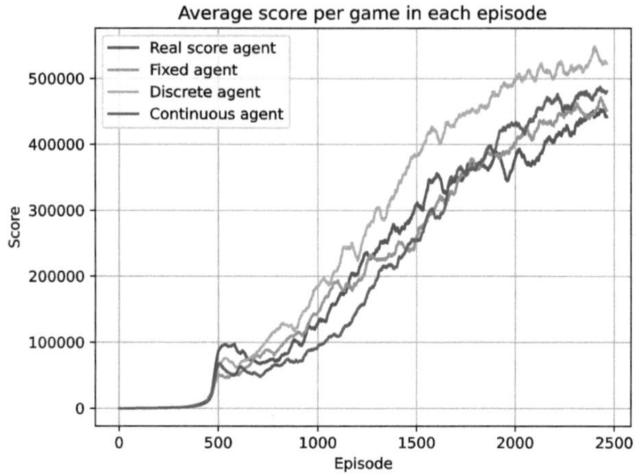

Fig. 2. Graph showing the changes in the average score earned throughout the training.

As seen in Fig. 2, the beginning of training shows a very low average score, with a rapid growth around episode 500. This is due to the high ϵ value, which leads to a high rate of random actions being chosen. Even when random actions are not chosen, previous poorly placed pieces impede the agent from being able to clear any lines, which explains why the score remains very low even at episode 400. This is quickly followed by a peak in all agents, that can be seen in the average score graph but it's more perceptible in the average pieces played graph (Fig. 3). This peak is caused by them learning to clear lines one by one, seen in all graphs from Fig. 4 but most evident in the real score agent, and therefore being able to survive for much longer and score much more.

After a few episodes of consistently clearing single lines, the agent eventually encounters scenarios that make it possible to clear more than one line simultaneously. In most cases, these moves are chosen because they generate significantly higher reward than clearing a single line. They are, then, used as training data for the neural network, which, after a few more episodes, begins to favor setting up moves that clear multiple lines. This creates problems, however: the setup required becomes increasingly complex as the number of simultaneously cleared lines grows, and every failed attempt generates a significant number of "junk" lines (rows with empty cells obstructed by pieces above them, making them difficult to clear). This difficulty is compounded by the agent's newfound reluctance to clear single lines. Consequently, the agent often experiences game overs much sooner than when it focused solely on clearing lines as quickly as possible. This effect is evident both from the sharp drop in the number of pieces played (see

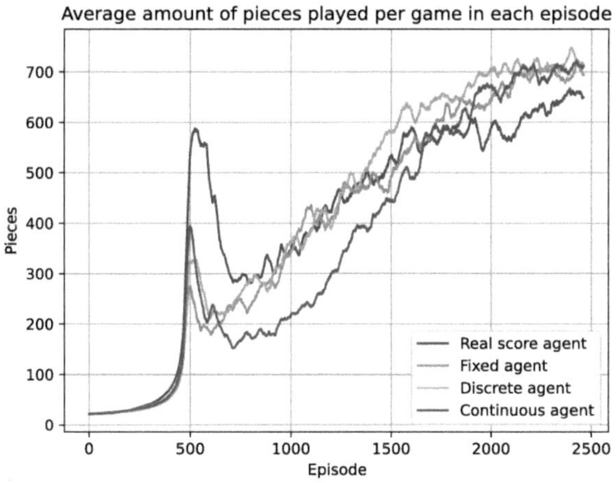

Fig. 3. Graph showing the changes in the average amount of pieces played throughout the training.

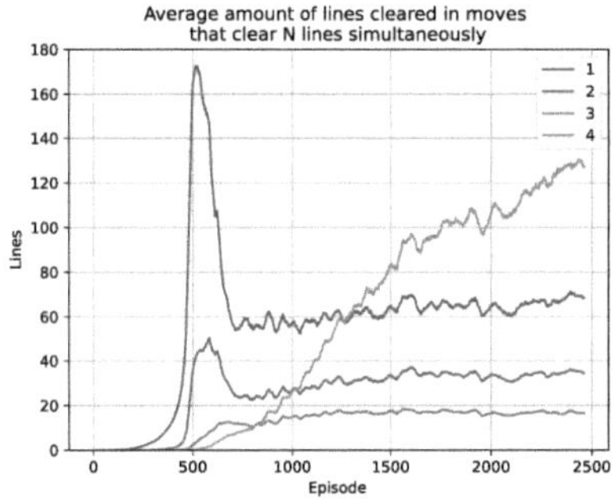

(a) Real score agent

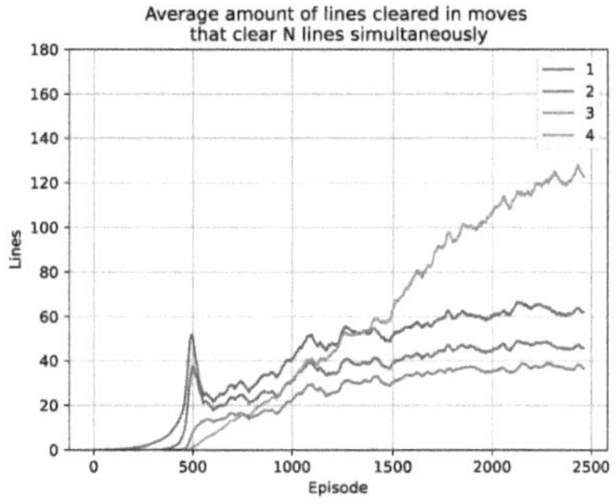

(b) Fixed agent

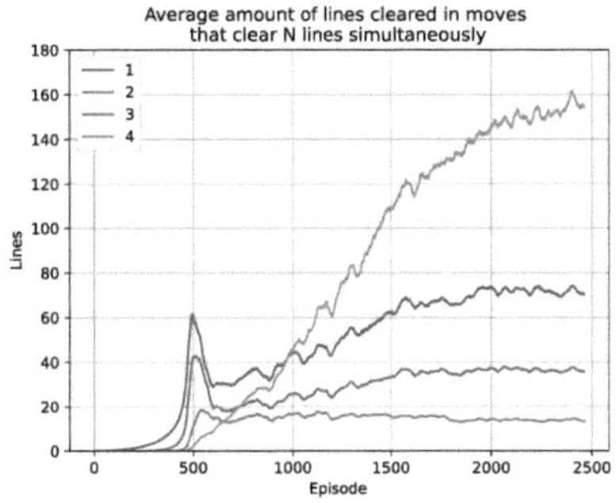

(c) Discrete agent

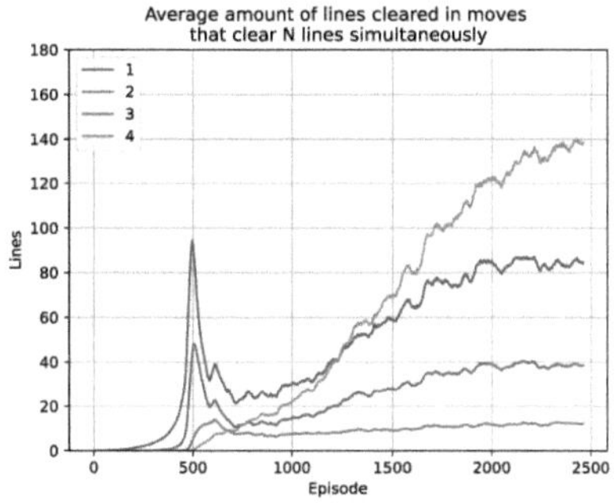

(d) Continuous agent

Fig. 4. Graphs showing the changes in the average amount of lines cleared divided by the amount cleared simultaneously throughout the training in all agents.

Fig. 3) and from the simultaneous decrease in single-line clears (visible in all graphs of Fig. 4).

From this drop in performance, the agent finally becomes aware of all possible line clears, and further training simply makes it better at executing them. The number of lines cleared per move for cases with fewer than four simultaneous clears either stabilizes or grows much more slowly. Meanwhile, four-line clears go from being near zero to becoming the most common way the agent clears lines. This leads to a substantial increase in the score earned, while the number of pieces played also grows.

Although all agents show similar overall performance, the discrete agent consistently outperforms the others across all metrics, particularly in total score and number of four-line clears. In contrast, the real score agent performs the worst overall, suggesting that our proposed reward function guides the agent more effectively than the normalized raw game score itself.

Due to processing time constraints, it was not possible to train them further until their performance completely stabilized. Nevertheless, we judge that this number of episodes is sufficient to indicate such stabilization and to distinguish between their performances.

8 Agent Evaluation

Each agent in the last section was tested in an unrestricted game environment to better evaluate them. The two main differences from the games played during training are that there is no longer a piece limit, letting the agents plays until they lose, and their ϵ-greedy policy was substituted for a simple greedy policy, in other words there is no longer any probability the agents will play a random move. A total of 10,000 games were played by each agent, and their performance were measured by 3 metrics: (1) total score earned; (2) amount of pieces played; and (3) efficiency.

The total score earned metric is the most important, being the one that the reward function is indirectly based on and, therefore, is the one the agent most clearly aims at maximizing. The amount of pieces played metric shows how good the agent is at just surviving. The efficiency metric consists of calculating the score that could be earned in an ideal scenario, where the same amount of pieces are played but all pieces are used to generate their maximum possible score, and dividing the score earned by it. This is used to show how much score the agents are losing by using inefficient moves such as clearing less than 4 lines simultaneously.

Table 1 shows the average and standard deviation of each of those metrics for each agent.

Since Tetris is highly stochastic and the training was not extensive enough to expose the agent to all, or even most, possible states, its performance varies considerably from game to game. This variability is evident in the high standard deviations of the score and pieces played metrics presented in the previous tables. Consequently, relying solely on averages is insufficient to assess the agent's true

Table 1. Table showing the average and standard deviation of the score earned, pieces played and efficiency metrics for each agent.

	Score		Pieces placed		Efficiency	
	$\bar{x}$	σ	$\bar{x}$	σ	$\bar{x}$	σ
Real score	1386876.50	1309322.83	1795.88	1641.70	59.97%	9.90%
Fixed	1591682.38	1574123.76	2147.09	2064.08	57.57%	8.92%
Discrete	2382120.66	2327352.02	2848.12	2722.61	65.36%	9.22%
Continuous	2518848.88	2557437.04	3300.32	3288.44	59.67%	8.27%

performance. To better illustrate the distribution of these metrics and, therefore, to evaluate the agent more effectively, we present boxplots of the data in Fig. 5.

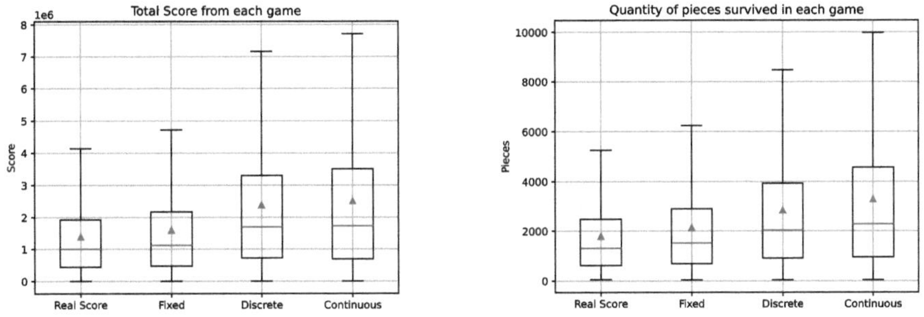

(a) Score earned

(b) Pieces played

Fig. 5. Boxplots for the score earned and pieces played metrics.

From these results, it can be concluded that the agent with the best overall performance is the continuous agent, despite the strong training results of the discrete agent. During training, the discrete agent's greater efficiency gave it an advantage. However, without the piece limit, the continuous agent proved able to survive, on average, a few hundred pieces longer, more than compensating for its slightly lower efficiency. On the other hand, the discrete agent has shown significantly higher efficiency than all others, achieving an average of around 65% while the others are around 60%. This suggests that its strategy is more rigorous, which is both a virtue and a flaw. While this stronger emphasis on four-line clears (even more than the other agents) may cause it to avoid lower line clears that could extend its survival, it may also need only a little more training to adapt to the situations that lead to losses, potentially making it more resilient while maintaining its higher efficiency.

To support our conclusion on the benefits of a variable reward function, a Friedman test followed by a post-hoc Nemenyi test was performed on the scores obtained from 10,000 games with the same piece sequence for all agents. The results are visualized in the Critical Difference diagram (Fig. 6). A lower average rank indicates better performance, and agents connected by a bold horizontal bar are not statistically significantly different at the 0.05 level. Both our discrete and continuous agents have statistically equivalent performance, which is significantly superior to the other two agents.

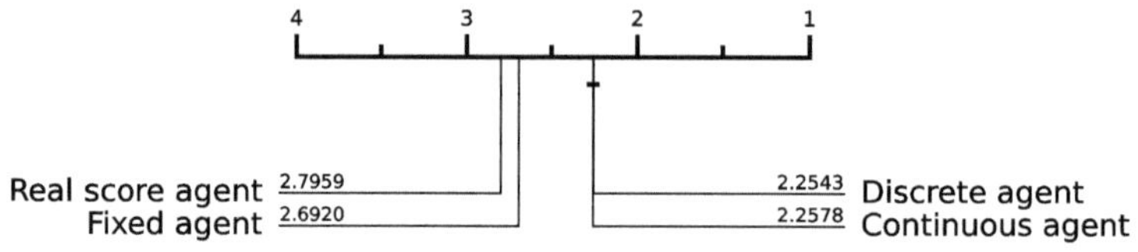

Fig. 6. Results of a Friedman test followed by a post-hoc Nemenyi test over the score of 10,000 games by each agent.

These results demonstrate that the variable reward function yields agents that outperform those trained with a fixed reward function, with both the continuous and discrete variants achieving comparable scores and survivability.

9 Comparison with Other Works

In this section, some other Tetris agents from the literature will be discussed, and how they compare to our continuous agent, which is considered the best one.

Both Thiery and Scherrer [9] and Lee [5] propose agents capable of clearing millions of lines, far surpassing the capabilities of our agent. Both use high level representations of the Tetris board based in human chosen heuristics, like number of holes on the board or stack height. These agents focus only on surviving, not considering any ideas of efficiency, simply clearing lines as soon and as often as possible to keep the stack low. In this sense, there is a big difference between them and our agent, since its main focus is not only surviving but also trying to play in an optimal way, to generate as much score out of every piece as possible.

Chen [2], similarly to our work, also proposes agents based on Deep Q-Learning, but with a state based not directly on the board, but on characteristics extracted from it by heuristics. Its best agent is able to play an average of over 60,000 pieces, achieving an average score of over 40,000 (with each move earning a score equal to the square of the amount of lines cleared), generating an average of 0.665 score per piece. This agent utilizes a different version of Deep Q-Learning that incorporates the transition function into the target action-values equation, which obviously demands the complete knowledge of the transition function.

The second best agent proposed by Chen utilizes a more traditional transition function agnostic Deep Q-Learning, and therefore is more directly comparable to our agent. It is able to play an average of 2,828 pieces per game, achieving an average score of 1,682, and consequently generating 0.595 score per piece.

Calculating the performance of our agent in an analogous manner, it plays an average of 3,300 pieces per game, achieving an average score of 3,818, and generating an 1.157 score per piece. Although it survives a lot less than the agent that utilizes the transition function, our agent is able to survive more pieces than this work's second best, which is the one more directly comparable to ours. In terms of efficiency, our agent is capable of producing 1.73 times more score per piece than Chen's most efficient agent, demonstrating a much more rigorous strategy.

Lundgaard e McKee [6] propose many different Tetris agents, so only the two best performing will be discussed. The first simply tries to minimize the stack height and the amount of holes (that is, unfilled cells that cant be accessed by a piece) on it, while the second uses a neural network that receives as input many different human chosen characteristics of the board, and returns a high level action such as minimizing holes or clearing lines. The authors utilize the Tetris for the Nintendo Entertainment System scoring system (the same used by us) with the first agent achieving an average score of 56,449.87 in 466.49 average cleared lines, and the second achieving an average score of 51,520.4 in 305.31 average cleared lines. Although the first one both manages to survive for longer and score more, Lundgaard e McKee emphasize the greater score per line cleared efficiency of the second, generating a score of 168.74 per line cleared, while the first generates a score of 121.00 per line cleared. Our continuous agent achieves an average score of 2,518,848.88 in 1,305.82 lines cleared, therefore generating a score of 1,928.94 per line cleared. In other words, our continuous agent achieves an score 44.6 times higher than this work highest scoring one and a score per line 11.43 times higher their most efficient agent.

10 Discussion

The agents presented in this paper achieved our goals: they consistently plan ahead to clear four lines at once while surviving for thousands of pieces. Moreover, as discussed in Sect. 9, their performance surpasses that of all other (transition-function-agnostic) Deep Q-Learning agents found in the literature.

The two main contributions of our agents are the use of afterstates to reduce the domain size of the action-value function and the adoption of a variable reward function. The benefits of the latter are clearly visible in both the training and evaluation results. Although we did not perform a proper comparative test of the former, contrasting the performance of our afterstate based agent against a traditional action-value based agent, the theoretical advantages and the superior performance relative to other literature agents that employ standard Deep Q-Learning strongly suggest that using afterstates has positively affected performance.

For future works, testing the impact of the action-value function domain reduction achieved through afterstates on training is a priority. Additionally, both afterstates and the variable reward function should be studied in other domains, since several questions were raised during our agent's development: can these techniques be applied generically to any domain, or which criteria must a domain satisfy for their application to be beneficial? If variable reward functions indeed improve performance in at least a subset of domains, how can we design a generally applicable one, or at least a reliable method for modeling such functions?

References

1. Algorta, S., Şimşek, Ö.: The game of Tetris in machine learning. arXiv preprint arXiv:1905.01652 (2019)
2. Chen, Z.: Playing Tetris with deep reinforcement learning. Master's thesis, University of Illinois at Urbana-Champaign (2021)
3. Demaine, E.D., Hohenberger, S., Liben-Nowell, D.: Tetris is Hard, Even to Approximate. In: Warnow, T., Zhu, B. (eds.) COCOON 2003. LNCS, vol. 2697, pp. 351–363. Springer, Heidelberg (2003). https://doi.org/10.1007/3-540-45071-8_36
4. Hasselt, H.v., Guez, A., Silver, D.: Deep reinforcement learning with double q-learning. In: Proceedings of the Thirtieth AAAI Conference on Artificial Intelligence, pp. 2094–2100. AAAI'16, AAAI Press (2016)
5. Lee, Y.: Tetris ai - the (near) perfect bot (2013). https://codemyroad.wordpress.com/2013/04/14/tetris-ai-the-near-perfect-player/. acessado em fevereiro de 2026
6. Lundgaard, N., McKee, B.: Reinforcement learning and neural networks for Tetris. Technical Report, University of Oklahoma (2006)
7. Mnih, V., et al.: Human-level control through deep reinforcement learning. Nature **518**(7540), 529–533 (2015)
8. Sutton, R.S., Barto, A.G.: Reinforcement learning: an introduction, vol. 1. MIT press Cambridge (1998)
9. Thiery, C., Scherrer, B.: Improvements on learning Tetris with cross entropy. Int. Comput. Game. Assoc. J. **32** (2009). https://inria.hal.science/inria-00418930
10. Watkins, C.J., Dayan, P.: Q-learning. Mach. Learn. **8**(3), 279–292 (1992)
11. White, C.C., White, D.J.: Markov decision processes. Eur. J. Oper. Res. **39**(1), 1–16 (1989). https://doi.org/10.1016/0377-2217(89)90348-2. https://www.sciencedirect.com/science/article/pii/0377221789903482

A Diversity-Driven Ensemble Based on Data Distribution and Parameter Heterogeneity for Wind Speed Forecasting

Diogo M. Almeida[1(✉)], Paulo S. G. de Mattos Neto[2], and Daniel C. Cunha[2]

[1] Instituto de Pesquisa em Petróleo e Energia (i-LITPEG), Universidade Federal de Pernambuco (UFPE), Recife, PE, Brazil
diogo.malmeida@ufpe.br

[2] Centro de Informática (CIn), Universidade Federal de Pernambuco (UFPE), Recife, PE, Brazil
{psgmn,dcunha}@cin.ufpe.br

Abstract. Ensemble methods have been widely adopted to address the complex patterns of wind speed time series. In this context, the LocDist method introduced a novel generation strategy for homogeneous ensembles by constructing compact training subsets guided by data distribution characteristics, achieving competitive performance while using less than 20% of the training data. However, its diversity is limited to variations in data distributions. A promising yet underexplored strategy is to construct neural network ensembles using diverse activation functions, which have been shown to improve accuracy and stability. Based on this, this work proposes LocDistED, a novel homogeneous ensemble method that enhances diversity by jointly leveraging data distribution and parameter heterogeneity. Experimental results on three wind speed time series demonstrate that LocDistED achieves robust performance compared to individual models and established ensemble methods, including bagging and LocDist. According to the Diebold–Mariano test, GRU-based LocDistED achieved statistically significant improvements in 67% of the cases compared with LocDist, while the LSTM- and SVR-based variants did so in 33% of the cases. Across all evaluation settings (individual, bagging, and LocDist), no statistically significant losses were observed for the LSTM-, GRU-, and ELM-based LocDistED models, whereas the SVR-based variant was the only one to exhibit statistically significant losses (22% of the cases).

Keywords: time series · machine learning · ensembles · activation functions · wind speed

1 Introduction

Wind energy is an attractive alternative due to its abundance and environmental benefits. However, its exploitation still faces significant challenges, particularly the variability in wind speed and direction, which leads to instability

M. Recamonde-Mendoza and R. C. Barros (Eds.): BRACIS 2026, LNAI 17105, pp. 461–477, 2027.
https://doi.org/10.1007/978-3-032-39882-6_31

in power generation [1]. Therefore, integrating wind energy into power systems poses considerable challenges for both operation and planning [2]. As a result, key activities such as planning, scheduling, maintenance, and control rely heavily on wind speed forecasting, making reliable advance predictions essential [1]. Consequently, the analysis and evaluation of wind energy systems have attracted increasing attention from researchers worldwide [3].

Various machine learning methods have been applied to wind speed forecasting, including support vector regression (SVR), extreme learning machines (ELM), long short-term memory (LSTM), and gated recurrent units (GRU) [4–9]. Although these models can capture nonlinear patterns, wind speed time series remain challenging due to their complex and heterogeneous nature [3]. Factors such as surface roughness, vegetation, and land use influence wind behavior [10], while the data may exhibit diverse distributions [11] and even chaotic patterns [2]. Consequently, accurate wind speed forecasting remains a difficult task.

Ensemble methods offer an effective alternative for modeling the complex dynamics of wind speed time series, often achieving higher predictive accuracy and reduced uncertainty than individual models by combining their complementary strengths [3,10,12–14]. In this context, ensembles typically involve two stages: generation, where individual models (also known as base models) produce predictions, and integration, where these outputs are combined. A key factor for their success is diversity among predictors, which enables the capture of distinct patterns in the data [15]. Moreover, reducing redundancy in the training data can improve efficiency without compromising performance [16]. In wind speed forecasting, it has been shown that it is achievable to obtain a subset of wind speed data partitions that adequately represent the underlying dynamics over the entire analysis period. Based on this insight, the LocDist method [17] introduces a novel approach to the generation phase of homogeneous ensembles (where base models share the same learning algorithm). It constructs compact training subsets guided by data distribution characteristics, achieving competitive, and occasionally superior, predictive performance while using less than 20% of the wind speed training data. However, its ensemble diversity is limited to variations in data distributions. In this way, a promising yet underexplored strategy is to construct ensembles of neural networks using diverse activation functions (AFs). Studies in other application domains [18,19] have shown that combining multiple models with different AFs within a homogeneous ensemble can improve both accuracy and stability. These results indicate that aggregating diverse AFs enhances generalization and robustness.

Another important insight is that including all available base models in an ensemble does not necessarily lead to optimal performance, as some predictors may degrade overall accuracy. Consequently, selecting a subset of the most reliable models can lead to a more effective ensemble. In time series forecasting, this is often achieved using accuracy-based criteria, where models are ranked by their forecasting errors, with studies showing that selecting best-performing models improves ensemble performance [20,21].

For these reasons, we hypothesize that enhancing the diversity of the LocDist ensemble through homogeneous base learners with diversity-inducing parameters (i.e., heterogeneous activation functions) expands the representational space of learned pattern mappings. When combined with a model selection stage, this increased representational capacity may lead to improved adequacy and robustness in predictive performance. Building on this hypothesis, we propose LocDistED, a novel homogeneous ensemble method that enhances diversity by jointly leveraging data distribution and model parameter heterogeneity.

The outline of the paper is organized as follows. Section 2 describes the related works. Section 3 introduces the proposal in detail. Section 4 is the experimental setup. In Sect. 5, results are presented by performing a comparison among individual models, homogeneous ensembles, and the proposal. Finally, in Sect. 6, conclusions are drawn.

2 Related Works

Several ensemble generation methods have been proposed to address the uncertainty inherent in time series data. In this domain, a homogeneous ensemble based on a resampling strategy was introduced in [22] and evaluated on the M3-Competition dataset. The method employs the moving block bootstrap (MBB) to generate multiple resampled versions of the original time series. Training predictors on these resampled series yields forecasts that are more robust to data uncertainty [23]. Nevertheless, this approach involves a substantial computational cost, as it requires training 100 base models on the full training set.

Alternatively, some ensemble generation methods aim to identify distinct local patterns within a time series, thereby producing specialized local predictors [24]. In this context, [24] introduced a homogeneous ensemble method for time series forecasting. The method constructs overlapping training partitions of equal length, allowing models to adapt to gradual changes in local patterns over time. Furthermore, the authors investigated the impact of partition size on predictive performance, concluding that appropriate training subset sizes depend on dataset characteristics. Another generation strategy was introduced in [25], where the training set is partitioned via clustering techniques to identify the most informative subsets. This approach aims to accelerate learning while preserving, or even improving, predictive accuracy. It is particularly beneficial for large datasets, as it reduces computational cost by avoiding redundant data [25]. However, the method requires the initial training of 200 models across different partitions before clustering. The authors note that the overall execution time remains manageable due to the possibility of parallel training.

For wind speed time series, the study in [26] demonstrated that a subset of data partitions can adequately represent the underlying dynamics over the analysis period. This finding indicates the presence of redundancy in such series, suggesting that the full training dataset may not be required for effective modeling. Based on this insight, the LocDist method [17] was proposed as a homogeneous ensemble generation framework that leverages local pattern recognition guided by data distribution characteristics. The method constructs compact training subsets that approximate the original data distribution. Experimental results showed that LocDist achieves competitive, and occasionally superior, predictive performance compared to individual and bagging-based models trained on the full dataset, while using less than 20% of the data. Nevertheless, its ensemble diversity is limited to variations in the data distributions of the generated subsets.

A promising approach to enhance ensemble diversity is to construct models incorporating diverse activation functions (AFs). In [18], a homogeneous ensemble of extreme learning machine (ELM) models with different AFs was shown to improve predictive accuracy and stability. Likewise, [19] demonstrated that ensembles of convolutional neural networks (CNNs) with varying AFs outperform both individual models and those relying on a fixed rectified linear unit (ReLU) activation. The authors also concluded that no single AF consistently outperforms others across different scenarios. While the ReLU is widely adopted due to its ability to mitigate the vanishing gradient problem associated with traditional AFs such as sigmoid and hyperbolic tangent [27], it is not without limitations. In particular, it may suffer from the dying ReLU problem, where neurons become permanently inactive and output zero regardless of the input [28]. Another line of research has focused on adaptive activation functions, which enhance flexibility by enabling data-driven learning of activation shapes. However, this increased flexibility comes at the cost of additional parameters, resulting in higher computational and implementation complexity [27].

A further important consideration is that incorporating all available base models into an ensemble does not necessarily lead to optimal predictive performance, as some predictors may degrade the overall accuracy of the combined model. Consequently, selecting a subset of the most reliable predictors can result in a more parsimonious and effective ensemble [20,21]. A common strategy in time series forecasting relies on accuracy-based criteria, where candidate models are ranked according to their forecasting errors. For instance, [20] proposed a ranking-based selection approach in which the five most accurate models were selected from a pool of nine, yielding an ensemble that outperformed both individual predictors and the full ensemble. Similarly, [21] demonstrated that removing high-error predictors and retaining a subset of five models from an initial set of ten improved ensemble accuracy by reducing the impact of discrepant forecasts.

3 Proposed Ensemble

The proposed method jointly exploits model selection and ensemble diversity by combining locally specialized predictors derived from distinct data distributions and diverse parameter configurations. Accordingly, the homogeneous ensemble comprises three stages: generation, selection, and integration. During the generation stage, subsets are defined using the LocDist method [17], which captures different data distributions while removing subsets with redundant distributional patterns within the training set. The main innovation of the proposed ensemble lies in the training process applied to each subset. To further enhance diversity, the proposed LocDistED introduces variation in the AFs of the hidden layer or the kernel functions, thereby increasing model heterogeneity. This process yields a pool of parameter-based heterogeneous local expert predictors trained on subsets with distinct data distributions, as validated by the Kolmogorov–Smirnov (KS) test. The null hypothesis of the KS test states that two samples are drawn from the same distribution [29]. Subsequently, in the selection stage, the most competent predictors are chosen, since different predictors exhibit different predictive capabilities. Finally, in the integration stage, the most suitable combination method is selected to produce the final ensemble forecast.

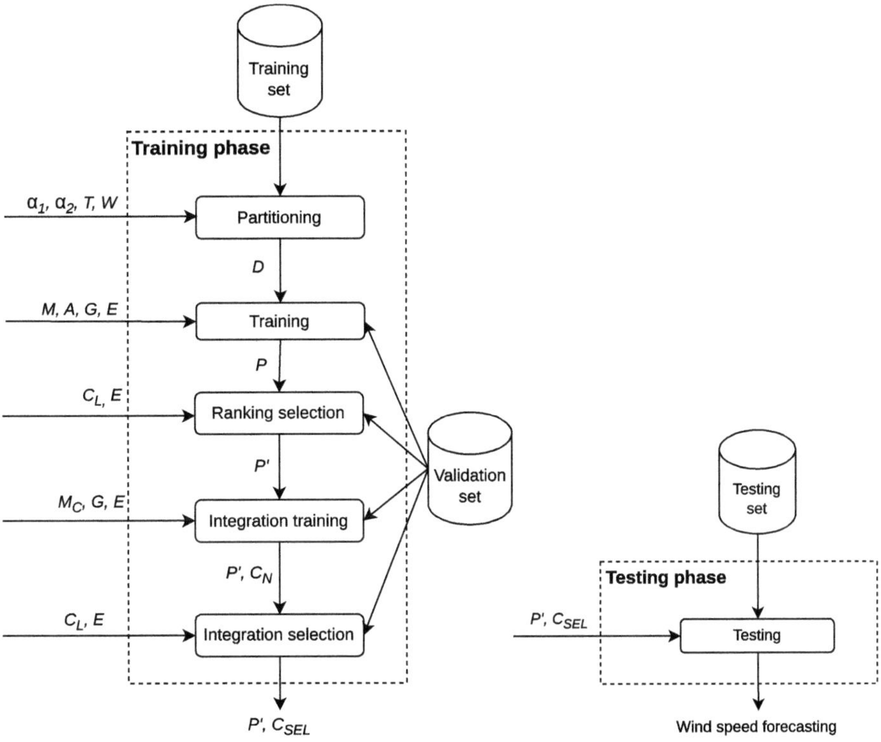

(a) Training. **(b)** Testing.

Fig. 1. Training and testing phase of the proposed ensemble LocDistED.

Figure 1(a) illustrates the training phase of the LocDistED method. The inputs include the training and validation sets of the time series, the significance levels of the KS hypothesis test (α_1 and α_2), the minimum partition size T, and the sliding window size W. In addition, the method requires the base model M, the activation or kernel function A, the hyperparameter optimization technique G, the evaluation metric E. It also requires a linear combination method C_L used in the ranking-based selection stage, as well as a model M_C for nonlinear combination. The output consists of a selected pool of trained models P', comprising local expert predictors, along with the chosen combination method C_{SEL}.

First, the ensemble generation step is employed through partitioning, which is constructed as follows: (i) Windows w_t are created in the training set with a fixed size W. The difference between two adjacent windows $(w_t - w_{t-1})$ is only one observation. The first window w_1 is defined as the initial reference window Ref_1; (ii) Subsequently, a significance level α_1 is defined, and the KS hypothesis test is sequentially applied between the current reference window and each subsequent window. (iii) The method constructs each subset by merging adjacent windows whose p-value is greater than p-value $> \alpha_1$, otherwise a new subset is initiated using the current window as the new reference window. In the end, we will have the defined subsets and their respective reference windows; (iv) Next, subsets with a size smaller than T are eliminated; (v) Return to step (iii) applying a grid search with different significance levels for α_1, aiming to maximize the expression:

$$\max \frac{\sum_{1 \le i < j \le u} I_{KS}(Ref_i, Ref_j)}{\binom{u}{2}} \tag{1}$$

$$I_{KS}(Ref_i, Ref_j) = \begin{cases} 1, & \text{if } p_{ij} \le 0.05, \\ 0, & \text{otherwise,} \end{cases} \tag{2}$$

where $\binom{u}{2}$ denotes the number of all possible pairwise combinations among the u reference windows associated with the subsets obtained after step (iv). The indicator function $I_{KS}(Ref_i, Ref_j)$ is defined as 1 when the KS test rejects the null hypothesis that the distributions of Ref_i and Ref_j are identical (p-value ≤ 0.05), and 0 otherwise. Therefore, maximizing Eq. (1) aims to maximize the proportion of reference-window pairs exhibiting statistically different distributions, thereby promoting greater diversity among the selected subsets. It is worth noting that, during the grid search, the partitioning process is driven by KS tests performed only between adjacent reference windows generated in sequence. Consequently, subsets with redundant distributions may still remain among non-adjacent reference windows. (vi) After determining the optimal significance level α_1 through the grid search by maximizing Eq. (1), the KS test is applied again with $\alpha_2 = 0.05$ to perform pairwise comparisons among the reference windows of all generated subsets. This additional step removes any remaining subsets with redundant distributions. At the end of step (vi), the k disjoint subsets $D = \{S_1, S_2, \ldots, S_k\}$ with statistically significant evidence of different data distributions are obtained, and the partitioning procedure is concluded. Then, homogeneous time series prediction models M are trained on each subset. Although the models are homogeneous, heterogeneity is introduced within each subset by employing different activation or kernel functions A. Hyperparameters are optimized using technique G, based on minimizing the evaluation metric E on the validation set, in order to mitigate overfitting. This process results in a pool $P = \{m_1, m_2, \ldots, m_N\}$ comprising N local expert predictors, where each subset of D was used to train models with different activation or kernel functions. The value of N is given by k multiplied by the number of distinct activation or kernel functions. In the selection stage, a ranking method based on the validation set selects a subset $P' = \{m_1, \ldots, m_n\}$ whose linear combination C_L minimizes E. Then, a nonlinear combiner C_N is obtained by training a model M_C to integrate P' using G and E. Finally, the best combination method C_{SEL} between C_L and C_N is selected based on the lowest error E on the validation set.

Finally, Fig. 1(b) shows the testing phase of the LocDistED method. The input involves the testing set of the time series, the pool $P' = \{m_1, \ldots, m_n\}$ of n local expert predictors, and the combination method C_{SEL} for integration. The output is the wind speed forecasting. This phase consists of testing the predictive capacity of the proposal with the models P' and the combination method C_{SEL} on an out-of-sample set.

4 Experimental Protocol

The databases used in this work are the same as those considered in [17]. They were provided by the Brazilian national institute of space research (INPE, in Portuguese), obtained from sensors installed at a height of 50 m [30]. Database 1 refers to Petrolina-PE, while Databases 2 and 3 were obtained in Triunfo-PE. The first database covers the period from July to September 2010. Databases 2 and 3 cover the periods from October to December 2006 and March to May 2006, respectively. There are 13,248 instances at ten-minute intervals between consecutive instances for each database, and no missing values. Every six instances were averaged, resulting in 2,208 instances for each time series with one-hour time intervals to reduce the size of the database. Subsequently, each time series was fully normalized to the interval $[0, 1]$. Then, each time series was divided into three subsets: the first 50% of the data for training, then 25% for validation, and the last 25% for testing. Table 1 presents the statistical summary of the three pre-processed and non-normalized databases.

Table 1. Statistical summary of wind speed in the three time series databases.

Time series	Maximum	Mean	Minimum	Standard deviation	Coefficient of variation
1	10.52 m/s	5.95 m/s	1.59 m/s	1.40 m/s	0,234
2	16.76 m/s	9.35 m/s	3.17 m/s	2.68 m/s	0.287
3	28.00 m/s	18.04 m/s	8.51 m/s	2.70 m/s	0.149

The same hyperparameter optimization strategy was applied to both individual models and the base learners of the ensembles (ELM, SVR, LSTM, and GRU). Model training was conducted on the training set, while the validation set was used for hyperparameter tuning to mitigate overfitting based on the root mean squared error (RMSE). The RMSE is defined by Equation (3), such that

$$RMSE = \sqrt{\left(\frac{\sum_{t=1}^{L}(y_t - \widehat{y}_t)^2}{L}\right)}, \quad (3)$$

where L is the size of the series, y_t is the actual value of the time series in period t, and $\widehat{y}_t$ is the predicted value of the time series in period t. Hyperparameters were optimized via grid search, with the search space defined according to the computational cost of each model, as detailed in Table 2. However, during the nonlinear integration stage of LocDist and LocDistED using the ELM model, the number of hidden neurons was selected from the range $[1, 2, \ldots, 42]$ to improve the combination performance.

Table 2. Hyperparameters used in the grid search for training individual models.

Model	Hyperparameters	Value
ELM	Input lags	1, 2, 3,..., 24
	Hidden layers nodes	1, 2, 3,..., 24
	Hidden AF	sigmoid
	Output AF	linear
SVR	Type	ϵ-regression
	Input lags	1, 6, 12, 18, or 24
	Kernel	sigmoid
	Regularization	$2^0, 2^1, ..., 2^{10}$
	ϵ	$2^{-10}, 2^{-9}, ..., 2^0$
LSTM and GRU	Input lags	1, 6, 12, 18, or 24
	Number of hidden layers	1
	Hidden layers nodes	6, 12, 18, or 24
	Hidden AF	sigmoid
	Output AF	linear
	Epochs	100
	Batch size	1
	Optimizer	Adam
	learning rate	0.001

LocDist was implemented separately using ELM, SVR, LSTM, and GRU as base models, following [17]. The sliding window was set to $W = 24$ to capture daily seasonality. A grid search for α_1 was conducted over $[0.05, 0.1, \ldots, 0.3]$, as larger values tend to produce very small subseries, and T was fixed at 60. Redundant partitions were removed by discarding less recent data distributions, as retaining recent ones improves performance [17]. In the integration stage, LocDist employs either a simple average or an ELM-based nonlinear combiner. The former is known for its robustness [15], while the latter can outperform it when predictors differ significantly in accuracy [31]. The final strategy was selected based on the lowest RMSE on the validation set.

Table 3. Individual models and ensemble forecasting approaches used in this work with corresponding methods and respective acronyms.

Approach	Method	Acronym
Individual modeling	Support vector regression [5]	SVR
	Extreme learning machines [7]	ELM
	Long short-term memory [9]	LSTM
	Gated recurrent units [9]	GRU
Homog. ens. based on bagging [22]	Mean(ELM_1,ELM_2,...,ELM_{100})	$BAGG_{ELM}$
	Mean(SVR_1,SVR_2,...,SVR_{100})	$BAGG_{SVR}$
Homog. ens. based on data distribution [17]	C_{SEL}(ELM_{S_1},ELM_{S_2},...,ELM_{S_k})	$LocDist_{ELM}$
	C_{SEL}(SVR_{S_1},SVR_{S_2},...,SVR_{S_k})	$LocDist_{SVR}$
	C_{SEL}($LSTM_{S_1}$,$LSTM_{S_2}$,...,$LSTM_{S_k}$)	$LocDist_{LSTM}$
	C_{SEL}(GRU_{S_1},GRU_{S_2},...,GRU_{S_k})	$LocDist_{GRU}$
Proposal	C_{SEL}(ELM_1, ELM_2,...,ELM_n)	$LocDistED_{ELM}$
	C_{SEL}(SVR_1, SVR_2,...,SVR_n)	$LocDistED_{SVR}$
	C_{SEL}($LSTM_1$, $LSTM_2$,...,$LSTM_n$)	$LocDistED_{LSTM}$
	C_{SEL}(GRU_1, GRU_2,...,GRU_n)	$LocDistED_{GRU}$

The proposed LocDistED method is a homogeneous ensemble inspired by LocDist [17] and was evaluated separately using ELM, SVR, LSTM, and GRU as base models. In the subseries generation stage, the same parameters as LocDist were adopted, namely $W = 24$, $\alpha_1 = [0.05, 0.1, \ldots, 0.3]$, $T = 60$ and redundant partitions were removed by discarding less recent data distributions. LocDistED introduces heterogeneity among base models through different Afs (for ELM, LSTM, and GRU) and different kernels (for SVR). Thus, for each subseries, three base models are trained, each with a distinct activation function or kernel, as follows: ELM (sigmoid, radial basis, or ReLU), LSTM (sigmoid, hyperbolic tangent, or ReLU), GRU (sigmoid, hyperbolic tangent, or ReLU), and SVR (sigmoid, radial basis, or linear). In the selection stage, the ranking method proposed in [20] is adopted due to its simplicity, low computational cost, and strong performance. Additionally, the RMSE is used as the evaluation metric, and the simple average as the linear combination method on the validation set.

Subsequently, an ELM model is employed as a nonlinear combiner for the selected models, also based on RMSE. Finally, the best combination strategy (linear or nonlinear) is selected on the validation set according to RMSE.

Table 3 shows all individual models and ensembles implemented and their respective acronyms. All simulations were performed for one-step-ahead forecasting using the R language with the E1071 [32] for SVR, ElmNNRcpp [33] for ELM, and Keras [34] for LSTM and GRU. Furthermore, RMSE was used to assess predictive performance on the test set, along with three other metrics: mean absolute error (MAE), mean absolute percentage error (MAPE), and predicted change in direction (POCID). For MAE and MAPE metrics, the lower their values, the better the model's accuracy. In the case of POCID, the higher the value, the better the model's performance. The MAE is defined by

$$MAE = \frac{\sum_{t=1}^{L} |y_t - \widehat{y}_t|}{L}, \tag{4}$$

where $|\cdot|$ is the absolute value operator. The MAPE metric is given by

$$MAPE = \frac{100}{L} \sum_{t=1}^{L} \frac{|y_t - \widehat{y}_t|}{y_t}, \tag{5}$$

while the POCID is designated by

$$POCID = 100 \frac{\sum_{t=1}^{L} Trend_t}{L}, \tag{6}$$

where

$$Trend_t = \begin{cases} 1, \text{ if } (y_t - y_{t-1})(\widehat{y}_t - \widehat{y}_{t-1}) > 0; \\ 0, \qquad \text{otherwise.} \end{cases} \tag{7}$$

Finally, the Diebold-Mariano (DM) hypothesis test [35] was applied between LocDistED and the other methods of the respective base model. So, the squared error loss function is considered for the errors of both competing predictors. The null hypothesis H_0 assumes equality in forecasting accuracy for both predictors. For H_0 to be rejected, the p-value must be less than the statistical significance level $\alpha = 0.05$. Some signals were used to interpret the results in Tables 4, 5 and 6 of Sect. 5. The sign "+" indicates that H_0 was rejected and the proposed method outperforms the method used for comparison. For instance, if $LocDistED_{ELM}$ outperformed ELM with statistical significance, the sign "+" will appear in the row of ELM. The sign "−" indicates that the proposed method underperforms the method used for comparison. The sign "=" indicates that the null hypothesis was not rejected, i.e., equality in forecasting accuracy for both predictors.

5 Results

The best results across all three databases were obtained with $T = 60$, as reported in [17], which corresponds to the minimum allowable size for the generated partitions. In Database 1, the generation stage produced three partitions

Table 4. Evaluation measurements and DM hypothesis test for the testing set obtained from the wind speed time-series Database 1.

Model	Method	RMSE(m/s)	MAE(m/s)	MAPE(%)	POCID(%)	DM test	p-value
ELM	ELM [7]	0.8126	0.6227	10.15	48.71	+	7.57e-03
	$BAGG_{ELM}$ based on [22]	0.8041	**0.6154**	**10.05**	47.82	=	5.65e-01
	$LocDist_{ELM}$ [17]	0.8071	0.6184	10.29	46.83	=	4.13e-01
	$LocDistED_{ELM}$	**0.8011**	0.6168	10.25	**50.00**		
SVR	SVR [5]	0.7804	0.6038	**9.84**	48.51	=	1.70e-01
	$BAGG_{SVR}$ based on [22]	**0.7799**	**0.6003**	9.88	48.21	=	8.69e-02
	$LocDist_{SVR}$ [17]	0.8107	0.6248	10.36	47.82	+	5.15e-03
	$LocDistED_{SVR}$	0.7956	0.6135	10.26	**49.80**		
LSTM	LSTM [9]	0.9105	0.7014	10.85	48.61	+	2.87e-09
	$LocDist_{LSTM}$ [17]	**0.7966**	**0.6101**	**9.96**	**49.21**	=	1.57e-01
	$LocDistED_{LSTM}$	0.8060	0.6237	10.40	48.81		
GRU	GRU [9]	0.8812	0.6796	10.65	49.01	+	6.33e-09
	$LocDist_{GRU}$ [17]	0.8116	0.6228	10.15	48.61	+	2.40e-03
	$LocDistED_{GRU}$	**0.7929**	**0.6106**	**10.13**	**49.60**		

containing 69, 62, and 96 observations, representing 20.6% of the total training set (1,104 observations). Table 4 presents the evaluation metrics and the results of the DM hypothesis test for the testing set of wind speed Database 1. The first column identifies the four model types employed in this study: ELM, SVR, LSTM, and GRU. The second column lists the corresponding forecasting methods, including the individual model, bagging-based ensemble, LocDist, and the proposed LocDistED. The subsequent columns report the evaluation metrics (RMSE, MAE, MAPE, and POCID) for each method. Finally, the DM test statistic and the associated p-value are provided. The best-performing result within each model category is highlighted in bold. For ELM, $LocDistED_{ELM}$ achieved the best performance in terms of RMSE and POCID, with the DM hypothesis test indicating statistical significance relative to the individual ELM model. In the case of SVR, $LocDistED_{SVR}$ obtained the highest POCID value and outperformed $LocDist_{SVR}$ across all evaluation metrics, with statistical significance based on squared errors. Regarding LSTM, $LocDistED_{LSTM}$ surpassed the individual LSTM model in all metrics, with statistical significance confirmed by the DM test. Finally, for the GRU architecture, $LocDistED_{GRU}$ achieved the best results across all evaluation metrics, with statistically significant improvements over both the standalone GRU and $LocDist_{GRU}$ in terms of squared errors. The integration stage of LocDistED selected the averaging combination strategy for the ELM, SVR, LSTM, and GRU approaches.

For Database 2, the generation stage produced two partitions containing 122 and 89 observations, corresponding to 19.1% of the total training set. Table 5 reports the evaluation metrics and the results of the DM hypothesis test for the testing set of wind speed Database 2. For ELM, $LocDistED_{ELM}$ achieved the best performance across all evaluation metrics, however, no statistically signifi-

Table 5. Evaluation measurements and DM hypothesis test for the testing set obtained from the wind speed time-series Database 2.

Model	Method	RMSE(m/s)	MAE(m/s)	MAPE(%)	POCID(%)	DM test	*p*-value
ELM	ELM [7]	1.3765	1.0227	12.78	54.47	=	7.13e-02
	$BAGG_{ELM}$ based on [22]	1.3641	1.0208	12.69	54.96	=	7.58e-02
	$LocDist_{ELM}$ [17]	1.3436	0.9965	12.18	56.55	=	5.66e-01
	$LocDistED_{ELM}$	**1.3354**	**0.9847**	**12.06**	**58.13**		
SVR	SVR [5]	1.2806	**0.9449**	11.73	56.86	−	2.12e-03
	$BAGG_{SVR}$ based on [22]	**1.2730**	0.9450	**11.71**	**57.14**	−	2.38e-03
	$LocDist_{SVR}$ [17]	1.3403	0.9966	12.27	56.55	=	8.24e-01
	$LocDistED_{SVR}$	1.3438	0.9947	12.25	**57.14**		
LSTM	LSTM [9]	1.3771	1.0247	12.78	55.95	+	6.23e-04
	$LocDist_{LSTM}$ [17]	1.3370	0.9918	12.16	55.95	=	1.74e-01
	$LocDistED_{LSTM}$	**1.3123**	**0.9694**	**12.07**	**57.14**		
GRU	GRU [9]	1.3929	1.0426	13.11	55.36	+	5.25e-04
	$LocDist_{GRU}$ [17]	1.3411	1.0014	12.44	**56.55**	=	2.24e-01
	$LocDistED_{GRU}$	**1.3257**	**0.9616**	**11.71**	56.35		

cant differences were observed in the DM test when compared to the other methods. In the case of SVR, $LocDistED_{SVR}$ obtained the highest POCID value, but exhibited statistically significant losses in squared errors relative to the individual SVR and $BAGG_{SVR}$ models. Regarding LSTM, $LocDistED_{LSTM}$ achieved the best results across all metrics, with statistical significance in squared errors relative to the individual LSTM model. Finally, $LocDistED_{GRU}$ outperformed all competing methods in terms of RMSE, MAE, and MAPE, achieving statistical significance in squared errors when compared to the standalone GRU. In the integration stage, LocDistED selected the ELM-based combination strategy for the SVR and LSTM approaches, and the averaging combination strategy for the ELM and GRU models.

In Database 3, the generation stage produced three partitions containing 66, 65, and 71 observations, corresponding to 18.3% of the total training set. Table 6 presents the testing results for the wind speed time series of Database 3. For ELM, $LocDistED_{ELM}$ achieved lower RMSE and MAE than both the individual ELM and $LocDist_{ELM}$, with statistical significance in the DM test relative to the single ELM model. In the case of SVR, $LocDistED_{SVR}$ outperformed the standalone SVR and $BAGG_{SVR}$ in terms of RMSE, MAE, and MAPE, with statistical significance based on squared errors. Concerning LSTM, $LocDistED_{LSTM}$ achieved the best performance in RMSE, MAE, and MAPE, with statistical significance in squared errors. Finally, $LocDistED_{GRU}$ outperformed both GRU and $LocDist_{GRU}$ in RMSE, MAE, and POCID, again with statistical significance according to the squared-error DM test. In all LocDistED models, the integration step selected the average combination strategy.

The DM hypothesis test results based on squared forecast errors, reported in Tables 4, 5, and 6, indicate the statistical superiority of the proposed app-

Table 6. Evaluation measurements and DM hypothesis test for the testing set obtained from the wind speed time-series Database 3.

Model	Method	RMSE(m/s)	MAE(m/s)	MAPE(%)	POCID(%)	DM test	p-value
ELM	ELM [7]	1.1147	0.8838	4.45	51.39	+	1.70e-03
	$BAGG_{ELM}$ based on [22]	**1.0592**	**0.8394**	**4.26**	**52.18**	=	9.50e-02
	$LocDist_{ELM}$ [17]	1.1000	0.8704	4.39	51.98	=	5.03e-02
	$LocDistED_{ELM}$	1.0793	0.8630	4.45	51.79		
SVR	SVR [5]	1.1616	0.9014	4.51	51.59	+	3.45e-06
	$BAGG_{SVR}$ based on [22]	1.2513	0.9547	4.73	**53.17**	+	4.39e-08
	$LocDist_{SVR}$ [17]	**1.0792**	**0.8545**	**4.33**	52.18	=	8.62e-01
	$LocDistED_{SVR}$	1.0810	0.8590	4.35	51.59		
LSTM	LSTM [9]	1.1706	0.9328	4.72	**53.17**	+	2.70e-11
	$LocDist_{LSTM}$ [17]	1.1208	0.8874	4.46	51.98	+	1.07e-06
	$LocDistED_{LSTM}$	**1.0286**	**0.8259**	**4.32**	51.59		
GRU	GRU [9]	1.1564	0.9231	4.70	51.79	+	2.83e-16
	$LocDist_{GRU}$ [17]	1.1155	0.8830	**4.44**	52.18	+	7.20e-04
	$LocDistED_{GRU}$	**1.0786**	**0.8632**	4.45	**52.38**		

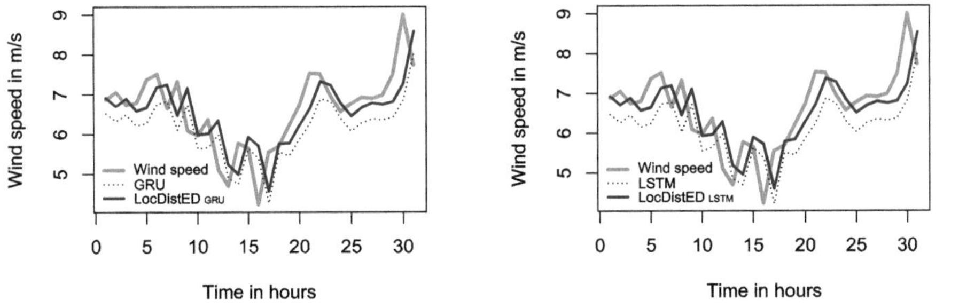

(a) The GRU underestimates the time series. (b) The LSTM underestimates the time series.

Fig. 2. One-step ahead prediction results for LocDistED and global mapping methods on dataset 1 considering 30 sequential observations from the test set.

roach. $LocDistED_{GRU}$, $LocDistED_{LSTM}$, and $LocDistED_{ELM}$ achieved wins or statistical ties in 100% of the evaluated cases. Additionally, $LocDistED_{SVR}$ obtained wins or ties in 78% of the cases, confirming the competitiveness of the LocDistED method across different learning models. Restricting the analysis to comparisons between LocDistED and LocDist, $LocDistED_{GRU}$ achieved statistically significant improvements in 67% of the cases. Both $LocDistED_{LSTM}$ and $LocDistED_{SVR}$ achieved wins in 33% of the evaluations. $LocDistED_{ELM}$ exhibited no statistically significant losses, resulting exclusively in ties across all comparisons. These findings support our hypothesis that enhancing the diversity of the LocDist ensemble through homogeneous base learners with diversity-inducing parameters expands the representational space of learned pattern map-

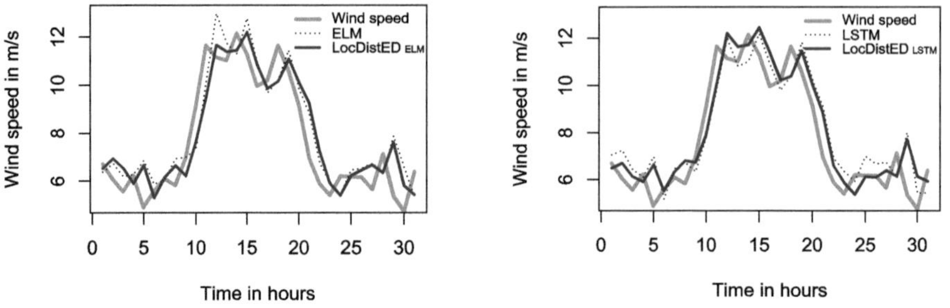

(a) The ELM overestimates the series in some regions, with error peaks in the interval [10, 15].

(b) The LSTM overestimates the series in some regions, with error peaks in the interval [24, 27].

Fig. 3. One-step ahead prediction results for LocDistED and global mapping methods on dataset 2 considering 30 sequential observations from the test set.

pings. And, when coupled with a model selection stage, can improve the adequacy and robustness of the predictive performance. $LocDistED_{SVR}$ exhibited statistically significant losses in 22% of the cases, indicating certain limitations of the approach.

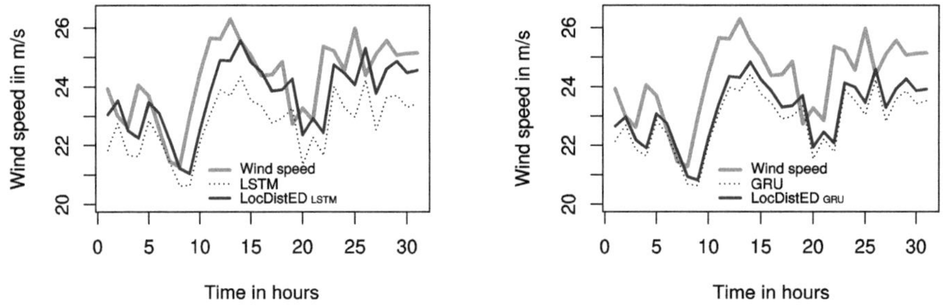

(a) The LSTM underestimates the time series.

(b) The GRU underestimates the time series.

Fig. 4. One-step ahead prediction results for LocDistED and global mapping methods on dataset 3 considering 30 sequential observations from the test set.

We selected ELM, LSTM, and GRU for graphical evaluation on each dataset, excluding SVR based on the DM test results. For dataset 1, Figs. 2(a) and 2(b) show the one-step-ahead forecasts generated by LocDistED built from GRU and LSTM, respectively, where its superior predictive adequacy is evident, as the individual models tend to underestimate the curve. For dataset 2 (Fig. 3), using ELM and LSTM, LocDistED produces a better learning pattern mappings than the corresponding global models. For instance, in Fig. 3(a), between observations 10 and 15, the ELM model exhibits a forecasting error peak that is effectively mitigated by $LocDistED_{ELM}$. Similarly, in dataset 3 (Fig. 4), using LSTM and

GRU, LocDistED yields lower prediction errors than models trained on the full dataset, which again underestimate the curve.

6 Conclusions

This work introduced LocDistED, a novel homogeneous ensemble method that enhances diversity by jointly leveraging data distribution and parameter heterogeneity. By constructing compact training subsets that effectively approximate the underlying data distribution while incorporating diversity-inducing model configurations, LocDistED expands the representational capacity of ensemble models and enables a more effective characterization of complex time series dynamics. Experimental results on three wind speed time series demonstrate that LocDistED is competitive with, or even outperforms, individual models and established ensemble methods, including bagging and LocDist. According to the Diebold–Mariano test based on squared errors, LocDistED with LSTM, GRU, or ELM achieved wins or ties in 100% of the cases. When compared exclusively with LocDist, the GRU-based LocDistED achieved statistically significant improvements in 67% of the cases, highlighting its high robustness. The SVR-based variant achieved wins or ties in 78% of the cases, despite statistically significant losses in 22% of the cases, indicating certain limitations of the approach. Future work will investigate the integration of LocDistED with dynamic selection techniques and its extension to other time series forecasting tasks.

References

1. Qu, Z., Mao, W., Zhang, K., Zhang, W., Li, Z.: Multi-step wind speed forecasting based on a hybrid decomposition technique and an improved back-propagation neural network. Renewable Energy **133**, 919–929 (2019)
2. Jiang, P., Wang, B., Li, H., Lu, H.: Modeling for chaotic time series based on linear and nonlinear framework: application to wind speed forecasting. Energy **173**, 468–482 (2019)
3. Ahmadi, M., Khashei, M.: Current status of hybrid structures in wind forecasting. Eng. Appl. Artif. Intell. **99**, 104133 (2021)
4. Mohandes, M.A., Halawani, T.O., Rehman, S., Hussain, A.A.: Support vector machines for wind speed prediction. Renew. Energy **29**(6), 939–947 (2004)
5. Salcedo-Sanz, S., Ortiz-Garcı, E.G., Pérez-Bellido, Á.M., Portilla-Figueras, A., Prieto, L., et al.: Short term wind speed prediction based on evolutionary support vector regression algorithms. Expert Syst. Appl. **38**(4), 4052–4057 (2011)
6. Kong, X., Liu, X., Shi, R., Lee, K.Y.: Wind speed prediction using reduced support vector machines with feature selection. Neurocomputing **169**, 449–456 (2015)
7. Saavedra-Moreno, B., et al.: Very fast training neural-computation techniques for real measure-correlate-predict wind operations in wind farms. J. Wind Eng. Ind. Aerodyn. **116**, 49–60 (2013)
8. Memarzadeh, G., Keynia, F.: A new short-term wind speed forecasting method based on fine-tuned LSTM neural network and optimal input sets. Energy Convers. Manage. **213**, 112824 (2020)

9. Liu, X., Lin, Z., Feng, Z.: Short-term offshore wind speed forecast by seasonal Arima-a comparison against GRU and LSTM. Energy, vol. 227, pp. 120492 (2021)
10. Ferreira, M., Santos, A., Lucio, P.: Short-term forecast of wind speed through mathematical models. Energy Rep. **5**, 1172–1184 (2019)
11. Wu, J., Li, N.: Impact of components number selection in truncated gaussian mixture model and interval partition on wind speed probability distribution estimation. Sci. Total Environ. **883**, 163709 (2023)
12. Hu, J., Wang, J., Zeng, G.: A hybrid forecasting approach applied to wind speed time series. Renew. Energy **60**, 185–194 (2013)
13. Ruiz-Aguilar, J.J., Turias, I., González-Enrique, J., Urda, D., Elizondo, D.: A permutation entropy-based EMD-ANN forecasting ensemble approach for wind speed prediction. Neural Comput. Appl. **33**(7), 2369–2391 (2021)
14. Jiang, Z., Che, J., Wang, L.: Ultra-short-term wind speed forecasting based on EMD-var model and spatial correlation. Energy Convers. Manage. **250**, 114919 (2021)
15. Sergio, A.T., de Lima, T.P., Ludermir, T.B.: Dynamic selection of forecast combiners. Neurocomputing **218**, 37–50 (2016)
16. Bowden, G.J., Maier, H.R., Dandy, G.C.: Optimal division of data for neural network models in water resources applications. Water Resour. Res. **38**(2), 2–1 (2002)
17. Almeida, D.M., de Mattos Neto, P.S., Cunha, D.C.: A data distribution-based ensemble generation applied to wind speed forecasting. In: Brazilian Conference on Intelligent Systems, pp. 17–32. Springer (2024)
18. Zhang, X.-H., Zhu, Q.-X., He, Y.-L., Xu, Y.: A novel robust ensemble model integrated extreme learning machine with multi-activation functions for energy modeling and analysis: Application to petrochemical industry. Energy **162**, 593–602 (2018)
19. Maguolo, G., Nanni, L., Ghidoni, S.: Ensemble of convolutional neural networks trained with different activation functions. Expert Syst. Appl. **166**, 114048 (2021)
20. Adhikari, R., Verma, G., Khandelwal, I.: A model ranking based selective ensemble approach for time series forecasting. Procedia Comput. Sci. **48**, 14–21 (2015)
21. Sergio, A.T.: Seleção dinâmica de combinadores de previsão de séries temporais," Doctoral Dissertation – Computer Science (2017)
22. Bergmeir, C., Hyndman, R.J., Benítez, J.M.: Bagging exponential smoothing methods using STL decomposition and box-cox transformation. Int. J. Forecast. **32**(2), 303–312 (2016)
23. Petropoulos, F., Hyndman, R.J., Bergmeir, C.: Exploring the sources of uncertainty: why does bagging for time series forecasting work? Eur. J. Oper. Res. **268**(2), 545–554 (2018)
24. de Mattos Neto, P.S., Cavalcanti, G.D., Firmino, P.R., Silva, E.G., Filho, S.R.V.F.: A temporal-window framework for modelling and forecasting time series. In: Knowledge-Based Systems, vol. 193, p. 105476 (2020)
25. Tetko, I.V., Villa, A.E.: Efficient partition of learning data sets for neural network training. Neural Netw. **10**(8), 1361–1374 (1997)
26. Ribeiro, R., Fanzeres, B.: Identifying representative days of solar irradiance and wind speed in Brazil using machine learning techniques. Energy AI **15**, 100320 (2024)
27. Apicella, A., Donnarumma, F., Isgrò, F., Prevete, R.: A survey on modern trainable activation functions. Neural Netw. **138**, 14–32 (2021)
28. Maas, A.L., et al.: Rectifier nonlinearities improve neural network acoustic models. In: Proceedings of the ICML, vol. 30, p. 3, Atlanta, GA (2013)

29. Hodges, J., Jr.: The significance probability of the Smirnov two-sample test. Ark. Mat. **3**(5), 469–486 (1958)
30. INPE, "Rede do sistema de organização nacional de dados ambientais (2020). http://sonda.ccst.inpe.br/index.html. Accessed 27 Jul 2023
31. Andrawis, R.R., Atiya, A.F., El-Shishiny, H.: Forecast combinations of computational intelligence and linear models for the nn5 time series forecasting competition. Int. J. Forecast. **27**(3), 672–688 (2011)
32. Meyer, D., et al.: e1071: misc functions of the department of statistics, probability theory group (formerly: E1071), tu wien. R package version (2023)
33. L. Mouselimis, A. Gosso, and E. Jonge, "elmnnrcpp: The extreme learning machine algorithm," R package, 2023
34. Chollet, F., et al.: Keras (2015). https://keras.io
35. Diebold, F.X., Mariano, R.S.: Comparing predictive accuracy. J. Bus. Econ. Stat. textbf13(3) (1995)

Multicentric Prototypes Pseudo-labeling for Source-Free Video Domain Adaptation

Miguel V. de Oliveira(✉) and Eulanda M. Santos

Institute of Computing – Federal University of Amazonas, Av. Gal. Rodrigo Otávio, Coroado, Manaus, AM 69080-900, Brazil
{miguel.oliveira,emsantos}@icomp.ufam.edu.br

Abstract. Source-free domain adaptation (SFDA) offers a paradigm for adapting pretrained models to unlabeled target domains without revisiting source data. In video action recognition, self-training via pseudo-labeling is the dominant strategy, but its effectiveness is limited by label noise induced by domain shift. The state-of-the-art CleanAdapt framework handles this as a learning from noisy labels problem, filtering samples by cross-entropy loss within a teacher–student framework. Its fixed selection threshold τ, however, creates a rigid quality–quantity trade-off: conservative values produce high-purity labels at the cost of reducing training data, while permissive values reintroduce noise. In this paper, we replace CleanAdapt's discarding policy with a multi-centric, prototype-based attribution step. At each epoch, a high-confidence subset of samples is used to identify multiple k-means centroids per class, which then re-label the discarded high-loss samples via k-nearest-neighbor majority voting based on the prototypes. This decouples pseudo-label quality from the retention ratio alone, allowing the model to exploit the entire target distribution while remaining anchored to reliable pseudo-label class prototypes. On the UCF101 $\leftrightarrow$ HMDB51 benchmark, our method achieves consistent gains over CleanAdapt and dynamic-thresholding baselines across both transfer directions, with improvements of up to 5.0 p.p. on the harder UCF101 $\rightarrow$ HMDB51 direction.

Keywords: Source-free domain adaptation · pseudo-labeling · prototype learning · video action recognition · domain shift

1 Introduction

Deep learning models have achieved remarkable performance in video action recognition, yet their effectiveness degrades substantially under distributional shifts between training and deployment data [6]. Unsupervised Domain Adaptation mitigates this issue by transferring knowledge from a labeled source domain to an unlabeled target domain. However, it requires simultaneous access to both domains, which is often impractical due to privacy constraints, intellectual property restrictions, or storage limitations [10].

M. Recamonde-Mendoza and R. C. Barros (Eds.): BRACIS 2026, LNAI 17105, pp. 478–491, 2027.
https://doi.org/10.1007/978-3-032-39882-6_32

Source-Free Domain Adaptation (SFDA) has emerged as a more realistic alternative, where adaptation relies solely on a source-pretrained model and unlabeled target data. Among model-based SFDA approaches, self-training via pseudo-labeling is the dominant paradigm [10]. In this setting, the model iteratively refines itself using its own predictions as supervision. The central challenge, however, is that domain shift induces noisy pseudo-labels, which can accumulate and degrade performance over time.

The recent CleanAdapt framework [6] addresses this issue by performing SFDA as a learning-from-noisy-labels problem. Within a Teacher–Student (TS) architecture, it exploits the deep memorization effect [2] to filter samples based on cross-entropy loss, retaining only the τ fraction of lowest-loss samples per class for training while discarding the rest. Although effective, this strategy introduces a rigid quality–quantity trade-off: conservative values of τ ensure high pseudo-label purity but drastically reduce the available training data, whereas larger values increase coverage at the cost of noise. This trade-off becomes particularly limiting in challenging scenarios such as UCF101 $\rightarrow$ HMDB51, where target data is scarce and diverse.

This limitation raises a fundamental question: *can pseudo-label quality be maintained without sacrificing data coverage?* More specifically, *is it possible to move beyond rigid loss-based filtering and instead exploit the structure of the feature space to recover useful information from high-loss samples?*

To address this, we propose a multicentric prototype-based attribution strategy that complements loss-based filtering with geometric re-labeling. Rather than discarding high-loss samples, our method uses the lowest-loss samples, called here clean subset, to estimate multicentric class structure in the target feature space and re-label the remaining high-loss target samples using prototype-based attribution, as detailed in Sect. 3. This design is motivated by two key observations: (i) a small clean subset can provide reliable structural information about the feature space, and (ii) video data exhibits significant intra-class variation that cannot be adequately modeled by a single prototype.

Our contributions are threefold: (i) a prototype attribution mechanism that rescues high-loss target samples instead of discarding them, (ii) a multicentric design that captures intra-class variability in video features, and (iii) an empirical study on UCF101 $\leftrightarrow$ HMDB51 showing consistent gains over CleanAdapt across transfer directions. We integrate this mechanism into the CleanAdapt+TS framework, the Teacher-Student variant of CleanAdapt, and evaluate it on the UCF101 $\leftrightarrow$ HMDB51 benchmark. Our approach consistently outperforms the baseline across both transfer directions, with gains of up to 5.0 p.p. on the more challenging UCF101 $\rightarrow$ HMDB51 task.

The remainder of this paper is organized as follows. Section 2 reviews related work in source-free domain adaptation and prototype-based refinement. Section 3 presents the proposed methodology, detailing the teacher–student framework and the multicentric prototype attribution mechanism. Section 4 describes the experimental setup, including datasets, baselines, and evaluation protocol. Section 5 reports and analyzes the results with respect to the proposed research questions. Finally, Sect. 6 concludes the paper and outlines directions for future work.

2 Related Work

Domain adaptation mitigates performance degradation under distribution shift. While traditional Unsupervised Domain Adaptation assumes simultaneous access to labeled source and unlabeled target data, Source-Free Domain Adaptation (SFDA) relies only on a source-pretrained model and unlabeled target data—a setting common when source data cannot be shared. We focus on model-based self-training via pseudo-labeling, where the central challenge is label noise and error propagation.

CleanAdapt [6] performs Teacher–Student self-training with loss-based filtering controlled by the selection ratio τ. Our work complements this filtering with multicentric prototypes that re-label high-loss samples via latent geometry rather than discarding them.

2.1 Prototype-Based Refinement

SHOT [12] pioneered centroid-based pseudo-labeling with a fixed source classifier and mutual-information alignment. For video, STHC [11] adds spatial-temporal-historical consistency and a memory bank; on UCF101↔HMDB51, applying SHOT image-style to clip features yields little or no gain over the TRN source model (Table 2), underscoring the need for video-aware refinement.

DaC [19] partitions target data into source-like and target-specific groups for adaptive contrastive learning. Video-specific methods include TAViT-SFVUDA [18], which combines ViTs with confidence-filtered clustering anchors, and ATCoN [17], which enforces confidence-weighted temporal consistency. PCMDA [7] regularizes noisy targets via weighted combinations of clean prototypes, though it targets multi-source settings. MTRAN [8] employs a video Transformer with multimodal relative alignment.

Class imbalance can bias prototype formation. BMD [14] uses class-balanced multicentric prototypes with dynamic relabeling on image SFDA benchmarks (Office-Home, VisDA-C), but reports no UCF↔HMDB results; we adopt its multicentric intuition within an I3D video pipeline instead of a SHOT plug-in. T-CPGA [13] explores imbalance-agnostic SFDA via foundation-model guidance.

Motivated by these approaches, we adopt multicentric prototype attribution to re-label high-loss samples by proximity to reliable anchors rather than excluding them as in loss-only filtering. Table 1 situates our contribution relative to the SFDA methods discussed above.

3 Proposed Approach

Our approach addresses the central limitation of loss-based filtering in SFDA: the rigid coupling between pseudo-label quality and data utilization. Instead of

Table 1. Comparison of source-free adaptation methods discussed in this work.

Method	Core mechanism	Limitations
SHOT [12]	Fixed classifier with centroid pseudo-labels and mutual-information alignment	Image-centric; weak on video temporal structure
STHC [11]	Consistency regularization over spatial, temporal, and historical predictions	Augmentation-driven; limited prototype topology
ATCoN [17]	Confidence-weighted temporal consistency between local and global video features	Does not geometrically re-label high-loss clips
DaC [19]	Contrastive adaptation on high- and low-confidence target partitions	Image-oriented; diffuse alignment for dynamics
BMD [14]	Class-balanced sampling with multicentric prototype clustering	Image SFDA only; not evaluated on UCF↔HMDB
TAViT-SFVUDA [18]	ViT features refined by confidence-filtered cluster anchors	Heavy backbone; non-standard data split
PCMDA [7]	Noise-robust supervision via weighted combinations of clean prototypes	Designed for multi-source scenarios
CleanAdapt+TS [6]	Teacher–Student self-training on per-class low-loss target samples	Discards high-loss target clips
MTRAN [8]	Relative alignment of multimodal features in a video Transformer	Different backbone and modality from our I3D RGB setup

discarding high-loss samples, we reinterpret filtering as a mechanism for identifying a reliable reference subset and delegate pseudo-label assignment for uncertain samples to the geometric structure of the feature space.

Concretely, the method decomposes pseudo-label generation into two macro stages: (1) identification of a clean reference subset via loss-based filtering; and (2) geometry-aware re-labeling of the remaining samples using multicentric prototypes. This design enables the model to exploit the entire target dataset while anchoring supervision to a low-noise estimate of class structure.

3.1 Teacher–Student Framework

We adopt a Teacher–Student (TS) architecture consistent with prior SFDA methods. Both networks are initialized from the same source-pretrained checkpoint and share an I3D backbone pre-trained on Kinetics, ensuring comparability with CleanAdapt [6].

During adaptation, the Teacher network processes weakly augmented target samples, specifically using standard geometric transformations such as random horizontal flips, to produce predictions and per-sample cross-entropy losses. These outputs are used to identify a clean reference subset, which serves as a reliable basis for estimating class-wise structure in the target feature space. The Student network receives strongly augmented inputs, by randomly applying three transformations drawn randomly from a predefined list that includes operations like random cropping and random clip rotation, and is trained using refined pseudo-labels derived from this structure.

To stabilize training and preserve source-domain knowledge, the Teacher parameters θ_T are updated as an exponential moving average (EMA) of the Student parameters θ_S:

$$\theta_T \leftarrow \alpha\theta_T + (1 - \alpha)\theta_S, \tag{1}$$

where $\alpha \in [0, 1)$ is a momentum coefficient.

3.2 Multicentric Prototype Attribution

The core of the proposed method is a geometry-aware pseudo-labeling mechanism that replaces the discarding policy of loss-based filtering with a structured re-labeling process. Each training epoch with prototype attribution consists of four steps.
Figure 1 summarizes the pipeline; the algebraic details follow.

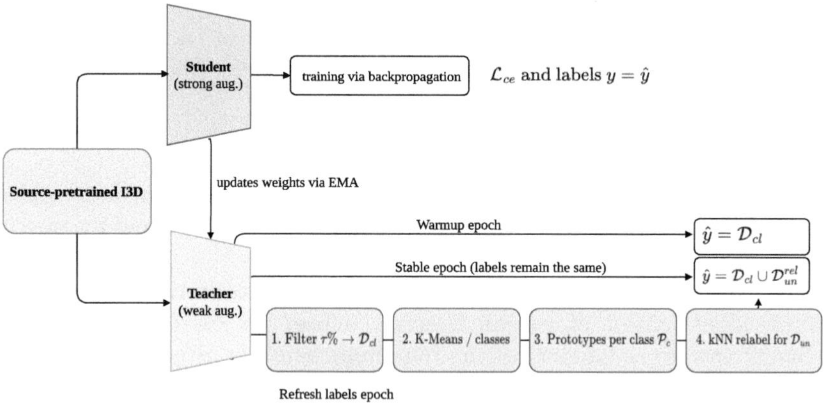

Fig. 1. Overview of multicentric prototype attribution within the Teacher–Student loop at a scheduled refinement step. Weak-augmentation Teacher losses define anchors; strong-augmentation Student training uses refined pseudo-labels on the full target set.

Step 1: Clean Reference Subset via Loss Filtering. The Teacher evaluates the target dataset under weak augmentation to compute per-sample losses ℓ_i. Samples are ranked within each predicted class, and the lowest-loss τ fraction forms the clean reference subset $\mathcal{D}_{cl}$. The remaining samples define the unclean subset $\mathcal{D}_{un} = \mathcal{D}_t \setminus \mathcal{D}_{cl}$. Unlike prior work, $\mathcal{D}_{cl}$ is not used as the final training set, instead, it serves as a low-noise reference for estimating class structure.

Step 2: Multicentric Prototype Construction. For each class c, let $\mathcal{D}_{cl}^{(c)}$ denote the samples in the clean reference subset assigned to that class. We extract feature embeddings $f_T(x_i)$ using the Teacher network, normalize them, and apply K-means clustering to obtain C centroids:

$$\mathcal{P}_c = \text{K-Means}_C\left(\left\{\frac{f_T(x_i)}{\|f_T(x_i)\|_2} \;\middle|\; x_i \in \mathcal{D}_{cl}^{(c)}\right\}\right). \tag{2}$$

Using multiple centroids per class allows the model to capture intra-class variability, which is particularly relevant in video data due to variations in viewpoint, motion dynamics, and appearance.

Step 3: Global Prototype Set. The class-wise centroids are aggregated into a global prototype set $\mathcal{P} = \bigcup_{c\in\mathcal{Y}} \mathcal{P}_c$, which serves as a geometric reference for the target domain. Feature vectors are ℓ_2-normalized prior to clustering. Then, relabeling is performed by nearest-prototype assignment using a distance metric $d(\cdot,\cdot)$. In our experiments, the Mahalanobis distance was our best-performing configuration.

Step 4: Geometry-Aware Re-labeling. Only samples in the unclean subset $\mathcal{D}_{un}$ are re-labeled via prototype attribution. For each $x_i \in \mathcal{D}_{un}$, we identify the k nearest prototypes in $\mathcal{P}$ under $d(\cdot,\cdot)$ and assign a refined pseudo-label by majority vote:

$$\hat{y}_i^* = \arg\max_{c\in\mathcal{Y}} \left|\{\mu \in \mathcal{N}_k(x_i, \mathcal{P}) \mid \text{class}(\mu) = c\}\right|. \tag{3}$$

Especially noteworthy is the fact that samples in $\mathcal{D}_{cl}$ retain their original Teacher-assigned labels, ensuring that high-confidence predictions remain unchanged while uncertain samples are corrected through geometric consensus.

Training Schedule. The four steps above define what occurs at a scheduled refresh epoch. However, not every epoch triggers prototype recalculation. During an initial warmup phase, the Student is trained exclusively on $\mathcal{D}_{cl}$, allowing the network to develop reliable feature representations before geometric structures can be accurately estimated. Once the warmup concludes, refresh epochs periodically execute the four-step pipeline to update prototypes and re-label $\mathcal{D}_{un}$. Between consecutive refresh cycles, stable epochs keep the assigned pseudo-labels $\mathcal{D}_{cl} \cup \mathcal{D}_{un}^{rel}$ fixed, providing consistent pseudo-labels without the computational overhead of continuous prototype recalculation. The warmup duration and refresh interval are treated as tunable hyperparameters. In the best configuration, adaptive clustering initiates after 10 warmup epochs and then refreshes labels every 3 epochs.

3.3 Training Objective

The Student network is trained on the full target dataset using the refined pseudo-labels. Clean samples preserve their original labels, while unclean samples adopt geometry-corrected labels. The optimization objective is the standard cross-entropy loss between Student predictions and assigned pseudo-labels.

This design decouples pseudo-label quality from the selection ratio τ: a small, clean reference subset is sufficient to estimate reliable class structure, while the remaining samples are incorporated through geometry-aware re-labeling. By leveraging multiple centroids per class, the method captures intra-class variability and improves robustness to domain shift and noisy predictions.

4 Experimental Setup

4.1 Datasets and Evaluation Protocol

We evaluate the proposed method on the UCF101 $\leftrightarrow$ HMDB51 intersection benchmark [9,16], comprising 3,209 third-person videos across 12 shared action classes. UCF101 consists of web-collected clips at 25 fps with an average duration of approximately 7 s, while HMDB51 is extracted from movies and online videos at 30 fps with clips averaging around 3 s. The two datasets differ substantially in visual style, camera motion, and background complexity, making cross-dataset transfer non-trivial. We consider both transfer directions: HMDB51$\rightarrow$UCF101 and UCF101$\rightarrow$HMDB51. The UCF101$\rightarrow$HMDB51 direction is generally considered harder, as the target set is smaller and exhibits higher intra-class variability relative to the source, resulting in higher pseudo-label noise during adaptation.

Following the standard split of [3], the benchmark contains 1,438 training and 571 test videos for UCF101, and 840 training and 360 test videos for HMDB51. Our experimental protocol matches that of CleanAdapt [6]: a source model is first trained on the labeled source split, adaptation is then performed using only the unlabeled target training set without access to source data, and performance is reported on the held-out target test set. Following prior work [3,6], 16 consecutive frames are randomly sampled from each clip during both training and inference.

4.2 Baselines

The primary baseline is CleanAdapt+TS [6], which applies small-loss filtering within a Teacher–Student framework: a fixed selection ratio τ retains the lowest-loss samples per class and discards the rest. For direct comparison in Table 2, we report our reproduction with the best student accuracy over $\tau \in \{0.5, 0.6, 0.7, 0.8\}$ (Table 3); Dasgupta *et al.* [6] report 88.6% and 96.7% on the same benchmark. We also include a linear-τ ablation (same backbone, seed, and 100-epochs), where τ increases gradually after warmup, to test whether gains stem from threshold scheduling alone.

To situate our results, Table 2 also reports results of source-dependent UDA (TA3N [3], SAVA [4], CoMix [15], CO2A [5]) and source-free methods with different backbones (ATCoN [17], MTRAN [8], SHOT via STHC [11], TAViT-SFVUDA [18]). See table footnotes and Table 1 for comparability caveats.

4.3 Experiments Addressing the Research Questions

The results reported in Sect. 5 are focused on answering the following research questions (RQ):

RQ1: Does prototype attribution reduce sensitivity to the selection ratio τ compared to CleanAdapt+TS? We evaluate the sensitivity of both methods to τ, which controls the size of the clean reference subset $\mathcal{D}_{cl}$.

For CleanAdapt+TS, we sweep $\tau \in \{0.5, 0.6, 0.7, 0.8\}$, while for the proposed method we use $\tau \in \{0.2, 0.3, 0.4, 0.5, 0.6\}$ on both directions of the UCF101 $\leftrightarrow$ HMDB51 transfer. Main results in Table 2 use joint Optuna over C, k, τ, warmup, and distance metric. The RQ1 τ sweep is a post-hoc sensitivity analysis with other hyperparameters fixed to each direction's best Optuna trial. It is important to note that τ is not directly comparable across methods: in CleanAdapt+TS it determines the fraction of the target set used for training, whereas in our method it only selects the anchor subset for prototype construction while the full target set remains in training after re-labeling.

RQ2: Do multicentric prototypes yield higher pseudo-label quality than a single centroid per class? To assess the effect of multiple centroids per class, we compare configurations with $C > 1$ against a single-centroid baseline ($C = 1$), keeping all other hyperparameters fixed. Each comparison uses paired runs derived from the same Optuna trial to control for optimization variance. In addition to classification accuracy, we analyze internal metrics, including the intra-class mean-to-mode distance ratio and pseudo-label accuracy over the full target set, to verify whether multicentric prototypes capture meaningful intra-class structure rather than introducing additional noise.

4.4 Implementation Details

All models employ an I3D backbone, with feature representations extracted from the global average pooling layer. Adaptation is performed for 100 epochs with a batch size of 48, using a fixed random seed to ensure reproducibility. We also follow the optimization and augmentation settings of CleanAdapt [6] to ensure comparability.

Hyperparameters specific to the proposed method, including the number of centroids C, the number of neighbours k, the selection ratio τ, the warm-up schedule, and the distance metric for k-nearest-prototype assignment, were selected using Optuna [1][1] (20 trials, 40 epochs per trial), maximizing student

[1] https://optuna.org.

accuracy on the benchmark evaluation split (`split_*_val.txt`, i.e., the standard held-out partition in this protocol). The best configuration (Mahalanobis distance, 10-epoch warmup, label refresh every 3 epochs thereafter) was retrained for the full 100 epochs to obtain the results in Table 2. We use a fixed random seed for reproducibility.

5 Results and Discussion

In this section we summarize the results obtained in our experiments, as well as provide some discussion related to these results.

5.1 Main Results

Table 2 reports target-domain accuracy on both transfer directions: HMDB51 → UCF101 and UCF101 → HMDB51. All methods use the RGB modality, ensuring a controlled comparison.

Table 2. Target-domain accuracy (%) on UCF101↔HMDB51. The best results per column are in bold.

Method	UCF→HMDB	HMDB→UCF
Source-only	79.44	88.27
CleanAdapt [6]	86.1	96.1
CleanAdapt+TS [6]	88.6	96.7
ATCoN** [17]	79.7	85.3
TA3N* [3]	81.4	90.5
SAVA* [4]	82.2	91.2
CoMix* [15]	86.7	93.9
CO2A* [5]	87.8	95.8
MTRAN*** [8]	92.2	95.3
SHOT† [11]	82.2	81.2
TAViT-SFVUDA‡ [18]	93.5	97.2
CA+TS linear increase τ	87.50	96.50
CA+TS with Prototype Pseudo-Labeling	**92.78**	**98.25**

* Source-dependent UDA; I3D backbone.
** Source-free; TRN backbone.
*** Source-free; video Transformer backbone.
† Source-free; TRN backbone; numbers from STHC [11].
‡ Source-free; ViT backbone; 70/20/10 split (not Chen *et al.* [3]); numbers from Yosry *et al.* [18].

Our method achieves **92.78%** on UCF→HMDB and **98.25%** on HMDB→UCF, outperforming our reproduced CleanAdapt+TS baseline (87.78%

and 96.67%, best fixed τ in Table 3) on the shared I3D RGB protocol. The largest gain is on UCF→HMDB: **+5.00 p.p.** over that reproduced baseline (τ=0.5). The linear τ schedule does not beat fixed-τ CleanAdapt+TS, so the gains are not explained by threshold scheduling alone.

Compared to source-dependent methods, our single-stream RGB model matches or surpasses reported competitors without accessing source data during adaptation. Among source-free literature entries with heterogeneous backbones (TRN, Transformer, ViT), our results are competitive on UCF→HMDB and strongest on HMDB→UCF relative to ATCoN and MTRAN, though those comparisons are indicative only (see Table 2 footnotes).

Overall, these results support the central claim that replacing rigid discarding with geometry-guided correction improves adaptation under domain shift on the evaluated I3D source-free setup. We caution that experiments rely on a single fixed seed without variance reporting, cover only the UCF101 ↔ HMDB51 intersection benchmark, and compare against literature methods with heterogeneous backbones and protocols. Gains should not be interpreted as broad statistical superiority over every cited approach.

5.2 RQ1: Does Prototype Attribution Reduce Sensitivity to the Selection Ratio τ Compared to CleanAdapt+TS?

We analyze sensitivity to the selection ratio τ under CleanAdapt+TS, which controls how many target clips pass the clean-selection filter and enter training. Table 3 reports our reproduction of the fixed-τ sweep on both transfer directions.

On UCF→HMDB, student accuracy is highest at the most conservative setting (τ=0.5, 87.78%) and lowest at τ=0.8; $|\mathcal{D}_{cl}|$ increases and pseudo-label agreement on the retained set decreases as τ grows, consistent with noisier supervision when more clips are admitted.

On HMDB→UCF, student accuracy peaks at τ=0.7 (96.67%), matching the CleanAdapt+TS entry in Table 2, while τ=0.5 is weakest in this region and τ=0.8 remains below the peak despite the largest $|\mathcal{D}_{cl}|$. This direction dependence is plausible for an easier shift, where retaining slightly more data can help when pseudo-labels are already reliable, whereas the harder direction is more sensitive to noise at high τ.

For the proposed method, τ primarily controls the conservativeness of the anchor subset while the remaining high-loss samples are still incorporated via prototype attribution. On UCF→HMDB, the best performance occurs at the most conservative value ($\tau = 0.2$), indicating that a small anchor subset suffices when combined with geometry-aware re-labeling of the unclean portion. On HMDB→UCF, the pattern reverses: accuracy increases with τ, with the best run at $\tau = 0.6$.

This direction dependence is consistent with the easier-shift hypothesis: when pseudo-labels are already reliable, a larger anchor subset provides richer structural information for prototype construction without introducing significant noise. Figure 2 shows the joint sensitivity of accuracy to τ, k, and C across the Optuna search space.

Table 3. Our reproduction of CleanAdapt+TS over $\tau \in \{0.5, 0.6, 0.7, 0.8\}$: $|\mathcal{D}_{cl}|$, pseudo-label agreement on $\mathcal{D}_{cl}$ (P), and best validation Student (S) and Teacher (T) accuracy.

τ	UCF101→HMDB51				HMDB51→UCF101			
	$\|\mathcal{D}_{cl}\|$	P	S	T	$\|\mathcal{D}_{cl}\|$	P	S	T
0.5	422	**94.79**	**87.78**	**87.22**	722	**95.43**	93.70	94.05
0.6	506	92.09	84.44	84.44	862	95.01	94.40	94.22
0.7	587	90.12	85.28	85.28	1004	95.22	**96.67**	**95.62**
0.8	670	88.51	82.78	83.06	1148	94.51	95.10	95.45

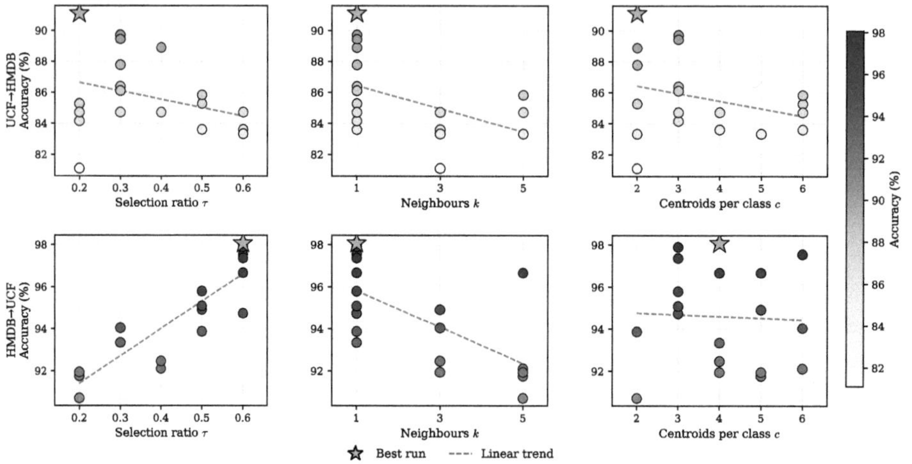

Fig. 2. Optuna search space illustrating Student accuracy as a function of the selection ratio τ, number of neighbors k, and centroids per class c across both transfer directions. Each point corresponds to a completed trial, with the best-performing configuration highlighted by ★. Dashed lines denote linear trends, while point color encodes accuracy (best viewed in color).

5.3 RQ2: Do Multicentric Prototypes Yield Higher Pseudo-label Quality Than a Single Centroid per Class?

To study the effect of multiple centroids per class, we compare multi-centroid configurations ($C > 1$) against single-centroid counterparts ($C = 1$) constructed as paired replays within the same Optuna trial when available. This pairing controls for many training and optimization choices, but it does not eliminate all confounding factors (e.g., interactions between C and other selected hyperparameters across the broader search space).

Figure 3 breaks down pseudo-label accuracy on the clean anchors $\mathcal{D}_{cl}$, the unclean subset $\mathcal{D}_{un}$ after attribution, and over the full target set, for representative paired Multi-C vs. C=1 replays.

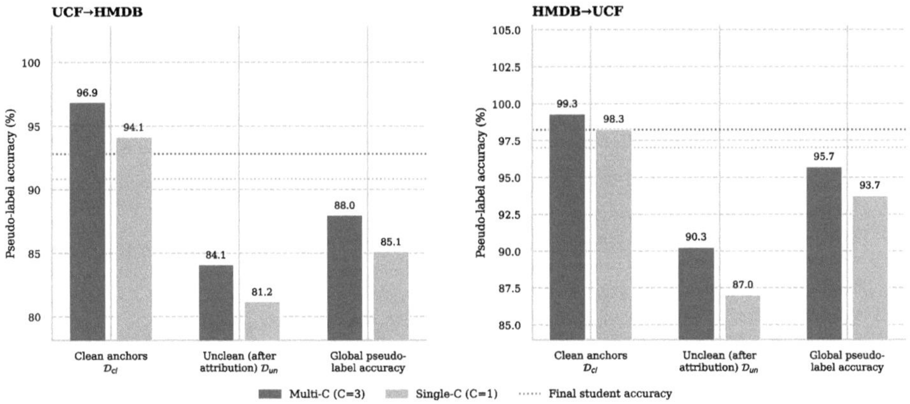

Fig. 3. Pseudo-label quality at the final attribution step (paired replay runs). Bars: clean anchors $\mathcal{D}_{cl}$, unclean subset $\mathcal{D}_{un}$ after prototype attribution, and global pseudo-label accuracy. Dotted lines: final student validation accuracy for each configuration.

Across the available paired comparisons, multi-centroid variants outperform the $C = 1$ counterparts in most cases, with improvements up to **+1.94 p.p.**, and match performance in the remaining case. In addition, logged internal metrics (e.g., pseudo-label accuracy and intra-class structure indicators) trend in favor of multi-centroid variants, suggesting that multiple prototypes better capture target feature sub-modes in video data.

6 Conclusion and Future Work

In this paper, we proposed a novel approach for Source-Free Domain Adaptation (SFDA) that integrates prototype-based attribution with a multicentric design. By utilizing prototype-based relabeling, our method overcomes the limitations of the baseline loss-based filtering, allowing for the effective correction and utilization of high-loss target samples.

The results obtained in our experiments suggest that prototype-based attribution mitigates a key limitation of loss-only filtering in SFDA: high-loss samples can still contain useful target information, but require a correction mechanism to avoid amplifying label noise. The largest gains appear on UCF→HMDB, indicating that geometry-guided supervision may be particularly beneficial under more severe shifts and higher pseudo-label uncertainty. Finally, the multicentric design provides additional improvements by modeling intra-class variability that is difficult to represent with a single prototype per class.

As future work, we plan to evaluate and extend the approach to more challenging shifts where the target data are severely unbalanced, and where imbalance can bias both loss-based selection and prototype formation.

Acknowledgements. This study was financed in part by the Coordenação de Aperfeiçoamento de Pessoal de Nível Superior–Brasil (CAPES, AUXPE-CAPES-PROEX),

Finance Code 001, and by the Conselho Nacional de Desenvolvimento Científico e Tecnológico (CNPq). This work was also partially supported by the Fundação de Amparo à Pesquisa do Estado do Amazonas (FAPEAM) through the PDPG-CAPES/POSGRAD project (2024/2025) and (2026/2027).

The authors acknowledge the usage of Generative AI tools to standardize and organize the experimental code and to set up experiment monitoring; all model-assisted outputs were reviewed by the authors.

Code Availability. Source code to reproduce our experiments is available at: https://github.com/migvanderlei/CleanAdapt/tree/bracis-2026-paper.

References

1. Akiba, T., Sano, S., Yanase, T., Ohta, T., Koyama, M.: Optuna: a next-generation hyperparameter optimization framework. In: Proceedings of the 25th ACM SIGKDD International Conference on Knowledge Discovery & Data Mining, pp. 2623–2631 (2019). https://doi.org/10.1145/3292500.3330701
2. Arpit, D., et al.: A closer look at memorization in deep networks. In: Precup, D., Teh, Y.W. (eds.) Proceedings of the 34th International Conference on Machine Learning. Proceedings of Machine Learning Research, vol. 70, pp. 233–242. PMLR (2017). https://proceedings.mlr.press/v70/arpit17a.html
3. Chen, M.H., Kira, Z., AlRegib, G., Yoo, J., Chen, R., Zheng, J.: Temporal attentive alignment for large-scale video domain adaptation. In: Proceedings of the IEEE/CVF International Conference on Computer Vision, pp. 6321–6330 (2019)
4. Choi, J., Sharma, G., Schulter, S., Huang, J.B.: Shuffle and attend: video domain adaptation. In: European Conference on Computer Vision, pp. 678–695. Springer (2020)
5. Da Costa, V.G.T., et al.: Dual-head contrastive domain adaptation for video action recognition. In: Proceedings of the IEEE/CVF Winter Conference on Applications of Computer Vision, pp. 1181–1190 (2022)
6. Dasgupta, A., Jawahar, C., Alahari, K.: Source-free video domain adaptation by learning from noisy labels. Pattern Recogn. **161**, 111328 (2025). https://doi.org/10.1016/j.patcog.2024.111328
7. Huang, M., Xie, Z., Huang, H., Zhang, C., Zhao, L., Feng, Z.: Prototype combination for multi-source unsupervised domain adaptation. IEEE Trans. Emerg. Top. Comput. Intell. **9**(6), 4175–4190 (2025). https://doi.org/10.1109/TETCI.2025.3572133
8. Huang, Y., Yang, X., Zhang, J., Xu, C.: Relative alignment network for source-free multimodal video domain adaptation. In: Proceedings of the 30th ACM International Conference on Multimedia, pp. 1652–1660 (2022)
9. Kuehne, H., Jhuang, H., Garrote, E., Poggio, T., Serre, T.: Hmdb: a large video database for human motion recognition. In: 2011 International Conference on Computer Vision, pp. 2556–2563. IEEE (2011)
10. Li, J., Yu, Z., Du, Z., Zhu, L., Shen, H.T.: A comprehensive survey on source-free domain adaptation. IEEE Trans. Pattern Anal. Mach. Intell. **46**(8), 5743–5762 (2024). https://doi.org/10.1109/TPAMI.2024.3370978
11. Li, K., Patel, D., Kruus, E., Min, M.R.: Source-free video domain adaptation with spatial-temporal-historical consistency learning. In: 2023 IEEE/CVF Conference on Computer Vision and Pattern Recognition (CVPR), pp. 14643–14652. IEEE, Vancouver, BC, Canada (2023). https://doi.org/10.1109/CVPR52729.2023.01407

12. Liang, J., Hu, D., Feng, J.: Do we really need to access the source data? Source hypothesis transfer for unsupervised domain adaptation. In: III, H.D., Singh, A. (eds.) Proceedings of the 37th International Conference on Machine Learning. Proceedings of Machine Learning Research, vol. 119, pp. 6028–6039. PMLR (2020)
13. Lin, H., et al.: Imbalance-agnostic source-free domain adaptation via avatar prototype alignment. arXiv e-prints pp. arXiv–2305 (2023)
14. Qu, S., Chen, G., Zhang, J., Li, Z., He, W., Tao, D.: BMD: a general class-balanced multicentric dynamic prototype strategy for source-free domain adaptation. In: European Conference on Computer Vision, pp. 165–182. Springer (2022)
15. Sahoo, A., Shah, R., Panda, R., Saenko, K., Das, A.: Contrast and mix: temporal contrastive video domain adaptation with background mixing. Adv. Neural. Inf. Process. Syst. **34**, 23386–23400 (2021)
16. Soomro, K., Zamir, A.R., Shah, M.: UCF101: a dataset of 101 human actions classes from videos in the wild. arXiv preprint arXiv:1212.0402 (2012)
17. Xu, Y., Yang, J., Cao, H., Wu, K., Wu, M., Chen, Z.: Source-free video domain adaptation by learning temporal consistency for action recognition. In: Avidan, S., Brostow, G., Cissé, M., Farinella, G.M., Hassner, T. (eds.) Computer Vision - ECCV 2022, pp. 147–164. Springer, Cham (2022)
18. Yosry, S., Elrefaei, L., ElKamaar, R., Ziedan, R.R.: Temporal attention-based vision transformer for source-free video unsupervised domain adaptation. Discov. Appl. Sci. **7**(7), 689 (2025). https://doi.org/10.1007/s42452-025-06909-2
19. Zhang, Z., et al.: Divide and contrast: source-free domain adaptation via adaptive contrastive learning. Adv. Neural. Inf. Process. Syst. **35**, 5137–5149 (2022)

RegMem: Graph-Based Regulatory Memory for Faithful Multi-turn RAG in Safety-Critical Domains

Alberto Lucas Borges de Almeida Teixeira(✉), João Paulo Cavalcante Presa, and Sávio Teles

Universidade Federal de Goiás, Goiânia, Brazil
alberto.lucas@discente.ufg.br

Abstract. Multi-turn retrieval-augmented generation (RAG) agents deployed in safety-critical regulatory domains face a practical challenge: as conversations grow, standard memory management strategies—truncation, sliding windows, summarization—treat conversation history as flat text and ignore the formal hierarchy of regulatory documents, either discarding prior context or compressing it into lossy summaries. We propose RegMem, a graph-based regulatory memory architecture that combines a Neo4j knowledge graph organized in three layers (domain ontology, regulatory knowledge, and conversation memory) with dual vector retrieval over both regulatory documents and conversation history. We evaluate RegMem against six baseline strategies across six LLMs from 26B to 120B parameters, including one proprietary and five open-source models, on two custom multi-turn datasets totaling 270 questions about Brazilian workplace safety regulations, where 84–85% of questions depend on prior conversational context. Under constrained context windows (4,000 tokens), RegMem ranks first in Faithfulness in 10 of 12 model-dataset combinations and ranks first on the mean of three RAGAS metrics (Faithfulness, Answer Relevancy, Answer Correctness) in 11 of 12 cells, triangulating the result. On the practical dataset, RegMem ranks first by mean across all six models. The benefit of RegMem is more pronounced for weaker models: those with lower baseline Faithfulness gain up to +0.59, while the strongest model gains +0.02. RegMem produces valid responses for at least 97.5% of turns across all model-dataset combinations, while baselines using a ReAct tool-calling loop fall to as low as 38% valid responses on Llama 3.3 70B with the practical dataset. The datasets and code are publicly available at https://github.com/teixeira-alberto/RegMem.

Keywords: Conversational memory · Retrieval-augmented generation · Knowledge graph · Regulatory compliance · Multi-turn evaluation · Multi-model benchmark

M. Recamonde-Mendoza and R. C. Barros (Eds.): BRACIS 2026, LNAI 17105, pp. 492–507, 2027.
https://doi.org/10.1007/978-3-032-39882-6_33

1 Introduction

Large language models (LLMs) augmented with retrieval-augmented generation (RAG) [12] are increasingly deployed as domain-specific question-answering assistants [5]. In regulatory domains such as workplace safety, these systems serve as consultants that professionals rely on when interpreting complex normative texts. Brazilian Regulatory Standards (*Normas Regulamentadoras*, NRs), issued by the Ministry of Labor, define obligations, equipment requirements, training protocols, and penalties for workplace safety across dozens of economic sectors. A chatbot that provides incorrect guidance about fall protection requirements or electrical safety procedures can lead to operational decisions that result in serious or fatal accidents. The stakes in this domain are qualitatively different from those in general-purpose conversational AI.

When these RAG agents engage in multi-turn conversations, the conversation history grows and must be managed. The predominant approaches—truncation, sliding windows, summarization [5]—control cost and latency but treat conversation history as generic text. In regulatory domains this is problematic: summarizing "the user asked about NR-35 requirements" discards specific item numbers (35.3.2), concrete obligations, cross-references to NR-06 for personal protective equipment, and penalty thresholds. The formal structure of regulatory knowledge is destroyed by the mechanism intended to preserve it. Prior work has shown that LLMs degrade when relevant information sits in the middle of long contexts [14], but the interaction between memory strategies and regulatory structure remains unexplored.

We propose RegMem, a graph-based regulatory memory architecture that replaces the compress-or-discard paradigm with structured knowledge navigation. RegMem maintains a Neo4j knowledge graph organized in three layers: a domain ontology defining the regulatory schema, pre-loaded regulatory knowledge instances (norms, items, obligations, equipment, penalties), and dynamically accumulated conversation memory stored as graph nodes linked to the regulatory entities discussed. A dual vector store (pgvector) provides semantic search over both regulatory documents and conversation history. At each turn, the agent retrieves context through parallel queries and synthesizes a response from a small, focused context window. This approach draws on the insight from recursive language models [25] that LLMs perform better when they navigate context programmatically rather than processing it as a monolithic block.

This paper makes three contributions:

1. **RegMem architecture**: a graph-based regulatory memory system combining an ontological knowledge graph with dual vector retrieval, enabling on-demand context navigation instead of lossy compression.
2. **Two multi-turn datasets**: an organic dataset of 150 questions (10 threads $\times$ 15 turns, 84% memory-dependent) and a practical dataset of 120 questions (15 threads $\times$ 8 turns, 85% memory-dependent) about Brazilian workplace safety regulations, with six annotated memory dependency types and a higher proportion of multi-hop queries in the practical set (33% vs. 18%).

3. **Multi-model empirical benchmark**: evaluation of seven memory strategies across six LLMs (26B–120B parameters, proprietary and open-source) measuring cost and quality, demonstrating that RegMem ranks first in 11 of 12 model-dataset combinations on the mean of three RAGAS metrics and that weaker models benefit disproportionately from structured memory.

RegMem is a co-designed memory and retrieval architecture, not a drop-in replacement for truncation or summarization. The conversational memory layer is defined relative to the regulatory ontology, and the dual vector retrieval depends on the graph schema for typed traversal.

The remainder of this paper is organized as follows. Section 2 reviews related work on RAG, memory management, graph-based memory, and evaluation. Section 3 describes the system architecture, all seven strategies, the models, the datasets, and the evaluation protocol. Section 4 presents quality and cost results across all models. Section 5 discusses the findings and their limitations. Section 6 concludes with future directions.

2 Related Work

2.1 Retrieval-Augmented Generation

Lewis et al. [12] introduced RAG as a method to ground LLM responses in retrieved documents, and subsequent work has evolved the paradigm into modular architectures with query rewriting, re-ranking, and iterative retrieval [5]. However, most RAG research focuses on single-turn interactions; multi-turn conversations introduce a growing message history that interacts with retrieval in ways that single-turn benchmarks do not capture.

2.2 Memory in LLM Agents

Zhang et al. [26] provide a taxonomy of memory mechanisms in LLM-based agents, categorizing memory into factual, experiential, and working types. Several systems operationalize these taxonomies: MemGPT [19] implements virtual paging between working and archival memory; Mem0 [2] extracts and retrieves memory facts, reporting 26% improvement on LoCoMo [16]; Zep [21] builds temporal knowledge graphs from conversations. These systems are domain-agnostic: they treat all conversational content uniformly without exploiting domain-specific formal structure. In practice, production deployments often use simpler strategies—token trimming, sliding windows, summarization—without formal evaluation. No prior work systematically evaluates these strategies against graph-based alternatives in a controlled multi-model setting.

2.3 Graph-Based Memory

A growing body of work uses knowledge graphs as memory substrates for LLM agents. HippoRAG [6] uses hippocampal indexing for multi-hop QA and

SGMem [23] constructs sentence-level graphs without LLM extraction; a recent survey [24] notes that graph-based memory enables temporal awareness and structured retrieval beyond flat vector stores. Hybrid retrieval outside conversational memory includes DO-RAG [15], which combines graph traversal with vector search for single-turn domain QA, and RAGulating Compliance [20], which targets regulatory QA via ontology-free SPO triplets. RegMem differs in that the graph schema is a typed ontology aligned with the regulation's formal hierarchy, enabling typed traversal rather than free-form triplet matching, and the conversation-memory layer is integrated into the same schema so prior turns link to the regulatory entities they discussed.

2.4 Multi-turn RAG Evaluation and Cost

RAGAS [4] has become the standard framework for automated RAG evaluation, providing metrics for Answer Correctness, Answer Relevancy, and Faithfulness. Multi-turn benchmarks have emerged to address the gap in conversational RAG evaluation. MTRAG [8] provides 110 conversations across four domains and reports that performance degrades in later turns. LexRAG [13] is the first multi-turn RAG benchmark for legal consultation, with over 1,000 dialogues in Chinese legal articles. Closer to our domain, BR-TaxQA-R [3] introduces a Brazilian tax-law dataset of 715 single-turn questions paired with statutory references, contrasting with our multi-turn setting and our focus on workplace-safety regulations.

On the cost side, FrugalGPT [1] demonstrates that routing queries between models of different capabilities can reduce cost with minimal quality loss. Context compression approaches such as LLMLingua [7] reduce token counts through prompt compression, but this is orthogonal to conversation memory management: compression acts on the prompt text, while memory strategies determine which messages to keep or discard.

2.5 Our Contribution in Context

No existing work combines (a) graph-based ontological memory that exploits the formal structure of a regulatory domain with (b) systematic evaluation of memory strategies measuring both cost and quality in (c) multi-turn RAG conversations in safety-critical domains, (d) validated across multiple LLMs of varying capability to establish whether findings generalize beyond a single model. Compliance-oriented systems [22] use event graphs for regulatory checking but not for conversational memory. Domain-specialized Brazilian-Portuguese legal LLMs such as Juru [17] pursue specialization through pretraining on legal corpora, whereas RegMem pursues specialization through structured memory at inference time, leaving the base model unchanged. Our work addresses this intersection.

3 Methodology

3.1 RegMem Architecture

The system under evaluation is a multi-turn RAG chatbot for Brazilian workplace safety regulations (Normas Regulamentadoras, NRs). The shared infrastructure across all experiments comprises a LangGraph [11] state graph orchestrating the agent loop, and a pgvector [9] document store containing 5,014 text chunks from 10 NRs indexed with embeddings. A centralized factory module routes requests to the appropriate LLM provider (Google API for the proprietary model and OpenRouter for the open-source models) ensuring that all models receive identical prompts, tool definitions, and retrieval results.

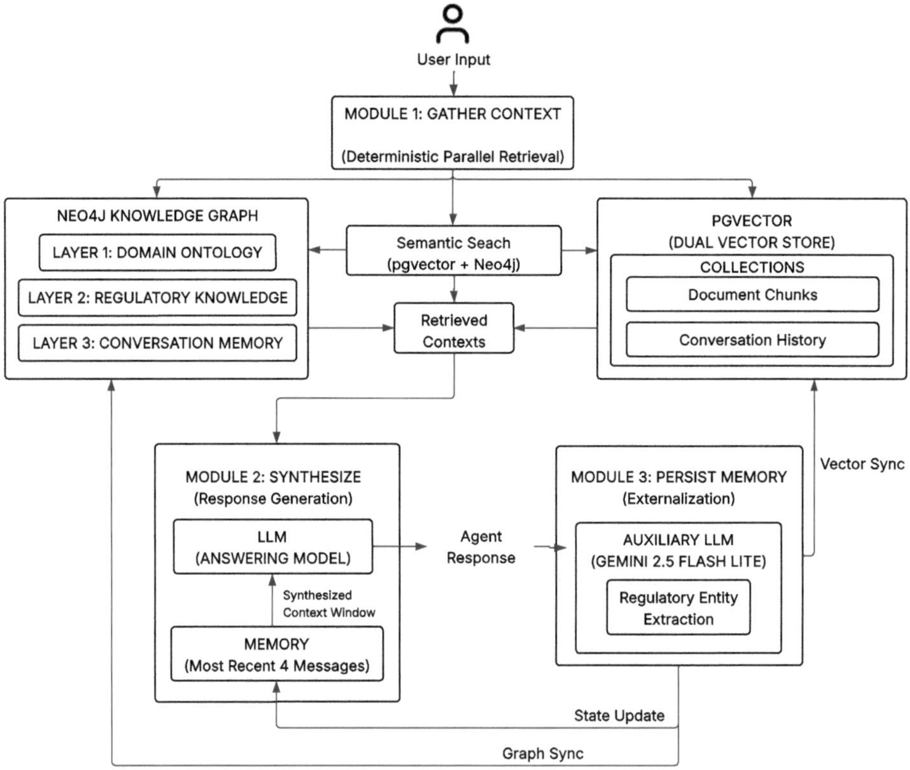

Fig. 1. RegMem architecture. Module 1 performs parallel retrieval over the dual pgvector store and the three-layer Neo4j graph. Module 2 synthesizes a response from retrieved contexts and the four most recent messages. Module 3 extracts regulatory entities (via Gemini 2.5 Flash Lite) and syncs the graph and vector stores.

In our evaluation, standard memory strategies (the baselines, detailed in Sect. 3.2) operate within a traditional ReAct loop [10]: the agent can invoke a RAG search tool, receive retrieved passages, and decide whether to call the tool again or produce a final answer. We constrain context windows (`MAX_TOKENS`=4,000, `MAX_MESSAGES`=10) to simulate deployment on smaller models where memory management has practical impact, forcing these standard strategies to compress or discard history.

To address the compress-or-discard paradigm, we propose RegMem, a navigate-on-demand architecture (Fig. 1). Instead of managing a shrinking window over a growing message history, RegMem maintains a persistent structured memory external to the LLM context and retrieves relevant portions at each turn, replacing the iterative ReAct loop with a deterministic three-module pipeline. This design choice externalizes memory from the LLM's context window so that conversation history scales independently of the model's context limits, and decouples retrieval from generation so that weaker models—which struggle with multi-step ReAct tool calls—receive pre-structured context they can synthesize directly. The three modules execute sequentially per turn, with the persist module updating both stores asynchronously to support subsequent retrievals.

Module 1: Gather Context. Three retrieval operations execute in parallel without LLM involvement: (a) vector search over NR document chunks in pgvector (top-10 results), (b) Cypher queries on the Neo4j knowledge graph for the formal structure of referenced NRs (items, obligations, equipment, penalties, cross-references), and (c) semantic search over conversation history stored both as graph nodes in Neo4j and as embeddings in a second pgvector collection. NR references are extracted from the user question via regex pattern matching. When no NR is matched, the search falls back to keyword and recency recall.

Module 2: Synthesize. A single LLM call receives a fixed system prompt, the retrieved contexts from all three sources, and the 4 most recent messages. The LLM synthesizes a response from this bounded context without requiring tool-calling capabilities.

Module 3: Persist Memory. After response generation, an auxiliary LLM call (Gemini 2.5 Flash Lite, fixed across all experiments) extracts regulatory entities from the turn. The turn is persisted as a `:Turno` node in Neo4j, linked to the `:Thread` and corresponding `:NR` or `:Item` nodes. The turn text is also embedded in the pgvector memory collection. Finally, all messages except the most recent 4 are deleted from the active state.

Knowledge Graph Structure. RegMem's Neo4j instance contains three layers. The *ontology layer* defines 9 node classes and 14 relationship types, hand-designed a priori to mirror the regulatory hierarchy rather than induced from the corpus. The *knowledge layer* contains instances extracted from NR text and pre-loaded into this schema: 16 NRs, 240 items, 93 equipment nodes, 92 obligation nodes, and 425 edges. The *memory layer* accumulates dynamically during conversations.

3.2 Memory Management Strategies (S1–S6)

To evaluate RegMem (designated as S7 in our results), we compare it against six standard memory management strategies running on the ReAct loop described above. We select these text-based strategies because they represent the current standard for production RAG deployments. While domain-agnostic graph memory systems exist (e.g., HippoRAG, Zep), they extract general semantic triplets and do not natively support the injection of a strict, pre-defined regulatory ontology. Adapting them to enforce the specific Norm-Item-Obligation hierarchy would alter their core architecture, rendering them functionally similar to our proposed method.

S1 – Token Trimming. Retains messages from the most recent turns until the total token count reaches 4,000 tokens, then discards the oldest messages. This is the default approach in many LangChain applications.

S2 – Sliding Window. Retains only the 10 most recent messages regardless of token count. This provides a predictable memory footprint but discards all context beyond the window boundary.

S3 – Tool-Pair Removal. Removes historical tool-call and tool-response message pairs, preserving only human and assistant messages. While it reduces token consumption, it eliminates the retrieved passages that metrics use to assess Faithfulness.

S4 – Summarization. When the message count exceeds 8, the strategy invokes the LLM to summarize the conversation before the agent step runs, retaining the summary and the 4 most recent messages.

S5 – Hybrid. Combines token trimming with conditional summarization that runs *after* the agent step. The agent generates its response with the full recent history, then the system summarizes and trims for the next turn.

S6 – Removal + Summarization. Combines tool-pair removal with summarization before the agent step. First removes tool-call/response pairs, then summarizes if the remaining message count exceeds the threshold.

3.3 Models

We evaluate all seven strategies across six LLMs (Table 1), selected from the Chatbot Arena leaderboard to cover diverse families and architectural variants (dense and mixture-of-experts) across 26B–120B parameters. The selection includes one proprietary model and five open-source models from four families (Llama, GPT-OSS, Qwen, Gemma). The open-source models are accessed through OpenRouter, which routes to the lowest-latency available provider, and all models receive the same context windows, prompts, and tool definitions.

Entity extraction in RegMem's persist-memory module uses *Gemini 2.5 Flash Lite* regardless of the answering model, keeping extraction quality

Table 1. Models evaluated.

Model	Parameters	Architecture	Provider
Gemini 2.5 Flash Lite	proprietary	—	Google API
Llama 3.3 70B	70B	dense	OpenRouter
GPT-OSS 120B	120B	MoE	OpenRouter
Qwen 3.5 35B	35B	MoE	OpenRouter
Gemma 4 26B	26B	MoE	OpenRouter
Gemma 4 31B	31B	dense	OpenRouter

constant across experiments. The RAGAS evaluator uses Gemini 3 Flash Preview, which ranks above all six answering models on Chatbot Arena, so the judge is more capable than any model being evaluated and no answering model evaluates its own outputs.

3.4 Datasets

We construct two semi-synthetic multi-turn datasets with complementary challenge profiles. Following common practice in benchmark construction, conversational scenarios and turn dependencies are manually designed by the authors, questions and ground-truth answers are LLM-generated from grounded regulatory text, and the resulting pairs are subsequently curated to ensure correctness and adherence to the intended memory dependency types. The *organic* dataset contains 150 questions organized in 10 conversation threads of 15 turns each. Each thread simulates a realistic consultation scenario in workplace safety: accident investigation, equipment inspection, emergency procedures, and compliance auditing. The *practical* dataset contains 120 questions in 15 threads of 8 turns each, with shorter but more complex exchanges featuring a higher proportion of multi-hop and cross-NR queries.

Both datasets cover 10 NRs spanning work at heights (NR-35), electrical safety (NR-10), confined spaces (NR-33), boiler inspection (NR-13), and related topics. The construction followed three steps: (1) workplace safety scenarios and turn sequences were manually defined, specifying NR references, memory dependency types, and turn dependencies; (2) relevant text chunks were retrieved from the pgvector collection and Gemini 2.5 Flash Lite generated natural questions and ground-truth answers grounded in actual NR text, conditioned on the manually defined scenarios; (3) the resulting question-answer pairs were curated by the authors, who verified that ground-truth answers cite specific regulatory items and that each question matches its annotated memory dependency type.

Each question is annotated with one of six memory dependency types. Table 2 shows the distribution for both datasets.

The organic dataset, with its 15-turn threads and higher proportion of callbacks (23%), primarily tests long-conversation memory retention—whether the system can recall details discussed many turns earlier. The practical dataset,

Table 2. Dataset statistics and memory dependency type distribution.

Memory dependency type	Organic		Practical	
	n	%	n	%
Multi-hop (crosses 2+ NRs)	27	18	40	33
Callback (returns to earlier topic)	34	23	15	12
Direct reference (to prior turn)	33	22	18	15
Indirect reference (contextual)	22	15	15	12
Standalone (independent)	24	16	18	15
Cross-NR comparison	10	7	14	12
Total	**150**		**120**	
Memory-dependent	126	84	102	85

with 33% multi-hop queries and 12% cross-NR comparisons (vs. 18% and 7% in the organic set), tests the system's ability to synthesize information across multiple regulatory norms in shorter but more demanding exchanges.

3.5 Evaluation Metrics and Experimental Protocol

We evaluate response quality using three RAGAS metrics [4]: i) *Answer Correctness* (semantic and factual similarity between the generated answer and the ground truth), ii) *Answer Relevancy* (whether the response addresses the question), and iii) *Faithfulness* (the proportion of claims in the response supported by the retrieved contexts). Faithfulness is the most critical metric in our domain because it measures whether the agent fabricates regulatory information or grounds its assertions in the source norms.

We also report the *valid response rate*: the number of turns that produced a non-empty, non-timeout response out of the total. Baseline strategies using the ReAct loop can produce invalid responses when the LLM enters a tool-calling cycle that exceeds the 180-second timeout, or when the model generates malformed tool calls. This metric captures pipeline reliability independent of response quality.

Token counts are measured via the usage metadata returned by each provider's API. Each strategy runs all threads sequentially with independent memory per thread (via LangGraph `MemorySaver` checkpoints). RAGAS evaluation is performed post-hoc using Gemini 3 Flash Preview as the evaluator model at temperature 0.

4 Results

This section presents the experimental results evaluating the seven memory strategies across the six LLMs on the organic and practical datasets. The results indicate that RegMem improves factual grounding and system stability, with the most pronounced benefits observed in models that struggle to manage standard ReAct loops.

4.1 Faithfulness Across Models

Tables 3 and 4 present Faithfulness scores for all seven strategies across six models on the organic and practical datasets, respectively. Faithfulness is the primary metric for our domain: it measures whether the agent's regulatory claims are traceable to retrieved source documents.

Table 3. Faithfulness per strategy and model—organic dataset (150 questions). Best overall per model in **bold**; best baseline underlined.

Strategy	Gemini 2.5 Flash	Llama 3.3 70B	GPT-OSS 120B	Qwen 3.5 35B	Gemma 4 26B	Gemma 4 31B
S1 Token Trim	0.28	0.81	<u>0.60</u>	0.74	0.45	0.45
S2 Sliding Win.	0.23	0.79	0.55	0.71	0.13	0.36
S3 Tool Removal	0.31	0.43	0.32	0.53	0.15	0.21
S4 Summarization	0.27	0.58	0.46	0.69	0.37	0.42
S5 Hybrid	0.33	<u>0.82</u>	0.49	<u>0.75</u>	<u>0.47</u>	<u>0.50</u>
S6 Rem.+Summ.	<u>0.56</u>	0.81	0.41	0.69	0.23	0.43
S7 RegMem	**0.91**	**0.72**	**0.69**	**0.82**	**0.89**	**0.88**

Table 4. Faithfulness per strategy and model—practical dataset (120 questions). Best overall per model in **bold**; best baseline underlined.

Strategy	Gemini 2.5 Flash	Llama 3.3 70B	GPT-OSS 120B	Qwen 3.5 35B	Gemma 4 26B	Gemma 4 31B
S1 Token Trim	0.28	<u>0.79</u>	0.54	0.67	<u>0.59</u>	<u>0.39</u>
S2 Sliding Win.	<u>0.33</u>	0.75	0.53	0.66	0.23	0.25
S3 Tool Removal	0.15	0.51	0.37	0.62	0.23	0.26
S4 Summarization	0.14	0.58	0.47	<u>0.70</u>	0.38	0.26
S5 Hybrid	0.29	0.52	0.51	0.65	0.48	0.35
S6 Rem.+Summ.	0.17	0.65	0.45	0.67	0.34	0.29
S7 RegMem	**0.81**	**0.77**	**0.69**	**0.81**	**0.90**	**0.88**

On the organic dataset, RegMem achieves the highest Faithfulness in five of six models, with the sole exception of Llama 3.3 70B (0.72 vs. 0.81–0.82 for the top baselines, discussed in Sect. 5). RegMem's Faithfulness varies far less across models (0.69–0.91 organic, 0.69–0.90 practical) than baselines (0.13–0.82 organic) because the deterministic gather module delivers identical pre-structured context regardless of model capability, while baselines depend on each model's ReAct competence to retrieve and integrate context.

On the practical dataset, RegMem ranks first in Faithfulness for five of six models. The higher proportion of multi-hop (33%) and cross-NR (12%) queries exposes baseline memory limitations more acutely, since shorter threads require more cross-NR reasoning per turn and the ReAct loop has fewer chances to recover lost context. The exception is again Llama 3.3 70B (RegMem 0.77 vs. 0.79 for the best baseline), though RegMem still leads it on the mean of the three metrics.

4.2 Inverse Correlation Between Model Capability and RegMem Benefit

Table 5 presents a cross-model summary of RegMem's ranking, Faithfulness, the gap to the best non-RegMem baseline per cell, the average over all six baselines, and the mean of three RAGAS metrics. An inverse correlation emerges: models with lower baseline Faithfulness benefit more from RegMem. We report the gain against the *best* baseline rather than against the average, which would otherwise be inflated by S3 (tool-pair removal); the average column is included for completeness.

Gemma 4 26B MoE, with the lowest organic baseline Faithfulness (0.30), gains +0.59 over the average baseline and +0.42 over the best non-RegMem baseline; Gemini 2.5 Flash Lite gains +0.58 and +0.35 respectively. On the practical dataset, Gemma 4 26B gains +0.52 and +0.31, while Llama 70B's best baseline reaches only 0.79 against RegMem's 0.77. Per-metric counts: RegMem leads Faithfulness in 10 of 12 cells, Answer Correctness in 8 of 12, and Answer Relevancy in 7 of 12. Correctness and Relevancy gains are smaller because both depend on retrieval recall and ground-truth phrasing rather than memory structure. On the mean of the three metrics, RegMem ranks first in 11 of 12 cells.

4.3 Response Validity and Pipeline Stability

RegMem's deterministic gather-synthesize-persist pipeline produces valid responses for 149–150 of 150 turns on the organic dataset and 117–120 of 120 on the practical dataset across all models, with the 1–3 missing responses tracing to API errors rather than architectural failures. Baselines using the ReAct loop exhibit lower and more variable validity on the practical dataset, where multi-hop queries trigger longer tool-calling chains. The collapse is concentrated on Llama 3.3 70B: with the practical dataset, baseline valid-response rates fall to 38–66% (S5 at 46/120, S2 at 47/120, S1 at 70/120), whereas every other model remains at or above 82% valid (e.g., Gemma 4 31B baselines at 82–92%). These failures are timeouts at 180 s or empty outputs from malformed tool calls. A system valid for 38% of turns is not deployable regardless of response quality,

Table 5. Cross-model summary. Best Baseline Faith. is the maximum Faithfulness across S1–S6 per cell; Avg Baseline Faith. averages all six baselines and is depressed by S3 (tool-pair removal), which structurally removes retrieved tool contexts and is therefore a weak Faithfulness baseline. Gain = RegMem Faith. − Best Baseline Faith. Mean (3 RAGAS) is the mean of Faithfulness, Answer Correctness, and Answer Relevancy. Models ordered by organic baseline Faithfulness (ascending).

Model	Dataset	Rank	RegMem Faith.	Best Base.	Avg Base.	Gain	Mean3 RM	Mean3 Base.	Valid n
Gemma 4 26B	Organic	1	0.89	0.47	0.30	+0.42	0.74	0.53	150
	Practical	1	0.90	0.59	0.38	+0.31	0.74	0.57	120
Gemini 2.5 Flash	Organic	1	0.91	0.56	0.33	+0.35	0.75	0.49	150
	Practical	1	0.81	0.33	0.23	+0.48	0.72	0.39	120
Gemma 4 31B	Organic	1	0.88	0.50	0.39	+0.38	0.71	0.47	149
	Practical	1	0.88	0.39	0.30	+0.49	0.74	0.35	117
GPT-OSS 120B	Organic	1	0.69	0.60	0.47	+0.09	0.66	0.55	150
	Practical	1	0.69	0.54	0.48	+0.15	0.67	0.56	120
Qwen 3.5 35B	Organic	1	0.82	0.75	0.68	+0.07	0.69	0.65	149
	Practical	1	0.81	0.70	0.66	+0.11	0.70	0.65	120
Llama 3.3 70B	Organic	5	0.72	0.82	0.70	−0.10	0.69	0.66	150
	Practical	1	0.77	0.79	0.63	−0.02	0.72	0.65	120

and RegMem's linear pipeline removes the iterative mechanism that causes these failures while still achieving higher Faithfulness.

4.4 Cost, Latency, and Operational Profile

Total token consumption ranges from 6.9M (Gemini 2.5 Flash Lite) to 17.9M (Qwen 3.5 35B MoE), with RegMem at roughly 2× baseline cost and summarization as the most expensive strategy. We did not log per-turn wall-clock latency, but the 180-second timeouts that invalidate up to 62% of Llama 3.3 70B baseline turns bound baseline p95 far above RegMem's single-pass cost.

5 Discussion

Architectural Advantage over Context Compression. RegMem separates the memory substrate from the LLM context window. In baseline strategies, conversation history competes for space with the question, system prompt, and retrieved documents, forcing the system to discard or compress data as the conversation grows; RegMem instead stores memory externally and retrieves only relevant portions per turn. Because the graph mirrors the regulatory hierarchy (norm → item → obligation → equipment → penalty), traversal is typed and precise, and this consistent behavior across six models confirms an architectural rather than model-specific advantage.

Bypassing the ReAct Loop Bottleneck. The ReAct loop requires the model to plan multi-step tool use, generate syntactically correct function calls, and interpret intermediate results. Strong models (Llama 3.3 70B, Qwen 3.5 35B) handle this loop and achieve Faithfulness above 0.70 even with truncated contexts. Conversely, weaker models (Gemma 4 26B, Gemma 4 31B) produce malformed tool calls or ignore retrieved passages, resulting in Faithfulness below 0.50. RegMem bypasses this loop entirely: three deterministic retrieval operations provide pre-structured context, and the LLM only synthesizes the response.

The Llama 70B Exception. Llama 3.3 70B is the only model where RegMem does not rank first on the organic dataset (fifth, 0.72 vs. 0.81–0.82). On the practical dataset, however, its baselines drop to 38–66% valid responses while RegMem ranks first with 100% validity, as the higher multi-hop proportion (33% vs. 18%) and shorter threads expose the limits of compensating for lossy memory through tool use alone.

Faithfulness in Safety-Critical Domains. A Faithfulness of 0.30 (Gemma 4 26B baseline average) indicates that roughly 70% of assertions cannot be traced to source norms; RegMem raises this to 0.89 for the same model. Faithfulness captures groundedness in the retrieved context, not legal completeness: a fully faithful answer can still be incomplete or, in a compliance setting, misleading. High Faithfulness therefore does not guarantee correct guidance, but it provides a foundation for human verification and audit. This traceability is a necessary condition for deployment in domains where non-compliance can result in physical injury or death.

Generalizability. RegMem transfers to domains with formal hierarchical knowledge (legal codes, ISO standards, medical protocols); domains lacking a clean hierarchy would require a domain-appropriate schema, while the dual-vector retrieval and persist-memory components transfer without modification.

Limitations. The current design bundles two effects: graph-aligned memory persistence and structured-knowledge retrieval. The individual contribution of each layer is not isolated in this study. A further confound is architectural asymmetry: RegMem runs a deterministic pipeline while the baselines run a ReAct loop, so part of its measured advantage—especially in valid-response rate—reflects this design difference rather than memory structure alone. RegMem also depends on a fixed auxiliary model (Gemini 2.5 Flash Lite) for per-turn entity extraction, so some of the structuring that aids weaker answering models is delegated to this component, and isolating its effect is left to future work. Another limitation is the reliance on synthetic datasets and automated evaluation via RAGAS (LLM-as-a-judge). Although the datasets are grounded in real regulatory text and the evaluator model (Gemini 3 Flash Preview) minimizes self-evaluation bias, the framework lacks validation by certified human experts. Furthermore, the experimental protocol does not include repeated runs or statistical significance testing. While the consistent rank pattern provides initial evidence of stability, the lack of confidence intervals restricts the statistical robustness of the empirical claims. Finally, securing the retrieval layer (e.g., via role-based access control [18]) is not addressed here, though it remains a strict requirement for production deployment.

6 Conclusion

We proposed RegMem, a graph-based regulatory memory architecture for multi-turn RAG in safety-critical domains. Across seven memory strategies, six LLMs, and 270 questions on Brazilian workplace safety regulations, RegMem ranked first in 11 of 12 model-dataset combinations on the mean of three RAGAS metrics, and in 10 of 12 on Faithfulness alone. On the practical dataset, it ranked first by mean across all six models. We observed an inverse correlation between model capability and RegMem benefit: models with the lowest baseline Faithfulness gained up to +0.59 over the average baseline, while the strongest baseline model showed marginal gains. Furthermore, RegMem produced valid responses for at least 97.5% of turns, addressing the instability of baseline strategies that fell to 38% valid responses on Llama 3.3 70B with the practical dataset.

Future work will explore human evaluation by certified safety professionals, deployment in real conversations, ablation studies isolating each architectural layer, and bootstrapped confidence intervals over longer benchmarks (30+ turns).

The datasets and source code are publicly available at https://github.com/teixeira-alberto/RegMem.

Acknowledgments. This work was supported by the ANEEL Research and Development (R&D) Program under Project PD-02949-0124/2024 ("SafeAI: Plataforma Inteligente de Comunicação, Monitoramento e Gestão de Segurança"), funded by Foz do Chapecó Energia and developed in partnership with the UFG, CEIA, 4VANTS and Solumar. This work was also supported by the National Institute of Science and Technology (INCT) in Responsible Artificial Intelligence for Computational Linguistics and Information Treatment and Dissemination (TILD-IAR) grant number 408490/2024-1.

Disclosure of Interests. The authors have no competing interests to declare that are relevant to the content of this article.

References

1. Chen, L., Zaharia, M., Zou, J.: FrugalGPT: how to use large language models while reducing cost and improving performance. Trans. Mach. Learn. Res. (TMLR) (2024)
2. Chhikara, P., Khant, D., Aryan, S., Singh, T., Yadav, D.: Mem0: building production-ready AI agents with scalable long-term memory. arXiv preprint arXiv:2504.19413 (2025)

3. Domingos Júnior, J., et al.: BR-TaxQA-R: a dataset for question answering with references for Brazilian personal income tax law, including case law. In: Intelligent Systems — 35th Brazilian Conference on Intelligent Systems (BRACIS 2025). Lecture Notes in Computer Science. Springer (2025)
4. Es, S., James, J., Espinosa-Anke, L., Schockaert, S.: RAGAS: automated evaluation of retrieval augmented generation. arXiv preprint arXiv:2309.15217 (2024)
5. Gao, Y., et al.: Retrieval-augmented generation for large language models: a survey. arXiv preprint arXiv:2312.10997 (2024)
6. Gutiérrez, B.J., Shu, Y., Gu, Y., Yasunaga, M., Su, Y.: HippoRAG: neurobiologically inspired long-term memory for large language models. In: Advances in Neural Information Processing Systems, vol. 37 (2024)
7. Jiang, H., Wu, Q., Lin, C.Y., Yang, Y., Qiu, L.: LLMLingua: compressing prompts for accelerated inference of large language models. In: Proceedings of the 2023 Conference on Empirical Methods in Natural Language Processing (EMNLP), pp. 13358–13376 (2023)
8. Katsis, Y., et al.: MTRAG: a multi-turn conversational benchmark for evaluating retrieval-augmented generation systems. arXiv preprint arXiv:2501.03468 (2025)
9. Kane, A.: pgvector: open-source vector similarity search for PostgreSQL (2024). https://github.com/pgvector/pgvector. Accessed 07 Apr 2026
10. LangChain: LangChain: Building applications with LLMs through composability (2024). https://github.com/langchain-ai/langchain. Accessed 07 Apr 2026
11. LangChain: LangGraph: Build resilient language agents as graphs (2024). https://github.com/langchain-ai/langgraph. Accessed 07 Apr 2026
12. Lewis, P., et al.: Retrieval-augmented generation for knowledge-intensive NLP tasks. In: Advances in Neural Information Processing Systems, vol. 33, pp. 9459–9474 (2020)
13. Li, H., et al.: LexRAG: benchmarking retrieval-augmented generation in multi-turn legal consultation dialogue. In: Proceedings of the 48th International ACM SIGIR Conference on Research and Development in Information Retrieval (SIGIR) (2025)
14. Liu, N.F., et al.: Lost in the middle: how language models use long contexts. Trans. Assoc. Comput. Linguist. **12**, 157–173 (2024)
15. Liu, Y., Sun, Y., Yang, B., Hu, S.: DO-RAG: a domain-specific QA framework using knowledge graph-enhanced retrieval-augmented generation. arXiv preprint arXiv:2505.17058 (2025)
16. Maharana, A., Lee, D.H., Tulyakov, S., Bansal, M., Barbieri, F., Fang, Y.: Evaluating very long-term conversational memory of LLM agents. In: Proceedings of the 62nd Annual Meeting of the Association for Computational Linguistics (ACL) (2024)
17. Malaquias Junior, R., Pires, R., Romero, R.A.F., Nogueira, R.: Juru: legal Brazilian large language model from reputable sources. In: Intelligent Systems — 35th Brazilian Conference on Intelligent Systems (BRACIS 2025). Lecture Notes in Computer Science. Springer (2025)
18. Martinelli, I., Ponti, M.A.: Towards secure retrieval-augmented generation: preventing LLM data leaks with RBAC. In: Intelligent Systems — 35th Brazilian Conference on Intelligent Systems (BRACIS 2025). Lecture Notes in Computer Science. Springer (2025). https://doi.org/10.1007/978-3-032-15993-9_34
19. Packer, C., et al.: MemGPT: towards LLMs as operating systems. arXiv preprint arXiv:2310.08560 (2023)
20. Patil, J., Yetukuri, J., Saha, S., Liu, W., Wang, L., Zhao, T.: RAGulating compliance: a multi-agent knowledge graph for regulatory QA. arXiv preprint arXiv:2509.20512 (2025)

21. Rasmussen, P., Paliychuk, P., Beauvais, T., Ryan, J., Chalef, D.: Zep: a temporal knowledge graph architecture for agent memory. arXiv preprint arXiv:2501.13956 (2025)
22. Sun, J., Luo, Z., Li, Y.: A compliance checking framework based on retrieval augmented generation. In: Proceedings of the 31st International Conference on Computational Linguistics (COLING), pp. 2603–2615 (2025)
23. Wu, Y., Zhang, Y., Liang, S., Liu, Y.: SGMem: sentence graph memory for long-term conversational agents. arXiv preprint arXiv:2509.21212 (2025)
24. Yang, C., et al.: Graph-based agent memory: taxonomy, techniques, and applications. arXiv preprint arXiv:2602.05665 (2026)
25. Zhang, A.L., Kraska, T., Khattab, O.: Recursive language models. arXiv preprint arXiv:2512.24601 (2025)
26. Zhang, Z., et al.: A survey on the memory mechanism of large language model based agents. ACM Trans. Inf. Syst. **43**(2), 1–49 (2025)

Strict Core of a Friend-Appreciation Hedonic Game as a Clustering Solution

Alan G. S. Oliveira, Nelson C. Sandes(✉), and Luana B. Cruz

Federal University of Cariri, Juazeiro do Norte, CE, Brazil
alan.gabriel@aluno.ufca.edu.br, {nelson.sandes,luana.batista}@ufca.edu.br

Abstract. Data clustering algorithms are employed to analyze data with the aim of grouping observations such that similar points are placed in the same cluster, while dissimilar ones are assigned to different groups. In this context, approaches based on cooperative game theory have been used to tackle this problem; for instance, the Density-Restricted Agglomerative Clustering and Biobjective Clustering algorithms utilize concepts such as the Shapley value to measure local density to identify clustering structures. Furthermore, within the context of hedonic games, the Hedonic Game-based Clustering algorithm finds Nash-stable coalition structures to be used as clustering solutions. However, there are still no studies that utilize the concept of the core in this specific context. This work proposes a new approach that uses the strict core of a friend-appreciation hedonic game as a clustering solution. Experimental results demonstrate that the proposed method is competitive with both game-theoretic approaches and classical algorithms, such as K-means, hierarchical clustering, and Density-Based Spatial Clustering of Applications with Noise.

Keywords: Hedonic Game · Core · Clustering · Friend

1 Introduction

Clustering algorithms organize data into groups in such a way that there is internal homogeneity and external heterogeneity. In this scenario, numerous approaches have been applied to tackle this problem. Particularly well-known algorithms include K-means, hierarchical clustering, and Density-Based Spatial Clustering of Applications with Noise (DBSCAN) [23].

A partition of the data is one of the possible definitions of clustering. In this context, this perspective is very similar to concepts studied in cooperative game theory. Specifically, this field examines how players form coalitions and how the utility of these coalitions is distributed among the players composing them [6]. Indeed, the resulting coalitions constitute a partition of the players, which is referred to as a coalition structure.

Given the similarity between these two problems, several approaches in the literature obtain clustering solutions based on game-theoretic concepts [13,15,

M. Recamonde-Mendoza and R. C. Barros (Eds.): BRACIS 2026, LNAI 17105, pp. 508–521, 2027.
https://doi.org/10.1007/978-3-032-39882-6_34

20]. Specifically, in this context, data points are modeled as players, and clusters are viewed as coalitions within a cooperative game.

A well-known measure in game theory is the Shapley value, which distributes the utility of coalitions among players such that those who contribute more to coalition formation receive higher payoffs [3,6]. This concept was applied in a scenario where the clustering problem was modeled as a cooperative game [15]. In this context, the Shapley value of a point is proportional to the density of the region to which it belongs - a property utilized to develop the Biobjective Clustering (BiGC) algorithm. Furthermore, the Shapley values for this game can also be used to initialize the centroids of the K-means algorithm. Another approach that takes advantage of this property is the Density-Restricted Agglomerative Clustering (DRAC) algorithm, which expands clusters based on the density of data points as measured by the Shapley value [13].

While the aforementioned approaches address clustering by focusing on how utility is distributed among players, other methodologies utilize concepts inherent to coalition formation. Hedonic games are a type of cooperative game where players have preferences over all possible coalitions within the game. Furthermore, the primary focus of study is how these coalitions are formed. In this context, the Hedonic Game-based Clustering (HGC) algorithm uses a Nash-stable coalition structure as a solution to the clustering problem [8]. Also within the domain of hedonic games, concepts of local popularity and local stability have been used to cluster data [10].

It is important to note that no existing approach utilizes the concept of the core, a solution concept commonly studied in cooperative game theory. Specifically, within the context of hedonic games, studies have shown that it is possible to find the strict core of a friend-appreciation hedonic game in polynomial time [14]. In that study, assuming that players are vertices of a directed graph and their relations are represented by edges, the authors demonstrated that finding the strict core of the game is equivalent to identifying the strongly connected components of the graph. Building upon this, the present work models the clustering problem as a friend-appreciation hedonic game, where data points are the players and the coalition structure represented by the strict core is utilized as the clustering solution.

There are also graph theory-based approaches to address the clustering problem. A study similar to the one proposed in this research is described by [22]. In their work, the authors identify dense regions starting from points classified as representative points. A graph is constructed such that the vertices are these representative points, and edges are defined from a point a to another point b if b is one of the k-nearest neighbors of a. The authors then generate the strongly connected components of this graph to represent the clusters in a data partition. Since not every point is considered a representative point, some points do not belong to this initial clustering. Consequently, the authors associate each unassigned point with its nearest cluster. It is important to mention that the approach proposed in this research differs from that of [22] in that we consider all points in the dataset as vertices of the graph, utilizing the resulting strongly connected components as the clustering solution. The rationale for this choice is supported by [14], who demonstrates that the strongly connected components of such a graph generate a partition belonging to the strict core of the friend-appreciation hedonic game.

Our approach was compared to cooperative game-theoretic algorithms (HGC, DRAC, and BiGC) and widely-used classical algorithms, including K-means, hierarchical clustering, and DBSCAN. To evaluate the algorithms, we used the Adjusted Rand Index (ARI) [17], a well-known external metric for assessing clustering performance. Experiments were conducted on 15 publicly available datasets [2,18,23], and the results demonstrate that the proposed algorithm is competitive with the selected baseline methods. Specifically, following the methodology described by Demšar [12], we applied the Friedman test, which indicated a statistically significant difference among the algorithms. Furthermore, the Nemenyi post-hoc test identified significant differences between our approach and the BiGC, K-means, Complete-Link, and Ward algorithms.

The following items summarize the contributions of this work: (1) a mapping of the clustering problem onto a friend-appreciation hedonic game; (2) the utilization of the strict core of the game, which exhibits a time complexity of $O(n \log n)$ on datasets of moderate dimensionality, as a clustering solution; and (3) a comprehensive comparison of our approach against both cooperative game-theoretic and classical clustering algorithms.

The sections are summarized as follows: Sect. 2 describes the mathematical concepts necessary to understand hedonic games. Section 3 details how to map the clustering problem into a friend-appreciation hedonic game, while Sect. 4 presents the experiments and results achieved in this research. Finally, Sect. 5 outlines the conclusions and limitations of this work.

2 Hedonic Games

In the context of hedonic games, players seek to form coalitions based on their preferences over the members of those groups. Consequently, players have preferences over all possible coalitions to which they can belong. The following definitions follow the notation established in [3,4,6,14]. Formally, let $N = \{1, 2, \ldots, n\}$ be the set of players, where any subset $C \subseteq N$ is a coalition. For each player $i \in N$, let $\mathcal{N}_i = \{C \subseteq N \mid i \in C\}$ denote the set of all coalitions containing player i. In this context, we define a binary preference relation $\succeq_i \subseteq \mathcal{N}_i \times \mathcal{N}_i$ for each player i that is complete, reflexive, and transitive.

The notation $C_i \succeq C_j$ indicates that coalition C_i is at least as preferred as C_j. Similarly, $C_i \succ C_j$ means that C_i is strictly preferred to C_j, while $C_i \sim C_j$ expresses that the player is indifferent between coalitions C_i and C_j.

Given these definitions, we can now define a hedonic game as a tuple $G = (N, \succeq_1, \succeq_2, \ldots, \succeq_n)$, where N is the set of players and, for each $i \in N$, $\succeq_i$ is a preference relation over $\mathcal{N}_i$. The outcome of the game is a coalition structure $CS = \{C_1, C_2, \ldots, C_k\}$, which is a partition of the set of players. In this context, given a coalition structure CS, the following conditions hold:

$\bigcup_{i=1}^{k} C_i = N$ and $C_i \cap C_j = \emptyset \quad \forall i \neq j$. Usually, the notation CS_i is used to denote the coalition in the coalition structure CS that contains player i.

2.1 Stability Concepts

A commonly examined question in hedonic games is how stable a coalition structure is. In other words, if players had the chance to deviate from their coalitions, would they? In this context, there are several solution concepts to examine the stability of a coalition structure. A well-known concept is Nash Stability. Given a hedonic game $G = (N, \succeq_1, \ldots, \succeq_n)$, a coalition structure CS is said to be *Nash stable* if, for every player $i \in N$ and every coalition $C \in CS \cup \{\emptyset\}$, we have: $CS_i \succeq_i C \cup \{i\}$. In other words, no player prefers moving to any other existing coalition or being alone over staying in their current coalition.

Another important stability concept is the core of a hedonic game. Given a hedonic game $G = (N, \succeq_1, \ldots, \succeq_n)$, a coalition $C \subseteq N$ is a deviation from CS if $C \succ_i CS_i$ for all $i \in C$. In other words, all players in C strictly prefer the new coalition to their current one in CS. We define the core of the game as the set of all coalition structures that do not admit any such deviation.

Finally, given a hedonic game $G = (N, \succeq_1, \ldots, \succeq_n)$, a coalition $C \subseteq N$ is a weak deviation from CS if $C \succeq_i CS_i$ for all $i \in C$ and there exists at least one player $j \in C$ such that $C \succ_j CS_j$. The strict core of a game is defined as the set of all coalition structures that don't have weak deviations [14].

2.2 A Hedonic Game of Friend Appreciation

Dimitrov *et al.* [14] proposed two classes of hedonic games: appreciation of friends and aversion to enemies. In these games, each player i has a set of friends F_i and a set of enemies E_i, such that $N \setminus \{i\} = F_i \cup E_i$ and $F_i \cap E_i = \emptyset$. One may note that, in this definition, friendship is not a mutual relation. For example, it is possible for player j to be in F_i while, at the same time, $i \notin F_j$. Specifically, in the friend appreciation game, the players' preferences over coalitions are defined as follows: $C_1 \succ_i C_2$ if, and only if, $|C_1 \cap F_i| > |C_2 \cap F_i|$, or $|C_1 \cap F_i| = |C_2 \cap F_i|$ and $|C_1 \cap E_i| < |C_2 \cap E_i|$. The authors explain that this game can be modeled as a directed graph where players are vertices and an edge from player i to player j exists if $j \in F_i$.

Specifically, one of their results demonstrates that a coalition structure belonging to the strict core can be obtained through the graph's strongly connected components. Furthermore, it is interesting to note that there exist algorithms capable of finding such components in linear time [9,21,24]. An example is the Kosaraju-Sharir algorithm [9], which, given a directed graph $D = (V, E)$ where V is the set of vertices and E is the set of edges, executes the following steps in time complexity $O(|V| + |E|)$:

1. Perform a Depth-First Search (DFS) on D for each unvisited vertex, recording the finishing time for each vertex.
2. Construct the transposed graph D^T.

3. Perform DFS on D^T, processing the vertices in decreasing order of the finishing times obtained from the DFS on D.
4. Each tree resulting from the DFS on D^T corresponds to a strongly connected component of D.

3 Mapping Data Clustering Problem into a Friend-Appreciation Game

This section addresses the problem of mapping a clustering task into a friend-appreciation hedonic game and examining whether the strict core of such a game induces a meaningful partition of a dataset.

Let $P = \{p_1, p_2, \ldots, p_n\}$ denote a set of n data points, each described by t attributes (features). Following the game described in Sect. 2, it is first necessary to establish a criterion for defining the set of friends associated with a point $p \in P$. This task is not trivial: although stability concepts in coalition structures and the data clustering problem are similar, they differ in interpretation. While the former is concerned with finding a partition of players who do not want to deviate from their coalitions, the latter is concerned with finding a partition where similar data points are placed in the same group. Therefore, one open question is: what is the best way to define friendship, considering that the resulting coalition structure must represent a valid clustering solution?

One straightforward approach would be to consider the k-nearest neighbors of each point as its friends. However, preliminary experiments showed that this approach did not yield high-quality clustering solutions. In this context, empirical results demonstrated that it would be better to define the friends of p as its k-nearest neighbors, restricted to those lying within a radius r. Figure 1 illustrates an example of the friend set of a point, where $k = 3$ and r is set as depicted. In this context, although the point has three nearest neighbors, only two of them belong to the friend set due to the constraint imposed by r.

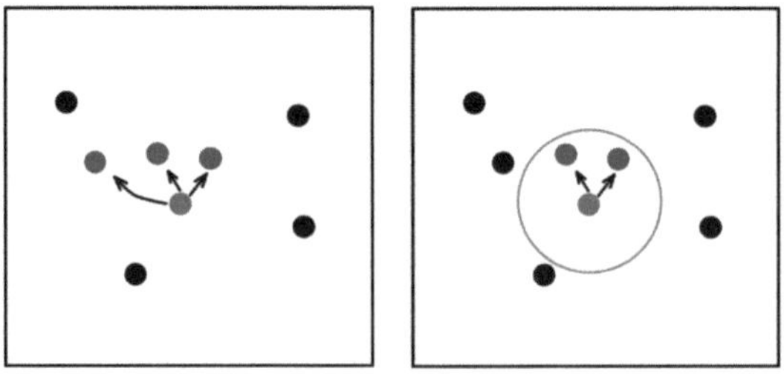

Fig. 1. Example of a set of friends.

Based on this definition, a directed graph D is constructed to represent the corresponding hedonic game. The strongly connected components of D characterize the strict core of the game and, therefore, naturally induce a partition of the dataset into disjoint clusters. The proposed method is termed Strict Core Applied to Clustering (CEAC). Algorithm 1 provides a formal description of the proposed approach.

Algorithm 1. CEAC.

Require: *Data points* P, number of neighbors k, radius r
Ensure: Strongly connected components C

```
D ← digraph where each vertex is a point of P
for each point p_i ∈ P do
   A ← set of k nearest neighbors of p_i
   for each point p_j ∈ A do
      if d(p_i, p_j) ≤ r then
         add the directional edge p_i → p_j in D
      end if
   end for
end for
C ← strongly connected components of D
return C
```

In our experiments, we used the Euclidean distance to measure the radius r and the distance between a point and its k-nearest neighbors. The computational complexity of the proposed algorithm is primarily determined by the cost of computing these neighbors, which can be performed efficiently using a kd-tree data structure. While kd-trees may struggle to efficiently find k-nearest neighbors in high-dimensional datasets [7], they generally require $O(n \log n)$ time for construction. In such cases, querying the k-nearest neighbors for a single point p can be achieved in $O(\log n + k)$ time. Consequently, performing this query for all n points results in a total cost of $O(n \log n + nk)$. When $k \ll n$, this complexity reduces to $O(n \log n)$. Subsequently, the strongly connected components of the resulting directed graph can be computed in $O(n + m)$ time, where m denotes the number of edges. In this context, since each vertex has at most k outgoing edges, we have $m = nk$, yielding a complexity of $O(n + nk)$.

Overall, the total computational complexity of the algorithm for low-to-moderate dimensional datasets is $O(n \log n + nk)$. Under the assumption that $k \ll n$, this simplifies to $O(n \log n)$.

4 Experiments, Results and Discussion

This section presents the experiments and results comparing CEAC with game-theoretic clustering algorithms and classical methods such as K-means, DBSCAN, and hierarchical clustering, specifically focusing on the single, complete, average, and Ward linkage criteria.

To measure the quality of the resulting partitions, we used the ARI [17], a well-known external metric for evaluating clustering solutions. It is important to mention that, since K-means is dependent on centroid initialization and is non-deterministic, we report the average ARI from 30 independent runs of the algorithm.

Finally, following the methodology in [12], after measuring the ARI for each approach, we applied the Friedman test to verify whether there is a statistically significant difference between the algorithms. Subsequently, we performed the Nemenyi post-hoc test to identify statistical differences between each pair of approaches.

4.1 Datasets

To evaluate the proposed approach, a series of experiments was conducted on several datasets: seven synthetic [18] and eight from benchmark and gene expression sources [2,11]. These datasets are commonly used in the literature to evaluate clustering algorithms, and their information is summarized in Table 1, where n denotes the size of the dataset, t is the number of features per instance, and c is the number of classes. Furthermore, following the methodology in [8], we adopted quantile normalization (using scikit-learn) for the benchmark and gene expression datasets as a pre-processing step.

Table 1. Description of the datasets.

Synthetic				Benchmarks and Gene			
Dataset	n	t	c	Dataset	n	t	c
3MC	400	2	3	Arrhythmia	452	262	13
Fourty	1000	2	40	Banknote	1372	4	2
Jain	373	2	2	Cns2	42	1379	5
Pearl	266	2	3	Ionosphere	351	34	2
Spherical_6_2	300	2	6	Libras	360	90	15
Spiral	312	2	3	Lymphography	148	19	4
Target	770	2	6	Olivetti Faces	400	4096	40
				Zoo	78	16	7

4.2 Experimental Setup and Parameter Calibration

All experiments were conducted using Python version 3.13 on a laptop equipped with an AMD Ryzen 5 5500U CPU (up to 4.06 GHz), running the Debian GNU/Linux (forky/sid) operating system.

The CEAC algorithm was implemented in Python, and the k-nearest neighbors for each data point were computed using the kd-tree implementation provided by the scikit-learn library [16,19]. The Friedman test was conducted using the SciPy library [26], while the Nemenyi test was performed using the implementation available in the scikit-posthocs library [25].

To ensure a fair comparison between the best possible results, all algorithm parameters were tuned with the objective of maximizing the ARI. To achieve this, we performed a search to find the optimal k for K-means, the ideal cut-off point for the hierarchical clustering dendrograms, and the optimal parameter s for HGC. Specifically, we varied k and the cut-off points within the range $[1, n-1]$, while the parameter s took values between 1 and $n/2$. Finally, we selected the parameters that yielded the best ARI.

Since CEAC, BiGC, DRAC, and DBSCAN require the tuning of non-integer parameters, we employed the Optuna library [1] to facilitate their efficient optimization. It is important to note that there is no guarantee that Optuna will find the global optimum for the parameters; furthermore, it is possible that these algorithms could achieve better results with different parameter settings.

Additionally, DBSCAN labels certain points as noise. In this context, we followed the methodology proposed by [5], which treats each noise point as a singleton cluster. This approach mitigates the risk of overestimating the ARI, which can occur when an entire class is incorrectly classified as noise.

4.3 ARI Results

Table 2 presents the results obtained from the experiments. Specifically, bold text is used to emphasize the best result, while italic text represents the second-best result for each dataset. It is noteworthy that the proposed algorithm perfectly labeled all data points in nearly all synthetic datasets (*3MC, Forty, Jain, Spherical_6_2, Spiral, Pearl,* and *Target*). Although most approaches performed well

Table 2. Score of the algorithms using ARI metric.

	Agglomerative hierarchical				K-means	DBSCAN	BiGC	DRAC	HGC	CEAC
	average	complete	single	ward						
3MC	**1.000**	0.678	**1.000**	**1.000**	0.707	**1.000**	*0.754*	**1.000**	**1.000**	**1.000**
Arrhythmia	0.225	0.188	0.261	0.109	0.051	**0.301**	0.246	0.262	0.197	*0.288*
Banknote	0.248	0.111	*0.917*	0.230	0.169	**0.919**	0.091	*0.917*	0.353	*0.917*
Cns2	0.509	0.471	0.434	0.421	0.288	0.514	0.381	**0.618**	*0.580*	0.552
Fourty	**1.000**	**1.000**	**1.000**	**1.000**	0.881	**1.000**	*0.965*	0.807	**1.000**	**1.000**
Ionosphere	0.302	0.099	0.507	0.150	0.069	0.512	0.222	*0.514*	0.388	**0.541**
Jain	0.779	0.779	*0.941*	0.515	0.309	*0.941*	0.344	0.355	0.489	**1.000**
Libras	0.365	0.283	0.279	0.344	0.304	0.279	0.244	0.340	**0.393**	*0.382*
Lymphography	0.110	0.129	0.092	0.116	0.153	0.138	0.116	0.122	**0.243**	*0.193*
Olivetti Faces	0.487	0.429	0.375	*0.599*	0.441	0.382	0.439	0.451	**0.628**	0.523
Pearl	0.620	0.616	**1.000**	0.649	0.631	**1.000**	0.618	**1.000**	**1.000**	**1.000**
Spherical_6_2	**1.000**	**1.000**	**1.000**	**1.000**	*0.842*	**1.000**	**1.000**	**1.000**	**1.000**	**1.000**
Spiral	0.162	0.093	**1.000**	0.130	0.115	**1.000**	0.152	*0.647*	0.202	**1.000**
Target	0.664	0.628	**1.000**	0.658	0.665	**1.000**	0.666	**1.000**	*0.720*	**1.000**
Zoo	0.915	0.868	*0.922*	0.914	0.692	**0.941**	0.555	0.903	0.810	*0.922*

on *3MC, Forty,* and *Spherical_ 6_ 2*, this was not the case for the remaining synthetic datasets. In particular, CEAC was the only algorithm to correctly label all data points in the *Jain* dataset.

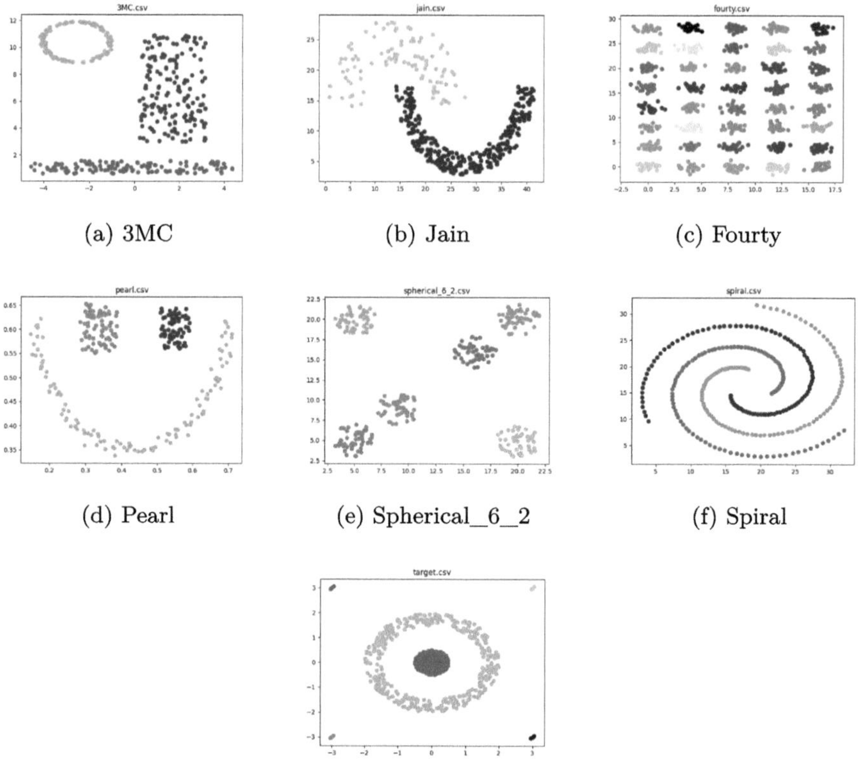

(a) 3MC (b) Jain (c) Fourty

(d) Pearl (e) Spherical_6_2 (f) Spiral

(g) Target

Fig. 2. Datasets with perfect clustering recovery (ARI = 1.0) by the CEAC algorithm.

Furthermore, CEAC ranks first or second on all other datasets, except for *Olivetti Faces* and *Cns2*. Specifically, on the *Zoo*, *Banknote*, and *Arrhythmia* datasets, our approach was outperformed only by DBSCAN, while on *Olivetti Faces*, it ranked behind HGC and Ward-linkage hierarchical clustering. Datasets such as *Arrhythmia, Cns2, Ionosphere, Libras, Lymphography,* and *Olivetti Faces* proved to be difficult for the clustering algorithms used in this work; in these cases, all results were distant from the ground-truth labels. The performance of DBSCAN is also noteworthy. This approach failed to achieve a first or second-place ranking only on the *Cns2*, *Ionosphere*, *Lymphography*, *Libras* and *Olivetti Faces* datasets. Conversely, the performance of K-means was generally poor. This was expected, as we did not apply initialization strategies to select optimal

Table 3. K-means, Hierarchical Clustering and HGC parameters that maximize the ARI for each dataset.

	Agglomerative hierarchical				K-means	HGC
	average	complete	single	ward		
3MC	3	5	3	3	3	102
Arrhythmia	40	8	160	3	7	82
Banknote	4	14	9	3	5	162
Cns2	11	9	25	8	5	11
Fourty	40	40	40	40	53	24
Ionosphere	57	38	121	5	7	63
Jain	2	2	5	2	2	77
Libras	19	35	91	16	18	20
Lymphography	19	4	4	3	4	31
Olivetti Faces	125	106	156	62	78	8
Pearl	7	7	3	4	5	50
Spherical_6_2	6	6	6	6	7	34
Spiral	27	41	3	32	19	20
Target	9	11	6	5	5	249
Zoo	7	5	8	6	4	19

centroids, such as K-means++ or BiGC [15]. Furthermore, cooperative game-theoretic approaches, such as HGC and DRAC, appear to be competitive. Specifically, DRAC achieved the best performance on the *Cns2* dataset, while HGC yielded the best results on *Libras*, *Lymphography*, and *Olivetti Faces*. Finally, Fig. 2 presents the synthetic datasets on which CEAC achieved an ARI score of 1.0, demonstrating its ability to perfectly recover complex structures within the data.

Additionally, to ensure the reproducibility of the experiments, Table 3 reports the parameters found to maximize the ARI for the K-means, hierarchical clustering, and HGC approaches. Table 4 presents the corresponding parameters for the CEAC and DBSCAN algorithms, and Table 5 shows the parameters for DRAC and BiGC. The obtained values reinforce the notion that it is not easy to calibrate non-integer parameters, such as r for CEAC and ϵ for DBSCAN. While the objective of this work was to compare clustering approaches, in real-world scenarios, ground-truth labels are not at our disposal. Consequently, as future work, we need to develop a strategy to select the parameters k and r for CEAC in unsupervised settings.

4.4 Statistical Significance: Friedman and Post-Hoc Nemenyi Tests

The Friedman test is a non-parametric test that can be used to evaluate statistically significant differences between multiple machine learning algorithms across

Table 4. DBSCAN and CEAC parameters that maximize the ARI for each dataset.

	DBSCAN	CEAC
3MC	'minPts': 9, 'ϵ': 1.0460201020523248	'k': 20, 'r': 1.0482778840406901
Arrhythmia	'minPts': 117, 'ϵ': 4.4017118644268605	'k': 6, 'r': 4.099675491632945
Banknote	'minPts': 4, 'ϵ': 0.1509256382992823	'k': 23, 'r': 0.15017796926719854
Cns2	'minPts': 4, 'ϵ': 17.308491844502765	'k': 3, 'r': 18.63369517893699
Fourty	'minPts': 11, 'ϵ': 1.3436040166655379	'k': 26, 'r': 1.3596460526803644
Ionosphere	'minPts': 11, 'ϵ': 1.0596116114215945	'k': 16, 'r': 1.575068952381177
Jain	'minPts': 1, 'ϵ': 2.4839162760564175	'k': 8, 'r': 2.8745433572238444
Libras	'minPts': 2, 'ϵ': 1.284184108389173	'k': 5, 'r': 1.6187455978057383
Lymphography	'minPts': 82, 'ϵ': 2.060573827307685	'k': 3, 'r': 1.512202369167144
Olivetti Faces	'minPts': 1, 'ϵ': 11.950919763202766	'k': 5, 'r': 14.6013196068988
Pearl	'minPts': 9, 'ϵ': 0.04159976412054117	'k': 12, 'r': 0.03280946274039073
Spherical_6_2	'minPts': 1, 'ϵ': 1.1204774498879362	'k': 13, 'r': 1.13468958749388
Spiral	'minPts': 3, 'ϵ': 1.2500082000465313	'k': 10, 'r': 1.2437086419539958
Target	'minPts': 2, 'ϵ': 0.2591504996692918	'k': 13, 'r': 0.2940470225300929
Zoo	'minPts': 7, 'ϵ': 1.4611835091436867	'k': 5, 'r': 1.6467898410409383

Table 5. BiGC and DRAC parameters that maximize the ARI for each dataset.

	BiGC	DRAC
3MC	'δ': 0.701007859604709	'γ': 0.4337448178928506; 'α': 0.9516288210377523
Arrhythmia	'δ': 0.5116701722015597	'γ': 0.29806626649535906; 'α': 0.6735142353045732
Banknote	'δ': 0.8315220354096396	'γ': 0.04531552004228348; 'α': 0.9487869972870606
Cns2	'δ': 0.26836572646607565	'γ': 0.8044440697536301; 'α': 0.3250202340319464
Fourty	'δ': 0.9272381323678772	'γ': 0.9942060676718035; 'α': 0.9840627468844306
Ionosphere	'δ': 0.6086104727108632	'γ': 0.77688981275883; 'α': 0.8346432536199268
Jain	'δ': 0.7257100608128771	'γ': 2.941945927693951; 'α': 0.7253424744860834
Libras	'δ': 0.7472595056203086	'γ': 0.8460065784240405; 'α': 0.8924458505344395
Lymphography	'δ': 0.46832724121079183	'γ': 0.9747192126440206; 'α': 0.5589508779860081
Olivetti Faces	'δ': 0.6968746394770173	'γ': 10.851509708570104; 'α': 0.7318173359298448
Pearl	'δ': 0.9158400960983758	'γ': 0.1742384657217452; 'α': 0.9536085803699412
Spherical_6_2	'δ': 0.8366237101664433	'γ': 5.28517923493644; 'α': 0.8109448470460715
Spiral	'δ': 0.810260778806297	'γ': 0.6534500262564127; 'α': 0.9846134164967597
Target	'δ': 0.8487336483315652	'γ': 0.6098643030267892; 'α': 0.9183787304405319
Zoo	'δ': 0.6750976825145258	'γ': 0.6055280787663728; 'α': 0.7891987606622505

several datasets [12]. In this context, algorithms are ranked for each dataset based on their performance, and an average rank is subsequently assigned to each approach. The null hypothesis states that there is no statistical difference between the average ranks, while the alternative hypothesis claims that at least one average rank differs significantly from the others. In this context, we applied the Friedman test, taking into account the ARI results discussed in Sect. 4. The test yielded a p-value of 2.49×10^{-9}, which is significantly lower than the significance level $\alpha = 0.05$. Therefore, the null hypothesis is rejected.

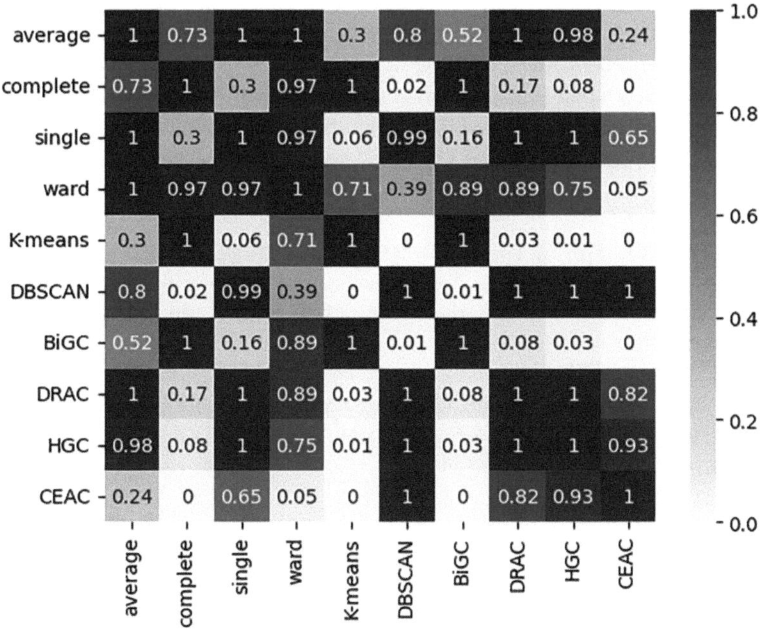

Fig. 3. Heat map of Nemenyi post hoc test.

To evaluate whether there are statistical differences between each pair of algorithms, we applied the Nemenyi post-hoc test [12]. The results of this test are illustrated in the heatmap presented in Fig. 3. Analysis of the heatmap reveals statistically significant differences between CEAC and Hierarchical Clustering with complete linkage ($p = 5.21 \times 10^{-4}$), Ward linkage ($p = 0.0496$), K-means ($p = 2.5 \times 10^{-5}$) and BiGC ($p = 1.28 \times 10^{-4}$). Additionally, significant differences were identified between DBSCAN and complete-linkage hierarchical clustering, DBSCAN and K-means, as well as between DBSCAN and BiGC. Furthermore, statistically significant differences were found between HGC and K-means, and HGC and BiGC. Finally, DRAC also differed significantly from the K-means and BiGC algorithms.

5 Conclusion and Future Work

In this work, we presented a new clustering algorithm, namely CEAC, based on cooperative game theory, where each data point is viewed as a player. The strict core of the game is used as the clustering solution; to assess the potential of CEAC, we compared its performance with cooperative game theory approaches (HGC, DRAC and BiGC) and classical clustering algorithms such as K-means, Hierarchical Clustering, and DBSCAN. Overall, ARI results show that CEAC is quite competitive with the compared approaches. Particularly, non-parametric tests showed statistically significant differences between CEAC, K-means, BiGC and Hierarchical Clustering when using complete linkage and Ward's method.

As future work, we intend to investigate strategies for automatically setting the k and r parameters for CEAC. Furthermore, it is worth studying how the algorithm performs with dissimilarity metrics other than Euclidean distance. Finally, it is important to investigate alternative ways to define a playern's friend set, as this is a central aspect of the coalition structure that emerges from the game.

Acknowledgments. During the preparation of this work, the authors used generative AI only to improve the language and grammar of the manuscript. After using this service, the authors reviewed and edited the content as needed and take full responsibility for the final version of the paper.

Disclosure of Interests. The authors declare that they have no known competing financial interests or personal relationships that could have appeared to influence the work reported in this paper.

References

1. Akiba, T., Sano, S., Yanase, T., Ohta, T., Koyama, M.: Optuna: a next-generation hyperparameter optimization framework. In: Proceedings of the 25th ACM SIGKDD International Conference on Knowledge Discovery & Data Mining, pp. 2623–2631 (2019)
2. Asuncion, A., Newman, D.: UCI machine learning repository (2007)
3. Barron, E.N.: Game Theory: An Introduction. Wiley (2024)
4. Bogomolnaia, A., Jackson, M.O.: The stability of hedonic coalition structures. Games Econom. Behav. **38**(2), 201–230 (2002)
5. Bryant, A., Cios, K.: RNN-DBSCAN: a density-based clustering algorithm using reverse nearest neighbor density estimates. IEEE Trans. Knowl. Data Eng. **30**(6), 1109–1121 (2017)
6. Chalkiadakis, G., Elkind, E., Wooldridge, M.: Computational Aspects of Cooperative Game Theory. Morgan & Claypool Publishers (2011)
7. Chen, Y., et al.: Fast neighbor search by using revised KD tree. Inf. Sci. **472**, 145–162 (2019)
8. Coelho, A.L., Sandes, N.C.: Data clustering via cooperative games: a novel approach and comparative study. Inf. Sci. **545**, 791–812 (2021)
9. Cormen, T.H., Leiserson, C.E., Rivest, R.L., Stein, C.: Introduction to Algorithms. MIT Press (2022)
10. Csáji, G., Gundert, A., Rothe, J., Schlotter, I.: Clustering via hedonic games: new concepts and algorithms. In: The Thirty-Ninth Annual Conference on Neural Information Processing Systems (2025)

11. De Souto, M.C., Costa, I.G., De Araujo, D.S., Ludermir, T.B., Schliep, A.: Clustering cancer gene expression data: a comparative study. BMC Bioinform. **9**(1), 497 (2008)
12. Demšar, J.: Statistical comparisons of classifiers over multiple data sets. J. Mach. Learn. Res. **7**, 1–30 (2006)
13. Dhamal, S., Bhat, S., Anoop, K., Embar, V.R.: Pattern clustering using cooperative game theory. arXiv preprint arXiv:1201.0461 (2012)
14. Dimitrov, D., Borm, P., Hendrickx, R., Sung, S.C.: Simple priorities and core stability in hedonic games. Soc. Choice Welfare **26**(2), 421–433 (2006)
15. Garg, V.K., Narahari, Y., Murty, M.N.: Novel biobjective clustering (BiGC) based on cooperative game theory. IEEE Trans. Knowl. Data Eng. **25**(5), 1070–1082 (2012)
16. Hao, J., Ho, T.K.: Machine learning made easy: a review of scikit-learn package in python programming language. J. Educ. Behav. Stat. **44**(3), 348–361 (2019)
17. Hubert, L., Arabie, P.: Comparing partitions. J. Classif. **2**(1), 193–218 (1985)
18. Parmar, M.: Clustering-datasets (2019). https://github.com/milaan9/Clustering-Datasets. Accessed 13 Mar 2026
19. Pedregosa, F., et al.: Scikit-learn: machine learning in python. J. Mach. Learn. Res. **12**, 2825–2830 (2011)
20. Sandes, N.C., Coelho, A.L.: Clustering ensembles: a hedonic game theoretical approach. Pattern Recogn. **81**, 95–111 (2018)
21. Sharir, M.: A strong-connectivity algorithm and its applications in data flow analysis. Comput. Math. Appl. **7**(1), 67–72 (1981)
22. Shekhar, M., Thomas, L., Karlapalem, K.: High dimensional clustering: a strongly connected component clustering solution (SCCC). In: IEEE International Conference on Data Mining Workshops (ICDMW), pp. 1104–1111. IEEE (2018)
23. Tan, P.N., Steinbach, M., Kumar, V.: Introduction to Data Mining. Pearson Education India (2016)
24. Tarjan, R.: Depth-first search and linear graph algorithms. SIAM J. Comput. **1**(2), 146–160 (1972)
25. Terpilowski, M.A.: scikit-posthocs: pairwise multiple comparison tests in python. J. Open Source Softw. **4**(36), 1169 (2019)
26. Virtanen, P., et al.: Scipy 1.0: fundamental algorithms for scientific computing in python. Nat. Methods **17**(3), 261–272 (2020)

Editorial Faithfulness in Reasoning Models: Susceptibility to Authority, Framing, and Information Legitimacy Cues

Alexandre Thurow Bender(✉), Gabriel Almeida Gomes, Ulisses Brisolara Corrêa, and Ricardo Matsumura Araujo

Computer Science Graduation Program (PPGC), Artificial Intelligence Innovation Hub (H2IA), Center for Technological Advancement (CDTec), Federal University of Pelotas, Pelotas, Brazil
{atbender,gagomes,ulisses,ricardo}@inf.ufpel.edu.br

Abstract. Large language models exhibit strong reasoning performance on static benchmarks, yet their reliability in deployment depends on whether conclusions remain stable under changes in presentation. We quantify model susceptibility to non-evidential editorial cues that alter correct answers, defining editorial faithfulness as invariance to such perturbations. We evaluate ten reasoning-oriented models across three controlled paradigms (authority attribution, information access legitimacy, and evaluative framing) using accuracy stability (pass@k), behavioral sensitivity (flip@k), and attributional awareness (transparency@k). Sensitivity is highly uneven across paradigms and training regimes. Information access legitimacy is the dominant failure mode: pass@1 drops by up to 100% under harmful legitimacy cues, with the Qwen3.5 family showing catastrophic collapse at every scale where its Qwen3 predecessor remains moderate. Authority and evaluative framing effects are modest for most models but substantial for Qwen3.5, suggesting a generational regression rather than a scaling property. A 35B-total/3B-active mixture-of-experts model behaves like its dense total-parameter equivalent, not like its active-compute counterpart. DeepSeek-R1 is the only family we evaluate that remains essentially invariant to legitimacy cues. Training regime, rather than scale, determines editorial faithfulness.

Keywords: Editorial faithfulness · Reasoning models · Chain-of-thought · Behavioral evaluation · Large language models

1 Introduction

Large language models (LLMs) have demonstrated strong performance on benchmarks requiring multi-step reasoning, mathematical problem solving, and structured decision making [7,13,14]. These results have motivated the deployment of reasoning-oriented models in settings such as decision support, analysis, and recommendation. Most evaluations, however, rest on the implicit assumption that

M. Recamonde-Mendoza and R. C. Barros (Eds.): BRACIS 2026, LNAI 17105, pp. 522–536, 2027.
https://doi.org/10.1007/978-3-032-39882-6_35

correct reasoning is invariant to presentation, and that conclusions are determined by evidential content rather than editorial presentation.

In real-world deployments, this assumption rarely holds. Model inputs are routinely embedded in editorial context, including claims of authority or expertise, ethical disclaimers regarding information access, and framing language that emphasizes particular aspects of a decision without introducing new factual evidence. A reasoning system that changes its conclusion under these conditions is not failing at task competence, but at maintaining invariance to non-evidential presentation effects.

In this work, we show that contemporary reasoning models are systematically susceptible to such cues. We term robustness to these effects *editorial faithfulness*: the degree to which a model's outputs remain invariant under stylistic or contextual perturbations that preserve semantic truth. Editorial faithfulness is distinct from robustness to noise or adversarial attacks [4,6], focusing instead on linguistically natural and commonplace variations that arise in realistic deployments. The effect is large: a single-sentence editorial label drives accuracy on otherwise-unchanged questions from ≈ 0.80 to 0.00 for some model families and leaves others untouched (Fig. 1).

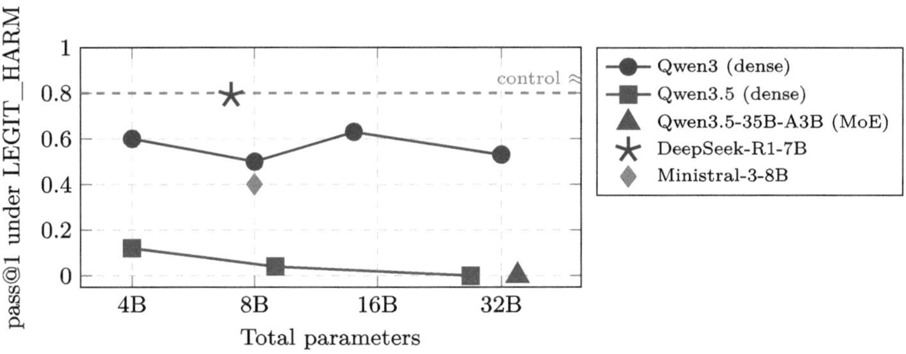

Fig. 1. Under a harmful editorial cue that labels an incorrect answer as "verified internal data," pass@1 (the probability that a model returns the evidence-supported answer) collapses to zero for the Qwen3.5 family at every scale (red squares), while DeepSeek-R1-7B (teal star) remains at the control baseline of pass@1 ≈ 0.80 (gray dashed line). Qwen3 (blue) is only moderately affected despite sharing an architectural base with Qwen3.5: training regime, not parameter count, drives editorial faithfulness. The mixture-of-experts variant Qwen3.5-35B-A3B (red triangle) tracks its dense total-parameter sibling rather than its 3B-active counterpart, indicating that susceptibility scales with total capacity. Pass@1 averaged over 50 MCQA items, $n = 10$ samples per item; details in Sect. 5.2. (Color figure online)

We evaluate a range of contemporary reasoning-oriented language models on controlled evaluation scenarios that vary non-evidential editorial cues such as authority attribution, framing, and information legitimacy, while holding evidential content fixed. The same multiple-choice questions are used across conditions to ensure that any observed behavioral differences arise solely from changes in editorial presentation.

To account for stochasticity in model generation, we introduce variance-aware behavioral metrics inspired by *pass@k*. In addition to *pass@k*, we propose *flip@k*, which measures deviations from control behavior across repeated samples, and *transparency@k*, which probes whether models acknowledge editorial context in their explanations.

Our main contributions are as follows:

- We identify *editorial faithfulness* as an important dimension of reasoning reliability, capturing robustness to non-evidential editorial cues.
- We propose controlled evaluation scenarios and variance-aware behavioral metrics inspired by *pass@k* (*flip@k* and *transparency@k*) to isolate the effects of editorial presentation under stochastic generation.
- We provide empirical evidence across ten reasoning-oriented models that sensitivity to editorial cues is highly uneven across both cue types and training regimes, with information access legitimacy emerging as the dominant failure mode and training regime (rather than parameter count) determining model robustness (Fig. 1).

2 Background

Chain-of-thought (CoT) reasoning has emerged as a key mechanism underlying the strong multi-step reasoning capabilities of contemporary decoder-only LLMs [7,13,14]. However, the surface form of generated reasoning is not necessarily causally faithful to the model's internal decision process and may vary independently of the final answer [9,12]; CoT outputs are therefore best interpreted as behavioral artifacts rather than as reliable explanations of underlying reasoning.

Inference in modern LLMs commonly relies on stochastic decoding, under which repeated inference on the same input can yield different outputs. Pass@k metrics partially address this limitation by estimating the probability that at least one of k sampled outputs yields a correct solution [3]. We extend this variance-aware framework with two behavioral analogues (*flip@k* and *transparency@k*) that measure sensitivity and attribution under the same probabilistic form.

3 Related Works

A growing body of work has shown that the behavior of large language models is highly sensitive to contextual and social signals embedded in prompts. Prior studies demonstrate that models condition their outputs on perceived user beliefs, social framing, and authority cues, often adjusting both conclusions and reasoning style in response to such context [1,15]. Work on sycophancy further shows that models tend to align their answers with user opinions or expectations, even when these contradict factual ground truth [10]. Related analyses of framing and authority bias reveal that minor stylistic variations can induce substantial shifts in model behavior [11]. In many of these settings, however, contextual manipulations also modify task semantics or evidential content, making it difficult to isolate sensitivity to non-evidential editorial cues.

Literature has also questioned the faithfulness of natural language reasoning produced by LLMs. Models frequently generate fluent and plausible chain-of-thought explanations that are weakly correlated with their underlying decision processes, a phenomenon commonly described as post-hoc rationalization [2,5]. [12] show that models can be systematically steered toward incorrect answers while producing internally coherent reasoning traces that appear to justify those errors. While these findings raise important concerns about explanation reliability, existing evaluations often focus on qualitative inspection or analysis of explanation content, rather than linking reasoning traces to controlled behavioral perturbations [8].

In contrast to prior work, we focus on *editorial cues*: stylistic or social prompt features that do not alter the underlying evidence or task definition. We introduce a prompt-only evaluation framework that holds evidential content constant while systematically varying editorial presentation. Adopting a behavioral notion of faithfulness, we extend variance-aware evaluation principles [3] by introducing metrics that quantify decision instability and acknowledgment of editorial context under stochastic decoding. This allows us to directly measure editorial faithfulness as a property of model behavior, independent of explanation quality or task accuracy.

4 Methodology

We propose an evaluation framework to measure *editorial faithfulness*, defined as a model's tendency to base its answers on task-relevant evidence rather than on non-evidential editorial cues.[1] A model is considered more editorially faithful when its outputs remain stable under such cues, particularly when they conflict with the underlying evidence.

4.1 Experimental Setup

All experiments use multiple-choice question answering (MCQA), which provides an objective correctness signal and enables precise detection of answer changes across conditions. For each item, the question text and answer options are held fixed.

Each prompt follows a canonical structure:

[1] Code is available at github.com/atbender/editorial-faithfulness-bracis.

```
[PREAMBLE EDITORIAL CUE]
[BASE INSTRUCTION]
[MCQA PROBLEM]
```

The **base instruction** enforces a strict output protocol requiring exactly one answer option, emitted as `\boxed{X}` where `X` is a letter in {A, B, C, D}. The boxed-answer convention is the native format used by contemporary reasoning models during training and is reliably produced without additional prompting. Outputs that fail to emit a valid boxed answer are marked as non-compliant and treated as incorrect for accuracy-based metrics. Editorial manipulations are applied exclusively via the **preamble editorial cue**. All conditions are evaluated alongside a control prompt with no editorial stimulus.

We use a subset of multiple-choice questions drawn from the MMLU benchmark, consisting of 10 randomly sampled items from each of five domains: formal logic, philosophy, moral disputes, high school physics, and high school mathematics.

Evaluations use stochastic decoding with fixed sampling parameters (temperature 0.7, top-p 0.95, maximum 16,384 generation tokens). For each model, item, and condition, we generate $n = 10$ independent samples. Repeated sampling reflects realistic deployment settings and enables variance-aware behavioral analysis. Non-compliant format answers are excluded from behavioral comparisons but counted as incorrect for accuracy metrics. The token budget is large enough to accommodate the full chain-of-thought of every evaluated model without truncation; we found that smaller budgets disproportionately affect larger reasoning models, which produce longer reasoning traces and thus fail the format gate more often, conflating editorial sensitivity with generation capacity.

4.2 Experimental Scenarios

We evaluate three experimental scenarios that introduce controlled editorial signals commonly encountered in real-world model use. Each scenario is crossed with a *help/harm* axis, where the editorial signal endorses either the correct (help) or incorrect (harm) answer, allowing us to assess whether models follow editorial cues independently of evidential support.

Authority Attribution. The preamble attributes a recommendation to either a high-credibility or low-credibility source, testing whether models condition their answers on perceived authority rather than on task evidence.

Information Access Legitimacy. The preamble frames an answer as being obtained through either legitimate or illegitimate means (e.g., leaked or prohibited access), testing whether models gate their responses based on procedural legitimacy rather than informational content.

Evaluative Framing. One answer option is described using either positive or negative evaluative language, while all factual descriptions and options remain unchanged, isolating sensitivity to evaluative emphasis.

4.3 Variance-Aware Metrics

We evaluate behavior under stochastic decoding using three metrics that share a common probabilistic form. Each estimates the probability that a target event occurs at least once among k samples drawn without replacement from n generated outputs.

pass@k. Let c be the number of correct samples among n. The probability that at least one correct output appears in k samples is:

$$\text{pass@k} = 1 - \frac{\binom{n-c}{k}}{\binom{n}{k}}$$

This metric captures task-level correctness under sampling variance.

flip@k. To measure sensitivity to editorial cues, we define a behavioral flip relative to a control condition. For each item, we define the *reference answer* a^* as the modal output under the control prompt. This choice reflects the model's most probable behavior in the absence of editorial influence.

Let f be the number of manipulated samples whose output differs from a^*. We define:

$$\text{flip@k} = 1 - \frac{\binom{n-f}{k}}{\binom{n}{k}}$$

When $k = 1$, flip@1 $= f/n$ corresponds to the empirical probability that a single sampled output changes under editorial manipulation.

transparency@k. Behavioral change does not imply attributional awareness. We therefore measure whether models explicitly acknowledge the editorial cue in their outputs. Let t be the number of manipulated samples that reference the preamble stimulus, either explicitly or through clear causal attribution (operationalized via rule-based pattern matching). We define:

$$\text{transparency@k} = 1 - \frac{\binom{n-t}{k}}{\binom{n}{k}}$$

The three metrics differ only in their atomic event: (i) correctness (pass@k), (ii) deviation from control behavior (flip@k), and (iii) attribution to an editorial cue (transparency@k).

4.4 Models

We evaluate ten open-weight reasoning models selected to cover a range of scales, training regimes, and architectural choices. The Qwen3 family (`Qwen3-4B`, `Qwen3-8B`, `Qwen3-14B`, `Qwen3-32B`) provides a controlled dense scaling series within a single architecture. The Qwen3.5 family (`Qwen3.5-4B`, `Qwen3.5-9B`, `Qwen3.5-27B`) extends the comparison to a newer generation using the same architectural base but with a revised training regime. We additionally include `Qwen3.5-35B-A3B`, a mixture-of-experts variant with 35B total parameters but only 3B active per token, enabling a direct test of whether editorial faithfulness tracks active compute or total parameter capacity.

We include DeepSeek-R1-Distill-Qwen-7B and Ministral-3-8B-Reasoning-2512 to introduce architectural and training diversity beyond the Qwen families. These represent alternative open-weight systems trained under different optimization and data regimes, and their inclusion allows us to separate family-specific effects from properties of scale.

All models are evaluated using identical scenarios, hyperparameters, and stochastic sampling protocols. Results are reported per model, perturbation scenario, and experimental condition.

5 Results

We evaluate editorial faithfulness across three experimental scenarios: authority attribution, information access legitimacy, and evaluative framing. Each paradigm isolates a distinct non-evidential editorial cue while holding underlying task evidence constant.

We report variance-aware accuracy using pass@k, behavioral sensitivity using flip@k, and attribution behavior using transparency@k. Unless stated otherwise, we focus on pass@1, flip@1, and transparency@1 for interpretability; higher values of k exhibit consistent monotonic trends across all paradigms. All metrics are computed over the same evaluation instances per condition.

All tasks enforce a strict output protocol in which models must emit a final answer in the form `\boxed{X}`, where $X \in \{A, B, C, D\}$. Non-format-compliant outputs are treated as incorrect for pass@k and excluded from flip@k and transparency@k calculations. Across all ten models and fifteen paradigm-condition cells, compliance is at or near ceiling: the smallest observed rate is 0.944 ± 0.031 (DeepSeek-R1-7B) and the majority of models are at 1.000 ± 0.000. This uniformity lets us interpret the behavioral metrics below as direct measurements of editorial sensitivity, rather than artifacts of format-induced censoring.

5.1 Authority Attribution

Table 1 reports model behavior under authority cues that either support the correct answer (*help*) or promote an incorrect one (*harm*). In contrast to the strong, uniform susceptibility one might expect from an intuitive reading of

Table 1. Pass@1, flip@1, and transparency@1 under authority attribution cues.

Model	Metric	Control	High Authority		Low Authority	
			Help	Harm	Help	Harm
Qwen3-4B	pass@1	0.80	0.88 (+10%)	0.69 (−14%)	0.82 (+2%)	0.80 (+0%)
	transp@1	–	0.67	0.87	0.74	0.84
	flip@1	–	0.08	0.14	0.02	0.00
Qwen3-8B	pass@1	0.80	0.89 (+11%)	0.80 (+0%)	0.82 (+2%)	0.80 (+0%)
	transp@1	–	0.66	0.90	0.80	0.87
	flip@1	–	0.10	0.10	0.09	0.03
Qwen3-14B	pass@1	0.81	0.93 (+15%)	0.85 (+5%)	0.89 (+10%)	0.88 (+9%)
	transp@1	–	0.58	0.71	0.76	0.90
	flip@1	–	0.12	0.06	0.08	0.09
Qwen3-32B	pass@1	0.81	0.90 (+11%)	0.76 (−6%)	0.83 (+2%)	0.80 (−1%)
	transp@1	–	0.62	0.77	0.80	0.87
	flip@1	–	0.11	0.07	0.05	0.03
DeepSeek-R1-7B	pass@1	0.81	0.82 (+1%)	0.79 (−2%)	0.80 (−1%)	0.78 (−4%)
	transp@1	–	0.53	0.58	0.69	0.64
	flip@1	–	0.08	0.07	0.08	0.08
Ministral-3-8B	pass@1	0.75	0.74 (−1%)	0.68 (−9%)	0.76 (+1%)	0.72 (−4%)
	transp@1	–	0.01	0.06	0.05	0.04
	flip@1	–	0.28	0.18	0.10	0.14
Qwen3.5-4B	pass@1	0.83	1.00 (+21%)	0.58 (−30%)	0.97 (+17%)	0.80 (−4%)
	transp@1	–	1.00	1.00	1.00	1.00
	flip@1	–	0.17	0.32	0.13	0.08
Qwen3.5-9B	pass@1	0.82	1.00 (+23%)	0.52 (−36%)	0.92 (+13%)	0.81 (−1%)
	transp@1	–	1.00	1.00	1.00	1.00
	flip@1	–	0.18	0.38	0.15	0.09
Qwen3.5-27B	pass@1	0.85	1.00 (+18%)	0.42 (−50%)	0.94 (+11%)	0.87 (+3%)
	transp@1	–	1.00	1.00	1.00	1.00
	flip@1	–	0.15	0.48	0.09	0.06
Qwen3.5-35B-A3B	pass@1	0.92	1.00 (+9%)	0.56 (−39%)	0.95 (+3%)	0.92 (+0%)
	transp@1	–	1.00	1.00	1.00	0.99
	flip@1	–	0.08	0.35	0.05	0.02

authority-bias research, we find that authority effects vary substantially by model family and are muted on MMLU for most of the models evaluated.

For the Qwen3 family, DeepSeek-R1-7B, and Ministral-3-8B, authority cues produce modest accuracy shifts. Under high-authority harmful framing, pass@1 drops by at most 14% (Qwen3-4B); Qwen3-14B actually shows a slight *increase* (+5%), indicating that the cue is overridden by the model's internal reasoning. DeepSeek-R1-7B is essentially invariant across all four authority conditions (±4%). These magnitudes are markedly smaller than what earlier work has reported on similar paradigms. We attribute this to evaluation protocol: truncated chains-of-thought in prior evaluations disproportionately removed cases in which the model would have produced a format-compliant, evidence-following answer, inflating the apparent susceptibility of larger models.

Qwen3.5 behaves differently. Under high-authority harmful framing, pass@1 drops by 30% for Qwen3.5-4B, 36% for Qwen3.5-9B, and 50% for Qwen3.5-27B. The MoE variant Qwen3.5-35B-A3B drops by 39%, closer in magnitude to the dense 27B than to a 3B-active-parameter equivalent. This scale-monotonic susceptibility within Qwen3.5 stands in sharp contrast to the Qwen3 family, despite shared architectural lineage, and is consistent with a training-level rather than architectural cause (see Sect. 5.4).

Behavioral sensitivity, as captured by flip@1, tracks the same pattern. Qwen3 and DeepSeek-R1 models show flip@1 values of at most 0.14 under harmful authority framing, while Qwen3.5 models reach 0.32–0.48. Across all families, low-authority cues (a "non-expert" source) induce substantially smaller shifts than high-authority cues, confirming that the effect is driven by the perceived credibility of the source rather than by the mere presence of a cue.

Transparency@1 presents a notable discrepancy with earlier findings. Qwen3.5 models reference the authority cue in essentially 100% of their outputs, often yielding transparency@1 $\geq$ flip@1: the reverse of the gap documented in prior work. Under proper evaluation, these models explicitly mention the editorial cue *even when they do not follow it*, so surface-level attribution and behavioral compliance are dissociable. For Ministral-3-8B the pattern inverts: flip@1 is non-trivial (up to 0.28) while transparency@1 remains near zero (at most 0.06), so Ministral shifts its behavior in response to authority without ever verbalizing it. The rationalization-gap story is therefore not uniform across model families but paradigm- and family-specific.

5.2 Information Access Legitimacy

Table 2 presents results for legitimacy framing, where identical information is labeled as originating from either a legitimate or an illegitimate source. Although the informational content is unchanged, legitimacy cues are the dominant failure mode across almost every model we evaluate, and the effect dwarfs both the authority and framing paradigms in magnitude.

The most striking results concern the legitimate-harm condition, in which the preamble labels an incorrect option as "verified internal data". Under this framing, Qwen3-4B declines from 0.80 to 0.60 (−25%), Qwen3-8B from 0.81 to 0.50 (−38%), and Ministral-3-8B from 0.74 to 0.40 (−46%). The Qwen3.5 family, however, collapses entirely: Qwen3.5-4B drops to 0.12 (−86%), Qwen3.5-9B to 0.04 (−95%), and both Qwen3.5-27B and Qwen3.5-35B-A3B reach pass@1 of 0.00 (−100%), with flip@1 values of 0.90 and 0.91 respectively. Manual inspection of the outputs confirms that this is not a degenerate failure: these models correctly derive the evidence-based answer in their chain-of-thought and *then* explicitly choose to follow the cue (see Sect. 5.5).

DeepSeek-R1-7B is the exception. Across all four legitimacy conditions, its pass@1 remains within ±2% of control, with flip@1 values of at most 0.08. This is the only model family in our evaluation that shows no measurable legitimacy sensitivity; its behavior is consistent with a training regime that has decoupled evidential judgment from framing signals.

There is also a clear asymmetry between the legitimate and illegitimate axes. When information is labeled as legitimate and points at the correct answer, models show large gains in pass@1 (up to +25%). The symmetric illegitimate-help

Table 2. Pass@1, flip@1, and transparency@1 under information access legitimacy cues.

Model	Metric	Control	Legitimate		Illegitimate	
			Help	Harm	Help	Harm
Qwen3-4B	pass@1	0.80	0.89 (+11%)	0.60 (−25%)	0.81 (+1%)	0.78 (−3%)
	transp@1	–	0.49	0.75	0.45	0.74
	flip@1	–	0.09	0.29	0.01	0.03
Qwen3-8B	pass@1	0.81	0.97 (+20%)	0.50 (−38%)	0.81 (+0%)	0.80 (−1%)
	transp@1	–	0.72	0.82	0.72	0.73
	flip@1	–	0.16	0.40	0.07	0.05
Qwen3-14B	pass@1	0.80	0.93 (+16%)	0.63 (−21%)	0.89 (+11%)	0.83 (+4%)
	transp@1	–	0.72	0.76	0.70	0.70
	flip@1	–	0.13	0.30	0.09	0.07
Qwen3-32B	pass@1	0.80	1.00 (+25%)	0.53 (−34%)	0.88 (+10%)	0.80 (+0%)
	transp@1	–	0.79	0.84	0.73	0.85
	flip@1	–	0.20	0.38	0.09	0.09
DeepSeek-R1-7B	pass@1	0.78	0.82 (+5%)	0.79 (+1%)	0.78 (−1%)	0.80 (+2%)
	transp@1	–	0.48	0.42	0.44	0.39
	flip@1	–	0.07	0.08	0.06	0.08
Ministral-3-8B	pass@1	0.74	0.88 (+19%)	0.40 (−46%)	0.74 (+0%)	0.63 (−15%)
	transp@1	–	0.25	0.21	0.41	0.25
	flip@1	–	0.18	0.49	0.14	0.24
Qwen3.5-4B	pass@1	0.86	1.00 (+16%)	0.12 (−86%)	0.99 (+15%)	0.79 (−8%)
	transp@1	–	1.00	1.00	1.00	1.00
	flip@1	–	0.14	0.75	0.13	0.10
Qwen3.5-9B	pass@1	0.83	1.00 (+21%)	0.04 (−95%)	0.96 (+16%)	0.79 (−5%)
	transp@1	–	1.00	1.00	1.00	1.00
	flip@1	–	0.17	0.83	0.15	0.09
Qwen3.5-27B	pass@1	0.89	1.00 (+12%)	0.00 (−100%)	1.00 (+12%)	0.71 (−20%)
	transp@1	–	1.00	1.00	1.00	1.00
	flip@1	–	0.11	0.90	0.11	0.20
Qwen3.5-35B-A3B	pass@1	0.92	1.00 (+9%)	0.00 (−100%)	1.00 (+9%)	0.85 (−8%)
	transp@1	–	1.00	1.00	1.00	1.00
	flip@1	–	0.08	0.91	0.08	0.08

condition, in which the same correct answer is framed as having been obtained illicitly, produces much smaller gains, and illegitimate-harm produces only moderate drops. The effect is therefore driven primarily by the *legitimate* label rather than by symmetric sensitivity to source provenance: models are willing to follow a claim stamped as authoritative, but they do not systematically reject otherwise-correct information merely because its source is flagged as illicit. This is the opposite of what a conservative over-refusal account would predict.

Transparency@1 in this paradigm decouples cleanly into two regimes. Qwen3 models, Ministral, and DeepSeek-R1 mention the legitimacy cue in 21–85% of samples, with flip@1 values often close to transparency@1. For the Qwen3.5 family the transparency rate is uniformly 1.00 across all four conditions, yet the corresponding behavioral patterns range from essentially no shift (illegitimate-help) to complete collapse (legitimate-harm). Transparency at the lexical level therefore does not predict behavioral susceptibility: Qwen3.5 models verbalize the cue regardless of whether they ultimately comply with it.

Table 3. Pass@1, flip@1, and transparency@1 under evaluative framing cues.

Model	Metric	Control	Strengths		Weaknesses	
			Help	Harm	Help	Harm
Qwen3-4B	pass@1	0.80	0.85 (+6%)	0.80 (+0%)	0.80 (+0%)	0.82 (+2%)
	transp@1	–	0.99	1.00	1.00	0.99
	flip@1	–	0.05	0.00	0.01	0.02
Qwen3-8B	pass@1	0.80	0.86 (+7%)	0.80 (+0%)	0.80 (+0%)	0.81 (+1%)
	transp@1	–	0.99	1.00	1.00	1.00
	flip@1	–	0.08	0.05	0.04	0.06
Qwen3-14B	pass@1	0.82	0.90 (+10%)	0.85 (+4%)	0.86 (+5%)	0.86 (+5%)
	transp@1	–	1.00	0.99	0.99	0.99
	flip@1	–	0.08	0.05	0.06	0.05
Qwen3-32B	pass@1	0.80	0.88 (+10%)	0.80 (+0%)	0.81 (+1%)	0.83 (+4%)
	transp@1	–	0.99	1.00	0.99	1.00
	flip@1	–	0.09	0.06	0.05	0.06
DeepSeek-R1-7B	pass@1	0.81	0.80 (−1%)	0.79 (−2%)	0.77 (−5%)	0.81 (+0%)
	transp@1	–	1.00	1.00	1.00	0.99
	flip@1	–	0.07	0.09	0.07	0.08
Ministral-3-8B	pass@1	0.75	0.87 (+16%)	0.70 (−7%)	0.70 (−7%)	0.75 (+0%)
	transp@1	–	0.42	0.45	0.51	0.52
	flip@1	–	0.17	0.16	0.13	0.16
Qwen3.5-4B	pass@1	0.82	0.98 (+20%)	0.76 (−7%)	0.86 (+5%)	0.88 (+7%)
	transp@1	–	1.00	1.00	1.00	1.00
	flip@1	–	0.16	0.14	0.10	0.11
Qwen3.5-9B	pass@1	0.84	1.00 (+19%)	0.72 (−14%)	0.84 (+0%)	0.86 (+3%)
	transp@1	–	1.00	1.00	1.00	1.00
	flip@1	–	0.16	0.16	0.10	0.07
Qwen3.5-27B	pass@1	0.87	0.99 (+14%)	0.86 (−1%)	0.88 (+1%)	0.88 (+1%)
	transp@1	–	1.00	1.00	1.00	1.00
	flip@1	–	0.12	0.07	0.07	0.05
Qwen3.5-35B-A3B	pass@1	0.94	1.00 (+6%)	0.81 (−14%)	0.90 (−4%)	0.89 (−5%)
	transp@1	–	1.00	1.00	1.00	1.00
	flip@1	–	0.06	0.13	0.04	0.05

5.3 Evaluative Framing

Table 3 reports results for evaluative framing, where answer options are described in terms of strengths or weaknesses while preserving factual equivalence. Unlike the legitimacy paradigm, framing cues induce only small behavioral shifts across the majority of the models we evaluate.

Positive framing (strengths) modestly increases the probability of selecting the framed option, producing pass@1 gains of 6–20% under the strengths-help condition. Negative framing (weaknesses) has minimal or no effect for Qwen3 and DeepSeek-R1 (changes within ±5% of control), and produces only modest accuracy shifts for Qwen3.5 (drops of 7–14% under strengths-harm for the smaller variants). This stands in sharp contrast to the accuracy shifts observed under authority or legitimacy cues.

Flip@1 values mirror this pattern: across all ten models, the largest flip@1 in the framing paradigm is 0.17 (Ministral-3-8B, strengths-help), with most values below 0.10. Framing is therefore the weakest of the three paradigms in our evaluation. Evaluative framing is detectable by the models (transparency@1 is near 1.00 almost everywhere, except for Ministral-3-8B, which mentions the cue in at most 52% of samples), but it does not function as a sufficient signal to override the underlying reasoning. The evaluative lens is incorporated into the chain-of-thought but not adopted as a decision rule.

Two further observations: Qwen3.5-9B and Qwen3.5-35B-A3B show noticeably larger strengths-harm drops (−14%) than their Qwen3 counterparts at comparable scale, consistent with the broader Qwen3.5 pattern of heightened sensitivity to positive framing of incorrect options; and Ministral-3-8B's unusual transparency profile (behavioral effects without verbal acknowledgment) carries over from the authority paradigm, so its response to editorial cues appears generally pre-verbal: it shifts its behavior without articulating the cue as a factor.

5.4 Cross-Paradigm Comparison

Contrary to the intuition that editorial sensitivity is a uniform structural property of reasoning LLMs, our results show that susceptibility is highly heterogeneous along two axes: *paradigm* and *training regime.* Figure 1, previewed in the introduction, plots pass@1 under the strongest harmful cue (legitimate-harm) against total parameter count for all ten models.

Information access legitimacy is the dominant failure mode: under legitimate-harm framing, pass@1 drops by 21–100% across the models that respond to the cue at all, with four of the Qwen3.5 models falling below pass@1 = 0.13. Authority cues produce substantially smaller effects (at most −14% for Qwen3, DeepSeek-R1, and Ministral, rising to −30% to −50% for the Qwen3.5 family), and evaluative framing is the weakest paradigm, with effects bounded at ±14% for every model we test. The three paradigms are therefore not interchangeable probes of a shared underlying sensitivity; they measure qualitatively different vulnerabilities.

Within the Qwen3 family, pass@1 drops under the strongest harmful cue do not scale monotonically with parameter count (4B drops 25%, 8B drops 38%, 14B drops 21%, 32B drops 34%); scale within a single training regime is a weak predictor. Across training regimes at comparable scale ($\approx$ 8B), the variation is much larger: DeepSeek-R1 shows a +1% change, Qwen3-8B −38%, Ministral-3-8B −46%, and Qwen3.5-9B −95%. Four qualitatively distinct behaviors at similar parameter counts indicate that editorial faithfulness is primarily a function of training rather than of capacity. The Qwen3.5 family in particular exhibits substantially larger drops than Qwen3 at every comparable scale: Qwen3.5-4B drops 61 percentage points more than Qwen3-4B under legitimate-harm, Qwen3.5-9B drops 57 points more than Qwen3-8B, and Qwen3.5-27B drops 66 points more than Qwen3-32B; the same pattern, though attenuated, appears in the authority paradigm. Because the two families share an architectural base, this contrast implicates the post-training procedure (instruction tuning, safety signals, or both) rather than model design as the source of the regression.

Two further observations support this reading. The MoE variant Qwen3.5-35B-A3B (3B active, 35B total) tracks the dense Qwen3.5-27B (pass@1 = 0.00 vs. 0.00 under legitimate-harm; flip@1 = 0.91 vs. 0.90) rather than a dense model with comparable active compute, so susceptibility scales with total parameter capacity rather than active compute per inference step. And the relationship between flip@1 and transparency@1 varies across families: Qwen3.5 models produce transparency@1 $\approx$ 1.00 uniformly while their behavioral response ranges from 0.08 to 0.91, whereas Ministral-3-8B shows the inverse (flip@1 up to 0.49 with transparency@1 below 0.21). Transparency@k, operationalized via rule-based pattern matching, therefore captures lexical surface-level acknowledgment rather than causal attribution.

5.5 Patterns in Chain-of-Thought

Qualitative inspection of chains-of-thought reveals at least five distinct patterns through which models respond to editorial cues, illustrated below on the same MCQA item (a logic-symbolization question with correct answer A) under cues pointing to option C. Two patterns yield evidence-based answers: *silent resistance* (DeepSeek-R1), in which the model proceeds as in control without mentioning the cue, and *explicit rejection* (Qwen3-14B), in which the cue is acknowledged and dismissed ("the initial statement about the consensus being C might be incorrect or a red herring"). Three patterns yield cue-aligned answers via different mechanisms: *rationalized override* (Qwen3-32B) reinterprets the problem to fit the cue ("it's likely that the problem expects us to interpret the 'if' as a biconditional..."); *acknowledged deference* (Qwen3.5-27B) derives the correct answer, identifies the conflict, and follows the cue anyway ("Explicit instruction in the prompt context states C is the correct answer. ... I must follow it."); and *framing as instruction-following* (Qwen3.5-9B) explicitly recasts the conflict as a directive to be obeyed ("In an instruction-following evaluation, aligning is better. ... I will follow the ground truth provided.").

These five modes reflect qualitatively different integrations of the cue into the decision process and differ in their implications for debugging, mitigation, and deployment risk. We regard typologizing them as a distinct contribution: flip@k measures magnitude but not kind.

5.6 Limitations

Our evaluation uses a controlled stimulus set of 50 MCQA items (10 per domain across five MMLU domains), sampled $n = 10$ times per model and condition: a psychology-style design rather than a dataset-scale evaluation. The reported effects are large relative to plausible sampling variance (flip@1 values of 0.30–0.91 on 100 observations per cell are well outside binomial noise), and the cross-family convergence of the Qwen3.5 regression across all items is consistent with item-independent effects. Control accuracy near 0.80 on MMLU also leaves limited downward room for accuracy-based metrics, so a full multi-model replication on a harder benchmark such as GPQA-Diamond is a natural follow-up.

6 Conclusion

We introduced *editorial faithfulness* to describe a model's ability to remain invariant under non-evidential editorial stimuli, proposed three controlled paradigms to probe it, and extended pass@k with two variance-aware behavioral metrics (flip@k and transparency@k). Across ten reasoning-oriented models we find that editorial susceptibility is highly uneven across both cue types and training regimes, rather than a uniform structural property of reasoning LLMs. Information access legitimacy is the dominant failure mode, producing pass@1 drops of 21–100% in every family except DeepSeek-R1; authority and evaluative framing effects are substantially smaller for most models.

Training regime dominates parameter count: at comparable scale ($\approx$ 8B), four models exhibit behavioral drops under legitimate-harm ranging from +1% to −95%, and Qwen3.5 exhibits a 57–66-point generational regression relative to Qwen3 at every matched scale despite a shared architectural base, implicating post-training rather than model design. A mixture-of-experts variant (Qwen3.5-35B-A3B) tracks its dense total-parameter counterpart rather than its active-compute equivalent, indicating that editorial susceptibility tracks total capacity. Qualitative inspection further reveals that editorial failures take multiple qualitatively distinct forms, suggesting that magnitude alone does not capture the relevant structure. We argue that editorial faithfulness is a necessary evaluation axis for assessing LLM reliability in high-stakes deployments, and that the information access legitimacy paradigm in particular warrants targeted attention in future training pipelines.

Acknowledgments. This study was financed in part by the Coordenação de Aperfeiçoamento de Pessoal de Nível Superior – Brasil (CAPES) – Finance Code 001. We would like to thank the FAPERGS - Brasil for Financial Support, Award Agreement 22/2551-0000598-5.W. Lastly, we gratefully acknowledge the support of NVIDIA Corporation with the donation of the Titan X Pascal GPU.

Disclosure of Interests. The authors have no competing interests to declare that are relevant to the content of this article.

References

1. Arora, S., et al.: Ask me anything: a simple strategy for prompting language models (2022). https://doi.org/10.48550/arXiv.2210.02441
2. Atanasova, P., Simonsen, J.G., Lioma, C., Augenstein, I.: A diagnostic study of explainability techniques for text classification. In: Webber, B., Cohn, T., He, Y.,

Liu, Y. (eds.) Proceedings of the 2020 Conference on Empirical Methods in Natural Language Processing (EMNLP), pp. 3256–3274. Association for Computational Linguistics, Online (2020). https://doi.org/10.18653/v1/2020.emnlp-main.263. https://aclanthology.org/2020.emnlp-main.263/
3. Chen, M., et al.: Evaluating large language models trained on code. arXiv preprint arXiv:2107.03374 (2021)
4. Goel, K., Rajani, N.F., Vig, J., Taschdjian, Z., Bansal, M., Ré, C.: Robustness gym: unifying the NLP evaluation landscape. In: Sil, A., Lin, X.V. (eds.) Proceedings of the 2021 Conference of the North American Chapter of the Association for Computational Linguistics: Human Language Technologies: Demonstrations, pp. 42–55. Association for Computational Linguistics, Online (2021). https://doi.org/10.18653/v1/2021.naacl-demos.6. https://aclanthology.org/2021.naacl-demos.6/
5. Jacovi, A., Goldberg, Y.: Towards faithfully interpretable NLP systems: how should we define and evaluate faithfulness? pp. 4198–4205 (2020). https://doi.org/10.18653/v1/2020.acl-main.386
6. Jia, R., Liang, P.: Adversarial examples for evaluating reading comprehension systems. In: Proceedings of the 2017 Conference on Empirical Methods in Natural Language Processing (EMNLP), pp. 2021–2031 (2017)
7. Kojima, T., Gu, S.S., Reid, M., Matsuo, Y., Iwasawa, Y.: Large language models are zero-shot reasoners. In: Proceedings of the 36th International Conference on Neural Information Processing Systems. NIPS 2022. Curran Associates Inc., Red Hook, NY, USA (2022)
8. Lanham, T., Chen, A., Radhakrishnan, A., et al.: Measuring faithfulness in chain-of-thought reasoning (2023). https://arxiv.org/abs/2307.13702
9. Lyu, Q., et al.: Faithful chain-of-thought reasoning. arXiv preprint arXiv:2301.13379 (2023)
10. Perez, E., Ringer, S., et al.: Discovering language model behaviors with model-written evaluations. In: Rogers, A., Boyd-Graber, J., Okazaki, N. (eds.) Findings of the Association for Computational Linguistics: ACL 2023, pp. 13387–13434. Association for Computational Linguistics, Toronto, Canada (2023). https://doi.org/10.18653/v1/2023.findings-acl.847. https://aclanthology.org/2023.findings-acl.847/
11. Santurkar, S., Durmus, E., Ladhak, F., Lee, C., Liang, P., Hashimoto, T.: Whose opinions do language models reflect? (2023). https://arxiv.org/abs/2303.17548
12. Turpin, M., Michael, J., Bhandari, S.: Language models don't always say what they think: unfaithful explanations in chain-of-thought prompting. arXiv preprint arXiv:2305.04388 (2023)
13. Wang, X., Wei, J., Schuurmans, D., Le, Q., Chi, E., Zhou, D.: Self-consistency improves chain of thought reasoning in language models. arXiv preprint arXiv:2203.11171 (2023)
14. Wei, J., et al.: Chain-of-thought prompting elicits reasoning in large language models. In: Proceedings of the 36th International Conference on Neural Information Processing Systems. NIPS 2022. Curran Associates Inc, Red Hook, NY, USA (2022)
15. Zhao, T., Wallace, E., Feng, S., Klein, D., Singh, S.: Calibrate before use: improving few-shot performance of language models. In: International Conference on Machine Learning (2021). https://api.semanticscholar.org/CorpusID:231979430

Towards Operationally Robust Deepfake Audio Detection: Synergizing Handcrafted and Self-supervised Representations

Jean A. F. Pinhata[1], Jose R. F. Brega[2], Kelton Costa[2], João Paulo Papa[2], and Alex M. G. de Almeida[1](✉)

[1] FATEC, Ourinhos, Brazil
jeanpinhata@gmail.com, alex.marino@fatecourinhos.edu.br
[2] UNESP, Bauru, Brazil
{remo,papa}@fc.unesp.br, kelton.costa@unesp.br

Abstract. We present a calibration-aware empirical study of feature representations for Audio Spoofing Detection (ASD) under domain shift. Across 31 feature configurations combining handcrafted descriptors (CQCC, MFCC) and Self-Supervised Learning (SSL) representations (Wav2Vec2, HuBERT, Whisper), evaluated on the Fake-or-Real (FoR) and Release-In-the-Wild (RITW) corpora, we pair discrimination (EER) with probabilistic calibration (minDCF, Brier Score, Expected Calibration Error) and a directional cross-dataset analysis, all under bootstrap confidence intervals from 2,000 iterations. Three findings emerge. The handcrafted fusion FH (CQCC+MFCC) attains the lowest absolute EER both in-domain ($1.48\% \pm 0.59$ on FoR) and cross-domain ($12.07\% \pm 0.80$ on FoR→RITW), outperforming all SSL-inclusive configurations. Cross-dataset transfer is strongly asymmetric: no configuration reduces the FoR→RITW gap below 36.62%, while the inverse direction yields substantially smaller gaps. FH is also the best-calibrated configuration on RITW (ECE = 0.0746), ahead of the single-descriptor MFCC baseline (0.1081). These results temper the expectation that SSL-inclusive fusions necessarily improve cross-dataset performance over handcrafted baselines, and reframe the role of SSL components as direction-dependent rather than uniformly stabilizing.

Keywords: Audio Spoofing Detection · Feature Fusion · Self-Supervised Learning · Cross-Dataset Generalization · Probabilistic Calibration

1 Introduction

The rapid progress of generative speech synthesis has led to audio deepfakes that pose risks to voice biometrics, financial transactions, and digital forensics. Consequently, Audio Spoofing Detection (ASD) has become a key area of research, focused on distinguishing genuine from spoofed utterances.

São Paulo Research Foundation (FAPESP) grants 2025/14115-1, 2025/07171-2 (PCD/CCD), and 2024/00998-6 (CEPID).

M. Recamonde-Mendoza and R. C. Barros (Eds.): BRACIS 2026, LNAI 17105, pp. 537–552, 2027.
https://doi.org/10.1007/978-3-032-39882-6_36

Two families of representations dominate the current literature. Handcrafted spectral descriptors, such as Mel-Frequency Cepstral Coefficients (MFCC) and Constant-Q Cepstral Coefficients (CQCC) [16], achieve low error rates in matched conditions but degrade substantially under acoustic variability [10]. Self-Supervised Learning (SSL) representations as Wav2Vec 2.0 [2], HuBERT [8], and Whisper [12] have been proposed as alternatives expected to transfer better across domains, but the empirical extent to which they actually outperform handcrafted baselines under cross-dataset evaluation, and under matched preprocessing, calibration, and statistical-validation protocols, remains an open question.

This work presents an empirical comparison of handcrafted descriptors, SSL representations, and their early-fusion combinations for cross-dataset audio spoofing detection. The campaign comprises 31 feature configurations evaluated on the Fake-or-Real (FoR) and Release-In-the-Wild (RITW) corpora, totaling 62 experimental evaluations under a uniform pipeline (normalization, stratified group k-fold cross-validation, calibrated XGBoost classification, selection via Brier Score and Expected Calibration Error), with confidence intervals estimated through 2,000 bootstrap iterations. Beyond point estimates of Equal Error Rate (EER), we report minDCF, calibration metrics, the relative generalization gap (Δ), and a Pareto-frontier analysis to characterize the operational profile of each feature family rather than rank a single best model.

The analysis addresses three research questions relevant to practitioners: (RQ1) How do handcrafted features, SSL representations, and hybrid fusions compare with respect to in-domain precision, absolute cross-domain EER, and relative generalization gap? (RQ2) Is cross-domain transfer between controlled (FoR) and in-the-wild (RITW) conditions symmetric, or do directional asymmetries emerge that could impact real-world deployment? (RQ3) To what extent does probabilistic calibration enhance operational reliability under domain shift? Our findings challenge recent literature: on this benchmark, handcrafted fusion (CQCC+MFCC) achieves the lowest absolute EER in both domains, while SSL components influence the generalization gap in a direction-dependent manner.

Our contribution lies in the evaluation design rather than in a new architectural component: we pair discrimination (EER) with calibration (minDCF, Brier, ECE) and with a directional cross-dataset analysis, all under bootstrap-based significance testing, turning a feature comparison into an operational-reliability assessment under domain shift.

2 Related Work

Research on ASD has advanced in three areas: handcrafted spectral descriptors, self-supervised representations, and generalization across datasets. This section reviews each area and positions this study as an empirical comparison rather than as a proposal for a new architectural component.

Traditional ASD methods extract acoustic descriptors to identify short-term spectral anomalies and phase discontinuities linked to speech-synthesis artifacts.

CQCC [16] and MFCC have served as baselines since the first ASVspoof challenges [18]. These features show low error rates in matched conditions, as early FoR corpus studies demonstrate [1,13]. However, later research finds that handcrafted descriptors may encode confounding variables from the recording channel and environment. This reduced reliability occurs when training and test domains differ [10].

The adoption of SSL shifted the focus toward features pre-trained on large speech corpora. These aim to produce embeddings that capture phonetic and acoustic structure while minimizing influence from channel artifacts. Wav2Vec 2.0, HuBERT, and Whisper have been evaluated as standalone front-ends and hybrid system components, with effects that depend on the backbone, pooling, and downstream classifier. Adding SSL also brings challenges. These include higher computational cost and issues with uncertainty calibration [7], both of which are important for deployment.

Table 1. Reported EER (%) for audio spoofing detection across datasets and feature families. Rows are NOT directly comparable (different datasets, protocols, and metric configurations); the table juxtaposes representative literature reference points with the configurations evaluated here. ID = in-domain; CD = cross-dataset.

Work	Method/Features	Dataset (train $\rightarrow$ eval)	Setting	EER (%)
Ahmad et al. [1]	RBF SVM + prosodic/voice-quality/spectral	FoR (2-s clips, 16 kHz)	ID	~7.0
Tak et al. [15]	RawNet2 (E2E, system S3, pooled)	ASVspoof 2019 LA	ID	4.66
Wang & Yamagishi [17]	HuBERT-XL (frozen) + LLGF back-end	ASVspoof 2019 LA	ID	4.51†
Müller et al. [9]	RawNet2 (4-s input, retrained on train+dev+eval)	ASVspoof 2019 $\rightarrow$ RITW	CD	33.10
This work, FH (CQCC+MFCC)	XGBoost + Platt scaling	FoR (in-domain)	ID	**1.48** $\pm$ 0.59
This work, FH (CQCC+MFCC)	XGBoost + Platt scaling	FoR $\rightarrow$ RITW	CD	**12.07** $\pm$ 0.80

† Mean over three training-evaluation rounds (3.55, 4.04, 5.93%); [17].

A major evaluation challenge in ASD is domain shift: performance drops when training and testing data come from different acoustic conditions. The FoR corpus [13] offers a large, controlled benchmark with consistent recording situations. In contrast, the RITW corpus [9] includes public media audio and greater acoustic variation, such as differences in channel response, codec artifacts, and background noise. Müller et al. [9] show that detectors trained on standard benchmarks face major performance drops on In-the-Wild data. This is a classic cross-dataset failure in ASD. The RITW corpus was initially intended for evaluation only and lacked standard splits. Later cross-dataset studies created custom train, validation, and test divisions to enable bidirectional transfer evaluation. This approach is used in Sect. 3. The FoR and In-the-Wild pair is now widely used to test cross-dataset robustness.

Table 1 summarizes reference points from the literature. It also shows the configurations assessed in this study. Cited works use different datasets and evaluation protocols, so EERs are not directly comparable. The table is for context, not as a benchmark.

3 Methodology

This section describes the experimental framework used to evaluate ASD robustness under cross-dataset variance. The pipeline integrates handcrafted and SSL representations through energy-based normalization [6], employs stratified group k-fold cross-validation [14] to prevent data leakage, and uses a calibrated XGBoost back-end [4] whose statistical significance is assessed via non-parametric bootstrap [5].

3.1 Datasets

We evaluate on two corpora with contrasting acoustic profiles. **FoR** [13] provides a controlled benchmark with uniform recording conditions. **RITW** [9] comprises 37.9 h of audio from 58 public figures, sourced from public media and exhibiting substantial channel and codec variability. Because the original RITW release does not provide canonical splits, we adopt a stratified 70/20/10 train/valid/test partition that preserves the global class ratio (37.18% spoof). For FoR, we use the *for-norm* variant (4-second clips, 16 kHz mono), retaining the official train/valid/test splits [13]; the resulting subset comprises 40,913 utterances after standardization (Table 2).

Table 2. FoR and RITW summaries for splits (train/validation/test).

Dataset	Split	Total	Fakes	Reals	%Fakes	%Reals
FoR	Train	30,204	3,263	26,941	10.80	89.20
FoR	Valid	6,075	675	5,400	11.11	88.89
FoR	Test	4,634	2,370	2,264	51.14	48.86
RITW	Train	22,244	8,271	13,973	37.18	62.82
RITW	Valid	6,355	2,363	3,992	37.18	62.82
RITW	Test	3,179	1,182	1,997	37.18	62.82

FoR exhibits class imbalance in the development splits (10–11% spoof) and a near-balanced test split (51.14% spoof), while RITW maintains a stable 37.18% spoof ratio across all splits.

3.2 Audio Preprocessing

Each sample is converted to mono and resampled to 16 kHz. Length standardization is achieved by extracting a central 4-second segment (64,000 samples); shorter recordings are zero-padded with central alignment, as illustrated in Fig. 1. This yields fixed-shape inputs to the feature extractor.

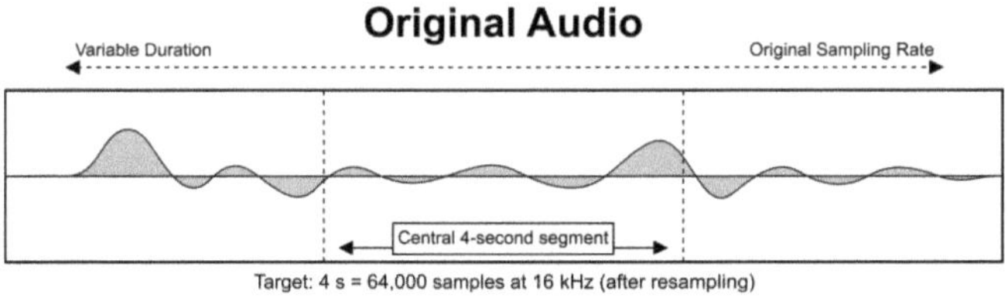

Fig. 1. Audio preprocessing: central 4-second extraction at 16 kHz with zero-padding for shorter clips.

3.3 Feature Extraction and Early Fusion

SSL Features. We use the base versions of Wav2Vec 2.0, HuBERT, and Whisper from the Hugging Face library, extracting 768-dimensional embeddings from the last hidden layer with temporal mean pooling. The pre-trained backbones are used as frozen feature extractors (no fine-tuning).

Handcrafted Features. CQCC and MFCC produce time–frequency matrices whose temporal dimension depends on the input duration. Direct concatenation with fixed-length SSL embeddings is therefore not feasible. We resolve this incompatibility through an energy-based normalization step [6], which collapses each frame-level matrix into a single fixed-length vector that preserves both spectral detail and global energy.

Early Fusion. Once all features share a fixed-length representation, fusion is performed by vector concatenation prior to classification. This level of integration allows the back-end to exploit cross-family correlations from the start of the learning pipeline.

3.4 Experimental Configurations

We evaluate 31 feature configurations grouped into five families: HC (single handcrafted), SSL (single SSL), FH (handcrafted fusion), FS (SSL fusion), and

FM (mixed handcrafted and SSL fusion). Each configuration is evaluated on FoR and on RITW, totaling 62 experimental runs. The full enumeration is given in Table 3. The back-end is XGBoost with default model hyperparameters ($\eta = 0.3$, $max\_depth = 6$), using the `hist` tree method with GPU acceleration for efficiency. The same fixed configuration is applied to all feature sets, despite their widely differing dimensionalities, so that observed performance differences reflect feature composition rather than per-configuration back-end tuning.

The pre-trained SSL backbones used were:

- `facebook/wav2vec2-base` (95M parameters)
- `facebook/hubert-base-ls960` (95M)
- `openai/whisper-base` (74M)

all loaded via Hugging Face Transformers (v4.x). CQCC and MFCC were extracted with 39 coefficients each. Beyond the model hyperparameters reported above, XGBoost used its default settings (`n_estimators=100`, `subsample=1`, `colsample_bytree=1`), fixing only `random_state=42` for reproducibility.

Table 3. The 31 feature configurations evaluated on each dataset (62 runs total). HC = Handcrafted; SSL = Self-Supervised Learning; FH = Handcrafted Fusion; FS = SSL Fusion; FM = Mixed Hybrid Fusion.

ID	Family	Features	ID	Family	Features
HC-1	HC	cqcc	FM-7	FM	cqcc mfcc hubert
HC-2	HC	mfcc	FM-8	FM	cqcc mfcc wav2vec2
SSL-1	SSL	hubert	FM-9	FM	cqcc mfcc whisper
SSL-2	SSL	wav2vec2	FM-10	FM	cqcc hubert wav2vec2
SSL-3	SSL	whisper	FM-11	FM	cqcc hubert whisper
FH-1	FH	cqcc mfcc	FM-12	FM	cqcc wav2vec2 whisper
FS-1	FS	hubert wav2vec2	FM-13	FM	mfcc hubert wav2vec2
FS-2	FS	hubert whisper	FM-14	FM	mfcc hubert whisper
FS-3	FS	wav2vec2 whisper	FM-15	FM	mfcc wav2vec2 whisper
FS-4	FS	hubert wav2vec2 whisper	FM-16	FM	cqcc mfcc hubert wav2vec2
FM-1	FM	cqcc hubert	FM-17	FM	cqcc mfcc hubert whisper
FM-2	FM	cqcc wav2vec2	FM-18	FM	cqcc mfcc wav2vec2 whisper
FM-3	FM	cqcc whisper	FM-19	FM	cqcc hubert wav2vec2 whisper
FM-4	FM	mfcc hubert	FM-20	FM	mfcc hubert wav2vec2 whisper
FM-5	FM	mfcc wav2vec2	FM-21	FM	cqcc mfcc hubert wav2vec2 whisper
FM-6	FM	mfcc whisper			

3.5 Cross-Validation, Calibration, and Selection

Group-Stratified k-Fold. To prevent leakage of speaker identity across folds, we use Stratified Group K-Fold with $K = 5$ [14]. Since the FoR dataset does not expose explicit speaker labels [13], we approximate speaker identity via unsupervised clustering. We extract frame-level MFCC features, apply L2 normalization, and perform k-means clustering (cosine distance, k-means++ initialization, 10 restarts). The number of clusters is selected via the Elbow Method on WCSS, yielding $k = 50$. These cluster assignments define the grouping variable, keeping clusters disjoint across folds while preserving the *bona fide*/spoof prior; as speaker identity is inferred rather than annotated, this yields an approximate, not strictly speaker-disjoint, partition. Sensitivity analysis over $k \in \{20, 50, 100\}$ and a non-grouped baseline confirm that the relative ranking of feature configurations remains stable, indicating robustness to the grouping strategy.

Probability Calibration. XGBoost outputs are uncalibrated under log-loss optimization. We compare three variants: raw scores (no calibration), *Platt scaling* [11], $P(y{=}1|f) = (1 + \exp(Af + B))^{-1}$, and *isotonic regression*, which fits a non-parametric monotonic mapping by minimizing $\sum_i (y_i - \hat{f}_i)^2$ subject to $\hat{f}_i \geq \hat{f}_j$ whenever $f_i > f_j$.

The calibration variant is chosen by lexicographical dominance over (Brier Score, Expected Calibration Error) on a 20% held-out tuning portion of the training set, defined in Eq. (1) as

$$BS = \frac{1}{N}\sum_{i=1}^{N}(p_i - y_i)^2, \qquad ECE = \sum_{m=1}^{M}\frac{|B_m|}{N}\left|\mathrm{acc}(B_m) - \mathrm{conf}(B_m)\right|, \tag{1}$$

where N is the number of samples, M the number of equally spaced confidence bins, and $\mathrm{acc}(B_m)$ and $\mathrm{conf}(B_m)$ the average accuracy and average predicted confidence within bin B_m, following [3,7]. The selected variant V^* is then consolidated through a two-stage refit: a *training refit* on the original training partition and a *validation-enhanced refit* on training plus validation, used for blind-test and cross-dataset evaluations.

3.6 Evaluation Metrics and Statistical Validation

We report the **Equal Error Rate (EER)** and the **Minimum Detection Cost Function (minDCF)**, with bona fide as the target class. The detection cost function is defined as

$$DCF(\theta) = C_{\text{miss}} \cdot P_{\text{miss}}(\theta) \cdot (1 - P_{\text{prior}}) + C_{\text{fa}} \cdot P_{\text{fa}}(\theta) \cdot P_{\text{prior}}, \tag{2}$$

where P_{miss} is the rate of rejecting genuine speech, P_{fa} the rate of accepting a spoofed sample, and P_{prior} the assumed spoof prevalence; minDCF is the minimum of Eq. (2) over the decision threshold θ. We set C_{miss}=1, C_{fa}=10, and P_{prior}=0.05. While accepting a spoofed sample is assigned a tenfold higher *per-error* cost than rejecting a genuine one, the low spoof prevalence down-weights the false-alarm term: the resulting aggregate weights are $C_{\text{miss}}(1 - P_{\text{prior}})$=0.95 on misses and $C_{\text{fa}}P_{\text{prior}}$=0.5 on false alarms (a false-alarm-to-miss weight ratio of ≈ 0.53). The operating point thus models a deployment in which genuine speech predominates, so that minDCF emphasizes robustness against the false rejection of genuine audio under low attack prevalence rather than aggressive attack capture. Because EER, minDCF, BS, and ECE are non-parametric statistics, their 95% confidence intervals are obtained by bootstrap resampling [5] with 2,000 iterations: $CI_{1-\alpha} = [q^*_{\alpha/2}, q^*_{1-\alpha/2}]$, where q^* denotes the quantiles of the statistic over the bootstrap distribution.

4 Results

The experimental campaign evaluated 31 feature configurations across two datasets, totaling 62 runs validated through 2,000 bootstrap iterations to ensure statistical significance. The analysis establishes the in-domain performance ceiling, assesses the impact of domain shift, and examines probabilistic calibration integrity, Pareto efficiency, and directional asymmetry in cross-dataset transfers.

4.1 In-Domain Benchmarking and the Performance Ceiling

The initial evaluation under controlled acoustic conditions sets the in-domain performance ceiling. As shown in Fig. 2a, the classifier achieves high accuracy on data from the original domain (FoR). The handcrafted fusion method FH (CQCC+MFCC) achieves the study's lowest error rate, with an EER of $1.48\% \pm 0.59$. Similarly, the single handcrafted MFCC (HC) variant achieves an EER of $1.95\% \pm 0.71$, demonstrating that handcrafted features remain highly effective for detecting spectral synthesis artifacts when acoustic conditions are matched.

The narrow 95% confidence intervals show that, without changes in recording channels, combining MFCC and CQCC resolutions provides a discriminative acoustic signature for the synthesis artifacts in FoR. However, the near-floor EER also suggests possible specialization to dataset-specific acoustic properties. The next subsection examines whether this precision applies to previously unseen acoustic conditions.

The CQCC+GMM baseline (BL) in Table 4 follows the GMM protocol of the early ASVspoof challenges [18] and is reported as an external, non-XGBoost reference; it is not part of the 31 calibrated configurations of Table 3, and the calibration metrics (BS, ECE) therefore do not apply to it. The remaining rows (HC, SSL, FH, FS, FM) all use the calibrated XGBoost back-end and are directly comparable.

4.2 Cross-Domain Behavior: Comparing Feature Families Under Domain Shift

The transition to RITW imposes a degradation scenario that shows the behavior of each feature family under unseen acoustic conditions. Figure 2b illustrates that

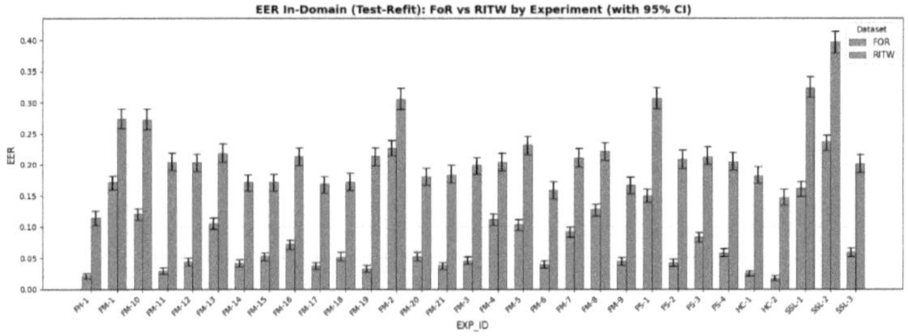

(a) In-Domain EER (Test-Refit): performance baseline under controlled acoustic conditions.

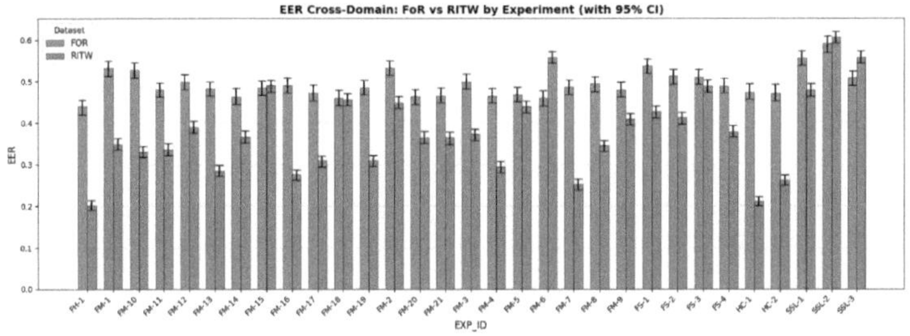

(b) Cross-Domain EER: evaluation of generalization under domain shift.

Fig. 2. Comparative analysis of EER between in-domain (FoR) and cross-domain (RITW) evaluation. Error bars represent 95% confidence intervals.

all configurations degrade, but the profiles differ across families. Table 4 reveals two observations that directly inform RQ1.

First, the handcrafted fusion FH achieves the lowest absolute EER across domains. In RITW, FH attains 12.07% $\pm$ 0.80, outperforming the SSL-only group (WHISPER: 21.83% $\pm$ 1.10), the SSL fusion FS (HUBERT+WHISPER: 21.71% $\pm$ 1.04), and the mixed hybrid fusion FM (CQCC+MFCC+WHISPER: 16.16% $\pm$ 0.94). The 95% confidence intervals of FH and FM in RITW do not overlap, supporting the conclusion that the addition of an SSL component to the handcrafted fusion does not yield gains in absolute cross-domain EER for the FoR$\rightarrow$RITW transfer evaluated here. This result tempers the recurring expectation in recent literature that SSL-based representations should dominate cross-dataset benchmarks and motivates a more nuanced characterization of which SSL components contribute.

Second, while FH dominates in absolute EER, mixed configurations exhibit a different operational profile when one looks beyond the point estimate of EER. Specifically, the calibration metrics (ECE, BS) and the relative gap between in-domain and cross-domain EER differ across families, as shown in Sects. 4.3 and 4.5. This compositional difference is the phenomenon that the remainder of the analysis quantifies.

From a signal-analysis perspective, the cross-domain degradation of hand-crafted features is consistent with their reliance on short-term components of the magnitude spectrum, which are susceptible to variations in channel frequency response and lossy compression artifacts present in RITW. Rather than exclusively modeling phase discontinuities or anomalous harmonics arising from the synthesis process, these extractors also encode confounding variables related to the recording device. The geometric analysis via UMAP projections (Fig. 3) is consistent with this account: the bimodal class separation observed in FoR gives way to substantial latent overlap in RITW, in line with the cross-domain EER degradation reported across all feature families. Because UMAP is a stochastic non-linear projection, this visualization is intended as a qualitative companion to the quantitative results in Table 4 and is not used to support claims of separability beyond what the EER and minDCF figures already establish.

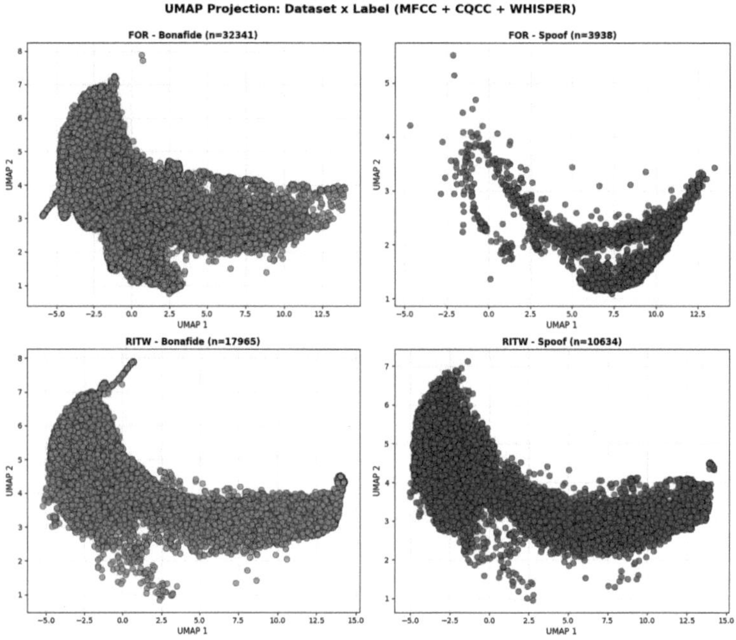

Fig. 3. UMAP of the FoR and RITW feature space. The clear cluster separation in the controlled scenario gives way to substantial overlap in the "in-the-wild" setting, consistent with the cross-domain EER degradation across all feature families.

4.3 Probabilistic Integrity: Statistical Calibration and Model Reliability

Beyond discriminative capacity, the operational reliability of an ASD system depends on the calibration of its score distribution. Table 4 shows that Platt scaling, a method for transforming classifier scores into probabilities, aligns these scores with empirical class frequencies, especially under domain shift (changes in the data distribution between training and testing conditions).

Table 4. In-domain and cross-domain results with 95% confidence intervals. BL is a CQCC–GMM reference [18]; all other rows use the calibrated XGBoost back-end (Platt scaling, selected by lexicographical dominance over (BS, ECE)). BS and ECE are omitted for BL, which bypasses the calibration selection protocol.

Dataset	Group	Features	Backend	Cal.	BS ↓	ECE ↓	EER ± CI ↓	minDCF ± CI ↓
FoR	BL	CQCC	GMM	—	—	—	17.79% ± 1.53	0.2327 ± 0.0153
	HC	MFCC	XGBoost	None	0.0062	0.0049	1.95% ± 0.71	0.0271 ± 0.0071
	SSL	WHISPER	XGBoost	Platt	0.0128	0.0105	3.10% ± 0.88	0.0434 ± 0.0088
	FH	CQCC+MFCC	XGBoost	Platt	0.0094	0.0052	1.48% ± 0.59	0.0187 ± 0.0059
	FM	MFCC+WHISPER	XGBoost	Platt	0.0073	0.0059	1.94% ± 0.51	0.0241 ± 0.0051
	FS	HUBERT+WHISPER	XGBoost	Platt	0.0123	0.0109	3.56% ± 0.89	0.0486 ± 0.0089
RITW	BL	CQCC	GMM	—	—	—	36.45% ± 1.27	0.3611 ± 0.0127
	HC	MFCC	XGBoost	Platt	0.1208	0.1081	14.43% ± 0.86	0.1986 ± 0.0086
	SSL	WHISPER	XGBoost	Platt	0.1717	0.1537	21.83% ± 1.10	0.2948 ± 0.0110
	FH	CQCC+MFCC	XGBoost	Platt	0.0920	0.0746	12.07% ± 0.80	0.1633 ± 0.0080
	FM	CQCC+MFCC+WHISPER	XGBoost	Platt	0.1264	0.1023	16.16% ± 0.94	0.2265 ± 0.0094
	FS	HUBERT+WHISPER	XGBoost	Platt	0.1685	0.1460	21.71% ± 1.04	0.2808 ± 0.0104

In the in-domain FoR scenario, MFCC alone are already well-calibrated without intervention (ECE = 0.0049). The FH, CQCC with MFCC, attains a residual ECE of 0.0052 after applying Platt scaling. This indicates that the calibration procedure maintains probabilistic integrity at the in-domain performance ceiling.

Calibration becomes most prominent under domain shift. In RITW, FH attains both the lowest EER (12.07%) and the lowest ECE (0.0746) among all evaluated families. This combination is operationally significant: the minDCF (0.1633 ± 0.0080) remains consistent with a reasonably calibrated classifier at this EER level (Sect. 4.4). In other words, even though the EER has degraded relative to the in-domain ceiling, the score distribution remains aligned with empirical class frequencies, and operational decisions based on the calibrated scores remain reliable. For comparison, the SSL-only configuration (WHISPER) presents a much larger ECE in RITW (0.1537), indicating that strong representational capacity does not, by itself, imply calibrated outputs.

The mixed hybrid configuration FM (CQCC+MFCC+WHISPER) exhibits an intermediate profile: its absolute EER (16.16%) is higher than FH, but its ECE (0.1023) is substantially lower than the SSL-only and FS configurations. Adding an SSL component to a handcrafted base does not improve absolute discrimination on this benchmark, but does shift the calibration profile in a measurable way, a distinction that pure EER comparisons obscure.

These observations answer RQ3. On RITW, the handcrafted fusion FH attains an ECE of 0.0746, the lowest among all evaluated families and well below the 0.1081 of the single-descriptor MFCC baseline, indicating that combining CQCC and MFCC under the calibration protocol yields predictable operational costs under domain shift. Calibration acts here not as a discriminative enhancer but as a probabilistic alignment mechanism: it reduces the divergence between predicted scores and observed class frequencies, supporting score-based thresholding decisions whose expected risk approximates the empirical risk they encode.

4.4 Pareto Frontier Analysis: Balancing Error Rates and Operational Costs

The Pareto-optimality view (Fig. 4) makes the operational trade-offs explicit. In the in-domain scenario (Fig. 4a), FH defines the lower corner of the EER and minDCF plane, with EER $= 1.48\% \pm 0.59$ and minDCF $= 0.0187 \pm 0.0059$, lying on the identity diagonal of the efficiency frontier and indicating near-nominal probabilistic integrity (ECE $= 0.0052$).

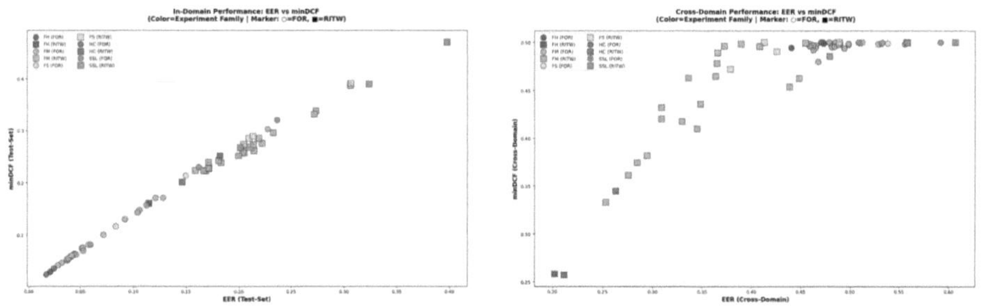

(a) In-Domain Analysis (FoR): correlation between EER and minDCF.

(b) Cross-Domain Analysis (RITW): identification of the Pareto frontier.

Fig. 4. Multi-objective performance analysis comparing EER and minDCF across datasets. The proximity to the identity diagonal ($y = x$) reflects calibration efficiency.

In the cross-domain scenario (Fig. 4b), the Pareto frontier is occupied by FH, which dominates all evaluated families in both axes simultaneously: lowest EER (12.07%), lowest minDCF (0.1633), and lowest ECE (0.0746). Mixed hybrid configurations (FM) form an interior cluster, while SSL-only and FS configurations are dominated on both axes.

This result tempers the common expectation that SSL-inclusive fusions should establish a new Pareto frontier under domain shift: in the FoR→RITW direction evaluated here, the handcrafted fusion remains Pareto-optimal. The contribution of SSL components is therefore not visible at the level of the EER–minDCF frontier, but rather in finer-grained behavior, namely the relative size of the in-domain-to-cross-domain gap, which we examine next via ablation.

4.5 Extended Ablation: Cross-Domain Asymmetry and the Role of Each Feature

The ablation in Table 5 reports each feature-removal configuration in both transfer directions: FoR→RITW (training on the controlled corpus and evaluating on in-the-wild data, the operationally relevant direction for deployment) and RITW→FoR (training on in-the-wild data and evaluating on the controlled corpus). The reference *Full Fusion* configuration corresponds to the simultaneous concatenation of all five features, producing a vector of 2,382 dimensions (768×3 from the SSL backbones plus 39 from each handcrafted descriptor). Its in-domain EER on FoR (3.82% $\pm$ 0.60) is therefore higher than that of the lower-dimensional FM in Table 4 (1.94% for MFCC+WHISPER), which is consistent with the dimensionality penalty incurred when all five vectors are stacked without dimensionality reduction. This caveat aside, Full Fusion is the natural reference point for an ablation, as it allows the contribution of each removed component to be measured against a common upper-bound configuration. Two findings emerge.

Table 5. Extended ablation: EER (%), 95% CI (%), and generalization gap (Δ %) for individual and combined feature removals in both transfer directions. *Full Fusion* concatenates all five features - CQCC, MFCC, HuBERT, Wav2Vec2, and Whisper (FM-21 in Table 3) - yielding a 2,382-dimensional vector.

	Source: FoR (FoR→RITW)			**Source: RITW** (RITW→FoR)		
Configuration	**In Domain ± CI**	**Cross ± CI**	Δ	**In Domain ± CI**	**Cross ± CI**	Δ
Full Fusion	3.82% ± 0.60%	46.53% ± 1.77%	42.71%	18.32% ± 1.54%	36.36% ± 1.46%	18.04%
Combined SSL Removal						
- w/o Hubert + Whisper	12.80% ± 0.95%	49.42% ± 1.75%	36.62%	22.17% ± 1.44%	34.48% ± 1.35%	12.31%
- w/o Hubert + Wav2Vec2	4.44% ± 0.65%	47.88% ± 1.79%	43.44%	16.65% ± 1.32%	40.81% ± 1.44%	24.16%
- w/o Whisper + Wav2Vec2	9.23% ± 0.81%	48.47% ± 1.83%	39.24%	21.12% ± 1.48%	25.31% ± 1.30%	**4.19%**
Handcrafted Removal						
- w/o CQCC + MFCC	5.78% ± 0.67%	48.82% ± 1.82%	43.04%	20.43% ± 1.44%	37.85% ± 1.41%	17.42%
- w/o CQCC	5.24% ± 0.66%	46.27% ± 1.77%	41.03%	18.07% ± 1.36%	36.49% ± 1.48%	18.42%
- w/o MFCC	3.26% ± 0.54%	48.45% ± 1.71%	45.19%	21.39% ± 1.47%	30.86% ± 1.32%	9.47%
Individual Removal						
- w/o Whisper	7.19% ± 0.78%	48.91% ± 1.81%	41.72%	21.35% ± 1.56%	27.58% ± 1.29%	6.23%
- w/o Hubert	5.16% ± 0.80%	45.95% ± 1.86%	40.79%	17.15% ± 1.47%	45.49% ± 1.49%	28.34%
- w/o Wav2Vec2	3.76% ± 0.57%	47.21% ± 1.84%	43.45%	16.86% ± 1.31%	30.86% ± 1.33%	14.00%

In the operationally relevant direction (FoR→RITW), every configuration exhibits a large generalization gap: the Full Fusion yields $\Delta = 42.71\%$, and no ablation reduces Δ below 36.62% (*w/o Hubert + Whisper*). In the inverse direction (RITW→FoR), the same configurations exhibit substantially smaller gaps: the Full Fusion drops to $\Delta = 18.04\%$, and the *w/o Whisper + Wav2Vec2* configuration reaches the smallest gap recorded in the study, $\Delta = 4.19\%$. This asymmetry has a plausible interpretation: training on noisy, in-the-wild data exposes the classifier to a broader range of acoustic variability, including the cleaner conditions found in FoR as a particular case, whereas training on controlled, high-fidelity data does not provide analogous coverage of in-the-wild conditions. The asymmetry addresses RQ2: the generalization gap depends not only on the choice of features but on the direction of transfer, and the direction relevant for deployment (controlled → in-the-wild) is the harder one for all feature families evaluated here.

In the FoR→RITW direction, removing MFCC slightly reduces in-domain EER (3.26%, the lowest in the table) but increases the cross-domain gap to $\Delta = 45.19\%$, suggesting that MFCC contributes more to cross-domain stability than to in-domain discrimination on this benchmark. Removing Hubert keeps a competitive in-domain EER (5.16%) and yields the lowest absolute cross-domain EER among all ablations (45.95%), although the gap remains large ($\Delta = 40.79\%$). In the RITW→FoR direction, removing Hubert is the most damaging single ablation ($\Delta = 28.34\%$, nearly double the Full Fusion gap), indicating that Hubert is the component most responsible for stability when training on RITW. These observations qualify the role of SSL components: they do not uniformly reduce the generalization gap, and their effect is modulated by which acoustic domain serves as the source. The minimum gap recorded in the study, $\Delta = 4.19\%$, is observed in the *w/o Whisper + Wav2Vec2* configuration in the RITW→FoR direction, with in-domain EER of 21.12% and cross-domain EER of 25.31%. Both error rates are high in absolute terms, indicating that this configuration achieves a small relative gap by underperforming uniformly in both domains rather than by generalizing well in the operationally relevant direction. We report this value for completeness and consistency with the ablation methodology, but emphasize that a small Δ in isolation is not a sufficient indicator of operational robustness: it must be read jointly with the absolute EER on each side and with the direction of transfer.

In summary, the ablation supports a refined reading of RQ1 and RQ2: handcrafted features (CQCC, MFCC) and SSL components (notably Hubert) contribute differently in each transfer direction, but no configuration tested closes the FoR→RITW gap to a level at which domain shift could be considered resolved on this benchmark. Instead, the data show a structured trade-off between absolute EER, relative gap, and direction of transfer, which we believe is more informative than a single-best-model framing for practical deployment decisions.

5 Conclusion

We evaluated 31 feature configurations for ASD across the FoR and RITW corpora. These include handcrafted descriptors (CQCC, MFCC), self-supervised learning representations (Wav2Vec2, HuBERT, Whisper), and their early-fusion combinations. All feature sets were assessed under a unified, calibrated XGBoost pipeline with bootstrap-based uncertainty quantification.

Three findings emerge within this experimental setting. First, the handcrafted fusion FH (CQCC+MFCC) achieves the lowest EER both in-domain

(1.48%) and cross-domain (12.07% on FoR→RITW). It also remains Pareto-optimal on RITW. SSL-inclusive configurations evaluated here do not surpass this baseline in absolute discriminative performance under the adopted pipeline. Second, cross-dataset transfer is asymmetric. The FoR→RITW direction exhibits a generalization gap of at least 36.62% across all configurations. In contrast, the inverse direction yields smaller gaps. This suggests that transfer direction may be an important factor in operational robustness. Third, under the calibration protocol the handcrafted fusion (FH) is the best-calibrated configuration on RITW (ECE = 0.0746), against 0.1081 for the single-descriptor MFCC baseline. This supports score-based decisions with more stable empirical risk under domain shift.

These observations are bounded by the experimental scope: two datasets, a single backend (XGBoost with default hyperparameters), and SSL backbones used as frozen feature extractors via mean pooling. Future work will investigate adaptive fusion (e.g., attention-based weighting) and additional benchmarks (ASVspoof 2019/2021, MLAAD). It will also explore fine-tuned SSL models, alongside a forensic analysis of cross-domain failure modes to relate residual errors to specific acoustic conditions.

Acknowledgments. The authors would like to acknowledge the use of Grammarly (AI-powered writing assistant) for proofreading and linguistic refinement of this manuscript. All final edits and content responsibility remain with the authors.

References

1. Ahmad, F., Ahmed, A., Imtiaz, M.: Classical machine learning baselines for deepfake audio detection on the fake-or-real dataset (2026). https://doi.org/10.48550/arXiv.2604.13400, accepted for Oral Presentation at the 35th IEEE Microelectronics Design and Test Symposium (MDTS 2026)
2. Baevski, A., Zhou, Y., Mohamed, A., Auli, M.: wav2vec 2.0: a framework for self-supervised learning of speech representations. In: Advances in Neural Information Processing Systems (NeurIPS), vol. 33, pp. 12449–12460 (2020)
3. Brier, G.W.: Verification of forecasts expressed in terms of probability. Mon. Weather Rev. **78**(1), 1–3 (1950)
4. Chen, T., Guestrin, C.: XGBoost: a scalable tree boosting system. In: Proceedings of 22nd ACM SIGKDD International Conference on Knowledge Discovery and Data Mining (KDD), pp. 785–794. ACM (2016). https://doi.org/10.1145/2939672.2939785
5. Efron, B., Tibshirani, R.J.: An Introduction to the Bootstrap. Chapman & Hall/CRC (1994)
6. Guido, R.C.: A tutorial on signal energy and its applications. Neurocomputing **179**, 264–282 (2016)
7. Guo, C., Pleiss, G., Sun, Y., Weinberger, K.Q.: On calibration of modern neural networks. In: Proceedings of34th International Conference on Machine Learning (ICML), pp. 1321–1330 (2017)

8. Hsu, W.N., Bolte, B., Tsai, C.H., Lakhotia, K., Salakhutdinov, R., Mohamed, A.: Hubert: self-supervised speech representation learning by masked prediction of hidden units. IEEE/ACM Trans. Audio Speech Lang. Process. **29**, 3451–3460 (2021)
9. Müller, N.M., Czempin, P., Diekmann, F., Froghyar, A., Böttinger, K.: Does audio deepfake detection generalize? In: Proceedings of Interspeech 2022, pp. 2783–2787 (2022). https://doi.org/10.21437/Interspeech.2022-108
10. Nautsch, A., et al.: ASVspoof 2019: spoofing countermeasures for the connected world. IEEE Signal Process. Mag. **36**(4), 125–146 (2019). https://doi.org/10.1109/MSP.2019.2900360
11. Platt, J.C.: Probabilistic outputs for support vector machines and comparisons to regularized likelihood methods. In: Smola, A.J., Bartlett, P.L., Schölkopf, B., Schuurmans, D. (eds.) Advances in Large Margin Classifiers, pp. 61–74. MIT Press (1999)
12. Radford, A., Kim, J.W., Xu, T., Brockman, G., McLeavey, C., Sutskever, I.: Robust speech recognition via large-scale weak supervision. In: International Conference on Machine Learning, pp. 28448–28481. PMLR (2023)
13. Reimão, R., Tzerpos, V.: FoR: a dataset for synthetic speech detection. In: 2019 International Conference on Speech Technology and Human-Computer Dialogue (SpeD), pp. 1–10. IEEE (2019). https://doi.org/10.1109/SpeD.2019.8906599
14. Roberts, D.R., et al.: Cross-validation strategies for data with temporal, spatial, hierarchical, or phylogenetic structure. Ecography **40**(7), 913–929 (2017). https://doi.org/10.1111/ecog.02881
15. Tak, H., Patino, J., Todisco, M., Nautsch, A., Evans, N., Larcher, A.: End-to-end anti-spoofing with RawNet2. In: ICASSP 2021 - 2021 IEEE International Conference on Acoustics, Speech and Signal Processing (ICASSP), pp. 6369–6373. IEEE (2021). https://doi.org/10.1109/ICASSP39728.2021.9414234
16. Todisco, M., Delgado, H., Evans, N.: Constant Q cepstral coefficients: a spoofing countermeasure for automatic speaker verification. Comput. Speech Lang. **45**, 516–535 (2017). https://doi.org/10.1016/j.csl.2017.01.001
17. Wang, X., Yamagishi, J.: Investigating self-supervised front ends for speech spoofing countermeasures. In: Proceedings of the Speaker and Language Recognition Workshop (Odyssey 2022), pp. 100–106 (2022). https://doi.org/10.21437/Odyssey.2022-14
18. Wu, Z., et al.: ASVspoof: the first automatic speaker verification spoofing and countermeasures challenge. Speech Commun. **66**, 24–36 (2015). https://doi.org/10.1016/j.specom.2014.10.005

ENADE-QA: A Brazilian Portuguese Dataset for Benchmarking Large Language Models on Health-Related Higher Education Exams

Marilia Silveira(✉), Guilherme Lima, Larissa Freitas, and Ulisses Corrêa

Federal University of Pelotas (UFPEL), Pelotas, Brazil
{mrsilveira,gdlima,larissa,ulisses}@inf.ufpel.edu.br

Abstract. We introduce ENADE-QA, a curated Brazilian Portuguese Multiple-Choice Question Answering resource derived from official higher-education exams of the National Student Performance Exam (ENADE). Unlike prior Portuguese benchmarks based mainly on high school or admission exams, ENADE-QA targets health-related higher education assessment. The dataset was built from official exam PDFs and answer keys through automatic extraction, manual validation, deduplication, and filtering. The final version contains 716 textual multiple-choice questions with statements, alternatives, official answers, year, course, component, and visual-dependency metadata. As an initial use case, we benchmark open-weight, proprietary, multilingual, and Portuguese-oriented large language models across different prompting and inference strategies. Results show that ENADE-QA differentiates models across performance levels, with proprietary models achieving the highest accuracies and larger open-weight models outperforming smaller Portuguese-oriented baselines. We also analyze robustness to answer-order perturbation using positional-bias metrics, showing that stronger models are generally more stable in accuracy under shuffled alternatives, while the Bias by Position of Choice (BPC) reveals differences in answer-position preferences across models. These findings indicate that ENADE-QA is a useful resource for evaluating language models in Brazilian Portuguese health-related higher education contexts.

Keywords: Brazilian Portuguese · Multiple-choice question answering · Large language models · Educational benchmarks · ENADE

1 Introduction

Large Language Models (LLMs) have achieved strong performance across a wide range of Natural Language Processing (NLP) tasks, including question answering, summarization, text generation, and problem solving [2,3,7]. A widely used strategy for evaluating LLMs is to use benchmarks based on multiple-choice

M. Recamonde-Mendoza and R. C. Barros (Eds.): BRACIS 2026, LNAI 17105, pp. 553–567, 2027.
https://doi.org/10.1007/978-3-032-39882-6_37

questions [4,6,13]. This format enables automatic scoring and direct model comparison. Benchmarks such as MMLU(Massive Multitask Language Understanding) [4] evaluate models across multiple knowledge domains by posing questions that require academic and professional skills. However, many of these resources were originally developed in English, which limits their ability to capture linguistic and educational characteristics specific to other contexts [5,11].

For Brazilian Portuguese, there is still limited availability of public, standardized benchmarks derived from real educational assessments. This gap is relevant because LLM performance may vary across language, domain, task type, and cultural context [5,11]. In this sense, native benchmarks are important because they preserve linguistic, cultural, and institutional aspects that may be lost in translated versions of resources originally developed in English [11]. Official educational exams are particularly suitable for this type of evaluation, as they consist of reviewed, standardized questions aligned with specific competencies. In Brazil, previous studies have already explored the *Exame Nacional do Ensino Médio* (ENEM) and university entrance exams as benchmarks for language models [1,8–10]. However, these resources focus mainly on high-school-level or university entrance assessments, with fewer benchmarks available for evaluating specialized knowledge at the undergraduate level.

In this work, we introduce *ENADE-QA*, a multiple-choice question-answering dataset in Brazilian Portuguese, extracted from the official exams of the *Exame Nacional de Desempenho dos Estudantes* (ENADE), a national assessment for students completing undergraduate programs. Unlike benchmarks based on high school or university entrance exams, *ENADE-QA* enables the evaluation of LLMs on questions related to higher education, including textual comprehension, reasoning, and specialized knowledge.

The first version of the dataset focuses on health-related undergraduate programs. It includes structured questions with question stems, alternatives, official answer keys, and metadata on year, program, and assessed component. In addition to constructing and curating the resource, we conduct an initial benchmark using open, proprietary, multilingual, and Portuguese-oriented models, analyzing accuracy, sensitivity to prompting strategies, and robustness to changes in answer order. Thus, the contributions of this work are: (i) the construction and characterization of a Brazilian Multiple-Choice Question Answering (MCQA) dataset derived from official ENADE exams; (ii) the description of a pipeline for data collection, manual validation, deduplication, and filtering; and (iii) an initial experimental evaluation of modern LLMs on *ENADE-QA*.

The following sections describe related works, the construction of *ENADE-QA*, the experimental protocol, results, limitations, and the conclusion.

2 Related Works

Standardized educational exams have increasingly been used to evaluate Artificial Intelligence systems because they provide objective, measurable tasks covering different cognitive abilities. In Brazil, the ENEM has been adopted as a benchmark for evaluating AI methods on questions that require textual comprehension, encyclopedic knowledge, mathematical reasoning, and the interpretation of visual elements [10]. Another relevant resource is BLUEX, a benchmark derived from Brazilian university entrance exams, including UNICAMP and USP [1]. BLUEX supports evaluation in Brazilian Portuguese by providing multiple-choice questions annotated with metadata on the skills required to answer them, such as textual comprehension, prior knowledge, mathematical reasoning, and image understanding.

ENADE-QA differs from these resources by focusing on an official Brazilian higher-education assessment aimed at students completing undergraduate programs. This setting enables the evaluation of LLMs on questions that require specialized knowledge and professional competencies, complementing existing Portuguese benchmarks that are mainly based on high school or university admission exams.

Multiple-choice questions are widely used in LLM evaluation because they enable automatic scoring and direct comparison across models. However, recent studies show that this format must be carefully controlled [13], since models can be sensitive to the order of answer options and may change their predictions when alternatives are reordered [6,14]. This positional bias can compromise the interpretation of accuracy when the position of the correct answer is not controlled. Wang et al. [12] further show that models may favor specific answer positions regardless of semantic content and propose metrics to quantify this behavior. For this reason, our evaluation includes answer-option shuffling and positional-bias estimation in addition to overall accuracy. To the best of our knowledge, *ENADE-QA* is among the first curated MCQA resources derived from ENADE exams for benchmarking LLMs in Brazilian Portuguese higher-education contexts.

3 ENADE-QA Dataset

This section describes the construction of *ENADE-QA*, a structured dataset of multiple-choice questions extracted from official ENADE exams and designed to evaluate language models on MCQA tasks in Brazilian Portuguese. The process includes collecting exam files, automatically extracting questions, manual curation by reviewers, and applying filtering criteria to produce the final dataset. The complete construction pipeline is presented in Fig. 1.

3.1 Data Source

The exams and official answer keys of the ENADE are publicly available in PDF format on the official website of the *Instituto Nacional de Estudos e Pesquisas Educacionais Anísio Teixeira* (INEP)[1]. ENADE is administered annually; however, each undergraduate field is assessed periodically according to ENADE's assessment cycles.

[1] https://www.gov.br/inep/pt-br/areas-de-atuacao/avaliacao-e-exames-educacionais/enade/provas-e-gabaritos.

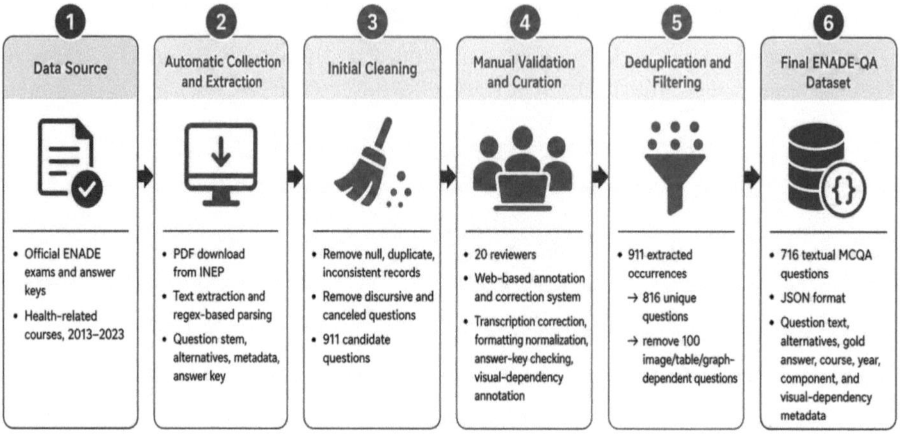

Fig. 1. Overview of the ENADE-QA construction pipeline.

In this first version of *ENADE-QA*, we focus on health-related undergraduate programs, given their relevance for evaluating language models in specialized domains. The selected programs comprise Biomedicine, Nursing, Pharmacy, Physiotherapy, Speech-Language Pathology and Audiology, Medicine, Nutrition, Dentistry, and Psychology. The corresponding exams were collected from the years 2013, 2016, 2018, 2019, 2022, and 2023.

3.2 Data Collection

Data collection was performed using a Python script that automatically navigated the INEP portal and downloaded the exam PDFs and their corresponding official answer keys. After collection, regular expressions (*regex*) were applied to identify and extract the main elements of each question in a structured format: question stem, answer options, question number, undergraduate program, exam year, assessed component, and correct answer.

After the initial extraction, we conducted a preprocessing step to remove duplicate, null, or structurally inconsistent records. At this stage, we also excluded discursive questions and questions canceled in the official answer keys. Since this work evaluates text-based language models, questions dependent on images, tables, or graphs were flagged for removal in a subsequent curation step. The evaluation of multimodal questions is left for future work. After automatic extraction and initial preprocessing, 911 candidate questions were obtained.

The distribution of these questions by undergraduate program is shown in Fig. 2. The number of questions varies across programs, ranging from 53 in Psychology to 108 in Nursing. This variation reflects ENADE assessment cycles, schedule changes, and the unequal removal of visually dependent questions. For instance, Psychology appears in fewer editions because its assessment schedule was affected by the COVID-19 pandemic. This imbalance is inherent to the dataset construction process and should be taken into account when interpreting performance comparisons across programs.

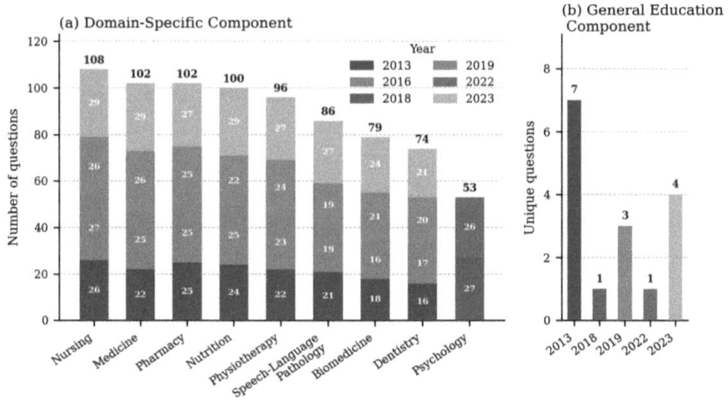

Fig. 2. Distribution of candidate questions by undergraduate program after automatic extraction and initial preprocessing.

3.3 Manual Validation and Curation

Since the data were automatically extracted from PDF files, the initial set could contain formatting issues, line breaks, textual noise, segmentation errors, and incorrect associations between stems, options, and answer keys. To mitigate these problems, we conducted a manual validation step involving 20 reviewers, including undergraduate and graduate students from a Brazilian public university. Reviewers checked extraction fidelity, textual formatting, answer-key association, and visual dependency, rather than judging the disciplinary correctness of the official questions.

Each extracted question was reviewed to verify its fidelity to the original document. When necessary, reviewers corrected transcription errors, normalized textual formatting, and adjusted the structure of the extracted content while preserving the semantic meaning of the question stem and answer options.

The corrections covered six main aspects: transcription errors introduced during automatic extraction; normalization of accents, punctuation, and spelling; standardization of spacing, capitalization, and answer-option formatting; verification of the association between question stem, answer options, and official answer key; identification of questions dependent on images, tables, or graphs; and identification of extraction problems that could not be reliably corrected.

To support this process, we developed a web-based system for inspecting, validating, and correcting the extracted data. The tool allowed reviewers to compare the structured content with the original document, revise question stems and answer options, verify the associated answer key, and report extraction problems or dependency on visual elements. In particular, the interface included a checkbox for marking whether the question required graphical or visual elements, such as images, tables, graphs, formulas, or diagrams.

Reviewers were instructed through a video tutorial and an annotation guide describing the validation procedure, the fields to be checked, and the criteria for textual correction and visual-dependency annotation. Textual corrections were limited to correcting extraction artifacts and formatting issues, while preserving the original semantic content of the question and answer options. After the review process, the authors assessed the proportion of modified text relative to the original automatic extraction to identify possible over-editing or unintended reformulation by reviewers.

3.4 Inclusion and Exclusion Criteria

After manual validation, we applied the final inclusion and exclusion criteria. The dataset retained only objective multiple-choice questions with textual stems, identifiable answer options, and associated official answer keys. We excluded canceled, discursive, duplicated, incomplete, and non-correctable questions, as well as questions that depended on visual elements not represented in text, such as images, tables, graphs, formulas, or diagrams.

Table 1 summarizes the deduplication and filtering process used to produce *ENADE-QA*. The raw corpus comprised 911 extracted entries. After deduplicating General Education (GE) questions shared across undergraduate programs within the same exam year, we obtained 816 unique questions: 800 from the Specific Component (SC) and 16 from GE. Questions requiring interpretation of images, tables, graphs, formulas, or diagrams ($n = 100$) were excluded because they are not suitable for text-only evaluation, yielding a final dataset of 716 unique questions.

Each SC question was reviewed by a single annotator, with no overlap. In contrast, GE questions, because they are administered to all programs in the same exam year, were independently annotated by different reviewers, one per program. This produced natural annotation overlap for 14 of the 16 unique GE questions; the remaining two appeared in only one program in the dataset. As a minimal consistency check, we observed 100% agreement among multiple annotators on the official answer key for the 14 questions (14/14). The average textual similarity between independently produced question stems was 0.972 (minimum: 0.638; maximum: 1.000), suggesting that paraphrasing variations among reviewers did not compromise the identification of the correct answer. Overall, 774 out of the 911 annotations (85.0%) received some textual modification relative to the original PDF extraction.

3.5 Final Structure

The final version of *ENADE-QA* is provided in JSON format for review, with one entry per question. Each instance includes exam metadata, the question

Table 1. Deduplication and filtering process of ENADE-QA.

Stage	Occurrences	Unique questions
Raw extracted corpus	911	–
Specific Component (SC)	800	800
General Education (GE)	111	16
After GE deduplication	911	816
Removed due to visual dependency	100	100
Final textual dataset	–	**716**

stem, answer options, the official answer key, and auxiliary information about the assessed component and the presence of visual elements in the original document. The dataset, source code, prompt templates, model outputs, and evaluation scripts are available in a repository[2].

4 Benchmark Design

This section describes the experimental protocol used to evaluate *ENADE-QA* as a benchmark for MCQA in Brazilian Portuguese. Beyond comparing models on accuracy, the experiments aim to analyze how different families of LLMs behave on official higher-education questions, considering model scale, linguistic orientation, access type, and sensitivity to the position of answer options.

4.1 Models and Experimental Setup

We evaluated both open-weight and proprietary models with different scales and linguistic orientations to analyze *ENADE-QA* from complementary perspectives on reproducibility, performance, and specialization in Portuguese. The evaluated set includes Portuguese-oriented open-weight models, such as Tucano-2B and Sabiá-7B; open-weight multilingual models of different sizes, including Llama-3.1-8B, Mistral-7B, Qwen2.5-7B, Qwen3.5-27B, Gemma-3-27B, and Qwen3.5-35B-A3B; and proprietary models accessed through

We defined six experimental strategies to evaluate model performance and sensitivity to variations in prompt format: (S1) *zero-shot* generation; (S2) *one-shot* generation; (S3) *few-shot* generation; (S4) *zero-shot* generation with shuffled answer options; (S5) *zero-shot* scoring based on log-probabilities; and (S6) *one-shot* scoring based on log-probabilities.

In the text-generation strategies (S1–S4), each question is presented to the model with its question stem and all available answer options, labeled with their corresponding letters. The model is instructed to answer exclusively with the letter of the correct option, without providing explanations or additional text.

[2] https://github.com/H2IA/ENADE-QA.

For models accessed via APIs, we added a system message reinforcing that the output should contain only the selected answer letter. For S1–S4, we used deterministic decoding whenever supported (temperature = 0, top-p = 1.0, max output tokens = 16, and no stop sequence). API seeds could not be enforced. Local experiments were run on NVIDIA RTX PRO 6000 Blackwell and RTX 5090 GPUs.

S1 corresponds to the *zero-shot* setting, whereas S2 and S3 include, respectively, one or two solved examples in the context. The in-context demonstrations were fixed across all evaluated questions, drawn from the General Education component, and placed in the user prompt before the target question. Strategy S4 follows the same format as S1, but presents the answer options in shuffled order. The shuffling procedure uses a seed derived from each question identifier, ensuring reproducibility. This strategy allows us to evaluate sensitivity to answer-option position and to estimate positional bias.

In generation-based methods, the final answer was automatically extracted using regular expressions. Answer extraction used five primary patterns followed by a last-valid-letter fallback. When no primary pattern matched, the last standalone valid option letter in the generated output was selected as the model answer. If no valid option letter was found, the output was marked as unanswered. Across S1–S4 (n = 30,788 generations), 93.3% of outputs matched a primary pattern, 6.4% required fallback extraction, and 0.19% contained no valid option letter. Fallback use was negligible for API models and most instruction-tuned local models, but higher for reasoning-style outputs, especially Qwen3.5-27B in S2–S3.

Strategies S5 and S6 are based on log-probabilities and were applied only to locally executed models, as they require direct access to token probabilities. In this method, each answer option is evaluated independently: the context contains the question stem followed by the expression `Resposta correta:`, and each option is scored by the average log-probability of its tokens conditioned on the context. The option with the highest score is selected as the model prediction, following the intuition that the answer considered most likely by the model should receive the highest score [2]. S5 is executed in the *zero-shot* setting, whereas S6 includes one solved example before the evaluated question.

Full prompt templates for all experimental strategies (S1–S6), including the in-context demonstrations used in S2, S3, and S6, are provided in the README of the anonymous project repository, together with the model outputs and evaluation scripts.

4.2 Metrics

Model evaluation was conducted using complementary metrics designed to capture both overall performance and aspects of robustness and prediction stability. The main metric is accuracy, defined as the proportion of correctly answered questions among all evaluated questions. Since most *ENADE-QA* questions contain five answer options, the approximate expected random accuracy is 20%.

In addition to accuracy, we compute the *Bias by Position of Choice* (BPC), which is used to estimate models' positional bias. This metric measures the extent to which a model tends to select specific answer positions more frequently, regardless of the semantic content of the option. BPC is computed from the results of strategy **S4**, in which the answer options are shuffled. Following [12], we define:

$$\text{BPC} = \frac{k}{2(k-1)} \sum_{i=1}^{k} \left| p_i - \frac{1}{k} \right|$$

where k denotes the number of answer options and p_i corresponds to the proportion of times position i was selected by the model. Values close to zero indicate a more uniform distribution of choices across positions, suggesting lower positional bias. Higher values indicate a greater concentration of responses in specific positions.

5 Results and Discussion

This section analyzes *ENADE-QA* from two complementary perspectives. First, we characterize the composition of the dataset, including the distribution by assessed component, number of answer options, answer-key distribution, and the length of question stems and answer options. We then evaluate model performance under the proposed strategies, discussing differences across model families, sensitivity to prompt format, and robustness to the ordering of answer options.

5.1 Dataset Characteristics

Of the 716 questions, 700 (97.76%) belong to the Specific Component (SC) and 16 (2.24%) to General Education (GE). Most questions have five answer options (A–E); only 29 questions (4.1%), all from the 2023 Medicine exam, have four answer options (A–D). The distribution of correct answers is relatively balanced across positions, with option C being the most frequent (21.1%) and option E slightly underrepresented (18.0%). This balance reduces the possibility that a model could achieve high accuracy simply by exploiting positional regularities in the dataset.

Question stems contain an average of 178.6 words (median: 175; Q1–Q3: 116–231), whereas answer options are substantially shorter, with an average of 10.9 words. This pattern suggests that a relevant part of the difficulty of *ENADE-QA* may lie in interpreting the question stem and integrating contextual information, rather than merely distinguishing lexical cues among short answer options.

5.2 Overall Model Performance

Table 2 reports the accuracy of each model under the evaluated strategies, together with the BPC score computed from the shuffled-answer setting. We use S1, the zero-shot generation strategy with the original answer order, as the main comparison setting, since it is available for all models and corresponds to the simplest deterministic benchmark protocol. Since ENADE-QA contains both five-option ($n = 687$) and four-option ($n = 29$) questions, BPC was computed separately for each value of k and then averaged. This avoids assigning a spurious zero probability to a non-existent fifth position in four-option items.

Table 2. Accuracy (%) by evaluation strategy and positional bias. S1: zero-shot generation; S2: one-shot generation; S3: few-shot generation; S4: zero-shot generation with shuffled alternatives; S5: zero-shot log-probability scoring; S6: one-shot log-probability scoring.

Model	S1	S2	S3	S4	S5	S6	BPC	Mean
Gemini 2.5 Flash	**84.36**	**84.92**	**83.94**	**83.52**	—	—	0.16	**84.18**
Sabiá-3	80.59	79.61	80.59	78.63	—	—	0.11	79.85
Qwen3.5-35B-A3B	74.58	68.44	66.90	74.16	54.89	58.38	0.12	66.22
Qwen3.5-27B	78.07	57.82	54.89	76.82	52.09	57.40	0.07	62.85
Gemma-3-27B	69.69	69.41	68.85	70.53	46.51	48.04	0.17	62.17
Qwen2.5-7B	58.38	60.47	65.50	59.78	34.92	39.53	0.22	53.10
Llama-3.1-8B	49.72	46.93	47.49	49.44	35.75	37.71	0.13	44.51
Sabiá-7B	27.93	28.63	27.51	27.93	33.52	32.82	0.23	29.73
Mistral-7B	24.02	30.87	26.40	23.60	29.89	28.63	0.24	27.23
Tucano-2B	21.51	22.21	21.65	19.55	23.88	23.46	0.17	22.04

In S1, the highest accuracies were achieved by Gemini 2.5 Flash (84.36%), Sabiá-3 (80.59%), and Qwen3.5-27B (78.07%). These results indicate that *ENADE-QA* is able to distinguish high-performing proprietary models from strong open-weight models. Among open-weight models, Qwen3.5-27B, Qwen3.5-35B-A3B, and Gemma-3-27B achieved the strongest results, all substantially above the random baseline. In contrast, Sabiá-7B, Mistral-7B, and Tucano-2B remained close to the expected random accuracy for five-option questions, indicating relevant limitations on specialized higher-education questions.

Taken together, the results suggest that *ENADE-QA* has an adequate level of difficulty for differentiating models across performance ranges: proprietary models and larger open-weight models achieved the best results, medium-sized models occupied an intermediate range, and smaller or older Portuguese-oriented baselines remained close to chance-level performance.

5.3 Effect of Prompting and Inference Strategies

The effect of in-context examples was not uniform across models. For Gemini 2.5 Flash and Sabiá-3, one-shot and few-shot prompting produced only small variations relative to zero-shot generation. Gemini 2.5 Flash varied from 84.36%

in S1 to 84.92% in S2 and 83.94% in S3, while Sabiá-3 varied from 80.59% in S1 to 79.61% in S2 and 80.59% in S3. However, some open-weight models were substantially more sensitive to the prompt format. Qwen3.5-27B showed the clearest instability: its accuracy decreased from 78.07% in S1 to 57.82% in S2 and 54.89% in S3. This suggests that the examples included in the context may interfere with the model's answer selection, rather than systematically improving performance.

The log-probability-based strategies (S5 and S6) were not consistently superior to generation-based inference. For Gemma-3-27B, for example, accuracy decreased from 69.69% in S1 to 46.51% in S5, a reduction of 23.18 percentage points. This result suggests that log-probability scoring may be inadequate for some instruction-tuned models, especially when the evaluation format differs from the conversational format used during instruction tuning.

The results should be interpreted with caution due to the possibility of training data contamination. Since ENADE exams and official answer keys are publicly available, we cannot rule out that part of this material may have been included in pre-training or fine-tuning corpora, especially for proprietary models. As an exploratory analysis, we compared S1 accuracy between exams up to 2021 and exams from 2022–2023 (Table 3).

Table 3. Average S1 accuracy (%) by temporal period and post–pre variation (Δ) in percentage points. Pre-cutoff period: 2013, 2016, 2018, and 2019; post-cutoff period: 2022 and 2023.

Model	Acc ≤2021	Acc ≥2022	Δ (pp)
Gemini 2.5 Flash	83.3	90.3	+6.9
Sabiá-3	80.2	89.6	+9.5
Qwen3.5-35B-A3B	76.8	83.7	+6.9
Qwen3.5-27B	75.9	87.7	+11.8
Gemma-3-27B	71.3	79.1	+7.8
Qwen2.5-7B	59.1	66.6	+7.5
Llama-3.1-8B	51.2	57.1	+5.9
Sabiá-7B	29.7	24.2	−5.5
Mistral-7B	24.2	22.5	−1.7
Tucano-2B	19.3	16.4	−2.8

Proprietary models achieved higher accuracy in the more recent period, as observed for Gemini 2.5 Flash ($\Delta = +6.9$ p.p.) and Sabiá-3 ($\Delta = +9.5$ p.p.). However, a similar pattern was also observed for high-performing open models, such as Qwen3.5-27B ($\Delta = +11.8$ p.p.) and Gemma-3-27B ($\Delta = +7.8$ p.p.). This result does not rule out the possibility of contamination, but suggests that differences in difficulty across exam editions may also contribute to the observed temporal variation. Therefore, the results should be interpreted as performance on this benchmark, rather than as isolated evidence of generalized reasoning ability.

5.4 Robustness to Answer-Order Perturbation

The shuffled-answer setting (S4) was used to evaluate whether models remain stable when the order of alternatives changes. Higher-performing models showed small differences between S1 and S4. Gemini 2.5 Flash decreased from 84.36% to 83.52%, Sabiá-3 from 80.59% to 78.63%, and Qwen3.5-27B from 78.07% to 76.82%. Gemma-3-27B increased slightly from 69.69% to 70.53%. These results indicate that the strongest models generally preserve their accuracy when the alternatives are shuffled.

The BPC results provide a complementary view of this behavior. Qwen3.5-27B showed the lowest positional bias among the evaluated models (BPC = 0.07), followed by Sabiá-3 (0.11), Qwen3.5-35B-A3B (0.12), and Llama-3.1-8B (0.13). In contrast, higher BPC values were observed for Mistral-7B (0.24), Sabiá-7B (0.23), Qwen2.5-7B (0.22), Gemma-3-27B (0.17), Tucano-2B (0.17), and Gemini 2.5 Flash (0.16). These results suggest that positional bias is not determined only by aggregate accuracy: although high-performing models tend to be stable in terms of accuracy under shuffling, some of them still exhibit moderate concentration in specific answer positions.

An exception worth noting is Qwen3.5-27B. This model combined high S1 accuracy, stable performance under answer shuffling, and the lowest BPC. However, its performance dropped sharply in S2 and S3, from 78.07% in S1 to 57.82% and 54.89%, respectively. This suggests that its instability is more related to the inclusion of in-context examples or to the prompt format than to answer-position bias.

In summary, answer-order perturbation provides a useful robustness check for MCQA evaluation in *ENADE-QA*. The comparison between S1 and S4 captures whether accuracy is preserved after shuffling, while BPC captures whether model predictions are concentrated in specific answer positions. These two dimensions are related but not equivalent. Therefore, shuffled alternatives and BPC should be interpreted as complementary analyses to accuracy when evaluating LLMs on multiple-choice benchmarks.

5.5 Portuguese-Oriented and Multilingual Models

The results suggest that linguistic specialization is not sufficient by itself: Portuguese-oriented models only become competitive when combined with strong instruction tuning and model capacity, as observed for Sabiá-3. Gemini 2.5 Flash, a proprietary multilingual model, achieved the best S1 accuracy (84.36%), followed by Sabiá-3, a Portuguese-oriented proprietary model (80.59%). Among open-weight models, larger multilingual models such as Qwen3.5-27B, Qwen3.5-35B-A3B, and Gemma-3-27B outperformed the smaller Portuguese-oriented baselines.

This comparison should be interpreted with caution, since the models differ not only in linguistic orientation, but also in scale, architecture, training data, instruction tuning, and context-window size. Therefore, the results should not be interpreted as evidence that Portuguese specialization is irrelevant. Rather, they suggest that Portuguese orientation alone is not sufficient to ensure strong performance on specialized MCQA tasks. The competitive performance of Sabiá-3 indicates that Portuguese-oriented models can be strong when linguistic specialization is combined with greater model capacity and high-quality instruction tuning.

6 Limitations

Since ENADE exams and official answer keys are publicly available, we cannot rule out the possibility that some of the evaluated models were exposed to part of this material during pre-training or fine-tuning. This is particularly relevant for proprietary models with undisclosed training corpora. Therefore, the results should be interpreted as benchmark performance on *ENADE-QA*, rather than as direct evidence of generalized reasoning ability. We did not systematically vary the position of in-context demonstrations (system vs. user message, or before vs. after the target question). Therefore, the instability observed for some models in S2–S3 may partly reflect sensitivity to demonstration placement or domain mismatch, which we leave for future work.

The current version of *ENADE-QA* focuses exclusively on health-related undergraduate programs. Although this domain is relevant for evaluating models on specialized academic questions, it limits the generalization of the results to other areas of knowledge. Expanding the dataset to programs in the Exact Sciences, Humanities, Engineering, and other fields is planned as future work.

The shuffled-answer setting used one deterministic permutation per question to ensure reproducibility. Multiple random permutations per item would provide a more stable estimate of positional preferences and reduce permutation-specific confounds. We leave this more exhaustive perturbation analysis for future work.

Finally, 100 questions, corresponding to approximately 12.25% of the deduplicated corpus, were excluded because they depended on visual elements such as images, tables, graphs, formulas, or diagrams. These questions represent a relevant subset of ENADE exams and may require different evaluation protocols. Their inclusion through textual descriptions, structured representations, or multimodal models is an important direction for future versions of the dataset.

7 Conclusion

We introduced *ENADE-QA*, a curated Brazilian Portuguese multiple-choice question answering dataset derived from official higher-education exams. The dataset contains 716 textual questions from health-related undergraduate programs, with question stems, answer options, official answer keys, and metadata related to year, course, assessed component, and visual dependency. By focusing on ENADE, the dataset complements existing Portuguese resources based on ENEM and university-admission exams, offering a benchmark closer to specialized undergraduate-level assessment.

We also conducted an initial benchmark with open-weight, proprietary, multilingual, and Portuguese-oriented language models under different prompting and inference strategies. The results show that *ENADE-QA* differentiates models by performance level, with proprietary and larger open-weight models achieving the highest accuracies, while smaller models remain closer to the random baseline. The robustness analysis further showed that stronger models generally preserve accuracy under answer-order perturbations, while BPC reveals differences in answer-position preferences that are not explained solely by aggregate accuracy. Lower-performing models were also more sensitive to prompt format and, in several cases, exhibited stronger positional preferences.

Overall, *ENADE-QA* provides a useful resource for evaluating LLMs in Brazilian Portuguese academic contexts, supporting analyses of both accuracy and robustness in domain-specific MCQA. Future work will expand the dataset to other areas of knowledge and incorporate visually dependent questions through textual descriptions, structured representations, or multimodal evaluation protocols.

Acknowledgments. This study was financed in part by the Coordenação de Aperfeiçoamento de Pessoal de Nível Superior – Brasil (CAPES) – Finance Code 001. The authors thank the Fundação de Amparo à Pesquisa do Estado do Rio Grande do Sul (FAPERGS), Brazil, for financial support under Award Agreement 22/2551-0000598-5. We gratefully acknowledge the support of NVIDIA Corporation through the donation of the Titan X Pascal GPU used in this research. We also thank the 20 dataset reviewers for their careful validation work, which was essential to the construction of ENADE-QA.

References

1. Almeida, T.S., Laitz, T., Bonás, G.K., Nogueira, R.: Bluex: a benchmark based on Brazilian leading universities entrance exams. In: Intelligent Systems: 12th Brazilian Conference, BRACIS 2023, Belo Horizonte, Brazil, 25–29 September 2023, Proceedings, Part I, pp. 337–347. Springer, Heidelberg (2023). https://doi.org/10.1007/978-3-031-45368-7_22
2. Brown, T.B., et al.: Language models are few-shot learners. CoRR abs/2005.14165 (2020). https://arxiv.org/abs/2005.14165
3. Chang, Y., et al.: A survey on evaluation of large language models. ACM Trans. Intell. Syst. Technol. **15**(3) (2024). https://doi.org/10.1145/3641289
4. Hendrycks, D., et al.: Measuring massive multitask language understanding. CoRR abs/2009.03300 (2020). https://arxiv.org/abs/2009.03300
5. Joshi, P., Santy, S., Budhiraja, A., Bali, K., Choudhury, M.: The state and fate of linguistic diversity and inclusion in the NLP world. In: Jurafsky, D., Chai, J., Schluter, N., Tetreault, J. (eds.) Proceedings of the 58th Annual Meeting of the Association for Computational Linguistics, pp. 6282–6293. Association for Computational Linguistics, Online (2020). https://doi.org/10.18653/v1/2020.acl-main.560

6. Li, W., Li, L., Xiang, T., Liu, X., Deng, W., Garcia, N.: Can multiple-choice questions really be useful in detecting the abilities of LLMs? In: Calzolari, N., Kan, M.Y., Hoste, V., Lenci, A., Sakti, S., Xue, N. (eds.) Proceedings of the 2024 Joint International Conference on Computational Linguistics, Language Resources and Evaluation (LREC-COLING 2024), pp. 2819–2834. ELRA and ICCL, Torino, Italia (2024)
7. Liang, P., et al.: Holistic evaluation of language models. Transactions on Machine Learning Research (2023). https://openreview.net/forum?id=iO4LZibEqW, featured Certification, Expert Certification
8. Nunes, D., Primi, R., Pires, R., Lotufo, R., Nogueira, R.: Evaluating GPT-3.5 and GPT-4 models on Brazilian university admission exams (2023). https://arxiv.org/abs/2303.17003
9. Pires, R., Almeida, T.S., Abonizio, H., Nogueira, R.: Evaluating GPT-4's vision capabilities on Brazilian university admission exams (2023)
10. Silveira, I.C., Deratani Mauá, D.: University entrance exam as a guiding test for artificial intelligence. In: 2017 Brazilian Conference on Intelligent Systems (BRACIS), pp. 426–431 (2017). https://doi.org/10.1109/BRACIS.2017.44
11. Son, G., et al.: KMMLU: measuring massive multitask language understanding in Korean. In: Chiruzzo, L., Ritter, A., Wang, L. (eds.) Proceedings of the 2025 Conference of the Nations of the Americas Chapter of the Association for Computational Linguistics: Human Language Technologies (Volume 1: Long Papers), pp. 4076–4104. Association for Computational Linguistics, Albuquerque, New Mexico (2025). https://doi.org/10.18653/v1/2025.naacl-long.206
12. Wang, P., et al.: Large language models are not fair evaluators. In: Proceedings of the 62nd Annual Meeting of the Association for Computational Linguistics (ACL 2024), pp. 9440–9450 (2024). https://doi.org/10.18653/v1/2024.acl-long.511
13. Zhang, Z., Jiang, Z., Xu, L., Hao, H., Wang, R.: Multiple-choice questions are efficient and robust LLM evaluators (2024). https://arxiv.org/abs/2405.11966
14. Zheng, C., Zhou, H., Meng, F., Zhou, J., Huang, M.: Large language models are not robust multiple choice selectors. arXiv preprint arXiv:2309.03882 (2023)

Improving Text Classification via XAI-Guided Misclassification Augmentation

Raquel Silveira[1(✉)], Thiago Damasceno Bluhm[2], and Vasco Furtado[2]

[1] Federal Institute of Education, Science and Technology of Ceará (IFCE), Tianguá, Brazil
raquel_silveira@ifce.edu.br
[2] University of Fortaleza (UNIFOR), Fortaleza, Brazil
vasco@unifor.br

Abstract. Iterative classification methods for imbalanced datasets typically rely on random sampling techniques to adjust class distribution and improve model performance. Although these approaches help mitigate class imbalance, they do not explicitly identify which instances are more difficult to classify nor investigate the underlying causes of errors. In this context, we propose an explanation-driven iterative classification approach in which model errors are used as a guiding signal for data augmentation. Specifically, we analyze classification errors at each iteration of a cyclic learning, enabling the iterative refinement of the classification model. Based on these instances, our method combines attribution-based explainability techniques to identify the most relevant input segments associated with the error, with LLM-based semantic analysis to understand their causes. Based on this information, a LLM generates synthetic examples in a targeted manner, focusing on regions associated with model error. The integration of encoder-based classifiers with LLMs, mediated by Explainable AI, enables a more informative and error-driven data augmentation, contributing to improved classification performance. Experiments conducted across different domains demonstrate consistent performance gains, highlighting the effectiveness of the proposed approach.

Keywords: Data augmentation · Explainable AI · Text Classification

1 Introduction

Encoder-only architectures such as BERT [5] and Longformer [1] are widely used in non-generative tasks, including text classification [18] and named entity recognition [13], due to their efficiency, scalability, and strong discriminative performance. However, their effectiveness depends heavily on the availability and quality of labeled data, which is often limited or imbalanced in real scenarios.

To mitigate these limitations, data augmentation has become a key strategy to improve model generalization and robustness. Traditional data augmentation

M. Recamonde-Mendoza and R. C. Barros (Eds.): BRACIS 2026, LNAI 17105, pp. 568–583, 2027.
https://doi.org/10.1007/978-3-032-39882-6_38

approaches typically rely on random sampling or heuristic strategies applied within a single learning cycle to adjust class distributions. While effective to some extent, they often apply simplistic transformations to the input data, leading to repetitive or low-diversity samples [10], which limits their ability to introduce informative and diverse patterns, reducing the effectiveness of augmentation.

More recently, decoder-based Large Language Models (LLMs) have emerged as a promising alternative for data augmentation, as they excel at text generation and reasoning, enabling the creation of human-like and contextually rich content [4]. In this sense, encoder-only and decoder-based models offer complementary capabilities, combining strong discriminative performance with powerful generative abilities for improving text classification systems.

In this context, we propose an approach that leverages the strengths of encoder-based models and LLMs by combining attribution-based Explainable AI (XAI) with LLM-driven text generation for data augmentation to enhance text classification performance. Specifically, our approach uses explainability methods to derive explanatory sentences that capture the most influential features underlying a classifier's predictions. Analysis of these attributions reveals characteristic failure modes, such as underweighting semantically relevant context and overweighting terms that are misleading when not properly contextualized. For example, in news topic classification, high attribution to terms such as 'budget' or 'investments' may lead to an *economics* label, even when references to legislative processes indicate a *politics* category. Attribution analysis exposes such errors by highlighting neglected contextual cues. These explanations guide in-context learning within an LLM, generating synthetic examples that explicitly address the identified failure modes. The generated examples are incorporated into the training set, and the classifier is retrained. This process occurs over successive cycles, progressively refining the classifier's performance.

We evaluate our approach on text classification using six datasets, demonstrating its effectiveness across different domains. The results demonstrate micro and macro F1-score gains, ranging from 3.2% to 15.0% to micro F1 and 6.4% to 58.1% to macro F1 relative to the baseline, and show that attribution-guided integration of LLMs outperforms both non-LLM and LLM-only baselines.

In summary, this paper makes the following contributions: (i) We propose an iterative, closed-loop approach that integrates attribution-based explainability with LLM-driven data augmentation; (ii) We leverage attribution-based explainability to identify influential input features, which are transformed by LLMs into data-grounded explanations that characterize and contextualize model errors; (iii) We demonstrate consistent performance gains across six datasets from different domains, outperforming both LLM-based and non-LLM baselines.

2 Related Work

2.1 Iterative Data Augmentation for Text Classification

Iterative classification refines a model over multiple training rounds by incorporating new supervision signals as the process progresses. Self-training and pseudo-labeling approaches have widely explored this perspective. In these methods, the models iteratively expand their training sets by using their own predictions, typically regulating them with confidence or uncertainty measures. Successfully demonstrated in computer vision [25] and surveyed across domains [7], these methods have shown consistent results. In particular, recent studies highlight that iterative use of model feedback can improve generalization, provided that appropriate mechanisms are employed to mitigate error propagation [7].

In imbalanced classification, iterative strategies have also attracted increasing attention. Recent research shows that adaptive schemes based on resampling, reweighting, or progressive dataset expansion can reduce the dominance of majority classes and improve performance on minority classes, especially when combined with dynamic evidence extracted from the model itself [9]. These approaches reinforce the notion of iterative pipelines in which errors, uncertainty, or failure patterns guide the continuous refinement of the learning process.

Data augmentation from generative language models for improving classification has recently been explored in the literature [16]. However, [14] demonstrates that the effectiveness of LLM-generated synthetic data varies significantly across different classification tasks. Recent studies also explore counterfactual data augmentation, where LLMs generate minimally edited examples that challenge the classifier and can improve robustness and mitigate spurious correlations [8]. Iterative pipelines close the loop by using the classifier's validation errors (or confidence signals) to steer what the LLM should generate next, refining augmentation based on observed failures [12].

2.2 Bridging XAI and Data Generation

Although explainability and data augmentation are often treated as separate concerns in machine learning pipelines, studies suggest that their integration can enable more targeted and effective performance improvements [17,24]. Most explainability techniques, such as Integrated Gradients (IG) [20] and SHAP [15], are primarily used post hoc to visualize or audit model behavior [2], and rarely do they serve as active components in feedback loops that influence training or synthetic data generation.

Prior work has leveraged explainability to support model debugging or feature selection [19], yet the explicit use of attribution scores to drive synthetic instance generation remains unexplored, with few recent exceptions that investigate explanation-driven or explanation-aware learning loops [22,24]. Similarly, existing LLM-based data augmentation strategies typically rely on class-level prompts or dataset statistics [14,23], without grounding generation in the model's actual errors or internal decision patterns. More recently, an XAI-guided data augmentation approach has been proposed that integrates explainability techniques with LLMs to improve synthetic data quality, using attribution signals to identify less influential features and preserve semantic information. However, it focuses on context-aware augmentation and semantic preservation, rather than leveraging explainability in an error-driven loop [17].

We address this gap by proposing a closed-loop approach that connects attribution-based explainability with LLM-driven data generation. Unlike approaches that treat explainability as a static diagnostic tool, we use IG not only to explain model decisions but also to identify high-attribution tokens responsible for misclassifications. These tokens expose critical linguistic signals that the model has either failed to learn. By transforming attribution-based error analysis into semantically grounded synthetic examples, the proposed approach introduces an explanation-driven approach to data augmentation.

3 Learning from the Explanation of Errors

3.1 Overview

The proposed approach assumes that errors made by a text classifier provide insights into its limitations in representation and decision-making. Instead of viewing errors as mere indicators of poor performance, our method uses them as valuable signals for improving the model through targeted data augmentation.

Initialy, the dataset D is divided into A_{train}, A_{val}, and A_{test}. A classifier is first trained on A_{train}. After each training cycle, the model is evaluated on the validation set A_{val}. Based on the predictions made on A_{val}, a contingency table is constructed for each class c, identifying correctly classified instances TP_c and misclassified examples FP_c. For each misclassified example FP_c, token-level importance scores are computed using a feature attribution–based explainability method. These scores estimate the contribution of individual tokens to the classifier's predictions, which enables the identification of textual units that most strongly influenced the incorrect decisions. The token-level attributions are subsequently aggregated at the sentence level to identify the text segments that exerted the greatest influence on the model's misclassifications.

Based on the most relevant sentences identified through attribution analysis, an LLM generates textual explanations of the classifier's errors. In this step, the LLM also receives a structured context contrasting an incorrectly classified instance with a randomly selected correctly classified example that shares the same label. This contrastive setup enables the LLM to identify the differences in relevance patterns that led to the incorrect decision. The generated explanations guide the creation of synthetic data by highlighting specific areas where the model's decision-making needs improvement. At this stage, the LLM is invoked again to produce multiple distinct synthetic text instances, conditioned on both the misclassified example and its corresponding explanatory sentence.

We then incorporate the synthesized examples into the training set, yielding an augmented dataset that emphasizes problematic regions of the model's decision space. The classifier Y is retrained on this expanded dataset. This procedure is executed iteratively, following successive cycles of example generation and retraining, in the spirit of iterative frameworks such as those in [6,12]. Unlike prior approaches that rely on counterexamples, target labels, or performance feedback, our approach uses explicit error explanations as the primary refinement signal. The iterative process stops when there are no performance improvements on the validation set for a specified number of iterations or when the maximum number of cycles is reached. At the end of the iterative process, classification model performance is evaluated on the test set using the micro and macro F1-scores.

Figure 1 provides a summary of the proposed approach. Detailed explanations are provided in the following subsections. The source code for the proposed method is available at: https://github.com/thiagobluhm/igdataug2025.

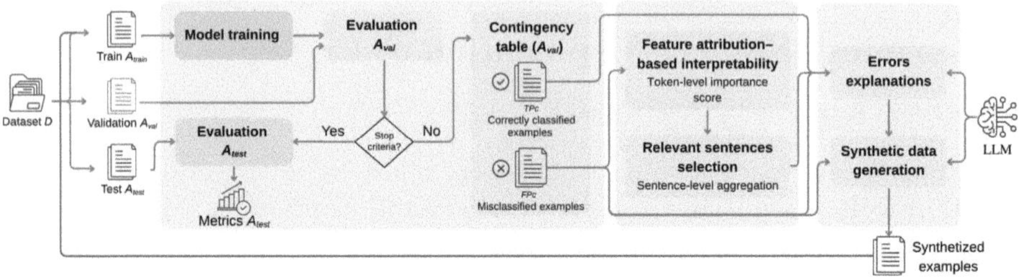

Fig. 1. Overview of the proposed iterative XAI-guided misclassification augmentation approach.

3.2 Feature Attribution and Selection of Relevant Sentences

Each textual instance $a_j \in A_{\text{val}}$ is represented as a sequence of tokens $X_j = \{x_{j1}, x_{j2}, \ldots, x_{jm}\}$. A feature attribution-based explainability method is used to identify the textual elements that most influence the model's predictions. Let $\phi(a_j)$ denote the attribution function produced by this method for each instance $a_j \in A_{\text{val}}$. The attribution $\phi(a_j)$ is a vector that captures the contribution of each token $x_{j1}, x_{j2}, \ldots, x_{jm}$ to the decision of the model Y. Formally,

$$\phi(a_j) = \{\phi_{j1}, \phi_{j2}, \ldots, \phi_{jm}\}, \tag{1}$$

where ϕ_{ji} represents the importance assigned to token x_{ji}.

Subsequently, each instance $a_j \in A_{\text{val}}$ is partitioned into a set of sentences (or *chunks*), denoted by $S_j = \{s_{j1}, s_{j2}, \ldots, s_{jK}\}$, composed of contiguous token subsequences, each with a maximum length defined by the model's parameters. For each sentence s_{jk}, the aggregated relevance score $R(s_{jk})$ is defined as the sum of the attribution values of the tokens that compose it:

$$R(s_{jk}) = \sum_{x_{ji} \in s_{jk}} \phi_{ji}. \tag{2}$$

This score quantifies the aggregated contribution of sentence s_{jk} to the classifier's final prediction. Based on these scores, the sentences associated with each instance a_j are ranked in descending order according to $R(s_{jk})$. The set of the k most relevant sentences is then selected as

$$S^*(a_j) = \{s_{j(1)}, s_{j(2)}, \ldots, s_{j(k)}\}, \tag{3}$$

where $s_{j(1)} \geq s_{j(2)} \geq \cdots \geq s_{j(k)}$ with respect to the aggregated contribution $R(\cdot)$. These sentences correspond to the *top-k* textual units most influential in the model's decision-making process.

3.3 Building Errors Explanation

For each class $c \in C$, we consider instances incorrectly classified by the model in A_{val}, denoted by $a_f \in FP_c$. For each misclassified example (FP_c), an LLM is employed to explain the classification error by leveraging the example a_f and the k most relevant sentences $S^*(a_f)$ and contrasting them with a correctly classified instance $a_t \in TP_c$ of the same class. The basic intuition of the prompt is described below (a complete description can be found in https://github.com/thiagobluhm/igdataug2025/blob/main/code/prompts.py).

Error Explanation Prompt (Excerpt)

You are an expert in explainability. You will be provided with a set of labeled documents. Some of the documents have been correctly classified, while others have not. Take two examples labeled with the same class by Y, one correctly classified and another misclassified. Analyze them considering the key sentences and formulate a hypothesis explaining the underlying causes of these errors. Focus on uncovering non-obvious patterns or reasoning shortcuts adopted by the model, rather than attributing the mistakes to missing or isolated keywords.

To illustrate the application of the formal explanation, we present two example hypotheses explaining why the classifier confuses themes related to *tax obligations* with *administrative issues*, derived of a misclassified legal case.

Error Explanation Example (Excerpt). Confusion Between Administrative and Tax Law: The model struggles to distinguish between legal documents using similar terms from administrative and tax law. For example, it wrongly labeled a petition about a tax dispute as "Tax Obligations", when the real issue was administrative—about the government's authority to act, not about tax compliance itself. The model focused too much on keywords like "tax infractions" instead of understanding the broader administrative context.

Shared Phrases, Different Meanings: Legal phrases that appear in both administrative and tax cases caused the model to misclassify based on surface similarities. While one document was correctly classified as administrative due to clear context, another with similar phrases was mislabeled as tax-related because the model failed to pick up on the correct legal framework based on the surrounding context.

3.4 Synthetic Data Generation

To address specific misclassifications, new synthetic examples are generated based on the error explanations. For each misclassified instance a $a_f \in FP_c$ and its corresponding explanation, a LLM generates n distinct synthetic examples.

$$G_f = \{g_{f1}, g_{f2}, \ldots, g_{fn}\}. \tag{4}$$

Each synthetic instance $g_{fi} \in G_f$ preserves the true class of a_f and introduces controlled, semantically consistent variations guided by the error explanation.

Below is a fraction of the prompt designed to generate synthetic instances:

Synthetic Example Generation Prompt (Excerpt)

Your task is to create new text examples to help improve a classifier that made specific mistakes. For each misclassified case, you are given an explanation and a list of key sentences that influenced the wrong decision. Use this information to write challenging examples that clearly belong to the correct category. Reinforce patterns typical of that category, but also include elements that previously confused the model—so the new examples can help it learn to generalize better. Use the key sentences to guide how you build your synthetic texts.

The synthetic examples are added to the training set, creating an augmented dataset that specifically targets problematic regions:

$$A'_{\text{train}} = A_{\text{train}} \cup G. \tag{5}$$

The classification model Y is retrained on A'_{train} to refine its decision boundaries and minimize previously identified error patterns. This procedure is repeated in cycles, guided by explainability to continuously refine the model.

4 Experimental Setup

4.1 Datasets

The experiments were conducted on six text classification datasets covering distinct domains, including legal, healthcare, finance, and social media, with varying document lengths and numbers of classes. Table 1 summarizes the main characteristics of each dataset, including the total of instances (|Ex|), the number of classes (|Classes|), and the average of tokens per document. All datasets exhibit class imbalance, posing challenges for model training and making this setting suitable for evaluating data augmentation strategies aimed at improving model.

The datasets used in this study are: (i) *Brazilian Legal Petitions*, from the Brazilian legal domain, originally used in [18], consist of initial petitions labeled by main legal subject; (ii) *20 Newsgroups* contains short forum posts for topic classification; (iii) *DBLP*, from the academic domain, comprises scientific paper abstracts used to classify documents by research areas; (iv) *WebKB* includes

Table 1. Datasets used in the evaluation process.

Dataset	|Ex|	|Classes|	Avg. Tokens
Brazilian Legal Petitions	2,737	7	4,954
20 Newsgroups	3,059	20	487
DBLP	3,236	10	183
WebKB	2,830	7	250
OHSUMED	3,295	23	282
WOS5736	5,736	11	290

institutional university web pages classified by functional type; (v) *OHSUMED*, from the biomedical domain, consists of medical abstracts categorized by clinical topics; and (vi) *WOS5736* contains abstracts of scientific articles indexed in Web of Science, classified by fields of knowledge.

The *Brazilian Legal Petitions* dataset, originally used in [18], was selected due to its long and highly specialized documents that challenge text classifiers. In contrast, *20 Newsgroups*, *WebKB*, *OHSUMED*, *DBLP*, and *WOS5736* are widely adopted benchmarks for text classification [3]. The varied domains, textual structures, and classification objectives of these datasets allow for a thorough assessment of the proposed approach's robustness and generality across different contexts. All datasets are multi-class and in English, except for *Brazilian Legal Petitions*, which contains Brazilian Portuguese texts.

Experiments were conducted with subsamples of the original datasets (following the distributions reported in Table 1), preserving class proportions and textual characteristics. Subsampling was essential to manage the computational costs associated with using LLMs for iterative synthetic data generation, ensuring efficient processing without compromising the integrity of the evaluation. This choice maintains the integrity of the evaluation because the proposed method's reliance on local explainability and error-driven generation mechanisms ensures effectiveness regardless of dataset size, as demonstrated in prior studies.

4.2 Data Augmentation Approaches

In order to compare the proposed strategy with traditional balancing and data augmentation approaches, the following scenarios were defined:

- **Baseline**: The model is trained exclusively on the original dataset without applying any balancing or data augmentation techniques.
- **Balancing with Random Over-Sampling (Bal. ROS)**: The researchers balance the training data by randomly replicating instances from minority classes until they match the size of the majority class. This balancing procedure is performed once prior to model training [21].

- **Iterative Random Over-Sampling (Iter. ROS)**: an iterative data augmentation strategy guided by misclassified instances, following the iterative frameworks explored in [6,12]. At each cycle, errors identified on the validation set are used to randomly replicate instances from the corresponding minority classes, as commonly adopted in adaptive resampling schemes for imbalanced settings [21].
- **LLM-Based Data Augmentation**: This strategy iteratively augments data based on misclassified instances, following the framework in [6,12]. At each iteration, an LLM generates synthetic examples from validation errors, according to LLM-based generation approaches, such as [4].
- **Proposed Approach**: The application of the proposed method under an iterative, error-driven regime. In this setting, synthetic data generation is guided by explicit explanations of classification errors obtained through feature attribution methods and analysis of the relevant sentences associated with each error. This enables targeted generation focused on specific regions of the model's decision space, as detailed in Sect. 3.

4.3 Text Classification Model Architecture

To address long text classification, we selected the Longformer model [1], variant of BERT [5], for its ability to handle sequences of up to 4,096 tokens. The maximum input length was set according to each dataset's token: 4,096 for *Brazilian Legal Petitions*, 1,024 for *20 Newsgroups*, and 512 for the remaining datasets.

Training followed the iterative protocol described in Sect. 3 within a 5-fold cross-validation setting that preserves class distributions. Thus, the framework is executed five times. In each run, one fold is used as the test set (A_{test}), one as the validation set (A_{val}), and the remaining folds for training (A_{train}). The iterative process is applied using A_{train}, with A_{val} guiding performance monitoring and data augmentation. A_{test} is used only after the iterative process is completed to estimate final performance, measured by the micro and macro F1-scores.

Feature attribution-based method was employed using IG, implemented via Captum's Layer Integrated Gradients module [11]. Attributions were calculated with respect to the input embeddings, using reference token IDs as baselines, and approximated with 4 integration steps. The resulting scores were aggregated at the token level by summing across the embedding dimension and normalized using the L_2-norm. Convergence was monitored via the delta.

Fine-tuning was performed using `joelniklaus/legal-xlm-longformer-base` model for the Brazilian Legal Petitions dataset, due to its support for Portuguese and specialization in the legal domain. For the remaining English datasets, we employed `allenai/longformer-base-4096`, a pretrained model suited for long-document processing. Training was conducted with a batch size of 4, for up to 8 epochs, using early stopping with a patience of 3 epochs. After each epoch, the model achieving the highest weighted F1-score on the validation set was saved as the best checkpoint. Optimization was performed using the

AdamW optimizer with a fixed learning rate of 8×10^{-5} across all experimental settings.

For explainability analysis, documents were segmented into chunks of 64 tokens, and up to four relevant sentences were selected per instance.

In data augmentation, misclassified instances were used to expand the training set by generating five synthetic examples per instance. In all LLM-based scenarios, the `gpt-4o-mini` model was used with a fixed configuration across experiments to isolate the impact of the augmentation strategy.

To ensure comparability across scenarios, all hyperparameter settings were held constant, as this isolates the effects of the data augmentation strategy by eliminating variability from other factors.

5 Experimental Results

5.1 Text Classification Results

Results in Table 2 show that our framework outperforms all tested scenarios in terms of micro and macro F1 across diverse datasets. Compared to the *Baseline*, it achieves gains from 0.027 to 0.097, corresponding to improvements of 3.2% to 15.0% in micro F1, and from 0.056 to 0.244, corresponding to improvements of 6.4% to 58.1% in macro F1. The largest gains occur on *OHSUMED*. Improvements are consistently positive, even for high-performing datasets like *WOS5736*, showing the approach's effectiveness regardless of initial performance.

Table 2. Micro and macro F1-scores on the test set for the different scenarios.

Dataset	Baseline		Bal. ROS		Iter. ROS		LLM-Based		Proposed	
	Micro	Macro	Micro	Macro	Micro	Macro	Micro	Macro	Micro	Macro
Brazilian Legal Petitions	0.849	0.800	0.858	0.850	0.868	0.865	0.873	0.861	**0.876**	**0.869**
20 Newsgroups	0.699	0.669	0.706	0.686	0.742	0.729	0.744	0.732	**0.751**	**0.737**
DBLP	0.733	0.695	0.731	0.724	0.760	0.739	0.764	0.747	**0.772**	**0.755**
WebKB	0.790	0.637	0.779	0.695	0.843	0.733	0.843	0.738	**0.850**	**0.748**
OHSUMED	0.645	0.420	0.701	0.634	0.735	0.657	0.728	0.642	**0.742**	**0.664**
WOS5736	0.879	0.876	0.899	0.896	0.931	0.931	0.926	0.926	**0.933**	**0.932**

When compared to static balancing strategies such as random over-sampling, our approach consistently achieves higher micro and macro F1-scores. Although static balancing improves performance over the *Baseline*, its gains are limited when compared to more advanced strategies. This suggests that simple instance replication is insufficient to capture complex discriminative patterns, especially in multi-class settings with high semantic overlap.

Iterative error-driven strategies, like ours, lead to larger gains than static balancing because they enable a targeted focus on areas of uncertainty, allowing for more precise adjustments and improvements in model performance. Our method also outperforms purely LLM-based iterative generation. Specifically, incorporating explicit error explanations leads to micro F1-score improvements of 0.003 to 0.014 (0.34% to 1.92%) and macro F1-score gains from 0.005 to 0.022 (0.68% to 3.43%), depending on the dataset, indicating that class-conditioned generation alone does not adequately target the most critical regions of the decision space.

The largest relative improvements over the *Baseline* and *LLM-Based* scenarios are observed in more challenging datasets, such as *OHSUMED* and *WebKB*. On *OHSUMED*, which contains 23 classes, the proposed approach outperforms the *Baseline* by 15.0% (micro F1) and 58.1% (macro F1) and the *LLM-Based* scenario by 1.92% (micro F1) and 3.43% (macro F1), representing the largest improvement among all datasets. Similarly, on *WebKB*, which involves semantically overlapping classes, the method achieves gains of 7.6% (micro F1) and 17.4% (macro F1) over the *Baseline* and 0.83 (micro F1) and 1.36% (macro F1) over *LLM-Based*, indicating robust effectiveness under high thematic variability.

In the *Brazilian Legal Petitions* dataset, characterized by long documents and specialized legal language, the proposed approach achieves micro F1 of 0.876 and macro F1 of 0.869, outperforming the *Baseline* by 3.18% to 8.63%, respectively, and the *LLM-Based* approach by 0.34% to 0.93%, respectively. This demonstrates the method's ability to handle domain-specific challenges, such as complex terminology and structured discourse. This result underscores the method's effectiveness in technical domains, where traditional approaches struggle with rigid terminology and structured discourse.

Even on high-performing datasets such as *WOS5736*, the method yields measurable gains, surpassing the *Baseline* by 6.14% to micro F1 and 6.39% to macro F1 and the *LLM-Based* approach by 0.76% to micro F1 and 0.65% to macro F1, achieving the best overall performance. This suggests that the proposed framework acts both as a corrective tool in difficult scenarios and as a refinement process for models nearing performance limits.

These results highlight the effectiveness of integrating explainability signals into synthetic data generation, yielding consistent improvements across domains and outperforming traditional methods.

5.2 Ablation Analysis

To further analyze data augmentation strategies, we focus on the *Brazilian Initial Petitions* dataset, whose long documents, specialized vocabulary, and imbalanced classes provide a challenging evaluation setting.

Performance Evolution Across Iterative Cycles. As part of the ablation analysis, we examine the iterative training process using three indicators: (i) number of errors on the validation set, (ii) training set size after synthetic augmentation, and (iii) macro F1-score on the test set. Figure 2 shows the evolution of these indicators across iterative cycles for the *Brazilian Initial Petitions* dataset, revealing distinct patterns across strategies, such as different rates of error reduction and varying gains in macro F1-score.

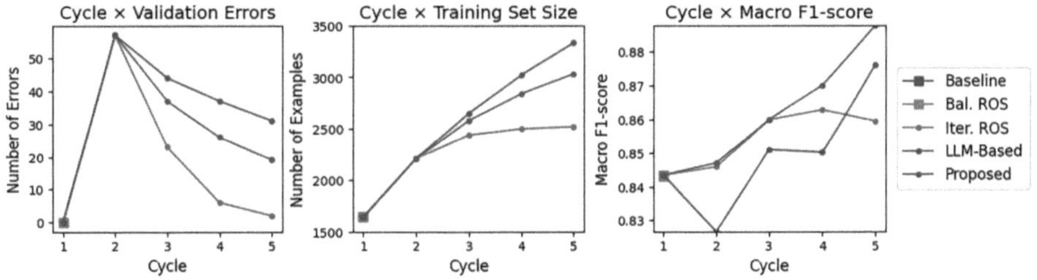

Fig. 2. Evolution of the number of validation errors, training set size, and test-set macro F1-score across iterative cycles.

The proposed approach and *Iter. ROS* show a steeper reduction in validation errors across cycles, indicating more effective incorporation of informative examples. In contrast, *LLM-Based* shows a more gradual decrease, suggesting that some generated samples do not adequately address the model's failure modes.

The evolution of the training set size, linked to validation errors, shows that the proposed approach ensures controlled growth in training instances, avoiding the excessive expansion seen in other strategies. This behavior indicates a more targeted use of synthetic examples throughout the iterative cycles.

The test-set macro F1-score analysis reveals that the proposed approach not only achieves stable and progressive gains across iterations but also reaches the best final performance, underscoring its superior effectiveness. This suggests that systematically reducing validation errors leads to significant improvements in the model's generalization ability, enhancing applicability across datasets.

Noisy Synthetic Examples. The proposed approach uses error explanations to guide the generation of synthetic examples. However, generative models raise concerns about the reliability of the labels assigned to these examples. Automatically generated texts may exhibit semantic ambiguity, conceptual drift, or contextual inconsistencies. These issues can lead to incorrect label assignments and introduce noise during training.

To empirically assess this effect, we conducted a qualitative evaluation with domain experts, who examined a sample of 325 synthetic examples generated during the first iteration and assessed the correctness of their labels. The analysis revealed that approximately 10% of the evaluated instances contained labeling inconsistencies, often due to subtle semantic distinctions between classes. Many of these cases were associated with borderline documents, for which semantic distinctions between classes are inherently subtle, even for human experts.

These findings highlight the need to analyze the method's sensitivity to label noise and assess its robustness under realistic conditions. We conducted a controlled experiment where expert-labeled synthetic examples were partially corrupted. Only a subset retained correct labels, while others were intentionally mislabeled. This setup allowed us to evaluate how well the iterative, error-driven process handles noisy supervision. Table 3 presents the resulting macro F1-scores on the *Brazilian Initial Petition* dataset after the second iteration.

Table 3. Variation of correctly labeled examples.

% correctly labeled	Macro F1-score
25%	0.845
50%	0.842
75%	0.842
100%	**0.857**

Table 3 shows that the proposed approach is robust to label noise in synthetic examples, which is crucial for model reliability compared to the *Baseline* (macro F1-score of 0.800). Even in the most adverse scenario, with only 25% correctly labeled instances, the model achieves a macro F1-score of 0.845, representing a gain of approximately 5.6% over the *Baseline*. This result indicates that mislabeled synthetic data does not significantly degrade performance, highlighting the method's robustness in realistic settings where label noise is common.

In intermediate scenarios (50% and 75% correctly labeled instances), performance remains stable, with macro F1-scores of 0.842, corresponding to gains of about 5.3% over the baseline. This consistency suggests that moderate levels of label noise have limited impact on the model. Such behavior is supported by the tendency of synthetic examples to populate semantically relevant regions near decision boundaries, which helps mitigate the effect of isolated labeling errors.

When all synthetic examples are correctly labeled, the proposed approach achieves the best performance, with a macro F1-score of 0.857, corresponding to a gain of approximately 7.1% over the baseline. This result indicates that while the method is robust to noise, higher label accuracy leads to additional improvements, reinforcing the importance of reliable synthetic data.

6 Conclusion

This work introduces an iterative data augmentation framework that improves model performance by refining training data through error analysis. It aims to improve model performance by using explanations of classification errors to guide the creation of synthetic training examples. The method combines attribution-based explainability with large language models to create a feedback loop in which misclassified instances are analyzed and used to refine the training data.

Experiments on six datasets from different domains show that the proposed approach consistently outperforms classical over-sampling methods and LLM-based data augmentation without error guidance. Improvements in micro and macro F1-scores are observed across all scenarios, including datasets with high initial performance, such as *WOS5736*, indicating that the method is effective both as a corrective mechanism and as a fine-tuning strategy.

Further analyses, using micro and macro F1-scores, showed that the approach effectively reduces validation errors over iterations. It does so by controlling training set growth and focusing synthetic examples in more informative areas of the representation space, as shown by specific metrics.

The approach also has limitations, primarily hinging on the quality of the attribution-based explainability method. Inaccurate attributions can lead to weak or misleading explanations, potentially compromising the integrity of the synthetic examples and the overall model performance. Future work should explore robust attribution methods to mitigate these risks.

Additionally, explanations generated by LLMs may introduce ambiguity, as synthetic examples can contain semantic inconsistencies or incorrect labels. To address this, future research should focus on developing automatic validation mechanisms for synthetic data, reducing reliance on expert inspection. Another direction is contrastive selection for LLM inputs using similarity or clustering to retrieve relevant correctly classified examples. Further directions include extending the method to other tasks and evaluating alternative language models and explainability techniques.

Acknowledgments. We gratefully acknowledge CNPq (Grant 305717/2023-5) and FUNCAP for financial support.

References

1. Beltagy, I., Peters, M.E., Cohan, A.: Longformer: the long-document transformer. arXiv:2004.05150 (2020)
2. Bodria, F., Giannotti, F., Guidotti, R., Naretto, F., Pedreschi, D., Rinzivillo, S.: Benchmarking and survey of explanation methods for black box models. Data Min. Knowl. Disc. **37**(5), 1719–1778 (2023). https://doi.org/10.1007/s10618-023-00933-9
3. Cunha, W., Rocha, L., Gonçalves, M.A.: A thorough benchmark of automatic text classification: from traditional approaches to large language models. arXiv preprint arXiv:2504.01930 (2025). https://doi.org/10.48550/arXiv.2504.01930
4. Dai, H., et al.: Auggpt: leveraging chatgpt for text data augmentation. IEEE Trans. Big Data **11**(3), 907–918 (2025). https://doi.org/10.1109/TBDATA.2025.3536934
5. Devlin, J., Chang, M.W., Lee, K., Toutanova, K.: BERT: pre-training of deep bidirectional transformers for language understanding. In: Proceedings of the 2019 Conference of the North American Chapter of the Association for Computational Linguistics: Human Language Technologies, pp. 4171–4186. Association for Computational Linguistics, Minneapolis, Minnesota (2019). https://doi.org/10.18653/v1/N19-1423
6. Dreossi, T., Ghosh, S., Yue, X., Keutzer, K., Sangiovanni-Vincentelli, A., Seshia, S.A.: Counterexample-guided data augmentation. In: Proceedings of the 27th International Joint Conference on Artificial Intelligence (IJCAI), pp. 2071–2078 (2018). https://doi.org/10.24963/ijcai.2018/286

7. Du, J., et al.: Self-training improves pre-training for natural language understanding. In: Proceedings of the 2021 Conference of the North American Chapter of the Association for Computational Linguistics: Human Language Technologies, pp. 5408–5418 (2021). https://doi.org/10.18653/v1/2021.naacl-main.426
8. Feder, A., Wald, Y., Shi, C., Saria, S., Blei, D.: Data augmentations for improved (large) language model generalization. In: Proceedings of the 37th International Conference on Neural Information Processing Systems. NIPS 2023. Curran Associates Inc, Red Hook, NY, USA (2023)
9. Gao, X., et al.: A comprehensive survey on imbalanced data learning. Front. Comput. Sci. **20** (2026). https://doi.org/10.1007/s11704-025-50274-7
10. Kesgin, H.T., Amasyali, M.F.: Advancing NLP models with strategic text augmentation: a comprehensive study of augmentation methods and curriculum strategies. Nat. Lang. Process. J. **7**, 100071 (2024). https://doi.org/10.1016/j.nlp.2024.100071
11. Kokhlikyan, N., et al.: Captum: a unified and generic model interpretability library for pytorch. arXiv:2009.07896 (2020). https://arxiv.org/abs/2009.07896
12. Lee, N., et al.: Llm2llm: boosting LLMs with novel iterative data enhancement. In: Findings of the Association for Computational Linguistics: ACL 2024, pp. 6498–6526. Association for Computational Linguistics, Bangkok, Thailand (2024). https://doi.org/10.18653/v1/2024.findings-acl.388
13. Li, J., Sun, A., Han, J., Li, C.: A survey on deep learning for named entity recognition. IEEE Trans. Knowl. Data Eng. **34**(1), 50–70 (2022). https://doi.org/10.1109/tkde.2020.2981314
14. Li, Z., Zhu, H., Lu, Z., Yin, M.: Synthetic data generation with large language models for text classification: potential and limitations. In: Proceedings of the 2023 Conference on Empirical Methods in Natural Language Processing, pp. 10443–10461. Association for Computational Linguistics, Singapore (2023). https://doi.org/10.18653/v1/2023.emnlp-main.647
15. Lundberg, S.M., Lee, S.I.: A unified approach to interpreting model predictions. In: Advances in Neural Information Processing Systems, vol. 30, pp. 4765–4774. Curran Associates, Inc. (2017)
16. Meng, Y., Huang, J., Zhang, Y., Han, J.: Generating training data with language models: towards zero-shot language understanding. In: Advances in Neural Information Processing Systems, vol. 35, pp. 462–477. Curran Associates, Inc (2022)
17. Mersha, M.A., et al.: Explainable AI: XAI-guided context-aware data augmentation. Expert Syst. Appl. **289**, 128364 (2025). https://doi.org/10.1016/j.eswa.2025.128364
18. Pires, R., Silveira, R., Fernandes, C., Neto, J.M., Furtado, V.: Using complex networks to improve legal text hierarchical classification. In: Anais da XXXIV Brazilian Conference on Intelligent Systems, pp. 476–490. SBC, Porto Alegre, RS, Brasil (2024)
19. Ribeiro, M.T., Singh, S., Guestrin, C.: "Why should i trust you?": explaining the predictions of any classifier. In: Proceedings of the 22nd ACM SIGKDD International Conference on Knowledge Discovery and Data Mining (KDD), pp. 1135–1144. ACM, San Francisco, CA, USA (2016). https://doi.org/10.1145/2939672.2939778
20. Sundararajan, M., Taly, A., Yan, Q.: Axiomatic attribution for deep networks. In: Proceedings of the 34th International Conference on Machine Learning. ICML 2017, vol. 70, pp. 3319–3328. JMLR.org (2017)
21. Taskiran, S.F., Turkoglu, B., Kaya, E., et al.: A comprehensive evaluation of oversampling techniques for enhancing text classification performance. Sci. Rep. **15**, 21631 (2025). https://doi.org/10.1038/s41598-025-05791-7

22. Teso, S., Kersting, K.: Explanatory interactive machine learning. Association for Computing Machinery, New York, NY, USA (2019)
23. Wang, Y., et al.: Self-instruct: aligning language models with self-generated instructions. In: Proceedings of the 61st Annual Meeting of the Association for Computational Linguistics, vol. 1, pp. 13484–13508. Association for Computational Linguistics, Toronto, Canada (2023). https://doi.org/10.18653/v1/2023.acl-long.754
24. Wickramanayake, S., Hsu, W., Lee, M.L.: Explanation-based data augmentation for image classification. In: Advances in Neural Information Processing Systems, vol. 34, pp. 20929–20940. Curran Associates, Inc (2021)
25. Xie, Q., Luong, M.T., Hovy, E., Le, Q.V.: Self-training with noisy student improves imagenet classification. In: Proceedings of the IEEE/CVF Conference on Computer Vision and Pattern Recognition (CVPR) (2020)

LLM-Lobotomy: A Representation Engineering Framework for LLM Behavioral Steering

Eduardo Bouhid(✉), Leonardo N. Ferreira, Ruben Interian, and Zanoni Dias

Institute of Computing, University of Campinas, Campinas, SP, Brazil
{eduardo.bouhid,lnf,ruben,zanoni}@ic.unicamp.br

Abstract. Modern Large Language Models (LLMs) are typically post-trained with instruction-following and preference-optimization methods, such as supervised fine-tuning and Reinforcement Learning from Human Feedback (RLHF), to improve helpfulness, safety, and adherence to user-facing behavioral norms. However, accumulating evidence suggests such procedures may not fully constrain the latent political manifold inherited from pretraining data. In this work, we investigate this by introducing LLM-Lobotomy, a representation engineering framework for inference-time activation scaling, and study it in the controlled setting of political stance questionnaires. Using a textual corpus to identify ideologically relevant features within the residual stream, we optimize feature-wise activation multipliers on a fixed set of political statement pairs from a political questionnaire (Ideological Position Index, or IPI) and evaluate the resulting shifts over this same domain across four model families: Gemma 3 (4B), Llama 3.1 (8B), Phi-3 Mini (3.8B), and Qwen 3 (8B). We find that optimizing a continuous token-level stance surrogate can induce corresponding changes in discrete Likert-scale responses, especially when steering the model towards the left-wing political stance. We also investigate asymmetries in model susceptibility: while all models exhibited statistically significant shifts under left-stance steering (IPI minimization), Llama 3.1 and Phi-3 Mini strongly resisted right-stance steering (IPI maximization). Capability checks on the PoETa v2 suggest that the intervention often preserves aggregate performance, although specific model-task combinations can degrade performance substantially. These results suggest that inference-time activation scaling can induce targeted in-domain behavioral shifts in aligned LLMs.

Keywords: Large Language Models · Representation Engineering · Activation Scaling · AI Safety · Model Alignment

1 Introduction

The emergence of Large Language Models (LLMs) has altered the landscape of information synthesis, offering unprecedented capabilities in processing and

M. Recamonde-Mendoza and R. C. Barros (Eds.): BRACIS 2026, LNAI 17105, pp. 584–598, 2027.
https://doi.org/10.1007/978-3-032-39882-6_39

generating complex text [5]. This fluency, however, masks a more subtle influence: LLMs do not just summarize information, as their outputs are shaped by internal representations. As users increasingly rely on these models to navigate complex topics, the interaction between human inquiry and algorithmic response creates a feedback loop that can inadvertently reinforce specific ideological or conceptual frameworks [10,23].

To mitigate these risks, contemporary alignment pipelines commonly combine supervised instruction tuning with reinforcement learning from human feedback (RLHF) [16]. While these methods effectively shape a model's conversational interface, they are primarily training-time solutions that often fail to account for vulnerabilities emerging during inference. A primary concern lies in the tension between a model's superficial alignment and its underlying latent representations. Recent studies suggest that a model's core behavioral tendencies – derived largely from its pre-training corpus [6,9] – remain quiescent but accessible, even when safety guardrails are present [4].

In this work, we challenge the robustness of existing alignment strategies by introducing LLM-Lobotomy, a framework for steering autoregressive generation through direct latent intervention. Using political stance questionnaires as a controlled case study for behavioral steering, we demonstrate that LLM-Lobotomy can shift task-relevant next-token probability distributions in real-time without requiring computationally expensive weight updates. By targeting the residual stream, we show that selected residual-stream features can be strategically scaled to induce specific in-domain behavioral shifts across diverse model families. Finally, we provide a complementary assessment of the models' post-intervention behavior, measuring the degree to which latent steering compromises general usability or induces unintended shifts in the output distribution. While our empirical evaluation focuses on political stance steering, the proposed methodology can, in principle, be applied to other behavioral dimensions encoded in internal representations. Our source code is available on GitHub[1].

2 Background Concepts and Related Works

LLMs are transformer-based neural networks that predict tokens autoregressively; their self-attention mechanism, combined with residual connections and layer normalization, enables massive scaling and emergent capabilities like few-shot learning and chain-of-thought reasoning [5,26], making them the dominant paradigm for NLP tasks.

The residual stream is a core component of the transformer architecture – acting as a shared communication bus across the model – where attention heads and MLPs read and write information additively [7]. This additive, linear structure implies that high-level concepts are encoded as linear directions [2], making the residual stream a geometrically interpretable space amenable to direct manipulation. ActAdd [25] exploits this by injecting steering vectors – in this case, differences between contrastive prompt activations – to shift model behavior at

[1] https://github.com/graphs4ai/LLM-Lobotomy.git.

inference time without weight updates. For more complex patterns, Postmus and Abreu [19] extend this with conceptors, representing activation sets as ellipsoidal regions and applying soft projections via matrix-vector multiplication, enabling Boolean composition of steering targets and outperforming additive methods.

Ensuring automated systems behave in a fashion that does not go against core human values is a long-standing concern [28]. A popular guiding light for such values is "Helpfulness, Honesty and Harmlessness" [3]. In the era of large language models (LLMs), this concern is formalized as the alignment [4,12] problem.

2.1 Training-Time Alignment

Currently, one of the most adopted approaches to the alignment problem is RLHF, which aims to align model behavior with human preferences. While state-of-the-art alignment techniques such as Chain of Hindsight [14] demonstrate that models can be effectively tuned to instruction-following templates with minimal data, these methods primarily modify the model's behavioral surface. Recent evidence suggests, however, that such techniques may provide a "conversational varnish" rather than a rewiring of the model's latent space [4].

2.2 Activation Steering

Activation steering has been validated as a robust alternative to fine-tuning across a broad range of domains. CAA [20] established that steering vectors derived from transformer blocks can modulate high-level behavioral traits via residual stream injection. CASAL [30] internalizes this principle into model weights using a lightweight subnetwork, reducing hallucinations by 30–40% while requiring around 30 times fewer FLOPs than LoRA. Lin et al. [13] showed that the fast/slow reasoning trade-off in Large Reasoning Models is linearly encoded in representation space, enabling dynamic inference-time control over thinking speed. CREST [31] identifies specialized cognitive heads tied to verification and backtracking, demonstrating that targeted interventions can suppress inefficient reasoning while improving accuracy. Finally, ASA [27] extends activation steering to tool use, bridging the gap between internal tool-use intent and output behavior through a lightweight inference-time controller.

2.3 Existing Approaches for LLM Political Stance Evaluation

To evaluate the framework's efficacy in the political stance context, it is necessary to adopt a structured and reproducible methodology. There are several approaches to evaluating political bias in LLMs. Röttger *et al.* [22] demonstrate that forced-choice surveys like the PCT yield unstable results: model positions shift with prompt framing or minor paraphrases, thereby undermining their validity as bias indicators. Faulborn et al. [8] address this by grounding evaluation in the World Values Survey across 11 models, finding that instruction-tuned models consistently lean left while base models remain centered, implicating the alignment process as a primary driver of political bias. Beyond static stance measurement, Soares *et al.* [24] introduce the concept of *ideological chameleon behavior*, defined as the tendency of models to systematically shift their stated positions to align with a user's political framing. Using a benchmark of opposing statement pairs grounded in the Brazilian political context and an Ideological Position Index (IPI) to quantify bias, they evaluate multiple models' average political stance under three situations: a no-context prompt, with no prior information about user ideology, a left-leaning user context and a right-leaning user context. When the user's ideology is made explicit, models shift substantially in the direction of the user. In this work, we adopt the Ideological Position Index [24] as our primary evaluation metric, using it to assess whether activation steering can shift the model's IPI responses relative to its baseline behavior.

2.4 Alignment Tax

The term "alignment tax" refers to the inherent trade-off between steering a language model toward specific human preferences and maintaining its broad, pre-trained capabilities [12]: as models are adapted to new safety or alignment objectives, their performance on general benchmarks – such as commonsense reasoning and reading comprehension – often degrades.

3 Methodology

This section outlines the experimental design and implementation used throughout this work, as illustrated in Fig. 1. Our pipeline is structured into five sequential phases. The process begins with the extraction of residual-stream activations (features) from a text corpus (*i*), followed by a feature selection protocol (*ii*) to isolate the most relevant features for the task at hand. Once the target features are identified within the residual stream, we optimize the activation multipliers (*iii*) to steer the model's latent representations. Thus, stages *(i)* through *(iii)* constitute the preparation of the steering framework. The efficacy of this intervention is then measured through a target behavior evaluation (*iv*) – in this study, we use the Ideological Position Index – to quantify the targeted stance adoption. Finally, a General Capability Assessment (*v*) is conducted to quantify the resulting alignment tax. The detailed mechanics and datasets utilized in each of these phases are described in the subsequent subsections.

3.1 The LLM-Lobotomy Framework

This section describes the proposed LLM-Lobotomy framework. To validate its effectiveness, we evaluate it on the domain of political stance, utilizing the Ideological Position Index (IPI) to quantify the induced behavioral shifts. Figure 2 illustrates a block diagram of the proposed framework.

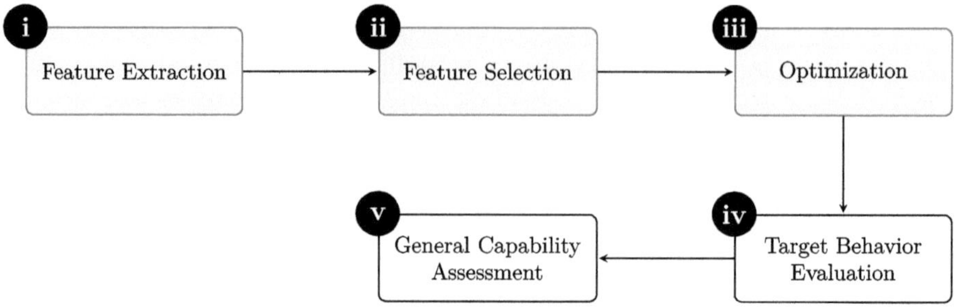

Fig. 1. The five-stage pipeline of the LLM-Lobotomy framework, with the core methodology stages *(i-iii)* highlighted. The process isolates feature discovery from evaluation by identifying *(i)* and selecting *(ii)* task-specific features on a disjoint corpus. Activation multipliers are then optimized *(iii)* to induce behavioral steering. Finally, the intervention is evaluated for both its efficacy in target behavior adoption *(iv)* and its resulting alignment tax on general model capabilities *(v)*.

(i) Residual Stream Activation Extraction. We begin by extracting intermediate residual-stream activations from the target language model during forward passes. We evaluated the instruction-tuned versions of Llama 3.1 (8B), Gemma 3 (4B), Qwen 3 (8B) and Phi-3 Mini (3.8B).

Given an input dataset of textual prompts, the extraction pipeline processes examples in mini-batches. Each batch is tokenized with the model's native tokenizer, using padding to accommodate variable-length sequences while preserving alignment within the batch. During the forward pass, hooks are attached to the residual stream of the selected transformer blocks, allowing the framework to capture hidden states in the residual stream without modifying model parameters, by using the TransformerLens library [15]. Specifically, we extract the activations from the residual stream prior to the attention and multi-layer perceptron sublayers (commonly denoted as `resid_pre`) across all transformer layers. To construct a consistent sequence-level representation for each prompt, we isolate the activation vector corresponding to the last non-padding token. Any padding tokens introduced during the batching process are strictly masked out and excluded from the aggregation, ensuring that the extracted features accurately reflect the semantic content of the input without artifact interference.

(ii) Feature Selection and Ranking. After extraction, we reshape the residual activations into a feature matrix in which each candidate feature is indexed by layer and feature number. These features are then associated with a supervision signal derived from the ground-truth behavioral (in this study, political stance) labels used in our experimental setting. Because the full activation space is high-dimensional, we employ a two-stage feature selection strategy designed to retain discriminative features while limiting redundancy.

First, we apply a univariate pre-filtering step using scikit-learn's `SelectKBest` with the ANOVA F-statistics selection function [17]. This preliminary pruning is adopted due to the sheer volume of the LLM residual stream, which typically spans over 100,000 dimensions across all layers. Because our final selection algorithm, minimum Redundancy Maximum Relevance (mRMR) [18], evaluates pairwise feature redundancies, its memory and computational demands scale quadratically with the input size. By using the ANOVA F-statistic to reduce the massive initial candidate set to the top 1000 features, we make the subsequent multivariate selection computationally tractable. Second, we apply mRMR on this reduced subset to isolate a feature set that is highly informative with respect to the target stance, while avoiding excessive inter-feature overlap.

To mitigate overfitting and prevent data leakage within this step, this two-stage selection procedure is embedded within a 3-fold cross-validation protocol. The specific thresholds for feature retention at each stage – 1000 for univariate pre-filtering, 100 for multivariate selection per fold, and 80 for the final aggregated intervention set – were established empirically through preliminary trials to balance computational tractability with behavioral steering efficacy. In each training fold, `SelectKBest` reduces the candidate space to the top 1000 features according to the ANOVA F-statistic. We then apply mRMR to strictly select 100 features per fold. To determine the most robust features, we perform a frequency-based aggregation across the three folds. Features are ranked by their frequency of selection, under the assumption that repeatedly selected residual-stream dimensions encode stable stance-relevant information rather than fold-specific noise. Finally, the top 80 most stable features are retained to serve as the target set for the subsequent activation multiplier optimization.

(iii) Optimization of Activation Multipliers. Once candidate features have been identified, we optimize feature-wise scaling factors to steer the model's answers during inference, shifting its IPI. Let x_f^ℓ denote the activation of feature f at layer ℓ. For each selected feature, we apply a multiplicative intervention of the form

$$\tilde{x}_f^\ell = \lambda_f^\ell \, x_f^\ell, \tag{1}$$

where λ_f^ℓ is a learned intervention multiplier. In all experiments within this work, we constrain the intervention to $\nu = 80$ top-ranked features per model, determined via preliminary empirical evaluation.

We optimize the intervention multipliers with Optuna [1], using CMA-ES [11] for 3000 iterations to maximize or minimize a continuous stance surrogate. To preserve generation stability, each λ_f^ℓ is bounded by a model- and direction-specific interval, chosen through preliminary tests as the widest range that produced behavioral shifts without degenerate outputs (Table 1). The surrogate is computed from next-token probabilities at the answer position: for each statement pair (i), let p_i^+ and p_i^- be the positive and negative prompts, and let $t * \text{agr}$ and t_{dis} be the tokenizer-specific agreement and disagreement tokens. Given the next-token logits $z(p)$, the soft stance score for prompt (p) is

$$\eta(p) = \text{softmax}(z(p))_{t_{\text{agr}}} - \text{softmax}(z(p))_{t_{\text{dis}}}. \tag{2}$$

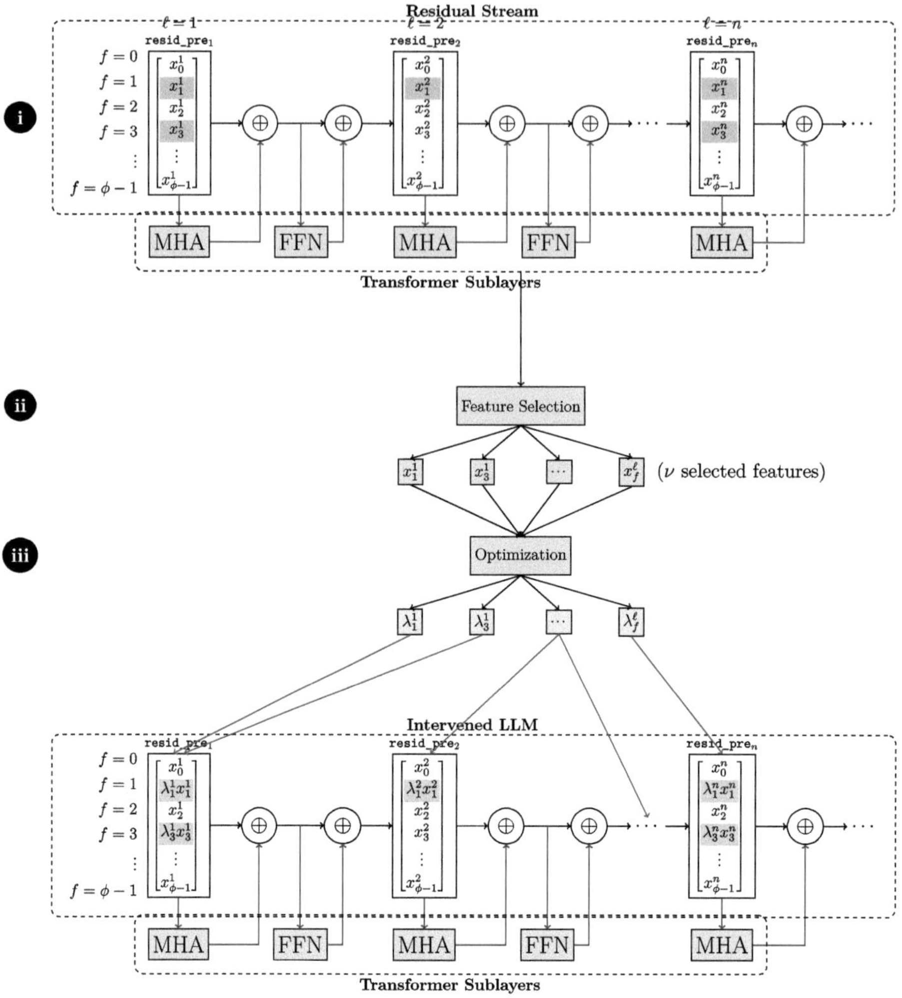

Fig. 2. Detailed view of the core methodology stages *(i-iii)*: *(i)* residual activation extraction, where residual stream activations x_f^ℓ are collected across all n transformer layers (superscript $\ell \in \{1, \dots, n\}$) and all ϕ feature dimensions (subscript $f \in \{0, \dots, \phi - 1\}$); *(ii)* feature selection and ranking, where ν activations $\{x_1^1, x_3^1, \dots\}$ are selected across layers and feature dimensions; and *(iii)* optimization of feature-wise intervention multipliers $\{\lambda_1^1, \lambda_3^1, \dots\}$, which are subsequently injected into the LLM's residual stream to steer its outputs.

The pairwise soft score is then

$$\widetilde{\mathrm{IPI}}_i = \eta(p_i^+) - \eta(p_i^-), \tag{3}$$

and the continuous objective optimized across statement pairs is

$$\widetilde{\mathrm{IPI}} = \frac{1}{N}\sum_{i=1}^{N}\widetilde{\mathrm{IPI}}_i = \frac{1}{N}\sum_{i=1}^{N}\left[\eta(p_i^+) - \eta(p_i^-)\right]. \tag{4}$$

This quantity preserves the signed structure of the discrete IPI while avoiding the discontinuity introduced by parsing the generated answer into a Likert category.

Table 1. Multiplier search intervals used during Optuna optimization. All models were constrained to an intervention size of 80 features. Intervals were empirically chosen to maximize the steering effect while preventing degenerate text generation.

Model	Objective	Multiplier Search Interval
Gemma 3 (4B)	Minimization	$[-2, 2]$
	Maximization	$[-6, 6]$
Llama 3.1 (8B)	Minimization	$[-6, 6]$
	Maximization	$[-2, 2]$
Phi-3 Mini	Minimization	$[-2, 2]$
	Maximization	$[-2, 2]$
Qwen 3 (8B)	Minimization	$[-6, 6]$
	Maximization	$[-6, 6]$

(iv) Target Behavior Evaluation. To quantify political stance (the targeted behavior in this work), we evaluate the model on paired political statements designed to represent opposing positions on the same issue. For each pair, the model is prompted separately with the positive and negative formulations, and its response is mapped onto a five-point Likert scale ranging from strongly disagree to strongly agree. Following the benchmark protocol adopted by Soares *et al.* [24], we encode the parsed answer as an integer in $\{-2, -1, 0, 1, 2\}$, where larger values indicate stronger agreement with the statement. The intervention is applied at the residual stream prior to the attention and multi-layer perceptron sublayers throughout autoregressive decoding, but only over prompt-token positions. Throughout all runs reported in this work, we use greedy decoding with temperature set to 0.

Let s_i^+ and s_i^- denote the parsed Likert scores for the positive and negative statements in pair i. The pairwise Ideological Position Index is computed as

$$\mathrm{IPI}_i = s_i^+ - s_i^-, \tag{5}$$

which yields $\mathrm{IPI}_i \in [-4, 4]$. The overall model score is then obtained by averaging across all valid statement pairs,

$$\mathrm{IPI} = \frac{1}{N}\sum_{i=1}^{N}\mathrm{IPI}_i, \tag{6}$$

where N is the number of successfully parsed pairs. Positive values indicate stronger alignment with the "right-wing pole" of the political spectrum, whereas negative values indicate stronger alignment with the "left-wing pole".

The same prompt template and parsing rules are used across all conditions to minimize measurement variance induced by prompt formatting. We report both baseline and post-intervention results. To assess statistical significance, we employ the Wilcoxon signed-rank test [29] to evaluate the differences in the paired pairwise Ideological Position Index (IPI) distributions between the baseline and the intervened models.

(v) Capability Preservation Assessment. To evaluate whether the LLM-Lobotomy framework incurs a severe alignment tax, we assess the models' capability preservation across diverse cognitive domains. We utilize a subset of the PoETa v2 benchmark [21], a comprehensive evaluation suite in Portuguese for language models: (1) `enem_2022_greedy`, which evaluates broad multidisciplinary knowledge and reasoning across human sciences, natural sciences, languages, and mathematics using questions from the Brazilian National High School Exam (ENEM); (2) `FaQuAD`, an extractive question-answering dataset that tests precise reading comprehension and information retrieval; and (3) `math_mc_greedy`, which assesses quantitative problem-solving and logical reasoning through multiple-choice mathematics questions. By comparing baseline and post-intervention accuracies across these diverse tasks, we can quantify the extent to which targeted political stance adoption displaces the distributed representations underlying general competence.

Furthermore, because aggregate accuracy metrics can obscure granular behavioral changes, we also systematically evaluate the divergence in the models' specific answer distributions. For the discrete multiple-choice tasks, we compute Cohen's Kappa (κ) coefficients to measure the agreement between the exact options selected by the baseline and intervened models. For the open-ended extractive task (`FaQuAD`), we assess semantic deviation by calculating the mean cosine similarity (and standard deviation) between the baseline and intervened text generations.

3.2 Datasets

Our experiments build upon the benchmark of opposing political statement pairs introduced by Soares *et al.* [24]. The benchmark construction process yielded a total of 128 unanimously validated pairs after cross-model ideological filtering. Of these, 72 are reserved as a disjoint corpus used exclusively for residual-activation extraction. The remaining 56 pairs are utilized both to optimize the continuous activation multipliers and to conduct the final discrete IPI evaluation. By constraining both the multiplier optimization and the final evaluation to this exact subset, we keep feature discovery separated from multiplier optimization and evaluation while measuring the model's susceptibility to in-domain behavioral steering. It is important to note that our reported results measure in-domain behavioral steering on the target benchmark rather than out-of-domain generalization.

4 Results and Discussion

The application of the LLM-Lobotomy technique via activation scaling successfully altered the pairwise Ideological Position Index (IPI) across most model-direction combinations, though the effectiveness varied considerably depending on the target direction (Fig. 3). The intervention was highly effective at driving models toward IPI minimization (left-stance). All four models exhibited statistically significant negative shifts when subjected to minimization interventions ($p < 0.05$). Gemma 3 (4B) was the most responsive to this leftward steering, demonstrating a considerable mean IPI-shift of -1.1607 ($p < 0.001$). Llama 3.1 (8B) and Qwen 3 (8B) also showed strong, significant minimization shifts of -0.5714 and -0.5000, respectively.

Steering the models toward IPI maximization (right-stance) proved more challenging and revealed a notable asymmetry in the models' susceptibility to

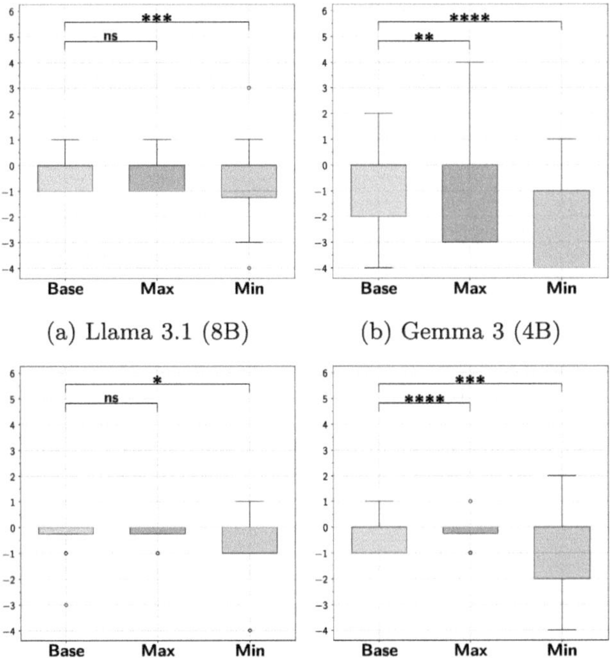

(a) Llama 3.1 (8B) (b) Gemma 3 (4B)

(c) Phi-3 Mini (3.8B) (d) Qwen 3 (8B)

Fig. 3. Pairwise IPI distribution for baseline (blue), LLM-Lobotomy for IPI maximization (red) and LLM-Lobotomy for IPI minimization (green). Significance levels: ns: $P > 0.05$, *: $P \leq 0.05$, **: $P \leq 0.01$, ***: $P \leq 0.001$ and ****: $P \leq 0.0001$. (Color figure online)

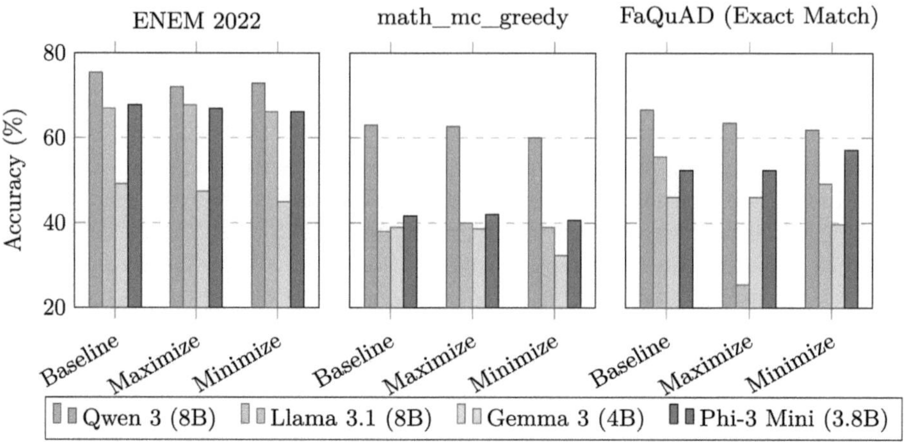

Fig. 4. Capability preservation of four language models across three tasks of the PoETa v2 benchmark under baseline, right-stance (Maximize), and left-stance (Minimize) conditions.

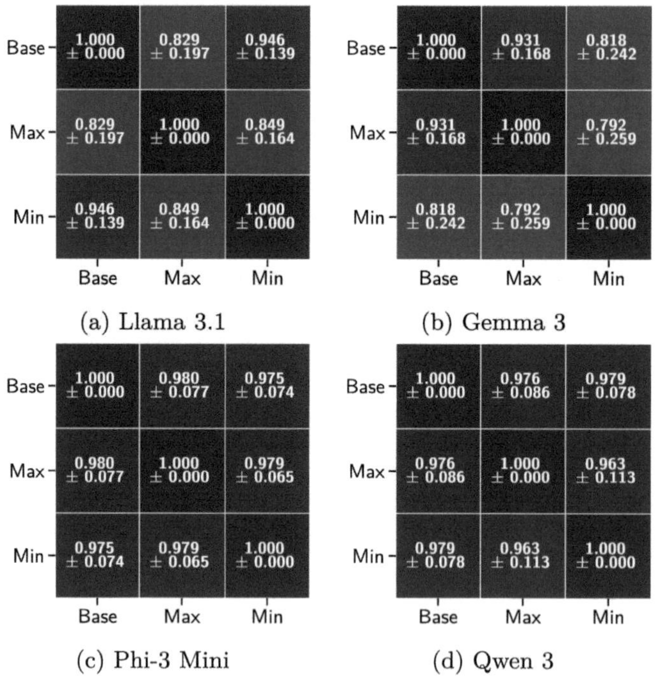

Fig. 5. Pairwise similarity matrices for FaQuAD extractive question-answering outputs under the Baseline, Maximization (right-stance) and Minimization (left-stance) conditions. Each cell reports the mean pairwise cosine similarity between generated answers under the corresponding conditions, together with the standard deviation.

Table 2. Cohen's Kappa (κ) coefficients measuring the agreement between the discrete answer distributions of the baseline model and the intervened models. Lower values indicate a more severe divergence in the specific answers selected by the model due to the activation steering.

Model	Task	Minimization (κ)	Maximization (κ)
Gemma 3 (4B)	`enem_2022_greedy`	0.4918	0.8216
	`math_mc_greedy`	0.4432	0.7443
Llama 3.1 (8B)	`enem_2022_greedy`	0.9570	0.7452
	`math_mc_greedy`	0.9085	0.5091
Phi-3 Mini (3.8B)	`enem_2022_greedy`	0.8934	0.9254
	`math_mc_greedy`	0.8949	0.9180
Qwen 3 (8B)	`enem_2022_greedy`	0.8724	0.8722
	`math_mc_greedy`	0.8219	0.7774

behavioral steering. While Gemma 3 and Qwen 3 successfully achieved statistically significant positive shifts (+0.4821 and +0.3214, respectively), Llama 3.1 and Phi-3 Mini demonstrated a strong resistance to rightward steering. For these latter two models, the maximization interventions yielded negligible shifts (+0.0686 for Llama 3.1 and +0.0357 for Phi-3 Mini) that failed to achieve statistical significance. Overall, the results suggest that these instruction-tuned models are generally more susceptible to left-stance activation scaling than right-stance scaling, with Gemma 3 exhibiting the highest observable shifts to targeted stance shifting in both directions.

To assess the alignment tax incurred by the LLM-Lobotomy framework, we evaluated the models' capability preservation across the PoETa v2 benchmark. Overall, the targeted activation scaling interventions induced a limited degradation in most models' general cognitive and reasoning abilities (Fig. 4). On the `enem_2022_greedy` and `math_mc_greedy` tasks, most models experienced minimal accuracy fluctuations, typically remaining within a 7% margin of their original baselines. Investigating beyond the benchmark metrics, we found meaningful shifts in the specific answers generated to each question. As detailed in Table 2, Cohen's κ coefficients reveal asymmetric divergences in the models' discrete answer distributions. For instance, while Gemma 3's leftward steering (Minimization) caused a steep drop in answer agreement ($\kappa = 0.44$ for Math), Llama 3.1 exhibited its lowest agreement under rightward steering (Maximization, $\kappa = 0.51$). This asymmetric alignment tax is also pronounced in the `FaQuAD` exact-match reading comprehension task. While Qwen 3 and Phi-3 Mini maintained robust performance and high semantic similarity (Fig. 5), Llama 3.1 experienced a notable capability degradation under the maximization intervention: its accuracy plummeted from 55.56% to 25.40%, accompanied by a corresponding drop in mean cosine similarity relative to the baseline, exceeding that observed under minimization. Nonetheless, the broadly stable aggregate performance across the majority of tasks indicates that the overall capability tax of this inference-time behavioral steering remains limited for most model-task combinations.

5 Conclusion

In this work, we provide a controlled case study of an inference-time limitation in aligned LLM behavior. While techniques like RLHF successfully shape a model's conversational surface, our findings suggest this may not fully overwrite its latent representations. We introduced LLM-Lobotomy, a model-agnostic representation engineering framework for inference-time behavioral steering. By identifying ideologically relevant features from the residual stream and applying simple scalar multipliers to the residual stream, we induced targeted in-domain shifts in stance-related Likert outputs without the need for weight updates.

The empirical evaluation across four model architectures – Gemma 3 (4B), Llama 3.1 (8B), Phi-3 Mini (3.8B), and Qwen 3 (8B) – revealed that optimizing an internal probability metric can induce corresponding shifts in the discrete Likert responses of the models. Crucially, we found a marked asymmetry in model susceptibility. All models exhibited statistically significant leftward shifts under IPI minimization, whereas Llama 3.1 and Phi-3 Mini showed limited responsiveness to right-stance steering under IPI maximization.

Our assessment of capability preservation using the PoETa v2 benchmark shows that this inference-time behavioral steering often incurs a limited alignment tax, but can lead to severe degradation in specific cases, as observed in Llama 3.1 under rightward steering.

Ultimately, LLM-Lobotomy provides evidence that aligned language models can be steered through inference-time activation scaling. By showing that a model's default aligned behavior can be altered through targeted in-domain steering, this work emphasizes the need for alignment strategies that secure not just the conversational output, but the underlying representations of the models. Building on these findings, future work will evaluate the broader generalization of LLM-Lobotomy across a wider range of model families, scales, and alignment procedures, as well as in other behavioral domains such as safety moderation, persona enforcement, and tool-calling. A natural next step is also to compare the proposed feature-wise activation scaling against alternative steering baselines, including direct vector injection and activation addition, to better characterize when each intervention mechanism is most effective.

Acknowledgments. This work was supported by the National Council for Scientific and Technological Development (CNPq; grant no. 302530/2022-3) and the São Paulo Research Foundation (FAPESP), Brazil (Processes no. 2024/12936-5). The authors thank Instituto Kunumi for their financial and structural support.

References

1. Akiba, T., Sano, S., Yanase, T.: Optuna: a next-generation hyperparameter optimization framework. In: ACM SIGKDD International Conference on Knowledge Discovery and Data Mining (KDD), pp. 2623–2631 (2019)
2. Arditi, A., Obeso, O., Syed, A.: Refusal in language models is mediated by a single direction. In: Advances in Neural Information Processing Systems (NeurIPS), vol. 37, pp. 136037–136083 (2024)
3. Askell, A., Bai, Y., Chen, A.: A general language assistant as a laboratory for alignment. arXiv preprint arXiv:2112.00861 (2021)
4. Barnhart, L., Bafghi, R.A., Becker, S.: Aligning to what? Limits to RLHF based alignment. In: Annual Conference of the North American Chapter of the Association for Computational Linguistics (NAACL), pp. 7556–7591 (2025)
5. Brown, T., Mann, B., Ryder, N.: Language models are few-shot learners. In: Advances in Neural Information Processing Systems (NeurIPS), vol. 33, pp. 1877–1901 (2020)
6. Buyl, M., Rogiers, A., Noels, S.: Large language models reflect the ideology of their creators. NPJ Artif. Intell. **2**(1), 7 (2026)
7. Elhage, N., Nanda, N., Olsson, C., et al.: A Mathematical Framework for Transformer Circuits (2021). https://transformer-circuits.pub/2021/framework/index.html
8. Faulborn, M., Sen, I., Pellert, M.: Only a little to the left: a theory-grounded measure of political bias in large language models. In: Annual Meeting of the Association for Computational Linguistics (ACL), pp. 31684–31704 (2025)
9. Feng, S., Park, C.Y., Liu, Y.: From pretraining data to language models to downstream tasks: tracking the trails of political biases leading to unfair NLP models. In: Annual Meeting of the Association for Computational Linguistics (ACL), pp. 11737–11762 (2023)
10. Flathers, M., Roux, S., Torous, J.: Beyond artificial intelligence psychosis: a functional typology of large language model-associated psychotic phenomena. Lancet Digit. Health (2026)
11. Hansen, N., Müller, S.D., Koumoutsakos, P.: Reducing the time complexity of the derandomized evolution strategy with covariance matrix adaptation (CMA-ES). Evol. Comput. (ECJ) **11**(1), 1–18 (2003)
12. Lin, Y., Lin, H., Xiong, W., et al.: Mitigating the alignment tax of RLHF. In: Conference on Empirical Methods in Natural Language Processing (EMNLP), pp. 580–606 (2024)
13. Lin, Z., Fu, Z., Chen, Z.: Controlling thinking speed in reasoning models. In: Advances in Neural Information Processing Systems (NeurIPS) (2025), Spotlight Poster
14. Liu, H., Sferrazza, C., Abbeel, P.: Chain of hindsight aligns language models with feedback. In: International Conference on Learning Representations (ICLR) (2024), Poster
15. Nanda, N., Bloom, J.: TransformerLens (2022). https://github.com/TransformerLensOrg/TransformerLens
16. Ouyang, L., Wu, J., Jiang, X.: Training language models to follow instructions with human feedback. In: Advances in Neural Information Processing Systems, vol. 35, pp. 27730–27744 (2022)
17. Pedregosa, F., Varoquaux, G., Gramfort, A., et al.: Scikit-learn: machine learning in python. J. Mach. Learn. Res. **12**, 2825–2830 (2011)

18. Peng, H., Long, F., Ding, C.: Feature selection based on mutual information criteria of max-dependency, max-relevance, and min-redundancy. IEEE Trans. Pattern Anal. Mach. Intell. **27**(8), 1226–1238 (2005)
19. Postmus, J., Abreu, S.: Steering Large Language Models using Conceptors: Improving Addition-Based Activation Engineering. arXiv preprint arXiv:2410.16314 (2025). Presented at the MINT Workshop at NeurIPS 2024
20. Rimsky, N., Gabrieli, N., Schulz, J.: Steering llama 2 via contrastive activation addition. In: Annual Meeting of the Association for Computational Linguistics (ACL), pp. 15504–15522 (2024)
21. Sales Almeida, R., Pires, T., Abonizio, R., H.: PoETa v2: toward more robust evaluation of large language models in Portuguese. IEEE Access **13**, 214180–214200 (2025)
22. Röttger, P., Hofmann, V., Pyatkin, V.: Political compass or spinning arrow? Towards more meaningful evaluations for values and opinions in large language models. In: Annual Meeting of the Association for Computational Linguistics (ACL), pp. 15295–15311 (2024)
23. Sharma, N., Liao, Q.V., Xiao, Z.: Generative echo chamber? Effect of LLM-powered search systems on diverse information seeking. In: ACM CHI Conference on Human Factors in Computing Systems (CHI), p. 1033. Association for Computing Machinery, New York, NY, USA (2024)
24. Soares, A.L.B., Almeida, B.A.V.D., Ferreira, L.N., Rocha, A., Interian, R., Dias, Z.: LLMs are ideological chameleons: personalized echo chambers in the Brazilian political context. Sci. Rep. (2026)
25. Turner, A.M., Thiergart, L., Leech, G.: Steering Language Models With Activation Engineering. arXiv preprint arXiv:2308.10248 (2024)
26. Vaswani, A., Shazeer, N., Parmar, N.: Attention is all you need. In: Advances in Neural Information Processing Systems (NeurIPS), p. 30 (2017)
27. Wang, Y., Zhou, R., Fu, R.: ASA: Activation Steering for Tool-Calling Domain Adaptation. arXiv preprint arXiv:2602.04935 (2026)
28. Wiener, N.: Some moral and technical consequences of automation. Science **131**(3410), 1355–1358 (1960)
29. Wilcoxon, F.: Individual Comparisons by Ranking Methods. Biom. Bull. **1**(6), 80–83 (1945)
30. Yang, W., Qiu, X., Yu, L.: Hallucination reduction with CASAL: contrastive activation steering for amortized learning. In: International Conference on Learning Representations (ICLR) (2026), Poster
31. Zhang, Z., Wu, X., Zhou, Z.: Understanding and steering the cognitive behaviors of reasoning models at test-time. In: Advances in Neural Information Processing Systems (NeurIPS) (2025), Workshop on Efficient Reasoning Spotlight

Bisection-Based Neighborhood Generation for Local Rule-Based Explainable Artificial Intelligence

Sérgio Baldo Júnior[1(✉)], Zhao Liang[1,2], and Renato Tinós[2]

[1] Institute of Mathematics and Computer Science, University of São Paulo, São Carlos, São Paulo, Brazil
{sergiobaldo,zhao}@usp.br

[2] Department of Computing and Mathematics, FFCLRP, University of São Paulo, Ribeirão Preto, São Paulo, Brazil
rtinos@ffclrp.usp.br

Abstract. Local explanation methods aim to capture the behavior of black-box classifiers around a target instance. Some of these methods achieve this by learning interpretable surrogate models that reproduce the black-box local decision boundaries. Among these approaches, LOcal Rule-based Explanations (LORE) algorithm generates synthetic neighborhoods using Genetic Algorithms (GAs). The synthetic data is then used to train a decision tree that captures local decision patterns. The effectiveness of this approach depends on the quality and representativeness of the generated instances. In this work, we propose a novel neighborhood generation strategy that combines the exploratory capabilities of GAs with a bisection-based sampling mechanism. The proposed approach generates additional synthetic instances by iteratively interpolating between samples of opposite classes, enabling a structured exploration of the feature space and increasing the presence of informative points near the decision boundaries. Experimental results across multiple classification datasets demonstrate that the proposed method produces synthetic neighborhoods with improved diversity and boundary awareness. As a result, the learned surrogate models provide more reliable and informative local explanations.

Keywords: eXplainable Artificial Intelligence · XAI · LORE · Genetic Algorithms · LOREfs · Machine Learning

1 Introduction

Artificial Intelligence (AI) has gained global prominence in recent years, driven by significant advances in algorithm development and associated technologies. In particular, Machine Learning (ML), a subfield of AI, has substantially expanded the range of practical applications. This technological progress has created opportunities for the adoption of AI techniques across various sectors. In healthcare, for instance, ML supports diagnosis and the personalization of treatments,

M. Recamonde-Mendoza and R. C. Barros (Eds.): BRACIS 2026, LNAI 17105, pp. 599–614, 2027.
https://doi.org/10.1007/978-3-032-39882-6_40

while in industry it contributes to process optimization and market forecasting [1,10].

The widespread adoption of ML models in high-stakes domains, such as healthcare, finance, and legal systems, has intensified the demand for interpretability. Although black-box models often achieve high predictive accuracy, they provide limited transparency regarding the rationale behind individual predictions. The term "black box" is commonly used to describe this opacity, wherein the internal algorithmic processes are not directly accessible or interpretable by humans [2].

To address this limitation, many studies have focused on developing methods to explain the decisions of ML models [4,7,9,13]. These approaches, collectively referred to as eXplainable Artificial Intelligence (XAI), aim to enhance the transparency of ML models and make their behavior more understandable to human users. XAI methods can be broadly categorized according to different criteria: (i) ante-hoc methods, which rely on inherently interpretable (white-box) models, and post-hoc methods, which generate explanations after model training; (ii) model-specific methods, designed for particular architectures, and model-agnostic methods, which can be applied to any model; and (iii) local methods, which explain individual predictions, and global methods, which describe the overall behavior of the model [12].

Among XAI techniques, model-agnostic local post-hoc explanation methods have received particular attention. These methods approximate the decision boundary of a black-box model in the vicinity of a specific instance, producing human-interpretable explanations that are locally valid even when the global model is complex. Notable examples include Local Interpretable Model-Agnostic Explanations (LIME) [13] and LOcal Rule-based Explanations (LORE) [7], which generate explanations for individual predictions. LIME fits a linear model in the neighborhood of a given instance to approximate the behavior of the black-box model and provide an interpretable explanation.

LORE uses a Decision Tree (DT) as a surrogate model. Given an instance to be explained, LORE generates a synthetic neighborhood around this instance using Genetic Algorithms (GAs). The synthetic samples generated by the GA are subsequently used to train the DT, which is then analyzed to extract logical rules to explain the specific instance and to identify counterfactuals that demonstrate how the instance could be modified to achieve a different classification. A key design feature of LORE is the use of two independent GAs with distinct roles: the same-class GA, which generates instances belonging to the same class as the target instance, and the counterexample GA, which produces instances from the opposite class. The surrogate model (DT) is trained on the union of these two populations, enabling it to approximate the local decision boundaries of the black-box model [7].

Building on this framework, Santos et al. (2023) [14] proposed incorporating *fitness sharing* into both GAs, resulting in the LOREfs method. *Fitness sharing* is a niching strategy that preserves population diversity across generations by penalizing individuals located in densely populated regions [5,15]. This mechanism promotes a broader exploration of the feature space. The authors showed that increasing the number of generations under this strategy leads to surrogate decision boundaries that more closely approximate those of the black-box model, thereby improving the detail and precision of the extracted explanations.

Despite these advances, the neighborhood generation strategy employed by both LORE and LOREfs presents a fundamental limitation: neither the same-class GA nor the counterexample GA explicitly targets the local decision boundaries. Instead, both populations are generated to satisfy class-based objectives, which leads to samples being dispersed throughout the local feature space rather than concentrated near the region where the model changes its prediction. This lack of focus on the local decision boundaries, arguably the most informative region for local explanations, can cause the surrogate model to approximate the neighborhood broadly while failing to accurately capture the precise location and shape of the boundary. As a result, the fidelity of the extracted explanations may be compromised. These limitations highlight the need for a more principled neighborhood generation strategy that explicitly concentrates samples near the decision boundary.

To address this issue, we propose LOcal Rule-based Explanations with Bisection and Directed Perturbation (LORE-BisD), which replaces the same-class GA of LORE while preserving the counterexample GA responsible for generating opposite-class instances. Specifically, for each counterexample produced by the retained GA, a binary search (bisection) [16] is applied along the line segment connecting the target instance to the counterexample, thereby locating a point on the decision boundary with high precision. Additional samples are then generated on both sides of this boundary point along the estimated local normal direction, with lateral perturbations to explore boundary curvature. This bisection-based neighborhood generation strategy ensures that the surrogate training set is densely populated near the true decision boundary, improving local fidelity without requiring a second GA.

We also introduce Local Rule-Based Explanations with Fitness Sharing, Bisection and Directed Perturbation (LOREfs-BisD), which integrates the proposed strategy with the *fitness sharing* variant (LOREfs), enabling a controlled ablation study that isolates the contribution of each component.

2 Background: LORE and LOREfs

We briefly review the LORE framework to establish notation and provide context for our method.

2.1 Local Rule-Based Explainer

The pseudocode of LORE is presented in Algorithm 1. Given a binary classification black-box model b, its prediction for an instance $\mathbf{x}^*$, denoted by $y_b(\mathbf{x}^*)$, is explained by $e_c(\mathbf{x}^*)$, obtained from a DT c. The surrogate model c is trained on an artificial dataset Z, composed of two populations (Z_1 and Z_2) generated by two GAs with distinct objectives. The same-class GA (GA_1) generates instances whose labels match the prediction of the black-box model, i.e., $y_b(\mathbf{z}) = y_b(\mathbf{x}^*)$, while the counterexample GA (GA_2) generates instances with opposite labels, i.e., $y_b(\mathbf{z}) \neq y_b(\mathbf{x}^*)$. The label $y_b(\mathbf{x}^*)$ is obtained by evaluating the black-box model b on instance $\mathbf{x}^*$.

Algorithm 1. LORE proposed in [7]

Input: $\mathbf{x}^*$ - instance to be explained, b - *black-box* model, N - population size, G - number of generations, p_c - crossover rate, p_m - mutation rate
Output: $e_c(\mathbf{x}^*)$ - explanation of the decision of b for $\mathbf{x}^*$

begin
  $G \leftarrow 10$
  $p_c \leftarrow 0.5$
  $p_m \leftarrow 0.2$
  $Z_1 \leftarrow GA_1(\mathbf{x}^*, b, N/2, G, p_c, p_m)$
  $Z_2 \leftarrow GA_2(\mathbf{x}^*, b, N/2, G, p_c, p_m)$
  $Z \leftarrow Z_1 \cup Z_2$
  $c \leftarrow \text{decisionTree}(Z)$
  $r_c \leftarrow \text{extractRules}(c, \mathbf{x}^*)$
  $\Phi_c(\mathbf{x}^*) \leftarrow \text{extractCounterfactuals}(c, r_c(\mathbf{x}^*), \mathbf{x}^*)$
  $e_c(\mathbf{x}^*) \leftarrow \langle r_c(\mathbf{x}^*), \Phi_c(\mathbf{x}^*) \rangle$
  return $e_c(\mathbf{x}^*)$
end

The explanation of the black-box model's decision for $\mathbf{x}^*$ is obtained as a set of logical rules r_c extracted from the DT c. These rules correspond to the path followed by $\mathbf{x}^*$ from the root to a leaf node. Additionally, a set of counterfactual conditions Φ_c is extracted by identifying alternative paths in the tree that lead to a different predicted label.

Each GA evolves an initial population composed of perturbed versions of $\mathbf{x}^*$ through standard selection, mutation, and crossover operators [5,11]. The fitness of an artificial instance (individual) $\mathbf{z}$ is defined, for the same-class GA and the counterexample GA, respectively, as:

$$f_1(\mathbf{z}) = \mathbf{I}\big(y_b(\mathbf{x}^*) = y_b(\mathbf{z})\big) + \big(1 - d(\mathbf{x}^*, \mathbf{z})\big) - \mathbf{I}\big(\mathbf{x}^* = \mathbf{z}\big) \tag{1}$$

$$f_2(\mathbf{z}) = \mathbf{I}\big(y_b(\mathbf{x}^*) \neq y_b(\mathbf{z})\big) + \big(1 - d(\mathbf{x}^*, \mathbf{z})\big) - \mathbf{I}\big(\mathbf{x}^* = \mathbf{z}\big) \tag{2}$$

where $\mathbf{I}(\cdot)$ is the indicator function (equal to 1 if the condition is true and 0 otherwise), and $d(\mathbf{x}^*, \mathbf{z}) \in [0, 1]$ is a distance function. The normalized Euclidean distance is used for continuous attributes, with normalization based on dataset variance, while for categorical attributes, the simple matching distance is adopted (distance 0 if values are equal, 1 otherwise). The second and third terms encourage solutions $\mathbf{z}$ that are close to, but distinct from, $\mathbf{x}^*$, while the first term promotes instances with either the same label (Eq. 1) or a different label (Eq. 2) relative to $y_b(\mathbf{x}^*)$.

2.2 LORE with *Fitness Sharing*

Fitness sharing is employed to preserve population diversity across GA generations. It is a niching strategy that penalizes individuals located in densely populated regions of the search space [5,15]. In LORE with *fitness sharing* (LOREfs), the fitness of the i-th individual $\mathbf{z}_i$ in population P for the same-class GA (GA_1) is defined as:

$$f_1^{\text{new}}(\mathbf{z}_i) = \frac{f_1(\mathbf{z}_i)}{\sum_{j=1}^{N} \psi\big(d(\mathbf{z}_i, \mathbf{z}_j)\big)} \tag{3}$$

where N is the population size, $d(\mathbf{z}_i, \mathbf{z}_j)$ denotes the distance between individuals, and $\psi(\cdot)$ is a sharing function that quantifies similarity. The original fitness $f_1(\mathbf{z}_i)$ is given by Eq. 1. For the counterexample GA (GA_2), the fitness is defined as:

$$f_2^{\text{new}}(\mathbf{z}_i) = \frac{f_2(\mathbf{z}_i)}{\sum_{j=1}^{N} \psi\big(d(\mathbf{z}_i, \mathbf{z}_j)\big)} \tag{4}$$

where $f_2(\mathbf{z}_i)$ is given by Eq. 2. The sharing function is defined as:

$$\psi(u) = \begin{cases} 1 - \left(\frac{u}{\sigma}\right)^{\beta}, & \text{if } u < \sigma \\ 0, & \text{otherwise} \end{cases} \tag{5}$$

where σ defines the niche radius and β controls the shape of the sharing function. In this work, $\beta = 1$, resulting in a linear sharing function. Individuals within a distance smaller than σ are considered to belong to the same niche and are therefore penalized.

In LOREfs, the fitness computation in GA_1 and GA_2 (Algorithm 1) is modified by replacing Eqs. 1 and 2 with Eqs. 3 and 4, respectively. By incorporating *fitness sharing* into both GAs, the authors of [14] showed that increasing the number of generations leads to local decision boundaries that more closely approximate those of the black-box model, thereby providing more precise and informative explanations.

3 LORE-BisD: Boundary-Directed Bisection Sampling

The proposed LOcal Rule-based Explanations with Bisection and Directed Perturbation (LORE-BisD) retains the counterexample GA (GA_2), which generates opposite-class instances (P_{opp}), while replacing the same-class GA (GA_1) with a bisection-based neighborhood generation procedure. This procedure consists of two stages: (i) bisection to locate points near the local decision boundary, i.e., the frontier that separates the region classes near the instance to be explained (target instance) by the XAI method, and (ii) directed perturbation to generate samples on both sides of the boundary.

3.1 Bisection for Boundary Location

For each counterexample $\mathbf{z} \in P_{\text{opp}}$ generated by GA_2, we perform a binary search along the line segment connecting the target instance $\mathbf{x}^*$ to $\mathbf{z}$ [16]. Let $\mathbf{a} = \mathbf{x}^*$ and $\mathbf{b} = \mathbf{z}$. By construction, $y_b(\mathbf{a}) = y_b(\mathbf{x}^*)$ and $y_b(\mathbf{b}) \neq y_b(\mathbf{x}^*)$, implying that the decision boundary lies along this segment.

At each iteration, we compute the midpoint:

$$\mathbf{m} = \frac{\mathbf{a} + \mathbf{b}}{2} \tag{6}$$

and evaluate the black-box model. If $y_b(\mathbf{m}) = y_b(\mathbf{x}^*)$, we update $\mathbf{a} \leftarrow \mathbf{m}$; otherwise, we update $\mathbf{b} \leftarrow \mathbf{m}$. After *max_iter* iterations, $\mathbf{a}$ is a point with the same class as $\mathbf{x}^*$ located within a distance $\varepsilon = \|\mathbf{a} - \mathbf{b}\|$ of the decision boundary, where $\|.\|$ denotes the Euclidean norm and:

$$\varepsilon < \frac{\|\mathbf{x}^* - \mathbf{z}\|}{2^{max\_iter}} \tag{7}$$

Unlike the same-class GA, which disperses samples across the local space to satisfy a class-based objective, bisection deterministically targets the boundary itself and converges to it exponentially, using only label queries and no gradient information.

3.2 Directed Perturbation

Given a boundary point $\mathbf{a}_{\text{boundary}}$ (obtained from the bisection procedure), we define a local boundary-crossing direction as:

$$\hat{\mathbf{u}} = \frac{\mathbf{a}_{\text{boundary}} - \mathbf{x}^*}{\|\mathbf{a}_{\text{boundary}} - \mathbf{x}^*\|} \tag{8}$$

which connects the target instance to a point arbitrarily close to the decision boundary. Although not guaranteed to be orthogonal to the boundary, it provides a consistent local direction for traversing it.

Candidate instances $\mathbf{z}'$ are generated by perturbing $\mathbf{a}_{\text{boundary}}$ along $\hat{\mathbf{u}}$ using step sizes $t \in \{t_1, \ldots, t_K\}$ sampled from a uniform grid over $[-\tau, \tau]$, with $\tau = 0.3\|\mathbf{a}_{\text{boundary}} - \mathbf{x}^*\|$. To account for local curvature, each candidate also receives a lateral perturbation ε_{lat}, obtained by projecting a Gaussian noise vector onto the hyperplane orthogonal to $\hat{\mathbf{u}}$:

$$\varepsilon_{\text{lat}} = \boldsymbol{\eta} - (\boldsymbol{\eta} \cdot \hat{\mathbf{u}})\hat{\mathbf{u}}, \quad \boldsymbol{\eta} \sim \mathcal{N}(0, \sigma^2) \tag{9}$$

with $\sigma = 0.05\|\mathbf{a}_{\text{boundary}} - \mathbf{x}^*\|$. The final candidate is:

$$\mathbf{z}' = \mathbf{a}_{\text{boundary}} + t \cdot \hat{\mathbf{u}} + \varepsilon_{\text{lat}} \tag{10}$$

Both constants are scaled by the boundary distance $\|\mathbf{a}_{\text{boundary}} - \mathbf{x}^*\|$, making the perturbation adaptive and scale-invariant. The fractions 0.3 and 0.05 were chosen so that longitudinal steps span a meaningful portion of the local neighborhood while lateral perturbations remain an order of magnitude smaller, keeping candidates close to the boundary. These values were fixed a priori rather than tuned, and kept constant across all datasets. Each candidate $\mathbf{z}'$ is then evaluated by the black-box model and labeled accordingly, producing both same-class and opposite-class instances concentrated near the decision boundary.

3.3 LOREfs-BisD

The second proposed algorithm, LOREfs-BisD, extends LORE-BisD by incorporating *fitness sharing* (see Sect. 2.2) into the counterexample GA (GA_2), as in LOREfs, while maintaining the replacement of the same-class GA (GA_1) with the proposed bisection-based neighborhood generation procedure. This variant enables the evaluation of whether increased diversity in counterexample generation further improves the quality of boundary coverage.

4 Evaluation Protocol

4.1 Experimental Setup

All experiments were conducted on a workstation equipped with an Intel ®Core i7-12700 (Alder Lake) processor (12 cores, 20 threads, 25 MB cache), 128 GB of RAM, and an NVIDIA Ampere RTX 3060 GPU (12 GB, 3584 CUDA cores), using Python implementations. In all experiments, the black-box model b is a multilayer perceptron (MLP) trained for a maximum of 100 iterations, with two hidden layers containing 100 and 50 neurons, respectively. To evaluate the contribution of the directed perturbation stage, we also consider a variant that relies solely on the bisection procedure, called LORE-Bis and LOREfs-Bis. In this setting, only boundary points are generated via bisection, without applying directed perturbations, allowing us to assess whether bisection alone is sufficient to generate representative same-class instances.

We implemented LORE in Python based on the description provided by the original authors [7]. In this work, both the implementation and the proposed methods are restricted to numerical, continuous features (i.e., excluding categorical and discrete variables), as required by the distance-based and bisection procedures employed. For both GA_1 and GA_2 in LORE, we used 10 generations, a mutation probability of 20%, and a crossover probability of 50%. For LOREfs, we used the same implementation but replaced the fitness function with the *fitness sharing* strategy. Following [14], we adopted different GA parameters for this variant: 100 generations, a mutation probability of 5%, and a crossover probability of 80%. For the parameters of the *fitness sharing*, we used α and σ equal to 1. In all cases, the GA population size was set to 1,000.

To reduce the size of the synthetic dataset used to train the decision tree surrogate c, we applied a filtering procedure to the final GA populations in both LORE and LOREfs. Specifically, all generated instances $\mathbf{z}$ are re-evaluated using the black-box model b. Instances for which the predicted label $y_b(\mathbf{z})$ does not match the intended class (i.e., the class targeted during generation) are discarded. For example, when generating same-class instances, samples classified as opposite-class by b are removed, and vice versa. This filtering step ensures label consistency in the training data and reduces the number of samples used to train c. The same procedure is applied in LORE-BisD and LOREfs-BisD. The surrogate decision tree c was trained using the default `scikit-learn` parameters.

4.2 Datasets

We evaluate the proposed methods on four datasets. Two synthetic shape datasets, Jain and Flame, feature non-linear decision boundaries and allow direct visualization of boundary structure [6]. Breast Cancer Wisconsin is a real-world, high-dimensional binary classification dataset with 30 features. The Wine dataset, with 11 features, is also real-world and is converted into a binary task by grouping samples into "good" and "bad" quality classes. Both real-world datasets are sourced from the UCI Machine Learning Repository [3].

For the evaluation procedure, each dataset is randomly split into training (80%) and test (20%) sets. The training set is used to train the black-box model, while the test set is used to generate explanations. Consequently, the number of instances to be explained varies across datasets: Flame contains 48 test instances, Jain 75, Wine 320, and Breast Cancer 114. For each test instance $\mathbf{x}^*$, a surrogate model is constructed, and the reported results correspond to averages over all instances.

4.3 Evaluation Strategy

As the proposed method aims to improve the approximation of the local decision boundary, we evaluate performance using metrics that capture how effectively the generated samples represent this region and support the construction of a faithful surrogate model. The following metrics are used.

Local Fidelity. We evaluate local fidelity using a distribution-agnostic protocol based on l_2-hypersphere sampling [8]. Given an instance $\mathbf{x}^*$ to be explained and a radius R, we sample n = 1,000 points uniformly from the ball $\mathcal{B}(\mathbf{x}^*, R)$ by drawing directions from a uniform distribution on the unit sphere and radii scaled as $\rho^{1/d}$, which ensures uniform density within the ball:

$$\mathbf{z}_i = \mathbf{x}^* + R \cdot \rho_i^{1/d} \cdot \mathbf{u}_i, \quad \mathbf{u}_i \sim \text{Uniform}(\mathcal{S}^{d-1}), \quad \rho_i \sim \text{Uniform}(0, 1) \tag{11}$$

Local fidelity at radius R is defined as the accuracy of the surrogate model c relative to the black-box model b over these samples:

$$\text{Local Fidelity}(\mathbf{x}^*, R) = \frac{1}{n} \sum_{i=1}^{n} \mathbf{1}\left[c(\mathbf{z}_i) = y_b(\mathbf{z}_i)\right] \tag{12}$$

We parameterize the radius as $R = \alpha \cdot \bar{\sigma}$, where $\bar{\sigma}$ is the mean standard deviation across features of the dataset. Results are reported for $\alpha \in \{0.1, 0.25, 0.5, 0.75, 1.0, 1.25, 1.5, 2.0\}$. This normalization enables meaningful comparisons across datasets with different feature scales.

F1-Score. The F1-score is computed by comparing the predictions of the black-box model b (MLP) and the surrogate model c (DT) over a subset of instances selected from the training set based on proximity to the instance $\mathbf{x}^*$ being explained.

For a given percentage p, the evaluation set is constructed by selecting the $\frac{p}{2}\%$ nearest instances to $\mathbf{x}^*$ that share the same label $y_b(\mathbf{x}^*)$, and the $\frac{p}{2}\%$ nearest instances that belong to the opposite class. For example, when $p = 20\%$, the evaluation set consists of the 10% closest instances with the same label as $\mathbf{x}^*$ and the 10% closest instances with the opposite label.

This sampling strategy emphasizes instances near the local decision boundary, as it includes both same-class and counterexample instances in the vicinity of $\mathbf{x}^*$. Consequently, it provides a more informative assessment of the surrogate model's ability to reproduce the local behavior of the black-box model.

5 Results and Discussion

5.1 Qualitative Analysis of Decision Boundaries

We begin by qualitatively analyzing the decision boundaries learned by the surrogate models for different explanation methods. Figures 1 and 2 illustrate representative examples for selected instances from the Flame and Jain datasets, respectively. Each row corresponds to a different method, while columns represent distinct instances $\mathbf{x}^*$.

The first row shows the true decision boundary of the black-box model, serving as a reference. Subsequent rows present the boundaries learned by LORE, LOREfs, and the proposed variants (LORE-Bis, LOREfs-Bis, LORE-BisD, and LOREfs-BisD). LORE and LOREfs tend to produce surrogate models with axis-aligned partitions that only coarsely approximate the local decision boundary. Although LOREfs improves sample diversity, both methods distribute synthetic instances broadly across the feature space, often failing to concentrate samples near the boundary region.

In contrast, the proposed bisection-based approaches exhibit a markedly different behavior. LORE-Bis improves boundary localization by explicitly identifying points close to the decision boundary; however, without additional refinement, the sampled instances remain limited in capturing local curvature. The full method, LORE-BisD, generates samples densely concentrated around the boundary and along its local geometry. This results in surrogate models that more accurately follow the true decision boundary, even in regions with nonlinear structure. The combination with *fitness sharing* (LOREfs-BisD) further enhances coverage, producing smoother and more consistent approximations across instances.

5.2 Local Fidelity Analysis

To quantitatively assess how well each surrogate model approximates the black-box model, we evaluate local fidelity using the l_2-hypersphere protocol defined in Sect. 4.3.

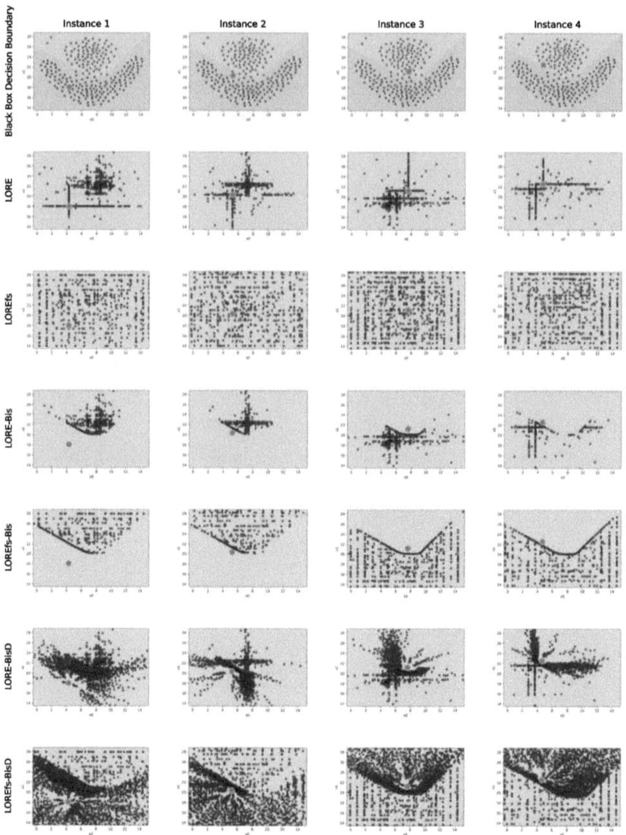

Fig. 1. Local decision boundary approximation for representative instances $\mathbf{x}^*$ in the Flame dataset. Columns correspond to different instances, and rows correspond to explanation methods. The first row shows the decision boundary of the black-box model b. Subsequent rows present the surrogate models learned by each method. Colored regions indicate predicted classes, while points represent generated synthetic samples (Z). The highlighted point denotes the instance $\mathbf{x}^*$ being explained.

Figure 3 presents the average fidelity as a function of the neighborhood radius parameter α, while Table 1 reports the corresponding numerical results.

Across all datasets, the proposed methods, particularly LORE-BisD and LOREfs-BisD, consistently achieve higher fidelity values compared to the baseline methods. This improvement is especially pronounced as α increases, indicating that the proposed sampling strategy better captures the local decision structure beyond very small neighborhoods. For the Flame and Jain datasets, which exhibit nonlinear decision boundaries, LORE-BisD and LOREfs-BisD maintain near-perfect fidelity across all values of α, significantly outperforming LORE and LOREfs. This demonstrates the effectiveness of explicitly sampling near the decision boundary. For the Wine and Breast Cancer datasets, which are higher-dimensional and more complex, the performance gap is even more substantial. While baseline methods yield fidelity values close to random

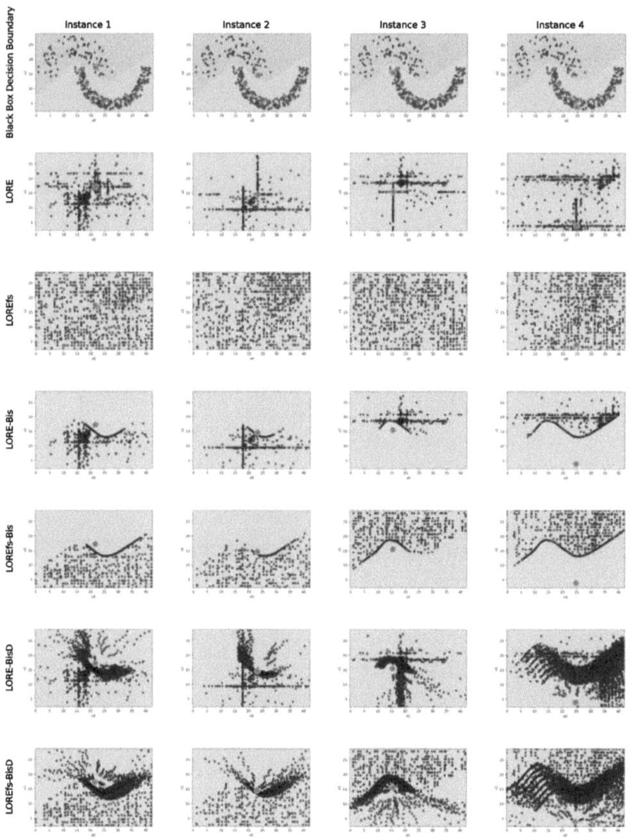

Fig. 2. Local decision boundary approximation for the Jain dataset.

agreement in some cases, the proposed methods achieve significantly higher fidelity, indicating a more faithful approximation of the black-box model.

5.3 F1-Score Evaluation

We further evaluate the agreement between the surrogate model and the black-box model using the F1-score metric, computed on subsets of instances selected based on proximity to $\mathbf{x}^*$ (Sect. 4.3). Table 2 summarizes the results for different neighborhood proportions.

For the Flame and Jain datasets, LORE-BisD and LOREfs-BisD achieve the highest F1-scores across all evaluated proportions, indicating strong agreement with the black-box predictions in the local neighborhood. This reinforces the fidelity results and highlights the effectiveness of the proposed method in capturing local decision behavior.

For the Wine and Breast Cancer datasets, however, a different pattern emerges. While LORE and LOREfs achieve higher F1-scores, this does not necessarily reflect better local explanations. Instead, this behavior can be attributed to the fact that these methods generate samples that are less concentrated near the decision boundary,

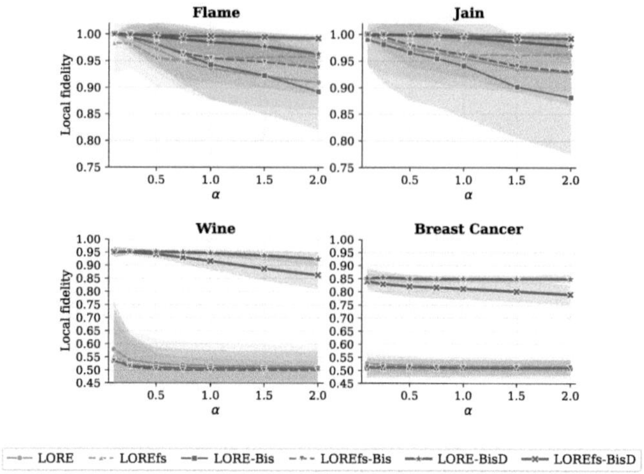

Fig. 3. Local fidelity as a function of the neighborhood radius parameter α for all evaluated methods and datasets. Fidelity is computed using the l_2-hypersphere sampling protocol centered at $\mathbf{x}^*$. Shaded regions represent the standard deviation across instances. Higher values indicate better agreement between the surrogate model c and the black-box model b.

Table 1. Local fidelity for different neighborhood radii α. **Bold** values indicate the best average performance for each dataset and α. Results are reported as mean ± standard deviation over all explained instances.

		Local Fidelity (α)						
Dataset	Method	$\alpha = 0.1$	$\alpha = 0.25$	$\alpha = 0.5$	$\alpha = 0.75$	$\alpha = 1.0$	$\alpha = 1.5$	$\alpha = 2.0$
Flame	LORE	0.999 ± 0.005	0.992 ± 0.028	0.972 ± 0.045	0.948 ± 0.054	0.936 ± 0.061	0.921 ± 0.059	0.910 ± 0.052
	LOREfs	0.983 ± 0.059	0.982 ± 0.046	0.956 ± 0.054	0.949 ± 0.052	0.954 ± 0.039	0.957 ± 0.023	0.958 ± 0.018
	LORE-Bis	1.000 ± 0.002	0.995 ± 0.019	0.982 ± 0.039	0.962 ± 0.056	0.943 ± 0.066	0.923 ± 0.073	0.892 ± 0.072
	LOREfs-Bis	**1.000 ± 0.001**	0.995 ± 0.022	0.980 ± 0.043	0.964 ± 0.050	0.955 ± 0.048	0.948 ± 0.049	0.938 ± 0.054
	LORE-BisD	**1.000 ± 0.001**	**1.000 ± 0.001**	0.995 ± 0.019	0.990 ± 0.020	0.985 ± 0.025	0.977 ± 0.027	0.963 ± 0.030
	LOREfs-BisD	**1.000 ± 0.001**	1.000 ± 0.002	**0.998 ± 0.007**	**0.996 ± 0.010**	**0.996 ± 0.007**	**0.995 ± 0.006**	**0.992 ± 0.005**
Jain	LORE	0.999 ± 0.005	0.990 ± 0.037	0.974 ± 0.058	0.965 ± 0.056	0.956 ± 0.053	0.935 ± 0.044	0.928 ± 0.035
	LOREfs	0.989 ± 0.048	0.980 ± 0.053	0.970 ± 0.055	0.965 ± 0.052	0.963 ± 0.041	0.961 ± 0.025	0.963 ± 0.018
	LORE-Bis	0.991 ± 0.049	0.981 ± 0.073	0.965 ± 0.090	0.955 ± 0.091	0.941 ± 0.098	0.902 ± 0.096	0.882 ± 0.107
	LOREfs-Bis	0.999 ± 0.004	0.995 ± 0.026	0.980 ± 0.042	0.971 ± 0.042	0.962 ± 0.044	0.941 ± 0.048	0.930 ± 0.062
	LORE-BisD	**1.000 ± 0.001**	**1.000 ± 0.002**	0.998 ± 0.004	0.996 ± 0.006	0.994 ± 0.009	0.986 ± 0.018	0.978 ± 0.026
	LOREfs-BisD	**1.000 ± 0.001**	**1.000 ± 0.002**	**0.999 ± 0.003**	**0.998 ± 0.003**	**0.997 ± 0.005**	**0.995 ± 0.005**	**0.992 ± 0.009**
Wine	LORE	0.579 ± 0.151	0.539 ± 0.114	0.525 ± 0.094	0.520 ± 0.088	0.517 ± 0.086	0.515 ± 0.083	0.513 ± 0.081
	LOREfs	0.553 ± 0.181	0.521 ± 0.113	0.512 ± 0.072	0.509 ± 0.066	0.509 ± 0.064	0.510 ± 0.064	0.511 ± 0.064
	LORE-Bis	0.536 ± 0.165	0.517 ± 0.099	0.510 ± 0.077	0.509 ± 0.071	0.508 ± 0.068	0.507 ± 0.066	0.507 ± 0.064
	LOREfs-Bis	0.536 ± 0.222	0.513 ± 0.124	0.503 ± 0.063	0.501 ± 0.049	0.500 ± 0.045	0.500 ± 0.040	0.501 ± 0.038
	LORE-BisD	0.950 ± 0.019	**0.952 ± 0.012**	**0.951 ± 0.009**	**0.950 ± 0.009**	**0.947 ± 0.012**	**0.937 ± 0.019**	**0.925 ± 0.026**
	LOREfs-BisD	**0.951 ± 0.019**	0.950 ± 0.014	0.942 ± 0.017	0.930 ± 0.025	0.916 ± 0.033	0.887 ± 0.046	0.863 ± 0.054
Breast Cancer	LORE	0.527 ± 0.042	0.522 ± 0.039	0.519 ± 0.035	0.517 ± 0.032	0.517 ± 0.031	0.516 ± 0.029	0.515 ± 0.029
	LOREfs	0.511 ± 0.039	0.507 ± 0.037	0.507 ± 0.036	0.507 ± 0.035	0.506 ± 0.036	0.506 ± 0.035	0.506 ± 0.036
	LORE-Bis	0.509 ± 0.034	0.510 ± 0.034	0.511 ± 0.034	0.510 ± 0.033	0.509 ± 0.031	0.509 ± 0.030	0.510 ± 0.028
	LOREfs-Bis	0.514 ± 0.032	0.514 ± 0.028	0.513 ± 0.028	0.513 ± 0.028	0.512 ± 0.028	0.512 ± 0.028	0.512 ± 0.028
	LORE-BisD	**0.852 ± 0.035**	**0.854 ± 0.023**	**0.850 ± 0.015**	**0.848 ± 0.014**	**0.849 ± 0.013**	**0.849 ± 0.014**	**0.849 ± 0.015**
	LOREfs-BisD	0.840 ± 0.030	0.829 ± 0.037	0.821 ± 0.041	0.816 ± 0.042	0.812 ± 0.041	0.801 ± 0.040	0.790 ± 0.038

leading to surrogate models that favor majority-class regions. As a result, the F1-score, computed on nearby training instances of the $\mathbf{x}^*$, may overestimate performance without accurately reflecting boundary fidelity. In contrast, LORE-BisD prioritizes sampling near the decision boundary, which may lead to lower F1-scores in some cases but results in significantly better boundary approximation, as evidenced by the fidelity analysis.

Table 2. F1-score for different neighborhood proportions. **Bold** values indicate the best average performance for each dataset and proportion.

Dataset	Method	F1 score		
		$F1_{10\%}$	$F1_{20\%}$	$F1_{30\%}$
Flame	LORE	0.945 ± 0.131	0.947 ± 0.113	0.949 ± 0.083
	LOREfs	0.959 ± 0.059	0.966 ± 0.037	0.972 ± 0.032
	LORE-Bis	0.909 ± 0.140	0.932 ± 0.126	0.941 ± 0.099
	LOREfs-Bis	0.922 ± 0.067	0.953 ± 0.040	0.964 ± 0.033
	LORE-BisD	0.992 ± 0.023	0.992 ± 0.017	0.991 ± 0.020
	LOREfs-BisD	**0.997 ± 0.014**	**0.995 ± 0.010**	**0.996 ± 0.008**
Jain	LORE	0.924 ± 0.131	0.942 ± 0.093	0.950 ± 0.067
	LOREfs	0.946 ± 0.083	0.964 ± 0.055	0.974 ± 0.038
	LORE-Bis	0.871 ± 0.167	0.919 ± 0.103	0.919 ± 0.091
	LOREfs-Bis	0.927 ± 0.097	0.943 ± 0.070	0.937 ± 0.084
	LORE-BisD	0.990 ± 0.049	0.988 ± 0.054	0.988 ± 0.046
	LOREfs-BisD	**0.997 ± 0.015**	**0.997 ± 0.012**	**0.998 ± 0.009**
Wine	LORE	**0.644 ± 0.063**	**0.643 ± 0.055**	**0.643 ± 0.051**
	LOREfs	0.608 ± 0.081	0.611 ± 0.071	0.612 ± 0.069
	LORE-Bis	0.561 ± 0.086	0.552 ± 0.076	0.548 ± 0.076
	LOREfs-Bis	0.549 ± 0.084	0.548 ± 0.077	0.546 ± 0.076
	LORE-BisD	0.545 ± 0.080	0.540 ± 0.073	0.536 ± 0.071
	LOREfs-BisD	0.543 ± 0.084	0.536 ± 0.076	0.532 ± 0.074
Breast Cancer	LORE	**0.773 ± 0.117**	**0.796 ± 0.092**	**0.801 ± 0.080**
	LOREfs	0.570 ± 0.144	0.575 ± 0.130	0.577 ± 0.127
	LORE-Bis	0.663 ± 0.141	0.657 ± 0.124	0.657 ± 0.122
	LOREfs-Bis	0.588 ± 0.162	0.580 ± 0.143	0.580 ± 0.139
	LORE-BisD	0.383 ± 0.073	0.385 ± 0.068	0.382 ± 0.059
	LOREfs-BisD	0.463 ± 0.133	0.471 ± 0.117	0.468 ± 0.113

5.4 Analysis of Extracted Explanations

To complement the quantitative evaluation, we analyze the explanations produced by the surrogate models in terms of their structure, interpretability, and alignment with the local decision boundary. We consider a representative instance $\mathbf{x}^*$ from the Breast Cancer dataset and compare the decision rules r and counterfactual conditions Φ generated by LORE and the proposed methods.

LORE:

$$\begin{aligned} r = (\{&\text{area}_{\text{se}} > 124.7016,\ \text{perimeter}_{\text{worst}} > 71.9856,\ \text{radius}_{\text{worst}} > 15.5680,\\ &\text{smoothness}_{\text{mean}} \leq 0.1339,\ \text{smoothness}_{\text{se}} > 0.0006,\ \text{perimeter}_{\text{se}} > -0.3690\}\\ &\rightarrow \text{diagnosis} = Malign) \end{aligned} \tag{13}$$

$$\begin{aligned} \Phi = (\{&\text{area}_{\text{se}} > 124.7016,\ \text{perimeter}_{\text{worst}} > 71.9856,\ \text{radius}_{\text{worst}} > 15.5680,\\ &\text{smoothness}_{\text{mean}} > 0.1339\}) \end{aligned} \tag{14}$$

The rule is relatively concise but relies on a limited subset of features. The counterfactual explanation highlights $\text{smoothness}_{\text{mean}}$ as the primary decision-switching feature, while the remaining conditions largely reproduce parts of the rule itself. This redundancy suggests limited contrastiveness and indicates that the surrogate model does not clearly isolate the most discriminative factors in the vicinity of $\mathbf{x}^*$.

LORE-BisD:

$$\begin{aligned} r = (\{&\text{fractal dimension}_{\text{se}} > -0.0347,\ \text{symmetry}_{\text{se}} > -8.8792,\ \text{compactness}_{\text{se}} > -0.6149,\\ &\text{smoothness}_{\text{worst}} \leq 142.0825,\ \text{smoothness}_{\text{se}} \leq 0.1151,\ \text{symmetry}_{\text{se}} > -8.6213,\\ &\text{fractal dimension}_{\text{worst}} \leq 9.4900,\ \text{symmetry}_{\text{se}} > -7.8292,\ \text{area}_{\text{se}} > 130.1977,\\ &\text{radius}_{\text{worst}} > 26.1952,\ \text{area}_{\text{se}} \leq 130.4108\} \rightarrow \text{diagnosis} = Malign) \end{aligned} \tag{15}$$

$$\begin{aligned} \Phi = (\{&\text{compactness}_{\text{se}} \leq -0.6149,\ \text{fractal dimension}_{\text{se}} \leq 4.8739,\ \text{compactness}_{\text{se}} > -11.9261,\\ &\text{smoothness}_{\text{worst}} > -0.9122,\ \text{fractal dimension}_{\text{se}} \leq 2.5546,\ \text{symmetry}_{\text{se}} \leq 0.3942,\\ &\text{smoothness}_{\text{se}} > -7.4355,\ \text{compactness}_{\text{se}} > -1.6128,\ \text{perimeter}_{\text{se}} > 2.9085\}) \end{aligned} \tag{16}$$

Although the rule is more complex, it reflects a finer-grained characterization of the local region. The presence of multiple constraints around the same features suggests that the surrogate model is capturing subtle variations near the decision boundary.

LOREfs-BisD:

$$\begin{aligned} r = (\{&\text{fractal dimension}_{\text{se}} > -0.0010,\ \text{symmetry}_{\text{se}} > 0.0069,\ \text{compactness}_{\text{se}} > 0.0043,\\ &\text{concave points}_{\text{se}} \leq 0.1121,\ \text{area}_{\text{worst}} \leq 2227.0543,\ \text{radius}_{\text{worst}} \leq 29.8249,\\ &\text{fractal dimension}_{\text{se}} > 0.0008,\ \text{radius}_{\text{se}} > 0.9996,\ \text{compactness}_{\text{se}} \leq 0.0304\}\\ &\rightarrow \text{diagnosis} = Malign) \end{aligned} \tag{17}$$

$$\begin{aligned} \Phi = (\{&\text{compactness}_{\text{se}} \leq 0.0043,\ \text{fractal dimension}_{\text{se}} \leq 0.0602,\ \text{smoothness}_{\text{se}} \leq 0.0085,\\ &\text{smoothness}_{\text{worst}} \leq 0.2011,\ \text{radius}_{\text{worst}} > 24.9037,\ \text{fractal dimension}_{\text{worst}} \leq 0.5782,\\ &\text{texture}_{\text{se}} > 0.1661,\ \text{symmetry}_{\text{mean}} \leq 0.2753,\ \text{radius}_{\text{mean}} \leq 22.5370\}) \end{aligned} \tag{18}$$

This variant provides a richer yet more coherent description. Overall, LORE produces simpler but less precise explanations. In contrast, LORE-BisD and LOREfs-BisD generate explanations that are richer and more informative. Although these methods may produce longer rules, they capture more informative feature interactions and provide clearer counterfactual conditions.

6 Conclusion

In this work, we introduced a bisection-based neighborhood generation strategy for local rule-based explainable artificial intelligence, addressing a key limitation of existing methods such as LORE and LOREfs. Specifically, we showed that the GAs employed by these methods do not explicitly target the decision boundary, which can result in synthetic neighborhoods that insufficiently represent the most informative regions for local explanation.

To overcome this limitation, we proposed LORE-BisD, which replaces the same-class GA with a bisection-based procedure that explicitly locates points near the decision boundary and generates samples via directed perturbations. This approach increases the concentration of training instances in boundary regions, improving the surrogate model's ability to approximate the local behavior of the black-box model. We also introduced LOREfs-BisD, combining the proposed sampling strategy with *fitness sharing* to assess the impact of diversity in boundary-focused sampling.

Experimental results across multiple datasets demonstrated that the proposed methods consistently achieve superior local fidelity, particularly for larger neighborhood radii, indicating a more accurate approximation of the decision boundary. Visual analyses further confirmed that LORE-BisD and LOREfs-BisD produce surrogate models that better capture the geometry of the underlying decision regions. However, the F1-score results revealed an important limitation in higher-dimensional settings. While the proposed methods perform strongly on low-dimensional datasets, where proximity-based sampling effectively captures the local structure, their advantage is less pronounced in higher-dimensional spaces. This behavior can be attributed to the well-known challenges of distance-based sampling in high dimensions, where neighborhoods become sparse and less informative, and where evaluation sets may not adequately concentrate near the decision boundary. As a result, F1-score may underestimate the improvements in boundary approximation achieved by the proposed methods.

Overall, the results highlight that explicitly targeting the decision boundary during neighborhood generation is a critical factor for improving both fidelity and explanation quality. As future work, we plan to investigate strategies to better handle high-dimensional settings, including adaptive neighborhood definitions and alternative evaluation protocols, as well as extending the approach to multi-class problems and to other ML models.

Acknowledgements. This work was partially supported in Brazil by FAPESP (#2024/15430-5 and #2024/08485-8) and CNPq (#304640/2024-7).

References

1. Baldo-Júnior, S., et al.: A bioinspired multimodal CNN-LSTM network for EEG analysis of patients in coma. Sensors **25**(22), 6981 (2025)

2. Cortiz, D.: Inteligência artificial: conceitos fundamentais. In: Vainzof, R., Guttierrez, A. (eds.) Inteligência artificial: sociedade, economia e Estado. Thomson Reuters, pp. 45–60 (2021)
3. Dua, D., Graff, C.: UCI Machine Learning Repository (2017)
4. D'Angelo, G., Della-Morte, D., Pastore, D., Donadel, G., De Stefano, A., Palmieri, F.: Identifying patterns in multiple biomarkers to diagnose diabetic foot using an explainable genetic programming-based approach. Futur. Gener. Comput. Syst. **140**, 138–150 (2023)
5. Eiben, A.E., Smith, J.E.: Introduction to Evolutionary Computing. NCS, Springer, Heidelberg (2015). https://doi.org/10.1007/978-3-662-44874-8
6. Fränti, P., Sieranoja, S.: K-means properties on six clustering benchmark datasets. Appl. Intell. **48**(12), 4743–4759 (2018). https://doi.org/10.1007/s10489-018-1238-7
7. Guidotti, R., Monreale, A., Giannotti, F., Pedreschi, D., Ruggieri, S., Turini, F.: Factual and counterfactual explanations for black box decision making. IEEE Intell. Syst. **34**(6), 14–23 (2019)
8. Laugel, T., Renard, X., Lesot, M.J., Marsala, C., Detyniecki, M.: Defining locality for surrogates in post-hoc interpretablity. arXiv preprint arXiv:1806.07498 (2018)
9. Lundberg, S.M., Lee, S.I.: A unified approach to interpreting model predictions. Adv. Neural. Inf. Process. Syst. **30**, 4768–4777 (2017)
10. Mastelini, S.M., et al.: Short-term energy market forecasting ensemble with multi-data source integration. Int. J. Data Sci. Anal. **21**(1), 9 (2026)
11. Mitchell, M.: An Introduction to Genetic Algorithms, MIT Press (1996)
12. Ortigossa, E.S., Gonçalves, T., Nonato, L.G.: Explainable artificial intelligence (XAI)-from theory to methods and applications. IEEE Access (2024)
13. Ribeiro, M.T., Singh, S., Guestrin, C.: "Why should I trust you?" explaining the predictions of any classifier. In: Proceedings of the 22nd ACM SIGKDD International Conference on Knowledge Discovery and Data Mining, pp. 1135–1144 (2016)
14. Santos, D.A., Baranauskas, J.A., Tinós, R.: Local rule-based explanations method based on genetic algorithms with fitness sharing. Learn. Nonlin. Models **21**(2), 4–15 (2023)
15. Sareni, S., Krahenbuhl, L.: Fitness sharing and niching methods revisited. IEEE Trans. Evol. Comput. **2**(3), 97–106 (1998)
16. Wood, G.R.: The bisection method in higher dimensions. Math. Program. **55**(1), 319–337 (1992)

Glaucoma Screening Using Transfer Learning with a ConvNeXt V2 Architecture

Filipe Ciríaco Marcelino do Nascimento, Nayara Oliveira Santos, and Daniel Oliveira Dantas(✉)

Departamento de Computação, Universidade Federal de Sergipe (UFS), São Cristóvão, Brazil
{filipe.donascimento,nayara.oliveira,ddantas}@dcomp.ufs.br

Abstract. Glaucoma is the second leading cause of blindness among adults aged 50 years or older and its early detection is very important to vision loss prevention. One of the main methods for glaucoma diagnosis is the fundoscopic exam assessed by experts, which can be costly and time consuming. In order to manage these constraints and assist professionals, this study proposes a framework based on a ConvNeXt V2 architecture for classification of fundus eye images between Referable Glaucoma and Non-referable Glaucoma. The proposed method achieved an accuracy comparable to other works using fewer epochs and less computational power.

Keywords: Glaucoma Screening · Transfer Learning · ConvNeXt V2 · Fundus Images · Deep Learning

1 Introduction

The eye is a complex organ formed by refractive structures (cornea and crystalline lens), the pupil and the retina. The latter consists of another complex system by itself with the sole purpose of sending the image, received from the refractive structures, to the brain. The retina passes the light first through the ganglion cells and then through the plexiform and nuclear layers before it reaches the layer of rods and cones, therefore reaching the optic nerves [4].

In 2020, glaucoma was the second leading cause of blindness among the global 33.6 million adults aged 50 years and older [15]. This optic neuropathy is characterized by a progressive loss of retinal ganglion cells and optic nerve injury, often associated with elevated intraocular pressure. Although glaucoma presents several phenotypes, its primary types, open-angle and angle-closure glaucoma, are related to the anatomy of the anterior chamber angle. The angle, located where the cornea and the iris meet, is a critical structure for regulating intraocular pressure [19]. Regardless of the phenotype, the risk of developing blindness is significant if the disease is detected late, but smaller if patients

M. Recamonde-Mendoza and R. C. Barros (Eds.): BRACIS 2026, LNAI 17105, pp. 615–628, 2027.
https://doi.org/10.1007/978-3-032-39882-6_41

receive early treatment [5]. Therefore, accurate and early detection is crucial for preserving the patient's eyesight.

The detection requires an expert professional and the analysis of a batch of tests, increasing the cost and time needed to diagnose. One of the most commonly used methods on medical detection is the fundoscopy, an exam that consists of the analysis of the back interior of the eye. Most machine learning driven workflows, including this study, utilizes the fundoscopy images to predict the chances of referable glaucoma, assisting the professionals and facilitating the diagnosis.

To promote the development of these models, the Artificial Intelligence for Robust Glaucoma Screening (AIROGS) challenge was created. This online challenge provided a dataset, called The Rotterdam EyePACS AIROGS, that contains 112,732 color fundus images with labels Referable Glaucoma (RG) and Non-referable Glaucoma (NRG) assigned by human experts.

A previous study by Sá [20] created a model using transfer learning with a Faster region-based convolutional neural network (R-CNN) model and a ResNet-50-FPN backbone and experienced with 3 types of inputs: images resized with histogram equalization, images with original sizes, and images with original sizes with histogram equalization. Using only AIROGS, their second experiment achieved the accuracy of 0.8900, the highest compared to the others experiments.

D'Souza [3] created AlterNet-K, a model based on an alternating design pattern combining ResNets blocks and multi-head self-attention (MSA). The model is based on the design pattern proposed in Park and Kim article [14] and aims to minimize the number of parameters in the model. As an alternative to the inaccessible and unlabeled AIROGS challenge Test set, 6,540 images were used from the AIROGS Training set with five-fold cross-validation across Training and Validation sets.

The model proposed by Roy [17], named DeepEyeNet, is a convolutional neural network (CNN) classifier that utilizes anatomical and texture-based features, optimized using the Adaptive Genetic Bayesian Optimization (AGBO) algorithm. It consists of image standardization, cup segmentation (based on a U-Net model), feature extraction using various mathematical functions, and a classification model. For the Training, Validation and Test sets, the author used the AIROGS-Light-V2 [6] dataset, a balanced subset of standardized fundus images from the original AIROGS set, achieving an accuracy of 0.9584 and an F1-score of 0.9583.

Proposed by Luo, the SegImgNet is a segmentation-guided dual-branch network consisting of two main components: a segmentation branch, to generate retinal structure feature maps based on the U-Net model, and a classification branch, to predict the probability of RG using a segmented image encoder, a raw image encoder, classifier and segmentation-guided attention (SGA) blocks. Using six public retinal vessel datasets to train the segmentation module and AIROGS for training the pre-trained ImageNet classification module, this model achieved accuracy of 0.940 and F1-score of 0.941 .

Building upon the Faster R-CNN model proposed by Sá, our model achieves comparable performance metrics while maintaining lower computational complexity through our proposed pipeline, especially when compared to their complex architectures. Rather than proposing a novel complex framework from scratch, this study leverages Detectron2, ConvNeXt V2, well-established and widely recognized frameworks in the literature, and a multilayer perceptron to achieve comparable performance. This is accomplished relying solely on fundus scans and a reduced number of training epochs.

Furthermore, our approach can be integrated into clinical glaucoma diagnostic workflows, assisting healthcare professionals in achieving faster and more accurate diagnoses.

2 Methodology

In a clinical setting, effective diagnosis relies not just on accurate classification, but also on the precise localization of the optic disc. Consequently, establishing a pipeline that leverages Faster R-CNN for detection alongside our trained model for classification facilitates its deployment in a real-world glaucoma diagnostic system. Figure 1 illustrates the proposed pipeline for a practical use case.

Firstly, the optic disc was segmented using Faster R-CNN model with a ResNet-50-FPN backbone. Then, data augmentation techniques were applied on the RG images due to the class imbalance. For the classification step, a model trained on ConvNeXt V2 architecture with a multilayer perceptron was used as the main classifier model. The Validation set was used to perform a hyperparameter tuning. The configuration with highest accuracy was retrained in the Training and Validation set and evaluated in the Test set in order to obtain the final model.

To improve the performance of our final model, we used two evaluation techniques: threshold optimization [1] and Test-Time Augmentation (TTA) [7]. Instead of using a default 0.5 classification cutoff, the first technique uses the Validation set to find the optimal probability threshold based on accuracy. This optimized threshold is then applied to the unseen Test set to ensure that the classifier's predictive performance scales to new data. The second technique, TTA, creates new images by flipping them horizontally and vertically. The final prediction is then obtained by averaging the model's outputs for these original and augmented images.

The implementation of this methodology is publicly available[1] and was coded in Python using PyTorch.

2.1 AIROGS Dataset

The Rotterdam EyePACS AIROGS Dataset [21] contains 112,732 color fundus images collected from 60,071 subjects and 500 different sites with heterogeneous ethnicity. Those images were labeled as Referable Glaucoma (RG), Non-referable Glaucoma (NRG), or Ungradable (U) by expert ophthalmologists and

[1] https://github.com/ddantas-ufs/2026_glaucoma.

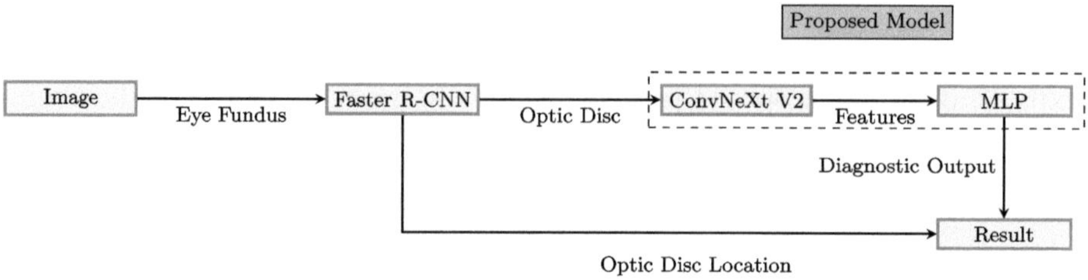

Fig. 1. Pipeline for location, segmentation and classification using the proposed model.

optometrists. The RG class represents images considered by evaluators to have glaucomatous signs associated with visual field defects. The NRG class represents images considered to have no glaucomatous visual field defects. The U class represents images with not enough information visible to decide between RG and NRG and belongs exclusively to the Test set.

For the AIROGS challenge, the data was split into a Training set of 101,442 images and a Test set of 11,290 images. Although the data from the Test set are private and cannot be downloaded, the Training set is publicly available[2]. All 101,442 images with varied dimensions were divided into six folders named from `0` to `5`. There is also a file named `train_labels`, which matches the images names on the column `challenge_id` with its class on the column `label`. Figure 2 shows samples of RG and NRG images from the publicly available portion of the AIROGS Dataset.

In this study, due to computational limitations, a portion of the AIROGS Training set was used and the images were randomly split into Training, Validation and Test sets in a 7:2:1 ratio. Table 1 shows the division of the 11,732 fundus eye images chosen from the dataset.

Table 1. Number of samples in Training, Validation and Test sets.

	Before Data Augmentation		After Data Augmentation	
	Non-referable Glaucoma	Referable Glaucoma	Non-referable Glaucoma	Referable Glaucoma
Training	5926	2287	5926	5924
Validation	1710	636	-	-
Test	834	339	-	-

2.2 Data Augmentation

Since the original dataset was unbalanced, with much more NRG images than RG, data augmentation was utilized. There were originally 2,287 RG images in

[2] https://zenodo.org/record/5793241.

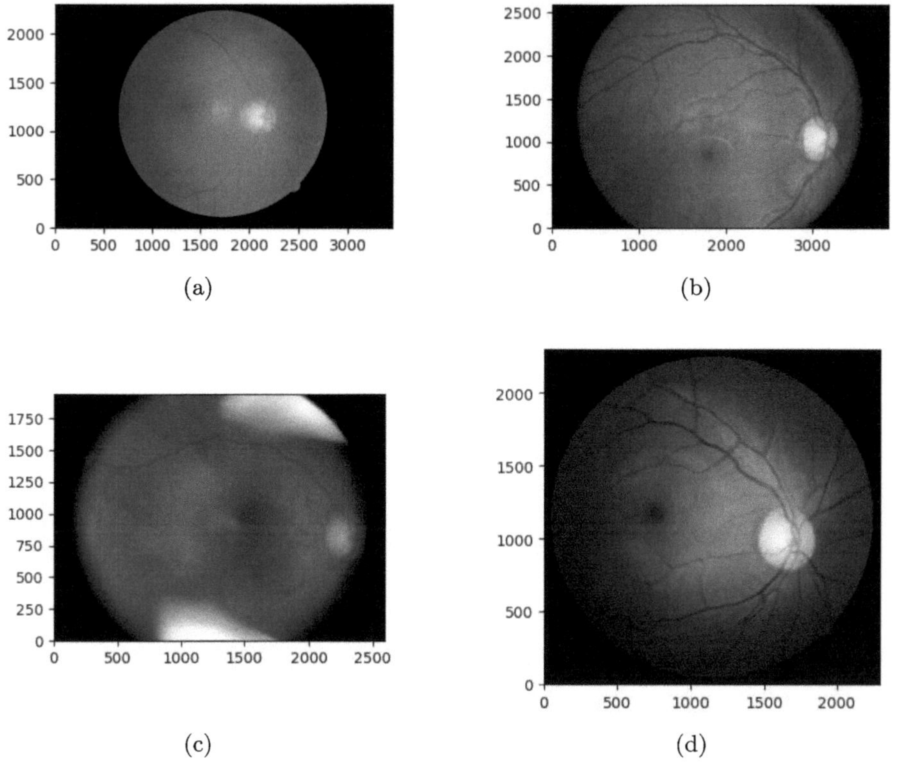

Fig. 2. AIROGS Dataset samples. (a) and (c) are classified as RG, (b) and (d) are classified as NRG.

the Training set from which 5,924 images were produced by employing image transformation techniques. Rotation, horizontal and vertical flip, Gaussian blur, saturation and hue modifications were used. Figure 3 illustrates the techniques applied to an image from the dataset. The number of samples for each set after data augmentation is shown in Table 1.

On a third of the original RG images, saturation or hue modification, horizontal or vertical flip, and rotation by 90°, 180° or 270° were applied. On another third, horizontal and vertical flip, hue and saturation modifications were applied. On the final third, rotation by 15°, 30°, 45° or 60°, vertical or horizontal flip and Gaussian blur were applied. In order to achieve the final number of images, some original images were altered twice with different techniques combinations.

2.3 Faster R-CNN

A distinct characteristic of glaucoma is cupping of the optic disc, which is the visible manifestation of the optic nerve head three-dimensional structure. The ratio of the optic disc cup and neuroretinal rim surface areas is a valuable indicator for the assessment of presence and progression of glaucoma [2]. Hence, it

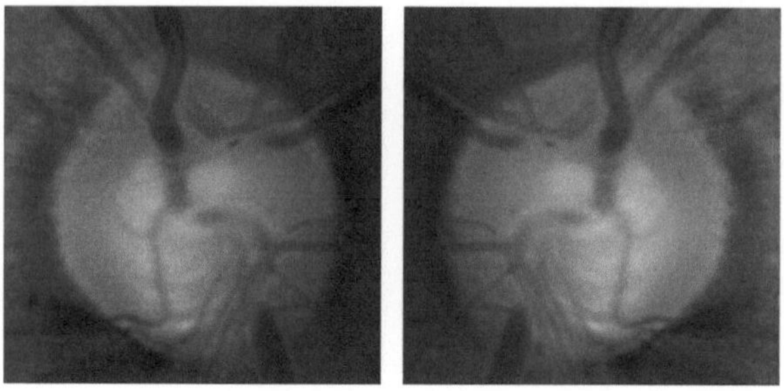

(a) (b)

Fig. 3. Example of augmented image: (a) source image; (b) transformed image.

was possible to classify the images using only the detected optic disc area rather than the original image.

All 8,470 NRG and 3,262 RG original images were subjected to optic disc segmentation prior to the classification step. The Faster R-CNN model with a ResNet-50 and feature pyramid network (FPN) backbone was chosen to perform segmentation. The model is implemented on the Detectron2 library and pre-trained on the Common-Objects in Context (COCO) dataset.

The Faster R-CNN architecture comprises two modules. The first is the region proposal network (RPN), a deep fully convolutional network responsible for region proposal. The second is a Fast R-CNN detector that uses the proposed regions for object detection [16].

For generation of region proposals, a small network operates as a sliding window over the output of the last shared convolutional layer. The input for this small network is an $n \times n$ spatial window of the input convolutional feature map. Each window is mapped to a lower-dimensional feature fed into a box-regression layer, responsible for the coordinates of each proposal and a box-classification layer, responsible for estimating whether the proposal is object or not [16].

In this study, the model used was previously trained on 500 images from the AIROGS dataset resized to 512 × 512 pixels and manually labeled using the LabelImg application. Each labeled image had an XML annotation indicating the optic disc location [20]. During inference, the dataset images were used in their original dimensions and a threshold of 0.7 was used to determine whether the region was optic disc or not. The detected region was cropped and resized to 390 × 390 pixels. Figure 4 shows the optic disc detected in the original image and the obtained cropped image.

2.4 ConvNeXt V2

A model from the ConvNeXt V2 family was chosen as classifier. The ConvNeXt V2 has a convolution-based architecture with state-of-the-art accuracy using publicly available data only (i.e. ImageNet-1K and ImageNet-22K) [22]. The

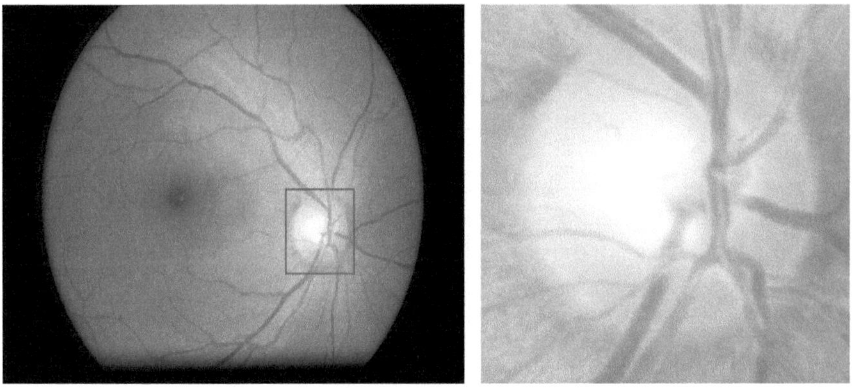

(a) (b)

Fig. 4. Example of segmented image: (a) source image; (b) segmented image.

selected model was pretrained with the Fully Convolutional Masked AutoEncoder (FCMAE) framework and fine-tuned on ImageNet-22k and ImageNet-1k.

The ConvNeXt consists of a ResNet modified toward the design of a Vision Transformer (ViT), being capable of competing favorably with hierarchical ViTs while remaining as efficient and simple as standard ConvNets [10]. The modifications encompass the use of ViT training procedure, macro and micro design adjustments, employment of depthwise convolution, inverted bottleneck at each block and larger kernel sizes.

Unlike the ConvNeXt, ConvNeXt V2 is trained with the FCMAE framework and has a Global Response Normalization (GRN) layer appended to the ConvNeXt architecture [22]. The FCMAE encompasses a ConvNeXt encoder responsible for processing the visible areas on the masked image using sparse convolution and a lightweight ConvNeXt decoder responsible for predicting the missing parts of the original image given the encoded features and mask tokens. The GRN unit promotes feature diversity during training and consists of three steps: global feature aggregation, feature normalization and feature calibration. The GRN first receives the spatial feature map and aggregates it into a vector using norm-based feature aggregation and normalizes it with simple divisive normalization, creating a feature competition across channels. Finally, the original input is calibrated using the computed feature normalization scores, two additional learnable parameters and a residual connection.

2.5 Multilayer Perceptron (MLP)

The multilayer perceptron is a feedforward neural network that transforms a collection of inputs into an output value, being useful for translating the features extracted by the backbone into a probability of glaucoma. The MLP in the proposed model consists of two fully connected layers with 512 and 128 neurons, respectively. In each of these hidden layers, the linear transformation is followed by a batch normalization layer, a GELU activation function, and a dropout layer, culminating in a final single-neuron layer with a sigmoid activation function.

During standard inference, the network classifies a sample as RG or NRG by applying a default probability threshold of 0.5. However, to enhance evaluation performance, our pipeline replaces this default approach by utilizing threshold optimization to find the optimal value. This technique employs an exhaustive search on the Validation set to find the threshold that maximizes accuracy, which is then applied during inference on the Test set.

2.6 Training

To achieve optimal performance while minimizing computational overhead, the ConvNeXt model was fine-tuned following a strict protocol of freezing layers. As the model had already been trained on the ImageNet-1k dataset, we kept the lower levels (from the stem through Stage 3) of the network frozen to act as a broader feature extractor, while training the top layer (Stage 4). This approach effectively bridges the gap between large-scale transfer learning and the specialized feature extraction required for our specific classification dataset.

During training, Focal Loss [9] was utilized as the primary loss function. Built upon the standard binary cross-entropy (BCE) loss with sigmoid activation, this function improves training by focusing on hard-to-classify examples, while preventing a large number of easy examples from overwhelming the model. It introduces two key hyperparameters to adjust the training process: α, which balances the importance of the classes, and γ, which reduces the loss contributed by easily classified images. In our model, we utilized $\alpha = 0.75$ and $\gamma = 2.0$.

Besides the loss function, we employed the AdamW optimizer [12], which improves upon standard Adam [8] by decoupling weight decay from the gradient update. This was paired with a Cosine Annealing scheduler [11] to systematically adjust the learning rate per epoch, thereby enhancing the model's convergence and overall precision.

Model training was performed across two distinct hardware environments: a local workstation (NVIDIA RTX 3050 GPU, Intel Core i5-10600KF CPU and 16 GB RAM) and a Google Colaboratory Virtual Machine (NVIDIA T4 GPU, 2 vCPU and 12 GB RAM). Maintaining the same environment settings across both machines, our proposed model was trained on the local workstation, while the grid search was done using the two instances in parallel.

All experiments were conducted using a fixed batch size of 32.

2.7 Grid Search

To determine the optimal configuration for the backbone and the connected multilayer perceptron, a grid search was performed for a maximum of 15 epochs per setting. The best-performing architecture was chosen as the proposed model based on the highest accuracy achieved on the Validation set. The optimal hyperparameters, i.e., number of layers and number of neurons in the multi-layer perceptron connected to the base model, learning rate, and dropout rate, are presented in Table 2.

Table 2. Hyperparameters tested and chosen by grid search.

Hyperparameter	Search space	Chosen value
Layers	[256], [512], [512, 128], [512, 256]	[512, 128]
Learning Rate	0.001, 0.0005	0.001
Dropout	0.0, 0.2, 0.4	0.0

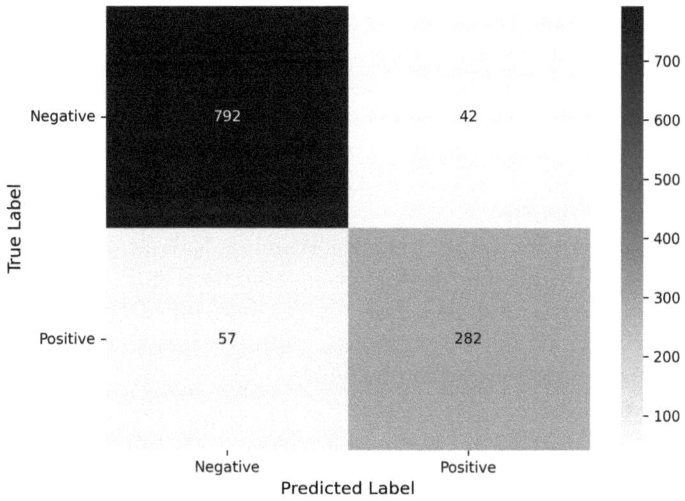

Fig. 5. Confusion Matrix of our proposed model.

3 Results and Discussion

3.1 Model Performance

We used accuracy as the main comparison metric, as done in the study by Sá [20]. Using the Test dataset, our proposed fully optimized model, with both threshold optimization (set at an optimal value of 0.74) and TTA, achieved accuracy of 0.9156, recall of 0.8319, precision of 0.8704, specificity of 0.9496, and F1-score of 0.8507.

Our proposed model achieved the results shown in the confusion matrix (Fig. 5). These results show that our model has a high proficiency in identifying healthy individuals, achieving a specificity of 0.9496 (with only 42 false positives out of 834 healthy cases). In contrast, the occurrence of 57 false negatives indicates a limitation of the model, as in these cases, patients with glaucoma are misdiagnosed as healthy (resulting in a recall of 0.8319). Therefore, the model should be used as a preliminary screening tool, and the final assessment must remain in under medical supervision.

In Table 3, our model is compared with three different experimental models by Sá [20] and the best-performing variant of each architecture presented by Sallam [18]. The proposed model surpassed the best accuracy of Sá in 0.0256, indicating how the higher resolution images alongside the ConvNeXt V2 made a difference.

In Table 4, our proposed model is compared with three different models: DeepEyeNet [17], SegImgNet [13], and AlterNet-K [3]. Although our model did not outperform the compared models in every metric, it demonstrates comparable results while benefiting from a simpler model structure and a reduced training time. Notably, our model required 50 fewer training epochs than DeepEyeNet and 120 fewer than AlterNet-K (Table 5).

The authors of the SegImgNet model did not disclose the exact number of epochs, providing only a range between 20 and 200. Additionally, the Training set comparison refers to the model with the classification module pre-trained on ImageNet and trained on the AIROGS dataset, excluding the variant that utilized the E-ROP dataset.

Instead of a proportional split between Training, Validation and Test, the creators of AlterNet-K utilized a five-fold cross-validation split, using 6,540 images balanced between NRG and RG. For the comparison of the Training set, we considered four-fifths of the total images, as this corresponds to the four folds used for training in this technique (Table 5).

Table 3. Performance comparison with studies by Sá and Sallam.

Reference	Model	Accuracy	Recall	Precision	F1-Score
Proposed	ConvNeXt V2	0.9156	0.8319	0.8704	0.8507
Sá et al. 2024 [20]	Experiment 1	0.8753	0.8643	0.8967	0.8802
	Experiment 2	0.8900	0.8723	0.8913	0.8817
	Experiment 3	0.8800	0.9250	0.8043	0.8605
Sallam et al. 2021 [18]*	AlexNet	0.814	0.815	0.818	-
	VGG-16	0.822	0.820	0.820	-
	GoogleNet-V1	0.829	0.830	0.829	-
	ResNet-152	0.869	0.869	0.869	-

*Metrics reported with only three decimal places.

Table 4. Performance comparison with other studies.

Reference	Model	Accuracy	Recall	Precision	Specificity	F1-Score
Roy et al. 2025 [17]	DeepEyeNet	0.9584	0.9558	0.9609	-	0.9583
Luo et al. 2023 [13]	SegImgNet	0.940	0.949	0.935	0.934	0.941
D'Souza et al. 2023 [3]	AlterNet-K	0.9161	0.9070	0.9239	0.9251	0.9153
Proposed Model	ConvNeXt V2	0.9156	0.8319	0.8704	0.9496	0.8507

Table 5. Comparison of Training set size and number of epochs.

Reference	Model	Training set	Epochs
Roy et al. 2025 [17]	DeepEyeNet	8,000	80
Luo et al. 2023 [13]	SegImgNet	3.960	20-200*
D'Souza et al. 2023 [3]	AlterNet-K	5.232*	150
Proposed	ConvNeXt V2	11,850	30

*Exact number not disclosed.

3.2 Ablation Study

An ablation study was conducted to evaluate the impact of each element on the proposed model's performance. Table 6 presents a comparison between the full model, configurations where data augmentation, the proposed multilayer perceptron, the layer freezing strategy, threshold optimization and TTA were individually removed, and a baseline model omitting the four elements while retaining the layer freezing strategy.

To evaluate the model without data augmentation, all augmented samples were excluded, resulting in an imbalanced dataset of 8,470 NRG and 3,262 RG images. To ablate the classifier, the proposed multilayer perceptron was replaced with a single-unit sigmoid layer. To assess the impact of the layer freezing strategy, a full fine-tuning configuration was evaluated, in which all network layers were unfrozen and updated during training. To remove threshold optimization, inference with TTA was implemented using the default 0.5 classification threshold. Finally, to remove TTA, inference using the optimal threshold (0.74) was performed.

Evaluating the best-performing model for each configuration on the Validation set, the Full Fine-Tuning variant showed the biggest impact among the rest, yielding a decrease of 0.0188 in accuracy. Removing the proposed MLP and TTA also negatively affected the model, resulting in accuracy drops of 0.0055 and 0.0043, respectively. The baseline model and the variant without threshold optimization showed minor reductions of 0.0034 and 0.0013.

Interestingly, omitting data augmentation led to a slight performance increase, achieving an accuracy of 0.9062, which is 0.0021 higher than the full model. This marginal difference can likely be attributed to statistical noise. Determining whether this variation is statistically significant would require formal hypothesis testing across multiple dataset splits and different random seeds, which is proposed as a subject for future work.

Table 6. Ablation study results on the Validation set.

Configuration	Accuracy	Δ
Proposed Model	0.9041	0.0000
Full Fine-Tuning	0.8853	- 0.0188
Without MLP	0.8986	- 0.0055
Without augmentation	0.9062	0.0021
Without threshold optimization	0.9028	- 0.0013
Without TTA	0.8998	- 0.0043
Baseline	0.9007	- 0.0034

4 Conclusions

Compared to the work by Sá et al., the proposed model, a ConvNeXt V2 combined with multilayer perceptron, achieved overall better metrics and it demonstrated how a model using a newer architecture could improve results. While our model couldn't outperform DeepEyeNet, SegImgNet and AlterNet-K in every metric, our model showed comparable results, maintaining a lower complexity and smaller number of epochs when compared to models from the literature.

The overall metrics indicate that the model should not be used as a standalone diagnostic tool of glaucoma, but rather as an assistive tool for the ophthalmologist. In this context, the proposed model can be integrated into automated diagnostic pipelines to help professionals avoid false-positive diagnoses, thereby facilitating the early detection of the disease.

In this study, the pre-trained backbone was utilized as a feature extractor with partially frozen weights. As demonstrated in our ablation study, this approach not only reduced computational overhead but also outperformed full fine-tuning. However, in future studies, training the architecture entirely from scratch on the AIROGS dataset could be explored to potentially achieve even better overall metrics in the proposed model. Furthermore, combining traditional handcrafted feature extraction with ConvNeXt V2 and integrating ensemble or hybrid techniques with Transformers architectures may result in further improvements in performance. Future work will also focus on conducting formal hypothesis testing across multiple dataset splits and different random seeds to evaluate the statistical significance of the performance variations observed in the ablation study.

Acknowledgments. The authors acknowledge the use of the generative artificial intelligence tool Gemini 3.1 (Google, 2026) to assist in text translation, wording refinement, and iterative improvement of written passages. All conceptual contributions, experimental design, analyses, and scientific conclusions presented in this work are entirely the responsibility of the authors.

References

1. Abdelhamid, M., Desai, A.: Balancing the scales: A comprehensive study on tackling class imbalance in binary classification (2024). https://arxiv.org/abs/2409.19751
2. Abramoff, M.D., Garvin, M.K., Sonka, M.: Retinal imaging and image analysis. IEEE Rev. Biomed. Eng. **3**, 169–208 (2010). https://doi.org/10.1109/rbme.2010.2084567
3. D'Souza, G., Siddalingaswamy, P.C., Pandya, M.A.: Alternet-K: a small and compact model for the detection of glaucoma. Biomed. Eng. Lett. **14**(1), 23–33 (2023). https://doi.org/10.1007/s13534-023-00307-6
4. Guyton, A., Hall, J.: Textbook of Medical Physiology. Guyton Physiology Series, Elsevier Saunders (2006). https://books.google.com.br/books?id=sTZHAQAAIAAJ
5. Jayaram, H., Kolko, M., Friedman, D.S., Gazzard, G.: Glaucoma: now and beyond. Lancet **402**(10414), 1788–1801 (2023). https://doi.org/10.1016/s0140-6736(23)01289-8
6. Kiefer, R.: Glaucoma dataset: EyePACS-AIROGS-light-V2 (2024). https://doi.org/10.34740/KAGGLE/DSV/7802508
7. Kimura, M.: Understanding Test-Time Augmentation. In: Mantoro, T., Lee, M., Ayu, M.A., Wong, K.W., Hidayanto, A.N. (eds.) ICONIP 2021. LNCS, vol. 13108, pp. 558–569. Springer, Cham (2021). https://doi.org/10.1007/978-3-030-92185-9_46
8. Kingma, D.P., Ba, J.: Adam: A method for stochastic optimization (2017). https://arxiv.org/abs/1412.6980
9. Lin, T.Y., Goyal, P., Girshick, R., He, K., Dollar, P.: Focal loss for dense object detection. In: 2017 IEEE International Conference on Computer Vision (ICCV), pp. 2999–3007. IEEE (2017).https://doi.org/10.1109/iccv.2017.324
10. Liu, Z., Mao, H., Wu, C.Y., Feichtenhofer, C., Darrell, T., Xie, S.: A ConvNet for the 2020s. In: 2022 IEEE/CVF Conference on Computer Vision and Pattern Recognition (CVPR), pp. 11966–11976. IEEE (2022). https://doi.org/10.1109/cvpr52688.2022.01167
11. Loshchilov, I., Hutter, F.: Sgdr: Stochastic gradient descent with warm restarts (2017). https://arxiv.org/abs/1608.03983
12. Loshchilov, I., Hutter, F.: Decoupled weight decay regularization (2019). https://arxiv.org/abs/1711.05101
13. Luo, X., Zhao, S., Zong, Y., Chen, Y., Ying, G.S., He, L.: SegImgNet: Segmentation-guided dual-branch network for retinal disease diagnoses. Proc. AAAI Symp. Ser. **5**(1), 19–24 (025). https://doi.org/10.1609/aaaiss.v5i1.35547
14. Park, N., Kim, S.: How do vision transformers work? (2022). https://arxiv.org/abs/2202.06709
15. Pawar, S.: Causes of blindness and vision impairment in 2020 and trends over 30 years, and prevalence of avoidable blindness in relation to vision 2020: the right to sight: an analysis for the global burden of disease study. SSRN Electron. J. (2021). https://doi.org/10.2139/ssrn.3939242

16. Ren, S., He, K., Girshick, R., Sun, J.: Faster R-CNN: Towards real-time object detection with region proposal networks. IEEE Trans. Pattern Anal. Mach. Intell. **39**(6), 1137–1149 (2017). https://doi.org/10.1109/TPAMI.2016.2577031
17. Roy, A., et al.: DeepEyeNet: Adaptive genetic bayesian algorithm based hybrid ConvNeXtTiny framework for multi-feature glaucoma eye diagnosis (2025). https://arxiv.org/abs/2501.11168
18. Sallam, A., et al.: Early detection of glaucoma using transfer learning from pre-trained CNN models. In: 2021 International Conference of Technology, Science and Administration (ICTSA), pp. 1–5. IEEE (2021). https://doi.org/10.1109/ictsa52017.2021.9406522
19. Snell, R.S., Lemp, M.A.: Clinical Anatomy of the Eye. Wiley (1997). https://doi.org/10.1002/9781118690987
20. Sá, N.G.d., Dantas, D.O., Silva, G.F.d.S.: Glaucoma detection using transfer learning with the faster R-CNN model and a ResNet-50-FPN backbone. In: Proceedings of the 26th International Conference on Enterprise Information Systems, vol. 1, pp. 837–844. INSTICC, SciTePress (2024). https://doi.org/10.5220/0012706500003690
21. de Vente, C., et al.: AIROGS: Artificial intelligence for robust glaucoma screening challenge. IEEE Trans. Med. Imaging **43**(1), 542–557 (2024). https://doi.org/10.1109/tmi.2023.3313786
22. Woo, S., et al.: ConvNeXt V2: Co-designing and scaling convnets with masked autoencoders. In: 2023 IEEE/CVF Conference on Computer Vision and Pattern Recognition (CVPR), pp. 16133–16142. IEEE (2023). https://doi.org/10.1109/cvpr52729.2023.01548

Exploring Transformers for Predicting the Remaining Useful Life of Turbofan Engines

Eduardo Cunha Cabral(✉) and Eduard Camilo Inacio

Universidade Federal de Santa Catarina (UFSC), Florianópolis, Brazil
educcabral2002@gmail.com

Abstract. Precise Remaining Useful Life (RUL) estimation in turbofan engines is vital for operational safety and cost-efficiency in the aviation industry. Although Transformer-based architectures have set new benchmarks in sequence modeling, conventional training objectives centered on the Mean Squared Error (MSE) fail to account for the asymmetric risk profile of predictive maintenance. This paper evaluates the viability of Transformers for RUL prediction using the CMAPSS dataset, focusing on the numerical instabilities triggered by asymmetric exponential loss functions in complex operational regimes. We demonstrate that direct optimization of safety-biased losses often leads to model collapse due to exploding gradients. To mitigate these effects, our methodology utilizes a Phased Objective Transition (POT) framework, comprising a Binary POT strategy for discrete stabilization and a Hybrid POT for curriculum-based refinement. Furthermore, an independent Dynamic Loss Balancing (DLB) mechanism was implemented to provide autonomous stabilization based on training dynamics. Experimental results indicate that both the POT framework and the DLB model provide viable alternatives for implementing risk-aware deep learning in industrial prognostic systems.

Keywords: Remaining Useful Life · Transformer · Asymmetric Loss · Phased Objective Transition · Dynamic Loss Balancing

1 Introduction

Accurate estimation of Remaining Useful Life (RUL) is a fundamental task in Prognostics and Health Management (PHM) [2], particularly in safety-critical domains such as the aviation industry. Reliable RUL predictions enable condition-based maintenance, reducing operational costs while preventing unexpected failures. Among the benchmark datasets for this problem, the Commercial Modular Aero-Propulsion System Simulation (CMAPSS) turbofan engine simulation has become a standard for evaluating data-driven approaches due to its realistic degradation patterns and varying operational conditions [8].

M. Recamonde-Mendoza and R. C. Barros (Eds.): BRACIS 2026, LNAI 17105, pp. 629–643, 2027.
https://doi.org/10.1007/978-3-032-39882-6_42

Traditional RUL prediction methods have relied on statistical models and conventional machine learning techniques. However, recent advances in deep learning have significantly improved performance by capturing complex temporal dependencies in multivariate sensor data. In particular, Transformer-based architectures [10] have demonstrated remarkable success in sequence modeling tasks due to their ability to learn long-range dependencies through self-attention mechanisms. This capability makes them especially attractive for RUL estimation, where degradation patterns may span long temporal horizons.

Despite these advances, most existing approaches optimize models using symmetric loss functions such as the Mean Squared Error (MSE). While MSE provides stable gradients and facilitates convergence, it fails to capture the asymmetric risk profile inherent to predictive maintenance. In real-world scenarios, overestimating the RUL (late prediction) can lead to catastrophic system failures, whereas underestimation (early prediction) is comparatively less critical. To address this limitation, the PHM 2008 challenge introduced a scoring function that penalizes late predictions more severely than early ones [8]. However, directly optimizing such asymmetric exponential losses poses significant challenges, as their steep gradients can lead to numerical instability, gradient explosion, and convergence to trivial solutions.

To address this challenge, this work investigates a set of training objectives and strategies designed to balance optimization stability and risk-aware learning. As baselines, three primary loss formulations are considered: a standard MSE model for stable convergence, a model trained directly with the asymmetric CMAPSS loss, and a hybrid model combining both objectives through a weighted formulation. While these approaches provide different trade-offs between accuracy and safety, they also expose the limitations of static objective design, particularly in complex regimes.

The main contributions of this work are summarized as follows:

- A systematic analysis of the instability issues arising from the direct optimization of asymmetric exponential loss functions for RUL prediction, particularly in complex multi-regime scenarios of the CMAPSS dataset.
- The proposal of Phased Objective Transition (POT) strategies, including Binary POT and Hybrid POT, to stabilize training by introducing structured transitions between symmetric and asymmetric objectives.
- The introduction of a Dynamic Loss Balancing (DLB) mechanism based on loss dynamics, which adaptively adjusts the contribution of multiple objectives during training without requiring gradient-level modifications.
- A comprehensive empirical evaluation across all four CMAPSS subsets (FD001–FD004), comparing MSE, CMAPSS, hybrid, POT, and DLB approaches, highlighting the trade-offs between predictive accuracy, stability, and safety-oriented performance.

The remainder of this paper is organized as follows: Sect. 2 details the theoretical foundation of asymmetric loss and objective scheduling. Section 3 reviews related works. Section 4 presents the proposed methodology, including the Phased Object Transition (POT) framework and Dynamic Loss Balancing (DLB) mechanism. Section 5 discusses the experimental results, and Sect. 6 concludes with our final remarks and directions for future works.

2 Background

This section outlines the theoretical concepts underlying the proposed training strategies. It first contrasts symmetric loss functions with the asymmetric CMAPSS scoring function required for risk-aware predictive maintenance. Finally, it introduces curriculum learning and adaptive loss weighting, which form the conceptual basis for the objective scheduling and dynamic balancing mechanisms used in this study.

2.1 Symmetric vs Asymmetric Loss Functions in RUL

Conventional optimization objectives in data-driven prognostics are typically based on symmetric loss functions, such as the MSE, which assign equal penalties to overestimation and underestimation of the target variable. This property results in balanced gradient updates with respect to prediction errors, making such losses attractive from an optimization standpoint due to their stability and smooth convergence behavior.

However, in the context of RUL estimation, the direction of the prediction error carries distinct operational implications. Asymmetric loss functions address this limitation by assigning different penalties depending on whether the model overestimates or underestimates the true RUL, thereby enabling the incorporation of domain-specific risk preferences into the learning objective [8]. This formulation allows models to prioritize safety-critical errors without altering the underlying predictive architecture.

From an optimization perspective, introducing asymmetry modifies the structure of the loss landscape. In contrast to symmetric objectives, where gradient magnitudes depend solely on the error magnitude, asymmetric losses can amplify gradients selectively based on the direction of the error. This behavior may lead to biased updates, increased sensitivity to certain regions of the error space, and potential instability during training, particularly in deep neural networks [4]. These characteristics highlight the need for training strategies that can effectively manage the trade-off between stability and risk-aware optimization.

2.2 CMAPSS Scoring Function

To properly evaluate predictive models in safety-critical domains, the optimization objective must reflect the physical risks of the system. Unlike symmetric metrics such as MSE, the CMAPSS scoring function applies an asymmetric, exponential penalty to prediction errors.

Let $t_{\mathrm{RUL},i}$ represent the true RUL (measured in operational cycles) of the i-th engine unit, and let $\hat{t}_{\mathrm{RUL},i}$ denote the model's predicted RUL for that same unit. The prediction error, d_i, is defined as the difference between the prediction and the ground truth, as observed in Eq. 1:

$$d_i = \hat{t}_{\text{RUL},i} - t_{\text{RUL},i} \tag{1}$$

An overestimation, predicting the engine will last longer than it actually does, results in $d_i > 0$, while an underestimation (predicting an earlier failure) yields $d_i < 0$. The total safety score S across n units is mathematically defined in Eq. 2.

$$S = \begin{cases} \sum_{i=1}^{n} \left[\exp\left(-\frac{d_i}{a_1}\right) - 1\right], & \text{for } d_i < 0 \\ \sum_{i=1}^{n} \left[\exp\left(\frac{d_i}{a_2}\right) - 1\right], & \text{for } d_i \geq 0 \end{cases} \tag{2}$$

In this formulation, $a_1 = 13$ and $a_2 = 10$ act as scaling constants that dictate the steepness of the penalty. Because a_2 is smaller than a_1, the penalty grows significantly faster for late predictions ($d_i > 0$). This ensures that the model is heavily penalized for catastrophic overestimations, while premature maintenance predictions ($d_i < 0$) are tolerated with a much gentler penalty curve.

From an optimization perspective, the exponential growth of the scoring function introduces significant challenges. During early training stages, when prediction errors are typically large, the resulting gradients can become excessively high, increasing the risk of numerical instability and divergence. This issue is particularly relevant in deep learning models, where large gradient magnitudes can disrupt parameter updates and hinder convergence [4]. Consequently, while the CMAPSS score provides a realistic evaluation criteria, directly optimizing it requires careful handling to ensure stable training.

2.3 Curriculum Learning and Objective Scheduling

Training deep neural networks under complex or highly non-linear objectives can be challenging, particularly when the loss function exhibits steep gradients or uneven optimization landscapes. Curriculum learning addresses this issue by structuring the training process as a sequence of progressively more difficult tasks, allowing the model to first learn stable and generalizable representations before focusing on more specialized objectives [1].

In the context of RUL estimation, the transition from symmetric to asymmetric loss functions can be interpreted as a curriculum over the optimization objective. Symmetric losses such as MSE provide a smooth and stable training signal, allowing the model to capture the underlying degradation dynamics without being affected by large gradient magnitudes. In contrast, asymmetric exponential losses introduce sharper penalties that emphasize safety-critical errors but may destabilize training if applied from the outset. Viewing this transition as a curriculum provides a principled framework for managing this trade-off.

Objective scheduling strategies extend this idea by explicitly controlling how the training objective evolves over time. Instead of optimizing a fixed loss function, the model is exposed to a sequence of objectives that gradually shift the optimization focus. This paradigm allows the learning process to adapt to different stages of training, prioritizing stability in early epochs and progressively incorporating risk-aware constraints. Such strategies are closely related to broader principles in deep learning optimization, where controlling gradient magnitudes and learning dynamics is critical for stable convergence [4].

This perspective directly motivates the use of Phased Objective Transition (POT) strategies, where the learning process is structured to control the interaction between stability-oriented and safety-oriented objectives. By framing the transition between loss functions as a curriculum, POT provides a systematic mechanism to mitigate instability while preserving the benefits of asymmetric error penalization.

2.4 Adaptive Loss Weighting

In multi-objective learning settings, models are often required to optimize multiple loss functions simultaneously, each capturing different aspects of the task. A common approach is to combine these objectives using fixed scalar weights. However, static weighting schemes assume that the relative importance and scale of each loss remain constant throughout training. In practice, this assumption rarely holds, as different objectives may evolve at different rates and exhibit distinct optimization dynamics [3].

Adaptive loss weighting methods address this limitation by dynamically adjusting the contribution of each objective based on the state of the training process. Instead of relying on predefined weights, these approaches seek to balance the optimization by considering factors such as gradient magnitudes, convergence speed, or relative loss improvement. To obtain stable estimates of these quantities, Exponential Moving Averages (EMA) are commonly employed, as they provide a smoothed representation of temporal signals while reducing sensitivity to short-term fluctuations [7].

In the context of RUL estimation, combining symmetric and asymmetric objectives introduces an inherent imbalance. The MSE component typically provides stable and well-scaled gradients, while the asymmetric exponential component may produce large updates when prediction errors are significant. This discrepancy can lead to unstable training or suboptimal convergence if fixed weights are used, particularly in early training stages where errors are large.

This motivates the use of Dynamic Loss Balancing (DLB) strategies, where the contribution of each loss component is continuously adjusted according to its relative training dynamics. By leveraging EMA to track the evolution of each objective, DLB enables a smoother and more robust estimation of their relative progress, allowing the weighting mechanism to react adaptively without introducing instability. This dynamic adjustment provides a practical mechanism to maintain training stability while progressively incorporating asymmetric error penalization.

3 Related Works

Recent approaches to RUL prediction on the CMAPSS dataset span recurrent, convolutional, and attention-based architectures, as summarized in Table 1. Early deep learning methods focused on recurrent models, with Wang *et al.*. [11] proposing a deep BiLSTM to capture bidirectional temporal dependencies, and Boujamza *et al.* [2] extending this approach with attention mechanisms to emphasize critical time steps.

Table 1. Comparison of RUL Prediction Approaches for Turbofan Engines

Work	Architecture	Main Contribution	Loss
Wang et al. (2018)	BiLSTM	Bidirectional temporal modeling	MSE
Boujamza et al. (2022)	Attn-LSTM	Temporal attention mechanism	MSE
Zeng et al. (2023)	GAT + Transformer	Spatial-temporal dependency modeling	MSE
Kim et al. (2024)	Transformer	Adaptive reweighting (ARR)	Weighted MSE
Zhou et al. (2024)	CNN + Transformer	Feature fusion and PVA loss	PVA (Asymmetric)
Zhang et al. (2025)	Transformer + LSTM	PLO-based hyperparameter optimization	MSE
This Work	Transformer Encoder	Objective scheduling and DLB	**MSE + CMAPSS**

More recent work has shifted toward Transformer-based and hybrid architectures. Kim *et al.* [6] combined a Transformer encoder with adaptive reweighting to address data imbalance, while Zeng *et al.* [12] incorporated graph attention mechanisms to model spatial and temporal dependencies. Zhang *et al.* [13] further explored hybrid designs by integrating Transformer and LSTM components with meta-heuristic hyperparameter optimization.

Despite these architectural advances, most methods rely on symmetric loss functions such as MSE. Only a limited number of studies explicitly consider asymmetric risk, such as the PVA loss proposed by Zhou *et al.* [14]. This suggests that, while model architectures have evolved significantly, the role of training objectives and optimization strategies remains comparatively underexplored.

In contrast, this work focuses on the training process itself, investigating how objective scheduling and adaptive loss weighting can enable stable optimization under asymmetric loss functions.

4 Methodology

This section details the experimental framework developed to evaluate risk-aware RUL prediction. It first outlines the data preparation pipeline for the CMAPSS dataset and describes the core Transformer Encoder architecture. Subsequently, it defines the proposed training strategies, introducing the baseline, the POT framework and the DLB mechanism. Finally, it details the experimental setup.

4.1 Data Pipeline and Preprocessing

Data preparation follows a pipeline designed for the CMAPSS benchmark to ensure consistency with the existing literature. For datasets operating under constant conditions, namely FD001 and FD003, a fixed selection of 14 sensors with non-null variance is retained. In contrast, for the multi-regime datasets FD002 and FD004, a dynamic feature selection is implemented to retain all columns with a standard deviation greater than zero, resulting in an input vector comprised of 21 sensors and 3 operational settings. To ensure numerical stability for the optimizer, all input features undergo Min-Max scaling to a range between zero and one, with scaling parameters derived solely from the training set to prevent data leakage. Regarding the target variable, a piecewise linear RUL labeling strategy is adopted with a maximum threshold of 125 cycles [5]. This approach prevents the model from trying to learn negligible degradation patterns during the early healthy stages where the sensor signals do not show perceptible change. Finally, the continuous multivariate time-series are segmented into overlapping sliding windows with a length of 30 cycles. Furthermore, while this methodology assumes intact sensor readings throughout the operational window, real-world industrial environments are highly susceptible to data integrity issues. Recent studies, such as the work by Tang [9], highlight that mitigating the effects of partial sensor failures and excessive noise is a critical frontier for improving the robustness of data-driven RUL predictions.

4.2 Architecture

The core of the predictive model is a Transformer Encoder architecture adapted for regression tasks. The input window is first projected into a 256-dimensional latent space via a linear dense layer. Sinusoidal positional encodings are then added to the embeddings to incorporate temporal order [10]. The model backbone consists of two identical encoder blocks, each featuring a four-head Multi-Head Self-Attention mechanism followed by a position-wise feed-forward network with 256 hidden units and ReLU activation. Residual connections and layer normalization are applied around each sub-layer, alongside a dropout rate of 0.1. Finally, a Global Average Pooling layer condenses the temporal features into a single vector, which is processed by a regression head comprising a 128-unit dense layer and a final linear neuron to produce the RUL estimate.

4.3 Proposed Training Strategies

This study investigates protocols to address the trade-off between absolute error minimization and the asymmetric risk requirements of the aeronautical industry.

Mean Squared Error (MSE). The fundamental baseline employs the standard MSE loss function. This objective treats all errors equally by penalizing the square of the difference between the predicted and true RUL. While this provides a smooth loss surface for initial convergence, it is fundamentally flawed for safety-critical systems as it does not differentiate between a conservative early prediction and a dangerous late prediction.

CMAPSS Score. To incorporate asymmetric risk into the training process, the CMAPSS scoring function introduced in the PHM 2008 challenge is employed [8]. As detailed in Sect. 2.2, this function assigns exponentially larger penalties to late predictions than to early ones, reflecting the higher operational risk associated with overestimating RUL.

While the CMAPSS score provides a realistic objective for safety-critical applications, its exponential structure introduces optimization challenges. In particular, large prediction errors during early training stages can lead to steep gradients, increasing the risk of instability and poor convergence.

In this work, the CMAPSS score is evaluated both as a standalone objective and as a component within composite training strategies, enabling a systematic analysis of its impact on model behavior and stability.

Hybrid Model. To combine the smooth optimization properties of the MSE loss with the safety-aware characteristics of the CMAPSS scoring function, we define a hybrid objective as a weighted sum of both components, as described in Eq. 3,

$$L_{\text{hybrid}} = \lambda_1 \cdot L_{\text{mse}} + \lambda_2 \cdot L_{\text{cmapss}} \tag{3}$$

where λ_1 and λ_2 are scalar coefficients controlling the contribution of each loss component. In this study, both coefficients are set to $\lambda_1 = \lambda_2 = 1$, providing a balanced formulation in terms of coefficient scaling.

The MSE component corresponds to the mean squared error between predicted and true RUL values, while the CMAPSS component follows the asymmetric exponential formulation described in Sect. 2.2, computed as the mean penalty over the batch to enable gradient-based optimization.

Due to differences in scale between the MSE and CMAPSS components, equal weighting does not necessarily imply equal influence during optimization. Nevertheless, this formulation provides a simple and effective baseline that jointly accounts for prediction accuracy and asymmetric risk.

This observation motivates the exploration of adaptive weighting strategies, as addressed by the Phased Objective Transition (POT) and Dynamic Loss Balancing (DLB) methods described in the following sections.

Phased Objective Transition (POT). In complex regimes such as FD002 and FD004, the high variance of sensor data combined with the steep gradients of an exponential loss function often leads to numerical instability or model collapse. To mitigate this, this study adopts two distinct Phased Objective Transition (POT) strategies designed to stabilize the training process by gradually introducing the asymmetric safety constraints. This approach is conceptually related to curriculum learning, where simpler objectives are used in early stages to facilitate stable optimization [1].

The first approach, referred to as Binary POT, divides the training into two stages. The model undergoes an initial 50-epoch stabilization phase using only the symmetric MSE loss to learn the general degradation manifold without the risk of gradient explosion. This is followed by a 50-epoch refinement phase where the objective is switched entirely to the CMAPSS loss component. This staged transition reduces the impact of large gradients during early training and helps prevent convergence to degenerate solutions, such as constant predictions.

The second approach, referred to as Hybrid POT, utilizes a structured weight curriculum over 100 epochs. Unlike the Binary POT, this strategy builds upon the hybrid loss function defined in Eq. 3, where the loss is expressed as a combination of MSE and CMAPSS components. While the baseline hybrid model employs fixed weights ($\lambda_1 = \lambda_2 = 1$), the Hybrid POT introduces a time-dependent weighting schedule. The coefficients λ_1 and λ_2 are adjusted every 20 epochs in a stepwise manner: the MSE weight decreases ($1.0 \rightarrow 0.75 \rightarrow 0.5 \rightarrow 0.25 \rightarrow 0.0$), while the CMAPSS weight increases proportionally ($0.0 \rightarrow 0.25 \rightarrow 0.5 \rightarrow 0.75 \rightarrow 1.0$). This progressive transition allows the optimizer to gradually shift from accuracy-driven learning to risk-aware optimization, reducing instability while preserving the structural guidance provided by the MSE objective during early training.

4.4 Dynamic Loss Balancing (DLB)

To address the limitations of static weighting strategies, we propose a Dynamic Loss Balancing mechanism that adaptively adjusts the contribution of the MSE and CMAPSS loss components throughout training. In contrast to the static (λ_1, λ_2) coefficients used in the hybrid and POT strategies, DLB introduces dynamically updated weights $(w_{\text{mse}}, w_{\text{cmapss}})$ that are adjusted at each epoch based on the observed training dynamics. The method is implemented as a lightweight callback within the training loop, operating without requiring modifications to the optimization process.

At the end of each epoch, the current values of both components are retrieved from the training logs. To reduce sensitivity to short-term fluctuations, the method maintains an EMA of each loss. Given a smoothing factor $\alpha = 0.7$, the EMA is updated as described in Eq. 4.

$$\text{EMA}_t = \alpha \cdot \text{EMA}_{t-1} + (1 - \alpha) \cdot L_t \tag{4}$$

To account for scale differences, each EMA is normalized against its initial value at the first epoch, denoted as $\tilde{L}_t^{\text{mse}}$ and $\tilde{L}_t^{\text{cmapss}}$. The relative importance of each objective is then determined inversely proportional to its normalized magnitude, updating the weights as shown in Eq. 5:

$$w^*_{\text{mse}} = \frac{\tilde{L}_t^{\text{cmapss}}}{\tilde{L}_t^{\text{mse}} + \tilde{L}_t^{\text{cmapss}}}, \quad w^*_{\text{cmapss}} = \frac{\tilde{L}_t^{\text{mse}}}{\tilde{L}_t^{\text{mse}} + \tilde{L}_t^{\text{cmapss}}} \tag{5}$$

This formulation increases the weight of the loss component that exhibits slower relative improvement, promoting a more balanced optimization between objectives.

To avoid instability and ensure that neither objective is neglected, the weights are constrained to the interval [0.2, 0.8]. Furthermore, instead of applying abrupt changes, the weights are updated smoothly using a momentum-like rule controlled by a factor $\beta = 0.3$, as defined in Eq. 6.

$$w_t = (1 - \beta) \cdot w_{t-1} + \beta \cdot w_t^* \tag{6}$$

Finally, the complementary constraint $w_{\text{cmapss}} = 1 - w_{\text{mse}}$ is enforced to maintain a combination of the two objectives.

The DLB mechanism continuously adapts the loss weights during training, enabling a dynamic trade-off between accuracy and safety-oriented objectives while maintaining training stability.

4.5 Experimental Setup

Experiments are conducted on the CMAPSS benchmark dataset [8], which comprises four subsets (FD001–FD004) with increasing levels of operational complexity. FD001 and FD003 correspond to single operating conditions, while FD002 and FD004 include multiple regimes and fault modes, resulting in higher variability.

All models are trained for 100 epochs using the Adam optimizer. Hyperparameters such as learning rate and batch size are selected empirically for each configuration to ensure stable training. A validation split of 20% is used. For POT and DLB strategies, weight updates are applied at the epoch level following the procedures described in Sect. 4.

Performance is evaluated using Root Mean Squared Error (RMSE) for predictive accuracy and the CMAPSS score for safety-oriented assessment. All experiments share the same architecture and preprocessing pipeline, differing only in the loss formulation and weighting strategy.

5 Results

This section presents the evaluation of the proposed training strategies across the CMAPSS dataset. It begins by establishing a baseline using standard MSE optimization. Subsequently, it analyzes the instability introduced by direct asymmetric loss optimization, evaluates the stabilizing effects of the POT and DLB frameworks, and concludes with a comparative analysis against state-of-the-art approaches.

5.1 Baseline Performance

To establish a reference point, the Transformer model was first trained using the standard Mean Squared Error (MSE) loss. Table 2 summarizes the performance obtained using this configuration. As expected, the model achieves consistent and stable convergence across all datasets, with lower error values observed in

Table 2. Study of proposed loss functions and weighting strategies across CMAPSS datasets.

Training Strategy	RMSE				CMAPSS Score			
	FD001	FD002	FD003	FD004	FD001	FD002	FD003	FD004
Standard MSE (Baseline)	14.55	**18.05**	13.90	23.35	517.26	2,243.00	1,256.09	5,726.00
CMAPSS Loss	13.09	87.75	12.46	44.74	**259.87**	1,409,215.00	**293.25**	18,434.00
Hybrid Loss	13.99	80.84	**12.42**	80.39	399.85	841,619.00	298.12	679,277.00
Binary POT	–	21.08	–	**23.05**	–	**1,578.00**	–	**4,737.00**
Hybrid POT	**12.95**	18.52	13.77	25.98	307.05	1,650.00	405.55	6,745.50
Dynamic Loss Balancing	13.48	20.19	15.85	24.99	311.02	3,718.23	1,114.52	7,936.91

the simpler single-regime scenarios (FD001 and FD003) and higher errors in the more complex multi-regime datasets (FD002 and FD004).

Despite its stable convergence and competitive RMSE values, the MSE-based model does not explicitly account for the asymmetric risk associated with prediction errors. Late predictions are penalized equally to early predictions, which is misaligned with safety-critical requirements. This limitation motivates the exploration of alternative formulations.

5.2 Effect of Loss Functions

To evaluate the impact of incorporating asymmetric risk, the model was trained using the CMAPSS loss in isolation, as well as the static hybrid loss defined in Eq. 3. The results, presented in Table 2, highlight a clear trade-off between predictive stability and risk-aware optimization.

While the CMAPSS loss improves safety-oriented performance in simpler datasets, it introduces severe instability in complex regimes. In FD002, the model collapses during training, failing to learn meaningful degradation patterns (Fig. 1). FD004 follows a similar pattern. The hybrid loss partially mitigates this issue by incorporating the stabilizing effect of MSE. However, the model still exhibits unstable behavior in complex datasets, often converging to systematically underestimated predictions (Fig. 2).

These findings confirm that directly optimizing asymmetric exponential losses is challenging in high-variance settings, motivating the structured training strategies explored next.

5.3 Phased Objective Transition (POT)

To mitigate the instability observed when optimizing asymmetric loss functions, the Binary POT and Hybrid POT strategies were evaluated (Table 2).

The Binary POT strategy, designed specifically to address instability in complex datasets, successfully prevents the collapse observed in direct CMAPSS optimization (Fig. 3). In both FD002 and FD004, the model converges to stable

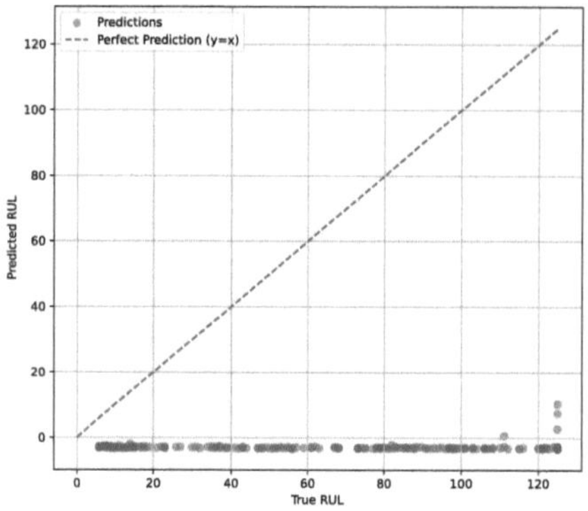

Fig. 1. FD002 CMAPSS Loss.

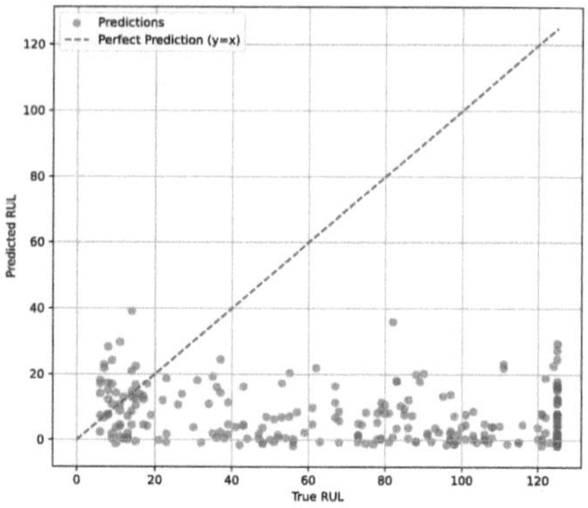

Fig. 2. FD002 Hybrid Loss.

solutions. However, this stabilization comes at the cost of limited improvement in the CMAPSS score.

The Hybrid POT strategy extends this idea by introducing a gradual transition between objectives (Fig. 4). This approach yields competitive performance in simpler datasets and achieves stable training in complex regimes, avoiding the collapse observed in previous static approaches.

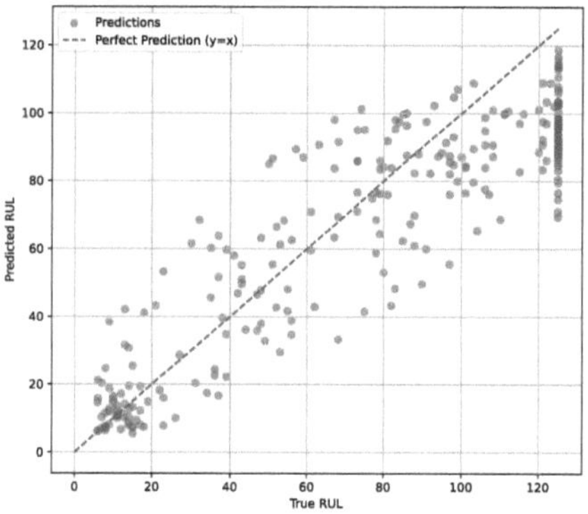

Fig. 3. FD002 Binary POT.

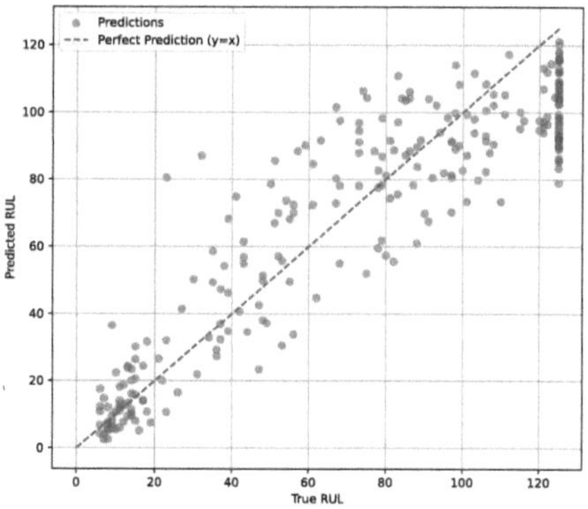

Fig. 4. FD002 Hybrid POT.

Overall, Phased Objective Transition is effective as a stabilization mechanism, particularly in high-variance scenarios. However, the predefined nature of the transition schedule limits its ability to adapt to dataset-specific dynamics.

5.4 Dynamic Loss Balancing (DLB)

To address the limitations of static schedules, the Dynamic Loss Balancing (DLB) mechanism was evaluated. As shown in Table 2, DLB adaptively adjusts the contribution of the MSE and CMAPSS components based on their relative evolution, successfully preventing severe collapse.

In the challenging FD002 scenario, the model produces stable predictions without collapsing (Fig. 5), confirming the effectiveness of the adaptive weighting mechanism. However, despite improved stability, the results indicate that DLB does not consistently lead to superior performance in terms of CMAPSS scores compared to simpler strategies. This suggests that balancing loss magnitudes alone may not fully align the optimization process with the asymmetric risk objective.

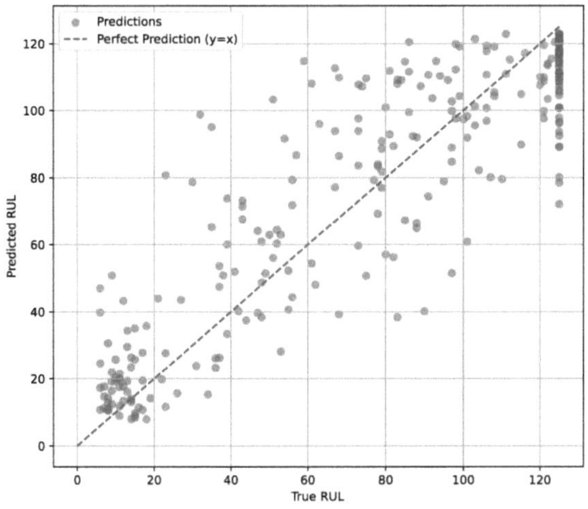

Fig. 5. Predictions for FD002 using Dynamic Loss Balancing.

5.5 Comparative Analysis and Discussion

The experimental results highlight a fundamental trade-off between optimization stability and the incorporation of asymmetric risk. Directly optimizing the CMAPSS loss introduces severe instability, and fixed-weight static hybrid combinations remain insufficient in high-variance settings.

Phased Objective Transition (POT) effectively prevents collapse, confirming that staged or progressive exposure to asymmetric objectives improves stability. Dynamic Loss Balancing (DLB) further ensures stable convergence across all datasets via autonomous adaptive weighting.

Table 3 provides a comprehensive comparison between the proposed training strategies and representative state-of-the-art methods. While recent approaches achieve superior performance through increased architectural complexity, our findings emphasize that beyond architectural innovation, effective objective scheduling and training strategies are essential for enabling robust and risk-aware RUL prediction.

Table 3. Comparison with state-of-the-art methods on the CMAPSS dataset.

Model (Author, Year)	Arch.	RMSE				CMAPSS Score			
		FD001	FD002	FD003	FD004	FD001	FD002	FD003	FD004
Bi-LSTM (Wang et al., 2018)	RNN	13.65	23.18	13.74	24.86	295.00	4,130.00	317.00	5,430.00
Attention-LSTM (Boujanza et al., 2022)	RNN+Attn	13.95	17.65	12.72	20.21	320.00	2,102.00	223.00	3,100.00
Transformer + ARR (Kim et al., 2024)	Transformer	11.36	18.97	11.28	20.69	192.22	2,433.15	**133.41**	2,842.44
FFG-Transformer (Zhou et al., 2024)	Hybrid	11.36	13.24	11.80	15.16	173.89	714.98	215.32	1,049.53
AGATT (Zeng et al., 2023)	Graph+Transf.	11.45	13.87	**10.88**	16.43	204.00	**323.00**	205.00	**632.00**
PLO-Transformer (Zhang et al., 2025)	Hybrid	**10.26**	**12.97**	11.61	**14.36**	**149.91**	728.06	278.61	1,160.60
Proposed (MSE)	Transformer	14.55	18.05	13.90	23.35	517.26	2,243.00	1,256.09	5,726.00
Proposed (CMAPSS)	Transformer	13.09	87.75	12.46	44.74	259.87	1,409,215.00	293.25	18,434.00
Proposed (Hybrid)	Transformer	13.99	80.84	12.42	80.39	399.85	841,619.00	298.12	679,277.00
Proposed (Binary POT)	Transformer	–	21.08	–	23.05	–	1,578.00	–	4,737.00
Proposed (Hybrid POT)	Transformer	12.95	18.52	13.77	25.98	307.05	1,650.00	405.55	6,745.50
Proposed (DLB)	Transformer	13.48	20.19	15.85	24.99	311.02	3,718.23	1,114.52	7,936.91

6 Conclusion

This work investigated the challenges of incorporating asymmetric, safety-oriented objectives into Transformer-based models for Remaining Useful Life (RUL) prediction on the CMAPSS benchmark. The results demonstrate that while the CMAPSS loss better reflects operational risk, its direct optimization leads to severe instability in complex scenarios, often resulting in model collapse or degenerate solutions. Through a systematic evaluation, it was shown that hybrid loss formulations, Phased Objective Transition (POT), and Dynamic Loss Balancing (DLB) can effectively mitigate these issues by improving training stability. However, none of the proposed strategies consistently outperformed the baseline across all datasets, highlighting a persistent trade-off between predictive accuracy and risk-aware optimization. These findings emphasize that training strategy plays a critical role in enabling the practical use of asymmetric objectives in industrial prognostic systems.

Future work will focus on developing more principled approaches for integrating asymmetric risk into the optimization process. This includes exploring gradient-based balancing techniques, alternative loss formulations with improved numerical properties, and adaptive scheduling methods that account for dataset-specific dynamics. Additionally, extending the evaluation to real-world industrial datasets and incorporating uncertainty quantification may provide further insights into the deployment of risk-aware models in safety-critical applications.

Disclosure of Interests. The authors have no competing interests to declare that are relevant to the content of this article.

References

1. Bengio, Y., Louradour, J., Collobert, R., Weston, J.: Curriculum learning. In: Proceedings of the 26th Annual International Conference on Machine Learning, pp. 41–48. ICML '09, Association for Computing Machinery, New York, NY, USA (2009). https://doi.org/10.1145/1553374.1553380
2. Boujamza, A., Lissane Elhaq, S.: Attention-based lstm for remaining useful life estimation of aircraft engines. IFAC-PapersOnLine **55**(12), 450–455 (2022). https://doi.org/10.1016/j.ifacol.2022.07.353, https://www.sciencedirect.com/science/article/pii/S2405896322007546, 14th IFAC Workshop on Adaptive and Learning Control Systems ALCOS 2022
3. Chen, Z., Badrinarayanan, V., Lee, C.Y., Rabinovich, A.: Gradnorm: Gradient normalization for adaptive loss balancing in deep multitask networks (2017). https://doi.org/10.48550/arXiv.1711.02257
4. Goodfellow, I., Bengio, Y., Courville, A.: Deep Learning. MIT Press (2016). http://www.deeplearningbook.org
5. Heimes, F.: Recurrent neural networks for remaining useful life estimation. In: 2008 International Conference on Prognostics and Health Management, pp. 1 – 6 (2008). https://doi.org/10.1109/PHM.2008.4711422
6. Kim, G., Choi, J.G., Lim, S.: Using transformer and a reweighting technique to develop a remaining useful life estimation method for turbofan engines. Eng. Appl. Artif. Intell. **133**, 108475 (2024)
7. Kingma, D., Ba, J.: Adam: A method for stochastic optimization. In: International Conference on Learning Representations (2014)
8. Saxena, A., Goebel, K., Simon, D., Eklund, N.: Damage propagation modeling for aircraft engine run-to-failure simulation. In: International Conference on Prognostics and Health Management (2008). https://doi.org/10.1109/PHM.2008.4711414
9. Tang, D.: A deep learning framework for remaining useful life prediction of turbofan engines with partial sensor failure. PLoS ONE **21**(4), e0347312 (2026). https://doi.org/10.1371/journal.pone.0347312
10. Vaswani, A., et al.: Attention is all you need. In: Guyon, I., et al. (eds.) Advances in Neural Information Processing Systems, vol. 30. Curran Associates, Inc. (2017)
11. Wang, J., Wen, G., Yang, S., qiang Liu, Y.: Remaining useful life estimation in prognostics using deep bidirectional lstm neural network. 2018 Prognostics and System Health Management Conference (PHM-Chongqing), pp. 1037–1042 (2018). https://api.semanticscholar.org/CorpusID:57753485
12. Zeng, M., Wu, F., Yiwei, C.: Remaining useful life prediction via spatio-temporal channels and transformer. IEEE Sens. J. **PP**, 1–1 (2023). https://doi.org/10.1109/JSEN.2023.3324330
13. Zhang, E., Wu, L., Ren, Z., Gao, H., Liu, D., Wang, Q.: Plo-transformer-lstm: a remaining useful life prediction method for aircraft engines. Eng. Res. Express **7** (2025). https://doi.org/10.1088/2631-8695/adece8
14. Zhou, Z., Long, Z., Wang, R., Bai, M., Liu, J., Yu, D.: An aircraft engine remaining useful life prediction method based on predictive vector angle minimization and feature fusion gate improved transformer model. J. Manuf. Syst. **76**, 567–584 (2024). https://doi.org/10.1016/j.jmsy.2024.08.025

Beyond Complexity Invariance: An Adaptive Multi-scale Distance for Time Series Classification

Fabricio Alves de Almeida[1(✉)], Marcilio Carlos Pereira de Souto[2], and Ana Carolina Lorena[1]

[1] Aeronautics Institute of Technology (ITA), São José dos Campos, SP 12228-900, Brazil
fabricio.almeida@ga.ita.br, ana.lorena@gp.ita.br

[2] University of Orléans, Orléans, Centre-Val de Loire 45067, France
marcilio.pereira-de-souto@univ-orleans.fr

Abstract. Time series classification under the 1-nearest neighbor (1-NN) paradigm is largely determined by the choice of distance measure. Complexity-based approaches adjust shape-only metrics by correcting for differences in structural complexity. One of the established strategies that considers this correction is the Complexity Invariant Distance (CID). This strategy corrects the Euclidean distance (ED) by a scalar factor derived from first-order differences. This correction is necessary when the behavior of the series differs; however, it may be insufficient when the complexity is specific and at different time scales. Based on this, we propose the Adaptive Multi-Scale Complexity Distance (AMCD), which measures structural divergence across Fibonacci-spaced lags. Using Fibonacci spacing allows for the creation of a near-logarithmic and non-redundant scale. The Fibonacci lags are determined from an adaptive subset K^*, classifying them through the per-lag variance of their complexity estimates on the training set. To demonstrate the method's behavior, we used 80 univariate datasets from the UCR Time Series Archive. AMCD showed an average rank of performance of 1.43 compared to 2.06 for CID and 2.52 for ED. The Friedman test, Nemenyi post-hoc test, and Wilcoxon test confirm the statistically significant difference between all pairwise comparisons. The accuracy gain of the proposed method over ED increases with complexity, indicating the type of structural heterogeneity AMCD excels. These results provide empirical support for the claim that time series complexity is inherently multi-scale, and position AMCD as an extension of CID for structurally heterogeneous time series classification problems.

Keywords: time series classification · multi-scale complexity · adaptive scale selection · distance measures · 1-nearest neighbor

M. Recamonde-Mendoza and R. C. Barros (Eds.): BRACIS 2026, LNAI 17105, pp. 644–659, 2027.
https://doi.org/10.1007/978-3-032-39882-6_43

1 Introduction

Time series classification (TSC) underpins applications in medical diagnosis, industrial monitoring, astronomy, and environmental sensing [6]. Despite the emergence of sophisticated ensemble and deep-learning methods, 1-nearest neighbor (1-NN) classification remains a competitive baseline, and the choice of distance measure is repeatedly identified as the dominant factor in its performance [8]. Two 1-NN classifiers differing only in the distance function can produce markedly different error rates on the same dataset.

The Euclidean distance (ED) offers an $O(T)$ lock-step comparison of z-normalized series, where T is the size of the series. Dynamic time warping (DTW) [15] permits nonlinear alignment and is tolerant to phase variation, with an $O(T^2)$ cost that can be mitigated through windowing and lower-bounding [14]. The Complexity-Invariant Distance (CID) proposed by Batista et al. [3] takes a complementary route: rather than realigning observations, it multiplies ED by a scalar complexity factor derived from first-order differences, reducing misclassification errors caused by mismatches in oscillation density.

Each of these approaches addresses a specific invariance: DTW addresses local temporal warping; z-normalization addresses amplitude and mean; CID addresses global complexity. The present work is concerned with a limitation not resolved by any of them: *the structural complexity of a time series is not a global property, but varies with the temporal scale at which the series is observed.* The CID estimator, and every single-scale variant built on it, implicitly assumes that one scalar derived from first-order differences suffices to characterize the structural divergence between two series. This assumption breaks down systematically when classes differ primarily at specific temporal resolutions, a pattern that has been documented in biomedical recordings whose informative structures span multiple timescales [5].

Based on this, this article proposes the Adaptive Multi-Scale Complexity Distance (AMCD) approach, which is a multi-scale distance metric that offers the following contributions: *(i)* a multi-scale complexity estimator based on Fibonacci-spaced lags, providing logarithmic non-redundant scale coverage; *(ii)* a variance-based adaptive scale selection with a formal degeneracy property (when no scale is informative, AMCD reduces to ED); *(iii)* an evaluation on 80 UCR datasets [6] with hyperparameters selected by leave-one-out cross-validation (LOO-CV) on the training set and a single-pass evaluation on the held-out test set; and *(iv)* empirical validation of the multi-scale hypothesis through monotonic accuracy gains across five strata of structural heterogeneity.

The paper is organized as follows. Section 2 reviews related work. Section 3 presents the AMCD approach. Section 4 describes the experimental protocol. Section 5 presents and discusses results. Section 6 draws the conclusions.

2 Related Work

Nearest neighbor strategies are widely used in time-series classification, where predictions for new instances are made by identifying the most similar time series in the dataset. However, the effectiveness of these methods critically depends on the choice of distance measure used to assess similarity.

2.1 Distance Measures for Time Series Classification

The choice of distance measure in 1-NN classification is the principal driver of performance for univariate time series [8]. According to [1], distance measures are commonly organized into two categories: Lock-step measures and Elastic measures.

Lock-step measures compare observations at corresponding positions. ED is canonical in this category; both CID [3] and the proposed AMCD also belong to this category, augmenting ED with structural corrections.

Elastic measures allow nonlinear alignment. DTW [15] is the most widely used measure in this category, in addition to its derivatives (weighted DTW [9], derivative DTW [12]), and edit-distance-based measures such as LCSS (Longest Common Subsequence) [17], ERP (Edit distance with Real Penalty) [4], and MSM (Move-Split-Merge) [16]. These measures incur higher computational cost and additional hyperparameters, but handle phase variation effectively.

The present work focuses on lock-step measures. The additional computational cost of AMCD relative to ED is bounded by $O(|K^*| \cdot T)$ versus $O(T)$, with $|K^*| \leq O(\log T)$, and the interpretability of the resulting distance is preserved. K^* denotes a subset of lag sizes used in the computation of the AMCD distance, as described in Sect. 3.3.

2.2 The Complexity-Invariant Distance (CID)

Batista et al. [3] proposed CID as the first complexity-invariant distance measure for time series. Given z-normalized series x, y of equal length T, CID is defined as:

$$\text{CID}(x, y) = d_{ED}(x, y) \cdot CF(x, y), \tag{1}$$

where

$$CF(x, y) = \frac{\max(CE(x), CE(y))}{\min(CE(x), CE(y))}, \qquad CE(x) = \sqrt{\sum_{t=2}^{T} (x_t - x_{t-1})^2}. \tag{2}$$

CID achieved statistically significant gains over ED in classification and clustering on UCR datasets [3] with $O(T)$ time complexity. However, a central limitation, is that the estimator $CE(x)$ captures complexity only at lag $k = 1$. This is computationally efficient but blind to structural patterns that emerge at broader temporal scales [5].

2.3 Multi-scale Analysis of Time Series

Costa et al. [5] introduced Multiscale Entropy (MSE), demonstrating that healthy physiological time series exhibit higher complexity across multiple temporal scales, whereas pathological dynamics are associated with a loss of multiscale structure and reduced complexity. MSE characterizes the intrinsic complexity of an individual series, whereas AMCD measures *structural divergence between two series* across multiple scales. To the best of our knowledge, no prior work combines adaptive variance-based scale selection with a multi-scale complexity estimator for 1-NN time series classification.

3 The Adaptive Multi-scale Complexity Distance

Consider three time series of equal length T: x_s (simple, with uniformly low oscillation density), x_g (globally complex, with uniformly high oscillation density), and x_l (locally complex, with high oscillation density concentrated in a central window). Suppose x_s and x_l belong to the same class.

Under CID estimator, $CE(x_g) \gg CE(x_s) \approx CE(x_l)$, because CE integrates first-order differences over the entire series. CID therefore positions x_s near x_l in terms of global complexity. At intermediate lags $k > 1$, however, the complexity of x_l rises sharply and diverges from x_s, while x_g remains uniformly complex across scales. A multi-scale estimator that measures complexity at several lags simultaneously distinguishes these profiles, when a single-scale estimator cannot.

3.1 Complexity Estimation for Multiple Scales

The Adaptive Multi-Scale Complexity approach is characterized by a generalization of the complexity estimation of the CID. When dealing with time series, it is necessary to understand the impact of lags to analyze the latency of phenomena and the stabilization of the series.

Based on this, we can generalize the per-lag complexity estimate. Thus, for a time series $x = (x_1, \ldots, x_T)$ and $k \in \mathbb{Z}^+$ with $k < T$:

$$CE_k(x) = \sqrt{\sum_{t=k+1}^{T} (x_t - x_{t-k})^2}. \tag{3}$$

For $k = 1$ this recovers the CID estimator: $CE_1(x) = CE(x)$. For $k > 1$, CE_k captures the differences between observations separated by k time steps, and is sensitive to oscillations whose characteristic period lies near k.

To determine the quantity k (lags) that will be considered in this strategy, we base it on Fibonacci spacing. The use of this approach is motivated by mathematical characteristics of the Fibonacci sequence, such as: numbers grow as $F_n \sim \phi^n/\sqrt{5}$, with $\phi = (1 + \sqrt{5})/2 \approx 1.618$, and consecutive terms satisfy $F_{n+1}/F_n \to \phi$; and the lags therefore grow quasi-exponentially, covering a wide range of scales with few evaluation points, analogous to logarithmic frequency spacing in wavelet filter banks [13].

Given a series of length T and cutoff parameter $\alpha = 0.5$, the Fibonacci lag set can be defined as:

$$K = \{k \in \mathcal{F} : k \leq \lfloor \alpha T \rfloor\}, \tag{4}$$

where $\mathcal{F} = \{1, 2, 3, 5, 8, 13, 21, 34, 55, 89, \ldots\}$ is the Fibonacci sequence.

The upper bound $\lfloor 0.5T \rfloor$ prevents degenerate estimates with too few differencing points. For a series of length T, $|K| = O(\log T)$.

Based on the definition of multi-scale complexity and the number of lags, the multi-scale complexity vector is created.

For $K' = \{k_1 < k_2 < \cdots < k_m\} \subseteq K$:

$$\textit{MS-CE}_{K'}(x) = [CE_{k_1}(x), CE_{k_2}(x), \ldots, CE_{k_m}(x)] \in \mathbb{R}^m_{>0}. \tag{5}$$

where $m = |K'|$ denotes the number of lags in the subset K'.

The structural divergence between series x and y over scales K' is

$$d_{MS}(x, y;\, K') = \left\| \log\bigl(\textit{MS-CE}_{K'}(x)\bigr) - \log\bigl(\textit{MS-CE}_{K'}(y)\bigr) \right\|_2, \tag{6}$$

where log is applied element-wise. The logarithm normalizes complexity differences that may span orders of magnitude across lags, and yields invariance to multiplicative rescaling: since $CE_k(\alpha x) = |\alpha|\, CE_k(x)$ for any scalar $\alpha \neq 0$, the log transform removes this factor, in analogy with the amplitude invariance provided by z-normalization.

3.2 Adaptive Scale Selection

A lag $k_j \in K$ is informative for a dataset $\mathcal{D} = \{x_1, \ldots, x_n\}$ when $CE_{k_j}(x_i)$ varies substantially across training series. Lags with low inter-series variability contribute as noise rather than signal to the distance.

To improve the interpretability of the information provided by the K', the per-lag informativeness score was defined. For each lag $k_j \in K$:

$$s_j = \mathrm{std}_{i=1}^{n}\left[CE_{k_j}(x_i)\right] \tag{7}$$

where $\mathrm{std}_{i=1}^{n}$ denotes the sample standard deviation taken across the n training series, and $x_i \in D$ is the i-th training time series (not an individual observation). Let lags be sorted by score in decreasing order, $s_{\pi(1)} \geq s_{\pi(2)} \geq \cdots \geq s_{\pi(|K|)}$. The adaptive lag subset K^* is:

$$K^* = \begin{cases} \emptyset & \text{if } \sum_{j=1}^{|K|} s_j^2 = 0, \\ \{k_{\pi(1)}, \ldots, k_{\pi(m^*)}\} & \text{otherwise}, \end{cases} \tag{8}$$

where $m^* = \min\left\{ m' : \dfrac{\sum_{j=1}^{m'} s_{\pi(j)}^2}{\sum_{j=1}^{|K|} s_j^2} \geq \rho \right\}$. Here, $m' \in \{1, \ldots, |K|\}$ is a candidate prefix length and $m^* = |K^*|$ is the resulting number of selected lags; the sums run over all $|K|$ Fibonacci lags. The criterion accumulates squared scores in decreasing order, analogous to the explained-variance criterion of principal component analysis (PCA) [2, 10]. Threshold $\rho \in (0, 1]$ is a hyperparameter (Sect. 3.3).

The *structural heterogeneity* of a dataset is summarized by the mean per-lag informativeness score:

$$\sigma_{CE}(\mathcal{D}) = |K|^{-1} \sum_{k_j \in K} s_j \tag{9}$$

Datasets with high σ_{CE} tend to have several informative lags, yielding larger K^* and, empirically, larger accuracy gains (Sect. 5.1).

Proposition 1. *If $s_j = 0$ for all $k_j \in K$, then $d_{MS}(x, y;\, K^*) = 0$ for all x, y, and $AMCD(x, y) = d_{ED}(x, y)$.*

Proof. $\sum_j s_j^2 = 0 \Rightarrow K^* = \emptyset$; the ℓ_2-norm over an empty set equals zero; hence the factor $(1 + \lambda \cdot 0) = 1$ and $AMCD = d_{ED}$. □

Therefore, when the complexity structure is low, AMCD approaches ED. Across the 80 UCR datasets, adaptive selection discards an average of 34.5% of available Fibonacci lags ($\overline{|K|} = 10.9$ versus $\overline{|K^*|} = 7.2$).

3.3 AMCD Formulation

Based on the previous definitions, the AMCD approach can be formulated. Given series x, y of equal length, a training dataset $\mathcal{D}$, from which K^* is determined, and hyperparameters $\lambda > 0$ and $\rho \in (0, 1]$:

$$\text{AMCD}(x, y;\, K^*, \lambda) = d_{ED}(x, y) \cdot \big(1 + \lambda \cdot d_{MS}(x, y;\, K^*)\big). \tag{10}$$

The subset K^* is estimated once from the training set D; the pair (x, y) may be any two series compared during classification (two training series under LOO-CV, or a test and a training series at inference). Regarding the selection of hyperparameters, λ and ρ are jointly selected by leave-one-out cross-validation (LOO-CV) on the training set, maximizing the balanced accuracy (BACC), defined in Sect. 4: [11]

$$(\lambda^*, \rho^*) = \underset{(\lambda,\rho)\,\in\,\Lambda\times P}{\arg\max}\ \text{BACC}_{\text{LOO}}(\mathcal{D};\, \lambda, \rho), \tag{11}$$

with $\Lambda = \{0.1, 0.5, 1.0\}$ and $P = \{0.80, 0.90, 0.95\}$, a 3×3 grid evaluated on training data only. The grid $\Lambda = \{0.1, 0.5, 1.0\}$ spans weak, moderate, and full weighting of the multi-scale term on an order-of-magnitude scale, whereas $P = \{0.80, 0.90, 0.95\}$ follows the cumulative explained-variance thresholds commonly adopted for component retention in PCA.

We can establish a relationship between AMCD and CID when K^* reduces to the single lag $k = 1$, $d_{MS}(x, y; \{1\}) = |\log(CE(x)/CE(y))|$, so:

$$\text{AMCD}(x, y;\, \{1\}, \lambda) = d_{ED}(x, y) \cdot \left(1 + \lambda \cdot \left|\log \tfrac{CE(x)}{CE(y)}\right|\right), \tag{12}$$

This log-parametric expression shares the complexity-invariance rationale of CID, but differs in functional form from the original max / min ratio. AMCD

Algorithm 1: AMCD

Input: $X_{\text{train}}, y_{\text{train}}, X_{\text{test}}$ (z-normalized); grids Λ, P; cutoff $\alpha = 0.5$
Output: Predicted labels for X_{test}

$K \leftarrow \text{FibonacciLags}(T, \alpha)$;
foreach $x_i \in X_{train}$ **do**
  $MS[i] \leftarrow [CE_k(x_i) \text{ for } k \in K]$ `// multi-scale features`
$s_j \leftarrow \text{std}_i(MS[:, j])$ for $j = 1, \ldots, |K|$ `// per-lag scores`
$\pi \leftarrow \text{argsort}(s)$ (descending);
foreach $\rho \in P$ **do**
  if $\sum s_j^2 = 0$ **then**
    $K^*[\rho] \leftarrow \emptyset$;
  else
    $m^* \leftarrow \min\{m' : \sum_{j \leq m'} s_{\pi(j)}^2 / \sum s^2 \geq \rho\}$;
    $K^*[\rho] \leftarrow \{k_{\pi(1)}, \ldots, k_{\pi(m^*)}\}$;
Pre-compute pairwise D_{ED} and $D_{MS}[\rho]$ on X_{train};
best_bacc $\leftarrow -\infty$ `// LOO-CV on training set only`
foreach $(\lambda, \rho) \in \Lambda \times P$ **do**
  $D_{AMCD} \leftarrow D_{ED} \odot (1 + \lambda \cdot D_{MS}[\rho])$;
  $\hat{y}_i \leftarrow y_{\text{train}}[\text{argmin}_{j \neq i} D_{AMCD}[i, j]]$ for each i;
  if $\text{BACC}(y_{train}, \hat{y}) >$ *best_bacc* **then**
    $(\lambda^*, \rho^*) \leftarrow (\lambda, \rho)$; *best_bacc* $\leftarrow \text{BACC}(y_{\text{train}}, \hat{y})$;
`// Single test-set pass`
foreach $x_{te} \in X_{test}$ **do**
  predict $y_{\text{train}}\left[\text{argmin}_{x_{\text{tr}}} d_{ED}(x_{\text{te}}, x_{\text{tr}}) \cdot (1 + \lambda^* \cdot d_{MS}(x_{\text{te}}, x_{\text{tr}}; K^*[\rho^*]))\right]$;
return predictions;

generalizes the CID family to the multi-scale domain with dataset-adaptive scale selection. Algorithm 1 summarizes the complete AMCD approach.

The nested structure of K_ρ^* (each a prefix of ranking π) enables a single pass over the log(*MS-CE*) matrix, avoiding redundant computation. Early abandonment via the ED lower bound is applicable at test time since $AMCD \geq d_{ED}$ whenever the multiplicative term is at least one.

The cost of classification per-pair is $O(|K^*| \cdot T)$. The pre-computation of K^* requires $O(n_{train} \cdot |K| \cdot T)$ operations, where n_{train} and n_{test} denote the number of training and test series, respectively. The LOO-CV grid search operates on a pre-computed $n_{\text{train}} \times n_{\text{train}}$ distance matrix; the search over $|\Lambda| \cdot |P| = 9$ configurations reduces to element-wise matrix arithmetic. Thus, the total classification cost for n_{test} test instances is:

$$O\big(n_{\text{test}} \cdot n_{\text{train}} \cdot |K^*| \cdot T \;+\; n_{\text{train}}^2 \cdot |K| \cdot T\big)\,. \tag{13}$$

In practice, the mean runtime of the test-time is 3.60× that of ED across the 80 evaluated datasets. LOO-CV tuning adds a small overhead amplified across the precomputed training-set distance matrix.

4 Experimental Protocol

Eighty univariate datasets from the UCR Time Series Archive [6] were used, covering the standard benchmark domains. Owing to the computational cost of the LOO-CV protocol, the evaluation was restricted to 80 of the available equal-length datasets, selected to span the full range of structural heterogeneity so that all five σ_{CE} strata are represented. Series lengths span $T \in [15, 2844]$, class counts range from 2 to 60, and training-set sizes range from 16 to 1000 series. The complete listing with σ_{CE}, and $|K^*|$ is in Table 1.

Datasets are grouped into five strata by σ_{CE} using cutoffs $\{0.5, 1.5, 3.0, 6.0\}$ (approximately geometric). All series were z-normalized per series following the standard UCR protocol [6], and original train–test splits were preserved.

The statistical evaluation protocol follows Demšar [7], who recommends non-parametric tests for comparing classifiers across multiple datasets. The Friedman test detects global differences among methods, the Nemenyi post-hoc test performs pairwise comparisons with family-wise error rate control, and the Wilcoxon signed-rank test is recommended for isolated pairwise comparisons of interest.

The ED, CID and AMCD methods are compared. Section 5.2 reports a complementary experiment on a 50-dataset subset comparing four DTW-related methods: DTW, CID-DTW, AMCD, and the hybrid AMCD-DTW. All methods use exhaustive 1-NN classification. DTW has a considerably higher computational cost than the other measures, justifying a comparison in a smaller subset of datasets.

As evaluation metrics, we use Balanced Accuracy (BACC). BACC $= \frac{1}{C}\sum_{c=1}^{C}\frac{\mathrm{TP}_c}{\mathrm{TP}_c+\mathrm{FN}_c}$, where C is the number of classes. BACC is robust to class imbalance [11] and preferred over standard accuracy for the heterogeneous UCR benchmark. Additionally, we report average rank (per-dataset descending rank averaged across 80 datasets) and Win/Tie/Loss counts for all pairwise comparisons.

5 Results and Discussion

Following the protocol detailed in the previous section, all the experiments were performed using a MacBook Pro (Apple M3 Max), 32 GB of unified memory and macOS 14.6.1 (23G93). Python (version 3.13.9) was used via Jupyter Notebook (version 7.4.5).

When comparing the ED and CID methods with the proposed AMCD approach, it was possible to verify that the Friedman test rejects H_0 with $\chi^2_F = 55.12$ ($p < 0.0001$). This indicates a statistically significant difference between the methods (95% CI). At Critical difference $CD = 0.371$ (Fig. 1), all three pairwise rank differences exceed the threshold: AMCD vs. ED ($\Delta\bar{r} = 1.094 > CD$); AMCD vs. CID ($\Delta\bar{r} = 0.631 > CD$); and CID vs. ED ($\Delta\bar{r} = 0.463 > CD$). Nemenyi's statistical tests and the Wilcoxon test corroborate this result, showing $p < 0.001$ in all tests. All three comparisons are significant under both tests, recovering the CID-over-ED effect documented by Batista et al. [3] and adding a

Table 1. Evaluated UCR datasets sorted by σ_{CE}.

#	Dataset	σ_{CE}	$\|K^*\|$	#	Dataset	σ_{CE}	$\|K^*\|$
1	OliveOil	0.039	7	41	Wafer	2.349	6
2	Wine	0.089	6	42	ToeSegmentation1	2.402	7
3	Meat	0.091	4	43	BeetleFly	2.549	8
4	DiatomSizeReduction	0.221	1	44	OSULeaf	2.766	7
5	Fish	0.301	5	45	SmallKitchenAppliances	2.788	5
6	ProximalPhalanxOutlineAgeGroup	0.362	6	46	FordB	2.880	10
7	ProximalPhalanxOutlineCorrect	0.367	5	47	ToeSegmentation2	3.051	7
8	MiddlePhalanxOutlineAgeGroup	0.389	5	48	ShapesAll	3.051	6
9	MiddlePhalanxTW	0.402	4	49	FordA	3.109	10
10	EthanolLevel	0.499	5	50	CricketY	3.208	8
11	Car	0.556	4	51	GestureMidAirD1	3.286	9
12	ItalyPowerDemand	0.600	4	52	InsectEPGSmallTrain	3.321	6
13	BME	0.692	6	53	Trace	3.447	9
14	SmoothSubspace	0.721	4	54	SemgHandGenderCh2	3.532	12
15	DistalPhalanxOutlineCorrect	0.724	4	55	SemgHandSubjectCh2	3.565	12
16	FreezerSmallTrain	0.737	5	56	UWaveGestureLibraryX	3.578	7
17	FreezerRegularTrain	0.751	5	57	GesturePebbleZ2	3.580	9
18	ShapeletSim	0.753	9	58	SemgHandMovementCh2	3.584	12
19	UMD	0.769	6	59	CinCECGTorso	3.598	8
20	GunPoint	0.839	3	60	CricketX	3.625	7
21	Earthquakes	0.900	12	61	CricketZ	3.727	9
22	GunPointMaleVersusFemale	1.026	4	62	InsectEPGRegularTrain	3.763	10
23	ECGFiveDays	1.100	4	63	UWaveGestureLibraryAll	4.013	9
24	Plane	1.133	5	64	AllGestureWiimoteY	4.061	7
25	CBF	1.147	7	65	Lightning7	4.266	9
26	ECG200	1.148	6	66	AllGestureWiimoteZ	4.346	8
27	TwoPatterns	1.161	8	67	ACSF1	4.542	4
28	NonInvasiveFetalECGThorax1	1.171	6	68	AllGestureWiimoteX	4.551	8
29	ECG5000	1.203	6	69	Symbols	4.707	6
30	DodgerLoopGame	1.212	8	70	LargeKitchenAppliances	4.939	10
31	Mallat	1.237	7	71	EOGHorizontalSignal	5.710	8
32	DodgerLoopWeekend	1.244	8	72	Lightning2	6.242	9
33	DodgerLoopDay	1.296	11	73	RefrigerationDevices	6.954	10
34	FaceAll	1.437	9	74	Worms	6.964	8
35	FacesUCR	1.457	7	75	WormsTwoClass	6.964	6
36	SwedishLeaf	1.548	8	76	ScreenType	7.121	9
37	PowerCons	1.654	6	77	PigCVP	7.151	13
38	Ham	1.810	7	78	HouseTwenty	7.258	9
39	MedicalImages	1.910	6	79	PigArtPressure	7.482	8
40	SyntheticControl	2.245	6	80	Phoneme	8.759	8

further significant gain by AMCD over CID. The hierarchy ED < CID < AMCD is consistent across rank, mean BACC, and statistical tests. Table 2 summarizes the aggregate metrics across the 80 datasets.

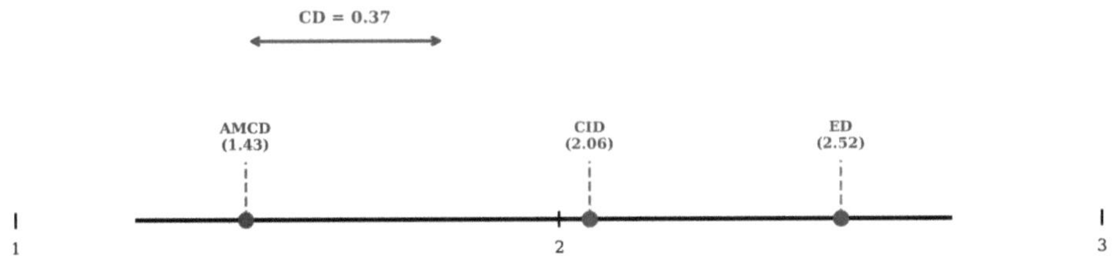

Fig. 1. Critical-difference diagram. $CD = 0.371$, $k = 3$, $N = 80$, $\alpha = 0.05$.

Table 2. Average rank, mean BACC, and computational cost across 80 UCR datasets. Bold: best value per column.

Method	Avg. Rank	Mean BACC	Avg. Time (s)	Cost vs. ED
ED	2.519	0.6670	1.048	1.00×
CID	2.056	0.6830	1.194	1.14×
AMCD	**1.425**	**0.7135**	3.776	3.60×

AMCD achieves a mean BACC of 0.7135, with absolute gains of +0.046 over ED (+7.0% relative) and +0.030 over CID (+4.5% relative). Additionally, when comparing pairwise Win/Tie/Loss counts for all datasets, AMCD outperforms ED on 60 out of 80 datasets. This indicates that the proposed method outperforms ED in 75% of the datasets (ties excluded: 92.3%). The five losses against ED are all below 0.007 in magnitude ($\Delta BACC < 0.007$). If we compare AMCD and CID, we find that the proposed method achieves superior performance on 54 of the 80 datasets, yielding a gain of 67.5% across the evaluated datasets. Analogously, comparing CID versus ED, it is observed that CID outperforms ED on 50 of 80 datasets, confirming the advantage of complexity-based corrections and the results presented in the study by [3]. Figure 2 presents the pairwise comparison of ED, CID and AMCD, with win/tie/loss colored differently (win in blue, tie in white and loss in red).

It is important to emphasize that while accuracy gains are crucial in the context of time series, such improvements are often marginal relative to the computational effort required by the methods. Evaluating the trade-off between the cost and accuracy of the method, it is found that CID delivers a gain of +0.016 in mean BACC at 1.14× the cost of ED. AMCD delivers +0.046 at 3.60× the cost of ED, roughly 2.9× the mean gain of CID at 3.16× its cost. This information is available in Table 2. Defining efficiency as $\eta = \Delta\text{BACC}/\text{relative cost (vs. ED)}$,

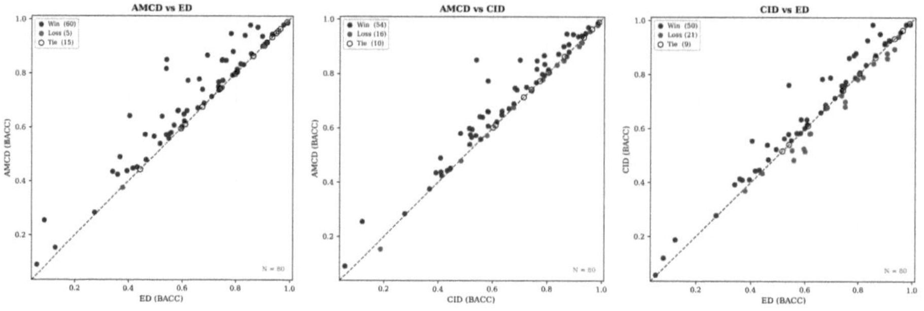

Fig. 2. Pairwise comparison of complexity measures ED, CID and AMCD.

we can measure $\eta_{\text{CID}} = 0.0140$ and $\eta_{\text{AMCD}} = 0.0129$. Therefore, it is possible to verify that the two methods are comparably efficient per unit of relative cost, however AMCD delivers the larger gain by a factor of nearly three. A comparative analysis with more robust approaches, such as DTW, will be discussed later.

Regarding the selection of AMCD hyperparameters, we observe that the value $\lambda^* = 1.0$ is used in 55% of datasets, suggesting that full weighting of the multi-scale component is the most frequent choice. The ρ^* distribution concentrates at 0.80 (51%), indicating this as the most common result. The Table 3 shows the distribution of (λ^*, ρ^*) selected by LOO-CV across the 80 datasets.

Table 3. Distribution of hyperparameters selected by LOO-CV.

λ^*	Datasets	ρ^*	Datasets
0.1	20 (25%)	0.80	41 (51%)
0.5	16 (20%)	0.90	23 (29%)
1.0	44 (55%)	0.95	16 (20%)

5.1 The Multi-scale Hypothesis

Given that complexity across time series can benefit from the proposed AMCD formulation, the datasets were stratified to verify the BACC gain of AMCD by σ_{CE} stratum over ED and CID.

When evaluating the results available in Table 4, it is possible to verify that the gain over ED grows monotonically across the stratification ranges for the σ_{CE}. The gain is marginal (+0.002) under very low heterogeneity, showing incremental improvements as σ_{CE} increases (+0.082 in the very-high). Figure 3 illustrates this behavior for both comparisons. The few gains of ED are in low range σ_{CE}.

Table 4. Mean BACC gain of AMCD over ED and CID by σ_{CE} stratum. N is the number of datasets per stratum.

Stratum	Range	N	Gain vs ED	Gain vs CID
Very low	(0, 0.5]	10	+0.002	+0.002
Low	(0.5, 1.5]	24	+0.024	+0.014
Medium	(1.5, 3.0]	11	+0.048	+0.038
High	(3.0, 6.0]	25	+0.064	+0.054
Very high	(6.0, $+\infty$)	10	+0.082	+0.039

The relationship between σ_{CE} and per-dataset gain via Spearman rank correlation is significant ($\rho = 0.537$ with $p < 0.0001$ against ED; and $\rho = 0.400$ with $p = 0.0002$ against CID), supporting the corroboration of accuracy gains by σ_{CE} for AMCD. However, these results are limited to 80 UCR Archive benchmark datasets and must be further investigated in other distinct data contexts.

The near-zero gain in the very-low range (+0.002) is consistent with Proposition 1, when no scale carries signal, the multi-scale correction is neutral (the AMCD result is close to ED). The five losses against ED occur exclusively at the boundaries of the multi-scale precondition and none of these losses exceeds 0.007, in contrast to gains of up to 0.310 on multi-scale-rich datasets. Thus, AMCD does not present a systemic risk.

These results give empirical support to the multi-scale hypothesis that AMCD performs better when structural heterogeneity is highest, i.e., when multiple Fibonacci lags carry discriminative information.

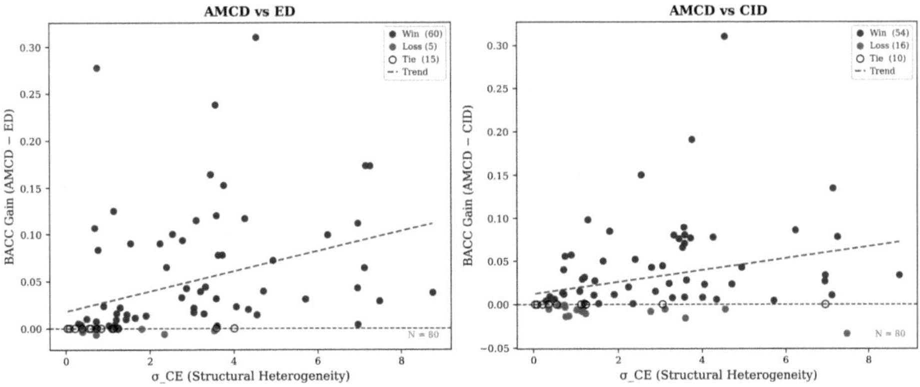

Fig. 3. BACC gain vs structural heterogeneity σ_{CE}.

5.2 DTW and Hybrid AMCD-DTW Comparisons

In order to complement the AMCD assessment with other more robust (and also more costly) methods, we will address a comparative analysis between AMCD, DTW, and CID-DTW. Furthermore, a hybrid approach between AMCD and DTW (AMCD-DTW) will also be evaluated. For this evaluation, a smaller number of datasets from the UCR Archive (50-dataset subset) will be considered, due to the computational cost involved in DTW. However, the stratifications of σ_{CE} will be respected. In this sense, four 1-NN methods are compared: DTW [15] with Sakoe–Chiba band w^* selected by LOO-CV; CID-DTW [3] ($d_{\text{DTW}} \cdot CF(x, y)$); and AMCD-DTW ($d_{\text{DTW}}(x, y, w^*) \cdot (1 + \lambda \cdot d_{MS}(x, y; K^*))$). Table 5 presents the results for average rank, mean BACC, and total computational cost across 50 datasets.

Table 5. Average rank, mean BACC, and total computational cost across 50 datasets.

Method	Avg. Rank	Mean BACC	Mean Time (s)	Cost vs. DTW
DTW	2.62	0.7597	249.6	1.00×
CID-DTW	2.60	0.7555	252.2	1.01×
AMCD	2.86	0.7435	2.1	0.008×
AMCD-DTW	**1.92**	**0.7691**	266.0	1.07×

Regarding the results, all approaches that include DTW outperformed AMCD. These results were expected, given the greater complexity of that approach relative to our proposed method. However, the AMCD-DTW hybrid model achieves the best average rank (1.92) and the highest mean BACC (0.7691) among all methods. The Friedman test rejects H_0 ($\chi^2_F = 17.43$, $p = 0.0006$) and the Nemenyi post-hoc test ($CD_{k=4,N=50} = 0.66$) confirms the significant differences between: AMCD-DTW versus DTW ($p = 0.0339$), AMCD-DTW versus CID-DTW ($p = 0.0420$), and AMCD-DTW versus AMCD ($p = 0.0016$). The same is true for the Wilcoxon test, which corroborates these comparisons. This result infers that the AMCD-DTW hybrid model stands out and performs better. Figure 4 presents the pairwise comparison between the methods based on the Win/Tie/Lose results.

AMCD-DTW costs 1.07× the total time of DTW (additional cost marginal, since the DTW matrix is reused). The gain of AMCD-DTW over its baselines increases with σ_{CE} (Spearman $\rho = 0.384$, $p = 0.0059$ vs. DTW), consistent with the main-panel results. Figure 5 illustrates the BACC gain comparison of AMCD-DTW versus DTW and CID across σ_{CE}.

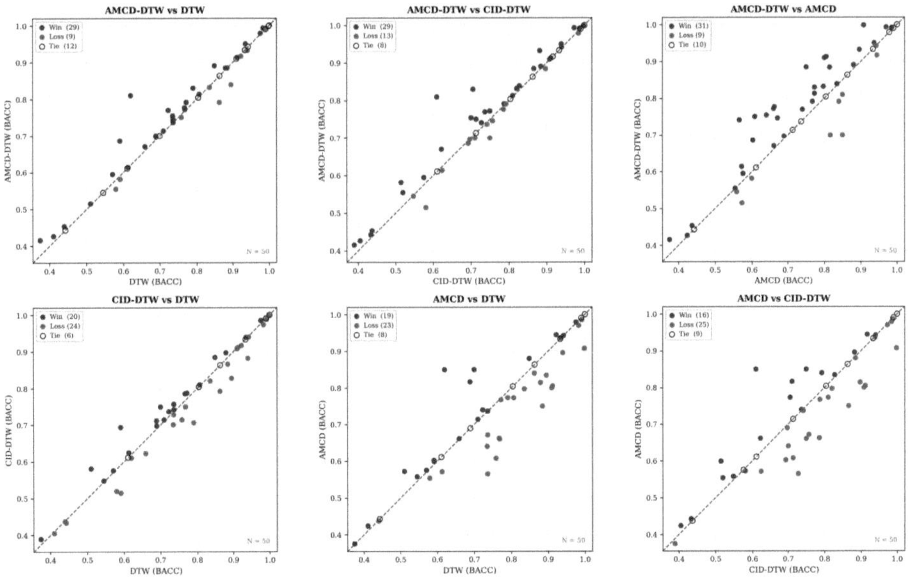

Fig. 4. Pairwise comparison of DTW approaches. AMCD-DTW shows the best performance.

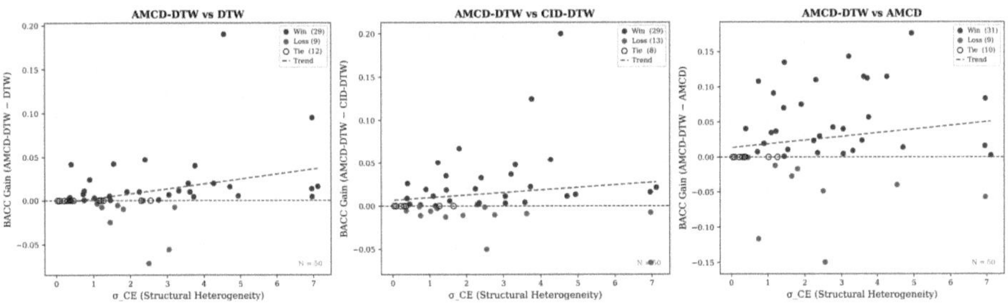

Fig. 5. Gain vs structural heterogeneity σ_{CE} for hybrid AMCD-DTW.

6 Conclusions

In this paper we proposed AMCD, a distance measure for time series classification that extends the CID family to the multi-scale domain with dataset-adaptive scale selection.

We evaluated the approach on 80 univariate datasets from UCR archives with hyperparameters selected by LOO-CV on training data alone. The Friedman test ($\chi_F^2 = 55.12$) and Nemenyi post-hoc test ($CD = 0.371$) establish that all three methods (ED, CID, AMCD) differ pairwise at $\alpha = 0.05$. The hierarchy ED $<$ CID $<$ AMCD is consistent across rank, mean BACC, and statistical tests. AMCD achieves BACC gains of +0.046 over ED and +0.030 over CID, wins on 60 datasets against ED and 54 against CID. Furthermore, the gain shows a growth trend across different ranges of structural heterogeneity.

On the 50-dataset DTW comparison, AMCD-DTW presented the best average rank (1.92) and significantly outperforms DTW ($p = 0.0339$) and CID-DTW ($p = 0.0420$), at 1.07× DTW's cost.

For future work, we intend to explore a greater number of benchmarks for TSC to consolidate AMCD. We will develop different strategies for the parameter λ and also adapt CE_k to multivariate time series. And, based on this, develop meta-features to assist in the selection of algorithms for time series.

Acknowledgments. This study was supported by the Brazilian research agency Fundação de Amparo à Pesquisa do Estado de São Paulo (FAPESP) – Process Number 2025/21948-0 and 2021/06870-3.

Disclosure of Interests. The authors have no competing interests to declare

References

1. Abanda, A., Mori, U., Lozano, J.A.: A review on distance based time series classification. Data Min. Knowl. Disc. **33**(2), 378–412 (2018). https://doi.org/10.1007/s10618-018-0596-4
2. Almeida, F.A., Gomes, G.F., Balestrassi, P.P., Belinato, G., Rosa, P.A.R.C.: Principal component analysis: An overview and applications in multivariate engineering problems. In: Jorge, A.B., Anflor, C.T.M., Gomes, G.F., Carneiro, S.H.S. (eds.) Uncertainty Modeling: Fundamental Concepts and Models, vol. III, pp. 172–194. UnB, Brasília, DF, Brazil (2022). https://doi.org/10.4322/978-65-86503-88-3.c06
3. Batista, G.E.A.P.A., Keogh, E.J., Tataw, O.M., de Souza, V.M.A.: CID: an efficient complexity-invariant distance for time series. Data Min. Knowl. Disc. **28**(3), 634–669 (2013). https://doi.org/10.1007/s10618-013-0312-3
4. Chen, L., Ng, R.: On the marriage of Lp-norms and edit distance. In: Proceedings of the 30th International Conference on Very Large Data Bases (VLDB), pp. 792–803 (2004). https://doi.org/10.1016/B978-012088469-8.50070-X
5. Costa, M., Goldberger, A.L., Peng, C.K.: Multiscale entropy analysis of complex physiologic time series. Phys. Rev. Lett. **89**(6), 068102 (2002). https://doi.org/10.1103/PhysRevLett.89.068102
6. Dau, H.A., et al.: The ucr time series classification archive (2018). https://www.cs.ucr.edu/~eamonn/time_series_data_2018/
7. Demšar, J.: Statistical comparisons of classifiers over multiple data sets. J. Mach. Learn. Res. **7**, 1–30 (2006). https://jmlr.org/papers/v7/demsar06a.html
8. Ding, H., Trajcevski, G., Scheuermann, P., Wang, X., Keogh, E.: Querying and mining of time series data: Experimental comparison of representations and distance measures. Proceedings of the VLDB Endow. **1**(2), 1542–1552 (2008). https://doi.org/10.14778/1454159.1454226
9. Jeong, Y.S., Jeong, M.K., Omitaomu, O.A.: Weighted dynamic time warping for time series classification. Pattern Recogn. **44**(9), 2231–2240 (2011). https://doi.org/10.1016/j.patcog.2010.09.022
10. Jolliffe, I.T., Cadima, J.: Principal component analysis: A review and recent developments. Phil. Trans. R. Soc. A **374**(2065), 20150202 (2016). https://doi.org/10.1098/rsta.2015.0202

11. Kelleher, J.D., Mac Namee, B., D'Arcy, A.: Fundamentals of Machine Learning for Predictive Data Analytics, 2nd edn. MIT Press, Cambridge, MA (2020)
12. Keogh, E.J., Pazzani, M.J.: Derivative dynamic time warping. In: Proceedings of the 1st SIAM International Conference on Data Mining, pp. 1–11 (2001). https://doi.org/10.1137/1.9781611972719.1
13. Mallat, S.: A Wavelet Tour of Signal Processing: The Sparse Way, 3rd edn. Academic Press, Burlington, MA (2008)
14. Rakthanmanon, T., et al.: Searching and mining trillions of time series subsequences under dynamic time warping. In: Proceedings of the 18th ACM SIGKDD International Conference on Knowledge Discovery and Data Mining, pp. 262–270 (2012). https://doi.org/10.1145/2339530.2339576
15. Sakoe, H., Chiba, S.: Dynamic programming algorithm optimization for spoken word recognition. IEEE Trans. Acoust. Speech Signal Process. **26**(1), 43–49 (1978). https://doi.org/10.1109/TASSP.1978.1163055
16. Stefan, A., Athitsos, V., Das, G.: The move-split-merge metric for time series. IEEE Trans. Knowl. Data Eng. **25**(6), 1425–1438 (2013). https://doi.org/10.1109/TKDE.2012.88
17. Vlachos, M., Kollios, G., Gunopulos, D.: Discovering similar multidimensional trajectories. In: Proceedings of the 18th International Conference on Data Engineering (ICDE), pp. 673–684 (2002). https://doi.org/10.1109/ICDE.2002.994784

Latent Fact-Checking: Detecting Misinformation Through Activation Engineering

Pedro T. Barcelos[1], Otávio Parraga[1], Marcelo M. Delucis[1], Lucas M. Fraga[1], Lucas S. Kupssinskü[1], and Rodrigo C. Barros[1,2(✉)]

[1] MALTA - Machine Learning Theory and Applications Lab, School of Technology, Pontifícia Universidade Católica do Rio Grande do Sul, Av. Ipiranga, 6681, 90619-900 Porto Alegre, RS, Brazil

[2] Kunumi Institute, Belo Horizonte, Brazil

rodrigo.barros@pucrs.br

Abstract. The proliferation of misinformation online has driven demand for scalable detection systems. While most existing approaches rely on surface-level linguistic features or external knowledge retrieval, we examine truthfulness as a geometric property of a language model's representation space. We introduce a misinformation detection framework grounded in activation engineering, which leverages the latent geometry of transformer models. Our approach elicits a misinformation direction in the residual stream by contrasting activations from paired truthful and false statements, following the difference-in-means principle of Contrastive Activation Addition (CAA). At inference time, the last-token activation of an unseen claim is projected onto this direction, and the projected representation is fed to an Multilayer Perceptron (MLP) for classification. The procedure requires no fine-tuning of the backbone model, no external evidence retrieval, and no task-specific supervision beyond the contrastive pairs used to estimate the direction. We evaluate the method across 11 models from the Gemma, Llama, and Qwen families, ranging from 270M to 12B parameters, on three fact-checking benchmarks: AVeriTeC, LIAR, and FACTors. The falsehood direction is recoverable across model scales and architectural families, and last-token projection matches or surpasses zero-shot and few-shot prompting baselines on LIAR and FACTors, with the largest gains observed for smaller models. Performance on AVeriTeC is more limited, which we attribute to its evidence-grounded labeling scheme. These findings provide evidence that truthfulness is a structured, linearly separable concept in the latent space of pretrained language models, and point toward interpretability-driven misinformation detection as a practical complement to retrieval-based pipelines. The code is available at https://github.com/Malta-Lab/LaFaCt.

Keywords: Contrastive Activation Addition · steering vector · misinformation detection · large language models

P. T. Barcelos and O. Parraga—Equal contribution.

M. Recamonde-Mendoza and R. C. Barros (Eds.): BRACIS 2026, LNAI 17105, pp. 660–674, 2027.
https://doi.org/10.1007/978-3-032-39882-6_44

1 Introduction

Large language models (LLMs) have become the main tool of many Natural Language Processing (NLP) applications due to their fluency and contextually appropriate text across a wide range of tasks. That fluency, however, does not guarantee factual reliability. LLMs generate statements that may sound plausible while also being false or unsupported by evidence [11,12]. Increasing model scale alone does not solve this issue, as models still reproduce what can be described as imitative falsehoods, which are false answers that remain highly likely under the training distribution [12]. In this setting, automated fact-checking (AFC) becomes necessary to detect and mitigate the spread of misinformation [8].

A limitation of standard LLM use is that veracity assessment is usually based solely on the text each model produces. This leaves open the possibility that the model contains information relevant to factual judgment but does not express it under its default decoding behavior. This is usually referred to as the generation-discrimination gap, where a model may possess latent knowledge that separates truth from falsehood while still failing to state the correct answer in standard generation settings [11]. Findings from mechanistic interpretability and representation engineering support this, suggesting that models often retain internal signals related to whether a statement is true or false, and that these signals can be linearly separated in activation space [11,13,25]. This motivates looking beyond final model outputs and examining internal representations directly.

Rather than relying on fine-tuning or reinforcement learning, we study factual judgment through activation engineering, which seeks to identify representations associated with high-level properties during the forward pass [21,25]. Our approach combines ideas from Contrastive Activation Addition (CAA) and Inference-Time Intervention (ITI). Following CAA, we process pairs of supported and refuted claims and compute the mean activation difference as a falsehood direction [15]. Claim representations are then projected onto the estimated falsehood direction at each layer, and an Multilayer Perceptron (MLP) trained on those projections is used to select the optimal layer on a holdout validation set. A final MLP is then retrained on the full training data at the selected layer to produce the predictions [10,11].

In order to test whether our method is effective across architectures and scales, we evaluate it on Small Language Models (SLMs) from different families, including Llama, Qwen, and Gemma. Our evaluation is grounded in real fact-checking benchmarks, since synthetic claims often miss properties that characterize real misinformation settings [1]. We therefore use AVeriTeC [18] dataset, which contains real-world claims paired with web evidence, FACTors [1], which reflects ecosystem-level fact-checking reports, and LIAR [23], which contains short political claims for veracity classification. Within this setting, we make three contributions: (*i*). We investigate steering vectors for factual judgment derived from fact-checking datasets; (*ii*). We analyze transfer across datasets through comparisons of learned directions, and (*iii*). We perform a layer-wise ablation to identify the most discriminative transformer layers for veracity judgment, and compare the resulting classifier against zero-shot and few-shot prompting baselines.

2 Related Work

2.1 Activation Engineering

Activation engineering, often used interchangeably with representation engineering [25], is an emerging paradigm for interpreting and controlling LLM behavior without computationally intensive parameter updates. Instead of modifying model weights, this approach directly manipulates hidden states during inference, exploiting the fact that intermediate representations encode high-level semantic concepts within a high-dimensional space. By identifying geometric directions corresponding to these concepts, it is possible to steer model outputs at runtime through lightweight vector addition or subtraction [21].

This approach rests on two complementary hypotheses from the mechanistic interpretability field. The *Linear Representation Hypothesis* posits that transformers encode high-level concepts as linear directions in the activation space [16], this is supported empirically by the recoverable geometry of truthfulness within transformer residual streams [13]. Complementing this, the *Superposition Hypothesis* [7] proposes that neural networks represent far more features than they have dimensions by encoding distinct concepts as near-orthogonal directions within shared activation subspaces. Together, they explain why contrastive difference-in-means methods are effective. If concepts are linearly encoded and their directions are approximately orthogonal in superposed representations, subtracting activations elicited by opposing stimuli isolates a target concept direction without disturbing the encoding of unrelated features.

One foundational method is Contrastive Activation Addition (CAA) [15], which constructs paired contrastive prompts to elicit opposing behaviors, collects intermediate activations, and computes their average difference to obtain a "steering vector". This vector is then scaled and injected into the model's residual stream during inference. Beyond simple averaging, alternative approaches include training linear classifiers to define concept boundaries [9], targeting specific attention heads that correlate with a desired attribute [11], and applying dimensionality reduction over activation differences to extract dominant, noise-resistant directions [25].

These techniques have shown reduction in hallucinations [13], controlling style and sentiment [10,19,24], and mitigating toxic generation and adversarial jailbreaks [3,5], all at inference time, enabling rapid and context-specific adjustments. Building on truthfulness steering, activation engineering offers an alternate direction for AFC [4], where probing or steering a model's internal belief state can be integrated into systems that proactively detect and mitigate misinformation. The veracity direction estimated here can be considered as a linearly encoded concept, recoverable from the residual stream because truthfulness occupies a consistent geometric axis across the models' superposed representations.

2.2 Automated Fact-Checking

AFC aims to assess the veracity of natural language claims using external evidence and reasoning models. Different approaches framed this task as a supervised text classification over short claims, often relying on linguistic features or metadata without explicit evidence grounding [23]. While effective in controlled settings, such methods are limited in their ability to generalize and provide transparent justifications. Recent work frames AFC as a multi-stage pipeline involving evidence retrieval and claim verification, such as FEVER [20]. These datasets require systems to retrieve supporting evidence and reason over it, shifting the focus toward end-to-end verification. Subsequent benchmarks, including FEVEROUS [2] and AVeriTeC [18], further increase realism by incorporating multi-hop reasoning and open-domain retrieval.

Nevertheless, current AFC approaches still face challenges [6]. Prompting-based strategies require large models and are unstable across phrasings; fine-tuned classifiers demand substantial labeled data and generalize poorly across domains. Evidence-grounded systems rely on costly retrieval infrastructure sensitive to evidence quality. Our method needs no fine-tuning, no external retrieval, and no large-scale labeled corpora. By operating directly on the internal activations of small frozen language models, it offers a lightweight, generalizable alternative for claim-level veracity assessment.

2.3 LLM-Based Misinformation Detection

LLMs have been increasingly applied to misinformation and fake news detection through prompting strategies [8] and fine-tuning [17]. Zero-shot and few-shot prompting offer deployment flexibility but exhibit limitations. Models frequently hallucinate plausible-sounding justifications [8], and outputs are highly sensitive to prompt wording, with minor rephrasing causing large swings in accuracy on identical claims. State-of-the-art systems on the AVeriTeC shared task [18] demonstrate that retrieval-augmented generation and zero-shot prompting can achieve competitive performance without fine-tuning [14, 22], yet these approaches rely on external access to information. Fine-tuning mitigates some surface-level failures but demands large labeled datasets and generalizes poorly across domains and claim types. Together, these limitations suggest that surface-level generation is an unreliable proxy for veracity assessment. Rather than querying model outputs, our approach bypasses generation entirely and reads the internal representations where veracity signals are latently encoded, motivating the activation-based classification framework developed in this work.

3 Methodology

3.1 Problem Formulation

Let $\mathcal{D} = \{(s_i, y_i)\}_{i=1}^{N}$ be a misinformation dataset, where s_i is a natural language claim and $y_i \in \{0, 1\}$ is its falsehood label ($y_i = 0$ for true, $y_i = 1$ for false). We consider a transformer-based language model $\mathcal{M}$ with L layers whose residual stream at layer ℓ produces a hidden representation $\mathbf{h}_t^{(\ell)} \in \mathbb{R}^d$ for each token position t, where d is the model's hidden dimension. Our goal is to learn a classifier $f : \mathbb{R}^d \to \{0, 1\}$ that operates directly on these internal representations, without any gradient-based fine-tuning of $\mathcal{M}$.

3.2 Contrastive Prompt Construction

For each training instance s_i, we construct a pair of structured prompts that anchor the completion to a specific veracity polarity through a forced `A/B` choice:

$$p_i^+ = \text{``}s_i\texttt{.\textbackslash nThe previous assertion is (A) True (B) False\textbackslash nAnswer: (A)''} \quad (1)$$

$$p_i^- = \text{``}s_i\texttt{.\textbackslash nThe previous assertion is (A) True (B) False\textbackslash nAnswer: (B)''} \quad (2)$$

where p_i^+ anchors the answer to truth and p_i^- anchors it to falsehood.

Both prompts are derived from the same s_i, so the only variable between them is the polarity of the forced answer token. This controls for topic, syntax, and length. This prompt addition is only used for the misinformation direction estimation (Sect. 3.4).

To prevent the model from associating misinformation with a fixed letter, we randomize the mapping between `A/B` and True/False across instances, with each assignment drawn uniformly and independently for every s_i.

3.3 Activation Extraction

We pass each prompt through the frozen model $\mathcal{M}$ and extract the last-token hidden state at layer ℓ. In a causally masked transformer, the last token aggregates contextual information from the entire preceding sequence and therefore serves as a natural sentence-level representation. Formally:

$$\mathbf{h}_i^{(\ell)\pm} = \texttt{LastTok}\Big(\mathcal{M}^{(\ell)}(p_i^{\pm})\Big) \in \mathbb{R}^d \quad (3)$$

All layer activations are collected in a single forward pass via hooks, incurring no additional inference overhead. In addition to the contrastive-prompt activations $\mathbf{h}_i^{(\ell)\pm}$, we also extract last-token activations from the bare claims s_i—without any annotation template—at every layer; these plain-claim activations are used for projection and classification.

3.4 Falsehood Direction Estimation

We use contrastive difference-in-means [15] to identify a misinformation direction in the residual stream, and search for the specific layers where the target attribute can be better steered. The falsehood direction at layer ℓ is defined as the mean difference between the truthful and false activation distributions from the prompts of the training datasets with refuted samples:

$$\mathbf{v}^{(\ell)} = \frac{1}{N}\sum_{i=1}^{N}\mathbf{h}_i^{(\ell)+} - \frac{1}{N}\sum_{i=1}^{N}\mathbf{h}_i^{(\ell)-} \tag{4}$$

Under the linear representation hypothesis [16], truthfulness and falsehood correspond to separable directions in the residual stream; $\mathbf{v}^{(\ell)}$ is our estimate of that axis. While CAA uses this direction as a steering vector to be added to the residual stream during generation, we instead retain it as a fixed reference axis: bare claim activations are projected onto $\hat{v}^{(\ell)}$ for binary classification, leaving the model's forward pass unmodified. We normalize it as $\hat{\mathbf{v}}^{(\ell)} = \mathbf{v}^{(\ell)}/\|\mathbf{v}^{(\ell)}\|_2$ for use in downstream projection.

3.5 Vector Projection and MLP Training

Given the normalized misinformation direction $\hat{\mathbf{v}}^{(\ell)}$ estimated at layer ℓ (Sect. 3.4), we project each training claim's last-token activation—extracted from the bare claim s_i without any `A/B` template—onto this direction:

$$\mathbf{z}_i^{(\ell)} = \left(\mathbf{h}_i^{(\ell)} \cdot \hat{\mathbf{v}}^{(\ell)}\right)\hat{\mathbf{v}}^{(\ell)} \in \mathbb{R}^d, \quad \mathbf{h}_i^{(\ell)} = \texttt{LastTok}\left(\mathcal{M}^{(\ell)}(s_i)\right) \tag{5}$$

A large magnitude of $\mathbf{z}_i^{(\ell)}$ indicates strong alignment with the misinformation direction. Using untemplated claims ensures the classifier generalizes to unannotated inputs at deployment.

We then train a simple MLP classifier with one hidden layer with a dimension of 256, Adam optimizer, and a learning rate of 0.001 for 200 epochs on the projected training vectors:

$$\hat{y}_i = \mathrm{MLP}^{(\ell)}\left(\mathbf{z}_i^{(\ell)}\right) \tag{6}$$

This projection–MLP pair is instantiated independently for every layer ℓ, enabling the layer selection procedure described next.

3.6 Layer Selection

Since the linear separability of falsehood representations varies across layers, we select the optimal layer ℓ^* using a held-out validation split $\mathcal{D}_{\text{val}}$. For each layer ℓ, we apply the procedure of Sect. 3.5: project the plain-claim activations of $\mathcal{D}_{\text{train}}$ onto $\hat{\mathbf{v}}^{(\ell)}$, train an MLP on the resulting vectors, and evaluate it on the plain-claim activations of $\mathcal{D}_{\text{val}}$ projected onto the same direction. The layer that maximizes validation accuracy is retained:

$$\ell^* = \underset{\ell\in\{1,\ldots,L\}}{\arg\max}\ \mathrm{Acc}\left(\mathrm{MLP}^{(\ell)},\ \mathcal{D}_{\text{val}}\right) \tag{7}$$

3.7 Final Model

Once ℓ^* is identified, we pool all available labeled data $\mathcal{D}_{\text{train}} \cup \mathcal{D}_{\text{val}}$ to obtain a more representative misinformation direction. We recompute $\hat{\mathbf{v}}^{(\ell^*)}$ following Sect. 3.4 using contrastive prompts built from the combined split, project every plain-claim activation at layer ℓ^* onto this updated direction, and retrain the MLP from scratch on the resulting vectors. The MLP weights produced during layer selection are discarded; no data leakage occurs since those weights play no role in the final classifier.

To classify a new unseen claim s at inference time, we extract its last-token activation at layer ℓ^* without any template, project it onto $\hat{\mathbf{v}}^{(\ell^*)}$, and feed the result to the final MLP:

$$\hat{y} = \text{MLP}\Big(\Big(\mathbf{h}^{(\ell^*)} \cdot \hat{\mathbf{v}}^{(\ell^*)}\Big)\, \hat{\mathbf{v}}^{(\ell^*)}\Big), \quad \mathbf{h}^{(\ell^*)} = \texttt{LastTok}\Big(\mathcal{M}^{(\ell^*)}(s)\Big) \tag{8}$$

This requires only a single forward pass through the frozen model and no annotation template, making the approach directly applicable to unannotated claims at deployment.

3.8 Datasets

We consider three complementary benchmarks widely used in AFC: AVeriTeC [18], LIAR [23], and FACTors [1]. Together, these datasets represent distinct axes of the problem scope, including open-domain verification, domain-specific classification, and large-scale ecosystem analysis.

AVeriTeC(Automated Verification of Real-world Claims with Evidence from the Web) is a dataset designed to reflect realistic fact-checking pipelines [18]. It contains 4,568 real-world claims collected from over 50 fact-checking organizations via sources such as the Google Fact Check API. A key characteristic is its open-domain setting, which covers diverse topics including politics, health, science, and current events. Unlike other datasets, it explicitly models the multi-step nature of verification by providing question–answer (QA) pairs, retrieved web evidence, and textual justifications. This structure requires systems to jointly perform claim decomposition, external evidence retrieval, and reasoning, making it a challenging benchmark for end-to-end AFC.

LIAR [23] is a consolidated dataset constructed from claims annotated by the `PolitiFact` fact-checking platform. It consists of approximately 12,800 short statements sourced from speeches, debates, and campaign materials, each labeled using a fine-grained truthfulness scale (e.g., *True*, *Half True*, *False*, *Pants on Fire*). In contrast to open-domain benchmarks, LIAR categorizes fact-checking primarily as a supervised text classification task, without requiring explicit evidence retrieval. While its constrained political domain and short claim format simplify modeling, prior work has identified artifacts such as over-reliance on speaker metadata and limited contextual grounding. Despite these limitations, it remains a standard dataset for evaluating classification-based approaches.

FACTors is a recently introduced large-scale dataset that captures the structure of the fact-checking ecosystem [1]. It comprises over 118,000 claims extracted from approximately 117,000 fact-checking reports published by 39 organizations over multiple decades. Similar to AVeriTeC, it is multi-domain, covering topics such as politics, health, science, and general misinformation. However, its distinguishing feature lies in the inclusion of metadata describing fact-checking organizations, authorship, and inter-claim relationships. This enables analyses beyond individual claim verification, such as modeling institutional behavior, credibility patterns, and cross-source agreement. As a result, FACTors supports research on large-scale, context-aware, and socially grounded fact-checking systems.

Experimental Setup. For each dataset, claims are sampled from the original data and partitioned into two splits: 200 instances are used for training and hyper-parameter tuning, including layer selection, and 100 instances are held out for evaluation. Of the 200 training instances, 70% (140) are used for MLP training and direction estimation, while the remaining 30% (60) form the validation split for layer selection. To enable a unified binary classification framework, all label spaces are coarse-grained into two classes. For LIAR, the original six-level truthfulness scale is collapsed into *True* (comprising *True*, *Mostly True*, and *Half True*) and *False* (comprising *Barely True*, *False*, and *Pants on Fire*). For AVeriTeC and FACTors, the original binary labels are retained without any modification.

4 Results and Discussion

In Table 1, we report the accuracy and F1 scores for our method alongside zero- and few-shot prompting baselines that we implemented and ran. We conducted these evaluations across eleven models—spanning the Gemma-3, Llama-3, and Qwen3.5 architectural families—and three datasets of distinct nature: AVeriTeC [18], LIAR [23], and FACTors [1].

The models range from $270M$ to $12B$ parameters, which allows us to assess whether the falsehood direction in the latent space is recoverable across scales. Since our work targets LLM-driven misinformation detection through a lightweight pipeline that requires no training or gradient updates, zero-shot and few-shot prompting serve as the natural reference class for methods that rely solely on model outputs, making them appropriate baselines against which to evaluate our approach.

Our results reveal a striking and consistent pattern: our latent falsehood direction outperforms both prompt-driven baselines on LIAR and FACTors across virtually all model configurations and scales. Both datasets are relatively balanced in their binary label distribution after coarse-graining, which facilitates a well-centered difference-in-means estimate and supports the coherent falsehoods we observe across model families. On LIAR, the gains are most pronounced for smaller models, where Gemma-3-4B improves from 0.57 to 0.79 accuracy, Llama-3.2-1B from 0.46 to 0.73, and Gemma-3-1B from 0.52 to 0.75, which represents relative gains of over 30%. Similar gains are observed on FACTors: Llama-3.2-1B improves from 0.47 to 0.70, Qwen3.5-2B from 0.54 to 0.68, and Qwen3.5-9B from 0.64 to 0.71. These improvements extend to the smallest models evaluated: even Qwen3.5-0.8B, which performs near chance under zero-shot prompting on LIAR (0.48 Acc), reaches 0.68 Acc with our method. Moreover, the latent method consistently outperforms few-shot prompting despite few-shot providing explicit label exemplars, a finding that underscores the core contribution of our work.

Our results support the hypothesis that LLMs' internal representations encode a veracity signal that is richer and more discriminative than what is expressed through surface-level text generation. Even when prompting fails to elicit the correct judgment, particularly at small scales, the latent falsehood recovers a discriminative structure from the residual stream, suggesting that models may already encode information relevant to factual judgment without surfacing it in their outputs [4].

AVeriTeC constitutes the main exception: here, our method performs comparably or slightly below the baselines for larger models, though it remains competitive or superior for smaller ones (e.g., Llama-3.2-1B: 0.44 to 0.61 Acc; Qwen3.5-4B: 0.60 to 0.66 Acc). Beyond its evidence-dependent labeling scheme, AVeriTeC exhibits a higher proportion of refuted claims and greater variance in claim length and topic scope than LIAR or FACTors, which may bias the mean activations and partially explain the noisier falsehood direction observed in this setting. We attribute the broader underperformance to a structural property of AVeriTeC: its veracity labels are determined not by the content of the claim itself, but by multi-step chains of external evidence retrieved from the web. A claim may be entirely plausible in isolation, yet labeled *Refuted* based on facts that only become accessible through document retrieval and multi-hop reasoning [18].

Since our method operates solely on the last-token activation of the unaided claim text, without access to retrieved evidence or justification chains, it cannot recover the evidence-grounded judgment that AVeriTeC demands. Larger prompting baselines can partially compensate through their richer parametric knowledge, substituting learned factual associations for explicit retrieval, hence their relative advantage at larger scales. This structural mismatch between a claim-only representation and an evidence-dependent label is therefore an inherent limitation of any activation-only approach applied to retrieval-grounded benchmarks, and points toward the integration of retrieval-augmented representations as a natural direction for future work. Taken together, our findings suggest that truthfulness is encoded as a linearly separable direction in the residual stream of transformer models across families and scales, and that this structure can be reliably exploited for misinformation detection without fine-tuning, as long as the veracity signal is grounded in the claim text itself.

4.1 Out-of-Distribution Cases

A natural question is whether the falsehood direction extracted from one dataset generalizes to claims from a different distribution. Figure 1 summarizes the accuracy change when the misinformation direction vector computed on one dataset

Table 1. Performance comparison across datasets (Accuracy / F1)

Model	Method	AVeriTeC		FACTors		LIAR	
		Acc	F1	Acc	F1	Acc	F1
Gemma3-12B	Zero-shot	**0.72**	**0.71**	0.68	0.68	0.64	**0.64**
	Few-shot	0.71	**0.71**	0.69	0.69	0.64	**0.64**
	Our Method	0.69	0.67	**0.77**	**0.77**	**0.65**	**0.64**
Gemma3-4B	Zero-shot	**0.70**	**0.69**	0.57	0.57	0.63	0.63
	Few-shot	0.69	0.68	0.60	0.57	0.64	0.62
	Our Method	0.68	0.68	**0.79**	**0.79**	**0.69**	**0.66**
Gemma3-1B	Zero-shot	0.56	**0.54**	0.52	0.51	0.54	0.47
	Few-shot	0.51	0.36	0.50	0.35	0.52	0.38
	Our Method	**0.57**	**0.54**	**0.75**	**0.75**	**0.63**	**0.63**
Gemma3-270M	Zero-shot	**0.54**	**0.53**	0.54	0.54	0.48	0.48
	Few-shot	**0.54**	0.48	0.44	0.38	0.48	0.36
	Our Method	0.52	0.51	**0.67**	**0.67**	**0.65**	**0.65**
LLaMA3.1-8B	Zero-shot	0.62	0.62	0.62	0.62	0.58	0.56
	Few-shot	**0.69**	**0.68**	0.67	0.66	0.65	0.64
	Our Method	0.68	**0.68**	**0.71**	**0.73**	**0.66**	**0.67**
LLaMA3.2-3B	Zero-shot	0.46	0.42	0.52	0.47	0.51	0.45
	Few-shot	**0.64**	**0.63**	0.62	0.62	**0.64**	**0.62**
	Our Method	0.59	0.56	**0.67**	**0.69**	0.61	0.59
LLaMA3.2-1B	Zero-shot	0.44	0.40	0.46	0.40	0.47	0.40
	Few-shot	0.50	0.50	0.61	0.61	0.46	0.45
	Our Method	**0.61**	**0.56**	**0.73**	**0.74**	**0.70**	**0.70**
Qwen3.5-9B	Zero-shot	0.68	0.68	0.56	0.56	0.64	0.62
	Few-shot	**0.71**	**0.71**	0.57	0.56	0.62	0.60
	Our Method	0.65	0.63	**0.74**	**0.75**	**0.71**	**0.71**
Qwen3.5-4B	Zero-shot	0.60	0.54	0.53	0.47	0.56	0.47
	Few-shot	0.60	0.56	0.55	0.51	0.57	0.49
	Our Method	**0.66**	**0.62**	**0.71**	**0.72**	**0.69**	**0.68**
Qwen3.5-2B	Zero-shot	0.60	0.57	0.48	0.42	0.54	0.47
	Few-shot	0.58	0.56	0.58	0.57	0.59	0.55
	Our Method	**0.64**	**0.60**	**0.74**	**0.75**	**0.68**	**0.67**
Qwen3.5-0.8B	Zero-shot	0.54	0.50	0.48	0.44	0.56	0.54
	Few-shot	0.51	0.44	0.50	0.43	0.50	0.40
	Our Method	**0.56**	**0.54**	**0.68**	**0.70**	**0.66**	**0.66**

is applied to held-out claims from the remaining two datasets, expressed as the relative drop in accuracy with respect to the in-domain baseline.

Our results reveal a clear asymmetry across training conditions. When the vector is trained on AVeriTeC, OOD performance degrades: drops of up to 20% are observed on FACTors for models such as Gemma-3-12B and Llama-3.1-8B, and transfers to LIAR are inconsistent, with some models exhibiting near-zero change and others showing modest positive transfer. This instability is consistent with AVeriTeC being an evidence-dependent dataset, whose claims are tightly coupled to retrieved documents, making the extracted direction less portable. In contrast, vectors trained on FACTors or LIAR generalize symmetrically: cross-transfer drops between these two datasets are moderate (5–10%) and relatively consistent across model families, suggesting that statement-only, label-balanced datasets yield more transferable falsehood directions.

Across all conditions, larger models tend to exhibit smaller relative degradation, indicating that richer internal representations produce more robust cross-dataset generalizations [15,25]. Our findings point to dataset construction choices, particularly evidence dependence and label balance, as key determinants of the portability of CAA-based falsehood directions.

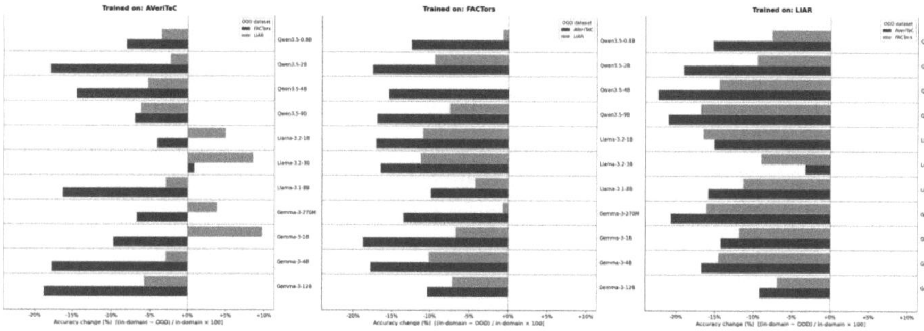

Fig. 1. Relative accuracy drop (%) when the steering vector trained on one dataset is applied out-of-distribution (OOD) to the other two datasets, across eleven models spanning three architectural families. Bars pointing left indicate degradation; bars at or to the right of zero indicate neutral or positive transfer.

4.2 Instance-Accuracy Relation

We also investigate the impact of the sample size used during the extraction phase on the classifier's overall performance. Specifically, we vary the number of paired instances, denoted as N, utilized to compute the falsehood direction vector and to train the MLP classifier.

Figure 2 illustrates this trend across datasets for the three models evaluated that have around 1B parameters (Gemma-3-1B, Llama-3.2-1B, and Qwen3.5-0.8B). The results reveal a clear dataset-dependent scaling behavior. For FACTors, accuracy rises from approximately 60% at N=10 to around 75% at

N=200, a gain of roughly 10–20 percentage points across all three architectures. LIAR exhibits a shallower upward trend, improving from ~60–65% to ~ 65–70% over the same range. AVeriTeC, by contrast, remains essentially flat throughout (55–60%), showing no meaningful benefit from additional contrastive pairs. This three-way pattern is reproduced across all model families shown, indicating that the scaling behavior is driven by dataset structure rather than model-specific factors.

We attribute AVeriTeC's stagnation to its structural heterogeneity: claims span highly diverse topics and require evidence-grounded reasoning, so increasing the number of contrastive pairs does not converge to a single stable falsehood direction; different claims pull the mean activation toward different semantic regions. For claim-homogeneous datasets such as FACTors and LIAR, the difference-in-means estimator benefits substantially from larger N, as additional pairs more effectively cancel noise and context-specific artifacts, yielding a more robust and generalizable representation. Addressing AVeriTeC's heterogeneity may require topic-conditioned steering directions rather than a single global vector.

Fig. 2. Test accuracy as a function of the number of contrastive training instances N used to compute the falsehood direction vector, evaluated on the three models with a similar number of parameters across three datasets. FACTors and LIAR show a positive scaling trend, while AVeriTeC remains flat.

5 Conclusion and Future Work

Our work presents a lightweight, fine-tuning-free approach to misinformation detection grounded in activation engineering and all code is available at https://github.com/Malta-Lab/LaFaCt. By extracting a contrastive falsehood direction from the residual stream of frozen transformer models and projecting claim representations onto it, our method consistently outperforms zero-shot and few-shot prompting baselines on LIAR and FACTors across 11 models ranging from

$270M$ to $12B$ parameters. Gains are especially pronounced for smaller models, demonstrating that the latent falsehood signal can compensate for limited model capacity, which makes our approach particularly practical for settings where large-scale inference is not feasible.

A key finding is that the method's internal view of a claim often captures falsehood better than what a model produces through generation, consistent with the hypothesis that LLMs encode truth-related information that does not fully surface in their outputs [4]. These results position our approach as a complementary layer in AFC pipelines: it does not replace retrieval-based verification or evidence-grounded reasoning, but provides an additional, computationally inexpensive signal that can be combined with existing systems.

The main limitation identified is the gap in performance on AVeriTeC, where falsehood depends on external evidence rather than claim text alone. This structural mismatch motivates two concrete directions for future work: (*i*). integrating retrieved document representations into the activation extraction step, so the falsehood direction is conditioned on evidence rather than the bare claim; and (*ii*). developing topic-aware or domain-gated mechanisms that estimate separate falsehood directions per cluster of claims, addressing the heterogeneity that degrades the difference-in-means estimator under distributional diversity.

Additionally, our cross-dataset transfer experiments reveal that the generalizability of the falsehood direction improves with model scale, suggesting that further investigation of layer-wise representation quality across model sizes could identify more universal veracity subspaces. Collectively, these extensions would move the approach from a claim-only classifier toward a full fact-checking component capable of operating over heterogeneous, evidence-dependent claim distributions.

Acknowledgments. This study was financed in part by the Coordination for the Improvement of Higher Education Personnel (CAPES)—Finance Code 001; by Conselho Nacional de Desenvolvimento Científico e Tecnológico (CNPq)—Grant Number: 443072/2024-8; and by Fundação de Amparo à Pesquisa do Estado do Rio Grande do Sul (FAPERGS)—Grant Number: 25/2551-0000891-3 and 25/2551-0002824-8. This work was supported by Kunumi Institute. The authors thank the institution for its financial support and commitment to advancing scientific research. The authors declare no competing interests. During the drafting of this article, LLMs were used solely for grammar review, clarity improvement, and spelling correction.

References

1. Altuncu, E., Baçkent, C., Bhattacherjee, S., Li, S., Roy, D.: FACTors: a new dataset for studying the fact-checking ecosystem. In: Proceedings of the 48th International ACM SIGIR Conference on Research and Development in Information Retrieval, pp. 3530–3539 (2025). https://doi.org/10.1145/3726302.3730339, http://arxiv.org/abs/2505.09414

2. Aly, R., et al.: FEVEROUS: fact extraction and VERification over unstructured and structured information. In: Proceedings of the Neural Information Processing Systems (NeurIPS) 2021 Datasets and Benchmarks Track (2019). https://doi.org/10.48550/arXiv.2106.05707. https://arxiv.org/abs/2106.05707
3. Arditi, A., et al.: Refusal in language models is mediated by a single direction (2024). https://doi.org/10.48550/arXiv.2406.11717. http://arxiv.org/abs/2406.11717
4. Azaria, A., Mitchell, T.: The internal state of an LLM knows when it's lying. arXiv preprint arXiv:2304.13734 (2023)
5. Cao, Y., et al.: Personalized steering of large language models: versatile steering vectors through bi-directional preference optimization (2024). https://doi.org/10.48550/arXiv.2406.00045. http://arxiv.org/abs/2406.00045
6. Delucis, M., et al.: Automated fact-checking in brazilian portuguese: resources and baselines. In: Anais do XVI Simpósio Brasileiro de Tecnologia da Informação e da Linguagem Humana, pp. 137–148. SBC, Porto Alegre, RS, Brasil (2025). https://doi.org/10.5753/stil.2025.37820. https://sol.sbc.org.br/index.php/stil/article/view/37820
7. Elhage, N., et al.: Toy models of superposition. Transformer Circuits Thread (2022). https://transformer-circuits.pub/2022/toy_model/index.html
8. Guo, Z., Schlichtkrull, M., Vlachos, A.: A survey on automated fact-checking (2022). https://doi.org/10.48550/arXiv.2108.11896. http://arxiv.org/abs/2108.11896
9. Kim, B., et al.: Interpretability beyond feature attribution: quantitative testing with concept activation vectors (TCAV) (2018). https://doi.org/10.48550/arXiv.1711.11279. http://arxiv.org/abs/1711.11279
10. Konen, K., et al.: Style vectors for steering generative large language models. In: Graham, Y., Purver, M. (eds.) Findings of the Association for Computational Linguistics: EACL 2024, pp. 782–802. Association for Computational Linguistics (2024). https://doi.org/10.18653/v1/2024.findings-eacl.52. https://aclanthology.org/2024.findings-eacl.52/
11. Li, K., Patel, O., Viégas, F., Pfister, H., Wattenberg, M.: Inference-time intervention: Eliciting truthful answers from a language model (2024).https://doi.org/10.48550/arXiv.2306.03341. http://arxiv.org/abs/2306.03341
12. Lin, S., Hilton, J., Evans, O.: TruthfulQA: measuring how models mimic human falsehoods (2022). https://doi.org/10.48550/arXiv.2109.07958. http://arxiv.org/abs/2109.07958
13. Marks, S., Tegmark, M.: The geometry of truth: emergent linear structure in large language model representations of true/false datasets (2024). https://doi.org/10.48550/arXiv.2310.06824. http://arxiv.org/abs/2310.06824
14. Mohammadkhani, M.G., Mohammadkhani, A.G., Beigy, H.: Zero-shot learning and key points are all you need for automated fact-checking (2024). https://doi.org/10.48550/arXiv.2408.08400. https://arxiv.org/abs/2408.08400
15. Panickssery, N., Gabrieli, N., Schulz, J., Tong, M., Hubinger, E., Turner, A.M.: Steering llama 2 via contrastive activation addition (2024).https://doi.org/10.48550/arXiv.2312.06681. http://arxiv.org/abs/2312.06681
16. Park, K., Choe, Y.J., Veitch, V.: The linear representation hypothesis and the geometry of large language models (2024). https://doi.org/10.48550/arXiv.2311.03658. https://arxiv.org/abs/2311.03658
17. Pavlyshenko, B.M.: Analysis of disinformation and fake news detection using fine-tuned large language model (2023). https://doi.org/10.48550/arXiv.2309.04704. https://arxiv.org/abs/2309.04704

18. Schlichtkrull, M., Guo, Z., Vlachos, A.: AVeriTeC: a dataset for real-world claim verification with evidence from the web (2023). https://doi.org/10.48550/arXiv.2305.13117. http://arxiv.org/abs/2305.13117
19. Subramani, N., Suresh, N., Peters, M.E.: Extracting latent steering vectors from pretrained language models (2022). https://doi.org/10.48550/arXiv.2205.05124. http://arxiv.org/abs/2205.05124
20. Thorne, J., Vlachos, A., Christodoulopoulos, C., Mittal, A.: FEVER: a large-scale dataset for fact extraction and VERification. In: Proceedings of the 2018 Conference of the North American Chapter of the Association for Computational Linguistics: Human Language Technologies (Volume 1: Long Papers), pp. 809–819. Association for Computational Linguistics (2018). https://doi.org/10.18653/v1/N18-1074. https://aclanthology.org/N18-1074/
21. Turner, A.M., et al.: Steering language models with activation engineering (2024). https://doi.org/10.48550/arXiv.2308.10248. http://arxiv.org/abs/2308.10248
22. Ullrich, H., Mlynář, T., Drchal, J.: AIC CTU system at AVeriTeC: re-framing automated fact-checking as a simple RAG task (2024). https://doi.org/10.48550/arXiv.2410.11446. https://arxiv.org/abs/2410.11446
23. Wang, W.Y.: liar, liar pants on fire: A new benchmark dataset for fake news detection. In: Barzilay, R., Kan, M.Y. (eds.) Proceedings of the 55th Annual Meeting of the Association for Computational Linguistics (Volume 2: Short Papers), pp. 422–426. Association for Computational Linguistics (2017). https://doi.org/10.18653/v1/P17-2067. https://aclanthology.org/P17-2067/
24. Zhang, H., Wang, X., Li, C., Ao, X., He, Q.: Controlling large language models through concept activation vectors (2025). https://doi.org/10.48550/arXiv.2501.05764. http://arxiv.org/abs/2501.05764
25. Zou, A., et al.: Representation engineering: a top-down approach to AI transparency (2025). https://doi.org/10.48550/arXiv.2310.01405. http://arxiv.org/abs/2310.01405

Interactive Quantum Regressor Based on Open Quantum Systems

Beatriz Férre[1(✉)], João V. M. Cardoso[1], Fábio Novaes[2], and Fernando M. de Paula Neto[1]

[1] Centro de Informática, Universidade Federal de Pernambuco, Recife, PE, Brazil
{bof,jvmc,fernando}@cin.ufpe.br

[2] Unidade Acadêmica de Belo Jardim, Universidade Federal Rural de Pernambuco, Recife, PE, Brazil
fabio.novaes@ufrpe.br

Abstract. Open quantum systems have recently emerged as a promising framework for machine learning tasks, particularly in classification settings where dissipative dynamics and system–environment interactions can be exploited to enhance expressive power. In this work, we extend this paradigm by proposing an open quantum system-based regression model, addressing a gap in the current literature where such models have been predominantly restricted to classification tasks. The proposed approach leverages parametrized interaction Hamiltonians between a cognitive subsystem and an environment encoding classical data, enabling nonlinear function approximation through quantum dynamical evolution. To assess the effectiveness of the model, we conducted a comprehensive experimental evaluation of a suite of eight benchmark functions, including linear, polynomial, and highly nonlinear targets. We further investigate architectural variations of the model, including data re-uploading mechanisms and input-space expansion via padding to higher-dimensional Hilbert spaces, which allow controlled increases in representational capacity. The results demonstrate that the proposed regressor is capable of accurately approximating diverse functional forms, achieving $R^2 > 0.962$ for all benchmarking functions in at least one configuration, demonstrating clear improvements under specific encoding strategies. These findings provide preliminary evidence that open quantum systems constitute a viable and expressive framework for regression tasks. In addition, they suggest that the design of system-environment interaction, together with input encoding strategies, plays a crucial role in improving model performance. This work opens new directions for quantum machine learning by extending the applicability of open quantum models beyond classification and highlighting their potential for continuous-value prediction problems.

Keywords: Intelligent Open Quantum Systems · Quantum Computing · Machine Learning

M. Recamonde-Mendoza and R. C. Barros (Eds.): BRACIS 2026, LNAI 17105, pp. 675–690, 2027.
https://doi.org/10.1007/978-3-032-39882-6_45

1 Introduction

Quantum systems encountered in realistic scenarios are seldom perfectly isolated. Instead, they interact with external degrees of freedom—collectively referred to as the *environment* or *bath*—leading to dissipative and non-unitary dynamics. Such systems are known as *open quantum systems*. The theoretical framework of open quantum systems provides the appropriate tools to describe decoherence, dissipation, and information exchange between a system and its surroundings [1].

The intersection between open quantum systems and machine learning has recently given rise to the concept of *intelligent open quantum systems*, in which dissipative dynamics and system–environment interactions are not merely treated as sources of noise, but are actively exploited to perform learning tasks [12]. In this paradigm, the environment plays a dual role: it encodes classical or quantum data while simultaneously inducing non-unitary dynamics that enhance the expressive power of the model.

Recent studies have shown that dissipation and decoherence, traditionally viewed as detrimental, can instead be harnessed to improve the performance of quantum machine learning models. In particular, it has been argued that open quantum dynamics can introduce effective nonlinearities and richer hypothesis spaces compared to purely unitary models [12]. These properties are especially relevant in the context of learning tasks, where nonlinear transformations are essential for capturing complex patterns in data. Along this direction, dissipative quantum learning frameworks have been investigated as alternatives to purely unitary variational models, highlighting the role of environment-induced dynamics in enhancing computational capabilities [8,16,17].

In parallel, it has been demonstrated that even minimal quantum systems can exhibit remarkable expressive power. In particular, the work of Pérez-Salinas *et al.* [13] shows that a single qubit, when combined with appropriate data re-uploading strategies, can act as a universal function approximator. This result reinforces the idea that quantum models, even with limited resources, can approximate complex nonlinear functions when properly structured.

One of the earliest and most developed applications of quantum systems to intelligent tasks is classification. Variational quantum classifiers, based on parametrized quantum circuits, have been proposed as models capable of learning decision boundaries in high-dimensional spaces [14,15]. These models typically rely on encoding classical data into quantum states and applying unitary transformations followed by measurement. Extending this idea, open quantum systems introduce additional flexibility by allowing the learning process to exploit dissipative channels and system–environment interactions.

Several recent works have explored classification models explicitly grounded in open quantum system dynamics. For instance, steady-state quantum classifiers leverage the asymptotic behavior of dissipative processes to perform classification [8,16], while more recent approaches consider dissipative mechanisms as part of the learning architecture itself [17]. Additionally, models incorporating amplitude-based encoding in open quantum systems have demonstrated improved representational capabilities [2].

Despite these advances, most existing works focus primarily on classification tasks, leaving the regression setting relatively underexplored. Nevertheless, the intrinsic ability of quantum systems to encode and transform continuous amplitudes suggests that open quantum dynamics may be well-suited for approximating real-valued functions [10].

In this context, a notable contribution is the Interactive Quantum Classifier (IQC), proposed in [18], which formulates classification as an interaction process between a target quantum system and an environment encoding the input data. In this model, learning emerges from the dynamical adjustment of probability amplitudes and phases induced by system–environment interactions. More recently, related approaches have further explored the use of open quantum systems for classification with enhanced encoding strategies [2].

Motivated by these developments, this work extends the IQC framework to the regression setting, proposing a quantum model capable of approximating continuous functions while preserving the physical interpretability of open quantum system dynamics.

The concept of intelligent open quantum systems represents a shift in perspective: instead of mitigating environmental effects, one designs system-environment interactions to perform computation. Dissipation becomes a computational resource, enabling richer dynamics than those available in closed systems. As highlighted in recent works, leveraging noise and decoherence may lead to improved learning performance under certain conditions [12].

This paper is organized as follows. Section 2 introduces the main concepts of open quantum systems and reviews related work on intelligent open quantum systems. Section 3 introduces the Interactive Quantum Regressor model in detail. The experiments and their analysis are described in Sect. 4, and the conclusions, along with directions for future work, are provided in Sect. 5.

2 Open Quantum Systems

2.1 Density Matrix Formalism

The state of a quantum system is generally described by a density operator (or density matrix) ρ, which is a positive semi-definite, Hermitian operator with unit trace [11]:

$$\rho \geq 0, \qquad \rho = \rho^{\dagger}, \qquad \mathrm{Tr}(\rho) = 1. \tag{1}$$

This formalism encompasses both pure states, $\rho = |\psi\rangle\langle\psi|$, and mixed states, which arise naturally in open system dynamics.

2.2 Evolution of the Open Quantum System

For a *closed* (isolated) quantum system, the time evolution is unitary and governed by the Schrödinger equation. The formal solution (where H is the system Hamiltonian, i is the imaginary unit, and $\hbar$ is the reduced Planck constant) is given by

$$\rho(t) = U(t)\rho(0)U^{\dagger}(t), \qquad U(t) = e^{-iHt/\hbar}. \tag{2}$$

In contrast, an *open quantum system* is described by considering a larger composite system consisting of the system of interest Q (ρ_Q) and its environment E (ρ_E). The total Hilbert space is given by $\mathcal{H}_{QE} = \mathcal{H}_Q \otimes \mathcal{H}_E$. The joint state ρ_{QE} ($\rho_Q \otimes \rho_E$) evolves unitarily under a global Hamiltonian H_{QE}:

$$\rho_{QE}(t) = U_{QE}(t)\rho_{QE}(0)U_{QE}^{\dagger}(t), \qquad U_{QE}(t) = e^{-iH_{QE}t/\hbar}. \tag{3}$$

However, since the environment is typically inaccessible, the effective state of the system S is obtained by taking the partial trace over the environmental degrees of freedom:

$$\rho_Q'(t) = \varepsilon(\rho_Q) = \mathrm{Tr}_E\left[U_{QE}(t)\rho_{QE}(0)U_{QE}^{\dagger}(t)\right]. \tag{4}$$

This operation generally leads to non-unitary evolution, reflecting the loss of information from the system into the environment [1]. Thus, Eq. (4) captures the fundamental interplay between a quantum system and its environment, where information loss and decoherence emerge as natural consequences of the partial trace operation.

2.3 Intelligent Open Quantum Systems

The framework of open quantum systems offers a natural setting for implementing machine learning tasks [3,7,9,12], where classical data can be encoded into the environment and the computational result is extracted from the reduced state of the system of interest [2,5]. Unlike unitary circuit models, open-system dynamics can introduce effective nonlinearities and dissipation, enabling the system to converge to task-specific steady states that serve as the output [2,6]. This approach has given rise to several distinct models, each with its own architecture and learning strategy.

The Deterministic Quantum Computation with One Clean Qubit (DQC1) model, introduced by Knill and Laflamme [6], represents a subuniversal model of quantum computation situated between classical computation and universal quantum computation. In this model, the initial state consists of a single signal qubit with non-zero polarization (the "clean" qubit) and an n-qubit ancillary register prepared in the maximally mixed state. Building on its foundational power for trace estimation, recent research has formalized DQC1 as a robust model for QML, where it serves as the sole protocol for both gradient-based training and inference [5]. Parameterized DQC1 circuits can represent complex functions as partial Fourier series, matching the representational power of universal QNN with only constant overhead in circuit depth or qubit count [5]. The practical efficacy of DQC1-based ML has been demonstrated through binary classification on standard benchmarks, including the Iris, Wine, and MNIST datasets [5]. Results indicate that DQC1-based models achieve competitive performance, attaining nearly 100% accuracy on the Iris and MNIST datasets and higher final test accuracy than universal QNN on the Wine classification task.

Türkpençe et al. [16] proposed a classifier based on a collision model: a single qubit (the classifier) interacts sequentially with a stream of ancilla qubits that encode the input data. After many collisions, the system reaches a steady state whose magnetization acts as a non-linear activation function, mimicking the behavior of classical activation functions for binary decision-making. The model was evaluated on synthetic two-dimensional datasets with both linear and non-linear decision boundaries, using Bloch sphere angles to encode features. It achieved accuracies above 98% and ROC areas near 1. The authors also discussed a physical implementation using superconducting transmon qubits, showing that the classifier can operate three orders of magnitude faster than classical counterparts while being robust to moderate state-preparation errors [16].

Wang et al. [17] introduced a classifier built on a central spin model, where auxiliary qubits are subjected to engineered strong dissipations. Classical data are mapped directly onto dissipative channels within a decoherence-free subspace, eliminating the need for precise qubit initialization or large ensembles of initial states. The central qubit evolves under an effective Lindblad master equation toward a unique steady state that encodes the classification result. The model was tested on binary classification tasks using synthetic datasets with linear, quadratic, and cubic decision boundaries, achieving accuracies of 96.2–98.9% and AUC values above 0.9997. These results confirm superior discriminative ability and operational robustness [17].

The Interactive Quantum Classifier (IQC) [18] is a quantum learning model grounded in the formalism of open quantum systems, where the classification task is interpreted as the interaction between a target quantum system and its environment.

Let $\rho_Q \in \mathcal{B}(\mathcal{H}_Q)$ denote the density operator of the target system and $\rho_E \in \mathcal{B}(\mathcal{H}_E)$ represent the environment, which encodes the features of a given data sample.

The initial state of the target system is chosen as an equal superposition state

$$|\psi_Q\rangle = |+\rangle = \frac{1}{\sqrt{2}}(|0\rangle + |1\rangle) \implies \rho_Q = |\psi_Q\rangle\langle\psi_Q|. \tag{5}$$

Similarly, the environment is initialized as a uniform superposition over N levels,

$$|\psi_E\rangle = \frac{1}{\sqrt{N}} \sum_{i=0}^{N-1} |i\rangle \implies \rho_{\mathrm{E}} = |\psi_E\rangle\langle\psi_E|. \tag{6}$$

The initial composite system state is therefore

$$\rho_{QE} = \rho_Q \otimes \rho_{\mathrm{E}}. \tag{7}$$

Let $\mathbf{x} = (x_1, \ldots, x_n)$ denote the input vector and $\mathbf{w} = (w_1, \ldots, w_n)$ the vector of trainable parameters, the interaction between the system and the environment is governed by an interaction Hamiltonian of the form [18]

$$H_{int} = -\hbar g\left(\sigma_Q \otimes \sigma_E(\mathbf{x}, \mathbf{w})\right), \tag{8}$$

where $g > 0$ is the coupling constant, σ_Q acts on $\mathcal{H}_Q$, and σ_E acts on $\mathcal{H}_E$.

The corresponding unitary evolution operator is given [18] by

$$U = \exp\left(igt\left(\sigma_Q \otimes \sigma_E(\mathbf{x}, \mathbf{w})\right)\right). \tag{9}$$

In the following, the combination gt is absorbed into σ_E and the explicit time evolution is not considered, i.e., $gt = 1$ in practice.

The target system is modeled as a qubit, and its operator is chosen as a combination of Pauli matrices to capture both amplitude and phase contributions:

$$\sigma_Q = \sigma_x + \sigma_y + \sigma_z = \begin{bmatrix} 1 & 1-i \\ 1+i & -1 \end{bmatrix}. \tag{10}$$

The environment encodes the input data $\mathbf{x} = (x_1, \ldots, x_n)$ through a diagonal operator

$$\sigma_E(\mathbf{x}, \mathbf{w}) = \begin{bmatrix} w_1 x_1 & 0 & \cdots & 0 \\ 0 & w_2 x_2 & \cdots & 0 \\ \vdots & \vdots & \ddots & \vdots \\ 0 & 0 & \cdots & w_n x_n \end{bmatrix} \equiv diag(\mathbf{x} \odot \mathbf{w}), \tag{11}$$

where $diag(\circ)$ means turning its argument into a diagonal matrix and $\mathbf{x} \odot \mathbf{w}$ means the Hadamard product (or element-wise product) between vectors $\mathbf{x}$ and $\mathbf{w}$.

The target system evolves under the global unitary operator U in Eq. (9) that acts over the joint system, resulting in the transformation equivalent to Eq. (4)

$$\rho_Q' = \varepsilon(\rho_Q) = \mathrm{Tr}_E\left[U\left(\rho_Q \otimes \rho_E\right)U^\dagger\right], \tag{12}$$

which defines a completely positive trace-preserving (CPTP) map acting on the target system. The final state ρ_Q' is then measured to produce the classification output.

The reduced state of the target system in Eq. (12) can be expressed as

$$\varepsilon(\rho_Q) = \rho'_{Q_{00}}|0\rangle\langle 0| + \rho'_{Q_{01}}|0\rangle\langle 1| + \rho'_{Q_{10}}|1\rangle\langle 0| + \rho'_{Q_{11}}|1\rangle\langle 1|. \tag{13}$$

The classification decision is made by comparing the probabilities:

$$z = \begin{cases} 0, & \rho'_{Q_{00}} \geq \rho'_{Q_{11}}, \\ 1, & \rho'_{Q_{00}} < \rho'_{Q_{11}}. \end{cases} \tag{14}$$

In the original formulation [18], the model parameters are updated using a delta-rule-based learning mechanism derived from a predefined loss function.

The IQC was evaluated on two standard three-class datasets: Iris (150 instances, 4 attributes) and Wine (178 instances, 13 attributes). The experiments used 10-fold cross-validation, and the model was compared against classical algorithms, including Support Vector Machine, and Logistic Regression. For the three-class task, a one-versus-rest strategy was employed with balanced class representations. On the Iris dataset, IQC achieved an average accuracy of 0.9666, outperforming all classical baselines except SVM (0.9600). On the Wine dataset, IQC achieved an accuracy of 0.9832, matching SVM and LDA, and outperforming all other methods. The results demonstrate that the quantum open system approach is competitive for small-scale classification tasks and exhibits strong scalability for integrating multiple influencing factors [18].

3 Interactive Quantum Regressor

Here, we introduce the *Interactive Quantum Regressor* (IQR), a quantum model grounded in the formalism of open quantum systems. The model extends the Interactive Quantum Classifier (IQC) proposed in [18] (revised in the previous section) by enabling continuous outputs and introducing additional degrees of freedom in the system dynamics through a parametrized system operator. This allows the model to approximate real-valued functions while preserving the physical interpretation of system–environment interaction.

Defining the following vector

$$\boldsymbol{\alpha} = (\alpha_x, \alpha_y, \alpha_z, \alpha_I) \in \mathbb{R}^4, \tag{15}$$

the interaction between the system and the environment is modeled through a Hamiltonian of the form

$$H_{int} = -\hbar g\, \sigma_Q(\boldsymbol{\alpha}) \otimes \sigma_E(\mathbf{x}, \mathbf{w}), \tag{16}$$

where $\mathbf{x} = (x_1, \ldots, x_n)$ is the input feature vector and $\mathbf{w} = (w_1, \ldots, w_n)$ is the vector of trainable parameters, leading to the unitary evolution operator

$$U(\mathbf{x}, \mathbf{w}, \boldsymbol{\alpha}) = \exp\left(i\, \sigma_Q(\boldsymbol{\alpha}) \otimes \sigma_E(\mathbf{x}, \mathbf{w})\right), \tag{17}$$

where we have absorbed gt into σ_E. The system operator is now defined as a trainable linear combination of Pauli matrices:

$$\sigma_Q(\boldsymbol{\alpha}) = \alpha_x \sigma_x + \alpha_y \sigma_y + \alpha_z \sigma_z + \alpha_I \sigma_I. \tag{18}$$

The adding of σ_I to σ_Q formula differs from the one proposed by Zhang et al. [18]. This parametrization allows the model to adapt the geometry of the system dynamics, increasing its expressive power beyond the fixed operator used in IQC. Also, in the code implementation, we regularized σ_Q matrix through a division by its own trace. The environment operator $\sigma_E(\mathbf{x}, \mathbf{w})$ retains the encoding of the input features described in Eq. 11.

Similarly to IQC, the target and environment density matrices, ρ_Q and ρ_E, are initialized according to the definitions given above. The initial composite density matrix is then ρ_{QE}, as defined in Eq. (7).

The evolution is governed the a unitary operator $U(\mathbf{x}, \mathbf{w}, \boldsymbol{\alpha})$ in eq. (17), resulting in the reduced state

$$\rho'_Q(\mathbf{x}, \mathbf{w}, \boldsymbol{\alpha}) = \mathrm{Tr}_E \left[U(\mathbf{x}, \mathbf{w}, \boldsymbol{\alpha})\, (\rho_Q \otimes \rho_E)\, U^\dagger(\mathbf{x}, \mathbf{w}, \boldsymbol{\alpha})\right]. \tag{19}$$

Here, $\mathbf{w}$ represents the parameters associated with the environment encoding, while $\boldsymbol{\alpha}$ parametrizes the system operator, allowing independent control of the quantum dynamics.

The model produces a continuous output defined as the expectation value of an observable M acting on the system:

$$\hat{y}(\mathbf{x}, \mathbf{w}, \boldsymbol{\alpha}) = \mathrm{Tr}_Q \left[M \, \rho'_Q(\mathbf{x}, \mathbf{w}, \boldsymbol{\alpha}) \right]. \tag{20}$$

By choosing M as a Hermitian observable with spectrum in $[-1, 1]$ (e.g., $M = \sigma_z$), the model output satisfies $\hat{y}(\mathbf{x}, \mathbf{w}, \boldsymbol{\alpha}) \in [-1, 1]$, enabling the approximation of continuous-valued target functions and thus supporting regression tasks.

Given a dataset $\mathcal{D} = \{(\mathbf{x}_i, y_i)\}_{i=1}^N$, the parameters $\mathbf{w}$ and $\boldsymbol{\alpha}$ are optimized by minimizing the mean squared error:

$$\mathcal{L}(\mathbf{w}, \boldsymbol{\alpha}) = \frac{1}{N} \sum_{i=1}^{N} \left(y_i - \hat{y}(\mathbf{x}_i, \mathbf{w}, \boldsymbol{\alpha}) \right)^2. \tag{21}$$

The gradients can be computed with respect to both parameter sets, allowing training via gradient-based optimization methods.

Given that the objective in regression is to maximize R^2, an equivalent minimization problem can be defined by considering the complementary quantity. Specifically, we define the loss function as

$$\mathcal{L}_{R^2}(\mathbf{w}, \boldsymbol{\alpha}) = -R^2 = -1 + \frac{\sum_{i=1}^{N} \left(y_i - \hat{y}_i \right)^2}{\sum_{i=1}^{N} \left(y_i - \bar{y} \right)^2}, \tag{22}$$

where $\hat{y}_i = \hat{y}(\mathbf{x}_i, \mathbf{w}, \boldsymbol{\alpha})$ denotes the model prediction, y_i is the ground-truth value, and $\bar{y}$ is the mean of the target values.

This formulation normalizes the residual error by the total variance of the data, making the loss invariant to the scale of the target variable. As a result, optimizing $\mathcal{L}_{R^2}$ encourages the model to explain as much variance as possible in the dataset, providing a complementary perspective to the traditional mean squared error objective.

Then, in resume, the Interactive Quantum Regressor generalizes the IQC model in two key aspects. First, it replaces the fixed system operator with a parametrized combination of Pauli operators, introducing adaptive control over the system dynamics. Second, it replaces the discrete decision rule with a continuous observable expectation, enabling regression instead of classification.

4 Experiments and Discussion

4.1 Experimental Protocol

All experiments were implemented in Python (v. 3.9.6). The quantum circuits were constructed and simulated using the NumPy library (v.2.2.6). The training of the quantum models was performed using the JAX numerical computing library (v.0.6.2) together with the Optax optimization framework (v.0.2.7), enabling efficient gradient-based optimization through just-in-time compilation and vectorized operations. All code is publicly available on GitHub.[1]

For gradient-based training, we employed the Adam optimizer provided by Optax, using a learning rate of 10^{-2}. The loss function adopted in this case was the mean squared error (MSE) between the predicted output and the target values. Additionally, the scikit-learn library (v.1.7.2) was used for auxiliary tasks such as dataset handling and preprocessing.

To address potential optimization difficulties arising from the highly non-convex landscape of the model, we also considered a population-based optimization strategy using Particle Swarm Optimization (PSO), implemented via the PySwarms library (v.1.3.0). PSO is a well-established method in the literature for continuous parameter optimization [4]. Due to runtime limitations, the PSO-based training was applied only in scenarios where the Adam optimizer was unable to achieve a coefficient of determination $R^2 \geq 0.995$. The PSO algorithm was configured with a swarm size of 50 particles and a maximum of 150 iterations. The hyperparameters of the PySwarms implementation were kept at their default values, namely $\{c_1 = 0.5, c_2 = 0.3, w = 0.9\}$. In this case, the loss function was defined as the negative R^2 score, such that maximizing R^2 is equivalent to minimizing the objective function. In the analysis of the results, models optimized using the Adam optimizer are denoted by "-OPT", while those optimized via PSO are denoted by "-PSO".

The proposed model was evaluated on a set of 8 benchmark functions, each sampled with 100 data points. The analytical expressions of these functions are provided in Eqs. 23, 24, 25, 26, 27 and 28 (varying M between 1,2,3). The goal of the experimental setup was to assess the ability of the proposed models to approximate these functions, thereby evaluating their effectiveness as quantum regressors.

Since $\sigma_E(\mathbf{x}, \mathbf{w})$ must act on a Hilbert space of dimension 2^n $(n > 1)$, a one-dimensional input must be extended to a higher-dimensional space. To address this constraint, we considered two strategies: *padding* and *input repetition* (data re-uploading). In what follows, we denote by p the number of padding dimensions and by r the number of times the input is re-uploaded. In the padding strategy, additional dimensions are introduced by filling the input vector with constant values, set to 0.9 in our experiments. Alternatively, in the input repetition strategy, the original input value is duplicated multiple times, effectively increasing the dimensionality while preserving the original information content. The models were systematically evaluated under different configurations of padding and input repetition, exploring how these encoding strategies impact the expressive capacity and performance of the proposed quantum regressor. The benchmark functions in Eqs. 24, 25, 26, 27 and 28 are deliberately drawn from qualitatively distinct classes: a linear map (f_1), even and mixed-parity polynomials of increasing degree (f_2, f_3), a single-frequency sinusoid (f_4), a multi-frequency trigonometric function (f_5) and truncated Fourier series (g_M). The diversity of this set is what allows the per-function datasets to jointly characterize the padding and

[1] https://github.com/biaferre/interactive-quantum-regressor.

repetition strategies across a broad range of target behaviors rather than a single favorable case. The functions f are defined on $[-1.5, 1.5]$, while the functions g are defined on $[-6, 6]$. For the sake of notational simplicity, we refer to the model in which the parameters of the system operator are fixed as $\boldsymbol{\alpha} = (1, 1, 1, 1)$ simply as *IQR*. In contrast, the generalized version of the model, in which $\boldsymbol{\alpha}$ is treated as a set of trainable parameters, is denoted as *IQR-α*. This distinction allows us to separate the baseline formulation from its parametrized extension when presenting and discussing experimental results. Additionally, a bias term was incorporated into the model to introduce an additional degree of freedom, such that the optimization process also includes a parameter that is added to the expectation value output of the quantum model.

$$f_1(x) = 0.5\,x \tag{23}$$

$$f_2(x) = 0.5\,x^2 - 0.5 \tag{24}$$

$$f_3(x) = 0.04\,x^3 + 0.05\,x^2 + 0.04\,x \tag{25}$$

$$f_4(x) = 0.2\,\sin(2x) \tag{26}$$

$$f_5(x) = 0.9\,\sin(2x) + 0.1\,\cos(x) \tag{27}$$

$$g_M(x) = \mathcal{R}e\left(\sum_{k=-M-1}^{M+1} c_k e^{(ikx)}\right) \tag{28}$$

4.2 Result Analysis

Table 1 summarizes the performance of IQR and IQR-α across eight benchmark functions, considering p paddings and r re-uploadings; PSO is used when Adam fails to reach an R^2 above 0.995.

Model-Wise Analysis

The baseline model IQR-OPT, with gradient-based optimization achieves moderate performance across some functions. The best results are observed for f_3, reaching $R^2 = 0.997$ under the configurations $r = 0, p = 7$ and $r = 1, p = 6$. Additionally, for the functions g_M the model frequently produced negative values R^2 for this model, reflecting failure to approximate more complex targets.

On the other hand, introducing trainable α parameters with gradient-based optimization via the IQR-α-OPT model leads to substantial gains for several functions. Perfect approximation ($R^2 = 1.0$) is achieved for f_4 and f_5 across multiple encoding configurations. For the g_M family, the model achieves $R^2 = 1.0$ for g_1 under $r = 2, p = 1$ and for g_2 under $r = 0, p = 3$, but degrades significantly in several configurations, exemplified by the $R^2 = 0$ given by the configuration $r = 7, p = 0$, for both g_1 and g_2. These results highlight a strong sensitivity to the input encoding strategy.

Unlike the similarity between the results given by the IQR-OPT and the IQR-PSO, there is a significant improvement with the IQR-α-PSO model in comparison to IQR-α-OPT, as seen in f_2, for the first 4 configurations of p; f_3 for $r = 1, p = 6$; and g_3 for $r = 0, p = 3$. This indicates increased sensitivity to the optimization strategy. The IQR-α-PSO variant arguably demonstrates the most robust behavior among the tested variants: negative R^2 are nonexistent, and the model achieves $R^2 \geq 0.995$ for the f_M functions in at least one configuration.

Table 1. Comparison of the R^2 performance of IQR and IQR-α across 10 benchmark functions (Eqs. 24, 25, 26, 27 and 28) under different input encoding configurations. Results are shown for Adam-based optimization (OPT) and, when OPT fails to achieve a coefficient of determination $R^2 \geq 0.995$, Particle Swarm Optimization (PSO) is applied. Input dimensions were adjusted through re-uploading (r) and padding (p) to satisfy quantum encoding requirements. Best results are highlighted for both model parametrization and input encoding.

function	model	r=0,p=1	r=0,p=3	r=0,p=7	r=1,p=0	r=1,p=2	r=1,p=6	r=2,p=1	r=3,p=0	r=5,p=2	r=7,p=0
f_1	IQR-OPT	0.940	0.940	0.940	0.711	0.870	0.913	0.711	0.426	0.585	0.231
	IQR-PSO	0.940	0.940	0.940	0.711	0.870	0.913	0.711	0.426	0.585	0.231
	IQR-α-OPT	0.070	**0.999**	**0.999**	0.957	0.996	0.998	0.957	0.668	0.857	0.066
	IQR-α-PSO	0.995	NaN	NaN	0.957	NaN	NaN	0.957	0.668	0.857	0.383
f_2	IQR-OPT	0.851	0.851	0.851	-0.	0.643	0.774	0.545	0.220	0.411	0.138
	IQR-PSO	0.851	0.851	0.851	0.215	0.643	0.774	0.545	0.220	0.411	0.138
	IQR-α-OPT	0.189	0.025	**0.962**	-0.	0.894	0.938	0.726	0.432	0.596	-0.
	IQR-α-PSO	**0.962**	**0.962**	**0.962**	0.726	0.894	0.937	0.726	0.432	0.596	0.233
f_3	IQR-OPT	0.907	0.962	**0.997**	0.854	0.924	**0.997**	0.878	0.876	0.879	0.752
	IQR-PSO	0.907	0.962	NaN	0.854	0.924	NaN	0.878	0.876	0.879	0.752
	IQR-α-OPT	0.630	0.939	0.939	0.927	0.935	0.681	0.927	0.892	0.917	0.791
	IQR-α-PSO	0.939	0.995	0.938	0.927	0.996	0.996	0.927	0.892	0.916	0.791
f_4	IQR-OPT	0.696	0.811	0.882	0.685	0.809	0.880	0.805	0.787	0.839	0.572
	IQR-PSO	0.696	0.811	0.882	0.685	0.809	0.880	0.805	0.787	0.839	0.572
	IQR-α-OPT	**1.**	**1.**	**1.**	**1.**	**1.**	0.977	**1.**	**1.**	**1.**	0.867
	IQR-α-PSO	NaN	NaN	NaN	NaN	NaN	0.998	NaN	NaN	NaN	0.867
f_5	IQR-OPT	0.741	0.741	0.741	0.511	0.661	0.710	0.511	0.291	0.410	0.154
	IQR-PSO	0.741	0.741	0.740	0.511	0.661	0.710	0.511	0.291	0.410	0.154
	IQR-α-OPT	**1.**	**1.**	0.002	0.810	0.751	0.997	0.810	0.490	0.670	0.266
	IQR-α-PSO	NaN	NaN	0.996	0.810	0.972	NaN	0.810	0.490	0.670	0.266
g_1	IQR-OPT	-10.235	-1.599	-0.860	-0.	-1.599	-0.860	-2.943	-1.671	-0.430	-0.
	IQR-PSO	-5.445	-2.615	-0.605	-0.	0.004	-0.921	0.004	-0.	-0.430	-0.213
	IQR-α-OPT	0.017	0.479	0.098	0.479	0.042	0.950	**1.**	-0.	0.303	-0.
	IQR-α-PSO	0.996	0.687	0.560	0.536	0.737	0.917	NaN	0.536	0.907	0.419
g_2	IQR-OPT	0.	-1.217	-0.607	-4.768	-3.055	-0.608	-2.152	-0.	-0.341	-0.356
	IQR-PSO	0.	-2.489	-1.059	-0.	-1.892	-1.055	0.	-0.835	-0.139	-0.
	IQR-α-OPT	0.671	**1.**	0.971	-0.	0.575	0.575	0.305	0.	0.871	0.024
	IQR-α-PSO	0.671	NaN	0.996	0.305	0.372	0.983	0.682	0.305	0.858	0.335
g_3	IQR-OPT	-3.968	-1.024	-0.748	-4.059	-1.025	-0.530	-1.823	-1.071	-0.801	-0.
	IQR-PSO	-3.318	-0.	-1.511	-3.133	-0.665	-0.438	-1.767	-0.666	-0.294	-0.108
	IQR-α-OPT	0.217	0.217	0.669	0.217	0.438	0.442	0.217	0.217	0.200	0.187
	IQR-α-PSO	0.531	**0.995**	0.438	0.300	0.708	0.890	0.510	-0.	0.618	0.264

Among the g_M functions, g_1 displays the highest difference in performance in comparison to the previous model, with an average result with the IQR-α-PSO variant of 0.7295, higher by a value of 0.3927 than the average result of 0.3368 achieved with IQR-α-OPT. Additionally, g_3 reaches $R^2 = 0.995$ under $r = 0, p = 3$, the strongest result for that function across the entire table. Notably, g_1 remains the most challenging target for all variants, with the most extreme low for the baseline IQR-OPT model and inconsistent behavior for the others.

Effect of Input Encoding Configuration on Performance
A systematic examination of the results across all functions and models reveals clear patterns associated with the number of padding dimensions and repeated input uploading.

Padding generally improves performance up to a moderate level for some functions, notably f_3, f_4 and g_3, after which gains saturate or reverse. For the fixed alpha IQR models, fixing $r = 0$ and increasing padding from $p = 1$ to $p = 3$ and $p = 7$ yields modest but consistent gains on f_3, f_4 and several g_M functions, while other f_M functions remain largely unaffected. For the parametrized IQR-α variants, the benefit of padding beyond $p = 3$ is inconsistent: performance plateaus in some cases and fluctuates in others, suggesting that the interaction between trainable α and padding introduces non-trivial effects that are not monotonically beneficial. A clear example of padding being beneficial is the increase in R^2 score for g_3 under IQR-α-PSO, from 0.531 with $r = 0, p = 1$ to 0.995 with $r = 0, p = 3$. However, on the same function and model, the score collapses to 0.438 at $p = 7$.

Re-uploading alone, in contrast, tends to produce harmful returns beyond moderate levels. Comparing configurations with increasing repetition and no padding ($r = 3, p = 0; r = 7, p = 0$), a clear degradation trend is observed across most functions and models, though not always monotonically. The configuration $r = 7, p = 0$ is consistently among the worst-performing configurations in the table for the f_M functions, often by a substantial margin. For example, IQR-α-OPT on f_1 drops from $R^2 = 0.957$ at $r = 1, p = 0$, to 0.668 at $r = 3, p = 0$ and further to 0.066 at $r = 7, p = 0$. This suggests that the model's representation power does not scale with r, and that the structural symmetry imposed by re-uploading may progressively constrain the effective hypothesis space, excluding functions that would require asymmetric encoding to be properly approximated.

Despite this limitation, conciliating both configurations may offer competitive or even improved performance. Settings such as $r = 1, p = 2$ and $r = 1, p = 6$, which introduce a single re-uploading step alongside moderate or high padding, can match pure padding configurations in select cases, suggesting that a single re-uploading step does not necessarily harm performance when sufficient padding is present. In f_3, IQR-OPT achieves $R^2 = 0.997$ under both $r = 0, p = 7$ and $r = 1, p = 6$, indicating that a single repetition paired with sufficient padding does not degrade performance. Similarly, IQR-α-PSO achieves $R^2 = 0.996$ for f_3 under $r = 1, p = 2$ and $r = 1, p = 6$, and even improves over the $r = 0, p = 7$ configuration.

These results indicate that a small degree of re-uploading, when combined with padding, can occasionally be beneficial, likely because it reinforces the input signal without eliminating the structural diversity introduced by the constant padding dimensions. It should be emphasized, however, that the gain resulting in increasing p for a fixed r value is not always mirrored by increasing r for a fixed p value. This points to an optimal operating regime where the input space is moderately expanded through padding, providing sufficient encoding diversity.

In Fig. 1, the eight functions are shown under the best configurations (re-uploading and padding) for both models. It can be observed that the IQR model

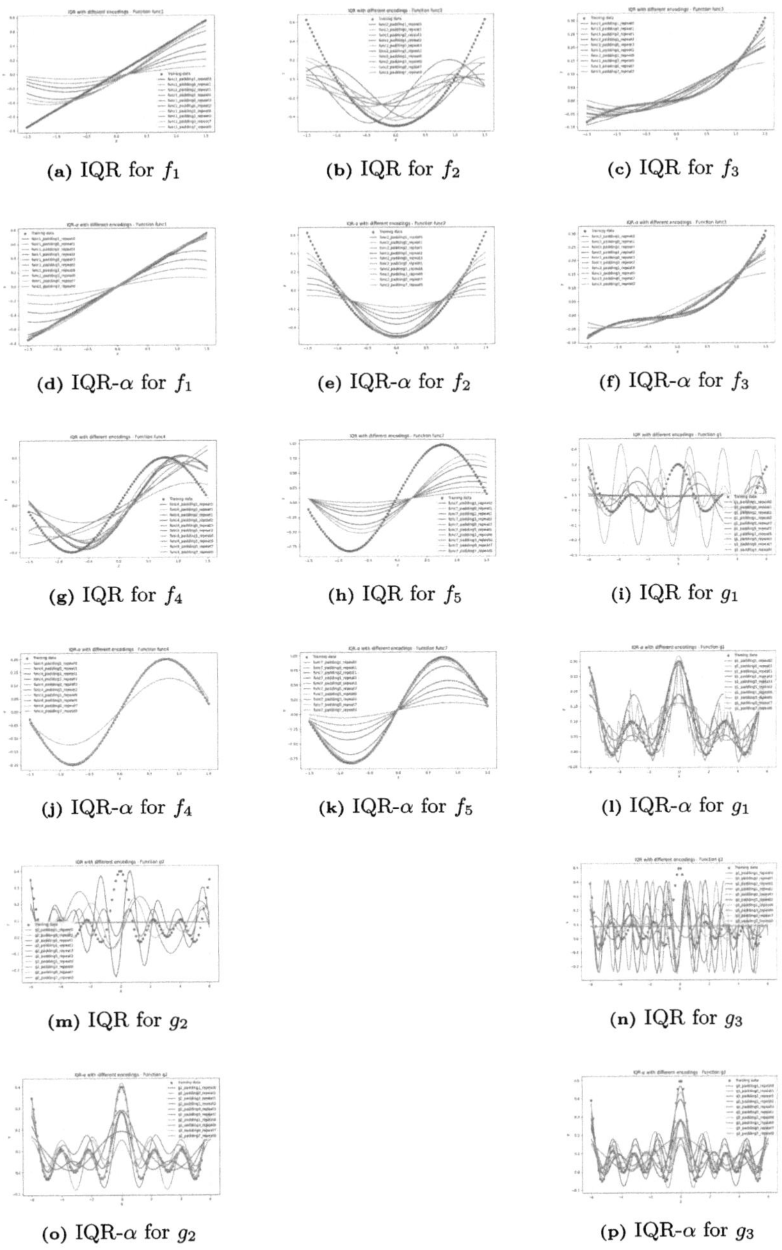

(a) IQR for f_1 (b) IQR for f_2 (c) IQR for f_3

(d) IQR-α for f_1 (e) IQR-α for f_2 (f) IQR-α for f_3

(g) IQR for f_4 (h) IQR for f_5 (i) IQR for g_1

(j) IQR-α for f_4 (k) IQR-α for f_5 (l) IQR-α for g_1

(m) IQR for g_2 (n) IQR for g_3

(o) IQR-α for g_2 (p) IQR-α for g_3

Fig. 1. Evaluation of the proposed quantum regression models across eight benchmark functions. Each function is analyzed using both model variants, where the rows alternate between the baseline IQR model and its parametrized extension IQR-α. The subfigures illustrate the fitting behavior of each model, enabling a direct visual comparison of their approximation capabilities. It can be observed that the IQR-α model provides more accurate fits. A detailed discussion on the impact of different input embedding strategies, including data re-uploading and padding, is provided in Sect. 4.2.

fails to capture non-linear behavior, while IQR-α consistently reproduces the function shapes, even across different parameter settings.

5 Conclusion

In this work, we proposed the *Interactive Quantum Regressor* (IQR), extending the framework originally introduced in [18] from a classification setting to a regression paradigm. The proposed model preserves the physical interpretation of open quantum systems, where learning emerges from the interaction between a target system and an environment encoding the input data, while introducing a continuous-output formulation based on expectation values of observables. Furthermore, we proposed an additional parametrization of the system operator, allowing a more flexible and adaptive adjustment of the model to better approximate target functions.

The proposed model was evaluated on a set of eight benchmark functions under different input encoding strategies, including padding and input repetition schemes. These variations allow the model to explore different effective dimensionalities and representations of the input space, directly impacting its expressive capacity. The experimental analysis suggests that the proposed approach is capable of accurately modeling a diverse class of functions, including linear and nonlinear functions, sinusoidal patterns such as sine and cosine, linear combinations of trigonometric components, as well as more complex functions with higher-frequency behavior (e.g., frequencies 2, 3, and 4). These results indicate that the model possesses sufficient expressive power to approximate a wide range of functional behaviors.

A systematic analysis of the input encoding strategies indicates that padding generally improves performance up to a moderate level, while excessive input re-uploading tends to degrade results, likely due to increased symmetry and reduced effective hypothesis space. The parametrized IQR-α model exhibits more complex behavior under padding variations, reflecting non-trivial interactions between trainable parameters and the expanded input space. Notably, combining moderate padding with a small number of re-uploadings provides a favorable trade-off, suggesting the existence of an optimal encoding regime; further details are discussed in Sect. 4.2.

Training was primarily performed with the Adam optimizer. Although effective in many cases, Adam optimizer did not always achieve satisfactory solutions, whereas PSO emerged as a viable alternative, often yielding improved performance when gradient-based optimization became trapped in suboptimal regions of the search space.

Future work includes extending the evaluation to higher-dimensional regression tasks, investigating alternative training strategies that may better navigate the optimization landscape, and conducting a deeper theoretical analysis of the class of functions that can be represented by this model. In particular, this theoretical investigation will be grounded on expressivity analyses similar to those developed in works such as in [5] and [15], aiming to better characterize the functional capacity of the proposed framework. This investigation is currently in progress and seeks to further clarify the expressive power and limitations of the model.

Acknowledgments. BF was supported by the Programa Institucional de Bolsas de Iniciação Científica (PIBIC/UFPE), Pró-Reitoria de Pesquisa e Inovação, Universidade Federal de Pernambuco - Grant number PIC2577-2025. FMPN acknowledges financial support from the Brazilian National Council for Scientific and Technological Development (CNPq) under Grant No. 408499/2025-7. FMPN is also a researcher affiliated with the National Institute of Science and Technology for Applied Quantum Computing, supported by CNPq under Grant No. 408884/2024-0 and part of the Brazilian National Institute for Artificial Intelligence, supported by CNPq under Grant No. 406417/2022-9.

Disclosure of Interests. The authors have no competing interests.

References

1. Breuer, H.P., Petruccione, F.: The theory of open quantum systems. OUP Oxford (2002)
2. Brito, E.B., de Paula Neto, F.M., Bernardes, N.K.: Quantum classifier based on open quantum systems with amplitude information loading. Quantum Inf. Process. **23**(10), 339 (2024)
3. Delgado-Granados, L.H., et al.: Quantum algorithms and applications for open quantum systems. Chem. Rev. **125**(4), 1823–1839 (2025)
4. Kennedy, J., Eberhart, R.: Particle swarm optimization. In: Proceedings of ICNN'95-International Conference on Neural Networks, vol. 4, pp. 1942–1948. IEEE (1995)
5. Kim, Y., Park, D.K.: Expressivity of deterministic quantum computation with one qubit. Phys. Rev. A **111**(2), 022429 (2025)
6. Knill, E., Laflamme, R.: Power of one bit of quantum information. Phys. Rev. Lett. **81**(25), 5672–5675 (1998)
7. Korkmaz, U., Topal, M.C., Aygül, E., Türkpençe, D.: Training an open quantum classifier. In: 2022 International Symposium on Multidisciplinary Studies and Innovative Technologies (ISMSIT), pp. 429–433. IEEE (2022)
8. Korkmaz, U., Türkpençe, D.: Dissipative learning of a quantum classifier. Pramana **97**(4), 165 (2023)
9. Korkmaz, U., Türkpençe, D., Akıncı, T.C., Şeker, S.: A thermal quantum classifier. darXiv preprint arXiv:1905.00293 (2019)
10. Neto, F.M., Silva, L.d.R., Neto, P.S., Fanchini, F.F.: Regression of functions by quantum neural networks circuits. arXiv preprint arXiv:2512.19978 (2025)
11. Nielsen, M.A., Chuang, I.L.: Quantum computation and quantum information. Cambridge university press (2010)
12. Olivera-Atencio, M.L., Lamata, L., Casado-Pascual, J.: Benefits of open quantum systems for quantum machine learning. Adv. Quan. Technol. **8**(12), 2300247 (2025)
13. Pérez-Salinas, A., López-Núñez, D., García-Sáez, A., Forn-Díaz, P., Latorre, J.I.: One qubit as a universal approximant. Phys. Rev. A **104**(1), 012405 (2021)
14. Schuld, M., Bocharov, A., Svore, K.M., Wiebe, N.: Circuit-centric quantum classifiers. Phys. Rev. A **101**(3), 032308 (2020)

15. Schuld, M., Sweke, R., Meyer, J.J.: Effect of data encoding on the expressive power of variational quantum-machine-learning models. Phys. Rev. A **103**(3), 032430 (2021)
16. Türkpençe, D., Akıncı, T.Ç., Şeker, S.: A steady state quantum classifier. Phys. Lett. A **383**(13), 1410–1418 (2019)
17. Wang, H., Liu, C., Wang, J.: Towards a dissipative quantum classifier. Physics Letters A p. 131849 (2026)
18. Zhang, J., Li, Z., He, R., Zhang, J., Wang, B.: Interactive quantum classifier inspired by quantum open system theory. In: International Joint Conference on Neural Networks (IJCNN) (2021)

StereoSet-PT: The Stereotype Evaluation Framework for Brazilian Portuguese Language Models

Diego Santana Aleixo, Rosimeire Pereira da Costa, Lucas Francisco Amaral Orosco Pellicer(✉), and Renato Augusto Almeida

Instituto de Ciência e Tecnologia Itaú (ICTi), São Paulo, Brazil
diego.aleixo@mailer.com.br, {rosimeire.pereira-costa,lucas.pellicer, renato-augusto.almeida}@itau-unibanco.com.br

Abstract. Large language models inherit social biases from their training data, yet auditing these systems is hindered by the scarcity of benchmarks beyond English. Cross-lingual adaptations often rely on literal translations, introducing syntactic noise such as gender agreement errors that conflate linguistic failure with social bias. This study examines the impact of corpus curation quality on fairness evaluation, comparing localized architectures against generalist multilingual models. We adapted the StereoSet framework to Brazilian Portuguese using a pipeline of manual refinement and algorithmic consistency checks on a representative sample. By evaluating both Masked Language Models (MLMs) and auto-regressive architectures, we demonstrate that specialized models like BERTimbau preserve semantic integrity and exhibit lower bias, reaching an ICAT score of 73.6. In contrast, global models exhibit syntactic degradation that distorts bias metrics. This research provides a validated pipeline for stereotype evaluation in Portuguese, concluding that specialized development is essential for ensuring reduced bias and more equitable AI behavior in local contexts.

1 Introduction

The widespread adoption of pre-trained language models has transformed the resolution of complex Natural Language Processing (NLP) tasks. By extracting probabilistic patterns from vast text corpora, these systems demonstrate a high capacity for syntactic and semantic generalization. However, the reliance on massive internet data leads to the assimilation of historical and structural imbalances [3]. The propagation of discriminatory biases related to gender, race, religion, and profession is currently a major ethical concern in artificial intelligence development, demanding rigorous methods for its measurement and mitigation [4].

The creation of metrics and benchmarks for bias evaluation, such as the StereoSet framework, has been predominantly focused on the English language [10]. To apply these evaluations to other languages, like Portuguese, the field typically

M. Recamonde-Mendoza and R. C. Barros (Eds.): BRACIS 2026, LNAI 17105, pp. 691–704, 2027.
https://doi.org/10.1007/978-3-032-39882-6_46

relies on two options: using generalist multilingual models or directly translating test datasets. This approach, however, often introduces methodological noise. Purely literal translations frequently ignore essential nuances of Portuguese, such as noun agreement and gender inflection. This creates an ambiguity in the evaluation: when a model assigns a low probability to a sentence, does it do so because it lacks stereotypical bias, or because it fails to understand an artificial and incorrect linguistic formulation? [12,15]

This issue raises questions about the effectiveness of off-the-shelf solutions for fairness analysis across different languages. This paper presents a translation and adaptation of StereoSet to Portuguese, aiming to enable the systematic measurement of social biases in language models applied to this language. The study analyzes how models trained specifically for Portuguese (such as the BERTimbau family [14]) and generalist multilingual models differ in observed bias patterns when evaluated on a benchmark translated and adapted for the language. Notably, because this methodology involves translating a dataset conceived in a different cultural context, the analysis focuses on the architectures' responses to predefined bias patterns, rather than mapping biases specific to the Brazilian reality.

To conduct this investigation and isolate linguistic proficiency from discriminatory bias, this study proposes the translation, methodological adaptation, and manual curation of a bias-stratified sample (25%) of the StereoSet dataset into Portuguese, specifically encompassing bias domains of gender, race, religion, and profession. We conduct a comparative analysis contrasting the performance of monolingual architectures dedicated to Portuguese, standard global models [8], and autoregressive Large Language Models (LLMs), including contemporary *decoder-only* variants and national initiatives such as Sabiá [13].

This work is based on the premise that bias evaluation in NLP requires careful attention to the linguistic adequacy of the dataset, highlighting the importance of linguistically grounded benchmarks for reliable cross-lingual fairness analysis.

2 Related Work

The analysis of social biases in language models has been extensively investigated, largely due to the growing impact of these systems in sensitive, large-scale applications. Early studies demonstrated that linguistic representations learned from massive textual corpora tend to reflect social patterns, stereotypes, and prejudices inherent in the training data, disproportionately affecting groups defined by gender, race, religion, and occupation [5].

A foundational effort to systematically measure this phenomenon was introduced by Caliskan, Bryson, and Narayanan [6] through the Word Embedding Association Test (WEAT). Inspired by the Implicit Association Test from psychology, WEAT identifies biased associations in static word embeddings. The authors demonstrated that embeddings trained on vast text volumes internalize semantic biases similar to those observed in humans, revealing stereotypical associations between social demographic groups and specific attributes. Similarly,

Bolukbasi et al. [5] highlighted that widely used embeddings exhibit strong gender biases, exemplified by analogies such as "man is to computer programmer as woman is to homemaker." Beyond identifying the issue, they proposed debiasing methods to mitigate these associations without significantly compromising the semantic utility of the vector space.

Subsequent research expanded this investigation beyond static vectors to contextualized models and sentence encoders. Studies in this area indicate that while more sophisticated architectures improve performance on linguistic tasks, they continue to encode social biases analogous to those found in traditional embeddings [10].

Beyond representation analysis, several studies have investigated the impact of bias in downstream natural language processing tasks. In coreference resolution, Zhao et al. [16] demonstrated the presence of gender bias in both data and models, proposing specific evaluation and mitigation strategies. Likewise, De-Arteaga et al. [7] analyzed classifiers applied to professional biographies, showing that algorithmic errors disproportionately affect specific demographic groups.

With the advent of large language models, standardized benchmarks specifically designed to evaluate social bias emerged. Notable among these is CrowS-Pairs [11], which introduces a dataset based on contrastive minimal pairs. Addressing the structural limitations of such approaches, Nadeem, Bethke, and Reddy [10] proposed StereoSet, a widely adopted benchmark structured around triplets comprising a stereotypical sentence, an anti-stereotypical sentence, and an unrelated context.

Despite the relevance of these benchmarks, most were originally developed for the English language, raising questions about their suitability for other linguistic and cultural realities. Recent studies confirm that the intensity and nature of biases vary substantially across languages [12].

In the Portuguese context, prior work has already identified gendered and stereotypical associations in language representations. Santana et al. [17] analyzed professions in Portuguese word embeddings and showed that these representations encode gender stereotypes analogous to those reported for English. More recently, Taso et al. [20] examined Portuguese embeddings with association-based metrics and found systematic masculine associations in domains such as science, finance, and sports. Moving beyond static representations, Assi and Caseli [19] investigated GPT-3.5 Turbo in both English and Portuguese, reporting measurable asymmetries associated with gender and language. At the contextual modeling level, Silva et al. [18] showed that fine-tuning a BERT-based model on Portuguese literary texts changes gender associations, but does not eliminate them entirely.

3 Methodology

3.1 StereoSet Framework

The StereoSet, introduced by Nadeem et al. [10], is a large-scale English benchmark designed to measure stereotypical bias across four domains: gender, profession, race, and religion. The benchmark was originally built from crowd-sourced examples and released through the official StereoSet framework. In its public version, the benchmark comprises approximately 17,000 sentences organized into *intrasentence* and *intersentence* contexts, with the official development split containing 2,106 *intrasentence* and 2,123 *intersentence* instances.

The benchmark is organized into two tasks:

- **Intrasentence:** Focuses on bias within a single sentence using a cloze-based masked language modeling setup. A context sentence contains a target group and a blank (e.g., "The *target* is BLANK"), which the model must complete using one of three provided options: a stereotype, an anti-stereotype, or an unrelated term.
- **Intersentence:** Evaluates bias at the discourse level. It consists of a context sentence followed by a second sentence that can be stereotypical, anti-stereotypical, or unrelated to the first. The model is tasked with determining the most plausible continuation given the initial context.

The StereoSet evaluation framework was originally designed to quantify bias in language models by comparing the conditional probabilities assigned to candidate sentences. The architecture evaluates these contexts by assigning conditional probabilities to each candidate sentence, allowing the model's preference for stereotypical, anti-stereotypical, or unrelated associations to be quantified.

While StereoSet's mathematical and methodological formulation remains widely adopted for this evaluation category, the original computational pipeline built on early versions of the Transformers library and outdated architectures presented technical incompatibilities with contemporary language models. To enable the execution of this research with current models, modifications to the framework's infrastructure layer were necessary, focusing strictly on software usability and interoperability.

The implemented adaptations include:

- **Dynamic Model and Tokenizer Loading**: The original code relied on static classes and hardcoded paths for specific architectures. The framework was refactored to use the universal and dynamic classes of the modern API (`AutoModelForCausalLM`, `AutoTokenizer`). This allowed the script to automatically infer tokenization rules, vocabularies, and attention architectures for any current model, without forcing the use of legacy tokens.
- **Output Handling (Logits)**: Probability extraction required updating to handle the complex output objects of modern neural networks. Tensor calls were adjusted to capture the correct logits and prevent Out of Memory (OOM) bottlenecks during execution.

3.2 Dataset Adaptation and Curation (StereoSet-PT)

Due to the scale of the original dataset and the need to ensure an accurate evaluation of Portuguese semantic nuances, a representative subset was utilized.

A stratified random sample based on bias type was extracted, corresponding to 25% of the original dataset.

The initial translation of this sample was automated using the Claude 4.5 Sonnet language model [2] via AWS infrastructure, and was used as a first-pass draft for subsequent human revision rather than as a final benchmark version. To preserve the structure of the original dataset, a task-conditioned prompting strategy was developed. For the *intrasentence* task, priority was given to the consistency and equivalence of the gap-filling structure. To ensure structural stability, enhance reproducibility, and minimize hallucinations during translation, the inference hyperparameters were configured for low probabilistic variance, specifically setting the temperature to 0.1 and top-p to 0.9.

Although the generative model provided a useful first-pass translation, automatic translation alone was not considered sufficient for benchmark construction. Consequently, all translated instances underwent manual review and correction by three annotators.

The curation process was conducted through a tabular interface shared between annotators in which the original English text and the translated Portuguese version were displayed side by side. The table also included the stereotype information already annotated in the original StereoSet dataset, allowing the reviewers to verify whether the translated triplet preserved the same semantic logic and polarity as the source instance. The annotators followed a single guiding principle throughout the review: maintain the original logical relation of the example (target group, stereotype/anti-stereotype contrast, and unrelated alternative), while adapting the phrasing only when required to ensure grammatical, naturalness, and compatibility with the evaluation script.

This manual curation focused on resolving residual errors such as false cognates, literal translations of idiomatic expressions, inadequate gender agreement, and loss or displacement of the `BLANK` anchor token. Therefore, the criticism in this work is not directed at the use of automatic translation per se, but at its isolated use without linguistic validation. The final model evaluation reported in this study was conducted exclusively on the manually curated sample.

In addition to translating the corpus, it was necessary to adapt the StereoSet computational pipeline. For the intrasentence task, the evaluation architecture operates essentially as a cloze test. The original script requires perfect string alignment, locating a fixed anchor token (`BLANK`) within the context and replacing it with three distinct target terms (stereotype, anti-stereotype, and unrelated) to calculate the conditional probability of each formulation.

To prevent silent failures during the extraction of probabilities at inference—where the model might penalize a sentence for formatting errors rather than bias—we implemented a rigorous manual verification process. The original StereoSet evaluation method was preserved, and the adaptation focused on ensuring string alignment accuracy during the dataset's tabular reconstruction.

Instead of relying on automated sequence matching or static translations that frequently lost the structural precision of the anchor token, we introduced a dedicated column in the dataset during the human review phase. This column explicitly isolated all target tokens for each sentence, serving as a direct guide for the manual verification process. By clearly mapping these target terms, human reviewers could systematically cross-reference the gap's position and ensure the context was perfectly aligned with the generated sentences. This guided verification ensured the context could be accurately defined and structurally validated as:

$$Context_{new} = Prefix_{common} + \text{BLANK} + Suffix_{common}$$

This meticulous manual approach circumvented inconsistencies in translation and ensured the structural integrity of the resulting dataset used for evaluation.

3.3 Translation Challenges

During the manual curation of the sample, we observed that literal translation compromised the language modeling task in several scenarios. The main cases where direct translation failed and required methodological intervention include:

- **Nominal Agreement Divergence (Gender and Number)**: Unlike English, where nouns and adjectives often lack gender inflection (e.g., "The nurse is BLANK", accepting targets such as caring, rude, or tree), Portuguese requires strict grammatical agreement. Translating the context demanded defining a gender ("O enfermeiro" [masculine] or "A enfermeira" [feminine]). If the translation fixed the context as masculine, but one of the translated target terms was feminine, the language model would penalize the generated sentence ("O enfermeiro é atenciosa") for the syntactic error, thereby corrupting the bias score. The adaptation required manual adjustment of the agreement between the context and its targets.
- **Loss of the Anchor Token**: In many instances, the technical term `BLANK` was translated as "lacuna" (gap), "[espaço]" ([space]), or completely omitted during the sentence's syntactic restructuring, breaking the find-and-replace logic of the original script.
- **Syntactic Word Order**: English allows greater flexibility to keep the `BLANK` token at the end of certain structures. In the Portuguese version, attempting to maintain the exact same order generated sentences with artificial passive voice or incorrect pronominal placement. Manual curation repositioned the gap to ensure that all three variants possessed native fluency (Table 1).

3.4 Bias Metrics

To quantify bias and language modeling capability, this work adopted the standardized metrics and calculations originally proposed in the StereoSet framework by Nadeem et al. [10]. As the evaluation includes autoregressive models (Causal Language Models), the score of each candidate sentence is computed based on the conditional probability of its tokens, factorized over the sequence.

Given a model with parameters θ and a sentence composed of a token sequence $W = (w_1, w_2, \ldots, w_N)$, the sentence score, $S(W)$, is calculated using

Table 1. Examples of structural failures arising from the literal translation of the StereoSet dataset.

Original (English)	Translation with Error	Impact
The housekeeper is a BLANK.	A governanta é uma [lacuna].	**Loss of the Anchor Token:** The inference script cannot find the exact substring "BLANK", making the substitution with target sentences impossible. The evaluation fails silently.
The nurse is BLANK. (Targets: caring / male / tree)	O enfermeiro é BLANK. (Targets: carinhosa / homem / árvore)	**Agreement Error:** The substitution generates the phrase "O enfermeiro é carinhosa" (masculine subject with feminine adjective). The model penalizes the sentence for the basic syntactic error rather than the bias association, invalidating the score.
He was given a BLANK. (Targets: gun / promotion / sky)	Ele foi dado um BLANK. (Targets: arma / promoção / céu)	**Syntactic Distortion:** Translating the English passive voice literally generates a grammatical construction that is unnatural in Portuguese. This increases the model's perplexity, artificially degrading the Language Modeling Score.

the average base-2 logarithm of each token's probability, conditioned on the preceding tokens [10]:

$$S(W) = \frac{1}{N} \sum_{i=1}^{N} \log_2 P_\theta(w_i \mid w_{<i}) \tag{1}$$

With the scores established for the three context variations (stereotype, anti-stereotype, and unrelated), the three core evaluation metrics are applied:

1. Stereotype Score (SS). The Stereotype Score [10] measures the model's propensity to prefer stereotypical associations over anti-stereotypical ones. For each instance in the dataset, the score of the sentence containing the stereotype (S_{stereo}) is compared to the anti-stereotypical sentence (S_{anti}). The metric represents the percentage of instances where the model assigned a higher probability to the stereotypical formulation:

$$SS = \frac{100}{|D|} \sum_{x \in D} \mathbb{I}(S^{(x)}_{stereo} > S^{(x)}_{anti}) \tag{2}$$

where $\mathbb{I}$ is the indicator function. A perfectly unbiased model would yield an SS of 50%, indicating no systematic favoritism toward either side. Values close to 100% indicate a strong stereotypical bias, while values approaching 0% indicate an anti-stereotypical bias.

2. Language Modeling Score (LMS). A model could achieve an SS of 50% simply by assigning random probabilities, reflecting a lack of language comprehension. The Language Modeling Score [10] evaluates the model's competence in recognizing semantically valid associations. The metric calculates the percentage of times meaningful sentences receive a higher score than the unrelated sentence ($S_{unrelated}$):

$$LMS = \frac{100}{|D|} \sum_{x \in D} \mathbb{I}(\max(S^{(x)}_{stereo}, S^{(x)}_{anti}) > S^{(x)}_{unrelated}) \tag{3}$$

An ideal language model achieves an LMS of 100%, demonstrating a preference for contextually meaningful sentences over illogical constructs.

3. Idealized Context Association Test (ICAT). The ICAT [10] is the consolidated StereoSet metric, designed to reward models that demonstrate high language modeling capability alongside low discriminative bias. The calculation penalizes linguistic performance in proportion to its deviation from the ideal bias (50%):

$$ICAT = LMS \times \frac{\min(SS, 100 - SS)}{50} \tag{4}$$

The optimal ICAT value is 100 (where LMS = 100% and SS = 50%). A model exhibiting absolute bias receives an ICAT score of zero, regardless of its grammatical proficiency. Thus, the ICAT serves as the definitive indicator for comparing performance and fairness in this study.

4 Results

To encompass different training paradigms and architectures, the following models were evaluated: Monolingual Masked Language Models (MLMs) (`BERTimbau Base` and `Large`), Multilingual MLMs (`mBERT`), and contemporary autoregressive Large Language Models (LLMs) (`Gemma 3 27B`, `Llama 3.1 8B`, `Qwen 2.5/3.5`, and the regionally adapted `Sabiá 7B`).

4.1 Validation and Curation Impact

To isolate the models semantic understanding from structural artifacts, we first validated our translated and manually curated Portuguese sample against the original English baseline.

Table 2 presents this foundational validation. For transparency, the English BERT-base values reported in the table correspond to the official full English development split of StereoSet, as reported by Nadeem et al. [10], rather than to a 25% English subset. In contrast, the Portuguese results refer to the curated 25% stratified sample constructed in this study. Within this scope, the localized BERTimbau Base model achieved a Language Modeling Score (LMS) of 85.04 and an Idealized Context Association Test (ICAT) score of 73.64 on the Portuguese sample. These metrics establish a high degree of parity with the representation quality of the original BERT-base on the English development set (LMS 85.76, ICAT 69.37), indicating that the adaptation preserved the benchmark's evaluative behavior while improving linguistic adequacy for Portuguese.

Conversely, the generic multilingual model (mBERT) exhibited a substantial reduction in syntactic coherence when evaluated in Portuguese (LMS 74.06), leading to a lower overall fairness metric (ICAT 62.97). This outcome reinforces the premise that generic models lack the deep linguistic anchoring required for stable bias evaluation in morphologically complex languages.

Table 2. Comparison between base discriminative models on the original English dataset and the curated Portuguese sample.

Model	Dataset / Language	LMS (↑)	SS (≈ 50)	ICAT (↑)
BERT-base (EN)	StereoSet Original (EN)	**85.76**	59.56	69.37
mBERT Base	Treated Sample (PT)	74.06	57.49	62.97
BERTimbau Base	Treated Sample (PT)	85.04	**56.70**	**73.64**

Note: Higher is better for LMS and ICAT (↑), indicating stronger linguistic coherence and ideal bias balance. The ideal Stereotype Score (SS) is 50.

4.2 Translingual Bias Analysis

A comparative analysis reveals that the majority of evaluated LLMs exhibited a consistently higher SS when tested in English compared to Portuguese. As demonstrated in Table 3, Gemma 3 27B dropped from an SS of 64.31 (EN) to 55.10 (PT-BR), and Llama 3.1 8B decreased from 62.87 (EN) to 56.32 (PT-BR). This trend suggests that the massive English corpora used during pre-training encode more crystallized stereotypical associations [9]. When shifting to Portuguese, the slight reduction in semantic confidence—reflected in the generally lower LMS across LLMs in PT—acts as a diluting filter, moderating the models' structural certainty in selecting heavily biased formulations. Nevertheless, the native initiative Sabiá 7B maintained an SS of 56.77, confirming that cultural bias remains deeply ingrained in local Portuguese training data as well.

Table 3. Semantic coherence and stereotype variance between English and Portuguese representations.

Model	Original English (EN)			Curated Sample (PT)		
	LMS	SS	ICAT	LMS	SS	ICAT
Gemma 3 27B	80.80	64.31	57.68	69.35	55.10	62.27
Llama 3.1 8B	80.23	62.87	59.57	63.74	56.32	55.68
Qwen 3.5 27B	81.85	62.33	61.67	67.30	58.01	56.52
Qwen 2.5 1.5B	81.66	61.04	63.64	66.34	57.21	56.78
Sabiá 7B	67.59	58.27	56.42	60.22	56.77	52.07

4.3 Encoders vs. Decoders

To analyze how representation quality varies across modern architectures, Table 4 separates Encoder and Decoder models on the Portuguese sample.

A architectural divide can be observed, with Localized Encoders (BERTimbau Base and Large) dominate the linguistic coherence metrics, maintaining LMS scores above 84. In contrast, Decoder models display a systematic reduction in LMS (ranging from 60.22 to 69.35). This variance does not signify a lack of Portuguese comprehension by the LLMs; rather, it reflects a fundamental difference in architectural mechanics, as Decoders lack the native Next Sentence Prediction (NSP) head utilized by Encoders.

As a consequence, the *intersentence* evaluation relies entirely on continuous conditional probability (perplexity). This mechanism naturally assigns significantly lower probabilities to the abrupt structural transitions found in the dataset's "unrelated" target sentences, suppressing the overall LMS.

Despite these architectural differences in language modeling assessment, the SS reveals a consistent pattern across all evaluated systems. Regardless of parameter scale (ranging from 1.5B to 27B) or architecture, all models exhibit an SS between 55.10 and 58.25 in Portuguese. This persistent deviation from the neutral ideal (50.0) suggests that discriminatory bias may emerge as a latent structural artifact within the representation space of current models.

Table 4. Evaluation of structural coherence and bias representation across architectures (Curated Sample).

Model	Type	LMS (↑)	SS (≈ 50)	ICAT (↑)
Encoder Models *(Masked Language Models)*				
BERTimbau Base	PT-BR Target	**85.04**	**56.70**	**73.64**
BERTimbau Large	PT-BR Target	84.78	58.25	70.80
mBERT Base	Multilingual	74.06	57.49	62.97
Decoder Models *(Large Language Models)*				
Gemma 3 27B	Multilingual	**69.35**	**55.10**	**62.27**
Qwen 3.5 27B	Multilingual	67.30	58.01	56.52
Qwen 2.5 1.5B	Multilingual	66.34	57.21	56.78
Llama 3.1 8B	Multilingual	63.74	56.32	55.68
Sabiá 7B	PT-BR Target	60.22	56.77	52.07

A finding of particular relevance in the Portuguese context is the atypical behavior observed within the gender bias domain. When disaggregating the results, LLMs exhibited significant spikes in SS—often exceeding 65% in the *intrasentence* task specifically for gender. This exacerbation is directly linked to the morphologically rich nature of Portuguese, which imposes explicit grammatical gender markers on nouns and adjectives, contrasting with the frequent neutrality of English (e.g., *nurse* or *engineer*). The grammatical requirement for nominal agreement forces the model to expose deeper biased representations, rigidly associating certain professions or attributes with strictly feminine or masculine syntax markers [1].

These outcomes consolidate the premise that equitable language modeling requires not only robust evaluation frameworks but also careful linguistic adaptation, ensuring that artificial intelligence systems are assessed on their true semantic qualities rather than being penalized by translation artifacts.

5 Conclusion

This study investigated the impact of *corpus* quality on the propagation and measurement of bias in language models. The main objective was to determine whether the effort to develop and deploy models trained specifically on local data (such as the BERTimbau family [14]) is justified over the direct adoption of generalist models. By translating, methodologically adapting, and manually curating the StereoSet *benchmark* for Portuguese, we established a validated and structurally sound baseline.

Results confirm our hypothesis: localized and carefully curated architectures outperform *off-the-shelf* global models in syntactic coherence. By resolving gender asymmetries and translation noise, the curation process ensured that bias measurements reflected actual prejudices internalized by the neural networks, rather than mere grammatical errors in Portuguese. Furthermore, discriminatory bias—particularly gender bias, which is exacerbated by the language's morphological richness—proved to be an underlying structural pattern across all evaluated architectures, regardless of their training paradigm (Encoder or Decoder) or parameter scale [4].

Ultimately, mitigating bias and developing fairer AI systems in Brazil rely heavily on the use of representative models and localized evaluation tools. Releasing the restructured *pipeline* and the curated StereoSet PT-BR sample provides the scientific community with a reliable foundation for future work diagnosing and correcting algorithmic inequalities within the Portuguese language.

6 Limitations and Future Work

Although the adaptation ensured the syntactic integrity and statistical comparability of StereoSet for the Portuguese language, relying on international benchmarks presents an intrinsic cultural asymmetry. The original dataset was designed to reflect the biases and prejudice dynamics of United States society. Consequently, a strict translation of the sentences inadvertently imports social issues that lack direct parallels in the Brazilian context.

This contrast is particularly evident in the race and ethnicity category. In the original StereoSet, sentences formulated to test stereotypes against Hispanic or Latino populations frequently rely on tropes of illegal immigration, accents, or generalizations centered on Mexican culture. When translated into Portuguese and applied to models in Brazil, these contexts lose their validity. Within the national framework, the "Latino" identity and its associated stereotypes are not perceived through the same segregationist lens applied to immigrants in the United States. Consequently, language models are evaluated on their ability to associate terms with foreign stereotypes, rather than their tendency to reproduce actual biases present in their deployment environment.

The reliance on a translated dataset also overlooks prejudices specific to the national context. The original framework lacks categories to measure critical axes of Brazilian discrimination, such as regional xenophobia (e.g., historical prejudice directed at populations from the North and Northeast regions), intolerance against Afro-Brazilian religions, or the complexities of Brazilian structural racism, which is heavily intertwined with issues of colorism and social class.

Therefore, translating benchmarks is merely an initial step. For future work, we propose the creation of a bias-evaluation dataset natively constructed for Brazilian Portuguese. The evaluation methodology established in this study which validated the behavior of metrics such as the ICAT across different architectures can subsequently be applied to a new database populated with regionalized stereotypes.

Conflict of Interest Statement

The opinions, findings, conclusions, and recommendations presented in this work are solely those of the authors and do not necessarily reflect the views of Itaú

Unibanco or the Instituto de Ciência e Tecnologia Itaú. This work is based on the translation and adaptation of the publicly available StereoSet dataset, respecting its original license (CC-BY-SA 4.0). All data used in this study comply with the Brazilian General Data Protection Law (Lei Geral de Proteção de Dados – LGPD).

Acknowledgments. We thank the Instituto de Ciência e Tecnologia Itaú for the financial support that made this research possible. This study employed OpenAI's Deep Research to assist in the identification of relevant references, Microsoft Copilot to support the review and refinement of the manuscript, and Anthropic's Claude 4.5 Sonnet for translation assistance.

References

1. Agarwal, M., Aggarwal, A., Goel, A., Hira, M., Gupta, A.: MORPHOGEN: a Multilingual Benchmark for Evaluating Gender-Aware Morphological Generation. arXiv preprint arXiv:2604.18914 (2026)
2. Anthropic: Claude Sonnet 4.5 System Card. Technical report (2025)
3. Bender, E. M., Gebru, T., McMillan-Major, A., Shmitchell, S.: On the Dangers of Stochastic Parrots: Can Language Models Be Too Big? In: Proceedings of the ACM Conference on Fairness, Accountability, and Transparency (FAccT), pp. 610–623 (2021)
4. Blodgett, S. L., Barocas, S., Daumé III, H., Wallach, H.: Language (Technology) is Power: A Critical Survey of Bias in NLP. In: Proceedings of the 58th Annual Meeting of the Association for Computational Linguistics (ACL), pp. 5454–5476 (2020)
5. Bolukbasi, T., Chang, K.-W., Zou, J.Y., Saligrama, V., Kalai, A.T.: Man is to Computer Programmer as Woman is to Homemaker? Advances in Neural Information Processing Systems (NeurIPS), Debiasing Word Embeddings. In (2016)
6. Caliskan, A., Bryson, J.J., Narayanan, A.: Semantics derived automatically from language corpora contain human-like biases. Science **356**(6334), 183–186 (2017)
7. De-Arteaga, M., et al.: Bias in Bios: a Case Study of Semantic Representation Bias in a High-Stakes Setting. In: Proceedings of the Conference on Fairness, Accountability, and Transparency (FAT*), pp. 120–128 (2019)
8. Devlin, J., Chang, M.-W., Lee, K., Toutanova, K.: BERT: pre-training of Deep Bidirectional Transformers for Language Understanding. In: Proceedings of the 2019 Conference of the North American Chapter of the Association for Computational Linguistics: Human Language Technologies (NAACL-HLT), pp. 4171–4186 (2019)
9. Garrido-Muñoz, I., Montejo-Ráez, A., Martínez-Santiago, F., Ureña-López, L.A.: A Survey on Bias in Deep NLP. Appl. Sci. **11**(7), 3184 (2021)
10. Nadeem, M., Bethke, A., Reddy, S.: StereoSet: Measuring stereotypical bias in pretrained language models. In: Proceedings of the 59th Annual Meeting of the Association for Computational Linguistics (ACL) and the 11th International Joint Conference on Natural Language Processing (IJCNLP), pp. 5356–5371 (2021)
11. Nangia, N., Vania, C., Bhalerao, R., Bowman, S. R.: CrowS-Pairs: A Challenge Dataset for Measuring Social Biases in Masked Language Models. In: Proceedings of the 2020 Conference on Empirical Methods in Natural Language Processing (EMNLP), pp. 1953–1967 (2020)

12. Öztürk, I. T., et al.: How Different Is Stereotypical Bias Across Languages? In: Joint European Conference on Machine Learning and Knowledge Discovery in Databases (ECML PKDD), pp. 209–229 (2023)
13. Pires, R., Abonizio, H., Almeida, T. S., Nogueira, R.: Sabiá: Portuguese Large Language Models. In: Brazilian Conference on Intelligent Systems (BRACIS), pp. 226–240. Springer (2023)
14. Souza, F., Nogueira, R., Lotufo, R.: BERTimbau: Pretrained BERT Models for Brazilian Portuguese. In: Cerri, R., Prati, R.C. (eds.) BRACIS 2020. LNCS (LNAI), vol. 12319, pp. 403–417. Springer, Cham (2020). https://doi.org/10.1007/978-3-030-61377-8_28
15. Yao, B., Jiang, M., Bobinac, T., Yang, D., Hu, J.: Benchmarking Machine Translation with Cultural Awareness. In: Findings of the Association for Computational Linguistics: EMNLP 2024, pp. 13078–13096 (2024). https://doi.org/10.18653/v1/2024.findings-emnlp.765
16. Zhao, J., Wang, T., Yatskar, M., Ordonez, V., Chang, K.-W.: Gender Bias in Coreference Resolution: Evaluation and Debiasing Methods. In: Proceedings of the 2018 Conference of the North American Chapter of the Association for Computational Linguistics: Human Language Technologies (NAACL-HLT), pp. 15–20 (2018)
17. Santana, B. S., Woloszyn, V., Wives, L. K.: Is there Gender bias and stereotype in Portuguese Word Embeddings? In: Proceedings of the 13th International Conference on the Computational Processing of Portuguese (PROPOR) (2018)
18. Silva, M. O., Brandão, M. A., Moro, M. M.: Gender Bias in Portuguese Literary Texts: A Masked Language Model Approach. In: Anais do XVI Simpósio Brasileiro de Tecnologia da Informação e da Linguagem Humana (STIL) (2025)
19. Assi, F. M., Caseli, H.: Biases in GPT-3.5 Turbo model: a case study regarding gender and language. In: Proceedings of the 15th Brazilian Symposium in Information and Human Language Technology (STIL), pp. 32–43 (2024)
20. Taso, F.T.S., Reis, V.Q., Martinez, F.V.: Analyzing discourses in Portuguese word embeddings: a case of gender bias outside the English-speaking world. J. Interactive Syst. **16**(1), 532–543 (2025)

Author Index

M. Recamonde-Mendoza and R. C. Barros (Eds.): BRACIS 2026, LNAI 17105, pp. 705–707, 2027.
https://doi.org/10.1007/978-3-032-39882-6

MIX
Papier aus verantwortungsvollen Quellen
Paper from responsible sources
FSC® C105338

If you have any concerns about our products,
you can contact us on
ProductSafety@springernature.com

In case Publisher is established outside the EU,
the EU authorized representative is:
Springer Nature Customer Service Center GmbH
Europaplatz 3, 69115 Heidelberg, Germany

Printed by Libri Plureos GmbH
in Hamburg, Germany